John Pocock
Wellington / Baltimore 1995

REDEMPTION SONGS

'Wherever Te Kooti went – wherever he step foot from one area to another – he's singing!' This biography traces the songs, the narratives and the pathways by which the 19th-century Maori leader Te Kooti Arikirangi Te Turuki sought to give the land and his people new life.

REDEMPTION

A life of

E koro, Te Turuki tirohia mai au, he morehu tangata no runga
i nga puke i puta mai i te whare i Rangiatea.

O sir, Te Turuki, look at me, a survivor of the people from the hills,
who came from the house at Rangiatea.

Waiata sung at Te Wainui, 1895

SONGS

Te Kooti Arikirangi Te Turuki

Judith Binney

AUCKLAND UNIVERSITY PRESS
BRIDGET WILLIAMS BOOKS

First published 1995
Auckland University Press
with Bridget Williams Books
University of Auckland
Private Bag 92019
Auckland, New Zealand

ISBN 1 86940 131 X

Published with assistance from Creative New Zealand (Arts Council of New Zealand Toi Aotearoa) through Te Waka Toi, and from the Historical Branch of the Department of Internal Affairs.

Internal design by Afineline, Wellington
Typeset in CG Bem by Archetype, Wellington
Printed by Kings Time Printing Press, Hong Kong

For Sebastian

This book is dedicated to the memory of my two outstanding teachers,
Sir Monita Delamere and Sir Keith Sinclair, who died within a month of each other
in 1993. In turn, it is offered in all humility to those who hold the stories
that are yet to be told.

CONTENTS

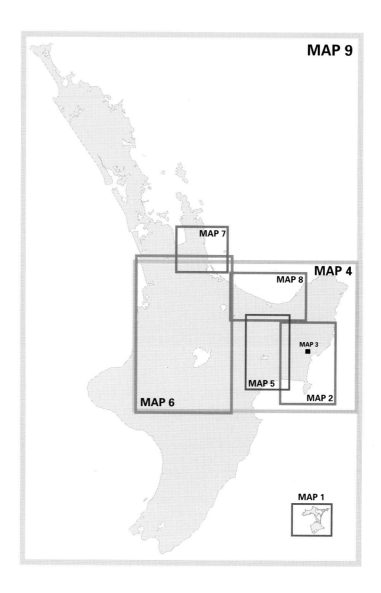

MAPS

ABBREVIATIONS

AD	Army Department
AGG A	Agent General Government, Auckland Province
AGG HB	Agent General Government, Hawke's Bay Province
AIM	Auckland Institute and Museum
AJHR	*Appendices to the Journals of the House of Representatives*
APL	Auckland Public Library (Auckland City Libraries)
AS	*Auckland Star*
ATL	Alexander Turnbull Library, Wellington
AU	University of Auckland
AWN	*Auckland Weekly News*
BPT	*Bay of Plenty Times*
CL	Crown Law Office
CM	Canterbury Museum
CMS	Church Missionary Society
CPL	Canterbury Public Library
CT	Contemporary translation
DOSLI	Department of Survey and Land Information
DSC	*Daily Southern Cross*, Auckland
DT	*Daily Telegraph*, Napier
ECHR	*East Coast Historical Records*
EP	*Evening Post*, Wellington
GBPP	*Great Britain Parliamentary Papers*
GLNZ	Grey Letters, New Zealand, Auckland Public Library
GM	Gisborne Museum
GNZMA	Grey New Zealand Maori Letters, Auckland Public Library
GS	*Gisborne Standard*
GT	*Gisborne Times*
HB	Hawke's Bay Province
HBH	*Hawke's Bay Herald*
HBM	Hawke's Bay Museum, Napier
HL	Hocken Library, Dunedin
IA	Internal Affairs Department
J	Justice Department
JHR	*Journals of the House of Representatives*
JP	Justice of the Peace
JPS	*Journal of the Polynesian Society*
Le	Legislative Department
LT	*Lyttelton Times*
MA	Maori Affairs Department
MHR	Member of the House of Representatives
ML	Mitchell Library, Sydney
MLC	Maori Land Court
MONZ	Museum of New Zealand Te Papa Tongarewa, Wellington
MP	Member of Parliament
MSS	Manuscripts

NA	National Archives (Wellington)
NZH	*New Zealand Herald*
NZLR	*New Zealand Law Reports*
NZM	*New Zealand Mail*
NZT	*New Zealand Times*
OLC	Old Land Claims
OS	Oral source
P	Police Department
PBH	*Poverty Bay Herald*
PBS	*Poverty Bay Standard*
PD	*New Zealand Parliamentary Debates*
QEIIAM	Queen Elizabeth II Army Museum, Waiouru
RM	Resident magistrate
WC	*Wanganui Chronicle*
WI	*Wellington Independent*
WT	*Waikato Times*

MEASUREMENTS

As imperial measures were used in the 19th century, these have generally been retained. For those for whom these scales of measurement have no meaning, metric conversions are listed below.

Linear measure

1 inch	= 25.4 millimetres
1 foot = 12 inches	= 0.3048 metre
1 yard = 3 feet	= 0.9144 metre
1 mile = 1760 yards	= 1.609 kilometres

Square measure
1 acre = 4840 square yards = 0.405 hectare

Weight

1 pound	= 0.4536 kilogram
1 ton	= 1.016 tonnes

INTRODUCTION

This account is an interpretative biography of the founder of the Maori faith known today as the Ringatu, or the Upraised Hand. It is the oldest of the surviving, indigenous, scripturally based religions in Aotearoa, the means by which Maori analysed their colonial situation in the 19th century. The original name of the faith was Te Wairua Tapu, the Holy Spirit.[1] It was born out of a time of conflict between Maori and Pakeha, but it also evolved extensively during the lifetime of its founder, Te Kooti Arikirangi Te Turuki. Today there are three main branches, each with a separate constitution and name. One has taken the founder's name, Te Haahi o Te Kooti Rikirangi; and one retains the older name, Te Haahi o Te Wairua Tapu. The earliest registered church (1929) is Te Haahi Ringatu. These divisions indicate that different interpretations of the religious teachings have evolved. They indicate too that rivalries of mana (leadership and authority) grew after the death of Te Kooti in 1893. There can be no single truth about such a man; and this book contains many histories.

This is not a history of the faith. I have written a biography, but it is not conceived as though there is a single understanding of its subject and his significance. Te Kooti is a figure in Maori 19th-century history around whom conflicting traditions have developed. These conflicts operate at several levels, and they also infuse the different sources upon which the historian must draw. There have been quite different 'received truths' co-existing in the community at large. There is one body of thought, shared by an increasing number of both Maori and Pakeha, that Te Kooti was a martyr, unjustly imprisoned by a colonial system which brought war to Maori tribes in order to dispossess them. There is another quite different view, extensive until very recent times, that he was the most ruthless of Maori leaders. This view was shared by many Pakeha of his time (but not by all who knew him) and also by some of the Maori leaders and hapu who fought against him. Te Kooti is also for many, including descendants of Maori who opposed him during the wars, the centre of a living religious tradition which still identifies him with Moses, as leader of the Maori people in their time of captivity and 'exile'. His predictions for their ultimate deliverance explain and shape events in the present day. He is also understood to stand in the long line of Maori leaders who spoke for the mana motuhake, the independent and continuing authority of Maori in their own land.

His own history has been, and still is, told in different forms. In the Maori oral traditions, there are narratives whose purpose is to confirm the religious truths and the beliefs the narrators maintain about Te Kooti's role as their prophet. Even their earliest stories about him as a rebellious and troublesome young man serve, purposively, to show the importance of God's intervention in his life. These stories are not neutral. They belong to the parable tradition of the scriptures, which reinforced the traditions from the Maori oral world, where stories are narrated — and recast down the generations — for a purpose. The stories are told and retold so as to reveal their meaning for the present time, and we can recognise the human truth they contain, even if the stories themselves may be 'historically untrue'. There are many oral narratives belonging to different kin-groups. If the main battle in the history of any colonised people is over their lands, the historical narratives which the people retain locally are all concerned with the means of holding, or recovering and protecting, the land. Almost all the Maori stories that are still told of Te Kooti place him as the guardian of the land, and of the people's autonomy.

In addition to these oral narratives, there are numerous written sources deriving from the faith itself. Te Kooti kept his own notebooks of his religious visions and his early kupu whakaari, the predictions and promises of God to him, standing in the line from Adam, Abraham, Moses, David and Christ. He believed that God had visited him with the promise that he would redeem his people 'from bondage & oppression'.[2] Two diaries, written in his own hand, have survived (and there were others, which may still exist). In addition, during the course of research over 60 letters written by Te Kooti have been uncovered. Most of these have never been seen or cited previously by any historian, Maori or Pakeha. They form only a tithe of what once existed, for Te Kooti had a profound belief in the written word. There are also over 90 songs composed or adapted by Te Kooti, or in some cases by people closely associated with him, which also consciously tell aspects of this history and which were written down on Te Kooti's instructions. They were recorded by one of his three secretaries, Hamiora Aparoa, and a manuscript book of the waiata, written in Hamiora's beautiful copperplate script, has survived. From internal evidence it appears to have been compiled (or completed) about 1907, although this manuscript does not include the last songs composed by Te Kooti during 1890–93.[3] These additional waiata — some 20 song texts — exist in transcript copies held by the Haahi Ringatu. I was generously given access to them. Almost none of this material has ever been looked at historically.

As well as these original sources, there are the texts of the Ringatu faith: not simply the prayers (inoi), hymns (himene), and the panui (scriptural texts), but the predictions, the sayings in glossolalia, and the records of the Ra (the particular sacred days) and of the places where these were held. Te Kooti's decision to keep records in writing was deliberate. He had three secretaries, often called the three 'cornerstones': Hamiora, Petera Te Rangihiroa (Petera Tawhana) and Matiu Paeroa. Petera had been a prisoner with Te Kooti on Wharekauri (Chatham Island); Matiu and Hamiora both belonged to the Ngati Porou communities of exiles, who gathered at Mataora and Wharekawa on the east coast of the Coromandel peninsula in the late 1860s, and who gave vital support to Te Kooti during the wars and afterwards. Both Hamiora and Matiu lived with Te Kooti after

1872, in the years of his 'second exile' in the King Country, the Rohe Potae of Ngati Maniapoto. Matiu was the recorder of the religious sayings, while Hamiora was more the 'minute secretary', keeping notes of speeches in a Maori shorthand and writing them up in full thereafter.[4] Records deriving from both men have survived, together with some transcripts of material attributed to Petera.

Matiu's original book of sayings and predictions exists in a transcript copy made in 1930 at Wharekawa. The book begins with the date 11 April 1885 and states that, 'On this day we have committed to writing the sayings contained in this book, as a source for study and contemplation' ('Ko te ra tenei i tuhia ai enei korero ki roto ki tenei pukapuka mau ai, hei titiro hei whakamahara hoki').[5] All the original manuscript books kept by Hamiora Aparoa were destroyed on Te Kooti's orders. This was done, it is recalled, because of a hara (sin) of violence which Hamiora committed when he struck his own wife in a quarrel. After Te Kooti's death, however, Hamiora rewrote the books from memory.[6] Some of these manuscripts have survived with the Haahi Ringatu at Te Wainui in the Bay of Plenty; others have been scattered among different families. Hamiora's records also form part of a great compilation of texts made in 1927 from the three secretaries' books, as well as other sources, by Rapata Peene (Robert Biddle), the secretary of the Haahi Ringatu. There are also other books of kupu whakaari, compiled and copied by different tohunga within the Ringatu faith, which contain many of the same texts or, in some instances, variant texts and different versions. All these books record the predictions and sayings of Te Kooti, along with a wealth of other material. Much of this material is, of course, intrinsically difficult and deceptive, for many of the recorded statements are intentionally opaque. As the Ringatu elder Wiremu Tarei stated in 1974, referring to the book of prophecies which he held in trusteeship, 'I still can't translate them properly even if I spent all week!'[7] For the historian seeking clarifications of the past from these sources, there are many difficulties.

Set against this huge body of Ringatu material, all of which has its own purposes and concerns, there are other kinds of sources. One vast grouping of manuscripts is the official and unofficial records of the military phase of Te Kooti's life, some of which were published by the government in the annual *Appendices to the Journals of the House of Representatives*. The thrust of this material is, of course, quite different. When it has been used by historians previously (and much of it has not), it has been largely to depict a 'Boys' Own' adventure story account of the wars, with predictable colonial heroes. Unquestionably the worst example is the only previous full-length biography of Te Kooti, published by W. Hugh Ross in 1966. The opening sentence labels Te Kooti as the 'arch-rebel' who plunged the centre of the North Island into a 'blood-bath'.[8] Hidden within the colonial military material is, in fact, a wealth of information which can contribute towards another understanding entirely — that is, the internal logic of the wars Te Kooti fought, the alliances he forged, and the enemies he made. It also contains explanations for much of the last part of Te Kooti's life, when he sought reconciliation with both the past and his former enemies.

There are settler traditions, songs and fantasies as well. Te Kooti became a figure in the European popular imagination, generating both fear and admiration, not always in equal proportions. His extensive journeys, undertaken after his pardon in 1883, took him to many parts of the North Island. Family stories were told of the occasions when 'grandma' met the 'old villain', but Te Kooti appears in many guises in the European stories, just as he does in the Maori narratives. He is certainly paraded in stereotype portrayal as a 'drunken ruffian', and he was used as the 'bogeyman' to frighten small children in Poverty Bay in the later 19th century,[9] but at other times he is remembered as a very intelligent and abstemious leader. He was most often seen as a threat to peace and Maori 'progress'. But at least one of his former wartime antagonists, Gilbert Mair, writing in 1884, saw him as 'a wonderful man [who] still exercises great influence over his large following'.[10] Te Kooti's lawyer, William Napier, placed such high personal value on the two greenstone mere which Te Kooti gave him that he itemised them in his will in 1925 and bequeathed them to one of his sons.[11] Others who had known Te Kooti during the wars, such as Gilbert Mair's brother William, never forgot their hostility. In 1889, when Colonel Thomas Porter finally arrested Te Kooti, Porter boasted that Te Kooti had predicted to his followers, '"When Porter and I meet face to face my end is near." (Ka mate ahau)'.[12] Porter had to wait a few years for his satisfaction. His biography of Te Kooti, which he published in serialised form in 1914, consolidated many of the stereotypes of Te Kooti by its use of phrases like 'rebel prophet' and founder of a 'fanatic war cult'. Nevertheless, Porter's narrative contains some genuine insights, and even in 1889 he was critical of those who tried to strip Te Kooti of all dignity. Porter's close association with Maori, particularly the leading tohunga of the Ringatu faith, Eria Raukura, also gave his published account a breadth of understanding that few other Pakeha written sources reveal.[13] Eighty years later, largely because of Eria's involvement, it stands as one of the better published sources about Te Kooti.

Te Kooti Arikirangi Te Turuki continues to live in oral narrative, and his influence is far from ended. In death as in life, multiple ambiguities surround him. The oral histories, and the understandings they carry, have engendered history in their turn, as they set — and may still set — further events in motion. Te Kooti's burial-place is unknown; it is claimed by several regions — itself a testimony to his importance to Maori groups. In one continuing oral tradition an essential task for his successor is to recover his bones. This tradition states that, with the fulfilment of this quest, the One foretold by Te Kooti to complete his work and redeem the people will then be revealed. Te Kooti also continues to live in many individual memories. To some he is a figure who generated profound loyalties and great empathies, yet to others, both Maori and Pakeha, he was a man without magnetism. These different histories cannot be reconciled, nor should their differences be smoothed away.

Nor can the various kinds of historical sources simply be interwoven. I have conceived of my task, as an historian, as being to juxtapose these different ways of recording and narrating history so that each retains its integrity, its purpose and its autonomy. In the process of writing, of course, manifest untruths and prejudices are not given any weight. The normal criteria for judging historical accuracy are not suspended — that is, that there are better versions, more careful transcripts, original diary entries and eye-witness descriptions, which must take precedence over reminiscence, speculation, ill-founded opinion and rumour. But there are also competing understandings. I have determined to let these different understandings remain, while giving the greatest emphasis to recovering previously ignored Maori interpretations of this part of their history. Their understandings are formed by a different past than that experienced by Pakeha families who have roots in the middle of the 19th century.

There has been a debate in New Zealand society about the writing of Maori history. As Angela Ballara commented thoughtfully in her recent essay, 'Pakeha uses of Taki-timutanga: who owns tribal tradition?', Maori objections to Pakeha dominance in historical writing have been intended not so much to claim an absolute ownership or monopoly over their history, nor to claim a right to censor (as is sometimes presumed), but rather to ensure that Maori understandings and values be given their full weight.[14] The debate is about the narrating of history in ways which are meaningful to Maori. For while written historical accounts can usually inform, misconceived assumptions about who possesses 'the truth' and what are the appropriate ways of assessing, analysing and judging have been set up and perpetuated with the pre-eminence of European historical writers. The debate about 'who' should write 'what' history, however, can never rest on grounds of religion, race or gender. Any prescriptions couched in such terms, being openly deterministic, are ill-considered. Such views are prescriptive of learning and imagination; on the one hand they tie us within patterns of polemical thought and, on the other, make us prisoners of personal experience alone. They also deny the important fact that the historian must aspire to be independent, otherwise written history becomes merely a series of self-referential statements.

The debate must be about the ability to understand the issues involved, and the strength of the ideas developed in the writing. Every historian brings individual perceptions and judgments to bear, including their selection of what is important from that myriad of data which is the past. The act of writing history can be conceived as an encounter between the multifaceted human past and the individual who is constructing the present narrative. This construction of history as literature, however, is very different from self-representation by the participants. The act of historical reconstruction allows different voices to speak; it reveals people in their own times and contexts, which are not our own and should not be seen to be like our own. The question which can be legitimately asked of any such work of historical reconstruction is whether its perceptions and procedures are of value to an audience whose own experiences and cultural understandings will themselves be diverse. But no one owns the past; no one owns that complexity of shared experiences and human and cultural exchange. The past is inhabited by all our ancestors. In 19th-century Aotearoa our ancestors are entwined. The representations of this past must attempt to uncover their values and tropes, the cultural referentials by which they variously acted. They may sometimes be very different, but at times they are also very similar.

If we who live in the present in Aotearoa can discuss our shared history in the 19th and 20th centuries, then we may gain from that past. If we cannot do this, then we will have learnt nothing from the past and we will have exchanged nothing between each other. In the representations of the past in the late 20th century the dialogue must be between each other: that is, it must transcend both self-representation and those European notions of claiming uniquely to possess the historical language which establishes an analytical truth. It must be a discussion which offers intellectual benefits to both Maori and European. As the Ringatu elder Reuben Riki said, the sharing of his knowledge had to have purpose 'for me and my next of kin to come'.[15]

Te Kooti emerged from the shadows as a leader not because of his rank or lineage but as a result of the experiences he underwent as a man born in a land which was being colonised by another people. His life spanned both the world of war, where he sought to hold the land and the mana Maori, and a pact of peace, made with the government in 1883. His vision was essentially religious, for he strove to direct the energies of Maori within a framework of thought which applied the scriptural teachings to their particular situation. This was the language of analysis he acquired from his times. His messages were couched in the prophetic terms of the bible and he used the catechetical method of asking unexpected questions, thereby teaching people to see, judge and act. Similarly, he drew on the Maori oral world, whereby knowledge from the past is conceived as lying before one and encompassing one, helping to shape decisions and actions in the present. This ever-broadening past threads back to the ancestors but it is also reinterpreted for the present. Te Kooti fought a long guerrilla campaign with strategic brilliance, but he was never overtly a political leader. He came into sharp conflict with many of the dominant Maori figures, as well as rival Maori prophets, throughout his life. Like all prophet–leaders he was a man of friction. His goal was the collective redemption of the people and the recovery of their land into their own hands. His belief was that God had made a promise not to forget those who were lost and whose land had been taken. Te Kooti sought to direct all his followers' actions in this world towards the fulfilment of this vision.

As a Maori leader he was not a tribal figure. Te Kooti saw himself as one who had been rejected in his homelands, by Maori as well as by Pakeha. He lived always in exile. He was protected by many and claimed by many; but in reality he belonged to no one. His relationship with Tuhoe, who gave him shelter in his time of great need and who mostly became his converts, was profound, but he also chose not to live with them, despite their wishes. Probably above all other 19th-century Maori leaders, Te Kooti transcends any tribal claims.

In writing this biography I have been helped and guided by several of the senior Ringatu elders. They felt that it was critical to differentiate between the man and his life, and the faith he founded. As the tohunga and secretary of the Haahi Ringatu, Robert (Boy) Biddle of Kutarere, put it, it is 'important to avoid making the man into a demi-god' and to avoid venerating him, rather than what he created, 'otherwise it gets cloudy'.[16] It is, as Biddle also said, important to test later views and opinions against the evidence of the times and from clearly stated sources. He spoke critically about 'the conglomerations' which have come through as sources in his own world, texts and sayings which have been melded together for a particular purpose and infused with preconceived ideas as to what they should mean.[17] He warned that a biography might be challenged, partly because of the different understandings and interpretations of Te Kooti's words within the various segments of the faith. This biography rests on the personal knowledge of elders from several sections of the faith, and their informed oral accounts, but it rests also on the contemporary historical data of the archival collections, texts written by many hands. In attempting this biography, I hope that it will reveal some of Te Kooti's many complexities and clarify the major issues of his time. I do not intend to close discussion; quite the reverse, I should like this biography to open dialogues and enable further understandings to come forth.

My debt for the knowledge and support from some of the senior elders within the Ringatu world is without end. What they retain is what they choose to retain; what they shared they chose to share as they themselves deemed appropriate. I wish particularly to thank Robert (Boy) Biddle, with whom I have had many long conversations over more than 12 years and who has ever patiently endured my questions. My gratitude to the late Monita Delamere of Whitianga and Opotiki is equally great; his support, generosity and breadth of vision were constant. Both made available to me written texts belonging to their fathers, respectively the secretary and the Poutikanga (Main Pillar) of the Haahi Ringatu. The late Wiremu Tarei of Te Teko also generously permitted me access to material from a different branch of the faith, Te Haahi o Te Kooti Rikirangi,[18] although his unexpected death curtailed our personal dialogue. This material was collated by the late Frank Davis and is now deposited, under controlled conditions of access, at the Alexander Turnbull Library in Wellington. The knowledge of these three Maori elders is unparalleled. Educated within the faith, they also belong to the last of the generation whose grandparents knew Te Kooti.

There are also many others to be thanked. First and foremost, Tihei Algie, who as the senior great-granddaughter of Te Kooti is the head of his whanau. Her biography appeared in an earlier book, *Ngā Mōrehu: The Survivors*, which I published with Gillian Chaplin in 1986 (revised in 1990). We initially went to visit Tihei with the view of writing the life of her ancestor, and our friendship grew from that first encounter. Others from Gisborne and neighbouring areas also gave advice and support, in particular the late Ned and Heni Brown of Whatatutu, who made available to me the manuscript book of the Ringatu tohunga Tawehi Wilson. Tupae (John) Ruru, the leading elder within Te Haahi o Te Wairua Tapu, and Reuben Riki, the former assistant secretary of this branch of the faith, also generously shared with me some of their extensive knowledge.

There are others to be remembered or thanked for their advice and their knowledge. In many instances my debts to them will be seen in the citations in the book, but here I would like particularly to acknowledge: Tairongo Amoamo, Te Riaki Amoamo, Tiwai Amoamo, Pat Aramoana, Angela Ballara, James Belich, Bruce Biggs, George Brown, John Bryce, Arnold Butterworth, David Collier, Caroline Daley, Frank Davis, Ken Gartner, Paul Goldsmith, Gil Hanly, Russell Hargreaves, Paki Harrison, Layne Harvey, Dick Hauraki, Laura Hiku (Taupeki), Charlotte Hitaua, David Holmes, Bill Hook, Tawhaki Horomona, Horopapera Tatu, Kino Hughes, Kanea Huitoroa, John and Waipiro Ihe, Witi Ihimaera, Rutene Irwin, Kevin Jones, Te Maaka Jones (Delamere), Moana Jones (Pouaka), Himiona Kahika, Te Huinga (Jack) Karauna, Faith Keenan, Pare Keiha, Michael King, Mac Kurei, Paroa (Jack) Kurei, Emma Lemuel Te Urupu, Irene Lister, Taua McLean, Eruera Manuera, Buddy Mikaere, Paetawa Miki, Wharehuia Milroy, David Napier, Roger Neich, W. H. Oliver, Putiputi and Tumeke (Mac) Onekawa, Claudia Orange, Patrick Parsons, Merimeri Penfold, Norman Perry, Erina (Lena) Pohatu, Chris Pugsley, Ema Rogers (Delamere), Heta and Te Paea Rua, Hillman

Rua, Mau and Miria Rua, Te Akakura Rua, Terepu (Jack) Ruru, Anne Salmond, Maurice Shadbolt, D. R. Simmons, Don and Margaret Sinclair, Jeffrey Sissons, Pat Smith, Takerangi Smith, Kendrick Smithyman, Keith Sorrenson, Don Stafford, C. K. Stead, John Sullivan, Heni Sunderland, Nan Symons, Awhina Tamarapa, Niko Tangaroa, Joe Te Maipi, Heneriata (Nellie) Te Moananui, Ultima Te-Urupu, C. G. Thomas, Rose Thompson, Tuaru (Henare) Tuwhangai, Anton v'd Wouden, Ranginui Walker, Alan Ward, Kati Wharepapa, Amelia Williams, Haare Williams, John and Rose Williams, and Heni Wiremu. There are also special debts: to Gillian Chaplin, who travelled with me much of the way (in many senses), and without whom the book could never have been started. Dave White was, as ever, a tower of strength; so too were Margaret Rapana and Michael Neill. Judith and Michael Bassett made it possible for me to go to Wharekauri. Ruth Harley and Michael Volkerling again put up with me and my obsessions with sustaining enthusiasm. There are many others, too, with whom I have talked or from whom I have sought information or guidance, too numerous to be included, and I hope they will accept this acknowledgment of my appreciation to them.

I have drawn extensively on the Army Department records for the war period (1865–72). I have consistently used the original manuscripts at National Archives in Wellington instead of the versions of the reports and letters which were sometimes published contemporaneously in the *Appendices to the Journals of the House of Representatives*. I have, however, indicated in the notes where the published version may be found (if I have traced it), because that will generally be more accessible to readers. The main issue is not censorship but inaccurate transcriptions, particularly of Maori names. The published texts are also only a fraction of what exists.

There will inevitably be some mistakes in this book, given the extent and complexity of the task undertaken: even a 'thrice-told tale' is not free from imperfections, as all story-tellers know. Te Kooti's life touched those of many people living in different parts of this land. I have had to enter into complex tribal histories, and it is not possible for anyone to be familiar with them all. I have had to seek to establish identification for people about whom nothing has been written. I have had to make some deductions based on logic, without firm confirmation. A crucial example is the case of Te Paea Tiaho, sister of King Tawhiao, who I have deduced was the woman Te Paea Iho sent by the Kingitanga to weave a peace between Ngati Kahungunu of Wairoa and Tuhoe in 1870. Nothing in Te Paea's entry in the *Dictionary of New Zealand Biography*, Volume II (1993) touches on this sequence of negotiations, nor does any historian of the wars mention her intervention. Nothing seems to be known about her two husbands, who were also involved, and the *Dictionary* was unable to get help from her kin when compiling her life. These are the sorts of problems encountered when attempting to reconstruct the Maori world historically. In the 19th century (and indeed later) Maori people often changed their names to record important events or to remember others who had died by adopting their names, and it is not always possible to be attuned to these changes. Personal names were also frequently abridged. One writer cannot seek out all the appropriate elders and families who may well hold family knowledge and who will be the only source for this kind of information and confirmation. I therefore ask Maori readers to have tolerance — 'hei ko te ngawari' in the words of the ancestor — and to let me know of any errors they find, so that these can be corrected. Other writers will come after me, too, building on, adding to and changing some of the material here. They will use new sources, and they will have different insights and different perceptions. That is the nature of history, whether written or oral.

The quotations from the Maori manuscript sources are cited, following usual historical practice, as they are found in the original. I am particularly indebted to Jane McRae and Peti (Betty) Woodard of the Maori Studies Department, University of Auckland, who put much thought, time and skill into translating the Maori texts. Peti translated the waiata, other than those for which I had a working translation from Frank Davis's research dossier. Jane translated every prose text cited here, except where it is specifically stated otherwise. Where contemporary translations do exist I have retained them; they are indicated by 'CT' in the notes. I decided to do so in order to indicate what European recipients of letters understood at the time, but where there were errors or serious distortions of sense the necessary corrections have been made, on Jane's advice. Where a change from the original has been made it is indicated in the notes. We decided to standardise word and particle breaks in order to render the 19th-century Maori texts understandable for modern readers, who might otherwise find them confusing. Again, I am greatly indebted to Jane, who took the difficult decisions. The long vowel marker has not been inserted in quotations, which remain in this respect as they are in the original, however erratic the marking. Some minimal punctuation markers, however, have been added to indicate the decisions taken in dividing phrases and sentences. The capitalisation of proper names and place names has also generally been standardised, although some names have been left when it seemed more important to retain their original form. On the rare occasions where the double vowel was systematically adopted (in recent published texts), it has been standardised to the macron. In quotations from oral interviews the long vowel is marked by the macron.

In 1985 I was awarded the John David Stout Research Fellowship in Wellington, which allowed me to commence the archival research for this book (and to complete *Ngā Mōrehu*). Subsequently, in 1991, a research grant from the Foundation for Research, Science and Technology enabled me to take a year away from teaching at the University of Auckland in order to complete the research for and to begin writing this book. Without this support the task would have been impossible; that statement itself indicates my gratitude to both institutions. The book took three further years in the writing. Throughout the entire project, I have had assistance from the University of Auckland. A book of this nature, with its large photographic, travel and translation costs, is more than any individual can carry, and university research grants have covered a substantial portion of these. The remaining costs in all these areas I have borne myself. There are, of course, places I had hoped to see and people with whom I had hoped to talk, but there comes a time when one has to say — enough. I would here like to thank my colleagues in the history department at the university who have had to put up with some of my oddities during the long processes of research and writing. I would also like to thank the secretarial staff of the department, who have helped in many ways, both directly and indirectly (although word-processors have shifted the role of typist back to the author). I would also like to acknowledge the assistance of librarians, archivists and curators in many different repositories, without whose skills this book would have been the poorer. As in almost all public educational institutions today, they are vastly overworked but have remained consistently helpful. I would like here to mention particularly John Laurie of Auckland University Library, Peter Hughes, Gordon Maitland, Mick Pendergrast and Rose Young of Auckland Institute and Museum, David Colquhoun and Philip Rainer of the Alexander Turnbull Library, Ruth Robinson and Jeremy Cauchi of National Archives, Wellington, Stuart Park of the Museum of New Zealand, S. M. Patterson of Queen Elizabeth II Army Memorial Museum, Joy Axford of Hawke's Bay Museum, Sheila Robinson and Robert de Z. Hall of Gisborne Museum, Jinty Rorke of Tauranga Public Library, Cath Bidwell of Canterbury Public Library, and Jo-Ann Smith of Canterbury Museum, all of whose initiatives helped to uncover material. I am grateful also to the cartographers Barry Bradley, Philip Carthew, Tony Fraser and John Williams of the New Zealand Historical Atlas project for drawing the maps, and to the Atlas editor Malcolm McKinnon for advice on their design and for permission to use and adapt Map 4, created originally for the Historical Atlas. Simon Cauchi undertook the daunting task of compiling the index. Finally, I would like to express my gratitude to Bridget Williams and Andrew Mason, who have given support, advice and encouragement throughout, ensuring that the original vision was able to be achieved.

Judith Binney,
January 1995

CHAPTER 1

THE SHADOW OF PREDICTION

Te Kooti Arikirangi Te Turuki was born under the shadow of prediction which set him apart from all other men. The words that foresaw his birth were ominous, associating him with darkness and the coming of strangers to the land:

> Tiwha tiwha te pō.
> Ko te Pakerewhā
> Ko Arikirangi tenei ra te haere nei.

> Dark, dark is the night.
> There is the Pakerewhā
> There is Arikirangi to come.

This song is the first recorded in Te Kooti's book of waiata, written out in the clear hand of his secretary, Hamiora Aparoa.[1] The song was composed by the matakite (visionary) Toiroa Ikariki (Ikarihi) of Nukutaurua on the Mahia peninsula; it was 'for his grandchild' ('mo tana mokopuna'), Arikirangi, and it is dated 1766 in the manuscript book. In the oral narratives it is remembered how the spirit of prophecy entered Toiroa that day: his back arched and the fingers of his raised hands splayed out as he became a lizard (papateretere). The lizard is a bearer of both life and death in the Maori cosmogony; it is a sign of belonging to the spirit world and used as such in ancestral carvings. As Toiroa spoke he made a lizard's quick darting movements. And thus it is also said of Te Kooti himself that, when he spoke, he was 'like a lizard'.[2]

In the traditions of the East Coast, Toiroa is remembered as having foreseen the coming of the strangers, with their red or white skin, like the earthworm, titipa.[3] Toiroa named these people 'Pakerewhā', possibly alluding to 'rewha', disease, which they brought. He drew images of them in the sand, with their ships and carts and horses, although he did not know these names, and he wove items of their clothing out of flax. He made a little basket and when it was finished he put it on his head and called it a taupopoki (hat). He slit a cloak and turned it into trousers (pukoro) which he wore. He made a strange article of stone, its stem a branch of the kokomuka shrub, and puffed smoke from a dried pohata leaf through it. He named it 'he ngongo' (a pipe). He made a wooden sailing boat, with a rudder. Then he took a small black mussel shell (hanca) and set a fire burning within it. It was the funnel for the steamer, which he called, wryly, 'ngatoroirangi' ('the fires of heaven'), after the ancestor and seer from whom he directly traced his descent, Nga Toro i Rangi, the great tohunga of the Arawa canoe. It was Nga Toro i Rangi who had called up the fires of Tongariro. All these tokens of a changing world Toiroa transported to the nearby villages, including those of Turanganui-a-Kiwa — where James Cook would soon make his first landfall, and where Te Kooti would later be born.

In one version of Toiroa's narrative, written down about 1931 by Paora Delamere, the Poutikanga (Main Pillar) of the Ringatu church founded by Te Kooti, it is said that after Toiroa had rested at Turanganui he spoke again with a new vision. This concerned two children who would be born to two cousins ('he turanga whanau raua') within Ngati Maru, a large hapu of the Rongowhakaata people living there. After their birth, strangers would arrive bringing their new god:

> Te ingoa o to ratou Atua, ko Tama-i-rorokutia, he Atua pai, otira, ka ngaro ano te tangata.

> The name of their God will be Tama-i-rorokutia (Son-who-was-killed), a good God, however the people will still be oppressed.[4]

At the end of his speech, Toiroa sang the first waiata of Arikirangi.

In the Ringatu manuscripts collated from 1927 by Robert Biddle senior (the secretary of the church) from the originals kept by Te Kooti's three secretaries, there is another version of Toiroa's narrative. Here, the text specifically says:

> 'Na ko ahau (Te Kooti) te kai whakaatu i matakitetia mai ai e ia, a ki te whanau ahau ka tae mai he iwi hou ki tenei motu. He Atua ano to ratau, ara ko Tama-i-rorokutia he Atua pai otira ka ngaro te tangata.'

> 'Now I (Te Kooti) was the one to reveal what he [Toiroa] prophesied, that when I was born a new people would come to this land. They would have another God, that is Tama-i-rorokutia, a good God, however the people would be oppressed.'[5]

This quotation is annotated as having been directly taken from Te Kooti: 'T.K.' It must have been derived from a written manuscript, for chapter references are also given. This manuscript was clearly known to Paora Delamere, for some key phrases and statements in his extended history are worded identically, confirming the existence of an original text. Te Kooti explained that Toiroa lived at Nukutaurua, and was a 'matakite' as well as an ancestor of his ('He tipuna ano nooku'). Nukutaurua is famous in the history of the East Coast peoples, for it was the final landing-place of the Takitimu canoe, as well as the site of an early whare wananga (school of learning) associated with that canoe, from which both the Rongowhakaata and Kahungunu tribes trace their descent. Te Kooti's lineage from the two eponymous ancestors Kahungunu and Rongowhakaata is shown in Whakapapa A (page 14). Nukutaurua is overlooked and protected by the famous pa Maunga-a-Kahia, and the story of its defence by Kahungunu explains as well the origins of Te Aitanga-a-Mahaki, the descendants of Mahaki, the grandchild of Kahungunu and the ancestor with whom Te Kooti would later compare himself.

This passage in the manuscripts shows that the entire body of tradition concerning Toiroa, which is seminal to the Ringatu faith, derives directly from Te Kooti. It was his narrative in origin; it is his tradition. This is not to say it was a fiction. Toiroa was widely known as a visionary and as one associated with the hope of establishing a lasting peace in the land. Another pupil of Toiroa, Hamiora Mangakahia, who was the first Premier of the Kotahitanga Maori Parliament in 1892, also considered that he had been chosen to fulfil Toiroa's quest for peace, which Toiroa had called for in 1858. Hamiora quoted a prediction of Toiroa that it would be 'the distant descendant' ('te Miha') who would, one day, bring about this peace.[6] In this manner, the lines of authority descending from Toiroa's mana were similarly woven into the Kotahitanga movement and its search for Maori political autonomy.

Te Kooti's quoted text is quite brief and lacks many of the details of Delamere's longer narrative, although most of the main elements are contained there. In Paora Delamere's narrative, Toiroa was asked by the people of Turanganui to explain the conduct of the two children. He answered that they would be conceived on the same day. But it might be that the child of the younger man, Te Turuki, kinsman to Te Kooti's father, would be born first. The inverse sequence of the births would itself be a premonition of disorder. For Toiroa said:

> Tena, ki te riro ko ta te teina ki mua whanau mai ai, hei muri ko ta te tuakana whanau ai, na, he iwi kino taua iwi hou, ina tae mai ki tenei Motu.

> But, if it happens that the [child] of the younger is born first, and that of the elder afterwards, then the newcomers will be an evil people, when they arrive in this Land.[7]

Another version of this narrative was told by Eria Raukura, who in 1866 had been a prisoner with Te Kooti on Chatham Island (known to Moriori as Rekohu and to Maori as Wharekauri). Eria later became the leading tohunga of the Ringatu church, and in his account three children are named: Te Huiakama, Te Whanau a Rerea and Rikirangi. In this narrative, the first two are associated with goodness and life (ora) for the people; but Rikirangi would be surrounded by evil and calamity.[8] In the telling and retelling of this persistent narrative (as with all oral traditions), some details become lost or, alternatively, are expanded. But the inner core — in this case, the warning of the times of trouble and the naming of the one child of trouble — has been retained.

In Paora Delamere's narrative there are only two children, who are both named: Te Huiakama and Arikirangi. They are predicted to grow and then suffer an illness which would cause them great pain. The inverse order of their births would determine their survival, for from this illness the first-born, of the younger line, Te Huiakama, child of Te Turuki, would not recover. Toiroa then sang a lament concerning the death of this child — and his throat was dry. Toiroa's lament (waiata apakura) is recorded by Delamere.[9] It is also recorded in the manuscript which quotes Te Kooti's narrative of these events.[10] It was similarly transcribed, apparently in association with the year 1866, into Hamiora's book.[11] 1866 could be said to be the year in which the evil that Toiroa had foreseen commenced, for it was the year when Te Kooti was arrested and sent into exile to Wharekauri, the beginning of the dark years of trouble and conflict.

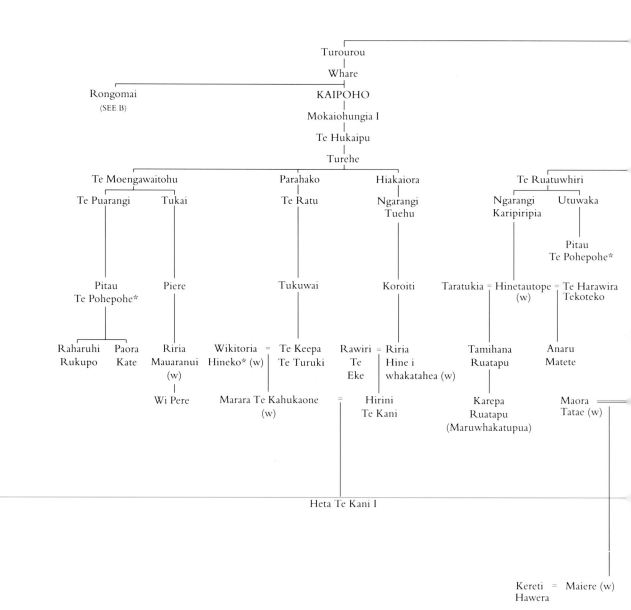

Turourou
|
Whare
|
Rongomai   KAIPOHO
(SEE B) |
       Mokaiohungia I
       |
       Te Hukaipu
       |
       Turehe

Te Moengawaitohu   Parahako   Hiakaiora   Te Ruatuwhiri

Te Puarangi   Tukai   Te Ratu   Ngarangi   Ngarangi   Utuwaka
                        Tuehu   Karipiripia

                                             Pitau
                                             Te Pohepohe*

Pitau   Piere   Tukuwai   Koroiti   Taratukia = Hinetautope = Te Harawira
Te Pohepohe*   (w)   Tekoteko

Raharuhi   Paora   Riria   Wikitoria = Te Keepa   Rawiri = Riria   Tamihana   Anaru
Rukupo   Kate   Mauaranui   Hineko* (w) | Te Turuki   Te   Hine i   Ruatapu   Matete
                   (w)   Eke   whakatahea (w)
                   |
                   Wi Pere   Marara Te Kahukaone   =   Hirini   Karepa   Maora
                                  (w)   Te Kani   Ruatapu   Tatae (w)
                                                            (Maruwhakatupua)

Heta Te Kani I

Kereti   =   Maiere (w)
Hawera

Whakapapa A

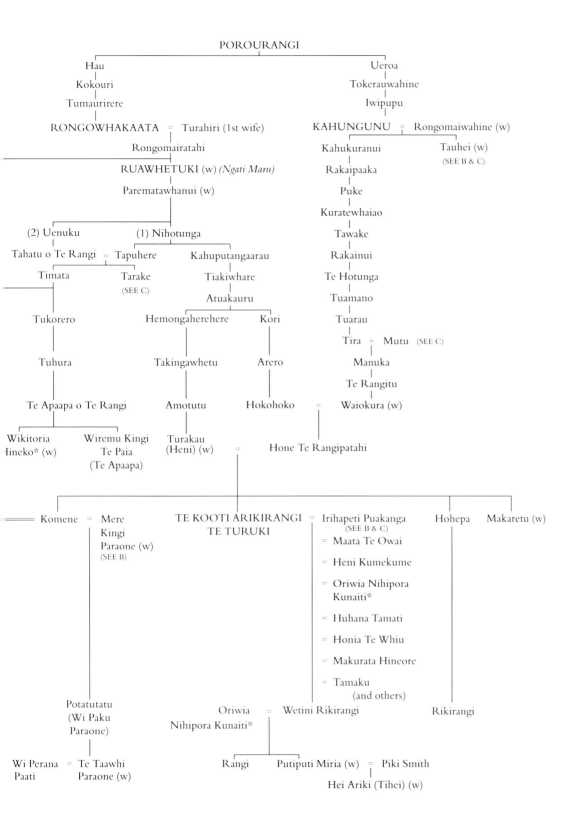

POROURANGI

Hau
Kokouri
Tumaurirere

RONGOWHAKAATA = Turahiri (1st wife)

Rongomairatahi

RUAWHETUKI (w) *(Ngati Maru)*

Parematawhanui (w)

(2) Uenuku   (1) Nihotunga

Tahatu o Te Rangi = Tapuhere   Kahuputangaarau

Timata   Tarake   Tiakiwhare
                (SEE C)

Tukorero   Atuakauru

Tuhura   Hemongaherehere   Kori

Te Apaapa o Te Rangi   Takingawhetu   Arero

Wikitoria   Wiremu Kingi   Amotutu   Hokohoko   =
Hineko* (w)   Te Paia
                     (Te Apaapa)   Turakau
                                          (Heni) (w)   =   Hone Te Rangipatahi

Ueroa
Tokerauwahine
Iwipupu

KAHUNGUNU = Rongomaiwahine (w)

Kahukuranui   Tauhei (w)
                     (SEE B & C)
Rakaipaaka

Puke

Kuratewhaiao

Tawake

Rakainui

Te Hotunga

Tuamano

Tuarau

Tira = Mutu   (SEE C)

Manuka

Te Rangitu

Waiokura (w)

═══ Komene = Mere   TE KOOTI ARIKIRANGI = Irihapeti Puakanga   Hohepa   Makaretu (w)
            Kingi   TE TURUKI   (SEE B & C)
            Paraone (w)   = Maata Te Owai
            (SEE B)
                                             = Heni Kumekume

                                             = Oriwia Nihipora
                                               Kunaiti*

                                             = Huhana Tamati

                                             = Honia Te Whiu

                                             = Makurata Hineore

                                             = Tamaku
                                               (and others)

Potatutatu   Oriwia   =   Wetini Rikirangi   Rikirangi
(Wi Paku   Nihipora Kunaiti*
Paraone)

Wi Perana = Te Taawhi   Rangi   Putiputi Miria (w) = Piki Smith
Paati   Paraone (w)
                                             Hei Ariki (Tihei) (w)

* Indicates person appears elsewhere on this whakapapa

Toiroa had also said:

> Na, te ritenga o tetahi o aua tamariki nei — mo te kino ano ki runga o tenei Motu. E
> kore te pai e roa e haere ana, kua timata te kino, no reira i huaina ai to tera ingoa ko
> Ariki-Rangi.

> Now the behaviour of one of those children will relate to the trouble in this Land. The
> time of prosperity will not last long before the trouble begins, hence that one is to be
> named Ariki-Rangi.[12]

In this tradition and in all its sources, the details are consciously structured into a
predictive pattern, in terms of both time and the sequence of events. Exactly 100 years
exist between the prophecy, its date ascribed as three years before Cook's landfall, and its
fulfilment in 1866. Te Kooti's birth date is stated by Delamere as being 1814. 1814 is the
year in which the new God was first brought to the land by the Anglican missionaries.
This event the Ringatu narrative tradition also remembers — as the coming of the God
Tama-i-rorokutia.[13] Te Kooti was born to the elder of two cousins, Te Rangipatahi, and
it was Toiroa who named him Arikirangi.

The tradition is structured, but its purpose is not undermined by those facts which
contradict it. Te Kooti Arikirangi was born at Te Pa-o-Kahu, a large Ngati Maru settlement on the seaward coast of the Awapuni lagoon, by the old mouth of the Waipaoa
river.[14] His actual date of birth is unknown, but it was probably in 1832. He gave his
age as 35 when he married on Wharekauri in July 1867, which suggests this year of
birth.[15] Edmund Tuke, formerly of the prison guard there, also estimated his age at
about 35 years when he was on the island,[16] and this was accepted at the time by other
Europeans who knew him, including Thomas Porter. However, the various physical
descriptions of him are often contradictory — like most aspects of his life.

Although it is certain that Te Kooti had no facial moko, he was often described as
bearing his name tattooed on his chest and arms — a common 19th-century practice for
Maori men and women. However, the accounts are somewhat confused as to the actual
names he had chosen to have inscribed. Tuke stated that he had 'Te Kooti Rikirangi' on
his left breast; Porter claimed at the time that this was wrong, although later he stated
that, in 1889, he saw the name 'Rikirangi' engraved in blue lines when Te Kooti dramatically exposed his chest to him at the time of his arrest.[17] Another later version, narrated
by an elderly Tuhoe man, is that the name 'Rikirangi' was 'graved in thin green scars' on
his breast.[18] In 1869 Porter wrote that those who knew Te Kooti from childhood had
said that he bore the name Te Kooti on the inside of his right arm below the elbow. This
would conform to a practice of the missionaries, who often lightly marked the forearm
of their converts with their new name. On the outside of Te Kooti's left arm, below the
elbow, Porter said he bore the name 'Ko Maieri'; Maiere was a family name.[19] The name
of his first wife, Irihapeti, appeared on his right arm.[20] In yet another account, from
Tawhai, who had fought alongside Te Kooti, he was described as having the name 'Te
Turuki', 'an old family name', branded on his right arm.[21]

Some, perhaps all, of these physical details will be correct. 'Te Kooti' is understood to
be his Christian baptismal name. The first known reference to him in European sources
is April 1852, when this name was used, indicating that he was already baptised.[22] By

Eria Raukura (Tutara-kauika), Ringatu tohunga, July 1913. He is wearing his own particular frockcoat, which was edged in gold braid. On the collar were the words 'Hahi Tapu', while the same words in English, 'Holy Church', appeared on the cuffs. Photograph probably by James McDonald.

C258, MONZ

his own account, given to the historian James Cowan in 1889, he took the name 'Coates' from official notices he had seen on a trading trip to Auckland.[23] The Reverend Thomas Grace, who taught Te Kooti at the Anglican mission at Whakato in Poverty Bay between 1850 and 1853, said that he had been named after the lay secretary of the Church Missionary Society, Dandeson Coates.[24] In early letters he simply signed his name 'Tekoti' or 'Tekooti'.

In 1867, when Te Kooti married his second wife, Maata Te Owai, in a civil wedding, he signed his full name on the certificate as 'Tekoti Rikirangi'.[25] He would also continue to use the name 'Rikirangi' in later correspondence. He himself never used the fuller form 'Arikirangi'; it was, however, used in Te Kooti's lifetime by his secretary, Hamiora Aparoa.[26] Te Kooti adopted his 'uncle's' name, Te Turuki, quite early. At first he used it in conjunction with Te Kooti, but increasingly he dropped his baptismal name except when writing to Pakeha. The first time he used Te Turuki in his correspondence was in December 1868; it seems that he took this name upon his return from exile. As well as being a name within his 'family', it was understood to convey a new spiritual growth and leadership.

In Paora Delamere's account, Te Turuki was the name of his father's younger kinsman.[27] It is possible that this man was Te Keepa Te Turuki, who signed the Treaty

Pa Tarata, settlement on the Waipaoa river, Turanga, in January 1838. This was the world into which Te Kooti was born. Pencil drawing by William Colenso.   HBM

of Waitangi at Turanganui (Poverty Bay) in 1840 as 'Te Turuki'.[28] He was kin to Te Kooti's father, as is shown in Whakapapa A and D (see pages 14 and 34).[29] Te Turuki, Te Kooti's kinsman in the narratives, appears in the events surrounding Te Kooti's rejection by his father; it was he who took the boy in when his father left him for dead.

These narratives are central to the predictive history of his life, beginning with Toiroa's visions. Delamere told the story of Hone Te Rangipatahi's attempt to kill his son many times. He taught it to the Maraenui schoolchildren, who sent their version to the magazine *Te Ao Hou* in November 1957.[30] Their story describes how Te Kooti was so troublesome that his father determined to get rid of him. He decided to dig a well at the pa (or, in other versions, a kumara pit). The site was near the fortifications of the pa, and the well was dug in the sand and boxed in with wood. Te Rangipatahi sent the boy down to dig and, when he thought he had enough kits of sand, he suddenly threw them at his son, knocking him down and burying him. But the wooden boxing protected the boy, and he found a way into an old trench that ran to the pa. He reached the house of his 'uncle' ('tana matua') and climbed up into the pataka. As he crouched hidden, he heard his father and uncle talking, his father telling lies as to his whereabouts. His uncle became certain that he had come to some harm, and began to lament for him.

> No tenei, katahi a te Kooti ka heke iho i te pataka awhihia ana e tana matua keke ano he tangata i hoki mai i te mate.

> At this, Te Kooti came down from the pataka, to be embraced by his uncle as one returned from the dead.[31]

In another version, written down by Delamere, there are many more significant details. In particular, Te Rangipatahi's younger brother or cousin, Te Turuki, is named. The text states clearly that he was 'the younger relation of his own Father, his very own, of Te Rangipatahi' ('ko te taina o tona ake Pāpā, tipu ake o Te Rangi-patahi'). The mischievousness of Arikirangi is both enjoyed and moralised on, particularly his rejection of the Anglican prayers and his constant thieving from Maori and Pakeha. The description of the well varies, the boy being saved here by the flat stones of the natural spring, but a central point is reiterated: that the boy escaped by his own ingenuity. Most important, the connection is made with the larger narrative of prediction: for when the news came to Toiroa of Te Rangipatahi's treachery, Toiroa already knew about his grandchild who had been buried alive. He went at once to Te Pa-o-Kahu. He wept over his grandchild, but said nothing about the burying.

> Na, i tetahi ra mai, ka Hāea (Tohi) e ia taana mokopuna [a] Ariki-rangi. Tona tikanga o tera mahi o te Hāea, he karakia na te Maori, hei mea kia mau ai nga korero, nga tikanga, me nga karakia a te tohunga i te tamaiti e akona ana.

> Then, one day he performed a Hāea (Tohi) ceremony over his grandchild Ariki-rangi. The function of that Hāea ceremony, a prayer-service of the Maori, was intended to fix in the young child under tuition the words, rites and prayers of the tohunga.[32]

It was also Toiroa who later dedicated Arikirangi to the god of war and humankind, Tu-matauenga, feeding him with a stone as food so that he would retain the knowledge. This detail was a conscious reference to the Maori rituals of learning in the whare wananga. The narrative states, 'Tū was the name of that Stone' ('Ko Tū te ingoa o taua Kohatu').[33] In these ways, Toiroa is stated to have performed both the naming and the dedication ceremony for the child. As the narrative continues it records that there were very many Maori prayers — and that they were not learnt by Toiroa's 'grandchild', Arikirangi. But the majority of the old man's talks, and some of his songs, he did retain. Thus, the narrative indicates that, while Te Kooti was taught much of the knowledge of the Maori world, his prayers would be the new prayers (inoi), prayers of the new God, who had yet to reveal himself directly to Te Kooti.

After these events, Te Kooti's behaviour became even stranger. His thieving increased and he seemed possessed, unable to control his body or to sit quietly. Then, the little bit of good that remained in his heart remembered something. He went to Nukutaurua to visit Toiroa. He asked Toiroa to drive out these works ('enei mahi') that he had taught him, which were 'evil' ('he kino'). But Toiroa refused. He told Te Kooti, however, that he would not die, as he had feared.

It was after Te Kooti's return from his visit to Nukutaurua, Paora Delamere relates, that Arikirangi entered the Anglican missionary church and was baptised as Te Kooti. But, before his baptism, he had returned to some of his old ways, particularly his thieving. He stole from both Pakeha settlers and his kinsmen at Turanganui. He also travelled, crewing on the schooner, the *Queen* (*Kuini*), which one day he found being repaired at his village. Maori-owned, it took cargoes of wheat and animals to Auckland. At this time, he married his first wife, Irihapeti, daughter of Te Waaka Puakanga of Te Whanau-a-Ruataupare, a hapu of Ngati Porou at Turanganui. According to this narrative, their union was a difficult one, for she was the widow of a kinsman and also a Roman Catholic believer. Consequently, they moved from the district, and under her influence Te Kooti entered into the Catholic church. Toiroa came to them. He told Te Kooti that, although he had been 'bewitched on account of her' ('te makututia koe mona'), he would find a new God and see him in person.

> A, ka korero mai ano ia ki a koe, penei me au e korero atu nei ki a koe.

> And he will speak to you, just as I am speaking to you now.[34]

But before entering into this purposeful account of Te Kooti's first religious visions, other sources must be juxtaposed to discover more about the young Te Kooti.

In 1889 Te Kooti told Cowan that he had, in the early days, the days of peace, crewed on various schooners. One vessel with which Te Kooti is associated in local tradition is the schooner *Henry*, which in the late 1850s and early 1860s sailed the coast between Turanga (later Gisborne), Wairoa and Napier until it was wrecked off Mahia peninsula in 1867. The Maori schooner the *Queen* (3500 tons) was also trading from 1854 until June 1866, when it was wrecked off Portland Island. It regularly brought mail and supplies for the European settlers at Turanga.[35] One of its chiefly owners in the early 1860s was another of Te Kooti's uncles, Te Warihi Potini,[36] whom he would later execute on the voyage of escape from Wharekauri. Te Kooti was also involved with Waaka Puakanga and one of the most senior chiefs of Rongowhakaata, Raharuhi Rukupo, in another Maori schooner, the *Adah*. This was badly damaged in an autumn gale in 1858, and by December they were all striving to pool their individual earnings from the Auckland trade to help pay the debt Rukupo still owed on the vessel.[37] Te Kooti also travelled to Auckland on the *Whetuki*, and said he was the supercargo, the man who attended to the business side of the vessel's voyage. The *Whetuki* (or, to give it its full name, *Ruawhetuki*) was named after the founding ancestress from whom Ngati Maru trace their line. It too was a Maori vessel, bringing cargoes back from Auckland for the community in competition with the major storekeeper and trader at Turanga, Captain George Read. Two other rival traders, settled even earlier than Read, John Harris and John Hervey, were particularly antagonistic towards Te Kooti, as their correspondence will show. Te Kooti's sailing skills would later be used on Wharekauri, where he was the steersman of the government whaleboat — and in planning and directing the prisoners' escape on the schooner *Rifleman*.

During visits to Auckland, Te Kooti at some time attended the Wesleyans' Native Institution at Three Kings, founded in 1844.[38] There he encountered the 'experimental religion', as it was called by its teachers. It was probably at this institution that he also acquired his ability to read English,[39] for the Wesleyans expressly made English a part of the curriculum because this was a school for potential leaders. Thus, by the early 1850s, Te Kooti had been in direct contact with the three major Christian sects in their competitive battle for Maori converts.

His own detailed mastery of the scriptures, both the Old Testament and the New, is unquestionable. It is evidenced in his diary, which dates from 1867.[40] At the Whakato Anglican mission at Turanga he was taught by Grace, as well as by Samuel Williams and the Reverend William Williams.[41] Through Grace in particular he was encouraged, as were all Grace's pupils, to develop the skills and knowledge for Maori economic self-sufficiency. Grace urged them to 'take the plough in their own hands', and to build and sail their own trading vessels to keep control of the prices they received for their goods. Grace thereby earned the hostility of the local settlers and traders, and also that of William Williams, who ensured his dismissal from Turanga in 1853 for too great an emphasis on 'worldly' matters. It was undoubtedly under Grace's influence that Te Kooti aspired to become a minister in the Anglican church. This move, popular European tradition recalls, Williams refused. According to Sarah Dunlop, who knew Te Kooti from her childhood and was sympathetic to him, even though he had been involved in the Anglican church for seven or eight years and was a lay preacher, Williams still threw him out after he attended church one Sunday, drunk.[42] Conversely, Grace had encouraged the young man and thought him one of his outstanding pupils. He took Te Kooti on his journey to Taupo to select the site of his new mission in December 1853,[43] and according to the family Te Kooti worked for a while as a shepherd for the missionary. Te Kooti remembered this early friendship when, in about 1883, he met Grace's son and commented that if he had encountered Grace during the wars he would never have harmed him.[44]

By early 1852 Te Kooti had become notorious to Harris as one of a group of young men living at Makaraka with the outspoken Rongowhakaata and Ngai Tawhiri chief Kahutia, who were causing trouble in the district. This 'trouble' involved protest over local land rights and was supported by Grace, who considered that both the government's and the settlers' overwhelming aim was 'to possess themselves of the land altogether regardless of the real interests of the natives'.[45] The group's notoriety took the form of charging for pasturage, or seizing horses and cattle that were being grazed without agreement on Maori land, and of levying anchorage dues in the river. The rangatahi, the young men of the district, took on the role of 'social bandits'[46] when they found no other effective means of redress against the squatters. The protest — and the tactics — was replicated in many parts of the colony. On 8 March 1852 a group of six, including Te Kooti, broke into the home of Thomas Norcross, a bullock driver at Makaraka, and stripped it: this was a taua muru (plunder party) in reprisal for a dispute over the ownership of a pig. Kahutia was also in confrontation with Read about the latter's occupation of some unsold land. It is significant that Kahutia was closely associated with the Roman Catholic faction at Turanga, for at this time Maori Catholic groupings often formed as conscious opposition to the established Protestant leaders. Kahutia defended the actions of the 'troublemakers' before a 'committee' or runanga called by the chief Rukupo, at Makaraka. Rukupo wrote:

> Ka korero ahau kia whakahokia mai nga taonga. Katahi a Kahutia ka whakatika mai ka korero kino kia patua nga pakeha.

> I said that the goods should be returned. Then Kahutia stood up and said rudely that the pakeha should be killed.[47]

Rukupo told Harris that the protests were part of a wider movement to recover occupied land and to set up a 'coalition' against the government. Messengers, he said, had been sent all along the coast. This was probably a reference to the early attempts to establish a Maori king, when Te Kani a Takirau, the paramount chief at Turanga and Uawa, was sought out (in vain) to undertake the task. Although Te Kani was not prepared to accept the idea of a Maori kingship, he was himself involved in serious dispute with the Anglican mission. The argument left their new church still unfinished at the end of 1852 and, for a while, all the roads to Turanga were rendered tapu on Te Kani's instructions.

These conflicts within the community did not cease. In July 1853 the government wrote, in response to continuing complaints, to Rukupo and to Anaru Matete, the emerging younger leader of Ngati Maru, and to other senior Turanga chiefs about their 'young men', who were 'in the habit of plundering' the houses and vessels of the settlers. The chiefs were urged to continue to work with the settlers through the runanga to settle these disputes.[48] But Te Kooti's pa — as the young men's settlement was apparently now being called — was attacked that year because he and those with whom he associated 'had become a terror to the district'.[49] The youthful chief Wi Pere, who was to maintain an ambivalent relationship with Te Kooti all his life, claimed to have led this assault by young warriors on young warriors. He said Te Kooti's faction were taking all the horses, pigs and cattle they could lay their hands on. They had made great hauls of grog from the Pakeha, and generally raided the district, taking in the young Maori women: 'Their only reply to the protests of angry husbands was to point to their loaded guns.' Te Kooti's pa by the river had become a place of sanctuary for young 'malcontents': those who had angered the runanga, the committee of senior chiefs.[50] The pa was taken in an attack by Te Aitanga-a-Mahaki, Wi Pere's tribe, and their prisoners were brought to Whakato and handed over to the Rongowhakaata chiefs. But Te Kooti escaped — his second daring escape. He swam across the river at the point where the Bridge Hotel now stands, and got away. However, his pigs and cattle were all sold off by the 'church committee', realising £1000 for the damage he had caused.[51] Expeditiously, Te Kooti went to visit Taupo with Grace, and he probably stayed away from the district for a time. This was a pattern of moving in and out of the area that he was beginning to develop, for he was back again, and again notorious, in 1858. The attention of the first resident magistrate, Herbert Wardell, was drawn that year to a group of young men known as 'Koti Rikirangi's party', who had a reputation for thieving and being 'great drinkers of grog'. The man who raised the objections, Petera, was trying to persuade his brother, who was living with the group, to sever his association with them.[52]

A further episode involving Te Kooti occurred later that year. The illicit sale of spirits to Maori was a major issue; Wardell and the senior chiefs were all trying to stop this spiralling trade. On 19 November Te Kooti purchased two cases of gin from the settler George Johnson. He bought them for a woman living at Patutahi and paid for them by taking wheat to Johnson. He was in trouble twice over, for not only was the trade in spirits illegal but selling to settlers was banned by the runanga, which was trying to stop the Europeans profiteering as middlemen in the Auckland trade. Te Kooti paid his fine to the runanga (a cow), while his older brother Komene, who had been with Te Kooti when they took out the load of wheat at night, was persuaded to lay a formal charge against Johnson. Johnson, enraged, threatened the magistrate, saying, '"I'll go and see Koti. I would a damd. sight rather give Five pounds to him than to the Queen any day."'[53] The bribe achieved its aim, as Wardell's diary makes clear:

Koti swore positively he had 'never had either a glass, a bottle or a case of Spirits from Johnson.' I believe a more deliberate case of perjury was never committed — he having said the case produced was one he got from Johnson & that it was sent from Patutahai [*sic*] as he received it full of goods, not Spirit.[54]

The illegal alcohol trade at Turanga was channelled through particular agents, as Wardell also noted: 'Johnson gave it to Koti — [George] Read to Rangiwh[a]itiri'.[55] However, the trade was controlled from October 1860, when the young chief of Rongowhakaata, Hirini Te Kani, who had himself acquired a reputation as a drinker, managed to achieve a collective tribal agreement with Read and thus to curb the sales. A marked improvement in the Maori community was observed from this time, and this change establishes a context for Te Kooti's reformation.

One other first-hand reference exists of Te Kooti's presence in Turanga in these early years. It comes from C. George Goldsmith, two of whose children were executed on Te Kooti's orders in 1868. Goldsmith affirmed (in 1889) that he had employed Te Kooti as a labourer at various times between 1855 and 1864, and on several occasions had caught him in the act of theft.[56] However, Louise Margaret U'ren of Makaraka remembered him differently. He had been employed as a youth by her grandmother, Margaret U'ren, to work on their farm, and they had included him in their family prayers. They taught him, she said, to read the bible.[57] Te Kooti was also recollected as having laboured near Napier, in charge of a group of men clearing the Turirau swamp by Puketapu hill. There is a strong tradition that he lived there and worked in this capacity for the early settler, John Heslop. Heslop and his sons migrated to New Zealand in 1857 and began clearing at Puketapu about 1860–61, although Heslop legally leased the land only in 1867. The tradition concerning Te Kooti in the Heslop family is connected (in the telling) to the period from 1860 to 1864, when the Puketapu school opened. The story was in circulation in the 1890s, published in 1908, and is still told among those who worked for the Heslops, who became one of the district's great runholding families in the later 19th century. In these accounts Te Kooti's name was 'Hiroki', which he continued to use when he sent messages to Heslop and his sons during the time they fought for the government. Hiroki could have been a name by which he was known before his missionary baptism, or it could have been one he had adopted, for it simply means 'lean' or 'thin'. In the earliest known version of this story he is said to have had this name marked on his left arm and a bracelet on the other.[58] Thus the different stories are woven and cannot always be unstitched. The persistence of this tradition is, however, marked.[59]

Popular European tradition in Gisborne also retains a number of narratives of Te Kooti's activities, in particular his dexterous thefts. After he was thrown out of the church by William Williams, he was, according to Sarah Dunlop, for a while very 'disagreeable', and always stealing rum. Goldsmith was undoubtedly a source of some of these stories, for a frequently told tale of this time is about the rum which regularly vanished from the hogshead casks kept at Goldsmith's store at Kairourou, Matawhero. Goldsmith stated in his affidavit for the Crown, submitted to the Court of Appeal against Te Kooti, that when Te Kooti had earlier worked for him, he was 'then addicted to drink' and was more than once caught in the act of thieving.[60] The oral versions remember how he was discovered hopping over the fence one night and his method of extracting the liquor was then revealed: a hollow stem of toetoe plugged into the bottom of the barrel to drain it through the floorboards of the store. In November 1868, this store would be destroyed and two of Goldsmith's children killed in the reprisals exacted by Te Kooti against those whom he saw as the cause of his forced exile in 1866. Hidden inside this 'popular' narrative, therefore, is a history of conflict between the early European trade monopolists and a man whose 'theft' was probably an act of reprisal against them, as he sought to keep economic control in the hands of the tribal communities. The stories have become 'entangled objects'[61] as different meanings are appropriated from them. The popular European tales about Te Kooti's notoriety are transformed in the predictive history of Te Kooti, as narrated by Paora Delamere. Conversely, the economic conflict between coloniser and colonised is obscured in the 'simple' stories of Te Kooti's dexterity, just as old nursery rhymes and fairy tales may hide, in the retelling, many harsh original experiences.

Other narratives recollect Te Kooti's philandering, and one version directly attributes his being named as disloyal in 1866 to revenge for his adultery with the wife of the chief Hamiora Whakataka (Kaiwhakataka). His outrageous behaviour as a tangata puremu (adulterous man) is recalled in the frequently told story of the occasion when he smuggled his willing lover out of the kainga where she was living, trussed up like a pig in a roll of canvas thrown across his saddle-bow. Again the narrative admires his dexterity — especially his role as a trickster — and it morally condemns him. This incident is told by Porter as being the trigger for the attack on Te Kooti's pa of 'malcontents' in 1853.[62] The story was widely known among Ngati Porou, who undoubtedly were Porter's informants, and it was recounted by Tuta Nihoniho as the underlying cause of the first accusations laid against Te Kooti to the government.[63]

In the Ringatu narratives there is a purpose to the stories about Te Kooti's riotous early life. They are intended to show the intervention, and ultimate power, of divine forces over the disorder in his life. Among the seminal narratives of Toiroa and Te Kooti, there is one concerning Te Kooti's visit to Nukutaurua when still a young man. Te Huitau Te Hau, a Ringatu elder, wrote down this story for Paora Delamere. It is still retained in the oral traditions of Nukutaurua, where it was related to the author by the Ngati Kahungunu elder, Bill Hook, in 1982. It also appears in the manuscript account directly attributed to Te Kooti and dated there as February 1865.[64] Two versions (Te Huitau Te Hau and Bill Hook) record how Toiroa commanded Te Kooti to visit him, when the young man was not yet 'possessed of the spirit' — that is, when he was still turbulent and difficult. Toiroa then predicted to Te Kooti that he would see him coming from Turanga, weeping, and disappearing on a raupo raft beyond Papahuakina (Table Cape). But soon he would return, bearing the prayers of the faith with his hand up-raised. Thus, in this narrative, Toiroa foresaw the coming of the new faith, the Ringatu or Upraised Hand, which was to be born on Wharekauri during Te Kooti's imprisonment. Then, when the time came for the young man to depart from Nukutaurua, in Te Huitau's account, Toiroa called out:

> tahitahia mai nga kirikiri o taku kainga, kei awhi nga rimurimu o te kainga nei i a koe.
>
> sweep off the gravel of my village lest the seaweed of the village encircles you.[65]

Te Kooti swept the gravel from his feet, as he had been told, before he entered his canoe and returned to his own village. In the Ringatu narratives of Te Whanau-a-Apanui of the East Coast, the people of the seaweed are the Maori spirits. Maaka Jones, daughter of Paora Delamere and herself a Ringatu tohunga, described them as the 'seaweed people, sea-gods, atuas in the form of people', who were possessed of Maori mana.[66] The reference then suggests that the seaweed is Toiroa's spiritual world, which Te Kooti must finally leave behind.

In Bill Hook's version of this narrative, the cryptic saying contained a different prediction. Toiroa called out to the youth:

> 'Wipe the sand and the seaweed of my beaches from your feet.' And Arikirangi laughed for he knew then that if he goes to Wharekauri, this would be the only place he will never invade — on his return. And he did wipe his feet before he got on the canoe.[67]

Thus the oral story told at Nukutaurua, albeit the same narrative, carries quite different implications. The text derived directly from Te Kooti states:

> 'Noku ka eke ki te poti ka rere mai ia ka hopukia oku waewae ka mea, — Ruia iho nga kirikiri o to tipuna o Papa-i-a-nuku, kia waiho ai tenei waahi hei taanga manawa mo o tipuna me o mātua.'

> 'When I climbed onto the boat, he [Toiroa] ran up to me, caught my feet, and said, — Shake off the gravel of your ancestor Papa-i-a-nuku, so as to leave this place as a space for spiritual inspiration for your ancestors and elders.'[68]

Each version, then, possesses its own message. In this last, the oldest text, the reference is specifically to the land: that Nukutaurua will be a place which will for ever belong to the Maori ancestors. Indeed, it is said of Nukutaurua that a handful of sand from Hawaiki had been carefully placed there by the captain of the Takitimu canoe when it landed. Now what belonged there, remained there; that knowledge was to be left there with the ancestors. Te Kooti would ultimately find another fount of knowledge; he did not take it from Nukutaurua. 'What he did elsewhere was what he did elsewhere', as Boy Biddle explained. 'But', he added, 'a lot of the Ngāti Kahungunu people still don't believe that.'[69] Thus meaning is ascribed, and 'texts' live and relive in the telling, so that what most closely pertains to the narrator's and the particular community's understanding of the significance of the story is brought out. Essentially, this is the parable form of narrating history. In this way, orality keeps tradition alive. But the tradition itself is not necessarily fixed, nor is it frozen in time or meaning.

Te Kooti's predictions, which began with his exile on Wharekauri, have similarly acquired different interpretations for each tribe and for each region. The oral narratives of the elders, and the kupu whakaari (words of foresight and promise), allow for independent understandings, and these different understandings co-exist. Meanings are ascribed according to the place, the context and the narrator. This is the strength and scope of orality, which the printed page sometimes circumscribes and inhibits.

However, this warning having been given, it can also be seen that there are often common sequences and central elements within the Maori oral narratives. In Paora

Delamere's narrative, the sequence of the important events is carefully maintained. The first apparition of the new God to Te Kooti is specifically stated to have occurred after his marriage to Irihapeti. The narrative states also that this encounter with God occurred as Te Kooti wandered 'into the wilderness, into the mountains' ('ki te tahora ki te maunga').[70] At this time Te Kooti had seemed to others struck with madness, and they cast him out. When he came in his wanderings to the mountains, he saw spread on their ridges a strange covering of white seaweed. As he drew nearer a spirit person ('wairua') emerged, straightening itself and standing forth from the seaweed. It was a man in form, but from his hat sprang rays of light like the sun, and his clothes were as white clouds. The apparition told him to look at himself, and he found that he recognised the white blanket in which he was dressed and he realised that the affliction of madness had passed from him.

The spirit told him to be peaceful and the new god of whom Toiroa had spoken would appear before him. This new god Toiroa had named Kahutia Te Rangi. And then this god first revealed himself, but he was as yet unnamed in the narrative. He too was in the form of a man but he bore a wooden weapon (taiaha) and his cloak was the aristocratic puahi (made of dogskin). Kahutia Te Rangi is the great ancestor of the East Coast tribes. He was the chiefly son of Uenuku, conceived on a superior sleeping-mat, and challenger to Uenuku's god, Tu-matauenga. His teachings were of peace. Toiroa's vision was, therefore, that the new god was also the spiritual ancestor of the people, but that he appeared in challenge to the ancestral god of war. Kahutia Te Rangi is understood to be Toiroa's god.[71]

In the narrative recorded by Delamere, it was the spirit who arose from the seaweed who destroyed this as yet unnamed god. The narrative also states that the spirit told the god that in the beginning he had created the god, but now on this day he cursed him. The god tried to strike him down, but instead disappeared like a burning fire: 'me te korakora ahi nei te ahua o te ngaromanga o tera Atua'.[72] The narrative is describing a contest of mana, a contest of ultimate power, which results in the destruction of the ancestral divinity by the spirit.

Then the spirit spoke to Te Kooti. The narrative states that this encounter took place on the mountain, thus according with both scriptural tradition and some accounts of the ancestor Tawhaki, the bearer of knowledge to humankind in the Maori world. It was on the mountain that 'this great Spirit God' ('tenei Wairua Atua nui') told Te Kooti that, as Te Kooti had seen him completely, revealed in all his power, he would now never be driven away from him. This particular narrative sequence — that is, the description of the spirit who rose out of the seaweed on the mountain and this consequential promise by God — is also recorded in the account given in Te Kooti's own words.[73]

The 'Spirit God' also gave Te Kooti certain signs. As Paora Delamere narrated the story, for three years Te Kooti would be denied issue. In the fourth year, he would conceive a child. The narrative adds here '1857 perhaps' ('1857 pea'). The other sign would be two dead bodies, whereupon a man would come for him the following day, and the spirit would instruct him what to do. Thus he would know that 'I am a God who saves people' ('Ko reira koe mohio ai, he Atua whakaora tangata ahau'). He also warned Te Kooti that Te Kooti would revert to his evil ways until the fourth year came around. The 'Spirit God' said he was not like the gods of the Maori ancestors, because the new people were a people who had been foreseen, and that he was a new god.

He then told Te Kooti that he did not come freely but was one who is summoned. When Te Kooti asked him if he was Kahutia Te Rangi, the god of whom Toiroa had foretold, he would not answer. Thus Te Kooti had not yet understood the meaning of the contest of mana. Finally, the spirit warned him again that there would be a time when Te Kooti would be lost in darkness, his home a cave, his sleeping companion the sound of the whip (te whiu) and

> e mongamonga noa iho ou iwi i te taumaha o [o] mahi i a ratou. A, ko reira ano ahau mahara ai ki a koe, a, ka tino mohio koe i taua wa he Atua whakaora tangata ahau.

> your tribes will be completely crushed by the weight of your deeds against them. But, then too I will remember you, and you will know for certain at that time that I am a God who saves people.[74]

Delamere's narrative then traces the sequence of these predicted events. It tells that Te Kooti returned to his village and describes how, at the break of day, a man came to take him to a kinsman who lay dead, surrounded by wailing mourners. Te Kooti cleared the mourners from the house and, placing his hands on the head of the lifeless corpse, said, 'Arise, because you have been brought back by the hand of the living God on high' ('E ara, no te mea he mea paihere koe na te ringaringa o te Atua ora i runga rawa').[75] He raised the second body later the same day. The narrative states that this second man was one of two bodies lying together, and that the other was quite dead. It thereby implies that an epidemic (like measles) had struck the community, an only too frequent occurrence at this time. A circling whirlwind struck the house, one body fell to the floor, and Te Kooti lifted it up by its hands, using the same words. The two who were thus raised are named: Eruera Pouto and Hemi Taihuka of Turanga, and it may be noted that the latter was sent as a prisoner to Wharekauri in 1866, just before Te Kooti. However, Te Kooti returned to his evil deeds and, although he was skilled in healing, many who came to him died.

Then, in the third year, the spirit returned in the form of the figure on the mountain. He told Te Kooti that his child, who would be born in the next year, was to be named 'Kahutia-te-Rangi'. After the child's birth another new god would appear, to whom the tribes at Turanga would kneel. But Te Kooti himself would reject him. When this event came to pass, Te Kooti would recognise the meaning of the prediction. These words are understood to be a premonition of the advent of the Pai Marire religion — the religion Te Kooti claimed always to have rejected — and the consequent onset, in 1865, of the civil war on the East Coast. Finally, the figure now told his name to Te Kooti: he was Mikaere, the archangel of God and sent by him. In Te Kooti's own account the text reads simply:

> Na ko taana meatanga mai ki au 'He mea kua kitea nuitia nei ahau e koe, e kore ahau e whakarere i a koe. Tooku ingoa ko "*Mikaera*"'.

> And what he said to me was 'Since you have seen me openly, I will not abandon you. My name is "*Michael*"'.[76]

In Delamere's narrative, it was Mikaere who gave Te Kooti the sign that would be integral to the Ringatu faith: te kopere, the rainbow. Its manifestations, he told him, could be read. If it stood cut short, in a great glow of red, it was a warning of danger and death; if its form was complete, it was a sign of life and hope. To Te Kooti he gave one particular sign to protect him. It was the white lunar rainbow called 'rehita'. It is the light in the darkness.

Embedded in this narrative is a predictive history, which leads to war. The archangel Michael is God's messenger of war in the scriptural traditions. He is the high chief ('te rangatira nui' in the Maori bible), who takes the part of the people in the time of their greatest trouble (Daniel 10:13; 12:1). In popular tradition, Michael has been equated with the Holy Spirit,[77] and is specifically so in this narrative. The Ringatu elders say, quite directly, 'It is Mikaere who appears to Te Kooti'.[78] Or, as the written narrative of the Ringatu tohunga Tawehi Wilson from Waikaremoana and Poverty Bay recorded, equally directly, 'The angel, who was called Michael, appeared to him' ('Ka puta te anahera ki a ia e kiia nei ko Mikaere tona ingoa').[79]

Delamere's narrative also contains a predictive history of the birth of Te Kooti's only son by his wife Irihapeti. The narrative here places the event as 'perhaps' 1857. Te Kooti and Irihapeti's son was known as Wetini Rikirangi. When he died, on 3 October 1928, he was said to be 68 years old. This would place his birth at around 1860. Wetini's relationship with his father would be dramatically severed in 1868 when, as a small boy, he was taken prisoner by those fighting against Te Kooti. He was then brought up by his father's opponents among Ngati Porou.[80] The predictive history is silent about the child; it states only that, just before he was born, the white rainbow stood over the place and that 'All was well with the birth of that child into the world of light' ('Pai tonu ano hoki te whanautanga mai o taua tamaiti ki te ao marama').[81] There is no sequence, no comment, thereafter.

The Ringatu tradition, which was initiated by Te Kooti himself, tells the history of his early life with a focus on the intervention of God on behalf of the Maori people at the time of their greatest calamity. Te Kooti is portrayed as a man of 'evil' and even of 'madness', but also as one predestined to greatness. In the teachings of the old tohunga Eria Raukura, the framework of this history is stated quite precisely:

> I te tau 1766, e toru tau i mua atu o te taenga mai o te pakeha ki tenei motu, ka whakaaturia e Toiroa a Ariki-rangi me nga ahuatanga katoa o tona oranga i tenei ao. Nana tenei Kawenata i whakahou ano, i whakahangai [*sic*] hoki ki runga i ta te wairua arahitanga. Kua rereke haere nei i nga tipuna i te roanga haeretanga o roto i nga tau. Kua neke atu nei i te 1000 tau mai ano a taua hekenga mai i Kanaana.

> In 1766, three years before the arrival of the pakeha in this land, Toiroa spoke out about Ariki-rangi and all the aspects of his life in this world. He [Toiroa] renewed the Covenant and conducted it according to the guidance of the Spirit. It had been altered by the ancestors over the years, [for] more than 1000 years had passed since that migration out of Canaan.[82]

In this way Eria yoked the most distant ancestral past to the early Christian teachings. The union of the two traditions would be understood as being completed only on

Wharekauri, with the revelations there of the Ringatu covenant and the prophetic sayings of the angel ('anahera') who appeared again to Te Kooti.[83]

These narrative traditions, transformed in different ways by European and Maori perspectives, are built upon a framework of facts. That framework includes a genealogy which can be reconstructed. It is important to realise that Te Kooti Arikirangi Te Turuki had been born in a line of descent collateral to the senior chiefs of Ngati Maru of the Rongowhakaata tribe (see Whakapapa A, B and D, pages 14, 30 and 34). His father was descended from their eponymous tribal ancestor, Rongowhakaata, and his senior wife, Turahiri. Te Kooti's paternal grandmother, Waiokura, was descended from Kahungunu and his pre-eminent wife, Rongomaiwahine, from whom many of the people of Turanganui and the Mahia peninsula trace their descent. Toiroa of Nukutaurua was an elder kinsman of Te Kooti from Kahungunu, and he was also of Ngati Maru.[84] Waiokura herself belonged to Ngati Ruapani, the founding tribe of Poverty Bay who trace their descent from Kiwa and Paoa, the canoe captains after whom the bay (Turanganui-a-Kiwa) and the great river (Waipaoa) are named (see Whakapapa A and C, pages 14 and 32). Te Kooti also traced his descent from Ruapani through his mother, Turakau (Heni).[85] Ngati Ruapani claimed the inland territory of Turanganui from Paparatu to Waikaremoana, and were closely intermarried with Tuhoe, the people of the Urewera, as well as with Ngati Kahungunu living in the upper Wairoa.[86] All these descent lines and ties of kinship enabled him to forge some critical alliances in the wars. It cannot be said that he was of low status, although that was the common European view of the time, reinforced by statements about Te Kooti made by some senior Turanga chiefs. He had challenged the leading chiefs of Ngati Maru and Rongowhakaata when he acted as a wild boy and 'social bandit', and he certainly gained their enmity. They were instrumental in the decision to send him as a prisoner to Wharekauri in 1866. In this, their interests coincided with those of the dominant traders and government officials. It is to this world of intrigue and war that we now turn.

PAOA   KIWA
| |
Hineakua (w)   =   Kahutuanui
|
Hauakiterangi
|
Aniukitaharangi
|
Ngoreoterangi
|
Ue a Ngore
|
Tahungaehenui
|
Ruatepupuke
|
RUAPANI   =   Wairau (1st wife)
|
(w) Ruarauhanga   =   KAHUNGUNU   =   Rongomaiwahine (w)
| |
Ruaroa   Tauhei (w)
| |
MAHAKI
|
Te Nonoikura (w)   =   Te Ranginui a Ihu
|
Whakauaki
|
Te Kuru (w)   =   Rongomaimihiao
|
TAWHIRI
|
Mate ————————————————— = —————
|
Rongoteuruora
|
Te Rangihiria
|
Mokaiohungia II   Taringa
| |
Rangirukuhia   Te Maangakaiota (*Te Whanau-a-Iwi*)
| |
Ngetengeteroa   (SEE C)   Te Kapa
| |
Pita Te Hukinga   Ruku   Te Nanati =
| (Te Nonoti)
Te Waaka   Ana   =   Paratene   Kahutia
Puakanga   Pototi
                             (Turangi)*

TE KOOTI   =   Irihapeti   Henare   Riperata Kahutia (w) ══
ARIKIRANGI   Puakanga   Turangi
TE TURUKI*   (Kakapango)
                                           Heni Materoa =

Wetini Rikirangi
(SEE A)

Whakapapa B

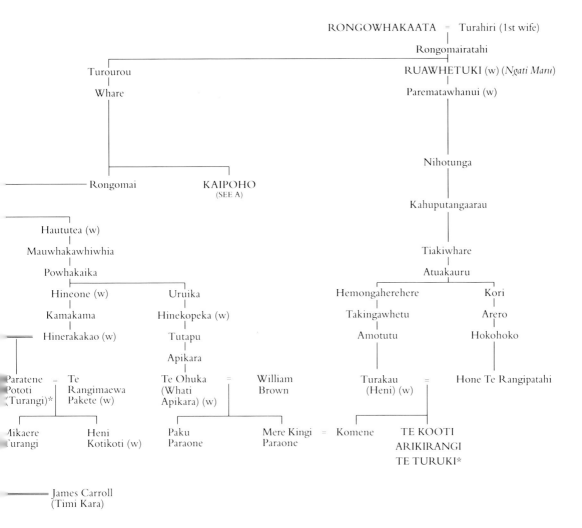

RONGOWHAKAATA = Turahiri (1st wife)

Rongomairatahi

Turourou

Whare

RUAWHETUKI (w) (*Ngati Maru*)

Parem018atawhanui (w)

Nihotunga

Rongomai — KAIPOHO
(SEE A)

Kahuputangaarau

Hautūtea (w)

Mauwhakawhiwhia

Powhakaika

Tiakiwhare

Atuakauru

Hineone (w)   Uruika

Kamakama   Hinekopeka (w)

Hinerakakao (w)   Tutapu

Hemongaherehere   Kori

Takingawhetu   Arero

Amotutu   Hokohoko

Apikara

Paratene = Te   Te Ohuka = William
Pototi   Rangimaewa   (Whati   Brown
(Turangi)* Pakete (w)   Apikara) (w)

Turakau = Hone Te Rangipatahi
(Heni) (w)

Mikaere   Heni   Paku   Mere Kingi = Komene   TE KOOTI
Turangi   Kotikoti (w)   Paraone   Paraone   ARIKIRANGI
                                                                TE TURUKI*

James Carroll
(Timi Kara)

* Indicates person appears elsewhere on this whakapapa

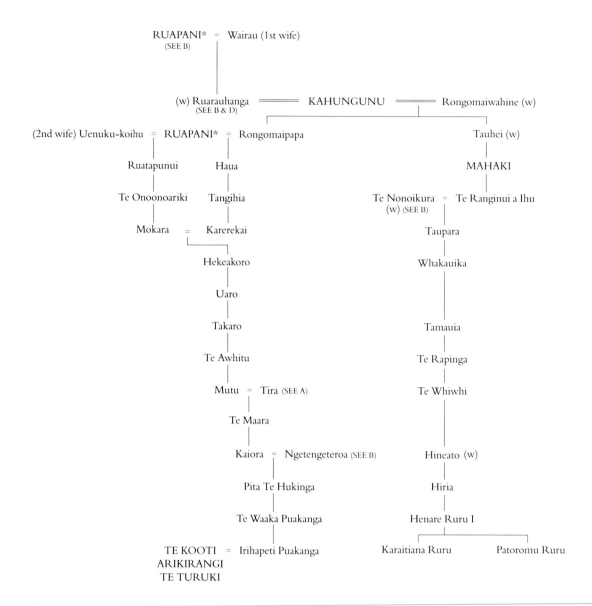

RUAPANI* = Wairau (1st wife)
(SEE B)

(w) Ruarauhanga ═══════ KAHUNGUNU ═══════ Rongomaiwahine (w)
(SEE B & D)

(2nd wife) Uenuku-koihu = RUAPANI* = Rongomaipapa   Tauhei (w)

Ruatapunui   Haua   MAHAKI

Te Onoonoariki   Tangihia   Te Nonoikura = Te Ranginui a Ihu
                                          (w) (SEE B)

Mokara = Karerekai   Taupara

Hekeakoro   Whakauika

Uaro

Takaro   Tamauia

Te Awhitu   Te Rapinga

Mutu = Tira (SEE A)   Te Whiwhi

Te Maara

Kaiora = Ngetengeteroa (SEE B)   Hineato (w)

Pita Te Hukinga   Hiria

Te Waaka Puakanga   Henare Ruru I

TE KOOTI = Irihapeti Puakanga   Karaitiana Ruru   Patoromu Ruru
ARIKIRANGI
TE TURUKI

Whakapapa C

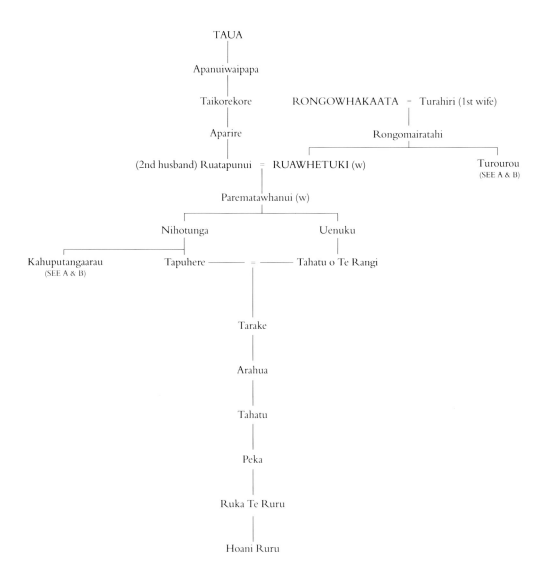

TAUA

Apanuiwaipapa

Taikorekore

RONGOWHAKAATA = Turahiri (1st wife)

Aparire

Rongomairatahi

(2nd husband) Ruatapunui = RUAWHETUKI (w)

Turourou
(SEE A & B)

Parematawhanui (w)

Nihotunga

Uenuku

Kahuputangaarau
(SEE A & B)

Tapuhere ——————— = ——————— Tahatu o Te Rangi

Tarake

Arahua

Tahatu

Peka

Ruka Te Ruru

Hoani Ruru

*Indicates person appears elsewhere on this whakapapa

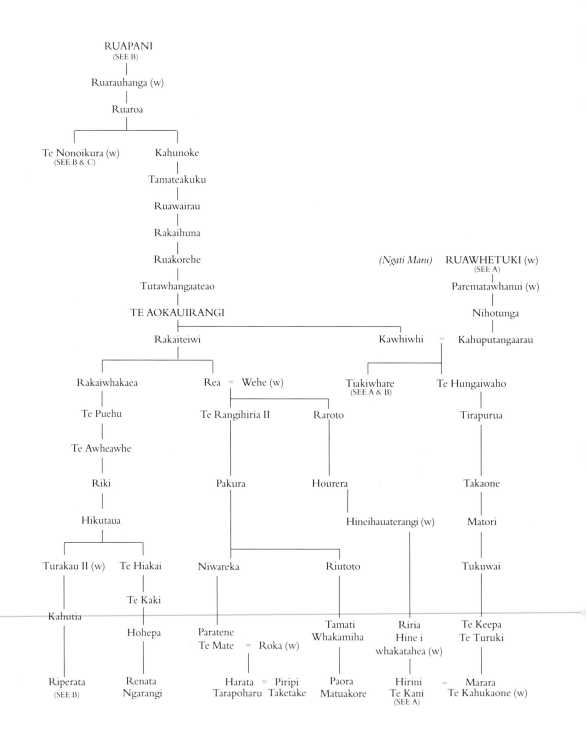

RUAPANI
(SEE B)

Ruarauhanga (w)

Ruaroa

Te Nonoikura (w)   Kahunoke
(SEE B & C)

Tamateakuku

Ruawairau

Rakaihuna

Ruakorehe

Tutawhangaateao

TE AOKAUIRANGI

(Ngati Maru) RUAWHETUKI (w)
(SEE A)

Parematawhanui (w)

Nihotunga

Rakaiteiwi   Kawhiwhi = Kahuputangaarau

Rakaiwhakaea   Rea = Wehe (w)   Tiakiwhare   Te Hungaiwaho
(SEE A & B)

Te Puehu   Te Rangihiria II   Raroto   Tirapurua

Te Awheawhe

Riki   Pakura   Hourera   Takaone

Hikutaua   Hineihauaterangi (w)   Matori

Turakau II (w)   Te Hiakai   Niwareka   Riutoto   Tukuwai

Te Kaki

Kahutia   Hohepa   Paratene   Tamati   Riria   Te Keepa
Te Mate = Roka (w)   Whakamiha   Hine i   Te Turuki
whakatahea (w)

Riperata   Renata   Harata = Piripi   Paora   Hirini   =   Marara
(SEE B)   Ngarangi   Tarapoharu Taketake Matuakore   Te Kani   Te Kahukaone (w)
(SEE A)

Whakapapa D

CHAPTER 2

THE HINGE OF FATE

Te Kooti grew up at a time when the first European settlement was occurring at Turanganui. The major chiefs entered into arrangements with these early settlers, accepting them into their communities for the trade benefits they brought. Men like John Harris, William Brown, James Wyllie, George Read and William Greene took Maori wives and were given land for themselves and their children. In the early days many of these land and grazing arrangements were quite informal, for the understanding on the Maori side was that the settlers were a part of their communities. Sarah Dunlop, whose family arrived in 1850 and soon settled near Whakato at Te Arai, commented that their first encounter with Te Kooti was when he arranged to take a calf each year as payment for the grazing of stock.[1] As a lease of Maori land, this was technically illegal, but it was typical of the transactions of the time. Te Kooti was also party to a later agreement (made in 1865) allowing Greene to fence some land at Matawhero which Te Kooti (and others) had given to Greene for his half-Maori children. Te Kooti sold him the 200 fence posts that he needed.[2] This agreement soon led to conflict with Read, who claimed a part of the land. He disputed both the boundary and just who among the Maori had the right to dispose of it. Te Kooti lived and worked in regular contact with the settlers: he is remembered as having a whare for a long period on the western bank of the Waipaoa river, 'opposite the blacksmith's shop on the right bank' near the present Bridge Hotel.[3] His whare was in the area generally known as Te Ahipakura. Te Kooti also lived at Tarere, on the upper Taruheru river near Makaraka, where William Brown had his home.[4]

There is no doubt that Te Kooti became involved in the politics of land as they evolved in Turanga during the 1850s and early 1860s. His association with Kahutia is one indication. Kahutia, who had made some early land transactions, soon emerged as the leader of the 'redemption' movement, which from 1851 sought to take back lands that had been alienated at Turanga and to return the payments — horses or cattle — made for their use. In other words, the European claims to 'sales' (together with some of the illicit leases) were being rejected, and usufructory rights, which in the local Maori understanding were often all that had originally been negotiated, were being cancelled.[5] Te Kooti was one of those named by Harris in 1852 as acting as the 'bother boys' of the redemption movement. By 1859, when the early 'purchases' in the district were being investigated, the redemption movement had become the 'repudiation' movement, and Raharuhi Rukupo of Ngati Maru and Ngati Kaipoho hapu was its prime instigator. Kahutia himself confessed to the Old Land Claims' Commissioner that he had been mistaken in making land transactions, and for this error he had been threatened with exile. Now the generally shared objective was to repossess the lands. When the governor visited Turanga shortly after this inquiry, he was told sharply that, unless his purpose in coming to see the tribes was to restore the lands of which they had been 'cheated', they had no wish to see him at all.[6] Herbert Wardell, the magistrate, reached the opinion that the Europeans lived there only 'on sufferance'. He observed that Turanga Maori had no intention of parting with their lands and were, therefore, 'exacting in their demands, and arbitrary in their mode of enforcing them'. But, he also noted, 'personal violence was scarcely ever offered to Europeans'.[7] By 1860 Harris considered that the entire district was in sympathy with the Maori King — not in the acceptance of his authority, that is, but in the shared objective of stopping all land sales and, if possible, 'to reclaim that already sold', including that sold 'with the knowledge of the Tribes, and never disputed' previously[8] — as he put it somewhat evasively, as his own claims were at the centre of the protests. Nevertheless, by 1864 splinters in Maori solidarity were appearing. Soon after Kahutia's death, his hapu, Te Whanau-a-Iwi living at Makaraka, was the first of the anti-land-sellers to fragment.[9]

Te Kooti himself does not emerge from the background in these early disputes. There are no further references to him in European correspondence until 1865, and it is quite probable that he had again temporarily left the district. But in 1865–66 he reappears, and to the settlers John Harris and John Hervey he was nothing but a packet of trouble. From Hervey's point of view he was an inveterate thief — as were all Ngati Maru, who lived at the mouth of the Waipaoa river and who, he complained, ever since he had moved among them, 'robbed and plundered me in every shape imaginable'.[10] George Goldsmith's store at Matawhero was also plundered at this time,[11] and this may well be the occasion when he was robbed of his rum. That Ngati Maru's opposition to Hervey's store near their settlement was political is evidenced by the leadership Hervey cited as responsible for the constant raids upon it: Anaru Matete, the active young leader of Ngati Maru, and Renata Tupara, of the same hapu. Both men were considered significant figures in Poverty Bay, and both had been closely involved with the Anglican church for a long time. Anaru, whom Te Kooti considered as his chief, had been a lay reader and was highly thought of by William Williams, who had included him in the first synod for the region, in 1861. But in 1865 Anaru and Renata both became converts in the new movement that reached the East Coast: the Pai Marire faith.

The Turanga chiefs had maintained a policy of neutrality during the wars which engulfed Taranaki and Waikato from 1860. The runanga they held regularly made their position very clear: they were independent leaders. In 1858, they had held a series of meetings with two purposes. The first was to establish fixed local prices for the goods they sold to Pakeha because, as Wardell commented, they felt they were being 'done' both by the traders and by the missionaries with their low payments for goods. For a while they banned sales entirely.[12] At the second meeting, held in May, Queen Victoria's authority was discussed. Paratene Pototi, the old and senior chief of Ngai Tawhiri, a

Hirini Te Kani, the leading chief
of Turanga in 1865. Oil on canvas,
date unknown. Photographed, by
permission of Heni Sunderland,
by Gillian Chaplin, 1984.

TE MANA-O-TURANGA, MANUTUKE

hapu of Rongowhakaata, spoke firmly: 'We are not the remnant of a people left by the
Pakeha; we have not been conquered: the Queen has her island, we have ours'. Kahutia
stated equally clearly: 'We will exercise our own authority in our country. . . . I had the
mana before the pakeha came and have it still.'[13] During the governor's visit in January
1860, the chiefs, led by Rukupo, objected to the Union Jack being hoisted over the house
where he was staying. These attitudes of independence ensured their refusal to join the
Kingitanga and, equally, their determination to try to control the processes of European
settlement at Turanga. The penetration of Pai Marire in 1865, and the deep divisions
among Maori it caused, has to be understood in this context.

The Pai Marire religion and its new God, Tama-Rura (Son-Ruler), was deliberately
brought to the East Coast by the emissaries sent by the Taranaki prophet, Te Ua
Haumene. The emissaries, called the Tiu or Jews, also carried with them the preserved
head of a young, fair-haired and bearded soldier,[14] one of five who had been killed and
decapitated at an ambush in Taranaki on 6 April 1864. The Tiu sought out the young
chief Hirini Te Kani, who, by his lineage and as the adopted son and successor of Te
Kani a Takirau, was the chief of Te Aitanga-a-Hauiti and paramount at both Turanga

Patara Te Raukatauri, Pai Marire
missionary to the East Coast.
ALBUM 14, HBM

and Uawa. Te Ua had instructed them: 'Let it [the head] be carried properly' ('Kia tika te hari'), and there let it end its journey. It was to be given to Hirini so that 'Hirini may deliver it to his English friends at that place' ('kia tae pai ai ki a Hirini maana e hoatu pai ki ona whanaunga Pakeha i reira').[15] The purpose of this strange ritual was to seal a broad Maori unity under the new faith and a new 'King', for Te Ua was asking Hirini to protect the religion and to accept its teachings. The emissaries sent by Te Ua were Patara Te Raukatauri and Kereopa Te Rau. Although their message was one of peace underlaid by a grim warning, they were preceded by news of the execution of the Anglican missionary Carl Volkner on 2 March 1865 at Opotiki. If his death was instigated by Kereopa's preaching, as it appeared to have been, the message of peace had become blurred. The pentecostalist preachings of Pai Marire, from their first appearance on the East Coast, were accompanied by confusion and death.

There was a wide divergence of attitude among Maori of Turanga as to the message and intentions of the new faith. Another of their missionaries who came from Opotiki,

Aperahama Tutoko (Te Rangituatahi) of Te Aitanga-a-Mahaki, who first brought the explanation of Volkner's death to Turanga in 1865. He was later wrongly accused of complicity in it. This photograph was taken about 1880.　AIM

Aperahama Tutoko, told a large gathering of the Turanga chiefs at Te Poho-o-Mahaki meeting-house at Waerenga-a-Hika in March 1865 that they worshipped 'Jehovah, the Angel, Christ, & the Holy Spirit'. He explained the killing of Volkner by the Whakatohea people. It was, he said, because Volkner had acted as an informer on his own congregation, 'going backwards & forwards to the Town' (Auckland), stirring up the Pakeha to fight. But, Aperahama said, 'choose for yourselves, if you do not approve, let the Whakatohea alone be the Titi (Titi is the mutton bird which flies towards the flame of a large flame [*sic*] kindled for the purpose & is then killed).'[16] The Pai Marire message of salvation was not a declaration of war with the settlers or the European missionaries. As William Williams himself observed, commenting on Te Ua's original letter of instructions: 'If this is the only instruction given there is no sanction in it to murder.'[17] A similar letter of instructions from Te Ua to Kereopa and Patara was quite explicit in its directives: 'don't do anything at all to the pakeha' ('kaua e aha ki te pakeha').[18] Thus Anaru Matete said in a deputation of the Hauhau leaders of Turanga to Harris on 25 July:

Te Waru Tamatea, high-ranking chief of inland Wairoa. He always wore his long hair bound up in a koukou, or top-knot, adorned with feathers. His main settlement was at Whataroa. He fought at Orakau in 1864, and at Wairoa in 1865–66. But because he surrendered and signed the oath of allegiance in May 1866, he was not sent to Wharekauri. He would become a major supporter of Te Kooti after his return in 1868.   ALBUM 3, HBM

Stay. Why leave your places? We have joined the Hauhau because we think by so doing we shall save our land (te Ao) and the remnant of our people. We have no quarrel with the settlers, we are not bringing trouble on you .... All our chiefs with Lazarous (Rukupo) say the settlers shall and will be protected.[19]

But others were less convinced of either the peaceful purposes or the truth of the Pai Marire (Hauhau) teachings. In April a party of Pai Marire converts from Te Whanau-a-Hinemanuhiri tribe of upper Wairoa, led by the high-born chief Te Waru Tamatea,[20] had come to Nukutaurua. When old Toiroa learnt that they were on their way, he instructed the people to assemble at Oraka and said that their stay would be determined by the lasting of the food. He told them to place the food in a line, which would serve as a division between the tangata whenua (the local people) and the strangers. The speeches became heated, and the meeting dragged on. The following day, 'the Hhau began to call out for more kai but they were told that there was none at hand and that they were all faring alike and they were obliged to go to the rocks for kuku and paua'. When the party went on to Nuhaka, the Hauhau were received in silence, while the people of Nukutaurua, who had accompanied them, were greeted and welcomed. When the strangers asked for an explanation, they were told they had no right to expect to be welcome. They were then given food, but they discovered it had been prepared as alternate layers of cooked and raw kumara. When his portion was brought to Te Waru, he was greatly insulted.[21]

Toiroa rejected the new faith and its bearers. Nor did he change his opinion. In August 1865 the plainest words possible were brought from Nukutaurua: 'Toiroa said, he did not like the Hauhau' ('ki a Toiroa, e ki ana ia kaore ia e pai ki te Hauhau').[22] Nor was Te Kooti a convert. As he told George Grey in 1879, equally plainly, 'I would not accept the Hauhau God' ('Kahore hoki ahau i pai ki te Atua hauhau').[23] But he witnessed the slow slide into civil war at Turanga between March and November 1865. We know that to some extent he also participated, attending a huge meeting of the Pai Marire priests held at Taureka in July to initiate new converts.[24] Many who attended said they only went to listen,[25] and Te Kooti seems to have been one of them. He took the Dunlop children home when the rituals of initiation (called 'pooti', or going to the post), held around the niu pole erected by a portion of Ngati Maru at Te Arai, became too feverish. The family relied upon him to whisk their children out of trouble — and apparently he did. Te Kooti was a man whom the Dunlops trusted, and such recollections of him are unique at a time of rapidly mounting tension among the settlers.[26] Fear was so high that William Williams and a part of his family fled from Turanga at the beginning of April, although Harris reported at the same time that he did not yet anticipate any confrontation with the Europeans. He trusted the assurances of the senior chiefs.[27]

The Pai Marire preachers insisted that they came in peace. They offered a religion which was independent of the missionaries, and which seemed to empower Maori. Its spread was dramatic at Turanga. The inland tribe Te Aitanga-a-Mahaki were among the first converts. By early April Henry Williams junior estimated at least a third of all the Turanga Maori were believers, with another third calling themselves neutral.[28] Yet the polarisation into hostile factions, which the senior Turanga chiefs were seeking desperately to avoid, occurred when Mokena Kohere, a major leader of Ngati Porou from the East Coast, came in May to Turanga. He set up a flagstaff and hoisted the Union Jack upon it as a statement of defiance of the great niu poles, with their flags and banners.[29] Although he did this with the consent of Ngai Te Kete, the small tribe upon whose headland, Titirangi, he erected the flagstaff, Hirini Te Kani (who also shared ownership of the land) threatened to tear the pole down.[30] Hirini was not committed to Pai Marire, but he was also not prepared to have Ngati Porou make claims on the mana of the territory of Turanga,[31] any more than the chiefs had accepted the flag above the resident magistrate's house during the governor's visit of 1860.

In 1858, when the Turanga chiefs had decided neither to join the Kingitanga nor to choose a king from among themselves, there had been talk of erecting their own flagstaff, which should itself be called 'King'.[32] It was their statement of their autonomy. Flagstaffs and flags were potent images for Maori, for the post (and the flag) claimed the land. Te Kooti's prophetic dream about Anaru Matete, which is attributed to 1864, states his rejection of the authority of the niu poles:

The niu pole at Puketi, a Pai Marire community in south Taranaki. This pencil drawing is from 'Ua Rongopai', a notebook recording the teachings of Te Ua. It shows the characteristic fenced area at the base of the pole, described in Te Kooti's dream. The lower flag was a flag for New Zealand, 'Nui Tireni'. The emblems are of the three islands in unity.　GNZ MMS 1, APL

Na, ka puta mai he moemoea ki a Te Kooti Ariki-rangi. Ko te moe tenei: —
　　Titiro rawa atu ia ko tetahi pa tino nui i runga i te Maunga. Kikii tonu a roto i taua pa i te tangata, he whero katoa o ratou kakahu. A, ko te ingoa o taua iwi, he Tu-rehu. A, ka kite atu ia ko tetahi pou nui, he roa e tu ana i waenganui o taua iwi me te Haki ano e rere ana i runga, me te nama ano o te Haki. Kihai i rite ki nga nama Haki a te Pakeha, i rereke noa atu ano.
　　Na, tana tirohanga atu ki taua iwi, toro tonu o ratou ringaringa ki runga ki te aronga o tau pou. A, i reira tonu ano, ka kite ia i a Anaru Matete, hei karanga Matua ano ki a ia. Na, e mau ana ano a Matete i te Haki. Pera ano te ahua me te Haki i runga i te pou ra. A, haere tonu atu a Anaru ki tau[a] pou ra, toro tonu atu tona ringaringa ki te aronga ki runga o taua pou ra.

Now a dream came to Te Kooti Ariki-rangi. This was the dream: —
　　He was looking intently at a very large pa on top of the Mountain. Inside the pa it was crowded with people, all in red clothes. Those people were named Tu-rehu (Fairy). And he saw a large, high pole standing in the midst of the people and a Flag with a number on it flying at the top. It was not the same as the numbers on Pakeha Flags, it was quite different.
　　Now, while he was looking at the people, they suddenly stretched their hands up towards the pole. And also there he saw Anaru Matete, a relative and Elder of his. Matete was also holding a Flag, just like the one on the pole. Anaru went straight up to the pole and stretched his hands up towards the top of it.[33]

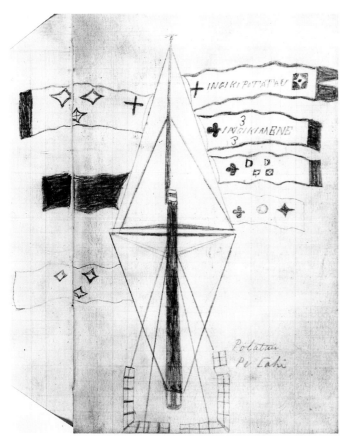

The niu pole at Te Putahi, Taranaki, with flags showing the same emblems as those adopted by Anaru Matete. They indicate this community's loyalty to King Potatau ('Ingiki Potatau'), the second Maori King. The second flag has the message 'Ingiki Mene' ('King of Men'), and shows the fallen club and 3, the latter apparently invoking the Trinity. This is probably the 'number' described as being marked on the Pai Marire flags in Te Kooti's dream. Pencil drawing from 'Ua Rongopai'.   GNZ MMS 1, APL

In his dream, his spirit sang a waiata to the spirit of Anaru. This waiata is recorded, and it is a song of ill omen. The song describes the 'karakia Parirau Hauhau', or the flapping wing of the Hauhau faith.[34] The image is of the volatile and transitory nature of the faith, while the text comments on the 'quivering of the hands of some of the priests, they looked like the trembling of a bird's wings in flight' ('no te aroarohakitanga o nga ringaringa o etahi o nga porewarewa, ka tu ahua aroarohaki rere a parirau manu tonu te ritenga').[35]

Then the narrative continues:

> Na, titiro atu ia e porotiti ana taua iwi katoa i raro o te pou ra. Kaore ia i mohio atu ki ta ratou korero, a, oho ake ana ia i tona moenga. . . . Haere tonu atu ia i taua ra ano ki te korero i tana moemoea ki a Anaru Matete. Ko ia hoki te tumuaki o raua iwi, he tangata matau hoki ia ki nga mea katoa. A, oti katoa i a ia te korero taua moe ki a Anaru, a oti ana ano i a Anaru te whakarite, te tikanga mo taua moe. Ko tana kupu tenei mo taua moe: Ae, tera e puta mai he Atua hou ki konei, a, ka tahuri katoa nga iwi o konei ki taua tikanga. Na, mo te waiata tona tikanga he mate, ara, he whenua mate.

> Now, he saw all the people in a circle at the base of the pole. He did not understand what they were saying, and then he woke up from his sleep. . . . On that same day he went at once to tell Anaru Matete of his dream. He was the leader of their tribe, and a man learned in all things. When he had quite finished describing his dream to Anaru,

and Anaru had also finished his interpretation of its meaning, this was his word about it: 'Yes, a new God will emerge here, and all the local tribes will turn to that faith. As for the waiata, its meaning is misfortune, that is, misfortune for the land.'[36]

This Ringatu narrative goes on to establish Te Kooti's rejection of the Hauhau teachings, and all its rituals. It states that most of Ngati Maru were converted, but that ten remained aloof. One named was Te Kooti, and another was his senior chief, the elder half-brother of Anaru, Tamihana Ruatapu, who indeed consistently stood apart.

> Na, katahi ratou ka matakitaki ki nga whakahaere o taua karakia e mahia. E mahia ana e nga iwi o Turanganui. Whakaarahia ai he rakau roa tiketike kia tu ki runga hei iringa mo nga kara. Ka karangatia te ingoa o taua pou kara he Niu. Ka taiawhiotia te taiepa i te take o te Niu. Na, ka karakia ano ka toro nga ringa ki runga o te Niu hei whakanui ki a ratou Atua.
>
> Katahi ia, a Te Kooti, ka titiro atu ki ta ratou mahi. Rite tonu ki te mea i kitea ra e ia i roto i tana moemoea. No reira, ka korero ia ki tona iwi, ki a Ngati-Maru, ka mea: – E hika ma, kaati kaua e tahuri atu ki tena Atua horihori, ka raru koutou akuanei. Koi[a] ana akuanei te ritenga o te moe nei, tae noa ki te waiata. He raruraru he mate tona mutunga iho.

> Now, they watched the practices of that church as performed by the tribes of Turanganui. A lofty log was erected for flags to hang on. That flagpole was called a Niu. A fence encircled the base of the Niu. Now [they] prayed and stretched their arms up to the Niu, in praise of their God.
>
> Te Kooti then saw that what they were doing was just as he had seen in his dream. So he spoke to his tribe, to Ngati-Maru, and said: – My people, stop this, don't turn to that false God, or soon you will be in trouble. Before long it will be like the dream and the song – trouble and death their conclusion.[37]

But Mokena's erection of the flagstaff on 20 May 1865, to flout the niu, served only to arouse the anger of most of Rongowhakaata. He had deliberately placed the pole on Titirangi hill and fortified it. In response, Hirini immediately erected a new pa at the base of the hill to defend, he said, the bones of his father, Rawiri, who was buried there. Leonard Williams soon realised that the flagstaff had become the focal issue: 'They do not like the flagstaff'. As he said, 'the soreness in people's minds' was the insistent behaviour of the government Maori faction, the Kawanatanga, led by Mokena, 'and nothing else'.[38] Hirini, who had earlier refused to allow the Pai Marire to fly their flags, called 'Riki' and 'Tamarura', at his settlement, now threatened to join Pai Marire. Two of the leading chiefs among the Kawanatanga, Paratene Pototi and Te Waaka Puakanga, father of Te Kooti's wife Irihapeti, in turn wrote urgently to the government:

> . . . kua tae mai to matou tohu, ara, te kara kei te wahapu o Turanganui e tu ana. Kua hiahia nga rangatira Maori o Turanga ki te patu i a matou, a Hirini Te Kani, a Raharuhi Rukupo, kei whai tohu a te Kuini ki runga ki a matou. . . . Kua kore matou e pai kia hinga to matou kara Kuini. Koia te take o te riri ki Turanga.

> . . . our signal has arrived, that is, the flag standing at the mouth of Turanganui. The Maori chiefs of Turanga want to kill us, Hirini Te Kani and Raharuhi Rukupo, so that

Te Poho-o-Rawiri, fortified. The meeting-house was erected by Hirini Te Kani at the foot of Titirangi (Kaiti) hill. It was turned into a temporary magazine and garrisoned from 15 September 1865. Photograph probably by Leonard Williams, 1866.   RHODES ALBUM, F110529 1/2, ATL

> the Queen will not have control over us. . . . We will not consent to our Queen's flag coming down. This will be the reason for fighting at Turanga.[39]

They stressed that they were small in number, and asked Donald McLean, as the agent for the general government, to come there. From this moment, the situation began to escalate.

McLean's arrival on 5 June (seemingly forewarned on the previous evening by the sight of a fiery meteor in the east, 'as large as Venus at her brightest'[40]) ensured that the issues would now be seen increasingly in absolute terms. He demanded an oath of loyalty, and on 7 June, 'at the fstaff pa', some 40 or 50 were prepared to take the oath.[41] But Hirini refused while the flagstaff stood. The complexity of the situation grew as pa building intensified in the district. Some pa were consciously identified as Pai Marire, and others as kupapa, or neutral, but both were in opposition to Mokena's government pa. The niu poles spread, tall giants claiming the land in the names of Son-Ruler ('Tamarura') and his warrior angel, 'Riki', the archangel Lord ('Ariki') Michael.

The rites of initiation at the 'pooti' continued and spread. Ngati Maru, for the most part, committed themselves early in July. On 20 and 23 July two huge meetings took place. The 'Queen's Maori' (Kawanatanga) met at Whakato marae on 20 July, excluding from the runanga both Hauhau and kupapa. They erected a pole and flew their flags surmounted by the red ensign, for, as Henare Ruru argued, just as the mana of the

Hauhau lay in their flag Tamarura, so theirs now lay in the Queen's flag. The senior unconverted Ngati Maru chief, Tamihana Ruatapu, warned of war and spoke of the Pai Marire prophecy that in August they would separate themselves from all others and sweep all before them across the land. But, although the mood was ominous, most of the chiefs still felt that they could continue to govern themselves and protect their Pakeha settlers. Hapi Kiniha observed sharply that they certainly did not wish to be governed from outside — as were the Hauhau.[42] On 23 July the Pai Marire summoned their own runanga. Although some, like Wiremu Kingi Te Paia, talked of erecting a niu pole at Whakato in front of Ngati Maru's church, and others suggested swapping the flags on Mokena's flagstaff so that it could become a niu, the thrust of the meeting was not aggressive. The Pai Marire chiefs sought to reassure the settlers that they need not leave. They urged that their adoption of the new faith was not in itself a threat. War would come to Turanga only if the government took the first step — by sending troops. The delegation of Pai Marire leaders, including Wiremu Kingi, Anaru Matete and others from Ngati Maru, went to Harris with their decision. Kingi urged him, 'Don't listen to what you are told by the Queenites, the Hauhau here will not molest you.' Anaru also assured him that Hirini Te Kani would be sufficient protection, and that on this matter all the chiefs were agreed.[43]

The war came to Turanga in precisely the manner the Pai Marire chiefs had feared. In June, civil war had broken out in the Waiapu district of the East Coast among Ngati Porou. In a series of fights, to which the government committed troops, the Pai Marire converts were driven south. There was much debate among the Pai Marire at Turanga as to whether or not to rush to their aid. Several, including Wiremu Kingi, left in August in a vain attempt to mediate for peace.[44] On 6 September, old Toiroa sent a message to Rukupo and the other Pai Marire leaders urging them to stay quietly at home. He feared that the war would come to them, without their going 'elsewhere to seek for it'.[45] But already some had set off to support their kin. In particular, Te Aitanga-a-Mahaki from inland Poverty Bay left on 3 September for Uawa, to avenge the death of their prophet, Raniera Rangakaheke, who had gone to Tokomaru to proselytise and been killed in the subsequent fighting. They thus ensured that the war could no longer be contained.

At the same time, Pai Marire refugees from the East Coast sought out their kin at Turanga. On 14 September, 400 Pai Marire — men, women and children — sought sanctuary in the newly constructed Pai Marire pa at Waerenga-a-Hika, which was built in part of an older pa, belonging to Te Aitanga-a-Mahaki, located on the river bank near the mission. At Turanga, Hirini Te Kani still struggled to retain his autonomous control, for the thing he most feared was the arrival of troops — joined by the Ngati Porou fighters — in pursuit of the fugitives. He was now finally prepared to seek guns from the government, and to take a small body of military settlers under his protection. He also made it clear to Raharuhi Rukupo that he would share the arms and the men equally with him — thus, of course, heightening the settlers' fear of his ambiguous loyalty.[46] Rather, he was trying hard to hold a balance of power and to sustain the chiefs' authority in the district, so as to prevent invasion. But he was fully aware that the presence of the refugees ensured that Ngati Porou would come in their wake. Mokena

Wiremu Kingi Te Paia (Wiremu
Kingi Te Apaapa), a chief of Ngati
Maru and of Te Aowera hapu of
Ngati Porou at Turanga. He was
a convert to Pai Marire in 1865.
He went with Te Kooti in 1868,
but expressed doubts about him
and his faith. Rephotographed, by
permission of Heni Sunderland,
by Gillian Chaplin.

Te Mana-o-Turanga, Manutuke

had already announced that the support which had come from Turanga to the Pai Marire
of Ngati Porou would bring him back to destroy them.[47]

By the beginning of November, the atmosphere was of increased tension and rising
disorder. The settlers had begun to panic, and talked of the 'rebellion'. Some had come to
live in sled-houses close by the newly established military settlement at Hirini's fortified
pa. They closed up their own homes, which were then ransacked. Anaru Matete was
present as a witness to these acts, even if not directly participating, and Ngati Maru were
among those seen carrying off the plunder. For, as Karauria Te Ua explained, the ture
(law) was now 'broken & they might as well help themselves as they pleased'.[48] Rukupo
tried hard to mediate, offering compensation and sending delicacies (sweet kiekie in
calabashes) to the party of militia officers now stationed at Te Poho-o-Rawiri, who
rejected them. The militia refused to negotiate with him in any way, saying that McLean
and the troops would soon be there to settle everything.[49] As anticipated, it was the
arrival on 9 November of Mokena and 260 Ngati Porou, together with Donald McLean
and the government troops, which brought war.

McLean set arbitrary terms for 'peace', which were impossible for most of the

Turanga leaders to countenance. All Maori had to take an oath of allegiance; all malefactors and those who had 'fought against the Government' were to be surrendered; everyone who did not belong to the district was to be expelled; and all arms were to be surrendered. If these terms were not complied with, then the 'lands of the promoters of disturbance' would be confiscated.[50] McLean refused to negotiate or discuss his terms. The Poverty Bay tribes were being treated as rebels before they had become so.[51]

McLean's ultimatum expired on 16 November. Two or three days before that some signed the oath of allegiance. 'Tamihana Ruatapu's Party' was one. There were 53 signatories in this 'Party', but they did not include Te Kooti.[52] The major portion of Ngati Maru instead withdrew to Patutahi, a community which identified with the Pai Marire, to show their rejection of the terms.[53] Seventy-nine of them declared their intention to fight. On 16 November, with the expiry of the ultimatum, the assembled government forces moved to lay siege to the refugees sheltering at Waerenga-a-Hika with the Te Aitanga-a-Mahaki people. This assault was 'the hinge of fate' for the East Coast.[54] It forced war upon the tribes of Turanga, and it also ultimately created a 'rebel' leader from a man who had not been one: Te Kooti Arikirangi Te Turuki.

Te Kooti always claimed that he fought with the government forces at Waerenga-a-Hika, and he also said (in 1873) that he had killed two Pai Marire fighters during the siege.[55] The siege was a prolonged one, for the pa fell only on 22 November. But Te Kooti was arrested one day earlier. In a hastily scribbled 'PS' to a letter dated 21 November, the commander of the attacking forces, Major James Fraser, added: 'I have made just now a prisoner of a native called Koti on suspicion of being a spy.'[56]

It was this episode which set in motion the chain of events that led to Te Kooti's exile. There is little doubt that most of Rongowhakaata fighting with the government were extremely ambiguous about the siege. Lieutenant J. C. St George recorded in his diary many details about their lack of co-operation and their passing information to the defenders. His account is of a siege enforced by reluctant allies. He wrote on 20 November:

> Tuke today saw some of our Native allies (Hirini Te Kani's men) throwing away their bullets and firing blank cartridges during the attack this morning — I believe every one of Hirini's & Pototi's men would turn against us on the slightest reverse.[57]

Fraser also commented on the ambiguity of those who 'called themselves friendly natives' and observed, on 21 November, 'Master Hirini has not shown his nose since the fighting commenced'.[58] Captain Reginald Biggs had already noted that all of Paratene Pototi's men (about 40) were in constant communication with the Hauhau.[59] St George said, at the end of the siege, they found out from the prisoners that 'they knew of our movements almost as soon as we made them — They knew of the Gun coming up before we did — this they learnt from some of our allies (Hirini's men).'[60]

That information was smuggled into the pa is unquestionably true. That Te Kooti had kinsmen fighting with the besieged is also true. One of these was his elder brother, Komene,[61] with whom he had been living recently and who may have joined the besieged from Patutahi. On 18 and 19 November those within the pa had been massively reinforced from Patutahi. Throughout 18 November, 200 or 300 Maori had

The ruins of Waerenga-a-Hika pa, February 1866. This new pa was on the site of the present Anglican Maori cemetery on the edge of the old river bank (it was incorrectly located by James Cowan in the diagram in his history of the wars). In the background is Bishop William Williams's house, which was sacked by Mokena Kohere's assaulting troops. As John Harris noted (on 25 November): 'The Pai Marire have not done us one tenth part of the damage inflicted by Morgan and his men.' In the foreground (left) lies the niu pole, which was cut down by the troops. A few of the palisades of the pa are still visible. Photograph by Leonard Williams.   Rhodes album, F110531 1/2, ATL

watched the siege from the hilltop pa Pukeamionga, which looks down on Patutahi and the surrounding river flats. That evening one party, disguised by wearing the white calico arm badges of the government forces, infiltrated Waerenga-a-Hika pa. The next day another huge support-group of about 200 appeared, led by Anaru Matete. They divided into three forces and carried with them white calico flags, marked with a red cross in the upper corner and, in some cases, a crescent moon.[62] These were the Pai Marire fighting flags, Riki ('Lord' Michael). This kokiri (fighting party) was joined by men issuing out from the pa. The government forces immediately opened fire upon them 'before they could come up with us',[63] although some still thought the white flags might have been flags of truce. It was in this atmosphere of ambiguous loyalties and covert strategies that Te Kooti's arrest took place.

There are four main accounts of Te Kooti's actions, all recorded retrospectively. One is the diary of Paratene Ngata (father of Apirana Ngata), who came to Turanga with the Ngati Porou fighters under Mokena and Ropata Wahawaha on 9 November. In 1924 he recorded his memories of the siege at Waerenga-a-Hika. In the midst of it, he said,

> I and 24 other young men were sent to Makaraka to guard and escort the carts of stores and casks of powder that were being unloaded from a boat. Te Kooti Rikirangi and

Pencil drawings of Pai Marire flags from 'Ua Rongopai'. The first, an oblong flag (above), shows some of the emblems commonly used: X and crescent moon. It has also the fallen club, which stands for the Kingdom of David which is to come again. The second (below) has the bust of a soldier on it. This bust appears (in its style) to be an image of respect.

GNZ MMS I, APL

many others were there. They were catching horses and selling them to the Pakeha soldiers at Turanganui. They helped us to transfer the cargo from the boat to the waggons. After that, Te Kooti and his companions left, and we harnessed the bullocks to the carts. When we got to Makauri, along the track which lay through heavy whitepine bush, a messenger from the Ngai Tahupo Loyalists arrived. He urged us to hurry because Te Kooti had gone to the Hauhaus at Pukeamionga (Patutahi) and suggested that they come and waylay the convoy.

I instructed the messenger to proceed to Waerengaahika and give Ropata the message and also to ask him to send 50 soldiers to meet us on the track between Tapui and Makauri.

When he left we turned off towards Taruheru. . . . Those in the rear did all they could to obliterate the wheel marks.

We travelled all night . . . . About 8 am we arrived at Waerenga a Hika. Te Kooti was apprehended and held in a room of the Bishop's residence. My soldiers took turns, in pairs, every four hours, to guard the prisoner, until the 22nd November, 1865, when the Hauhaus surrendered. He was then included with other prisoners and escorted to Turanganui.[64]

Ngata's account is given support by a Ngati Porou manuscript history of the fighting. Here, the anonymous author remembered that at the end of the siege, when the Pai Marire emerged, they did not look human, so dirty were they and so long was their hair. It was then that

kua rangona te kupu a te Kooti Rikirangi mo nga kaata paura a te Kawanatanga i te haerenga o aua kaata ki Waerengaahika — i ki a te Kooti kia murua aua kaata paura — korero whakapae tera.

Te Kooti Rikirangi's statement was heard about the Government's powder carts on the way to Waerenga-a-Hika — that Te Kooti had said to steal them. That was the accusation made.[65]

A third account is that of W. Leonard Williams, published posthumously in 1932. He stated that Te Kooti had been charged with having communicated with the enemy and for giving ammunition to one man. 'He acknowledged that he had been in communication with his brother', Komene, but only with a view to extricating him from the war.[66] This account was certainly in circulation in 1868, when a version of it was published in the *Daily Southern Cross*.[67] There it was said that he had gone to fetch Komene from Pukeamionga, the Pai Marire pa near Patutahi, where the Ngati Maru fighters had gathered from 12 November, fearing that it would be the next place attacked by the government forces.[68] The chronology of the 1868 narrative is, however, inaccurate, for Te Kooti is said to have successfully warned his brother after the fall of Waerenga-a-Hika on 22 November — when he was already a prisoner.

The fourth account, which is the most widely known, was told first by Thomas Gudgeon in 1879, and more fully by Porter in his serialised history of Te Kooti, published in several newspapers in 1914.[69] Porter's first chapter began with the famous words, 'Ko Rikirangi! Puhia! Patua!' ('It is Rikirangi! Shoot him! Kill him!').[70] The shout came from one of three men, who had surrounded 'a young man dressed as a "friendly"'.

Porter wrote that he immediately recognised one of them, 'a fine looking old chief with a white beard, his face partially covered with the blue tattoo lines of the "moko"', who held his revolver to the young man's head. He was 'the loyal old Chief Paora Parau'. Time has distorted Porter's memory, for Paora Parau was then a young man who had been active as an informant and spokesman for the government's views since October.[71] He belonged to Te Aitanga-a-Hauiti and was, as well, a kinsman to Wi Tako Ngatata of Waikanae, and like him a strong opponent of the Pai Marire.[72] The incident is described as having taken place in the thick flax bushes at the front of the pa, near the besiegers' lines. Parau accused Te Kooti of supplying 'the rebels' with ammunition. Porter wrote:

> There was no time then to discuss the question of the prisoner's guilt or innocence, and I directed Parau to take him to head-quarters and hand him over to the guard for safe custody and await trial. This the old chief did, marching his captive off to the guard-room in the Mission-house, our present base, with his revolver still held in hand ready.[73]

None of these accounts is incompatible, but all show traces of distortion. Paratene Ngata stated that Te Kooti was then formally tried and sent to the Chathams, which is incorrect; he also claims a surprisingly large role for the 16-year-old he then was. But his account of Te Kooti has some corroboration. It seems that a form of inquiry was held, and that Te Kooti was then released, quite quickly, for want of evidence.[74] According to another version, Te Kooti was freed on the testimony of Ensign Ogilvie Ross, who later married Sarah Dunlop. Ross was badly wounded (shot through the head) on 17 November. He was not expected to live. But apparently he testified that Te Kooti was alongside him with the government forces through the thick of the siege.[75] Certainly, in 1873 Te Kooti made a similar statement, referring the government agent James Mackay to Ross for confirmation.[76] Although Ross had fought against Te Kooti in 1868, he remained friendly with him and Te Kooti wrote to Ross in 1873 seeking his help to obtain a pardon.[77] Sarah Dunlop's own account is somewhat different. She said that Te Kooti took no part in the war: 'he was down at the redoubt with us. He would fight for neither side, saying he didn't wish to'.[78] While she was probably expressing his views accurately enough, her comment cannot, in itself, be taken as correct.

The siege came to an end with the surrender of about 200 men and another 200 women and children. Seventy-one Turanga Maori died there.[79] Some of those who had been taken prisoner during the fighting were kept at the Kohanga Karearea redoubt while others were transferred into the hands of the Rongowhakaata at Oweta, under the leadership of Tamihana Ruatapu. Te Kooti was not among either group. But there were those at Poverty Bay who maintained that he should have been held and sent away. On 14 April 1866, John Harris wrote to McLean:

> There are several parties here, who ought to be got rid of — Koti & his brother Komene both known thieves. — broke into Bloomfield's house at Matawhira and have killed cattle &c. on several occasions and the former is known to have been a spy all through the opperations carried on here.[80]

Paora Parau. He was one of the Maori police guards who took the third party of prisoners, which included Te Kooti, to Wharekauri in June 1866. He remained on the island for a while, when this photograph was taken.

A different portrait of him, when slightly older but still in military uniform, has inscribed on the back: 'Paora Parau Good friend & chief but an awful drinker' (carte de visite, ATL).

It is interesting that Harris also named Wi Pere, the young leader of Te Aitanga-a-Mahaki, who had certainly been equivocal in his attitudes towards the Pai Marire. According to Harris, Wi Pere had supplied caps to the Hauhau at Waerenga-a-Hika, and had 'avowed Riki and Rura, by encircling the niu'. Harris claimed that Wi Pere had passed on as much information as he could and, at the last minute, 'came with his friends' to Tamihana's pa at Oweta. Hervey, writing two days after Harris, chose to single out for government attention Renata Tupara, the Ngati Maru chief, calling him both the expert thief who had picked his locks and Anaru Matete's 'right hand man'.[81]

Te Kooti had, in actuality, been seized again before either of these letters was written: on 3 March 1866. That he was, as he sang in his waiata, included in the group of prisoners who were seized on that day[82] seems to be confirmed by a letter written on 5 March: that among those who had been bundled onto the *St Kilda* was 'one that was [first] apprehended some time ago for communicating with the enemy after he had surrendered at the fight at Waerenga a hika.'[83]

It was the arrival of McLean and the governor, Sir George Grey, at Poverty Bay on 3 March which had set these events in motion. Grey brought with him Te Ua as a prisoner on display so as to destroy his mana in the region. This idea had been put to the government by the senior Hawke's Bay chiefs, Karaitiana Takamoana and Renata Kawepo.[84] Grey's arrival at Turanga coincided deliberately with that of McLean and the *St Kilda*, chartered by the government to take the East Coast Pai Marire prisoners to Napier and Wharekauri. The idea had first been mooted by the Minister for Defence, Colonel T. M. Haultain, when he visited Turanga on 20 February. McLean's appearance was the first indication locally that this policy was about to be enforced. A hurried meeting was called with a select group of the Kawanatanga chiefs. McLean apparently told them that the length of time the prisoners would remain on Wharekauri would be determined by their behaviour there, although earlier a term of about 12 months had been mentioned.[85] The proposition was approved by the chiefs, according to Leonard Williams, and embarkation began at once. In less than four hours, and before darkness fell, there were as many on board as the 75-foot schooner could accommodate: 42 (or 44) men and 48 women and children, making a total of about ninety.[86] They were all Te Aitanga-a-Mahaki prisoners[87] — except Te Kooti.

Te Kooti was summarily seized that day. According to one body of tradition, he was working in his taro patch or, variously, he was out pig-hunting at Repongaere when he was trapped.[88] Yet another version has it that he was peacefully carting timber, on contract, for an officer's residence being built at Napier.[89] A first-hand, though retrospective, version is given in George Goldsmith's affidavit of December 1889, where he testified that he was one of the militia volunteers who arrested Te Kooti in 1866 at 'Taratukia'; by implication this was the reason for the reprisals which Te Kooti exacted against him and his family in 1868.[90] A fourth account names James Wyllie, who was also one of the militia volunteers and was notorious for his abusive language and behaviour. Wyllie said, when he saw Te Kooti sitting on the beach at Muriwai, '"Take this man too."'[91]

What exactly Te Kooti was accused of still remains uncertain. There are two distinct versions. One is derived from Tuta Nihoniho's account of the 'tangata puremu', the adulterous man. Tuta stated that it was the cuckolded Rongowhakaata chief Hamiora Whakataka who seized the opportunity and laid the 'concocted' charge to the European officers and the Kawanatanga chiefs that he had seen Te Kooti supplying gun-caps to the Hauhau at Waerenga-a-Hika. Te Kooti was then seized and flung

> like a dog into a boat taking Hauhau out to the steamer. Te Kooti asked, 'For what reason am I put in the boat with the Hauhau? I am not a Hauhau!' But what cared Biggs, and Wilson, and Paratene Turangi [Pototi], and other Native chiefs? All they said to Te Kooti was, 'Go on to the boat; go on to the boat.'[92]

In this narrative is embedded the rationale for Te Kooti's reprisal in 1868: for the three men named there would all be executed.[93] Two Maori, Ihimaera Hokopu and Pera Taihuka, attributed with having reported that they had seen Te Kooti supplying ammunition to the Pai Marire at Waerenga-a-Hika, would also be killed in the attack on Turanganui in 1868.[94] Elsdon Best understood that Te Kooti's re-arrest had been because some former Pai Marire, held as prisoners, had given this information about him.[95] But it was Paratene Pototi whom Te Kooti particularly remembered for the contempt with which he kicked him onto the boat and into exile, his words parroting the voices of the Pakeha officers: 'Go ona te poti'.

The other version derives from the statement of Captain George Preece that a letter had been intercepted from Te Kooti to his chief Anaru Matete, warning him of an ambush: 'Wednesday is the day, and Te Reinga is the place.'[96] Anaru had escaped from the pa at Waerenga-a-Hika and with about 100 men had made his way to inland Wairoa. There they were again pursued, and attacked.[97] By early January they had been driven inland, from Te Reinga across to Waikaremoana. However, Anaru again escaped and he had remained in direct communication with Poverty Bay. On 17 February Leonard Williams described the message that Anaru had sent back:

> First there is going to be a great runanga held in England to enquire into the reasons why the Maories are being killed off by the Pakeha. This runanga is going to be conducted by 'Te Tuuka' (?Duke of Newcastle). Hare R[eweti] [C. O. Davis] blames ML. [McLean] for having rushed into war on this coast, & the Bishop of Waiapu comes in also for his share. There was no necessity for fighting anywhere but at Opotiki, as these people had done nothing in these other places but turn Hhaus, & the Hhau religion shd be tolerated just as well as any other religion. The Maori Kawanatanga will go to the wall yet & Hauhauism will gain the day, and the time will en[sue] when Anaru Matete will return triumphantly to Turanga and apportion the land to the people who are to occupy it, and carry all before him.[98]

Anaru had become the leader of a significant movement of dissent on the East Coast. At Te Reinga he had linked up with Te Waru, who with a party of kinsmen had also fought with the Pai Marire at Waerenga-a-Hika and had similarly escaped. This renewed alliance brought about the beginning of the Wairoa war in December 1865. Although the Pai Marire had been driven inland by January, they had gathered in strength at Waikaremoana.

McLean's decision to take prisoners at Turanga on 3 March was made in this context, combined with his belief that there were still 'fugitives' at Turanga, capable of attack on Europeans.[99] In May Te Waru capitulated and took the oath of allegiance, but the Tuhoe resistance at Waikaremoana to the Ngati Kahungunu government forces still appeared as a major threat to McLean, and directly influenced his subsequent judgments at Napier,[100] including his disregard of Te Kooti's written pleas for a hearing.

The war was also brought to Hawke's Bay. The final defeat of the Pai Marire on the East Coast occurred there, on 12 October 1866, with great losses among the Hauhau, who were besieged at Omarunui and Petane. Some of the prisoners taken that day indicated that, although their own prophet–leader, Panapa, had established direct links with Anaru, Anaru was not the instigator of war nor of the Pai Marire cause in the district[101] — though he had been widely believed to be so. Rather, he had radically changed both his tactics and his objectives.

In May 1866 Anaru had got through the Urewera country and gone to King Tawhiao. In the past Anaru had always rejected association with the Kingitanga in favour of a policy of independence and neutrality for Turanga.[102] But now, from Taupo, Anaru sent out Tawhiao's proclamation to all the East Coast tribes, which invited them to take shelter within his house. In an accompanying letter dated 7 June and carried to Turanga by Anaru's daughter, Harata Hinepoka, and her escort, Maaka Taina (Younger Brother), Anaru described the errors of the two original Pai Marire messengers, Kereopa and Patara. These included the attempt to set up Hirini as a challenge to Tawhiao as King. Anaru now rejected Rura and Riki. He talked of the transfer of power in Taranaki to new prophetic leaders there, Te Whiti, Tohu Kakahi and Taikomako. He stated that God now stood with them, and also with Tawhiao. He said that the Lord ('te Ariki'), the appointed prophets, Tawhiao and 'I too will retain the land and it will not be taken away' ('kei ahau ano hoki te Whenua e pupuru ana e kore e riro').[103] Anaru and his followers had turned their back on war, although this was not understood at the time. The message was also obscured by Maaka's stressing the need for extensive planting of potatoes along the road to Te Reinga, apparently in preparation for the renewal of war in the spring.[104]

It was because the government considered Anaru to be the instigator of a broad Maori alliance, reaching to the Kingitanga, to Taranaki and to Tuhoe, that he was thought to be so dangerous. It was Anaru's conduct and his apparent sustained association with Kereopa and Patara which ensured that Te Kooti would also continue to be judged as a treacherous 'spy'.

The policies of land confiscation on the East Coast were being developed inside this framework. The means were not yet determined, but were certainly being discussed locally in January and February 1866.[105] Read was already seizing the opportunity to panic Maori into selling in advance.[106] A Native Land Court was expected to be held at Turanga, and the question of what was to be 'done' with the 'Hauhau land' would be considered then.[107] In fact, the legislation for the East Coast area was brought into place only in October. It empowered the court to inquire into title and seize any land of those engaged in 'rebellion'. But as early as March the government agents had certainly had it on their agenda to remove all potential troublemakers. As Leonard Williams stated, when Haultain had first introduced the idea of deportation at Turanga, the object was to have the prisoners 'out of the way until the question of the confiscation of land should be settled, as the people had been warned beforehand that they would be punished in this way' by McLean's ultimatum.[108] Anaru Matete's message of February also makes it clear that the 'division of the land' had become the focus of renewed local discontent. He promised the reassertion of Maori control and the triumphant reapportioning of the land.

Te Kooti's arrest took place as these events began to burgeon and intersect. There were clearly a number of settlers and Turanga Maori leaders who were happy to see him kicked onto the boat. But he himself always protested his innocence. There seems no question that he was not a convert to the Pai Marire religion. That he acted out of kinship loyalties and a growing commitment to the cause of the land of Turanga, together with a concern for his younger chief, Anaru, seems very likely. It is certain, however, that he was never brought to trial for any of the charges made. It was abuse of power which finally engendered Te Kooti's imprisonment — and his subsequent actions.

In the waiata he composed telling of his exile as starting on 3 March, he sings only of his sadness at being taken from his home. He also speaks of his rejection of the Pai Marire God 'Tamarura', who had brought all the trouble upon them.

> Ka tu au ka korikori
> Ka puta te rongo o Taranaki e hau mai nei.
> Ka toro taku ringa ki te Atua e tu nei
> Ko Tamarura, ka mate i te riri ki Waerengahika.
> I te toru o Maehe ka whiua atu au ki runga i te kaipuke.
> Ka tere moana nui au nga whakaihu ki Waikawa,
> Ka huri tenei te riu ki Ahuriri hei a Te Makarini,
> I whiua atu au ki runga ki a Te Kira au e noho nei.
> Ka tahuri whakamuri he wai kei aku kamo e riringi nei.
> Hanganui Hangaroa[109] nga ngaru whakapuke, kei Wharekauri,
> E noho. E te iwi tu ake ki runga ra tiro iho ki raro ra
> Awangawanga ana te rere mai a te ao ra runga i Hangaroa
> I ahu mai Turanga i te wa kainga kua wehea
> Na konei te aroha e te iwi kua a haere nei kupapa
> E te iwi ki raro ki te maru o te Kuini,
> He kawe mo tatau ki runga ki te oranga tonutanga.
> Kaati ra nga kupu i māka i te wa i mua ra
> Tena ko tenei e te iwi whakarongo ki te ture kawana
> Hei whakapai ake mo te mahi a Rura naana nei i raru ai e.

Here only a literal translation of this song is attempted:

> I stand and bestir myself,
> The news, brought here from Taranaki, is out.
> My hand reaches forth to the God standing here,
> Tamarura (Son-Ruler), defeated in the fighting at Waerenga-[a]-Hika.
> On 3 March I was flung on board the ship.
> I was borne across the great ocean, by the headlands to Waikawa,[110]
> Sent on, and dropped off at Ahuriri,[111] to McLean,

Then thrown on board the *St Kilda*, there to remain.
I turned back, the tears welling from my eyes.
Hanganui, Hangaroa,[112] the waves rise up, to Wharekauri,
There to remain. O people, arise and look to the north
The clouds flying towards us over Hangaroa bring grief.
They come from Turanga, the distant home from which we are separated
Causing such yearning, o people. We will continue quietly now,
O people, under the shelter of the Queen,
That we may all be carried to the prosperous life.
Enough of the words recited in the days gone by,
This is it, o people, obey the law of the governor,
Which will set to right the troublesome work of Rura.[113]

The waiata recalls Toiroa's earlier prediction: that he would one day see him sail from the bay, the tears welling from his eyes, and separated from those he loved. Toiroa lived to see all these events, for he died on 16 July 1867, when Te Kooti was on Wharekauri.[114] Te Kooti's last visit to the old man is remembered as being in the month of February (and quite possibly in 1865), when Toiroa warned him he would not now remain long at the village at Turanga and that misfortune would strike the land and the people.[115] It is significant that in the waiata, which is written in the form of a song of yearning, Te Kooti, following the spirit of the old man's teachings, urges the people to obey the government and the law, despite all the events they had experienced.

The prisoners on the *St Kilda* were taken first to the Napier immigration barracks and there placed under guard. The intention was to send them immediately to Wharekauri, but McLean soon discovered that a number of them had not been directly involved in the fighting at all. Only 39 of the men were sent in the first batch of prisoners to Wharekauri, with ten women and 19 children.[116] Te Kooti was not included. Of those who remained behind, some were still held over in Napier, while yet others were brought home again on the *St Kilda*. Harris's letter of 14 April (quoted earlier), which named Te Kooti and Komene among the 'several parties here, who ought to be got rid of', was written to complain about those who had just been sent back. They had arrived at Turanga on the previous day. He said: 'Some of those returned are great scamps. I did hope we had seen their backs for some time.'[117] He then named one elderly man, Paora Te Arawharuke, as 'one of the worst' of these, and he continued with a descriptive list of those he considered should be got rid of. Te Kooti and Komene are the first mentioned and the context implies that they had just been brought home.

The *St Kilda* had returned to Poverty Bay not merely to take these prisoners back but also to round up a fresh selection of the 'worst' of Te Aitanga-a-Mahaki, defined as those who had refused to accede to terms until taken prisoner at Waerenga-a-Hika.[118] It seems unlikely that Harris would not have known whether Te Kooti had been arrested and retained in Napier. However, all is uncertain. Te Kooti may have been held over in Napier because of the degree of suspicion about him. He may have been kept on the boat and transferred from one ship to another, as oral tradition has it.[119] Or he may have been returned and then re-arrested — for a third time.

In Te Kooti's own account, given in 1873, he refers to two distinct arrests only. He also cited another player: Captain George Read. Te Kooti told James Mackay that shortly after the fight at Waerenga-a-Hika he was arrested on a trumped-up charge of horse stealing, brought by Read in revenge for Te Kooti's independent trading activities, which had reduced Read's business with Maori. There was a magisterial inquiry, he said, and the case was dismissed. 'Then they said I was a Hauhau and a spy for them. Captain Reid [*sic*] used his influence, and I was made a military prisoner and sent to Napier.'[120] This account does not explain the sequence of events accurately, but it does reinforce the evidence of the vitriolic hostility towards Te Kooti shared by the traders, all of whom were in regular contact with McLean. This hostility towards a sharp-witted economic competitor certainly contributed to his arrests, however many there were.

The second batch of prisoners was gathered up at Poverty Bay on 16 April and sent on to Wharekauri from Napier a week later. They were almost all from Te Aitanga-a-Mahaki. The batch sent on to Wharekauri did not include Te Kooti — nor any of the Rongowhakaata prisoners.[121] They were being held back for the third sailing of the *St Kilda*.[122] A list of the prisoners originally intended for the second sailing of the *St Kilda* has also survived.[123] It included the 48 males who were sent, and an additional ten men from Rongowhakaata who were not. Nine of the ten were sent with the third batch; one individual seems not to have been sent at all. But Te Kooti was not among these ten.

On 15–22 May McLean again visited Turanga to administer the oath of allegiance. There, on the last night, George Read threw a 'grand dinner' for him and the officers of the garrison.[124] McLean wrote afterwards that, during this visit, he had not considered it necessary to take any more prisoners from Poverty Bay, with the exception of two natives 'who acted as spies during the war'.[125] This may well be a reference to Te Kooti's re-arrest. If so, the decision was influenced as much by Anaru's continuing resistance as by the local vendettas directed against Te Kooti.

He was certainly held in the Napier gaol in early June. On 4 June he wrote urgently from there to McLean:

> E hoa, he ki atu naku mo te taha ki a au e noho nei i roto i te hauhau. Me whakaatu mai taku hara kia marama ai i a au. Hua noa hoki au me wakawa. Heoi ano. Na Tekoti, kuini maori.

> Friend. This is what I have to say about my staying amongst the Hauhau. Explain to me what I have done wrong so that it is clear to me. I also think I should be brought to trial. That is all. Te Koti, Queen's Maori.[126]

In a second letter, dated 6 June, he and his brother Komene together wrote to McLean:

> E hoa, tena koe. Tenei taku kupu ki a koe ko nga tangata kino i waiho e koe, ara, te kino ko te hoatu tingara ki nga tangata, ko Te Rire ko Waere. He pu he tingara na Waere enei na Te Rire he tingara. Ko nga maori kawana ko Himiona Katipa, ko Pera Kararehe [Pera Taihuka], ko Te Otene Puru, ko Te Watene Tangiori, ko Hare Turi, ko enei tangata

Te Kooti's letter to Donald McLean, 4 June 1866, asking for a trial.   HB4/13, NA

he hoatu tingara pu ki te hauhau. Pono rawa tena korero. Heoi ano. Na Tekooti raua
ko Komene.

Friend. Greetings. My message to you concerns certain bad men whom you have let be,
Read and Wyllie, whose misdeed was to give percussion caps to other men. Wyllie [gave
away] guns and caps; Read percussion caps. The government Maori who gave per-
cussion caps to the Hauhau were Himiona Katipa, Pera Kararehe [Pera Taihuka], Te
Otene Puru, Te Watene Tangiori and Hare Turi. That information is absolutely true.
That is all. Te Kooti and Komene.[127]

In a third, undated, letter to his 'tuakana' (elder brother or cousin), Te Matenga
Tukareaho,[128] Te Kooti again protested his innocence and asked Te Matenga to intervene
on his behalf with McLean. He stated that the Hauhau all knew that he was a 'Queen's
man' ('ko au he kuini au') right up to the engagement at Turanga, when he fought those
who ran into the bush. He added that he and his hapu, whom here he named as being
Ngai Te Kete, were all loyal to the Queen. (Ngai Te Kete were the small hapu of
Rongowhakaata who had consented to Mokena's erection of the flagstaff at Turanga;
they are usually identified as the same people as Ngai Tawhiri, old Paratene Pototi's
hapu;[129] Te Kooti's somewhat distant kinship with them is shown in Whakapapa B on
page 30.) Te Kooti complained that none of those on the Queen's side had come to see
him while he was held prisoner. He said that it was thought that there would be trials
held at Turanga, and that it was perhaps for this reason that some from the second batch
of prisoners had been held back, men like Te Waaka Rongotu and Heremaia Kohukohu,
whom he here named. (Te Waaka Rongotu was, significantly, Raharuhi Rukupo's only
son, and he would be sent to Wharekauri with Te Kooti in the third batch of prisoners.)
Te Kooti urged again that he be given a trial, so that the error could be brought out.[130]

His protests and his naming of the local merchant gun-runners were of little use. His
citing of information against his kinsmen, an unpleasant act of desperation, and his
claim of primary tribal allegiance to those who had helped erect the flagstaff were
equally in vain. F. E. Hamlin, the government interpreter at Napier at the time,
commented later, in the context of Te Kooti's appeal to Grey in 1879, that Te Kooti had

persistently requested a trial, saying to him frequently in prison, '"my great desire is to be tried for my offences"'.[131] Hamlin commented that his understanding was that Te Kooti had been held, not because he had actively taken up arms against the government, but that 'the great accusation against him was that he supplied the rebels with arms and ammunition and also acted not only as a spy but also as an adviser to the rebels.'[132] If this was so, it is already clear that he was far from alone in these actions in a situation where most of the Turanga Maori had consistently rejected the absolutist divisions of 'loyal' or 'disloyal' which had been foisted upon them. Neither Te Kooti nor any of the Rongowhakaata men held back were tried. Nor were Te Kooti's appeals seriously considered — merely filed. One reason may have been that they coincided with the letters sent out by Anaru Matete to the senior chiefs of Hawke's Bay and Turanga, urging their coalition under the King.

The first of these letters had been sent on 17 May from Tauranga on the shores of Lake Taupo. This was where Te Kooti would seek to make his new home when he first returned from exile in 1868. Anaru wrote to the leading Hawke's Bay chiefs, Karaitiana Takamoana, Renata Kawepo and Paora Kaiwhata, telling them that the land had been saved and that the King movement was absolute. He therefore urged them to 'return ashore' ('hoki mai ki uta') with him, likening the King to the high ground on which the people might take refuge.[133] The second group of letters was sent on 7 June to Rukupo and to Paratene Titore. The letter to Paratene was intercepted by McLean, who showed it to Leonard Williams at Napier on 12 June, just after Te Kooti had been sent to Wharekauri.[134] These later letters were sent from Ruatahuna, where Anaru had renewed links with the most feared tribe of all — because they were so unknown — the Tuhoe of the mountainous Urewera. To Rukupo, Anaru wrote:

> E ta, kua ora te motu kenana. . . . Kua mau te motu, kei uta te whenua kei uta te tangata. Kei te ringa o te Ariki, kaha rawa, kei te ringa o Tawhiao, kei te ringa o tana Tekaumarua e pupuri ana te motu katoa.

> Sir, the land of Canaan is safe. . . . The land is retained, the lands and the people ashore. The whole land is being held in the hands of Almighty God, in the hands of Tawhiao, and in the hands of his Tekaumarua [the Twelve apostles of Tawhiao].[135]

He added that he had given up all the lands of the East Coast from Wairoa to Uawa into the hands of the Lord, and to 'his blessed leader, Tawhiao' ('ko tana manaaki ko Tawhiao'). He signed the letter with the insignia 'X 3'. These were the same religious emblems as had been used on the Pai Marire flags: they were probably signs for the Lord and the Trinity respectively. The Kingdom of David, promised to be restored on earth, was now interpreted to be the establishment of the Kingdom of Tawhiao. The Poverty Bay chiefs, in a collective letter signed by Hirini Te Kani, Paratene Pototi and Waaka Puakanga (among others), rejected Anaru's claims outright. They told him that the land was not in his hands, nor those of Tawhiao. The land, they said, belonged to the Queen — and to them. It rested in their hands. They asked pointedly, 'Where is ashore?' ('Kei hea a uta?'). They urged him instead to end the war, to stop the killing deep within the forests, and to return to his home.[136]

Maori prisoners on Napier's stony foreshore below the prison, waiting to embark on the *St Kilda* for Wharekauri. This group is said to be the third batch of prisoners (47 people), which included Te Kooti. Photograph probably by Charles Robson, 1866.   118691 1/2, ATL

These letters reveal the deep divisions which had now developed among the tribes of the East Coast. Te Kooti's position at this time was probably still closer to that of the Turanga chiefs than that of Anaru. His waiata of exile, composed for himself and for his people, witnesses his continued belief in the righteousness of the law — despite the fact that it was composed after he had been sent to Wharekauri.

Te Kooti and his brother Komene were despatched on the *St Kilda* with the third group of prisoners, nearly all Rongowhakaata people. They embarked on 5 June, the day before the date given on their joint letter of appeal. The decision was probably taken without McLean ever having considered their pleas. Their inclusion had almost certainly been urged by Reginald Biggs, the newly appointed commander of the Turanga militia, who was in Napier at this time[137] and who clearly wanted to be rid of potential trouble-makers. Te Kooti always blamed Biggs for his exile.

The new batch of prisoners, a party of 30 men, nine women and eight children, landed on the island on 10 June.[138] The years of the Exile had begun.

CHAPTER 3

EXILE
(JUNE 1866–JULY 1868)

———————————

The prisoners were sent to an island which was ill-prepared for their arrival. No housing had been arranged: each party had to 'hut themselves'.[1] They were stationed at Waitangi, on the western coast of Wharekauri, and batch 'No 3' spent June and July, the mid-winter days of 1866, constructing long communal houses out of ponga and flax in the separate compound established for the prisoners.[2] Then they joined the others in build-ing the barracks and the redoubt and digging the surrounding trenches, at the other end of the little bay. A further large batch of prisoners arrived on 23 October, consisting of those who had been captured at Omarunui and Petane: 52 men and eight women.[3] A final group landed on 28 December, also prisoners from the Hawke's Bay war: 21 men, 12 women and seven children.[4] For the most part, the women and children were accompanying their husbands or fathers and, according to the instructions, were not to be treated as prisoners.[5] However, the eight women who were sent in October were prisoners, and they alone of the women are named in the prison lists. These five parties were the whakarau: the 'political offenders',[6] as they were described, kept on the island without trial. Their imprisonment was later admitted to have been illegal.[7] They were primarily, but not entirely, from the East Coast — Te Aitanga-a-Mahaki, Rongowhaka-ata, Ngati Hineuru and Ngati Kahungunu — and most of them had been believers in the Pai Marire faith.

They had all found the 500-mile voyage from Napier harsh, and they were unaccus-tomed to the extreme cold of the island. Most of them had quite inadequate clothing. Some became very ill, and 28 are known to have died on Wharekauri.[8] A hospital was finally completed in May 1867, built by the prisoners out of ponga and 'tohitohi' (flax). Consumption was one of the killers, but there were also deaths directly related to the hard work. They were poorly equipped for the task of growing their food, which was expected to supplement, and ultimately replace, the government rations. Fishing was also difficult, as they were not experienced in putting out from these rough shores. They grew some potatoes but, at first, were given neither ploughs nor seed for wheat, the government seeing these as only leading to demands for a mill.[9] Early in 1868, however, they got the ploughs and in the oral traditions it is still remembered how they had to yoke one another, including women and children, to the ploughs so as to pull them.[10] They hated the indignity so much that they regularly broke their tools. One of the

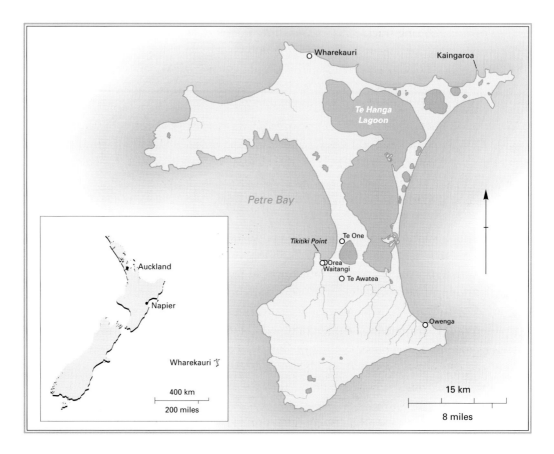

Map 1. Wharekauri (Rekohu) (Chatham Island)

Wharekauri settlers, Tom Ritchie, wrote that the blacksmith had told him how the prisoners

> would stand and get their feet on their spades & work them into the ground doing nothing till Elliott [the head guard] & Finmore [Fynmore, the sergeant] came round they would catch the handel of the buried spade & break it so the reason of their not working was their[s] was broken & so they were sent to my shop with their spades & blow the bellows if required untill they were repaired the same with their ploughs. The ploughs were so often broken Capt Thomas told Child [the blacksmith] he would not pay for any more ploughs broken unless he garranteed them for a month. . . . Alright I look out no broke for a month . . . & the next day the afore said plough was broken the same with other things. Hau Haus had a holiday helping I around [?] while the plough was being mended.[11]

Earlier, some prisoners were hired to labour for the few European settlers on various parts of the island, and one ponga log hut, built by them, still survives on the Wharekauri estate.[12] They were paid for this labour, and at first (from December 1866) it was 1s 6d a day. But as the money was kept 'in trust' until their return to New Zealand, they saw little profit from it, and were reluctant to work in this manner. Most were used on roadmaking and cutting tracks on the island after the redoubt and the gaol were finished.

Te Kooti soon became quite ill, and his name recurs in the medical reports from December 1866. He was treated for chronic asthma. In March 1867 the doctor, John Watson, reported that Te Kooti was 'unfit for work', and that he suffered from asthma of 'fifteen years standing'.[13] He was seriously ill from 7 December 1866 ('cough and cold' for a fortnight) right through to May 1867; that is, the period in which he underwent the visionary experiences which he recorded in his diary. He was ill for a week in September 1867, and also in June 1868, just before the escape. This last occasion was again reported as 'asthma'. The missionary stationed on the island, J. G. Engst, described him in 1868 as a 'sick, miserable man', and added that he often gave him money, because of his need.[14]

It is probable that, in fact, Te Kooti was suffering from tuberculosis, which had not yet been medically identified as a bacillus. TB was very common among Maori in the 19th century, and it took many forms. It flourished particularly in situations of privation: poverty, overcrowding and malnutrition. It was also contagious. Its general symptoms are a long drawn-out fever and a wasting away, and Te Kooti's illness was described by his Maori companions as 'he pararūtiki', a form of paralytic fever.[15] But it is also possible for patients to recover from TB of the lungs, even of an advanced nature, and this seems to have been precisely what happened to Te Kooti.

Edmund Tuke, one of the military guards on the island, said that 'one morning after the boats had returned from a fishing expedition' (Te Kooti was the principal steer-oar in the whaling boat), 'I found Te Kooti in a very bad state — spitting blood.'[16] He was put on the sick list, and was so ill that he was taken to a separate whare to die. The prisoners got his winding-sheet ready,[17] and began to prepare a coffin. One of the seminal Maori oral traditions springs from this time. He was looked after only by an old woman, 'his aunt',[18] probably Wikitoria Topa, wife of Te Warihi.[19] Te Kooti lay with a burning fever, watching the fire in his hut. The fire became a ngarara (lizard) and each of its limbs was a burning brand as it started to crawl towards him. He cried out to God, and the lizard became a fire again. After this test of Te Kooti's faith, the second test occurred when the hut became flooded with water, which rose almost to his neck and threatened to engulf him. He again cried out to God, and the water drained away. After the third test, which the narrator of this story, Monita Delamere, could not recollect,[20] Te Kooti told his aunt, when she came to him with his food during the evening:

> 'This is what I want you to do. You go to the house' — there was a house there, a minister's house — 'and you see the minister sitting on his chair, at his table, and the light.' And he said, 'You see the books on his table, and you take the one on the right hand side and bring it.' Told her exactly, and she didn't want to go, because — but Te Kooti said, 'Haere, haere!' And she did. It went exactly as Te Kooti explained to her: 'You'll find that old fellow sitting there, all you do is go in, and bring the book out — he won't harm you.' But he made sure — 'Not the one on the left, but the one on the right.' So she went in and brought it, and that minister, when he saw her, he looked up and he was astounded — he couldn't do a thing! It was the Holy Bible. That's the one she took, and the karakias were formed from there. And the Tangi a Heremaia was the first hymn.[21]

This narrative traces the origin of the teachings of the Ringatu to Wharekauri and specifically to the texts of the scriptures. The Lamentation (Tangi) of Jeremiah is the original hymn of the faith. It describes the pain of bondage and exile. In its final lines the hymn says: 'Our own lands have been taken by strangers, but you will always be my Father, for ever' ('Kua riro to matou wahi tipu i nga tangata ke, ko koe tonu ia hei Matua tipu moku, ake ake').[22] The hymn also says, 'But let my heart and my hands be raised up in the search for my God' ('Aue kia ara atu toku ngakau me oku ringaringa, ki te whai i toku Atua').[23] The practice which would become particular to Ringatu and which gave the faith its name — the raising of the hand in praise of God at the end of each prayer — stemmed from these words. Today, and for as long as anyone can remember, the practice is to raise up the right hand. As Monita Delamere said simply, 'I think it began from there — from that hymn, Te Tangi a Heremaia'.[24]

Eria Raukura, who was to become the senior tohunga of the faith and who had come to the island with the fourth group of prisoners when he was about 32 years old,[25] listed for Porter the texts of Te Kooti's earliest teachings. The fount, and a part of the very first service which Te Kooti created on Wharekauri,[26] was Jeremiah 31:16–17:

> Thus saith the Lord; Refrain thy voice from weeping, and thine eyes from tears: for thy work shall be rewarded, saith the Lord; and they shall come again from the land of the enemy.
>
> And there is hope in thine end, saith the Lord, that thy children shall come again to their own border.

Walter Christie, who was a guard on Wharekauri in 1867, said that Te Kooti had borrowed his bible and copied out portions of it.[27] The remark suggests (as does Monita Delamere's narrative) that the text Te Kooti used was an English-language bible. Indeed, the complete Maori bible was published only in 1868. We know that Te Kooti read aloud portions from a 'large' English-language book in 1869: it may have been Christie's bible. It is also thought that Te Kooti owned a little pocket-book of English *School Songs, Sacred, Moral, and Descriptive*, published in 1859 for use in the day schools;[28] admonitory and self-improving in its tone, it probably derived from his days at the Three Kings Institution. He also owned a volume which contained together the Anglican Maori prayer-book and psalms of 1859 and the Maori New Testament of 1862.[29] It is possible that he had that volume with him on Wharekauri. Leonard Williams was told that, at first, Te Kooti had refused the Testament offered him when he was ill but took the prayer-book and 'read the psalms from it to himself with great avidity'.[30] Later, Williams also wrote that, during his convalescence, Te Kooti had studied the 'imprecatory passages in the Psalter',[31] and this prayer-book and Testament contains a few (but not many) annotations in what appears to be Te Kooti's hand, making deletions from the text and emphasising certain passages in the psalms and the scriptures.[32] In Te Kooti's Wharekauri diary there are many passages copied out from the scriptures, both the Old and the New Testaments. The translations of the Old Testament in his diary are close to (but not identical with) those in the 1868 Anglican Maori bible, which suggests that Te Kooti had had access to or had memorised passages from earlier Anglican translations of various sections of the Old Testament, which had

The first vision, 21 February 1867: the Voice ('Reo') of God speaks to Te Kooti. Two pages from Te Kooti's diary on Wharekauri.

C12471, ATL

been published in three separate parts by 1858. However, the juxtaposition of passages and verses, by which he created his services with their particular emphases, was entirely his own.

More significant, Te Kooti also recorded in his diary the visions he experienced during his feverish illness. The first entry is dated 21 February 1867:

> Ko te marama tenei i nui ai toku mate 21 o nga ra ka hemo au

> This was the month in which my sickness increased, on the 21st day I became unconscious.[33]

The Spirit of God ('te Wairua o te Atua') came to him and raised him up, telling him that he had been sent to make known the name of God 'to his people who are dwelling in captivity in this land' ('ki tona iwi e noho whakarau nei i tenei whenua'). Te Kooti wrote that his illness prevented him from recalling clearly what had then been said to him.

On 21 March he again became unconscious, and the Voice ('Reo') which had spoken a month before spoke again. When he looked, he could see nothing. He asked his friends, weeping over him, who it was that had spoken, but they did not know. 'I then surmised it was God himself' ('ano ahau ka mahara ko te Atua anake').

On 10 April he was smitten with the same illness and was, he wrote, 'like unto a tree that has been struck down by the wind, that looks never again to be joined to its root' ('ano te rite kei te rakau e tuakina ana ki raro e whatia ana hoki e te hau kahore nei ona maharatanga kia hoki ano ki tona putake'). On 21 April he again became unconscious, and again the voice spoke to him. It told him to fear not, for God had heard his crying. He said he would teach him the words which he had spoken to 'all your ancestors' ('koutou tipuna'), Abraham, Isaac and Jacob, and their descendants down to David. He told him that man's knowledge was from writing ('he reta'), and comes only from without; but that the knowledge he possessed was from within, and could not be seen by another. The words which he spoke, therefore, Te Kooti must teach the people. Then the voice appeared in bodily form, and he was like a man.

> Ko te ahua [o] ona waewae kei te kapua ma, ko tona kakahu kei te hukarere te ma, ko tona mahunga kei nga whetu nui, ko tona karauna kei te ra, ko tona whitiki kei te torengitanga o te ra kei te rerenga ake hoki, ko tona kowhiuwhiu kei te kopere, ko tona tokotoko kahore ano i kitea i tenei ao . . . .

> His feet appeared like a white cloud, his garments were like the whiteness of snow, his head like a myriad of stars, his crown like the sun, his girdle as the setting and rising of the sun, his fan was like a rainbow, and his staff was such as has never been seen in this world . . . .

The staff was of every colour, impossible to distinguish, and too bright to gaze upon. But the voice was as clear as crystal. This figure of God, undoubtedly derived from the Book of Revelation,[34] told him again to fear not ('kaua e wehi'), for he would not forsake him or his people. Then he instructed him. Te Kooti wrote:

> ko te nui o nga korero katoa me nga inoi me nga tangi, na mau katoa i roto i a au enei korero ahakoa nui, kahore hoki he pukapuka i toku taha i tau[a] ra i homai ai enei korero kia mahia e ahau. Katahi ia ka mea mai, Tuhituhia ki to ngakau no te mea e kore koe e mahue i a au a maku koe e whakaako.

> most of all that was said, including the prayers and the laments, I retained, despite the quantity and even though I had no book at my side on the day on which I was given these instructions to carry out. He then said, 'Inscribe this on your heart for I will not forsake you, and I will teach you.'[35]

On a later occasion, 21 May, the spirit again told him to reject books, as they were written by humans. In this text, then, is embedded the importance of orality to the foundation and rituals of the faith. The command also reinforced the Maori oral systems of transmitting knowledge directly from person to person, in contrast with Europeans' belief in written books, whose authority was considered uncertain. However, Te Kooti laboured over his diary and he would ensure that all his prophetic statements were recorded in writing. One of the whakarau also wrote down some of the first prayers which Te Kooti composed. Six inoi (prayers), written on the back of the 'Scale of Rations' for prisoners, have survived. The document seems to have travelled with the whakarau for it includes annotations referring to Opepe, Tauranga and Taupo, where fighting occurred in 1869. Some personal names, including that of Te Waru, who was not sent to Wharekauri, are also inscribed on it, and not by the government hand.[36] Te Kooti himself also wrote down 50 inoi in his later diary of 1869–70.[37]

Thus, while the faith is founded on the direct and immediate dialogue ('nga korero') between God and Te Kooti, the written word was also used, right from the beginning, to record oral teachings. For Te Kooti was told by the voice (on 21 May) that 'all the things I tell you of now may be set down' ('kia tuhia nga korero katoa i korero nei ahau ki a koe').

With the first apparition of the spirit in bodily form, on 21 April, Te Kooti was also given two signs ('tohu'). These were held in the hand of the spirit and he gave them to Te Kooti. As he stretched out his hand to receive them, he saw that the first was a lizard ('he ngarara'), but in a form which he had never previously seen, and he fell to the ground in fear. Thus, this awesome image suggests a new spirit world, into which Te Kooti was being inducted. The second sign that Te Kooti was given was the flame of light, which appeared upon his hand but did not burn.

He immediately began to make known the words of God to the whakarau. The sign of the flaming light he only revealed later, in church, on 18 June 1867.[38] The news of the new religion then spread rapidly, and reports of it reached Poverty Bay, brought by some of the returning Maori guards, within a month.[39] Almost a year later, the resident magistrate, Captain W. E. Thomas, was finally told about the sign of the flame by Te Warihi.[40] Thomas learnt that in the services Te Kooti had been conducting (with Thomas's permission and under the auspices of the Anglican church), he had been 'rubbing his hands with the phosphorus of matches to represent "Atua" before holding Service'. Te Kooti had obtained a profound influence over most of the prisoners and had, said Thomas, 'led them to the belief that the adoption of these practices will tend to deliver them from their bondage'.[41]

In his diary, Te Kooti recorded how, before revealing this sign, he had called on their lay reader ('kai karakia'), Karanama Ngerengere,[42] to bring forth his books so that he might know whether these things he had been told were to be found therein.[43] But when Karanama went to fetch the books they were no longer there. Te Kooti wrote 'his fetching of the book which had been taken was explained by the hidden one' ('tana tangohanga i te pukapuka na kua riro na te mea ngaro i whakamarama'). This passage hints at some episode similar to that related earlier concerning the minister's two books, in that it suggests that the appropriate books were searched for, but now they had vanished. As a consequence of this revelation, on 21 May 1867 Te Kooti and Karanama called together all the people. Te Kooti told them that *he* had been appointed as the mouth-piece of God ('ko koe hei reo moku'). All the things that he told them could now be set down.

For himself, however, the voice had said:

> ko koe ia kei whawha koe ki tetahi pukapuka, no te mea ko ena reta na te tangata he mea pouri, engari maku e korero ki a koe mau ki a ratou kia mohio ai ratou he reo ahau no te Atua. Ko te kupu i ngaro i a ratou mau e karanga ki te Atua, a maku e whaki atu.

> as for you don't touch any book, because the letters of men are dark, rather I will speak to you and you to them, so that they may know that I am the voice of God. The words that elude them you must ask of God, and I will make [them] known to you.

Thus Te Kooti was set apart; it was he who was the vehicle of direct communication with God. He alone spoke with God; he alone possessed the Word.

On 30 May Te Kooti was again instructed to call together the people. They assembled, and they were the same number as the date itself: thirty. On 4 June, the elders were summoned, and then, Te Kooti wrote, two manifestations of God were revealed — but what they were he did not record. On 18 June, God's fire was displayed. Te Kooti wrote:

> ko te ahi ka whakakite ia ki te whare karakia, ka kite te iti me te rahi, heoi ka tau tana manaaki ki tona iwi, ka oti hoki ana korero te mahi e te iwi katoa.

> the fire that he revealed in the church will be seen by great and small, and thus his blessing will light upon his people, and his sayings will be acted upon by all the people.[44]

From that date, he wrote, God began to strengthen him, and prepare his voice and body. He lost all fear of the great men, the chiefs ('nga rangatira'), and 'from this time began all those things which had been spoken of by him [God] to his servant' ('otira me nga mea katoa i korerotia e ia ki tona pononga'). To the whakarau, he appeared more than ever as a man who had risen from the dead.

Thus, the diary traces the sequence of Te Kooti's illness and the visions which led to the promulgation — and the first adoption — of the new faith in May–June 1867. The teachings were essentially scriptural, although one of the given signs was unquestionably Maori: the ngarara, which may be both life-threatening and life-giving. It is traditionally the sign of the man who walks on the 'taha wairua', the spiritual side of life.

The religion identified the people with the Israelites in their bondage. Their new prayers simply asked God for his mercy, so that they might return home.[45] The Pai Marire chants, incorporating pidgin-English phrases that many of them had once used, were all discarded. Te Kooti took the people back directly to the scriptures, which seemed to offer them the assurance that their escape from Pharaoh's soldiers was inevitable. They adopted the history of Exodus as their own, and the strength of Exodus history lies in its end: its *unconditional* promise of the return.[46] In Deuteronomy, or the fifth book of Moses, the whakarau read the essential message of the scriptures: that the words ('nga kupu') were for them:

> The Lord made not this covenant with our fathers, but with us, even us, who are all of us here alive this day.[47]

In his diary Te Kooti wrote out a portion of the Covenant of the Rainbow (Kopere). The rainbow is God's sign to Noah, and is declared to be eternal to every generation.[48] This promise is understood today as being the third of the eight covenants of the Ringatu faith, which are believed to have been revealed to Te Kooti on the island.[49] The kopere is the particular sign of God's covenant with the Ringatu, for, as Heni Brown put it, 'that's the sign of a Ringatū, you know. They always believe in the rainbow. This rainbow stands over Chatham Islands.'[50] Just as God had revealed himself to Moses in the Egyptian house of bondage, so it is believed that God revealed himself to his servant in the 'wharepononga' ('house of bondage') of the exiles on Wharekauri. According to the Ringatu teachings, the fifth covenant given by God to Te Kooti on Wharekauri was the 'Covenant with Moses', which showed them the way. It was derived directly from Exodus 20:2:

> I am the Lord thy God, which have brought thee out of the land of Egypt, out of the house of bondage.[51]

These teachings took hold precisely at the time when the prisoners first learnt that they were not to be released after a year, as they had expected. In April 1867, Major J. T. Edwards was sent to report on the prison and the general situation of the prisoners. He wrote that they told him that they had been promised they would be sent back, if they had behaved well, a few at a time, 'probably after they had been one year at the Chathams', and that all of them would be returned 'as soon as the war was over'. He recommended that this process begin.[52] Instead, however, Thomas was instructed in June to inform the prisoners that they would not now be repatriated until the East Coast land confiscations had been determined.[53]

This decision had been taken by McLean, on the advice of Reginald Biggs, the new resident magistrate at Poverty Bay. Biggs had informed McLean that he was encountering almost universal obstruction among Maori at Turanga, both 'loyal' and 'rebel', who were attempting to conceal all information about titles to the land. Allowing any of the prisoners to return at this juncture, he felt, would simply increase his difficulties.[54] In this manner, the prisoners learnt of yet another punishment: that confiscation was apparently to be rammed through, while their exile stretched endlessly before them.

It was this realisation more than anything else which crystallised the new faith and gave Te Kooti his following. As a consequence, in the religion of the Ringatu it is believed that on Wharekauri the sixth covenant, the Covenant with Israel, was then revealed to him. As Boy Biddle explained, 'This Covenant shows ways and means of gaining access to the Promised Land, no such provision having been made in the Covenant given to Abraham.'[55] The text is Deuteronomy 30:3–5, or the promises given to Moses:

> then the Lord thy God will turn thy captivity, and have compassion upon thee, and will return and gather thee from all the nations, whither the Lord thy God hath scattered thee. . . . And the Lord thy God will bring thee into the land which thy fathers possessed, and thou shalt possess it . . . .

Eria Raukura taught that it was the revelation of these covenants on Wharekauri which finally brought together the two religious traditions, Maori and Pakeha, which had become separated by the original departure from Canaan. The revelation of the covenants on Wharekauri was the completion of the first cycle of renewal, which had begun with Toiroa's predictions. It will be remembered that Eria said:

> I te tau 1766, e toru tau i mua atu o te taenga mai o te pakeha ki tenei motu, ka whakaaturia e Toiroa a Ariki-rangi me nga ahuatanga katoa o tona oranga i tenei ao.

> In 1766, three years before the arrival of the pakeha in this land, Toiroa spoke out about Ariki-rangi and all the aspects of his life in this world.

Eria had continued:

> . . . No Wharekauri ka puta mai nei te Anahera a te Atua ki a ia [Te Kooti]. Ka whaka-atutia mai nei ko te Kawenata Ringatu, me nga kupu whakaari katoa. Te kupu whakaari tuatahi, me nga tauira ano o te kupu whakaari o te hanganga mai o te Ao. Nga kupu ano mai i a Aperahama tae noa mai ki a Te Karaiti. . . . No te wa rawa i a Te Kooti katahi ano ka tino whakamaramatia te hononga o nga mea tuatahi ki nga mea o muri

nei, ara, ta te Maori maunga mai i a Io, ki ta te pakeha maunga mai i te rongopai o Ihu Karaiti.

> ... At Wharekauri the Angel of the Lord appeared to him [Te Kooti]. There the Ringatu Covenant, and all the prophetic sayings were revealed; the first prophetic saying, and examples of prophetic sayings since the creation of the World. Also the sayings from the time of Abraham and up to Christ. ... It was only in the very time of Te Kooti that the relationship was made clear between the first and later matters, that is, of the Maori holding to Io, and the pakeha holding to the gospel of Jesus Christ.[56]

Two religious traditions are seen as conjoined with Te Kooti: the world of the Maori and their supreme god Io (who perhaps journeyed with them from the Pacific), and the new gospel of their collective salvation, through Christ. The Israelite traditions of persecution and deliverance in the Old Testament, with which they now identified, became the source of a new strength. It was this faith which gave them their 'hope so close to certainty'[57] and provided the basis of their active rebellion against their captivity.

These beliefs crystallised fully in 1868. A year before Te Kooti had written home to the community at Te Ahipakura, by the Waipaoa river, to say that they were not living in any trouble on the island. It seems significant that in this letter, sent on 3 January 1867, just before his recorded visions commenced, he had said:

> Kotahi tonu te whakaaro a matau, ko te ata noho anake, ko te whakarongo hoki ki te ako a o matau rangatira. Ko tenei, nui atu to matau ata noho, ora hoki. Kaore a matau turoro, he parau ena korero.

> We are of one mind, and that is only to live quietly and listen to the teachings of our chiefs. This is it, that we are indeed very quietly settled, and in health also. We have no sick, that's false talk.[58]

This report seems to run counter to what we know of his own situation, and also that of other prisoners. It suggests, therefore, that the prisoners, at least in public, had initially accepted their position and tried to make the best of it. There are glimpses of these efforts in other sources too: an account of a 'grand feast' which the whakarau put on for all the local inhabitants, including the Europeans, and an improvised cricket match that they initiated in the early summer in 1866.[59] In April 1867 Major Edwards observed the cleanliness and neatness of their whare, each decorated with flowers, ferns, tokotoko (carved sticks) and mere, all the work of the prisoners.[60] (One of these tokotoko, 'beautifully carved', was recovered from Te Kooti's whare after the escape,[61] as was the wooden chest in which he had kept his papers and personal possessions.[62]) On 27 July 1867, Te Kooti married Maata Te Owai, one of the female prisoners from Te Aitanga-a-Mahaki, a widow who had probably accompanied her previous husband into exile. The wedding took place when Te Kooti was beginning to regain his health. He declared himself to be a bachelor. The civil ceremony was conducted by Thomas, and Te Kooti gave the prison doctor's little daughter, who acted as their bridesmaid, his light greenstone (inanga) oval pendant, inlaid with paua shell, which he had worn at his neck since being sent into exile. It was carved in the form of three birds' heads, and represented the three islands of Aotearoa in unity.[63] If the first months of 1867, then, were still times of acceptance of the prison situation, by 1868 the mood had unquestionably changed.

It began to alter as Te Kooti's words took hold. Thomas Ritchie senior first commented upon the change at the beginning of April 1868. He noted a new restlessness among the whakarau, a gradual but steady increase in their desire to quit the island.[64] Even the quieter ones, he observed only a few days later, were now determined to leave; to force them all to continue to remain would only serve to call up a resistance.[65] It is clear that at this time Te Kooti was conducting secret religious services. One place is remembered in the oral traditions from Wharekauri. Hidden in the sandhills of Petre Bay, to the east of Waitangi towards Te One, there is a little valley where Te Kooti used to preach in the evenings. Here, it is recalled, he made his prediction that the ships would come, or if not he would be given a rod, like Moses, to part the sea.[66] Tom Ritchie recorded and underlined this prediction in his diary: 'Te Kooti Prophetsized "*that the Government in the month of July (1868) would send a vessel to take them to N.Z. & if not God would empower him Te Kooti to strike the Sea with a rod & they would be able to walk to N.Z. on dry land*"'.[67]

The Ringatu date the giving of the covenants of the faith to Te Kooti on Wharekauri as 12 May 1868.[68] In Paora Delamere's account it is written simply:

> Ko nga tau, me te homaitanga ki a Te Kooti te Kawenata Ringatu e te Wairua o te Atua.
> 1. 1868. Mei 12   te homaitanga a te Wairua i te w[h]akapono Ringatu.

> The years, and the delivering to Te Kooti [of] the Ringatu Covenant by the Spirit of God.
> 1. 1868. May 12   the Spirit delivers the Ringatu faith.[69]

This belief is one of the reasons that the Ringatu celebrate the 12th of every month as their particular holy day. In Hamiora's transcript of one of Te Kooti's last speeches (5 February 1893), the sayings ('nga kupu') are also dated as beginning on 12 May 1868 and are stated there, by Te Kooti, as coming to an end in 1893.[70] One of Te Kooti's waiata is also dated 12 May 1868. The accompanying explanatory note in Hamiora's book says that it is the text of the very first words and prophetic sayings of the faith, produced on this day. But the song is no 'text' of sayings. Rather, Te Kooti mourns his exile 'in this never-ending night' ('ka roa nei ko te po'). He compares his lot with that of an adulteress ('he wahine toukohi'), who bears the mark of shame. The land of his birth ('taku whenua tipu'), where the sacred fires were burning and to which he yearned to return, is described as:

> Nona te wairua i hora mai ka atu atu [*sic*] ki kona.
> A wehi ana ahau, he punarua he tutetute ki te moenga.

> Hers is the soul spread out steadfast before me.
> I fear the omen, a second wife, a hustler to the bed.[71]

The song, then, is concerned with the way he was betrayed and his fidelity to the land. It also possibly draws upon his recent, second marriage for its metaphor of duality of commitment. It was a marriage which became sour.

There are no diary entries for 12 May; nevertheless it is certain that the critical

Waitangi, 1868. The redoubt and enclosed barracks can be seen on the scarp (left). On the beach below is the court-house (with the flagpole in front), and behind it is the gaol, built by the prisoners. To the right the large building behind a fence is the inn run by Isabella and John Alexander. On the scarp above and to the right is Orea flat, with the prisoners' compound. Pen and ink drawing by the surveyor S. Percy Smith.   Smith Sketchbook III, C19,667, AIM

teachings were promulgated at this time. For it was on 20 May that Te Warihi was finally stirred to inform Thomas about Te Kooti's practices. Thomas was also told by another prisoner, Keke, that Te Kooti had anointed Keke's wife with holy oil. Keke described the episode in some detail: Te Kooti had put the oil in a little pain-killer bottle made 'fast on his wrist'. When he held up his hand 'after taking out the cork crying Glory & [?] binding his Hand', the oil ran down onto her head as she knelt before him. He was exorcising Keke's wife of 'an Eval Spirit', in Tom Ritchie's understanding.[72] The woman was Te Warihi's daughter, and her husband, like her father, objected strongly.

Because Thomas at first doubted Te Warihi and Keke, both of whom he knew had previously quarrelled with Te Kooti, he made further inquiries. He learnt that the prisoners 'by their ploughing work had built some sheds for their nights lodgings, the place was about two miles from their camp, and at evenings they held their prayers, and . . . it was not the form of worship of the Church of England'.[73] When Thomas questioned him, Te Kooti apparently responded in challenge with the remark that Thomas should pray for his own soul before that of the Queen,[74] which could be read equally as a political or a religious jibe. It was undoubtedly a reference to the Anglican Maori prayer-book, in which a prayer for the Maori chiefs and their families had been replaced by a prayer for the Queen; it was a change much objected to in Poverty Bay and

Another view of Waitangi bay, looking west. The redoubt and its flagstaff are visible on the scarp, with the prisoners' compound behind. Two churches can be seen in the foreground: Waitangi church on the left, and a raupo chapel (probably the prisoners') standing above Petre Bay, on the right. Pen and ink sketch by Percy Smith, 1868.   Smith Sketchbook III, C19,670, AIM

had directly sparked the protests of 1858, when the chiefs had refused to accept the Queen's authority as being greater than theirs.[75] The 'Natives of the Island' confirmed Te Warihi's account: Te Kooti had been marking his hands with yellow phosphorus taken from match heads,[76] and he would hold them up in the darkness of the whare karakia so that they shone forth with an unearthly radiance. He also drew a cross, which he made luminous by the phosphorus mixed with gum from flax plants.[77] In one version, he raised this luminous cross slowly by a thread above the pulpit,[78] which would be seen as blasphemy in Anglican teachings. Thomas also discovered that three prisoners, who had been released during the early part of 1868, had been instructed by Te Kooti to conceal the new doctrines until the rest were allowed to follow them, and that one, Pehimana Taihuka, had been instructed to '"pikari te whenua" "scratch the land" in a direct line to Wharekauri as soon as he landed',[79] to mark the pathway for their escape.

On 8 June Thomas placed Te Kooti in solitary confinement in a hut 'at a distance from the others' on Orea flat.[80] Tom Ritchie added that Thomas had made Te Kooti build the hut for himself outside the redoubt.[81] In the oral traditions it is told how Te Kooti escaped every night from his confinement. He would then hold prayers in the compound, indicating his presence to the others by holding up his glowing hand — or simply vanish, and then reappear to tell them what he had been doing. One narrative from this time has survived in the memory of both Maori and Pakeha. Ned Brown, a Ringatu elder from Whatatutu, and his wife, Heni, related this story. It concerns (among others) Heni's great-grandmother, Meri Puru, who had been sent with her father, Hori Puru of Te Aitanga-a-Mahaki, in the first batch of prisoners to Wharekauri:

> *Ned*: Someone spoke out of turn and told a warden, 'O, Te Kooti's not in gaol, he was here with us, last night, talking to us.' 'No, he's still in gaol — you must be dreaming.' 'No he comes here, every night.' And before, he referred to this Angel, Michael, coming to rescue them. He said to them, 'Look, here's a stone! I want you people to eat it. If your faith is good, you can do it.' So I believe old Penehā[82] put it in his throat — couldn't get — almost choke — couldn't get it down — too big! So they had a session with one another, 'How we going to eat that stone?' Just saw old Peneti trying to perform how to swallow it, it won't work. So all right, 'Let's all put it to God. Tell God to help us.' . . . And when they went to sleep it was given to one of them in a dream. He woke up, startled, and he said, 'I've got it! I've got it!' And they all woke up, and said, 'What?' 'O, how to eat that stone!' And he got the stone and pounded it into dust. Got it all into dust — and he gave you a bit.
> *Heni*: And that's how they ate it.
> *Ned*: O, this will be fantastic, but that's how we were told.
> *Heni*: That's the sharing, too. 'Cos my great-grandmother ate that stone.
> *Ned*: 'Cause Te Kooti said, 'You people got to swallow that stone.' But they couldn't find an answer. But in a dream, after their prayers, the Lord blessed them. This particular person woke up, startled, and he said, 'I've got it, I've got it.' . . . And they pounded it all into powder. And every one of them had a bit. So, they were rescued.[83]

The Maori oral tradition narrates the riddle, or the task that is set and has to be solved before deliverance can be achieved. The solution found is jointly to partake of the stone of knowledge. This task recalls the practices of the whare wananga, where it was considered necessary to eat a small stone to 'fix' the learning. It was the practice Toiroa had used in his first initiation rites for the young Te Kooti.

Oral tradition from Wharekauri also recalls this story, but in a modified form. David Holmes, a resident at Waitangi since 1922, was told that Te Kooti had a small stone. Te Kooti asked the people, 'What should we do with it?' He had it ground into powder, and made everyone 'have a lick of that stone', each one taking the powder on their finger. If they had the faith, he said, they should do it. But Te Warihi had refused.[84]

Eria Raukura also narrated this story to Porter. It was 'a round white stone', he said, which Te Kooti produced at an evening service. Te Kooti explained that it was 'a holy one placed in his path by Te Atua, God'. The text behind this act was undoubtedly Revelation 2:17: 'To him that overcometh will I give to eat of the hidden manna, and will give him a white stone'. For six days the whakarau struggled with the riddle, until the illumination was given to Karanama Ngerengere, who said that the stone must be pounded into powder and 'as flour' eaten by all. Te Warihi alone refused to partake of it.[85] In these versions, the story also anticipates the death of Te Warihi, who was thrown overboard on the voyage home by Te Kooti because he had been a disbeliever and had acted as a 'spy'.

The prisoners' huts on Orea flat, overlooking Waitangi bay, 1886. Watercolour by Margaret O. Stoddart.
STODDART ALBUM, CM

It is in Te Kooti's Wharekauri diary that the earliest records he made of God's promises and predictions exist. The use of these sayings, each introduced by a word or phrase
in the strange tongue, 'te reo ke', was to develop as a recurring aspect of his teaching and
of the Ringatu faith in general. An entire body of texts has grown around the kupu
whakaari, or prophetic sayings, and they will be discussed later. But it is important here
to note that, on 1 January 1868,[86] Te Kooti recorded the first of these sayings, thereby
recording too the first New Year of the new faith. There are three strange words written
on this date: 'Aneko', 'Iperene' and 'Utiera'. Te Kooti wrote the 'interpretation' or
meaning of each; these particular words in 'te reo ke' would thereafter be used as a
referential system to the stated promises.

> Aneko: tona whakamaoritanga: A kua kaha toku wairua ki te whakaora i toku iwi, e
> kore tetahi atu ke atu e kaha ake i ahau. Awhi mai ki ahau i roto i te ponongatanga a
> maku koutou e whakateitei ake.

> Aneko: its interpretation: My spirit is empowered to save my people and no other shall
> be stronger than I. Draw near to me in your bondage and I shall raise you up.

> Iperene Kupu: I tenei wa ka whakahoki ahau i toku iwi ka whakatupu ahau i a ratou, e
> kore ano tetahi ringa e pa atu ki a ratou a muri nei.

> Iperene Word: At this time I shall return my people and I will nourish them, and no
> hand shall be raised against them after this.

> Utiera Kupu: U tonu taku riri ki nga iwi nana i whakamate toku iwi, ka whakamate
> ahau i nga matua a tae noa ki nga tamariki, e kore e takina e ahau taku [riri] ake ake.

> Utiera Word: My wrath shall always abide on those who oppress my people, I will
> punish the parents and even the children, my anger will never abate.

In these texts Te Kooti created the base of a religion of mercy, and also one for war. These first texts, 'A. I. U.', stand at the heart of the Ringatu teachings and have been copied and recopied into many private manuscript books of believers.[87] In Biddle's Index book to his manuscripts, he dated the three words 'A. I. U.', significantly, as 12 May 1868, which must have been the occasion of their promulgation by Te Kooti. These are the original teachings, born in the time of bondage. The teachings, and the texts, have in turn evolved according to time and context. Some, Te Kooti would later declare to have been fulfilled. The predictive history, which he consciously generated and recorded, was itself also modified and adapted by him over time.

These beliefs became focused for the first time early in 1868. The marked shift in mood among the prisoners also became evident. In January, William Rolleston had visited the island to assess the prisoners' situation. The whakarau complained particularly of the doctor, who, as Thomas admitted, was really 'physically incapable of attending to his duties'[88] because of alcoholism. The prisoners also told Rolleston that their prayers were interfered with by the guard, who often came in smoking during their services, and that they were forced to stand in line, both men and women, with their private parts exposed. Rolleston recorded the prisoners' speeches in some detail: Te Kooti is conspicuous by his absence.[89] Gilbert Mair, who accompanied Rolleston and commented at the time only that he found the prisoners' quarters 'very nice and tidy', later claimed that Te Kooti had made a 'most eloquent speech' of protest at every meeting they held, and particularly objected to the hindrance of the services.[90] The spokesmen recorded by Rolleston told him they were ordered to work when not well and were sometimes kicked and abused by the guard. A later account, written anonymously by one of the guards on Wharekauri to rebut a statement clearing them of misconduct, accused the head guard, Elliott, of regularly using a riding whip to lash the younger prisoners across the shoulders.[91] They worked on wet days and, as they had few clothes, in the climate of the island this was a great hardship. There were also complaints about the low rates of pay received when labouring for the settlers: in 1867 the rates had been reduced to 1s a day or, when shearing, £1 per 100 sheep. Although they were now allowed to keep and spend this money, the government suspended the rations of those who were employed. On road works they received no pay at all. But the issue was not simply the work; Rolleston's report makes clear that the standard of the military guard had markedly deteriorated, and that drunkenness and attendant abuses had become common.

Ritchie senior attributed the prisoners' change of attitude to Rolleston's visit and the subsequent implementation of some of his recommendations for a more humane (or lax, in Ritchie's eyes) regime. From the beginning of April, the military guard was discontinued; Rolleston had described it simply as a 'public nuisance'. In its place were half the number of Armed Constabulary men: that is, a senior sergeant, a corporal and nine constables. Edmund Tuke commented later that all surveillance was taken off the prisoners and they were allowed to go where they liked on the island. Roll calls were dispensed with, and they were no longer forced to work. Tom Ritchie said the same: the 'Hau Hau no more to work for settlers' but were instead expected to grow all their own food and grind their own wheat.[92] According to Tuke, however, most were left with nothing to do except 'concoct mischief'.[93]

One further explanation for the change in atmosphere is offered in Porter's account; it derives from the detailed knowledge he acquired from Eria Raukura. This was that the repatriation of some of the principal chiefs in January 1868 had given Te Kooti an authority with the prisoners which he had not, until this time, consolidated. Indeed, it was said that the prisoner Herewini Punairangi, a former lay preacher for William Williams, had revitalised an earlier influence and restored some of the Hauhau modes of worship.[94] The departure of nine chiefs, including Te Wirihana Tupeka, Hemi Taka Te Whiwhi, Wi Mahuika, Tiopira Tawhiao (Rangitawhiao) and Tipene Tutaki of Te Aitanga-a-Mahaki, created a vacuum of authority which Te Kooti filled. While there may be some truth in this view, it is also clear that at least one of the chiefs released was a supporter of Te Kooti. Te Wirihana was sent home, as Thomas later discovered, with Te Kooti's instructions to keep the faith secret.[95]

The escape, which Ritchie had half-anticipated, was planned — and predicted — by Te Kooti. Two documents were later found, left behind in one of the prisoners' houses:

> Ki nga kai hapai o te ture. Ki te Runanga o te whare nui. E hoa ma, rapua mai he oranga mo tatou. Kua kite au i to koutou tika i te timatanga iho ano o to tatou Karakia. E hoa ma, kia kaha ki te rapu i te mea ngaro hei ora mo tatou. Heoi.
>
> Na Te Kooti.
>
> Inahoki kua mahue tatou na te ngoikore. Inaianei kua puta mai ko ta te Tamaiti tikanga raua ko tona Matua. E te iwi, kia kaha, meake ka puta mai he kaipuke mo tatau. Ki te kore a Te Kira e homai e Te Atua mo tatau, he kaipuke ke atu. Koia tenei ko te kaipuke nei, ko taku taima tenei. E te iwi kia kaha.

> To the upholders of the law. To the Council of the big house. My friends, seek salvation for us. I have seen that you have acted properly since we began our Karakia. My friends, be strong in seeking out the hidden thing that is to save us (alluding to a riddle that he had given them). Enough.
>
> From Te Kooti.
>
> For it is on account of weakness that we have been forsaken. But now has come forth the direction (revelation) of the Son and of his Father. O people, be strong for soon a vessel for us shall appear. If the *St Kilda* is not given to us by God, there will be some other vessel. With this vessel, it will be my time. O people, be strong.

> He Ture.
>
> Tuatahi. Ki te puta he kupu a muri nei me whakamana tonu.
> Tuarua. Ko te tupato ki nga mahi kei runga i te tima. Ki te peka ki tenei mea ka mate. Ka mau ki te Atua he oranga kei reira.

> A Law.
>
> First. If word comes forth hereafter, let it immediately be given effect.
> Second. Be cautious about the work on board the steamer. If any one turns aside, it is death. In adhering to God there is salvation.[96]

These documents indicate not only Te Kooti's primary role in the escape but also that a governing structure had been set up among the prisoners. A council or runanga of the elders had been established for collective decisions, and Te Kooti had devised a code of laws for their guidance, as well as the riddle of the stone. Eria Raukura mentioned this

The 'Hauhau huts paddock', Te Awatea estate, Wharekauri. The ring of stones used to be near the rock outcrop in the middle. The huts were in the same area. Photograph by Judith Binney, 1989.

organisational structure to Porter.[97] It can be established that the council was set up in November 1867. In the notebooks compiled by Robert Biddle senior from the manuscripts kept by Te Kooti's secretaries, its origin and membership are described in detail. The council derived from a visitation by God ('Atua') to Te Kooti on 23 October (or perhaps 27 October),[98] and after 'one month of working, he spoke of it to all the people' ('a kotahi marama ia e mahi ana, ka korerotia e ia ki te iwi katoa'). Thirteen chiefs were appointed as 'Leaders of the Way' ('kai Whakahaere Tikanga'). Four of these chiefs, Tiopira Tawhiao, Pehimana Taihuka, Te Wirihana Tupeka and Horomona Tutaki, were subsequently released at different times and, as we have seen, at least one of them returned home with instructions from Te Kooti to keep the faith (and the plans) secret. The chiefs represented 13 tribes who had people imprisoned on the island.[99] The escape was therefore plotted with a high degree of organisation and collaboration.

The planning was precise, but the style predictive. The escape was anticipated in detail from at least the beginning of April 1868. Thomas Ritchie's shepherd Herewini, who had worked with him at Kaingaroa for over a year, gave his notice on 9 April, and Ritchie discovered that he had been urged in no fewer than seven letters to return to Waitangi.[100] Herewini told him he had to be back at Waitangi by 1 July: 'he was sorry to leave but he said he must obey Te Kooti'.[101] Some of the prisoners also warned the Ritchies that the shipment of wheat seed, sent by the government in April for planting, '"*they would never Eat*"'.[102] Rather, its arrival had been the catalyst for their actions — for it had shown them definitively that the government still had no intention of releasing them.[103]

It was the arrival of the *Rifleman*, a schooner, on Friday, 3 July which gave Te Kooti the opportunity for which he had planned with such great care for at least three months.

Tikitiki point, from where the exiles departed. Photograph by Judith Binney, 1989.

In harbour at the same time was a small ketch, the *Florence*, which was about to sail, its cargo already loaded. Te Kooti had forewarned that there would be two ships on the appointed day: it was the sign the whakarau were to look for.[104] In his diary Te Kooti had recorded some ship movements, and the length of time the vessels stayed in the port at Waitangi; whether he had advance information of this particular conjunction is unknown, but it seems possible. In the account narrated by Eria Raukura, the prediction concerning the two ships, one larger and one smaller, was made by Te Kooti on the previous Sunday, 28 June.[105]

The prisoners unloaded part of the *Rifleman*'s cargo of flour on the afternoon of its arrival, working in light drizzling rain. On the next day, Saturday, the rain was pouring down, and this, it is narrated, was the third sign to look for, which Te Kooti had given to indicate the appointed day.[106] According to Eria's detailed account, Te Kooti addressed the prisoners after karakia that morning: 'This is God's day for us, and the rain from heaven (te ua o te Rangi) is sent as a sign of our deliverance.'[107] Then he gave out the detailed instructions, particularly to the crews of the boats who were to unload the *Rifleman*. Thomas recorded in his report on the escape that, despite the heavy rain, the prisoners 'volunteered with greater alacrity than usual' for their duties getting firewood for the barracks, which they did every Saturday.[108] When this task was completed, some gathered at the store just outside the redoubt, while others, who had carried the firewood inside, remained within. Te Kooti himself came into the guardroom with a bundle of wood about five minutes before he gave the signal for action. 'Plenty of rain Bob', was all he said to the carpenter, who happened to be present when he arrived.[109] It was at about 2.30 in the afternoon when the prearranged sign was given: Te Kooti's flag, white with a red border, was raised over the prisoners' quarters.[110] Four constables and the carpenter were seized and bound with the unusually long flax ropes the prisoners had made for the firewood. All this had been planned: 'Tie them to the forms' they would be sitting on, Te Kooti had said.[111] At the same time, other prisoners broke open the magazine. Contrary to Te Kooti's instructions, however, one of the four constables in the guardroom was killed. This was Michael Hartnett, who was struck on the head with a tomahawk by Tamihana Teketeke (Tekateka), apparently in revenge for Hartnett's interference with his wife.[112] Tom Ritchie noted in his diary: 'Te Kooti was furious as his order was *no one was to be killed*'.[113] In every other respect, the rising was characterised not only by the 'precision, rapidity, and completeness with which the enterprise was planned and executed' but also by 'the moderation shown in the hour of victory'.[114] It was undoubtedly hoped that this moderation would influence the government's attitude to their escape. Here Te Kooti was wrong.

There are some delightful details, too. Anne Smith, wife of the surveyor S. Percy Smith, who was working on the island, described to her mother a few days later how the young man whom they employed, Kuare, had been particularly brisk and industrious that Saturday morning. He went off in the late afternoon as usual, but came back in a hurry for his wages. She gave him the £5 note she had, because he told her he wanted to purchase a cow and calf with it; he owed her a pound. He was immediately followed by his brother-in-law, Ohe, who wanted payment for some washing that had been done. Then a third man, who sold the family milk from his cow, asked for his money, by which time Anne had run out of change and she told him to get the money off Kuare. Off he went — as fast as it was possible for a man dying of consumption, she noted sadly.[115]

There is a place called locally 'the Hauhau huts paddock', on the Waitangi–Owenga road. It is on the old Te Awatea estate, which once belonged to Alexander Shand, who employed some of the prisoners to clear the bush. They lived in four ponga huts while working, hence the name. But, until at least the 1950s, there was also a large ring of raised stones, each regularly spaced.[116] The stones seemed placed as seats, quite wide apart, and perhaps it was a place for assembly and prayer. Associated with this tradition is another that says the gold of the 'Hauhau' is hidden there. It is claimed that 200 gold sovereigns are buried in the paddock, the hidden wages of the bushfellers, who were at Waitangi on the day of the rising and had no time to fetch them.[117] This is the first (in time) of the many stories of 'Te Kooti's hidden gold'. Inflation seems to have overtaken the daily wages that were being paid, but then that is the stuff of myth.

At the same time as the redoubt was seized, the *Rifleman* was taken by a second group of about 15 armed prisoners, led by Karanama Ngerengere. There is an oral story, retained by Te Kooti's family, which celebrates the role of the women prisoners in the capture of the *Rifleman*. The men came on board and began a haka, ostensibly to entertain the crew, and as the men dropped back the women came forward, singing, gyrating and 'shaking their bums' at the seamen. The sailors started to grab at them and were drawn into the middle of the group, where they were overcome.[118]

A third group, consisting of about eight armed men, captured the *Florence*. Its cargo of pigs was transferred to the *Rifleman*, its crew sent ashore and its cables cut, so that it would drift onto the rocks, thus preventing pursuit. Thomas was seized when he went

The schooner *Rifleman*, c.1871. Watercolour by Tom Ritchie.   Z MSS 36/5/1, CPL

The *Rifleman*, aground on Great Barrier Island, 29 August 1871. Pen drawing by Tom Ritchie.

Z MSS 36/5/1, CPL

up to the redoubt, after hearing that it had been taken. He was immediately tied up and, with some others, brought down to the gaol on the beach below the redoubt. The prisoners then took his keys, and Te Kooti opened the safe in the court-house next door. Some of the settlers' houses were also searched for money. Isabella Alexander (the inn-keeper) successfully hid the bag containing most of hers — 200 gold sovereigns in one version, whose symmetry appeals — in a boiling kettle.[119] S. Percy Smith lost only his single-barrel fowling piece, which was one of the 13 privately owned guns taken.[120] The only looting that occurred was in the house of the unpopular sergeant, Frederick Fynmore. But even that was limited, and was certainly not nearly as much as the settlers' rhetoric later suggested, for his claim for damages came to only £15 2s. Everywhere else, only money, arms and ammunition were sought, not reprisal.

The property taken by the whakarau was the remaining cargo left on the *Rifleman*, the pigs from the *Florence*, the money from Thomas's safe (£397 8s 2d) and £125 1s of private money from the settlers' houses. The prisoners also seized the arms and ammunition from the magazine in the redoubt: that is, 31 rifles and five revolvers, plus bayonets, belts and pouches; 4584 rounds of ammunition, 5195 caps and 200 rounds for revolvers. They took a bugle, which would become famous for its use as a military decoy, some spades, axes, adzes, knives, tomahawks and buckets, as well as some 'medicinal' wine and tobacco.[121]

While Thomas and others were still locked in the gaol, the whakarau went in orderly fashion on board the *Rifleman*. The women went first, some carrying children. In total, 298 people — 163 men, 64 women and 71 children — went out to the ship in small boats, launched from Tikitiki point. Four of the whakarau chose to stay behind, including Keke and his wife. By nightfall the cargo was trimmed and the vessel had set its sails. But the strong south-west winds were against them, and the ship was unable to beat its way out of the harbour. When the elderly blacksmith came down and broke the locks on the gaol to release Thomas and the others, they could all see it standing in the harbour mouth. Impotently, they watched the schooner return to its anchorage. The next day, Sunday, it got under way again, but spent all day trying to beat out of the harbour against the gale-force winds. The last Thomas saw of it was at dusk, in the channel near the north-west end of Wharekauri, attempting a direct course for the North Island.[122] By midnight, its lights marked the ship to be still only about four miles off shore, but the wind had turned to the east, taking the people away.[123]

The best-known story from the escape is the death of Te Warihi on the voyage. As the ship continued to struggle against strong head winds, Te Kooti ordered first that all their greenstone taonga — patu and heitiki — be gathered up in a blanket. This done, he threw them all over the side. These were objects which tied them to their past: 'objects of power which personified the ancient mana'.[124] When the sacrifice failed, Te Kooti sent for Te Warihi. The old man came up on deck and Te Kooti ordered his hands to be bound and for him to be thrown overboard. According to Eria Raukura, Te Warihi said, 'I am not unfaithful to God. It is the vindictiveness of that incorrigible [man] that causes my death. (Ko te mau-a-hara na tena nanakia e whakamate ana ahau).'[125] But he was lifted over the rails and tossed into the sea. He sank like a stone — 'Whenei me te Kohatu' — commented Peita Kotuku, one of the whakarau present.[126] Thus the informer was sacrificed: the Jonah, as Te Kooti said.[127] Te Kooti's second law for the escape had warned of death for any who turned aside. In 1879 he was to claim that Te Warihi's role as an informer had been discovered by the drawing of lots:[128] thus his destiny was made manifest. However, it is likely that Te Warihi's relationship with Thomas had been obvious to everyone. Indeed, as Te Kooti later said pragmatically, '"he had done nothing but croak, predicting an evil end to all of us, and had frightened

Ringatu elders gather at Te Wainui, Te Kooti's marae on the Ohiwa harbour, to bless a carved case, and also a greenstone patu, which formerly belonged to him, March 1979. The items were then taken on the elders' pilgrimage to Wharekauri and given to the museum at Waitangi.

Here, the case rests on Te Kooti's monument erected at Te Wainui. The elders are from Te Teko: Eruera Manuera, chief of Ngati Awa; Pareake Manuera; Parekura Tutua; Mere Tauhinga Ngaheu Brown; Te Uru Wimutu (Tihi); Aniheta Ratene; Ani Hohapata Stewart; (standing) Danny P. U. Mason. At the rear on the right: Wiremu Tarei, Ringatu tohunga. In front: Kakaho Te Ua, the carver; Matarena Reneti, who narrated her own history as a Ringatu in 1982. The text engraved on the plaque is Isaiah 61:1: 'he hath sent me to bind up the brokenhearted, to proclaim liberty to the captives, and the opening of the prison to them that are bound'.

The chest contains the patu, the covenants of the Ringatu faith and (on the right) a photo of the Ringatu elders at the unveiling of the monument in 1908. The chest is still in the Wharekauri museum. The greenstone patu was, however, reclaimed by a party from Whakatane and Te Teko in December 1987, and returned to the Ngati Awa descendants of Te Kooti's elder brother, Komene, for it was considered to be the inalienable taonga of the family. A tekoteko was given in its place, lest death resulted from this act.   *Whakatane Beacon, 6 March 1979*

some of the more timid men, so that they were almost ready to turn round"'.[129] Within two hours and after the saying of prayers and the singing of hymns, the gale died away. It was the 'test', the prisoners believed; and with this human offering to the Old Testament God the exiles were granted their fair and swift wind.[130] The next morning, said Peita Kotuku, they sighted land.

The voyage to New Zealand had taken four days. John Martin, one of the crew, described some aspects of it, for the *Rifleman*'s crew had all been kept on board (except the captain, who was ashore at the time of the seizure). They were retained to sail the ship away after the whakarau had made their landfall. The six crew were well treated, given meat and porter (a strong beer), although Te Kooti forbade alcohol for the whakarau. Edward Baker (Peka Te Makarini), one of the prisoners exiled in the same group as Te Kooti and who, according to Martin, had married Te Kooti's sister, cooked the meals and served them first. Te Kooti and four other chiefs lived in the cabin, and took their meals after the European crew: this was (and is) a conscious act of courtesy among Maori. Martin observed that, although there were 'five chiefs', Te Kooti was in command in every respect: 'whatever he said was law'.[131]

They sighted land on the morning of Thursday, 9 July 1868. Then there was porter, carefully rationed and shared, for the returning exiles.[132] They were off the cliffs of the East Coast, with the sacred mountain of Ngati Porou, Hikurangi, clearly visible. They steered the ship to a landing known to most of them: Whareongaonga, a stony beach set in rugged bush-covered hills a little way south of Turanga. It was used locally as a fishing cove, and was well hidden from both land and sea. It was there that they made their landfall: the exiles had finally returned home.

CHAPTER 4

THE RETURN
(JULY–NOVEMBER 1868)

It was late in the winter afternoon of Thursday 9 July when the whakarau made their landfall at Whareongaonga. The little settlement was largely deserted: the men were away, hunting pigeon, and only women and children were there.[1] There was no one to challenge them; no one to welcome them. The whakarau began to unload the vessel that afternoon, using local canoes and the ship's whaleboat. It was near noon on the following day before they finished and took their leave of the *Rifleman*. According to the seaman, John Martin, Te Kooti was the last to go ashore. An elderly Maori woman remembered later that he was dressed in a 'perfect masher suit and patent leather boots'; it is a memory which appeals.[2] He gave each of the crew £6 and told them they could come with him if they wished and he would say they had been taken prisoner. Or they could sail the vessel to 'Port Nick' (Wellington), or better still back to Lyttelton. The mate, John Payne, joked that he would take the vessel and sell it at Valparaiso: '"That is a very good idea," said Te Kooti.'[3] Tamely, the crew chose Wellington, but they carried with them a letter written by Te Kooti exonerating them from any involvement in his escape. That it was addressed to the resident magistrate in Lyttelton, the ship's home port, suggests that this was where Te Kooti had expected the crew to go, and he may have reached this agreement with them, hoping to buy some time.[4]

The narrative account of the landing collated by Robert Biddle senior reveals that the whakarau were uncertain as to the reception they might receive. Karanama Te Whare from Rongowhakaata was first sent ashore with a party of 50 to get the canoes they needed. Te Kooti instructed the kokiri (assaulting warriors) to surround the village completely and to make everyone prisoner. No one was to be killed and only their arms were to be captured. In the event, only five men were seized, and the women fled. But their guns were taken. Te Kooti also ordered that one fowl and one pig be taken and hung up until he landed; they were to be the sacrificial offerings made in thanksgiving for a safe landing.

Then he made a prediction which would pass down into the history of the Ringatu. The events which were about to occur would, he said, dictate their fortunes. In the pa there were, he said, three kegs of powder and 30 guns. In addition, a man of the pa, named Isaac, had been revealed to him in a vision. If this man died, then the pa would be surrendered to them and all within it taken. If neither Isaac nor his son died,[5] then those events would not come to pass: instead, 'We are the ones who will die' ('Ko tatau kua mate'). And he first uttered the prediction 'Enemeripi' for 'The village of the crossing' ('Te kainga o te whitinga mai'), Whareongaonga:

> Nga mate mo tatau Ko te Hoari
> Ko te Whakarau
> Ko te mate Uruta
> Ko te mate Kai.

> The deaths for us are: the Sword
> Captivity
> Epidemic
> Famine.[6]

Their hope was to be able to pass quickly through to the interior of the island, without conflict. If they failed in this objective, then all these forms of death would be the consequence. This kupu whakaari would be recalled and significantly expanded by Te Kooti at the terrible siege of Nga Tapa in December 1868.

The relative absence of the people of Whareongaonga is explained in oral stories told by the descendants of the chief Wi Kaipuke, who was living there at the time. Hamuera Toiroa, a seer who lived at Muriwai, had warned that Te Kooti was coming to Whareongaonga. In one narrative, Hamuera made the people eat most of their fowls and their pigs before the ship arrived, and their hostile nickname for the prisoners thereafter was 'pigs and hens', or that which they had consumed.[7] In another story, Hamuera

> had a walking-stick and he put his walking-stick into the ground at Muriwai and he said, 'Te Kooti will never ever come into Muriwai, he will never ever touch any people in Muriwai.' . . . Then Te Kooti arrived through there, came up through Whareongaonga and there was no one there, and he found their fires still burning, or just the embers there, and he knew they had just left. Which way did they go? He was confused then. He didn't know.[8]

The Whareongaonga people had fled some miles around the shore to shelter at Muriwai. This narrative, in its telling, anticipates November 1868, when many Maori from Turanga would also take sanctuary from Te Kooti's kokiri at Muriwai pa. Muriwai is always remembered by its own people as the place where blood would never be allowed to flow.[9]

At Whareongaonga, Te Kooti ordered that no one was to eat or drink or smoke until the task of unloading the ship was completed and all were safely ashore. The crew was then paid off and given the letter of exoneration. In it Te Kooti stated simply that Jehovah had intervened to deliver his people from their captivity. He also asked, in this his first communication with the government, that they be left in peace and not be pursued.[10] Then he told every man, woman and child to gather up firewood for the sacrifice of the offerings they were to make. Seven 'Sinners' ('Tangata Hara') were named, and told they could not undertake this task. But the sinners were not permanently cast aside, for one was Petera Te Rangihiroa, who later became one of Te Kooti's secretaries, and another was old Hotoma Kahukura, who would soon be captured by the

Terrain
− 500m +

Maungahaumi ▲

Mangatu ○

Uawa (Tolaga Bay) ○

Makihoi pa ▲

Wharekopae

TE AITANGA
–A–MAHAKI

NGATI
POROU

Te Karaka ○

Makaretu

Waipaoa

Nga Tapa ▲
Te Rere Falls

Okahuatiu ▲

Taureka ○

Waimata

Repongaere Lake

Hangaroa

Taruheru

RONGOWHAKAATA

Gisborne ● ▲

SEE INSET

Tiniroto Lakes

Te Waihau ○
Whenuakura ○
Te Ahi Manu
▲ Whakapunake
Te Koneke

Ruakituri

Te Arai

Muriwai ○

Paparatu ○

Te Reinga ○

Te Puninga ○

Maraetaha ○
Whareongaonga ○

20 km

10 miles

Wairoa ○

Nuhaka ○

Nukutaurua
*Maunga
–a–Kahia* ▲ ○
*Papahuakina
(Table Cape)*

Repongaere Lake

Waerenga–a–Hika ○

Te Pukepuke ○
Patutahi ○
Pukeamionga ○

Tarere ○

Matawhero ○
Pipiwhakao ○
Makaraka ○
Te Ahipakura ○

Kohanga
Kearea Redoubt ■
Te Pa–o–Kahu ○
Gisborne ○
Te Arai (Manutuke) ○
▲ Titirangi
*Awapuni
Lagoon*
Whakato ○
Oweta ○
*Turanganui
–a–Kiwa*

5 km

Pakirikiri ○

3 miles

Map 2. Turanganui (Poverty Bay)

government forces. Then Te Kooti instructed that newborn children be fastened to the firewood: it was the sacrifice of Abraham that he demanded. 'It was a test': the imposition of his absolute discipline over nearly 300 people.[11] Their commitment and unity demonstrated and sustained, the sacrificial offerings could then be made: that is, the fowl and the pig, just as Abraham had sacrificed the ram instead of the son he had promised.[12] As Reuben Riki commented directly, 'It was a cockerel they sacrificed, this time'. The burnt offering was made because 'it was the return to the home land. It *wasn't* the Promised Land.'[13]

Near the fire the whakarau were seen at worship, and the forms they used seemed strange to the observers: they stood before God and did not kneel, and they raised their right hands at the end of their prayers.[14] The Ringatu manuscripts state that, after the sacrifice of the burnt offerings, Te Kooti preached to them and said:

> Na, kaati ra te koropiko, engari whakaaratia te ringa, me toro te ringa me whakanui ki to tatou Kaihanga.

> Cease bowing down, but raise up your hand, stretch it out and praise our Creator.[15]

It is from this occasion that the Ringatu date the practice of the upraised hand, whose textual origins lie, as we have seen, in the Lament of Jeremiah. After the sacrifice and the prayers there was food; the fast they had sustained since the previous day was broken. Finally Te Kooti distributed all the goods from the ship: shirts, gowns, blankets, cloth and money, while those who were to carry the guns were chosen.

At Whareongaonga, the ark to carry the covenant was constructed, while the land was renamed. The hill at the southern end of the cove Te Kooti called Moriah, the place where Abraham had built his altar of sacrifice and where God had appeared before David and instructed him to build the house of the Lord. The part of the bay where the water was rough, and where the shelving reefs lay, Te Kooti named the Tablets of the New Law.[16] Even today, this area is considered tapu, because of its association with the return of the exiles; the waves are unpredictable, and the sea is never calm. If the kina are knocked from your hands by the waves, it is a warning to leave at once.[17] In such ways, Te Kooti bonded the people and the land into his restructuring of their history; and thus he applied his religious vision, by which their situation was analysed and by which he also promised them collective salvation.

In the afternoon of Friday, 10 July, an emissary appeared on the skyline. He was Ihaka Ngarangi One, whom they knew, but what he shouted they could not hear. It was Sunday morning, 12 July, when the first messengers of the government arrived at Whareongaonga. They were Paora Kate (Paora Katete), who was the younger brother of Rukupo and had acted as a guard on Wharekauri, Wi Mahuika, one of the prisoners who had been released, and another of the senior Turanga chiefs, Renata Whakaari. They had been sent by Reginald Biggs, the resident magistrate and commanding militia officer, with the message that the whakarau were to give up their arms.[18] They were offered no terms; they were told to surrender, and await the decision of the government as to their future.[19] Paora Kate's contemptuous manner did not help. He sneered, it was later reported, 'So it is you, Rikirangi te hianga [the deceiver]. I thought so; this is

The sheltered but stony cove of Whareongaonga, looking north. A steep track leads down the valley by Mount Moriah, at the southern end. This is the earliest aerial photograph of Whareongaonga, taken in February 1938.   NZ AERIAL MAPPING, SURVEY 78, G/2

your work.'[20] In reality he did not speak directly to Te Kooti at all. He stated, in sworn evidence, that he saw only Te Kooti's 'mouthpiece', as Te Kooti remained secluded in a house, stooping down out of sight when Paora glimpsed him. Paora told the whaka-rau that 'an investigation' would be held but he admitted, 'This is the word that I kept dark from them, viz., that the man who was the cause of their escaping would be apprehended.'[21]

It seems that very little was said by anyone. Paora reported to Biggs that the prisoners 'were very sulky and would not speak'. They also indicated that they did not wish for any further communication with Turanga Maori, whether 'Loyals or Rebels'.[22] Leonard Williams was told that the women and children were also totally silent, refusing, on Te Kooti's instructions, to greet the messengers as they entered the hastily constructed whare karakia.[23] In the Ringatu manuscript account, the three men brought only one message, which Te Kooti disdained:

> E Te Kooti, homai nga pū. Kaati, kaua koe e whakaara pakanga.

> Te Kooti: E pai ana a koutou korero, engari kaore e taea te whakarite o koutou hiahia. Haere, e hoki, korero atu kua ū mai matau ko nga whakarau katoa. Inahoki te kupu na, ka whakahokia atu ratau e ia ki te whenua i homai e ia ki o ratau matua i mua, a ka hoki atu hoki ratau ki reira.

> Te Kooti, give us the guns. Stop now, don't start a fight.

> Te Kooti: What you say is good, but your desires will not be fulfilled. Go, return and say that we, all the prisoners, have landed. For thus it is spoken: he returned them to the land which earlier he had given to their parents, and they returned there.[24]

Eventually Renata Whakaari asked if he could take home with him one of the children, a ten-year-old who could not talk. Renata, Leonard Williams wrote, returned the boy to his tribe, Te Aitanga-a-Mahaki.[25] This was the only exchange.

A few of the whakarau began to show themselves. Armed, some came to Muriwai but they refused to speak to anyone. Others appeared at J. W. Johnson's station in the hills some miles north of the bay, near Maraetaha, where they held a service in an old whare across the river from the homestead.[26] They were, said Maata Te Owai, Te Kooti's wife who would give evidence against him after she fled from the siege at Nga Tapa, the young men known as Te Kooti's 'Twelve Apostles'.[27] When they returned to Whareongaonga, they brought with them four Maori prisoners, two men and two women. The young men had also been searching for arms,[28] since the whakarau possessed only about 50 Enfield rifles, the vital weapon for their defence. Nevertheless, Biggs decided it was impossible for him to mount an attack upon them. His greater mistake was to pursue them when they began their long journey inland.

On 14 July the whakarau left Whareongaonga. They released the prisoners they had taken. Their passage was slow, burdened as they were with goods, and with the women and small children. Their goal was the King Country. As Leonard Williams heard it, 'The object they have in view in making for the Waikato country is to inaugurate a new order of things, the main feature of which is that there is to be no king'.[29] It is clear that Te Kooti intended to challenge Tawhiao because the King claimed to be the mouthpiece of God; Te Kooti told Paora Kate, 'We go to Waikato, there to dethrone the King and set up one that shall be the chosen of the Atua'.[30] It was a clash of mana; a struggle for religious authority. Some European commentators were too quick to interpret Te Kooti's challenge as a statement that he intended renewing the wars. Colonel G. S. Whitmore wrote in August, after talking with his prisoner Hotoma Kahukura: 'Koti talks of dethroning the King because he has mismanaged the war.'[31] Rather, Te Kooti hoped to make his way peacefully through to the interior, crossing the lands of Tuhoe into the upper Waikato and establish himself there. He said dryly he needed only 'a path 18 inches wide' and, commented Leonard Williams, had 'no doubt the atua will shew it to him'.[32]

To each of the government messengers sent to him Te Kooti made it clear that he would fight only if he was pursued and attacked.[33] According to Hotoma, he planned to send out letters to the Wairoa chiefs, Te Waru and Paora Te Apatu, asking for permission to enter their lands and perhaps to stop there. His final objective as to where they would reside was Taupo,[34] more specifically Tauranga, the village on the eastern shore of the lake where Anaru Matete had sheltered in 1866. Tauranga would remain in Te Kooti's mind for a long time. In March 1869, after he first successfully crossed through the Urewera country, the Tuwharetoa people recalled that 'Te Kooti has said that "Tauranga (on Taupo Lake) will be his resting place."'[35] This village was closely associated with the east Taupo chief Te Rangitahau (Tahau) of Waipahihi and Opepe, who had been captured at Omarunui and sent to Wharekauri with the fourth group of prisoners; he was one of the more formidable of the warriors among the whakarau. Te Rangitahau had also been a pupil of the great tohunga of Tuwharetoa, Werewere Te Rangipumamao, and was one of the more influential of Te Kooti's converts. The two men co-operated closely from 1868 and, in March 1870, they were again reported as trying to get back to Taupo, which was to be their 'permanent place'.[36] The reason lies in the explanation and prediction which Te Kooti gave the prisoners from Tuhoe at Wharekauri on the day before their escape:

> Te tapenakara mo te āka ki Taupo, tikarere tatau ko reira, a ki te tu taua tapenekara [*sic*] kaore he pakanga; otira ki te pai ano hoki te whakahaere.
>
> Otira mehemea ki te pakanga tatau ki te hoariri ina whiti tatau ki tawaahi, kaore hoki he aha, he iwi ano toku kei reira. Kaore engaro [*sic*] ka tae mai ratau ki a tatau i te wa ano e whiti atu ai tatau ki tawahi.

> The tabernacle for the ark will be at Taupo; we shall go directly there, and if that tabernacle stands there will be no fighting, however [only] if the planning goes well.
>
> But if we fight the enemy when we cross to the other side, it will not be without purpose, for they are also my people there. However, rather they will come to us at the time we cross to the other side.[37]

Te Kooti's task, then, was the journey 'into the wilderness', to set up the tabernacle for the ark of the covenant.[38] This was the first of the deeds that had to be fulfilled before the exiles could re-enter Canaan, their Promised Land. He or his spokesman apparently tried to explain this to Paora Kate, saying, 'we only ask an open path to the interior of the land. We will not molest Turanga.'[39]

As the whakarau began their journey, seemingly moving towards Lake Waikare-moana, they were watched to see what course they were taking. On 15 July, Wi Pere rode after them, and overtook some of the stragglers. He tried to persuade old Arapeta Taniwha to come away with him, but the 'old man said that their atua had bidden them to go and therefore he must go'.[40] At Te Puninga, a few miles directly inland from Whareongaonga, they rested and held an evening service. Afterwards, Te Kooti told the whakarau that, if they saw 'four people', those who were on sentry duty were not to shoot them but to capture them carefully and bring them to him.[41] On 17 July four (or six) messengers intercepted the party at Te Puninga. They included Karepa Maruwhaka-tupua, son of Tamihana Ruatapu, Ihaka Makahua of Te Mahanga near Mahia, Wi Kaipuke, the chief of Whareongaonga, sent by the prophet Hamuera Toiroa, and Wi Pere. These four men were specifically named in the Ringatu account of this meeting, while Wi Pere also recorded his own description of the encounter. He wrote that he had been persuaded by the Europeans to take a letter to Te Kooti in a final attempt to communicate with him. It apparently contained a statement that the whakarau would not be molested and that they could, as Paora Kate claimed he had also said, return to Turanga to live — if they surrendered their arms. Wi Pere wrote: Te Kooti 'replied angrily that he would not listen to me, that the Almighty was directing his actions'.[42] After this exchange, neither Wi Pere nor Wi Kaipuke was 'allowed to come back again' to negotiate by the whakarau.[43]

In the Ringatu account of this meeting it is Ihaka Makahua who is the central figure; indeed, Leonard Williams noted in his diary that Ihaka had been very 'impressed with the "mana" of Kooti's atua'.[44] He was given some money from the whakarau but he was not bought. The Ringatu history narrates that, when Ihaka finally got up to speak, his command was spurned by Te Kooti. First Ihaka told him to return to Nukutaurua:

> ina to ara ko to tipuna ko Toiroa kua kitea noatia atu koe, koi nei to ara i whiti mai ai koe ki tawahi nei, tenei; ka poua mai te tokotoko.
>
>   Te Kooti ka mea: . . . E kore au e pai ki to tokotoko. Kia rongo mai koe, ehara i taua tokotoko i whiti mai ai ki tawaahi nei. Ka mau tona ringa ki te tokotoko, ka mea ia, Titiro ei, ki te tika o to rakau. Ka poua ki te whenua ka noho iho ia ki runga, katahi ka mea: Nga Atua kihai nei i hanga i te Rangi i te whenua, ka ngaro ratou i runga i te whenua, i raro atu ano hoki i enei rangi. — Ka whati whatiia taua rakau. Ina kē toku Atua, ina ana korero, ka mamau te Rawiri i a ia ka whakaatu.

> since your way is [from] your ancestor, Toiroa, who has already predicted it for you. This is the way by which you crossed to this side, this; and he stood up the staff.
>
>   Te Kooti said: '. . . I don't agree with your staff. Hear this. It was not by that staff that I crossed over to this side.' He placed his hand on the staff and said: 'Look at the direction of your rod.' He pushed it into the ground, sat on it, and then said, 'The Gods who did not create Heaven [and] earth, they will be destroyed on earth, beneath these very skies.' — And he broke that stick into pieces. 'For it is instead from my God that these words come', and he took up the [Book of] David and showed it [to them].[45]

In this narrative, Te Kooti is shown to reject utterly the power of the divinatory rods or staffs (niu) of the old priests. These were believed to reveal the success or direction of journeys undertaken by the manner in which they fell and shifted on the ground. This text recapitulates Te Kooti's earlier challenge to the prophet Hamuera. An oral version of the same narrative, told at Muriwai, specifically states that Hamuera sent the staff to Te Kooti, along with a whip. The two items bore

> an implied question, 'Do you wish a walking stick to aid you on your path here, or a whip to drive the people?' Te Kooti's response was to take the stick, and break it in half,

take the whip and chop it in pieces, and to throw all in the fire. Then he gave his reply, to be conveyed to Hamuera: 'I want nothing to do with witchcraft.' [But] Hamuera had the last word, when he was told Te Kooti's reply. 'Then, since you do not come now, you will never come. Even until great forests have grown over you.' . . . And never did he set foot in Muriwai.[46]

This particular version of the story focuses on the fact that Muriwai would be a sanctuary from the shedding of blood at Turanga, rather than on Te Kooti's spiritual triumph over their prophet.[47] The death of Hamuera, as we shall see in the next chapter, will add yet another thread to this story.

From Te Puninga the trek continued, and by 19 July the whakarau had reached a high ridge, Te Rahui, commanding a view over the Te Arai river, which flows towards Turanga. On 14 July at Turanga, Biggs had taken the fatal decision to attempt to cut the party off at that river, knowing they would try to cross it on their route through to the Urewera.[48] But if the whakarau's slow passage could be tracked by the Maori forces he set trailing them,[49] the whakarau were also prepared to defend themselves. On the evening of 19 July, their scouts reported sighting a camp of Biggs's military volunteers at Paparatu, in the Te Arai valley.[50] That evening, as Eria narrated to Porter, the whaka-rau held an assembly of the chiefs. The men who spoke up for war included Karanama Ngerengere, Peka Te Makarini and Pera Te Uetuku of Nga Ariki Kaiputahi hapu from Mangatu.[51] Te Kooti then said, 'I expected this after my refusal to surrender our arms and selves again to the Government. . . . The taniwha lies across our path, and we must kill it or ourselves be killed.'[52] The preparations for an ambush were devised as Te Kooti divided the fighting men into two kokiri, one to be led by himself and the other by Karanama Ngerengere.

It was totally successful. On 20 July, the volunteers' scouts spotted a small group of the whakarau clustered together above them on a spur, apparently reconnoitring their position. Their real purpose was to divide the government forces. They fired over the heads of the government men and forced one section of them to move to a hill about '500 yds. on the flank'. But there the volunteers found themselves pinned down by 'well directed shots . . . crashing through the flax'.[53] The trap was well laid. The remainder of the volunteers (42 of the 66 Europeans under the command of Captain Charles Westrup) were caught in the valley. In the course of the fighting a party of Kawanatanga recruits from Ngati Maru, led by Tamihana Ruatapu, arrived at Paparatu camp. They unsaddled their horses, loitered about the camp, and for the most part refused to come to the aid of the besieged government men. The volunteers hemmed in on the hill could see the fight below. They heard the bugle, which Peka Te Makarini used to great effect to confuse Westrup's troopers, and heard the commands to attack them: 'Kokiri. Kokiri. Ka whati. Ka whati' ('Go forward, go forward. They are routed').[54] Te Kooti was seen throughout the day, holding the enemy's attention in the front and shouting commands, while the main assault came from the rear. Two of the volunteers died; the rest were put to flight. They abandoned their camp and its goods: food, rum, bedding, some ammu-nition, ten rifles and 80 good horses with packsaddles, saddles and bridles. But the whakarau had also suffered their first deaths in battle. Three bodies were found subsequently, two carefully hidden by their companions.[55] Death now walked with them on their journey into the wilderness.

In the aftermath, Westrup's report grossly exaggerated the force mounted against him: 150 rifles and guns.[56] What he did not exaggerate was the reluctance of the Maori contingents to fight alongside him. It is clear that there was widespread sympathy for the whakarau among Rongowhakaata, who were already being called 'double-faced' ('kei te angaanga rua nga whakaaro').[57] Only a few of Te Aitanga-a-Mahaki and Ngai Te Kete men were prepared to fight at all.[58] Noting all these events from Napier, the former missionary William Colenso wrote accurately and prophetically to McLean: '*I regret exceedingly* that the returned natives have been hunted. I think they might have been quietly managed. — But I fear it is too late now.'[59]

Eria described the next stage of the planning of the whakarau. After the victory at Paparatu, Te Kooti redivided them into two new parties. The younger men, now mounted on the government horses, were sent by a long bridle track, while the main body, guarded by the older men, went directly on foot through the mountains. They intended to reunite at Te Ahi Manu, near Whakapunake mountain, east of the Hangaroa river. Te Kooti spoke to them before they set out:

> God has again helped us and cleared our path. But the taniwha is not killed. It is only the head we have maimed, and although we have deprived it of some teeth, yet the body is still alive, and will pursue us again. We must haste to where he cannot reach us.[60]

The two parties left Paparatu on the morning of 21 July and reunited that evening. Their trail was picked up later, strewn with leaves from the tops of cabbage trees, used as food, while at one point a large unbroken looking-glass, presumably brought from the *Rifleman*, lay on the path, surreally reflecting the bush.[61] The following morning, the first major support and reinforcements reached them: Ngati Kohatu from Te Waihau, the people of the windy lakes. From them the whakarau learnt of a new government force coming inland from Wairoa to intercept them. Forewarned, Te Kooti again prepared for an ambush.

The whakarau went down to the waters of Te Waihau, where they camped. That evening, their scouts captured Biggs's despatch messenger, Paku Paraone, who was well known to them, for he was the part-Maori son of the Turanga trader William Brown. His family was particularly known to Te Kooti, for Paku's sister, Mere, had married his brother Komene. The government messages Paku brought were read over and precisely translated by Peka Te Makarini, who was completely bilingual. Paku was also questioned closely. Now well informed, the council of chiefs debated his fate. According to Eria, it was Te Kooti who ordered his death. This was the first deliberate execution of the war.

The man selected as executioner was Maaka Ritai, one of the whakarau, who was from Ngati Tuaraia of Waitotara, near Whanganui.[62] In 1872 he was brought to trial for this act. At the trial, three of the whakarau gave evidence that Maaka had been selected by Te Kooti to kill Paku. One of these witnesses was Maata Te Owai. She became one of the government's 'star witnesses' in the several trials held during the wars, and there seems to be some vindictiveness in her readiness to testify. In 1872, she stated that Te Kooti had appointed Maaka as his executioner just prior to the landing at Whareongaonga. He was to kill any whom Te Kooti ordered, regardless of kinship ties, although it is significant that he was not from Turanga. Maaka himself said that he was one of three who had been appointed to destroy those whom Te Kooti wished; otherwise they themselves would be killed.[63] The evidence given by the witnesses to the court in 1872 placed emphasis on the fear which Te Kooti commanded.[64] As a consequence, the jury recommended mercy and, although Maaka was sentenced to death, the punishment was commuted to life imprisonment. He was subsequently released in the 1883 amnesty.

Paku's body was deliberately left unburied. It was found by some of his kinsmen, who were with the government forces, and buried with a simple wooden headboard, 'This is Paku'.[65] This calculated execution created a significant issue of revenge among Rongowhakaata, for Paku was the son of Hine Whati o Te Rangi (Whati Apikara), and close kin to Kahutia. It was the first death which would make enemies for Te Kooti among his own people.

On 23 July, messengers from Ngati Kohatu of Te Reinga, who maintained both kinship and residential connections with Poverty Bay, defeated the rain and snow to bring to Te Kooti the news that the Wairoa expedition had reached Te Reinga. That evening Te Kooti spoke after the karakia: 'In front of us there is another tooth of the Taniwha. In the morning, let the cooking ovens be ready early, that we may move on again, and be strong to meet our enemy. God once more will give us power and make our foes weak in the morrow's battle.'[66] The whakarau now began their trek from Te Waihau along the high ridge, Te Koneke, on the eastern side of the lakes. They were intent on ambush, and that afternoon they trapped the Wairoa contingent. Te Kooti appeared on the top of the hill above them, wrote one of the troopers, 'attired in a loose flowing robe, and with the sun shining on him he seemed to me much as Moses of old appeared on Sinai, or as Joshua commanding the sun to stand still.'[67] The small party of government volunteers, led by Captain William Richardson, was caught down in the valley. The Maori Kawanatanga forces from the lower Wairoa tribes, led by Paora Te Apatu, largely managed to avoid participating in the fighting. Richardson claimed to have had only 20 men with him, four of whom were Maori, as he staged his retreat from Te Koneke. But it was here that Hotoma, who was acting as a scout, was captured, and two (or three) of the whakarau were killed.

From Te Koneke, the whakarau crossed the fast-flowing Hangaroa river in local canoes, the horses swimming behind. Thence they came to Whenuakura, a Ngati Kohatu village on the western side of the river, where they were welcomed by the chiefs of the community, Rewi Tipuna and Watekina Tukaiuru. Almost at once they were joined by the outstanding leader of Ngati Kohatu, Korohina Te Rakiroa, and some 15 or 20 of his men,[68] armed with the four rifles recently issued to them by the government. Te Rakiroa himself later claimed that he had been taken prisoner by Te Kooti after the battle at Te Koneke, but then chose to stay with him.[69] From Whenuakura, Te Kooti wrote to the two senior chiefs of Whataroa village, Nama and Te Waru; indeed, Hotoma said that Te Kooti had always planned to send letters to them once he reached Whenuakura. From these chiefs Te Kooti sought not merely shelter but further fighting support.

Te Waru replied, sending the whakarau messenger, Paora Te Wakahoehoe, back to Te Kooti with a tiwha, a gift as a request for support in a conflict of his own. Paora had previously acted as a messenger for Bishop William Williams when he carried gifts of the New Testament to the Maori prisoners in Napier gaol in 1866; this time he brought a famous greenstone mere named Tawatahi, and Te Waru's daughter Te Mauniko, to be Te Kooti's wife. In accepting these gifts, Te Kooti accepted the take, or cause, for which his help was sought: they were witness to his obligation. The issue was the deliberate execution of Pita Tamaturi, the adopted son of Raharuhi Rukupo, by Reginald Biggs. Pita had been a leader of Te Aitanga-a-Mahaki, who gave their support to the Pai Marire in the wars on the East Coast, and was taken prisoner at Hungahungatoroa pa on 11 October 1865. The Ngati Porou manuscript history of the 'Campaign against the Hauhau on the East Coast, 1865–70' tells what happened. Ropata Wahawaha had taken Pita prisoner when Biggs encountered them. Biggs asked who the man was, and whether he was a chief. When Ropata affirmed he was an important figure, 'Biggs killed that man' ('ka whakamatea e te Piiki taua tangata').[70] Such behaviour was not unprecedented in the East Coast wars: at Pakairomiromi, two months previously, no male prisoners were taken and the pa was burnt down.[71] Te Kooti accepted the gifts and their consequences. He kept the mere through most of the fighting; on 18 August 1871 he abandoned it in a desperate flight from his pursuers.[72] With this tiwha, Biggs's death was Te Kooti's to exact.

Te Waru and Nama were to join Te Kooti after the fight at the Ruakituri river. Both men had fought at Waerenga-a-Hika for the Pai Marire, and their overall motivation then was autonomy for themselves and their people. Now there was a more specific cause: their opposition to the land confiscations which Biggs had engineered in the upper Wairoa district in 1867 as reprisal for the Pai Marire wars.[73] It was this which brought them to Te Kooti. Even more specifically, four blocks of land, which should have been returned by the Crown after the confiscation settlement of 5 April 1867, had not, in fact, been given back.[74] At least two of these blocks, Ruakituri and Waiau, were Te Waru's tribal land. This issue, the seizure of land on the East Coast, was to be, as we shall see, a significant factor in Te Kooti's revenge at Turanga in November 1868. Te Waru and Nama must have been Te Kooti's major informants about the arbitrary manner and the extraordinary tactics which Biggs had adopted on the East Coast. These land issues would escalate over the next few months and would have a direct bearing on the war. They underlay all Te Kooti's conflicts.

At Whenuakura village, Te Kooti again committed himself to a path of war. According to Eria, he preached first from Exodus 14:30–31:

> Thus the Lord saved Israel that day out of the hand of the Egyptians; and Israel saw the Egyptians dead upon the sea shore.
> And Israel saw that great work which the Lord did upon the Egyptians: and the people feared the Lord, and believed the Lord, and his servant Moses.

Now was the moment for Te Rakiroa and his Ngati Kohatu followers to adopt the new religion: 'We will follow in your path; your Atua shall be ours also.' Most important, it was here, according to Eria, that Te Kooti first decided not only to continue the trek into the interior, but also that 'we will turn again upon our oppressors; all the land shall be ours.'[75]

However, as the party, now enlarged by Ngati Kohatu, left Whenuakura, they were still consciously undertaking the journey into the Wilderness, the 'Koraha',[76] the necessary stage before the people are ready and courageous enough to seek to return to Canaan.[77] As God had led the Israelites on divers paths in their journey from their house of bondage, so the experiences of these new children of Israel were considered as the testing of their faith. They crossed over the great mountain divide to the west and came down to the Ruakituri river. Then they followed the river path up towards its headwaters, crossing and recrossing the flooded waters. Many horses were lost on this treacherous route. Their progress was slow and the group became strung out, the rearguard eventually left two days behind the others. Finally, however, they arrived at their sanctuary, Puketapu (Holy Mountain), an ancient pa overlooking the river on the borders of the Urewera country. This was territory known intimately to Eria through his mother's people, whose land it was,[78] and this would be one reason why they had decided to go there. But it was land in which Te Waru and Te Kooti also had rights. Te Kooti would be included, along with Eria and Te Waru's eldest son, Tipene, as one of the original shareholders of the block when, much later, it was given a Crown title.[79] Puketapu had also been used already as a place of sanctuary in 1867 by those of Rongowhakaata who had refused to take the oath of allegiance;[80] now the whakarau planned to refortify the pa on their own land and defend themselves there from attack.

But the colonial forces, under the command of Colonel George Whitmore, were very close behind. On 8 August, 120 volunteers from Napier entered the bed of the Ruakituri river under the shadow of Holy Mountain, which was about half a mile away to the north. As the advance troops passed beside the high papa flat of the river edges, they were fired on simultaneously from the front and their right flank; scrambling up into the gorge, they were besieged by hidden fighters in the bush. Once again, Te Kooti had laid a carefully planned ambush. His men were concealed on the steep bush-covered banks above the river on both sides, and on an island in the middle. The volunteers were trapped among the huge boulders of the river bed. Whitmore wrote in amazement:

> the enemy fought very differently to any Natives I have yet seen engaged. He held a body of desperate men in reserve, to charge whenever he sounded the bugle. His fire was deliberate and never thrown away; every shot fell close to its mark if it did not reach it, and there was no wild volley discharge during the action. He began the fighting himself, and no opportunity was afforded me to summon him to surrender.[81]

Te Kooti's emphatic victory on the Ruakituri river was not without loss. He himself was wounded, shot in the ankle, and carried from the fight on the back of one of his wives — perhaps to preserve the state of tapu in which male warriors would have been placed for the duration of the battle. He also lost some men (three, according to his messengers sent to the Tuhoe; eight on Whitmore's least rhetorical estimate).[82] But Whitmore retreated in defeat. His £10 offer for Te Kooti's capture was unspent, and he had gained a new nickname, 'Witi koaha',[83] Witless.

Just as the fighting was ending, a messenger, Solomon Black, reached Whitmore with despatches. According to Thomas Withers (one of the volunteers), Black brought the government's instructions to cease the pursuit. It had apparently been decided that, if Te

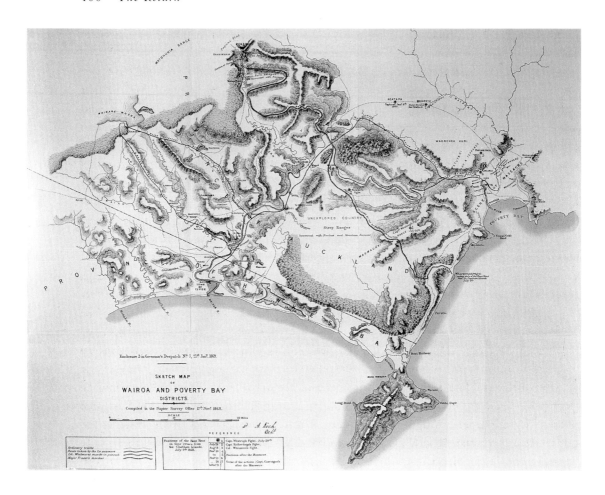

Sketch map enclosed in the governor's despatch of 21 January 1869. It accurately dates the landing of the whakarau and the end of the long siege at Nga Tapa. It also shows the location of the fight of 8 August under the shadow of Holy Mountain (Puketapu). Marked on the west bank of the river is the position taken by the Ngati Kahungunu chief, Paora Kaiwhata, who sustained fire on the island in the middle of the gorge, where Te Kooti's men were hidden. 'Papuni Flat', just north of the mountain, is the bed of the dried-up Papuni lake, at the northern end of which the small kainga Pokimi was located (see Chapter 5).

GBPP, FACSIMILES VOL. 15

Kooti was left unmolested, he might settle down.[84] This account of the message (else-where unreported, and no doubt unwelcome to Whitmore as he was being fired upon) seems to be supported by the fact that the government soon attempted to make overtures to the whakarau to prevent any further fighting. The tragedy was that these overtures were grossly mishandled.

On 7 October, in response to a telegram from Whitmore, the government authorised negotiations with Te Kooti. The terms offered were that, if the whakarau surrendered themselves and their arms, no further proceedings would be taken against them. In addition, 'Land will be found for them to live on', 'wherever it can be obtained'.[85] The negotiator was to be Father Euloge Reignier, a Roman Catholic missionary working in

Hawke's Bay. Many of the whakarau captured at Omarunui and Petane were known to him and had been part of his congregation.[86] He was to work with Hotoma, who had been captured at Te Koneke and who was now being used to negotiate with Te Kooti as a condition of his own release.[87] Their primary purpose, however, was to persuade the chief Nikora Te Whakaunua, one of the whakarau,[88] and his followers from Ngati Hineuru of Runanga to separate from Te Kooti and settle for peace. Whitmore had informed the government that Nikora felt aggrieved that he and his men had been left to sustain the rearguard fighting at Ruakituri when the others withdrew after Te Kooti was wounded. Nikora had sent out a message indicating his desire to negotiate for peace for his segment of the whakarau.[89]

Reignier had already made one abortive attempt to reach the whakarau in the Wairoa district in September. He had turned back because he lacked specific instructions and was afraid of the concessions that would be demanded of him.[90] He set out again on 13 October from Napier. At Te Pohue he met a government despatch rider from Runanga, where Reignier was intending to go. The trooper, a man called Hope, informed Reignier that he would not be able to get through as the upper Mohaka river was in flood and he could not cross it. Further, he said that only Te Kooti's supporters were being allowed through Ahikereru (the old mission centre in the Urewera near modern Te Whaiti) on the long route around to Puketapu. 'Only Hauhaus can pass through those places and only with the Hauhau flag', Hope said. All the people of Tarawera and Runanga had already left to join Te Kooti, he added. Reignier unwisely consulted local European opinion at Te Pohue, and upon their advice entrusted the despatches to Hope, who was due to return to Runanga shortly. Hope promised to send the messages through with Te Kooti's supporters, 'Hauhaus' as he called them, who regularly travelled from Runanga on to Taupo, and beyond, to Tawhiao in the King Country. Hope got back to Runanga on 19 October and the government despatches from Reignier were then sent through the Urewera to Puketapu.[91] Reignier's message invited Nikora and the Hineuru to come back to Runanga, or to any place of their choosing, 'if they were anxious for peace'.[92] This attempt to drive a wedge between groups of the whakarau could hardly have enhanced the credibility of the other offers. Reignier then returned to Napier, expecting nothing to come of his journey. He recognised that Te Kooti was gaining adherents, not losing them, in the wake of victory. Immediately upon his return to Napier on 17 October, he learnt of the execution of four Maori messengers sent from Wairoa in a simultaneous attempt to reach Te Waru and Nama before they committed themselves to Te Kooti. Reignier's loss of nerve will have probably seemed justified to him.

The bodies of the four messengers were subsequently recovered near Whataroa, Te Waru's settlement on the Manga-a-Ruhe river. They had intended to continue on to Puketapu, and for this reason they were seen as spies. All were men of note within Ngati Kahungunu; two of them, Karaitiana Rotoatara and Ahitana Karari, had been among the few Maori who were prepared to fight against Te Kooti at Te Koneke. Karaitiana, however, also had close ties with Te Waru, having been matua whangai (adoptive father) to one of his daughters. Te Waru was not at the settlement when the messengers arrived, but his brother Reihana (Horotiu) entertained them and lulled their sense of danger. They were killed in the night as they slept. Reihana cut out Karaitiana's heart for the

Maori god of war, Tu-matauenga. This was the 'whangai hau', the offering of the heart of the first man slain on a kokiri, and also an act of revenge for his participation in the fighting.[93] Reihana took the heart with him to Waikaremoana when he went to join Te Kooti, and placed it in the tuahu (separate sacrificial enclosure) at Matuahu pa. When Te Kooti in turn visited Matuahu, he ordered the tuahu and the heart destroyed: this was not his religion, nor his form of sacrificial offering.

Nevertheless, this killing created formidable enemies for Te Kooti among Ngati Kahungunu. It was widely believed that Te Waru had authorised the deaths (although this was incorrect), and certainly, by 20 October, it was known that Te Waru and Nama had joined up with the whakarau.[94] Their wars were now linked. Te Kooti will have been reminded of the consequences of his acceptance of Te Waru's tiwha; at the same time, however, Maori were becoming more divided as these deaths started to bring new motives into play. Requital for the loss of kin began to cry out to different family groups.

Te Kooti himself, after the victory on the Ruakituri river, retired to Holy Mountain. The old pa was cleared and refortified, while Te Kooti slowly recovered from his wound. 'Te Koti the prophet says he is sleeping now', Reignier was informed in October.[95] In actuality Te Kooti was sending letters across the land. He wrote to King Tawhiao, apparently seeking permission to enter the King Country. He also wrote to the Tuhoe chiefs. He sought their permission to enter the Urewera, and he also urged them to give up their form of karakia.[96] He wrote to Turanga asking his kin to remain 'outwardly loyal' to the government, but to try to gather arms for his support when he came down 'in the summer'.[97] It would seem, therefore, that immediately after the fight on the Ruakituri, he was still exploring the two possibilities: of continuing forward, or of turning back.

As Reignier had seen, Te Kooti was gaining new support. Te Waru and Nama and their followers reached him in September. So did some men from Turanga.[98] One of those who joined at this time was Matene Te Karo,[99] who would be charged (in 1869) with high treason. Te Kooti also learnt at this juncture that his first letter to Tawhiao had been intercepted 'by the Government Maori' ('i te Kawanatanga') at Te Waiparati and that a government attack upon Puketapu was planned.[100] He was therefore unlikely to take seriously the overtures for peace sent on through the trooper and message boy, Hope.

He was still debating his choices. His ultimate objective remained Taupo lake, as Frederick Helyar learnt from messengers who came from Puketapu to Runanga on 28 October. But Helyar also learnt then that Te Kooti was going back to Poverty Bay first: 'they say that they are merely obeying the orders of their God'.[101] Helyar's informants were Wirihana Te Koekoe, an emissary of Tawhiao and a leading chief from east Taupo, who was on his way home from Puketapu, and Hohepa Te Kate, one of the whakarau, on his way to find the King. In September Wirihana had brought Tawhiao's word to Te Kooti: he was not to fight, not to renew the wars.[102] Hohepa was setting out for the King Country with new messages for the King — but he was too late. The next night another messenger came to Runanga from Taupo with the news of Tawhiao's final decision for Te Kooti:

The king has refused to assist the exprisoners in the slightest degree and declares his intentions of repelling them if they encroach upon his territory in the least — He is incensed with the exprisoners because they listen to and obey the dictates of their prophet in preference to his own.[103]

Te Kooti had been waiting anxiously also for the decision of Tuhoe. At a meeting at Ahikereru in October, which a number of the whakarau attended, it was accepted that they could remain where they were, in the 'upper Wairoa' on the borders of the Urewera, and to hold 'the confiscated or ceded land there' as an occupying force.[104] Tuhoe made it clear that they opposed any attempt by the government to reach the whakarau at Puketapu through the Urewera.[105] A few Tuhoe from Te Whaiti also went to join Te Kooti at Puketapu. But as yet Tuhoe had not given their permission for Te Kooti to enter their lands.[106] It would not be until March 1869 at Tawhana (in the Waimana valley) that Tuhoe committed their land and their people to Te Kooti.[107]

By October 1868, Te Kooti was in actuality encircled. To go forward into the King Country invited certain conflict with Tawhiao. He had thrown down a challenge, and the King had picked it up. To go through the Urewera without the support of Tuhoe was to seek a war he did not want; he knew that he could not enter the area of their mana without their concurrence. It was in this context that Te Kooti decided to seek to recover Turanga. He had nowhere else to go. But the decision was construed (and understood) in prophetic terms. He told the whakarau, said Ema Katipa, who was taken prisoner by Te Kooti in November, 'that God would give the Turanganui country, and all the best places of the Europeans, back to him and his people.'[108] At Holy Mountain he started to prepare to take back what was his.

Eria Raukura narrated for Porter many of the details of the three months the whakarau spent at Puketapu. Porter also had access to a statement written down two years later by one of the whakarau (whom he had captured), and a manuscript notebook of Te Kooti, which dated from this time.[109] It was from this notebook that Porter recovered the scriptural texts whereby Te Kooti evolved his purpose. Shortly after the fight on the Ruakituri, Te Kooti had preached from Proverbs 23:35:

> They have stricken me, shalt thou say, and I was not sick; they have beaten me, and I felt it not: when shall I awake? I will seek it yet again.

Over these months he preached regularly, exhorting the people to strength, but also using fear as a weapon to harden their resolve. He told them that, if they were strong, God would restore the land to them; if not, it was they who would be given into the hands of 'the Government men'. He said he had been too merciful, asking 'only that our path should not be intercepted. They did not listen. Now we must turn and strike them. . . . Now Turanga shall be given us to dwell in!'[110]

It was at this time, according to Porter's account, that he took the name Te Turuki, and certainly it first appeared in his letters in December 1868. Porter did not understand the name, not realising that it was from Te Kooti's adoptive 'father' and kinsman. The significance of the act lay in his deliberate rejection of the missionary baptismal name, Te Kooti. The choice reclaimed his lineage among the Turanga chiefs; it was

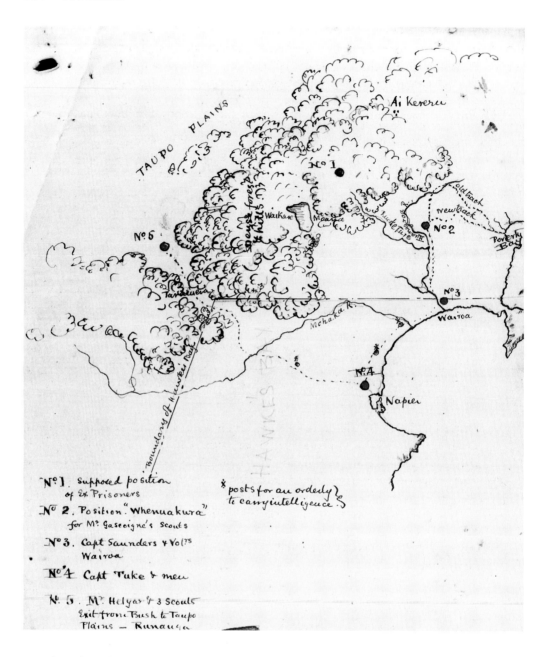

Map drawn by Colonel Whitmore, 5 October 1868, to explain his planned strategy. It locates Whenuakura ('No 2'), the Ngati Kohatu village, as being on the eastern side of the Hangaroa river, confusing it with Te Koneke. It very roughly locates the whakarau at Puketapu. It shows two possible routes that the whakarau might use in an attack on Turanga, which was already feared.   ADI 68/3306, NA

simultaneously a statement of a new spiritual birth. Thereafter, those who joined him, and stayed with him, like the Tuhoe, would always call him Te Turuki.

He recruited some significant support. By October he had a force of probably about 250 men. They came, as we have seen, primarily from the upper Wairoa, and from the north and inland of Napier. These areas had given support to the Pai Marire in 1865–66. But their anger had been rekindled by the land confiscations. In Hawke's Bay, a large area on the north side of the Esk river and stretching across the upper Mohaka river to Tarawera, had been confiscated in reprisal for the fighting. It included Petane, where the major confrontation had occurred in 1866, and most of the lands of Ngati Hineuru, who had fought both there and at Omarunui.[111] Now these lands were being reoccupied by those joining Te Kooti; this was a deliberate strategy by the people of Petane, who had returned to the confiscated Tangoio lands in September, and it was copied shortly afterwards by Ngati Hineuru as they reclaimed the Tarawera block.[112]

This was the time when Te Kooti learnt that confiscations were proceeding at Poverty Bay, and in the most arrogant way possible. The tactics adopted, and the muddle which had been created by the East Coast Land Titles Investigation Act of 1866, are most clearly expressed in a petition sent from Turanga dated 8 July 1867, bearing 256 Maori signatures. At first Biggs had tried to force the East Coast people to cede all their land to the Crown. He told them that much of it was going to be confiscated in reprisal for the Pai Marire wars, and that the rest would then be returned as a Crown grant to those who had been 'loyal'. He also told them it was necessary to have all their land brought before the Native Land Court to establish their titles. The court, to which the Turanga people were first summoned in September 1866, did not convene. Then, they said, the 'death-causing' words came: 'the land was taken' ('ko te kupu whakamate, ara, ko te tango whenua'). The petitioners wrote:

> i kaha tonu hoki a Te Piki ki te tohe i to matou whenua kia whakaaetia, kia tukuna, katahi matou ka whakaae atu ki a ia tetahi pihi whenua, he pihi nui noatu he iti rawa te wahi i mahue atu ki a matou . . . . otira te take i whakaae ai matou he hoha no matou ki tona tawainga i a matou, me te maha o nga kupu whakawehiwehi a te Kawanatanga ki a matou, kihai ia i pai ki ta matou i whakarite ai, ko tana i pai ai kia riro te raorao katoa i a ia, kia tere matou ki runga i nga maunga; heoi ka mea atu matou me waiho ma te Kooti Whakawa e whakaora i a matou, katahi ka puta mai tana ki a matou, ka mauria mai e ia te Kooti Tango whenua, katahi ano matou ka rongo i tenei ingoa mo te Kooti, miharo ana matou.

> Captain Biggs was urgent in asking us to consent to our land being ceded; then we consented to hand over a piece of land, it was a very large piece, leaving a piece for ourselves much smaller as compared with the other . . . . But we gave our consent only because we were wearied at his constantly teasing us, and because of the many intimi- dating words of the Government used towards us; but he was not satisfied with what we had agreed to. What he wanted was, to get all the level country, and we might perch ourselves on the mountains. Thereupon we told him it must be left for the Land Court to give us relief; then he replied, he would bring the land-taking Court. This was the first time we had heard such a name for the Court, and we were surprised.[113]

The muddle — and the pressure — continued, and resistance grew at Turanga to making any cessions at all, or to bringing any land before the court. It is clear from Biggs's letters that he continued to lean heavily upon the people,[114] despite a chaotic legal situation. The 1866 Act, under which he was operating, actually sought to take land from those who had *not* been in rebellion (the consequence of incompetent drafting).

The court was suspended because of this muddle, the Act was corrected in October 1867, and Biggs pressed on. He was trying to get before the court all the land in a vast block extending from Lottin Point, on the northern tip of East Cape, to the upper Wairoa. The government's objective was to determine title, and then seize all that which was deemed to belong to 'rebels'.[115] At Turanga, however, there was mounting opposition to this legislation, and J. C. Richmond had been told plainly, when he visited early in 1867 to try to hasten a settlement, that the people considered the deaths of the slain and the banishment of the prisoners to Wharekauri were 'sufficient punishment'.[116] Then, in February 1868, McLean visited Turanga and tried in vain — and in what, stretching credibility, he saw as a compromise — to persuade the chiefs to cede only a large block of land on the Waipaoa and Waimata rivers.[117] The government would then waive its claims to the rest. Conversely, he threatened that if they did not do this the land would all be taken by the Native Land Court. Hone Mohi Tawhai, the Maori assessor sent to Turanga, wrote, 'I, myself, heard these words from Mr McLeans own mouth. . . . This causes me to tremble . . . that the Court is a land-taking thing.'[118]

As a result of the escalating resistance, and the clumsiness of the existing legislation, on 20 October 1868 yet another confiscation Act was passed. This was the East Coast Act, which stated that, because a considerable number of natives in the district had been or were in rebellion, it was proper that land should be taken. Anyone who had been engaged in rebellion, singly or conjointly, or had counselled or advised such acts since 1863, would not be permitted to obtain title in tribal land. Moreover, the court was empowered to divide tribal land and to confiscate any that had belonged to 'rebels'; it would also award certificates of title to those who were not identified as rebels. This Act was purposefully different from the previous legislation in that it created an ostensibly acceptable framework for establishing claims to ownership, as well as being confiscatory. It aimed to defuse the protests by Maori that the court was simply land-taking, in order to gain their participation in its processes.[119] In fact, it created an environment where Maori contested ownership rights with one another. At the same time it sought to curtail any movement of sympathy for the whakarau by defining all supporters as 'rebels' and then punishing them by stripping them of their land. In such a manner, Te Kooti, along with so many others, was rendered landless.

Te Kooti had owned land in Poverty Bay. Its importance to him can be seen from the way he became involved in two separate disputes about adjoining pieces of land there. They were both at Matawhero, where it has been assumed in the historical dialogue that he had no particular claims. But it was there that the violation of his and his family's rights was most manifest. It is no accident that the only people to be killed in the November attack were those living on land at Matawhero which Te Kooti could properly consider his own.

These two land disputes, which were to become the cause for war (and the most frequently discussed conflict), need to be carefully outlined. During Te Kooti's exile on Wharekauri, both George Read and Biggs had taken land at Matawhero on which Te Kooti had once lived and which he had cultivated. Read's territorial expansion had brought him into a boundary dispute with his immediate neighbour, William Greene, and, at the same time, into argument with a group of Maori owners, who included Te

Major Reginald Biggs. He was appointed agent for the general government in November 1866, to carry out the East Coast land confiscations.   GM

Kooti, his brother Komene and Te Watene, an elder kinsman of Hirini Te Kani. They contested Read's ever-expanding claims. This group of owners had earlier given Greene his piece of land for his half-Maori children. The Maori vendors of Read's larger block joined in the argument in support of Read. This spiralling dispute at Matawhero was therefore multi-faceted: it was a conflict within Rongowhakaata about ownership rights and who could sell or transfer land, as well as being a quarrel with Read.

The contested boundary between Greene and Read was a newly dried-up bend in the Waipaoa river at Matawhero, defining the northern and eastern edges of a 27-acre block called Wainui 2.[120] The block had been given to Greene's children by their tupuna (their mother's kin). This was land where Te Kooti, Te Watene, and many others had had homes and gardens, which they left when Greene and his family settled there. While on Wharekauri Te Kooti had been contacted by the leaders of the nearby community at Te Ahipakura, where he had also lived, about the growing conflict over Wainui. He was told that one of their kinsmen, Renata Ngarangi of Te Whanau-a-Iwi, had sold the rich alluvial land of the dried-up river bed to Greene. Although the former river bed had already been added by the donors, Greene was prepared to purchase this large encircling valley, which effectively doubled the size of the block, in order, as he stated later, to guarantee that his land was complete.[121] Te Kooti wrote his reply on 3 January 1867, just before he fell seriously ill on Wharekauri. In it he mentions his little son 'Tini' (Wetini), who was with his mother:

> . . . mo Wainui: e hoa ma, kaore au e pai kia riro i a ia te hoko taua pihi. Ma koutou e tono kia utua e ia nga moni i kainga na e ia. Mehemea kei te ata whai ia i a Tini, e pai ana. Otira, kaore tonu e tika, no te mea kua oti i a au te korero ki a Wiremu Kirini. Kai a ia tonu taua pihi inai[a]nei. Tohea e koutou kia utua au moni e ia. Kaore au e pai. Ka huri.

> . . . about Wainui: friends, I do not agree that he [Greene] obtain that piece by sale. You should ask that he [Renata] pay [back] the money that he has used. If he looks after Tini, that's all right. However, it would still not be right, because I have already spoken to William Greene, and he himself has that piece now. Insist that he pays you your money. I won't agree. That's all.[122]

Despite the ambiguities created by the confusing pronouns, the letter clearly indicates that Te Kooti was upholding the gift of Wainui 2, which had been made to Greene and his family. In replying to the people at Te Ahipakura in this emphatic way he also indicates that it was within his (and others') authority to have made that gift, or the right of tuku whenua. He also indicates that Renata had a responsibility to care for Wetini, Te Kooti's son, especially after having taken money for a piece of their communally owned land. Renata Ngarangi would give evidence in 1869 that, urged on by the Ngati Porou chief Mokena Kohere, he had demanded (and received) £25 for the dried-up river bed from Greene. He knew that the piece had already been given to Greene, and he admitted that when his family heard about his actions they had protested strongly, blaming him for not getting their consent.[123] However, Renata was not the only person to sell the river bed to Greene.

On the formal award of title to Wainui 2, made to Greene's children in 1869 and containing the entire river bed circling its north-eastern boundaries, it is stated that a portion of the block had been acquired by a deed of gift dated 9 October 1865.[124] This deed survives. The first signature on it is that of Te Kooti ('Koti Rikirangi'); the second is that of his brother, Komene.[125] Greene gave evidence that the deed was drawn up at the outbreak of the Pai Marire troubles in Poverty Bay in order to confirm the earlier gift, made to the children by their kin, who were the extended family of Hirini Te Kani. The boundaries named on the deed were pointed out to Greene by the signatories,[126] as the deed confirms. The other portion (the former river bed) is stated in the award as having been acquired by purchase on 25 May 1866. The deed of this transaction also exists, recorded on the obverse side of the original. The 'sale' took place exactly three days after McLean had taken his last prisoners from Turanga — the two men who had acted, he said, as spies. The document suggests, therefore, that the land in dispute had been 'sold' the moment Te Kooti had been re-arrested and sent away. The original two signatures on this second deed are those of Mokena Kohere and Renata Ngarangi, and the wording on the deed is quite clear: 'We two have given away the valley beyond the home of William Greene the younger, at Wainui' ('Kua hoatu e maua te marua kei waho o te kainga o Wiremu Kirini tamaiti, ki Wai-nui'). Below their signatures, however, an additional signature was added later: that of Piripi Taketake. Piripi was married to Harata Poharu (Tarapoharu); she and her husband were the new claimants to this fertile alluvial land.[127] They would be executed by Te Kooti in November. Urged on by Read, they had insisted on their ownership and threatened to divide the river bed and sell the upper half to Read. Finally, Piripi and Harata 're-sold' the entire river bed to Greene, this time for £10.[128] In so doing they further inflamed the dispute with Read; Greene complained to the Native Land Court in August 1867 that Read had moved his (Greene's) fence at Wainui in order to cause him annoyance.[129] This act of sale simultaneously renewed the long-standing and bitter feud within Rongowhakaata between the land-sellers and the land-holders.

Sarah Dunlop knew of these tensions, knew that Te Kooti had formerly lived at Matawhero, and attributed his decision to strike there in November 1868 partly to a reprisal against the 'four natives who had taken and sold his land during his enforced absence'.[130] She particularly mentioned a 30-acre section of land belonging to Te Kooti, which Read had fenced in 'as a grazing paddock'.[131] This was another piece of contested land, which lay within Read's larger neighbouring block, Matawhero 4 (319 acres).[132] Matawhero 4 was the source of the second dispute, which must have festered in Te Kooti's mind during his exile. In fact, it had been partly responsible for his exile. It now becomes clear that Te Kooti and Komene's attack on Thomas Bloomfield's newly built house at Matawhero, as well as their cattle raids — the two episodes cited by John Harris in April 1866 to urge their exile — arose out of these arguments. Bloomfield had built his house within this block on Read's agreement. On 26 October 1864, Read had purchased half of Matawhero 4 from Harris and his sons, knowing that he had bought within it a disputed component, the area whose original sale was denied by Te Kooti.[133] Read had, as he himself admitted, thereby acquired Harris's 'risk'.[134]

The major argument was about the upper part of the block, which adjoined the river bed of Wainui 2 and extended to the east.[135] This area was called 'Otoma', after the old pa site at the northern corner of Matawhero 4; the name means place of burial, which indicates its significance.[136] The entire Otoma (Te Toma) block consisted of 150 acres, or at least so Harris claimed from the original deed of 'gift' ('kua homai noa') of 30 October 1843.[137] When Read bought this land from Harris, its boundaries had been pointed out to him by the faction who had long ago received a foaling mare in part-payment for it. Those who had then been promised a share of the mare's offspring but had received none rejected Harris's title.[138] Not only was the sale contested by some of the owners, it was in fact illegal: the original transaction had been made when only the Crown could purchase Maori land.[139] Harris's title to Otoma had been investigated by the Old Land Claims' Commissioner in 1859 and suspended until the dispute was resolved satisfactorily among the Maori owners. Tamati Tokorangi of Ngati Kaipoho, who was one of the two signatories to the original deed, gave evidence that there were many owners who should have received payment but the mare's offspring had gone entirely to the other signatory, Paratene Te Mate.[140] Edward Harris, John Harris's elder son, also admitted in 1859 that he knew that, if his family should try to occupy the

The deed of gift for Wainui 2. The land is given to William Greene, the elder of the two children of Greene and his wife Erena Kuha (Kuwha). The sketch roughly marks the sweep of the old river bed and shows the line to the furthest south-western point, where the tutu tree stood. The tree marked the boundary of Wainui 1, which was Ngati Maru land. The deed is dated Turanga 9 October 1865, and the text reads: 'Kua homai e matou ki a Wiremu Kirini, tamaiti a Wiremu Kirini raua ko Erena Kuha, tetahi pihi whenua kua whakaatu matou ki a ia i tenei rangi. Kei te tahataha tonu o Wainui te rohe, hangai ki te poro o te taiapa o Hori Korimete te timatanga, haere aa ki te pikitanga ki rawahi o to Hori Pokereni kainga. Ka tapahi whakaroto ki te tutu kua whakaatu matou ki a ia — a tapahi atu ano ki te timatanga o runga tahataha, ake ake.' ('We have given to William Greene, son of William Greene and Erena Kuha, a piece of land which we showed him today. The boundary is right on the Wainui slope, beginning at right angles to the end of George Goldsmith's fence, going on to the hill on the other side of George Poulgrain's home. It cuts inland to the tutu tree we showed him — and cuts back again to the beginning on top of the slope, right up.') The term used for giving, 'kua homai', is inclusive — that is, it still includes the donors within the gift, perhaps intending to indicate a continuing relationship between them. This is in contrast to the term used for the sale of the old river bed, written on the obverse of this document.

This is the earliest known signature of Te Kooti. It is followed by that of his older brother, Komene. The third signatory, Te Watene, was described in 1869 as a 'tupuna' ('grandparent') of Hirini Te Kani. Te Watene showed the land to Greene in 1865. The fourth signature appears to be written as 'By Hare' ('Na Hare'); his identity remains unknown. At the bottom Mokena Kohere has added his name, presumably when the 'sale' of the old river bed was made in 1866. The witness was George Goldsmith; the north-western boundary commenced at his block, Huiatoa. George Poulgrain's house was on the second disputed land block, Matawhero 4; Captain James Wilson acquired it from him and was living in it in 1868. The deed also gives the alternative name for Wainui, 'Waikowhai'.   Wainui 2, OLC 4/21, NA

The obverse side: the 'sale' of the old river bed. The deed is dated Turanga 25 May 1866, and the text reads: 'Kua hoatu e maua te marua kei waho o te kainga o Wiremu Kirini tamaiti, ki Wai-nui hei kainga ano mo raua ko tona matua. Te rohe timata ki te poro o te taiapa o Hori Korimete haere atu ki te taiapa a Hori Pokereni — me haere hoki te taiapa a Wiremu ki runga tahataha ki te taha mai ki Makaraka — Kua homai hoki a Wiremu Kirini, matua, e rua tekau ma rima paona hei utu mo taua pihi.' ('We two have given away the valley beyond William Greene the younger's home, at Wainui, as another residence for him and his father. The boundary begins at the end of George Goldsmith's fence [and] goes out to George Poulgrain's fence — William's fence must also go up the slope to the side facing Makaraka — William Greene, senior, has given twenty-five pounds as payment for that piece.') The deed is signed by Mokena and Renata Ngarangi; Piripi Taketake's signature was appended later.   WAINUI 2, OLC 4/21, NA

land, the objections would be renewed. An earlier attempt by another settler, Thomas U'ren, to erect a house there had already resulted in its being set on fire and destroyed; John Harris later named Te Kooti as one of the young men associated with that episode.[141] Consequently, Henry Harris, Harris's younger son, was happy to agree to his getting rid of the block to Read, for, as he said plainly to his father, 'I am Tired of waiting for the land I dont think it will be settled for some years yet to come'.[142]

This contested land was unquestionably one of the claims at the heart of the repudiation movement, upon which Harris had commented in general, and thereby evasive, terms to McLean. The Old Land Claims' Commissioner, F. Dillon Bell, had been much more forthright. Not only had he suspended the award of title to this block because of the dispute, he also recognised that Maori at Poverty Bay were united in their general determination to 'repossess themselves of the land', and that the settlers knew that to seek to survey any of the contested claims would be 'hazardous' in the extreme. Bell also said firmly that the government could not protect purchases or transactions made in violation of the law.[143]

This was the long-simmering conflict which lay behind Harris's intervention in 1866, successfully urging Te Kooti's exile. The family of original sellers, who had pointed out the boundaries again to Read in 1864, included, significantly, Piripi Taketake and his wife Harata Poharu, daughter of the chief Paratene who had signed the original deed for Otoma but who had refused to share the proceeds properly among all the owners.

The dispute within Rongowhakaata was about ownership rights. It had created an unending argument wherein the sale had been rejected by one section of owners. Read tried to annul the entire dispute by fencing in the whole of his claim in the winter of 1866, just after the whakarau had been exiled. This led to the entire area being marked loosely as 'Read's Claim and Native Land' in the first rough survey made, in July 1866– January 1867.[144] Read's long north-eastern fence line strides across the map, encompassing all the land within the large sweep of the Waipaoa river at Matawhero. At the time of the second survey, 1869, the surveyor himself admitted he had been directed to take the boundaries for Matawhero 4 from Read's fence, which by then completely encircled the property.[145] It was on a part of this disputed land, extending out from the north-eastern borders of Wainui 2, that Biggs built his own home (Biggs's 'hollow', as it was described[146]), and there he would be killed.[147] The uncompleted military redoubt, started in October 1868 at Toanga-Matawhero, was built by Read,[148] and he placed it close to the two disputed blocks. Its site had been chosen to defend his claims, as well as for the ease with which he had expected to be able to sell provisions to the garrison, although the redoubt was, in fact, never occupied. The boundless extent of Read's economic ambitions was observed by Captain William Newland, who was summoned to Turanga in 1868: 'The whole place', he said, 'seemed to belong to Capt Read who had several Vessels trading along the Coast. He had been a resident there for many years and had a Native wife who owned a large property in the Bay. All business seemed to go through Capt Read.'[149]

The news of all these developments would have reached Te Kooti at Puketapu through his informants from Poverty Bay. At issue was not only the economic power of monopolists like Read and Harris, and their illicit land-purchasing methods. There was also a deep-seated conflict among Rongowhakaata over shared ownership, intensified by the actions of those chiefs who either were prepared or were pressured to sell the land. Te Kooti's decision to attack Matawhero was far from random: it was a war to reclaim his land. This has been denied in previous discussions about the reasons for his attack on Matawhero. Such doubts derived, in part, from a failure to realise the extent of the suppression of ownership rights perpetuated through the processes imposed by the Poverty Bay Commission, with the consequence that most people remained ignorant of Te Kooti's close involvement with the land at Matawhero. All the evidence presented to the commission in 1869 was manipulated to meet the requirement of excluding

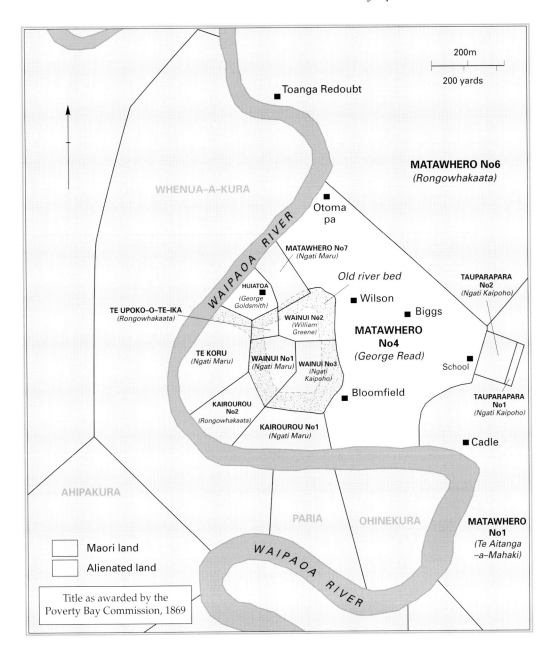

Map 3. Matawhero 1868–1869

'rebels'. The evidence would be given by Maori struggling to establish their loyalty — at the expense of others. They also acted out of a fear that, because all Poverty Bay was ceded to the government following the attack of November 1868, if the claims were not mounted the government would keep the land instead of giving out titles. There was a further, unspoken reason: to avoid any discussions which might directly connect the events of November with the previous land disputes. But the documentation pieced together reveals that Te Kooti's ownership rights were uncontestable. It also reveals how a suspended land title (half of Matawhero 4) came to be silently transferred into European hands by the commission's decision of 1869.[150] Finally, it shows that Te Kooti himself acted consistently, recognising and upholding land gifts and agreements which had been properly made, but rejecting the incomplete or manipulative sales.

A further take (cause) of which Te Kooti would have been informed was the removal of the great carved meeting-house Te Hau-ki-Turanga (The Spirit of Turanga) from Orakai-a-Pu, the old pa at Manutuke. This house had been built in 1842–43 by Raha-ruhi Rukupo (and others) in memory of Rukupo's elder brother, Te Waaka Mangere. In 1867 Biggs had engineered its removal to Wellington without proper agreement. This was when J. C. Richmond was visiting Poverty Bay to try to hasten the land settlement. He also wanted to obtain the house for the government, but he could not get Rukupo's consent. Rukupo sent his second petition of 8 July 1867 to Parliament in protest:

> ko to matou taonga nui ko to matou whare whakairo kua mauria huhua koretia, e te Kawanatanga, kihai matou i whakaae .... i te taenga mai o te Ritimona, ka tono mai kia hoatu e au te whare, kahore au i whakaae, mea atu ana ahau ki a ia, kahore, kei te iwi katoa te ritenga, ka mea mai ia ki au na ratou ranei te whare? mea atu ana ahau, kahore naku ano te whare erangi ko te mahi na matou tahi. Ko te whakahokinga mai a te Ritimona heoi ano ra, ka mutu taku tohe atu ki a koe: . . . ko Kapene Piki i haere mai, ki te tiki mai i te whare, ka mea mai ia ki au kia hoatu te whare mo te Kawana ki Poneke. Ka mea atu au ki a ia, kahore au e pai. Tenei ano etahi o nga kupu a taua Pakeha kei au, heoi ano, haere atu ana taua Pakeha ki te pakaru i te whare, mauria atu ana, heoi ra kahore aku kupu whakaae ki a ia.

> Our very valuable carved house has been taken away, without pretext, by the Government: we did not consent to its removal . . . . at the time of Mr. Richmond's visit here, he asked me to give up the house; I did not consent, but told him, 'No, it is for the whole people to consider.' He then asked me if the house belonged to them all. I answered, 'No, the house is mine, but the work was done by all of us.' To this Mr. Richmond replied, 'That is all; I will cease to urge you.' . . . Captain Biggs came to fetch away the house. He desired me to give it up for the Governor, to be taken to Wellington. I told him I did not agree to it. He said other things, which I have not forgotten. He then went to take down the house, and carried it off, but I did not give my sanction to it.[151]

Richmond himself had written privately that, 'The only great thing done [on his recent visit to Turanga] was the confiscation and carrying off of a beautiful carved house with a military promptitude that will be recorded to my glory.'[152] This account, if not the self-congratulatory tone, is accurate. Although the house was paid for, in that £100 was handed over by Biggs to ten unknown individuals, it is clear that the removal was 'by force' and under active protest. As Captain John Fairchild, who physically removed it on Richmond's orders, said in his evidence to a later parliamentary inquiry: 'They stood there, and objected to every stick that was touched. . . . I took it with the tomahawk against their will.'[153] The wily Ngati Porou chief Mokena Kohere, who claimed to be an owner of the house (just as he had the land at Matawhero), said that he approved of its removal, as 'one of the spoils of victory over the rebels'.[154]

Te Hau-ki-Turanga was Te Kooti's meeting-house and it belonged to Ngati Kaipoho and Ngati Maru.[155] It stood close to the new pa which grew at Whakato around the Anglican mission, founded there in 1844. Te Kooti would have watched the house as it was built and, as a youth being trained in carving (as he was), he had possibly even played a tiny part in its construction. He would have visited it many times, for Rukupo had lived in the house for a long period. He had finally left it in 1866, moving to Pakirikiri. But even Richmond, who considered Rukupo to be 'a leading rebel in the Poverty Bay district' and therefore liable to forfeiture of land, recognised him 'as representing the owners' and agreed that the 'house stood on Rahurui's land'.[156] This house is the oldest complete meeting-house in the country. It stands at present, with the self-portrait of Rukupo, one of the greatest of the master carvers, guarding its doorway, in the Museum of New Zealand in Wellington. In 1994, an agreement with Rongo-whakaata was sealed finally by the return home to Manutuke of six kowhaiwhai panels from Rukupo's Anglican church; this enabled Te Hau-ki-Turanga to be retained for the new Museum of New Zealand building by accord, and not by compulsion.[157]

Te Kooti had not merely been sent into exile without trial. He had also been deprived of the land where he had once lived and any chance to title in it. His former meeting-house had been carted off to Wellington for 'display', despite the protests of the man who carved it and lived in it and who, it was admitted, represented the owners. Rukupo had protested not only against this, but against both the 'propriety' of sending the prisoners to Wharekauri and the forfeiture of any land at Poverty Bay.[158] Rukupo's anger was Te Kooti's anger. He had been truly dispossessed of all that a man could value.

At Puketapu he came to his resolution. He would turn back to Turanga and Mata-whero. He would become Joshua, the warrior son of Israel, to whom the task had been given to bring the children of Israel into the land sworn unto them. The first steps for the return were made. In mid-October 1868 there was a thrust at Wairoa, which was an attempt both to persuade the senior chief, Paora Te Apatu, 'to leave the road clear', and to acquire more arms.[159] It caused hysteria in the region, because the intentions of the parties of Te Kooti's scouts seen in the hills behind Wairoa were unknown. The strategy served successfully as a feint, concentrating attention in the wrong quarter. It also seems to have had some effect on Paora Te Apatu, who received from Turanga the same warning message to stay clear.[160] But it did not get the guns.[161]

On 24 October at Puketapu, Te Kooti held a runanga of the principal chiefs, who now included Te Waru, Te Rakiroa and Nama, as well as the whakarau chiefs. He told them of his intention to strike at Turanga. He instructed them in classical fashion: 'The weapons in the right hand, the plunder in the left' ('Nga patu ki te katau, nga taonga ki te maui'). Turanga would be given to them to dwell in, he predicted. He also said that Auckland, Wellington and Napier would ultimately fall: that is, the three centres of government power where the legal decisions (which had dispossessed them all) were made, and from where the pursuit had been mounted. The next night, which was their last on Holy Mountain,[162] Te Kooti preached from Joshua 23:5–6:

> And the Lord your God, he shall expel them from before you, and drive them from out of your sight; and ye shall possess their land, as the Lord your God hath promised unto you.

This carving is said to be a self-portrait of Raharuhi
Rukupo. It stands as a guardian inside the doorway of
Te Hau-ki-Turanga. (It perhaps should be added that this
portrait may be of Rukupo's elder brother, Tamati Waaka
Mangere, for whom Rukupo built this house. However, there
are parallels for it being the artist's portrait in at least one
other carved house of this period.)   C. 597. MONZ

> Be ye therefore very courageous to keep and to do all that is written in the book of
> the law of Moses, that ye turn not aside therefrom to the right hand or to the left.

Thus strictly disciplined, and intent on war, the people left the mountain. They were
divided into four groups: scouts (nga toro), an advance guard (matamua), the main body
(matua) and a rearguard (tomuri). It was the combination of open conferences between
the leaders, followed by extremely detailed planning, and then strict codes of discipline
being imposed, which made Te Kooti's limited forces so effective. In this manner the
journey home from the Ruakituri river began.

On 3 November, a large government force, sent out from Wairoa to find the bodies
of the four Maori messengers killed by Reihana, reached Whataroa. They found the

settlement abandoned except for an old couple. They immediately shot the crippled old man and seized some letters he had hidden about his body, and they captured and tried to terrorise his wife, Marara Hinekino, into talking. She was the mother of Te Waru's wife, Horiana.[163] They got little from Marara, except one critical piece of information: 'that Kooti was come over to Turanga'.[164]

It is just possible that he was already there. If the two entries made by a Maori trooper in Te Kooti's Wharekauri diary for 4 November 1868 are correctly dated, they indicate that Te Kooti had already dropped the diary near Turanga. However, it seems more likely that the entries were backdated.[165] Nevertheless it is possible that Te Kooti had ridden secretly to see the Ngati Maru chief Tamihana Ruatapu, at whose pa the diary was probably first found. If so, he had come to threaten him. On 8 November, Leonard Williams (who had just heard the news from Whataroa) commented, 'Tamihana Ruatapu professes to be living in fear of his life'.[166]

That day, Sunday, the possibility of an imminent attack on Turanga was being discussed openly among some of the leading figures in the community. Biggs talked with Williams after the church service at Matawhero, for he had recently had a message from Opotiki, warning him that the Whakatohea leaders there had received a letter from Te Kooti and that the attack might be soon. He had written immediately to Wairoa asking to be kept well informed.[167] Paratene Pototi had also been told of fires lit a few days back by a party apparently moving from Puketapu in the direction of Okahuatiu, as though they were making a road in a sweep to the north through to the back of Patutahi. He had also dreamt the previous night that Whataroa had been abandoned, which he saw as ominous for Turanga.[168]

Biggs and Williams were fully aware, too, that there had been communication between Turanga and Puketapu. They knew that the senior chiefs, including Wi Pere, whom Te Kooti had rejected as a messenger, had written to protest against the continued pursuit and unjust treatment of the whakarau. They had said, correctly, 'the patu was raised by the government' ('ko te patu ka hapainga e te kawanatanga'). Therefore, the whakarau should be allowed to return and the whole issue fully inquired into.[169] On 9 November the chiefs wrote again, with some urgency, stressing that the problem lay with the government:

> This is about the escaped prisoners. That fault is not ours, but it is the fault of you (the pakehas). They came out of your hands, and arrived at Turanga. The law did not intervene to investigate their crime, for, what matter what their crime was, the law ought to have looked into it; but no, it was left for the sword . . . . Why did not the law investigate . . . ? The desire of Te Kooti was to return here to Turanga; he had no desire to fight; it was from here the fighting emanated; he would not even then turn to fight, but only warded off the blows (acted on the defensive). . . . [A]s the matter stands, the Government alone are to blame for following up those prisoners in a resentful manner.

The chiefs added there was also a precedent that could have been followed: 'Those prisoners who were left in our charge, they are still with us', and were thus peaceful witnesses of that better resolution. The letter contains no indication of foreknowledge of the events which were to occur that night; rather the reverse. They urged that, at

Turanga, 'here we are still adhering to the law', and asked for government agents to respond to their pleas. They stated that they had refrained from assisting the whakarau and had instead 'kept aloof from them', even though they 'are our own tribe'. Yet, they said, for this restraint all they had been offered by Biggs was the demand that they give over all their lands. And this, they warned clearly, they would not do.[170]

They expressed what were undoubtedly widely shared Maori views. But there was more than cogent sympathy for the whakarau in the air; for, despite the chiefs' statement, there were also indications of active support for them. Biggs had written a month before that Ngati Maru had suddenly started having large karakia meetings, 'from what I can learn because Kooti orders it'.[171] He was quite correct in this interpretation. Te Kooti's message had been sent to Karepa, Tamihana's son, and all Ngati Maru in August to 'Go to the people, to turn [them] to the prayers' ('Haere ki te iwi, kia tahuri ki te karakia').[172] Biggs also knew that Ngati Maru, with several other Turanga tribes (Te Aitanga-a-Mahaki, Te Whanau-a-Kai, Ngati Kaipoho and Ngai Tahupo), were all trying to obtain government rifles for Te Kooti.[173] He therefore considered the Poverty Bay Maori were 'not to be trusted a bit'.[174] However, it was his own actions which made this assumption a reality.

The possibility of an attack on Turanga had been floated since August; the questions were when it would take place and from what direction. It was James Wyllie's wife, Keita (sister of Wi Pere), who had already given Biggs the vital information about the direction, which he chose to ignore: that the route was to be from the north, through Patutahi.[175] Biggs had been told this on or before 5 November,[176] and the local settlers there had kept a voluntary watch on the heavily overgrown track and the crossing at the Patutahi ford during 6–7 November — against Biggs's advice.[177] He remained convinced that, logically, the push would be from the south, when it came. On 9 November, he was again forewarned of its imminence. Leonard Williams received a letter from his brother Samuel, telling him to expect the attack. This news came from Wirihana Te Koekoe, who had returned from Puketapu to Taupo, where he gave out detailed information of the plans. He was the same messenger whom Helyar had earlier encountered at Runanga, but Wirihana's news, sent on by Helyar at the end of October, had been discounted by the commanding officer of the militia at Napier.[178] Leonard Williams again warned Biggs, as Turanga's commanding officer. The same day Biggs wrote to McLean. He mentioned that there were often alarms about the closeness of the whakarau, and he described the fires his own scouts had seen moving in his direction from Puketapu. He said that it was supposed the whakarau were cutting a road through the bush. He concluded by discussing his plans to ram through a forced cession of 10,000 or 15,000 acres of flat land at Turanga at a meeting with the chiefs which he was due to hold in one day's time.[179] That night Te Kooti struck.

CHAPTER 5

AND JOSHUA FIT THE BATTLE OF JERICHO
(NOVEMBER 1868–JANUARY 1869)

The assault on Turanga was highly planned. The whakarau came through the rugged mountains to Hangaroa, from where they had intended to travel down the river track to Waerenga-a-Kuri, inland of Manutuke. But at Hangaroa Te Kooti was told that that track was being watched by the government scouts. He therefore arced up to the north, to come down the Okahuatiu-Waikakariki valley behind Patutahi. On Sunday 8 November, while the whereabouts of the whakarau was being earnestly debated after church at Matawhero, they entered Te Pukepuke, which commanded the head of the valley leading down to Patutahi.

There were about 60 of them mounted on horses (some dressed in uniforms taken from Wharekauri), and the rest on foot. Here they were joined by men of Turanga. Who exactly these were remains unknown. But Te Kooti had come, at least in part, in response to an exchange of letters. Biggs certainly knew that some of the Turanga chiefs were in contact with Te Kooti, and one letter was seized which had been sent from Turanga to Whakatohea seeking active support for him.[1] Te Kooti always entered a district by invitation — even his own. For, as Reuben Riki put it, 'There is a limitation of movement, in the old days. You cross over to another area, you cross over into another mana: another mana to another mana.'[2] Te Kooti invariably negotiated his entry into a region: this is a recurring pattern, although it was not always successful. Te Kooti also expected to find men waiting for him at Patutahi.

At Te Pukepuke, and with consultation, the final details for the attack were determined. That night, Te Kooti sent out a kokiri to Patutahi kainga (village), which had been re-occupied by Te Whanau-a-Kai since the fighting of 1865.[3] He expected a few of his kinsmen from Ngati Maru also to be living there, in accordance with an understanding he had made with them. Karepa was one of four men who were said to have been there under this agreement. Other accounts, however, have it that the pact had not, in fact, been fulfilled.[4] The kokiri seized many of Patutahi's inhabitants — men, women and children. Te Kooti had two purposes: to gain absolute control of the village beside the ford across the Waipaoa river; and to give a warning (and a choice) to his kinsmen. The prisoners were brought back to Te Pukepuke, five miles up the valley, and placed under guard. Te Kooti told them that he held them all in his hands, 'to spare or kill. . . . Some of you being relations I will not destroy, but let you now join with us —

the chosen of Te Atua.'[5] Again he was using fear as a weapon; this is recalled by many who joined him at Poverty Bay. Hoera Kapuaroa, who was taken at Patutahi, said he was offered the choice of either joining, or being placed in the front of battle to be killed.[6] Wiremu Kingi Te Paia, who went with Te Kooti from Oweta and was finally captured in 1870, said simply: 'The reason I followed in his footsteps was, that I feared him on account of the death of Paratene [Pototi]', whom Te Kooti executed there. Kingi also said that he believed then that Te Kooti 'had obtained power from his god, and was advised by him that the Kawanatanga would be by him utterly destroyed'.[7]

In control of Patutahi valley and thus the means of his escape, Te Kooti called a runanga of chiefs at Te Pukepuke. He had been given detailed descriptions of the location of all the houses at Matawhero by Karepa, who had been found at Patutahi by the kokiri. Te Kooti took him on one side and questioned him closely.[8] It was widely believed in Poverty Bay that Karepa gave this information voluntarily.[9] Nevertheless, Karepa's statement that he was made a prisoner was ultimately accepted by the government. Then, according to Porter's version of events (given to him by one of the whakarau captured in 1870), at the runanga Te Kooti chose a kokiri of about 100. The rest were to stay to guard the valley. This attacking party in turn would be split into two main contingents. One was to be led by Nama, who was to strike first at Captain James Wilson's home at Matawhero. The second, and larger, party was led by Te Kooti on horseback, and was to attack Biggs's home. These two men were targeted because they were Pharaoh's overseers, or the military commanding officers of the district, and both had played a part in the siege at Waerenga-a-Hika. Wilson had decided on some of the cases as to who was to be exiled, and in 1866, as the temporary customs agent at Turanga, had also blocked supplies to those considered to be 'rebels'. Further, Wilson's home was on the disputed land at Matawhero,[10] as was Biggs's 'hollow' to the east. The killing of Biggs became Te Kooti's particular task with his acceptance of the tiwha from Te Waru.

The attack was made on the Matawhero settlers: that is, all those who now occupied Read's claim or were on the Maori-owned lands on the eastern side of the Waipaoa river extending to the north of Makaraka. There was no attack on the western side of the river (with the exception of one sheep-run just north of the Patutahi ford), nor on Turanga itself. As Sarah Dunlop observed, the revenge was limited and quite specific.[11] Te Rakiroa, who was with the kokiri, also said that Te Kooti had himself stated precisely 'who were to be killed'.[12]

The party crossed the Patutahi ford on the evening of 9 November. They passed by James Wyllie's house, which was near the ford on its eastern side, and left it alone, to preserve their own secrecy. When they came to Matawhero, the group divided, as planned, into two parties, who then in turn divided. It was some time after midnight when they struck, and Wilson and his family were probably the first attacked. Te Kooti himself was riding with a party of about 25 men.[13] (It may have been precisely 22, the number he was said to use for a kokiri, or the 'twenty and two captains' of the house who fought for King David.[14]) He went directly to Biggs's home. Porter's informant rode with that group. He said that 'Te Piiki' was writing letters when they reached there and surrounded the house. When Te Piiki called out, 'Who is there?', Te Kooti replied dryly, 'Open the door and see.' Biggs got out his revolver, but the door was forced. He fired twice at Te Kooti, and missed.[15] He, his wife and young son were killed. The attack swept on through the straggling Matawhero settlement, reaching south and east to the sled-home of the trooper John Mann near Makaraka. He, together with his wife and child, was killed and bayoneted. This was the eastern limit of the attack. The attack was also extended at one place across the river to the homestead of Richard Peppard and George Dodd, who were killed on their vast sheep-run lying immediately north and west of the Patutahi ford. This was leased land, to which Te Kooti had legitimate claims.[16] Altogether 29 Europeans and part-Maori were killed that night, and one other European, Alice Wilson, died later of her wounds.

Before dawn, some of the houses were seen to be burning. Wilson's and Biggs's were among the first set on fire, but over the next 48 hours most of the houses and sheds at Matawhero and north Makaraka were burnt. The school- and church-house at Matawhero, which had been built with Kahutia's permission, was deliberately left untouched, however.

This is a bare outline of the initial attack, which has been described and elaborated on by many writers since. It has usually been forgotten that the attack was not solely directed at the European families at Matawhero. Te Kooti himself said that 18 Maori chiefs were killed at Turanga, and this seems to be the most accurate statement.[17] All in all, probably 22 Maori were deliberately killed. This figure is lower than some recent revisionist accounts have suggested.[18] The Maori deaths were specifically selected and were no more random than those of the Europeans.

Piripi Taketake and his family at Matawhero were taken prisoner that night and subsequently shot. Piripi and his wife, Harata Poharu, were deeply involved in the dispute over Te Kooti's land at Matawhero. They had asserted their ownership of the former river bed, and had supported Read in his claim there. Harata also had only recently 'sold' a portion of the disputed land, adjoining the boundary of Read's large property, to the Matawhero storekeeper, John Cadle, who was himself killed.[19] Old Tutere Konohi (Tutere Kapai) was also killed at his home at Waitaria, near a ford across the Waipaoa, having helped Wyllie, his wife, Keita, and others to escape that night. He had told them he expected to be killed, but was too ill to leave. During Te Kooti's exile Tutere, of Te Whanau-a-Kai, had brought the land at Patutahi to the Native Land Court to establish his title; he had been the very first to co-operate with the government (as the name he became known by, 'Kapai' or 'Agreeing', suggests). This was land on which Te Kooti had claims and from which he was dispossessed.[20] It was for this reason that Tutere was killed and bayoneted, while his wife, Miriama Whakahira, who was also at their home, was spared. Miriama later stated that Te Kooti was present when Tutere was put to death. He was killed by two men, Te Wairama and Renata Amuamu (Hamuhamu) of the Wairoa, who, she said, were the appointed executioners.[21]

By the morning of 10 November, Te Kooti held all the land to the east of the river to Makaraka. He had taken many Maori prisoners. Maria Morris and her husband, Pera Taihuka, whom Te Kooti had named to the government in June 1866,[22] were one of the Maori families living at Matawhero captured that night. Maria wrote an account of the events she had witnessed. She said that first she heard the firing, at about two in the morning. She and some others then ran to Cadle's store, but found his house surrounded by men. She heard their strange dialect as they spoke, became afraid and ran away. One of the men with her, Hoera Whakamiha, was shot and killed. They were then all advised to flee by Wi Pere and Himiona Katipa, the two chiefs who were present at Matawhero. Himiona himself had escaped from Te Kooti's men at the pa, Pukeamionga, at Patutahi the previous day; he would later be seized and executed. Like Pera, he had been included by Te Kooti in his list of double-dealers. Maria wrote that they flew in all directions in their night-clothes, but she was taken prisoner, along with Piripi and Harata, and Ema Katipa and several others. Her husband, Pera, escaped, but returned when he discovered that she and their child had been taken. They were held together in her house, and at six a.m. (after dawn had broken) Te Kooti rode over to see them. He had been at Cadle's store, had a bottle of brandy in one hand and a long stock-whip in the other. His knee was supported in the stirrup leather because of the wound to his foot, which still prevented him from walking. Harata greeted him formally, being herself of very high rank. He did not return the greeting. He divided the prisoners, setting Piripi, Harata, their children and Pera apart,[23] telling them to stand on the left. 'Some he placed on the left hand, and some he placed on the right hand. . . . Te Kooti ordered all those on the left hand to be shot.'[24] He said, '"God has told me to kill women & children, now fire on them"'.[25]

In this manner, Pera, Piripi, his wife and their children were killed on Te Kooti's orders.[26] Like all the others, they were shot and then stabbed with bayonet or sword. This use of the sword was deliberate; in the understanding of those who killed them it was in fulfilment of the scriptural mandate taken directly from Psalm 63:10, 'They shall fall by the sword'. Te Kooti then ordered the singing of this psalm and, when this was done, he told the men to take the rest as prisoners back to Patutahi, leaving the dead as 'a portion for foxes'.[27]

One of those rounded up at this time was the lame Paora Rangiatea, who had escaped with the whakarau but had been left behind as they began their trek.[28] He was recognised by the men at Biggs's house, who then said, 'they are prisoners we must not shoot them'.[29] A distinction was being clearly drawn between those who were to be killed and those who were not. Another of the prisoners taken that morning was Heni Kumekume (Heni Te Ahorou), the young half-Maori woman who was to become Te Kooti's favourite wife. Maria Morris said that Heni seized a roaming horse, which the half-Maori girl Maria Goldsmith had been riding when she was shot and bayoneted. Maria, who was 16 years old, was killed because of her father's actions. He was a former employer of Te Kooti, and one of the mounted militia volunteers who had arrested him in 1866. Goldsmith's store at Kairourou, Matawhero, had long been a target for systematic plundering, as it stood on Ngati Maru land. Moreover, the ownership of a portion of Goldsmith's own land, Huiatoa at Matawhero, which had been given to him and his children in 1854, was contested by Ngati Maru. It was the same boundary dispute as had developed over Wainui 2, and had been fostered in the same manner by Mokena Kohere's 'sale' of the old river bed to Goldsmith.[30] Heni mounted Maria's horse and rode straight into Patutahi and a life-long companionship with Te Kooti.

The prisoners reached Patutahi about midday. Maria Morris wrote that, after they

Maria Morris (Mere
Tawharawhara).

B16705, MONZ

arrived, Te Kooti's followers built a sacrificial fire and laid upon it greenstone ornaments
and cloaks. They placed gunpowder under the wood and then set the whole pyre ablaze.
These were sacrificial offerings and a deliberate rejection of the old taonga (treasured
objects), which were seen as outward and visible talismans of adherence to the Maori
gods. Later, Te Kooti also burnt some of the guns they captured at Oweta, because they
had been used in the siege of Waerenga-a-Hika and had, he said, thereby contracted 'a
"hara"', or sin.[31] (One of the ten rifles captured at the very first ambush, Paparatu, had
also been burnt, although the others were distributed to the unarmed men.[32]) Other
objects said to have been burnt at Patutahi were the captured watches, probably because
they recorded only 'an evil time' with which the sons of men are 'snared', whereas the
'wise man's heart discerneth both time and judgment'.[33] All these objects were burnt
offerings which, as the text in Exodus told, the Lord had demanded of Moses. The
burnt sacrifices signified rejection of the old images of power and, as the Lord told

Moses, where such sacrifices were made 'in all places . . . I will come unto thee, and I will bless thee.'[34]

On the following morning, 11 November, some of the chiefs from the surrounding district came to Patutahi. The first were three men who came directly from Oweta: Natana Tukurangi, Wi Rangi Whaitiri and Paora Te Wharau. Maria wrote, 'Natana brought Te Kooti's little boy — a child about 4 years of age to see his Father.'[35] This was Wetini, who had been with his mother throughout Te Kooti's exile. Maria said simply, 'They wished to make peace but Te Kooti took them all prisoners'. Shortly afterwards Wi Pere, Himiona Katipa and others, who had earlier escaped from Patutahi, returned. Himiona, whose wife Ema was already a prisoner, was seized. But Wi Pere and those associated with him were offered a choice by Te Kooti: they could go with him, or die. And thus, Maria said, 'we all joined Te Kooti with our lips to save our lives but not with our hearts.' Wi Pere, however, she believed, 'thought that Te Kooti was one of God's Prophets & trusted him fully'. A letter by Wi Pere was later found at Patutahi, and this confirmed Maria's judgment. Written to Te Kooti, it said that he supported him and his prayers.[36] But Wi Pere was a double-dealer. The ambivalence of his relationship with Te Kooti would shadow both men all their lives.

The next day, 12 November, Paratene Pototi, Te Waaka Puakanga and others of the Rongowhakaata chiefs also visited Te Kooti at Patutahi. They came to tell Te Kooti 'to commit no more murders, but to make peace'.[37] A fragment of a letter written to Te Kooti on 10 November at Oweta suggests Paratene's hopes that a resolution could be achieved. It said:

> Ta matou kupu ki a koe, ae, amine. Kahore a matou kupu ke ki a koe, ko tenei anake ae, amine.
>
> Our word to you, is yes, amen. We have no other word for you, only this, yes, amen.[38]

And it seems that some agreement of neutrality was made. According to Wi Pere, at Patutahi,

> they made an agreement in writing not to interfere with each other. Te Kooti said, 'If I break the treaty, your copy shall be a sword to slay me; and if you break it, my copy shall be a sword to slay you.' Paratene answered, 'It is well'; and Te Kooti took off his hat, bowed, and said, 'Amen.'[39]

The following day, 13 November, Te Kooti and all who were with him left Patutahi and went up the Okahuatiu valley to Te Pukepuke. Soon after they had camped, Te Kooti received a message from Paratene Pototi, inviting him to come to Oweta pa — in one version, in order to 'fetch in the remnants of the people' in conformity with the understanding they had reached.[40] Before Te Kooti left the camp at Te Pukepuke, he ordered the execution of the four chiefs he held prisoner: Natana, Himiona, Wi Rangi Whaitiri and Paora Te Wharau. They were to be shot as 'government men',[41] and in order to terrify potential betrayers. As Wi Pere described the procedure, if Te Kooti 'intends to put a man to death, he strikes him lightly with a hunting whip which he always carries'.[42] The victim was then simply taken away. Three of the chiefs named

Heni Kumekume. This photograph was taken by S. Carnell of Napier and dates from either her visit there in February 1883 or, more likely, when she came with Te Kooti in 1885, or again in 1886.

CANON NIGEL WILLIAMS COLLECTION, 27070 1/2, ATL

were executed. But the fourth, Natana, was not at that time killed: Maata Te Owai managed to keep him to help her look after the little boy, 'who was away from his mother & very fretful'.[43] Thus, the women begin to emerge from the shadows in this world of requital and reprisal in which the men dominated. Te Kooti's wives will play more than one part in this narrative.

As Te Kooti approached the pa, the partial evacuation of Oweta began in anticipation of his arrival. One boatload of women and children went across the river to Turanga. Some of the men also decided to get out, including Tamihana Ruatapu, who rode along the beach. Two boats set off to get the remainder of Paratene's people, but they were turned back by a party which had come from Muriwai. This new group was led by Wi Kaipuke, and he bore a message from the prophet Hamuera Toiroa (now sometimes called Hamuera Mataora). The people at Muriwai needed reinforcements, because most of those at the neighbouring pa, Whakawhitira, near the mouth of the Waipaoa, had gone to see Te Kooti, perhaps to join him. The messengers successfully dissuaded the men in the boats from continuing the evacuation and instead turned them to the task of making Muriwai safe, and the centre of resistance.

Old Paratene Pototi waited, deliberately unarmed, at Oweta pa for Te Kooti. On 14 November he came. He brought with him many of his followers and also a number of the prisoners taken at Patutahi. It was in the morning: 'He appeared beyond our Pa, and held prayers. After prayers he entered the Pa'.[44] The chiefs welcomed him 'as a guest, — and gave him food'.[45] Then the speeches began. Te Kooti gave a short address, followed by some prayers.[46] But when Paratene got up to speak, Te Kooti seized the chiefs who had invited him there. He took eight men as prisoners. They included Paratene, Te Waaka Puakanga (father of Te Kooti's wife Irihapeti), Renata Whakaari (who had been sent by Biggs to confront the whakarau at Whareongaonga) and Ihimaera Hokopu (who had married Komene's wife, Mere Kingi Paraone, while he was in exile on Wharekauri). Ihimaera had co-operated with old Tutere over the Patutahi land and had, Mere said, been one who accused Te Kooti of supplying powder to the Pai Marire at Waerenga-a-Hika.[47] Iraia Riki and Hira Te Kai were two of the four others seized. They were all placed under close guard.

The execution of Paratene took place that day. It was quite calculated, and it has never been forgotten at Turanga. As Tuta Nihoniho wrote, Te Kooti said to Paratene, deliberately mocking the old man's fatal words,

> 'Greetings, my father who said, "Go on to the boat; go on to the boat." Son, you go on to the axe.'[48]

Of the captured chiefs, four were shot at the same time as they sat in a group. Ihimaera, Renata and Iraia were killed immediately, and Hira was left mortally wounded. Te Waaka Puakanga was accepted as a prisoner, and he was taken with the others when they left the pa.[49]

Most of the people at Oweta were either taken prisoner or chose themselves to follow Te Kooti. It seems that several casks of powder were also given to him. According to Wiremu Kingi, the casks actually belonged to Te Kooti and Te Waaka Puakanga, as they had purchased them in Auckland before Te Kooti's exile.[50] Some of those in the pa did manage to flee, while Raharuhi Rukupo was permitted to leave. He had been there all through the morning;[51] Hori Karaka, younger brother of Paratene Pototi, described how, when he himself arrived at Oweta in the early afternoon, he found Te Kooti's party sitting in a circle, Te Kooti threatening Rukupo with death because he would not support him.[52] Te Kooti then gave a silver watch to Rukupo. It had been taken from Wharekauri, and he had originally sent it to Rukupo after the landing of the whakarau. It was one of a number of gifts he had sent to the Turanga chiefs.[53] But Rukupo had returned the watch to him at Te Pukepuke — in place of the sword that Te Kooti had asked for as confirmation of his support. Rukupo had called the watch a whakapatipati — a deceiving gift. Now Te Kooti handed it to him again, and with it he gave him a sword. Then he let his mentor go.[54]

Wiremu Kingi Te Paia was among those who joined Te Kooti at Oweta; he would fight alongside him for two years. He described the fear which bound them together after the death of Paratene, and said that, when they got to Te Pukepuke and learnt that Wi Rangi Whaitiri had also been killed, they became even more alarmed. But Te Kooti told them that anyone attempting now to return to Turanga would 'be put to the sword'.[55] There would have been many men like Wiremu Kingi, divided in their own minds. Hoera Kapuaroa was undoubtedly one. Although afraid, he accepted Te Kooti's revelations. He went to Oweta to see his father, and acted as a guard over the prisoners seized there. He urged others to join Te Kooti 'as his Atua was not a Hauhau Atua — but the real and true God'.[56] On the other hand, during the attack on Matawhero, Hoera had sent a warning which ensured that Keita and James Wyllie and their family escaped.[57]

From Oweta, the hugely expanded party was taken to the old redoubt, Kohanga Karearea, and then on to Te Pukepuke. And thus the journey into the interior was renewed. By now there were about 300 prisoners as well as the whakarau: 600 people — men, women and children — whom Te Kooti held together by the power of the word and the force of his calculated requitals.

When Te Pukepuke was reached, those who had remained there learnt of the execution of the five chiefs at Oweta. Wi Pere asked Te Kooti if he could go back to bury their bodies, which had been left lying in the middle of the road. Finally, Te Kooti consented that they could be moved to the side, but they were not to be covered with earth: 'just leave them for the fowls of the air to eat'.[58] There was one final execution at Te Pukepuke. When Te Kooti returned, he learnt that Maata Te Owai had saved Natana (who had been one of the scouts patrolling with Lieutenant Gascoyne and who had tried to give a warning of Te Kooti's presence near Patutahi just before the attack[59]). Te Kooti immediately ordered Natana to be shot at the place where the three other chiefs lay, their bodies also unburied in conformity with the Old Testament formulae that Te Kooti had adopted. Te Pukepuke was renamed Golgotha, the hill of skulls, by the government troops who made their own camp there later, on the way to the fight at Nga Tapa. This was the evening when Te Kooti made his second burnt offering: all the guns taken from Oweta pa.

As the journey to the interior was recommenced, it seems appropriate to pause before we too undertake this journey into renewed war, and try to assess the attack on Matawhero and what followed it. This was the series of events which engendered the popular image of Te Kooti as the man-slaughterer, 'the murderer', the one Maori guerrilla fighter who calculatedly entered a European settlement to kill.

The narrative above draws substantially on testimonies of Maori, some made under duress. These are the testimonies made in the treason trials brought against some of Te Kooti's followers in 1869 and 1870; the testimonies made in the Native Land Court in 1869 and 1870, where anyone who had supported Te Kooti willingly was to be excluded from the lists of owners; testimonies made by those captured by government soldiers in the wars; and testimonies by some who escaped from Te Kooti. They are, therefore, the statements of those who sought not to identify with Te Kooti, the testimonies of people trying to protect themselves. But the details are sharp and not orchestrated; and it is in the details that the strength of these several accounts lies. Leonard Williams commented on the clarity and forthrightness of Maata Te Owai's evidence given in the Land Court;[60] the *Evening Post* made the same observation about her during the treason trials.[61] The *Wellington Independent* was similarly struck by the self-possession and clarity of the evidence of the Maori witnesses, in marked contrast with the Europeans. It attributed this lucidity to an ability to note and recall the minutiae of everyday occurrences:[62] a characteristic of those who use memory and oral account, rather than the written record, to retain knowledge.

These testimonies focus on events which took place in the Maori world, not the European. They reveal the extensive control which Te Kooti had by then developed. The whakarau were bound into a system of religious explanation which Te Kooti had engendered and which had, until now, served them well. Te Kooti had also revealed an outstanding military ability, which he had never previously exercised. He was a brilliant strategist. He had anticipated his pursuers every step of the way. He was a man who possessed, as Sarah Dunlop recognised at the time, 'a restless energy, force of will, decision, and great ingenuity to plan, and determination to execute', to which Maori responded strongly.[63] He had already brought within the arc of his religious authority some chiefs of great mana, even men who had not shared the experience of exile on Wharekauri. Te Rakiroa had come to his side along with Te Waru and Nama. All three were men accustomed to exercising chiefly power in their own right. But they shared grievances over land with Te Kooti, for theirs had been confiscated. They were also closely linked in kinship with the Ngati Hineuru exiles, which also probably explains their early association with the whakarau. All three had, together with Te Kooti, devised a military strategy in counsel, to which they all then adhered. The high profile of Te Waru's people in the attack on Matawhero was noticed by a number of witnesses, although his own role remains undisclosed. Tipene, Te Waru's son, was one of the appointed executioners at Te Pukepuke, while the killings at Oweta were carried out by Te Waru's men.

To this fairly cohesive group as many people again had now been added. They were all kin; but for the most part they had been compelled to join by force. Yet it was more than fear that welded this diverse group together. Te Kooti linked them under the power of the predictive word. This would be another extraordinary achievement.

There were many women in the party. Some were clearly drawn to Te Kooti, while others were equally clearly afraid of him. On Wharekauri he had taken several wives, perhaps deliberately following the pattern of the Old Testament leaders. Maata Te Owai had been, as we have seen, married to him in 1867 in a ceremony conducted by the resident magistrate, at which John Watson, the doctor, and all his family had been present. It is also thought (because of what appears to be a celebratory entry in his diary) that he had a son by Hana, born on the island on 14 March 1868 (although Hana was the wife of Ratima Te Ami).[64] Tangimeriana was possibly another wife whom he took on Wharekauri; certainly her name appears in his diary in two lists of women's names compiled in May 1868, and she was remembered as his wife by the prophet Rua Kenana, who named one of his own daughters after her.[65] After the return of the whakarau, Huhana Tamati, who had been with them, joined Te Kooti as his wife at Puketapu and remained with him until her capture in 1870.[66] Maria Morris commented that Te Kooti was accompanied by three wives when he came to Te Pukepuke. It was near there that the most remarkable of them all found him: Heni Kumekume. She would remain with him all his life, through war and through peace. She died after him, in August 1898.

Te Kooti would take other wives as well. Oriwia Nihipora Kunaiti was brought to him by her father at this time. She was from Te Reinga and, as Aperahama Te Uetuku narrated, was given to Te Kooti as his wife at Turanga. In exchange, Te Kooti presented her father, Tuateneheni, with his sword.[67] Oriwia was certainly with Te Kooti at the siege at Nga Tapa,[68] and she was taken prisoner only in 1871. She returned to live with him in the King Country after the wars, but then finally left him. Maria Morris said that Te Kooti had also invited her to become one of his wives, but her uncle Nepia Tokitahi (who was one of the chiefs on the council formed at Wharekauri[69] and who would later be named by Maaka as one of the other two, with himself, nominated as executioners) warned her neither to be impudent in her refusal, nor to accept him, for '"he is a Devil"'.[70] Maata Te Owai, whom he threatened with death for her protection of Natana, escaped at Nga Tapa and bore witness against him thereafter. In the history of these women, then, there are many differences. Some were bound willingly into his power and his forceful personality. But Maata, who chose to flee, said, 'His was the authority over the people. I heard him threaten those who wanted to leave. His authority and intimidation was continually exercised over them.'[71]

It was this exercise of power in all its manifestations that held the diverse group together in the wilderness. That, in turn, rested on the religious authority Te Kooti had established. This was the framework of explanation and direction which yoked the people together. This framework was to be tested a thousand times, yet it never totally broke. It would also find new life in the years of peace after the wars. This system of explanation, and Te Kooti's constant elaboration and modification of it in the midst of changing circumstances, lay at the heart of his personal power.

The killings at Poverty Bay over the five days 10–14 November were not random massacres. They were, as the evidence has shown, very specific. The European males who were killed died because of their previous military roles: all of them had served in the militia forces. Some, most certainly Biggs, had been involved in the execution of prisoners. But they and their families were also killed because they were living on land which had belonged to Te Kooti and from which he had been dispossessed during his exile — an exile which, as the *Wellington Independent* said plainly, was 'admitted to have

This early photograph is labelled Te Kooti's wife (left) and the wife of Topia Turoa (right), who was Makarena Ngarewa. The date and the occasion are unknown, but the costumes suggest the war period. It seems probable that the woman on the left is Maata Te Owai. In September 1869, when she was in Wellington to give evidence at the treason trials, she was described as being particularly young and as having small and regular features, with 'an Asiatic appearance'. She was also considered, by the same reporter, as 'far from bad looking'.
11371 1/2, Brierley Collection, ATL

been illegal'.[72] The Maori who were killed were those who had fingered him as disloyal, or who had dispossessed him during that exile by seizing the opportunity to attempt sales or by their readiness to co-operate with the government's land schemes. Women and children were killed as members of the family — usual in warfare. However, some Maori women were chosen for death — and others exempted — because of who they were and how they had acted in these issues. Hirini Te Kani also commented, referring to the chiefs killed at Oweta and Te Pukepuke, that:

> Ko to ratou mate na ratou ano i haere ki a te Kooti ehara i te kaha o te ringa o te Kooti. Na ratou i karanga kia haere ki to ratou pa noho ai a te Kooti.

> Their death was because they themselves went to Te Kooti, it was not by the power of Te Kooti's hand. They decreed to go to their pa, which Te Kooti occupied.[73]

The revenge Te Kooti exacted was based in the scriptural texts from the world of the Israelites in their suffering. It was constructed with ritual, even as to the exact manner of death by the sword. The dead were left unburied, their flesh to be given to the 'beasts of the field'. The so-called 'mutilations' of the bodies, which have been dwelt upon by the settler-historians and which still form a prevalent assumption, were rather a consequence of these practices. Maria Morris said that the 'Hauhaus never fired twice upon an enemy': instead they were told to take the sword and cut the bodies after the first shot.[74] Then the dead were found by rats, the domestic pigs and the 'fowls of the air', the harrier hawks — as was observed uncomfortably at the time. There is no evidence whatsoever of any deliberate mutilation, and the primary military sources are quite clear on this.

All these painful events were interpreted, by Maori who had suffered, as the fulfilment of old Toiroa's ominous words, 'Tiwha tiwha te pō', dark indeed is the night of Arikirangi.[75] Thus meaning is exacted from prophecy in its due time. The whakarau believed that none of these events would have happened if they had been allowed to go unmolested on their journey into the wilderness, through to Taupo.[76] This Te Kooti said again and again.[77] He reaffirmed it in 1873,[78] when he also stated that he had sent a warning to Biggs. This must have been Wirihana Te Koekoe's intended role all along: he was to seed that information deliberately. For Wirihana was a chief of Tauranga on Lake Taupo, Te Kooti's hoped-for destination,[79] and he was considered to be the senior leader of the 'Taupo Hauhaus'.[80] He went to join Te Kooti and to invite him to live at Tauranga shortly after the attack on Poverty Bay.[81] Yet he had given a warning about that attack — first from Runanga, and then in much greater detail from Taupo. If there was an ulterior purpose to the warning, it was presumably to threaten the government into making a genuine offer of immunity for the whakarau, in exchange for peace. No such offer was forthcoming. The assault — in its forewarning, in its execution, and in its high degree of control — was all a carefully determined plan, which had been born of the unending pursuit of the whakarau.

The journey inland began on 19 November. It too was undertaken with intent. It was not a military withdrawal: it was the renewal of the trek. The objective of the attack on Turanga had largely been achieved: that is, the 'reclaiming' of the land and its people. The permanent occupation of Turanga was never intended at this time, although the hope of its ultimate recovery was certainly anticipated. Like Joshua before him, Te Kooti turned his back upon his enemy after his triumph over Jericho, and took 'the people of war' with him.[82] The new migrants — the whakarau and their prisoners — took with them large numbers of horses, sheep and cattle and they returned on the 'good road' they had made.[83] From Te Pukepuke they travelled up the Wharekopae valley; their goal, according to Wi Pere, was an old pa, Makihoi. It belonged to Te Aitanga-a-Mahaki (and was a famous pa associated with Mahaki himself); situated as it was on Rakauroa mountain above the Waihuka river, controlling the inland road through to Opotiki, they felt they could be secure there. Te Kooti was already making inquiries about the chief Wiremu Kingi Te Kawau of Ngai Tai in the eastern Bay of Plenty as to what 'character' he bore, and would later, as we shall see, write threateningly to him from Nga Tapa. By 22 November the last of the migrants reached Te Karetu, a small pa at the junction of the Wharekopae and Makaretu rivers and near where the track turned north.

Te Kooti knew that they would be pursued; indeed, the first Ngati Kahungunu troops had landed at Turanga on 13 November. By the time the migrants reached Te Karetu, he also knew that the pursuit had begun. Two of his rearguard scouts had been caught in the Okahuatiu valley on 20 November. He also recognised immediately that Te Karetu was not a good defensive position in which to make a stand. It was a beautiful and sheltered valley, but was encircled to the south-east by an arc of high ridges that were too extensive for him to control effectively. While temporary defences were being thrown up there, he went on to explore Nga Tapa. This was an ancient pa of Turanga[84] (probably belonging to Te Aitanga-a-Mahaki), situated on a formidable mountain peak about three miles to the north-west and would have been known to Te Kooti's forces. It was there that he decided to entrench, and he sent work parties to clear and repair the fortifications. In choosing this site, he made his first strategic miscalculation: for, although impregnable, it could ultimately be taken by that great ally of siege troops, starvation.

Nga Tapa was not yet ready when the first troops caught up with the migrants. On 23 November, the Ngati Kahungunu fighters (340 men) brought from Napier and Mahia, together with a contingent from Ngai Tahupo from Muriwai, reached Te Karetu. Te Kooti had fortified the high razor-back ridge with rifle pits and placed outlying pickets there, but the troops pushed over the ridge and broke through this line of defence. They could then see all the tents pitched in the little valley immediately below them, a complete 'Canvas Town' enclosed by a large ditch and parapet.[85] The Makaretu river ran behind the encampment. Te Kooti's forces set fire to the fern on the surrounding ridges in an attempt to dislodge and unsettle their attackers, but they remained in control of the ridges and launched an assault on the valley. This attack was successfully beaten off, however, and then, although significantly outnumbered — for Te Kooti had only about 150 men who had rifles[86] — his kokiri, attacking from different directions between the three small hills within the valley, drove their assailants back to the ridge tops. There the pursuing troops remained, in a stalemate.

One of those among the attackers to fall mortally wounded was the high-born leader Karauria Pupu. He was a nephew of Ngati Kahungunu's great fighting chief, Renata Kawepo, and his lineage linked him with all the major chiefs of Ngati Kahungunu. He had been one of the ariki who had earlier rejected the offer of the Maori kingship. His death created a take (cause for revenge) for Ngati Kahungunu that would be almost impossible to expiate. Karauria also carried with him the long, triangular, red silk banner newly made by the Roman Catholic nuns of Napier for Renata. In this manner, one of the most famous flags of all came to Te Kooti. He renamed it Te Wepu, the Whip, perhaps because of the cracking noise it made as it flew, and perhaps because of the Archangel Michael's warning words to him. Its iconography — the crescent moon, the cross, a snow-covered mountain representing Aotearoa, the pierced and bleeding heart, and the six-pointed star of David — appealed, for the images could well symbolise the suffering, and the hopes, of the exiles. Thereafter, Te Kooti flew that flag in battle. It flew in defiance of Ngati Kahungunu at Nga Tapa, and went in its leather case from there into the Urewera with the refugees. It was finally recaptured by the government in 1870, when Peka Makarini was killed with it on his back.

This flag has taken on its own mythic dimensions. There is one version, narrated by Gilbert Mair, who told how he gave it to the present Museum of New Zealand only to discover later that it had been cut up for dusters; James Cowan added in a separate account that he had seen it in the museum, shortened, but with its emblems still intact.

Te Karetu. In the foreground is the 'low hill' where Te Kooti sheltered. The rear of the pa drops steeply into the Makaretu river. Nga Tapa is visible on the central skyline. Photograph by Judith Binney, October 1991.

There is another version which says that it was stolen by a cleaning woman. There is yet another narrative (not incompatible with any of the previous accounts) which says that it still exists. This account says that the flag has been seen quite recently (1973), cut in two halves, and that both were brought to Hawke's Bay by the Ringatu. Thus Te Wepu itself lives as a symbol of the promise of renewed Maori unity and reconciliation. Its facsimile was flown even more recently — for the Otatara pa summer festival at Taradale, Hawke's Bay, in 1993–94.

Another significant figure among the attackers who was killed was the prophet Hamuera Toiroa of Muriwai. He had been held, as Leonard Williams observed, 'in great repute as a dreamer',[87] and in the events that had occurred at Turanga from the landing of the whakarau, he had been Te Kooti's foremost religious challenger. Hamuera had predicted Te Kooti's death, and that his own would follow after. Thus the reports came flying in that Te Kooti was dead, as his voice was heard shouting orders but then had ceased. Te Waru took command and was reported as calling out, 'As you have lost your head, I will be your chief'.[88] What had happened, in fact, was that Te Kooti received a shoulder wound. Hamuera's last prophecy had failed him.

The Ngati Kahungunu fighters refused to renew the attack. They maintained only an odd, half-hearted blockade of Te Karetu. Te Kooti's forces kept great freedom of movement; this was to extend to Nga Tapa when, as late as mid-December, he would send out another lightning raid on Turanga. But before then, on 27 November, a party

Te Wepu: it was 52 feet long. It has been said that Te Kooti interpreted (or reinterpreted) the iconography so that the crescent moon stood for the Old Testament, the cross for the New Testament, the bleeding heart for the Maori people, and the mountain for the land. Ink sketch from a drawing by Captain Gilbert Mair.   A173/31, ATL

of 22 men,[89] all mounted, having successfully avoided the Ngati Kahungunu entrenchments on the ridge tops, came down by Repongaere lake and seized most of the contents of the newly established government arms store at Patutahi. The sortie indicates their good sources of information as well as their strategic ingenuity. They took at least eight kegs of powder and ammunition (that was the officially admitted total) and a few 'stand of rifles'.[90]

During this strange siege, Te Kooti got messages out to the Urewera and the King Country, seeking active reinforcements. But Tawhiao had named 1867–68 as the years 'of the Lamb' ('te Reme') and 'of peace' ('te ngehe'), the two successive years in which the weapon was 'to be sheathed'.[91] There would be no support from the followers of the King. Te Kooti again threatened: according to Wi Pere's account, he said that, if Tawhiao 'persisted in keeping aloof, he would be cursed by Jehovah, who would command him (Te Kooti) to march to Tokangamutu, and put Matutaera [Tawhiao] and all his people to the sword'.[92] About 30 Tuhoe from Maungapohatu joined Te Kooti during this time, but the leading chiefs of the Ruatahuna-Te Whaiti districts, to whom he had written, remained as yet uncommitted. They waited on a runanga which they had called for January, and from which he would get his first substantial support from Tuhoe.

Some of the prisoners taken from Turanga had managed to escape at the end of the first day of fighting at Te Karetu. Wi Pere, Maria Morris, Ema Katipa and several others, who had hidden with most of the women and children under a low hill close by the river bank, took advantage of nightfall to escape. All that Maria remembered of the battle was that Te Kooti had sheltered with them and when the wounded were brought in he 'spat on his fingers, then touched each wound, repeating a prayer as he did so in an unknown tongue.' It was neither English nor Maori: it was 'te reo ke', the strange language, which some understood to be Hebrew. Then he sent the wounded down to the river to wash.[93] This is the first known evidence of his role as a faith healer, which he would develop extensively in the years of peace.

The military power balance at Te Karetu shifted early in December with the arrival of 180 Ngati Porou fighters under Ropata Wahawaha. On 2 December Ropata attacked; and discovered that Te Karetu was defended only by a rearguard of 80 men.[94] Te Kooti had, once again, vanished. The rearguard fought strongly, and about half were killed. One of the men who was caught here, wounded, was Nama. Ngati Kahungunu took their revenge for the death of Karaitiana at Whataroa, the planning of which was attributed to Nama. They tied ropes to him and dragged him ensnared ('i rorea') through a fire in the burning pa until he died.[95] Another of Te Kooti's fighters killed was Kenana Tumoana, who had probably come with the Tuhoe from Maungapohatu. He was the father of Rua, the prophet who would one day put on the mantle of Te Kooti (although not without opposition). Rua was born posthumously, and this was the history within which he was brought up. For it was at Nga Tapa, within the month, that Te Kooti first predicted the One to come after him who would complete his work. This was the inheritance that the still-unborn child would claim.

Te Karetu fell and was fired. Five kegs of ammunition were recovered by Ngati Porou, but it was not the outstanding victory it was purported to be. The valley had been largely evacuated on the previous day,[96] when the news of the reinforcements had been brought to Te Kooti.[97] The main body of migrants had all gone to Nga Tapa, whose existence had, until then, been utterly unknown to the pursuers,[98] despite the fact that it could be seen from some of the ridges. The majority of Te Kooti's fighters, along with the women and children, had gone to strengthen the already formidable fortifications of Nga Tapa. They had also taken up the sheep, gathered in food and supplies of fern root, and prepared for a lengthy siege. Te Kooti himself, his shoulder torn and his ankle injured again by the stones of the river, had been carried up to the pa on a litter.[99] Huhana and Peita Kotuku also took turns to lift him, piggy-back, at the worst points.[100]

Nga Tapa was an ancient hilltop fortress, surrounded by cliffs on three sides and dense bush on the 'front' side, as Richmond described it.[101] The pa occupied the triangular apex of the hill, 703 metres high. Major St John quite accurately compared the summit of the hill to a tadpole, its body inclined downwards at an angle of some 60 degrees, both sides 'being precipitous', and its tail forming the narrow saddle at the rear.[102] From the highest point of the pa Turanganui could be seen, only 30 miles away as the crow flies, while to the west the great backbone of Maungapohatu, at the heart of the Urewera, was also visible. Three pre-European trenches ran across the upper part of the triangle, where food storage platforms and several whare were built. After the first siege and assault on the pa in early December, Te Kooti added two new forward lines to these older lines of fortification. The new breastworks then became the main lines of his defence. The outermost breastwork was built only on 29–30 December and was the front line of the defence for most of the second siege.[103] It was constructed by filling in the existing rifle pits in front and then building an entrenchment and 'parapet, and, last of all, a strong earthwork' behind them.[104] This inner earthwork was placed immediately in front of the large building called the 'church'. The platform of the 'church' can still be identified in the aerial photograph: it is about 16 metres long and seven metres wide, roughly conforming with the contemporary site drawing (55 feet by 25 feet). This 'church' was, in fact, the meeting-house, or 'roomy whare', where the defenders were observed to hold lengthy discussions during the siege.[105] The attacking party were amazed by what they found as they overran Nga Tapa after the second siege:

> three great earth-banks, running from side to side of the hill, powerful palisades, and
> deep trenches parallel with the earth-banks, which were about 15 feet in height, and

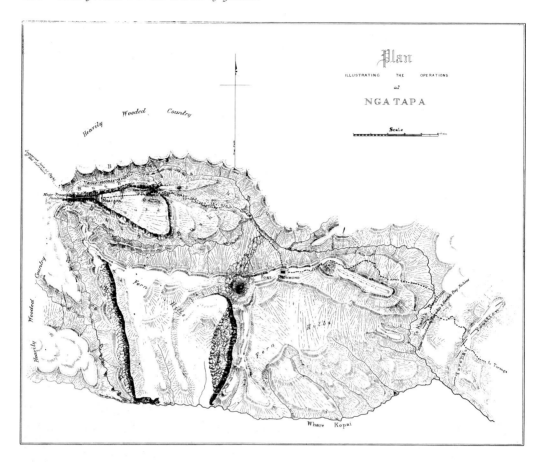

Plan illustrating the operations at Nga Tapa, by O. L. W. Bousfield, staff surveyor, 1869. It shows the manner in which the natural point of escape, running the length of the ridge at the apex of the triangle, was cut off by the two saps Fraser's forces placed there. The Crow's Nest (a small peak) is named and marked on the north-east edge of the hill, well below the defended upper triangle. At the very base of the hills, the site of the fight at Te Karetu is also shown. 'Tareha's Position' is the rifle-pitted ridge which commanded the valley (as well as the road from Turanga). Te Kooti and his people were camped along the Makaretu river, partially protected by three small hills within the valley. Original engraving.   [AP 32:71, NA]

placed one behind the other. There were also underground passages to facilitate communication between the trenches. The interior of the pa was a maze of rifle-pits, so arranged that a heavy fire could be concentrated upon any one pit, in the event of an attempt being made to storm the pa. Outside the pa, a space had been cleared for some distance in front by cutting down timber. The tree stumps had been left standing for three feet above ground, and the branches strewed between. The object was to prevent a night rush upon Ngatapa.[106]

After the fall of Te Karetu on 2 December, Ropata pressed on to Nga Tapa the following day.[107] But the attacking forces were now at odds among themselves, rendering the pursuit ineffectual. The Ngati Kahungunu leader, Tareha Te Moananui, had taken two men as prisoners, one of whom was his kinsman. Although this man was still able to bear arms, Te Moananui refused to kill him. Ropata Wahawaha interpreted this act as

An aerial photograph of Nga Tapa pa, showing the pre-European trenches at the apex, and a diagonal communication trench made by the defenders running up to them. The straight line at the base of this trench is the inner defensive breastwork built by Te Kooti's people. Just inside it is the flattened square which was the platform of the meeting-house. The communications trench leads out from this platform. At the south-west edge of this inner line is the large hole created when the attackers blew up the line, after the siege was over. From the centre of the natural scarp, marking the end of the triangle, an offensive sap built by the siege party runs up to the south-west end of Te Kooti's front line of defence, which was abandoned on the last day of the fighting. The mortar was placed near the middle of the natural scarp. Right beside it is the spring of water which the defenders had relied upon but lost on the second day of the fighting. Photograph dated 1 April 1952.   NZ Aerial Mapping, survey 542, 1642/13

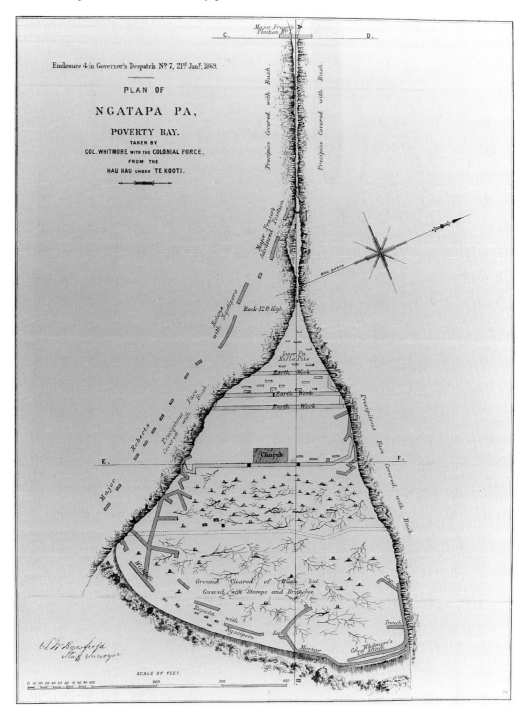

Nga Tapa pa, January 1869. The three pre-European trenches at the apex, to which rifle pits have been added, are shown clearly. The tail of the 'tadpole' leads into the small platform from where the escape took place, down the precipitous rock face to the north-east. This platform is separated from the rest of the ridge by another precipitous drop, and there Fraser's foremost men were stationed. Te Kooti's inner line of defence was the breastwork placed immediately in front of the 'church', or meeting-house. Once the siege party's saps came close to this breastwork, on the last day of the siege, they could not be effectively fired upon from above. Plan by O. L. W. Bousfield.   *GBPP*, Facsimiles Vol. 15 [AP 32:71, NA]

Nga Tapa

Nga Tapa, 1 January 1869. Pencil sketch by James Richmond from Fort Richmond, the military camp to the east of the pa.   PRIVATE OWNER, c/o ATL

an ill omen for them and, in the ensuing argument, Ngati Kahungunu withdrew from the field.[108] Consequently, Ropata's attack on 4 December was limited to about 150 men. They captured a rifle pit in front of the pa, but on 5 December, being short of powder (as well as men), Ropata abandoned the assault. James Richmond admitted that the expedition had not ended well.[109] Both Ngati Kahungunu and Ngati Porou had determined to go home, although not for the same reasons. Ngati Porou made it clear that they would fight again – but only if given adequate supplies and support. The expedition would have to be re-equipped and reorganised from scratch at Turanga.

Nevertheless, in these attacks upon Te Karetu and Nga Tapa, Te Kooti had sustained significant losses. Sixty rifles had been captured,[110] and in the combined fighting since 23 November at least 57 men had been killed.[111] One of these was his brother Komene;[112] another was Rihari Rikirangi, his 'uncle', captured and shot on 3 December.[113] Some of the Turanga prisoners had also escaped, and more of the women and children were heard escaping down the cliff after the siege was lifted at Nga Tapa.[114] Among the women who had got away was Mere Kingi Paraone, Komene's former wife, who had been taken prisoner at Oweta; when she reached Poverty Bay she reported that they had been reduced entirely to eating fern root, and that they had little powder and were making 'bullets of shot cast in a thimble'.[115]

Undoubtedly, the people in the pa were short of food and ammunition, but they certainly still had some supplies and they gathered in more once the siege was lifted. Moreover, the active planning continued. Te Kooti's strategies included the deliberate circulation of disinformation to the effect that the main body of his forces, including himself, had withdrawn directly from Te Karetu to Puketapu.[116] The purpose was to try to head off a second assault on Nga Tapa. At the same time, he wrote urgently to other chiefs demanding support, or at the very least neutrality. Three of these letters have survived. Two, dated 10 December, were sent to the eastern Bay of Plenty and were signed 'TeKooti te Turuki'. To Wiremu Kingi Te Kawau, he wrote:

> E hoa, tenei ahau te noho nei i runga i to tatou whenua. E hika, tenei te kupu ki a koe. Ko waho ou ki a Kawana, ki roto i a koe kia aroha ki nga morehu o nga tangata, ki te whenua hoki. Kei takahi koe i te iwi, i te whenua. Ka whai koe i te moni ki te pakeha hei oranga mou, nana ka mate koe. Engari kia rongo koe ki taku reta, me noho noa iho koe, me tou hapu. Kaua e haere mai i nga kokiri a te Kawana. Ehara te Atua i te tangata aroha ki te hunga tahae, me au ano hoki. E hoa, kia ora koe hei whetu mo Turanga, mo kona hoki. Ka ngaro o taina matua me o taua whanaunga i a au. E kore e whakaorangia[117] e ahau ake ake. Heoi ano.
>
> He kupu ke tenei. Ko Turanga kua pakaru, kua mate nga rangatira.

> Friend, I am here [Nga Tapa] living on our land. This is my word to you. Outwardly be of the Government, but inwardly be loving to the fugitives of the people and to the soil. Do not trample on the people or the soil. If you follow the money and the pakeha as a support by that you will come to trouble. Then listen to my letter and remain neutral. You and your people do not come with the war party of the Governor: the Atua is not a man of love to the thievish people (those who take land). Nor am I. Friend, may you live as a star for Turanga and for these (from our place). Also, your fathers and relatives, keep them out of my sight — I will not spare them hereafter. That is all.
>
> This is another word. Turanga has been broken (entered). The chiefs are dead.

Te Kooti then listed seven by name, and said he would not continue to name them. He told Wiremu Kingi that, altogether, 18 chiefs and 30 Pakeha had been killed at Turanga. He reminded him also that those who had pursued him had fallen — Ngai Tahupo, Rongowhakaata, Ngati Kahungunu, Wairoa and Ngati Porou — altogether 118, he said.[118] Wiremu Kingi received the letter in dread.

At the same time Te Kooti wrote to Hori Te Aunoanoa, a Ngati Porou refugee living with Wiremu Kingi. He wrote as his nephew ('iramutu'). He told him the same news, but the request was different:

> Haere mai koe, Hori. Me kore he hoa mou, mau hoki e tono atu he tangata ki nga mea e whakaaro ana ki te whenua. Kia tere mai i a Tihema nei, i a Hanuere ranei, kei roa koe.

> Hori come to me. If you have no companions it is for you to invite some persons among those who think about the land. Hasten during December or January. Do not delay.[119]

The third letter Te Kooti sent reveals the freedom of movement which he now had, but which, for the first time, he used disastrously. The letter was written later in December 'in search' ('whakataki') of Karanama Te Whare. It was left for him at Pokimi, a kainga just north of Puketapu mountain at the junction of the tracks from Maungapohatu and Nga Tapa. In it, Te Kooti reported on the second raid which he had personally led on Turanga, on 12–14 December. Four had been killed, as he told Karanama: a Pakeha, two half-castes and a Maori.[120] The attack had occurred on 12 December near Pipiwhakao, on Harris's property. Among the four killed were Wyllie's eldest son, William, a half-Maori, and Rewi Hapi, son of a Te Arai chief, Hapi Kiniha. The killings were not, however, the intended purpose of the swift raid. For, as both Harris and Richmond commented privately to McLean, Te Kooti had come for some ammunition, lead and bullets, which had been 'cache'd' in the long bush near Harris's place and which Waaka Puakanga had reported to Te Kooti. (The cache had, in fact, been found and removed.) It was 'not a planned murdering party', in either Harris's or Richmond's understanding, but it had unexpectedly encountered the four — to fatal ends. As a consequence, as Richmond noted, Te Kooti's men had retreated precipitately, dropping things all the way up the valley.[121]

Te Kooti's attack, with about 50 men, certainly took everyone by surprise. A combined Turanga and Wairoa force (just over 100 men) pursued them and encountered Te Kooti near Patutahi, but on seeing him the entire Turanga contingent, who made up most of the party, bolted. Ropata arrived with too few, too late.[122] Nevertheless, 37 prisoners, whom Te Kooti had also brought with him to his camp at Patutahi, managed to escape at this time. Among them were old Waaka Puakanga and his daughter Irihapeti, together with her son, the 'little boy of Kooti's'.[123] Wetini and Irihapeti, on Richmond's orders, were sent away to live with Ngati Porou, where the boy was brought up permanently alienated from his father.

Whatever the purposes of this second raid, it did not serve Te Kooti well. It confirmed that he remained a source of threat to the district, and that his base was, in fact, still Nga Tapa. Until then both Ngati Kahungunu and Ngati Porou had become convinced that his forces had dispersed and that Nga Tapa had been evacuated.[124] The campaign against him had actually been abandoned on 8 December — or at least, as Whitmore put it, '"No more at all until they first make a move"'.[125] The outside forces had been disbanded and were being sent away from Turanga.[126] With the raid, the campaign was immediately reborn: on the very day the reports of the raid were cabled through, the organisation for the assault on Nga Tapa began.[127] It was the second attack on Turanga which generated the terrible siege of Nga Tapa.

Te Kooti's letter to Karanama Te Whare was written before the siege had begun. He said that, despite the encounters they had had with the forces as they withdrew from Pipiwhakao to Te Pukepuke and then Okare,

> Kahore rawa he utu kihai kotahi. Heoi ano. Kei te tatari ahau ki a koe i tenei takiwa ki a Pera Tutoko hoki kei Waioweka. Kotahi whiu ki Turanga e toe nei. Nau i roa ai kia tere mai.

> There has been no reprisal at all, none. Enough. I am waiting for you in this place and for Pera Tutoko, who is at Waioweka. One drive to Turanga remains. The delay is on your account. Be quick.[128]

The letter indicates that some of the whakarau, in particular Pera (Aperahama) and Karanama, had been sent out on deliberate missions. Pera, who had been one of the original emissaries of the Pai Marire cause to Turanga in 1865, was very closely connected with Ngati Ira, the people living at Waioeka;[129] now he had been sent along with Timoti

Hakopa (Timoti Te Kaka), who had been a teacher in Volkner's church at Opotiki and was one of the whakarau, into the district of the Whakatohea tribe. Their mission was to persuade the Ngati Ira chief Hira Te Popoki (Hira Te Popo) to give them active support. That Pera got through is made clear in a letter sent in turn by Hira to the other hapu of the Whakatohea. Written about 18 December, Hira said:

> Friends, Pera Tutoko has arrived, friends do not persist in being deaf. The word of Te Kooti has come to us. January is the month when the whip will be applied to the disobedient children. Pera came to fetch us . . . . This is the month in which we will go. This January it turns.[130]

Karanama had been sent to Taupo seeking aid and, more specifically, to contact both Anaru Matete and Wirihana Te Koekoe. Karanama had been expected to return through Puketapu and Pokimi, where the letter had been placed for him to find. This letter also clearly shows that a third attack on Turanga was planned. Wiremu Kingi Te Kawau also understood this to be the reason for Pera's mission to Whakatohea.[131] Mere Kingi Paraone had warned of a planned attack when she reached Turanga on 11 December. Her warning, that there would be an attack in about three weeks' time, became confused by the flying raid on 12 December.[132] Waaka Puakanga also stated that Karanama Te Whare was 'intending to come to attack Turanganui'.[133] Old Pera Punahamua, who had been taken prisoner at Oweta, commented that Te Kooti's purpose in removing so many people at that time had been to clear the way for a future assault on his enemies. He then meant to bring back all those he had taken prisoner, so 'that they might occupy the land'.[134] This third attack, the planned reoccupation of Turanga, did not eventuate — presumably because the siege had been launched.

The forces reassembled by Whitmore did not reach Nga Tapa until 31 December. But on 24 December, at Nga Tapa, Te Kooti had predicted the outcome, and also the manner of his own 'capture'. This kupu whakaari has been copied down in many of the Ringatu books, and it is an adaptation and extension of the predictive saying that he had first uttered at Whareongaonga: 'Enemeripi'. This version is the text recorded by the Ringatu tohunga Tawehi Wilson:

> Ko nga tamariki katoa o te pae ka tukua atu ki te ringaringa [o] o tatou hoariri. E toru nga mate e pa mai ki a tatou.
> Ko etahi mate Hoari.
> Ko etahi mate Kai.
> Ko etahi ka whakaraua atu.
> Ahakoa hui te motu nei, e kore ahau e mau i a ratou, e kore hoki ahau e mate kia puta mai rano te tangata mo muri i au, maana ahau e hopu a, ka haereere ano ahau i tona aroaro a, mate iho ki raro i ona waewae.

> All the children of the region shall be given up into the hands of our enemies. There are three deaths which will strike us.
> Some shall die by the sword.
> Some shall die by starvation.
> Some shall be taken captive.
> Although this land gathers together, I shall never be seized by them, neither shall I die

until the man to follow me appears. He will capture me and I shall go about in his presence and die under his feet.[135]

This kupu whakaari is the first in a long sequence which looks towards Te Kooti's successor, one who he said would be greater than he. They will be discussed later. Here, the immediate point of the kupu is simply his survival: the survival of the leader until the 'next' appears, the one who will 'capture' him — as the government soldiers cannot — and whose identity is yet to be revealed. The kupu can also be understood, more directly, to predict the plan of action at Nga Tapa. Only Te Kooti and those who were closest to him would manage to escape: to have done this so secretly they must have been protected by the others' sacrifices.

The attack was launched on New Year's Day, 1869.[136] There were probably about 300 people in the pa. The siege party numbered more than 600: 250 Europeans in the Armed Constabulary divisions, 60 'detribalised' Arawa fighting under European officers, and over 300 Ngati Porou led by Ropata and Hotene Porourangi.[137] On the first day the attackers captured a small peak (which they named the Crow's Nest) from where they could see the defenders within the pa, hastily piling kits of sand in order to create firing loopholes in the defensive parapets. Major St John commented that they later discovered that the kits had been placed on the inner edges of the parapets, with the consequence that the muzzles of the rifles could not be sufficiently depressed to command the lower earthworks, which the attacking forces were to occupy.[138] This lack of precise knowledge about firing angles in pa and redoubt warfare would be a recurring problem for Te Kooti. It indicates that he had had little or no experience in rifle pa warfare. It also suggests that all those who were fighting with him also lacked that experience, or, more likely, were not able to challenge his military decisions because of the nature of his leadership. Given the previous military history of the Pai Marire fighters among the whakarau, lack of experience seems the less probable explanation.

Early on 2 January, the forces led by Major Fraser and Hotene cut off any line of retreat along the ridge behind the pa. Fraser's men had found a 'well beaten track' on a high narrow ridge leading to the rear of the pa and, sheltering among immense boulders just below the peak, managed to block the expected line of escape.[139] Ropata's men occupied the natural scarp line in front of the pa, where they found the pa's water supply: a hidden spring. A party of four men who attempted to come around from the rear of the pa to get water were captured and then shot. A sortie made towards the centre of the principal line of attack by a group of men, women and children, who must have been attempting to escape, was also driven back. By the third day the defenders were completely hemmed in, their only means of escape 'down a rocky precipice on the North side, which was considered far too steep for them to make their way down & was accordingly left unguarded'.[140] This decision was Whitmore's greatest error, for it robbed him of achieving the whole purpose of the siege. On the fourth day the heavy rain and mist, which had prevailed since the second evening and had turned the trenches into deep muddy holes, began to lift. The saps made by the siege party pressed forward remorselessly, but the defenders were quiet. There was very little response to the firing into the pa. Afterwards, the siege troops discovered that many of Te Kooti's followers' bullets were of pewter, made from spoons and 'run in thimbles', so short of ammunition were they.[141]

As the weather began to clear, the mortar started to pound the pa. However, some of its shrapnel ricocheted onto the front line of attack while other shots went right over the pa and landed among Hotene's men on the far side; consequently the firing had to be discontinued. On the fifth day the defenders attempted to throw out an earthwork, perhaps to hide the formation of an escape route down to the rock face. This movement was blocked by Arawa and Ngati Porou fighters, who climbed the rock face and reached the outer parapet, which protected them from the fire above. By dusk Te Kooti had abandoned this outer line of defence. But his fighters still maintained a 'galling fire' from the inner breastwork,[142] where later little pieces of white rag fluttering on sticks were found all along its length. A new offensive sap towards this rampart was begun, with the aim of blowing it up next morning. The men, women and children were now huddled inside the oldest part of the pa, jammed into the maze of rifle pits they had dug there. Arthur Kempthorne, a volunteer with the Turanga militia, wrote in his diary at the end of the day, 'we could hear them having their "karakia" or prayers, but on this occasion, only women's voices could be distinguished, the men wishing to keep their numbers secret'.[143]

In the early hours of the following morning, 6 January, the attackers heard a woman's voice calling from the pa: 'I am Meri Karaka, — there are no men left in the pa, — they are all gone!'[144] And thus it was that the siege party found the pa had been evacuated under the clear moonlight. Only a small group of 20, mostly women and children, some of whom had been prisoners, remained behind.

Beyond the apex of the pa, along the narrow saddle-back, the siege party discovered a stony outcrop, built up as an earthwork, called the '"Pah Puku" or women's retreat'. The very accurate firing which had damaged Fraser's forces had come from there.[145] This tiny 'pa on the knob' was accessible only by a flax ladder down a vertiginous rock outcrop at the apex of the hill. Whitmore had been warned about it:[146] it was the route of the escape down the cliff face to the north-east. Peita Kotuku, one of those who got away, described how he hauled himself down: 'When our position became desperate . . . we let ourselves down the cliff in rear of the pa by means of aka or forest vines, cut from the trees just outside the fort. The lowest part of the cliff where I went down on an aka vine was about sixty feet high.'[147] This daring feat was repeated by at least 190 people through the moonlit night, and it rendered Whitmore's capture of the pa a Pyrrhic victory. It also ensured that the attackers would seek a bloody revenge for being so manifestly outwitted.

Peita Kotuku said that the reason they evacuated the pa was that they had been cut off from the water supplies, thus fulfilling Te Kooti's prediction: '"I mate ai tera pa na te kore-kai, na te kore-wai"' ('"The deaths in that pa will be by lack of food, lack of water"').[148] Or, as Ropata himself said in the proverb he had sent to Richmond as his advice on tactics: '"Let food (ie hunger) fight slowly that the spirit may die."'[149] Indeed, at the end of the siege the whole pa gave out a horrible stench of death,[150] but the serious killing had only just begun. Ngati Porou set off in immediate pursuit. They brought back about 130 male prisoners captured in the bush and the gorges below the

The '"Pah Puku" or women's retreat', at Nga Tapa. This photograph is taken from the apex of the main pa looking along the 'tail of the tadpole'. At the end is the small stone platform near where Te Kooti is thought to have escaped, probably by going down within the curve of the cliff, which would have sheltered him from Fraser's watching forces at the rear. Photograph by Judith Binney, October 1991.

pa. The men were marched up the hill to the outer parapet of the pa, 'stripped of every vestige of clothing they possessed and SHOT — shot like dogs'.[151] Most of them, commented W. G. (William) Mair in a criticism of Whitmore's boasts, were in fact 'unarmed Turanga natives who had been taken prisoner by Te Kooti' and who had no chance with the 'indiscriminating Arawa or Ngati porou'.[152] In the end, only 80 prisoners were escorted out of the area, of whom 50 were women and 16 were children. Most of these were taken by Ngati Porou back to Waiapu as their own prisoners. One of the women captured and retained by Whitmore was Maata Te Owai, who would bear witness against her husband. A few male prisoners (about 14) were kept for the purposes of trial.[153]

In this killing, among those who died was Nikora Te Whakaunua, chief of the Ngati Hineuru exiles, who had stayed with Te Kooti despite Reignier's blandishments and who was one of Te Kooti's most feared fighters. Richmond admitted that he paid for Nikora's head;[154] some of the heads are known to have been taken back to Turanga for the money and then dumped in the river near the Armed Constabulary base.[155] Another who died here was Renata Tupara of Ngati Maru, husband of Meri Karaka.[156] He was among the first captured and was taken down to the camp at 'Fort Richmond' and shot.[157] His book of inoi (prayers) was later found within the pa.[158] It contained one prayer to God asking him to avenge the ill treatment 'we have received from our oppressors'; and another: 'Send thine angel to trample our enemies to the ground, and do thou cause all their bones to be utterly crushed'.[159] It also contained 'A prayer for loading a Gun':

> He inoi mo te puru Pu

> E Ihowa kia whakatata mai koe hei awhina i au i te ra o to matou hoariri. Meinga tau Anahera hei kai whakatika i taku hoari ina whiu atu e au ki a ratou 'mene tekere' ki tou ingoa tapu. Amine.

> O Jehovah, be thou near to help me in the day of my enemies. Let the Angel direct my sword when I strike at them. Mene tekere. [Glory] to thy sacred name. Amen.[160]

The phrase 'Mene tekere' was also written by another hand at the end of this prayer.[161] It was taken from 'the writing on the wall' in Daniel 5 (Mene, Mene, Tekel): 'God hath numbered thy kingdom, and finished it.'[162] It was a statement of resistance: it promised that the power arrayed against them would fall.

'Anatekere' is one of the words in 'te reo ke', the language of power which Te Kooti developed, and 'Anatekere' he used to indicate the words and appearance of God to the prophets.[163] Its root is God's message to the prophet Daniel, together with his promise of the future kingdom for the seed of Abraham. As the Ringatu elder Tupae (John) Ruru explained, 'All these things came out of the Book of Daniel, and the writing on the wall, Mene, Mene, Tekel. We call those inspirations "kupu whakaaris". And, just like in the Book of Daniel, he was formulating his church with them.'[164] Thus the early inoi were composed for a people who were desperate for the hope of survival, like those whom Daniel led, and in their prayers they too adopted a code language for their resistance.[165] During the siege Karanama Ngerengere, their priest and lay reader, had read scriptural passages from the Anglican Book of Common Prayer out loud to those on the parapets to help strengthen them: 'Praying was one of the guns', said Maata Te Owai simply.[166]

Most of the women and children found in the pa or the bush were taken away as prisoners. Kempthorne said, 'they looked very thin & emaciated & must have been nearly starving in the pa, the children especially looked like so many skeletons'.[167] At least one woman was shot — because, although she was merely wounded, 'all the Ngatiporou women refused to touch her'.[168] Within this war, then, there were many wars: and not the least was the retaliation of Ngati Porou against East Coast and Urewera tribal enemies.

A total of 136 men are known to have died at Nga Tapa: most of Te Kooti's fighting support. About 60 men escaped, together with some women and children.[169] At least five died in the bush of famine; their skeletons were found by a later expedition.[170] Among the women who escaped were three of Te Kooti's wives: Oriwia, Heni and Huhana. Among the men was Wiremu Kingi Te Paia. He described how he hid alone in the bush for three days without food or fire, and was nearly dead when he was found by some of the others. They gave him sustenance: cooked mamaku (tree fern), honey and kotukutuku. He also said that the very night they evacuated Nga Tapa, the messengers from Waioeka had reached them. Timoti Hakopa had returned to fetch them away.[171]

The mission to Whakatohea had been fulfilled: a place of sanctuary had now been offered.

And Te Kooti himself? Well, some tell that he had said that it would be where the rainbow ended that a way of escape would appear. In the early evening, as the storms finally cleared, the celestial bow, or the kopere, God's sign to them, rested on the sheer cliff at the rear of the pa. The rainbow was their pathway. Yet others say it was his white horse, the horse with spiritual powers ('te hōiho mā wairua') which bore him away on the great cliff face, despite the thousand rifles pointing straight at him.[172] For, as he had prophesied at Nga Tapa, 'I shall never die by their hand.' Rather, as one of his followers, Ned Brown, explained the kupu, 'I will go forth to the path of my creator, and I shall die under his feet.'[173]

Thus one of the great oral traditions which surrounds Te Kooti was also born: the legend of the white horse, swift as the wind, which will bear him away across mountains that not even a goat could traverse. The white horse will occur again and again in the narrative traditions that spring from the wars and which continue through the years of peace thereafter. His name, in some of the stories, is Pokai Whenua (Travel the Land)[174] and he is always the image of freedom.

By December 1868, it was being reported by the prisoners that there was only one horse among the whakarau, 'which Te Kooti himself rides'.[175] After the 12 December raid on Turanga the European military sources questioned this statement, and it was reported that, of the three horses the raiding party had, two were lost.[176] Only Te Kooti escaped on his horse. This then is the root of the story, for Te Kooti still could not walk at this time. But the story will be transformed. For the white horse is also the horse that bears the conqueror and saviour in the days of Revelation:

> And I saw heaven opened, and behold a white horse; and he that sat upon him was called Faithful and True, and in righteousness he doth judge and make war. . . . And he was clothed with a vesture dipped in blood: and his name is called The Word of God.[177]

CHAPTER 6

COVENANTS AND A KING
(JANUARY–AUGUST 1869)

Na koe e te ngakau e wawata tonu nei i ahau ka pau koe ko te toko atu te kupu a te Kuini e tu ana hau i te tohu o te hunga mate.

O you, my yearning heart within me, you are exhausted in supporting the word of the Queen, as I am marked for the ranks of death.

Me ui nga korero ki te rae kai au ki Waikato. . . . Ko wai au e tomina, kia ahatia hau nei?

Let the story be unravelled face to face, when I reach Waikato. . . . Who am I, and what is it I long to do?

SONGS OF TE KOOTI, C. 1869.[1]

The refugees from Nga Tapa scattered widely through the deep gorges of the mountains. Karepa Maruwhakatupua, who had been ill and had hidden in the bush before the siege, came across some of the survivors five days afterwards at the old pa, Makihoi. There were about 30 of them there, now debating what to do. Most of them intended to make their way to the head of the Motu river, which they knew to be Te Kooti's destination. Karepa and a few others turned aside, trekking painfully back to Turanga.[2]

Te Kooti had gone to Te Wera, the hidden country at the headwaters of the Motu river, which he would use more than once as a place of refuge. It was thick, heavily forested terrain, and it would not be penetrated by his pursuers until 1871. From there he planned to follow the Koranga river north-west to its junction with the Waioeka: this was the pre-arranged rendezvous, agreed at Nga Tapa before the survivors dispersed.[3] According to Karepa, who encountered further refugees as well as men from Whakatohea who had come to find Te Kooti, the latter had already sent a messenger to Opotiki to purchase supplies. He was using money from Wharekauri, which he had distributed when they first landed and which he now collected up again from the whakarau. He gave the messenger about £100 (as Wiremu Kingi Te Paia recollected), of which the messenger dared spend only £30 on clothing and rum, lest he draw attention to himself.[4] Then Te Kooti travelled on, following the mountainous river course into the Waioeka gorge. He was encountered there, on 27 January, by some men who had come up the Waioeka river carrying a letter for Hira Te Popo, the Ngati Ira chief. They found

Te Kooti camped across the river from the small settlement of Kaiota, at Maraetahi. He had arrived the previous day, and his party consisted entirely of whakarau (about 30 people). The letter-bearers noticed that he was still slightly lame. He told them that he was expecting men to come from Maungapohatu to join him. Hira, who had offered him sanctuary, now simply commented, '"I do not understand what this man's intentions are."'[5]

In fact, he waited on Tuhoe. What he would do depended on them. On 19 February he was joined by a small party of Tuhoe from Maungapohatu, together with a group of Ngati Porou traders and exiles who had been living on the east coast of the Coromandel since the 1850s. Some of these men had recently been sheltering at Tokangamutu with the King; they were led by Te Munu and Te Kewene, and were accompanied by Te Kooti's chief and kinsman, Anaru Matete.[6] It was also at this time that Wirihana Te Koekoe found them. He had come to fetch Te Kooti to Taupo, as he had promised. He sang for him a waiata composed by Te Heuheu Tukino II, the paramount chief of Tuwharetoa who died in 1846, which urged the people 'always to keep fast hold of the land'.[7] Te Kooti's support was beginning to regroup; he said he awaited a sign from heaven to determine his path.

This was his second period in the 'Koraha', the Wilderness. In 1870 Porter transcribed his prisoners' detailed accounts of their experiences, which probably depicted this time.[8] They arose every morning to prayers: either Psalm 32 ('Thou art my hiding place; thou shalt preserve me from trouble') or Psalm 34 ('Many are the afflictions of the righteous: but the Lord delivereth him out of them all').[9] Then the men went to hunt, and the ears of the first pig were cut and offered as a sacrifice to God. Strict rules of tapu were imposed: both eating and smoking were prohibited during hunting and when the party was on the move. Sometimes Te Kooti himself would start out alone in the early morning with a tame kaka sitting on his shoulder, a decoy to attract others. (One he had owned for a long time was captured in 1871 and became the pet of the provincial clerk of Napier, where it became famous for its capacity to bite through its thick brass chain.) Or he would search for wild honey in the hollow trees. He was noted for his continual reconnaissance of the terrain, climbing the ridges and the ranges, locating and mentally mapping the unknown landscape. When messengers arrived, they were brought immediately to his whare, and waited on his permission to enter; this deliberate separateness sustained his authority and also ensured that the news came to him first. At night, the last meeting for prayers (the fourth in the day) was held, and then total silence reigned until the dawn. He lived by the omens of the sky, thunder and the rainbow, and waited for the time that they told.

It was from Waioeka that Te Kooti uttered his next kupu whakaari. It is one of the most copied and recopied of all his predictions. The text below is from his diary, dated 6 March 1869. However, other versions are dated variously 1 February and 11 February, indicating that there was once another original source.[10]

> Te kupu whakaari ki Waioeka
> I   Eripi
> Ko ahau hei matua mo koutou ake ake
>   Tani

II

Ka whakaorangia e ahau te toenga o te tangata i hanga e toku ringa i te timatanga ake ake

III Ka pei ahau i te hunga kino. Ka whakahou ahau i nga rohe o Reneti = Hawira

The prophetic saying at Waioeka

I   Eripi

I shall be as father for you ever after

    Tani

II

I shall save the remnant of the people who were formed by my hand from the beginning and ever after

III I shall drive out the wicked. I will restore the borders of Reneti = Hawira.[11]

In the version in the Biddle manuscript, taken from Hamiora Aparoa's notebook, a further sentence is added:

Heoi ano kianga o te ingoa he whakarau koe. Tou ingoa ko Arohipene. To whenua ko Reneti Hawira.

There shall be no more naming you a captive. Your name shall be Arohipene. Your land Reneti Hawira.

The prediction was to be adapted and extended, and then, later still, claimed to have been completed. In the original forms of the kupu, the land is given a new name: Reneti Hawira. It is a name none of the Ringatu use today because it was consciously lifted from the land in 1885–86. It therefore went out of usage and its significance became lost.

When Te Kooti first returned, he had simply called the North Island Te Ika Roa, the Long Fish (of Maui), but this new name was one he now gave to both islands 'in Unity'.[12] Hawira is Havilah, the land in which the generations of Isaac dwelt, beyond Egypt. The scriptural text from which it comes (Genesis 25:18) had been copied out by Te Kooti at Te Papuni. He called Te Papuni '*Hawira* = the village of distraction' ('Ko te kainga o te potatutatu').[13] Havilah is also the land where the people were destroyed by Saul 'with the edge of the sword', saving only those whom he deliberately set apart.[14] Reneti = Hawira is literally Lent = Havilah. It would, therefore, seem to be a statement of the period of sacrifice, the 40 days of Lent, which itself commemorates the 40 years of exile of the Children of Israel. The overall name is like 'Israel' — that is, it is the area promised to them. The kupu from Waioeka is the pledge to the survivors, who have yet to enter their Promised Land. It assured them that God would intervene as their 'father'.

The kupu also promised the restoration of the land. On one level of meaning, the statement seems to refer to the area of influence and expansion of the faith itself: regaining the area of the faith and the recovery of their 'borders'.[15] But it also probably indicates that Te Kooti knew that finally a confiscation agreement had been rammed through at Poverty Bay on 18 December 1868. On that date the chiefs of Rongowhakaata and Te Aitanga-a-Mahaki had ceded all the land to the Crown, on account of the 'rebellion ... murders and burnings' ('te riringa ... me nga kohurutanga me nga tahutahunga').[16] The government had finally exacted its reprisals. Subsequently, in 1869, it would choose three substantial areas for itself and then attempt to adjudicate title in the remainder, recognising only those Maori who had given it support. All 'Hauhau' were intended to be dispossessed.[17]

In the additional text copied from Hamiora's manuscript, the people themselves were given a new name: Arohipene. It replaced the name of whakarau. It suggests their freedom, but its precise significance is unknown, except that it is thought to have been scriptural in origin.[18] The name seems never to have been used again.

There is another text from Waioeka, which in one source is dated 18 February 1869. This text looked to the construction of the faith. The version cited here is from the Biddle manuscript collection, which states that it was said at Tawhitinui, Waioeka, in that year:

1	Ko te Ture.	Ta te Ture he Hura.
2	Ko te Wairua.	Ta te Wairua he Hipoki.
3.	Ko te Haahi.	Ta te Haahi he pupuri, he whakarongo.
		Ko te ritenga tenei o te Ture o te Kawenata.

1	The Law.	The Law is a Divestment.
2	The Spirit.	The Spirit is a Cover.
3.	The Church.	The Church is an anchor and to heed.
		This is the meaning of the Law of the Covenant.[19]

In this kupu whakaari, the law is shown to be the dispossessor, but the faith and the church are the means of protection. Collective salvation lay only in the covenant made with God. This fundamental statement would be later reaffirmed in the days of peace as the foundation of the organised Ringatu church.

At Tawhitinui, words were also promulgated in 'te reo ke'. One, 'Tupeta', is explained: 'wehenga', 'separation':[20] it needs no further elaboration. This was the reality of their survival. The others were warnings of death: by epidemic and by the sword. On 20 February, the groups who had gathered at Waioeka separated and departed, carrying with them these words of direction.

Following on an invitation, Te Kooti had gone to Maungapohatu. So reported Hira Te Popo, writing from Tawhitinui to the young chief of Ngati Awa, Wepiha Apanui.[21] A few days later, Wepiha was also warned by the Tuhoe chief Rakuraku: the next strike would come at Ohiwa.[22] It was at Maungapohatu that Te Kooti formed an alliance with some of the Tuhoe leaders. The guerrilla wars were to be renewed. The chiefs who were now to come down to the Ohiwa harbour with him included Te Whenuanui and Paerau Te Rangikaitupuake, two of the leading chiefs of Ruatahuna.[23] Their alliance was forged on the back of the Hawke's Bay confiscations of 1867, which had taken the land of Tuhoe and Ngati Ruapani, Te Kooti's close kinsmen, by the southern shores of Waikaremoana. It was not until August 1872 that this land would be returned (that is, most of it), and then it was to Ngati Kahungunu, as the 'loyalist' tribe. Tuhoe would have to take their claim to the Native Land Court where, even as their rights were upheld, they were forced to sell the block back to the Crown, while Ngati Ruapani were utterly dispossessed.[24] In 1869, therefore, the inland Tuhoe and Ngati Ruapani chiefs were prepared to support Te Kooti — and also Te Waru, whom they had sheltered since

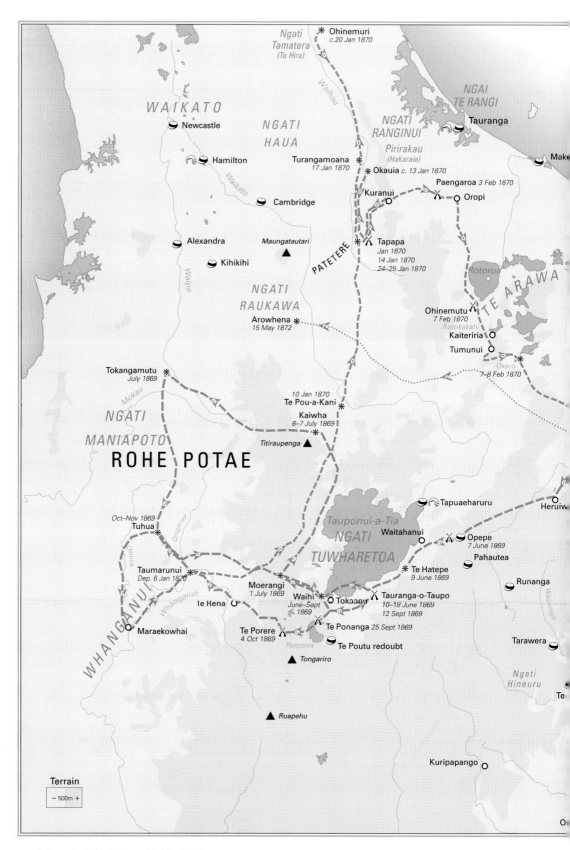

Map 4. The Wars, 1868–1872

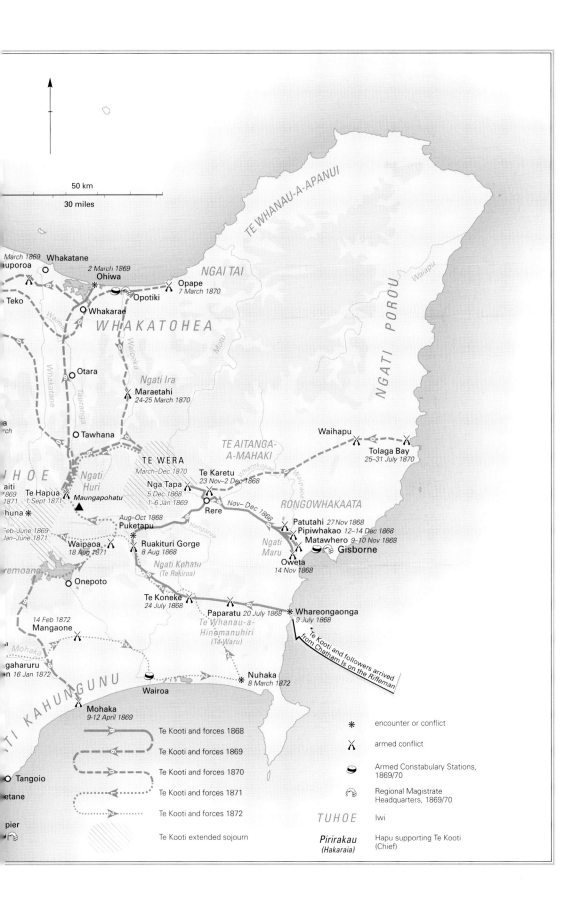

March 1869 Whakatane
uporoa Ohiwa 2 March 1869
Teko
Opape 7 March 1870
Opotiki
Whakarae

NGAI TAI

TE WHANAU-A-APANUI

NGATI POROU

Waiapu

WHAKATOHEA

Otara
Ngati Ira
Maraetahi 24-25 March 1870

Tawhana
Waihapu
TE AITANGA-A-MAHAKI
Tolaga Bay 25-31 July 1870

JHOE
Ngati Huri
aiti
1869
1871
huna

TE WERA *March-Dec 1870*
Te Hapua 1 Sept 1871 Maungapohatu
Nga Tapa 5 Dec 1868 1-6 Jan 1869
Te Karetu 23 Nov-2 Dec 1868
Nov-Dec 1868
Rere
RONGOWHAKAATA

Feb-June 1869
Jan-June 1871
Aug-Oct 1868
Puketapu
Waipaoa 18 Aug 1871
Ruakituri Gorge 8 Aug 1868

Patutahi 27 Nov 1868
Pipiwhakao 12-14 Dec 1868
Matawhero 9-10 Nov 1868
Gisborne
Ngati Maru
Oweta 14 Nov 1868

remoana
Onepoto
Ngati Kohatu (Te Rakiroa)

Te Koneke 24 July 1868
14 Feb 1872 Mangaone
Paparatu 20 July 1868
Whareongaonga 9 July 1868
Te Whanau-a-Hinemanuhiri (Te Waru)

Te Kooti and followers arrived from Chatham Is on the Rifleman

a
gaharuru
n 16 Jan 1872
Nuhaka 8 March 1872
Wairoa

KAHUNGUNU
Mohaka 9-12 April 1869

Tangoio
etane

pier

⁂	encounter or conflict
✗	armed conflict
	Armed Constabulary Stations, 1869/70
	Regional Magistrate Headquarters, 1869/70

Te Kooti and forces 1868
Te Kooti and forces 1869
Te Kooti and forces 1870
Te Kooti and forces 1871
Te Kooti and forces 1872
Te Kooti extended sojourn

TUHOE Iwi
Pirirakau (Hakaraia) Hapu supporting Te Kooti (Chief)

50 km
30 miles

the fall of Te Karetu. For his cause was theirs: the recovery of the land of upper Wairoa and Waikaremoana.

By the time that Te Kooti reappeared — at Otara, near the entrance to the Waimana gorge, at the beginning of March — he had equipped a force of 130–140 men with arms. William Mair also believed that Te Kooti had forged an understanding with the most remarkable fighter of Tuhoe in the eastern Bay of Plenty, Erueti Tamaikohatia.[25] Nor was he the only one to believe this: the chief Paora Hapi of Taupo was another who was convinced that the two worked together in 1869.[26]

Eru Tamaikoha had waged a singular guerrilla campaign in 1867–68 against the confiscations in the eastern Bay of Plenty, which had taken the only low-lying land that Tuhoe possessed. In 1866 the government had drawn a straight line on the map, as reprisal for the death of Volkner, although Tuhoe had had no part in that affair. This arbitrary line had cut Tuhoe off from the mouths of the Waimana and Ruatoki valleys and from access to the food-rich Ohiwa harbour. Tamaikoha's war had been against the injustices created by the exercise of law: the same cause as Te Kooti's. But Tamaikoha was not prepared to fight with Te Kooti. Although he had been specially invited, he had pointedly refused to attend the Tuhoe runanga in January. He remained utterly opposed to Te Kooti's religious teachings. Nevertheless, he did allow Te Kooti's passage through Tawhana, his settlement at the junction of the Tauranga and Tawhana rivers, which together form the Waimana river.

Moreover, it was at Tawhana that the pact with Tuhoe was made which sealed them for ever with Te Kooti. They gave him their land and their loyalty; he in turn swore his oath to them. This is what he said to Tuhoe, deliberately using the words God had uttered to Moses:

> Nau ahau i kukume mai i roto i te pouritanga. Kua tukua e koe te tangata i roto i te mura o te ahi, i roto i nga whakamatautauranga, mai ano o te ūnga mai e haere nei. Whakarongo, — *ko te kupu* tenei 'Ka tango ahau i a koutou hei iwi mooku a, ko ahau hei Atua mo koutou, a ka mohio koutou ko Ihowa ahau.'
>
> Ko koe hoki te iwi o te kawenata.

> You drew me out of darkness. You have sent the people into the flames of the fire, into the tests, since the landing [this] has gone on. Listen, this is what *I have to say*, 'I take you as my people, and I will be your God; you will know that I am Jehovah.'
>
> You are the people of the covenant.[27]

This text is derived from Hamiora Aparoa, and also from the old men ('koroua') of Tuhoe, including Te Purewa, a senior chief of Ruatahuna and Waimana. It is dated 20 March 1869 and is followed by Te Kooti's instructions for the attack on Ohiwa.

The date seems to be incorrect, for two reasons. On 20 March Te Kooti was in the headwaters of the Rangitaiki river heading directly inland for Ahikereru, where he would take sanctuary at Te Harema pa. It should probably read 2 March, when Te Kooti was reported as coming down from Tawhana and Otara into the Waimana gorge. Tawhana itself was well known to Tuhoe. It was accessible from Maungapohatu, and also from Nga Tapa and Waioeka on an old bush track.[28] On the night of 2 March Te Kooti occupied Whakarae pa, near the headwaters of the Ohiwa harbour. The pact at

Tawhana was made in the context of the early alliance he forged with Tuhoe and, although this alliance was unquestioningly reinforced by later events, this — the original agreement — specifically antedates the attack on Ohiwa.

These words are seen as the binding kupu which created the special relationship between Te Kooti and Tuhoe, which would grow. It states that it is they who are the people of the covenant; it is they upon whom the faith will rest. As one Tuhoe elder put it some years later:

> while the war was going on . . . [Te Kooti] entered into a covenant with the Tuhoe people, at Te Tawhana: it was to rest on the chiefs of Tuhoe, i.e. Kereru, Paerau, Te Purewa, Te Makarini Tamarau, Te Whenuanui, Te Ahikaiata, Tutakangahau, Te Haunui, & Te Puehu; these people gave their mana to be under the guidance of Te Kooti; and a piece of land including this block [Ruatoki], & extending from Waimana to Maungapohatu, was given over to Te Kooti. . . . Te Kooti said: 'Under this oath, let the people be one.'[29]

In this manner, Tawhana became the sacred place of Tuhoe. As a Tuhoe elder said:

> Ko te whenua tapu rawa ko Tāwhana. . . . Ahakoa a Maungapōhatu, engari ko Tāwhana te whenua o te oati ki te Atua, ake tonu atu. Ahakoa kotahi te tangata. 'Te whenua o te oati ki te Atua.' Koira te ingoa o Tāwhana.

> Tāwhana was a very sacred place. . . . Certainly Maungapōhatu, but Tāwhana is the land promised to God, now and for ever. Even if there was just one person [there]. 'The land promised to God.' That is the name of Tāwhana.[30]

The named chiefs were the most senior chiefs of Tuhoe. Conspicuous by his absence, however, is Tamaikoha, who is always remembered for his defiant statement to Rakuraku that he would rather put Te Kooti's atua in his pipe and use him as tobacco!

In 1869, Te Kooti was a man fighting for a future which could also conserve the past. He had allied with some (but not all) of the Tuhoe, whose cause was the rights of Maori in their own tribal lands. They saw themselves as the oppressed because of their recent experiences. They were not simply men living in the past: they had specific and legitimate grievances. Te Kooti offered a new order, and it seemed that he might achieve it. This new order rejected the Maori kingship as a failed experiment, already being eroded by whispering words from the government. This judgment was harsh, but it recognised that the King would no longer fight. Te Kooti instead sought to direct people through his vision, based in the covenant promises given to the Chosen of God. He also warned them of the consequences of faltering in the pursuit of this vision: their own destruction. It was a fearsome vision, to which many of the Tuhoe were drawn.

His war tactics were the tactics of disruption. The attacks were based, as all guerrilla campaigns must be, on highly accurate information as to where and when to strike. Te Kooti made the decision to come over to the eastern Bay of Plenty, where the Tuhoe leaders, together with Hira Te Popo, had extensive intelligence networks. He hoped that Whakatohea and Tuhoe would give him the connections he now needed.

From this time, Te Kooti would never go home again. He had to work with and through other tribes' leaders, and outside his own tribal territory. This makes him unique as a guerrilla fighter. His ability to continue the struggle, while retaining the authority of a prophet, was an extraordinary achievement, which will be analysed later. At this juncture, however, it is sufficient to say that the reasons he regained support, after such a significant loss as Nga Tapa, lay not only in his ability to project a vision but also in the fact that the cause was shared. The tribal support he gained invariably related to the land confiscations or to an abuse of law which the local people had experienced. The problem they faced was the extent of the military power that could be brought against them. The question was: what tactics would be most effective to force an acknowledgement of the injustices perpetrated?

The immediate purposes in the guerrilla raids which Te Kooti mounted in March–April 1869 were to gain arms and ammunition, and to persuade other Maori groups to his cause. Success would breed success, Te Kooti calculated, and those who wavered out of fear would be driven to join him. The object was to get men.[31] An insurgent movement could then be reborn. But the fear he engendered could also work against him.

The first strike came, as Rakuraku had warned, at Ohiwa. On 2 March a surveyor, Robert Pitcairn, was killed at the camp where he was living on Uretara island. Earlier on the same night, Rakuraku's pa, Whakarae, near the head of the Ohiwa harbour, had been taken. Miria Te Mautaranui, who was at the pa, said that the people were all made prisoners by Te Kooti without any resistance. The affair seems to have been orchestrated. Miria stated that she heard Te Kooti say he had come by Rakuraku's invitation, and Wiremu Kingi Te Paia added that Rakuraku gave all his guns and ammunition to Te Kooti. The occupation and patrol of the pa were to disguise Rakuraku's support, for his pa was on a high hill, clearly visible to a force of Arawa troops, whom the government had recently settled on the eastern shore of the harbour to watch over Tuhoe.[32] From Whakarae, a party (which included some of Rakuraku's men) was then sent to kill Pitcairn.

At the same time, a second contingent captured Hokianga island. The people there, Te Upokorehe, were taken prisoner and brought back to Whakarae. The next day Te Kooti told all of them, said Miria, that he would not interfere with Whakatane. The boundaries he set himself were the centre of the waters of Ohiwa, and from there he would turn his face eastwards again. J. A. Wilson, the commissioner of confiscated lands, wrote similarly: 'He has proclaimed that his Atua has given him the shores of that part of the Bay of Plenty to sweep as far as the East Cape.'[33] Te Kooti then stated that he would not harm those who did not oppose him; he would allow them 'to remain in quiet possession of their land'. Those who opposed him, however, he would sweep 'from the face of the earth'.[34]

The self-imposed boundaries seem to indicate that Te Kooti had yoked the cause of Tuhoe's and Whakatohea's land to his own. Hokianga island lay on the eastern side of the harbour. It was in the midst of the confiscated block and was cherished dearly by both Te Upokorehe and Tuhoe.[35] Immediately westwards lay Ngati Awa land, and Te Kooti did not have the support of Wepiha Apanui and Ngati Awa. He remained in occupation of Whakarae for several days. According to Miria, there was a total of about 200 people with him, including a core of whakarau, and all were well armed. He paraded the whakarau like soldiers, inspected them, and gave them orders. He was well armed himself with both revolvers and a sword. He was now, after all, a man with a price on his head: £1000.[36] The whakarau also had prices on their heads: vouchers in payment for their capture were being issued from 1869.

On 9 March Te Kooti struck again. He went westwards, in direct contradiction of what he had told Miria, who was the wife of the old chief Apanui. This pattern of sowing false military and strategic information he would adopt again and again. His objective was the Rauporoa pa on the west bank of the Whakatane river, the defended settlement of Ngati Pukeko. He appeared before the pa at about two in the afternoon, his leading men carrying a long white flag on a post. Some Ngati Pukeko were prepared to talk, but others slammed shut the pa gate and began to fire. After a two-day siege, Ngati Pukeko were forced to come to terms. On the morning of 11 March, their ammunition expended and two of their leading chiefs dead, they 'made a sort of a treaty with Te Kooti' and evacuated their pa.[37] At the same time as the siege of Rauporoa, Ngati Pukeko's mill and new redoubt on the eastern bank (built against Tuhoe) had been attacked. The kokiri sent against the redoubt was led by none other than Wirihana Te Koekoe, who had come through from the Urewera with Te Kooti. Although the redoubt and the mill fell, they were fiercely defended by Ngati Pukeko's manager, Jean Guerren, and Wirihana died in the fight. Without Wirihana, the road to Taupo and the sanctuary at Tauranga on the lake were now far less certain.

The fall of the redoubt and the pa gave Te Kooti temporary control of the Whakatane river mouth. Ngati Pukeko's mill and wheat fields were burnt, and the two European trading stores at Whakatane were also set on fire. When William Mair arrived on 11 March with the first troops (drawn from the local Armed Constabulary, together with Ngai Tai and Whakatohea from Opotiki), he recognised that Te Kooti had the advantage of him in both numbers and position.[38] Then the SS *Tauranga* arrived the next day, bringing ammunition but no men. Te Kooti was, for the moment, in complete control.

He could be observed from the ship's deck: he rode a grey horse and was dressed in a red shirt, boots and breeches, with four revolvers in his belt, and a sword at his side. He was everywhere, issuing instructions, while mounted orderlies galloped off, saluting, having received their orders from him 'in regular military fashion'.[39] But by the time the government reinforcements eventually arrived, he had gone. On 14 March he took prisoner the occupants of Paharakeke, a small pa on the Rangitaiki river. They consisted of about 40 people, including women and children. The evacuation of the pa had also been planned with their foreknowledge; the purpose was to clear the way for an attack on the major pa and redoubt nearby, Kokohinau. However, the position of Kokohinau's old chief, Te Rangitukehu, was reinforced with troops on the same day: the government had recovered control of the mouth of the Rangitaiki valley.

Te Kooti's forces had, however, been significantly increased by his prisoners. The primary object of the raids was men, and also ammunition and horses. Te Kooti then pushed inland up the river to Tauaroa, the Patuheuheu pa near modern Galatea. There, he found a people who were prepared to commit themselves to him. He probably entered the pa unopposed, and certainly Patuheuheu would fight for him for almost two years. From here, he sent out a mounted kokiri to bring in Ngati Manawa from their pa at Motumako. As the kokiri returned to Tauaroa, bringing a few prisoners with them, it

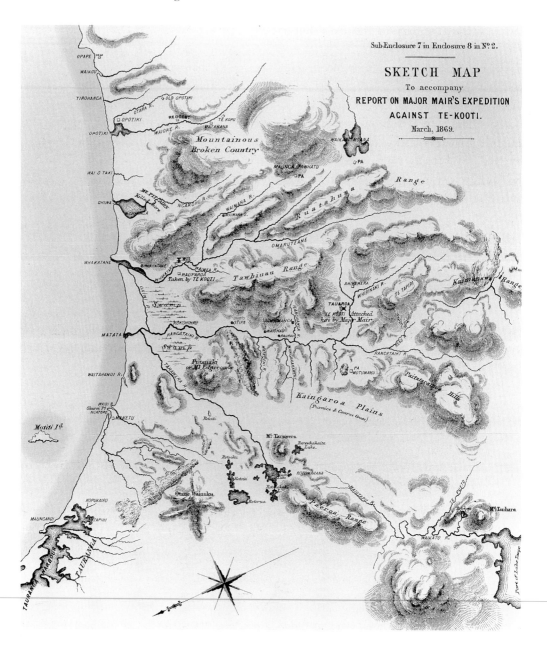

Map drawn by William Mair to explain the expedition of March 1869.   *GBPP*, Facsimiles Vol. 15

encountered a half-hearted siege that had been laid by the government forces before Tauaroa. However, Ngati Rangitihi from Lake Tarawera, who William Mair admitted were the only men he had with him who knew the terrain at all, refused to support it.[40] Consequently, in the darkness of the night, Tauaroa was successfully evacuated. At dawn on 19 March, the pa was empty and Te Kooti's rearguard could be seen high in the hills on their way through to Ahikereru. His objective was Te Harema pa, and there he would be given sanctuary by Ngati Whare hapu of Tuhoe.[41]

It was from Te Harema that Te Kooti sent out to Taupo, seeking support once again. The 'resting-place', he told the people at Te Harema, would be Tauranga on Lake Taupo.[42] On 26 March a letter written by Nepia Tokitahi,[43] Hemi Manu and Te Kooti, 'that is from all of us' ('ara na matou katoa'), was sent to Horomona and Pehimana, two chiefs of the upper Taupo district.[44] It said that 12 of their friends had died by the sword, though they themselves were well. In addition, five, whom they named in the letter, had been taken by an epidemic, thereby recalling Te Kooti's prophetic words, first uttered at Whareongaonga and more recently at Tawhitinui in the Waioeka. Influenza had begun to stalk them on their journey. It would also decimate the Tuhoe over the next three years. However, they said that, with these deaths,

> Kati. Ko tenei whakaora te Atua i te toenga o te tangata i hanga e ia, ka whakahou ia i nga rohe o Renetehauhira.

> That is all. For now God will save the remainder of the people whom he created, and he will renew the boundaries of Renete Hauhira.

They then recapitulated their first pursuit from Paparatu to Puketapu, where, they said, 'the gentleness' ('te ngawari') had ended. There the survivors ('nga morehu') from inland had joined them, and then the hardness ('pakeke') began. It had lasted from Turanga to Nga Tapa. But another stage had begun:

> Kei Ohiwa ka timata te ngawari — Whakatane, puta roa ki Rangitaiki, puta roa ki Tauaroa; no te ngawari katoa enei kua homai katoa enei pa e te Atua ki o matou ringa. Kati. Hei whakaaro ma koutou.
>
> E koro ma, te kupu ki a koutou tirohia te ra me te po te otinga o enei — kia hihiko mai koutou i te taenga atu o tena reta he reta powhiri haere mai i runga i te kaha o te Atua. Kia tere kia hihiko.

> At Ohiwa the gentleness started again — Whakatane, through to Rangitaiki, and Tauaroa; these pa were all given with ease by God into our hands. Well, that is for you to think about.
>
> Sirs, the suggestion to you is to consider day and night the conclusion from these things — so that soon after the arrival of this letter you [send] a letter of invitation to us, through the power of God. Be fast, be quick.[45]

On the same day, a somewhat contradictory letter written by Te Rangitahau (known as Tahau) and others at Te Harema was also sent to Tauranga on Lake Taupo. Addressed to Wi Te Wirihana, son of Wirihana Te Koekoe, and all the tribe, it spoke of the requital for Wirihana's death. The writers said reprisal had been fully taken with the deaths of the chiefs in the three pa that 'we destroyed' ('i horo i a matou'). They added: they would come to Tauranga with Te Kooti, and their word was: 'Stay there at Tauranga until we come to you' ('me noho tonu koutou i Tauranga naka a tae noa atu matou').[46]

Thus the long-term objective remained as it always had been: Tauranga on the lake, the place where the ark of the covenant and the tablets of the law were intended to rest, and the place from where Te Kooti had expected (and predicted) support would come. Yet his next strike, planned at Te Harema, would be in quite the opposite direction. His movements were dictated, he told the people, by the heavenly signs: the rainbow and thunder.[47] They were also based on the essential principle of guerrilla warfare, surprise. He knew that he was expected to come through to Waikato or to Taupo; his scouts, who were reported in the Taupo district in late March, would have told him that. Wirihana's widow was expecting him, and the people at Tauranga were known to be getting food ready.[48] Consequently, he turned back and came down on Mohaka in Hawke's Bay.

Three of his prisoners who had managed to escape from Ahikereru on 24 March reported to the government that Te Kooti was desperately short of ammunition. There were about 100 'good fighting men' at Te Harema, according to their account, and although they all had rifles, mostly Enfields, they were rationed to two or three caps each.[49] An appeal to the King for ammunition had been rejected. The purpose of the raid on Mohaka was to get supplies from the relatively well-equipped Kawanatanga tribes. The attack was also an exaction of revenge against Ngati Kahungunu for the war they had mounted against Te Kooti in 1868.

This kokiri crossed Lake Waikaremoana in the great lake-canoes of the Tuhoe; one overturned and 13 rifles were lost, but the men themselves survived. Then the party divided. Te Waru, who had been at Waikaremoana since the fall of Te Karetu and who had not taken part in the siege of Nga Tapa, led a diversionary party towards the upper Wairoa. Its purpose was to draw the Ngati Kahungunu alliance into a defence of that district, leaving the ammunition supplies at Mohaka largely undefended. Te Kooti led the main party down the Putere track to the Mohaka river. With him were the Tuhoe chiefs Te Whenuanui and Paerau, together with Anaru Matete. They reached the kainga at Te Arakanihi on the Mohaka on the night of 9–10 April and, according to Porter's Maori informants, the attack was deliberately timed to occur precisely on the same days of the month as the first assault on Poverty Bay.[50]

In the early hours of 10 April Te Kooti struck. The kainga was attacked: 31 bodies were later found there — men, women and children. The purpose was to ensure that the escape route up the Putere track remained clear, just as the control of Patutahi had been critical in the escape from Poverty Bay. In addition, some Tuhoe prisoners had recently been held at Te Arakanihi after a dispute.[51] Then the kokiri crossed down the river, passing through the properties of John Lavin and Alfred Cooper, killing both settlers, all of Lavin's family and an elderly farmhand — altogether seven people. Lavin, for one, had been part of the militia during the war in the upper Wairoa early in 1866: the raid was not just an attack on 'out settlers' but also reprisal for their participation in the fighting. As before, the bodies were bayoneted and left exposed, but they were not mutilated. The primary objectives of the raid were the two pa at Mohaka: Te Huki, on the eastern river flats, underneath the cliff terrace which protects the valley from the sea, and the larger pa, Hiruharama, which was high on the terrace, overlooking the whole valley.[52] Both were badly placed defensively, according to Leonard Williams, who visited Mohaka a few months later. It was possible for any attackers to stay under cover until quite close and, particularly at Te Huki, to come right up to the palisades without difficulty.[53]

The siege of Te Huki began in the afternoon and continued all night. In the morning Te Kooti offered to spare the lives of the inhabitants in return for their surrender. In one version (which seems the most credible) Ropihana, son of the senior chief of Ngati

Te Arakanihi, the Maori village at Mohaka, November 1855. Watercolour by Alfred John Cooper; it was annotated by his friend and neighbour, John Lavin, 'view of native settlement from our front window'. This was the site of the attack of 10 April 1869.   81210 1/2, ATL

Pahauwera, Paora Rerepu (who had been lured away with most of his fighters, as Te Kooti had hoped), concluded those terms with Te Kooti. He came with Te Kooti when they entered the pa that morning, but a Ngati Pahauwera warrior, Heta Te Wainoho, one of the few men in the pa, doubted the treaty and opened fire.[54] He shot at Te Kooti but the bullet passed through his clothing.[55] The surrender turned into slaughter: 26 people were killed, including Heta, but most were women and children. At Te Huki, Te Kooti gained the ammunition he needed to assault Hiruharama: there were three kegs of rifle cartridges in the pa, and they had been only lightly used in its defence.

But the siege of Hiruharama failed. Although an ambush set by Te Kooti successfully scattered a relieving force from Wairoa, that same morning (11 April), while he was still at Te Huki, another small party of men from Mohaka and the Wairoa managed to get through Te Kooti's lines on the north-east coast track. This party provided some reinforcement for the pa. A sudden explosion then revealed where the rest of the ammunition had been hidden, under a house in Te Huki pa, making a continuing attack on Hiruharama largely pointless. On Monday 12 April Te Kooti withdrew up the Mohaka valley to the camp at Arakanihi. Those within Hiruharama watched the departure of the siege party, their pack horses laden with stores. Te Kooti himself was remembered on the white horse he rode, said to have been newly stolen.[56] This is the first definite reference in the European historical memory to the white horse which inhabits the myth-narratives.

At Arakanihi, as Peita Kotuku recollected, Te Kooti allowed the kokiri to relax and enjoy the liquor they had taken from the Mohaka hotel. He had been angered by the fact that some men had got drunk during the night when Te Huki was under siege. Peita's account[57] is significant in that it reveals a leader who could control the use of alcohol. This is contrary to the reports which were starting to spread about him, and which would become a permanent part of the European stereotyping of Te Kooti. Tamati, one of the three prisoners who had escaped from Ahikereru, had said that Te Kooti had got very drunk at Te Harema: sometimes 'he quite forgets himself and rolls about all over the place'.[58] Rum (the 19th-century soldiers' drink) may well have provided a release, and many soldiers got drunk after and during battle. What Te Kooti was not doing was using rum for courage, nor to create the delusion of invincibility when fighting.[59]

From Arakanihi, the kokiri went back the way they had come. It was estimated that there were about 150 in the party. A significant portion of the men were Tuhoe and Ngati Hineuru, who had, as we have seen, old scores to settle with Ngati Pahauwera. Once again, within this East Coast war there were several wars. The kokiri reached Wairaumoana, the western arm of Tuhoe's wild and singularly beautiful inland lake. There, it reunited with Te Waru's contingent, which had also withdrawn, its diversionary task achieved. They celebrated with horse races on Onetapu beach by the straits of Manaia, which connects Wairaumoana with Waikaremoana. Then they crossed the narrows, their horses swimming behind the canoes, and re-entered the heartland of Tuhoe.

The raid on Mohaka was successful in that Te Kooti lost few men and gained a number of horses and some ammunition. The legend that he bore 'a charmed life'[60] grew ever more rapidly (particularly as his death at Mohaka had at first been wrongly reported). He had outmanoeuvred his opponents, and had again escaped pursuit. But now he had brought the war into the Urewera.

From mid-April the government put together the first Urewera expedition.[61] A three-pronged attack was to be mounted on Ahikereru and Ruatahuna: its purpose was to destroy Tuhoe's ability to shelter Te Kooti. It was with knowledge of the approach of war on an unparalleled scale (for the three expeditions totalled about 1300 men) that Te Kooti uttered the prediction concerning his own death. It is probably the most famous of all his kupu whakaari. It was also, consciously, 'the last supper', and he partook of it with Tuhoe.

At Ruatahuna there is a very old cabbage tree, growing a quarter of a mile from Oputao, near Umuroa pa. In the oral traditions of Tuhoe, this is the tree under which Tuhoe sat with Te Kooti and shared a meal from the one dish. As Eruera Manuera said in 1978, to this day the place is bare: the grass will not grow there again. The 'last supper' is marked on the ground for eternity.[62] It was there that Te Kooti spoke on 29 April 1869. He predicted his betrayal by those who sheltered him. In some versions of the narrative, this point is made very clearly. In William Greenwood's translation of one account, Te Kooti's words were: 'Listen! At present we are all eating out of one dish, but I say unto you here and now, that in the very near future you shall turn against me.'[63]

The most complete version, however, is that transcribed from Hamiora Aparoa's manuscript:

The cabbage tree near Oputao. In the background (right) is Te Poho-o-Parahaki, the Umuroa meeting-house. The boy and the man are Tuhoe, and the photograph was taken in the context of the story of Te Kooti at Oputao. The boy is holding a framed photograph of two people.   ELSDON CRAIG COLLECTION

Oputao — Ruatahuna.

Aperira 29. 1869. Whakarongo mai Tuhoe, me aku hoa whakarau o tawahi, mai o Whare-Kauri tae noa ki nga morehu katoa. Otira ki a koe e Tuhoe, he korero atu naku ki a koutou i tenei ra, he mihi he poroporoaki naku ki a koutou, a he whakaatu hoki i etahi kupu. . . . Heoi ano kite-kite-tanga o tatau i tenei ra,

    moetahitanga

    kai tahitanga

    noho tahitanga

    haerenga tahitanga

    korero tahitanga. . . .

A ko koutou ano e kai tahi nei tatau, ka tahuri mai ano ki te whawhai haere ki te hopu i au: hei tuku atu i au ki nga kai tukino i au . . . . Otira kaua hei pouri mo enei korero, no te mea ahakoa koutou whaiwhai i ahau i to koutou whanaunga, tae noa ki o tatau hoa e pakanga nei ki a tatau, puta noa ki te Kawana Pakeha, *e kore ahau e mau i a* koutou katoa. Heoi ano te tikanga, ko koutou tonu ka mawehe atu nei i au, na ka tonoa mai ano e te Kawana ki te whakarite i tenei kupu e korerotia atu nei e ahau ki a koutou i tenei ra. Ahakoa koutou whaiwhai haere i au me te Kawana ano hoki, e kore ahau e mau i a koutou. E kore hoki ahau e mate i a koutou, a *me mate Hau-aitu* noa iho he mate moku e mate ai ahau.

Oputao — Ruatahuna.

April 29. 1869. Listen Tuhoe, my prisoner friends from over there at Wharekauri and all the survivors. To you Tuhoe, I have this to say today — a greeting and a farewell to you, and a disclosure of some sayings. . . . We see ourselves this day,

> sleeping together
> eating together
> sitting together
> going about together
> talking together. . . .

And you yourselves, who eat together with us here, will turn to pursue and capture me, and to deliver me to those who ill-treat me . . . . But do not be upset by this talk, because although you pursue me with your relations, and our friends who fight us now, and even with the Pakeha Governor, *I will not be caught* by you all. But the outcome will be that you yourselves will separate from me and will be called upon by the Governor to fulfil this statement which I have made to you this day. Although you go in pursuit of me, even with the Governor, you will not capture me. Nor will you kill me, and it will simply be *through weakness* that I shall die.[64]

Boy Biddle has commented that the text foretells a death 'so silly, that you wouldn't ever believe what it is!'[65] As Te Kooti directed Tuhoe's ultimate tactics, he mocked the soldiers and he accurately predicted his own end. He then looked further into the future:

> A ko te wāhi o te MOTU nei e mate Hau-aitu ai ahau kei reira ano kei taua wāhi, kei taua takiwa ano te Tangata mo tatau mo nga iwi katoa. Ko ia ano hei whakahaere tikanga, a maana ano e whakaoti nga whakahaere mo tenei motu tae noa atu ki o tatau *whakatupuranga.*

> The place on this LAND where I shall die through weakness, there, in that place, in that district shall be the Man for us, for all the tribes. He alone will organise the way, and he too will complete the arrangements for this land for our *generations.*[66]

Thus the prediction looked to the completion of the work and the faith, and to Te Kooti's successor. The kupu consciously linked death to new life. It also linked the place of Te Kooti's actual death to the renewal and completion of the faith in the next generation. Different histories have evolved around these texts, and different interpretations have been given to them by the various claimants who have emerged since 1893. As a consequence, the texts have shifted both in memory and in written record, as their fulfilment has been sought in different regions of the land.

In May 1869, however, the issue was one of immediate survival. The first part of the government expedition, commanded by Whitmore, reached Te Harema on 6 May. Most of the men of the pa were either absent with Te Kooti at Ruatahuna and Waikaremoana, or in the valley 'collecting their crops'.[67] The pa was, nevertheless, attacked and, of the 50 prisoners taken, 40 were women and children. They were given to the Arawa troops under Whitmore and Te Pokiha Taranui to take as their own 'so that this hapu will be destroyed'.[68] It was a deliberate and remorseless unleashing of tribal hostilities by the government.

Whitmore's party then pressed on through to Ruatahuna, where they met with the second arm of the expedition, led by St John, who had come up through the Ruatoki valley. The two commanders now decided to observe an old whakatauki of Tuhoe known to them: 'If my neck is to be severed, it must be severed in Ruatahuna'.[69] All the settlements at Ruatahuna were destroyed. Oputao itself was burnt. Orangikawa, Paerau's pa at Tatahoata, and Tahora, Te Whenuanui's pa, were both taken by St John's force, although they had been evacuated. Te Whenuanui's great whare whakairo at Puhirake was fired. The very last act of the expedition before it withdrew on 18 May was the destruction of Te Harema. Whitmore boasted that every 'kainga of note', except those at Maungapohatu and Waikaremoana, was destroyed.[70] The cattle, horses, domestic pigs and potato crops were either killed or spoilt. Whitmore was to claim that destruction had been the main object of the expedition. As for the little potato gardens, which had been carefully enclosed, it was simply a matter of knocking down the fences and leaving the wild pigs to do the rest. This devastation was brought to bear on a people who were, even to Wiremu Kingi Te Paia's eyes, already very poor.[71] They themselves had scattered, rather than being caught like rats in a trap, and Whitmore remembered the mountains resounding with their lamentations.[72]

But the 'search and destroy' expedition failed in its real objective. On 11 May, on a track towards Waikaremoana, the Arawa contingent under Whitmore and Te Pokiha unexpectedly encountered an advance guard of Te Kooti's. But, alerted by the calls of their bugler, Peka Makarini, Te Kooti's men quickly vanished. They evaded a second encounter the next day, while the Arawa contingent refused to go beyond Ruatahuna to Waikaremoana or to Maungapohatu. They had imposed their own limits on this war. Perhaps it was because they remembered that the Tuhoe, in all former wars, had hunted their assailants 'out of the mountains with terrible loss';[73] more certainly it was because they refused to continue to work as 'slaves', fetching the powder and carrying the wounded, without their own chiefs acting as the controlling military leaders.[74] Once again, Te Kooti had escaped his pursuers. But it was Tuhoe who now told him that he must leave their land — for their own survival. 'They turned on him and caused him to leave Ruatāhuna: they drove him out. So he crossed the Kaingaroa plains, and emerged on the Taupō–Napier road at Ōpepe.'[75]

Indeed, he turned south-west: the long-delayed trek to Lake Taupo was now renewed. With about 200 people (50 mounted on horses and the rest travelling on foot), he came across the upper Rangitaiki river to the settlement at Heruiwi, on the edge of the ranges above the plains. Here he seized some prisoners and all the livestock, as the Ngati Hineuru elder, Peraniko Ngarimu, one of the whakarau, later recalled. Te Kooti took them with him to Taupo.[76] It was from Heruiwi, too, that they spotted the smoke from open fires at Opepe, which was Tahau's former kainga and which they knew should be

Te Harema (Salem) pa, where Te Kooti sheltered in March 1869. This was a modern rifle pa belonging to Ngati Whare of Te Whaiti. The pa is said to have been built in 1865; it was sacked by the Kawanatanga troops in May 1869. The outer wall was a defensive bank, with an inner ditch. (In this photograph the entire pa is surrounded by a bulldozed perimeter protection road, here partly cropped.) The platform of a large house can be seen within the protuding rectangle in the bottom right (south-east) section of the pa. Altogether, 16 house sites have been found in the pa. Rifle pits can also be seen at the bottom left (south-west perimeter). Photographed 1978.   DEPARTMENT OF CONSERVATION, ROTORUA FORESTRY SERVICE, 608/21

deserted. According to one of the survivors of the attack they launched, the 'careless' fires had been signals to Te Kooti set by a man who had acted as a guide for the cavalry scouts camped there.

Te Kooti, Karanama Te Whare and Nepia Tokitahi together led the attack. On the afternoon of 7 June, having secretly encircled the camp, Te Kooti wandered into it, calling out to the soldiers in a friendly manner. His Enfield rifle was, however, capped and cocked. Wiremu Kingi Te Paia said that Te Kooti was taken for an Arawa by the soldiers because of the 'silver-mounted' coat he wore, obtained in the raid at Whakatane. Most of the soldiers were asleep in the old houses of the kainga, and some had wet clothes drying by the fire. One of the cavalrymen came forward and shook hands with Te Kooti, and then the trap was sprung. Nine of the scouts were killed, but five managed to escape. All their arms and horses were taken. The bodies were cut with swords or tomahawks, and left exposed. None was mutilated. Opepe was not a 'massacre', as it has been called; again, it was a controlled military operation.

For Te Kooti it was a good omen ('tohu pai'): the first blood drawn in the new thrust towards Taupo. He left an equivocating letter to the 'government men' stuck in a forked stick at Opepe. It was found on 9 June:

> He whakaatu tenei naku ki nga Rangatira o te Kawana Pakeha Maori hoki kia ata mohiotia ai tenei parekura.
>
> Ko te take na Paora Hapi ahau i tiki ake ki Ruatahuna, na Hohepa Tamamutu na Poihipi Tukairangi, koia te take i pakaru ai Opepe. Te tuarua o nga reta o Paora Hapi tiki ake i a au i tutaki ki Heruiwi i te 8 o nga ra o Hune. Kotahi i mate o nga Pakeha kotahi i ora. Ko te pukapuka a Paora Hapi kei au tonu, nana i whakaatu nga kati moku kei Opepe kei Runanga, koia i tika ai taku whakamate i enei Pakeha awhekaihe hoki. No te 9 o nga ra o Hune ka hinga taku parekura, toko 9. Tokorua i ngaro, na te tata ki ro ngahere i ora ai. Hui katoa ko 10. Heoi ano.
>
> He kupu ke tenei — Kei rapu te whakaaro ko wai tenei taua. Ko te mea tono mai a te Atua hei whakaatu i tona kaha ki te ao ki te hunga kino ano hoki. Heoi ano tena reta.
>
> He kupu ke ano tenei me te patu i tae mai ki Kaingaroa. Na Paora Hapi ano tona kupu maku katoa nga tarutaru o Kaingaroa. Te rua — maku e patu nga Pakeha o konei. Koia toku kahanga i tae mai ai. He kupu pono ena. Ka huri te korero.
>
> Ki nga kawana katoa Pakeha Maori hoki.

Na Te Kooti Teturuki

Hune 10, 1869.

This letter is to enlighten you European & Maori chiefs that you may understand this fight.

> The reason is Paora Hapi fetched me from Ruatahuna & Hohepa Tamamutu and Poihipi Tukairangi — this is the reason for the fall of Opepe. The second letter that Paora Hapi wrote to fetch me I got at Heruiwi on the 8th day of June [6 June].[77] One Pakeha is killed and one saved. Paora's letter is with me. He fixed my boundary line at Opepe and Runanga — that is the reason why killing these Pakeha & halfcasts is right. These men fell on 9 June [7 June]. They were nine. Two escaped in the forest. Altogether ten were killed. That is all.
>
> This is another subject. You will wonder who were the fighting party. This is a

judgement of God to shew his might to the world and especially to the wicked. This is all of this letter.

This is yet another subject (or reason) why war should come to Kaingaroa. It was Paori Hapi's word that I should have all the grass of Kaingaroa. Secondly — That I should kill all Pakeha here — This is why I was prevailed upon to [be] cruel.[78] This is all truth. I have done.

To all government men, Pakeha & Maori.

Te Kooti Te Turuki

June 10, 1869.[79]

The letter was dated two days ahead, whether accidentally or by design is uncertain, although the inaccurate internal dates suggest the former. It referred to the killing of one of two Pakeha despatch carriers, who had been caught near Heruiwi by Peita Kotuku and his companions, and whose messages had confirmed the presence of cavalry in the district. The letter also deliberately implicated the three senior Taupo chiefs most closely associated with the government. It was, as the resident magistrate, Samuel Locke, soon deduced, carefully designed to throw suspicion upon them.[80]

Captain St George, who was stationed at Tapuaeharuru, the military base at Taupo, had previously been warned that both Paora Hapi and Poihipi had been in communication with Te Kooti. One of the three men who escaped from Ahikereru in March told him that both chiefs were trying to get access to government arms to give to Te Kooti.[81] While this was not the first time St George had been warned to this effect, he was disinclined to accept the information at face value in this world of intense rumour and slander. Nevertheless, he had made sure that Poihipi did not monopolise the ammunition supplies at Tapuaeharuru, and he had stayed alert to the possibility of a Janus-faced alliance with the Kawanatanga chiefs at Taupo. In the event, the letter proved to be deliberate disinformation.

It also referred to a speech that Poihipi had made at a hui held at Tapuaeharuru in early April, when it was expected that Te Kooti would come through to Tauranga, on the south-eastern shores of the lake. The Kingitanga chief of Tauranga-o-Taupo, Tukorehu, had spoken at the meeting: 'You govt. natives', he observed bitterly, 'have a very strong back. You have all the pakeha their guns ammunition &c. whereas we hauhau of Taupo have only ourselves — no one to back us.' He denied that they had ever invited Te Kooti to come: 'we wish to remain strictly neutral', he asserted. Poihipi's reply to him contained the words with which Te Kooti made play:

> We shall now draw a line from Opepe to Runanga & send out men to intercept any of Kooti's or other Hauhau's messengers. Take care we shall go out & we will catch these letter carriers.

St George moaned to himself: 'Master Poihipi let out every thing that we ought to have kept secret — the proposal to go and catch these 8 men [of Tauranga who had announced they were going to join Te Kooti] of course will go for nothing.'[82] An expedition to go into the Kaingaroa plains had, in fact, been agreed upon that night, but the next day Poihipi simply refused to go. The expedition set out only on 23 April. Poihipi

Peita Kotuku at Taringamotu, 1921.
Photograph by James Cowan.
COWAN COLLECTION, F31216 1/2, ATL

wrote two days later, 'we are guarding the roads of Te Kooti, Opepe & Runanga', but he complained about the purposelessness of the expedition, set up by the 'Colonel of Napier'.[83] It was abandoned on 28 April. The Kaingaroa plains had indeed been 'left' for Te Kooti. Subsequently, when St George tried again to persuade an expedition to go through to Heruiwi, Paora Hapi told him that the Taupo tribes would not cross the Kaingaroa 'owing to a superstition of death to any ope that [?] [tries to enter] the Urewera by this route'.[84]

Te Kooti was manipulating the news that he was getting about the actions and fears of the Kawanatanga leaders into a statement of their active support. By implicating the chiefs, he undoubtedly hoped to create even greater confusion and uncertainty than already existed locally.

In actuality, Te Kooti had come to Taupo 'because Paora Hapi had defied him', not because he had invited him.[85] Paora, as St George always recognised, intended to be on the winning side.[86] Poihipi also assured St George, when he showed him Te Kooti's letter, that his allegiance was to the Pakeha and that he 'remained firmly opposed to Te Kooti' ('e wakatete nei ki a Te Koti').[87] The third chief named, Hohepa Tamamutu, was in fact the initiator of the decision, which had been adopted by the Taupo Council of Chiefs (the Council of Forty) formed in December to prevent the 'Hauhau of Taupo' from supporting the whakarau, that they would oppose (if necessary by force) Wirihana Te Koekoe's invitation to the whakarau to come and live there.[88] Hohepa had not changed his views at all. Not one of these men gave Te Kooti their support when he struck at Taupo.

By the time Te Kooti reached the lake on 8 June, his original purpose, the pilgrimage, had turned into an encounter in a war zone. The party came through to Waitahanui, which belonged to Tahau's close kin and had been evacuated in advance, and then immediately turned south. The first settlement they entered was Te Hatepe, Paora Hapi's principal pa. Most of the people had hidden themselves, but one old man, Hona, was killed. On 9 June the entire settlement was burnt — thereby re-confirming its name for all time. From there Te Kooti went to Motutere, which was also set on fire. Then he journeyed on to Tauranga-o-Taupo, the seat of his objectives.

Exactly what happened here is not clear. Tukorehu had recently assured St George that the people there would remain 'quiet' and would not commit themselves to Te Kooti, because they did not want to be treated as Te Harema had been and be utterly destroyed.[89] It seems that some opposition may have been offered to Te Kooti when he first arrived at Tauranga. The earliest accounts were that an old man had been killed and some of the houses burnt, although this was probably a confusion with Te Hatepe.[90] Paora Hapi, who was at Runanga, soon heard that his own son and another man, Paora Te Tauri, had been taken prisoner.[91] Hohepa Tamamutu and a party of 20 men from Tapuaeharuru set out immediately for Tauranga on 10 June, but, finding themselves outnumbered, withdrew after a brief skirmish.[92] Thus Te Kooti stayed in occupation of Tauranga, while the major Maori Kawanatanga leaders all fled their villages 'in terror'.[93] The simultaneous discovery of the bodies at Opepe diverted the attention of the European military men, so there are no European reports of these events.

At Tauranga, Te Kooti sent out messages into the Maori world that 'the land is his'.[94] Paora Hapi reported on 18 June that Te Kooti was still at Tauranga, and that altogether six men and 15 women of the Tuwharetoa tribe had been killed.[95] In direct contrast, Wiremu Kingi Te Paia said that they had been received well at Tauranga and were given food. St George also understood that most of the people of Tauranga voluntarily joined Te Kooti[96] — as Te Kooti had originally anticipated. Nevertheless, it is clear that strains were affecting his party.

A number of the Tuhoe who had travelled with him turned back at this juncture: St George estimated about 100 people. Among them was Te Waru, ever an independent man. However, the reason for the back-tracking to the Urewera was probably not dissension but the arrival of troops at Waikaremoana. Lieutenant-Colonel Herrick's long-delayed expedition from Wairoa had occupied Onepoto, in the confiscated block on the south-eastern shores of the lake. He would remain there until July. However, some Tuwharetoa people, who were taken prisoner on the journey down the shores of Lake

Lieutenant-Colonel J. L. Herrick's expedition of June 1869 at Waikaremoana. This expedition was probably the reason that the Tuhoe chiefs turned back from Taupo. The soldiers spent their time building 'their Floating Coffins', as they dryly named the boats intended to take them across the lake to the fortified pa on the opposite shore. The boats were never used, and were sunk in the lake when the expedition was abandoned.   HBM

Taupo, also reported that Tahau had remonstrated with Te Kooti about the Tuwharetoa deaths, because the people were his kinsmen. He objected to any further killings and had reminded Te Kooti of 'the compact that had been entered in: whenever they happened to be in a district belonging to any chief who had joined him, such chief should have a voice in the operations'.[97]

It was possibly as a consequence of internal disputes that Te Kooti moved south, instead of remaining at the place he had always said would be his final destination. He composed a song on this occasion. It referred to his anxiety and concern about the quarrels, and it observed that the killing of many people had only just been averted. The song continued:

> Tohi atu ana taku haere ki te whakawhitiranga i Taupo. Te mauria rawatia ki nga take pa i Waihi. Ko wai ra kei roto ko Te Heuheu e tapu ra koe? Ka whanatu au ka haere ki te rapa i te pu-tere hou i a te Kingi, mana hau e whakahoki ki te kainga tipu.

> My journey is broken to bring the cause across Taupo, bringing it right up to the palisade posts of the pa at Waihi. Who is within but you, o sacred Te Heuheu? I shall leave in search of soldiers dedicated to the King, for he will return me to the place of my birth.

It concluded with a direct challenge to the paramount chief of Tuwharetoa, Horonuku

Te Heuheu Tukino IV, whose primary residence was at Waihi, at the southern end of the lake:

> Ka hinga to rahui tapu ko Taramai-nuku ko te puia i Tongariro taku te rae ii.

> Your sacred mark of protection, Taramai-nuku, the hot spring of Tongariro shall fall; the headland is mine![98]

Thus it is clear Te Kooti came in challenge to Waihi. There indeed he encountered, as he foresaw, Horonuku Te Heuheu. Horonuku had already been approached by Tawhiao, asking him to stay neutral but, if need be, to let Te Kooti pass unmolested.[99] Exactly what happened is again unclear, but Horonuku went with Te Kooti. He said he was taken prisoner. As he told his own people in October:

> I was left alone and forsaken by you. When I got to Tauranga I heard of the man who was killed I then got frightened. Te Kooti came when I got back. I was taken Prisoner, I have been such ever since.[100]

Certainly Te Kooti left Waihi with Horonuku in the ambit of his power. Five men who escaped from Waihi said that Horonuku and all the others were prisoners; Te Kooti 'did not kill any of them but prevents them getting away'.[101] They went westwards and inland, to Moerangi, a community which had already indicated its support for Te Kooti[102] and had been actively preparing for his arrival. In Te Kooti's own diary there are some fragmentary and opaque jottings concerning these events, which seem to confirm this analysis. For Te Kooti named Taupo 'Babylon' ('Papurona'), mentioned a gathering at Horonuku's pa, and then added:

> Moerangi ka mau a te Heuheu o matua ahu ki reir[a].

> Moerangi, where Te Heuheu will be caught, and your elders heaped up there.[103]

Wiremu Kingi Te Paia remembered the welcome they received at Moerangi: large calabashes containing 2000 pigeon preserved in fat, and three cows killed in their honour. The chief there, Te Wiripo Tohiraukura, sang a waiata which concerned the holding of the land and the persistence of their fight against the colonisers. But Horonuku spoke otherwise. While he gave welcome to the man from Te Tairawhiti (the East Coast), he refused to endorse the words of war that the others had uttered. At sunrise the next morning, however, Te Kooti spoke of his God and gave praise to him and, said Wiremu Kingi, Tuwharetoa then consented 'to adopt his religion'.[104]

If the balance of power seemed to have shifted dramatically, the dilemma remained: where should Te Kooti now go? From Moerangi he sent messengers to the upper Taupo chiefs, seeking their commitment. He also wrote to the communities along the western shores of the lake, who were closely involved with the Kingitanga. He threatened an attack on Tapuaeharuru, the government military post at the northern end of the lake, but his hopes were, in fact, pinned on the King at Tokangamutu (Te Kuiti). Te Kooti hoped that his own rising power would either force Tawhiao into alliance or topple him.

Some communication had already taken place between them. An invitation to Te Kooti from Tamati Ngapora, the King's senior adviser and his uncle, had been couched in clear warning terms: if he came in peace he was welcome; otherwise, he was not. To

Horonuku Te Heuheu at Tokaanu, October 1885. Photograph by Alfred Burton.   84 (BB 3779), MONZ

this rebuke Te Kooti had replied, according to one report, that he was coming to Tokangamutu regardless, and that he would 'assume himself the supreme authority which he coming direct from God was entitled to'.[105] This was a direct challenge to Tawhiao as King and as the prophet of God.

On 5 July the first report came through to the government that Te Kooti was on his way from Moerangi to confront Tawhiao. He travelled up the western shores of Taupo to Titiraupenga, a pa at the foot of the mountain of the same name, situated in the rugged bush-covered slopes which abut the Pureora forest. On 7 July, Ihakara Kahuao reported that Te Kooti was at Kaiwha, a little village of Titiraupenga. Ihakara had taken prisoner a man who had gone to capture pigs for Te Kooti and learnt that that day the ope was leaving for Tokangamutu.[106] The following day, the chief of Titiraupenga, Hitiri Te Paerata (a leading warrior from the battle at Orakau), wrote in terror to Taupo:

> E hoa ma, kua uru wehi matou ki a te Kooti. Kei Tokangamutu te huihuinga o nga iwi nei kei reira te urunga me te pakarutanga. E hoa, kia mau te puru o Kaingaroa, kia mau. Kaua te pakeha e tukua mai ma konei kei tupono mai ki a aku tamariki, me aku mea katoa.
>
> Friends, we have fearfully joined in with Te Kooti. The meeting of the tribes will be at Tokangamutu and there the joining in and the breaking away will take place. Friends, keep up the blockade of Kaingaroa, keep it up. Don't let the pakeha be sent this way, in case they fall on my children, and all my possessions.[107]

These accounts were soon confirmed by other reports which came flying in. At Kaiwha, Rewi Maniapoto had come to meet Te Kooti and to urge him to venture no further into the King Country — that is, into Maniapoto's tribal territory. But Te Kooti rejected his advice, and insisted he was continuing.[108] It was there also that he was joined by Hakaraia,[109] an old Arawa chief living in the Titiraupenga and Patetere districts, who would play a significant part in events to come. A great assembly was held in the evening at Pukerimu, a village of Titiraupenga,

> and Te Kooti got up to address the people, and especially Hakaraia. He spoke for five hours, and made quotations from a large book written in the English language. During this long address, which was listened to with great attention by every one, Hakaraia constantly said to me — 'Te Kooti is a true man. I thought I knew a good deal, but this man's knowledge is much greater than mine. I shall have to succumb to him.' His knowledge did not only relate to the things of the earth, but extended to those of heaven. Hakaraia agreed to accompany him to Tokangamutu.[110]

Hakaraia's support for Te Kooti from this juncture was the beginning of a critical alliance with tribes from the northern Bay of Plenty and Patetere, whose land had also been recently confiscated. It was the means by which Te Kooti would enter that territory, when all else failed him, in January 1870.

Another report came in from Titiraupenga shortly after Te Kooti had left. It was sent by Te Tatana, who belonged to Hitiri's small hapu, Ngati Te Kohera,[111] and who had watched the group's departure from Te Papa, at Titiraupenga, for Tokangamutu on 7 July. He noted that there were a number of important Tuhoe chiefs still with the party, including Paerau of Ruatahuna and Hapurona Kohi of Ahikereru, who had been one of the leaders of the Tuhoe contingent at Orakau. Horonuku was also with them, as well as many men from Tauranga, Waihi and elsewhere around the lake. Of the estimated 200 Tuwharetoa, half were not armed but were, he said, travelling with Te Kooti. This remark would seem to confirm their status as semi-prisoners. Te Tatana estimated the entire party to consist of 340 men, who had come through from the Urewera, as well as 200 men of Tuwharetoa, and a further 300 women and children.[112] He may have exaggerated, but the ope was clearly intended to be a major demonstration of Te Kooti's strength.

There are extensive oral narratives among Ngati Rereahu (the hapu of Maniapoto who live in the Tiroa district) about the challenges Te Kooti made as he entered their country, their area of mana. Each story relates to a specific place he visited. Those retold here come from this time, although Te Kooti also returned to the King Country through Taumarunui at the end of the year, and there are stories concerning that visit, too.

Henare Tuwhangai of Ngati Rereahu narrated how Te Kooti arrived at Paraharaha pa. Paraharaha is near to Titiraupenga, and Wiremu Kingi Te Paia's account indicates that the ope went there from Titiraupenga. Paraharaha itself is about a mile and a half from the sacred whare wananga (house of learning) of Ngati Rereahu, Te Miringa Te Kakara. The oral stories remember that Te Kooti was accompanied by many people, including Tuhoe, and that they came in a mood of challenge. Te Kooti punned on the name of the place, Paraharaha — flattened — and suggested that was exactly what he would do to them. As Henare told the story, it was the tohunga and chiefly leader, Te Ra Karepe, who thereupon confronted Te Kooti. When Te Kooti said to him, 'Surrender the mana of Maniapoto', Te Ra answered by extending his tongue in the manner of Maori defiance and saying, 'When you have this, my tongue, then you will have the mana of the land'.[113] In another version of the narrative, Te Kooti's words of challenge were, 'Homai o Atua kia kainga e au' ('Give me your Gods that I may consume them'), to which Te Ra replied, opening his mouth and pointing inside: 'Ae, haeremai: tikina!' ('Yes, welcome: come and fetch them!').[114] Te Kooti turned away, knowing it was a challenge to the death.

It is also told that one of Te Kooti's wives was left behind at Paraharaha. She was pregnant and was unable to continue travelling. She could not understand Ngati Rereahu's dialect, and was very lonely. She waited for Te Kooti to return for a long time, and she used to climb a kahikatea tree (which still stands today), from where she would gaze towards her homeland in the Urewera. The tree was therefore named Pikiwahine, Woman's Ascent. But finally she married a local man and became a part of his community;[115] in this story of displacement there is also resolution.

There is another recurrent story from this journey concerning a woman, and therefore it too is included. She was named Miriama and she had given birth to Te Kooti's son 'Tohou' as they travelled fast from Opepe to Waitahanui on 7–8 June. This man, it is said, became the first Maori killed at Gallipoli. This could be correct;[116] however, this part of the narrative may be a mythic structuring — rounding a cycle of sacrifice. Regardless of this dimension, one of the realities of the women's world — pregnancy in war — is briefly opened with these shifting, uncertain memories, only to be closed again.

Ngati Rereahu had previously consulted Te Ra as to how to treat the arrival of Te Kooti within their territory. Robert Emery of Ngati Maniapoto described Te Ra's response. At Te Miringa Te Kakara, their house of learning, Te Ra performed a ritual before the people. He took a flat totara slab and put it carefully on the ground. He poured two small piles of gunpowder onto it: one represented Te Kooti and his followers, the other themselves. '"Which ever one of the two explodes, they will surely suffer defeat"', he explained. Then he raised his right hand to the sky, and repeated the movement three times in front of their own pile. Only a wisp of smoke arose. Then he faced the pile which represented Te Kooti and, on the first movement of his arm, the little heap of powder burst into flames. Te Ra turned to the people and told them, '"Let no man of our people fire on Te Kooti first. Should Te Kooti or his followers fire the first shot they shall surely die by their own actions."' And so it was when Te Kooti came to the sacred place only words were exchanged. Therefore both survived, and Te Kooti went on his way to Tokangamutu.[117] The oral narratives convey the tension and ambivalence of the encounters in these communities, just as Hitiri's letter had done.

On 10 July Te Kooti reached Te Kuiti. He came first to Taupiri-o-te-rangi, Ngati Maniapoto's house (and settlement), where Rewi welcomed him as his kinsman. For the two men were related through Te Kooti's father, and this bond of kinship Rewi would honour through all his dealings with Te Kooti.[118] Te Kooti told Rewi that he came not to depose the King, as had been rumoured, but simply as 'a servant, sent to punish the wicked. The sword had been placed in his hands, and he would use it. He came to greet the King, and to rouse up the Waikato to take up arms.'[119] With him was the large party of Tuwharetoa, as well as a distinct core of 60 of his followers, and 'his five wives'. This war-hardened inner group, consisting mostly or entirely of the whakarau, were called a bodyguard or 'matua'. They were 'all mounted, and armed alike with breech-loading rifles, revolvers, and swords'.[120] The party, having greeted their hosts, then went to Tokangamutu, the portion of Te Kuiti which had been granted by Ngati Maniapoto to the King since the confiscation of his lands of Waikato. A large quantity of food had been gathered for a feast. It included the great delicacy of dried shark, as well as plenty of flour, said Maihi Pohepohe of Ngati Raukawa, who had travelled with his uncle, old Hakaraia. But

> Te Kooti said he should consider himself the host (tangata whenua), and that the Waikato were his visitors. He ordered his 500 men to load their guns with ball cartridges, and, when the Waikatos came within a short distance, he gave the word to fire over their heads. Great was the fear of the Waikato. They threw the food down and ran away. They retired a short distance, and were very angry.[121]

In this unexpected manner Te Kooti usurped the role of host and claimed his own independent authority. William Searancke, the resident magistrate in the Waikato, who was paid for undertaking 'secret service' during this visit of Te Kooti, observed that the Waikato people seemed 'to be partially paralyzed by Te Kooti's presence amongst them'. Searancke commented that they had nothing to say to Te Kooti; rather, they carefully watched and waited to see what he had to say.[122] And he, in his turn, waited for them.

Whalebone kotiate which once belonged to Te Kooti. The original was in the possession of Miss M. Lysnar of Gisborne, when it was photographed in 1943. Photograph by W. R. B. Oliver. AO 815, MONZ

According to Maihi Pohepohe, he waited a week — and still Waikato and the King would not see him.

Te Kooti remained determined to dominate. The Waikato people learnt that he had earlier ordered the Taupo communities to bring out all their greenstones — patu, heitiki and earrings — and to give them to him to be destroyed. Now he demanded this of them, as well: they must destroy the things of Baal, he said. He compared himself directly with Jehu, God's anointed king over the people of Israel, whose task was war. He reminded them of the narrative of Jehu's entry into the kingdom of Judah:

> So there went one on horseback to meet him, and said, Thus saith the king, Is it peace? And Jehu said, What hast thou to do with peace?[123]

Te Kooti's followers gave out that he was 'The sent of God [come] to declare his power to the world, and also to the men of sin'.[124] He demanded that he be recognised as the prophet for Waikato. They must accept his religion. Thus, as Henare Tuwhangai said plainly, he came to claim the mana, 'that is, the power of God'.[125] Of Maniapoto he asked directly that Orakau, on the borders of their protected land, should be given up to him as a sanctuary and 'as payment for the Uriwera who fell in its defence'.[126]

In every way it becomes clear that Te Kooti had come to challenge Tawhiao. Moreover, the hidden threat within the texts of Jehu, whose career he said he would now follow, was the death of the King himself.[127] He claimed that all the island could fall into their hands if Waikato and Maniapoto were prepared to join him, but if not they must fight it out among themselves for the leadership.[128] Consequently, Waikato urged Tawhiao to leave Tokangamutu while Te Kooti was present. But 'Tawhiao absolutely refused to consent. Te Kooti will not, however, be allowed to see him', Searancke reported to the government.[129] Tawhiao's meeting-house remained guarded throughout Te Kooti's visit; it was continuously patrolled by policemen on the outside, while the Tekaumarua (the Twelve), who formed Tawhiao's own bodyguard, remained inside the house and fully armed.[130] Te Kooti and his party were forced to camp on the roadside as all the houses were deliberately occupied by 'the men of the place', while the outhouses were taken up 'by the women'.[131] Hitiri Te Paerata, for whom the whole experience was a nightmare, was now to say that accompanying the spurned Te Kooti was like being with 'a decayed dog, with the decay striking the noses of the women, and the children' ('me te kuri pirau, tangi ana te pirau ki ihu o te wahine, o te tamaiti').[132]

Wiremu Kingi Te Paia was also filled with unhappiness for, as he said, 'I had no interest in visiting strange places, or killing strange people'. He gave his own description of the climax of their stay at Tokangamutu:

> Our number was not over 200. When we reached Tokangamutu we were welcomed by the people, and guns were fired in our honor. While they were at prayers we sat by the King's house, a large raupo whare. There the assembly took place. There were 200 Waikatos present. Manga [Rewi Maniapoto] arose and sung a waiata. I forget the waiata. But he spoke to hold the land and keep up the fighting. In concluding, he handed Te Kooti a sword, by which he was to sever Mangatawhiri and Hangatiki.[133] Te Kooti answered, 'There is the sword; take it back. I will remain in front of the King. If *he* gives me the sword, I will take it; if not, let him keep his sword, and I will go elsewhere. The King is in the centre with his sword, and I on the outside.'

But it was Tamati Ngapora who replied for Tawhiao:

> The answer was a refusal. The words were that the people did not consent to Te Kooti's proposals; and that his purpose in coming amongst them was to lower their chieftain-ship, and to destroy their Atua; and that they would not bow down to his Atua.[134]

The conflict of mana was out in the open. According to Wiremu Kingi, Tawhiao was enraged by this usurpation of his authority by Tamati. He said that he had plundered his dignity as King in speaking thus: 'Therefore, let me bear the name of Matita (driven on shore)' while Tamati is King, he shouted angrily.[135] Kingi also believed that Tawhiao himself was prepared to consider renewing war against the Europeans. His narrative indicates the deep divisions within the Kingitanga as to what policy to adopt at this critical juncture. Unquestionably, Tawhiao had initiated the policy of peace, which the Kingitanga had adopted since 1866. Only three months earlier, in April 1869, he had issued yet another proclamation: that the 'slaying of man by man [is] to cease' ('Ko te patu a te tangata i te tangata kaati'),[136] and this policy would continue to prevail. But whether he was being deprived of the decision-making power at this critical moment in order to sustain the peace policy is a significant question.

Rewi Maniapoto, great war-leader and chief of Maniapoto, was observing the whole situation with extreme care and attention. He had been at Lake Taupo just before Te Kooti's arrival there, and he had voiced his anger at the occupation of 'the interior of the Island' and at the destruction that had been wrought upon Tuhoe. He had urged the Taupo chiefs to let Te Kooti pass unopposed — that is, if his objectives were peaceful, as he had remarked pointedly to Horonuku.[137] Rewi was far too shrewd to involve Maniapoto in a war which would lead only to their destruction. But the issue was: could Te Kooti be the man who might alter the balance of power? Was he indeed Jehu?

For Rewi the question that must have lain in his mind was whether Te Kooti had the capacity to mount so strong a challenge to the government that it could bring about the restitution of the confiscated lands of Waikato. Could he achieve what Tawhiao had not been able to do? In 1869–70, this did not seem an impossibility. After all, the British government itself was urging the colonial government 'to cede the lands conquered by the Queen's troops and to *recognize Maori Authority*'. Sovereignty over the 'Native Districts' and the confiscated lands, it suggested, should be returned to Maori as the means of ending the protracted wars. The 'Queens Sovereignty' should be surrendered in those areas, and the King should be recognised as having an 'absolute dominion' within his own borders.[138] This was precisely the goal of the Kingitanga movement; the dilemma was the best method to achieve it. Or, as Henry Sewell observed when writing to Sir George Grey from London to report the British proposals, the Maori authority, which London was suggesting they should recognise, could be equally that of Tawhiao or Te Kooti.[139] Sewell was scathing about these suggestions; in Rewi's mind it is possible that a serious choice had been posed.

Rewi's relationship with Tamati Ngapora — now known as Manuhiri (Guest) — was uncomfortable and strained. He had no desire to subordinate his mana in his own lands to that of Tamati, who certainly was not King. He chose an independent path: he decided he would journey with Te Kooti to observe just what manner of man he was.

Te Kooti waited at Tokangamutu for a week, and still Tawhiao refused to see him. As he waited there, two informants sent a physical description of him to the government:

> About sixty nine to seventy inches high: hair dark, wavy, and parted in middle: slightly hooked nose: complexion clear but dark: no tattooing on face; whiskers thin; long black beard and mustaches; is considered good looking; is stout in bodily appearance, stoops slightly when walking; has dogged look when not excited . . . .[140]

He stayed determinedly until 20 July. Then he made his preparations to depart. His horses were saddled and ready when he was commanded to stop by Waikato. The next day, a panui (pronouncement) from Tawhiao was formally read to him and his followers: 'Kati te pakiki' — Cease bothering them. He would be escorted by Waikato and Maniapoto to the borders of the Rohe Potae (the closed lands of the Kingitanga), and then be sent back to Taupo.[141] The way through to the northern Bay of Plenty was blocked to him at the same time, for both Hakaraia and the pre-eminent tribe there, Ngati Raukawa, had decided at this point to support the King's decision.[142] Ngati Maniapoto also determined to block his path to Orakau.[143] Te Kooti was to be turned back.

It is clear that he protested. An offer of sanctuary was then made to him: he could live inland, on the Mokau river, under the protection of Maniapoto.[144] This offer would be renewed when he finally returned, seeking Maniapoto's shelter, in 1872. The offer was made by the senior Mokau chiefs, Wetere Te Rerenga and Tikaokao, whose sudden arrival at Tokangamutu had precipitated this entire discussion.[145] At this juncture, Te Kooti appointed a delegation of speakers of the principal men from his party to try to articulate their cause. Among these chiefs was Anaru Matete,[146] and another was Paerau, who was well known to Maniapoto, having fought for them at Orakau. The discussions went on all day on 22 July.[147] The visitors spoke one after another before the Waikato and Maniapoto chiefs and, according to Maihi Pohepohe, it was Paerau who finally persuaded some of the Maniapoto chiefs to journey with them. But their purposes remained obscure. Maihi believed that they had decided to commit themselves to Te Kooti and to the renewal of war.[148] But others reported that Te Kooti was, in fact, being escorted away from Maniapoto's land. Te Tatana wrote hastily to Perenara Tamahiki at Taupo on 26 July that Te Kooti was not at all liked within the boundaries of the King's territory.[149] Searancke similarly reported that 'Tawhiao and the Waikatos and Ngati-maniapotos are determined to, if possible, compel Te Kooti and his followers to return to Taupo by the same road that they came.'[150] Aihepene Kaihau wrote even more graphically: Te Kooti had been told, '"Presently you will be made to return back by the same road you came hither, and your sword will in a short time fall to the ground, your hands will tremble, and your body will lie flat on the earth."'[151]

Finally, on 25 July Te Kooti left Tokangamutu. He sent a greenstone heitiki to Tawhiao, possibly as an offering of peace, although in this context it could seem to be a deceiving gift for the god Baal. However it was intended to be understood, it was not received. One of the Maniapoto chiefs gave it to Ropata Kaihau of Ngati Teata, who in turn gave it to Searancke. The latter understood that it was intended as a gift for the governor, and that it was Waikato and Maniapoto's statement of peace and a rejection of any association with Te Kooti.[152]

Te Kooti left under surveillance. He was accompanied by Rewi and Horonuku, both of whose purposes remained unclear to outside observers. Horonuku had apparently spoken strongly in Te Kooti's favour at Te Kuiti, where (according to Searancke) he had 'danced about like a madman, with a brace of revolvers stuck in his belt.'[153] On 18–19 July the three men had also visited Louis Hetet, a French trader considered to be Maniapoto's Pakeha who was living at Otorohanga, a few miles north of Te Kuiti. Of Rewi, Searancke reported nothing, except that he abstained from alcohol; Te Kooti got very drunk. The latter talked at length about the events which had occurred since his return and made it clear that the attack on Turanga in 1868 was the direct consequence of Biggs's persistent pursuit: if unmolested, he said, the whakarau would have interfered with no one.[154] What Searancke did not know were Te Kooti's future intentions. This was probably because Te Kooti himself was waiting for signs of guidance.

Te Kooti travelled a few miles south-west from Tokangamutu towards the Mokau river. There he camped for over a week, near an old settlement which belonged to Reihana, the senior chief of the Mokau district, who had accompanied him as an escort. Hitiri, still travelling with Te Kooti, wrote to say that Maniapoto had journeyed with them thus far simply to drive out Te Kooti and all his followers.[155] Searancke also

Greenstone female heitiki named 'Maungarongo' (Lasting Peace, or Peacemaker), formerly worn by Te Kooti. This tiki is possibly the one which Te Kooti gave to Tawhiao but which was passed to the governor, Sir George Bowen, in 1869. Maungarongo once belonged to a tohunga of Wairau valley, near Cloudy Bay; Te Kooti is said to have worn it in 1868. It was purchased from the Eady collection by the present Museum of New Zealand in 1977.

ME 13454, MONZ

commented privately that Te Kooti was being hemmed in by his escorts, with only one road left open for him — back to Taupo. The 'poor devil does not know where to go or what to do'.[156] Te Kooti's party now consisted of about 200 men, of whom 60 were his bodyguard, and another 100 women and children.[157] It is certain that some men in the original party had stayed at Te Kuiti. Te Kooti had brought with him the five kegs of powder which he had carted all the way from Taupo. The place where he made camp was where the road to Taupo, through Tuhua, branched off. His choice was to go — or to stay on in a most uneasy and ambivalent sanctuary.

It was there that he took his decision. He would return to Tauranga-o-Taupo: the wars would be renewed. The first message, which reached Taupo on 2 August and gave warning of his intended return, said, 'His are the days — His are the months — His is the year.'[158] The omens had been read. On 6 August Te Kooti set out again for Taupo.

CHAPTER 7

THE RETURN TO BABYLON
(AUGUST 1869–FEBRUARY 1870)

Te Kooti returned to Taupo by the road which went through Tuhua and on to Lake Rotoaira. He arrived there on 18 August 1869. Petera, one of Hitiri's men who had travelled with the party from Tokangamutu, wrote urgently to Perenara Tamahiki to tell the people of Taupo that they had arrived. He said that Te Kooti's permanent abode would be at Waitahanui, Tahau's former home on the north-eastern shores of Lake Taupo. Then, Petera warned, Te Kooti would turn and attack the Maori settlements. Rewi was travelling with them:

> Ko te haere he titiro i nga mahi a Te Koti, tona kotahi, kaore he hoa, e haere tupato ana ia.

> He is going to have a look at what Te Kooti is doing, he [Rewi] comes alone, and has no companions. He is going cautiously.[1]

Nevertheless, the Tuwharetoa party under Horonuku still remained with Te Kooti; they had not broken away. Petera therefore warned all the Taupo people to be wary, 'for there is great strength in Te Kooti's ways' ('ka nui te kaha o nga tikanga a Te Kooti').[2]

Te Kooti remained at Rotoaira for the rest of August, in direct contradiction of Hitiri's information. He was reported (correctly) to be building a pa at the lake and at Moerangi, and also (equally correctly) to be seeking to return home to Turanga — if he was left unmolested. The military forces slowly gathered around him, in both the north and the south, trying to determine his intentions in this world of rumour, speculation and contradiction.

On the morning of 10 September (the same day of the month that Te Kooti had chosen twice before to initiate an attack), he struck at Tauranga on the lake, once the place of his vision of peace. Henare Tomoana, in charge of a Ngati Kahungunu contingent of 120 mounted men who had only just established themselves at the village two days previously, sent urgently (but in vain) for assistance, saying that they had been attacked by 80 mounted men and 200 on foot. On the afternoon of 11 September Te Kooti withdrew, taking nearly all Ngati Kahungunu's horses, together with much of their equipment. Henare Tomoana's rough sketch of the fight shows that he had been completely hemmed in by his attackers. The withdrawal was brief, however, and was probably in order to get food, for that night the assault was renewed, though unsuc-

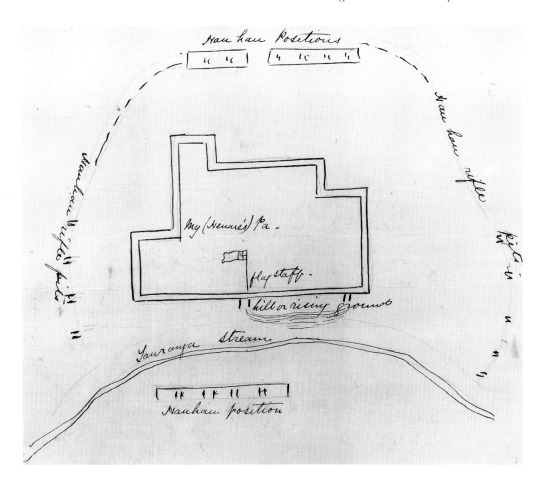

Henare Tomoana's diagram of the siege at Tauranga-o-Taupo, September 1869. The pa had been hastily thrown up by Tomoana's forces.   AD1 69/7112, NA

cessfully. Te Kooti failed to disperse the Ngati Kahungunu forces and was forced to retreat with the loss of five men.[3] He also abandoned Korohe, the nearby village which he had occupied. At the same time, however, a pa lying a few miles south of Rotoaira, which had been recently occupied by the Tuwharetoa chief Hare Tauteka in order to watch Te Kooti's movements, was attacked and burnt.[4] Te Kooti had split his forces in three, for simultaneously he also occupied Tokaanu, in the heart of Horonuku's (and Hare Tauteka's) territory.[5] By taking Tokaanu he had succeeded in separating the two arms of the government forces, camped respectively at Rotoaira and Tauranga. He also controlled the route south from Rotoaira into the upper Whanganui country, and it seems probable that he was opening up this route for himself as a passage into that vast wilderness.

However, he lacked the manpower necessary to sustain all his positions. His total forces were then estimated at between 300 and 400 men;[6] 300 was probably the more accurate figure. This was about the size of the contingent camped at Poutu on the southeast shores of Rotoaira and less than half the assembled forces of the government at

View from the pa at Tauranga-o-Taupo, December 1869, entitled 'the scene of Te Kooti's repulse by the Ngatikahunga in Sep: 1869'. Motutaiko island is in the centre (middle distance), and the mountain Tauhara dominates the skyline. Watercolour by W. H. Burgoyne.   WHANGANUI MUSEUM

Taupo (700).[7] Te Kooti therefore had to keep moving. His successes depended on his unpredictability, and on eroding the confidence of the government's Maori allies. He needed Maori recruits, but he could not risk a pitched fight. Thus he withdrew from Tokaanu on 14 September, taking the cattle and horses to Moerangi. Because Moerangi was considered a part of the King's territory it could not, according to the government's instructions at this time, be attacked. The great fear which conditioned — and inhibited — the government's military strategies at Taupo was that any attack on the Rohe Potae would bring about the alliance it dreaded most of all: a compact between Te Kooti and the Kingitanga.[8]

It was from the sanctuary at Moerangi that, on 25 September, Te Kooti made his second assault on Tokaanu. He struck from the densely forested hills behind the settlement with between 250 and 300 men. Lieutenant-Colonel Thomas McDonnell was later told by a prisoner that this was Te Kooti's entire force,[9] although it did not include Horonuku and those of Tuwharetoa who were accompanying him. They had remained at Moerangi with the women and children. Te Kooti personally led this major attack; and it failed. He was driven back into the ranges by Henare Tomoana's party and the government's Tuwharetoa contingents: 240 men in all. There they continued to fight, Te Kooti's men defending the rifle pits that they had earlier dug in the high saddle Te Ponanga, behind Tokaanu. McDonnell wrote that Te Kooti's forces 'fought well and contested every inch of ground, carrying off their dead and wounded to the fern-ridge above them, until forced to break.'[10] Privately he added, concerning the prisoners whom the government forces had taken, 'The wounded had their heads cut off and much trouble is thus saved'.[11] Hohepa Tamamutu, leader of the Tuwharetoa Kawanatanga contingent, thereby made plain his position: he would not be taking any male prisoners. Mana was at stake. Seven of Te Kooti's men were killed in the fighting; one was the whakarau Wi Piro, who was called 'the younger brother' ('te taina') of Te Kooti, and who had been standing beside him when shot.[12]

The defeat at Te Ponanga has often been described as critical, in that it ensured Rewi

Maniapoto would not ally with Te Kooti. It is unlikely, however, that he had ever intended to do so. Further, Rewi had already separated from Te Kooti before the fight at Te Ponanga took place. He had witnessed the two engagements with Henare Tomoana at Tauranga and their unsatisfactory outcome. He had always said that he would leave after escorting Te Kooti to Taupo,[13] and at this juncture he had gone. The weight of evidence makes it improbable that he had ever been prepared to fight alongside Te Kooti. Whatever thoughts Rewi may have toyed with, the events at Tauranga had determined the issue, however, and the news from Te Ponanga could only have confirmed it. Rewi went to the upper Whanganui, where he made contact with the crucial Kingitanga chiefs of the district, particularly Topine Te Mamaku of Maraekowhai.[14] It was he who controlled the upper Whanganui and of whom it was said, proverbially (and accurately), that he held 'the plug of Tuhua' ('te puru o Tuhua').[15] Te Mamaku, while insisting on his neutrality, now ensured that the way through the upper Whanganui would be closed to Te Kooti. Topia Turoa, the other leading Kingitanga chief of the upper Whanganui, joined Te Mamaku in this decision. Topia had been personally alienated by the killing of old Hona, his kinsman, on Te Kooti's orders at Te Hatepe in June.[16] In addition, four scouts had been seized at their own camp at Rotoaira on 7 September, one of whom was a priest or 'Papa' of Topia.[17] The scouts had been offered the choice of joining Te Kooti or being killed and, when they refused to join, were struck with swords or tomahawks, their bodies left ritually exposed. One of these men also had important Waikato connections, and letters were soon on their way to Tawhiao to inform him of their deaths. These letters were decisive. Topia and Te Mamaku travelled to meet with Rewi at Tuhua, and there they determined the policy of 'kati', or blockade. Te Kooti had failed to gain control in Te Kopu-o-te-ika-a-Maui, the Belly of the fish of Maui. There would be no alliance with the Kingitanga tribes of the upper Waikato or the upper Whanganui.

After the defeat on 25 September, Te Kooti withdrew again to Moerangi. It was from there that he prepared the earthwork redoubt at Te Porere-a-Rereao, near Papakai village on the bleak pumice lands at the edge of the bush, south of Moerangi and at the western edge of the Rotoaira basin. It is not clear who actually built the redoubt. There is a persistent tradition that the site was chosen by Tuwharetoa, and the redoubt built by them, as a test of Te Kooti's military skills. It has even been called a deliberate trap.[18] The suggestion derives from the well-known ambiguity of Tuwharetoa's support for Te Kooti, but Tuwharetoa would then have been trapping themselves. According to Porter's account, when Te Kooti was shown the pa he commented, 'Ziklag is the name for this Pa' ('Ko Tikaraka te ingoa mo tenei Pa').[19] The reference is to I Samuel 30:1–6, where it is told that the Amalekites, who were the people of Havilah (Hawira) against whom the Israelites contested, took Ziklag by fire 'on the third day' and captured all its women and children, including the two wives of King David. The prediction looks to the failure of the besieged in their fortress; it indicates Te Kooti's distrust of the redoubt's strengths. However, the prediction also anticipates David's successful pursuit of the Amalekites thereafter. The saying may, therefore, have been projected back onto events with the wisdom of hindsight; but this pattern of prediction is typical of Te Kooti, particularly in his later life. Each meeting-house he visited, especially those which were built for him, carried for him messages of warning, which he read in the carved

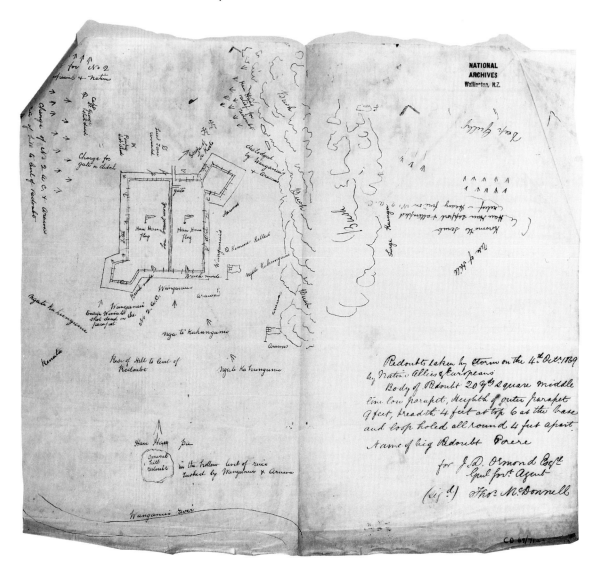

Te Porere, Te Kooti's redoubt. The route of Te Kooti's escape from the pa into the bush is marked. The only entrance to the pa was at this point, on the western side. The places where various of the government's fighters were killed or wounded are marked: 'Komene' was Ensign Komene of Te Arawa, who was shot there. Horonuku's small pa is also shown close to the Whanganui river. In two other versions of this drawing (one in McDonnell's press-copy letterbook and one in Whitmore's papers), this pa is clearly labelled 'Heu Heu's pa'. A complex of rifle trenches, it was taken at the same time as Te Porere by the Whanganui forces. Sketch by Thomas McDonnell.   AD1 69/7144, NA

work and pronounced to the people. If he did utter this remark at Te Porere, he was predicting a fearful doom for the besieged *before* battle, but also offering a later resolution.

The redoubt was built in the manner of a European fortification, and may have been taken from a standard military handbook of the time. The centre of the redoubt was about 20 yards square, and at two opposing corners there were flanking bastions, or angles, each just large enough to hold about 20 men. The walls were of sod and pumice earth, bound with layers of fern. The outer wall was nine foot high, and broader at the bottom than the top. It had loopholes for firing all around, placed about four feet apart, but their angle of declivity, as at Nga Tapa, was insufficiently sharp, so that men hidden close under the parapets were out of their reach. Nor did the flanking bastions adequately cover the outer walls. These faults suggest that lessons from Nga Tapa had not been learnt. It therefore raises the question as to who was in charge of the strategic planning: possibly men who had not been present at that siege. The pa also prepared for a style of fighting which Te Kooti had tried to avoid: the fixed battle. This suggests again that he was making his military decisions in conjunction with the local fighting chiefs, and here had been persuaded by his Tuwharetoa allies to attempt a direct defeat of the government forces from a fixed pa site. If so, he had not prepared well.

The weather was appalling in the last days of September, when the redoubt was being completed. It snowed hard, with driving winds and sleet continuing for several days.[20] The defences were probably never finished, for the outer ditch was incomplete in places. An inner wall, called a 'low breast work' in McDonnell's accompanying diagram, also seems pointless from a military point of view and was possibly unfinished.[21] However, it may have divided the pa into two political segments, Tuwharetoa and Te Kooti, each being marked by their own flags.

Between 2 and 4 October the government contingents, led by McDonnell, were brought up to Papakai, the nearby village, which Te Kooti himself had previously occupied but had abandoned. From there, the troops could see the redoubt, built on the edge of the bush and placed in a 'strong commanding position'.[22] 'On the third day', wrote Major Te Keepa Te Rangihiwinui, commander of the Whanganui contingent, 'we attacked', and thus, unconsciously, he recorded that the precise time of the scriptural prediction had been fulfilled.[23]

Thus began the battle at Te Porere, the second most serious of Te Kooti's military failures. Yet, as at Nga Tapa, he escaped, along with the core of his fighters. He was consequently also able to fulfil the second part of his prediction.

The conflict began on the morning of 4 October,[24] with a scouting thrust from the redoubt. The government forces went in with full force: 540 men. It was raining hard and Te Kooti's men were soon driven back to their redoubt. McDonnell wrote that the government's Ngati Kahungunu and Arawa forces had, in quite a short time, taken the trenches to the front and to the right of the redoubt, and from there, being protected by the parapets, could jump up and fire inside. They also stuffed the loopholes with lumps of pumice so that the defenders were unable to see except by exposing themselves over the parapets. Finally, the redoubt was taken by storm. Peita Kotuku said that, as St George led the charge on the redoubt (in which he died under Peita's fire), Te Kooti was inside in a rifle pit on the left flank of the redoubt (as drawn), surrounded by a 'bodyguard of women'.[25] The women were both shields for disguise and a fighting rearguard, as is evident from the heavy wounds that many of them sustained. Horonuku, who was also inside the redoubt, described how

> Te Kooti stopped in the Pa till just before it was taken when as he was putting his hand
> into his waist coat pocket for caps he was struck by a bullet which wounded his thumb

and second finger and cutting the third finger completely off and also passing through the fleshy part of his side.[26]

In great pain, Te Kooti fled the pa. In later years, these missing fingers would be noticed by those who attempted to sketch his likeness. This was the third wound Te Kooti had received; he told his followers that when he had received five he would then be 'invulnerable'![27]

Horonuku said that among Te Kooti's supporters with him at this time were 40 or 50 of the whakarau, Te Waru, a group of Tuhoe, and a number of the Tuhoe chiefs: Paerau, Hapurona, Te Makarini Tamarau, Rakuraku and Kereru Te Pukenui of Ruatoki. Although most of Te Waru's people and most of the Tuhoe had stayed to defend Waikaremoana, it is notable that both he and those Tuhoe chiefs had returned to Taupo.

Not all of them were present at the fight, however. Rakuraku was one who, together with Wiremu Kingi Te Paia and the east Taupo chief Tahau, after the loss at Te Ponanga had taken shelter at Retaruke, a pa in the upper Whanganui. Tahau, who had been a critical figure in Te Kooti's bid to make Taupo his home, is particularly conspicuous in his absence. It is clear that he had quarrelled with Te Kooti over the deaths at Taupo in June. When they returned to the lake in September, and Tahau was sent to occupy Tokaanu and Waihi, he deliberately held his men back from fighting against a party from his own tribe led by Hohepa Tamamutu. Poihipi Tukairangi narrated that when Te Kooti came to Tokaanu, and heard what had happened, he seized Tahau by the throat and said:

> 'I did not spare my own people from you. You killed women and children, and you try to protect your people.' Tahau answered 'It was not by my arrangement that we killed the people at Turanga. Nevertheless I will follow you and we will keep together — our cause is one.'[28]

Tuwharetoa oral tradition tells that the two went so far as to fight hand to hand at Waihi. Behind the kainga there, there is a great waterfall where they wrestled, but, their mana being equal, the fight was a stalemate. Te Kooti then left. This oral story clearly parallels that which tells of Te Kooti's contest with Te Ra Karepe at Paraharaha and, similarly, it asserts the independent mana of the local tribe.[29] This quarrel was not yet irrevocable, as Poihipi's account indicates, and Tahau would remain associated with Te Kooti and his men for some time to come. When the news of the defeat at Te Porere was brought to them, all at Retaruke fled together towards Taumarunui and the King Country.[30]

Nearly all the chiefs who were with Te Kooti at Te Porere also managed to escape. The pa had an excellent escape route into the dense bush lying immediately north and west where, as McDonnell's plan indicates, there had also been fighters hidden, who poured out 'galling' fire on his men. The site had been chosen for this reason — that is, its closeness to the bush, with its food supplies and shelter on an otherwise barren pumice plateau.[31] Indeed, Te Kooti's 'main camp' was a quarter of a mile from the redoubt in a bush clearing called Te Maro.[32] The redoubt was thus only one part of a larger strategy in which the overall safety of Te Kooti and his inner circle had been

Te Kooti.
Sketch made at
Te Teko. March 29th 1892.

Pencil and ink sketch of Te Kooti, 29 March 1892. It shows the missing fingers on his left hand. It also comments on his passion in later life for unusual hats, often described in newspaper accounts. He wears the greenstone earring shown in the photograph of his taonga (p.437). Drawing by Henry Hill at a hui at Te Teko.   COLLECTION OF MISSES D. & G. HILL, TAUPO, 82115 1/2, ATL

carefully considered. Nevertheless, he lost 37 people, including a younger brother or cousin, Mohi,[33] and more than 20 women and children were taken prisoner. Some of the women were severely wounded: they had been the last defenders of the pa. One of them was Te Waru's sister, Mere ('Mary'), who had been a wife of Te Kooti; she managed to escape again shortly afterwards.[34] Only one male prisoner, the chief Te Wiripo Tohiraukura from Moerangi, was taken and he was used immediately to open negotiations with Tuwharetoa's chief, Horonuku, who, sheltering in the bush, sent word on 5 October that he was prepared to surrender.

Te Kooti's losses at Taupo were severe. The government claimed to have found 52 bodies altogether, or about a sixth of Te Kooti's fighting force. Some of the women taken prisoner at Te Porere indicated the reluctance of Tuwharetoa to fight: Te Kooti had placed their women under a guard of his men, as hostages for Tuwharetoa's military commitment. On 7 October Horonuku came in and gave up his arms. The government ultimately accepted his statement that he had been a prisoner throughout, in part because it helped their cause by inhibiting any further support for Te Kooti at Taupo. They also recognised that it would be most injudicious to confiscate any land in the area. The government had come to realise, what it would never publicly admit, that the 'confiscation policy as a whole has been an expensive mistake'. To seek a 'cession' of some land instead was the more politic policy, and would bring far greater rewards, Donald McLean, the Native Minister, argued. He was both purposeful and blunt: this was the only policy which would 'not require a standing army to maintain possession' of the land.[35] The 'cession' that was finally won could be said to be Tongariro itself, transferred to the Crown by Horonuku in 1887.[36]

From the accounts of the prisoners, it seems that Te Kooti had been hoping to settle in the Taupo district. Near Papakai he had ploughed some land for potatoes, and he had a cart and horse team there. Nor had he destroyed crops or ploughs, unlike the Kawanatanga forces, as Hare Tauteka complained bitterly: 'Te Kooti did not act in this way for he thought these things would become his property' ('Kaore i penei a te Kooti i mahara hoki a ia mana ana mea katoa').[37] But 'Tauranga wahi o Taupo' (Tauranga belonging to Taupo) had proved to be an unobtainable goal. The ark would not rest there, and Te Kooti had to find friends where he could. From Te Porere he fled into the fastnesses of the forests at the uppermost headwaters of the Whanganui, to the east of the blockades being set by the Kingitanga.

When Te Porere fell, Te Kooti's flag flying in the redoubt came into the government's hands. It was captured by Lieutenant Wirihana Puna, in charge of a Whanganui contingent, and was given in 1870 to what is now the Museum of New Zealand. It bore the letters WI, which probably stood for the Holy Ghost, Wairua. The second flag which was flown at Te Porere was possibly Tuwharetoa's flag. The museum also holds a flag which was said to have been flown at Tokaanu when Te Kooti was there and to have been used by Tuwharetoa when fighting in company 'with Te Kooti'. It is a long, black, elegant, handmade flag with a white silk cross stitched onto its left-hand end (the head). This may have been the second flag flying at Te Porere, marking Tuwharetoa's area in the redoubt.[38]

Once again Te Kooti's people scattered and separated after defeat. McDonnell's Arawa

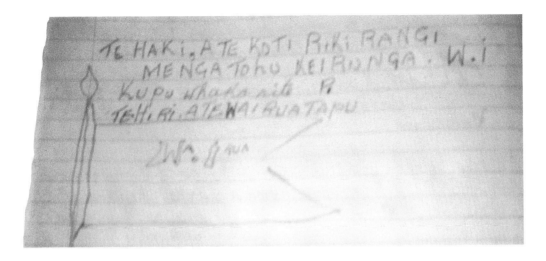

Drawing of Te Kooti's flag with the letters WI explained. Copied from a manuscript notebook held at Waikaremoana. The explanation reads: 'The flag of Te Kooti Rikirangi and the signs on it. W.I. Parallel saying Pi. The seal of the Holy Spirit. Wa. I rua'. Thus it suggests the sealing of the Holy Spirit upon Te Kooti. Pi is a reference in 'te reo ke' to a kupu whakaari. Its specific meaning is unknown. It could be a shortening of Eripi, that is the statement often reiterated by Te Kooti, 'I, Jehovah, am as a parent for you forever', but it was also used by itself, and different interpretations are given. Photographed by permission of Emma Lemuel Te Urupa, Raupunga, by Judith Binney, 1991.

and Whanganui troops pursued them to Moerangi and, finding this large settlement deserted, burnt it to the ground. In their sweep search for Te Kooti, one man captured was the young Petera Te Rangihiroa (Petera Tawhana) of Ngati Hineuru, who would later become one of Te Kooti's secretaries. Three Tuwharetoa men who surrendered told George Preece that Te Kooti himself was hiding out in a 'puni' (camp) in the bush, and the women and children had fled to the upper Whanganui river; yet others had gone through to Tuhua, where they knew they would be safe, for it was within the territory of Rewi Maniapoto, where no government troops could go.[39] The dilemma for Te Kooti remained: what reception would he now receive if he returned, defeated, into the Rohe Potae? For another net, this time cast by Rewi, was tightening around him.

On 9 November Rewi, together with Tamati Ngapora and other chiefs of the Kingitanga, met with Donald McLean. Rewi articulated what had been his policy all along: that should Te Kooti seek peaceful sanctuary within the Rohe Potae, 'I shall not molest him'. There were already, he said, 50 of Te Kooti's men living in sanctuary with him: 'do not you seek or attach blame to me for them (or have them tried for te Kooti's deeds)'. He had accompanied Te Kooti 'to get him out of my district'. If he were to enter it again and be 'troublesome I will give him to you', but he refused to agree to McLean's demands that he should surrender Te Kooti in any circumstances.[40] The Rohe Potae would be a sanctuary but on Rewi's own terms: the fighting had to end. He would take care of Te Kooti, but he would also keep him quiet: that was his resolve.[41]

Similarly, the upper Whanganui chiefs debated their own policies at a great hui held at Ohinemutu-o-Whanganui, the pa of the brothers Topia and Te Peehi Turoa, on 19–20

The Arawa fighting contingent at Kaiteriria pa, Rotokakahi (Green Lake), February 1870. Te Kooti's captured flag is displayed (rear). In the foreground, left, Captain Gilbert Mair stands beside three shovels, his right leg bent. Major William Mair reads a proclamation on the right. Both wear the kilts which were adopted for convenience in bush fighting. Photograph by D. L. Mundy.   20327 1/2, ATL

November. Among those assembled were men who had fought alongside Te Kooti, including Wiremu Pakau, a blind chief who had taken 12 men to join Te Kooti at Taupo, and also others who had gone to fight against him there. Topia himself had just returned from a visit to Tawhiao at Te Kuiti, and came bearing a letter from the King. He read it out to the chiefs: 'Te Kooti is to be cut off and his name is to be defiled'.[42] It was said that Te Kooti's attack on the Tauranga and Tokaanu settlements lay behind Tawhiao's decision to sanction 'Topia's following Te Kooti with the sword',[43] and this interpretation is supported by the date of Tawhiao's message to the Waikato, which reached Taupiri on 2 October. It stated that the one who would pursue Te Kooti had been chosen.[44] In deciding to try to capture Te Kooti, it was recognised that Tawhiao had broken the compact he had made with Te Whiti, the Taranaki prophet, that the sword should not again be unsheathed. The decision cannot have been taken with ease or pleasure.

Previous speakers at Ohinemutu had already made it clear that they were concerned that, if Te Kooti's people were allowed to come and live on the Whanganui, 'the window (matapihi)' of New Zealand (as it had been named by Tawhiao) would then be closed. War would ensue in their territory. For Te Peehi also there was a clear difference between the willingness of the people of upper Whanganui to shelter Titokowaru, the prophet and fighter of Taranaki, and their refusal now to give sanctuary to Te Kooti:

'the former was fighting for his land', he said. Topia announced here that he would start the search for Te Kooti. But, like Rewi, he set his own terms: 'I shall only take action against Te Kooti and his immediate followers — about thirty men.' And thus the policy was agreed upon: 'Let Kemp [Te Keepa] search from Taupo and I will search from this side, and let the roads be stopped.'[45] Further, as at least one of the government's Maori informants understood, Topia's aim was to seize Te Kooti if he could, but he would not hand him over to the government — for that indeed 'would be a "*Kohuru kino*"', an evil act of treachery.[46]

Nevertheless, the blockade was tightening. In the Tuhua district, immediately after the fall of Te Porere, Rewi had set a watching force of 300 on the road into the upper Waikato, while another smaller force of 80 guarded the route past Titiraupenga into the Patetere country. The upper Whanganui river, together with the Ohura river, which flows into it from Tuhua, were now barred. Te Kooti had no way out. He could not return by the north-west side of Taupo without encountering the government forces based at Tapuaeharuru.

Horonuku had reported that, when he left Te Kooti, the latter was hiding in the forest, his principal food being toi, the bush cabbage tree.[47] He was sheltered for a while by the major Tuwharetoa chief Nini (Matuahu), who had escaped with Te Kooti from Te Porere. Nini, unlike Horonuku, had refused to 'come in' to the government, despite overtures made to him, and he hid Te Kooti in the 'most inaccessible place' until his wounds healed.[48] Ngati Hikairo, the people of Te Rena, a village near the junction of the Whanganui and Whakapapa rivers, today say that Te Kooti took shelter with them at a nearby pa, Te Mako,[49] and this oral history supports the documentary evidence. For on 21 October McDonnell had learnt that Te Kooti was sheltering at Whakapapa, at the head of the Whanganui river, with the surviving core of the whakarau, and he set off immediately.[50] It was in this general area that his forces later stumbled across a bag of bullets, a whare containing old bandages and dressings, and some faded tracks leading towards the Tuhua district.[51]

By now Te Kooti's supply of ammunition was low. He had been resupplied upon his return to Taupo through purchases being made for him in the Coromandel and Thames by the Ngati Porou exiles living in the region.[52] Some ammunition had also been sent to him from the lower Whanganui, accompanied by a letter from the chief Te Oti Takarangi of Kaiwhaiki which asked Te Kooti to remember him when he 'came forth' ('i nga ra e puta ai koe').[53] Certainly, Te Kooti had had plenty of ammunition in the second attack on Tokaanu, and Ngati Porou had also brought him fresh supplies just before the fight at Te Porere. He must have been using the remaining Wharekauri money, which it was rumoured he still had with him in September.[54] He also had Napier bank notes and it was said he used them to buy ammunition from there.[55] According to Horonuku, all this ammunition had been distributed, as usual, just before the engagement. On the run again, Te Kooti had very little left.[56]

Yet from the wilderness he re-emerged. By late November he had got through to the Tuhua district and was living and moving in the fastnesses near that mountain. Petera, Hitiri's man, reported that when he left Te Kooti at Tuhua, on 28 November, Te Kooti had already gathered together a force of about 200 men.[57] They were living off the potato gardens made by local hunters in the bush clearings and they had also begun quite extensive planting themselves. Then, in early December, Te Kooti made a sudden raid down the Ohura river, seizing cattle belonging to Te Mamaku's people and threatening to attack them. However, this move did not drive allies to his side; rather, it served to ensure that Te Mamaku would give Topia his right of passage as he began the hunt for Te Kooti in December. The failure of intimidatory tactics was becoming a serious problem for Te Kooti. In a tribal society like Maori, threats will not necessarily gain supporters, particularly if the military power behind them is relatively limited. Only the 'ideology', the take (cause), can cut across the primary loyalties of kinship and tribe, and from the perspective of the Whanganui, the window of the island, the cause was unclear.

Petera and others said that Te Kooti's forces gathering near Tuhua included the Tuhoe chiefs and some of their men (about 100), and a few from Tuwharetoa. The core of whakarau, the 60, had also reassembled. It was at about this time that Te Kooti made contact with Titokowaru in Taranaki. Lucy Grey, kin to Titokowaru, described how Titokowaru counted up 30 men, and two of his senior fighting leaders, Toi Whakataka and Hauwhenua, had also volunteered to go. Titokowaru then warned them that if they went they should not return again. They must remain with Te Kooti: 'me noho atu ratou i a te Kooti'. Simultaneously, Tawhiao sent a message to tell them to stay away: 'it is for us to watch the actions of Te Kooti' ('tera nga mahi a te Kooti he matakitaki ma taua').[58] Consequently, although rumours flew about, the support for which Te Kooti waited did not come from Taranaki.[59]

But Petera commented that Te Kooti was also waiting at Tuhua for Hakaraia and his kinsman Kereopa Te Rau (the Pai Marire missionary to Opotiki and Turanga in 1865), as well as others from Patetere, to join him.[60] It was from that direction, to the north-east, that Te Kooti found the tear in the net woven around him.

The Tuhua chief Marino Te Hingohi wrote urgently in November to warn the chiefs of Taupo that Te Kooti talked of a return strike against them.[61] Other messengers reached Taupo shortly afterwards, bearing the same warning and the prophetic word that God had given Taupo to Te Kooti.[62] This was one useful stratagem, but there were others. Kereopa (and probably old Hakaraia), together with a small party, reached Te Kooti by 30 November. Kereopa brought with him some ammunition sent by the Ngati Porou exiles at Mataora, but his prime purpose was to persuade Te Kooti to come back with them and settle in the Patetere district at Tapapa, where he and Hakaraia lived. But Te Kooti seemed reluctant to make this decision. He was waiting for a sign. On 12 December it came.

Tawhiao's messenger, Aporo, reached him that day. The letter he bore told Te Kooti to sheathe the sword, and to come and live in peace at Tokangamutu. But Te Kooti 'contemptuously tore up the letter, threw it into the Wanganui River, and said to the messenger: "Return to Tawhiao and tell him I will not sheath the sword; that when I go again to Tokangamutu it will be to raise the sword, not to lay it aside."'[63] Kereopa was equally abrupt. He told Aporo that he did not recognise the King and that they would make their own laws.[64]

The challenge had been put down. Once again Te Kooti was on the move. Immedi-

The derelict meeting-house Te Kohera, at Te Kakaho, on the southern slopes of Titiraupenga, in which flags associated with Te Kooti were discovered in 1943. The tin trunk (arrowed left) contained a '30 ft Battle Flag'. This information accompanies the photograph. This flag is presumed to be the '30-foot' flag (it measures, in fact, 12.7 metres) deposited with the Auckland Museum by W. Hugh Ross in 1945 (Ethnology no. 28933), for Ross gave the information about the photograph to the Waikato Museum. Ross also deposited two other associated flags with the Auckland Museum in 1944. A fourth flag, also once stored in this house and linked by narrative with Te Kooti, was brought to the Museum of New Zealand in 1995. Photograph probably taken by Ross in 1943.   938, WAIKATO MUSEUM

ately after this confrontation both he and Kereopa left Tuhua and together journeyed north-east towards Maraeroa, in the Pureora forest near the foothills of Titiraupenga. On the same day, 12 December, the people of Maraeroa sent warning that the party was on the road, coming towards them with the object of going through to Titiraupenga and Patetere.[65] Possibly, Te Kooti's purpose was simply to test the way through to Patetere: would it be open? The party reached Maraeroa on 16 December, where they remained for several days in a situation of considerable tension. It was probably at this time that they stashed the four flags which were found, much later, in the meeting-house Te Kohera, near Titiraupenga. The flags were primarily red, white and khaki, and were emblazoned with many emblems, including white and red crescent moons, elongated crosses, four- and eight-pointed stars, and a variety of flower-like images (see Plates 4–5, 8).[66] A second message from Tawhiao reached Te Kooti there, and again he rejected the terms of peace and threatened to come to Te Kuiti in person.[67] And indeed Te Kooti turned back into the King Country, and got through to the upper Whanganui river, to the south-west of Taumarunui, in the latter part of December.

Topia Turoa. He became the paramount chief of the upper Whanganui after the death of Topine Te Mamaku. Topia and Te Keepa were paid £15,000 in 1870 for the Whanganui contingent against Te Kooti. They were paid at the rate of army field officers, and the men were paid as militia volunteers.　　90458 1/2, ATL

Tawhiao's messenger Aporo was now sent to Taumarunui in an urgent bid to avoid conflict between Topia's forces and Te Kooti. For Topia had set out from Ohinemutu-o-Whanganui on 13 December. He said repeatedly that he was acting in compliance with Tawhiao's wishes. But, as he journeyed up the river, the prospect of war within the Rohe Potae itself grew and this, above all, was what Aporo sought to avoid. He first tried to dissuade Topia from continuing. He met him on 24–25 December at Whakahoro, a pa at the river junction south of Te Mamaku's major settlement at Maraekowhai, and urged him to turn back. When that tactic failed, it seems that he chose to warn Te Kooti of Topia's imminent arrival. On both occasions he acted independently of the King and of Tamati Ngapora, who had given his support to Topia. A letter from Tamati, reiterating Tawhiao's word, reached Topia at Maraekowhai on 27 December. The fountain of life was in the right hand, Tamati wrote, while the fountain of blood had passed to the left: that is, the fighting had been brought to an end. 'Let there be no division' ('Kaua e wehewehea'), he said.[68] The letter was interpreted at Maraekowhai as entirely discrediting Aporo's stance that Topia's expedition should turn back. Then Te Mamaku, who had allowed Topia passage through to Maraekowhai, sent his own warning to Te Kooti of Topia's approach.

As Topia's forces soon observed, Te Kooti had dug extensive cultivations and rifle

Topine Te Mamaku, 17 May 1885.
Photograph by Alfred Burton.
BB 3701, MONZ

pits up the Whanganui river, north of Maraekowhai. These must have been made after the flight from Te Porere, for the pursuers found scattered stretchers and fresh graves as well as the little bush gardens.[69] Topia pushed on up the Whanganui river from Maraekowhai on 28 December with the understanding that Te Kooti was only about two days ahead. He was reluctantly accompanied by Te Mamaku and his men: so reluctantly, in fact, that Topia wanted to make them prisoners but he was restrained by Te Keepa. However, on the night of 31 December, as the river began to rise because of heavy rainfall, Te Mamaku and his party cleared out, leaving Topia surrounded by flood waters at Te Kakura. He remained trapped until 7 January; but the day before Te Kooti, alerted to the pursuit, had fled Taumarunui. Three days later Topia, Te Keepa and the combined force of 600 men finally reached the settlement, to find him gone.

Staff-sergeant Samuel Austin, who was with Topia's expedition, said that they were told by some women that Te Kooti had with him 90 fighting men, and about 200 women and children. He had also announced that he was going to the King, but after a short distance he had 'changed his rout[e] and took an other direction'.[70] This remark may well give the historical context for the oral story which Henare Tuwhangai narrated concerning Te Kooti's failure at Taumarunui. This story, in its structure, is very similar to that of Te Ra Karepe's earlier challenge, related in the previous chapter.

This time, however, it concerns the mana of Rewi Maniapoto and a challenge at Taumarunui. Te Kooti went to Taringamotu, a little settlement north of Taumarunui, where Henare's grandfather, Honuku, was then living. Between the meeting-house Te Puru-ki-Te-Tuhua at Taumarunui and the Tuwhenua pa near Taringamotu, Te Kooti raised up two posts. One he named Rewi, and the other he named for himself. He ordered his own men to fire at the post named for Rewi, and all 12 volleys missed. But the post he named for himself was smashed by the firing squad. The omens determined, he went back to Te Puru-ki-Te-Tuhua where everyone had gathered in challenge, with taiaha. Old Te Kuku, it is told, wanted to fight, taiaha against the gun, but Te Kooti turned away, and the party withdrew before the assembled wrath of Maniapoto.[71]

It is possible that this was the angry debate observed by two Maori scouts in the hills, sent from Taupo to watch Taumarunui. As they lay hidden on a ridge above Taumarunui they heard the speeches, and thus learnt that Te Kooti's intention was to travel west of the lake, on to Tapapa in the Patetere country.[72] Kereopa led Te Kooti and the whakarau by this route. On 10 January they arrived at Te Pou-a-Kani by the Waikato river, where Hitiri Te Paerata met them. Hitiri informed the Taupo chiefs that Te Kooti had 100 men with him, and about the same number of women and children.[73] With him still were the Tuhoe chiefs, Hapurona, Paerau, Te Makarini and Rakuraku, and also Nini of Tuwharetoa.[74] From there the party crossed into the Patetere district.

Te Kooti first appeared, unexpectedly, at Kuranui, a former Pai Marire centre where many from the district were gathered for a tangi. Those who were travelling with him on foot remained there to rest, while he rode straight on to the Okauia settlement, a few miles away, which he reached on 13 January.[75] According to a Ngati Haua prisoner, whom he had detained but who escaped that night, and also to several local Pirirakau informants, Te Kooti was accompanied by about 50 horsemen, all well armed, and was inquiring closely about the roads and passes and the disposition of the people.[76] From Okauia he circled back south to Tapapa. The party arrived there on 14 January and were welcomed by Hakaraia's small hapu (about 60 people). The leaders talked at length about the fighting 'and other evil talk', as Wiremu Kingi Te Paia put it.[77] But despite that account and the language of the messengers, who reported Te Kooti's intentions to the government in terms of war and challenge, it seems that, in reality, Te Kooti had come to Tapapa as a refugee.

All the evidence indicates that he was seeking a way to end the fighting while still retaining his freedom. Searancke recognised this change. He wrote to McLean privately from Hamilton on 17 and 18 January giving detailed information about Te Kooti at Okauia, thereby indicating that he had good sources. He also stated that Te Kooti was 'anxious to be allowed to live quietly if possible & would I think go gladly to any place when he could do so, but I presume this will not be allowed.'[78] He was probably correct on the first point and, unfortunately, also on the second.

As soon as Te Kooti reached Tapapa, he contacted the Matamata settler and runholder Josiah Firth, who had previously attempted to negotiate independently for the Kingitanga with the government (and had earned the name of a 'meddling fool' in St George's opinion[79]). On 16 January, Firth received a message from Te Kooti asking to meet him. Firth agreed and set the place: the monument for Wiremu Tamihana, the great

Plate 1. The redoubt built by the prisoners on Wharekauri in 1866. Major Edwards considered it 'weak, badly placed, and indefensible', while William Rolleston described it as 'practically useless for the purpose for which it was constructed'. Its walls were of sod; the buildings of ponga and flax (with the sensible exception of the square powder magazine built in the barracks courtyard). A marks the fort; B, the officers' quarters; C, the prisoners' quarters, although in fact they were not housed there but in a separate compound on Orea flat at the other end of Waitangi bay; D, the cook-house. This watercolour was sent by Captain Thomas in January 1867.   AD 31:15, NA

Plate 2. Painting on the rafter of a meeting-house built for Te Kooti at Te Houhi (near Galatea) by the Patuheuheu people, a hapu of Tuhoe. It shows the act of bayoneting, following Psalm 63, and this painting is understood to refer to the killings at Mohaka in 1869. Above is a figure in clerical garb and a full-face moko: perhaps a statement of the recovery of the control of religious teachings. Below is the sustenance of life for Tuhoe: snaring birds. The opening date of this house, Tama-ki-Hikurangi, is unknown; the house was moved in 1904, and re-opened at Waiohau in 1909, where it still stands. Photograph by Cliff Whiting, 1983.

Plate 3. Te Kooti's flag captured at Te Porere, October 1869. The flag is handmade, and the letters (made of pieces of cut fabric) are all handstitched onto the flag. The background was originally white. Its iconography has been much debated. The letters WI were used to mark the holy day (which, from the 1860s, was every tenth day in the Pai Marire calendar) in the King Country, and they probably stood for the Holy Spirit, Wairua Tapu. WI is also understood to refer to the Holy Spirit in the Ringatu faith. The large crescent moon was presumably a tohu (portent) of a new world; the red cross presumably the fighting cross of the Archangel Michael. These two elements, the moon and cross, reiterate the first two elements on Te Wepu, the captured flag of Ngati Kahungunu. It seems probable, therefore, that Te Kooti took these images and incorporated them into a flag of his own design. It is 1985 mm long and 830 mm wide, and is held by the Museum of New Zealand (ME 805).   B20507, MONZ

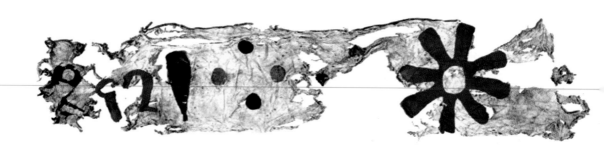

Plates 5a and b. The pair of flags deposited with the Auckland Museum by W. Hugh Ross in 1944 and associated at the time with Te Kooti's withdrawal from Taupo, after his defeat at Te Porere in 1869. The flag Plate 5a above is badly damaged; this portion is about 166 cm long. The iconography remains obscure. There is a large blue-green emblem, which might be a greenstone patu. The red number '2' stands beside an undecipherable emblem, alongside which there is another complex blue-green design. It could be a face with large eye circles. The eight-pointed red 'spoke-wheel' is suggestive of, though not the same as, the recurring 'spoke-wheel' design painted on some of the meeting-houses erected for Te Kooti after the wars.

E27291, AIM

HONORETIATOTATOUARANG

Plate 4. The huge triangular pennant from the meeting-house Te Kohera, first deposited with the Auckland Museum by W. Hugh Ross in 1945. It is 12.7 metres long; the white background material is of fine linen. The stitching is by machine. The staff end has white emblems on a white ground, including a crescent moon (or, possibly, a lunar rainbow). The division of the pennant — the first portion being entirely white, except for one eight-pointed red emblem, the second portion carrying red crosses and emblems on white — suggests a balance, or choice, for peace or war. The final portion contains the words (torn at the end), 'Whakahonoretia to tatou arang[a]' ('Honour to our leader').

The grouping of circles on this pennant is not dissimilar to Te Kooti's sketch of his dream, drawn in his diary (see photograph, p.532). There, eight circles (grouped in pairs) represented stars, and a diagonal cross was marked between the stars. It is possible, therefore, that the group of four circles on this flag depicts the southern cross constellation; the three circles, the three islands in unity.

E28933 (FORMERLY E27767), AIM

Plate 5b. The second flag of the pair deposited by Ross with the Auckland Museum in 1944. There are traces of a white band which was once attached below the central red section, but no evident traces of an upper band. The central red section is 235 cm long and 60 cm wide.

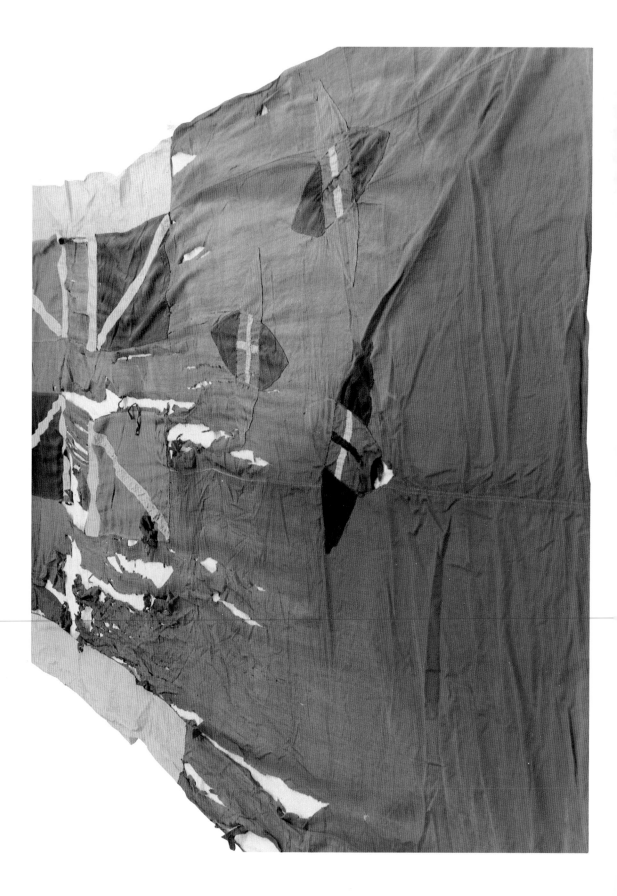

Plates 6 and 7. Flags from the Tapapa fighting: two almost identical flags held by the Whanganui Museum.

The first (and more battered) flag (above) was given to the museum in 1895 by Thomas McDonnell who identified it as Te Kooti's flag. The second has no provenance, but it too was labelled 'Te Kooti's battle flag'. In both, the Union Jack quarter is coloured green and dark brown (possibly originally black). The three four-pointed stars represent the three islands of New Zealand in unity and are made of the same colours as the Jack. This suggests that a deliberate statement was being made in rejection of red, white and blue — but not a rejection of a shared sovereignty. Both flags were about the same size: McDonnell's was stated as being over 16 feet long and nearly seven feet wide (it measures 4100 x 1840 mm), and as having a number of bullet holes in it.

At least one of these flags was flown in the fighting at Tapapa on 25 January 1870. Te Kooti's 'Battle Flag' — as described above — was reported (in 1933) as having been flown on several earlier occasions, including Matawhero in 1868 and Te Porere in 1869, though there seems to be no contemporary evidence. It is possible, however, that one of the flags was the second flag flown at Te Porere.

WHANGANUI MUSEUM

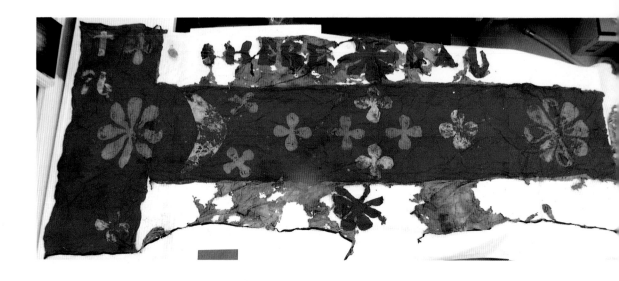

Plate 8. This flag was brought to the Museum of New Zealand in 1995. An accompanying letter (written in 1966) sets out its history. The flag was acquired about 1943 by the author of the letter; it was a gift from Turei Hohepa, the elderly guardian of the derelict meeting-house Te Kohera, at Te Kohatu. The flag is approximately 4 metres long and 1.7 metres wide.

The accompanying account states that, in 1943, '3 Hau Hau Flags' were known to be stored in a chest in Te Kohera. One (considered the best) vanished, taken to Auckland (with some carvings, which were returned); presumably flag 28933. It is possible that the flags were Kereopa's. However, by implication, the account connects this flag with Te Kooti, for it describes how, some time after the battle at Te Porere, Te Kooti visited Te Kohera, where the local people, a hapu of Tuwharetoa, agreed that there would be no fighting between them. It remembers that Te Kooti named a place in the district 'Ruamata', 'Bury the Lead', in confirmation of his intentions (and probably his actions).

This flag seems to have been a war flag and therefore was stashed. The words 'AHERE' and 'RAU', in red capital letters, are placed either side of the eight-petalled emblem in the upper portion. It is possible, therefore, that this was a signalling flag, raised for ambush and 'ensnarement': 'ahere' is used in this sense in the Maori bible. Elsdon Best related how Maori interpreted the alignments of the stars and moon to construct their fighting and ambush strategies, and the codes were possibly incorporated on war flags. This flag also has an undecipherable red emblem juxtaposed with what may be the number '6', suggesting a system. Three of the flags stored at Te Kohera show an eight-petalled flower, or sun, juxtaposed with a crescent moon to its right; the occluded side of the moon lies between them.

F3058, MONZ

'The meeting of Josiah Clifton Firth and Te Kooti'. This painting by Albin Martin was commissioned by Firth in 1873 and exhibited in 1876. Unfortunately, the landscape dominates the human presence. Firth, dismounted from his horse, stands talking with a group of three Maori men, one of whom is wearing a white feather — presumably Te Kooti. Te Huare also described Te Kooti at this time: he fought in different clothes on every occasion, no doubt for disguise, but in camp he chose usually to wear a red shirt, black trousers, and a kiwi mat (kahu-kiwi) upon his shoulders. Oil on canvas.   C17666, ATL

leader and mediator of the Waikato, with whose 'mantle of patience' Firth claimed he had been entrusted — and from whom he had leased land,[80] despite strong Kingitanga opposition. Firth's interests lay in peace in the Patetere district, where his runs lay. Firth described his meeting with Te Kooti, which took place on 17 January:

> About noon, some of my people observed a long line of dust on the road from Ohineroa. Immediately afterwards a messenger galloped up, and informed me that Te Kooti with forty attendants, would meet me, at 1 o'clock, at Thompson's [Tamihana's] monument at Turangamoana. . . . I arrived on the ground at 1 o'clock. As I approached the monument, a Maori advanced to meet me, raising his hat and saluting me as he approached. I dismounted on learning that Te Kooti stood before me. He was attended by two half-caste youths, fully armed; Te Kooti himself being unarmed. His height is about five feet nine inches; he is about thirty-five years of age, stoutly built, broad-shouldered and strong-limbed. . . . [His] jaw and chin convey the idea of a man of strong and resolute will. He has no tattoo; hair black and glossy; wears a black moustache and short black beard. His dress consisted of woollen cords, top boots, and a grey shirt; over the latter he wore a loose vest, with gold chain, and greenstone ornament. I noticed that he had lost the middle finger of the left hand.[81]

Firth told him that he came to listen, that he had no power to offer any terms: 'I am in the canoe, but I neither direct nor steer.'

> Te Kooti then replied: 'I have met you, the friend of William Thompson, the man who had a great regard for the people. I want to say to you that I will respect his last words spoken to you. I will not molest you or anything belonging to you, or to any of your people on this land. I wish also to say to you that I am weary of fighting, and desire to live quietly at Tapapa. If I am let alone I will never fight more, and will not hurt man, woman, or child.'

The two men continued to talk for some time, Te Kooti reiterating that he wished to live quietly with Hakaraia at Tapapa, but refusing to surrender to the government. Firth wrote:

> During this conversation his followers had formed in a half-circle at his back. They were all well armed — some with short Enfields, some with breech-loaders, and one or two double-barrelled fowling-pieces, all apparently in excellent order. A well-dressed woman, about twenty-five years old, of a handsome but melancholy cast of countenance, sat at Te Kooti's feet during the interview. I learnt afterwards that this woman was his wife.[82]

Firth had contacted Daniel Pollen, the agent for the general government in Auckland province, before he went to meet Te Kooti, and he then sent Pollen Te Kooti's offer to cease fighting if he was no longer pursued. Crossing with this telegram, however, was Pollen's reply that the government had no word for Te Kooti, except that if he surrendered he would be given safe conduct as a prisoner to Auckland. However, he promised that no military movement would occur until Firth had met with Te Kooti.[83] Te Kooti wrote to Pollen:

> Sir, I have seen your letter. My Word to you. I had already promised Hohaia [Josiah] to cease fighting. Afterwards your letter reached me and I have sent my word to you I will stop fighting, stop entirely. But as for me I will not go to Auckland, let me remain at peace (me noho ahau i runga o te pai). The killing shall cease, but if you follow me up let it be so.
> Sir, cease your punishing of me.
> This is all. From
> Te Kooti.[84]

Firth decided to go to Auckland to try to impress upon the government the possibility of a real chance of peace. Te Kooti wrote to him on both 18 and 19 January, reaffirming that he had agreed to cease the fighting. In the second letter, he asked Firth to persevere: 'I do not approve of war. Let me live in peace forever' ('Kaore au e pai ki te riri me noho au i runga i te rongo mau ake ake').[85] But the government was not interested: it was preparing for a large-scale confrontation. Te Kooti had long been judged as 'a midnight murderer of defenceless women and helpless infants'; 'repudiated and abhorred by the bulk of his own people'; and a man of 'atrocious cruelty and outrage'.[86] The Premier, William Fox, thought he had him trapped. He saw him as having only a small following and being 'evidently at his last gasp'.[87] Both J. D. Ormond, the general government's agent in Hawke's Bay, and Fox were irate that 'that meddlesome sweep Firth' should have been permitted by Pollen to promise that a period of military inaction would be allowed for the interview.[88] Fox ordered Pollen immediately to withdraw those orders and to cease from all interference with the military campaign, while Ormond simply instructed McDonnell to attack Te Kooti regardless of whether Firth was with him or not.

Te Kooti's final letter was sent to Firth and Pollen in Auckland urging that it was they who could 'make this peace' ('tenei houanga a rongo'). He asked Pollen to stop the government forces, who were on the hunt again, so that peace could be achieved.[89] But his words had no effect on the assembled majesty of the military men and the Premier. The chance to end the fighting was lost because the government wanted glory and a clear-cut victory. Nor would it waver in its righteousness, as it had simultaneously come close to a working alliance with the Kingitanga to block Te Kooti.

But Te Kooti was not without friends. The hidden agenda in the Taupo campaign had been the desire of men like Ormond, McDonnell and his brother, William, to open Lake Rotoaira, the Kaimanawa ranges and Ohinemuri to gold prospecting. Ormond had sent Samuel Locke in September 1869 to persuade the Taupo chiefs into an agreement to open the Kaimanawa lands, which he had succeeded in doing with McDonnell's help — in the midst of the military campaign.[90] Ormond's telegram to the Premier telling him of the victory at Te Porere had made the issue explicit: 'This engagement secures peace to Taupo, and opens Kaimanawa, which can now be tested.'[91] William McDonnell, who had already secretly lodged a claim for himself, had travelled with his brother and prospected along the way;[92] Thomas McDonnell, while complaining of inadequate rations, syphoned off army supplies to his brother's gold team,[93] who included some of the Whanganui Maori contingent. Gold-fever drove both the government and its agents; it also created alliances for Te Kooti from those trying to protect their lands.

Te Kooti had already made contact with old Te Hira Te Tuiri (Te Hira Wharewhenua) of Ngati Tamatera of Ohinemuri,[94] who had long resisted prospecting at the northern edge of the Kaimanawa ranges. Te Hira had supported Hakaraia in his invitation to Te Kooti to take sanctuary with them. Te Huare, who joined Te Kooti at Tapapa village, described how together they had ridden through to Te Hira at Ohinemuri, his settlement on the fast-flowing river at the base of the Coromandel peninsula. There the people welcomed them, unusually, by ringing a bell, a single solitary note; it was (or certainly became) the summons to gather, according to Te Kooti's teachings. Then 'Te Hira came and gave Te Kooti 7 kegs of powder and one bag of bullets about 2 feet long. It was just as much as one man could carry.'[95] For Te Huare this event was confirmation of Te Kooti's prescience, for he had predicted that they would be given powder there. For old Te Hira it was the sealing of an alliance with a man whose God had said 'that the Island may be theirs yet'.[96] He had already sent Te Kooti his word at Tokangamutu the previous July, when he compared him with the nest-cuckoo, Tawhiao: 'Go and do your work. You are a man of labour. There are two men in the Island: one is a man of labour, and the other of idleness', the squawking mouth in the nest.[97]

Te Kooti also found other sources of ammunition. Among the itinerant goldminers in the Hauraki district there were the 'Fenians', or Irish independence supporters, who were immediately suspected of giving or selling Te Kooti ammunition. It may well have been true. Horonuku had reported that a man named Michael O'Connor had been in touch with both Tawhiao and Te Kooti, and that he had brought some gun-caps for Te Kooti before the fight at Te Porere. O'Connor had said in his note to Te Kooti that his tribe was 'Aorihi' (Irish), thereby identifying Te Kooti's struggle with his own.[98] Te Huare also described to Gilbert Mair the occasion when Te Kooti predicted that he would be given 50 packets of caps, seven tins of powder, seven packages of ammunition and one revolver — at two in the afternoon. But they would have to journey a long way towards the Waikato to receive it. Forty of them rode to Peria (west of Matamata), where they found a European called Wira and another who Te Huare thought might have been called Hohaia (Josiah):

> Te Kooti placed his hand on his shoulder and one of the attendants drew a sword. Wira then came forward and threw down 50 to's of caps. 7 packets cartridges — 7 tins powder and a Revolver. Te Kooti then let them go. Hemi one of his troopers pulled out his watch, and it was just 2-o-clock.[99]

Te Huare's account focuses on Te Kooti's prescience. The government, however, would use it deliberately to discredit Josiah Firth, who, in the published version of Te Huare's narrative compiled by Gilbert Mair, became the threatened donor of the ammunition. Firth is described as unmanned, 'for his knees were shaking together through fear'. This text was undoubtedly manipulated for publication. Nevertheless, George Preece, who also saw Te Huare when he eventually surrendered, certainly gathered from him that Firth had given Te Kooti some caps and consequently joined in the tirade against Firth as a 'traitor to his own countrymen'.[100] But Firth himself adamantly denied that this later meeting had ever taken place, or that he had ever given ammunition to Te Kooti.[101]

Te Kooti had also developed networks of contact with the exiled Ngati Porou communities at Mataora and Harataunga (Kennedy Bay) on the Coromandel peninsula. He had, as we have seen, previously received assistance from them, with men travelling to join him under the leadership of Anaru Matete in February 1869. He had been in constant communication with them ever since,[102] and had received their ammunition at Tuhua and at Taupo. Another group from whom he would get support were the Pirirakau, a hapu of Waikato, who were settled in the ranges behind the Tauranga harbour. Unlike the main tribes of the Tauranga district, they had refused to surrender after the fighting in 1864 and did not recognise the legitimacy of the government's land confiscations there. The village of Kuranui was one of the places where they had settled and where Te Kooti would find shelter. Also living at Kuranui were more Ngati Porou exiles, whom Pirirakau had invited to take sanctuary with them; in fact, Kuranui had become a place of refuge for many people of different tribal origins from the mid-1860s.[103] Neither Waitaha nor Ngai Tapuika (the two Arawa hapu whom Hakaraia led), nor Pirirakau, nor even Ngati Raukawa of Patetere, had been acknowledged as having land rights in the negotiations with the government to establish tribal reserves within the confiscated block. In 1870 only Ngai Te Rangi had been recognised as the former landowners, with some consequent reserve rights.[104] Thus it was from these dispossessed tribes, and from the communities of exiles, that Te Kooti would draw his support.

Te Kooti also sought at the same time to come to an understanding with the region's tangata whenua, Ngati Haua. He visited young Tana Taingakawa, Wiremu Tamihana's son and now a leading figure within the Kingitanga, at Wairakau on the Waihou river. Tana wrote to the chiefs of Tauranga on 17 January:

> Hearken, Te Kooti has been to my place to bring his love to me and to Wiremu Tamihana. So I said to him, give Tauranga up to me.[105]

Te Kooti had pronounced that Waikato was the boundary that he now accepted: Tawhiao possessed one side, but his was to be Hauraki, Tauranga and Rotorua. Two Arawa hapu, Ngati Pikiao and Ngati Rangiwewehi, separating themselves from the government alliance, sang for Te Kooti their song of challenge: 'Who will eat those fish that parch the throat — rather let it be Rotorua', intimating their readiness to take the war into Rotorua on his behalf.[106] But Tana asked Te Kooti to leave him Tauranga (that is, not to bring the war there) and he understood that a compact was made between them. Thus Tana informed the governor, George Bowen, that he was not prepared to have the war imported into his land: 'Perhaps this command to fight is by you; if it is yours, I am not willing that my place and all these places should be trampled upon.'[107] Tana wrote urgently at the same time to the military commander of the Tauranga district, Colonel Moule:

> O friend, salutations to you, the man who is holding on to (keeping faith with) the last word of Governor Grey, William Thompson [Wiremu Tamihana], and Ihaia (Hohaia, Mr. Firth?) This is my peacemaking with you. Do not cover the peacemaking with a hat; it lies before us. . . . Leave the matter about Te Kooti to me.[108]

On the same day, 23 January, Te Hira wrote with equal urgency to McLean and with the same message: send the soldiers away from the boundaries of his land, Hauraki.[109]

But the dark clouds of war were gathering again. The government still clearly thought it had Te Kooti trapped. On 17 January, the date of Firth's meeting with Te Kooti, McLean held a meeting with Ngai Te Rangi to isolate Te Kooti and to persuade the tribe to support the government; simultaneously McDonnell and Te Keepa were ordered from Tapuaeharuru to join the attack. Part of Topia's Whanganui contingent also assembled with them, making a combined invading strength of 156 Arawa, 370 Whanganui and 96 Europeans gathered in Patetere by 20 January.[110] With these forces, McDonnell set up a base camp near Tapapa on 24 January.

The same day, Te Keepa set out from the camp in an attempt to move around to one side of the Tapapa village, on which a general attack was planned for the next morning. He found, however, that the kainga had already been evacuated: Te Kooti had moved out. Keepa seized and burnt an empty village. But later that day Topia's forces clashed with a picket from Te Kooti's party, close to the military camp, and in the early hours of the following morning the military camp itself was attacked. Te Kooti, returning from Ohinemuri with the ammunition given him by Te Hira, had seized the opportunity presented by a heavy fog to double back and strike at his pursuers. He was determined to surprise them. Te Kooti's party carried what appeared to be an English flag and, as McDonnell said, they 'were several times mistaken for friendlies'.[111] Te Huare, who fought there but fled afterwards, said he carried the flag. He also stated that Kereopa was one of the leaders of the attack,[112] commanding a group of his kinsmen, Ngati Rangiwewehi, the third Arawa hapu living in the Tauranga district.[113] One (or perhaps two) of Te Kooti's men fell, and the rest quickly withdrew. While this attack was taking place, Te Keepa reached Te Kooti's camp at Panetaonga, on the edge of the bush. He drove off its few defenders, captured 100 horses and shot another 20 or more, which were found tied up, cavalry style. These were presumably the horses of the raiding party, which had crept silently on foot in the fog to the soldiers' camp. Yet, despite this significant loss, Te Kooti's men all vanished into the countryside.

Now the hunt was on. McDonnell scoured the bush for the trail. On 29 January the combined forces moved north to Kuranui, and found there traces of Te Kooti's hiding-place: saddles and bridles hidden in potato pits, and fires still burning at a small kainga which had been hastily evacuated. A defensive rearguard also fired at them from the top of a nearby cliff that had just been searched.

Wiremu Kingi Te Paia's account confirms that Te Kooti had only just got away. Everyone had broken from the camp when they were surprised, and Te Kooti had been deserted. 'He only escaped by catching a horse' and riding off: the legend was being given new life. Five prisoners brought in from another village told them that Te Kooti and 200 men were in the bush above; among the five (who were quickly released by McDonnell) was Tana Taingakawa. The next day Te Keepa and Topia followed the trail to a rifle-pitted ridge, which had been well prepared for defence, and finally to a large encampment. It was big enough for 300, and had been occupied by a few the previous night. The trail led to a second encampment, and there the paths forked — south, and east towards Tauranga. The parties had separated.

At the same time, McDonnell was told that Tawhiao's secretary, Rewiti Te Atatu, with three friends, was at Kuranui when the troops arrived. Although Rewiti denied it,[114] there seems little doubt that he had brought a message for Te Kooti that all fighting must cease. Tana, Rewi, Tamati Ngapora and Tawhiao were all working hard at this time to contain the war. They sought to prevent any alliances being formed with Te Kooti east of the Waikato, which might draw the war into their borders or drive Te Kooti himself back into the Rohe Potae. Their messengers flew around the district — especially to Pirirakau and to Ngati Raukawa, whose sympathies were most likely to have been aroused. Aporo had been sent to Ngati Raukawa, on Tawhiao's orders, specifically 'to stop them joining Te Kooti',[115] while Tana, also on Tawhiao's instructions, was seeking Te Kooti in order to tell him to leave. Tana, as he told McLean graphically, wanted them all gone — the troops and Te Kooti — and gone now.[116]

Te Kooti evaded them all. On 2 February McDonnell came across what was undoubtedly the same encampment that Te Keepa and Topia had already discovered in the ranges near Kuranui. It was large enough for 300 to 400 and had been recently occupied by wounded men. McDonnell recovered a bag of blasting powder which the Whanganui contingent had missed, and a large 'Hauhau' flag wrapped in its cover. It was probably the one carried by Te Huare in the attack on the Tapapa camp on 25 January, or at least a similar flag. In one quarter there was a Union Jack, which had deceived the soldiers in the fog. Three four-pointed stars stood for the three islands in unity, and each bore a cross. This was a statement of a vision of shared sovereignty in Aotearoa: not an image of sedition.

Patu paraoa (whalebone patu), abandoned by Te Kooti in the flight from Tapapa. Purchased from the Reverend T. G. Hammond, it is in the present Museum of New Zealand (whalebone patu 377).
B 5172, MONZ

On 3 February there was a second close encounter. Major Fraser's newly arrived forces (236 men) were ambushed — by about 40 men — in the dense bush near Paengaroa. The attack was carefully planned and marked by the uncanny silence the attackers maintained throughout the skirmish. Fraser managed to extricate himself with the loss of three, but it was recognised that he had been completely outmanoeuvred. He soon discovered the reason for the attack: the main encampment of Te Kooti's people had been nearby. Fraser reported finding ammunition for Enfields and breech-loading rifles, and that upwards of 200 had been sleeping there 'in, about, and outside the whares in the fern'.[117] It was a sizeable camp, which had been recently expanded with long shelters, and had been in use for some days. Wiremu Kingi Te Paia said in a description of what must be the same encounter that 'again Te Kooti narrowly escaped. He was so closely pressed that he threw away everything but his shirt and trousers. We all bolted in the direction of Tauranga, and went into the bed of a gorge, so that our fires might be hid from view.'[118] On 5 February, their next encampment, near Oropi, was also discovered, 'so we had to run towards Rotorua'.[119]

This flight indicated a dramatic change of tactics. From the Kaimai ranges, Te Kooti suddenly appeared on 7 February at a garden behind the Ohinemutu settlement on Lake Rotorua. A party of Arawa women gathering potatoes there were surprised, and one was taken prisoner (probably in accordance with the codes of war in Deuteronomy 21

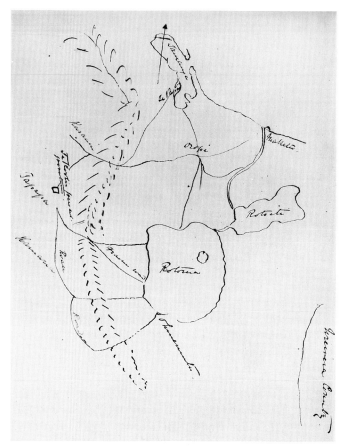

Sketch map drawn by the Arawa and annotated by H. T. Clarke, showing the various possible routes of escape open to Te Kooti from the western Bay of Plenty. 25 January 1870. MSS 32:217, ATL

regarding women who may be coveted). At the same time a part-Indian Canadian, Louis Baker, a naval deserter who had been living with Kereopa at Tapapa and had been closely associated with him, came in to Ohinemutu to tell the Arawa that Kereopa and Te Kooti were close by. The party was Te Kooti's entire force — 240 men and 100 women — and, he said, they were determined to get through to Ruatahuna.[120] It was the one path which Gilbert Mair had also just realised had been left open: the path back to the Urewera country.

Baker had apparently brought a letter to the Arawa chiefs signed by the Tuhoe leaders in flight with Te Kooti. In it they requested passage through Arawa's land — the right to enter into their mana whenua. Baker was seized and brought to Mair, who had just completed a forced march with the Arawa fighting contingent from Tapapa to Ohinemutu that morning. He said that he recognised the letter as being in Te Kooti's handwriting, although it carried the names of all the senior Tuhoe chiefs.[121] He immediately went in pursuit. In his official report he said:

> The enemy now lit large fires all along the edge of the bush, destroying the Arawa's houses and crops. About 1 o'clock I got up near the bush at the Paiaka settlement, and found that the Urewera had offered terms of peace to our people. Te Mamaku and Kepa Te Ahuru [a Tuhoe trooper with the Armed Constabulary] had been up to see Te

Kooti; the former returned with his younger brother Te Korowhiti, who had been taken prisoner by Te Kooti at Tauaroa in 1869. Petera Pukuatua, Paora Te Awahou, and some of the other [Arawa] chiefs believed in the sincerity of the proposals made by the Urewera, and were strongly opposed to an attack being made on Te Kooti's force. I saw at once that it was only a pretext to gain time by the enemy, and ordered the men to advance.[122]

In his diary he was even more explicit:

Petera, Paora, and others were making peace with the Uriwera on condition that Te Kooti was to go through unmolested. I dashed down the white flag and told the men to come on.[123]

The terms being negotiated were the right of passage. The senior chiefs of Arawa had accepted the request and were intending to invite Te Kooti into Ohinemutu. But Mair's intervention, as he knocked Petera over and tore down the flag he carried, brought instead a running fight. As Wiremu Kingi Te Paia said simply, 'We broke before the Arawa, and the chase commenced.'[124]

Mair wrote that Te Kooti had made good use of the delay created while the peace proposals were being discussed, and had already established a two miles' start. He also said that, as he himself ran into the bush after Te Kooti, he found a letter placed there, purporting to have been written by Kepa Te Ahuru and stating that he had gone freely with Te Kooti, but which he recognised to be in Te Kooti's hand. Unfortunately, it does not appear to have survived, although Mair enclosed it with his report.[125] This stratagem, if indeed it was that, did not ultimately discredit Kepa with the government. He would successfully play a double role in the following campaigns.[126]

Mair's chasing forces (120 men soon reduced to about 30 who were fleet of foot) caught up with the rear of Te Kooti's party and a heavy fight started, every inch of ground being contested. About a mile from where Mair had first seen Te Kooti's forces, the latter made a stand on the top of a small plateau. From there a party headed by Kereopa made a determined charge at their pursuers, and then retreated again, having bought time for the head of the party. Mair wrote:

We followed them up, but they travelled at such a rate that only a few of the fastest men were able to keep up with them, and, by making a short stand at every rise, they were enabled to keep their women in advance, and lead off the wounded. With my glass I plainly recognised Te Kooti and his wife both mounted in the advance . . . .[127]

They were being guided by Ihaia Te Mokomoko (Ihaia Te Waru) of Ngati Tahu of Waikato. His brother was one of the whakarau and Ihaia had long assisted Te Kooti with arms and information;[128] now, he took them through the broken land and deep swamps towards Lake Rotokakahi. Just after sunset, Mair came up close to the fighting rearguard, where he encountered an ambush led by Peka Makarini. Peka was carrying the bugle from Wharekauri, his little terrier dog (which he had captured at Mohaka) in a manuka basket, and the great flag, Te Wepu, on his back. Peka died here, protecting the rear of Te Kooti's party. He was left, 'a gibbeted thing', tied to a cabbage tree by the Arawa; later Ngati Pahauwera of Mohaka, in reprisal for the killings of 1869, took his

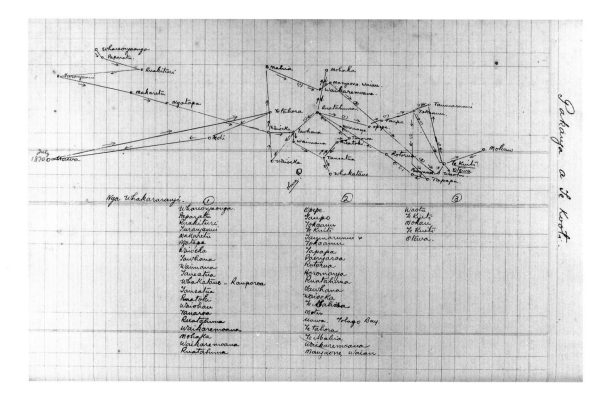

Te Kooti's battles. Page from a Ringatu manuscript book showing the 'pursuit across the land'. It lists the sequence of the fights and confrontations. It culminates in sequence 3 with the final flight to Te Kuiti in 1872 and then to Otewa, where Te Kooti moved after his pardon in 1883. Photographed by permission of Robert (Boy) Biddle.

bones and turned them into fish hooks and a flute.[129] Another who died in this fighting was Timoti Hakopa (Timoti Te Kaka), remembered as one of Te Kooti's designated executioners,[130] but who had also reached Te Kooti after the fall of Nga Tapa to bring him to the Waioeka. But Te Kooti never stopped. The party (about 200 people or fewer)[131] turned off the track suddenly, to the right, and plunged into the Tumunui bush as the darkness closed in. Pursuit was now impossible; the running fight of over eight miles had finished. But Te Kooti continued to travel through the night.

He came out to the shores of Lake Okaro to roast some potatoes, but was spotted there by a fresh scouting party sent out by Mair from Kaiteriria that evening. Warned by a dog, he was immediately on the move again, travelling at 'a tremendous pace'.[132] The trail now turned back into the dangerous thermal areas beside Lake Ngakoro, into Ngati Manawa's territory at Motumako, up the Horomanga gorge, and through to the Urewera. By nightfall of 8 February 1870, by a feat of extraordinary endurance, Te Kooti had reached Ahikereru and the shelter of Tuhoe.

CHAPTER 8

HE MANU TUTE AU KEI TE NGAHERE
(FEBRUARY–AUGUST 1870)

E kia tangi atu au ki te tane ka momutu ki tawhiti ka waiho i konei paheko ai hei ngaro.

I shall call out to the distant man: 'Remain here, joining us in being hidden.'

SONG OF TE KOOTI, C.1870.[1]

Immediately after Te Kooti's escape from Ohinemutu, Donald McLean as Native Minister announced a new policy. From 11 February 1870, Maori would control all the expeditions.[2] No European forces were to be engaged. The war in the Urewera and the East Coast, in its final phase, would be a Maori campaign, in both its manpower and its leadership. A large reward was set: £5000 for the capture of Te Kooti. There was to be no daily pay: just the prize offered — and the reminder that women and children should be saved. No word was said about the men, nor considered necessary.[3]

A three-pronged pincer movement was set in motion for the second time against Tuhoe: from Napier, from Turanganui, and from the eastern Bay of Plenty. Once again Tuhoe's land and crops were to be laid waste, and their chiefs driven to surrender. But Te Kooti himself was now continually on the move. He did not stop with Tuhoe. Rather, he crossed quickly through the Urewera and returned into the fastnesses of Te Wera, the vast and tangled country at the headwaters of the Koranga and Waioeka rivers.

It was in the darkness of this heavy forest that his followers first noticed that he carried with him the brightest light to guide their way. Ned Brown's narrative of Te Kooti's diamond begins:

> Te Kooti . . . used that diamond to go through a dense bush at Te Wera. And those that followed him saw it. It was in the form of a lamb: the diamond.[4]

This story of the diamond is a central portion of one of the seminal myth-histories about Te Kooti. It is first heard in the wars, its reverberations and ramifications continue into the years of peace, and it has generated new meanings for successive generations up to the present. It is told in many areas of the country, where different versions connect the narrative to the particular locality and to the particular people. The narrative has been published recently as a children's story in a version from the Mahia peninsula;[5] the present can treat the beliefs of the past as the dreams of childhood. From another region, Lena Te Kani Te Ua of Puha also remembered being told by her mother, Arihia, that, when Te Kooti rode on his white horse into Opotiki in the 1880s, he carried the diamond. It was 'as big as a duck's egg' and he wore it in a little flax kit tied at his neck. The kit now kept the light partially hidden, for otherwise people had to turn their faces away from the brightness of the stone.[6] In the version told by Ned Brown, the diamond was known not only for its blinding rays but also for its shape. It was fashioned in the form of 'Te Reme', the Lamb of God, and 'It lit the whole bush'.[7] This particular version establishes Te Kooti as Moses, and implicitly links him with Christ. He is *lux mundi*, the light of the world. As the children of Israel sacrificed the lamb in thanksgiving for their survival, the lamb is understood to be also the type of Christ: for he is the sacrificial 'Lamb of God, which taketh away the sin of the world'.[8] However Te Kooti was or has come to be seen, the bright diamond he carried is always the quintessential statement of Te Ao Marama, the Maori world of light and knowledge. Wherever he journeyed in the wars it will be seen too that he gave a portion of the diamond to place on the sacred mountains of the people for their protection.

From the fastnesses of Te Wera, and perhaps guided by the light, Te Kooti burst forth again. Having established several camps and stores of supplies in the headwaters of the Waioeka, he renewed his attack on the Maori communities of the eastern Bay of Plenty at the end of February. On 28 February he first attacked and burnt the mill belonging to the old Ngati Pahipoto chief, Te Rangitukehu (Tukehu) of Kokohinau, who had previously allowed his pa to be used as a government redoubt. Then, having given a warning of destruction, Te Kooti's raiding party swept up the Ruatoki valley, crossed over to the Waimana river, and travelled directly across to the Waiaua. From there, on 7 March the party, who were guided by Ngati Porou exiles over these tracks, struck again — at the pa at Omarumutu and the nearby settlement of Opape, two of the larger coastal dwelling-places of Whakatohea.

The purpose of the raid was to obtain both ammunition and men — the latter preferably as volunteers or, if not, then as prisoners. There was no other way now that Te Kooti could rebuild his fighting support. The need was urgent, for the government-orchestrated attack on Tuhoe had already begun. Ropata, setting out from Turanganui with the Ngati Porou contingent on 28 February, had entered their land, and on 13 March, Toreatai, the old pa at Maungapohatu, would fall before him. Whakatohea would have to provide the fighting force Te Kooti needed. Men who were taken back as prisoners 'became one of us soon after, and got arms', as Petera Te Rangihiroa explained.[9]

According to Wiremu Kingi Te Paia, Te Kooti had been in touch with Whakatohea the moment he reached Ruatahuna, and warned them of his coming. He added, 'There is not one of the Whakatohea, chiefs or otherwise, who has not been all for Te Kooti.' Pera, Whakatohea's messenger who had reached them at Ruatahuna, had said 'that the Whakatohea outside (*i.e.* the friendly Whakatohea) were prepared, waiting for Te Kooti.'[10] Later, the government forces found a letter from Te Ranapia Waihaku, a Whakatohea chief of Opape, inviting Te Kooti to make the raid. Te Ranapia himself would deny his involvement; the letter may have been written and left by Te Kooti to incriminate him.[11] It was certainly, however, with the understanding that he would gather in supporters that Te Kooti had launched his attack on the 'Whakatohea outside'. He himself led the raid on Opape. His men captured two kegs of powder and 30–40

Maraetahi pa. It is situated on the western bank of the Waioeka river, south of Oponae. This photograph looks across the river to the pa, which is marked by the rewa tree. Te Kooti's village spread from the pa down to the river. Photograph by Judith Binney, 1994.

stand of arms, but they deliberately touched no other property. Instead, they took the people — over 170 men, women and children.[12]

While some may have sympathised with Te Kooti, many were simply terrified. The women and children were taken as ransom so that their men would follow, and then also join Te Kooti's forces.[13] During this raid, Hetaraka Maihi, the son of the Arawa chief and early writer of Maori history, Wi Maihi Te Rangikaheke, was killed. His death created a formidable enemy for Te Kooti in his father and became another major factor in renewing Maori opposition to Te Kooti.

The raiding party withdrew quickly up the Waioeka river, taking their captives with them. They established themselves at the place Te Kooti had used as a refuge almost exactly a year before: Maraetahi, the pa and nearby village of Hira Te Popo. The two sites faced each other across the Waioeka river, immediately south of the junction of the Oponae stream. Te Kooti's village was built on the river flat at the foot of the old pa on the western bank. It consisted of 16 houses, with several others scattered a little higher up. When Te Kooti had departed from this village in 1869, he had given out that he would return, and he had left some people behind to plant the gardens. As Porter, who was with Ropata's expedition as military agent and adviser, commented, 'We found very large quantities of food planted here, some five acres of "taro," and many acres of maize, &c. It is the largest Native plantation I ever remember to have seen.'[14]

Te Kooti had also asked that a 'large house should be built for a *whare karakia*, or praying-house during his absence'.[15] He had said that God had told him that, after he had visited the King and Taupo, he would return there to rest.[16] At Maraetahi Ngati Ira had built a 'beautifully finished' house 84 feet long and 30 feet broad. It stood 'nine feet high at the eaves', and its beaten earth floor was covered with two long cross-plaited kiekie mats running the length of the building. At the centre of each mat, scriptural names had been worked in red wool, 'in letters six inches in depth'. In addition, there was a 'pretty little carved house' which had been built as Te Kooti's 'private abode'.[17] Altogether, there were 42 houses in and around this settlement, 'many of them large ones',[18] and it seems clear that Te Kooti had hoped that Maraetahi would be his sanctuary, should the pilgrimage to Taupo fail.

Soon after the kokiri and its prisoners reached the upper Waioeka river, the meeting-house was formally consecrated. Te Kooti told the people that here they might be safe from their pursuers, and he undoubtedly hoped this would be so. For it was now that he uttered his command of secrecy: 'Guard your Tongue' ('Tiakina tou Arero'). This very practical kupu from Te Tahora, Waioeka, is recorded in the second of his note-books to have survived.[19] At the same time he told the people to seek Jehovah, that they all might live. Maraetahi and Te Tahora (which was about a mile away upriver) were two of the hidden places in the upper Waioeka where he believed they might survive without discovery.

The war itself was now deep in Tuhoe lands. On 5 March, Te Keepa Te Rangihiwinui and a contingent of Whanganui and Ngai Tai fighters entered the Waimana valley. As they pushed up the river, they encroached upon the territory of Eru Tamaikoha, the leader of Tuhoe's resistance to the land confiscation. It was at Tamaikoha's settlement at Tauwharemanuka, high up the Tauranga river, that Te Keepa offered, after an exchange of warning shots, to negotiate peace. And thus a pact was sealed with Tamaikoha on about 10 March: that there would be neither surveys nor settlement on his remaining lands, but that he would cease to resist the government. Tamaikoha's neutrality had been won. Even more significantly, it becomes clear that the rongopai (peace) and its terms were to extend to the whole of Tuhoe.

For Te Keepa at once sent through a flag of truce to Tuhoe, who brought it to Ropata at Maungapohatu on 14 March, the day after the pa there, Toreatai, had fallen. Tamaikoha himself also came to Maungapohatu bearing a letter written by Te Keepa for Ropata, which set out the terms of their agreement. He too arrived just after the fall of Toreatai pa, and therefore left the letter for Ropata at a nearby pa, Tauaki, which had surrendered to Ropata on 13 March and had been abandoned. The terms were that Ropata's expedition should at once withdraw from the Urewera, and that all his Tuhoe prisoners should be released.[20] These terms infuriated Ropata, who saw it as a false peace and, more accurately, as one which rendered him powerless. However, he and Porter decided, although 'greatly against our wishes', that they must release the Tuhoe prisoners they had taken, and withdraw. Ropata made it clear to Tuhoe what *his* terms were: that they were not to shelter Te Kooti and that, if he had ever to return again, then they should fear him indeed.[21]

In sealing his pact with Tamaikoha, Te Keepa had given him a revolver and ammu-

Erueti Tamaikoha, senior Tuhoe
chief of the Tauranga river valley
in the eastern Bay of Plenty.

F73839 1/2, ATL

nition as the sign of his good faith: in a primarily oral society the gift, and its meaning,
seals the word. Tamaikoha, in his turn, had warned Te Keepa that Te Kooti was about
to attack the coastal settlements of Whakatohea. As a consequence, Te Keepa had immediately turned back to Opotiki, instead of continuing inland to Maungapohatu, as he
had originally intended. The day after he turned back, he learnt that Te Kooti had
already struck at Opape. The news had been delayed only because the Waimana river
was in flood for three days.[22]

Upon receiving the information of the rongopai, Ropata left Maungapohatu and
came down through the Waimana valley, looking for Tamaikoha. Although Porter's
diary is silent, in his retrospective account he indicates that at Tawhana, where the ope
stayed briefly, there was an 'angry passage of words between Ropata and Tama-i-koha,
almost leading to an open fight', but that Ropata, in the end, agreed to continue to
respect the peace.[23] He had brought with him as prisoners only the remnants of Ngati
Kohatu from upper Wairoa. Dispirited by the constant fighting, they had finally
separated from Te Kooti and had been sheltering at Maungapohatu — 49 people, of
whom half were children. Ropata intended to keep them as his personal captives, as they
were not covered by Tamaikoha's peace settlement.

Ropata reached Opotiki on 21 March, only to discover that the Whanganui contingents led by Te Keepa and Topia Turoa had left the previous night, pushing ahead of him up the Otara and Tutaetoko river valleys into the upper Waioeka river. They had gone in search of Whakatohea — Hira Te Popo and those with him who were still resisting the confiscation of their land. They were suspected, quite accurately, of giving support to Te Kooti. After reprovisioning his forces as quickly as possible, Ropata set out again late on 22 March. He went directly up the fast-flowing and boulder-strewn Waioeka river. At daylight on 25 March he unexpectedly encountered Te Kooti's guard as it came to relieve the sentries placed to watch the narrow gorge Te Karoro-a-Tamatea, downstream from Maraetahi pa. As he pushed them back up river to the pa, he still had no idea whatsoever that Te Kooti was there. The warning to guard the tongue had indeed been heeded. As Porter described it:

> On the 25th instant Ropata attacked Maraetahi under the impression that there were only Whakatoheas there. From the slight resistance offered, it was not guessed Te Kooti was present. After an hour's firing the pa was abandoned, the fugitives from it falling into the hands of Kemp [Te Keepa Te Rangihiwinui], who was marching down, after taking prisoners all the Whakatohea up river.[24]

Nineteen were said to have been killed in the attack on Maraetahi; Porter later admitted that they were all whakarau, 'who were summarily executed in the riverbed.'[25] Austin, who was with the Whanganui contingents which, on the previous day, had taken three other pa higher up the river, also reported the immediate execution (usually by tomahawk) of those former whakarau who had been identified during the fighting. One was a cousin of Te Kooti, Hakopa (Jacob); another was a Whanganui man who was said to have commanded the *Rifleman* because of his knowledge as a schooner captain.[26] Just over 300 people were taken prisoner: the vast majority were Whakatohea (218). They included all those whom Te Kooti had seized in his recent raid on the coast; there were more women than men, and many were children. The remaining 87 were Te Kooti's people: 23 men, 38 women and 26 children.[27] The high number of women and children among his people is also noticeable. The men were part of the fighting core of whakarau. It was Topia Turoa who now intervened, following the principles he had announced in accepting Tawhiao's mission, and prevented them from being summarily executed by Ropata.[28] Te Keepa similarly blocked the execution of some men whom his party had taken prisoner before their identity had been established and whom Ropata now wished to shoot.[29]

But Te Kooti himself and another 20 men (that is, 'rua tekau', a frequently used round number) had managed to escape. Porter learnt later that day, from a woman who had surrendered, that Te Kooti had indeed been present at Maraetahi. The firing from the picket guarding the entrance to the gorge immediately below the pa was heard and there were just 67 men in the pa at the time, she said, an extremely precise figure.[30] Her account is substantially borne out by that given later by Huhana Tamati, Te Kooti's wife, after her capture in July. Huhana said that the main body of people had not been at Maraetahi, but were in fact a little higher up the river at another pa, Raipawa, which was one of the pa that Te Keepa and Topia had taken.[31] At Maraetahi, everybody had immediately dispersed in different directions. According to Porter's informant, Te Kooti was abandoned and left alone in the pa. Porter wrote that, after the firing had nearly ceased,

> a man got up on the top of a whare and called out to us, 'Ko Wanganui tenei.' ['It is Whanganui.'] He then fired three times at us. I and Eru Rangiwaha ran up and fired two shots at close range at him, but little thought at that time it was Te Kooti himself.[32]

If this was indeed Te Kooti, for him to have escaped at this late stage of what was his greatest military disaster there must have been a very cogent escape plan. It is more likely, however, that the experienced tactician and survivor had got out earlier. Huhana suggested this in saying that she had run away with Te Kooti and all the others when they saw the government people approaching, but that they were fired upon by two men as they rested on a hill shortly afterwards. Everybody then fled, she said, leaving Te Kooti alone with only three men to protect him. Even so, he was certainly not unprepared.

Te Kooti, four of his wives, and the innermost group of about 20 men in fact got away. A uniform, said to be his, was found in the bush by his pursuers just after they had burnt Maraetahi pa: it had silver stripes on the trousers and silver braid on the vest,[33] and it may well have been the 'silver-mounted' uniform he had used to disguise his identity in the surprise attack on the troopers' camp at Opepe. Blank cheques were found in the pa itself; this, as Porter admitted at the time, was the first clue they got that Te Kooti had been at Maraetahi. Others who escaped from Maraetahi were the major local leaders: Hira Te Popo, and the Tuhoe chief, Rakuraku, who had been with Te Kooti for a year but whom Te Kooti had come increasingly to distrust, calling him the ngarara, or deceptive lizard.[34] Nevertheless, when Te Keepa had camped a night at Rakuraku's pa at the start of his expedition up the Waimana valley, the tracks of Te Kooti's raiding party to Opape (which would have been visible to Keepa in daylight) were kept hidden from him. Rakuraku's people (at least) had guarded their tongues.

The day before the sack of Maraetahi, 24 March, the principal pa taken by Te Keepa and Topia was Waipuna, about two miles up-river from Maraetahi. Many were sheltering there, including Hakopa, who was executed, and Kereopa and Hakaraia. Kereopa managed to escape, but old Hakaraia was shot trying to flee. The flag from Gate Pa, which he had brought all the way with him from Tapapa, was finally captured.[35] One man taken prisoner was Wiremu Kingi Te Paia. He soon afterwards dictated to Porter the long account of his experiences which has been quoted extensively in this book. Porter's own narrative of Te Kooti's life in the wilderness, which he first published in several newspapers in 1871, was composed from information he gained from the Maraetahi prisoners.[36] Porter's account of the attack on Matawhero in his serialised 1914 history of Te Kooti was also 'reluctantly related' to him by one of the whakarau captured at Maraetahi. Whoever this man was, Porter believed, despite his informant's denials, that he had actively participated in the deaths at Matawhero; by implication, the informant, having been squeezed dry, was then shot. For Porter wrote: 'he subsequently suffered the penalty for his misdeeds'.[37] It is possible, however, although extremely unlikely, that he was one of those who were sent for trial for rebellion.[38]

Now was the time, with so many captives at hand, for the government to set up a

Hori Puru. Te Ngawari meeting-
house, Mangatu. Rephotographed,
by permission of Tiwai Irwin, by
Gillian Chaplin.

second round of treason trials, partly to divert attention from the undeniable fact that Te Kooti himself had again escaped. The trials took place in Wellington in June and July 1870. In the dock were 34 prisoners who were Te Kooti's followers and had been taken by the Whanganui contingents in their sweep through the upper Waioeka settlements. Porter chose them as 'the worst of the male prisoners',[39] and several were former Wharekauri exiles. Among those who gave evidence for the Crown against them was Wiremu Kingi Te Paia, who took the opportunity to assert his inherited chiefly status in contrast with that of Te Kooti, thus helping to foster Pakeha stereotypes of Te Kooti as a dangerous upstart. Karanama Ngerengere, Te Kooti's priest and lay reader, was one of the men tried. Others of the whakarau included Hori Puru, who, when he finally returned home, became the first Ringatu tohunga at Mangatu, in inland Poverty Bay. Another was Aperahama Te Uetuku, who had been sent to Wharekauri with the first batch of prisoners, and who also would return to Mangatu and help to ensure the conversion of that community into one of the strongholds of the faith.[40]

Aperahama and Hori made a joint statement to Porter, starting from the landing of the whakarau at Whareongaonga and including accounts of the attacks on Matawhero and Oweta. But Porter did not use their joint statement in his published accounts, because the two men were trying to incriminate the Ngati Maru leaders Karepa and

Wiremu Kingi Te Paia as being hand in glove with Te Kooti from the moment of the return in 1868.[41] This was probably because Kingi was acting as witness against them. The fact of Karepa's and Kingi's active support for Te Kooti at Turanga remains unproven. They undoubtedly shared an ambiguity, as did many in Poverty Bay.

During these trials, witnesses stated that Te Kooti had repeatedly sworn that his purpose in fighting was 'to annihilate the *momokino*, "the bad breed"'. When pressed, it became clear even to the governor 'that the "bad breed" did not mean this man or that; it did not mean the *pakeha*, the foreigner ... but the Government people of both races.'[42] It was difficult, therefore, to argue that Te Kooti pressed a war against the whites. It was, however, faintly possible to claim that such a position, waging war against 'the bad breed', was seditious. Thirty of the 34 prisoners were indeed found guilty of levying war against the Queen. Most, in fact, had been pressured to plead guilty.[43] They were sentenced to death. But, as the judge had anticipated, the terms were commuted to imprisonment. Not one of them could be shown to have taken an active part in the attack on Poverty Bay, or any other 'atrocity' or 'murder', which was the only ground on which the governor was prepared to allow the death sentence to go forward. Those who were tried could be considered the lucky ones; most at least survived. While the colonial society could press for the confiscation of land, and turn a blind eye to river-bed shootings, it could not tolerate a public mass execution.[44]

The captives described to Porter their experiences in the upper Waioeka (the Tahora forest). They lived on wild honey and eels and ate them hunkered down, guns across their thighs, alert and listening for the slightest sound of a twig snapping.[45] Every two or three days they changed camp sites. They emphasised the strict disciplines which Te Kooti imposed, and the separateness he maintained for himself. He tested the courage of the men who were with him — as he had to in order that they might all survive. Paora Delamere once narrated the story of a man called Petera who was thus tested. Te Kooti placed him in charge of a separate kokiri, and then ambushed the men himself, firing upon them. Petera fled and hid in a tutu bush, but he was trembling so much with fear that the bush shook and gave his presence away. Petera was angry when he was told that the firing had been a test of his courage, but, as Delamere said, it was in this manner that Te Kooti retained the right to lead.[46] In a similar way, he sent out parties to search for supplies, or to locate other people, men and women; if the hunters failed to find food the blame was attributed to an offence they had given to God. The inspiration for decisions came to Te Kooti in dreams, which in the Maori cosmology were generally understood to be a means of communicating with the spirit world. Dreams, therefore, could convey warnings, or foreknowledge. For Te Kooti, dreams were the instructions of God, as were the signs from the heavens, thunder and the rainbow.

The captives' narratives to Porter conveyed the fear in which many of them lived. Porter confused this with his own prurient fascination with Te Kooti's exercise of '*le droit de seigneur*' on the women in the party:

> It is a practice with Te Kooti to have intercourse with his followers' wives by telling the men to send them to him, that his atua had said they should become *enciente* [sic]. Whatever men may think of this, they seldom dare refuse, or Te Kooti will, at some

future time, profess that his atua has revealed to him a traitor, and will request his death. He is never at a loss to find a pretext to dispose of anyone obnoxious to him.[47]

Porter had encountered the evidence of one such execution near Papuni, on Ropata's recent expedition into the Urewera. They had found the exposed body of Te Mano, a Urewera chief, together with that of his wife. Te Mano had joined Te Kooti from Maungapohatu, but Te Kooti came to distrust him. Porter was informed that Te Kooti had said that he had been warned against him by God: that he 'would cause his (Kooti's) death, and wanted to kill him'.[48] Earlier, William Mair had heard another version: that Te Mano had threatened to shoot some of the leading Tuhoe chiefs and that Te Kooti determined he should be put to death.[49] Te Mano escaped, but Te Kooti sent a kokiri to Maungapohatu to fetch him and his wife. They were executed by the sword, their bodies left ritually exposed in accordance with the commands of Psalm 63. Their deaths were not requited by either Tuhoe or Whakatohea (to whom Te Mano most closely belonged), suggesting that these executions were seen as having restored a balance. However, Porter commented in his diary when he discovered the bodies that one of his prisoners told them at camp that night of the 'fear in which he [Te Kooti] is held by them', because of such executions.[50]

Whether Te Mano had refused Te Kooti his wife is unknown. But Te Kooti's exercise of sexual power is made clear in other accounts. Maria Morris had been warned by her uncle Nepia Tokitahi, one of whakarau closest to Te Kooti, to refuse him. According to the prisoners, women captured by parties sent out on Te Kooti's directions were always brought directly to him. This command is found in the laws of Deuteronomy concerning war,[51] laws which Te Kooti had adopted in other ways. Religious authority may often be translated into sexual power: it is a characteristic of many prophetic movements. Te Kooti's waiata contain strong sexual metaphors of control, power and betrayal, which he used at times of crisis — as have other poets. In the context of the executions, Porter commented that those with Te Kooti now looked upon him as a god, who had to be obeyed.[52] Neither men nor women could deny him, lest they risk endangering the survival of everyone. They were linked to the wheel of their collective destiny. They had been instructed that it was obedience to his visionary commands which would determine their future; obedience was then the test of their faith. Obedience is the strength of all visionary movements, especially when under such remorseless pursuit as this one was. But the danger within such movements springs from the nature of the commands.

New identities were also bestowed on people who joined the group as converts. Each person was given a scriptural name, thus becoming incorporated in the new ways of seeing and interpreting. When they fought, they fought under Psalm 46, which they often recited before conflict: 'God is our refuge and strength'. To enter the group was to enter into a new society; the people became subject to new laws, a new theology and a new fellowship. In this the movement was very similar to several of the contemporary movements to resist colonialism which developed in central and east Africa, seeking to transcend tribalism by these codes of spiritual unity.[53] To explain their renewed flight into the 'Koraha', the Wilderness, Te Kooti composed a song of lamentation for his cause. Porter concluded his narrative in 1871 with this song:

E 'ha te putake
Te Kooti e whaiwhaitia nei?
Ana kei Waikato
Te putake e hu ae!

E toru tekau tonu
He waki nei te puihi;
Te kai-pupuri ra
I a Kenana e hu ae.

What is the reason
That Te Kooti is being pursued?
There at Waikato
Lies the reason.

There are just thirty
Walking in the bush;
The keeper
Will arise from Canaan.[54]

The song probably depicts Te Kooti's situation as he fled from Maraetahi. Certainly Porter, when he republished it in 1914 (with his translation), placed it in the context of Te Kooti's wanderings in 1870. Te Kooti was reduced, once again, to journeying with the 30 'walkers in the bush', the core of the whakarau. The blame for the continuing relentless pursuit Te Kooti placed on Tawhiao; it was Tawhiao who had committed Topia Turoa to the hunt. But if the song is of a shattered cause, as Porter described it, it still sings of rebirth in the land of Canaan.

Te Kooti fled into the Waioeka fastnesses. On 27 March one of his scouts, sent out to reconnoitre the camp of his pursuers, instead surrendered to them. He told Ropata that Te Kooti was sheltering in a potato clearing some distance from them, with only 20 men and a few women. The next day, as Ngati Porou set out in pursuit, they encountered a lone man to whom they called out, but he failed to respond, and vanished. Ngati Porou were unaccountably 'afraid of shooting him': 'Some of the men since say it was Te Kooti himself, because he had riding boots on.'[55] By now, the smallest event of war had the potential to become a part of the expanding legends of miraculous escapes.

There are several oral stories told of Te Kooti's escapes from death in these last phases of the fighting. Some clearly are based on episodes such as this. There are also stories narrated of deliberate attempts to kill him — some for the £5000 reward — all of which failed. John Ihe of Waiotahe told his version of the story of the man from Hamua, a Tuhoe hapu of Ruatoki, who attempted to ambush Te Kooti. This story is well known and undoubtedly rests on fact, as the different versions of it, which follow, underline. In John Ihe's account, the man, whom he did not name, told Te Kooti:

> 'I'm going to shoot you.' Not at that time. He said, 'When we get the war, I'm the man who [will] shoot you.' And Te Kooti said, 'That's all right.'
> They start off the war. And this fellow tried to catch up old Te Kooti, and he start to get past. But Te Kooti at the same time was telling his men this fellow [was] coming after him, trying to shoot him. 'That's all right; keep on, carry on.' This fellow got up

to Te Kooti and he said, 'That's it. I told you I'm going to shoot you!' And Te Kooti said, 'Yes, all right. But you shoot me — and if you don't kill me — there's something [going to] happen. But I'm not going to kill you.'

So this fellow got out this gun, shot it. And he [was] covered with smoke. When the smoke finish — he reckon the first time he's seen a gun like that smoking [after] only one shot — covered with smoke. He had a look: he's not there! He [Te Kooti]'s already gone about a couple of miles away! See! Then the old fellow [Te Kooti] turned round, and where he shot Te Kooti, the belt broke — cut the back. And old Te Kooti turned, and he said, 'That's good enough. I give you my belt, but after that you look out! There's going to be something wrong.' Well, he went down and picked up his [Te Kooti's] belt, and carried it. So he went.

That's a big family, so many people of that man, and every one of them when they are coming up 50 or 60, die by the gun. That's the thing he was telling them. That gun is going to turn back on your family. All nice people — but what happens, just going out shooting, got shot, getting through the fence, shot by the back. Always shot by the back.[56]

Taua McLean also told the story of the planned ambush of Te Kooti. It was his great-grandfather Whareteneti (Te Ahuru, of Ruatoki) who was the man from Hamua who attempted to kill Te Kooti. But the family was divided, for Whareteneti's son, Kepa Te Ahuru, was now fighting for Te Kooti. In this particular family account, it is narrated that Whareteneti had been caught by Te Kooti and was about to be killed:

> And Te Kooti said, 'Who's going to kill him?'
> 'His own son, eh?'
> Te Kooti said, 'No. Can't do that. Just let him go.' So they let him go. It was at Ruātoki. At Waikirikiri, the Hāmua people. They were going to kill Te Kooti. There is a curse on Hāmua for that.[57]

Boy Biddle told the same narrative as John Ihe but he named the man as Te Whetu of Hamua who ambushed Te Kooti, fired, and sliced Te Kooti's Sam Browne belt in two. As Te Whetu ran, Te Kooti called out his warning that the gun would be turned against his family. This curse, to which a series of accidental deaths by gunshot is attributed, was lifted only after a gathering was called at Ruatoki in 1950 to remove the words by prayer.[58]

Taua McLean narrated another apparently similar story, but this time about Te Kooti's escape from the siege at Te Karetu in 1868. Te Kooti was caught in the river bed at the Te Rere falls, where the steep banks are over eight feet high and where it seemed impossible that anyone could get out. He was being fired at by four or five men. Taua said:

> I can show you the place where they fired these shots at him; all they got was the belt! Eria [Raukura] was telling me this. He showed me the place. . . . When the smoke cleared up, he was galloping away on the other side, nearly half a mile away! And they went down to have a look — the belt was there, broken in half! With the bullet. Hard to believe, eh? He was on the white horse.[59]

The white horse, here named Pokai Whenua (Travel the Land), recurs in the war narratives and in the subsequent years of peace. In this story Te Kooti was trapped in the river, whose high banks no ordinary horse could have climbed. Only the white horse had the powers to bear him away.

John and Waipiro Ihe, in further stories from the wars, talked about the white horse — and also its dark shadow, the black horse of Te Kooti. The story is told first about how the people travelled through the bush; it then moves on to describe the waterfall through which they all escaped on the way from Tawhana to the uppermost reaches of the Waioeka:

> *John*: He had two horses: one black and one white one. The black one is the bad one. That's why they get two. . . . The black one, he only takes the saddle, and himself to get on that horse. Nothing else to get on that horse. Oh, very tapu that. Nobody allowed to get on that horse — the black one, no!
>
> *Question*: Why is the black horse 'bad'?
>
> *John*: It's very hard to explain; it's like tapu, church: when he comes out in this world, when Jesus gives him those things. But the black one is the one at the back — way at the back, when they go to war. You've got this special fellow to lead that horse. They sing out at the back, 'Keep him well away!' You've got to keep him away from the horse with the pack saddle, the food and all sorts. Got to keep him way at the back! No one can ride that black horse except Te Kooti. Never! If you rode that horse, then finish! For everybody. That horse is to keep the fellows getting shot at the back. If anybody shooting [at] you, that horse is at the back. If he goes at the front — oh boy — everybody get killed at the back!
>
> Of course he's got the white horse at the front. The white horse takes some of Te Kooti's stuff. The black horse, he never takes anything. The white horse he's got Te Kooti's walking stick and all his gears. Of course, they walk. He doesn't ride that horse. And looking at him, he's got no gun.
>
> *Waipiro*: But, in the war, when he gets wild, he pulls this walking stick out, it starts to look like a .22!
>
> *John*: It's a walking stick and it's a gun! He could pull this thing out and one shot, like that, and finish! . . . See, Te Kooti way at the front, and the black horse way at the back. Keeps it safe. All the soldiers are in the centre: warriors. Women at the back. And the black horse, way down at the back. They just walk, they walk with the soldiers, and the women. [Sometimes] he [Te Kooti] goes with the women, the old kuia, and the men. All mixed up. . . .
>
> Te Kooti was on the front, walking. And he keeps telling them to carry on. Because they'd be frightened when he got up to that big waterfall — oh, it's a high one — that's where the government's trying to jam them up, in there. When they get down there, they can't get to anywhere — they'll catch them there! So, when they start shooting, and Kooti just telling them to go. Kooti said, 'Just carry on.' One of them said, 'What about the waterfall?' He said, 'You carry on. Where the water's coming over.' When he got up to it, see, a big hole — oh, they can just walk through it, and this waterfall coming through. All 700 men just keep on going through it, Te Kooti standing there, watching. Everybody gets frightened — they don't know where to go, but he'd just point out to carry on. They stopped, and stand under the waterfall. You can't see nothing. All smoke, and you can't see nothing. They reckon he got the whole lot [out]. All gone through the waterfall and got out the other side![60]

The white and the black horse moved as a pair, both commanded by Te Kooti. They are two of the four horses of the Apocalypse. The red horse will appear in a later story; no one rides the 'pale' horse (the grey horse in the narratives), for that is death. He who sat on the black horse, however, 'had a pair of balances in his hand'.[61] Thus it is understood that the scales of measure and justice belong to the *sole* rider of the *black* horse. This long story therefore tells not only of the people's escape through Te Kooti's detailed knowledge of the land — one of his very great skills — nor only of his ability as a marksman, with his hidden walking-stick gun. It also makes clear that he holds the scales of measure in the final days of judgment.

These oral narratives record what the military men struggled with: Te Kooti's continual ability to elude them. Shortly after his escape from Maraetahi, F. E. Hamlin heard that Te Kooti was hidden at the head of the Waioeka in a great cave, the very cave which Kereopa had used when he fled in 1865 and to which he almost certainly took the refugees.

> This cave is said to be impregnable and of large size — so large that they have plantations at the bottom; the sides overhang, and they go down by a rope ladder. From the way the Natives describe it, it is like a basin upside down, with a smaller hole in the bottom which forms the entrance into it.[62]

The extraordinary realities generated the extraordinary stories. Hoani Te Paiaka, a chief from the upper Whanganui and Urewera, who had joined Te Kooti at Tuhua but who surrendered in April 1870, also described for Gilbert Mair the time after the flight from Maraetahi. They stayed first at Tahora and Te Pato, a short way up-river from Maraetahi, where there were small clearings in the bush and little potato gardens. Te Kooti told them then that if he was pursued he would go further up the Waioeka, to its very source. This is exactly what he did, but as he went into ever-wilder country, his spirit for the first time seemed to break. Hoani reported that Te Kooti

> is in a very desponding state, and says that his God has now forsaken him for the first time since he left Wharekauri. He has quite given up the idea of going to Waikato, as his influence over Waikato is quite gone, on account of his not having any men left. Hira te Popo . . . and eighteen or twenty of the Whakatohea are at Te Tahora. They have left Te Kooti . . . . They are mostly old men, and badly armed. Te Kooti, too, is almost without ammunition; he has plenty of powder, but no lead or caps.[63]

Hoani later expanded upon this account, describing the dissatisfaction emerging among Te Kooti's followers since the encounter at Tauranga on the lake in the previous September. He said, 'Kootis God left him at Tauranga (Taupo) and ever since nothing but reverses have followed them'.[64] The defeat at Maraetahi Hoani explained as being the consequence of Te Kooti's cursing his own people.

The particular issue was a quarrel which had arisen from the discovery of an act of adultery committed by Ruka, a nephew of Te Kooti. Adultery (puremu) in a war party violates the tapu of the group and immediately makes them vulnerable to death. Probably it had been the cause of Titokowaru's fall, when his fighting forces abandoned him in 1869, and it was outlawed in the circulated written codes of the Kingitanga fighters. Ruka had been killed by Hira Te Popo and others in the row which followed the discovery of his adultery. Then 'Te Kooti was heard praying that some evil might befall all his people for killing Ruka'.[65] Te Kooti's authority thus stood outside the old codes of tapu violation. While tapu warred with tapu and caused confusion among the ranks, the military consequence of the disaster at Maraetahi was that many groups abandoned him. Canaan became ever more distant as numbers dwindled.

One critical defection was a group of about 12 followers led by Nepia Tokitahi. They fled, in a separate party, into the Te Wera country and never rejoined Te Kooti. It seems clear that only a handful of the original whakarau survivors now remained with him. Hoani himself had been sent in mid-April from Te Pato to Ruatahuna with a letter from Te Kooti seeking, once again, the support of the Tuhoe. He asked them to '"build up the house", meaning for them to join him again'.[66] Hoani got through to Ruatahuna on 27 April, but the Tuhoe chiefs tore up the letter. The reply they sent was a refusal. They told Te Kooti to keep away, for if he came to Ruatahuna he would bring trouble upon them once again. The warning words of Ropata had indeed not been forgotten.

Immediately after the fall of Maraetahi, the intense pressure on both Tuhoe and Whakatohea was renewed in a bid to force those groups who might still give Te Kooti sanctuary to surrender. Among Whakatohea, the main objective was to persuade Hira Te Popo and those with him to come in. Hira was known as a chief of ability and integrity, who had played no part in Volkner's execution and for whom clemency could, therefore, be offered. The tactics were twofold. First, the relentless searches of his territory and, second, the offer of pardon and safety in exchange for his surrender, coupled with his assistance in the hunt for Te Kooti. These tactics worked partly because the fighting groups had fractured under the internal conflicts of religious codes.

On 17 June, 'Hira Te Popo and the greater portion of his hapu (Ngati-ira), viz., thirteen men, eleven women, and ten children, making a total of thirty-four, submitted' at Opotiki.[67] The numbers are so small; this is one of the pitiful truths revealed by the surrenders. At the heart of the 'resistance forces' were tiny hapu groups, who were usually no more than a few extended families. Against them were poised the organised Maori Kawanatanga forces, each of whom consisted of several hundred men. These men were fighting from a wide range of motives, extending far beyond the mercenary to the retention of their own lands. They too were autonomous, as we have seen. But the odds were incredibly out of proportion.

Hira told Ropata plainly:

> Ka hua hoki maua kei reira te ora mo te Iwi kaore ko te mate kei reira. . . . Ka mea ko te take i wehe ai matou kua mutu te whakaaro o te Kooti ki te whakahau ki nga tangata he mohio nona kua he ana ritenga kua omaoma noa hoki nga tangata i runga i a Tera mo te he o tona mahi. . . . Ka mea mai he matemate no nga tangata, he omaoma ka rua. Ko tona ki hoki ma tona Atua noa e whakamate te tangata. Katahi matou ka tatari kia whakamatea nga ope e tona Atua. Ehara kua teka ko matou anake e mate ana ko te Kawanatanga ko nga tangata i kiia ai e tera kia mate kihai i mate ara te Kawanatanga no reira matou ka mea, ka haere tatou ki waho noho tatou mo te mate haere mo te mate.

> When we joined (Te Kooti's rebellion) we believed at the time that the salvation of the people was in that direction, but instead of that we have found it to be the reverse. . . . The reason that led to our separation was this: Te Kooti had ceased to incite the Natives

Hira Te Popoki, chief of Ngati Ira
hapu of Whakatohea. The original
oil painting hangs in Irapuaia
house at Waioeka. Reproduced
by permission of Mac Kurei,
Waioeka.   CT 973, MONZ

in his cause; he discovered that his own schemes and devices had failed and broken
down, and that the Natives, his allies, were deserting him in all directions. . . . The chief
causes was [*sic*] the frequent deaths amongst his followers, and the frequent desertion
of the men. He (Te Kooti) had also stated, or led the people to believe, that his own
God had the power of destroying his enemies, and we waited to see whether his God
had the power of destroying the forces against him, but we found it to be all a false
statement, and that instead of the Government forces falling into his hands, it was, on
the other hand, we who suffered the loss, and then it was that we determined to separate
from him, for we reasoned thus: if we stay with him we shall die; and if we go, we
cannot fare worse: the risk is equal.[68]

He confirmed that, when he had parted from Te Kooti in early May, Te Kooti was
living at the headwaters of the Waioeka. There he was preparing a plantation, and there
a group of about 50 had re-formed around him: 'the *Morehu*', as they were now called,[69]
the Survivors and the Chosen Few. They had few guns and no powder or caps. (A cache
of 20 casks of powder and a bag of ready-cast bullets, which had been brought to Te
Kooti by Whakatohea and hidden in the bush at Maraetahi, had been revealed to Ropata
by one of his prisoners and taken away.[70]) They were living alone, said Hira, and without the support of Tuhoe.

Certainly, one by one the Tuhoe hapu were being pressured to surrender. In January, before Te Kooti's flight from Ohinemutu, Te Whenuanui had sent indication of his willingness to negotiate a peace. Now, the levers were being applied against all the Tuhoe chiefs to come in. And that was precisely what was meant: the chiefs and their hapu were expected to leave 'their mountain fastnesses' and come down to camp on a government reservation near Matata, or to live with nominated Kawanatanga chiefs of the Arawa or Ngati Awa tribes. Only those who surrendered voluntarily would be physically protected under the guarantee of the Kawanatanga chiefs.[71] At the same time, the third Urewera expedition was set in motion from early April: those who refused to surrender by 'coming in' could now expect no clemency whatsoever. This 'colonialist' strategy of domination is as contemporary as the American war in Vietnam, or the Maoist tactics of Sendero Luminoso in Peru. The ugly choice for Tuhoe was made more difficult by St John's unauthorised move, which violated the peace that Te Keepa had made with Tamaikoha.

The government had never sanctioned Te Keepa's treaty, even though Tuhoe (and Ropata) had abided by it. Nor had they informed Tamaikoha that they had not agreed to it.[72] But Tamaikoha had written to Te Keepa and Topia on 18 April, honouring its terms and informing them that, 'The Urewera will abide by their agreement.' Therefore, he said pointedly, 'If you invade me when Te Kooti is not here, there will be trouble.' He added that the Tuhoe had now all returned to their homes. He stated that only two hapu (whom he did not name) remained in association with Te Kooti — one of these was undoubtedly Ngati Huri (now known as Tamakaimoana) of Maungapohatu. He also warned finally of Te Kooti: 'Be watchful of that man.'[73]

On the same day Tamaikoha wrote to Ngati Awa and also to William Mair, and with the same message: the Urewera people 'have made a law' which they intended to keep. Te Kooti was not within their territory and, thus, any invasion of the Urewera was an unjustified act of war. To Mair he was particular: 'My friend, take care that you do not trespass within my district'.[74] Further, Tuhoe had posted notices of the peace on all the routes leading into the Urewera.[75] From Ahikereru in the heart of the Urewera, the Ngati Whare chiefs Hapurona Kohi and Hamiora Potakurua (who had been the Anglican head-teacher at the mission) also wrote to the Arawa to tell them that they were maintaining Te Keepa's peace and that they had no intention of being herded into forced encampments. Hapurona had fought for Te Kooti from Mohaka to Taupo; now he wrote:

> Kemp [Te Keepa] was a stranger (a man apart); his peace was good. Nothing satisfies you but taking us away bodily. . . . Friends, Te Kooti is not here, but at Waioeka still . . . Perhaps you have seen the proclamation of peace of Kemp's and Tuhoe's. It is stuck up at Te Taupaki (near Fort Galatea). Enough.[76]

All the evidence points to the fact that Tuhoe had determined, at least for the larger part, to maintain their neutrality and the agreed peace. But in the early hours of the morning of 25 April, St John attacked Tamaikoha 'and his mob', as he crudely put it, at Whakarae, by the Ohiwa harbour, where they were staying in order to bind the peace with Ngati Awa. Tamaikoha escaped the attack, but his old uncle Tipene was killed. It was, in Tuhoe eyes, treachery — 'a "Kohuru"', as the civil commissioner, Henry Clarke, rightly recognised.[77] St John lost his command in the Armed Constabulary, but great damage had been done. Hapurona was one of the several inland chiefs who grew afraid to negotiate, so distrustful had they become of the government. On 29 April, the Tuhoe wrote a collective letter to the Arawa stationed at Fort Galatea:

> Blood has been shed during the peace with Tamaikowha and now because of this go you back to the sea. Te Kooti is not here, but only me (the Urewera). I am at rest (lying down). Go your way. Enough.[78]

One by one, however, McLean managed to persuade Tuhoe that St John had violated a peace which he now intended to be kept — at least for those who came in willingly.

One of the first to come in, and one of the most critical, had been a small group of Ngati Whare fighters. Paraone Te Tuhi, who had gone with Te Kooti and had fought for him at Taupo and then parted from him in the flight from Ohinemutu, is remembered for the remark he made after he surrendered on 24 April: 'I am the rope, pull me and the horse will follow'.[79] St John's subsequent violation of the rongopai strained the rope, but gradually, as McLean hauled on it, others did follow. On 20 May all Ngati Whare finally surrendered, with 'old Hapurona dressed up to kill with a Dogskin mat on, feathers in his hair and taiaha in hand', leading them in. He stumbled over a tree stump as he entered the redoubt at Galatea and fell to the ground; those watching understandably exclaimed, '"He aitua he aitua" "an ill omen an ill omen"'.[80] But the surrender went smoothly, and Te Kooti had lost one of his primary bases of support in the Urewera.

Corporal Te Meihana of Ngati Manawa, who had acted as the mediator and negotiator with Hapurona and Ngati Whare, depicted accurately their situation just before they came in. He described how they had accepted Tamaikoha's peace but upon its violation had become too frightened to surrender, lest they in turn be killed. They had reiterated that Te Kooti was still in the Waioeka: 'The Urewera are all very badly disposed towards him. They have fixed a boundary for this man. They are all assembled waiting.'[81] Paraone Te Tuhi gave the same message: that Tuhoe lived in fear of the renewed war of destruction in their land, and that, for the most part, they had lost faith with Te Kooti because so many had died.

But the war in the Urewera had been reopened. A pincer movement from the East Coast and the Bay of Plenty was set in motion at exactly the same time as the overtures to surrender were being proffered. Tuhoe were being remorselessly squeezed. From 6 April two Arawa contingents, who, unlike the other Maori contingents, were led by European commanders, respectively George Preece and Gilbert Mair, maintained a regular skirmishing role. They operated out of Fort Galatea, on the Rangitaiki river, into the Urewera. It was to them that Ngati Whare and, later, the Patuheuheu hapu of the Horomanga gorge surrendered. At the end of April, two Ngati Kahungunu contingents from Mohaka and Wairoa set out to reoccupy Onepoto, on Lake Waikaremoana. The Wairoa arm of the expedition, accompanied by Hamlin, managed to get through on 6 May. Then, after temporarily quitting Onepoto, they returned and held that base from the middle of May. A little later Ropata launched the second Ngati Porou expedition into the Urewera, leaving from Turanga on 4 May. However, he turned back at Te Reinga, because of the appalling weather, on 16 May; he had correctly decided that to continue so late in the season was insane, and to renew before the spring 'a bad omen'.[82] However, he brought back with him more Ngati Kohatu prisoners, hauled in from Whenuakura and the sacred mountain, Whakapunaki. Ropata said pointedly: 'We have saved these prisoners, but it was the last time any one would be saved; on our future expedition, all would be killed.'[83]

It was the Wairoa expedition which placed the most direct pressure on Tuhoe. From Onepoto a series of attacks were mounted on the several pa on the northern side of the lake, in the mistaken assumption that Te Kooti was being sheltered there. On 7 June the Ngati Kahungunu forces (250 men) occupied Matuahu pa, which had been evacuated ahead of the attack, and then destroyed large quantities of potato stores and the gardens, newly made for next year's cultivation. A substantial quantity of toetoe and raupo collected for building fresh houses was burnt. Once again, the tactics were to wipe out the economic bases of Tuhoe's survival in this harsh land. Matuahu became the base for a series of sweeps to destroy all the plantations. On 15 June Hamlin, under a flag of truce, met with the chief Te Makarini Tamarau (Makarini Hona, Tamarau Waiari)[84] and began negotiations for the surrender of the Waikaremoana hapu. Makarini had been among those who fought at Mohaka and Taupo for Te Kooti. He expressed the Tuhoe fear of being made gaol-birds ('mokaikai') or, as Hapurona had said, of being deported to another island like Te Kooti himself. The other great dread, which Hapurona had also raised and which, he said, Te Kooti had warned them of when he was among them, was that their land would be taken away.[85] Indeed, Hamlin offered Makarini little except that 'it was not the wish of the Government to exterminate them'.[86] Perhaps the best indication of the plight of Tuhoe was Makarini's request that, next time they met, Hamlin could give them each a shirt, as it was so 'very cold'.[87] On 22 June Makarini surrendered.

Makarini and Hapurona, in turn, were used to persuade the leading Tuhoe chiefs of Ruatahuna to come in. On 11 July Hapurona, along with Hoani Te Paiaka and Hamiora Potakurua, arrived at Ruatahuna on a mission to bring in Paerau and Te Whenuanui. Rakuraku, who had himself recently surrendered, also joined these messengers. At a great hui held at Tatahoata, where all the people of Waikaremoana and Ruatahuna gathered, the Ruatahuna chiefs told the government emissaries, their close kinsmen, that Te Kooti was not with them. He was still, they said, in the upper Waioeka region. And they themselves were 'still firm in refusing him admittance to Ruatahuna.'[88] They also said that, although they were willing to surrender and to come out to the coast, they distrusted the government because of the treachery ('patipati') that it had used. Finally, on 16 July the Ruatahuna chiefs wrote collectively to the government. They said that they consented to the peace, and that they had nothing to add to it. But they would not come out. 'I will not go to you, because I am confused by the many words from you, the Government.'[89]

While this pressure was being brought to bear on Tuhoe, Te Kooti had remained for the entire time in the forest fastnesses of the upper Waioeka. The Morehu regathered there. Te Wera was the understood place of rendezvous, situated as it was midway

Map drawn by James Witty at Mohaka attempting to show Waikaremoana, and the military routes from Wairoa and Mohaka. Onepoto and Te Kiwi were the two main bases of the attacking forces. The map reveals the paucity of the geographical knowledge possessed by Europeans. Maungapohatu was a vague and mysterious place, always just off all maps! 21 April 1870.   ADı 70/2466, NA

between Ruatahuna, Waioeka and Nga Tapa. According to Paora Kunaku, who surrendered with Makarini, when he left Te Kooti in May Te Kooti had gathered about 50 men around him.[90] In July, when he made the plan for his raid on Uawa (Tolaga Bay), he had, according to Huhana, exactly 48 men with him, of whom 17 were too old to fight effectively.[91] No more had come to join him.

There had also been, as we have seen, some significant desertions. Nepia had gone because he believed too many had been sacrificed at Waioeka; most of those who had died there had been his kin. Nepia himself had gained the reputation among Maori of being a 'life-giving man' ('te kaiwhakaora tangata'), not a man of death.[92] He never rejoined Te Kooti and finally, in November, he surrendered to William Mair. The other major loss had been Te Waru, who had finally separated from Te Kooti during their flight from Ohinemutu. They had quarrelled fiercely at Taupo and, as Horonuku had already reported, all that Te Waru sought now was rest and an end to the killings. He took shelter with Tuhoe at Waikaremoana and Maungapohatu, and he, too, never rejoined Te Kooti. Finally, on 9 December, Te Waru surrendered to the government. Kereopa, who had separated from Te Kooti after the fighting on 25 March, had been expected to rejoin him at Te Wera, but failed to do so. He remained a refugee apart, alone and on the run.

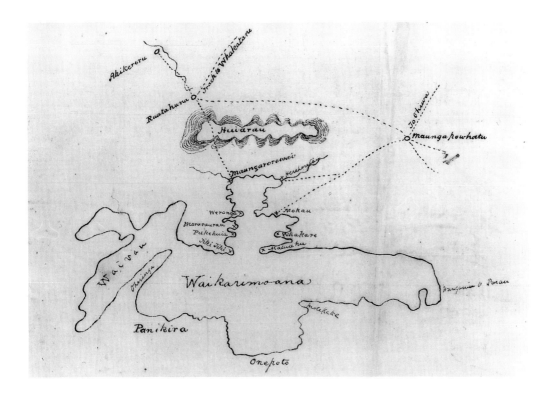

Map drawn by F. E. Hamlin of the Waikaremoana expedition, June 1870, showing the location of the main pa on the lake. Tikitiki and Matuahu (which is usually identified with Whakaari pa) surrendered to the Ngati Kahungunu expedition in June 1870. The location of Maungapohatu still remained vague.

AD1 70/2037, NA

Only three of the whakarau were definitely known to be with Te Kooti at the time of the July attack on Uawa. They were Paora Tu, Hirini Te Oiikau and Karanama Te Whare.[93] With him still, however, was his chief and friend, Anaru Matete. The majority of those still fighting for Te Kooti were Tuhoe; they had probably been with him for some time. Te Kooti had sent messengers to the Tuhoe asking for renewed collective support, but Huhana's account, given after her capture at Uawa, agrees with the statements of the Tuhoe chiefs that they had refused. The answer that Te Kooti received from Ruatahuna, she said, was that the Urewera would no longer join him. Thus Te Kooti had, yet again, to mount a kokiri to capture the men and ammunition he needed.[94]

Those who were with him at this time reported that he had indicated that his next attack might be upon Ngati Porou and that they would 'ultimately become his tribe'.[95] Te Kooti also told Kepa Te Ahuru, who had probably been taken as a prisoner at Ohinemutu but who had become so much a part of Te Kooti's group that he acted as 'second in command', that his objective was 'to capture a tribe that he wished to have with him'.[96] These were the tactics Te Kooti had used at Taupo and at Opape, relying in both places on some internal support. From Te Aitanga-a-Hauiti, the people of Uawa, he also expected to find hidden assistance; some of the whakarau came from there. That

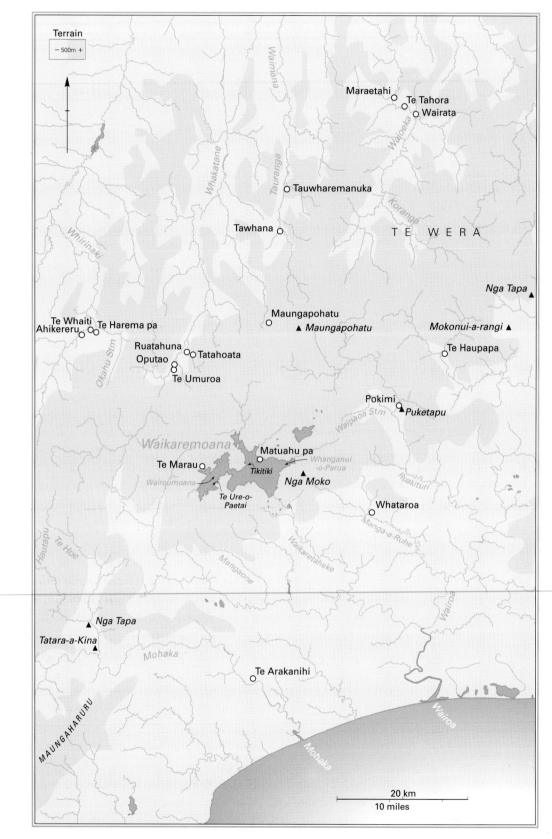

Map 5. The Hidden Sanctuaries

the people there were sympathetic towards him was known on the East Coast, for George Read had reported that the Tolaga Bay community would, if given its own choice, let Te Kooti into their pa.[97] Huhana's mother and brother lived at Mangakuku, and she was intended to be an intermediary with them.

As Huhana narrated the events, they left a party of 20 of the older men, and some of the women and children, at Te Wera, to make clearings and to plant in the bush. The kokiri which set out for Uawa consisted of only 28 men and five women. They included three wives of Te Kooti: Huhana herself, Oriwia and Honia (Nia) Te Whiu.[98] They went through country 'hitherto unknown to us', and it was only during the journey itself that Te Kooti informed them of their destination, so that none could escape and give warning to the place. He had told them, however, that the purpose was to get arms, people and clothing; no one, old or young, male or female, Maori or Pakeha, was to be killed. Those were instructions he had given Kepa Te Ahuru the day before they left Te Wera.

At one point on the journey they lost their way. They were forced to climb a high range from where, with Te Kooti's field glass, they could see the white cliff near Uawa. They set off again in that direction. On 25 July, Huhana and three others of the kokiri came to old Hone Pahoi's home, pretending to be Ngati Porou. Te Kooti soon joined them and told the old man he was none other than Major Ropata! After cooking and eating Pahoi's pig, the kokiri then set off for Mangakuku, taking their host with them as a prisoner. They split into two parties, one intended for Mangakuku and the other for Uawa. Early on 26 July, Huhana led one kokiri to Mangakuku, where she found her kin. She told them that Te Kooti had come to take them as prisoners, but that their lives would be spared. He also wanted their arms and ammunition. But her brother, Henare, decided that they could all escape to the pa at Uawa. Huhana said that she wished to escape with them, so Henare took her up on his horse. They raced away, but passing through a swamp she fell off and he left her behind.[99] One of the Tuhoe men found her and brought her back to Te Kooti. He threatened to shoot her for attempting to escape but, as he cocked his gun, one of them pushed it aside. Te Kooti kept her with them, tied up as a prisoner.

He had led the other kokiri. They surprised the family of Erimana Peka at their kainga at Mangahua, and took Ripeka, Erimana's wife, and his child as prisoners. But Te Kooti's attempt to force the pa at Uawa failed. It had been forewarned. The word, 'Huhana is here', had reached there and also her message, that 'Te Kooti had come to kill men and obtain powder'.[100] The message directly contradicted Te Kooti's instructions, but the pa was, as a consequence, well defended. Two local men were wounded in a skirmish outside the pa, but Te Kooti abandoned the assault. He had only about 20 men with him, and realised that the task was impossible once he no longer had the advantage of surprise. Paora, a local man who had been inside the pa, left it to survey the situation from a nearby hill. He first saw a part of the attacking kokiri on the ridge: seven men. Then he saw Te Kooti, who came up to him to greet him as kin. They pressed noses and Te Kooti said, '"welcome my father; come father to father, children to children."' He then said that he was alone, and told him, '"Go, salute your friends from me. I will not touch anything here."'[101]

Armed Constabulary hunting Te Kooti: two portraits from Tutamure house, Omarumutu. The house was opened in 1901. The officer wears a jaunty flower in his hat, and there is a red flower in a vase beside the constable. The two men face each other across the house, painted at the base of the first rafters at the front. A shadowy, bearded face, part painted-out, is to the left of the officer. Photographs by Roger Neich. Reproduced by permission of Te Riaki Amoamo, Opotiki.   F353, F354, MONZ

The attack had been a failure, because the killing days were over. Too many kin had died in these struggles. Nepia's flight had probably left its mark on all.

Te Kooti ordered the party to retire back inland, said Huhana, 'as we had failed to obtain what we came for'.[102] They retreated up the track by which they had come. In the early hours of the morning of 31 July, their camp at Waihapu (about 20 miles inland of Uawa) was attacked by the pursuing forces of 100 men, volunteers and Armed Constabulary hastily gathered together by Porter and William Richardson from Poverty Bay. Huhana said that the Tuhoe had gone on shortly before, and that she, Oriwia, Nia and Te Kooti and about seven men had remained behind. The men were cutting up pigs for food; Te Kooti and the three women were in a whare when some shots caught them

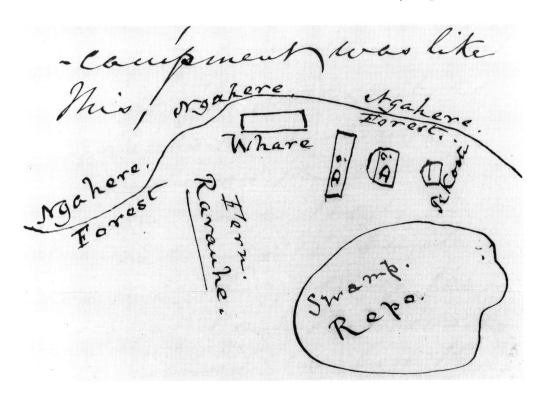

Te Kooti's camp from which he escaped after the flight from Uawa. This drawing was transcribed from the original report of Ruka Te Aratapu, who led a Ngati Porou expedition in search of Te Kooti. It depicts three whare on the edge of the forest, and Te Kooti's separate house. The swamp on the right was the path of Te Kooti's escape. 30 August 1870.   AD1 70/3334, NA

by surprise. The 'two or three shots'[103] were, as it turned out, fired without orders and before the camp had been fully surrounded: they were warning shots fired by one of the Uawa men. Te Kooti fled through a swamp into the bush; Huhana went towards the bush, but was caught. Porter said that he had seen a woman and three men fleeing on his left flank, one of whom had a carbine under his arm. It was Te Kooti, but Porter failed to recognise him — again. He acknowledged this, even in his retrospective account, saying that he thought the gestures the man was making were signals from one of the Uawa fighters. They were, in fact, gestures to Huhana as to how to get away. But she was seized by Porter.

The Morehu had had to abandon everything in their flight, including six Enfield rifles and Te Kooti's boots, shawl and blankets. The Tuhoe who had left the camp earlier had a total of only 14 rifles and three or four cartridges each. They too were seen by the government forces and fired upon, but also managed to flee, abandoning their food in their haste. Although the party was outnumbered and had so few guns or shots left, the entire kokiri got away. But Ripeka, their prisoner, fled from them. Huhana, who had only recently been untied by Oriwia, probably allowed herself to be captured.

The attack on Uawa was the last raid Te Kooti attempted to gather people to his cause. He may have believed that he would find substantial support there; he was undoubtedly thumbing his nose at Ropata. But the attack had not been a success. He fled back through the ranges of Mangatu. It is there, on the summit of the sacred mountain of Nga Ariki, Maungahaumi (Maungahaumia), that a portion of the diamond he had used to guide his way through the dark forests in all these journeys is now said to rest. It was given to them by Te Kooti as the mauri whenua to guard their land. But that, as they say, is another story.[104] In August 1870 Te Kooti was, once again, a restless bird flitting in the forest — 'he manu tute au kei te ngahere e whaiwhaitia nei' — and taking shelter within its vastness.

CHAPTER 9

THE SHELTER OF TUHOE
(AUGUST 1870–MAY 1872)

. . . Hoake rawa nei te rangi o te mahara. Kaore ka pau rawa te nuka.

. . . This day indeed will be remembered. The deception is certainly not
exhausted.

SONG OF TE KOOTI, 1872.[1]

Once again, Te Kooti faced the uncertainty of where to go, where to shelter. He had
still hoped, as late as March 1870, to get back to Taupo as 'his permanent place' ('tona
kainga tuturu').[2] The chief Hauraki, living at Huingaroa, had sent a new warning
through to Poihipi Tukairangi: 'Te Kooti is acknowledged at Taupo' ('heoi tenei tuturu a
te Koti ki Taupo').[3] Tahau and a group from Taupo and Patetere were said to be waiting
for him at Okauia, the pa where Te Kooti had first stayed when he reached the Bay of
Plenty in January. They had been separated from him in the flight from Tapapa, and
early in March Tahau had sent Ihaia Te Mokomoko to the Urewera with a message for
Te Kooti: he was to rejoin them in Taupo. He, Tahau, would appoint the day.[4] In May,
Te Kooti was reported as still hoping to link up with them.[5]

Despite this, Tahau's relationship with Te Kooti had been strained while they were at
Taupo, and he had become conspicuously inconspicuous there. Yet it is also clear that
Tahau had not defected.[6] He had sheltered with Wiremu Kingi Te Paia and others at
Retaruke pa, and Gilbert Mair tried to track him down as soon as he learnt that Tahau
was seeking to rejoin Te Kooti. Mair discovered that Tahau was trying to elicit renewed
support from Ngati Raukawa, but they had determined to stay 'quiet'. All Tahau could
say to them was: 'Your position is wrong. I, I will continue Te Kooti's work' ('E he ana
to koutou takoto. Ko ahau ka mahi tonu ahau i te mahi a Te Kooti').[7]

The only active encouragement came from old Te Hira, who sent Tahau some
powder and a red ensign for disguise, should he attempt to get through the military
lines to rejoin Te Kooti. Tahau and a party of 30 finally took refuge with Te Hira at
Ohinemuri in May. But by the middle of the year Tahau decided that he had had
enough of war. He began making inquiries about his chances of freedom, should he
surrender. Tahau's defection — albeit to a neutral position — damaged Te Kooti's cause
in the Maori world, for he had been one of the few high-born chiefs who had freely

Tahau and some of his followers. Portrait taken by Alfred Burton at Waipahihi-a-Tia, on the north-east
edge of Lake Taupo, probably in 1886.   BB 3741, MONZ

associated with Te Kooti, and at Taupo Te Kooti had few chiefly allies left. In November
1870, the missionary Thomas Grace encountered Tahau and a group of 60 hunting for
shellfish at the Katikati heads and he told Grace that he had left Te Kooti. He was now
'willing to come in', he said.[8] Grace added that he was astonished by the healthy appearance of this group, especially that of the women; he had become so accustomed to the
effects of war and malnutrition that he must have forgotten what well-fed people could
look like.

Without Tahau or Wirihana Te Koekoe, Te Kooti was now barred from Taupo. It was
also said that Te Kooti had come to hate the chief Horonuku Te Heuheu;[9] if this was
now true it was because this aristocratic leader had never aligned himself with him. Te
Kooti had failed to win over the senior men from the centre of the island, the powerful
leaders of the Kingitanga and the paramount chief of Tuwharetoa. Here again Te
Kooti's tactics of intimidation had not worked. He had miscalculated if he thought he
could frighten the aristocracy of the Maori world. His failure at Taupo had not been
so much a military defeat as a political failure: he had not gained the support that he
needed. His religious authority had not convinced these leaders; to them he was a man
of disturbance. Te Kooti's inability to attract the high-born chiefs to his cause,
'redeeming this Island for his people',[10] lay at the heart of his lack of success at Taupo.
Now, forced from the lands of Ngati Porou, who he predicted would 'ultimately
become his tribe'[11] (as indeed some would), he was alone again and on the run.

In this last phase of the wars Te Kooti becomes his most elusive — for a biographer as well as for the government. He would never gather any substantial fighting support again; but he also would never be betrayed. He flitted from sanctuary to sanctuary. He thus becomes a distant presence: watching, circling, tracking — and surviving. The oral stories recall some of his hidden places of shelter, together with his 'stepping stones' down the rivers, the virtually untrackable pathways through the land. This chapter is about survival, not about the recovery of authority or support. It is also about the extremes of duress to which he and many others were subjected. For the government's pressure on Tuhoe now significantly intensified. One by one the chiefs were being reined in. Rakuraku of Whakarae for a while tried to satisfy both sides. He told Te Keepa in early March that he had separated from Te Kooti and was willing now to make peace.[12] But he had, in fact, gone with Te Kooti's people to Maraetahi, from where he had escaped, and he had subsequently invited Te Kooti to shelter at Tawhana,[13] the place set apart by Tuhoe as their 'holy land'. But, as Te Kooti's diary indicates, he himself had grown to distrust Rakuraku, whom he saw as two-faced, like the taiaha.

By the beginning of July Rakuraku had decided to 'come in'. He then schemed with William Mair to persuade the inland Tuhoe chiefs to surrender, which was the condition for his own freedom.[14] The object was that there should be no sanctuary left in the Urewera for Te Kooti. It was hardly surprising that Te Kooti should send a messenger bearing cartridges to Ruatahuna, together with the words that they should be used to shoot Rakuraku.[15] Rakuraku's difficulties were compounded by the fact that his high-born wife, Hiria, had been seized by Te Arawa and was being held as a prisoner. The Tuhoe chiefs had, since May, refused to 'come out' from their lands until she was released,[16] and now they also said that they forbade any government troops to enter their territory by the road on which she had been betrayed. It was, as they sharply reminded Hapurona Kohi and the other chiefs sent as negotiators by the government, the road where the original peace had been sealed — that is, Te Keepa's route up the Waimana valley — on which she had been taken in violation of that agreement.[17]

On 27 July all the inland hapu of Tuhoe met at Ruatahuna with Hapurona and Rakuraku as the negotiators for the government. The Tuhoe were told that they must give up their arms, leave their lands, and come out to the coast: only then would their lives be spared.[18] In other words, the Urewera was to be denuded of its people, and they were to be brought to live for a while under the watching eyes of the coastal Maori tribes who had fought for the government. Tuhoe were assured that the government would take no more of their land by confiscation; but equally they learnt that the existing confiscation line would stand. The peace made by Tamaikoha and Te Keepa would be upheld. All the Tuhoe chiefs, including Tamaikoha, could surrender in safety, none — except Te Kooti and Kereopa — would be treated as criminals. Henry Clarke, the civil commissioner of the district, had written to Te Whenuanui, Paerau and Kereru: 'let your consideration of these words be clear. Do not hesitate about your land, which I ask you to forsake. "He kura kainga tena e hokia." (A proverb meaning that it is but leaving home to be again visited under more prosperous circumstances).'[19] These were the unpalatable terms which Hapurona and Rakuraku brought to Ruatahuna.

The Tuhoe were understandably divided in their responses. On 30 July Hapurona returned, bringing with him only the chief Te Haunui (one of the senior chiefs who had given Tawhana to Te Kooti in 1869) and a party of eight men and 12 women and children. They had deliberately left their mountains on the 'gentle side', the '*Taha Ngawari*' as they called it[20] — that is, Taupo — where they trusted they would not be killed because of Topia's principles. This was the only area where they were prepared to surrender; nowhere else did they feel safe. In a series of collective letters written in early August, the remaining Tuhoe chiefs reiterated to the government that Te Kooti was not with them: 'Te Kooti has been entirely forgotten by us in these days. Should you desire to follow after Te Kooti, go by outside (of our boundaries). Should Te Kooti come inside (our boundaries) we will advise you of it.'[21] They also wrote directly to Ngati Kahungunu, saying that they would not permit Te Kooti to enter their lands and that they had not set aside the peace made by Te Keepa; the death of Tipene, Tamaikoha's uncle, had been accepted as a 'peace offering for us both' ('hei maungarongo ma taua')[22] rather than needing a requital. (In March 1871, Tamaikoha would open a large meeting-house named Tipene at Tauwharemanuka for this 'rongo taketake', or binding peace.) The government's reply was brusque. Hamlin, together with the Ngati Kahungunu chiefs, informed the Tuhoe that they had no intention of listening to their demands: 'It remains for us to make choice of any road we like in pursuit of Te Kooti: if we think it right to travel through your district after Te Kooti we shall'.[23]

On 22 August the government sent Makarini back to Waikaremoana as the 'bearer of final terms of peace'.[24] With him went Te Paea Iho (Tiaho), sister of King Tawhiao, and her husband, Tiopira Hape. Both had been, and would continue to be, in contact with Te Kooti. Previously, in December 1868, when Karanama Te Whare (Karanama Moepuku) had been sent by Te Kooti to Taupo to find Wirihana Te Koekoe and Anaru Matete, the third person whom Te Kooti had asked him to contact for support at that time was Tiopira, who came from inland Wairoa. He had undoubtedly hoped then that Tiopira's sympathies for his kinsmen's plight, and the issue of their confiscated lands, might give him access to King Tawhiao. Te Paea herself was famous within the Maori world as a negotiator and mediator for peace.[25] She had earlier accompanied Makarini when he started his own negotiations with Hamlin in June. She had, however, found herself at the centre of a serious argument when she had been turned back in her canoe by a man from the Ngati Kahungunu forces, presumably because she was a woman and in disregard of her rank among the kahui ariki (the highest chiefs). This act had been considered a serious 'breach of Maori etiquette' and it had deeply offended Tuhoe, who had refused to continue to negotiate without her.[26] Te Paea returned with Makarini to reopen discussions on 27 June; now she was being sent back with him in one final effort to try to persuade the Tuhoe to leave their homes and come out to the coast. Her other task was to see Anaru Matete. He was believed to be sheltering at Ruatahuna with a group of about 20 of his original followers from Poverty Bay; Te Paea's purpose was to try to separate him from Te Kooti and to bring him in in peace. In this task she was pursuing the objectives of the pre-eminent Kingitanga leaders, who undoubtedly had sent her.

The Kingitanga chiefs were also attempting to reach Te Kooti, to persuade him to their policy of peace.[27] Their objective was to terminate the wars, and Tawhiao, Manu-hiri and Rewi were all working to this end. That Te Paea herself made direct contact with Te Kooti is evidenced by an exchange of letters between Te Kooti and two of the Ngati Kahungunu chiefs in November. On 10 November, Paora Te Apatu and the Reverend Tamihana Huata, senior chiefs of Wairoa, wrote to Te Kooti to tell him that the letter he had sent to Te Paea had reached them. They listed and commented upon three statements he had made to her: first, that a firm peace now existed between Te Paea and Ngati Kahungunu ('ko to kupu tenei he rongo tuturu tau ki a te Paea me Ngatikahungunu'); second, that even if he was still pursued by Maori, he would never turn back ('Tetahi o kupu ki te whai te Maori i a koe e kore koe e tahuri'); and finally that if his words were considered to be false, then they themselves could come to talk with him at Waikaremoana. The chiefs replied to him brusquely, saying that it was rather he who should come out to them — to live or to die. They told him the days of killing were over. Peace now prevailed at Ruatahuna and Waikaremoana.[28] Te Kooti answered in considerable anger. The letter challenges the duality of their commitments:

Noema 26 1/70

Ki a Tamihana Huata raua ko Paora te Apatu

E hoa ma, kua taemai ta korua reta whakaatu mo aku kupu e toru ki a te Paea. Ae, koia tena aku korero no te mea kei au ano te tikanga. Ehara ahau i te matuarua i te pena me korua.

    Heoi.

E hoa ma, kua kite ahau i ta korua reta kia haere atu ahau ki kona. E pai ana, ta te mea i tonoa mai ahau ki te motu kia whakakinoa kia tuahaetia kia whakamatea.

    Kihai ia nei ahau i hoatu e to tatou matua ki o koutou ringaringa, a, kihai koutou i hopu i whakamate i a au.

    Kaua ra e hipokina ki te kino ta koutou rongopai no te mea e mohiotia ana to koutou tinihanga ki te marama-tanga. E hara hoki i o tatou matua ake a koutou whakaaro engari he matua hou.

    Heoi.

E hoa ma, kua tae atu ahau ki kona, koia tena ko Rewi. Me aku kupu hoki, e kore tena kupu e mate ahakoa whai koe i a au, e kore au e tahuri atu.

    Heoi ano.

Mo ta korua kupu tuarua kua mutu nga ra patu tangata. Kahore, he nui te pakanga a o koutou matua hou kei muri ake nei, mo koutou mo matau hoki.

    Heoi ano.

Na to koutou hoariri

Na te Turuki.

November 26 1[8]70

To Tamihana Huata and Paora Te Apatu

Friends, your letter has arrived calling attention to my three statements to Te Paea. Yes, those were the things I said because I alone have the right. I am not one allied to many alike as you two are.

    That's all.

Friends, I have seen your letter [saying] that I should go there. That is all right because I was sent to the land to be mistreated, to be envied, and to be put to death.

[But] I was not given by our father [God] into your hands, and neither did you catch me nor put me to death.

Do not clothe your peace with evil because your deceit will come to light. Your thoughts are not from our own fathers, but from a new father.

That's all.

Friends, when I got there, Rewi was there. My words which will never die were — although you pursue me, I will not turn back.

That indeed is all.

As for your second statement that the days of killing people are over, no, the fighting of your new fathers will be great hereafter, for you and for us also.

That indeed is that.

From your enemy

From Te Turuki.[29]

He exults in his elusiveness; he challenges the chiefs' adoption of 'new fathers', that is, the government instead of God, which will be the path of more war, not less; and he insists that he is correct never to give up. It is a letter born of absolute commitment to his cause. If the reference to 'Rewi' is to Rewi Maniapoto, as seems likely, it also suggests that Te Kooti had again refused to take sanctuary with him, on Rewi's terms. This was the offer which, in the end, he would be driven to accept.

This exchange of letters suggests that Te Kooti understood that Te Paea had successfully negotiated an understanding with Ngati Kahungunu to cease their pursuit into the Urewera; certainly Ngati Kahungungu did not assemble an expedition in the spring of 1870, nor again thereafter. Te Kooti's letter was headed Waioeka, which, if correct, also supports Tuhoe's statements that he was not with them. Certainly, during October and November, this was the continuing thrust of the Tuhoe letters. Hoani Paiaka wrote from Ruatahuna to reaffirm that this was the 'decided word' of Tuhoe: 'That if Te Kooti comes to Ruatahuna that they will send him away and let us know — Lest he should climb over this holy barrier of peace that is now spread over the earth for man' ('Ki te tapoko mai a te Koti ki Ruatahuna ka peia atu ki waho ka whakaaturia ki a koutou. Kei pikitia mai te urungatapu tenei pai kua hora nei ki te whenua ki te tangata').[30] He explained that the only reason the remaining chiefs had not yet 'come out' ('kia puta ki waho') was a terrible sickness (probably influenza) which had spread among them that winter, causing many deaths. He thought perhaps 200 people had died, and a great many were ill and confined to their homes.[31]

The trickle of Tuhoe submissions continued throughout the last months of 1870. By the end of September all of Ngati Whare and Patuheuheu had surrendered, and there were 'now no people left at Ahikereru'[32] (this was not quite true, as we shall see). On 26 September, Te Whenuanui had come into Whakatane and soon after, in October, Paerau joined him. Te Whenuanui told McLean that he had fulfilled his laws and 'come under the wings of the bird of peace',[33] and he sealed the pact with a ritual exchange of gifts with William Mair. Te Whenuanui gave Mair two greenstone mere and two red garments (the colours of mana and tapu); Mair gave him a watch, a gold ring and a cloak, among other things. Te Whenuanui asked that he be given protection, lest he now be killed by Te Kooti. He and Paerau and all their people were sent to Napier in December, where they were to live temporarily under the control of Tareha Te Moananui. It was made clear that their return depended entirely on Te Kooti's capture and their assistance in this matter. The Urewera was being stripped piecemeal of its people by forced evacuation and by disease. But the land could never be as empty as the government wished.

On 16 October Tamaikoha had also formally met with Mair in the Waimana valley, and there confirmed his commitment to the peace that he had sworn with Te Keepa. He made his terms very clear: that Te Kooti could be pursued through his land, even to Maungapohatu, so long as he was informed beforehand and his kainga and plantations were respected. He himself would sustain the peace — unless his land was taken by force, or any of his pa surrounded in the night, or his people murdered by the government forces.[34]

During these months, Te Kooti's whereabouts remained a mystery to the government. It is almost certain that he did not, at this time, return to the Urewera, and that the Tuhoe were telling the truth. They were not sheltering him. But that some of them were in communication with him is also certain. As George Preece, commander of one of the two Arawa Flying Columns, observed, even if they did not actively resist, undoubtedly 'they will keep Te Kooti well informed'.[35]

Te Kooti had fled through the mountains of Mangatu back into the fastnesses of the upper Waioeka. It was thought that he might have gone to Te Wera, the area of sanctuary he had used after the flight from Maraetahi. But when, in January 1871, Ropata and Porter finally found his settlement there, on the uppermost reaches of the Waioeka (and only a few miles from the headwaters of the Motu), no one was there, and they concluded that it had not been occupied since the raid on Tolaga Bay.[36] It was a major kainga, with 27 comfortable whare, and there had been some recent burning of the forest to make plantations. The tracks of three men coming up the Waioeka from Maraetahi were also traced: it was they who had made the new clearings. They were three of a party of four men who had got lost after the dispersion from Tolaga Bay, and they too were searching for Te Kooti. Two days later, on 30 January 1871, Ropata discovered Rangiora, another pa where Te Kooti had sheltered after Maraetahi. It too was abandoned, but here he found two letters which had been left for Te Kooti. One was dated 15 May 1870 and had been written from Te Kakari, a community near Maungapohatu, by Maika Tuakana, one of the whakarau who was sheltering there, waiting for news.[37] It warned Te Kooti of the surrender of Paraone Te Tuhi and a section of Ngati Whare, who, it said, had gone over to the government. But the letter had not been collected.[38] It becomes clear that Te Kooti had not returned to his former sanctuaries within Te Wera district at all.

In January 1871, when Gilbert Mair got through to Ahikereru as part of the fourth expedition into the Urewera, which had been let loose that month, he discovered that a few of Ngati Whare were, in fact, still living there. They had been in contact with Ngati Kahungunu and had accepted a flag from them as a token of the peace which had been established between the two tribes — confirming Te Kooti's remarks about the success of Te Paea's negotiations. They told Mair that Te Kooti was at Te Wera, with about 20 men; and that he had written to Tuhoe 'saying that there would be one great cloud more arise, after which there would be peace. This is supposed to imply that he will shortly assume the offensive', Mair added in comment.[39]

Ngati Whare were wrong on both counts. In actuality, Te Kooti had taken sanctuary in the old areas he knew well between Papuni and Nga Tapa. One was Makihoi pa,[40] which had been a previous place of rendezvous. Another camp was at Te Haupapa (Te Houpapa), near Waimaha on the upper reaches of the Hangaroa river, which would be discovered in March 1871. This was land Te Kooti knew intimately: for it was his.[41] Te Haupapa lay beside the old inland track from Turanga to Maungapohatu; it was from there that, in January 1871, Te Kooti finally came through to Maungapohatu. There he found shelter with Ngati Huri, the people of the sacred mountain of Tuhoe. They were the hapu who had refused to come out to the coast the previous September and who, instead, 'ran away'![42]

The goal of the fourth Urewera expedition was the conquest of Ruatahuna and Maungapohatu. Once again, a pincer movement was planned: Ropata, accompanied by Porter, led the Ngati Porou contingent, which set out from Turanga on 14 January; Gilbert Mair started from Galatea with a smaller party from the Arawa Flying Column (45 men) one day later. Ropata's expedition found Te Wera and Rangiora, and he then decided to journey down the Waioeka river to Maraetahi. But it, too, was deserted. Ropata then crossed to the Waimana valley to confront Tamaikoha, while Porter went into Opotiki for supplies. On 9 February, Porter's returning party was challenged at the mouth of the gorge as they entered within Tamaikoha's sphere of power, his 'tino rangatiratanga'. They stripped to answer this challenge with their own tungarehu (war dance). However, it was only on Tamaikoha's terms that the combined Ngati Porou expedition of 200 men entered his lands: that he would escort them lest 'we accuse him of hiding Te Kooti'.[43] On 12 February they came to Tauwharemanuka, Tamaikoha's village on the Tauranga river. The Tuhoe chiefs, who had assembled there, would not help to search for Te Kooti, but they did promise their neutrality. However, from Maungapohatu Kereru had sent down his message of defiance to Tamaikoha and Ropata: that no 'booted feet' should pass the borders of Maungapohatu.[44]

Nevertheless, Ropata determined to press on. On 13 February, he came to Tawhana itself, still within the arc of Tamaikoha's chieftainship. Porter was struck by the appearance of the people: they seemed so fierce, even to an eye as habituated to Maori fighters as his. He wrote, 'they are true savages, and decorated with white feathers tied in their hair and forming a scalp lock similar to that of the North American Indians. Most of them were nude with the exception of a fancy worked mat round the waist.'[45] This image certainly implies that he was viewing them through mental stereotypes derived from the contemporary struggles of the Mohawk and the Cherokee, and setting them apart from the men he knew. In the speeches which followed, the Tuhoe told Ropata that they could not see the 'crimes' of Te Kooti, for it was the 'duty of every Maori to fight the foreigner, to with[h]old the island which was slipping into their hands'. Nor was the killing of women and children, for which Te Kooti was continually being held up as a 'murderer', exceptional in their view. It had always been their practice in war. Their views could not have been made more clear.

On 14 February a second letter arrived from Maungapohatu. It observed sensibly

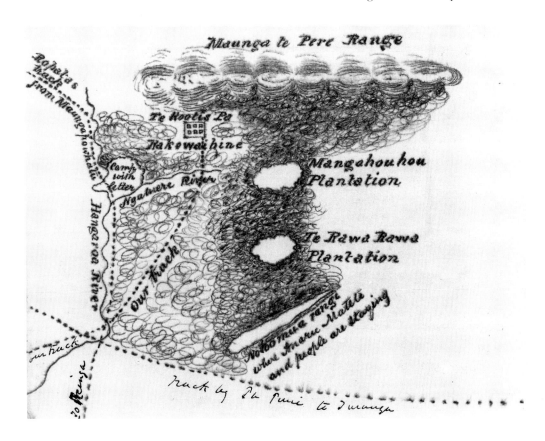

Porter's sketch of Te Kooti's refuge at Te Haupapa (Te Houpapa), March 1871. It shows the camp at the junction of the Hangaroa and Nga Tuere (Mutuere) rivers, where Te Kooti left the letter for Anaru Matete, as well as Te Kooti's 'Pa' at Kakewahine (Kakewaihine). Anaru Matete's separate pa was found later, at the peak of Mokonui-a-rangi, about three miles south-west of Nga Tapa.   AD1 71/377, NA

that, if the 200 men approached, the people would again run away! If only Ropata and Tamaikoha came, however, they would wait to see them. They reiterated that Te Kooti was not with them — 'yet you persist in coming with hundreds of men' ('tohe tonu mai koe me o rau').[46]

They did. On 16 February the old pa Tauaki at Maungapohatu was again occupied by Ropata and his men without opposition. Ngati Huri had withdrawn to Te Kakari, on the highest point of the ridge overlooking the track to Ruatahuna. From there they signalled that they would meet Ropata in peace. They welcomed him and Porter, as the guests of Te Whenuanui; but their words were barbed. The chief and principal speaker was Te Purewa (Renata Pohokorua). His was the second letter which had been left for Te Kooti at Rangiora and which Ropata had found there two weeks previously. In it, Te Purewa had told Te Kooti that he had his gun, brought to him by Atarihi, and which he had kept to protect himself. He had also written: 'Friend, may God protect you' ('E hoa, ma te atua koe e tiaki').[47] Now, he told Ropata that Te Kooti was not with them: 'seek him, and when you get him spare him as you spare us, and if you are able to bring peace among us do so.' He threw down his weapons, apparently as an indication of peace, and said that he would guide them through to Ruatahuna, where he would then leave them, as it was not within his chiefly domain, any more than Te Whenuanui had authority over them.

The speeches were deliberately ambiguous. On the next day, a party of Ropata's men encountered an old woman whose daughter was with Te Kooti; she, mistaking the strangers, asked after her. Ropata and Tamaikoha realised that Te Kooti had been there very recently (their conclusion was later confirmed by an account given to them by a prisoner). The offer to guide Ropata to Ruatahuna had been an offer to take him in quite the wrong direction. Ropata forced an old man of Ngati Kohatu, staying with the Maungapohatu people, into revealing that Te Kooti was hidden 'in the direction of Haupapa, near Waimaha'.[49] As the troopers set out to return to Maungapohatu and on to the Hangaroa river, they discovered the fresh tracks of Ngati Huri's messenger to Te Kooti. As they descended the path which passes along the northern edge of Maungapohatu, they found that a vast landslip had recently occurred, from just below its summit. It was over a quarter of a mile wide and a mile and a half long, and great forest trees and rocks had fallen jumbled together: 'The natives say it is an omen of the extermination of the Urewera tribe, as such a thing was never before known.'[49]

On 26 February, after a journey through the most fearsome country — a mass of forest that seemed impenetrable, with not a piece of flat land to be found — they came to the headwaters of the Hangaroa river. At its junction with the Nga Tuere stream they found a small camp site and there a letter written by Te Kooti, left for Anaru Matete. It read:

> Kia tupato. Te noho kia riro aneke [*sic*] maku (Te Kooti) te whakaaro. Kia tupato rawa. Kaore mohiotia taku hokinga atu.
>
> Be on your guard. Leave everything to me. Be very wary. I do not know when I may return.[50]

At this juncture, convinced that Te Kooti was hidden at Te Haupapa, the party went through to Te Reinga to supply themselves and to apply pressure on the 'old people' of Ngati Kohatu for information. Indeed, it was there they learnt that all their letters sent from Tawhana to Ngati Huri at Maungapohatu had been forwarded to Te Kooti. He had known their precise movements ever since they entered the Waimana valley. They also learnt who was one of the critical links between the people of Maungapohatu and Te Kooti: Te Whiu Maraki.

In the oral narratives of Tamakaimoana (the people from Maungapohatu and the Tauranga river valley), Te Whiu is the man to whom Te Kooti would entrust the stewardship of their people before he died. The stories associated with Te Whiu's guardianship remain a living part of their histories, and are told in Chapter 15. In 1871, Te Whiu was still a young man, aged between 25 and 27, and noted as a very fast runner.[51] But he was not only the swift messenger; he was also included in a list compiled for Porter by a prisoner, Tautata (whom he captured on 22 March), as one of the few people with Te Kooti who possessed a gun. Te Whiu was one of Maungapohatu's men travelling with Te Kooti, and Orupe was another — but Orupe did not have a gun.

Te Whiu Maraki, 1921.
Photograph by James Cowan.
F10981 1/2, ATL

But then, neither did Anaru Matete, nor Te Kooti himself, Tautata said;[52] this was certainly misinformation.

Of the 54 men named as being with Te Kooti at that time, only 25 were said to have guns. This probably does give some indication of the poverty and ill-equipped state of Te Kooti's supporters. Tautata said he had left Te Haupapa some two weeks previously, sent on a mission to Waikaremoana to find ammunition. His statement revealed that a few of the whakarau had survived and had rejoined Te Kooti. They included Karanama Te Whare, Maaka Ritai and Paora Tu. The majority of the men (33) were from Turanga; 13 were from Tuhoe (of whom four can be definitely identified as Maungapohatu people); the remainder (eight) came mostly from the upper Wairoa. This was the extent of Te Kooti's force. Tautata also told Porter that most of the men had been sent away at the same time as him to hunt pigs and collect wild honey. Te Kooti had set the northern boundary for the hunting expeditions as Te Karetu (about 12 miles north-east of Te Haupapa as the crow flies), lest they should fall into the hands of the government people. The few who had remained with Te Kooti at Te Haupapa were being tattooed. Tattooing was an extremely tapu process, partly because it involved shedding blood;

Tautata's remark suggests the deliberate revival of a practice which was associated, for males, with war and the assertion of their mana. Te Kooti himself was of the generation who had not been tattooed with traditional facial or bodily moko, and he remained so. In this he obeyed, it might be noted, the instructions of Leviticus 19:28. The decision for a few of the younger men to be tattooed (if the markings were traditional) must have related to their perception of themselves as chosen fighters, sent to 'redeem the land'. As the Tuhoe warrior Netana Te Whakaari, himself fully tattooed, said, you may lose everything you value through misfortune or war, but 'of your moko you cannot be deprived except by death. It will be your ornament and your companion until your last day.'[53]

Ropata and Porter had set out again from Te Reinga on 19 March for Te Haupapa, and their capture of Tautata raised their hopes that they finally had Te Kooti pinned down. They surrounded Te Haupapa in the early hours of the morning of 30 March. The 'only fault was the absence of an enemy or occupant of the place'![54] It was clear that the site had been unoccupied for some time, at least two weeks in Porter's esti-mation. In actuality, it must have been evacuated almost as soon as they had passed by on 28 February. For Ropata and Porter had taken the note left for Anaru and placed one of their own in the same clearing at the rivers' junction. This was intended as a ruse, suggesting that they were leaving the area; Tautata had found it just after the party had departed, when their fires were still warm, and had taken it immediately to Te Kooti. He seemed to have fallen for the trap, for the hunting parties were sent out (deliberately leaving their few guns behind to ensure they operated silently) and Tautata and others directed on their errand for ammunition[55] — but then Te Kooti vanished. As Pera Te Awahaka, who had been at Te Haupapa with Te Kooti and sent on the hunting ex-pedition, said simply: 'Te Kooti never tells us where he is going'.[56] Or, as Ropata put it much more graphically, 'perhaps he has made a mysterious jump, there is no knowing where, as it is not through idleness that he is not found'.[57]

Tautata took Ropata and Porter to a cave in the bush, 'a sort of magazine' for the few arms that were left. There they discovered some letters, which indicated that Te Kooti had been purchasing articles through Kawanatanga chiefs in the Wairoa. They also 'found secreted many of Te Kooti's valuables ... among the articles discovered were three rifles, two double-barrelled guns, and one single, two pouches of ammunition, two watches with gold chains, a sovereign, a shilling, old books, papers, and a prayer-book written by Te Kooti, and containing his cabalistic signs and revelations'.[58] This was probably the diary subsequently acquired by the former missionary William Colenso, and from which he published, later that year, his translations of some of Te Kooti's prayers.[59] It is discussed in Appendix A.

The camp consisted of three separate pa, or settlements. At Kakewahine, where Te Kooti's whare was, there were three large houses and four smaller; Rewarewa had seven houses; Mangahouhou was unfinished, but a large whare puni had been erected there. Altogether Te Haupapa was, Porter said, an unsurpassed hiding-place, which he could never have found without a guide, so hidden was it from view from anywhere in the surrounding countryside. Subsequently, he also discovered Anaru Matete's separate kainga at the peak of Mokonui-a-rangi, only a little way south-west of Nga Tapa itself.

Ropata Wahawaha, leader of the
Ngati Porou expeditions into the
Urewera, at Napier, 1871.

B12275, MONZ

Porter's approach had, however, been spotted by a woman on sentry duty and the people
fled from the pa. He captured several of the women and children, and two men, but
Anaru himself, together with his brother (or cousin) Hirini Te Ratu, who had been one
of the whakarau,[60] escaped by leaping over a cliff. Once again the leaders had got away
by a 'mysterious jump'.

The next day, however, Ropata rejoined Porter from his own search, bringing with
him some people whom he had captured from the hunting expedition. They had been
betrayed 'by the chattering of one of their pet kakas', and one of the waiata of these
events composed by Ngati Porou tells how they heard its clicking sound: 'He mokai
kaka ka rangona te ngetengetetanga i'.[61] Ropata had seized several of those named by
Tautata, including old Hotoma, who had never returned from his errand as government
messenger in October 1868. The leader of this group was Tamati Te Rangituawaru, a
Turanga chief, who had previously been taken prisoner at Waerenga-a-Hika. Altogether,
Ropata and Porter gathered in 12 men and 16 women and children as prisoners. They
also burnt all the settlements and plantations. But they had again failed in their primary
objective.

As a consequence, Te Whenuanui and Paerau were sent back to the Urewera on a
mission to bring in Ngati Huri of Maungapohatu. At a large hui held in early April at
Tatahoata, Paerau's pa at Ruatahuna, Tuhoe agreed that they would not shelter Te Kooti.

They had said this before; the significant change was the adherence of Kereru, pre-eminent chief of Ngati Rongo of Ruatoki, who had strong kinship ties with the people of Maungapohatu. Kereru wrote to the government:

> This is my word to you. In the day of Ropata Te Kooti will have no men; they will all come over to the Government, the Ngatihuri and Ngatirongo. Te Kooti is now by himself (or at a distant place). I am now living in quietness . . . .
>
> This is another word to you. Some of my people are with Te Kooti. I did not tell them to go, but he caught them. . . . I will go to fetch them, — I shall be strong to send them back.[62]

It was clearly the threat of Ropata's occupation of Ruatahuna and Maungapohatu which lay behind this agreement. The government's terms were carefully spelt out, lest there be any lingering misunderstanding. Any pa which harboured Te Kooti would be destroyed 'and its inhabitants carried away as before'. The return of all exiled Tuhoe was made conditional on Tuhoe's direct assistance in the hunt for Te Kooti.[63] This was the final message that Paerau and Te Whenuanui brought. Preece was soon able to add to Kereru's news some precise information, given him by Hapurona, who had come from the hui: that Te Kooti was said now to be at Mautaketake on the south-eastern shores of Waikaremoana, with about 40 people.[64]

The final combing of the Urewera began. Preece and Gilbert Mair, accompanied by Hapurona, set out from Fort Galatea on 25 May with 118 men, and went through to Tatahoata, where they met with Te Whenuanui and Paerau. At a runanga held there on 1–2 June, the Urewera chiefs made their position plain: they themselves refused to assist in capturing Te Kooti but should he enter their territory, they said, they would give information as to his whereabouts and prevent him from passing through to the King's country. They said that their refusal to assist was because they had been involved in the war for some years, and were tired of the whole thing. The last statement was undoubtedly true; but that Tuhoe would shelter Te Kooti also seems unquestionable. Ngati Huri held their runanga at Tauaki, Maungapohatu, on 20 June. Tamaikoha was present, as was Te Purewa and the little old chief Te Puehu. Mair commented in his turn: 'The Maungapowhatu Natives are a wild, restless set, with large shaggy heads of hair, and clad in mats made from the coarse fibres of the *toi* — they bore but small resemblance to civilised beings.'[65] Here, Preece and Mair were told plainly to go back, as Te Kooti was not with the people at Maungapohatu. In the end, after a long discussion, they said they would give no further assistance to Te Kooti.

Kereru had also been at Maungapohatu but had left as soon as he heard that the expedition was on its way there. He knew they had learnt that he (and Ngati Huri) had given Te Kooti, when he came to them in January, the Spencer repeating rifle which Wi Maihi Te Rangikaheke had earlier given to Tamaikoha as a statement of the end of their war.[66] The message intended by the new gift was support, not peace. Mair wrote: 'They sent two messengers after Te Kooti to get Tamaikowha's breach-loader, and to bring back the four Urewera, who still remain with him.'[67] But he did not learn where the messengers went.

There was clearly a network of covert assistance for Te Kooti, even though few now actually wished to fight along with him. The odds for victory through war were impossible. But the sympathy for his autonomous stand was extensive and included, as we have seen, some of the Kawanatanga chiefs, those whom the agent for the general government on the East Coast, J. D. Ormond, had considered to be 'in our confidence'.[68] Deliberate vagueness was one tactic adopted by Te Kooti's supporters. In early March, Porter had had confirmation from a prisoner, Kuare, who had been one of the whakarau and was being held in Napier, that Te Kooti indeed had plantations at Te Haupapa. But he also learnt that Kuare had told this to the Wairoa chiefs, in whose custody he was being held, but had said that the cultivations were at Te Wera, failing to state 'that Te Wera is a large tract of country and not a kainga'![69]

The delivery of muddied information, mingled with deliberately confused reports and slanderous assertions, was turned into an art form by Tuhoe. At the beginning of July the government suddenly heard from Makarini, the chief at Tikitiki, that Te Kooti had appeared at Waikaremoana and taken away some of the people there as prisoners. The story seemed credible, in that Te Kooti had used similar tactics previously to get the men and women he needed. The messenger Hirini, who brought this news, was full of stories he had heard from Te Aho, who had managed to escape from Te Kooti on 3 July. Te Kooti had boasted (probably accurately enough) to the prisoners that at one time, when Ropata was hunting for him in the bush, he lay within a few yards of him and heard every word Ropata had said.[70] But a woman, Apikara (Abigail), whom Makarini had also reported to have been taken prisoner at the same time and who also escaped, then denied that Te Kooti had ever been at the lake. She came down to Wairoa on 8 July and her statement was publicly accepted by the Wairoa chiefs, Tamihana Huata and Te Hapimana. Hirini then arrived, bringing a matchbox containing 68 percussion caps which, he said, Te Kooti had given him 'to forward to Govt. as he (Te Kooti) would not be a receiver of stolen goods, and as he got them from Makarini he was sure they were such'.[71] It was Makarini who was false. The objective of this tangled web of stories seems to have been to discredit Makarini, who had acted as an informant to the government. Not only Apikara but also Tamihana Huata had, in fact, been in communication with Te Kooti at Tukurangi, near Waikaremoana, at the end of June. Tamihana denied it, but he did admit that he had talked with both Hirini and Apikara at that time. Later, both Porter and Leonard Williams learnt that Tamihana had indeed met Te Kooti at the old redoubt there, and that Tamihana had also sent him food and clothing on three occasions; his acquaintance with Te Kooti went back to days at Turanga, where Tamihana had studied at the Waerenga-a-Hika mission.[72] At this meeting, Tamihana had prayed with him and given him a shawl, which later fell into the hands of the government men. Tamihana was an Anglican minister and it was also reported, probably correctly, that he had told Te Kooti that he would ultimately be taken (as would the Waikato): it was all a lost cause. Te Kooti had then replied that he would never be captured, and that he would fight this war even in the Waikato and for the King.[73] The ambiguity of his words about taking the war into the Waikato was left unchallenged, but the discussion between Te Kooti and Tamihana clearly echoes their earlier exchange, and the two men were no closer to an understanding than previously.

It can be established that Hirini had been a messenger from Te Kooti to the chiefs of the lower Wairoa since at least November 1870, seeking to win them over to neutrality.

On one occasion he bore a letter from Oriwia, Te Kooti's wife, to her kin.[74] It was subsequently discovered that Hirini had been a prisoner on Wharekauri and that he was close to Te Kooti.[75] He was, almost certainly, Hirini Te Oiikau of Te Aitanga-a-Mahaki and Ngati Kahungunu, whose wife was living at Waikaremoana; and in August he was again fighting alongside Te Kooti. As for Apikara, she returned to live with Te Kooti as his wife.[76] Later, a large whare in which they had both been living was discovered near the southern shores of Wairaumoana, in the Panekiri range. The communal house was described as being 50 feet long, and had been extensively used during the winter. There 'were evident traces of the woman Apikara, which shewed that she had slept in the whare after leaving the Lake'.[77]

Makarini had indeed reported correctly. Te Kooti had arrived at Te Marau, on the westernmost shores of Waikaremoana, on 30 June. Hirini later admitted that he had taken Te Kooti there. They had crossed the lake from the promontory on the southern shores, Te Ure-o-Paetai, in two canoes. Te Kooti's party consisted of about 40 men, women and children, and only some were armed. Te Kooti had talked to Hirini of returning to Tauranga (perhaps meaning Tauranga at Taupo) and reclaiming the support of the people there, but Hirini had not believed him.[78] At Te Marau, Te Kooti had captured some of Makarini's young men and women, sent by him to watch Te Kooti. Some of them may well have gone with him voluntarily; indeed, most of the people at Tikitiki were known to be sympathetic to Te Kooti and 'gave him every information and assistance' they could.[79] Nevertheless, Preece learnt later that Kereru had secretly visited Te Kooti and tried to persuade him to let Makarini's young men return home, but that Te Kooti had refused.[80] He needed them too much to let them go. Then, from Te Marau, he once again vanished.

However, he remained around the lake, flitting through the dense bush from one place to another. Fires were seen on 23 July, and eight days later two large canoes were found beached at the extremity of Whanganui-o-Parua, the eastern arm of the lake. The tracks which led from them were about a week old and went in several directions. A broken rifle stock was found in one of the canoes, which Makarini recognised as belonging to Pirihi, one of his young men. Heavy rain blotted out any further traces. The gale and snowfall which followed in the first days of August ended any immediate chance of pursuit.

About the same time, a small party of people from the upper Wairoa, who had supported Te Kooti in 1868 until Nga Tapa (when they had left him because too many had died), surrendered at Onepoto. Simeon, their leader, had recently seen Te Kooti for the first time since their defection. Makarini had told him where Te Kooti was, revealing that he too knew much more than he was saying to the government. Simeon commented that Te Kooti had 20 men with him at the lake, and another 15 men and eight women had joined him since.[81] He also said that Te Kooti had sent two messengers from Te Marau with letters to the King. One of the messengers was Karanama Te Whare (or Te Kani as he was now called).[82] He bore messages for Tahau and also for 'Kanara Peniana' (that is, 'O'Connor Fenian') at Ohinemuri.[83] From the latter Te Kooti was no doubt seeking ammunition, for Ohinemuri was a well-known place of supply, while Michael O'Connor was an equally well-known 'character in the Thames goldfield'.[84] Karanama was also to seek out the exiles sheltering at Ohinemuri. They included Paora Toki, the senior chief from Petane in Hawke's Bay, who had been a leader of the Pai Marire there and whose son, Turei, together with several kinsmen, had been captured and exiled to Wharekauri; in 1868 Paora had come to Te Kooti to see his son, and then joined the movement. He fought alongside Te Kooti at Mohaka.[85] Tahau and his party were similarly living under Te Hira's protection, as were the Ngati Porou refugees staying at Mataora.[86] Karanama's task was to try to get them to assist Te Kooti's escape into the Waikato. Makarini was told that Te Kooti was hoping to meet Karanama upon his expected return through the Kaingaroa plains in September.[87]

Karanama reached Patetere at the end of August and went first to Tahau at Waitoa. Tahau was recognised as the link between Tauranga and the Thames district, where Te Kooti's religious teachings were now rapidly spreading.[88] For all that Te Kooti was hemmed in and surrounded, his teachings had already begun to expand. This was Tahau's work, along with other refugees in the district. However, William Mair (now the resident magistrate at Alexandra in the Waikato and sent to watch the King Country) knew that, at the end of October, 'Tahau is waiting'.[89] It is certain, too, that Karanama returned again to see Tahau in November, immediately after he had visited the Rohe Potae. At that juncture, Tahau suddenly announced his return to Taupo. He deliberately came into Thames township to show himself, and to seek food. As the government's agent observed as he gave Tahau some flour, he was, like all the Ohinemuri people, 'very nearly starving'; Tahau's fortunes had turned again since Grace saw him a year ago. He stated that he was now going home.[90]

Yet it was clearly not the time for the renewal of open or active contact with Te Kooti. Te Hira himself had recently ended his long struggle to hold his territorial boundaries intact. He had announced that the telegraph wires, often seen by Maori as the first line of penetration, could cross his district to the Bay of Plenty coast.[91] Tahau's sudden return to Taupo at this juncture cannot be seen as a direct act of preparation for Te Kooti's welcome. It seems rather to be a discreet withdrawal, in the knowledge that Te Kooti would soon be attempting to break through the encircling net.

Having seen Tahau and Paora Toki in early September, Karanama had travelled on to Te Kuiti with his messages for Tawhiao. He reached there on 20 September, but, as both Wi Patene and William Mair wrote, he got a very mixed reception.[92] Tawhiao refused to reply to Te Kooti's letter, saying he would have nothing more to do with him.[93] But Manuhiri and Rewi were beginning to listen. Karanama's precise message is not known, but both chiefs soon wrote to the government seeking an end to the pursuit. On 13 October Rewi urged McLean to stop the Europeans and Maori from hunting Te Kooti and to work instead for peace.[94] Manuhiri wrote, 'the storm which broke the canoes and vessels has ceased, but the waves are still there': the Maori on the government side must be called off, he said, and McLean was the one man who could do so.[95] It was Rewi alone who announced publicly that he would send for Te Kooti to come and take shelter with Maniapoto. As he wrote to Mair plainly:

> That word [referring to a previous letter he had sent] is still strong. Cease the pursuit.
> — During the days of November my man (messenger) will go to bring him to Te Kuiti.[96]

During this lengthy time of waiting, Te Kooti was sheltering, throughout the worst
of the winter of 1871, in the Nga Moko ranges to the east of Waikaremoana. Tuhoe oral
tradition particularly remembers that he was secreted in a cave, Te Ana-a-te-kurinui-
a-Moko (The Cave of Moko's large dog), on the south-east shoulder of the highest
peak of the Nga Moko range. It was from this shelter that the little group hunted, using
old methods — snaring and spearing birds — which would later be illustrated in the
meeting-house Te Whai-a-te-motu, built by Tuhoe for Te Kooti. The hunters kept their
silence, and watched over the lake; and here the young women living with Te Kooti
were tattooed, presumably as a statement of their identity and beauty.

It was at this time that Preece and Gilbert Mair's Arawa search parties, setting out
from Whanganui-o-Parua on 6 August, discovered one of Te Kooti's camps. Preece
went with a group across the Nga Moko range and, on 7 August, they found a camp
near Papauma (about six miles from Whataroa). It appeared to have been left about four
days previously, but Preece heard footsteps during the night, and the party also captured
a dog. As they left in the morning, they had hardly gone ten yards when they were fired
upon. A brief skirmish resulted, and Preece followed the kokiri on a well-beaten trail
leading north-east to Papuni. But he had to turn back for lack of supplies. On 9 August

Mair and Preece returned together to the camp, where they found Te Kooti's letter left for them, 'stuck on a split stick in a very conspicuous position' in one of the huts.[97] It appeared to have been written that morning and it read:

Ki nga Kawanatanga katoa

E hoa ma, he kupu tenei naku ki a koutou. Me mutu te whaiwhai i a au no te mea kei toku nohoanga ano au e noho ana kei te puihi. Engari ka puta au ki te moana, whaia. Ko tenei mahi kohuru a koutou me te kiore te ketu ana i te hamuti. Me whakarere. He whai na koutou i a au tonoa mai he tangata kia haere atu au ki waho, na tatau riri ai. Ka pai.

Ki te kitea e koutou tena reta kei huna, hoatu ki nga rangatira katoa.

He kupu ke tenei. Ko taku mahara ko te maungarongo te oranga ko te mahi kai hoki. Kati kei te whakarite ahau i enei mahara kia oti.

E hoa ma, ko tena mahara a tatau ko te riri kaore ano i tae mai ki a au, engari ka tata ahau te whakarite i a koutou mahara. Engari kia tupato, kei ki koutou he kohuru, kahore. Heoi ano.

E hoa ma, i tonoa atu e au aku tamariki ki te kawe atu i taku pukapuka whakahoki mo koutou, tahuri ana koutou ki te whaiwhai. Kati, kauaka hai haku ki to koutou matenga.

Ko aua tamariki hoki ko Te Hata Tipoki, ko Epiha Puairangi, ko Patoromu Ruru. He tamariki ena i tohia ki te tohi o Tu i whangaia ki te Whatunuiarua, he tamariki hoki e whakaaro nui ana ki te whenua. Heoi ano.

Ki te kino koutou ki ena korero, me aha mo koutou na ana ia.

Na to koutou hoariri

Na Te Turuki.

To all the Government people

Friends, this is my word to you. Cease to pursue me because I am living in my own place in the bush. If I come out to the coast, then chase me. But this murderous work of yours is like a rat scratching in excrement. Leave off doing so. If you will chase me send someone to get me to come out to the coast and we will have a fight there. This would be good.

If you (anyone) find this letter do not hide it, give it to all the chiefs.

This is a different word. I think that in peace there is life and also in planting food, and I am putting these thoughts into practice so that they may be completed.

Friends, that thought of ours to fight has not yet come to me — but I will shortly fulfil your wishes (fight). Be on your guard, and do not say it is murder for it is not. That is all.

Friends, I sent my children to carry you a letter of reply, but you turned to chasing me.[98] Now do not complain at your death.

The names of these children: Te Hata Tipoki, Epiha Puairangi, and Patoromu Ruru. The children were consecrated by the tohi rites of Tu and were fed on the big kernel (stone) of Rua, and are children who think a great deal of the land. That is all.

If you despise these words who cares. They are for you.

From your enemy

From Te Turuki.[99]

The rituals described for the 'children' or young men of Turanga[100] were adapted from the Maori schools of learning. They were being 'fed' on knowledge: that is, the 'whatu' or 'kernel' of Rua, a complex rite which the chief Tutakangahau of Maungapohatu later described to Elsdon Best.[101] This ritual, combined with Tautata's earlier references to the tattooing of the young men — probably the very same youths, for two of the three, Patoromu and Epiha, Tautata had named as being with Te Kooti at Te Haupapa in March — suggests that Te Kooti had revived, or adapted, traditional practices relating to war, the destruction of enemies and imbibing of knowledge. The deity Tu-matauenga is particularly associated with war, and the tohi-a-Tu or tohi taua (warrior's baptism) was a ritual for men, which would be renewed before each expedition.[102] Toiroa had himself baptised Te Kooti as a young man with the tohi rites of Tu, and had sealed the ritual with a small stone, which Te Kooti had had to bite. This practice was intended to make the recipient strong and clear in mind for the tasks ahead, and it was generally used to confirm the rituals in the schools of learning. It was known as 'whatu whakahoro', referring both to the freeing from obstruction and, at a literal level, to the crumbling or shattering of the stone. To eat the stone was the task (and the riddle) which Te Kooti had set the whakarau in order to 'clear the way' for their escape from Wharekauri. The 'kernel' of Rua was here the large, hard and inedible stone of the hinau.[103] It was again possibly intended to represent the 'white stone' of Revelation, or the hidden manna given to 'him that overcometh'.[104]

Mair and Preece interpreted this letter as an overture for peace. One of its translators, Canon James Stack, saw the letter as a clear statement that it was the endless persecution by the government which alone had caused the killings. Nevertheless, Mair and Preece were very cautious in the reply they left for Te Kooti to find. Dated 9 August, their letter told him that he could come in if he wished, but they could not offer any terms: 'Leave it to the goodwill of the Government' ('Wai hoki te aroha o te Kawanatanga').[105] They were immediately warned by McLean to make no promises to Te Kooti other than that he would be tried 'for his crimes'. Above all, McLean said plainly, 'no pledge must be given that his life will be spared.'[106]

The Arawa expedition led by Mair and Preece attempted to follow the trail from the camp on 10 August, but the tracks indicated that the people had, once again, broken into small groups and scattered. As Mair commented, 'It is quite impossible to get near him [Te Kooti] by following his trail. His perfect knowledge of the country & wonderful skill in scouting would prevent our ever getting near him that way. . . . He runs at our approach, and no men can keep up with him.'[107] They decided to return to Onepoto for supplies (thereby losing a lot of time) and set out again, overland, on 15 August, heading for Lake Waikareiti. They managed to lose themselves and missed the lake, but on 18 August picked up the track they wanted, on the far side of the dividing range.

On the Waipaoa stream, which starts in the mountains north-east of the lake and runs down to join the Ruakituri river at Papuni, they discovered a camp which had been occupied only two or three days previously. They also found near there a letter scratched on a slab, written in haste, perhaps, or making a permanent mark:

> Orewha. Akuhata 1871
>
> Ki nga Kawanatanga katoa.
> E hoa ma. Me mutu ta koutou whaiwhai i au. He mahi kohuru kino tenei mahi a koutou. Ki te tohe tonu koutou. Heoi ano. Me pera ano hoki toku utu —
> Na Te Kooti Te Turuki

> Orewha. August 1871
>
> To all the Government people.
> Friends. You must cease your pursuit of me. This is evil treacherous work of yours. If you persist, very well, I will do the same (I will retaliate).
> Te Kooti Te Turuki.[108]

After a further two hours of tracking, Kepa Te Ahuru, the Tuhoe trooper who had parted from Te Kooti on the flight from Uawa and had then rejoined Preece in March 1871, saw a woman washing pikopiko (young shoots of fern) in the stream. He recognised her at once as Mere Maihi, who had been taken prisoner by Te Kooti at Opape, and from her they learnt that the camp was nearby. Most of the men, she said, were out hunting pigs and birds and would return at any time. Preece commented that they heard the sounds of chopping wood nearby and decided to attack at once.

They closed in carefully, and then 'rushed' the kainga, which was defended by a narrow ponga bridge across a small stream, as well as a strong fence made of tree-fern trunks. It was also 'situated so that it was impossible to surround it'.[109] The sentry at the gate was killed, and then Preece saw two men flee from a large hut inside the settlement and swim across the Waipaoa river. As they were climbing the cliff on the far side, one of the two was hit and fell back into the water. The other was Te Kooti. He dropped his blanket (which was later recovered with a bullet hole in it), turned, stark naked, at the top of the cliff, fired one shot and was gone.[110]

The man who fell was Paora Te Wakahoehoe, the messenger whom Te Waru had sent to Te Kooti with the greenstone mere Tawatahi when he sought the death of Biggs. At the camp by the river the mere was found, and with it Te Kooti's defence force shoulder ammunition belt (it was an officer's belt and was thought to have been taken from Wilson at Matawhero) and a cartridge box (which had belonged to Biggs), full of Spencer rifle ammunition.[111] This may well have been the ammunition for Tamaikoha's Spencer repeating rifle, but its discovery certainly reinforced the troopers' constant complaint that Te Kooti was getting some of the superior breech-loading weaponry, including the Snider-Enfield rifles using brass cartridges with which they themselves were not yet supplied, and which they considered essential for the wet bush-fighting conditions.[112] In the camp, they found nine Enfield rifles, as well as two breech-loading Terry carbines and several fowling pieces. There was also a watch with a gold chain, which may have belonged to Biggs;[113] it had not been burnt, unlike some of these worldly timekeepers taken previously.

This was a frustrating encounter, which may have been why it brought out some of the worst aspects of a colonial war. In a private letter describing the episode and probably written by Preece, the term 'niggers' appears,[114] which was rarely used — neither in army correspondence nor even in diaries. The party took four women and two children as prisoners, but they shot their only male captive. He was Wi Heretaunga, one of the whakarau who was considered to have played a major role in the executions at Poverty Bay. Kepa Te Ahuru, the grandson of Te Purewa and a most ambivalent young man, who was known as 'the brat',[115] claimed the right of executioner as Wi's nephew — perhaps to control the ramifications of utu, as he persuasively argued, and perhaps not.[116]

The party also discovered what Mere had said was true: most of the men were away hunting and had escaped their net — along with Te Kooti. In his diary for the following day, 19 August, Preece listed all the men and women then with Te Kooti, whose names he probably obtained from Mere. There were 31 men and 16 women. Among the men were still a few of the whakarau. One was Hirini Te Oiikau, who had almost certainly been Te Kooti's messenger and whose brother Hetariki had also been one of the whakarau, but who had been imprisoned for rebellion in 1869.[117] Others still with him were Paora Tu, Maika Tuakana and Maaka Ritai. Anaru Matete had also rejoined Te Kooti. The three young men, Epiha, Patoromu and Te Hata Tipoki, a grandson of Meri Karaka from Wairoa, were also with him. So were Te Whiu and Orupe from Maungapohatu. The women included his three known wives, Heni, Nia and Oriwia, but Apikara was not mentioned.

From this raid, Mair also acquired the words of two haka of defiance composed by Te Kooti. They are among the very few which have survived, because Te Kooti ordered the songs of violence to be destroyed after the wars.[118] Mair copied them into his field notebook in August 1871. The first haka sings of death. The metaphors are explicitly sexual:

> Te poho kapakapa noa.
> Te hikonui tupere mataku
> Hakiri hari, ka riro ia,
> Rewharewha a ha ha ha,
> . . . Ka wherawhera noa a Tuhoe i tana tume, kia matakitaki na e te Kawana.
> He aha ira tera, he puapua,
> He aha ira tera, he werewere,
> He aha i ara te mea tokomaha i puraurau mai i waenganui o te kiko taiariki ka pehia iho,
> e ka ka rekareka.

> The heart beats rapidly.
> The exploding awesome ejaculation
> Barely felt, he expires
> Silence — so there!
> . . . Tuhoe increases its circle, in defiance of the Governor.
> What then is this, [it is] a clematis (vagina),
> What then is this, [it is] a barnacle (vagina),
> What then is that [which] came to the centre of the body of invaders and pressed on them: oh how sweet!

The second Mair called a 'Puha', a song accompanied by a war-dance:

> Rangaranga, Rangaranga taua i a Pahauwera e
> Nau mai nei, hurihia ka ha —— e Hoa.
> Whakamau atu au ki Hangaroa, he ara kokiri na Porou.
> He hopu i a Te Kooti. Kahore kau e mau.
> Ka ha —— E Hoa.
> I Huiarau, he ara kokiri na Te Arawa.
> He kai tirotiro i Waikare i a Te Kooti.
> Kare kau e kitea ka ha —— E Hoa.
> Whakawehi mai te Kawana i tana Atua nei
> A te mini kaiwhara, i te Purukumu,
> Te hurihuri, napihia. Ka ha —— E Hoa.
> E Hoa i haramai nei te Kawana i Ruatahuna ki Maungapohatu.
> Ana to moho ko te oha a Kingi Hori.
> Akinga a iho ki runga ki to angaanga Kawana pokokohua, ka ha!

> Raise, Raise a war-party from [Ngati] Pahauwera,
> Come here, turn around — so there, my Friend.
> I am alert to Hangaroa, the path of attack by [Ngati] Porou,
> A snare for Te Kooti — who is not caught.
> So there, my Friend.
> At Huiarau, the path of attack by Te Arawa,
> A scout from Waikare after Te Kooti —
> Who is not seen. So there, my Friend.

> The Governor in fear of his God,
> Hugging Minie rifles at Purukumu (up his bum),
> Turning [them], clinging [to them]. So there, my Friend.
> Oh friend, the Governor came from Ruatahuna to Maungapohatu,
> With that treachery of the relic of King George.
> Rain down on your accursed Governor's head, so there![119]

This song exults in Te Kooti's elusiveness among the Urewera mountains. It tracks Ngati Porou on the Hangaroa river, and Te Arawa through the Huiarau range to the west; it remembers a scout sent from Waikaremoana, who failed to see the man watching him, the man he was seeking. It comments on the powerful and accurate 'Minie rifles', which fired the deadly, soft-lead, hollow Minie bullet. These were the long-range, breech-loading Enfields and Snider-Enfields, the major innovation in warfare from 1866. It seems to refer drolly to the government's desire to hoard the most recent models as an anal plug, rather than issue them to the bush fighters. This was certainly Preece's recurring complaint, for his poor weapons and wet ammunition defeated him in at least two critical encounters with Te Kooti. The last lines touch on the way in which the government's pressure had penetrated by stealth, even to Maungapohatu itself: that is, the way in which Tuhoe were being ensnared, one by one, to join the search for Te Kooti. It ends with absolute defiance: this was the haka of a man who would not surrender to any 'relic' of the King, George IV, who had never held authority over Aotearoa. It makes clear that the issue of sovereignty was being contested.

Preece may now have learnt more than he knew before, but he was still unable to pick up Te Kooti's trail. Snow and rain fell heavily on 19 August, and Preece lost any chance of immediate pursuit. However, he struck out towards Papuni, and it was on the Rangitata range, about nine miles north of the clearing, that he picked up the track again, on 25 August. He also encountered the Ngati Porou expedition (which had set out from Wairoa on 12 August) and it was they who took up the chase. The tracks divided and scattered in several directions, spreading out like a fan, but Porter, who accompanied Ngati Porou, found the point where the tracks all converged and they continued in their pursuit. The trail went east; the trail went west; the trail doubled back; the trail passed former camp sites — and the whole time it poured with rain. On 31 August Ngati Porou crossed the high dividing ranges of the Urewera country and, looking north, they could see the rivers running down into the Bay of Plenty. They had entered the headwaters of the Tauranga river, the upper reaches of Tamaikoha's territory, lying immediately north of Maungapohatu. A tiny scrap of smoke was spotted: Ngati Porou began to prepare a surprise attack on Te Kooti's camp, which was in a small clearing in the ranges. Sixty men were sent to surround it; there was to be no talking, no whistling and no coughing: absolute silence was to prevail. For communication they adopted the tactic of '"striking stars" from a centre', with Porter following the rays until they led him to the men lying in wait.[120]

The camp was in an old potato clearing of Ngati Huri, where there were a number of wharau (temporary shelters). In the middle of the clearing was a larger hut, built of totara bark: this was Te Kooti's. At daybreak on 1 September, the camp began to come to life and a dog started barking. Te Kooti called out from the larger whare asking why the dog was making the noise. An old woman came out from one of the huts saying that she did not know. She threw a stick at it, and Te Kooti called out to get the fires going as they must leave. Oriwia was seen emerging from Te Kooti's whare, starting to prepare food and going inside again. At that moment, a warning shot was fired by one of the men of the Ngati Porou expedition. The volunteer John Large, who accompanied them, guessed that the man was probably one of several who had once fought for Te Kooti.[121] Immediately, everybody in the camp scattered. Te Kooti emerged naked, a blanket in his left hand, said Porter in the only contemporary account known to have survived.[122] In his later retrospective account, he said that Te Kooti held a carbine, even though he also stated that the party lost all their weapons in their flight. Porter declared that Te Kooti stood for a moment behind a large tree and called out: '"It is the Ngati-porou! Escape who can!"' Accompanied by Heni Kumekume and several others, he leapt down a cliff — and once again evaded his pursuers.

In the hunt which followed, two of Te Kooti's wives, Oriwia and Nia, were brought in. Only Heni, who had been outside the whare when the alarm was given, managed to get away. Of Nia nothing more is known. Oriwia returned to live with her husband in exile in the King Country, although only for a time. By 1871 she was already known to be wanting to leave, and she finally did so. One man who escaped the net that day was Eria Raukura, who would become the senior tohunga of the faith when it was reborn in the new place of exile.

The attack on Te Hapua had once again failed in its primary objective. The pursuit continued, but the quarry remained elusive. Tamaikoha joined with Preece and Mair in early October. Together they found another abandoned camp of Te Kooti near Ahikereru on 12 October. Then, on 17 October, Preece, who had gone to Opepe to get supplies and left Tamaikoha to continue, heard the news that Te Kooti had been attacked that morning. The assault was by a Tuhoe expedition led by Hemi Kakitu, who had formerly joined Te Kooti at Whakarae in 1869; now his force consisted of a small party of Tamaikoha's and Te Whenuanui's men, who were bound by the terms set upon their lives and their lands by the government. The attack took place on the Okahu stream near Ahikereru, and one woman was taken prisoner. She was Huhana, Te Kooti's wife, who had earlier been captured on the flight from Uawa.

On the list of the names of 16 women which Preece had acquired from Mere Maihi on 19 August, a 'Huhana' (Susan) had been included but not there identified as one of Te Kooti's wives. Whether this woman was his wife or not, the fact of Huhana's return to Te Kooti about this time is significant, for she would have brought him military information. Both Porter and Westrup were reported, in December 1870, to be living with women who had been Te Kooti's wives; in Westrup's case, at least, the woman was one of many whom he took into his 'establishment'.[123] If Huhana was one of these wives, she would have sought out information for Te Kooti, as these women certainly were doing. Later still, Preece met Huhana and was impressed by her. She was by then married to an Armed Constabulary trooper named Brooking, and she told Preece the history of the prisoners' escape from Wharekauri and of their treatment on the island. He commented in sympathy: 'knowing the proud spirit of the natives, I do not wonder at their attempt and ultimate escape from ill treatment.'[124]

Now recaptured in October 1871, Huhana reported that Te Kooti had only 12 men with him; seven, she said, had left him. She added that he was trying to get through to the Waikato, but that 'some of his men were not willing to venture it'.[125] Two days later, on 21 October, Preece learnt more. Te Whiu Maraki came in to Ruatahuna to surrender after the fight. He reported that Te Kooti's waist belt and blanket had been cut in this skirmish — but once again he had vanished. This episode is one of the sources for the popular oral story (which, as we have seen, exists in several versions from different times) of Te Kooti's belt, broken by the shot fired by a man of Tuhoe. A contemporary account, sent to the *Hawke's Bay Herald*, described how Te Kooti had been surrounded by Hemi Kakitu's party as he sat on a log, his profile recognisable to the men, who all knew him well. One fired, contrary to Hemi's orders: 'The bullet struck his waist belt just beside the pouch, which he wore in front, and actually cut the belt in two. It is now in the hands of the Uriweras.'[126] This attempt to kill him, as Tuhoe narrate it, was a deliberate decision by a man from Ruatoki as the only way out of the terrible pressure on them, which 'had brought them to their knees' through starvation:

> So he ambushed him. And he fired at him — they say it was almost point blank where he fired at him. He [Te Kooti] used to have a Sam Browne — belonged to the Pākehās, he always wore this — perhaps the pouches where you carry the cartridges, hit there, and cut the belt off. But never knocked him down. So he turned round to this chap scrambling down, and he sang out to him, 'Come here! Come back, and we'll talk about it!' But he wouldn't. He bolted. So [Te Kooti] said, 'All right then, your family — your people — will die by the gun.'[127]

Despite this attempt to assassinate him, the Urewera country remained Te Kooti's shelter and some of its people his protectors. One, whom the Tuhoe oral narratives recall, is Makurata Hineore (Makurata Himiona), who became the wife of Paitini Wi Tapeka of Maungapohatu, Elsdon Best's informant and companion when he was living in the Urewera.[128] Makurata was referred to for many years as having been a wife of Te Kooti, and she helped to guide him on the hidden pathways known only to Tuhoe, and took him through to the Waikato. She was probably one of the women tattooed in the cave in the Nga Moko range in 1871. One well-known narrative recalls how, early in 1872, doubling back from Tutaepukepuke, where they had been hiding, they became lost crossing the high peak Te Whakaipu (near Te Whaiti) in the thick mist. Makurata became separated from the party and Te Kooti returned to help her, despite the close presence of his pursuers.[129] And 'these fellows fired. According to Gilbert Mair, he always cursed himself, because he didn't know why they couldn't hit Te Kooti — at that range!'[130] This was the occasion, however, as Tuhoe remember, that Te Kooti was wounded in his right hand. Te Kooti's droll remark to Mair, when they met in 1884, that he had escaped from him only by the 'breadth of the black of my finger nail',[131] may have been a literal as well as a metaphorical statement: two fingers on Te Kooti's right hand were broken and partly destroyed, although they remained usable.[132] It was probably Makurata, with Heni Kumekume, to whom Te Whiu referred when he said that there were 'two wives' with Te Kooti at the end of October 1871.[133] All the others known had been captured.

Makurata. She is remembered for having helped Te Kooti escape through the Urewera to sanctuary in the King Country. In this photograph her moko is clearly visible. The photo is from Elsdon Best's private collection and was taken about 1896.

At this time the first reports began to circulate that the Waikato people had determined 'to get Te Kooti to their country to give him shelter'.[134] This was undoubtedly Rewi's objective, for it seemed to be the only way to bring the agonising fighting to an end without surrendering Te Kooti to an inevitable death. Te Kooti's pursuers themselves became convinced that flight to the Waikato was his goal. Yet in actuality, from October 1871 until March 1872, he zigzagged through the Urewera and into the upper Wairoa and Mohaka forests to the south and east, rather than to the north and west. His pursuers were constantly amazed by the skills he used to evade them. As Makarini said dryly: 'Te Kooti . . . seems to like expeditions being sent after him but he takes care to follow the expedition instead of their following him, he marched after Ropata during his last visit, saw his men catching eels by torch light and threw a piece of wood into the water beside them.'[135] Captain Charles Ferris of the Armed Constabulary described how Te Kooti frequently hid his trail by walking in water and, when forced onto land, would scatter his small party in every direction; they then walked in circles until they came to a small branch creek, which they would follow in the water until it rejoined the main stream. There was no way, he said, that he could ever find these tracks, except for the fact that Makarini's people from Tikitiki were his guides. 'It is impossible to describe the numerous ways he [Te Kooti] endeavoured to hide his trail — by ascending perpendicular cliffs from the river, taking a long round and returning to within a short distance from where he left it — by following pig tracks in the densest bush where they would be obliterated by the pigs — by walking backwards and by every possible means he could think of'.[136]

By 'walking backwards' from the Waikato, he again outwitted his pursuers. Te Kooti reached the upper Mohaka district in December 1871 and sheltered there. Anaru Matete, who would finally surrender at Pakirikiri, near Gisborne, on 8 March 1872, said that Te Kooti had reunited with him in December on the Waiau river, not far from Te Putere, where he himself had been hiding after his flight from the attack of 18 August.[137] From there, both men journeyed south-west to the upper reaches of the Mohaka river. In local tradition, two pa in that district are associated with Te Kooti in flight. At the junction of the Te Hoe and Mohaka rivers there is a high rock mountain peak, Tatara-a-Kina (733 metres), which is today known as 'Te Kooti's Lookout'. Tall, carved and burnt totara posts of the palisading and whare puni remained there until the earthquake of 1931. The second pa was Nga Tapa, which lies about two miles to the north-west, on the junction of the Hautapu and Te Hoe rivers. This pa belongs to Ngati Hineuru — that is, Petera Te Rangihiroa's people. Oral tradition maintains that Te Kooti lived there for a while and that he used the nearby riverways as his stepping stones. The oral tradition is firmly supported by the military records: in late January 1872, Sub-inspector Northcroft found the tracks — following the river stones and then crossing and recrossing the Mohaka near Nga Tapa.[138] The oral history of Ngati Hineuru also recalls that Te Kooti came through at this time to Te Haroto, where he named their meeting-house 'Rongopai' (Peace), although this must be a telescoping of events with his later visit there in December 1885. But the link is clearly stated: 'Te Rangihiroa was the man'.[139]

A third pa associated with Te Kooti in this region is the huge 'boulder' pa at Maunga-nui station on the upper Mohaka river. It is recalled that Te Kooti travelled on a track which cut across the Te Hoe river and came down behind Rakaita mountain to a ford on the Mohaka. On the eastern side of the river (near the end of modern Boundary Road) stood an impregnable rock fortress, and it is said that he scaled the great rock face by means of a human ladder, ascending on the shoulders of his followers. It was probably from this pa that he struck at Philip Dolbel's sheep station at Maungaharuru on 16 January 1872: the last guerrilla raid of the war.[140] Dolbel himself had been a militia volunteer and his station had been used as a base during various sweeps of the upper Mohaka district. Te Kooti burnt down one house and the woolshed. The raiders also gained some basic food supplies, a breech-loading carbine, an Enfield rifle and five packages of Enfield ammunition, as Anaru Matete later described.[141]

The party consisted of nine men and three women — at least that was Preece's estimate, who followed up their trail. They certainly included both Te Kooti and Anaru. On 4 February, Preece picked up the tracks, which were apparently leading towards

Maungaharuru. He also found a camp site (with eight sleeping places, as he noted), as well as a letter by Te Kooti left behind for someone who was missing. The letter was unsigned but dated 1 February 1872.[142] Preece and the Arawa troopers found four further camp sites on a trail which appeared now to be heading back towards Te Kiwi and the southern shores of Waikaremoana: Anaru Matete said that the party had been trying to get through to the upper Wairoa to contact Tamihana Huata, the Anglican minister with whom they had previously communicated.[143] Their purpose was probably simply to obtain clothing and food: certainly that was all they asked for when they got through to Ngati Kahungunu in March. On 13 February the Arawa discovered a sixth camp and tracks, which seemed to them to be about a week old. Then, on the following day, when they crossed the Mangaone stream, they discovered fresh marks, bushes broken by hand, and an abandoned camp site where the embers were still warm. At the mouth of the Mangaone stream, about seven miles from the camp, they saw their targets scrambling up the cliff on the other side of the river. Preece's party fired but their ammunition had been ruined by the damp and the 'bruising' of the trek, and almost all their guns (Terry carbines) jammed. A running fight then took place over two miles and across several ridges. Two men were sighted crossing the last ridge at nightfall, heading towards the Waihi stream, when the troopers gave up the chase, exhausted and angry with their poor equipment. Te Kooti was one of these fleeing men. Anaru said that Te Kooti had escaped there, around the base of a hill, while he himself had hidden in the scrub. Anaru remained there all night, until the troopers left.[144] At the camp, the baggage which the refugees had been forced to abandon was found — tea, sugar, salt, and bacon taken from Dolbel's station. Once again, Te Kooti depended on the bush for survival.

This was the last definite encounter between Te Kooti and the troopers in the wars. He fled back towards Papuni, crossing the Waikaretaheke river, which flows south-east out of Waikaremoana, on 15 February. From there, on the following day, Charles Ferris picked up the pursuit. On 19 February, on the Mangapiopio stream (a branch of the Hangaroa river), some dogs wandered into the Armed Constabulary camp, smelling food. They were thought to be Te Kooti's, but the blinding rain blotted out the trail and prevented any pursuit. Ferris did not find Te Kooti. However, on 27 February, at Te Reinga on the Ruakituri river, he did capture four men, three of whom had been with Te Kooti for a long time. They said that they had separated from Te Kooti about two months before and had been living and planting in the ranges ever since. One was Maaka Ritai, who would later be tried for the execution of Paku Paraone: Ferris considered him one of the '"Kaipatus (butchers)"', and therefore almost 'as good a catch as Te Kooti'.[145] Another was Paora Tu, and one was a young man, Nikora Te Kiripaura, who had originally been taken as a prisoner at Turanga and who had gone with Te Kooti to the Waioeka. Paora said that after they had been attacked on 18 August the previous year they had all headed for Papuni, but that he and the youth with them, Hohepa (from Te Aitanga-a-Mahaki), were sent back to the Waipaoa stream to search out the troopers' path. At that point, Paora and Hohepa decided to leave Te Kooti. The pair went to Te Wera, where they met with Nikora, Maaka Ritai and Hirini Te Oiikau, who had all scattered after the fight near Maungapohatu on 1 September. They said that

Hirini had then left them to return to Waikaremoana, where his wife was, while they went to Te Reinga, where Ferris had encountered them. Their statements reveal the way in which, one by one, Te Kooti's supporters were leaving him to save their own lives.

An attempt by Te Kooti in January 1872 to capture new recruits at Maungaharuru pa was abandoned when one man was drowned, crossing at night over the colossal boulders of the Mohaka river, upstream of Willow Flat. The death was seen as an ill omen and Te Kooti turned back, according to an oral narrative still retained at Mohaka.[146] But in early March he appeared again — at Nuhaka, east of Wairoa, the territory of the old chief Ihaka Waanga, who had given his support to the government's expeditions from 1868.

On 10 March, Ihaka and Paora Apatu, senior Wairoa chiefs, wrote urgently: 'Te Kooti is here' ('Ko Te Kooti tenei'). Two days previously, Te Kooti had shown himself to Hare Houwaka, taken him prisoner and then sent him back to the chiefs with a message: that he would do them no harm — if they did not attack him. As he had treated Hare, so he would treat them. Ihaka and Paora interpreted the message as an offer of peace.[147] Hare reported that Te Kooti had with him four men (among whom was that staunch supporter, Hirini Te Oiikau), four children (or very young men), two women — and three guns. He said that Te Kooti had narrated the whole history of his pursuit from the moment of landing and emphasised how, when he finally turned his attention to war ('te whawhai') after he had been attacked at Puketapu, the government called it murder ('he Kohuru'). He asked Hare whether there were gardens where he could gather some food and, when Hare said there were none close by, told him to return in two days with food. The chiefs sent Hare back on 10 March, carrying a letter inviting Te Kooti 'to come in', and warning him that otherwise the pursuit would be immediately renewed — but he had, once again, vanished.[148]

Immediately this news reached Turanga, Paora Kate and Wi Pere joined Porter in an expedition to the Hangaroa river, hoping to block Te Kooti's passage back to the interior. But it was Ferris who picked up the trail, on 30 March, just one day old. He discovered that Te Kooti had, in the early hours of the previous morning, slipped through the long sentry line which had been set from Patutahi to Whenuakura (near Te Reinga). From a camp site near Paparatu, Te Kooti had got 'out from behind Whaka-punake right through the line of sentries posted to intercept him', Ferris wrote in angry frustration.[149] Te Kooti had clearly watched the liaison between the posted patrols and, at Kaikoura creek, flitted lightly between them in the darkness. He headed to the Hangaroa river and the land he knew intimately.

The trail Ferris now followed crossed and recrossed the Hangaroa, led to Papuni, and went down again to the Ruakituri river, the scene of Te Kooti's early victory of 1868. From there it passed through the dense bush to the eastern side of Waikaremoana. The trail covered about 150 miles, Ferris wrote, and Te Kooti never stopped for more than one night in any one place.[150] The pursuers sometimes saw where he had pulled wild honey from the trees in his flight; but they never saw him. Ferris deduced that Te Kooti would now seek to get through to the Waikato, as the Urewera was becoming less than ever a place of sanctuary.

In the aftermath of the attack on Te Kooti at Te Hapua on 1 September the previous

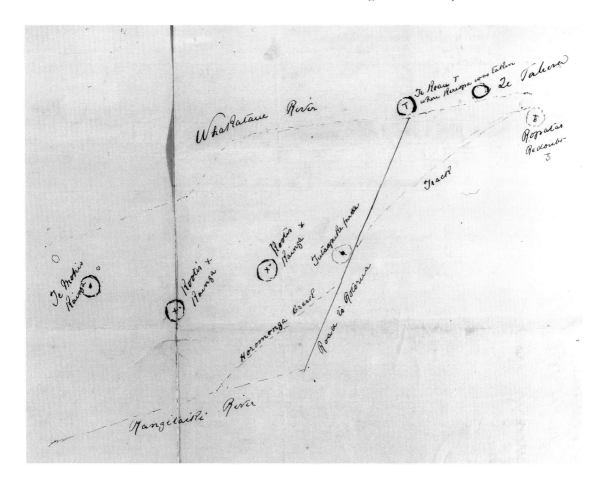

Map drawn 4 January 1872, showing where Kereopa was captured and also Ropata's redoubt at Ruatahuna. It marks the two kainga where Kereopa said that Te Kooti was hiding, in the deep bush north-west of Ruatahuna near Tutaepukepuke. The kainga lay on the east side of the Horomanga stream, which runs into the Rangitaiki river, and, according to Kereopa, the people there were sheltering Te Kooti. However, when Preece and Gilbert Mair followed up Kereopa's information, given the day before he was executed, they searched in vain.   AGG HB7/3, NA

year, the Maungapohatu chiefs, who had gathered to shelter in Tauaki pa when they heard the firing, had been forced to surrender 15 of Te Kooti's people who were, in fact, hiding with them. But they themselves still refused actively to help the government. Tauaki and Te Kakari were therefore attacked and captured by Ropata and Porter in late October, as part of the calculated policy of the 'pacification' of Ngati Huri. Both Maungapohatu and Ruatahuna were then held as occupied places, controlled by redoubts constructed on Ropata's orders. The first redoubt was built at Maungapohatu, and Ropata named it Kohitau (Gather in the Years) as his statement of the long path to their conquest.[151] Twice Makarini wrote in protest about Ropata's overbearing tactics 'within my boundaries' ('i roto i oku rohe'), burning houses, destroying cultivations and killing — all permitted by the government, as he observed sharply.[152] Te Purewa of Maunga-pohatu also tried to protest after the occupation of the pa, stating that the authority within Maungapohatu was his. He would have nothing to do with Ruatahuna: let Te Whenuanui and Paerau manage their people, and Tamaikoha his. Theirs was not the authority in Maungapohatu; the management of each hapu was its own, he stated firmly.[153] Finally, however, even the chiefs of Maungapohatu became the hunters. In exchange, however, they obtained what they had wanted: government recognition of the independent authority of the Tuhoe chiefs within their own separate districts.[154] Hetaraka Te Wakaunua of Maungapohatu then led a sweeping expedition through the land as far as Papuni and Erepeti in late February, and joined the search with Ferris in March. On this last patrol, there were 18 men from Maungapohatu as well as five from Tikitiki. Tuhoe had become the pursuers. Te Kooti's prediction — and instruction as to their final necessary tactics — had been fulfilled.

At the beginning of November, disgusted by the remorseless search, William Colenso had written to McLean in words which underscored the emerging narratives of Te Kooti's magical elusiveness. Nothing in the earlier wars compared with this bloody hunt, he stressed: nearly all Maori 'view this pursuit of Te Kooti and this killing of the Maoris with him as a set to against the race, & every event of this kind strengthens them, & the K[in]g party, wonderfully. — Would to God that 6 months ago you had made a *golden bridge* for Te Kooti to escape to Tawhiao! — that would have been the right thing.'[155] This was the bridge which Te Kooti finally trod; but it was not constructed by McLean.

In the last sweeps of the Urewera, the targets were just two men: Kereopa and Te Kooti. In November, Te Whiu and Hetaraka had led a Ngati Porou contingent to Kereopa's hiding-place at Te Roau, near Ruatahuna; as Kereopa said bitterly, it was the 'soldiers of Te Kooti's' from Maungapohatu who betrayed him.[156] But no one led Ngati Porou to Te Kooti. He still eluded the hunters, and he was helped on his way to safety. Late in April 1872 Ferris discovered his trail again, cutting across the Ruatahuna track, and it then seemed to Ferris to be once more heading south-west, towards the upper Wairoa or Mohaka.[157] However, at some point, Te Kooti turned back. He passed again through Heruiwi, where his dead trail was later found, and traversed the Rangitaiki river, passing close to the Galatea redoubt where, as he observed dryly, he had seen the soldiers playing cards at night.[158] He crossed the Kaingaroa plains, and on 15 May 1872 forded the Waikato river and entered Arowhena. There he slept the night: he had returned to the uneasy shelter of the Kingitanga.

Two women and six men accompanied him on the flight to Arowhena.[159] One of the women was Heni Kumekume. The other is unknown. She may have been Makurata, or possibly Oriwia. Maika Tuakana was one of the men, and Hirini Te Oiikau another.[160] This small, exhausted party went straight to Te Waotu, where Ngati Raukawa, who had been on the alert for them since October the previous year, were attending a hahunga, a ceremonial rite for the dead. They refused to receive them, broke up, and fled to their homes.[161] The little party then turned back again towards Te Kuiti and the King. They arrived there on 30 May, a group of battered refugees, in doubt as to their welcome. For, although Tawhiao had sent Aporo, his envoy, with an invitation of sanctuary to Te Kooti in July 1870 — just before the raid on Uawa — Te Kooti had, according to Huhana, distrusted the message and considered it simply a 'means of entrapping him'.[162]

Sleeping hut used by Te Kooti at Aotearoa pa, Arowhena. This tradition may date from the occasion of his flight into exile but more likely it dates from later times when he stayed there (as he did in June 1892). Photograph by W. R. B. Oliver, 1939.   A610, MONZ

But a second invitation, or karanga, had been proclaimed in November 1871 by Rewi, as we have seen. He would send a man to fetch him, he said. Rewi's terms were that there was sanctuary for Te Kooti with Maniapoto — if he came in peace. Although William Mair believed he had succeeded in dissuading Rewi from proclaiming it,[163] the call had certainly got through. On 8 November, at Whakatane, Preece heard that the Waikato people were determined to get Te Kooti to their country to give him shelter;[164] Ropata heard the same news only two days later at Maungapohatu.[165] If Te Paea had succeeded in pulling Ngati Kahungunu out of the hunt and into neutrality, it was Rewi's karanga which brought the wars to an end. It also ushered in the long years of Te Kooti's second exile.

CHAPTER 10

THE SHELTER OF MANIAPOTO
(MAY 1872–FEBRUARY 1883)

Hei konei tonu au taritari atu ai ki te ope tuarangi . . . .

Here am I still, awaiting the group from afar . . . .

SONG OF TE KOOTI, TE KUITI, c.1879.[1]

Te Kooti's reception at Te Kuiti was strained and uncomfortable. The news that he was seeking shelter reached there on 22 May 1872, and messages immediately summoned the leading Waikato chiefs to meet him upon his arrival. As expected, he came on 30 May, and it is still remembered how he sat on the hillside above Taupiri-o-te-rangi, Ngati Maniapoto's village, waiting while the deliberations, determining whether or not he would be invited to remain, dragged on.[2] Finally Maniapoto sent their messenger, Hone Taonui Hetet, to tell him that he could come in.

Te Kooti had entered their land at a time when the friction between Rewi Maniapoto (now called Mangamanga i Atua) and Tawhiao and the exiled Waikato leaders was again intensifying. Although the government had accepted the aukati, the encircling boundaries of the Rohe Potae which Pakeha could not enter without invitation, it was feeding the tension that existed between Ngati Maniapoto and their Waikato guests. In September 1871 Rewi had named William Mair 'Te Mea mataora roku' ('Mair, the weakening wedge'), recognising that his role was to lever them apart and the Rohe Potae open. McLean had begun to make approaches to Tawhiao from 1871, offering to recognise his authority 'within his own district'. The dilemma for Maniapoto was that this authority, if ever formally defined, would inexorably extend to legal control over their tribal lands. Tawhiao's perspective, as the homeless King, was that the *sine qua non* of any discussion with the government was the return of Waikato's confiscated lands: without this he would make no arrangements. Nevertheless, he was in a difficult position, for his support was slowly dwindling while his cause seemed ever more hopeless. Maniapoto, who were sheltering 2200 Waikato exiles living in or near Te Kuiti, also found the protracted role of host stressful. Rewi's offer of asylum to Te Kooti, whom Tawhiao had no desire to meet again, intensified the friction.

At first Tawhiao simply refused to see Te Kooti.[3] McLean quickly gathered that Te Kooti was living among the King's followers as 'no more than a prisoner at large during quiet behaviour'.[4] The tension increased as June went by, with Waikato jeering

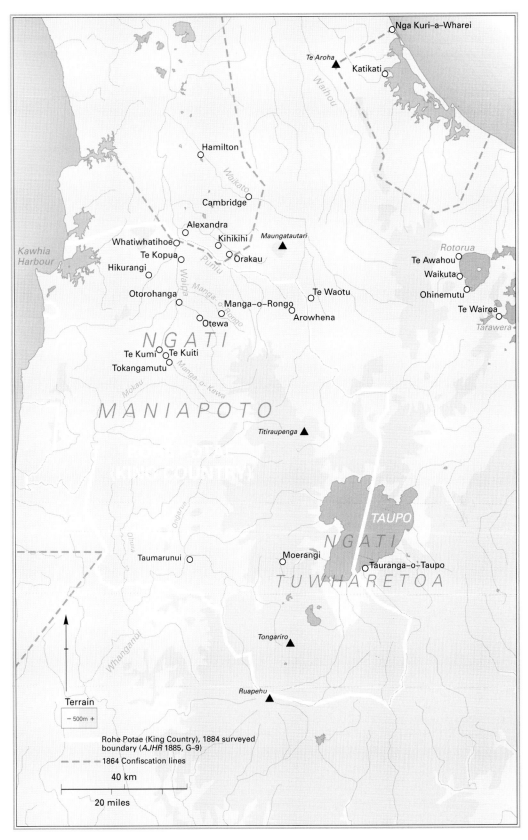

Map 6. *The Bounded Lands of Maniapoto*

Hone Taonui Hetet, the Ngati Maniapoto
messenger who was sent to Te Kooti to
invite him to enter Te Kuiti in May 1872.
Photograph from Tokanganui-a-noho,
Te Kuiti.   PORTRAITS 2/10,
      ANTHROPOLOGY DEPARTMENT ARCHIVE, AU

at Te Kooti and saying that he had been sent for by Rewi merely 'to keep him out of mischief'.[5] Tawhiao's messenger to the government, Aihepene Kaihau, who had recently married Te Paea, Tawhiao's sister, told the King to seize Te Kooti and make a slave of him if he saw him: 'me whakataurereka i a Te Kooti ki te kite koe i a ia'. He added brutally, let him 'be like a potato do not allow him any mana'.[6] By July, Mair reported that Te Kooti was saying that if the people there did not show him any more sympathy he would 'go back east'.[7]

Instead he was sent by Rewi to the upper Mokau river. It was dense bush country and would remain a '*terra incognita*'[8] to Europeans for many years yet. Te Kooti was reluctant to go there, objecting that he was being 'snubbed' at Te Kuiti not only by Tawhiao but also by Reihana Te Wahanui of the upper Mokau, the emerging leader of Maniapoto.[9] But Rewi and Te Wahanui escorted him there at the end of June, and it is clear that Te Kooti was being sent away. He was taken under a kind of 'safe conduct' as a refugee, and placed under the surveillance of the chief Tawhana.[10] When Tawhana said to Rewi, 'haere mai me to taonga' ('come to me with your treasure'), Rewi and Te Wahanui replied to him, 'ehara i te taonga' ('it is no treasure').[11]

Te Kooti remained in the Mokau district for a year, until May 1873. He settled at Mangaehu, near Te Poroporo, accompanied by about ten followers, and began culti-

Rewi Maniapoto (Mangamanga i Atua), December 1878.

vating the land. He also travelled down the river to the Mokau heads to get shellfish in the early spring. His appearance there coincided with a party of gold prospectors digging at the river mouth. The diggers were ordered off the land by Tawhiao, while Wetere Te Rerenga, the influential chief of upper Mokau who had led the attack on Pukearuhe redoubt in 1869, threatened a renewal of war against Ngati Mutunga for their apparent willingness to open up the coast to the prospectors. Te Kooti was said to have offered his support to Te Rerenga, but Tawhiao immediately sent messages for both of them to shut up.[12] Tawhiao also told Te Kooti that he must not travel to the coast again. The terms of sanctuary were an uncomfortable supervision until he submitted to Tawhiao's and Rewi's word that it was the time of peace, not war. This Te Kooti was still reluctant to accept. When Tawhiao came to the upper Mokau in December, Rewi sent for Te Kooti. He came 'with his seven followers & made a long speech & prayer — Tawhiao remained in his tent & made no sign whatever and Tk went away without eating the food prepared for him.'[13] It seemed to be an absolute fracture. Their reconciliation would not come about until the following year.

Pressured by this forced isolation, Te Kooti began to change. William Mair first gave the hint when he wrote in June 1873 that Te Kooti's desire was no longer to exert 'for evil' but rather 'to live at peace', and that through his sheer 'force of character' he was starting to recover a certain amount of influence.[14] In 1883 Te Kooti himself was to acknowledge:

> Ko te 10 tenei o nga tau i mutu ai i toku ringa te Hoari, i takoto ai ahau ki raro ki nga waewae o te Kingi, i ki ai ahau ka mutu i ahau te whawhai e haere nei tae noa mai ki tenei ra.

> This is the 10th year that has gone by since I ceased holding the Sword, which I laid at the feet of the King, when I said I have finished with the fighting going on [and have continued to do so] up to this day.[15]

Kereopa Te Apa of Aotea described the reconciliation of Tawhiao and Te Kooti. Tawhiao finally visited Te Kooti at Mokau about the middle of 1873. Before leaving Te Kuiti, Tawhiao spoke to his close kinsman Hotuhotu (Mohi) Purukutu, to whom he had given sanctuary after his slaying (in April 1873) of Timothy Sullivan, a Pakeha labourer clearing leased land inside the boundaries of the Rohe Potae. As a condition of his shelter, Purukutu had accepted Tawhiao's decree that there was to be no fighting and he had 'buried' his weapon at Te Kuiti.[16] Tawhiao summoned him,[17] and said:

> Kakahuria ou, e tu ki konei e haere ana ahau ki a Te Kooti.

> Put on your raiment and stay here, I am going to Te Kooti.

When he reached Te Kooti, he echoed his command:

> Kakahuria ou, takoto ki raro ki taku takahanga waewae.

> Put on your raiment; lie down at my footstool.[18]

With these words, Tawhiao offered Te Kooti his protection. Te Kooti, in response, accepted his command that these were the days of peace. In this manner the new era was initiated. It was the beginning of the period in which the new premises of the faith would emerge.

Te Kooti now came back to Te Kuiti to live. He arrived there in mid-September, and on 22 September Mair observed: 'Tk came to Kuiti to assist in building Tawhiaos house & is to remain there in future.'[19] He had come, Mair added a few days later, 'to superintend the carvings for the new house'.[20] Thus the sealing of the words of reconciliation was the carving and painting of the great meeting-house, now known as Tokanganui-a-noho, at Te Kuiti.

The house would, in fact, be substantially reconstructed by Te Kooti over a long period of time. He would transform it into one of the earliest and finest of the major carved and painted houses of the new era, whose purpose was to establish the 'Kotahitanga' or Unity of God's words. In September 1873 the original house was nearly finished and was being prepared for opening. It was being built by Ngati Haua of Waikato, 'in their portion of Kuiti', for Tawhiao.[21] There were 18 carved images (poupou) erected on the inside walls of the house. Its construction had, according to one account, been undertaken in the context of Tawhiao's planned move to Kawhia harbour. His intention was to leave the territory of Maniapoto and return to his kin living on the only southern lands remaining to Waikato. It was also being said that Te Kooti was to accompany Tawhiao and Ngati Haua on this journey of migration, and that he was to choose a site for his own kainga at Kawhia. This account seems to contradict Mair's earlier report that Te Kooti had come to reside at Te Kuiti. The house was being built, it was explained, in order 'to take charge of the place': it was to stand as a guardian for Waikato in the place they were leaving.[22] It was also being constructed as confirmation of Tawhiao's prediction of permanent peace, to which Te Kooti had now bound himself.

The innovations which were to extend and transform the house must be attributed largely to Te Kooti. The ancestral figures (expanded in number to 28 named figures on the two side walls with others on the front and rear walls) belong to different tribes, symbolising the gathering of the exiles at Te Kuiti. Their names were carved on their chests so that all could know them. They included the great founding heroes Maui and Paikea, as well as the eponymous tribal ancestors such as Maniapoto, Porourangi, Tuwharetoa and Tuhoe. The statement of reconciliation between Tawhiao and Te Kooti was further enunciated with the two poutokomanawa (central posts), which depict Mahina a Rangi and her husband Turongo, whose marriage had united the people of the East Coast and the Waikato. Most striking of all was the novel use of painted images both inside and outside the house. The tradition of painted scroll patterns on house rafters and canoes and paddles was strong in the art of Turanganui; here, this tradition from the East Coast was transformed into a figurative style, which would become particularly associated with the meeting-houses of the Ringatu. Tokanganui-a-noho was one of the first of the great meeting-houses in which brightly coloured naturalistic images of plants and flowers and stars and 'sea-beings' (marakihau), as well as painted portraits of living people, would be used.

Te Kooti's supervision of the paintings and carvings took place over two distinct periods. The original carved house was opened on 22 October 1873.[23] Then Te Kooti and Tawhiao travelled together to the Kawhia coast. They went to visit the Ngati Mahuta settlement at Te Taharoa and to open another new meeting-house there, but neither man remained at Kawhia.[24] Instead, Tawhiao returned to live for a while in the house at Te Kuiti, leading to it becoming known as the King's house. But he did not stay. After Tawhiao left Te Kuiti in 1875 Te Kooti brought in carvers from different regions to alter the house extensively and to create the new designs. Wiremu Kaimoana, a famous carver of Wairoa who was closely associated with Te Waru's people, described how he 'went to Waikato at the request of Te Kooti to build the "whare whakairo" for him at Te Kuiti — the name of the house being "Tokanganuianoho" — that work occupied a year & a half.' He said that this was in 1879,[25] but his memory from 1903 was probably a year or two out. As the renovations were nearing completion, the house was moved from its probable first site at Tokangamutu, the King's settlement at the northern end of Te Kuiti, to a new site at the mouth of the Manga-o-Kewa gorge in September 1882. A manuscript book, believed to have been kept by the Maniapoto elder Tomika Kereti, contains the following entry referring to this house:

Te Kuiti Hepetema 23 1882

He whakamahara tenei i te ra me te marama me te tau i maranga ai te whare whakairo i te Kuiti. Koia tenei ka timata i raro iho nei.

Te Kuiti, 3 June 1885. The house Tokanganui-a-noho, whose gable can be seen on the right, stands on the western bank of the river at the mouth of the Manga-o-Kewa gorge (south of modern Te Kuiti). This was the settlement where Te Kooti was known to be living early in 1883. The house was moved there in September 1882, before its reopening on 2 January 1883, when Te Kooti gave it to Ngati Maniapoto. It had been extensively re-carved and re-worked during 1881–82, under Te Kooti's direction. Photograph by Alfred Burton.

227, MONZ

No te 12 o nga haora o te po ka karia nga pou tahu. Tu tonu atu nga pou no te 14 ka iri te tahu ki runga.

Heoi ka maranga i konei te whare.

Te Kuiti September 23 1882

This is in memory of the day, month and year in which the carved house at Te Kuiti was lifted. It began as below.

At 12 o'clock at night the main posts were dug out. The posts were set apart, and on the 14th the ridge pole was placed upon them.

So the house was moved from here.[26]

Te Kooti's secretary Hamiora Aparoa stated in his records that the new work of

Tokanganui-a-noho, c.1887. The name of the carved head (koruru) on the front gable, 'Waho', is visible.
Later, the sign would be altered to 'Rawaho'; both are abbreviations for Rawaho o Te Rangi, a Maniapoto
ancestor. This name is not the original name of the house, as has recently been suggested. Henare
Tuwhangai and Robert Emery, senior Maniapoto elders, have both stated independently that the original
name of the house, given to it by Tawhiao, was Tokanganui-a-mutu, referring to the end of the hostilities
(or perhaps the Great Basket for those who have been cut off). The later name given to it was taken from
a Ngati Maniapoto house at Aotea (also erected in 1873), which had burnt down, and it referred to a
Maniapoto proverb; the name was transferred to the house at Te Kuiti on its reopening in 1883.

The photograph shows the painted figures of two warriors on the doorway. The figure on the left has
a topknot, and wears a huia feather, indicating high rank; the figure on the right has the short hair of the
new generation and he also wears a huia feather. Both hold a taiaha. Several paintings are also visible on
the posts and wall panels. One of the two large painted marakihau (sea-beings) can be seen on the right
of the doorway; they were described by S. Percy Smith in 1897 as standing between six and eight feet tall.
Linear patterns of leaves are also visible on the two upright boards on the left of the doorway, and stars
and 'spoke-wheels' can be seen to the right of the window. This use of painted images was innovatory.
All these figures and decorations are visible in Burton's 1885 photographs of the house, as is the named
koruru. These are undoubtedly the decorations of the 1881–82 reconstruction. What is missing in this
photograph is the large carved figure of a 'listener', which stood at the base of the post 1883–85: a male
figure with his right hand held up to his ear. This was the Ngati Mahuta ancestor Papaka, who would
reappear in the photographs of the house taken in 1899, shortly after its third move, which brought it to
its present site in Te Kuiti. He was possibly a free-standing figure, as was sometimes the case.
Photograph by F. Stewart.   B16499, MONZ

carving on Tokanganui-a-noho was begun on 9 October 1881 and completed on 20
December 1882.[27] Wiremu Kaimoana remembered correctly that he went home from
'the Waikato', the work completed, in 1883. The house was formally reopened on 2
January 1883, when Te Kooti gave it to the Maniapoto chiefs in gratitude for their

Interior of Tokanganui-a-noho in 1899. It shows the original earth floor and the two poutokomanawa,
Turongo and his wife Mahina a Rangi. The carved poupou have their names cut on their chests. This
photograph was taken after the removal of the house to its present site.

James Cowan, who knew the house, said that Te Kooti had constructed it with a secret door in the
rear wall. This was, he said, when the house was standing on its first site. Te Kooti used the door to
make 'miraculous appearances', having publicly left by the door at the front and then reappearing in the
smoky atmosphere from nowhere, at the rear of the house, with a prayer-book in his hands. Photograph
by James McDonald.   C156, MONZ

sanctuary. This history of the reopening of Tokanganui-a-noho in 1883, when it was so
named, is recorded in the Ringatu prayerbook:

> Na ka oti te whare whakairo o Te Kooti, i te Kuiti, i roto o nga ra o Tihema, i te 20 o
> nga ra, 1882. Muri iho ka taia te kawa a ka oti. Kua haere taua whakaatu ki nga iwi i
> runga i tana tikanga o te motu nei. Ko te kupu tera: Ko te ra tuatahi o Hanuere 1883, kei
> te Kuiti nei; me hui mai tatou ki konei whakarite ai i taua ra. Kia rongo ai i nga kupu,
> pehea ra te ahua.
> *Te Kuiti Hanuere 2, 1883.* Ka hui mai hoki nga rangatira o Ngati-Maniapoto, a N[g]ati-
> roora, ki roto i taua whare i taua ra, a Taonui raua ko Tawhana-tamaiti me etahi atu
> rangatira hoki. . . . Ki reira ratou ko Te Kooti ma korero tahi ai i a ratou korero mo nga
> iwi me te motu katoa hoki. A tukua atu ana e Te Kooti ma ratou e hua mai he ingoa mo

taua whare whakairo, a ko ana. Kupu tuku atu tenei: Haere mai e aku rangatira, haere mai ki to tatou taonga e tu nei. Kei kimikimi nga whakaaro, me aku nei whakaaro i mahia ai tenei whare hei taonga; heoi ano he aroha ki te tangata. Na ko tenei: ka tukua atu ki a koutou tenei whare i tenei ra ano. Kaati maku ko te mahi ma nga iwi nana i hanga tenei whare. Na to tatou taonga ki a koutou, ma koutou hoki e hua mai he ingoa mo to tatou taonga, ara mo tenei whare.

Now, the carved house of Te Kooti's was completed at Te Kuiti, in the days of December, on the 20th, 1882. Later, the ceremonies to remove the tapu were held [and] completed. That notice went out to the tribes under his faith in this land. It said: the first day of January 1883, at Te Kuiti — let us all gather here to fulfil that day and hear the words as to how it will be.

Te Kuiti January 2, 1883. The chiefs of Ngati Maniapoto and N[g]ati Roora also met in that house on that day; Taonui, Tawhana-tamaiti and some other chiefs too. . . . There they, together with Te Kooti and the others, had discussions concerning the tribes and also about the whole land. And Te Kooti allowed that they should give a name for that carved house, and his words delivered there were these: Welcome, my chiefs, welcome to our treasure which stands here. In case you are wondering about my intentions in building this house as a treasure, well, it was just love for the people. Now, there is this: this house is given to you on this very day. The work by the people who built the house is enough for me. Because it is our gift to you, you then must give a name to our treasure, that is, to this house.[28]

In this narrative, the name Tokanganui-a-noho was then chosen by the Maniapoto chief Taonui Hikaka. He spoke of Te Kuiti as the place of hemming-in and constriction (the literal, geographical meaning of Te Kuititanga), extending it to a larger statement of their present unhappy situation, and calling it the place where the survivors must gather together. It was, he said, consciously echoing Wiremu Kingi Te Rangitake's famous words about Waitara, the rock where the godwits could gather when all other places were consumed by the flowing tide of settlement. This house must be the perch. Therefore it was to be named, incorporating both an old Maniapoto proverb and the name of a former house built at Aotea in 1873 which had burnt down, the 'Great Basket for those who rested there'. But Te Kooti replied with one of his most famous predictions of warning:

No te mea koia na tonu te tikanga o a tatou mahara, ko te rapu tikanga mo te motu nei mo nga whenua me te tangata hoki. Otira e taea e ahau te pewhea, te take he kupu kua oti i au te korero i mua: 'Tenei ake nga ra kei te haere mai ka moana katoa tenei wahi ahu atu na ki roto o te awa nei puta noa ki waho, ka riro atu a konei i te Pakeha. A kati . . . kei te haere mai nga ra e whiowhio mai te Atua o te Pakeha i enei wahi; i tua ake ano, o te whare nei . . . rere tonu iho, tomo tonu mai i te roro o te whare nei, puta rawa atu i te tuarongo o te whare a, tera tonu koutou e kite e rarangi ana nga tutohu o te Atua whiowhio o te Pakeha i runga i nga hiwi tonu i tua tata ake nei o te whare nei. Na e kore e puta mai te tutukitanga o enei kupu o enei ra e korero nei ahau, engari kia hiki aku waewae i tenei wahi o Te Kuiti nei, ka moana a muri i au. A e kite ake ano aku kanohi i te raina e rere haere ana i muri i au. . . . Na ka kite ano iho aku kanohi i muri i au, e makenu ana te pawhatitang[a] o te huarahi o te Atua whiowhio haere o te Pakeha a ka waiho noa iho hei tangi noa ma te ngakau mokai'.

For this is the very reason for our thoughts, to seek the direction for this land, for the lands and the people too. But I will achieve this somehow — and the reason lies in the words already spoken of by me earlier: 'In days to come this place will be completely flooded, moving across into this river and right out to sea; [and] that will be taken by the Pakeha. And also . . . the day will come when the God of the Pakeha will whistle in these places; from far beyond this house . . . continuing right down to it, entering right into the porch of the house and coming straight through the back of it, and then at once you will see in lines the signs of the whistling God of the Pakeha along the very ridges which stand near this house. Now, the fulfilment of these words will not be achieved during the days in which I am speaking, but when I lift my feet from this place here in Te Kuiti, then the flood will come after I [am gone]. And my eyes will also see the line running along after me. . . . And my eyes will also see, after I [have gone] traces of the broken branches in the pathway of the whistling God of the Pakeha, which will just be left to be wept over by the foolish hearted'.[29]

The whistling God is understood as the prediction of the main trunk railway line, which would pass directly through Te Kuiti and force the removal of the house, for the third time, to its present site. The year 1883 marks the opening of the King Country to surveying, allowing the line to be built. Te Kooti's pardon was the final condition — of the several which Ngati Maniapoto laid down to the government — for the opening of the borders of the Rohe Potae. It would be met in February 1883.

Te Kooti's prophecy is retold from the King Country to Poverty Bay. It is a favourite tale because of the many implications, or layers of meaning, it conveys. The Ringatu elder from Poverty Bay, Reuben Riki, in 1982 told how Te Kooti had said to the King:

'I stand by and look back and I see a monster — a ngārara — it's behind my back, belching flames, and smoke.' That's the train. You see, where the pā is now, the government wants that place moved. They want the whole area for a marshalling yard — even today. I think that place has been moved two or three times to where it is now. And they want to move it again.[30]

The narrative extends right to the present: it suggests the constant pressure placed on the people and the land in the name of progress and development, which will directly touch their lives. In another version of the story, told by Boy Biddle, when 'they were standing in the middle of the bush — wasn't even a road there', Te Kooti said, 'when I lift my foot up, the Queen's belt will stretch through here'. The train itself is a metaphor of penetration by another authority. Its unswerving pathway through the land is the bite of European law or, as Boy Biddle added directly, 'how they were going to break Waikato's grip'.[31] Te Kooti's words predict a challenge to Tawhiao, and a warning of the end of the Rohe Potae. The story, then, confirms Te Kooti's understanding of the radical disruption that would follow from the very issue for which his pardon would be traded.

Tokanganui-a-noho in its 1883 form was one of the earliest houses built for the new Kotahitanga (Unity), 'concerning God's Words amongst all the tribes' ('mo wa te Atua Kupu ki waenganui i nga iwi katoa'), as Matiu Paeroa carefully described their

Taonui Hikaka. This portrait
hangs inside Tokanganui-a-noho.
PORTRAITS 2/34/40, ANTHROPOLOGY
DEPARTMENT ARCHIVE, AU

purpose.[32] These are the first meeting-houses which were built to be equally whare karakia (houses of worship). Faith and life were one; therefore, no separate houses of worship were built in Te Kooti's lifetime by his followers. The people were to pray within the encircling community of the ancestors; this is the organising principle in the structure of wharenui, which Te Kooti sustained. The house not only contains the images of the ancestors and expresses the group's identity; its actual structure represents the sheltering body of the 'parent'. This concept may well have stemmed from East Coast practices, such as placing the ancestors on the interior poupou of the house.[33] In building assembly houses that were also to be houses of prayer, Te Kooti engendered a new phase in the revival of the wharenui throughout the land.

According to Matiu's list, six other meeting-houses were built during the years Te Kooti lived within the Rohe Potae and before his pardon in 1883. They preceded the completion of Tokanganui-a-noho, and were all erected before Te Kooti was free to travel. The first five were all built on the Coromandel peninsula or at its base: Waikohu at Mataora (1877), Te Tahawai, near Katikati (1878), Katikati (1879), Waiau (1880)[34] and Te Makomako, Ohinemuri (1881). The names of these houses are not recorded in the list, and none survives today. The last, and most famous, however, is Ruataupare at Kokohinau, Te Teko. It was opened on 1 January 1882, and the oral traditions of Ngati Pahipoto state that Te Kooti sent the men who built and carved their house, and that he paid for all the construction costs as well.[35] The story of Kokohinau, and of some of the subsequent houses built for Te Kooti when he was at last able to travel beyond the bounds of the King Country, will be told in later chapters.

Tokanganui-a-noho probably introduced the naturalistic style of painting into meeting-house decoration. It was covered with trees, plants and flowers in cheerful, bright colours representing the land and its fruitfulness. On its exterior both the carvings and the painted panels were coloured white, black, red, green and blue, all hand-mixed from pipe-clay, charcoal and red ochre, melded in fish-oil.[36] The colours will have been intended to make symbolic statements, but we do not have their details now. The paintings of people included the living as well as the dead, and this was a break from most carving traditions. Portrayal of the living had begun earlier with Raharuhi Rukupo and his self-portrait carved in Te Hau-ki-Turanga (pictured in Chapter 4) and, at about the same time, Te Rangihaeata's self-portrait carved in a house he had built on Mana Island.[37] One might also add to this list Hongi Hika's carved self-portrait made in 1814. On the porch of Tokanganui-a-noho were images from the new world: a painted compass and the globe, together with a scene from a football match, with the players wearing the colours of the Auckland club.[38] On the rear wall of the porch was a painted panel of two people playing cricket and dressed for the part in European clothes. This style, depicting the new ways of measuring space as well as the ordinary, happy activities of 19th-century life, painted realistically, would be developed in many of the meeting-houses built for Te Kooti.

Roger Neich, in his recent study of the painted houses, has argued that an entirely new way of representing the world was born at Tokanganui-a-noho: that is, temporal narrative in painting, a conceptual change from the timeless presence of the ancestors in the carved houses.[39] Painting was developed because, unlike tattooing or carving, it was not bound by strict rules of tapu, nor did it require a lengthy period of training. The use of painted designs on and within the meeting-houses was not in itself an innovation; indeed, it was a strong part of the work of Rukupo, Te Kooti's mentor. But Te Kooti adopted it as an idiom to comment on the people's rapidly changing social and political histories. It was a form of episodic, visual narrative which recorded the history of the present and the actual people who had built the houses or donated the timber — living people. As the older meeting-houses had maintained the history of the ancestors and included the great figures from Maori cosmology, such as Maui and Paikea, now the houses carried as well painted symbols of the new world (the globe) and included illustrations of the domestic lives of the people. As the meeting-house is a place of encounter, where guests meet hosts, so too the histories confronted each other in the painted houses of Te Kooti. Two cultural spaces were depicted in the houses, the new jostling the old. Tokanganui-a-noho encompassed visually the ancient and the modern histories of all the tribes sheltering within the Rohe Potae. It was indeed the 'Great

Basket' of taonga (treasures) for all the people it protected, as the transfer of this name to the house was intended to convey.

This vision, a dialogue between the past and the present, was Te Kooti's. In a similar way he adapted the narrative songs. At the opening of Tokanganui-a-noho on 2 January, the Ringatu narrative records how, during his speech, Te Kooti sang two waiata, both of which he had adapted from older songs. In the second of these he told how, like weather-beaten Paikea, he had made his landfall to become a part of Maniapoto ('he pahi rawa au nou e Maniapoto, nou e Maniapoto'), as more than a spouse and more than a grandchild. These lines were reiterated from the original Ngati Kahungunu waiata aroha (love song). But at the end of this old song, he suddenly added a new warning for Maniapoto:

> me whakahoki atu nga moni ki te peeke nga moni ki te peeke, e mataku ana hau kei hou ki te whenua kei hou ki te whenua.

> return the moneys to the bank, the moneys to the bank, for I fear lest this land be bound up, lest this land be bound up.[40]

The speech, the songs (and probably the paintings too) contain premonitions of loss. The song warns of forced sales to banks and creditors, the standard device by which Maori land was acquired at this time. In later years, when Te Kooti travelled to open the new meeting-houses, he would invariably find the possibility of disruption or betrayal to which to alert the people. He often set tests or riddles for them to solve, based on the warnings he read from the house — its particular design, or the manner of its construction. The house would provide the image for the kupu whakaari. From the message of warning, he would then build the words and teachings of the new faith, precisely as he did at Te Kuiti on 2 January 1883. For, after he had sung his waiata warning of dispossession and the seductiveness of money, he told the people that the way forward belonged to God and the gospel, which would soon be broadcast among them. The way also belonged to 'the kind and forbearing heart' ('me te ngakau ngawari, manawanui'), the quality of the new and gentler faith, as he frequently described it. Then, he said, 'only then will it be completed, it will be fulfilled, and [we] will again have life' ('na katahi ano ka tutuki, ka rite ano hoki ka whiwhi ano hoki te oranga').[41]

Thus Te Kooti offered a collective salvation for the people through the teachings of the gospel or the new faith, whose essential quality and objective was 'kia ngawari', the journey towards tolerance and gentleness. 'Kia ngawari', as Ned Brown said in 1982 when discussing the history of the successive meeting-houses named 'Te Ngawari' built for Te Kooti at Mangatu, was to be peaceful and forbearing, in conscious rejection of the violent ways of the past.[42] This commitment to peace was undoubtedly the foundation of the faith developed by Te Kooti at Te Kuiti from 1874. Before tracing that history, however, we must first return to the political world which Te Kooti found himself inhabiting from the mid-1870s and to the ways in which he was seen in that world.

Quite soon after he came to Te Kuiti, Te Kooti made a concerted effort to obtain a pardon or, alternatively, a high court trial in England. He had consistently said, even in the last stages of his pursuit, that he was willing to be tried by the law.[43] On 17 October

This military-issue Snider carbine, manufactured in 1874, was acquired from Hamohana, who lived at Muriwai, Poverty Bay. It was reputed to have been once the property of a follower of Te Kooti. Red sealing wax has been used as an inlay in the carving, including the eyes of the figure on one side; on the other side the huia is carved in the realistic style associated with the Ringatu. Its provenance, combined with these particulars, suggest the gun might have been a peace-making gift. It was acquired by the Auckland Museum in 1934, along with other items from the East Coast. J. HALL COLLECTION, W752, AIM

1873 he went to Otorohanga, near the northern border of the Rohe Potae, where he met by prior arrangement his friend from Turanga, Ogilvie Ross, who was now living just across the Puniu river. Ross had earlier corresponded with Te Kooti, and Te Kooti's reply to him in February 1873 has survived. He wrote:

> Ko tenei, me whakaaro pumau nou kia kite koe i a au, e pai ana. Kei wehi koe, haere mai i runga o te aroha o te rangimarire. Kia wawe taua te kite me te korero tahi me te kawe tikanga ki te Kaiwhakawa nui. Ko koe tonu hei kawe ia [*sic*] aku kupu.

> If you are set on seeing me I agree to it. Don't be afraid, come in love and peace. Let us come together soon to see each other and talk together and take the case to the High Court judge. You yourself are to convey my words.[44]

To this letter he attached another to Sarah Dunlop, Ross's wife, whom Te Kooti, long ago, had looked after as a child. He sent his greetings and love to her and her children, and to her husband. He told her not to be afraid of him, for his love for them was constant. He asked her also to send him some clothes and medicine, and a couple of bottles of brandy: 'Girl, I will owe you for that' ('He nama naku ki a koe e hine').[45]

After this exchange of letters (carried for him by that staunch messenger, Hirini Te Oiikau), in May 1873 Te Kooti had sent his 'wife' (probably Heni, who would have been known to Ross) bearing a letter for McLean. In it Te Kooti asked for a pardon. Ross forwarded the letter,[46] but nothing more is known about it. He then came to meet Te Kooti in October, presumably with the government's knowledge. Afterwards Ross told William Mair that Te Kooti had treated his followers arrogantly but was humble, even 'cringing', to Ross. Te Kooti asked him to intercede on his behalf with the govern-

ment. He said he sought peace, and offered his revolver as the token of his intentions. Ross refused it. Mair's interpretation of all this, sent immediately to McLean, was that Te Kooti was 'demoralised & harmless'.[47] This view would not have helped any proposals which Ross brought. Yet Mair admitted that Te Kooti's 'urgent desire for pardon' was understandable and was also a significant move on his part. For, as he said, Te Kooti 'is an uncommonly shrewd fellow — we know — and as he sees the barrier breaking down it is only natural that he should speculate as to what will become of him' if the Rohe Potae were to be opened.[48]

Te Kooti's other strategy was to seek a trial in England, saying that only in that country was there any possibility of its being fair.[49] The experiences of the treason trials undergone by some of his followers in 1869 and 1870, and the hasty execution of Kereopa in 1872, bore him out in that respect. The inflamed stereotypes of Te Kooti being portrayed in most of the newspapers at this time would be accepted by the majority of European settlers, from whom any jury would inevitably be drawn. In popular imagery in 1873 Te Kooti was simply a murderer and violator of innocents, and no judge, however impartial, would be able to say otherwise. As the Napier *Telegraph* put it, in reference to both Te Kooti and Te Hata Tipoki, who was living in the King Country with him and who had expressed a wish to come to Poverty Bay to visit his mother: 'After our experience in hanging Kereopa, there would be no need to practise Calcraft's art on bags of sand. . . . A long rope and a short shrift will be all the honor' both should receive.[50]

From 1873 reports of Te Kooti's erratic behaviour also begin to appear. He was said to be drinking heavily — and from this time Pakeha descriptions usually portray him as a 'joker' and a drunk, and a man without mana. Yet all these reports contain their own contradictions. When James Mackay was sent that April to the King Country to try to persuade Tawhiao to surrender the men responsible for killing the labourer Timothy Sullivan, Te Kooti is described in the terms of the emerging stereotype, but other elements are present. Mackay was attacked by a young Waikato man at Te Kuiti on 6

May, and shortly afterwards, on the same morning, he unexpectedly encountered Te Kooti. As Mair reported the episode,

> T.K snatched off Mackay's hat . . . & putting it behind his back said 'taurekareka kei whea ahau kia mau i a koe: tena korero mai ki au' ['slave, when will I be caught by you; tell me']! They became good friends afterwards, but Mackay was about to play him only Rewi interposed saying 'Kati he haurangi' ['Enough, he's a drunkard'].

Mair commented that, although Mackay had not mentioned the encounter to him, he had said that Te Kooti was 'quite an insignificant looking little fellow, but has a good deal of influence with the young bloods; he is such a wag.'[51] The remark lightens the emphasis considerably, and provides an unexpected image of Te Kooti. Mackay also made no mention of the incident in his official report,[52] but he did describe it in some detail 16 years later. He had been attacked in his tent but immediately placed under Rewi's protection, and removed from the Waikato section of the settlement to Maniapoto's section. He was bathing his wound in the river when Te Kooti approached him, under the influence of alcohol. He wanted to shake hands but, when Mackay refused, he snatched Mackay's hat and hid it behind his back. Mackay then tried to wrestle it from him but Rewi intervened, fearing a fight. In Mackay's account, Rewi said warningly to Te Kooti, 'Mackay is my name now, all Ngatimaniapoto are named Mackay'.[53] In other words, leave him alone. The next day Mackay and Te Kooti met again by accident, just outside Te Kuiti. Te Kooti was quite sober. This second encounter was mentioned in Mackay's report, where he stated that Te Kooti appeared to have considerable influence with Maniapoto. Te Kooti told Mackay that he had dissociated himself from the Waikato exiles and the periodic attacks on Pakeha which had occurred. He emphasised that in all matters within the Rohe Potae he was guided by Rewi.[54] He then insisted on giving Mackay a lengthy account of the injustices he had experienced. He reiterated his conviction that it was Biggs's insistence on pursuit which alone had forced the fighting in 1868. He said, as was reported at the time by Leonard Williams and others, that he himself had always intended to try to get peacefully through to Te Kuiti. He also said clearly that he had subsequently sent word to Biggs that he would descend on Turanga, but that Biggs had simply not believed it.[55] He apologised for taking Mackay's hat and left, as 'an atonement', a small greenstone ear-drop.[56] When placed together these accounts reveal different facets of Te Kooti's personality, but they are not incompatible. They may reveal a man who takes his drink. They also show a man of quick intellect, of a stature which Mackay recognised, who was burdened with a strong sense of injustice.

Another encounter story stems from November 1873. An anonymous 'European' described his recent meeting with Te Kooti at the latter's settlement at Te Kuiti:

> Soon after we commenced our meal in came Te Kooti. He was dressed in good style, in fact, well got up — blue cloth military coat, handsomely braided and buttoned; trousers, Wellington boots, high top soft felt hat. I soon observed that the demon rum had taken him captive, and that he is no more the Te Kooti of former times. Physically, he is a wreck . . . . His name and fame have gained for him a deference and authority throughout Maoridom seldom accorded to Tawhiao. His intellect is like burnished steel — clear and bright. All questions of policy are referred to him, and his advice is

regularly carried out. 'Fighting,' he said, 'is bad for Maori and pakeha; and I never mean to fight again. If you doubt me, here is my revolver, which you can send to McLean, and say, 'This is Te Kooti's revolver, who wants to be at liberty to settle near the pakeha, where he can get eels and rum.' ... On retiring for the night, we found everything clean and comfortable — sheets, blankets, and quilt in proper European fashion. ... My reverie was suddenly dispelled by noises outside, where I distinctly heard Te Kooti discanting upon the folly of war. He said, 'Guns are bad; they shoot Maori and pakeha alike. Put away the guns! Plant corn! Catch the fish! And drink the rum! These are better than fighting.'[57]

Contradictions jostle each other in this account. The theme of drunkenness is set against the description of order, cleanliness, intelligence, authority, teachings based on the pursuit of peace, and a life based on the skills of planting and harvesting. This is not to say that Te Kooti did not get drunk, nor that he did not use alcohol for pleasure and also, more dangerously, to enhance his visionary experiences. Two years later, Rewi escorted an ex-trooper, who had once hunted Te Kooti at Mohaka, beside Te Kooti's kainga at Te Kuiti and cruelly commented (to indicate that the man had nothing to fear from an accidental encounter): '"he is a dog of mine and will not bark unless I set him on, but if he should say any thing to you, it will be simply because he will think that you have some rum with you."'[58] Alcohol was a problem, but that was not unique to Te Kooti. Alcohol was accessible in the King Country but, as a story told later in this chapter shows, Te Kooti was acutely aware of its dangers.

He was capable of sudden jests and sudden threats. His very unpredictability can make him seem inconsistent; like most prophets, he was a man of disturbance and not a custodian of order.[59] Early in 1875, Ropata received an unexpected letter from him. It asked contemptuously after his welfare, 'now that he is no longer in receipt of Government rations'. He wanted to know how 'Ropata is off for biscuits', or the pap food of the Pakeha.[60] At the same time, an even more puzzling letter was sent to Pera Tipoki of upper Wairoa, one of Te Kooti's former fighters who had been at Te Haupapa in February 1871, and who had escaped from there with him. The letter was sent to Wairoa in January 1875:

> Ki a Pera Tipoki
> Ki te iwi katoa
>
> Tena koutou. Heoi ano te kupu kia rongo mai koutou. Meake ka pa te whiiu ki te motu katoa.
> He paku tenei kua hore nei. Ko tenei nui atu.
> Ko te ra tena e tu ae [ai] ahau i te aroaro o nga hoa tautohe.
> Maku ano he whakaatu te ra e pa ae [ai] taua whiiu.
>
> Na Rikirangi te turuki
> alias Te Kooti.
>
> To Pera Tipoki
> To all the tribe
>
> Greetings to you. There is only one word for you to listen to. The whip will shortly be applied to the whole of the land.

What is past will be small compared to what is coming. It will be very great.

I will stand before the enemy on that day.

It will be for me to inform you of the day that that whip will fall.

From Rikirangi Te Turuki
alias Te Kooti.[61]

This letter is a copy; it is not written in Te Kooti's hand. The last line of the signature ('alias Te Kooti') suggests that it either was written for him or purports to have been sent by him. If the letter is genuine, it runs counter to the entire tradition, which Te Kooti stated so clearly in 1883, that he had become a man of peace from his reconciliation with Tawhiao. It is the first time the form Rikirangi Te Turuki appears in a signature, although he would use it in the future. It seems to promise renewed war, when the sound that will be heard again is the whip.

Earlier in the same month, the resident magistrate at Opotiki, Herbert Brabant, wrote that several letters from Te Kooti had recently been brought to his district, but he gave no account of their content. One particular letter which he forwarded in the original, and also in a copy, to McLean is no longer with the file.[62] However, it may have been the letter which now exists among the collated Maori correspondence in Donald McLean's papers, dated 25 October 1874. It was sent to Nepia Tokitahi and Tuahine (a woman), and other surrendered 'prisoners', who were being held under the surveillance of the Ngai Tai chief Wiremu Kingi Te Kawau at Torere and Tunapahore (Hawai), on the eastern edge of the Bay of Plenty. If this is the missing letter, it is very different in its mood from that sent to Pera Tipoki.

Ki a Tuahine, ara ki a koutou katoa, ki a Nepia, te ture, te whakapono, te Hahi, te aroha, te tangata, te mamae, te whenua, te mate, nga mea e noho ana i roto i te hunga whakaheke toto. Tena ra, tena ra koutou katoa.

Aue, aue te aroha i a au ki a koutou. Kei mahara kua mahue i a au te aroha, e kore e taea te wewete no te mea he roimata taku kai i te ao i te po.

Ki a koutou e noho mai na nga whakarau, tena ra koutou. Nga mea i wehea i roto i te tataritanga mo tatou katoa, tena ra koutou.

He waiata maori
    Taku turanga ake i te kuaha nei
    Whakaheke roimata
    He aroha noa ake ki te hau whakarua
    I hara mai ra koe i te iwi rae nona te moenga
    I ho kotahi aue he te aroha — ei.
Tena ra koutou.

He waiata na Rawiri 46
    Ko te Atua to tatau piringa me to tatau kaha he kaiawhina e tino tata ana i nga wa o te he.

    Ma konei ra tatou ka kore ai e wehi ahakoa kahakina nga maunga ki waenga moana.

Ma koutou e titiro tana tangi tae noa ki te mutunga.
    Ko aku korero ena ki a koutou ko tana waiata. Heoi ano.
    Ki a Nepia ara ki a koutou katoa. Ehara ia na i Turanga a kona te noho ai i kona ko

Turanga hoki tena ko nga tangata tena.

Heoi ano.

Na te Turuki.

To Tuahine, that is to all of you, to Nepia, the law, the faith, the Church, love, man, suffering, the land [and] death, the things which exist under the people who cause [our] blood to flow. Greetings, greetings to you all.

Ah, the love I have for you. Do not think that I have given up love, I can never be free of it because day and night tears are my sustenance.

To you living there who are prisoners, greetings to you. Those who are separated during this waiting time of ours, greetings to you.

Here is a Maori waiata

As I stand at this doorway,
My tears falling
It is simply love for the north-east winds
From whence you came, from the people gone to death,
One cry, love is perplexed — ei.

Greetings to you all.

Psalm of David, 46

God is our refuge and strength; a very present help in trouble.

Therefore will not we fear [though the earth be removed] and though the mountains be carried into the midst of the sea.

You should look at his lament, right to the end of it.

Those are my words to you [in] that psalm. That is all.

To Nepia, that is to all of you. That place is not Turanga that you should stay there, for if it were Turanga, then the people would also be there.

That is all.

From Te Turuki.[63]

If the letter concludes somewhat chastisingly, there is little doubt about the pain it expresses, and there is no doubt about the hope it offers: that 'the God of Jacob is our refuge'. It should be noted that God in Psalm 46 is the God who *destroys* the weapons of war and who causes the wars of destruction to cease 'unto the end of the earth'. He is the God who commands, 'Be still, and know that I am God'.

The letter written to Pera Tipoki seems to be the only evidence which runs counter to Te Kooti's teachings of peace. It seems unlikely to be a forgery, though that is possible. It may, rather, reflect a moment of anger, the flash of a desire to scourge the land with another friend and fighter. It is, however, inconsistent with all the teachings which Te Kooti was developing at Te Kuiti from 1874 and which are recorded by the Ringatu elders.

From that year, when he was living at Taramakiri, Te Kuiti, Te Kooti gradually developed the new calendar and rituals of the faith. The earliest instituted occasion was the First of January, which was created as a major ceremony of the faith and was celebrated initially on 1 January 1875.[64] This is the first of the four days (or Ra) which together stand as the four pillars of the Ringatu year. It was derived from Exodus 40:2:

'On the first day of the first month shalt thou set up the tabernacle of the tent of the congregation.' It is a gathering and love feast (hakari) held 'in remembrance of the Passover, ko te Kapenga', or the deliverance of the children of Israel.[65] The First of July was celebrated for the first time the next year. This day marks the beginning of the seventh month, and the practice was based on Leviticus 23:24, when the Lord commanded Moses to make of that day a sabbath and 'an holy convocation'. It celebrates the commencement of the cycle of renewal, coming out of death, and thus marks the rededication of the land to God at the very beginning of spring.

The First of January in 1875 and 1876, together with the First of July in 1876, were held at Waikohu, part of Mataora, among the Ngati Porou settled there. Te Kooti was not present. In December 1875 he explained why these gatherings were first held at Mataora: the celebration of 1 July had been initiated by Ngati Porou at Mataora in 1867, and thus it would start from there in its new, more defined form. It had also been proper, he said, to take the First of January there. The formal lists of the Ra and the places where they were held, which have been kept by the Haahi Ringatu, therefore always begin with the ceremony held at Mataora on 1 January 1875. From this time the Ra were regularly held at Mataora, but they were also held simultaneously at Te Kuiti, for Te Kooti could not yet travel outside the Rohe Potae. Once he was free to move, after his pardon in February 1883, the Ra of January and July would generally be 'called for' by other communities who had adopted the faith. This practice of passing the Ra from community to community then began to spread. From the mid-1880s the major celebrations of the faith began to circulate through the island. The First of January, in particular, was often combined with the opening of a new meeting-house built specially for Te Kooti. The Ra of 1 January 1877, held at Waikohu, Mataora, was the first example of this practice. Matiu Paeroa, who was one of the Ngati Porou settlers on the Coromandel, recorded that the Ra was taken on that occasion to Mataora so that the new house could be raised up ('hei whakaara').[66]

This was the first of the new houses built for the 'Kotahitanga' 'concerning God's Words amongst all the tribes'.[67] Its name is unknown; it was possibly the house (or its forerunner) Eripitani, which is remembered as the old Ringatu meeting-house at Mataora.[68] Eripitani, like the later and more famous house at Te Whaiti, Eripitana, was named for Te Kooti's early kupu whakaari of 1869 (Eripi/Tani), that is the promise of the salvation of the people. Then, in January 1878, Ngati Rangiwewehi (who had supported Te Kooti in the fighting in the Patetere district in 1870) took the Ra to Te Tahawai, north of Katikati, for the opening of their new house.[69] But Te Kooti himself did not attend any of these early ceremonies.

In 1879 he inaugurated the two festivals of planting and harvesting, which completed the four pillars of the year. Today they are generally (but not invariably) known as the huamata and the pure. The huamata is usually held on 1 June (but in some areas it is combined with the local First of July), and the pure is held variously on 1 November or 1 December, according to the region and its seasons. The pure completes the celebrations of the cycle of planting, by lifting the tapu from the growing crops. It is the harvest of the first fruits and is derived from Exodus 34:22 and Deuteronomy 26:2. These are the two celebrations which are today most lovingly remembered by those who were brought up as Ringatu, partly because the celebrations have often been abandoned as people have left their rural communities.

In 1880 Te Kooti also instituted the first of the month (called the new moon, 'Kohiti') as a day of prayer and a day of feasting.[70] This practice was also introduced among Ngati Porou on the Coromandel: at Wharekawa, for example, it was begun on 1 April 1882. The day and night which preceded it, the last day of the month, was named 'Po Takoto', the night of fasting and preparation.[71] The First was called a 'day of prayer to God, and a day of feasting, as in the days for the appearance of the new moon' ('hei ra karakia ki te Atua, hei hakari, pera ano me nga ra kowhititanga marama').[72] However, the practice was generally discontinued after 1885,[73] and in its place the Twelfths were introduced.

The Twelfths were first announced in December 1885, and at that time they were set alongside the First of the month. These were to be the two monthly pillars. Te Kooti said that the Twelfths were specifically for 'the manifestation of pain' ('ma nga putanga mamae mai').[74] But, in the end, the Twelfths replaced the first day of the month, and were formally instituted in 1888.[75] They stemmed most immediately from the occasion of Te Kooti's pardon on 12 February 1883, but they also recall other critical events. The day celebrates 12 May 1868, when the covenants of the faith, or 'All the prophetic sayings for Aotearoa' ('Nga kupu whakaari katoa mo Aotearoa nei'),[76] were said to have been fully revealed to Te Kooti on Wharekauri. The Twelfths also give thanksgiving for the Passover, the safe landing of the exiles at Whareongaonga, celebrated there on Saturday and Sunday 11–12 July 1868, which was thus the first 'Twelfth' held. They also recall the 12 tribes of Israel, with whom the people identified and from whom they traced their descent, and the 12 fruits on the Tree of Life in the Book of Revelation, an image to which we shall return. Twelve is thus the number in which certain seminal events in the experiences of the whakarau were reinforced by the symbolism of the number in the scriptures.

The number of services (the liturgical rituals) was expanded about this time from the original 12 to 34. The texts of these 34 panui (the compositions of scriptural lessons Te Kooti created for use in the services) are recorded in a copy of the book of the liturgy made in 1933.[77] Te Kooti also composed the sequence of the services, which were conducted with the prayers 'chanted by all standing, and Psalms were sung with right hand elevated',[78] the practice which ultimately gave the Ringatu their name. It seems that, at the same time as the liturgy was expanded, Eria Raukura was elevated as Te Kooti's chief preacher. This is certainly how Eria portrayed it to Thomas Porter. James Cowan, who knew Te Kooti when he was living in the Rohe Potae, also said that, in 1881, Te Kooti baptised Eria in the waters of the Manga-o-Kewa stream at Te Kuiti as the 'high priest' of the faith.[79]

As these rituals were developed over time, so the spirit of prophecy was revitalised. Exile sharpens this tradition; it had done so among the Jews. Exile also engenders writing — in the form of letters — but, even more important, forces the decision to record the people's history in their time of separation. As the explanations for the unhappy present are sought in past events, so too the resolutions for the future are sought in prayer and prophecy. These perceptions Te Kooti's secretaries recorded for the succeeding generations. Thereby, from the ashes of despair, the tradition of hope springs. This is the essence of the Ringatu faith: the commitment of the stout-hearted people ('te manawanui') to the future.

The kupu whakaari, the visionary predictions of Te Kooti, recommenced on 11–12 December 1877. This was precisely two years after the promulgation of 1 January and 1 July as the pillars of the year, and thus cannot be a random date. It was, of course, also a Twelfth. A waiata records the three new prophetic sayings,[80] and they were also written down later by Matiu Paeroa. After Te Kooti was pardoned, Matiu came from the Coromandel to live with him in the new community they built at Whakaarorangi, Otewa, and his book was begun there on 11 April 1885. It was the result of a collective decision to create a permanent record for themselves of 'the sayings that have been revealed to us' ('Kia mohio ai tatou ki nga kupu kua korerotia nei kia tatou').[81] The book, having set out its overall purpose, records that the kupu whakaari began again on 11 December 1877.

The prediction revealed that the observation of 1 January 1878 would be held at Te Tahawai, when 'the form of worship known by the name Morehu (Survivors)' ('nga karakia ki tenei ingoa e karangatia nei hei Morehu') would be explained.[82] The structure of the service was then set out. This was, however, preceded by the three prophetic words in 'te reo ke': 'Anata. Anaherehe. Anatekerehi.' These three terms were themselves explained on this predicted occasion at Te Tahawai:

> Anata. E kore ano hoki e tukua e ahau
> Anaherehe. A na taku herenga i a koutou
> Anatekerehi. Kia u ki aku tikanga.
>
> Anata. I will not release
> Anaherehe. Because I have bound you all
> Anatekerehi. Be true to my laws.[83]

Paora Delamere also noted, in the comprehensive list of the Ra he compiled, that the three prophetic sayings were pronounced at the gathering at Te Tahawai on 4 January 1878.[84] They were explained again almost a year after Te Kooti's pardon, on 10 February 1884 at Whakaarorangi, Otewa. The explanations were then hugely expanded. These new explanations have been transcribed in full, below, in order to show how the sayings were expanded, and the scriptural bases which underlie them. If they remain opaque, that is because opacity is an essential part of allegory.

A Jewish scholar wrote in the third century AD: 'all the divinely inspired writing, because of its obscurity, is like many locked rooms in a house. Beside each room lies a key which does not fit it . . . the greatest task is to find the keys and fit the right one to the room which it can open.'[85] It follows that there will be no exegetic finality for Te Kooti's sayings. Multivalence of meaning is a characteristic of all religious writings and sayings, and 'hermeneutic unendingness' (text upon text) occurs particularly in the Judaic tradition of religious commentary. It relates to the experience of exile. These ever-unfolding texts were, it has been suggested, the instrument of the 'improbable survival' of the Jews; in exile, the texts are 'homeland'.[86] To understand some of the hidden meanings is a task Te Kooti set the faithful — and the historian —

but to enter one locked room is, as has been warned, only the prelude to the discovery of another.

> 1. Anata) whakamaori[tanga]. E kore e tukua e ahau he roma nui kia waahi i runga i taku maunga tapu. No te haranga rano o te ao i whakapumautia e ahau taaku maunga, a, tae noa mai ki tenei ra ake ake.
> Whakamaoritanga — E kore e riro ke te hepeta o Hura me te kaiwhakatakoto tikanga o raro [o] ona waewae kia tae mai rano a Hiro ki a ia te huihuinga o nga iwi.
> 2. Anaherehe) A na taaku herenga i a koutou i whakaorangia ai koutou e ahau i roto i aku whiunga taimaha, he mea kia hoki mai ai koutou ki ahau. A, ka tahuri ka karanga ki tooku ingoa. Ko reira ahau mahara ai ki a koutou me taku maunga.
> [Whaka]maoritanga — Ko au ko au a Ihowa.
> 3. Ana Tekerehi) Kia u ki aku tikanga kia maharatia ai koutou e ahau a tena whaka-tipuranga, a tena whakatipuranga. Ko reira ano ahau mahara ai ki a koutou ki taaku kawenata. I hoatu e ahau ki a Aperahama, i hoatu ano e ahau he whenua mo ratou. Kia u ki aku kupu, kia hoatu ai e ahau to koutou whenua ki a koutou, ki o koutou uri i muri i a koutou. Kia mau ki aku tikanga.

> 1. Anata) interpretation. I will not let a great flood break over my sacred mountain. Because of the sins of the world, I will make fast my mountain, until this day and ever and ever.
> Interpretation — The sceptre shall not depart from Judah, nor a lawgiver from beneath his feet, until Shiloh come; and unto him shall the gathering of the people be. [Genesis 49:10].
> 2. Anaherehe) And by my hold on you, you will be saved by me from my heavy punishments in order to make you return to me. And [you] will turn and call my name. Therefore I shall remember you and my mountain.
> Interpretation — I, I am Jehovah.
> 3. Ana Tekerehi) Hold fast to my ways so that you will be remembered by me [in] each generation. Therefore I will remember you with my covenant. It was given by me to Abraham, I also gave some land for them. Hold fast to my words, so that I shall give your land to you, and to your descendants after you. Hold to my ways.[87]

The promise of the mountain (the icon of the people), sacrifice and fidelity: these are the recurring statements of God through the prophets in the scriptural traditions. Bind to the wheel of faithfulness, and the land will be restored: that is the essential message of these texts when placed in their historical context. The three prophecies which ushered in the new services for those who had survived — Nga Morehu — contain this hope. They stand, at the beginning of the renewal of the faith, as God's promise.

In Matiu Paeroa's book, these prophecies are themselves placed in an historical context, and that context, in turn, is commented upon. Thus a continuing dialectic is established between text and context, or between text, time and event. Both the past and the future are constantly being weighed and reweighed in the words of prophecy. Thus, in 1879, the Ra returned to Te Tahawai (both 1 January and 1 July), and there the 'sore affliction' ('he whiu mamae'), which was also said to have lain behind the establishment of these two days,[88] and 'a chastisement of mankind' ('i whiua ano nga tangata'), were predicted.

Ko te whiu mamae, ko te whiu hoari.

He hoari kei Tauranga, he hoari kei Hauraki, he hoari kei Waikato. Otira e kore te Kingi e pai kia puta enei raruraru, engari ko tana i pai ai kia kore he raruraru.

The sore affliction, the affliction of the sword.

There is at Tauranga a sword, a sword at Hauraki, a sword at Waikato. But the King will not consent to these troubles arising, rather he will approve there not being trouble.[89]

The text then comments that these troubles were brought to naught by God. 'The only thing that he permitted in this year was the taking into captivity of the peoples of Taranaki' ('Heoi rawa te mea i tukua atu e ia kia haere i te whakarau ko nga iwi o Taranaki, i roto i tenei tau').[90] The first arrests of the ploughmen of Parihaka were thus bound into the wheel of prophecy and explanation, while the mounting pressures on King Tawhiao had not yet led to an open rupture within the Kingitanga, nor yet to the breaking of his relationship with Te Kooti. Both would, however, occur subsequently.

This particular sequence continues as the arrests at Taranaki continued. The First of January for 1881 was held at Te Makomako, Ohinemuri, and the prophecy of affliction was enlarged upon. (Again it was the words which were taken there, for Te Kooti himself, as is clearly stated, did not go.[91]) The warnings were about the practice of sorcery as well as fear of the sword. However, at the very place of fighting, the spilling of blood would cease, it was said. In fulfilment of these words, that year 22 chiefs were claimed to have died through sorcery ('te mate whaiwhaia'), while the arrest of the prophets Te Whiti o Rongomai and Tohu Kakahi at Parihaka prevented the spilling of blood there. The kupu whakaari of the year were thus declared to have been realised.[92]

This sequence of kupu whakaari shows how the historical events of the time were sifted through the networks of paradox and interpretation that the prophetic tradition weaves. The kupu whakaari begin as great statements of renewal and promise, and they also invariably carry the threats of scourge and punishment. They may be applied to the immediate historical context, or understood to refer to happenings outside known human time. The events associated with these kupu were some of the critical happenings in the Maori world in the late 1870s and early 1880s: death by disease; death attributed to makutu; the forced break-up of the Parihaka community. It is a framework of thought that carries much persuasive power.

This system is embedded in the biblical narrative tradition where later events stand as the 'testimony' of the truth of the earlier spoken words. This is, after all, the essential relationship between the New Testament and the Old. There, as here, it was the testimonial interconnection between the opaque and equivocating utterances of the prophets of Israel and the later events that gave this system of explanation its authority. Prophecies are seen to be true when they are fulfilled by the unexpected occurrence. The discrete event fulfils the earlier promise, and the more unexpected the resolution of the prediction, the more it seems to confirm the far-seeing wisdom of the earlier words. The event (and the narrative which is then told about it) stands as testimony to God's word that he is moving with the people through time, and that he is indeed still speaking through their prophets. History is thereby understood pleromatically — that is, as being the narrative promise fulfilled.[93] It conforms (albeit in the most unexpected ways) to the hidden words, the words of prescience and foresight — in the Maori world, matakite.

Te Kooti so re-established this framework of thought in the years of his second exile that many Maori began to listen to him anew. From the Ringatu texts it is apparent that the first communities outside Te Kuiti who adopted the new rituals were those of the exiles living on the Coromandel — at Tairua and Hikuwai, at Paritu and Wharekawa, at Parakiwai and Mataora, and at Ohinemuri and Katikati at the base of the peninsula. These were the very people whom Karanama had been sent to find in 1871: the Ngati Porou exiles; Tahau and his people; and Paora Toki from Petane in Hawke's Bay. These kainga of exiles were among the earliest Ringatu communities, and the memory and evidence of these times still lingers at several of these places today.

At Otauru, immediately south of Tairua, where Te Kooti went in July 1884, an old Ringatu meeting-house still stands, although the house itself probably dates from a slightly later period than that visit. It is called Nga Tauiwi, the Strangers, for the exiles who lived there. This was also the name given to Paora Toki's followers as they sheltered with Te Hira; they were given some land at Cabbage Bay (on the western side of the Coromandel peninsula) by the government in 1871.[94] The Otauru settlement was founded by a Ringatu elder, Waiwera Hakaraia, and its people similarly called themselves Te Whanau-a-Pani, the Family of Orphans, for they had come from several tribes, particularly Te Arawa and Ngati Maniapoto.[95] Matiu Paeroa himself was one of a group of Ngati Porou exiles who acquired some land at Hikuwai (at the head of the Tairua harbour) from the local people, Ngati Hei, in 1872.[96] Their presence explains the growth of both Tairua and Hikuwai as important early centres of the Ringatu faith, which others would join during the 1880s.

At Paritu (now part of Opoutere on the Wharekawa estuary), where Te Kooti would come to celebrate the First of July 1885, there still stands a unique Ringatu church-house called Hurae (July) (see picture in Chapter 15). It was built in 1894 and named as a statement of lasting peace to fulfil one of Te Kooti's last predictive words.[97] Beside it there once stood also a little whare kawenata, a separate house for the bibles. Paritu was a Ngati Porou community, founded by Wharepapa Perepe from Te Karaka, Poverty Bay. Some Arawa exiles from Te Awahou came to live there too, including Tuhourangi who lost their lands after the eruption of Mount Tarawera in 1886.[98] Further south was Parakiwai, another large community of exiles. They too had strong kinship links with the Ngati Porou people living at Mataora. At Parakiwai Te Kooti set up a trading-store which served the many Maori gum-diggers who came to the district in the 1880s and which earned him income. He is remembered too in local Pakeha stories, particularly for having ensured the protection of the Parakiwai store belonging to his Pakeha rival on occasions when its owner was absent.[99]

Mataora was the earliest of all the Ringatu communities. There, as we have seen, the first First of January and the first First of July were held. Lying between Parakiwai and Mataora was yet another Ringatu settlement, Whiritoa, founded by Ngati Kahungunu refugees from the wars. It had the same origin as Te Makomako, near Paeroa, which became a Ringatu community under the influence of exiles who had fled there after the fighting in the northern Bay of Plenty in February 1870. Their escape into the Ohinemuri gorge was observed at the time,[100] and the present elder of Ngahu-toitoi marae, John Williams, told how his grandmother, Epera Hawea, from Nuhaka in Hawke's Bay, came there as a young woman. She had been in the fighting and fled to Ohinemuri. The party had only a few horses, so they held onto long ropes, four or five attached to each horse, to pull them along and speed their flight. Epera introduced the Ringatu teachings into the district, and with her came Tukua Te Ranga and his wife Anipeka, who were also Te Kooti's followers. They were Arawa people from the Tauranga district who had fought for Te Kooti at Tapapa. The first meeting-house built there, Te Nui-o-te-pa, is remembered by the local people, Ngati Tamatera, as being built by Te Kooti (or at the very least for him). Te Kooti named the house, and he stayed there when he came to visit[101] — as documented in July 1883 and February 1888. Its site, defined by an outlying trench, is still visible at the foot of Tapu-ariki hill. This sunken house, built of nikau and boards, and containing raupo tukutuku and carved ancestral pou, was almost certainly the house which was opened at Te Makomako on 1 January 1881, making it one of the earliest houses built for the Kotahitanga of the faith. After Te Kooti's death, it was abandoned as tapu and subsequently burnt (being seen as having 'turned round' on the people and thus a source of sickness). Nevertheless, the faith survived as an active part of the life of this community into the 1940s. The 'pure whaka-tō' and the 'pure hauhake' (the ritual planting on 1 June, and the lifting of the tapu ('whakanoa') with the gathering of the first fruits on 1 November) were maintained until that time.[102] The circuit of the Twelfths also revolved between these marae, going from Ngahu-toitoi to Mataora, from Mataora to Paritu, and from Paritu to Hikuwai, coming south to Ngati Maru at Thames, and then returning to Ngahu-toitoi.[103] In this region, the Ringatu faith was largely, though not entirely, a religion of exiles.

While the faith began to spread from the late 1870s, it kept a firm base at Te Kuiti. Te Kooti's teachings had begun to take hold there even before his arrival in 1872. The long-established trader in the district, Louis Hetet, informed McLean as early as November 1870 that Tawhiao seemed to be losing his hold while 'The Kooti's service & influence seems to be gaining ground.'[104] The exiles sheltering at Te Kuiti must have been responsible for the influence of the faith at this time. Once Te Kooti came to live there, the word began to spread more rapidly. The number of passing references to letters and messages being received from Te Kooti in many parts of the North Island — at Tarawera, at Wairoa, at Opotiki, at Maketu and at Te Whaiti — is striking. Hetaraka Te Wakaunua, who opposed him, wrote to inform both J. D. Ormond and McLean in December 1873 of 'what Te Kooti is up to here' ('tenei nga tikanga a te Koti kei konei e mahia ana'). All he had done was request Tuhoe to be earnest in their prayers, and more specifically to do penance ('kia whakamamae') on 29 November. That same day of penance (29 November) Te Kooti had also brought to the Mokau heads the previous year, urging the people to stay in their pa on this 'unlucky day'.[105] But Hetaraka also complained that those who believed wholly in Te Kooti's words — Ngati Huri of Maungapohatu — would no longer listen to the words of others: 'You should know that no one here goes by the laws of the Government, not one' ('Kia mohio korua kaore he tangata o konei e whakahaere ana i nga ture a te Kawanatanga, kore rawa atu kia kotahi').[106]

Te Nui-o-te-pa, the house built for Te Kooti at the base of Tapu-ariki hill on the Ohinemuri river. This photograph was brought to the opening of the house Te Awapu, the third of that name at Ngahu-toitoi, in December 1993. The old couple in the centre are Rehi Wiremu and his wife Herumate. Rephotographed, by permission of Amelia Williams, by Judith Binney.

From the later 1870s various resident magistrates also began to report the increasing adoption of 'Te Kooti's karakia' in their districts — the eastern Bay of Plenty, the upper Wairoa, and Poverty Bay. That intelligent missionary Thomas Grace visited Opotiki and Whakatane in October 1877 and in both places, he said, the people he met were all followers of Te Kooti and had adopted his prayers. He linked the spread of the beliefs in this area to the land confiscations. His annual letter to the Church Missionary Society for 1877 could be considerd the first significant 'biography' written of Te Kooti.

> Te Kooti (named after our former lay secretary)[107] who has without any competition been the greatest general on either side in the war, when he was a prisoner at the Chatham Islands compiled a sermon apparently to suit his circumstances and [it] is taken almost exclusively from the prayerbook — it consists chiefly of some of the collects & prayers and some of the Psalms and is only objectionable in what it omits — except that they have given up the Lords day and keep Saturday for their sabbath.
>
> When spoken to on this subject and asked why they have given up our old form of worship they maintain that they have not given it up that their worship is the worship of the prayer book. . . . Te Kooti's followers seem to have met with even more success than the Kings prophets — The whole of the Bay of Plenty two or three villages excepted — Tauranga included have become followers of Te Kooti — one or two places only adhering to the Kings form. I may here add that I have not been able to detect anything like a persecuting spirit both these parties (shall they be called sects) appear to

be on the best of terms and do not show any feeling or bitterness towards those who adopt the rival form or even to those who still adhere to us. And Te Kooti's people do not object joining our service or allowing us to preach to them. . . .

In early years they received Christianity (and I may say Colonization) at our hands, without doubting and to a great extent on credit. Colonization, war, Confiscation . . . have followed each other in quick succession; while the expectations anticipated from representations made when they signed the 'Treaty of Waitangi', have not been realized. And now they turn round and question their first advisers, and look at the whole of our connection with them as a scheme to get their lands from them . . . . These things, together with the course some of our brethren took in the war, has [*sic*] completely changed our position with these people.

Nor is the change less that has come over their own minds as regards the management of their religious affairs. Formerly, they consulted us in all matters connected with their teaching and worship . . . . Now, they assume the entire management of their own spiritual affairs and seem to consider they have a perfect [right] to do so. . . . They have clearly never intended to renounce Christianity − and go back to Heathenism − on the contrary. Whatever individual exceptions they may make − they have lost confidence in us as a body and look upon us with distrust and suspicion, and have determined to manage their own religious affairs.[108]

Grace restated these views forcefully shortly afterwards, when arguing against more complacent views such as those of the Reverend Seymour Spencer at Maketu: 'Missionary influence is below zero, all through the Bay of Plenty − Mr. Spencers 5000 Christians, are, I believe, to a man followers of Te Kooti, who while they use our prayers cut off the conclusion, when we ask all through our Lord Jesus Christ.'[109] Grace had no doubt that the new teachings were being widely accepted, particularly among young people who, as he pointed out, growing up during the 1860s had experienced virtually no other systematic teaching of religion.

Leonard Williams, who visited several of the Ringatu communities in the Bay of Plenty in 1878, commented similarly on Te Kooti's extensive influence, and the manner in which he was being consulted on all kinds of questions, people riding through to Te Kuiti to talk with him. The religion had been widely adopted by Whakatohea, Tuhoe and Ngai Te Rangi of Tauranga − all those who firmly believed that the missionaries 'had acted a deceitful part towards them'.[110] Williams was courteously received, however, and witnessed the Saturday services (and also, apparently, the Twelfths, although his two known accounts of this visit are retrospective[111] and he may have elided time, for the Twelfths were not formally instituted until 1885). He, like Grace, commented on the distinct emphasis Te Kooti's followers placed in their teachings, their prayers being addressed only to Jehovah. At Kokohinau, the chief Tiopira Te Hukiki, a former lay teacher of the Anglicans, told Williams sharply, '"You have not visited us for years, and now that you have come to us again you find that we have given up the way of the Son and have adopted instead the way of the Father"'.[112] This apparent division of the Godhead was understood, by clerics like Leonard Williams and James Stack, to be the result of a Maori identification with 'the sons of Shem, the family to which they believed themselves to belong'. Stack understood it to be not only a statement of autonomy from their former missionary teachers but also a powerful belief in their particular, unique relationship with God. Significantly, he described it in genealogical terms: a familial relationship with God, their Father, which Maori thought had been 'intentionally concealed from them by their English teachers for political reasons'.[113]

Similar reports multiplied. W. S. Gudgeon, now resident magistrate at Gisborne, wrote in 1879 of the strong hold the faith had gained in parts of the East Coast. He commented that, in January, a letter from Te Kooti had been sent to Waikaremoana, warning of a great pestilence that would soon befall the people. Te Kooti told them to leave their kainga, leave their road-making camps, leave all the camps of the Pakeha, and 'go out into the wilderness' for one month. This they had done.[114] The flight into the wilderness, the undergoing of penance, they believed, had averted the catastrophes threatened for that year.

From Napier, Wairoa and Opotiki the accounts continued to increase. Petane (the community of exiled Paora Toki, who now joined Te Kooti at Te Kuiti) and nearby Tangoio (the home of Maika Tuakana, who had journeyed with Te Kooti into exile in 1872) were both centres of the faith by 1881. The people of both places were in constant communication with Te Kooti, although there were also dissenters, who had recently constructed for themselves a separate church-house in the district. At Wairoa, Meri Karaka, who belonged to the most senior chiefly lines of Ngati Kahungunu and who, it will be remembered, had stayed behind in the pa at the siege of Nga Tapa, became one of the main promoters of the religion. She was in regular communication with Te Kooti from the late 1870s, despite being censured publicly for having visited him at Te Kuiti during March 1877.[115] All these people, wrote Preece, now the resident magistrate in Napier, were constantly visiting Waikato to see Te Kooti, and there 'is no doubt he has a great power over them'.[116] The most interesting account of all is the annual report for 1880 from the resident magistrate at Opotiki, Robert Bush. He stated that, although a number of the principal chiefs in the district were hostile to the new teachings — Wiremu Kingi Te Kawau, in particular — the people would not listen to the chiefs.

> I do not think the mere fact of their adhering to this form of worship indicates any desire on their part to act with hostility against the Government . . . but it is simply a belief that Kooti is something more than a human being. Many Natives have visited Kooti lately to consult him with respect to cases of sickness amongst them. Kooti is represented as telling them 'that it was no use their coming to him, as he was no god, but only a human being the same as themselves.' He, however, enjoined them to adhere to his form of worship.[117]

A man, not a god, and a faith which Grace had recognised as being little different from his own — except that it did not look to the Christian Saviour in its prayers. Rather, it looked directly to God. The penultimate prayer (inoi) of all Ringatu services is that known as the 'Pokaikaha', which was composed by Te Kooti. It is the fourth inoi in the earliest collection of his prayers which has survived — those written in his diary of 1869–70. It is the prayer for a people in confusion, that is, those who still await their Messiah. This prayer contains the essence of the original teachings of the faith:

> E te Atua tahuri mai ou taringa ki ta matou inoi, kei whakangaro atu koe ina tangi atu

matou. Anga mai, titiro mai hoki koe ki a matou e pokaikaha noa nei, e tangi nei hoki, koi matou e whakakororia nei ki tou ingoa tapu. Amine.

O God incline your ears to our prayers, lest you destroy us who sorrow here. Turn to us, and look down on us who are in confusion, and in sorrow, and who glorify your holy name. Amen.[118]

The faith of the Morehu was indeed built on the bible and the prayer-book, as Grace had said. Created from the scriptures, it was, however, essentially concerned with the problems of the colonised. It gave them the framework for analysing their own situation; it also offered them a unique relationship with God. It sought to bind them to him, and him to them. At this time, the Morehu certainly did not consider Christ to be their redeemer. Over time, this view has changed within sections of the Ringatu faith, and these changes can be traced to Te Kooti's last teachings, as will be shown later. The evolution of the faith, whereby the 'stages' of the bible came particularly to be emphasised and Moses interpreted as the type of Christ, began with Te Kooti himself. This emphasis would be extended and developed by the next generation of leaders. If Rua Kenana consciously re-enacted the whole history of the scriptures as the proclaimed Messiah, Paora Delamere was to teach belief in Christ.[119]

In the 1870s and early 1880s, the faith rested strongly on generating among the people a collective response to God's prophetic words. It certainly rested on the covenanted relationship between them and their God, or the politics of Exodus, whereby the destiny of the people is urged as being in their own hands.[120] The faith at this time also sent out its missionaries — in direct contrast to the practice of the Ringatu church today. Te Kooti announced this evangelical decision on 20 July 1878. He said he would send people to travel the island and carry the teachings to as many parts as possible: to Turanga, Wairoa, Porangahau, the Wairarapa, to the far north, and to the East Cape. Heni Kumekume and Hoani Pururu from Ngati Awa, who was considered Te Kooti's chief spokesman at this time, were to go to Te Kaha.[121] Two songs composed by Te Kooti refer specifically to sending Timo Mataora to preach in the Wairarapa in 1879, and to his return in the following year.[122] There had been some contact with and support for Te Kooti from the Wairarapa during the fighting in 1870,[123] and this connection, once renewed, would flourish. Kehemane (Gethsemane) marae at Tablelands became one of the centres of the Ringatu faith. The large meeting-house there, Takitimu (which the resident magistrate's reports indicate was being worked on as early as 1880 and which was finally opened by Te Kooti on 1 January 1891), was modelled on Tokanganui-a-noho. Its carvers were sent by Te Kooti and included Ngati Porou men from Turanga (and probably also from Mataora). This house was listed by Matiu as a part of the expanding Kotahitanga 'concerning God's Words'; it was the 19th and last house in his dated list (although not, of course, the last house built).[124]

One issue which confronted Te Kooti in the years after the wars was the continuing high Maori mortality rate. People needed explanations for the deaths. They came to Te Kuiti seeking them, and Te Kooti's reputation as a healer began to grow. Bush's account is probably the most accurate concerning the advice Te Kooti gave: to seek solutions in faith and prayer. Nevertheless, in the following year Bush also reported that Te Kooti

The meeting-house Takitimu at Kehemane, dated 7 August 1912. The house was 70 feet long and 20 feet wide. According to Ringatu sources, it was opened on 1 January 1891. It was constructed for Ngati Hikawera and work on it took place over a decade, as its erection was reported in 1886 as having been under way for some six years. Its side posts (amo) and barge-boards (maihi) are carved and painted in the style associated with Te Kooti. On the lower part of the two rear verandah posts (epa), one of which is just visible here, were the painted marakihau figures, with painted manaia placed above and below them. The house was carved by Ngati Porou carvers, among whom Hori Paihia is particularly remembered. They were followers of Te Kooti. On the right is the bell which was rung to summon people to worship. The house was given to the government by Ngati Hikawera in 1901 with the intention that it should be moved to Wellington; however, this did not eventuate and the house subsequently burnt down.

Te Kooti's words for this house when he visited Kehemane were remembered as '*Kai waho te mirimiri. Kai roto te rahurahu*', which could be translated as 'Beware of soothing flattery on the outside, for inside there is a roughness, or a hidden purpose'. It is a Ngati Awa proverb, here used to refer to ambiguous reasons for the construction of the house, which may have caused the delay in its opening. Te Kooti also told the people that only the wind would dwell in their house, which was interpreted by them that it should become a sacred house and stand apart.

MARTINBOROUGH LAPIDARY MUSEUM COLLECTION, F71282 1/2, ATL

was increasingly believed to possess the powers of healing and that he gave the reason for the continuing epidemics as makutu, or the practice of sorcery by Maori against Maori. The records of the Ringatu support this statement. From 1876 there is firm evidence that Te Kooti was insisting that makutu was being practised. On 21 December he wrote to Toha Rahurahu, a chief at Wairoa who had been his whaling master many years before, but who also helped to lead the last Ngati Kahungunu expedition against him in 1870. Te Kooti told Toha that the young high-born chief, Areta Te Apatu, sent from Wairoa, had reached Te Kuiti safely. He wrote:

> Our son has arrived in the Valley of Waikato, and I have seen him like an unclouded

sun. I have received your loving letter, and of your letter of caution on account of our son. It is good; I am not dark on the subject. Your words are not new that too much must not be said of big chiefs. He travelled here on my invitation and that of a man of low birth, but your word is good. My love is strong for our son and all the tribe on account of witchcraft. That is why I sent for him.[125]

In February, Areta returned to Wairoa, where he began to spread the 'new & mischievous doctrines', according to the resident magistrate, Dr Frederick Ormond.[126] Ormond was to report that, on two recent occasions, chiefs from Wairoa had visited Te Kooti to try to neutralise the power of certain 'supposed wizards' living in the district through 'a charm' that Te Kooti was believed to possess.[127]

From Opotiki Bush similarly described how a powerful individual might be named as having caused the death of another. In 1881 Te Kooti named Te Waru as a practitioner of makutu. Since 1874 Te Waru had been living in permanent exile at Waiotahe on the Ohiwa harbour, on land granted to him by the government after he had surrendered. When Leonard Williams met him there in 1878, he disclaimed any connection with the Ringatu faith — or indeed any other.[128] Te Kooti named Te Waru as being responsible for the death of Raiha, the youngest daughter of Apanui, the old chief of Ngati Awa, who himself had died only a year previously.[129] The family had recently suffered several deaths, which made them vulnerable to accepting this explanation. The accusation of makutu could be used dangerously against those who Te Kooti considered had betrayed him. It was a weapon he used against the 'big chiefs'.

But 'makutu', correctly used, is considered a power for good, not ill. It is believed to be a gift of God, bestowed upon some men and women; properly, it is the power of spiritual healing, and of life. The ambivalence of makutu is perhaps best shown in a story reported of Te Kooti in 1874. A young man of Ngati Porou, living with the exiles at Te Kuiti, returned to the East Coast for a great land meeting called by the old and very senior chief Iharaira Te Houkamau. There he was given a greenstone earring by another elderly Ngati Porou chief, Te Wikiriwhi Te Matehei. When the young man returned to Te Kuiti, he showed the earring to Te Kooti, who said that he must return it, or both Ngati Porou chiefs would die. Shortly afterwards, Te Houkamau (who had fought against Te Kooti) did indeed die, and Te Wikiriwhi, hearing of Te Kooti's warning, wrote urgently to get the earring back. Te Kooti in turn sent a message to Te Wikiriwhi telling him 'that he need not be afraid'.[130] If he claimed the power of makutu, here he chose not to use it for ill. Te Kooti instead exercised that power for healing.

He became known as a 'miracle-worker', and the numerous pilgrimages to Te Kuiti by people who were sick drew comment from 1877. The people came mostly from Urewera, Wairoa, Poverty Bay and the Bay of Plenty. The centenarian Moerangi Ratahi of Ngati Awa described (in 1971) how she was taken as a young child by her family to be healed of what she thought had probably been tuberculosis, for long only too prevalent in Maori communities. The entire family was ill, she remembered. They came to Te Kuiti, where Te Kooti was living in his own 'pa' under Rewi's protection: the time is thereby identified as being before 1883.

Te Kooti healed them all by the laying-on-of-hands, as in the Bible. He then prayed and they all regained their health.

That was why all her family became followers of the new religion. More than that, both she and her sisters stayed at Te Kuiti for some time, acting as nurses to the dozens of invalids who streamed in from all parts of the country. . . .

What was Te Kooti like? . . . 'He seemed to do much praying, particularly when he was healing. He made many people well again. Everybody thought him a good man.'[131]

Similarly, elders from communities along the East Coast rode to Te Kuiti on all manner of missions. They travelled on horseback over long roads to learn the teachings for the Morehu. They brought the 'Word' back to their own settlements. Each Ringatu community today possesses its own narrative of the elders who went, and the particular words that were given to them. Each elder — and each community — were set tasks by Te Kooti to fulfil. Ned Brown related the story of his grandfather, Te Hira Uetuku, who went to Te Kuiti about this time:

There was a lot of confusion with this land, Mangatū. So, my grandfather, he went. They said over here, 'Go and see Te Kooti.' So he went . . . and when he got there — Te Kooti had a habit of misleading people, to test you at all times to see how good your faith is. So, when he got there, what he had in mind, to ask Te Kooti, 'O what's going to happen to this land?' In other words, he's going there for his family in preserving and maintaining his rights to the land. So Te Kooti said to him, 'Well, now that you're here, I see you people are very tired, well, here's a bottle of whisky.' Well, my grandfather, his friends all got that bottle of whisky, all had a drink, but my grandfather refused. My grandfather said, 'No. I came for a purpose — and my mission is about Mangatū.' Then I think he put a curse on the ones that already had a drink —
Heni Brown: That's my family! My people! They're all dead now!
Ned: He [Te Kooti] said, 'Oh well, I'll give you — he mauri — he mauri mō te whenua' — pertaining to some powers unknown to us. That he will preserve your rights to the land. . . . 'Cos it is believed that it was part of the diamond that Te Kooti used — he used that diamond to go through a dense bush at Te Wera. And those that followed him saw it. It was in the form of a lamb: the diamond. Some say it is a portion or part of it, broken off from that, and given to my grandfather to plant on Maungahaumi. That is the mauri, to hold and preserve the family in the years to come. . . . Te Kooti said to him, 'You can sell the rest of Mangatū, but don't ever sell the mountain. Because that mountain, in days to come, your great-great-grandchildren will have a footing. It's better that than having no land.' So, Te Hira said to Te Kooti, 'Well, you can see my horse is used up. It's been a long ride from Mangatū to here, Te Kuiti. He'll never do this trip.' So, Te Kooti said to him, 'Well, you've got a mission — and it's got to be fulfilled — take my horse.' I believe my grandfather was the only one apart from Te Kooti rode that horse. The white horse. It took him only a day to come from Te Kuiti to Maungahaumia [*sic*] and back again, to fulfil his mission.[132]

The Ringatu tohunga from Poverty Bay, Tawehi Wilson, also recorded 'Nga Korero ki a Te Hira' ('The Words to Te Hira') in the manuscript book he kept of Te Kooti's various kupu whakaari. His text is a brief summary of the same story as Ned told. The white horse is there named Te Panerua, and the narrative is attributed to the Ra held at Te Whaiti in December 1883–January 1884.[133]

These stories, then, are old; they are retold and retained orally; and some of them are also written down. They preserve what is seen to be the critical relationship between the prophet and the community: the guidance that was given, the tests that were passed (or failed) and, as here, the protection Te Kooti placed on the sacred mountain of the people, so that they and their land will be preserved for ever.

From the late 1870s, the political environment for all the Te Kuiti exiles began to shift. We have already seen that Te Kooti sought a pardon, or alternatively a fair trial, in 1873, but his approaches were mainly ignored. Then in 1875 McLean made his definitive, and ultimately disruptive, offer to Tawhiao in an attempt to break the Kingitanga alliance and open up the block of territory which lay across the centre of the North Island. The government offered to accept Tawhiao's authority 'over the tribes within the district where he is now recognized as the head'.[134] It was also willing to return some of the confiscated land on the Waipa and Waikato rivers (those portions which had not yet been occupied), and to build Tawhiao a home at Kawhia. It was thought that he would gradually weaken; the mediators did not understand that Tawhiao would make no deals. He would accept only the return of all the confiscated land of Waikato. But it was from this time that Rewi began his own negotiations with the government which would culminate in the opening of the Rohe Potae in 1883. Rewi feared that the territory over which Tawhiao's authority might be recognised would encompass the tribal land of Maniapoto. He therefore sought different guarantees in order to conserve his people's lands intact. From the beginning of 1878 a series of major hui began, several of which Te Kooti attended. In the last analysis his fortunes — even his life — lay with Maniapoto, for it was they who were physically sheltering him, and it was they who insisted on an absolute amnesty for every one of the war refugees before there could be any negotiations over the main trunk line.

On 1 February 1878 the Premier, Sir George Grey, came to Te Kopua, within the northern boundary of the Rohe Potae, to meet with Tawhiao and Rewi. Purukutu and Te Kooti were both present, as the European observers noted. There are several descriptions of Te Kooti at this time, and they range from the commonplace to the bizarre. The reporter for the *Bay of Plenty Times* had a long story to tell which began:

> It was past midnight on Saturday last [2 February]. . . . I strolled over . . . on my way meeting a half-caste of my acquaintance. After a few words, he invited me to come and see Te Kooti, who was living with his two wives in a small tent about the centre of the encampment, not far from the tents occupied by Rewi and some other leading chiefs. . . . It was a small house tent just high enough to sit upright in, and it stood in a position which commanded the full view of our camp. . . . I waited outside until a light was struck, but could see through the opening, without being able to distinguish the objects within. . . . Very soon a match was struck, and I saw Te Kooti light a lamp, consisting of a pannikin containing fat. Then I crawled into the tent myself. Te Kooti had been lying across the tent, at the back and beside him, towards the door was one of his wives, and nearest the door another figure, which I had no doubt was the other wife. Te Kooti sat up: he had on a shirt, made of some material like a dressing-gown, and a blanket, almost a new one, covered his legs.[135]

Initially this seems to be a neutral enough description, but it soon becomes a tale of 'midnight horror' as the dark figure by the door was revealed to be yet another refugee and 'outlaw', Winiata, the murderer of 'poor Edwin Packer at Epsom', whose 'affrighted look' was 'like that of a wild beast suddenly roused from its lair'. One wild man sheltering another is the covert message, although the text pretends otherwise, denying that it is written 'as a mere sensational tale. *This is a plain record of facts*'. Another journalist described Te Kooti as a 'mild-looking man' and indicated that he was 'not tattooed'. He wore 'good clothes' and carried 'a valuable gold watch', he observed. But then he immediately surmised that the watch was loot 'from some person' whom Te Kooti had killed, and he recalled that the 'massacre' at Matawhero took place on Te Kooti's 'orders'. He also informed his readers that Te Kooti had said that, if the government did not treat Tawhiao justly, he would take up his arms again: Te Kooti 'claims considerable military skill, the possession of which he has indeed abundantly proved.' He was finally reported as drunk and dressed only in a 'breech-cloth', haranguing the crowd until a friend quietened him down and he returned to his tent.[136] These lurid images were the commonplaces to which the general public was becoming accustomed.

At the next meeting with Grey, held at Hikurangi in May 1878, Te Kooti was again described by European reporters. He arrived with a party of 30 followers, all of whom were said to be inebriated. They were ejected summarily, without being allowed food. Te Kooti was reported as having threatened to burn down the houses south of Te Kopua — that is, the homes of the Maori who had chucked him out.[137] Alcohol and violence are again stressed, and in this manner the crude stereotypes which spring from fear — or conversely from the sense of overwhelming power — were reinforced throughout the English-speaking community.

The Ringatu manuscripts, however, tell a very different story about this last episode. The occasion is remembered in two waiata which Te Kooti composed, and in a narrative transcribed from an original notebook kept by Hamiora, who had been living with Te Kooti at Te Kuiti since September 1877. Hamiora's narrative records how, after Te Kooti had arrived at Hikurangi and some of his party had gone into the bush to cut tent poles, Te Kooti went to Tawhiao's house. There he had placed a bottle of liquor in front of the King, in violation of Tawhiao's rules against the consumption of alcohol. Tawhiao seized the bottle and smashed it. Te Kooti left immediately, the others in the bush dropped their axes, and they all rode straight back to Te Kuiti. The story then moves into parable form — and it is Te Kooti who gains illumination. For the narrative goes on to relate how Te Kooti ordered everyone to pray through the night against the evil in man. Through a wild storm which raged as they prayed, Te Kooti himself wandered far afield (like King Lear), returning just before dawn. He was adorned with white albatross feathers, with only his face exposed. He entered like an old man, bent double, and coughing as he stumbled in. When he reached the centre post of the house, he stood with his head bowed and then told them all that, although goodness belongs to humans, humans will make it evil. Permanent peace was of God, not of humankind.

This narrative appears to be a parable of horror at himself; it also indicates his distrust of the political negotiations being undertaken. One of the songs composed suggests that the whole episode was a riddle ('He makitaunu') about who might be overturned ('kia hua ia ai'). The other waiata is a song of Te Kooti's own sorrow.[138] Hamiora concludes the story by describing how Te Kooti then left the house, telling the tohunga to stop the service. When the early morning bell rang, he returned to the house, now dressed in a shirt and kilt and the shawl he often wore. He carried a taiaha and a greenstone patu. He told the people in the house that the fighting had ended; he broke the taiaha in two and left it on the hearth. He placed the greenstone patu on top of it as a statement of peace, and went out. His final words were to reiterate that the peace of God was lasting, but that 'that made by Man which is still continuing' ('a ko ta te Tangata kai te haere tonu'), if it were to be broken, it would be the fault of man. These were the words that voices had spoken to him on that tempestuous night.[139] The story seems to test both Tawhiao and himself. It doubts the human negotiations, and seeks to bind the concerns of the people and the prophet to God. It reveals Te Kooti as a man who liked to use different guises and sudden strange appearances to sharpen his message. His startling reappearance clothed entirely in albatross feathers reinforced the statement of peace. He would use the device of unexpected guises again, and they would be remembered in oral stories from later years. Disguise was a favourite device of the great ancestor Tawhaki, who sometimes presented himself as an old man but who brought new knowledge and new ways of seeing to the land. In this narrative of Te Kooti it is clear that he was acting with reference to the past similarly to bring forth new understandings.

From this time another story tells of the rising tension between himself and Tawhiao. Ned Brown narrated how Te Kooti came to see Tawhiao and said to him boldly:

> 'Remove your hat! We will have a season of prayer.'
>
> And King Tāwhiao said, 'Who are you to come here and talk to a King? Nobody comes here and demand me to take my hat off!' Never removed his hat.
>
> So Te Kooti said to one of his followers, 'Sing "Te waiata a Rāwiri".' He start to sing the psalm of David, and he got to a certain section, and a whirlwind came in the room, from nowhere, spun around, and took King Tāwhiao's hat off! Took it away. And it disappeared! He was without that hat from that day to the day he died. That hat is still missing.
> *Heni:* That's the power Te Kooti had!
> *Ned:* And I said to these Waikato elders — jokingly — 'It's in my house now!'[140]

This narrative is about a challenge of mana. It not only anticipates the conflict of religious leadership which developed between the two men, but equally refers to the opening of the Rohe Potae, whose boundaries are often explained as being defined by the rim of Tawhiao's 'hat' (potae). This story probably belongs originally to the political negotiations of the late 1870s, which were to lift off Tawhiao's 'hat'.

At the end of the meeting in May 1878, during which Grey made a series of proposals to Tawhiao, Te Kooti immediately wrote to compliment Grey and the Native Minister, John Sheehan, on their policy, despite the fact that the government had made no offer of amnesty for those whom Maniapoto were sheltering. The letter seems very obsequious, although the translation probably over-emphasised that aspect. The original of the letter is now destroyed,[141] but it was part-published in 1899:

> You are the light (or the lamp) now, and you utter words of light, of goodness, and of

love to man. You all teach that troubles may not arise during your days. My word is
your management is very good, is exceedingly good. No man has taught in that manner
before. No trouble will now befall us. Salutations to you both, and to your Council.
Sufficient from your sinful slave, Te Kooti.[142]

The letter runs directly counter to the accounts of Te Kooti's distrust of the negotiations, and it cannot be readily reconciled with that evidence. But Tawhiao had expressed
some optimism at the end of the meeting, and Grey himself certainly left thinking that
he had laid the basis for a future settlement. Te Kooti's letter probably stemmed from
this temporary optimism. In the end, Tawhiao rejected the offered terms because they
included only a partial return of the confiscated land of Waikato.

Tawhiao was, however, still prepared to continue discussions, and Te Kooti was again
present at the next great hui, held a year later, again at Hikurangi. The familar intermingling of the serious with the bizarre continues in the local newspaper reporting, and
a story from this gathering also concerns a hat, but this time Te Kooti's. It was snatched
from his head by an elderly Maori woman, who then 'entwined her fingers in his locks
in such a fashion which threatened speedily to put him in old Uncle Ned's position, that
of having no wool on the top of his head, in the place where the wool ought to
grow'.[143] Hat-snatching must have been the favourite 19th-century device for ridicule,
but the report said 'Te Kooti took it very quietly', even though it was an intentional
attack on his personal tapu.

At this hui, on 8 May, Te Kooti wrote a long statement for Grey, setting out his
explanations for his arrest and exile. It is the first full account we possess of Te Kooti's
perception of the events, and it was the basis for his formal request for a pardon. He
talked first of the wars against the Pai Marire, which, curiously, he dated as beginning
on 1 February 1867. Perhaps he meant 1865. He stated clearly, 'I would not accept the
Hauhau God' ('Kahore hoki ahau i pai ki te Atua hauhau'). However, the morning after
the fighting in which the Hauhau were defeated (presumably a reference to Waerenga-a-
Hika), he was arrested by the government party, Maori and Pakeha, he said. He
described how he was released, then re-arrested, taken to the soldiers' barracks, and sent
to Napier. He depicted his several attempts to appeal to McLean for a trial, which
Hamlin also remembered (see Chapter 2). Te Kooti wrote at length about his time in
prison:

> E toru aku ra i tae ai ahau ki te whare whakawa (ehara i te mea tono na te tangata,
> engari naku ano i haere). He kaha no taku ngakau kia whakawakia au. I te ra tuatahi, ka
> tapoko ahau ki te whare, ka patai ahau ki te kai whakamaori o tana whare, ko Eruweti
> Hemara te ingoa, Kei whea a te Makarini? Tana kupu, He aha tau e patai na ki a ia? Taku
> meatanga atu ki a ia, Ko au kia whakawakia, kia marama ai taku hara. Na, tana
> meatanga mai ki a au, Hei te waru o nga Haora ka hoki mai ai koe, hei reira ia tae mai
> ai. I te waru o nga Haora ka tae au ki te whare ka patai ano ahau ki a ia, Kei whea a te
> Makarini? Na ka mea mai ano ia kei te raruraru engari mo apopo koe ka hoki mai hei te
> waru o nga Haora o taua ra i kiia mai ra e ia ka tae atu ano ahau. Na ka patai ano ahau
> ki a ia, Kei whea ano a te Makarini? Na ka mea mai ano ia ki a au, Kahore i tae mai kei
> te mate. Na taku meatanga atu ki a ia, Mau e ki atu apoapo [*sic*] ano ka hoki mai ahau
> kia whakawakia toku hara kia marama ai taku noho i te Whareherehere heoi kahore ia

i whakahoki kupu mai. I te ata i te waru o nga Haora ka tae ano au ki taua whare na ka
patai ano au ki a ia, Kei whea ano a te Makarini? Na ko tana meatanga mai ki a au, E hoa
me mutu te haere mai ki konei. Na taku meatanga atu ki a ia, Ka mahara ahau he whare
whakawa tenei mo te hara he aha ra te Pine i whakawakia ai tae ana ki a au kore ana e
whakawakia heoi. Ka puta atu ahau ki waho me te haere pouri ano ahau ki te kore oku
e whakawakia. Na ka kite au i a te Wirihana he Apiha taua tangata no matou i te
whawhaitanga o matou ki te Hauhau ki Waerengaahika. Ka mea atu ahau ki a ia, E hoa
me haere taua ki a te Makarini hei hoa moku kia whakawakia ahau. Na tana meatanga
mai ki a au, E wehi ana ahau i a te Makarini mutu kau tana kupu kua rongo maua i te
waha o te Makarini e riri ana ki a au. Tana kupu tuatahi, Tu atu haere atu. Kaore koe e
pai ki te haere mai ki te taone nei haere atu ki to koutou whare.

Heoi ano katahi ahau ka mohio kahore ahau e whakawakia. Na ka riro au ki
Wharekauri i te haerenga o nga Hauhau. He tino Kawana au kahore au i pai ki te
Hauhau kore rawa he nui te tohe a oku iwi kia tahuri ahau ki tana whakapakoko kihai
rawa au i pai. I Wharekauri au e noho ana ki timata taku ako ki oku iwi kia noho pai
kia kaha ki te whakapono. A i rongo katoa ratou i te ra i tata ai matou ki te hoki mai.

For three days I went to the court house (I was not requested to attend but I did so of
my own accord). My heart urged that I should have a trial. The first day I entered the
house I asked the interpreter of that court, Edward Hamlin by name, Where is Mr
McLean? He replied, Why do you ask for him? I answered him, I wish to be tried, so
that the crime that I have committed may be made clear. He thereupon told me, You
return at eight o'clock, for he will be here at that time. At eight o'clock I went to the
house, I again asked him, Where is Mr McLean? He replied, He is busy, but you come
back tomorrow at eight o'clock. At eight o'clock, of the day, I again returned, I again
asked him, Where is Mr McLean? He again replied, He has not come; he is not well.
Hereupon I said to him, You tell him tomorrow I shall return again, in order that my
crime may be investigated so that the reason I stay in prison may be clear. But he made
no word of reply. In the morning at eight o'clock I again returned to that house and I
again asked him, Where is Mr McLean? Then he said to me, Friend, you must cease
coming here. I then said to him, I thought this was a house in which crime is investigated. Why is [the theft of a] pin judged, but in my case no investigation is held? I
thereupon went outside the house, at the same time grieving because I could not get a
trial. Then I saw Mr Wilson. That person was an officer over us when we were fighting
against the Hauhau at Waerenga-a-Hika. I said to him, Friend. Let us both go to Mr
McLean so as to obtain me a trial. He said to me, I am afraid of Mr McLean. He had
just finished speaking when we heard Mr McLean's voice. He was angry at me. His first
word was, Stand aside, go away. It is not good that you should come to the town. Go
back to your house (the house of you and others).

That was sufficient. I then knew I would not be tried. I then was removed to Wharekauri with the Hauhau. I was a true Government man. I was not a Hauhau in any sense
of the word. My people begged of me strongly, that I should turn to their idol, but I
would not agree. Whilst I was on Wharekauri I commenced to teach my people to rest
quietly, and to put their trust in faith. They all heard of the day when we should soon
return.[144]

Te Kooti then briefly narrated the escape from Wharekauri, including the killing of
one of the guards by Tamihana Teketeke, and the decision, taken by drawing lots, as

he described it, to throw his uncle ('matua') into the sea. Without having done this, he said, they would have all perished. He then described how the government men came to them at Whareongaonga and demanded their arms. 'They also said that we would be arrested and put in gaol' ('Kia hoatu me te ki mai ano kia hopukia matou ki te Whare-herehere'). The messengers were two days persisting that the arms must be surrendered, and then, he said, on the third day, they were assaulted ('ka whakaekea'). This confrontation began the fighting ('Ko te whawhai tonu tenei'). As a consequence, and because they did not wish to fight, the whakarau tried to get through to the King. But they were pursued, and three times attacked by the government's forces. Twice, Te Kooti said, he sent a letter to the government saying that they should be left alone and not be killed. But after the third attack (the fight at Ruakituri),

> No reira ka tukua taku panui ki te Kawana Maori Pakeha hoki, E hoa ma ka whakae au ki te whawhi tatou no te mea ka toru a koutou whainga i a au ko tenei. Ko Noema te marama hei whawhaitanga ma tatou. Heoi aku kupu ka tupu te kino ka kiia e te Kawana he tangata kohuru ahau.

> On this account I sent a notice to the Government Maori and Pakeha, Friends, I agree that we fight for I have been followed up by you three times. Then November is the month in which we fight. Those are my words. Trouble will then arise. I was then called a murderer by the Government.

Thus he stated that he had warned everyone but, regardless, the attack on Poverty Bay had turned him into an outlaw.

Te Kooti's letter sets out his own perspective. He wrote it to obtain a pardon, but he does not distort the critical events or the critical sequence of those events. There seems to be some elision in his memory, particularly around his repeated arrests, and there is certainly narrative embellishment in his 'visits' to the courthouse, but there is no evidence of lying for the sake of a pardon. The reason he gives for attempting to reach the King Country is only a partial truth, but his intended challenge to Tawhiao belongs to another debate, not this one with the government. Overall his is a reasoned account, which is also largely borne out by other evidence.

The letter was taken seriously. Whitmore, at the time the Colonial Secretary in Grey's government, responded to the latter's request for an opinion with a telegram to state that Te Kooti must be considered a 'political offender'. All his acts, he said, had been committed 'in fair war and did not contravene Maori custom in war'. He certainly understood that any notion of an amnesty must include Te Kooti.[145] The government's interpreter, Hamlin, also wrote to say that, to the best of his knowledge, Te Kooti, in the early outbreak of war in Poverty Bay, 'never was known to actively take up arms against the Government, but the great accusation against him was that he supplied the rebels with arms and ammunition and also acted not only as a spy but also as an adviser to the rebels'. He recollected that Te Kooti had indeed asked to see McLean, and also to be tried — although the narrative of his several visits to the courthouse was an elaboration, as he was being held in the gaol. The letters Te Kooti wrote had been transformed into personal appeals. But Hamlin confirmed the essential point: Te Kooti 'said to me, my great desire is to be tried for my offences. Why am I not tried like other criminals. . . . I must confess he put the question [of the trial] to me several times.'[146]

However, everything remained unresolved. Grey sought to discover whether the governor's amnesty, pronounced as an act of clemency in March 1873 for all Maori then imprisoned for 'political offences', had ever been extended as a general amnesty. He learnt that it had not. The problem was compounded by the fact that some of the men sheltering with Maniapoto were not considered — in European eyes — to be political offenders at all. Purukutu was one; Winiata was certainly another. Obtaining special legislation for a pardon for these men would be a very thorny path to follow, for feelings were heated in the settler community after the killing of isolated individuals such as Sullivan and Packer. The government's negotiations with Tawhiao at Hikurangi had already collapsed on the issue of the confiscations, and Grey himself had left the meeting at Hikurangi on 13 May in a rage. Rewi's separate negotiations, which he initiated in June, also disintegrated when Grey refused to discuss or publish Rewi's terms. Grey's government fell shortly afterwards, and the whole matter was, once again, left in abeyance.

It was the urgent need for the North Island railway which dictated the final political settlement. The line from Auckland to Te Awamutu opened on 1 July 1880, and there it stopped. Maniapoto had to be wooed if the line was to continue, and for the Maniapoto leaders the terms were unequivocal: the establishment of a secure legal title for their lands once the border was opened, and a general amnesty for every one of the refugees they were sheltering. In July 1881 Tawhiao also signalled the end of his exile. On 11 July he crossed the border and formally entered Alexandra, the frontier military settlement, accompanied by 500 people. In the main street opposite Finch's hotel, he laid down his gun at the feet of William Mair. Seventy-seven other weapons were laid beside it. It was Tawhiao's statement of the end of war, and shortly afterwards he moved his settlement northwards. He came from Hikurangi, where he had been living since mid-1875, to Whatiwhatihoe, beside the Waipa river boundary. This was a move to end his isolation. Tawhiao now wanted Te Kooti to shift there with him, but both Topia Turoa and Rewi directly opposed this, saying it was better that Te Kooti stay at Te Kuiti until his pardon was agreed upon. At the same time, Rewi made it clear to the government that neither Waikato nor Maniapoto had any desire that Te Kooti should leave them; if he did, it would be only by his own decision. But Rewi also added, in words that were ominous for the future, that although he expected Te Kooti would indeed ultimately be pardoned the 'East Coast people will never forgive him'.[147] Indeed, Paratene Pototi's son, Henare Turangi, writing probably in response to a government inquiry, sent warning to the Native Minister that he did not want this 'Murderous Man' ('Kohuru Tangata') ever to come back to Turanga. If he does, he warned, then 'I will raise my hand against him' ('Ka pa taku ringaringa ki a ia').[148]

The Amnesty Act of September 1882 gave to the governor the power to extend a general pardon to Maori for all offences 'more or less of a political character' committed in war, or as a result of war. It also gave him the authority to exclude certain offences and certain Maori from these provisions. Whether the Act was intended to include Te Kooti — or to exclude him — remained unclear. During the parliamentary debates on the Bill, Te Kooti was emphatically mentioned by some speakers as the one Maori to

Whalebone mere said to have been given by Te Kooti to Bryce on the occasion of his pardon on 12 February 1883. This provenance derives from the section of the Bryce family who still hold the mere. It is also stated that Te Kooti gave Bryce a plain woven flax mat, which was subsequently donated to what is now the Museum of New Zealand. The provenance of the mere is not definite; however, it was lamented over by an elderly Maori woman from Te Kuiti, who came regularly to see it in the 1920s. The mere was photographed by the museum in 1985.   B16407, MONZ

whom the amnesty should not be extended. Rewi insisted that there must be no equivocation: the government must demonstrate that the Act, which was due to come into force by proclamation on 13 February 1883, included Te Kooti. As a consequence John Bryce, the Native Minister, accompanied by Rewi, came to meet Te Kooti at Manga-o-Rongo, a tiny settlement within the Rohe Potae, on 12 February. The meeting — and the pardon — was a political gesture aimed primarily at Maniapoto.

Te Kooti had agreed to the meeting, but he had also indicated his fear of betrayal. Winiata had been seized (for money) near Te Kuiti in June 1882, and subsequently hanged for murder. Since then, Te Kooti had closed his settlement to 'European and half-caste visitors'[149] for, as he told Bryce, 'He was as one of us, and I might have been taken in the same way'.[150] This fear of being sold, even by his own people, is also recorded in the prophetic literature specifically in this context. Te Kooti's prediction of betrayal (dated 1 January 1882 and described as a 'Kupu whakarite', an equivalent or confirming saying) was:

> Ko te tangata ka hokona. Ko ahau, ko te whare, ko te motu nei. Nga tangata katoa e noho nei i runga o tenei motu, ahakoa matua, tuakana, teina, tamaiti, ko ratou ano hei hoko i au.

> The man will be sold. There is myself, the house and this land. All the people dwelling in this land, whether they be parents, older brothers, younger brothers, or children, they shall indeed sell me.[151]

This prediction was understood to have been fulfilled with Winiata's capture and execution. But the threat remained, for the text surrounding the prophecy recalls that the government had tried to pressure the King to give up Te Kooti, and also states that 'some half-castes' ('etahi awhekaihe') had gone into the bush to try to capture him but had failed.[152] This distrust of marginal men, the men of ambiguous loyalties who can be bought by money, is a theme found in other Maori writing of this time.

Te Kooti was given firm assurances as to his safety, but he insisted that the meeting take place, not at Kihikihi as the minister had intended, but within the boundaries of the Rohe Potae. Bryce reached Manga-o-Rongo first, travelling by buggy across the rolling country south of Kihikihi to the kainga. About an hour and a half later, Te Kooti and a retinue of 30 mounted men arrived.

> Te Kooti was dressed in a long silk dust coat, white shirt, pants and leggings, and carried an umbrella. Physically, he was very little altered, betraying little if any anxiety or timidity, and to the Europeans who knew him in former days, very little changed.[153]

Bryce walked up to meet Te Kooti and they shook hands. Te Kooti then said, using the words of the Psalmist:

> Kua tutaki te mahi tohu raua ko te pono, kua kihi ki a raua te tika me te Rongomau e tipu ake te pono i te whenua e titiro iho te tika i te Rangi.

The government published their translation of this speech as

> Mercy and truth have met together; righteousness and peace have kissed each other; truth shall spring out of the earth, and righteousness shall look down from Heaven.[154]

The text is, in fact, Psalm 85:10–11. It is the song of celebration of the return of the people from captivity. It is one of the three psalms which are believed to have been given to Te Kooti by the Archangel Michael on Wharekauri. It is, explained the Ringatu elder Bill Hook, the psalm 'chosen by Michael to Te Kooti to act for anything he asked for'. When it is sung today in the services, 'It is the main one for revelation to you, to help you to overcome difficulties'.[155] In popular Christian traditions surrounding the Archangel Michael, Psalm 85 is often said to have been written by him.[156] Psalm 85 is, therefore, the song of the 'great prince' of whom it is promised that, at the time of the greatest trouble of the people, he will stand by them that they 'shall be delivered, every one'.[157]

After refreshments, the Maori who were present began to gather in front of the whare where Bryce and his party were seated. Te Kooti and his immediate followers walked to the centre of the Maori group, facing Bryce. Te Kooti stood a little apart, holding up his umbrella against the sun, as he often did. Bryce spoke first. He had, astoundingly, decided to seek evidence of 'repentance' and a statement of future peaceful intentions as the condition for freedom. Te Kooti replied to him directly:

> Ehara i a koe i hanga te pai moku engari naku ano. . . . Ehara i te mea na to pai e korero mai na i hanga ai e ahau te pai. Ko te 10 tenei o nga tau i mutu ai i toku ringa te Hoari i takoto ai ahau ki raro ki nga waewae o te Kingi. . . . No tenei ra katahi ano koe he mea

hoki kua oti noatu e au te ki e kore au e hoki atu ki tena mahi ki te patu tangata. Engari ka tuarua tia ano e au i tenei wa taku korero e kore ahau e hoki atu ki tena mahi. Engari ki te whakatara koe i au ka whakatara hoki ahau i a koe. Tau maungarongo na te tangata taku ia na te Atua, a ka mau ahau ki taku, a ka whakamatau i tau i ta te tangata. Ta te tangata maungarongo hoki ma te tangata ano e takahi. Otira e whakaae ana ahau, a muri ake nei hei runga o te Ture tooku nohoanga.

It is not you who created good for me but I myself. . . . It is not the goodwill you have spoken of to me which has made me good. This is the 10th year that has gone by since I ceased holding the sword which I laid at the feet of the King. . . . Today you have only just [spoken] of something which I had already ceased speaking about long ago, that I would not return to that occupation, to killing men. But today I repeat for the second time my statement that I will not return to that occupation. But if you challenge me, I also will challenge you. Your peace is from man; mine is that from God. I shall hold to mine, and I shall learn about yours, that of man. Only man himself will violate man's peace. But I agree, hereafter my dwelling will be upon the Law.[158]

This challenge to Bryce was not recorded in his report of their meeting. But it survives in Matiu Paeroa's transcription of the speeches made that day. Matiu's record also contains what became an essential dictum of the faith: that the people would live by the law. The peace of 12 February 1883 became a binding covenant for the Ringatu, and they refer to it always as the lasting peace: Te Maungarongo. It was the government which would violate it.

The news of Te Kooti's pardoning was given a very mixed reception throughout the society. Some newspapers, like the *Waikato Times*, endorsed it as removing an obstacle to the opening of the Maniapoto lands. The *Christchurch Star* noted the paradox that the pardon had been extended to Te Kooti by the 'bully of Parihaka, the oppressor of Te Whiti and his unfortunate people':[159] access to the land was the driving force behind Bryce's apparently inconsistent policies. The *New Zealand Herald* reprinted Walter Mantell's speech to the Legislative Council during the debate on the Amnesty Bill where he said, 'So far as I can remember the case, Te Kooti, great as his offences have been, was more sinned against than sinning, and if I endeavour to put myself in his place I cannot help thinking I should have been ten times as bitter in my revenge as he was'.[160] However, the *Lyttelton Times* was appalled that 'this monster' with so much blood on his hands had 'triumphed'.[161] In Napier, the settlers burnt Bryce in effigy. His image was 'placed on a white horse' (which Bryce was known to ride) 'at the head of a long procession, the town band playing the dead march': no saviour this, however. Taken to the river, the effigy was fixed to a stake at the centre of a pile of firewood, and then addressed (wrongly) 'as the first white man who had shaken hands with the arch-fiend Te Kooti for 14 years'. It was set alight, accompanied by a vast display of fireworks.[162] The peace of man was indeed an uncertain peace, and it would be severely tested in the years that followed.

CHAPTER 11

HOPES AND JOURNEYS
(MARCH 1883–JUNE 1886)

'The way of peace should be in the old war path, so that the footsteps made on it in anger may be effaced.'

MAORI PROVERB (QUOTED BY DONALD MCLEAN, MAY 1872).[1]

Whakarongo, e te iwi, ki te ture muru hara whārona i ara e te pono ki runga te ara mai o te tika . . . . I rokohanga atu ra e noho pupuru ana.

Listen, oh people, to the law granting amnesty, which has been reached by our faith upon the pathway of truth . . . . Stay keeping to it.

WAIATA COMPOSED BY TE KOOTI, DECEMBER 1884.[2]

Almost immediately after his pardon Te Kooti was presented with, and seized, the chance to demonstrate his gratitude (or sense of obligation) to the government. On 20 March the surveyor C. Wilson Hursthouse was captured at Te Uira, a tiny settlement just north of Te Kuiti, by the Tekaumarua (the sacred Twelve), whose leader was the Maniapoto prophet Te Mahuki Manukura. These men were disciples of the Parihaka visionary, Te Whiti o Rongomai; Te Mahuki had been one of the gaoled ploughmen of Parihaka. The Tekaumarua adamantly opposed Te Wahanui and Rewi's agreement that the government survey of the Rohe Potae for the railway could begin: they were extending Te Whiti's struggle to their own lands. Hursthouse, who had been the hated surveyor at Parihaka, was dragged from his horse by a hundred men, 'all naked to the waist', their 'faces painted' and with 'feathers stuck in their hair to show they meant business'.[3] He and his two companions were stripped and taken to Te Mahuki's settlement at Te Kumi. Hursthouse's capture was revenge for the destruction of Parihaka in November 1881, the Tekaumarua declaring that the Lord had finally delivered him into their hands. They fastened him with bullock chains and locked him in a cooking house. Three pigs were named, each for one of the prisoners taken; they were then killed and eaten, and Te Mahuki proclaimed, in a transformation of the scriptures, 'that this was the day that the Angels came down from Heaven to eat the flesh and drink the blood'.[4] It was a ritual intended to devour the mana of the captives and the mana of the missionaries' sacrament.

Wetere Te Rerenga of the upper Mokau had been guiding the survey party. He managed to escape and send out messages seeking help. On the morning of Thursday 22 March, a party of Wetere's people reached Te Kumi; at the same time, a small group, led by Te Kooti, arrived separately but equally intent on the release of the prisoners.[5] On one side of the cook-house the Maniapoto rescue party shouted that they were coming, while on the other Te Kooti called through the split-slab walls to the prisoners, '"It is I! It is I! my children."'[6] The door was then forced from outside by Maniapoto, and the captives released. Some of the Tekaumarua were tied up by the rescue parties, and Te Kooti took Hursthouse and his two companions back to his kainga at Te Kuiti. He clothed them, gave them food, and enabled them to get out telegrams describing their situation.

On Saturday a large gathering was held at Te Kooti's kainga, situated on the western bank of the river across from the main Maniapoto settlement, Taupiri-o-te-rangi.[7] Te Kooti's village was clustered around the newly reopened meeting-house, Tokanganui-a-noho, and well over 200 people came to discuss the affair. Te Kooti and Taonui had summoned the Tekaumarua by letter, saying that they were going to investigate their treatment of the prisoners. One hundred and three of the Tekaumarua — men, women and children — attended the gathering in Tokanganui-a-noho.[8] Taonui and other Maniapoto chiefs were there. Te Kooti himself played very little part in the heated discussions. He was acting simply as a facilitator, for this was Maniapoto's land and Maniapoto's politics.[9] Te Mahuki, who the previous day had appeared humble when the Maniapoto chiefs visited him, now spoke with considerable vitriol. He charged Bryce with having 'humbugged Te Kooti with a false pardon', and having 'humbugged' Tawhiao as well.[10] He called the government agents empty honeycombs, without any sweetness inside, and announced that he would go to Alexandra, and then on to Auckland. He would challenge the government men, who had driven him out of Parihaka. He told the gathering that 'his atua would protect him' against the Europeans,[11] and called to his people to follow him. He stormed out of the whare and 'tore up a Bible which he had to fragments, and then jumped on them'.[12] The view that Maori had been betrayed by the missionaries' versions of the scriptures could not have been made more clear.

After this dramatic departure, the discussion continued all night as to whether or not to restrain Te Mahuki. Most of the Maniapoto chiefs objected, saying that sufficient satisfaction (utu) had been given with the rescue of Hursthouse and the tying up — in deliberate retaliation — of some of the Tekaumarua. But it was agreed that Te Mahuki must be stopped from entering Alexandra. With that decision taken, Maniapoto — and Te Kooti — set out for Te Kopua, to block him if he tried to cross the river there. In the event, however, Te Mahuki and 22 followers were arrested on 26 March at Alexandra, having crossed the Waipa river by Tawhiao's 'new bridge' from Whatiwhatihoe. In the street opposite Finch's hotel (where Tawhiao had earlier laid down his guns), Te Mahuki stood and shouted angrily, '"Where is Bryce?"' When the cavalry commander, Lieutenant-Colonel William Lyon, and the new native officer, George Wilkinson, stepped forward, Te Mahuki stretched out his hand and called, '"Kia mate, kia mate; ma Ihowa raua ko Te Whiti e whakamate koutou katoa; kia mate, kia mate["] (Die, die; you shall all be destroyed by Jehova and Te Whiti; die, die)'![13] He then appealed to God to save him. But he and his men were immediately arrested by the concealed government forces. It was a hopeless mission of challenge, for which Te Mahuki found no sympathy — not from Maniapoto, nor from Te Kooti, nor from Te Whiti, who was himself newly returned to Parihaka after 18 months of exile without trial in the South Island. Te Mahuki was condemned simply as an irrational troublemaker.

On 27 March Te Kooti came to Alexandra to meet Bryce, at the latter's invitation. It is clear that Te Kooti considered that his recent behaviour had demonstrated his loyalty to those who had given him his pardon. While the press reported that nothing of importance transpired,[14] the Ringatu histories recorded the dialogue in some detail. Te Kooti expressed concern that his religious services were being obstructed in some communities. He said that the faith was not instituted without authority, 'For it is from within *the Scripture*' ('Engari no roto ano i *te Karaipiture*').[15] Bryce replied that he should persist with his church, as there was nothing wrong with it. Te Kooti must have welcomed the words, for they implied that he would not be molested by any government intrusion upon his teachings or his future journeys. It becomes quite clear that Te Kooti intended to travel widely on the new 'pathways' of peace, in order to convey the faith.

Bryce himself, however, was to make the first triumphal visit. He came to the Rohe Potae in April on a journey intended to announce that 'the King country may now be said to be open to the Pakeha'.[16] At Te Uira, where Hursthouse had been seized, Wetere invited Bryce to travel further and visit Te Kuiti. Bryce rode in on 17 April, and came first to Te Kooti's settlement. He was welcomed by the firing of guns from a group of 15 men assembled on the river bank, 'dressed in a semi-military style'.[17] He was formally received by Te Kooti's 'chief man', Hone (Hoani Poururu of Ngati Awa).[18] Only a few words were exchanged but Hone told Bryce, 'The journey you propose to make will be carried out. The Ngatimaniapoto will take care of you.'[19] Then he escorted Bryce into a white tent which had been specially prepared for his reception, with a 'splendid new floor mat' laid down. Te Kooti now appeared. He was dressed in black trousers and waistcoat, a black mourning cap with feathers, and a coloured blanket (or shawl) over his shoulders. He shook hands with everyone and invited them to take refreshments, which consisted decorously of tea and doughnuts. Notwithstanding, the *New Zealand Herald*'s reporter wrote 'the old man, who was looking very feeble, was under the influence of liquor, and smelt strongly of rum. He said very little'.[20] After taking tea, Te Kooti went out and sat in front of his whare, where he remained until the party left. Bryce crossed the river to see the Maniapoto chiefs. Taonui and Te Wahanui both expressed their concern about the message that Bryce's journey seemed to be giving. They wanted the country opened neither to settlers nor to prospectors, and they wanted their position to be understood. These territorial boundaries were still those of Maniapoto's authority. When Bryce passed back through Te Kooti's settlement the next morning, Te Kooti was still drunk.[21] It is probable that he, too, had real doubts about this processional parade into the Rohe Potae and had turned to the bottle. His erratic behaviour did not, however, put Bryce off. He sang Te Kooti's praises and drank his health in a toast of gratitude raised by Hursthouse at a banquet of celebration in New Plymouth a few days later.[22]

This description of Te Kooti as an 'old' and 'feeble' man, addicted to rum, directly contrasts with those given only two months before, when he had appeared to observers

Hoani Poururu (Hone Taupe): a photograph
taken about 1866, when he was held prisoner.
He was then aged thirty. Reproduced by
permission of H. M. Mead and Te Runanga
o Ngati Awa.

Te Murunga Hara: The Pardon, 1989

little changed from the active fighter. Now he was mourning a recent death, and he may
well have been ill. Indeed, George Wilkinson noted soon afterwards that Te Kooti was a
'victim to asthma, from which he suffers a great deal'. Writing in June, Wilkinson speculated that the disease, 'accelerated by drink', would probably kill him within a short
time.[23] Wilkinson was, in addition to his official functions, a publican at Kihikihi; he
supplied Te Kooti with the alcohol. He sold him food and drink to celebrate his pardon,
and would continue to do so; six years later he tried to sue Te Kooti for non-payment of
the remaining portion of this bill: £13 12s 6d![24] Te Kooti had a temporary camp at
Kihikihi, outside the restricting boundaries of the King Country where alcohol could
not legally be sold, and during October and November 1883 he gave away extensive
supplies of food and drink to celebrate his pardon; Wilkinson's description of him was
sour. Wilkinson was also wrong in his other presumptions: that the pardon would
ensure not merely Te Kooti's neutrality in any future confrontation but that 'if he takes
any side at all, [he] will take it with us'; and that Te Kooti's health was in serious
decline.[25] Instead, this man of mercurial temperament and powerful will was preparing
to move his settlement north from Te Kuiti to Otewa, and to begin the next stage in
the renewal of the faith.

The move was announced on 26 April, just a week after Bryce's visit. It is recorded in
Matiu's book:

He Kupu i puta i Otewa 26 o nga ra o Aperira 1883.

Ka mahue atu a te Kuiti me ona tikanga. He whenua hou tenei me ona tikanga. Kia hoū hoki, te mate kati i te Kuiti, ka mahue a Ihipi te kainga o te he, he whenua hou tenei kia hou hoki nga tikanga.

   Kaua hei whakaaro te ngakau ki te haere i a koutou hoki nga ra katoa, ki te whaka-aetia e te Kaihanga kia haere, ko nga mea toimaha me noho no te mea katahi ano hoki ahau ka haere.

The Word disclosed at Otewa, 26 April 1883.

Te Kuiti and its customs are left behind. This is a new land, with its rules. Let every-thing be renewed. Put an end to the prohibitions of Te Kuiti. Egypt, the abode of error, is left behind; this is a new land, so let all our customs be new.

   Do not ponder every day about the journey, for if the Creator agrees to the journey, the heavy things shall remain, because then I shall go.[26]

On 1 May a feast day was held for the departure from Te Kuiti and for the arrival at Otewa. The statement for that day was also recorded by Matiu:

Ko te ra tenei o to koutou hiritanga hei iwi tuturu ki te Atua.

This is the day that you are sealed as a people faithful unto the Lord.[27]

   The new settlement was at Whakaarorangi, Otewa, still within the lands of Ngati Maniapoto. There Taonui Hikaka had offered Te Kooti a place of residence, in gratitude for his gift of Tokanganui-a-noho.[28] Otewa lay immediately south of Manga-o-Rongo, where, just after the move, in May 1883 the traveller J. Kerry-Nicholls accidentally encountered Te Kooti. Kerry-Nicholls's description is of interest because it records Te Kooti's unbounded energy, in direct contrast with the earlier description an old, frail man. Te Kooti's party, about 50 riders headed by that skilful horsewoman, Heni Kume-kume, swept into the Manga-o-Rongo village, and there pitched their tents. Kerry-Nicholls described Te Kooti as an athletic man, aged about 50, with 'quick, dark, pierc-ing eyes' and a 'restless glance'.[29] This intense gaze was recalled by many people.[30] In a lengthy discussion which Kerry-Nicholls engineered about the future political relation-ships between Maori and European, Te Kooti was not at all swayed by his visitor's commonplaces about the establishment of good order and 'progress', depicted as the purpose of the system of authority which was developing in New Zealand. The pacific-ation of the land by road works and telegraph wires, freely described as the instruments of order and civilisation, was instead interpreted by Te Kooti and many other Maori in the 1880s as a hidden text for their conquest and dispossession — not least because of the discrimination in the various public works Acts applied to their lands since 1864. Maori experience made clear that substantive sovereignty was a confiscatory form of European rule. Te Kooti emphasised that, in his view, Maori must continue to hold their lands. Roads, rates and surveying, as he had already warned, were the things which consumed the earth,[31] while Maori experiences of government had been only a series of broken promises. He then burst forth in song, and the sudden animation of his features revealed to his visitor the power that he still possessed. This was no ageing, tired man;

Heni Kumekume, May 1883.
J. KERRY-NICHOLLS, *THE KING COUNTRY*, 1884

this was a man with life to live, with anger coursing in his veins, and who was distrustful of the politicians with whom he had recently negotiated.

A new series of revelations began at Whakaarorangi at Otewa. Te Kooti's journeying to other people and places also started at this time. He set out to spread his vision and to challenge those who opposed him. Matiu wrote:

> Hune 20. 1883. Ko te ra tenei i whakatika atu ai i Otewa i haereeretia ai e ia nga rohe o Reneti Hawira, i wahia ai e ia nga pa [o] ona hoa tautohe. 24 ka tae ki Ohinemuri 30 o nga ra o Hune ka whakaaturia te Kupu.

> 20 June. 1883. This is the day [they] set off from Otewa, and moved about the region of Reneti Hawira, and broke up the villages of those who opposed him. On the 24th, Ohinemuri [Paeroa] was reached, and on 30 June the Word was announced.[32]

The context of this statement is a series of prophetic utterances about the land being called 'Reneti Hawira', and Te Kooti's rivalry with the other major visionary leaders, particularly Tawhiao, and Te Whiti and Tohu of Parihaka. The move to Otewa announced openly Te Kooti's claim to be the prophet for the people of the whole land. He had left behind the patronage and the shelter of the King and was preparing to challenge his rivals.

The naming of the land as Reneti Hawira was initiated, as we have seen, in 1869. The name was maintained until 1885–86. The vision of 1883, as recorded by Matiu, meant that Te Kooti would now travel about the region of Reneti Hawira. His purpose was to expand the faith's area of influence, challenging hostility or indifference. The journeys of peace on the old pathways of war were also journeys of spiritual challenge; Te Kooti had already announced this intention at the Ra at Te Kuiti held at the opening of Tokanganui-a-noho.[33] He began immediately to travel, and at Te Makomako, Ohinemuri, at the end of June, he renewed his defiance of Tawhiao.

In a lengthy speech he narrated how the first Maori King, Tawhiao's father Potatau, had taught the people to reject Uenuku, the 'man-devourer' ('kai tangata'), the old god of the Waikato people, and instead to hold fast to Jehovah. He claimed that Tawhiao had put the teachings of his father aside through his new religion, Tariao, which, Te Kooti maintained, set Tawhiao up as God. As a result of abandoning Jehovah, both the people and the land had suffered. Te Kooti then abruptly predicted for 'Tawhiao the God' ('Ko Tawhiao te Atua') the end of his kingship in two years. He also told the people of Ohinemuri that, although they and he were divided in their worship and beliefs, 'each canoe paddling on its own' ('e hoe ana tena waka tena waka'), there was but one landing-place and three words, 'truth, love, and faith' ('ko te tikanga, ko te aroha, ko te whakapono').[34] These words, not the earthly kingdom, were the lasting message. Te Kooti then urged the people to cease working for different gods. He told them that the reason for all their suffering was the Pakeha: 'Te take o to tatou mate na te pakeha'. He described the pollution of the old ways and also of the new as being the causes of the sicknesses which had come among them. He argued that once they had been a tapu people, but with the coming of the Pakeha they had learnt to wash themselves with cooking water (hot water), and so now they had become a 'half-cooked' people ('tamaoatia ake'). Not content with breaking the proper order of the universe, the Christian ministers, who had urged this practice of washing in hot water, had then carelessly left their food or their pipes lying by the sacred books, the books of the covenant of David and the holy bible. They placed these books on dining tables, and the tapu of the books was thus removed ('whakanoa') through contact with cooked food.[35] Two of the major social practices of the Ringatu were laid out in this speech: their separation of cooked food from all occasions of prayer and worship, and their absolute refusal to wash in hot water. The premise behind these interdictions was the restoration of a balance or harmony which, it was understood, had existed within the Maori cosmogony and which the missionaries had violated by their casual practices and habits. The restitution of the principle of tapu pertaining to people — that is, sustaining the flow of divinity, which protects them and which alone makes human effort fruitful — lay at the heart of Te Kooti's words.

Alongside his injunctions, he also offered predictions. The 'kingship' lay not with Tawhiao — nor even with himself — for they were both mere men and, he said, Tawhiao will be 'as I am' ('Ka penei ano tona ahua me au nei'). There would, however, be another who would arise 'to lead us all' ('Ka ara ake ano tetahi tangata hei whakahaere i a tatou').[36] The prediction of the One who would come after him to complete the work was now renewed. But the meeting at Ohinemuri ended in confusion, as Te

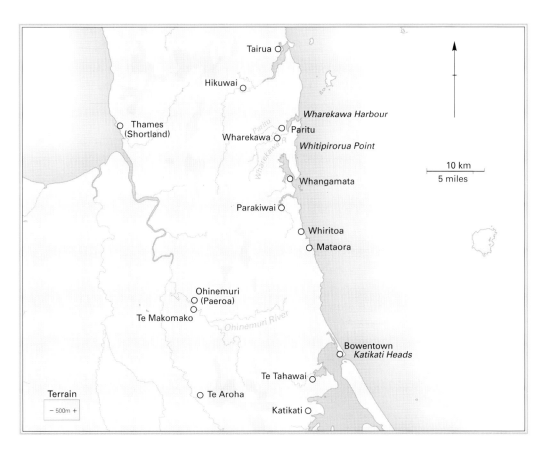

Map 7. South-East Coromandel Peninsula

Kooti's explanations were directly challenged that evening by Ropata (possibly Ropata Wahawaha). Because of this angry confrontation, it was said that the words for the Ra of 1 July at Te Makomako 'did not come forth' ('kihai i puta nga kupu o te ra').[37]

Despite this disruption at the first Ra he had held outside the Rohe Potae, Te Kooti continued to travel the boundaries of the land with his messages. His journey to and from Ohinemuri was briefly described in local newspapers. He was said to travel with a party of about 50 (sometimes called a 'body guard').[38] He had stayed at Omahu pa, near Te Aroha, on the way, and drank at 'Mr Coleman's bar' in the town. On his return through Te Aroha in July, he was again described visiting the town at Coleman's invitation. 'He came in a double-seated buggy, with three compatriots, a young native acting as charioteer.'[39] He was accompanied by a sizeable party of people, both mounted and on foot. He did not seem to be short of money, and he paid liberally for drinks with cash.[40] He manifested a triumphal procession: he was travelling through an area where a number of the refugees from the fighting of January 1870 were living, and where Tahau had sheltered. Despite encountering sharp opposition, Te Kooti was also reactivating many former ties.

This was the purpose of his journeys: both to renew the bonds and to attempt a

reconciliation with those who had fought against him. At the end of the year, he set
out for Tapapa and Rotorua. He arrived at Ohinemutu on 10 December accompanied
(according to a police observer) by 96 followers.[41] They came to the great carved house
Tama-Te-Kapua on the shores of the lake, where Te Kooti met with his former
opponents, Ngati Whakaue. He said to them:

> Do not refer to the sports we had yesterday; they are of the past, and let them be
> buried in the past; refer to them no more. Let the errors of our past life be a warning
> to us in the future. I am now travelling through the various districts of this island for
> the purpose of attaining two objects: first, to make peace, and secondly, to advocate
> submission to the laws.[42]

A written description of Te Kooti on this occasion seems to conform closely with
two drawings made of him in this meeting-house, which are the best images we have
of Te Kooti. The sketches have been attributed to the Reverend Richard Laishley, but
if they belong to this visit they are wrongly attributed. The *Bay of Plenty Times* published the description of Te Kooti and, although its image is unduly influenced by the
commonplaces of 19th-century phrenology, it does convey something of his personal
magnetism. The reporter thought, quite accurately, that he was about 50 years of age:

> In appearance he is noble and commanding, and possesses that indescribable something
> which irresistibly inspires respect and admiration in others. His countenance is ordi-
> narily mild; but when speaking, it assumes that sort of determined will which not
> unfrequently draws one under its magic influence. He has a large but well-proportioned
> head, and his forehead is particularly striking, being extraordinarily broad, indicating
> a possession of vast mental powers.[43]

Another report had earlier commented on his handsome appearance and the 'extremely
pleasant expression of his countenance' when he and a group of 200 had passed through
Cambridge at the start of this journey. It drew attention to Te Kooti's fine horse and
'very respectable costume' — and the fact that, despite this, he had been refused service
at one of the hotels. Cambridge people had turned their backs and, it noted, showed a
'strong aversion . . . to their presence'.[44]

At Ohinemutu and Te Awahou, however, Te Kooti was well received, and a nest for
the faith would be established in both places. At Ohinemutu, Tuhourangi also extended
an invitation for him to visit them while he was in the district.[45] A song Te Kooti
composed at Rotorua on 26 December contains a statement of developing harmony,
but it is also more equivocal:

> Kia haramai ana he pihāroa he torotoro taua ma Ngatikahungunu ki te putahitanga hei
> whakaahuru mai mo te manu a Tiki. Huia mai tatou kia kotahi te moenga e ei.

> We two are come here as a hatchet, an advance war party for Ngati Kahungunu, to
> clothe with feathers the bird of Tiki. We are all gathered here that there shall be one
> nest.[46]

The words suggest that the waiata was sung in Tiki, the little meeting-house built for
Te Kooti close by Tama-Te-Kapua at Ohinemutu. The song seems to be of unity, but

what transpired from the meeting was that the visitors, Tuhourangi, and their chief, Te Keepa Te Rangipuawhe, who had fought against Te Kooti in the Urewera in 1869, while being prepared to welcome him, backed away from support of his faith. Within days, therefore, Te Kooti would predict the destruction of their lands.

Leaving Ohinemutu, Te Kooti travelled to the Urewera to hold the First of January at Te Whaiti. There he opened the new carved meeting-house of Tuhoe called Eripitana. Paora Delamere annotated his listing of this occasion with the simple words: 'Whaiti. Good news. The Gospel extends' ('Whaiti. Rongopai. Ka nui haere te Rongopai').[47] Te Kooti's first prediction there was the equivalent or parallel saying ('whakarite') with which he returned to his vision of God's promise, originally uttered at Waioeka in March 1869. The text, as transcribed from Petera Te Rangihiroa's manuscripts, was

> 1 Tuihota 2 Ene 3 Keira 4 Houta.
>
> Whakarite. Ka mau taku pupuri i toku iwi me taku maunga, e kore e tukua e ahau te toenga o te Tangata i hanga nei e toku Ringa.
>
> 1 Tuihota 2 Ene 3 Keira 4 Houta.
>
> Parallel [saying]. I will retain my hold on my people and my mountain, I will not forsake the remnant of the People who were created by my Hand.[48]

Thus the Ra at Te Whaiti was marked by the reassurance of God's concern for the people. It was also the occasion of Te Kooti's first return to the land of Tuhoe, the people who had suffered so much for him. Here, then, were songs talking of old quarrels and new means of making peace:

> Ko te rongo-a-whare ko te rongo taketake ki mua ki te Atua ka whakahotu te riri.
>
> It is by negotiated peace, by the peace established before God that fighting is brought to an end.[49]

But songs of ill omen were also sung at Te Whaiti that January. One of these, not recorded by Hamiora but remembered by Tuhoe, was a waiata tohutohu (song of instruction) warning them not to sell their lands. It was probably composed in reply to their request that Te Kooti now take control of their lands.[50] In 1872 Tuhoe had formed the Union of Mataatua, or Te Whitu Tekau (The Seventy) as they called it, in order to protect their Rohe Potae (encircling boundaries), and at one of the early gatherings of Te Whitu Tekau, held in March 1874, the form of religious service adopted was stated to be 'Te Kooti's *karakia*'. The resident magistrate, Herbert Brabant, who was present at this hui, recognised the service as being largely portions of the psalms of David and prayers from the Anglican prayer-book.[51] Now, in January 1884, Tuhoe were seeking to place the mana of their land under Te Kooti's spiritual authority, in order to hold it. But his song reminded them sharply that there were three forms of authority, or mana, in the country: the mana of the Treaty of Waitangi; the mana of the Land Court; and, as well,

> Ko te mana tuatoru ko te Mana Motuhake,
> Ka kīa i reira ko te Rohe Pōtae o Tūhoe

Te Kooti at Rotorua 1887

Two portraits of Te Kooti, which have been attributed to Rev. Richard Laishley. However, both the attribution and the occasion are uncertain. Both sketches are dated 1887, and as the drawings are back to back on the same sheet of paper it seems certain that they were done at the same time and by the same artist. However, the dates and titles are added in a fine pencil and therefore the date could be incorrect. The profile portrait is annotated as being drawn at Tama-Te-Kapua. It is similar to a written description of Te Kooti made on the occasion of his visit there in December 1883. The problem is that Laishley was in England from February 1883 until January 1884.

Te Kooti's fondness for wearing 'a large straw hat' was noted by many other observers.

A114/4, ATL

Te Kooti or Turuki addressing Rotorua natives at Tama & Kapua in 1887

He rongo ka houia ki a Ngāti Awa.
He kino anō rā ka āta kitea iho
Ngā mana Māori ka mahue kei muri!

The third mana is the Separate Mana,
Hence the Rohe Potae of Tuhoe
And the peace made [by them] with Ngati Awa.
It would indeed be an evil thing
To abandon the mana of the Maori.[52]

Thus he was reminding them that the land was within their own authority, their mana, and that, as he said, 'he had not come for the purpose of acquiring lands'.[53] In the song he also warned them that, if they were tempted to accept the laws of the Councils ('te ture Kaunihera'), they would soon all be building roads and streets, the very things they opposed, for these were among the major agents of the government's invasive policy of pacification. He told them that his heart had searched out 'the Law' ('Nā taku ngākau i kimi ai ki te Ture') and it was for that reason that he knew it was wrong to sell. He was measuring the government laws against a higher concept of law, for he told them again:

Nōhia, nōhia!
Nō mua iho anō, nō ngā kaumātua! . . .
Hī! Hai aha te hoko!

Remain, remain [on the land],
It is from former ages, from your ancestors! . . .
Hī! Why sell![54]

Thus he was telling them to be watchful; it was a song warning of trouble. Indeed, Tuhoe would continue to involve him in their problems; just before his death in 1893 he was struggling to help them find peaceful ways to curtail and control the surveying of their land.

Hamiora recorded another waiata of prophecy and warning at Te Whaiti. This was Te Kooti's rendition of a song of Tuhourangi, which Hamiora stated was Te Kooti's prediction of the eruption of Mount Tarawera in 1886, which would destroy Tuhourangi's lands. The old lament began,

He aha ra kei toku ihu e waitohu noa nei
Te mutu noa i te rangi tahi?

What is this at my nose foreboding,
Nor ceases even a space?

And it continued,

Titiro ki Ruawahia ki Tarawera
No te mea i whakakopaia mai e Taraiti*
Ka mau te hu.**

Regard Ruawahia and Tarawera
Now that Taraiti has embraced you
The roar abates.

The house Tiki, erected at Ohinemutu as a 'Memorial of the Church of Te Kooti', 1 July 1913. It stands on the marae called Te Whakapono-a-Te-Kooti (The Faith of Te Kooti), and it was erected by Te Wharetoroa Tiniraupeka (Margaret Graham) and carved by Tene Waitere. It was built to replace an earlier house named Tiki, which had also been built for Te Kooti at Ohinemutu and in which, it is recollected, he used to stay. Te Wharetoroa transferred the ridge pole (that is, the supporting backbone — here, an old stockade post from the defence of Ohinemutu against the Waikato attack in 1836) from this house to the new house, sustaining their connection. The new house was for a while also a home for Gilbert Mair, who is buried at Ohinemutu; another, different, link. The house still stands, but the plaque in the porch stating its origins has been removed. Photograph by James McDonald, n.d.   B99, MONZ

This old song text was carefully glossed by Hamiora to show the hidden meanings in the words. Ruawahia at Tarawera was the place of the eruption of 10 June 1886, and when the mountain exploded, the homes of Tuhourangi were destroyed. Hamiora thus made notes of predictive explanation:

* ara. E te Atua, he ramahoki, he raiti a Taraiti.
**ara. Te Korohū. Te koropupu, te koroahu. ara. Ka mutu te hū, kaore e hū tonu a tau tini ana.

* that is. By God, Taraiti is a torch and a light.
**that is. The Steam. The boiling, the steam. In other words, when the roar ends, it will not sound for a very long time.[55]

There are different oral traditions explaining the reasons for Te Kooti's curse on Tuhourangi. The fact that the song was sung at the January 1884 gathering clearly relates his prediction to his recent visit to Tuhourangi. One tradition of what happened is retained among Tuhoe. This narrative says that Tuhourangi had refused to give Te Kooti a large English-language bible they had, saying to him that he would only use it for money. It was a huge old bible, 'so heavy with power and mana' that it could not be carried with ease. It had to be strapped on a person's back, an act which brought a particularly tapu portion of a man's body in contact with the holy book. This old bible was believed to have come from Israel; it was the bible (or covenant) which Tuhourangi later gave to the Tuhoe prophet Rua, when he came to them claiming to be the One whom Te Kooti had foretold.[56] They gave it to him then because of its past history and the curse that they believed Te Kooti had placed over them. It is quite likely that this continuing story stems from Te Kooti's visit to Tuhourangi in 1883.

For Tuhoe also, Te Kooti's visit in 1884 had its ambiguities. He came to open the house which he had instructed them to build for him, all the hapu in unity. But when he rode up to the finely carved house at Te Murumurunga, Te Whaiti, his horse shied and he saw the inverted figure of the ngarara on the poumua (the front pole), its wide mouth turned upside-down, ready to devour everything around it. Te Kooti then predicted:

> Kainga katoatia a ko te paepae o te whare nei ki roto [ka] kati tonu hei huihuinga mo nga morehu.
>
> It will be completely consumed, and only the threshold of this house inside will remain as the meeting place for the survivors.[57]

The warning was soon understood to concern the land. Thus it came to be remembered that Te Kooti had prophesied that, 'There will come a day when the people of Te Whaiti will lose everything, their land, their timber, and all that will be left to call their own will be the meeting houses.'[58]

Te Kooti named this house Eripitana (Eripi/Tani) in direct reference to his kupu whakaari of March 1869, first pronounced at Waioeka and renewed at Te Whaiti.[59] Eripitana was God's promise to the remnant of the people ('te toenga o te tangata') that they would be saved. The vision is derived from Isaiah 11:11.[60] The name 'Eripitani' was similarly used for the Ringatu meeting-house at Mataora, the community of the Ngati Porou exiles. But Te Kooti added a specific statement about the house at Te Whaiti:

> Ko te kai mo Eripitana te tapu o ngā tapu.
>
> The only proper thing for Eripitana is that it must be the holy of the holies.[61]

This house became extremely tapu as a consequence of these words (and because of the ill omen that Te Kooti had observed in the carving). It was abandoned and left to decay, and the house indeed soon became only its 'threshold'. Eripitana kept its lonely vigil for a long time, but later the house, which was known variously as the 'House of God' and the 'Holy of Holies', would be used as a place of worship for Ringatu gatherings. It was then considered to be a church rather than a meeting-house. A small whare was built at the rear of the house in an attempt to concentrate the tapu there. This little whare was

Eripitana, semi-derelict, 1900. A drawing of the house made in March 1891 by Thomas Ryan indicates that the words 'Ko Whakaari Eripi' were incised on the right-hand barge board (maihi). The upside-down ngarara (lizard), with its big devouring mouth, is visible at the base of the poumua (central support pole), beside which Hamiora Potakurua of Ngati Whare sits. Photograph by Augustus Hamilton.
32426 1/2, ATL

fenced in and its enclosure was seen as the centre of the holiness of the place. The offerings of coins and gifts (the sacrifices) were placed in the enclosure and in this way the larger house was intended to be freed for ordinary communal use. Despite this, it is still recalled that open-air services were held beside the river in preference to using the meeting-house.[62] For Tuhoe, Eripitana remained a place of fear and uncertainty for a very long time. Thus, although it was a house built for the Kotahitanga of the faith,[63] Tuhoe were left with an uncertain and difficult legacy.

From Te Whaiti, Te Kooti journeyed on, reaching Kokohinau marae at Te Teko about 10 January.[64] He stayed at the meeting-house, Ruataupare, which had also been built for him and for which he had sent the builders and the carvers, just as he had directed the construction of Tokanganui-a-noho. Ruataupare had been ritually opened on 1 January 1882 but, as Paora Delamere noted, Te Kooti had not been able to be there.[65] He had instead sent a waiata, as was often his practice. It was a lament for the confiscated land of Ngati Awa, part of the Matahina block, and while mourning its loss he told the people not to linger on memories of it, but instead to turn inland to their forests for their sustenance and life. But the song also warned that they would sell the birds of their forest for the froth of beer ('te huka o te pia') around their mouths.[66] It was a typical song of Te Kooti's, its purpose being to jolt the people into an awareness of future circumstances.

The oral history concerning Te Kooti and this house was retold by the Ringatu tohunga Wi Tarei at its centenary. Tarei was quoting the warning words which Matiu had recorded for the opening of the house; it is possible that they sprang rather from Te Kooti's recorded visit in 1884. Te Kooti said:

> Ae, e hoa ma, ka pai to koutou whare. Oti ano te raruraru, e titiro ake nei ahau, kei te whawhai tetahi o nga pakitara ki tetahi o nga pakitara, te whatitoka ki te tuarongo, te taina ki te tuakana, te tamaiti ki te matua.
>
> A, titiro ake hoki ahau ki nga kai o te whare nei he kohatu, he kirikiri, he tataramoa engari te one matua.

> Yes, my friends, what a beautiful house you have. The only trouble with it, as far as I can see, is that one wall is arguing against the other, the door against the back wall, the juniors against their seniors, the children against their parents.
>
> And I look at the contents of this house and I see stones, sand, and bush lawyer, but beyond them is the rich, fertile ground.[67]

As Wi Tarei commented, these sayings were very unpleasant to hear. In effect, Te Kooti was pronouncing that the people would fight and quarrel, back and forth, up and down, one side against the other. But, along with these words of cursing, there were also words of caring (just as there had been for Tuhoe). Te Kooti was speaking in parables, and the man whom Ngati Pahipoto of Kokohinau know as 'the mortal father' or 'the godly person' ('te matua tangata') also had words for them other than the warnings. These were 'sacred words' ('nga korero tapu'), which he uttered in the strange language:

> When the word of God came through to him, when the spirit entered him, then he was different. He became what the Ringatū call even today, he matua tangata, a godly person.[68]

On this occasion the sacred words were 'HERI ONO REI.' Wi Tarei explained that these were visionary words, brought to Te Kooti by the same spirit who had appeared before him long ago on Wharekauri announcing that he would be his source of wisdom. It was he who spoke the words in the 'different tongue' to Te Kooti. These three words were a reference to the scriptural parable of the man who sowed the seeds, some of which would fall on fertile ground.[69] The three words were then followed by the scriptural text Isaiah 55:6–7, and another riddling utterance:

> He pani nei hoki ratau kaore he whenua.
> He pouaru kaore he matua.
>
> They are orphaned without land.
> They are widowed without parents.[70]

Te Kooti always turned logical relationships upside down, but in so doing he was opening up fresh pathways. He was forcing the people to think, and if the will of the children was strong, as Wi Tarei argued, they would find a way out from within the unpleasant words.[71] As the text in Isaiah reminded, 'Seek ye the Lord while he may be found'. The words put the people to a test: it was for *them* to find the way to change, or to avoid the dark sayings. Te Kooti's waiata composed for this house was also a riddling song: it rudely suggested that owls and hens were more knowledgable than the people — in other words, these birds could distinguish the dark from the light. But his song also contained its own resolution: persistence in seeking would enable the people of the marae to differentiate evil from good.[72] The waiata is understood to be derived from the words of the prophet Jeremiah.[73]

Thus, at each of the marae Te Kooti visited on this long journey, he challenged the local people. To Tuhoe he gave a warning — and clear advice — on holding the land; for Tuhourangi, he seems to have used the weapon of a curse, often a 'natural weapon' of prophet–leaders,[74] which was effective because it was so feared within the Maori world. To Ngati Pahipoto of Kokohinau he had set the task of deflecting future quarrels.

Kokohinau had supported the government during the fighting of 1869 and had been used as a government military base thereafter. But it lay within the confiscated land block of the eastern Bay of Plenty, and by the later 1870s its people had largely become followers of Te Kooti for precisely this reason. Division had been their history, but now Ruataupare had been built as one of the earliest houses erected for the 'Kotahitanga' of the faith.[75] Its purpose was to reunite the people. Oral memory directly connects its construction with Te Kooti. As the old chief Eruera Manuera said, plainly enough, 'He had a crew, he brought them in, and they built it!' The carvers were from many areas — from Thames, from Ngati Porou, Ngati Awa and Tuhoe, as Eruera described them — creating a deliberate universality. Te Kooti also paid for all the building costs.[76] Eruera commented, when being interviewed by Frank Davis, that Te Kooti had directed its design, choosing 'one particular pattern' to predominate.[77] Unfortunately, the point was not elaborated, but Eruera's remark makes it clear that Te Kooti intended every aspect of the painted decorations of the meeting-houses to have meaning.

From Kokohinau, Te Kooti came to Whakatane, where he met Wiremu Kingi Te Kawau, who had himself arrived from Torere for a Land Court hearing. It seems likely that this was the occasion when Te Kooti gave Wiremu Kingi the large greenstone mere called Te Maungarongo (The Peacemaker), now held by the Auckland Museum.[78] These two former enemies exchanged speeches in which both upheld the principle of working within the law and under its protection. Te Kooti would never shift from this position — despite all the harsh experiences to come. He would maintain this principle even as he lay dying: one of the most famous of all his statements are the words of April 1893:

> Ko te waka hei hoehoenga mo koutou i muri i ahau, ko te Ture, ma te Ture ano te Ture e aki.

> The canoe for you to paddle after me is the Law. Only the Law can be pitched against the Law.[79]

From this meeting with one former opponent, Te Kooti travelled through to Matata where, on 12 January, he accidentally encountered another: Gilbert Mair. Mair wrote of their meeting with great enthusiasm: 'I received a tremendous demonstration from Te Kooti who gave me a very pretty mat, making me the most complimentary speeches. He is a wonderful man'.[80] When, later, Mair sent this shoulder mat (kinikini) for Augustus Hamilton to view, he described how Te Kooti had thrown it around him with the moving words, '"Even though this mat was too small to cover you, my love enriches your body from head to foot."'[81] Thus, in Maori terms, Te Kooti had extended his mana and his protection over Mair, reinforcing their mutual reconciliation. James Cowan, who later talked with Mair about the encounter, described how the two former antagonists then played soldiers. Te Kooti assembled the 30 men who were riding with him, borrowed a few shotguns and rifles, and they presented arms to Mair. He, in turn, ceremonially inspected the 'troops'. Later that day Te Kooti sent a message to Mair at the Horse Shoe Inn asking if he could send a bottle of rum up to him at the Arawa kainga. (Te Kooti, like all Maori, was not able to buy alcohol at an off-licence.) Mair supplied it 'and thus did the two old warriors exchange their pledges of aroha', wrote Cowan.[82] It was upon this old soldiers' encounter that Kendrick Smithyman based his droll poem, 'Meeting at Matata', included in Appendix B.

The next morning Te Kooti was gone, heading north with a following of 150 to Maketu, Hairini, Judea and Bowentown. The reporter for the *Bay of Plenty Times* thought that he seemed 'depressed and cast down', without life or energy, when he was camped outside Maketu on 13 January.[83] But the party made an impressive entrance when they rode onto Hairini marae, led by a standard-bearer with a large white flag, which had the Jack in one corner and the message 'Te Rongo Pai' (The Gospel, or Good Tidings) emblazoned in large gold letters upon it. At Hairini, Te Kooti simply refused to talk about the past again to the inquiring reporters. He stressed instead that he had come in peace. At the end of the month, when the party rode from Te Tahawai to Bowentown to visit Otawhiwhi, the marae of Te Whanau-a-Tauwhao, they had garlands in their hats and their horses were all decorated.[84] Each man also joyfully wore a fuchsia flower 'instead of the usual earring', noted the farmer's wife Adela Stewart, from whose summer garden at Athenree the flowers had been garnered, and where they had all been invited in for a cup of tea.[85] C. K. Stead's sesquicentennial poem, cast in Adela's voice, in turn remembers this occasion; it too is included in Appendix B. For Te Kooti, the journey may have been exhausting, but it was largely a triumphant tour of reconciliation. He had trodden the former paths of war and had graced them with the hopes of peace.

As soon as he returned to Otewa, Te Kooti reopened his inquiry with the government about a land grant at Orakau, which was where he wanted to live. The hope that Orakau would become his home went back to his request to Maniapoto in July 1869 that Orakau be given to him and his followers as requital for the sacrifice of Tuhoe, who had provided many of the fighters there, in that final siege of the Waikato war. As he told John Bryce when he met him in Alexandra in March 1883, he wished for that block 'on account of the presence of the dead there (killed in the Fighting)' ('ara i runga i te ahua o te hunga mate kei reira (i mate i te Pakanga)').[86] He hoped that this, being a sacred site, could become the home for the covenant. In his mind Orakau had clearly replaced Tauranga-o-Taupo, where in September 1869, as the Ringatu texts recall, 'the Sword was put in' ('Ka poua te Hoari').[87] Te Kooti had asked Bryce for a piece of land

Wiremu Kingi Te Kawau, who remained opposed to Te Kooti's teachings. Reproduced by permission of Joe Honatana, Torere.

at Orakau, to be taken from the confiscated block. It was, in one sense, the quid pro quo for his support in the Hursthouse affair; but from Te Kooti's perspective it was not just a deal. The grant of land would be an act of settlement, the exchange by which their reconciliation was sealed. From a Maori perspective, it would end any utu account: the gift of land, tuku whenua, would seal their new relationship of peacefulness. The move to Otewa had been intended as only temporary; Te Kooti went there as an invited guest. He was living on land to which, as was recognised, he had 'no claim'.[88]

He had already written to Bryce in July 1883, asking him for a decision about Orakau as soon as possible.[89] In August, Bryce promised to effect it.[90] However, the matter became clogged with political wrangles of nightmarish proportions. First, it proved 'impossible' to find any remaining Crown land which could be set aside as a 'native reserve' (except one block, which was too close to Kihikihi township for Pakeha comfort, and which the Waikato hapu Ngati Apakura had rightfully claimed but which was being withheld from them because they had rejected other, poorer, sites). It then became a matter of purchasing a block of private land suitable for Te Kooti and his followers — about 100 people, including women and children, as he informed the government.[91]

Thus, in November 1883, Te Kooti wrote suggesting a block of land which he himself had found. It was owned by a local farmer, Alexander Kay, who was willing to sell.[92] Much of the private land beside the government road from Kihikihi to the confiscation line near Orakau was swampy, but Kay stated that there was no less than 100 acres of dry and cultivable land within this particular block, Ngamoko No. 2. It consisted of about 260 acres, and actually lay just over the eastern side of the confiscation line, having been purchased by Kay from its Maori owners. It becomes clear that Kay was jumping at a chance to get rid of the land and he deliberately misled Te Kooti as to its cultivatability. When George Wilkinson went to look at it, in February 1884, he was disturbed by the extent of the swamp. He suggested that the government could purchase a portion of the swamp, which lay beside the Manga-o-hoe stream and which would give a supply of fish and timber, and, in addition, a further 25 or 30 acres of good farming land in an adjoining block (also owned by Kay). This last block lay along the confiscation line and led to the government road. Te Kooti came to look at the blocks at the end of February. He too now had doubts about the first piece. He asked if the government could, in place of Ngamoko No. 2, purchase an entirely different block, Lot 55A, consisting of about 100 acres (again owned by Kay). It lay to the east of the government road, was close to Orakau pa 'where his people are buried',[93] and was within the confiscated area. Te Kooti was anxious that his piece should be within the confiscated block so that there would be no subsequent dispute about the title, he said. He also had 'prophesied' that this last block would be given to him.[94] However, he indicated that he was still prepared to accept the original block, provided it remained undivided as it was almost entirely swamp.[95]

In September 1884 the government purchased Ngamoko No. 2 from Kay for £600, with the intention of dividing the block in half. Te Kooti was to be offered the choice of which portion he took. When, in November, he asked for the legal title to his half (even though, as he observed, the dry land in the block was sufficiently large for all of four people to live on, and the water could not be drained away[96]), it was withheld by the government.

The reason for this sudden change of policy was Te Kooti's desire to return to Turanga, first expressed in 1884, which had become a political hot potato.[97] When, in February 1885, Te Kooti met the new Native Minister, John Ballance, in connection with this new source of tension, the Orakau land grant was discussed. Te Kooti's secretary, Petera Te Rangihiroa, said then, 'Am I an eel that I should have been placed by Mr. Bryce in the water to reside?'[98] Petera asked again for the entire block. He also asked for an additional 40 acres of government land, the site of the Orakau blockhouse, a little to the south-east of the old pa.[99] Ballance now agreed that the block the government had purchased was uninhabitable. Therefore, he promised to try to find some dry land at Orakau. He did so partly in an attempt to keep Te Kooti in the Waikato district and to deflect him from attempting to return home. In April, Te Kooti again requested the 40-acre government block.[100] Ballance decided to grant him 30 acres (and to set apart the remaining ten acres of Orakau pa as a public reserve). However, Ballance's decision to give this land to Te Kooti was blocked in Parliament. The initial legislating clause was first altered at the committee stage from an outright grant to a

The large greenstone mere Te Maungarongo, given by Te Kooti to Wiremu Kingi Te Kawau, seeking to establish peace between them. The shallowness of the incisions on the hasp indicate that it was a 'modern' presentation mere.   E331, AIM

conditional right of occupancy 'during good behaviour'. The whole clause was then thrown out. The attack on it was led by none other than John Bryce, who defended his purchase of the original block as being perfectly adequate and the labour of drainage as being 'work to which the Maoris in that district are accustomed'.[101] The clause under which Te Kooti's 'good behaviour' right of occupancy had been awarded was therefore struck clean out of the Special Powers and Contracts Bill on 16 September 1885.[102] Political rivalry had combined with prejudice to prevent even this compromise solution.

Therefore, in June 1886, Te Kooti again asked for the title to the entire wetlands, Ngamoko No. 2.[103] After an abortive attempt at occupying it, he informed the government in November that the land was uninhabitable and impossible to drain.[104] Te Kooti would never receive title to this land. The Crown maintained ownership until 1923, when it was sold.[105] The government's promise to Te Kooti for land near Orakau was abandoned.

As a consequence of these appalling muddles, Te Kooti himself put down a deposit of £10 on some farm land owned by Kay. In the late spring of 1887, he ploughed and planted 15 acres of Kay's land. This was about the time when the young James Cowan first met Te Kooti, for Kay's land was near Cowan's father's property. Cowan remembered that Te Kooti had 'a neat camp of thatched whares and fished for eels in the swamp' on Kay's land.[106] Te Kooti was hoping to purchase the farm, or to exchange it for land he owned at Poverty Bay. He invited Kay to travel to Poverty Bay with him at the end of 1887 to view it.[107] But this journey Te Kooti never took. The government dissuaded him from it in 1887 and stopped him in 1889: any idea of an exchange fell through.

During this time, Te Kooti was seeking another piece of government land, 50 acres on the Coromandel peninsula. It was on the coast near Wharekawa, and he wanted it both as a place to live and as a run to graze cattle.[108] Soon after a disastrous fire in February 1888, which destroyed all Te Kooti's possessions and houses at Whakaarorangi, he erected a house on this Coromandel property. It was close to the communities of the Ngati Porou exiles who had given him support for so long and whom he visited quite regularly.[109] He applied to the government for a land title. This they were prepared to grant, so long as the land was not gold-yielding and the local Maori did not object to his presence.[110] Whatever the reason, no title seems to have been awarded. Certainly, the search for land shifted, in the following year, to the Ohiwa harbour in the eastern Bay of Plenty. There, a second block would ultimately be set aside by the government for Te Kooti and his followers: this story belongs to a later chapter. However, there never would be a permanent home for Te Kooti. He remained forever an exile. At Whaka-arorangi, he stayed only on sufferance. He yearned always for a place where he could settle, and where he could build the ark for the covenant. This would be realised at Ohiwa — but only after his death. The song composed by Te Araroa of Ngati Pahipoto, where she refers to the confiscated land of that tribe, recalls Te Kooti's pain:

> . . . Ka noho pani nei
> I pani ki te whenua
> I pani ki te tangata
> Au tangi kau iho i te po
> Ka whakatu ki hea te aroha
> Te tōnga o te ra ki a Rikirangi
> Ko tooku whanaunga ia tera
> Ina te ahua i mihi ki te whenua
> I tangi ki te tangata
> Ka noho wairangi nei. . . .

> . . . For I live like an orphan
> An orphan upon the land
> An orphan among the people.
> I cannot help but weep at night
> For where can I build my memorials?
> As the sun set on Rikirangi
> Likewise I am his kin,
> Like him, I greet the land
> And I weep for the people
> Who are confused and perplexed. . . .[111]

Te Kooti's hopes to return to the East Coast were first publicly voiced in 1884. His desire to visit Turanga (now called Gisborne) was indicated in a letter he had sent home early that year. The immediate and strong European opposition was picked up by the press in mid-April.[112] George Wilkinson was thereupon instructed to advise Te Kooti against such a visit.[113] But Te Kooti had been invited to Wairoa by Areta Te Apatu (Areta Te Rito o Te Rangi), who, it will be remembered, had stayed with Te Kooti at Te Kuiti a few years before. This invitation was a statement of reconciliation, for Areta's father, Paora Te Apatu, had been one of the senior Ngati Kahungunu chiefs fighting (albeit in his case with a noted lack of commitment) against Te Kooti. Areta, who also belonged to Ngati Maru, Te Kooti's hapu, had been trying to extend his invitation to include Poverty Bay.

Heni Kumekume, accompanied by Areta and Te Wahapango (a part-Maori chief from Petane), had herself visited Gisborne in February 1883, at the time of Te Kooti's pardon. They were bringing home the bones of kin who had died at Te Kuiti. The party stayed at Whakato marae at Oweta, and people from Muriwai and Pakirikiri, also former centres of opposition to Te Kooti, had come to welcome them.[114] Heni's visit was undoubtedly intended as a prelude to, and preparation for, Te Kooti's return.

The objections to his return did not come solely from the European community. At Wairoa, the senior chiefs openly expressed their opposition, particularly as the preparations for Te Kooti's visit, planned for December 1884, began. Renata Kawepo placed a notice in the local paper forbidding Te Kooti entry into his pa, Omahu,[115] and followed up with a letter to the Gisborne Maori newspaper, *Te Waka Maori, o Aotearoa*, expressing his hostility.[116] On 30 October, Toha Rahurahu, together with the Reverend Tamihana Huata of Wairoa and Henare Turangi (Paratene Pototi's son), wrote a joint letter asking the government to dissuade Te Kooti from visiting.[117] Two long petitions from Ngati Pahauwera of Mohaka, both collected at their request by their chief, the Anglican minister Hone Te Wainoho, were also sent in early November, urging the government not only to prevent the visit but also to give them arms to protect themselves. They had already constructed 'a fighting Pah' to be ready 'for any contingency',[118] while the destroyed Te Huki pa was renewed in readiness. At the same time Thomas Porter wrote from Gisborne to say that he could not be answerable for Te Kooti's life, if he returned.[119] Ropata was quoted as saying dryly that, if he came, he would 'treat him as a rangatira and give him his choice of deaths'.[120] But by the time these petitions and warnings had been received, Te Kooti had already decided, under persuasion from the government, to abandon his visit.[121]

He wrote, deliberately recalling the words he had spoken to Bryce when they met at Manga-o-Rongo at the time of his pardon:

> E kore au e takahi i te tika kua potaea nei ki toku mate me nga taonga papai kua homai nei e te Kawanatanga tuatahi raua ko te Paraihi: te Ture te Aroha te Maungarongo, te Kotahitanga me te Rongopai. Kati. Kua hamumu mai na koe he whakaae ana ke te kupu atu. Kati. Ko te whare hei nohoanga moku ko te mana o te Kuini me te Kawanatanga tae atu hoki ki te Ture . . . .

> I will not trample underfoot the goodness (or righteousness) that has been placed as a covering (cap) over my sickness (evil deeds), nor the precious gifts that have been given to me by the late Government and Mr. Bryce, viz., the Law, Affection, Peace-making,

the making one or joining together and the Gospel. Let it end (his persistence in wishing to go to the East Coast). You have spoken to (advised) me. All that I have to reply is that I agree to your suggestion. The only house in which I will reside shall be the authority of the Queen and the Government, including the Law . . . .[122]

At the same time Areta himself wrote to the government to express the views of those who had invited Te Kooti. The letter is worth quoting because it conveys their intentions, which were overruled:

> Au me toku iwi kia aroha koe ki te tangata kua horoia nei e te Ture a ka tuku kia haere mai ki konei ki te Wairoa nei kia kite i ona whanaunga e kore rawa e puta he kino i roto i te haere a te Kooti he mau[ng]arongo tana haere ki enei takiwa — he whai tana i te tika i te pai me te puta ki te ao marama o enei takiwa. Kati, kaua koe te Kawanatanga e kaiponu atu i tena ora o te tangata.

> I and my tribe wish you to shew pity on the man who has been cleansed by the Law and allow him to come to the Wairoa to see his relations. No evil whatever will arise out of Te Kooti's coming. He comes in peace to these districts seeking what is right and good and to come into these parts where everything is clear. Well then! do not you the Government with-hold that which would be of benefit to man.[123]

The party of travellers to Wairoa set out from Otewa on 12 December. Te Kooti journeyed with them as far as Te Waotu — and then he turned back, just as he had told Wilkinson he would. He therefore did not go to open the new meeting-house (probably the house known as Hikurangi) which had been constructed (or, more correctly, moved and rebuilt) for him at Te Waihirere. A group of over 150 people, mostly Tuhoe and Waikato shearers, had assembled at Tarawera in early December on Te Kooti's instructions, to journey with him to Wairoa. They were stopped at Mohaka, where they were challenged by Ngati Pahauwera, who had armed themselves and assembled along the Mohaka river bank. Once they learnt that Te Kooti was not with the party, however, they let them cross the river unopposed.[124]

Te Kooti himself had written to Wilkinson in November, asking the government to reconsider its request not to go. He implied that he would travel only to Wairoa where, as he said, he had been specifically invited. The hostility towards him existed elsewhere, and not there; and therefore he asked them to reconsider:

> Moumou to ratou whare me to ratou aroha ko tenei me haere mai, heoi ano a ratou kupu. . . . Ko tenei ehara i te takahi kupu. . . . Ehara au i ki atu kia aroha mai kia [hanga] nga whare hei kitenga ano ratou i a au he koa no ratou ki tenei maungarongo tena ra. Hori ata tukua ahau ki te hapai i te maramatanga i potaea nei e koe ki runga kia au. . . . Me tuku mai te tahi hoa moku ki te kore me tuku mai i te tahi reta hei tiaki moku.

> The house they have built in commemoration of my going to visit them, and their affection for me will all be wasted, and they say that I am to go there. . . . This is not with the intention of trampling under foot the word (of Government regarding myself). . . . I did not tell them to show this affection towards me, or to build a house in commemoration of their seeing me (again). But it is because of their joy in consequence of this peacemaking (my having been pardoned) that they did it. Now then George, let me go to uphold this enlightenment (or clearness) that has been placed as a

cap over me by you (the Government). . . . Send some person to accompany me; or in lieu of that, let me be furnished with a letter (from Govt.) as a protection.[125]

He wrote again on 2 December, sending a 'hymn' to the government. It was a Ngati Maniapoto lament:

> Moe hurihuri ai taku moe ki te whare
> Kei whea te tahu i aropiri ra
> I nga rangi ra o te tuatahitanga
> Ka haramai tenei ka tauwehe . . . .

> Restlessly within my house I sleep,
> Where is the loving companion who, in
> former days embraced me?
> But who now is from me severed . . . .[126]

He told Wilkinson that the letter could be published, if he wished. Yet, despite these pleas that he should be able to return to the land and the people from whom he had been cut off, Te Kooti finally observed the government's request.

From the government's perspective, it was the potential number of travellers which made the group so dangerous. Its officials knew that Te Kooti was free to journey wherever he wished, and that he was entitled to protection. But they argued that a large group might provoke 'a breach of the peace'. As Monita Delamere commented, to Europeans the party could look quite frightening, for they journeyed as 'a big mob', loaded into carts and buggies, accompanied by all their animals, chickens, dogs and horses, and sometimes using the beaches as their pathways: 'no one else travelled this way'.[127] There was also, more threateningly, the speculation that they would be armed. Although this supposition was denied in every report the government received from the police and the district native officers, the rumours spread like poison in the soil and ultimately affected the government's objectivity. It was finally on the probability of a 'breach of the peace', through actions by Te Kooti's *opponents*, that the government pressured him not to go.[128]

The First of January at Te Waihirere was held without the presence of the man for whom the occasion had been created. Three songs which he composed and sent for the gathering are very specific in their references to the importance of the law and of maintaining the established peace. The first wondered whether Te Kooti would ever set his eyes again on Mohaka, banned to him by Hone Te Wainoho, who had not accepted the amnesty; and the third concluded unequivocally,

> Ka kuhu au ki te ture hei matua mo te pani.

> I am entered within the law, that the orphaned shall have a parent.[129]

Although the desire to return to Turanga was now always in Te Kooti's mind, 1885 brought new demands and, with them, new journeys. But, whatever the uncertainties that these brought in turn, Te Kooti's decisions were always motivated by two concerns: a wish to spread the faith, and a determination to maintain the peace. On 3 February he met Ballance at Kihikihi to discuss the land grant at Orakau. Accompanying Te Kooti were several figures of significance: his two secretaries Matiu Paeroa and Petera Te Rangihiroa, Tutakangahau, chief of Maungapohatu, and Areta Apatu, who had renewed the invitation to Wairoa. Ballance assured Te Kooti, 'The forgiveness was complete, the pardon was also complete'.[130] He was, he said, free to travel; and there could and would be no interference in his religion. Ballance insisted that the government had advised him against going to the East Coast because of 'the existing state of feeling', but it had not prohibited him. 'The Government had no objection, and have none now, to your visiting the East Coast.' He added banally, and incorrectly, 'Time heals all wounds'. Ballance assured him that the government would continue only to advise: 'they will not interfere with the exercise of your liberty. It will be a matter left entirely with yourselves.'[131] He accepted Te Kooti's gifts — a dogskin cloak and a whalebone mere — as a statement of loyalty. The principles had been restated, and the exchange had been made. Petera said forcefully, 'The only canoe that I shall make use of to convey me to Wairoa will be the law'.[132] That canoe would ultimately prove to be untrustworthy for Te Kooti.

The Maori communities themselves were divided in their attitudes towards Te Kooti's visits. Not all responded to him and his religion. After he visited the Ringatu settlement at Paritu on the Coromandel to hold the First of July 1885, he travelled north to Harataunga (Kennedy Bay), another Ngati Porou trading settlement on the eastern coast of the peninsula which he had also visited in July the previous year. But the people would not adopt the new doctrines, preferring their Anglicanism. An old Ngati Kahungunu waiata which Te Kooti sang on this later occasion was pointed: it tells of the journey of Whatitata who found, on his return from extensive travels, that his wife had been unfaithful to him.[133]

In May–June 1885 Te Kooti had made yet another pilgrimage, first to Te Kuiti to fetch the bones of the Ngati Awa chief Te Hura Te Tai, and then east to carry them home to Matata and Kokohinau. Te Hura had been sentenced to death (with nine others) for the killing of James Te Mautaranui Fulloon, a government interpreter and informant, in 1865. Te Hura's sentence had subsequently been commuted to life imprisonment, from which he had then been released. However, he had died at Te Kuiti without ever returning home. Thus he became one of Ngati Awa's martyrs, arrested and sentenced as an act of war. Bringing home his bones was an occasion for lamentation. Te Kooti used it to extend his influence in the eastern Bay of Plenty, as the bones were taken to Ngati Awa's settlement Otamauru, on the Orini river north-west of Whakatane, and displayed there in mourning on the cabbage trees by the marae.[134]

At the start of this journey Te Kooti passed through Rotorua on 25 May, where his classic Maori gesture of defiance — extended tongue and rolled eyes — to the huge, noisy crowd which had gathered to watch his buggy was written up as coon humour by the local newspaper.[135] That evening he camped by the lake, and his visit coincided with a Land Court hearing being held by his old enemy, William Mair. Early the following morning Te Kooti came to see Mair and make his farewells, but Mair's gruff entry in his diary indicates his stubborn refusal (unlike his brother) to be reconciled: 'Te Kooti came and poropoaki to me at daylight but I would not show up.'[136]

Te Kooti arrived at Kokohinau on 1 June, travelling in his buggy at the head of a long cavalcade of 60 mounted riders.[137] Although the local teacher, Robert Donaldson, automatically described the party as the '*Te Kooti mob*', he admitted that Te Kooti him-self was 'an ordinary quiet looking man', who politely stepped up to him and shook his hand. He observed that there was '*no outrage*' of any kind during their stay at Te Teko, despite the extensive feasting which took place both at the pa and in front of the local hotel, where Te Kooti stayed.[138] This choice of the hotel, rather than the marae, enabled him to keep himself apart, as was his habit.

One of Te Kooti's main advisers and negotiators at this time was Hoani Poururu.[139] He too had been convicted for the murder of Fulloon and later released, and had lived at Te Kuiti under Rewi's patronage. Poururu had become a prominent figure in that community in the late 1870s, and he acted as Te Kooti's main emissary to the eastern Bay of Plenty. It was he who helped develop Otamauru as a Ringatu centre for the district. Not only were many of Ngati Awa and Whakatohea now converts to the faith: Matata and Maketu, both largely Te Arawa communities and former centres of opposition to Te Kooti, adopted the rituals in 1885.[140] The 'Po Takoto', the night of preparation and fasting held on the eve of the First of the month, was becoming a marked feature in nearly all the eastern Bay of Plenty communities.[141] The notable exception was Wiremu Kingi's community at Torere, where the faith had been stamped upon by the old chief.[142] The resident magistrate in the district, Robert Bush, sensed an urgency in the promulgation of the religion in this year. He commented that Te Kooti seemed particularly determined to spread the faith through to the East Coast, and had recently sent emissaries from Tuhoe in the hope that, if his prayers and rituals were widely instituted, he himself could then come home.[143]

Te Kooti's interrupted journey to Petane and Wairoa was renewed in December 1885. Hoani Poururu had informed the government that the party was travelling unarmed, and in accordance with 'good tidings of the Law' ('i runga i te rongo pai a te Ture').[144] They came through east Taupo, where they stayed with Tahau, and then on to Tarawera and Te Haroto, where again a large gathering was assembled to accompany Te Kooti to the coast. On 23 December, the party entered Petane in triumphant display. Two hundred people marched, three abreast, out from their overnight camp on the river flat. They were 'headed by a standard bearer carrying a white flag, having the Union Jack in the corner, and the words "Te Kooti" in black letters on the body of the banner'.[145] The Petane chief, Te Wahapango, had himself asked for a 'government' flag to fly during the visit, in order to make a similar statement of his loyalty.[146] The hosts at Petane, Ngati Hineuru and Ngati Matepu, who had had many men sent to Wharekauri in 1866, were spearheaded by 30 armed and naked warriors, who fired five volleys of gunfire in challenge and welcome. Te Kooti travelled at the centre of the marchers as they entered Petane pa in splendour. He was seated in his buggy, dressed in European clothing and, as he often did, held an umbrella over his head against the sun. He was attended by three uniformed men, while six mounted aides rode beside him. Two buggies, laden with food and clothing, accompanied him as his koha for the marae.

This was Te Kooti's first return to the East Coast, to the people who had given him so much support. His journey had been marked by a series of kupu whakaari, those utterances starting out in the strange language, 'te reo ke', which he pronounced at each of the places where he stopped: Tarawera (19 December), Te Haroto (21 December) and then Petane, on 26 December. The 'gospeller' Matiu carefully recorded them all.[147] These sayings would continue, and would be expanded upon, as Te Kooti travelled on to Wairoa to hold the First of January 1886. They were essentially scriptural promises of God's fidelity, and they culminated at Wairoa.

The journey itself was peaceful. Te Kooti passed through Napier on 23 December, from where Inspector Robert Bullen had been ordered by the Minister of Defence to accompany him to Wairoa. Bullen reported that the Europeans were 'mixing freely' with the party as it went through the town, and were conversing with Te Kooti. He was 'remarkably quiet', Bullen said; when questioned on current political matters, such as prospecting in the King Country and the main trunk line, Te Kooti commented simply that he had no power in these things, adding only that he concurred with the government. At Napier, he refused absolutely to have his photograph taken.[148] This is the first recorded instance of this stance, which he would sustain. His refusal ever to be photographed was due to the knowledge that his image would be misused, reproduced in profane contexts (on teatowels and cake tins) and displayed and handled in places where food was eaten. It was quite logical that he should refuse, although Heni Kumekume accepted a similar offer at Napier (see her photograph in Chapter 5). It was not a 'primitive' fear of the camera as a 'devil', sucking out the mauri, the life force of the individual, as has sometimes been argued, but a rational fear of abuse of the image which led Te Kooti, like Te Whiti, to reject photographers.

After he reached Petane, Te Kooti telegraphed the Native Department to tell them that Te Waru's son was travelling with him to Wairoa. This man was probably Tipene Te Waru. Te Kooti told the government because he feared that he would meet opposition from Maori at Mohaka and Wairoa.[149] On the advice of Areta, he had already told Reihana (Te Waru's brother) to turn back at Petane, because of his responsibility for the death of Karaitiana in 1868. Tipene travelled in the place not only of his exiled, now dead, father,[150] but also in the place of Reihana to seek an end to enmity at Wairoa. Bullen accompanied the party, and they all (225 people) crossed the Mohaka river in the early morning of 28 December. Bullen cabled to say that they 'passed the pah without a word being spoken on either side'.[151] Te Kooti's party rode behind the white flag they had carried into Hairini, bearing the words 'Te Rongo Pai'.[152]

The men in the pa by the road at Mohaka were on the alert, and armed. Old Paora Rerepu was present, dressed in his uniform and wearing his sword of honour, but the travellers went straight by. A kit of potatoes was sent out from the pa with instructions for them to pass on, and the reference was understood by all to be to Romans 12:20: 'Therefore if thine enemy hunger, feed him . . . for in so doing thou shalt heap coals of fire on his head.' In answer to a child's question, a woman with Te Kooti's party merely said, '"We are the Israelites."'[153] Another part of this exchange of scripture was Hone Te Wainoho's warning sent to Te Kooti, whom he compared to the man Shimei, pardoned by King Solomon, who had been told he must remain at Jerusalem and not wander abroad. There were four places where Te Kooti must not 'trespass', Te Wainoho said: Turanga, Whakatane, Wairoa and Mohaka, the places of killing. The warning was, if Te Kooti crossed the 'brook of Kidron', then he too must similarly expect death.[154]

However, the party was well received when it reached Te Waihirere at Wairoa, on 29

December. The local newspaper described the occasion as the travellers jogged in the early morning along the river bank. They rode three abreast, again in ceremonial display. In the front was Petera,[155] and with him in this first group of three rode the standard-bearer. Again he bore the flag 'Te Rongo Pai', and it would fly over the meeting-house throughout the time that Te Kooti stayed at Waihirere 'as the emblem of their mission'.[156] This time Te Kooti journeyed at the back of the cavalcade, accompanied by the three uniformed guards. He wore a suit, and a straw hat tied with a muslin puggaree to keep off the sun. After the initial challenge, mounted by the firing of guns and a haka, Te Kooti passed through the body of his followers and entered the new meeting-house alone. The local reporter noted that this house was the 'newest' of 'the two new houses' built by Areta Te Apatu at the marae. His observation is confirmed by the Ringatu list of the houses built for their Kotahitanga, which indicates that a second house was built at Wairoa, after the opening of the earlier one the year before.[157] This second house was probably Takitimu. When Te Kooti entered the house, no speeches of welcome had yet been made. Instead, the bell was rung for the prayers of the Ringatu service, in which all participated, both guests and hosts. The service seems to have taken place outside the house, in the open air, while Te Kooti remained inside. Then he came out and stood in front of the whare, while the food was made ready. Finally, after the hakari came the speeches of welcome,[158] which were all peaceful, for the senior chiefs who had opposed Te Kooti's visit stayed away.[159] The government's letters to influential local figures like Edward C. Williams, the Bishop of Waiapu, as well as their instructions to the police, had emphasised the legitimacy of Te Kooti's visit and the peacefulness of his intentions. They had been effective in defusing the local tension, while Te Kooti himself, as we have seen, kept Ballance informed of his movements and intentions.[160]

The Wairoa hosts spoke first. The speakers included men who had not supported Te Kooti, such as the Reverend Tamihana Huata, and also those who, like Te Rakiroa, had joined him in 1868. Only one speaker raised the issue of the death of Karaitiana, and he stated directly that that death was the blood of a kinsman, which could never be forgotten. Then the visitors spoke. They included the Tuhoe chiefs Rakuraku and Makarini, as well as Te Wahapango and Petera Te Rangihiroa. They all stressed that their mission was of peace. Panapa Waihopi, who had fought against Te Kooti at Nga Tapa and who had brought a party of Te Aitanga-a-Mahaki to Wairoa, stated that, as the government had pardoned Te Kooti, they too were welcoming towards him. Te Kooti spoke last. He was, observed the local paper, 'a forcible speaker'.[161] He referred to the past: he said again that it was the government's pursuit of him which had caused the killings; now 'peace had returned with him'.[162]

One story which is recalled from this occasion again reveals the kind of challenges that Te Kooti set wherever he travelled. As usual, he slept apart, here in a separate tent which was erected for him. But when he entered the meeting-house and Tamihana Huata greeted him, expecting him, as his guest, to sit on the visitors' side of the house, Te Kooti objected:

> You shall occupy the main side of the meeting house, and I the small side of the house. You are the visitor and guest, therefore the main side is yours. I am the host, and I must occupy the small side. I, as your host, must supply you with food.[163]

Te Kooti was fond of using this riddle. He had adopted it at Te Kuiti in 1869, with similar intent. An identical story is told about Kokohinau at Te Teko, where he claimed the small side of the house, 'te taraiti o te whare'. But there it was understood as being a modest statement: 'Let all the other churches have the important side of the house, and I can just tuck myself in behind the door here. Perhaps one day we can all work together.'[164] When Boy Biddle told the story of Wairoa's riddle, however, he emphasised the existing tension: every morning during Te Kooti's stay, when Tamihana arrived

> on his buggy, with people dragging him, not horses, and he'd stop, and jump down, and rant and rave there — and Te Kooti wouldn't bark, wouldn't bite. This started to annoy Thompson [Tamihana], being tangata whenua — but Te Kooti wouldn't answer his challenges to speak scriptures, to speak law, to speak whatever.[165]

The story is linked here to a protracted confrontation, like that with Tawhiao. It is interpreted not as a personal conflict between the two men but as a conflict of religious beliefs. Tamihana's odd behaviour was, presumably, a statement about his ties to his people; but Te Kooti then said that there was no point in their discussing scripture as Tamihana was 'tied up so tightly' by his own ideas.[166] Te Kooti's insistence on being placed as tangata whenua inside the house became understood as his statement that the Ringatu faith was the indigenous religion. The Anglican church, in which Tamihana was an ordained minister, was rather the stranger and guest and therefore should occupy the right-hand side of the house, the taranui. Yet others have questioned this understanding of the riddle. It has been noted that, if Te Kooti were indeed asserting this claim, he could have sat at the rear of the house — the tuarongo — with the local tohunga, which would have been locally appropriate. Thus again the meaning shifts according to different regional perceptions.

This same puzzle is narrated in another story, this time of the visit of Te Kooti to Koriniti on the upper Whanganui in January 1892. There the old chief Teki Kanara (better known in his younger days as Haimona Hiroti) is said to have welcomed Te Kooti by dramatically pulling down part of the wall of the meeting-house, Te Waihere-here, and saying,

> Haere mai, kei te rahi te whare mō tātou. Ko te Katorika ki tētehi taha, ko te Ringatū ki tētehi taha, ko te Mihingare kei te awarua.

> Welcome, there is ample room here for us all. The Catholics will occupy one side while the Ringatu the other and for myself, the Anglican, I will remain in the aisle.[167]

This narrative portrays the resolution of the riddle by the chief, who acts as the conciliator. In a much more dramatic version of the story of the arrival of the faith at Koriniti, it was Te Kooti himself who, riding his white horse at full force, burst open the rear wall of the raupo meeting-house and claimed his space in the centre aisle.[168] Thus, there are versions of the story which emphasise his power and versions which emphasise his modesty. Each contains a resolution which is deemed appropriate by the narrator.

Associated with the story of challenge to Tamihana at Wairoa are instructions Te Kooti is said to have issued later on the same day. The children were not to attend any of the revived mission schools, nor to be baptised or married by those churches, and

One of the two meeting-houses built at Te Waihirere, Wairoa, for Te Kooti, 1884–85. A welcoming text 'Haeremai ki te whare' is woven in tukutuku beside the door. This photograph was labelled by the school inspector Henry Hill, 'Pa at Wairoa built to receive Te Kooti. Government policy prevented him going to it 1883 [*sic*].' This building seems to be the painted house at Wairoa which Roger Neich has called (for convenience, as its name is unknown) 'Hikurangi'. It is thought to be the house 'Te Hau-te-ananui-[?o-Hikurangi]'. If so, it had been moved to Wairoa from Waiohiki in southern Hawke's Bay, and then extensively altered. Another photograph of this house shows a named ancestor painted on its porch: he was Areta Te Apatu's great-great-grandfather, Te Rangi Haere a Hiku, which seems to confirm the identification.

The other house erected at Wairoa was Takitimu, which was moved from its original site at Wairoa and rebuilt at Te Waihirere for Te Kooti. It is recalled that two houses called Takitimu and Hikurangi stood side by side at Te Waihirere, and that Takitimu was shifted to stand alongside Hikurangi. Te Kooti did not attend the opening of the first house built for him in 1884, but in the following year he went to Wairoa and opened the second house, newly prepared by Areta Te Apatu. On this occasion Te Kooti was reported as saying as he departed, 'You, Te Waihirere, shall become befogged, but in time you will again emerge' ('Ko koe e Te Wai-hirere ka pokia e te kohu a he wa ano tona ka puea'). The house Takitimu came to be considered extremely tapu, and fell into decay. It was burnt by the people between c.1898–1901. Hikurangi was also abandoned out of fear, and it too was burnt. After Areta's death, which occurred shortly after this second fire, the marae itself was abandoned. However, another house named Takitimu would be opened on the same site in 1938, thus allowing the prediction of the re-emergence of the people to be fulfilled.

383, ALBUM III (FORMERLY BELONGING TO HENRY HILL), HBM

they were to abstain from the sacraments they offered.[169] This exclusiveness runs directly counter to other messages of reconciliation, which are recorded. The comments upon the Ringatu practices made in the 1870s by interested Anglican clergymen like Thomas Grace and Leonard Williams also explicitly deny any such exclusiveness. Nevertheless, there seems to have been a time when Te Kooti was urging the protection of the children from external influences. The inspector-general of the new native schools certainly understood by 1882 that Te Kooti was preaching against them:

> He denounces our schools, because he fears the religious principles of the children of his followers may be injuriously affected if these children come into contact with pakeha masters and pakeha children. I hear also that he has declared that physical evils, such as disease and death, will overtake the children whose parents disobey his commands on this point. However this may be, Te Kooti's interference injudiciously affects the attendance at many of the schools.[170]

Te Teko was one school singled out as having its attendance affected by Te Kooti's hostility in the early 1880s. However, Bush, the resident magistrate, thought that the root of its particular problems — lax discipline and poor results — lay elsewhere.[171] He did not consider that the native schools in his district suffered because of Te Kooti's teachings.[172] Nevertheless, there is some evidence of parents taking their children out of school because of Te Kooti's influence. At the Waioeka school, which was attended by children from Hira Te Popo's settlement as well as by a number of Tuhoe families who lived and worked in the area, in 1889 the teacher noted that the three children of Wi Akurangi had been removed because their 'Father returned from Te Kooti's & does not wish his children at school'.[173] In the following year, Bush made the same connection between the reluctance of Tuhoe to send their children to the schools and the fact that they were followers of Te Kooti;[174] he therefore seems to have changed his mind within the year.

The extensive visits made by Te Kooti to various Maori communities in the 1880s certainly disrupted the school schedules. The children attended these gatherings, and helped prepare for them for days on end. The feasts also drained the communities of their stored food supplies; families then often scattered to plant or hunt, particularly during winter. This was a recurring observation by a number of schoolteachers after Te Kooti visited their area.[175] Any large-scale absence of children seems, in practice, to have been tied to the movements of their parents and the inadequate food resources rather than to a mass exodus caused by specific instructions to leave. But that Te Kooti sowed ideas about the protection of the children is unquestionable. As Eruera Manuera understood the message, Te Kooti had said to them:

> I have a school of my own, just as good as any other. Nevertheless, let the children attend school, so that they may learn to write their names and add up their money — then bring them back. If you leave them too long, perhaps they'll get too clever, and start robbing their own people.[176]

At the First of January 1886 at Wairoa, Te Kooti's predictive words for the year were revealed. They were: 'Awhenata, Opakeiata'. Matiu recorded their explanations and also the word which followed, that is, the word for the chiefs of Wairoa: 'Pioote'. The component parts of these sayings, as set out by Matiu, make clear the constant emphasis within the faith: that Jehovah was their God, and that he, and only he, would bring them to a collective salvation. The teachings also focus on the search for unity, and Te Kooti's marked hostility to the established, or senior, chiefs. Thus Matiu wrote:

Awhenata   Opakeiata

Awhe. Haere mai koutou katoa ki au e mauiuitia ana e toimahatia ana a maku koutou e whakaokiokio.

2. Ko au ko au a Ihowa kahore atu hoki he kai whakaora ko ahau anake.

3. Kei whakarerea e koe te atawhai me te pono.

Nata. He whakahi he whakapehapeha te ingoa o te tangata e korero ana i tona matauranga.

2. He kanga na Ihowa kei roto i te whare o te tangata kino he mea manaaki ia nana te nohoanga o te hunga tika.

Opakeiata

Opa. Kei tahuri koutou ki nga whakapakoko kei whakarewaina hoki tetahi Atua mo koutou ko Ihowa ahau ko to koutou Atua.

2. Nga Atua kihai nei i hanga i te rangi i te whenua ka ngaro ratou i runga i te whenua i raro atu ano hoki i enei rangi.

Kei. I te timatanga te kupu a i te Atua te kupu.

Ko te Atua ano hoki tana kupu.

2. A ka whai ahau i te kotahitanga, ko reira ra ano ahau whakau au i taku maunga.

Ata. E tangi koutou e aue ki o koutou mate.

Awhenata   Opakeiata

Awhe. Come to me all of you who are wearied by labour and weighed down; I shall bring you rest.

2. It is I, it is I who am Jehovah; no other brings life, save me alone.

3. Do not abandon mercy and faith.

Nata. Boastfulness, conceit are the names of the person who speaks about his knowledge.

2. The curse of Jehovah rests upon the house of the evil doer; the dwelling place of the righteous receives his blessing.

Opakeiata

Opa. Beware of turning to make images and elevating them as Gods, for I am Jehovah, your God.

2. Those Gods which did not fashion heaven nor earth are lost above the land and beneath the heavens.

Kei. In the beginning was the word, and the word was with God, and the word was God.

2. I shall pursue unity, for in it truly I shall establish my permanence (my mountain).

Ata. Then lament, cry out to your dead ones.[177]

The strange particles and phrases were a cryptogram for the central texts and tenets of the faith. They form an extensive reference system to the scriptural promises. The particular sayings are also understood to belong to the place where they were uttered, that is, they are the sayings for the local people. Thus the sayings have become fragmented in memory. People remember their own kupu and not those of others. But they were part of a system of reference created by Te Kooti. The component phrases were sometimes rearranged, too: thus 'Awhe' and 'Kei' had been joined to construct the saying for Tarawera on 19 December 1885. The meaning given then was consistent with the later explanations of the same two phrases at Wairoa: in the beginning was God, and he it is who lives for ever.[178] But the ascribed meanings also shift. 'Pi' and 'Kei' had been joined as the word Te Kooti sent out to Waihirere for the previous year.[179] The meanings ascribed to 'Pikei' (in another version 'Pi'), which were announced at that gathering, are cited completely differently in two manuscript versions of that particular kupu.[180] They cannot be reconciled; clearly, the respective recorders understood the intended meaning quite differently.

Te Kooti's use of 'te reo ke' maintained a necessary mystery. Secrecy is power. Those who know secrets can withhold them — or reveal them. For Te Kooti, the explanation, or revelation, and the expansions, when he pronounced them, were almost invariably scriptural. He was seeking always to direct the people into the unity of the faith, and to take hope from its promises for the future. Nevertheless, the faith which he held out before them he also veiled with the screens he erected. They acted as tests of the people's commitment. 'Te reo ke' was one kind of screen; it indicated that he possessed a knowledge which only he could divulge. Narrative by parable was another screen. The gospel of Saint Matthew taught this form of secrecy:

> Therefore speak I to them in parables: because they seeing see not; and hearing they hear not, neither do they understand.
>   . . . That it might be fulfilled which was spoken by the prophet, saying, I will open my mouth in parables; I will utter things which have been kept secret from the foundation of the world.[181]

Te Kooti's words could be ominous about the immediate future. They were certainly critical of the contemporary Maori leaders. At Wairoa, the words for the chiefs were:

> Pioote

> Pi. Ko te mea e herea i te whenua ka herea ano i te rangi.
> Oote. Kua oti te tatau nga ra o nga rangatira takirua rangatira o tenei wahi o tenei wahi e mate i roto i tenei tau.

> Pioote

> Pi. That which is bound up with the land is also bound up with heaven.
> Oote. The days of the chiefs have been counted; in this year, and in twos the chiefs of each place shall die.[182]

Thus, while Te Kooti saw the land as central to Maori concern, he chastised and threatened the hereditary chiefs as men of limited vision who must fall, and he considered the other prophet–leaders to be his rivals. He called Tawhiao, Tohu and Te Whiti 'the *three* houses of *resistance*' ('nga whare *whakakeke e toru*').[183] He scorned Tawhiao's recent visit to England, an attempt to take his petition of Maori grievances to Queen Victoria, as being fruitless. The song he sang to Tawhiao on the occasion of his departure in 1884 was a lament which is normally sung to a dead body. He cruelly greeted Tawhiao with the proverb, '"Great is your departure, insignificant will be your return"' ('"He nui to haerenga atu he iti to putanga mai"').[184] In a second waiata, he spoke contemptuously of the toboggan ('te papa-reti') in which Tawhiao had travelled to England and argued, quite correctly, that the power now resided with Ballance and Parliament in Wellington. Therefore, he said, 'Let my skin be tattoo-carved with peacefulness' ('Kia uhia mai taku kiri ki te rangimarie'). He also scathingly suggested that the law which Tawhiao should try to observe was, rather, the 'Blue Ribbon' ('Puruu-ripine') of temperance.[185] Thus, although he was himself consistent in his goal of peaceful co-operation, he was unquestionably a source of friction to other established Maori leaders.

After the First of January at Wairoa, with all its jostling and jousting words, Te Kooti set out to return to Otewa. He had exhausted all his funds. He was also living in fear of an attempt on his life after a dream that had been recently reported to him, in which the dreamer had seen two Europeans and a half-caste waiting to shoot Te Kooti.[186] This fear was based on Winiata's betrayal, and on a distrust of marginal men. It was not unrealistic, although there was no longer a price on Te Kooti's head. During his later years he would never drink from a glass for fear of being poisoned; it is said he drank only from a freshly opened bottle. In October 1885, just before he set out for Wairoa, he had written to the captain of the Kihikihi Armed Constabulary, seeking uniforms for six men. He wanted coats, trousers, hats — and ammunition — for them, so that they could act as a guard. He explained, again, that the purpose of the journey was to establish peace, but that ill-will existed on the East Coast from the past fighting.[187] The request was, understandably, turned down by the Defence Minister, and Te Kooti's three uniformed companions had been clothed from his own resources. But the fear of assassination clearly remained in his mind.

Te Kooti's return journey was probably less triumphant and more nerve-racking, but it passed peacefully enough. Mohaka remained as watchful as ever, and still refused to acknowledge him. There is an oral tradition which tells that the local people tied up their dogs when Te Kooti returned past their pa as a 'silent' protest, lest even their barking be interpreted as a form of welcome.[188] He reached Whakatane on 19 January 1886, and there he telegraphed the government for food. Earlier, he had vainly sought government money to meet the ferry fares of his large party for their return across the Wairoa and the Mohaka rivers;[189] now they were also, as he told Ballance, extremely short of food.[190] It was not the absence of hospitality — for he had been welcomed at Kokohinau — but the scarcity of supplies. The huge travelling parties drained the local communities of the surpluses they had garnered. This was a common observation by the native officers in their pious utterances about Maori 'improvidence', but this time Te Kooti's letter indicates the reality of such comments: that Maori communal wealth was constantly soaked up by the political and social roles expected of these small villages. Kokohinau had simply run out of food, just as Te Kooti had exhausted his own supplies with the gifts he had made during his long journey of reconciliation.

The last stage of the journey from Whakatane took the party of travellers by Lake Rotorua. One episode, which was recorded after the eruption of Mount Tarawera in June 1886, possibly occurred at this time, although it seems equally likely that the story belongs to Te Kooti's earlier visit to Tuhourangi in December 1883. On one or other occasion, he stayed at Te Ariki, on the southern arm of Lake Tarawera. This was a small Tuhourangi settlement, and its chief, Te Rangiheuea, had fought against Te Kooti in the Rotorua campaign of 1870.[191]

When Te Kooti's visit was approaching a termination, he said to his host that he had started rather unprovided with funds, and that he would like [it] if Rangiheuwea would accommodate him with £10 or £12. The chief answered, after the manner of many pakehas, that really he himself was pressed, and he could not oblige his friend however willing he was to do it. He said, however, that he would send his son round amongst the tribe to see if the money could be raised. The lad went, but utterly failed. He made, indeed, two attempts, but with no success. Te Kooti said nothing, but when he was mounting his horse to go he said to Te Rangiheuwea, 'Take my advice, and clear out of this place. Something is going to happen. I cannot tell you when it will happen — it may be soon, or it may be late — but come it will.'[192]

Te Rangiheuea died in the eruption of Tarawera. It was probably with some irony that Te Kooti gave £10 2s 1d to the Tarawera eruption relief fund.[193] It had been collected by the Otewa community and it was the first donation to the fund made by Maori in the King Country.[194]

It was probably on this same visit that Te Kooti went to Te Wairoa on the western shore of the lake. There the famous meeting-house Hinemihi stood, the eyes of its carved ancestral figures filled not with paua shells but with gleaming coins, gold sovereigns and half-sovereigns, florins and sixpences, all a showy demonstration of local wealth earned from tourism. In one oral version, which echoes Te Rangiheuea's narrative but also shifts it, it was Tuhourangi of Te Wairoa who refused to give Te Kooti what he had asked of them: ten shillings to lift the curse from the house which had been placed on it because of their greed. (At the time, ten shillings was the standard fee the Tuhourangi guides charged to take visitors to the famous Pink and White Terraces.) Heta Rua, who told this story, explained: 'That's all he wanted, to take that curse away from that meeting-house'.[195] But Tuhourangi would not give the money to him. Instead, 'They looked at him, "Oh, mate moni", that means he's hungry for money!'[196] 'This old man wants some money for some beer for himself. Ignore him!' ('Kei te hiahia te kaumātua nei tētahi moni hei kai pia māna. Hai aha mā tātau e aro atu ai!')[197] It is said, in what is still a widely told tradition, that the eruption of Tarawera was in revenge for this episode.

Te Kooti's prediction was recorded by Matiu and is dated 6 May 1886:

> O U E Keirana. Te Kupu. A maku e tuku iho i te rangi te tahi kapua mangu he ahi nei kei roto i a ia. A maku ano e tono ake tetahi kapua ona i runga i te whenua ka tutaki raua ki te takiwa o te rangi me te whenua ko reira ahau rui atu ai i te ahi ki runga i taua kapua a ka wahi ahau i to whenua ka whakamate ano hoki i nga mea katoa i hanga e toku ringa tae noa ki te tangata kia mohio ai te tangata ko Ihowa ahau.

> O U E Keirana. The Word. I shall release from heaven a black cloud with fire within it. I shall also send a cloud up from the land, and they shall meet in the region between heaven and earth. There I shall cast forth fire upon that cloud, indeed, I shall destroy your land. I shall cause to die all things made by my hand, including mankind, so that man shall know that I am Jehovah.[198]

When the Ringatu tohunga Wi Tarei from Te Teko quoted this prophecy, he also narrated how, on 9 June, as Te Kooti lay sleeping, a voice spoke to him and 'an angel

Hinemihi and the land covered in mud from the eruption. Photograph taken on 13 June 1886 by A. A. Ryan (Burton Bros. 4067). 706, MONZ

appeared to him'. It told him to arise, go outside the house, and look to the east, where he would see the things which had been spoken of come to pass. When Te Kooti came to the doorway he saw that there was a great cloud in the east, and that the sky was indeed filled with flame.[199]

Thus it was, during the early hours of the morning of 10 June 1886, that the people of Te Teko saw the flash of the eruption and the huge red fragments of rock as the volcano at the side of Lake Tarawera blew up. The flames and burning fireballs were etched brightly against the pitch-black sky, while the scoria, ash and dust rained down on their houses. The eruption destroyed the large whare karakia they had built,[200] and it buried Hinemihi. The people at Te Teko also saw

> this person standing on the edge of it with a red sword, flaming on the sword. Every time he puts the sword down into the mouth of that red crater, she goes up. They could see the outline of a person, standing on the edge of it. According to most of the Maori people, it *is* one of these angels. It was the one that rides the red horse.[201]

Thus it was the Archangel Michael, 'the one that travelled in between God and human', the angel for the time of anger, who appeared to the watchers, according to this oral account. The explanation for the eruption lay in the intervention of God's avenging angel. And there is no doubt that many Maori, in 1886, saw the eruption as a calamity wrought by 'The Hand of God' ('Te Ringa o te Atua') for they wrote to say so.[202]

The eruption destroyed the village of Wairoa and rendered the lands of Tuhourangi uninhabitable. Ngati Rangitihi of Lake Tarawera ordered all their lands closed, as well as those of Tuhourangi, on account of the deaths which had occurred. This rahui was binding on Maori and Pakeha alike.[203] The thick, lethal layers of pumice and sand had fallen also over the Urewera and the eastern Bay of Plenty, contaminating water supplies, destroying crops and poisoning the land. Farm animals and horses died in the following months for lack of pasture. At Te Teko and all along the Rangitaiki and Whakatane river valleys, extensive flooding occurred after the eruption, forcing people from their homes and destroying some settlements.

Te Kooti immediately sent out instructions to his followers in the Rangitaiki valley to flee inland, to escape the sickness ('mate').[204] It was dangerous to continue to live in that dust, he told them, very sensibly.[205] So they went to Te Whaiti and Ahikereru, obeying his words, and refused all other local offers of help.[206] The people at Te Teko left in a mass exodus at the end of July. They carried with them only a few tents and, according to the local schoolteacher, had 'very little to cover them from the wet'. They had also run out of food and had given every '*penny*' they had, including the subscriptions which had been raised for them, to Te Kooti.[207] They were undertaking a pilgrimage inland for their salvation. According to one account (which may be unreliable), Te Kooti had proclaimed, 'He is going to reconquer the land and each of his followers are to have new land'.[208] It seems like a messianic promise of a new world born out of the destruction of the old.

The famous Maori scholar Hamiora Pio from Rotomahana, who himself fled first to Te Teko and then to Matata as a refugee, was critical of the people who had left their homes because of the words of, as he put it, 'Te Kooti's Prophet' ('te Porohete a te Kooti'). He added:

> Na te Atua o te Porohete, i mea me heke i taua mate i mea mai ki a matau taua kupu kia haere hoki matau. Kaore au i whakaae ki taua mahi a taua tangata taku kupu. Ko Hehuketo, te Porahete te Kiingi o nga Kiingi, te Ariki o nga Ariki, o te Hahi.

> All the rest have been urged by the God of the Prophet to emigrate to avoid the pending doom. The same word was also sent to us to do the same, but I refused to listen to such advice. Hehuketo is the Prophet. He is the King of Kings and Lord of Lords in the Church.[209]

This seems to be a statement of the second coming, which Hamiora spurned. But the oral accounts have retained the real fear of the times. They link the arbitrary event into the myth-histories of the hidden power of Te Kooti and the warrior angel Michael, who was understood to be his guardian. At the very least, these oral narratives remind us that Te Kooti's journeys of reconciliation had not always proved to be that.

On the journey home in January 1886, Te Kooti had stayed at Te Awahou, on the north-western shore of Lake Rotorua.[210] It was a Ngati Rangiwewehi community, and its senior chief was none other than Wi Maihi Te Rangikaheke, who had fought deter-minedly against Te Kooti in the wars. But some families of Ngati Rangiwewehi had given Te Kooti support, particularly during the fighting in 1870 in the western Bay of

Plenty, where many from this divided hapu were living. By 1886 Te Awahou was the main Ringatu centre in the Rotorua district. There, on 28 January, Te Kooti spoke to the people about the land. The kupu whakaari for them was 'Peneetao', or simply, and reassuringly, that this land, and humankind, were everlasting.[211] The kupu stands in direct contrast with the harsh words directed at Tuhourangi. From Te Awahou, Te Kooti also telegraphed the government to say that he had been kindly treated by every tribe. Therefore he was returning to Otewa.[212] His first journey to the East Coast was now complete; its consequences were to follow.

CHAPTER 12

WHERE DOES THE FREEDOM LIE?
(FEBRUARY 1886–MARCH 1889)

Kaore hoki e te kino nei ko te tohe roa mai. Tukua atu au kia haere ki Turanganui ra, pae whenua hai taka whenua hai maunga rongopai.

How evil is this long-abiding dispute. Release me, that I may journey to Turanganui there, beyond the land's horizon, to make my land a place of abiding peace.

WAIATA COMPOSED BY TE KOOTI, TAPAPA, 12 FEBRUARY 1889, ON HIS ABORTED JOURNEY TO GISBORNE.[1]

For Te Kooti the return to Otewa in February 1886 ushered in a period of extensive religious activity interspersed with bouts of depression. He had journeyed to the East Coast, but had still been unable to go home. The land grant, which the government had originally intended to allow him to reside permanently in the Waikato and, they hoped, keep him away from the coast, had been blocked in Parliament by the lethal combination of John Bryce's self-defensiveness and settler prejudice. Although Te Kooti had been well received at Petane and Wairoa, he had also encountered continuing resistance to his teachings among Tuhourangi. The periods of acute depression, which have been hinted at, are also remembered in oral stories of people who lived at Otewa.[2] But then Te Kooti would suddenly take his white horse and ride like the wind: and together they leapt carelessly over the fences and ditches and boundaries as if they did not exist. This restless energy was ever and again rechannelled into new tasks and into creating new structures for the faith.

The community at Otewa had become a large, active settlement during the 1880s, situated as it was on the path to Manga-o-Rongo and Kihikihi. Cowan described it in 1886 as 'a place of well-built nikau and raupo houses, with large cultivations of wheat, maize, potatoes, kumara and fruit'.[3] Te Kooti built the road from Otewa to Manga-o-Rongo so that horses and carts could travel to the European market at Kihikihi.[4] Both he and Heni emerge in unexpected roles in Waikato society: she won prizes for her kiekie hats at Te Awamutu, while he took his reward at the Woodlands Annual Sports in 1885, coming second in both the half-mile handicap and the 'Four Part Race'.[5]

From 1883 Te Kooti was constantly seeking ways of acquiring carts and buggies to make it easier for the people to travel and trade. Hoani Poururu had in vain asked the government for a spring-cart to enable the community to trade with Kihikihi, as they

The bill for Te Kooti's sprung-cart, with two seats and 'wrench'. A name-plate with 'Te Kooti' on it was also included. The bill was sent to C. Wilson Hursthouse in May 1889.

89/1159, MA 23/8c, NA

could not afford one.[6] Early in 1885, Te Kooti wrote to Hare Pati (Harry Bird)[7] asking to borrow his buggy, as at the time he was unable to ride. But Hare had got rid of his. Later Hare sent him £8, which Te Kooti placed as a down-payment on a new buggy, his old one having collapsed.[8] It was after his arrest in 1889 that the government finally bought him a spring-cart, with two seats and his name engraved on plates. If this was conscience money, it is tempting to call it weregeld, for the buggy took him to Ohiwa on his last, fatal journey in 1893.

Just before the move to Otewa in 1883, Te Kooti's relationship with his wife Oriwia Nihipora had ended abruptly and in a manner which would scar him. Twice, in 1877 and 1878, she had returned to Wairoa to visit her kin and to re-establish links with the rapidly growing numbers of believers there. On her second visit, in February 1878, she was escorted by Reihana and the Wairoa prophet Te Hapi, who was himself returning from a visit to Te Kooti. Oriwia's visits caused some stir in Wairoa and led the chief Toha Rahurahu to write to the government saying that he wanted to try to capture her.[9] In March 1882 Te Kooti discovered that she had committed adultery with his son, Wetini. Te Kooti must have attacked her violently, for he told Maaka Ritai that he had killed her.[10] Nevertheless, Oriwia was still with Te Kooti in March 1883,[11] but shortly afterwards she fled to Auckland and sought help from the government to return to Gisborne.[12] There she was to live with Wetini as his wife, and bear him two children,

Rangi Rikirangi and Putiputi Miria.[13] Te Kooti's bitterness, and the curse he is said to have placed on his son and his issue to the fourth generation, explains why the couple concealed Wetini's identity from their own grandchildren for a long time. The facts of this relationship were acknowledged by Tihei, Putiputi Miria's daughter, as she recounted her life story for inclusion in *Ngā Mōrehu* but, in that book, while not obscured neither were they emphasised. This family history partly explains why Tihei grew up not knowing for a long time who she was.[14] Her ignorance was not simply the result of long-lasting hostility towards Te Kooti in the Gisborne community, as has been assumed by most commentators.

The bouts of depression directly influenced Te Kooti's religious pronouncements. Almost immediately after his return from Wairoa, he prophesied the abandoning of the faith. This negative view appeared in predictions and advice, and also in the songs. The gloss of the first song of 11 February 1886 states that it was an extension of the sayings uttered at Wairoa. The song clearly reflects Te Kooti's temporary despair:

> Kaore te po nei tuarua rawa e. Ko wai tohu ai e hokia mai hoki te mea ano au ka whiua ka maka ka waiho i konei ki kona e. Te ngutu wani noa mai ai he koha ra naku ko au. . . .

> Indeed this is the second night. Who was it that directed that I be returned, a thing flung, thrown, abandoned — from here to there. Parting words for me, uttered by harsh-speaking lips. . . .

He concludes with an angry sexual metaphor evoking a coupling with death:

> Tukua mai ki a ahau he po kotahi . . . Kei te raupine au kei te ohia noa e raro i au ki te ai ma taku teke i te rau o te ure ka horo katoatia e Hine-Nui-Te-Po. Ko te reka i whaia wiri ana aku papa.

> Give me a single night . . . I bind together; below me proves that coupling is my objective — the penis projects — all is swallowed up by Hine-Nui-Te-Po. My buttocks tremble with the sweetness.[15]

The gloss states that the song prophesied the desertion of the faith in his lifetime; the waiata contains echoes, in its expression of sexual anger, of the song announcing the faith in 1868. The gloss also says that Te Kooti warned of three prophets who were to come with signs and wondrous things; and, if that occurred, the people who held to the word and the faith would be deceived by them. This statement, dated 11 February 1886, was also recorded at length in the manuscript books of Robert Biddle. The prophets were tempters ('whakamatautau'), even of the cautious: the only answer was to trust in God.[16] The conclusion of all things was drawing near.[17]

Yet on the following day, the Twelfth, Te Kooti formally farewelled several of his followers with a different emphasis. These messengers included Petera Te Rangihiroa and Matiu Paeroa (his two long-standing secretaries), Meha Te Moananui (who had once fought against him),[18] Hoani Poururu, Te Whiu, and Rutene Koia Uru Te Rangi. At first Te Kooti spoke warnings to them that 'the Way will be abandoned and only I will remain' ('Ka mahue te Tikanga ko ahau anake te toenga').[19] He then sang a second waiata foretelling misfortune and trouble. This was for Rutene, and also for Meha.[20] But

Wetini Rikirangi and Oriwia Nihipora, with their family, 9 December 1914. They are (from rear left): Wetini; Te Kahukaone, wife of their son Rangi Rikirangi, holding her baby, Hori; Putiputi Miria, their daughter, with her daughter Tihei; Oriwia, with her adopted baby Meretene (Mary) Himoa. In front are the two older children of Rangi and Te Kahukaone, Hariata (Charlotte) and Rongo. Photograph by T. Thomas, Makaraka, Gisborne. Rephotographed, by permission of Tihei Algie, by Gillian Chaplin.

along with his admonitions, more practically he told them to be steadfast and tolerant in their planning. The making of strict regulations and laws must now cease, he said: 'let the Ture [the teachings, or the laws] be gentle' ('kia ngawari noa iho nga Ture').[21] It is apparent that they were being sent out as missionaries of a new, and 'gentler', faith. They were leaving behind the days of Moses; the harsh codes that belonged to the times of exile were being softened, as the Ringatu elder Tupae (John) Ruru of Puha carefully explained.[22] Similarly, when Ned Brown spoke of the house built at Mangatu named 'Te Ngawari', he said:

> Ā, ngā kōrero i kōrerongia e Te Kooti ki a rātau, 'Kauaka e kai hākari i tō koutou whakapono! Tukuna tō koutou whakapono kia haere, kia ngāwari, tukuna kia haere mo te pani, mo te pouaru, mo te rawakore.'

> The words that Te Kooti spoke to them were, 'Don't feast on your faith! Let it go out, be flexible, let it go out for the orphaned, the widowed, and the poor.'[23]

From a dark mood induced by the return to Otewa, combined with the realisation that he had, in fact, been prevented from reaching Turanga, new words about the faith came forth: now the emphasis was to be on tolerance and making the teachings accessible to those who had suffered.

It was at about this time, too, that the earlier sayings, in which the land had been named 'Reneti Hawira', were brought to an end. A new cycle for the faithful had begun. Two major statements are recorded: one uttered in 1885 and the other in 1886. The first, dated 25 January 1885, was spoken at Otewa:

> Te kupu whakaari mo te maungarongo. I mua to whenua ko Reneti Hawira kua rite i tenei ra e korerotia nei e koutou i te waiata, inahoki na te kuare i whakahaere i tenei ra, e ki nei ka karangatia koe ko Hepetipa, to whenua ko Peura, no te mea ka hua reka a Ihoa i a koe, a ka whai tahu to whenua.

> The prophetic saying concerning the abiding peace. In the past your land was Reneti Hawira. It is so today, as is spoken of by you in the song, for ignorance rules today; [and] it says you shall be called Hephzibah and your land Beulah, for the Lord is well pleased with you, and your land shall have a spouse.[24]

The second statement, dated 14 August 1886, was again uttered at Otewa. It referred directly back to the original promise, 'Eripitani', revealed at Waioeka in 1869 to the people in flight. This was God's eternal word, which lay at the very foundations of the faith, indicating that he would save those who remained:

> I Waioeka
> Eripitani
> Ka whakaora ahau i te toenga o te tangata i hanga e toku ringa. Ka pei ahau i te hunga kino ka whakapaia e ahau nga rohe o Reneti Hawira. E rua nga tikanga o roto o tenei kupu kua oti katoa. Ko te Rongopai te tahi kua oti tera, me tana riri ki te ao.

> At Waioeka
> Eripitani
> I shall restore the remnant of the people created by my hand. I shall drive away the wicked, and I shall restore the boundaries of Reneti Hawira. There are two meanings of this statement and both are completed. One is the gospel and that is completed, and also his anger towards the world.[25]

Taken together, the statements suggest the beginning of a new stage in the teachings of the faith. The text which lies behind the first statement is Isaiah 62:4. It is the promise that the land shall no longer be desolate but shall again become fruitful. Thus the land was to be renamed Peura, or Married; and he who was its spouse would complete the tasks set. It was for this reason that the Tuhoe prophet Rua Kenana, who would claim to be Te Kooti's successor, was baptised with the name Hepetipa by Eria Raukura. Eria, as high priest, baptised him in 1906 in the waters of the Waipaoa river which flowed through Turanga — the waters to which Te Kooti had never been able to return, the waters in which he had never again been able to cleanse his spirit.

The second statement came forth at a time when Te Kooti was surrounded by major problems. Nevertheless, the statement contains the unconditional promise that God's anger towards the world was over. This could be a reference to the last recent 'event' of anger: the eruption of Tarawera. Most prophecies — at least in their primary meaning

— intentionally relate to the lifespan of their audience. The statement, therefore, seems to be binding the people together within the sanctuary of new years of peace. It is in this sense, perhaps, that the boundaries of Reneti Hawira were restored. Hereafter, there is no further reference to this name for the land. As stated earlier, none of today's Ringatu elders knows the precise significance of the name. If it is akin to Israel, it indicates that the faith was no longer confined and constrained, but was now bearing fruit.

It was also precisely at this time that the followers of Te Kooti in the eastern Bay of Plenty, most particularly Tuhoe, were changing their names. The resident magistrate commented, in relation to the census of 1886, that hardly anyone bore the same name as they had in the census of 1881, and that this deliberate and universal re-baptism was the statement of a new era. He surmised that it was due to the fact that Te Kooti had been pardoned, and that everyone was therefore commencing 'a new and different life'.[26]

Te Kooti's wish to return to Turanga to complete this cycle of peace-making was to become a major issue from this time. His return would seal the land in unity; this was a pilgrimage which had to be made. The first reference to the building of a meeting-house there to receive him was October 1886. Paora Parau, who had once acted as a guard over Te Kooti, wrote to Ballance to say that a house was being erected for Te Kooti's accommodation when he came to Poverty Bay, so as to allow 'the public an opportunity of seeing what sort of man he is' ('kia matakitakiti[a] hoki e te ao katoa tona ahua').[27] For Paora, this was a surprisingly neutral remark, and suggests the widespread influence that Te Kooti was beginning to have on the East Coast. However, the visit was shelved again that year: a new momentum would grow during 1887.

Te Kooti was invited to Porangahau, in southern Hawke's Bay, for the First of January 1887. He used this opportunity again to test the responses to his returning home. At the beginning of December he set out with a following of 50 people, travelling through Taupo, Tarawera and Te Haroto, and reaching Petane on 19 December. After pausing there to rest among friends, he began the journey south to Te Aute and Waipawa on 21 December, accompanied now by another 200 people from the surrounding districts of Hawke's Bay.[28] At Te Aute he was received politely (but not warmly) with a feast, but at Waipawa and Waipukurau, as Te Kooti informed the government, both settlers and Maori showed their hostility.[29] At Waipawa, two of Te Kooti's guards, wearing 'policemen's coats', tried to push back and control a group of young Pakeha men, many of them armed, who had gathered near the Waipawa railway station in the early morning to jeer. Te Kooti's supporters were waiting for a protective police guard to escort them through the town. Once again it was Inspector Bullen; he got off the train, closed the hotel, and took the party straight across the river to continue their journey, accompanied by hoots, groans and hisses from the townsfolk. The pa at Waipawa had refused to welcome the party; the local hapu had also been conspicuously absent from the earlier welcome at Te Aute.[30] Pakeha racism was revealed in the *Hawke's Bay Herald*: the closure of the hotel was ordered, it said, to stop 'the niggers' grog',[31] not to defuse the situation, as was in fact Bullen's purpose. The party was similarly escorted through Waipukurau, Sergeant O'Malley riding with Te Kooti at the rear in his trap while Bullen went ahead by train to ensure that the hotels there were also closed.

There is an oral story which remembers how the party passed peacefully through Waipukurau, despite the local opposition. Boy Biddle tells it this way:

> The Pākehās there said, 'Well, here's this rat-bag coming now. We'll fix him one and for all!' So the night before, as they came along the road — he's got a song about it[32] — the township had got word he was coming, and they'd worked out their strategy. So he worked out his. He sent his men out to catch a hawk and a seagull. Well, you try and catch a hawk! But when Te Kooti said something, he expected it to be done! Don't hang around and doubt him! 'Go and catch a hawk and a seagull!' So these fellows all rode away, laughing to themselves, 'How do you catch a hawk? Even another hawk can't catch it!' Lo and behold, this hawk was sitting on the post. His back turned to them; sitting on a post. When they all saw it, they all had the same idea: 'There's the hawk!' Everybody stopped, very quiet, and one jumped off his horse, and sneaked up, and he said that the funny thing was, when he got hold of the hawk it never even tremored. He brought him back. So, down ahead of them was the beach. They rode on . . . and they got to the beach. A lot of seagulls there, and a lot of driftwood. This particular seagull was sitting on the driftwoods. And as the other ones flew away, he didn't fly away. So he got the same idea: jumped off their horses, everybody keeping quiet, and sneaking up — caught it! Took him back to Te Kooti.
>
> They used to put up a tent for him. He's by himself. So, he's got these two birds, and he's got them fighting. They pick away at each other — and the hawk would knock the seagull down. Separate them, do it again. Three times. He said, 'Well, let the hawk go. Let both of them go.' This fellow [Eru Matawha, one of Te Kooti's personal guards], he reckoned he was holding the hawk and, man, there was no way you could hang on to it. He kicked, scratched and bit! They let him go! He said to them, 'The reason why I got those birds, I told you yesterday there's going to be trouble at the town. Now, it's all right. There's going to be trouble, but there will be nothing come of it.'
>
> So, in the morning, when they went up, they got all the women in front, with the kids, and then the elderly people. Te Kooti always rode a white horse. So he said to this chap that caught the hawk, 'You ride the white horse.' This fellow thought, 'Oh, blow that! These fellows'll be after the white horse!' So Te Kooti said, 'No, you ride the white horse. I'll get on the buggy.' So, he's sitting up in the buggy, driving along. All the Pākehās went, 'There it is; there's the white horse!' Missed the man; see, he's gone past! This chap took off in all directions, and they chased it, and chased it. When they caught him, there was a Pākehā fellow among them who actually had seen Te Kooti, and he was that disgusted. He said, 'Man, that's not Te Kooti.' He said, 'The blighter's gone!'[33]

There is another version of the decoy who was passed off as Te Kooti as the party journeyed through Waipukurau, and it is much more grim. Hannah Callan Young remembered, or misremembered, the man who was tied behind a horse, with a rope around his neck which pulled him. He was heavily 'guarded because the whites were trying to lynch him' and 'he was struggling to get free'. She (aged nine at the time) was told that he was Te Kooti — a man with long hair and a heavily tattooed face. She remained convinced all her life that she had seen Te Kooti captive that day at Waipukurau.[34] He may have been a planned stalking-horse for the mob to pelt.

Thus Te Kooti reached Porangahau, where the huge preparations had been under way for weeks. The *Daily Telegraph* observed the houses which had been built, including a

Plate 9a. The polychrome carvings of Ruataupare, the house built by Te Kooti at Te Teko in 1882. This photograph shows the back wall, with the rear door which was added in 1960 for the comfort of older people. Eruera Manuera said at the time, in reply to critics of this innovation, that Te Kooti was a progressive leader and would have approved of it. The ancestral figures on the centre pou are Rangitihi (bottom), Kahungunu (centre) and Tapora (top). The house contains painted carvings of the ancestors of many tribes, in the same manner as Tokanganui-a-noho. Ruataupare, after whom the house is named, was a Ngati Porou ancestress of the East Coast peoples; Te Whanau-a-Ruataupare was the hapu of Te Kooti's first wife, Irihapeti. Photograph by Lynne Logan, 1990.

Plate 9b. Portrait of the ancestress Hakirirangi, dressed in contemporary 19th-century clothing, in the interior of Rongopai. Witi Ihimaera wrote of this house, 'The walls and ceiling enclosed you in a strange dream world . . . . the dream was of . . . the new Eden'. On 15 January 1888, Te Kooti sang this song for the gathering that had taken place there without him: 'I sleep restlessly in the house tossing and turning. Where is my loved one who should be close to me?' ('Moe hurihuri ai taku moe ki te whare. Kei whea te tau i aropiri ra.') CT 510, MONZ

Plate 10a. Baptism, or blessings, portrayed on
the rafters of the house Tama-ki-Hikurangi,
built for Te Kooti. Photograph by Cliff
Whiting, 1983.

Plate 10b. Painting within the house Te Purei in the Ringatu style. It shows the canoe 'Te Arawa',
flanked by two kiwi in the left panel, and a huia on the branch of a tree to the right. The painting makes
a statement about the uniqueness of this country, as well as the arrival of the local people. Kowhaiwhai
painting on the interior rafters can also be seen. Photograph by Judith Binney, 1991.

Plate 11a. Possibly the flag of Te Whitu Tekau, the union of Tuhoe. A flag with the 'bust' of a man, coloured black (but said to be on a red ground), was flying before the meeting-house during the hui at Ruatahuna in March 1874. It was described as 'the Te Kooti standard' and the red ensign flew alongside it. The flag illustrated may be the Te Whaiti version of the Tuhoe flag, which (according to Elsdon Best) had a black figure on a white ground. The man's collar is royal blue; blue is Tuhoe's colour of life. It is possibly an image of the archangel Michael. Compare it with the images painted on the lintel of the house Tuwhare (p.438).

This remarkable flag was deposited with the present Museum of New Zealand by Sir George Grey in 1879. It is recalled that, about 1936, a Tuhoe delegation came to claim this flag but were persuaded to leave it with the museum. The flag is handmade, with the images stitched carefully onto the white ground, and bordered in red. In full length it is a long, triangular pendant measuring nearly 6 metres.

ME 796, MONZ

Plate 11b. Te Turuki. Alan Taylor. Oil on board, c.1986.   JUDITH BINNEY

Plate 12a. Tauakira, the meeting-house at Otoko. Built in 1870, it was re-named by Te Kooti 'Te Parakuihi' (The Breakfast). The kowhaiwhai panels trace the people's genealogies. The prophet Wi Raepuku began his quest to open the 'seven seals' from this marae in 1921. Photograph by Judith Binney, 1994, by permission of Niko Tangaroa.

Plate 12b. The plaque placed on the meeting-house Te Ohaki for the centenary of Te Kooti's death in April 1993. The legend reads: 'Ko te whakapumautanga i te manawanui i runga i te kupu oati' ('The sealing forever of the strong-hearted people with the promised word'). Photograph, by permission of Robert (Boy) Biddle, by Judith Binney.

gabled villa for the most honoured guest, Te Kooti, and the tarpaulin city which had grown for others less esteemed. There were many tons of flour and thousands of crayfish, as well as pigeons, shark, Christmas puddings, whisky and brass bands — all gathered in for the Christmas festivities.[35] But on the marae Te Kooti was greeted ambiguously by Henare Matua, one of the principal chiefs of Porangahau and an important figure in Hawke's Bay. He was the founder of the Repudiation movement (against land sales), and that which had grown from it, the Kotahitanga (Unity) movement for a Maori Parliament. Henare was an ambitious man and a figure of contention. He made it clear that Te Kooti had been invited by a portion of the tribe and his brother Wiremu, but not by himself. However, he extended his hospitality, and he told Te Kooti that houses had been set apart for him and his party. But, he added, he still had a 'big bone' to pick before Te Kooti left the district. At this juncture, Te Kooti turned his back on Henare. In his speech in reply, he also refused to address himself to Henare, and he refused the houses which had been offered for his party's accommodation. Instead he kept himself secluded in a tent, guarded by four of his own men.[36]

Tension grew over the following days. In the first exchanges, Te Kooti suggested that they should play a game of draughts,[37] which was interpreted as accepting the challenge to argument. Henare agreed, when they could put an equal number of players on the board — the implication being that Te Kooti was not a worthy opponent. His speech on 27 December denigrated Te Kooti absolutely. Henare stressed his chiefly lineage, which he recited on his own marae, and told Te Kooti that the latter was 'a nobody', for he was 'not descended from a line of chieftains. I heard of you in the distance that you were going to save this island. What has been the outcome? You[r] supposed natural enemies and Europeans, together with those of our own race, lost their lives.'[38] Now, he would accept the challenge to the game of draughts, the argument. He mocked the fears of those who were saying that Te Kooti had bewitched their meeting-house, which was being opened at this time:[39] 'I have given up all such old-time things, and such stories were not true. I am not afraid of you.'[40] On the next day the argument continued openly on the marae. Henare spoke again, for about two hours, challenging Te Kooti. He said that Te Kooti's time was over. He denigrated him as a man without a home, in words that appear deliberately rude as well as paradoxical:

> 'I am standing on my own land. Those whom you say are trying to dispossess us are here around us. I live upon my land. Where is yours? You can see for yourself the falsity of such idea that anyone is trying to dispossess the Maoris of their land. Give me the island now.' meaning let law and order prevail.

After further debate about the many religions based in the scriptures and the several rival prophets, a debate in which many other speakers participated, Henare then extended the tips of his fingers to Te Kooti, who got up to speak. On the first day, Te Kooti had addressed the problem of alcohol, admitting his own weakness and urging others not to follow him. He had stated then (at least according to one report) that he used spirituous liquors 'to be inspired'.[41] This time he said to Henare:

> All you have said is correct. I have nothing to say against it. My mission is one of peace and good will. I am a sick man, and will retire.[42]

He muttered something inaudible to the koruru, the carved ancestral figure on the meeting-house, and then was silent.

Undoubtedly he was ill; there was evidence of acute asthma attacks which made him look, to passing observers, old and frail. The *Daily Telegraph* described him at Waipawa as 'a decrepit looking old drunkard', and as a very different man from the one who had visited Petane and Wairoa the previous year.[43] Bullen said the same, commenting that he seemed very 'asthmatical' and much more dependent on alcohol, adding that he 'was often the worse of it during this trip'.[44] Te Kooti knew his own weakness, and his first speech on the Porangahau marae had addressed his problems with drink. His reply to Henare was also honest, for Henare's speech largely expressed Te Kooti's stance since 1883: solutions lay within the law, not outside it. Was Henare challenging the past rather than the present? Te Kooti seemed not to have the strength to take issue with him.

But the meeting was not yet over. Two unfortunate episodes occurred which, at a time of heightened consciousness of makutu, introduced into the debate right at the beginning, enhanced Te Kooti's mana and increased the fear with which some regarded him. On 29 December a little girl, daughter of Henare Te Atua, was drowned when swimming in the river at Porangahau.[45] It was a lovely summer's day, but one on which Te Kooti had warned some ill would befall the marae, it is narrated orally. When the child drowned, he then said:

> I told you to be very careful of the kids. I did not say be careful of you people. So now you know what I meant. Now bury her.[46]

His apparent brutality shocked the community. Then, on 4 January, the day after Te Kooti left, Henare Matua himself was thrown from his buggy as he journeyed from Porangahau towards Waipawa and seriously injured. It was said of Te Kooti at his arrival that he had 'bewitched' some of the traps;[47] Henare's fall was now directly attributed to the contempt and defiance he had shown to Te Kooti.[48]

For, before he left, on 1 January Te Kooti had challenged the high chiefs in his prophetic announcement for the year. He warned that 20 chiefs would die, and he also stated that the suffering in the land was due to their arrogance, their failure to show compassion, and their desire for wealth. The kupu whakaari was 'Oro Pariera':

> 1. Wehenga tikanga, wehenga tangata, ka patu te tamaiti ki te matua, te matua ki te tamaiti te Rangatira ki tetahi Rangatira. Heke rawa te toto. Te putake mo te whenua e kore e kore tenei toto. Ka heke ano i runga i nga whakaaro a te Rangatira.

> 1. The ways are divided, the people divided, the child strikes parent, and the parent strikes the child, the Chief strikes Chief. Blood is shed. The essential issue is the land [and] there should not be this bloodshed. It shall flow again because of the plans of the Chief(s).

He warned that, unless the direction of the chiefs was good, there would be no First of July observances. The prediction continued:

> 2. Nga rangatira e mate i roto i tenei tau e 20. Te putake o tenei mate he whaiwhaia i runga i nga whakahawea a te rangatira ki nga kuare.

Te kupu tohutohu, kaua e whakahawea ki nga tutua, tena he whakaaro tona engari arohaina ka kite i tena tutua e noho ana ka hoatu.

Te putake o tenei mate na nga tutua mo te whenua i runga i nga whakahawea a nga rangatira ki nga kuare.

2. The chiefs shall die this year, 20 in number. The cause of this calamity is the chiefs pursuing their contempt for the lowly.

A word of guidance: do not despise the common people, for they have their opinion, but rather show compassion. When you see a lowly one, give to him.

The cause of this suffering of the common people on account of the land lies in the contempt of the chiefs for the low born.[49]

He also warned against a false prophet, who would emerge in the year, bringing evil. He spoke of a possible epidemic, because of which, should it occur and anyone die, the people should leave their settlement. As at this period cycles of infectious viral diseases — measles, influenza and typhoid — struck the Maori communities again and again, the advice was practical. Te Kooti concluded by telling the people to pray for an end to the suffering and to prevent these dreadful events, which he, as they, hoped not to see happening. He urged them to engrave his words upon the tablet of their hearts.

That the kupu whakaari sprang from the local conflict with Henare is evident. However, its roots went deeper. Te Kooti was outlining the great division between the hereditary aristocratic leaders of the Maori tribes and the 'marginalised' men, like himself — men who were prepared to challenge the chiefs from a different base of power. This was what made the prophets dangerous to the established Maori political leaders. And in a world where sudden accident and epidemic cycles could occur unexpectedly, predictive words acquire persuasive authority. It is the inevitability of unforeseen occurrences which gives the 'seeing words' such a powerful hold over humans.

It was the aristocratic leaders generally whom Te Kooti had been least successful in attracting to his cause, for they had their own bases of authority. Those chiefs who had joined him in the guerrilla wars, like Te Waru, had done so when their cause (their confiscated lands) and his (injustice) coincided. But Te Waru remained independent in his actions, and finally he had not accepted Te Kooti's religion. While the great hope of 'redeeming the land' was shared by many Maori, the idea was fraught with difficulties, not the least being how to determine the correct path. A later waiata of Te Kooti's directly addressed this problem. In this song, composed in 1890, he asked those whose inner desire was to see the 'return of Aotearoa' ('kia hoki mai Aotearoa') to consider this question: 'How could a country be returned; if it was taken away out to sea, who could control that act of consummation in the night' ('No whea ra e hoki mai he motu ka riro atu ki waho ki te moana ma wai ranei e pupuri i moea ki te po')? It was not the pursuit of a lost sovereignty which should preoccupy them; rather, it was the division of the land into pieces which was wrong. The emergence of this error ('tenei hē') would lead again to a season of war, he warned. Thereafter, 'the Person of the revelations shall arrive at this place' ('Kei kona ka tae mai te Tangata, ko te kupu whakaari tena') to restore the peace.[50]

Te Kooti's vision was a religious solution, the redemption of the people through faith and sacrifice. He found explanation for failure, and the continued suffering, in certain human actions and human frailties — at this time, chiefly arrogance. Now he was consciously appealing to the 'lowly', and to those who, for one reason or another, distrusted their established leaders. Inevitably, Te Kooti came to be seen by many of the established hereditary leaders as a force for division. He would remain one.

Te Kooti left Porangahau and travelled back through Te Aute to Napier and Petane. As the party passed through Napier on 6 January, they were described as looking extremely well, their horses fat and their carts laden with food.[51] Once again Te Kooti had been transformed, and his ill health forgotten. The party hurried past Napier, because the government had received a protest from the leading chiefs there, Renata Kawepo, Henare Tomoana and Paora Kaiwhata. They warned that, if Te Kooti tried 'parading' near their settlements, they would take it as a direct challenge.[52] Bullen informed Te Kooti of their complaint and, though Te Kooti expressed his irritation with them, saying '"I come only to speak peace to the Maori and the Pakeha"',[53] he avoided their settlements and went directly through Napier to Petane. Bullen commented, 'he is fearful of any obstruction & obeys any suggestion from me willingly'.[54]

There is an oral story still told by a Napier family of a time when Te Kooti passed through, which almost certainly stems from this occasion. C. G. Thomas (aged 85 in 1991) narrated his grandmother's story of how Te Kooti's party (some 30 people, as she remembered) stopped at her house by the junction of the road to Taradale from Napier. They licked the window panes with their tongues and pointed at their mouths to indicate their thirst on the hot summer's day. The water tanks were padlocked, but she went out, somewhat fearfully, to give them water to drink. After the party moved on, she found little woven flax baskets, filled with kumara and potatoes, left behind in gratitude.[55] The party (50 people, according to the police) passed on directly to Petane, where Te Kooti remained to hold the Twelfth of January. Here the chief Henare Pohio welcomed him, and the new kupu whakaari described the place as a sanctuary. The phrase in the strange language, 'te reo ke', was identical with that from Porangahau:

> Oro Pariera
>
> He wehewehenga tangata. Tenei kupu whakaari mo tenei whenua. Ko te rohe tenei kua manaakitia tenei wahi i haeretia mai nei e tatou tae noa mai ki konei no te mea ko te rohe ano tenei o te pakanga kihai te whawhai.

> Oro Pariera
>
> A division of people. This revelatory saying is about this land. This is the region which was blessed, this place to which we came up until now, because this is also the region of the relative who did not fight.[56]

This statement must have stemmed from Henare Matua's pursuit of them (for whatever purpose), which had ended in his being thrown from his buggy. But now they had entered the friendlier territory of Ngati Hineuru and Ngati Matepu, who had committed themselves to the faith for some time.

A later account of the sayings from this Twelfth at Petane recorded that Te Kooti spoke warmly of the place as 'the side which had been cared for on this land' ('Kua manakitia te taha ki runga i tenei whenua').[57] This saying was glossed with the secret word written as 'Aroparia', indicating an 'oral proximity', a frequent corruption in transmission. Te Kooti then spoke severely to those people who were still stubborn ('whakatoitoi') towards him. The quarrel on the East Coast was with him, as he said, but the forthcoming July celebration would be the time when the 'fight for the mana' would be known ('Kei a Hurae mohiotia ai te pakanga mana ra'). He asked them, if they were divided, how could there be resolution? And he also warned evasively that either the parent, or the child, would die.[58]

Thus the forthcoming July gathering was intended to be a test of conflicting powers within the Maori world. His parting words for the senior chief of Petane, Henare Pohio, were also uncomfortable: 'Soon is the time that your descendants will hang on this poplar' ('Me ake nei te wa e iri o uri ki runga i te papara nei').[59] Te Kooti would refer again to the poplar tree, growing at Petane. In 1891, he warned harshly that it might be the only thing left there, a foreign plant. Nevertheless, the poplar can also stand for renewed life, because of its capacity to spring into leaf from a dry stick, and Te Kooti would use it elsewhere as a metaphor with this meaning. The statement therefore possibly offered the promise of renewal out of loss. Again Te Kooti warned — and again equivocated.

This was Te Kooti's second journey to the East Coast, and the rising speculation about the likelihood of his return to Poverty Bay led the government to make an active change of policy. The joint issues of his freedom of movement and his safety, which had shaped the police tactics of maintaining an unobtrusive and generally protective presence, were to be subordinated to a new policy of suspicion and surveillance. On 10 February, Inspector Kiely of Hamilton was sent instructions to exercise a close watch over Te Kooti, on the orders of the Native Minister. He was told that he was to try to obtain 'an influence over' Te Kooti personally or, failing that, 'by means of those you are hereby authorised to employ'.[60]

Kiely tried to do his stuff. He met Te Kooti when he came to Kihikihi and attempted to talk with him, but, as Kiely possessed no command of Maori and Te Kooti little of spoken English,[61] communication between them remained limited and depended on an interpreter. Kiely reported that Te Kooti and his people caused no disturbance in Kihikihi, nor were they molested by Europeans there. On the contrary, Te Kooti had recently made a down-payment to a local storekeeper, James Farrell, for a one-acre section where he hoped to build a house for them all to stay in when they came to town. The money he had came from trade and donations raised for him, especially in Napier and other parts of the East Coast. Te Kooti visited Kihikihi regularly, was friendly with the Europeans there, and treated them with 'great hospitality' when they, in turn, visited Otewa.[62] When he came to town he was usually accompanied by five or six men, who rode alongside his buggy, but they caused no trouble. They merely watched Te Kooti protectively on the occasions when he had 'taken liquor', Kiely reported.[63] In fact he had nothing untoward to describe.

Consequently, Kiely sent Constable Jones from Alexandra to Otewa with instructions to observe all the passes and roads leading to and from the settlement, to count the population, and observe their activities. He also told Jones to be tactful: Te Kooti, he said, had always been friendly towards him. Jones rode there on 26 February. His report must have irritated the government for he, too, could find nothing to be alarmed about. He was met with friendliness by Te Kooti, who appointed one of his followers to act as interpreter. Jones described the community as 'by far the best and most flourishing looking Maori settlement I have seen in the district'. It was, he said, very compact, consisting of about 60 whare, made of raupo, standing close together and housing about 200 people. He thought that they had about 100 acres in cultivation, the principal crop (in February) being maize. Another source of income for the community was gum-digging in Hauraki and Ohinemuri, and many of the men were currently away at this occupation. Jones added:

> the fences, *whares*, cultivations, &c are in first class condition, and the people seem a much superior class to the usual run of Natives. They were all well clothed and exceedingly clean and everything indicated that they must have plenty of money. They are all East Coast Natives, and mix very little with the Ngatimaniapoto living in the adjoining settlements.[64]

Other descriptions of Whakaarorangi at this time reinforce this view. Even the *Poverty Bay Herald*, when discussing Te Kooti's intended visit to Gisborne in 1889, found space to reprint an account of the settlement as an ordered and hard-working community, where everyone (man, woman and child) had to do eight hours' labour each day and spend two further hours at prayer. Other reports noted the big 'Church', that is the meeting-house, with its 'handsome carvings' and a large bell suspended over its door-way, which was used to summon the community to prayers. The whare kai had its walls neatly lined with tukutuku, and its big tables were carved and polished. These buildings were destroyed by the fire of February 1888. Te Kooti himself was described as a 'remarkably clever and intelligent man, and a thorough organiser', who had 'reclaimed many outcast natives', giving them a focus for their lives at Otewa.[65]

Jones's account, written in the late summer of 1887, reinforced Kiely's observations about the relative lack of communication between Te Kooti and the Maniapoto chiefs, including Rewi, and indicated his absolute separation from Tawhiao. Te Kooti had been at Otewa the previous November, but alone of all the Maori leaders of note in the district he had not attended the tangi of Tawhiao's oldest son, Tu Tawhiao, held at Whatiwhatihoe, and his absence had been noted. All of Te Kooti's business was con-ducted through the frontier town of Kihikihi, rather than through Otorohanga. Jones's report gives the impression of an industrious, relatively prosperous community of exiles, living somewhat uncomfortably within the bounds of the Rohe Potae. The people had left Te Kuiti as soon as they could in 1883; resentments had built up against them as 'squatters', despite the gift of Tokanganui-a-noho. Kiely was also informed that, once the title to the land at Otewa was established through the Native Land Court, Te Kooti and his followers would have to leave, 'or pay for the land'.[66] Their isolation within Maniapoto's lands was also commented upon by George Wilkinson, the native officer,[67] and this undoubtedly increased as Otewa became a centre for the political revitalisation of the Kingitanga. Te Kooti's continual search for another home was intensified with these mounting pressures.

The invitation to hold the July 1887 gathering at Maraenui in the eastern Bay of

Plenty was, therefore, a great pleasure, and it was seen as an important omen of change. Te Whanau-a-Apanui had formerly been opponents of Te Kooti, but by 1885 they too were following the faith.[68] The two chiefs of Maraenui, Te Tatana Ngatawa (Nga-atawai) and Paora Ngamoki, invited Te Kooti there for the reopening of their meeting-house, Te Poho-o-Apanui, as a Ringatu house of prayer.[69] This renewal of their large carved house, which had been built by Te Tatana in 1872,[70] followed the practice already established with the reopening of Tokanganui-a-noho. This practice of renewal and reopening had also been adopted at Wairoa. The houses were all partially recarved and spiritually rededicated to the Kotahitanga of the new faith.

Two songs composed and learnt on the journey to Maraenui express Te Kooti's gratitude to the chiefs of Te Whanau-a-Apanui, and celebrate the decline of the influence of the old Ngai Tai chief, Wiremu Kingi Te Kawau:

> (1) Tera te haeata. Ka rere te whakaihi ra runga ana mai o Tarakeha ra ia kei tua Te Kawau he tangata kawana. Kauaka pea ra e tu mai ki te riri, kihai koe i rongo he mana no Kuini. Tenei te haere nei he maungarongo.
> (2) Akuanei au ka takahi i te ara noho ana hoki au i Maraenui ra ia hei hapai kupu ma hau e Te Tatana. Tu noa hoki au i te akau ra ia nou tou pono e Paora Ngamoki.

> (1) There is the dawn. The spell over Tarakeha[71] is dispersed; it was established by Te Kawau, a man of the government. Refrain from rising to do battle — perhaps you have not heard of the power of the Queen. This journey is in peace.
> (2) Soon I shall tread the path to stop at Maraenui, to bring the word to you, Te Tatana. I merely stand on that rocky shore, oh man of faith, Paora Ngamoki.[72]

The songs speak of Wiremu Kingi's inability to continue blocking the spread of the faith to Te Whanau-a-Apanui and along the East Coast. People from Te Whanau-a-Apanui had already ridden to see Te Kooti to hear about the teachings: one man who came to see him was Te Kohi Delamere, whose family was to be central in establishing Maraenui as a stronghold of the faith. Monita Delamere, Te Kohi's grandson, told the story of how Te Kohi invited Te Kooti to visit the people at Maraenui. Te Kohi, who had fought in the wars for the government, journeyed to the King Country to learn about Te Kooti's teachings, but

> you couldn't get near him because of the bodyguards and so many fellows protecting him. And yet there was this feeling within Te Kooti himself, that this fellow wants to see him. On the journey — they were travelling on horseback — he *raced* his horse up to beside the old fellow, Te Kohi, gave his horse a kick, and more or less signalled to follow him. And they followed flat out, before the others realised what was happening, but they were away, way ahead, and then they ducked round a corner, and the soldiers and everybody went flat out past them, and that's where they talked. And the old fellow said, 'We really want the Rā; bring it to Maraenui.' And this is all he [Te Kooti] said, 'Ara! Kei te pai.' And that's where he composed the waiata, 'He pā tō reo e Te Tai Rāwhiti'.[73]

This song was recorded by Hamiora. It was composed on the journey, along with the previous two waiata, and the travellers sang them as they went:

E pa to reo e Te Tai Rawhiti e
Pa-katokato ana te aroha i ahau
Me tika taku rori, me tika ki Maketu ra e
Hangai tonu atu te rae kai Kōhi
Kai atu aku mata, kai atu ki Motu ra e
He huihuinga mai no nga iwi katoa
Hoki atu e te kino, hoki atu ki to nohanga e
Kei te haere tonu mai nga ture
He aha rawa te mea e tohe riria nei e
He tuahae kei korerotia te rongo pai.
Me tu ake au i te marae o te whare nei e
Ki te whakapuaki i te kupu o te Hurae.
He aroha ia nei ki nga morehu o te motu nei e
Mo nga kupu whakaari e panuitia nei.
Ma koutou tatou e kawe ki te wai wehe ai e
Kia mutu ake ai te aroha i ahau.

Your voice calling from Tai Rawhiti touches me,
Forlorn still the love within me.
Straight is my road, straight to Maketu there,
Then forward on to the headland at Kohi
My eyes gaze on, over to Motu there,
A gathering place of all the tribes.
Go back evil, return to your dwelling place,
For the laws will continue to come.
What is this thing that causes constant quarrelling?
It is jealousy lest the gospel be preached.
Let me stand up at the marae of this house,
To speak the message of July.
My concern is for the remnants of the people of this land, and
For the words of revelation being proclaimed here.
May you take us to the water to sprinkle ourselves,
So that my distress may cease.[74]

Once again the police were instructed to watch the travellers, as they set out for Maraenui on 15 June. Te Kooti was accompanied by a group of about 30–50 people, some of whom had ridden from the Bay of Plenty to escort him. They included Ngati Awa and Tuhoe.[75] At Opotiki, the local constable described the party's ride through the town. He explained why he had sent a telegram before his written report: he feared that the press would, as usual, give an exaggerated account of the affair. He reported instead the 'orderly' ride of over 500 people through the main street in the middle of the morning of 27 June. They passed in a formation of about six abreast, led by the Waiotahe community, consisting presumably of Reihana and the other exiles from Wairoa, who were living there. Te Kooti and those who had come with him from Waikato rode after; the main body followed in turn. They were all local people from the surrounding communities of Te Whanau-a-Apanui and Whakatohea, many of whom Te Kooti had once taken as prisoners. They cantered at a slow pace, their horses held under

Te Kohi Delamere, who brought Te Kooti to Te Whanau-a-Apanui. This portrait hangs in Tutawake, the meeting-house at Whitianga. Rephotographed, by permission of Te Maaka Jones, by Gillian Chaplin.

close restraint.[76] Thus they came in full ceremonial procession to Maraenui, where the preparations for the Ra had been under way for months.

The visit was a major turning-point for the Ringatu. Te Whanau-a-Apanui's invitation had been discussed at length at a hui held at Pakirikiri, near Gisborne, in late February, and many people from Gisborne and Wairoa, as well as the eastern Bay of Plenty, had indicated then that they would be attending.[77] This Ra at Maraenui was the first major inter-tribal gathering held for Te Kooti; moreover, it had been summoned by people who had once opposed him. It indicated, as Wiremu Kingi Te Kawau commented when expressing his strong opposition, the rapid spread of the faith, which had now been adopted by most of the chiefs and tribes of the eastern Bay of Plenty and the Urewera. Wiremu Kingi feared not guns but 'the plans, and talk' ('Ko te pu anake te mea e tae nei otira ehara te pu i te mea nui ko nga kinga me nga korero te mea nui');[78] but what he meant precisely he did not say. It was left to the resident magistrate to spell out the message as he had heard it: 'that God has appeared to him [Te Kooti], and informed him, that the confiscated lands will again revert to the Maoris'.[79] Wiremu Kingi was anxious that this prediction could not be fulfilled without the renewal of war.

The kupu whakaari uttered for Maraenui on the First of July, 'Eneteri Awhata', was nevertheless quite orthodox. It contained words of reassurance, reminding the people of Jehovah's promise that he was their God, and that he would 'raise them up' ('e whakaara').[80] But the words for the house itself were less reassuring: their 'whare tapu', the renewed Te Poho-o-Apanui, would be neglected, while the place itself would become not Maraenui but 'Maraekōhatu', the marae of stones.[81] As the house decayed, so would the people depart from the faith and become deaf and unthinking, like stones. These words, like those for the house at Kokohinau, were to lie as a terrible burden upon it. The drowning of 16 schoolchildren from Maraenui and Omaio in 1900 would be attributed by some (although, it must be said, not by others) to this warning.

The background here was that a Land Court discussion would take place in the meeting-house in 1898, which retrospectively was seen to be a misuse of it. Te Whanau-a-Apanui had managed to dispossess Ngai Tai, their near neighbours, of a block of land which had long been disputed between them. The issue was festering in 1887–88, when Te Kooti visited them. On behalf of Te Whanau-a-Apanui, Te Kooti wrote to Wiremu Kingi Te Kawau in July 1888, asking him to cease surveying this block, Tunapahore, 'lest it be a cause of trouble in that district' ('kei waiho hei take raruraru mo tena takiwa').[82] Kingi saw Te Kooti's involvement in the case as a threat rather than an attempt to make peace. Te Whanau-a-Apanui filed a counter-claim; the subsequent use of Te Poho-o-Apanui for the hearing was then interpreted as an error. The outcome was recognised as unjust and it had then to be rectified;[83] the land was partitioned between the two tribes. Then came the deaths of the children. Te Poho-o-Apanui was demolished shortly afterwards in an attempt to exorcise the danger which it now seemed to present. The burden of its reconstruction then fell on the next generation; Monita Delamere recalled several abortive efforts to rebuild it during the 1920s. Finally, it was his father, as Poutikanga (Main Pillar) of the Haahi Ringatu from 1938, who built the little whare karakia at Maraenui, which stands today. Thus Te Kooti's words of warning were remembered and then acted upon by Paora Delamere in his renewal of Maraenui as a centre of the faith. These words generated an entire history, into which were woven many events.

When he visited Maraenui Te Kooti tested the people in other ways, too, and those tests are also remembered. In one version it is told how, when Te Kooti arrived for the Ra in 1887, he did not wait to be called or welcomed. He broke the ceremonial procession and rode the great white horse straight across the marae, whooping and waving like a cowboy. Then, later that night, during prayers in the house, he burst into a haka, and Te Whanau-a-Apanui fined him for violating the rules he himself had instituted.[84] In another version of this story, Te Kooti secretly tested Te Kohi Delamere by arriving at night and trying to catch the people unaware:

> Grandpa didn't know he was out on the marae, but he saw a cloak, just the flashing of a cloak — someone entering and flashed out again! And he looked up; he knew it was Te Kooti.

Three times, as the story goes — for three is a common number of completeness in oral tales — he visited Te Kohi in this way, but he never caught him asleep. The third time he visited, Te Kohi told the people to hide in the house:

Māoris in those days used to be able to foretell that someone was coming in: Grandpa had that gift of God. He knew Te Kooti was coming to test them. He said to his people to prepare themselves, and if Te Kooti arrived on the marae, instead of receiving him, there was not to be a child nor an adult outside the house. They all had to go in and remain inside until Te Kooti had left. And everybody asked him, 'Why?' He said, 'Well, he's coming here to test Te Whānau-a-Apanui.' And Te Kooti came outside, he did a haka and things like that, outside. And he performed; he tried to draw them out, but they didn't! And he left. And he said to my grandfather, he'd never catch them shirking! His faith will live for ever more.[85]

Thus these narratives establish the most important truth for the different narrators: that Te Whanau-a-Apanui passed the tests Te Kooti had set them.

The return journey from Maraenui in July 1887 passed peacefully. The huge party (now estimated at 600) stayed for a few days with Hira Te Popo at Waioeka. Te Kooti slept in separate quarters: they were roped off and guarded by a few sentries outside the barrier. The sentries carried stout riding whips, but no arms.[86] Matiu Paeroa and Hoani Poururu were there, the former being referred to as Te Kooti's 'principal tohunga'.[87] Both got rather drunk one night and fell off their horses on the way back to the camp, but Te Kooti was not part of this revelry. At Maketu, the police were sent to investigate a malicious report about Te Kooti's behaviour, which they soon dismissed as 'purposely exaggerated'.[88] The 'very worst' that could have been preferred against Te Kooti, wrote the Inspector, Samuel Goodall, was 'a charge of being drunk whilst in charge of a horse' and that, he added, would never have been contemplated against a European in similar circumstances. Te Kooti had simply got on to his horse, which then mounted the pub's verandah, but he did not use any 'offensive words or actions and went quietly away'. As Goodall said, an exaggerated account had been given to the press by a settler, 'who no doubt had motives of his own for so doing'.[89] Similarly, the resident magistrate, Robert Bush, wrote in his account of the whole visit:

The conduct of the natives was most excellent, considering that such a large number of them were here, and I think Kooti deserves great credit for maintaining such good order. Kooti in his speeches, enjoined on the people to live peacefully, to shew kindness to those in want, and refrain from selling land. He also appeared anxious not to be misrepresented, and for this purpose asked Wi Kingi [Te Kawau] . . . to accompany him to Kokohinau so that he might hear what he said to the people.[90]

However, it was now that the preparations for Te Kooti's return to Poverty Bay began in earnest. Bush believed, quite correctly, that that had always been Te Kooti's chief aim; with each visit, he observed, 'he seems to get nearer to that place'.[91]

The oral narratives from Turanga recall how a group of eight elders from the East Coast rode through to Te Kuiti to ask for a Ra — a January or a July — to be held there.

And this is what he said: 'Hoki atu. Whakahaungia te rongopai i runga i te ngāwari me te aroha. [Go back. Proclaim the gospel, the gentler faith, and the love of God.] Let the rich have their Rās, one day they'll get tired and that's when you shall come in.'[92]

The elders journeyed back, somewhat puzzled by the command. But, as they represented four communities within the district, each group took one word for its own meeting-house. And so four houses were built for Te Kooti in Poverty Bay, each possessing one of those directives as its name. The first to be built, as John Ruru narrated the story, was Whakahau, the Command, erected at Rangatira, near Te Karaka. This house belonged to the Haronga family of Te Aitanga-a-Mahaki, whose elders are remembered as having ridden to Te Kuiti.[93] Then Wi Pere (who is also recalled as one of the eight riders), together with his younger son, Moanaroa, who was for a while a secretary for Te Kooti, built the most famous of the four: Rongopai at Repongaere (near Waituhi), which was constructed during 1886 and 1887. After that came Te Ngawari, erected at Mangatu by the family of 'old' Peneha,[94] who had been a prisoner on Wharekauri and whose story of the stone of knowledge (narrated by Ned Brown) appears in Chapter 3. The fourth house, Te Aroha, was built at Puha by Oriwia Tuturangi Whaitiri, the only woman among the riders.[95] Thus, as John Ruru said, there are four marae in Poverty Bay to 'keep the words which Te Kooti said'.

The construction of Rongopai can be dated precisely from a reference early in February 1887 to the house that was being built under Wi Pere's direction at Repongaere to receive Te Kooti.[96] It was finished by late October 1887.[97] It is also known as Eriopeta, from a saying in 'te reo ke'; the precise meaning of this name is uncertain, and it is not understood locally any more.[98] 'Eri' was consistently the gloss for God's creation of heaven and earth; 'Peta' was a reference to Genesis 28:1 and 12, that is to Jacob, upon whose ladder to heaven the angels descended and ascended. 'Peta' was also, as the Ringatu manuscript glosses state, the reference to Genesis 49:10, with its prediction of the coming of the Messiah, there named Shiloh (Hiro), to whom Te Kooti had referred when he expanded upon his prophetic sayings in February 1884.[99] Thus 'Peta' is stated to be the blessing, the ladder and the sceptre.[100] The saying Eriopeta probably combines these scriptural promises.

The house Rongopai is a brightly painted garden. Moanaroa Pere, its architect, is portrayed on the exterior porch; its tohunga, Pa Ruru (Patoromu Ruru, Te Kooti's supporter from the last days of the fighting), also appears on one of the exterior rafter beams, hunting with his dog. Inside there is a wondrous, and populated, Eden. There are the important ancestors of Turanga, such as Hine Hakirirangi (wearing a pretty European dress and carrying a red rose), who planted the kumara, and Tauhei, who is established as the daughter of Kahungunu, for his fortress, Maunga-a-Kahia at Nukutaurua, is painted at her feet.[101] Her name and her female moko identify her, for otherwise she is depicted as a male warrior. There is Mahaki, with whom Te Kooti would soon compare himself, driven into exile. The young murdered twins, Tarakitai and Tarakiuta, are woven, and separately painted, as watching eyes within the tukutuku. This weaving of ancestral figures in tukutuku was unusual, but had occurred in Tokanganui-a-noho. The extensive use of painted images was firmly rooted in the local traditions of the Turanga artists, and indeed they may have originally taken it to Te Kuiti. Whatever the regional origins, the intermingling, the florescence and unexpected transformations of figures are the striking qualities about the house.

The portrait of Wi Pere, like those on the porch, broke with the usual tradition of incorporating images only of the dead. His mother, from whom his Maori mana

This photograph of the interior of Rongopai shows (on the left) Wi Pere, and his mother Riria Te Mauaranui (Mauharanui) perched on his shoulder. The chair signified his position as MHR; his tattoo is ahistorical, but represents his Maori status. On the right is Mahaki, the eponymous ancestor of Te Aitanga-a-Mahaki, with whom Te Kooti compared himself in his forced exile. Mahaki is represented without a facial moko, which he would have possessed. These painted pou are on the rear wall of the house. The photograph was taken before restoration. Reproduced by permission of the late Mahanga Horsfall, Waituhi.

descended, perches on his shoulder like a guardian owl. The painted chair behind him indicates his position as a member of the 1887 House of Representatives.[102] There is also a racehorse and its jockey (with the finishing flag marked 'Hape' (Crooked)), said to express the racing enthusiasms of the Pere family. The four emblems from the card deck are painted on one end of a rafter beam and elsewhere in the house. The spade is upside down: the fall of the cards is a recurrent image in many of the painted Ringatu houses. They represent the changing balances of political power — here, the toppling of the independent Maori world — and a new world that, in turn, was to come. (Maori code systems using playing cards were known; one cypher exists, transcribed by an elder from Wharekawa into his diary for 1875.[103]) Similarly, draughtboard patterns worked in the tukutuku at Rongopai represent Maori land blocks, swapped under Pakeha law. There is a boxing match, perhaps an image of controlled conflict, perhaps just for sheer fun. There are painted vases filled with flowers, and intertwining vines, and a Tree of Life with its 12 separate flowers. Little painted birds fly amongst the bright foliage of this fertile but no longer innocent garden of delights.

Amid all this profusion of history and life, there was also a painting of a purple thistle. It is often said to have been an image for Te Kooti,[104] possibly because, as Raniera Te Iho o Te Rangi once wrote of the Pai Marire faith, it spread 'like the scotch thistle, self sown . . . whose down is about to float away to all parts of the village.'[105] However, in one explanation, it is told that Te Kooti himself said,

> 'That side is beautiful: except the thistle! Why put the thistle there? It's only to sting people!'
>
> *Question*: But he never saw Rongopai?
>
> No. He could see it in his mind's eye. And he composed a song, quite a nice song, one of those quarter-tones, for that meeting-house. That's 'E hine tangi kino' ['O girl crying bitterly']. A predictment for that house — of what's going to happen.[106]

The thistle of Waituhi thus came to be seen as heralding misfortune. Of it, it was said forcefully, the thistle only draws blood. In later times, therefore, it was washed over with white paint on the advice of the tohunga and spiritual healer, Hori Gage.[107] If Rongopai itself ultimately became a house of healing, it was one which Te Kooti himself would never enter.

The issue of Te Kooti's return to Poverty Bay had been debated extensively at the Pakirikiri hui in February 1887, held to open the new meeting-house erected there, which was dedicated to Rukupo's memory. Another purpose of this gathering was to debate the claims of the four religions, including Ringatu, now established in the region and known by that name.[108] Raniera Turoa, who opened the lengthy discussions, spoke strongly against Te Kooti. In 1868 he had been living at Oweta, and he had married Paratene Pototi's daughter, Heni Kotikoti. Now he urged:

> let Te Kooti remain in Waikato. Never should he set his foot in Poverty Bay. The people of the East Coast were not asked that peace should be made with Te Kooti. It was Bryce's work. Te Kooti must not come here.[109]

Wiremu Kingi Te Paia spoke as well, saying that he too preferred that the people remain steadfast to the religion of the missionaries, the Anglican faith. A variety of teachings and beliefs meant trouble, and gave rise to prejudice among themselves. He spoke for unity. Wi Pere publicly endorsed his remarks. But, despite this façade, the Ngai Tai chief Wiremu Kingi Te Kawau, who reported on the hui to the government, warned of him:

> Kaua tenei korero e whakaatutia ki a Wi Pere e mohio ana ahau ki a ia kei taua taha. Ka rua ona taenga ki a te Kooti.
>
> Do not shew this to Wi Pere, or inform him of it, because I know he leans to that side. He has visited Te Kooti twice.[110]

As Wiremu Kingi Te Kawau must have known, Wi Pere and his family were at the time constructing Rongopai for Te Kooti. But Wi Pere's ambiguity in his public persona, as noted previously, would continue to stalk Te Kooti; and his ambiguity in some of his other activities, particularly his trusteeship of East Coast tribal lands, was observed at this gathering. James Carroll would take Pere's parliamentary seat from him in 1887 because of this concern and because of Pere's manifest self-interest. For all that, Wi Pere remains an ambivalent figure, hard to pin down, for he undoubtedly tried to juggle the conflicting interests and the high community expectations that were placed upon him with some scruple as well.

Hoani Ruru, who was living at Oweta and belonged to Ngati Maru, openly protested against Te Kooti's return. He said that he still felt bitter about the killing of his kin, as well as the Pakeha deaths. Only two men were reported as speaking for Te Kooti. One was Te Ao Pakurangi of Te Aitanga-a-Mahaki, a well-known carver. He would build the fifth house in the district at Te Kooti's request, Te Poho-o-Pikihoro, erected at Te Karaka in 1888–89. He proclaimed himself a follower of Te Kooti and emphasised that his teachings were for peace. The other man, Taake, said that he had been present when Bryce and Te Kooti met, and had heard what passed between them. What was being said about Te Kooti was very ill informed:

> The peace was made in Waikato. God is supporting Te Kooti. . . . The Government are upholding Te Kooti. . . . There were many things to be done for God's sake, but of all these Charity was the greatest.[111]

Te Ao stressed the humbleness and the meekness of those who followed the new faith. He, like Taake, emphasised that their numbers were few when compared with those who still followed the missionaries' teachings, and that they were modest in their stance, seeking no conflict. He suggested that it was perhaps because they were insignificant in number, and also mostly young, that they were being derided.

The long debate revealed the tensions within the Maori settlements at Poverty Bay and on the East Coast. Immediately after the hui, letters of protest and petitions began to pour into the Native Minister's office. The first was a settlers' petition, initiated by none other than Captain Charles Westrup, who had been so badly outmanoeuvred by Te Kooti in 1868. Signed by himself and 31 others, it was drawn up after a meeting on 14 February 1887. It adopted scaremongering tactics, attributing some 'recent Native murders' to the advice of Te Kooti, emphasising the already large numbers of Maori who regularly travelled to seek his guidance and to be healed, and asking that the government stop him from ever returning home.[112] The government responded by informing Te Kooti of the petition and advising him not to go; at the same time it told the petitioners that they were incorrect in their accusations against Te Kooti as an instigator of murder. But Westrup and some of the settlers wrote again in October,[113] and by that time the Maori letters of protest had commenced. On 17 October, Raniera Turoa, Hoani Ruru and several others petitioned the government. They claimed to speak for Ngati Maru, Ngai Te Kete and Ngai Tawhiri, and asked that Te Kooti be prevented from visiting them, for they had not yet forgotten 'the blood of our relatives' ('nga toto o matou whanaunga') and of their European friends.[114] Apiata Parekahika, another senior figure in Poverty Bay, wrote directly to Ropata, asking him what he intended to do about it. Apiata said:

> Mereana Paraone raua ko tana tamaiti me tana mokopuna kei Waikato kei te tiki i a Te Kooti Rikirangi,[115] ko te wha tenei o nga wiki tekau ma ono o nga ra o tenei marama

The hui at Pakirikiri, February 1887. The meeting was called by Te Otene Pitau, adopted son of Rukupo and a chief of Rongowhakaata, to discuss the question of the competing religious faiths in the district. The new meeting-house, Poho-o-Rukupo, also opened on this occasion, is in the background. (The house was moved in 1913 to its present site at Manutuke.) The photograph opposite shows the scale of the preparations for the great hui. Photographs by William F. Crawford, Gisborne's first mayor and local publican.

WFC A306, A308, GM

ano. . . . He mea tono a Mereana na te aitanga a Mawhaki, ko te ra, hei tetahi o nga ra o Tihema.

Mereana Paraone, with her son and grandchild, has gone to Waikato for the purpose of bringing Te Kooti Rikirangi to Gisborne. They will be gone four weeks on the 16th of this month. . . . Mereana was deputed by Te Aitanga-a-Mahaki — and the date fixed [for Te Kooti's departure] is 1 December.[116]

Mere Paraone was close kin to Te Kooti. Her son, by Te Kooti's dead brother Komene, was Potatutatu, who had been adopted and raised by Te Kooti at Te Kuiti. Potatutatu's eldest daughter, Tawhi, was also adopted by Te Kooti. Despite the past (for Mere's second husband, Ihimaera Hokopu, had been executed at Oweta in 1868, her brother Paku had been killed, and Mere herself been taken prisoner), the family were now Ringatu believers. As Heni Sunderland said, when talking about Mere Paraone (who was to bring up Heni in her turn), '*I never ever heard her say dreadful things about Te Kooti, I didn't.*'[117] Mere Paraone was sent by two chiefs of Te Aitanga-a-Mahaki: Panapa

Waihopi of Te Karaka, who had fought for the government at Nga Tapa and given evidence for it in the trials, and Tiopira Tawhiao, one of the former whakarau and a senior Anglican leader. It was they who had invited Te Kooti,[118] as a statement of reconciliation from that tribe. They were bringing Te Kooti home. This was precisely what Te Kooti had asked Panapa to do when he met him at Wairoa nearly two years previously. He said then that he would return — *if* he were invited.[119]

In direct contrast to this attempt at reconciliation, the *Poverty Bay Herald* waxed hysterical. So extreme were its utterances in an editorial on 24 October that Leonard Williams felt obliged to take up his pen to correct a number of fallacies. He reminded Gisborne that Te Kooti had 'a most substantial grievance against the Government' for his unlawful deportation to Wharekauri. Importantly, and contrary to widespread beliefs, he also stated that there was no good ground of which he was aware 'for supposing that any of the victims [of 10 November 1868] were subjected to torture or wanton outrage before they were put to death'. He wrote as one who did not favour Te Kooti's return, but who in all justice felt that he must check the misinformation that was being propagated.[120] Thomas Porter, now military commander of the East Coast district, also acted responsibly. He learnt from Maori informants that Te Kooti had no intention of returning without the clear sanction of the government. Hirini Te Ratu, one of the whakarau who had just returned from visiting Te Kooti at Otewa, told Porter on 3 November that Te Kooti was not coming at all, because of the danger, and certainly would not come without government approval: his 'preachers', including Matiu, would be there instead, to take his place.[121] Porter made sure that this information was published in the *Poverty Bay Herald* the next day.

But before this Porter had urged the government not to permit the visit;[122] the government in its turn placed pressure directly on Te Kooti. It could not prohibit him from going: this it knew. It stated this fact carefully in all its replies to letters and petitions. Nevertheless, in direct response to Porter's urgings, and Westrup's second petition, the new Minister for Native Affairs, Edwin Mitchelson, wrote to Te Kooti on 1 November, once again advising him not to go. It was also discovered that Rewi Maniapoto had agreed to travel with Te Kooti, and as a consequence pressure was brought to bear on Rewi. He was informed that the government was 'very much opposed' to the visit, as it might generate trouble; he was asked to intervene to deter Te Kooti.[123] George Wilkinson was sent to talk with both men.

At first, Rewi told Wilkinson that he had decided to go with Te Kooti so that, if Te Kooti were seized or molested ('hopukia'), he too would have to be taken. But, in response to the government's telegram, he agreed to try to persuade Te Kooti against the visit.[124] Wilkinson, who had been instructed to present the government's letter of advice to Te Kooti 'in a formal manner',[125] talked with Te Kooti again on 16 November. Te Kooti had sent a telegram on 3 November to inform the prominent chieftainess of Te Aitanga-a-Mahaki, Rawinia Ahuroa (whom one report called 'his sister-in-law'), that he and Rewi would now be setting out together on 8 December.[126] That he seems to have had doubts even then is suggested by the account Hirini Te Ratu gave to Porter on the very same day. To Wilkinson, Te Kooti now said simply: 'My Reason for wishing to go to Gisborne is because that is the only place at which I fought that I have not been to & made peace with the people.' He claimed that he had had satisfactory communication with Ropata on behalf of Ngati Porou. When Wilkinson stressed that the government's concern was for his safety, he answered, though not in submission to their request, 'Yes, I look upon the government and the law as my saviour & as my parent'.[127]

On 17 November Te Kooti wrote to Wilkinson, saying that he wished to go and was waiting to hear from the government:

> Kaore au e pai kia waiho ko te kino hei rangatira mo te ao. Engari i hanga te Ture me te Kawanatanga hei takahi i nga kino katoa i te ao. Me he mea ka waiho e ia te kino kia tupu ana e hara i te kino te he engari nana i whakaae. Ka mahara hoki a ahau mana e whakamana te maungarongo me te rongopai hei takahi i te kino.
>
> I am not willing that evil should be in the ascendant in the world. On the contrary, Law and the Government were instituted to keep down all evil. If they allow evil to exist then the evil should not be blamed for what happens but they [law and the government] should be blamed that allow it. I thought that they would give effect to the peace-making and to good report to the end that evil should be subdued.[128]

As Wilkinson commented, Te Kooti meant by 'evil' those who spoke ill of him and wished him harm; Te Kooti's mission was to make peace. The letter was really, he said, a request to the government and the law to support him in his decision. However, all Te Kooti received was another letter of dissuasion. On 23 November he finally telegraphed to say that, in compliance with their request, he would not go. He added, however, that he would yet be in Turanga 'at some future day' ('a enei ra e takoto mai').[129]

When Ropata was sent a copy of this telegram, he wrote that this phrase, 'at some future day', would cause unease. It was, he said, 'a very hard word' ('He kupu pakeke rawa tena').[130] Indeed, behind it lay the most famous of all Te Kooti's predictions. When he had accepted the government's advice not to travel to the East Coast in December 1884, he had then uttered a prophecy which would be remembered and its fulfilment endlessly speculated upon. This kupu whakaari, dated 14 December 1884, was pronounced at Otewa:

> a kua puta te kupu a te Kawana mo te kino, kaua ahau e haere ki Turanga ki te kawe i te Rongopai. Otira kei te pai. Ahakoa rua toru wha oku waewae, takoto ahau i roto i te papa rakau ko te tae ko tae ano ahau ki Turanga.

> the Governor has spoken about the trouble, that I should not go and carry the Gospel to Turanga. Well, all right. Although I have two, three, or four feet, or I am lying in a wooden box, I will still reach Turanga.[131]

'Two, three, or four feet' is interpreted as walking, hobbling along on a stick, or riding triumphantly on horseback. The wooden box is self-explanatory. This prophecy lies behind the continuing narratives that Te Kooti's body has been brought home — or one day will be.

Once again, Te Kooti had been dissuaded from travelling to Turanga. This time he was bitter. He had been told, by various Maori sources, that it was the Native Minister who had stirred up the protests, and also the threats against his life, of which, as Inspector Bullen realised, he lived in constant fear. The 'threats' might have been Westrup's; certainly, rumours were flying around Gisborne that Westrup planned to seize Te Kooti 'at all risks' for the 'murder' of Te Warihi in 1868.[132] Even more likely, they had been attributed to Porter. A great furore had developed after a speech he made to the Gisborne militia, in which he was reported as saying he would 'very quickly settle matters' with his old enemy, and furthermore advised his shooting.[133] Porter quickly denied the whole account, arguing that he had been grossly misquoted by the press. But Te Kooti understood that Mitchelson had admitted to Ropata, who went to see him in Wellington, that Mitchelson himself was behind these whirling threats. Te Kooti asked Wilkinson:

> Friend is this a good work to kill people with whom peace has been made that he agreed to it. Mr Bryce & Mr Ballance never spoke of me in that way. I am very dark indeed because the Minister has sanctioned killing in the face of the good feeling that is present in existence.[134]

He added that, if he had known of this deceit, he would never have acceded to the government's request. The government assured him that the reports were false, but the damage had been done. A strong sense of betrayal marks Te Kooti's famous lament, 'Pinepine Te Kura', which he composed for the gathering at Rongopai on 1 January 1888, the gathering that he did not attend.

The party of travellers to Gisborne left Otewa without him. They passed through

Opotiki on 17 December, and with them too came the spreading rumour that Te Kooti was travelling after them, in disguise.[135] Indeed, Bullen had already learnt that many influential Maori at Poverty Bay believed that Te Kooti would come secretly to Waituhi. The fear was that, if he were identified, then terrible trouble would follow.[136] The story that Te Kooti secretly returned to Turanga has entered oral tradition, and this 'fact' has been narrated to the author on several occasions. But Te Kooti did not travel to Gisborne in 1887.

Instead, he remained at Otewa, and 'only the people went' ('engari kaore a te Kooti i haere, ko nga iwi anake i haere'), as Hamiora's text introducing Te Kooti's lament carefully states.[137] On 21 December Te Kooti wrote to Tiopira Tawhiao about the house:

> E pa, ka manaakitia ano te whare i tenei ra. Kotahi ra ka ngaro atu i a koe i runga i o koutou mahara i o koutou, i nga rangatira. Ki te riro ko te whare o te tangata, ko te tikanga, ko te whakapono hei whare tuturu ake ake.

> Sir, the house is taken care of today. One day [however] it will be forgotten by you on account of your thoughts of yourselves [and] those of the chiefs. If the house of the people is taken away, the way [and] the faith [will remain] as a permanent shelter ever after.[138]

Thus the letter reminded, somewhat like the song 'E hine tangi kino', that the house might be forgotten and abandoned, left to cry alone. But the letter also stated that it was the faith, and not the house, which was finally important. Te Kooti then apparently referred to himself: he talked of the prisoner ('te herehere') and of one who 'is turning back and forth. I am that one in the hands of the tribes of all the island' ('Ko te tahuri atu, ko te tahuri mai tetahi. Ko ahau ra tena kei roto i te ringaringa o nga iwi o te motu katoa').[139] The letter, which is very opaque, does suggest that Te Kooti saw his fate as lying in the hands of the people — like Christ's. The song he composed for the gathering at Waituhi conveys this acute sense of betrayal by the government, the law, and the people:

> Pinepine te kura, hau te kura. . . .
> Tenei te tira hou tenei haramai nei,
> No te rongo pai no te rangimarie.
> Nau [mai] ka haere taua ki roto o Turanga
> Ki whakangungua koe ki te miini
> Ki te hoari ki te pu-hurihuri
> Nga rakau kohuru a te Pakeha e takoto nei. . . .
>
> Whakakake e te ture i te kiinga o to waha
> No runga rawa koe
> No te mana o Kuini e tu nei
> Na Rangi-tu koe na te kotahitanga
> Na Taane rawa koe nga pure tawhiti
> Te kaunati hikahika
> Te kaunati a to tipuna a Rawiri
> I haere ai i tere i nui ao,

Ka hika i tona ahi, kimihia e te iwi
Te ara o te tikanga i pai ai te noho i te ao nei.

Kei Turanganui he mata pu
He patu i te tangata kia mate.
Na te maungarongo hoki ra i haere ai i te ara . . . .

Karokaro i te tae-turi oo koutou taringa
Kia areare ai, me te whakarongo mai
Ki nga ki atu kaua ahau e patua.
Moku anake te ārai o Turanga
Te matenga o Mahaki i mau ai te rongo patipati . . . .
Whiti ke mai koe ki ra-i-nahi nei.

Te ai o mahara ka mate au i Waerenga-a-Hika.
Te ki mai koe me whakawa marire
Hopu ana koe i ahau kawe ana ki Wharekauri.
Ka manene mai au ki ro te wai
Ka u ana ko Whare-ongaonga.
Ka pa ko te waha o te Kawana.
E hika ma e! Ina ia te kai.
Tooia ki uta ra haehaetia ai
Tunua hai te manawa ka kainga ka pau,
Mo Koro-timutimu, mo Tauranga-koau.
Koia te riri pokanoa,
Ka kai ki te waipiro ka kai ki te whakama ki te mau-a-hara,
Me whakarere atu ena mahi kino e hika ma.

Little tiny treasure, treasure of renown. . . .
A new company of travellers is setting out
A people of faith and peace.
Let us travel on to Turanga
Where you shall parry the Minie rifle[140]
The sword and the revolver
The murderous weapons of the Pakeha lying everywhere. . . .

You the law, push on up as you proclaim
You are supreme
Even above the power of the Queen,
From Rangi-tu, the Sky above, from the unity,
From Taane himself, the ancient *pure* rites
From the fire-generating stick
The fire-stick of your ancestor David
Employed as he travelled the wide world,
Generating his fire; you the people
Seek the path of righteousness that we can live peacefully in this world.

In Turanganui are to be found bullets for guns
With which to kill man.
But it was in peace that I travelled the pathways . . . .

> Clean the wax from your ears
> That there might be no obstruction, then you will hear me
> When I say do not destroy me.
> Mine alone is banishment from Turanga
> The fate of Mahaki, a deceiving peace was made . . . .
> You, the recent arrivals
>
> You wrongly thought I would perish at Waerenga-a-Hika.
> And instead of judging me fairly
> You seized and shipped me to Wharekauri.
> But I slid into the water
> To make my landfall at Whareongaonga.
> Where I heard the voice of the Governor saying,
> 'Oh my friends! Here is food.
> It has been hauled ashore and cut to pieces
> The heart has been cooked, to be eaten and consumed,
> For Koro-timutimu and Tauranga-koau'.
> Hence this needless strife,
> Which comes from the consumption of liquor, from shame, from hatred.
> Therefore, I say, abandon these evil ways, my friends.[141]

The song is complex, and elegantly allusive. It plays on the text of the original Ngati Kahungunu lullaby (oriori), in which Turanga was described as a seat of warfare.[142] Its bewitching spells ('matawha') had driven others into exile previously; now it was Te Kooti's turn, exiled by the 'spell' of guns ('mata pu'). Like his ancestor Mahaki, he had been betrayed. The song comments on Te Kooti's long pursuit by Ngati Kahungunu, for Korotimutimu was a tipua (supernatural creature) who devoured men at Napier and at Taurangakoau, a landing-place for canoes at Cape Kidnappers. In this manner Te Kooti was referring to those who had formerly hunted him — and to whom he was to have been 'fed'. A note in Hamiora's manuscript commenting on the word 'shame' ('whakama') in the penultimate line states that it was a direct reference to those who still nurtured ill-will towards Te Kooti — that is, it says, Hoani Ruru and others, as well as some Pakeha, those whose kin had been executed at Poverty Bay in 1868 or who had fallen in the fighting at Nga Tapa.

'Pinepine Te Kura' is the best known of all Te Kooti's waiata, and it is sung on many occasions. It conveys the tragedy of Te Kooti's betrayal — both by the law, and by his own people. A second waiata Te Kooti composed at the same time is even more direct, and equally sad:

> Tera ia nga te po taua te taka noa mai ra e. Kei Turanganui e hau nei i te rongo, rongo rawa atu au e i te kupu korero. . . . Ka nui au te aroha. E hoa ma, e whakaponohia mai e naku hoki te mahi kai whakarere atu ko te wehenga ano e o aku makau tipu kei te toko-rau atu. Katahi taru kino e. Ko te whakatata atu ka kite au i te huhi mo te taringa kore ra ki te whakarongo mai i te kupu o te ture kei whakapai iho e mo te maungarongo a Te Paraihe.
>
> This then is the night we two meet failure. In Turanganui the news is spread; I hear the word spoken. . . . Great is my love. Friends, believe me — it is my doing, the abandon-

ment, the parting from my firm and fixed desire. How bad it is! In coming closer, I perceive the covered ears that do not listen to the word of law which sets in place the abiding peace of Bryce.[143]

The song indicates that it was finally his own decision not to go. He sang to Wi Pere, who had hoped to bring him home, or to people collectively, those who had supported him. A gloss to the last line makes it clear that by the 'abiding peace' Te Kooti was referring to the pardon of February 1883.

This mood of sorrow can only have been extended by the fire which destroyed all his property and houses at Otewa in February 1888, forcing him to ask for government assistance. His petition, sent to Parliament, was simply passed over without response.[144] It seemed as if all the world conspired against him: shortly after the fire, visiting Te Makomako, he took as his text Christ's words of despair: 'Oh God, why hast thou forsaken me?' ('E te Atua he aha koe i wha[ka]rere ai i a au?')[145] But again this sorrow was soon translated into action.

When Te Kooti was at Maraenui in July 1887, the Ra for the succeeding July had been called for Waioeka, Hira Te Popo's community in the eastern Bay of Plenty.[146] Thus Te Kooti came to the coast again. This time it was to open the great carved ancestral house, Tane Whirinaki, which had been built also for the Kotahitanga of the gospel.[147] He reached Whakatane on 21 June 1888, accompanied by about 80 riders. His arrival would almost certainly have been announced by the messenger whom he named 'Ramanui', the Great Torch: Tamati Te Ao Turoa of Te Teko, who often rode ahead of Te Kooti to proclaim his forthcoming visits.[148] At Whakatane they were joined by people from Ngati Awa and Tuhoe, and together they all travelled to Waimana and then to Opotiki, where they arrived on 24 June. They were joined by further parties from Turanga and Wairoa (people of Te Aitanga-a-Mahaki and Ngati Kahungunu), and a hundred Te Whanau-a-Apanui from the East Coast. All in all, some 500 visitors gathered at Waioeka pa on 24–25 June, to be greeted by another 500 from Whakatohea itself.[149] It was a great celebratory occasion, which Bush, the resident magistrate, described as being conducted with absolute propriety. Alcohol was banned from the marae on Te Kooti's instructions, and Te Kooti himself was sober the entire time. Bush commented directly that this was 'a new feature in Te Kooti, as hitherto he has drunk freely, though urging on the natives the advisability of abstinence. The conduct of the natives, both visitors and local, was excellent.'[150]

The Whakatohea elder, Paroa (Jack) Kurei, narrated how Hira Te Popo, his grandfather, had built the carved house for Whakatohea, and had invited Te Kooti to open it. But when Te Kooti arrived

he went up to the door of the meeting-house and opened it — and just peeped in. He never went in. He turned round to the people and said, 'Where am I to sit?' The people think, 'What's wrong now!' 'Where am I to sit? The place is full of people!' He means the carving — the wooden ones, standing there. Oh well. They sat there and talked, and he said, 'Oh well. Leave this as a coffin for me.' That's what he said. And today we try to understand what he meant by that. No one seems to know. There's a meaning to it, of course. Of course, other words he left to other places, to all the people, they came true. Well, people tried to find out what he means; we can't seem to find what the meaning of the word is. So they build a little one, a smaller meeting-house.

We, the people, used Tāne Whirinaki after as a church house. Even to our time, this generation. The old people, they used to go up to church in there, but we, as children, didn't like that house — all dark and gloomy, with all those carvings in there. Oh, make your hair stand up! The bell used to hang on Tāne Whirinaki, and at night-time they used to send us to ring the bell. Oh — but I had two or three mates — can't go by yourself! Too frightened! Anyway, two or three times — then I had a brainwave: in daytime, get flax, and tied him together to the bell. That night, oh one night anyway, 'Oh, better have a church. Run and ring the bell!' 'I can do it! I'm not frightened!' I got half in; I'd brought the flax line half way down the marae, went and pulled that flax! Oh, my mates: 'Cunning fellow, eh!'[151]

In the written records of the faith there is another version of Te Kooti's words for the house. This one is also narrated today. Once again, the kupu was unhappy for the people:

Opeke, Waioeka
Hurae. 1. 1888.
Ka mea a te Kooti: Ko te kupu tenei i tenei ra mo tenei whare. Tenei ake nga ra, kei te haere mai, ka pokapoka ia tenei whare e te kiore, kia pūareare a ka puare. Ka pokaia mai hoki e nga kiore i te Tuarongo puta rawa i te kuaha.

Ka rere mai te kaahu, ka titiro, a ka kite i nga kiore e karikari ana i tenei whare, i tenei waahi, ka hiahia ki te hopu; kia mau aua kiore. Ka mea te kaahu ki te hiahia ki te hopu, a heoi ka rērēre tonu mai te kaahu ki tenei waahi ki te tirotiro.

Opeke, Waioeka
July. 1. 1888.
Te Kooti said: This is the saying today for this house. The days will come when this house will be gnawed by rats so that it is opened up and exposed. It will be dug out by the rats from the back right to the door.

A hawk will fly in, look, and when it sees the rats digging in this house, at this place, then it will wish to catch and carry off those rats. The hawk will think that if he wants to catch [them], then it will have to continue to fly to this place to watch.[152]

These words of 1 July are interpreted as warning of the later division and erosion of the faith by false leaders, the 'rats' gnawing at the rear. The watching hawk needs to be vigilant.

The reporter for the *Bay of Plenty Times* observed that Te Kooti's disclosures ('whaka-kaukau') for the day were all being carefully recorded in writing. Much of what was said was deliberately enigmatic, most certainly to him. There was, however, one clear warning that the reporter understood: an epidemic, a skin disease, would strike in the coming months. Te Kooti urged prayer to help avert that calamity. According to the reporter, this occasion was the only one at which Te Kooti spoke in public, and it was to a huge audience, estimated at being 1200 people.[153] But the reporter noted that he also conducted baptisms of children during his stay.

The storm clouds were now beginning to gather around Te Kooti again. Directly after this Ra, Te Kooti went to Whakatane for the uhunga (final burial rites) for Wepiha

Tane Whirinaki, the house at Waioeka pa carved for Te Kooti, but which he never entered. This house was considered extremely tapu and was ultimately demolished. Because of the fear in which it was held, the carvings (which were multi-coloured in the style developed by Te Kooti) were left to decay. Subsequently they were placed in storage, and they now await another house. Among them are the two ancestral figures which bore the ridge pole: Muriwai and her son Tane Whirinaki, after whom the house was named. In this photograph, the house is boarded up. The bell hung inside the porch, on the left-hand side of the house when facing it — that is, the host's side. Photograph by C. Troughton Clark, c.1920.   B7099, MONZ

Apanui, the senior chief of Ngati Awa. It would not be long before he was accused by Maori opponents of having caused Wepiha's death by makutu. To this charge another would soon be added: the death, in August, of old Wiremu Kingi Te Kawau.[154] These deaths were attributed not simply to the conflicts between Te Kooti and those chiefs who had opposed him and his teachings, but also to his earlier prophecy that he would '"destroy" the chiefs' ('i nga kupu a te Kooti ka mate nga rangatira i a ia').[155] To these charges were attached others: that he was creating a movement whereby he, and he alone, claimed the mana over the land and the people. The statements attributed to him were becoming overtly more political, as his chiefly opposition also organised itself.

Not long before he died, Wiremu Kingi Te Kawau had written to tell Ropata that, during Te Kooti's stay at Whakatane and Waimana, the latter had come to an understanding with Urewera, Ngati Awa and Ngati Pukeko of Whakatane that their lands would be handed over to him as a guardian ('kua tukua . . . o ratou whenua ki a te Kooti mana e tiaki').[156] Hohepa Te Wharepu and five others of Ngati Pukeko, whose lands at Te Poroporo, Whakatane, were being entrusted to Te Kooti against their will, also wrote to Parliament. They voiced their objection that Te Kooti's 'church' had freely granted the authority over the lands and people at Whakatane to Te Kooti, including the land on which they were living. They were making him 'the Lord of Whakatane', the translator emphasised; they had complained, 'Ko te Kooti hei rangatira mo Whakatane'.[157] Rewiri Parera, the chief of Te Patuwai, a hapu of Ngati Pukeko, immediately constructed a pa to defend the land against Te Kooti. Te Patuwai informed Bush that Te Kooti had written to Tuhoe urging them to claim and occupy these lands, and that the hapu would resist any such attempt by Tuhoe.[158]

The issue was not simply rival claims over land areas between competing family and hapu groups, exacerbated by the extension of a new mana over these lands. The significant political aspect of Te Kooti's guardianship over tribal lands was that he instructed that they were not to be brought before the Native Land Court. The purpose was to ensure that the lands would be retained and not broken up by the inexorable process of survey, subdivision and individuation of title, which the procedures of the court fostered and which he opposed. Te Kooti had assured Wiremu Kingi, on what must have been the last occasion they met, that his policies concerning the land were to promote peace, not conflict and division, between the hapu.[159] For some leaders, however, this policy directly denied their own mana and independence, as well as preventing them from capitalising on their resources. These opponents of Te Kooti were also the hapu and chiefs who particularly objected to the fact that all the supplies of the communities vanished in support of the great feasts to welcome Te Kooti, leaving the people ill-provided for the winter months. They talked of the neglect of the children and the old people, for whom little could be found after the extravagant consumption of the communal resources in the hui.[160] The objectors also stated that Te Kooti was making his adherents collect money for him, and to do that they were being forced to sell their crops and animals to raise the cash, as well as to provide food for these feasts. Such views were reinforced by the native officers and schoolteachers in their various reports to the government about the social effects of Te Kooti's visits at this time. They reflected the predominant Pakeha stereotype of the wastefulness of the great feasts, but it should be noted that the unfortunate consequences — the draining of the community's resources, and the malnutrition evident among the children — were observed with concern not only by Pakeha.

Politically more dangerous was the information that Te Kooti had predicted that the confiscated lands would be returned. Hohepa Te Wharepu's petition to Parliament stated that:

> I te ki a te Kooti ka hoki mai nga whenua ki nga Maori ka ora i a ia te tangata koi nei.
>
> Te Kooti says that all the lands will come back to the Natives and that he is to be the Saviour of the Natives.[161]

Bush was even more explicit. The 'one danger in Kooti-ism', in his opinion, was that Te Kooti was now telling his adherents that the confiscated lands would be returned. In Bush's view, that event could occur only in one way, 'by driving out the pakeha from the country'; he saw this, therefore, as the implicit but widely understood content of Te Kooti's message.[162] That it was his own construct seems never to have occurred to

Tane Whirinaki and the two marae at Waioeka. The date of this photograph is unknown but it is before 1904, when the present meeting-house Irapuaia was opened. Here, a small raupo meeting-house stands on the exact site of Irapuaia, facing onto the second open marae (centre right). A long raupo dining shelter is partly obscured by the bright tin roof of Tane Whirinaki. A small shelter (or house) stands on the marae beside Tane Whirinaki; similarly, the tent suggests important guests were present. The photograph was taken from the burial mountain behind the marae, looking north-west across the Waioeka valley.   WHAKATANE MUSEUM

Bush. The Maori letters of protest emphasised, rather, that Te Kooti was claiming the mana over the land and over the people, and that the East Coast tribes had responded to him by placing their lands under his guardianship.[163]

The political emphasis of the messages being sent to the government altered the atmosphere in which the question of Te Kooti's return to Poverty Bay was being discussed. The petitions against his return were renewed once it was learnt that he had announced at Waioeka that he would go to Gisborne in March 1889. Wiremu Kingi Te Kawau and Te Hata Te Kakatuamaro both wrote immediately to Ropata, telling him that Te Kooti had instructed Te Aitanga-a-Mahaki to build a meeting-house at their new settlement at Te Karaka, and that he had urged them to finish it quickly in order to receive him at that time.[164] Wiremu Kingi believed that Te Kooti had chosen the date deliberately as a time when Parliament would not be in session, and so would be unable to respond quickly to his journey. This may have been so, but no deceit was involved: Te Kooti wrote to the government a month before he set out and informed them of his intention and of the date when he would depart from Otewa.[165]

Once the news that he intended to return in 1889 reached Poverty Bay, the protests began again. Hoani Ruru had already sent a petition to Parliament in June 1888, requesting the government to prevent Te Kooti from coming. Eighty-nine signatures, in addition to his own, were attached. The petitioners argued on the grounds of past history: the killing of Te Warihi, the executions at Matawhero, Patutahi and Oweta, and the 'loss of our goods and lands for Te Kooti's deeds' were among the several causes listed for the bitter feelings which remained in the local Maori community towards Te Kooti.[166]

The last reference, to the loss of land, was to the confiscations at Poverty Bay, which had been forced through in 1869. Three blocks had been taken, including about 50,000 acres at Patutahi. There was much confusion and discontent over both the extent and the location of the confiscated blocks. It had been understood, including by some present at the 1869 hearing, that only 5000 acres (not 50,000 acres) had been ceded at Patutahi. However, a large chunk of the 'back country' (estimated by the government's agent at the time as about 40,000 acres) was intended to be included, and this — and more — was added to the block.[167] The grievance over the confiscations had become a long-festering sore in the district, and it would continue well after Te Kooti's death. A common view was that the land had been taken after the siege of Nga Tapa in direct reprisal for 'the guilt of the Hauhaus'.[168] In this petition, the blame was laid directly upon Te Kooti.

A counter-petition was drawn up and presented by Karaitiana Ruru of Te Aitanga-a-Mahaki at Te Karaka, the people who had decided to build the meeting-house there for Te Kooti. Karaitiana was Patoromu Ruru's elder brother. Their father, Henare (now dead), had received government payment for the capture of whakarau in 1869. Thus the family history typically reflected both the divisions and the efforts at reconciliation being made in Poverty Bay. Two hundred and twelve others signed Karaitiana's petition — many more than Hoani Ruru of Ngati Maru had managed to collect. Karaitiana's petition was sent by the Gisborne solicitor, E. H. Ward, on behalf of the signatories; it was tabled by the Native Minister on 12 July, although he did not give it his support. The petitioners urged that Te Kooti be allowed to return to his birthplace, and be treated in a friendly way by Europeans and Maori alike. They stressed that the tensions and disputes in the Maori community would be eased, rather than aggravated, by his home-coming. Those who protested would then realise that he came in peace to the Crown's loyal subjects.[169] But the government made no recommendation. At the same time, it replied to others who wrote expressing opposition — even to Te Kooti's return to the eastern Bay of Plenty after the death of Wiremu Kingi Te Kawau, as James Carroll, the new member for Eastern Maori, had done — that it could only persuade Te Kooti that it was inadvisable for him to travel there.[170] The government also stated firmly to other petitioners that the killing of Te Warihi, which Westrup was thrusting forward as a device to challenge Te Kooti's legal right to freedom, was included under the amnesty proclamation of 1883.[171]

On 1–3 January 1889, Te Kooti held the Ra at Te Awahou. The government had been forewarned that 5000 people were expected to attend this occasion, called a Po Takoto.[172] Here too a new meeting-house had been built for Te Kooti, and it was opened at this gathering.[173] The house stood in challenge to Wi Maihi Te Rangikaheke's elaborately carved house, Whakaue, which had been opened at Te Awahou only four years earlier. Te Kooti's words were ominous. Matiu recorded them; they referred to the

Portrait of the prophet Rua Kenana, in front of Tane Whirinaki. When Rua claimed the mantle of Te Kooti's predicted successor, he visited all the sacred places associated with Te Kooti. This photograph dates from the late 1920s.   WHAKATANE MUSEUM

new house thus: 'The services, and this house, shall be abandoned' ('Ka mahue ano nga karakia me tenei whare ano hoki').[174] Indeed, this house was soon to be abandoned, as a photograph recorded. The house was possibly Te Purei, which once stood at Te Awahou and was sold and moved; it has the same proportions, and it still contains some of the naturalistic paintings associated with the Ringatu houses.[175]

The kupu whakaari for the gathering at Te Awahou were recorded by Matiu, Petera and Hamiora, in three separate texts. Their texts overlap but do not always agree, like the gospels of the New Testament. Here Te Kooti directed the people's faith towards Jehovah, warning of an imminent time of 'sore affliction' ('he whiu mamae').[176] He spoke of forthcoming bloodshed, greater even than that he had indicated for the previous year, 'that is, the blood for the sake of the land' ('ara te toto mo te whenua te putake').[177] This prediction ultimately reached the ears of Bush, who reported it to the government.[178] But Te Kooti had also told the people to arise and give their sacred offerings ('he patunga tapu') to God, for all their weariness and sickness ('nga mauiuitanga katoa'). He reassured them with God's words: 'Heaven is my throne, and the earth my standing place' ('Ko te Rangi taku torona ko te whenua toku turanga

The beautiful little meeting-house Pukeko, built by a section of Ngati Pukeko for Te Kooti. It was opened on 16 June 1884. It is said that Te Kooti was present at its dedication, and his kupu whakaari for the house is recorded as 'Oniihi'. It simply instructed the people to look to the faith as their guardian: 'Kia mau ki te whakapono. Ko te whakapono hei matua mo koutou.' Photograph by Judith Binney, 1993.

waewae'). He said finally that those who dwelt in the gospel and love 'are directed by us' ('te kai tono ko tatou').[179]

Thus Te Kooti urged faith and sacrifice. His words again warned of trouble and dissent, perhaps reflecting his mood. Six new prophets would arise, he said, of whom three would be greater than the others and they would take some of the people away. He spoke of a possible disaster for the Rotorua district, whereby the lake would become a sea and sweep all away before the year 1894. But in the version recorded by Hamiora, Te Kooti also gave the promise:

> Whata. E kore e ngaro te tangata hei whakahaere mo tatau, ko au hoki he karere — ki te tae au ki a ia, ko ia tera.

> Whata. The person to lead us will not be hidden; I am just a messenger — when I reach out to him, he will be that one.[180]

Thus he comforted his listeners, and promised them a resolution, probably in their time. He did not refer to the prospective journey — at least not in the words recorded. But everyone was aware of it, for Ropata had already warned Ngati Rangiwewehi that he would, if necessary, come and fight.[181] Moreover, when Te Kooti wrote soon afterwards to Ropata, suggesting that he might visit him at Waiomatatini, on the occasion of the opening of Ropata's carved meeting-house, Porourangi, Ropata replied that indeed he was welcome, for he would '"provide him with land for settlement 6 x 3, neither more nor less."'[182]

Te Kooti's opponents accused him not only of gathering the Arawa into his church and under his mana at this time, but of consenting to a petition devised by the Roman Catholic missionaries in the district to appeal to the Pope to intervene over Maori lands. Whititera Te Waiatua claimed to have a copy of the petition, which Te Kooti had signed.[183] Whititera was probably exaggerating, for he stated that the petitioners had transferred the 'mana' of their lands to the Pope, who would repeal the laws pertaining to Maori lands, yet at the same time he complained that Te Kooti was setting himself up as a new 'mana', or authority, for New Zealand. He seems to be creating two 'enemies' for the establishment. However, that a petition to the Pope was being circulated is not unlikely. A petition from the Roman Catholic Maori community at Matata would be sent only a few years later, asking the Pope to intervene on their behalf, for, as they said, 'We dwell without authority over our lands, which have been confiscated by the European' ('Ko matau e noho ana i runga i te mana kore whenua kua riro o matau whenua i te raupatu a te pakeha').[184] In the 1880s and early 1890s, many Maori were looking for other, higher authorities to whom they could appeal over the head of Parliament; the presence of Hirini Taiwhanga MHR at the January hui might well have stimulated such an appeal to the Pope, for Hirini had already tried in vain to visit Queen Victoria. That the hui discussed land issues is clear: recent legislation setting up rates on Maori land was a major grievance. Representatives from many tribal areas were present, including a large delegation from the Wairarapa. They said, however, that they had come particularly to learn about the new faith, and to take its rites home. Thus the gathering was a blend of religion and politics, as all hui were (and are): Te Kooti's importance is defined by what each person and community took from his words.

Immediately upon his return to Otewa Te Kooti wrote, on 12 January 1889, the first Twelfth of the New Year, to inform the government of his intention to travel to Gisborne. He would set out, he said, on 10 February,

> ki te kawe i te Ture i te Maunga-Rongo ki oku whanaunga e noho ana i reira ahakoa Maori Pakeha, kia kotahi tonu te haere ko te aroha me te mana o Te Kuini me te Whakapono, kia kaua he raruraru e hangaia ki runga o te Rongo Pai.
>
> to take the Law and Peace to my relations living there, whether Maori or Pakeha, so that there is a unified path in love, the authority of the Queen and the Faith, and so that no trouble is created over the Gospel.[185]

Three days later he wrote to Porter to inform him personally. It was a similar letter, expressing the hope 'May the chief spirit of lasting Peace protect us all' ('Ma te Ariki o te Maungarongo tatau katoa e tiaki').[186] Wilson Hursthouse, now resident magistrate at

Te Awamutu and on good terms with Te Kooti, also informed the government that he understood Te Kooti's purpose was 'to bind the peace', not to break it.[187]

At this juncture, the government's policy was still to give advice: that it was unwise for him to go. Edwin Mitchelson, the Native Minister, informed Te Kooti to this effect on 23 January.[188] The focus still remained his own safety, as the Police Commissioner, Walter Gudgeon, explicitly stated on 12 February in a letter to the Minister of Defence; this was despite the more watchful policy Gudgeon had initiated in 1887. He was particularly concerned that Te Kooti had been threatened by Ropata and Ngati Porou, and he directed that two uniformed constables should be sent from Wellington to accompany Te Kooti on the last stage to Poverty Bay, and to remain near him at all times. Porter, as the military officer commanding the East Coast, was to be asked to restrain the Ngati Porou chiefs.[189] The commissioner was following the government's original instructions to try to avoid a calamity.[190]

Before this, Mitchelson decided to ask Te Kooti to come to see him. On 7 February, Te Kooti and Heni Kumekume journeyed to Auckland. Te Kooti met Mitchelson and then the Premier, Harry Atkinson. Mitchelson had already intimated to Hursthouse that he would arrange to exchange the uninhabitable swamp near Orakau for a land grant at Ohiwa, out of the confiscated coastal lands of the eastern Bay of Plenty. He also revealed the tactics by which he hoped to stop the journey: that if a disturbance occurred at Poverty Bay, he would not make the grant.[191] Notwithstanding this threat, Mitchelson set the offer in motion, as he promised Te Kooti he would in Auckland.[192] He also tried to dissuade Te Kooti from returning to Poverty Bay. Mitchelson said the interview was cordial and friendly but Te Kooti had made it clear that this time he was determined. He had put the visit off from year to year at the request of the government, and now he was getting old. He had, moreover, given a pledge to go, and the dangers did not weigh with him for 'it would be his own body only that would suffer'. He had 'told his followers that if he were killed they must not avenge him'; the law alone would punish the offenders.[193] Therefore, he would make no promise to the government. As a token of his good will, he said, he surrendered a small revolver he carried, which he later stated had been intended as a 'present' for his son, Wetini.[194] It was an 1878 gun, named the 'Guardian American Model': there may have been irony in the remark — as there undoubtedly was in the intended gift.[195] However, he assured Mitchelson that he and his followers would travel unarmed.

The government's subsequent reversal of policy stemmed from the Premier, and the pressure that was brought to bear upon him when he went to Poverty Bay later in the month. Te Kooti left as planned, riding through Kihikihi on 12 February with about 20 people, of whom half were women and children.[196] They went on to Tapapa, where he composed the waiata quoted at the start of this chapter. The accompanying gloss to the song was the prediction that he would be captured:

> Ka whāwhātia ano ahau e te ringa tangata i roto i tenei haere. A, ka raruraru te iwi. Otira kia manawanui te ngakau, kaore e mate.

> I shall be taken by the hand of man in the midst of this journey. And the people will be troubled. However, be of stout heart, for I shall not die.[197]

Te Kooti's abandoned 'Prayer House' at Te Awahou. There are conflicting traditions about its fate. It may have been burnt, but Roger Neich has suggested that this house is Te Purei, which formerly stood at Te Awahou. Its name, The Isolated Rock, indicates its separateness, and indeed Te Kooti's house stood in conscious rivalry to Wi Maihi Te Rangikaheke's two large carved houses, Whakaokorau and Whakaue, built at Te Awahou in the 1880s.   James Cowan collection, 44567 1/2, ATL

He was watched every step of the way. Te Kooti stayed the night of 14 February at Te Awahou, and from there he journeyed to the coast, reaching Matata on 18 February. By then about 70 people were accompanying him, many of whom were women and children. They did not stop; they passed straight through to stay with Te Kooti's close followers at Kokohinau at Te Teko. Te Kooti was clearly trying to avoid conflict and he bypassed all settlements where there might be trouble, as Bush noted.[198]

It was at Poverty Bay on 18 February that the trouble really started. The local newspaper, the *Poverty Bay Herald*, had already given some very contradictory signals in its editorials. On 16 February, it stated clearly that there was no cause to believe that Te Kooti and his followers would 'take the initiative in committing a breach of the peace. The leader says he comes in peace, and wishes to depart in peace.' But then it added categorically that, if he were shot on this visit, the 'general verdict would be that it served him right'. A tumultous meeting of 500 settlers gathered on 18 February at Makaraka, where the victims of Matawhero lay in a collective grave. There the events of 1868 and 1869 were dwelt upon at length, and it was decided to form an armed 'vigilance committee' to prevent Te Kooti from reaching Poverty Bay. Westrup was the driving force behind this committee, which agreed to place itself under his orders. Several Maori were present, who spoke in favour of stopping Te Kooti. Hoani Ruru was one, and Hapi Kiniha, whose son, Rewi Hapi, was one of the boys killed in the attack of 12 December 1868, was another. Both joined this 'committee'. The lone spokesman for

Te Kooti was Arthur Desmond, who lived at Te Karaka and knew the people who had erected the new meeting-house to receive Te Kooti. Desmond was a socialist, a follower of Henry George. He had already stood unsuccessfully for Parliament on a platform of land nationalisation, not a popular view in a district where Te Kooti's return was being directly linked with the blocking of any future land sales by Maori.[199] Two Native Land Courts were sitting in Gisborne from January to June 1889: 'the first opportunity of getting the lands through the Court', as was observed.[200] Te Kooti's visit was seen as potentially obstructionist, which was hardly surprising. Among the many significant cases being heard was an attempted further subdivision of Pa-o-Kahu, Te Kooti's place of birth beside the Awapuni lagoon. This had been initiated by Hoani Ruru, and the hearing proved to be a classic example of a trustee trying to set up an immediate ancestor of his own as the recognised line of descent, in order to exclude others of Ngati Maru whose claims were equally valid.[201] Later Desmond wrote to the Wellington *Evening Post*, whose editorials had challenged the legality of the government's actions in arresting Te Kooti. Desmond supported the paper's stand, and argued that the 'whole agitation is a sham', got up by the local land speculators against a man who believed 'in using land for the production of wealth, but not in buying and selling it like a pig' for profit.[202] At Makaraka, he was shouted down by these 'respectable' settlers, although he said he had come forward simply to stop bloodshed. Desmond's rousing ballad exulting in Te Kooti was later published in the *Sydney Bulletin*. He wrote it in direct retaliation for 'The Settlers' Song', attacking Te Kooti, which the *Poverty Bay Herald* published. Both songs appear in Appendix B.

But no balladeer could deflect the settlers' manifestations of angry righteousness. By 19 February, over 200 men had enrolled in the vigilance committee, and Westrup cabled the Minister of Defence seeking (fortunately in vain) 300 rifles and 20,000 rounds of ammunition.[203] As a direct consequence of this 'unlawful assembly' (as the settlers knew themselves to be[204]), Mitchelson telegraphed Te Kooti. He asked him to turn back because of the formation of an 'armed party' at Gisborne.[205] Bush took the cable to Te Kooti at Te Poroporo, Whakatane, where he was staying on the night of 19 February. Te Kooti said simply that it had all been discussed with Mitchelson in Auckland; he was getting old, he had friends to see, and he could no longer delay. However, the experienced seaman within him gave him a metaphor which would allow him to change his mind: 'he was like the master of a vessel who looked out for breakers ahead when crossing a bar — If too heavy a sea, he put back.'[206]

The breakers did grow higher. On 20 February a telegram, signed by chiefs of Ngati Porou and other Maori at Turanga, warned the government that they would rise up and stop Te Kooti if he were not turned back at Opotiki.[207] Among the ten signatories were Hapi Kiniha, Raniera Turoa and Henare Turangi, Paratene Pototi's son, who had also spoken against the visit at the Makaraka meeting. Another signatory was James Carroll, whose aristocratic wife, Heni Materoa, was Paratene's granddaughter. The Native Department replied to them immediately, asking them to permit Te Kooti a short visit to Gisborne.[208] But on 21 February Atkinson himself arrived, at the settlers' request. He immediately conferred with the local justices of the peace (among them Westrup) and came to the conclusion that everyone had lost their heads in Gisborne.

The six-shot revolver given by Te Kooti to Mitchelson in 1889. It had been intended as a 'present' for Wetini. The model name is on the cylinder. The arms registration number is 38005.48.   AIM

He then proceeded to lose his. From this time on, Atkinson determined policy above the authority and advice of the police.[209] It was he who brought the armed constables and artillery to Poverty Bay, and it was he who determined that Te Kooti should be arrested. As Inspector Kiely wrote in his report: 'On the 23. 2. 89 it was well known in Gisborne that the Government would prevent Te Kooti from coming to the district and that forces were in motion'.[210]

Atkinson's armed constables ensured that the vigilance committee disbanded voluntarily, but it still set the government's policy. As the chairman, W. K. Chambers, had told the *Poverty Bay Standard* on 21 February, if the government did not act within 48 hours, the committee itself would act as if there were no government.[211] This threat brought the 18 special constables and 45 artillerymen to Gisborne, on Atkinson's orders. They arrived at 2 a.m. on 24 February. At first light they set out towards Te Karaka with the local militia (the East Coast Hussars), the police and Ropata's hastily resurrected Ngati Porou contingent, all under the direction of Porter, as the local military commanding officer. With them went Inspector Kiely and Sergeant J. H. Bullen, carrying the warrant for Te Kooti's arrest for 'unlawful assembly'. This had been issued on the direction of the Premier, after consultation with his notoriously conniving Solicitor-general, Frederick Whitaker, the previous evening.[212] Atkinson then joined the police and militia on the night of 25 February, and upon his command the combined forces (133 men) were ordered on 'a secret night march' to Opotiki, bearing the warrant.[213] In this manner, the law was set against Te Kooti. The hysteria of the settler

Hoani Ruru of Ngati Maru, who
opposed Te Kooti's return to
Turanga. Photograph by Margaret
Matilda White.

1535.380, WHANGAREI MUSEUM

community at Poverty Bay and the bitterness of some of his kin had turned against
him the instrument of government in which he most believed.

Nothing justifies this act. In the eastern Bay of Plenty, the tension developing
between Ngai Tai and Te Kooti's supporters had already been defused. Ngai Tai had
gathered at Opotiki for a Land Court hearing on 14 February, as had many followers
of Te Kooti from Whakatohea and Tuhoe. There, threats of makutu had been voiced
against Ngai Tai. It was said that Te Kooti had predicted the deaths of four senior
chiefs who had opposed him, and indeed three had died in 1888: Wiremu Kingi Te
Kawau, Renata Kawepo and Horonuku Te Heuheu.[214] The taunts concerned the fourth:
would it be Te Hata, the new leader of Ngai Tai, or perhaps Ropata? Ngai Tai armed
themselves and set out for Whakatane, but they returned to Torere on 18 February, in
compliance with Bush's instructions. When Te Kooti reached Whakatane, there was
no opposition waiting. Instead, Moanaroa Pere had ridden from Gisborne to greet
him. His father, no longer bound by political circumspection, having lost his
parliamentary seat to his rival, James Carroll, in July 1887, also sent a message from
Opotiki to say that he was waiting there, so as to remove any opposition. Bush
commented it was 'generally supposed Wi Pere is pushing Kooti through'.[215]

Hapi Kiniha, another opponent of
Te Kooti's return to Turanga.
Close kinship is certainly
suggested by the photographs of
these two men. Photograph by
Margaret Matilda White.

1535.383, Whangarei Museum

However, Wi Pere's presence in Opotiki related to a different, though not uncon-
nected, matter. A protracted Land Court hearing for the vast, inland Tahora No. 2
block, in which Te Kooti himself was involved as an owner, had brought Wi Pere and
many of the Tuhoe elders into town. This complex hearing had been initiated by a claim
to the whole block laid by just two men of Whakatohea. The counter-claims defended
the interests of the inland Poverty Bay tribes, including Ngati Maru, Te Whanau-a-Kai,
Ngati Kahungunu of upper Wairoa, Tuhoe and many others of Whakatohea as well.
This was a prime case of dragging elders into the Native Land Court because of the
actions of a compliant or greedy minority. Wi Pere, Tipene Te Waru and many of the
senior Tuhoe chiefs gave evidence through the entire period of Te Kooti's visit and
arrest, and well beyond. This extensive hearing, set in motion by the few, forced the
cutting of the land into pieces in the following year.[216]

Te Kooti passed through Opotiki township on the morning of Friday, 22 February,
accompanied by about 200 men and youths, and 50 women. He rode his 'white charger'
30 yards in front of the cavalcade,[217] and the rest of the procession followed 'quietly . . .
through the township', jogging three abreast.[218] There were several laden packhorses,
too, one of which carried a large object hidden in 'American oil-cloth'.[219] Much later,

and only in the context of Te Kooti's trials, the police suggested that this parcel was hidden arms; it was more probably the ark of the covenant.[220]

Bush was present as the party passed, as was Major F. Swindley, the commanding military officer and a large landholder in the district. Swindley joined Te Kooti in the Opotiki Hotel, where the latter was described as having 'his usual refreshment, Schiedam schnapps'.[221] Then they travelled together in Te Kooti's buggy to Omarumutu, where the road turned inland to connect with the Motu river and through to Poverty Bay. Te Kooti planned to stay for two days at Omarumutu, for he would not journey on the Saturday sabbath. Accompanying him at this stage were a number of the senior Tuhoe leaders, including Rakuraku, Kereru Te Pukenui, Te Makarini Tamarau, Te Whiu and Hemi Kakitu, all of whom had been with him at some point during the wars. With them also came Reihana and Tipene Te Waru, living at Waiotahe. The visit to Gisborne was indeed intended as 'a sort of . . . pilgrimage', as the *New Zealand Herald*'s reporter realised,[222] but it was different from his expectations in one critical respect: all the riders were unarmed.

Wi Pere also came with Te Kooti to Omarumutu, bringing with him the keys to the new meeting-house at Te Karaka. But he had also received a series of telegrams from his elder son in Gisborne reporting on the developing situation: the formation of the vigilance committee and its rapidly escalating numbers, together with the threat of the ten chiefs who had said that they would rise up to stop Te Kooti: 'ka whakatika tonu matou ki te arai atu i a Te Kooti'.[223] On the evening of 22 February, Atkinson sent a telegram ordering Te Kooti to turn back; he replied, saying that he had made up his mind to continue.[224]

Late that night, Te Kooti also received a telegram from a senior chief at Te Karaka, Paora Haupa, advising him that he should not now come — a communication with which others at Te Karaka strongly disagreed.[225] Matiu Paeroa, in his carefully kept account of the journey (commencing at Kihikihi on 12 February and which he called the 'Disruption at Opotiki' ('Potatutatu ki Opotiki')), described the telegram:

> 23. Noho tonu i reira: Ka tae mai te waea, kua puta a Wi Paraone, a Panapa, a Karaitiana Ruru, 'Ki waho o te whare kua mahue te whare i Turanga.'

> 23 [February]. Stayed on there [Omarumutu]: A telegram came [saying] Wi Paraone, Panapa [Waihopi], and Karaitiana Ruru 'had come out of the house, the house at Turanga had been forsaken.'[226]

The report was incorrect, for the people stayed at Te Karaka to welcome Te Kooti and did not leave the marae, as the accompanying photograph, taken the next morning, indicates. Great 'indignation' that the telegram had been sent was also expressed at Te Karaka on 23 February.[227]

An oral tradition at Te Karaka remembers, however, that disagreement did arise between the elders of the house. It is narrated that Te Kooti had predicted, when they had ridden to tell him that their house was ready, that their families would separate over this decision: 'That house is divided against me. If it is not why is the lion living in the house?' The elders were extremely puzzled by the remark at the time. It was only on their return to Gisborne that they discovered, painted under the window-sill inside the

Waiting for Te Kooti at Te Karaka, Sunday, 24 February 1889. The photograph shows the house, Te Poho-o-Pikihoro, built to receive him. The porch contained painted (not carved) poupou, and the interior was painted as well as carved. The house was 66 feet long, 33 feet wide and 22 feet high; its exterior walls and roof were of corrugated iron, a new and practical development. It was said that the house had taken three months to build, and no iron or nails had been used on which there was any sign of rust or tarnish.

The *Poverty Bay Herald* described the Sunday gathering: 'Visitors are arriving in hundreds, in buggies and on horses, and the place looks like a canvas township of the digging days. Every family has its appointed place, and the scene at night is very picturesque — the tents lighted up, the camp fires blazing . . . . The bell rings for church in the usual manner, and everyone gathers on the open space before the large new house, sit down, and pray and chant in the same style as is customary with Europeans.' Inspector Kiely, who was in charge of the police expedition, also praised the Te Karaka chief, Panapa Waihopi, who had invited Te Kooti, for his co-operation, and commented: 'The Te Karaka natives displayed an excellent feeling towards the police. The patrols visited the place every day.' The people at Te Karaka, in their turn, wryly named their marae Takepu, Stack of Guns, for the arms of the government forces stacked there. Photograph by William F. Crawford.   WFC A314, GM

house, the British coat of arms with the lion rampant. Its unexpected appearance was retrospectively interpreted (by some) as an omen of a house divided.[228]

Pere and Bush went together to see Te Kooti on Saturday morning, 23 February. He was still adamant that he would continue the journey. He compared himself to Christ, killed out of jealousy. Bush commented that Te Kooti appeared to be 'under some Religious spell and acts as one who does not care what becomes of his body if Soul saved'.[229] When Bush threatened that if he continued he would now be certain to be arrested, Te Kooti replied, 'I would be glad to be arrested at the hands of my father because he would then break through his own peace making with me.'[230] This was his only retaliatory 'threat'. From his perspective, he would have been freed from the constraints of the pledge that he had made to uphold the law, not in the sense of initiating armed resistance but in the sense of releasing him to challenge the legitimacy of those laws which had dispossessed him and circumscribed his rights. If the government broke the Maungarongo (the lasting peace) of 1883, then he would be the innocent party, and his stature enhanced in the Maori community. But he was still not seeking confrontation, nor did he instigate his betrayal by the government.

Te Kooti was officially told by the Opotiki police on the night of 23 February that an armed expedition was assembling at Gisborne. He was also told that the expedition would arrest him, should he attempt to proceed to Gisborne.[231] The *New Zealand Herald*, which had sent its own reporter to Opotiki, added that Te Kooti then offered to disband his entire party and to continue on alone. Again he was told that he must return to Waikato.[232]

The waiata he composed on 23 February is understandably bitter: it sings of the scourges sent against him. It cries how his heart was close to being scooped out for the multitude to devour: 'ka tata te ngakau te aohia ki waho kia kai mai e tini o runga'; it tells of the many-pointed fishing spear, fashioned to be driven into his flesh: 'he mata-rau hei tia mai mo taku kiri'; and of the mouths of angry women, seen muttering that he should be beaten with thorns and nettles (like Christ), and his penis split and severed: 'ki te ngutu o te wahine e komeme ana mai ki te harirau mai ki te tumatakuru ki te taraonga he hae kia te ure kai hautopea'. His anger spilt over into sexual oppositions; the pain is that he would be destroyed, utterly bereft of heartwood ('kohiwi').[233] On the following day, 24 February, Te Kooti announced his decision to turn back.[234]

It was immediately rumoured that he intended to send Petera Te Rangihiroa in his place to attend the opening of the meeting-house, set for 12 March.[235] Certainly, various people went through during the next few days, including a party of 12 sent on 25 February. They went partly as a 'blind', a strategy intended to protect Te Kooti,[236] and to carry messages. But the military blockade, set by Atkinson on the night of 23 February where the single-span bridge crossed the Motu river, inhibited their movements. One man was arrested there on 24 February, and while the block remained few slipped through although there were no further arrests.[237] The oral tradition grew that Te Kooti himself was among those whom the soldiers questioned at this barrier, asking, '"Where's Te Kooti?" And they said, "Oh, he's not far behind." Little did they know they were talking to Te Kooti himself!'[238] In actuality, it seems that Te Kooti received no communication in response to any of his messages until late on 26 February. Then, that night, Patoromu Ruru, who had managed to elude the government's sentries at the blockade, got through to Waioeka. He was accompanied by Te Kooti's returning messengers, and he brought news from Gisborne.

All public and press telegraphic communication from Gisborne to Opotiki had been cut from the evening of 25 February. This was done on Atkinson's orders, coinciding with his order for the 'secret night march'. Most newspapers carried the report that the stoppage was to prevent Te Kooti's messengers cabling news of the military movements to him. Only the Wellington *Evening Post*, which was very critical of Atkinson's massive exercise, modified its report that the line had been cut, saying that the single wire from Gisborne simply could not carry all the messages being sent and, therefore, telegrams had been refused for a period.[239] That may have been true; but the reporter from the *Auckland Star* complained that his cables were also refused by the telegraph office at Opotiki, so as to ensure the secrecy of the government's intentions and the troop movements from that end. In addition, certain passages in his reports were deleted before they were accepted by the office.[240] Press censorship was certainly operating. The wire, if not actually cut, was not available for public use. This entire military-scale campaign (which cost the country £2610[241]) was orchestrated by the Premier. Secret orders from the Ministry of Defence flew around the country between 22 and 26 February requisitioning men and arms from as far away as Lyttelton, Dunedin, Napier and Auckland. The 81 naval volunteers who were sent from Auckland to Opotiki conceived of themselves as going 'to the front' to 'fight Te Kooti'.[242]

Te Kooti himself partly collapsed under the strain. He went to the Opotiki Hotel on Monday, 25 February, and was massively drunk by the end of the day. He had gone to Waioeka pa the previous evening to seek the advice of old Hira Te Popo. As Boy Biddle narrated simply, 'Te Kooti asked him, "What shall we do?" His answer was very clear. He said, "My neck only gets tangled in the supplejack once."'[243] It was not only Hira who advised Te Kooti that he must now turn back; Wi Pere and others from Gisborne said exactly the same — to the extent that, when Te Peka Kerekere congratulated him on the wisdom of this decision, Te Kooti chucked him out of his tent, saying he was a fool.[244] The same advice, however, was consistently maintained, and Hira Te Popo wrote to Bush on 26 February affirming that Te Kooti had 'given out' that he was returning to Waikato.[245]

Nevertheless, Te Kooti himself contributed to a growing atmosphere of uncertainty. The first doubts about his intentions were raised by his delay at Waioeka. More significant, he had made some drunken assertions on 25 February to the effect that he was still going to Turanga. When Bush visited Te Kooti at Waioeka the next day, Te Kooti then told him that he would go back as far as Ohiwa and stay on the land the government had promised him there.[246] It was a logical, although somewhat equivocal, remark on Te Kooti's part. Early that same evening he wrote directly to Bush to state that he would 'positively return'.[247] Then, that night, Patoromu arrived bringing the news that, although the road to Gisborne was guarded, it should still be possible to get through.[248] At this juncture Te Kooti changed his mind and decided to continue on.

It was reported early on 27 February that he was leaving that day for Gisborne. Bush cabled at midday, 'Kootis conduct that of a lunatic one day going next not. He is leaving for Gisborne today followers straggling through . . . he not present though'.[249] Wi Pere also reported directly to Atkinson. Caught in this mesh, Pere cabled, '"Te Kooti was a man of two words"', declaring in the morning that he would go to Gisborne but retracting again later that afternoon.[250] Bush then observed some of Te Kooti's party, with swags, riding from Waioeka through Opotiki, and heading along the road for Gisborne. More important, Matiu Paeroa's account confirms that Bush was correct in supposing that they were testing the route. On 26 February Matiu had certainly understood that they were turning back:

> Ka whakaatutia e Rakuraku te kupu, apopo tatau hoki ai.

> The message was given out by Rakuraku — tomorrow we will return.

But, the next day, he wrote:

> Ka puta te kupu: Tatau ko Turanga i tenei rā, me haere ko nga wahine i mua, ko nga tohunga ki muri mai. Ko nga kati e rua, kei te taone tetahi, kei Omarumutu tetahi. Ki te hopukia mai to mua, haere tonu atu, ki te hopukia mai to muri haere tonu atu. A ko ahau mo muri. . . . Me haere inaianei, engari kia pai te haere.

> The message came: We are [for] Turanga today. The women must go in front, the priests behind. There are two barriers, one in the town, one at Omarumutu. If those in front are taken, keep on going; if those in the rear are taken, keep on going. I [Te Kooti] am [to come] later. . . . Go now, may the journey go well.[251]

Matiu then described how he set out, with others, although the main body remained behind at Waioeka with Te Kooti. He also described how, when they arrived at Omarumutu that afternoon, they discovered that Porter and Ropata had beaten them there from Gisborne and were searching the pa for Te Kooti.

This manoeuvre by the Gisborne armed force proved to be decisive. Te Kooti's final statement was the letter he sent — through the police — to Bush later that day. It was written in reply to Bush's communication, dictated by Porter, informing him that the troopers had reached Opotiki and that Porter would be coming to visit him next morning. In reply Te Kooti stated simply, 'I will not go on to Gisborne, but will return to the Waikato.' He said he would leave the following day.[252] He also told the *Auckland Star*'s reporter, who visited him early that evening at Waioeka, that he would be returning to Waikato the next day.[253]

Later that night Te Kooti slipped secretly out of Waioeka pa and cut across country by an old bush track to Waiotahe, the little community of the Wairoa exiles headed by Reihana. He was accompanied by two or three men and three wives, one of whom was Heni Kumekume and another was his youngest wife, Tamaku.[254] Once again, Heni and Te Kooti were fugitives. The flight was finally from martyrdom; or, as he described it to Hira: a flight to prevent any reprisals for his death.[255] What was thought at first to be an attempt on his life had occurred the previous day at Waioeka: a Maori, said to be armed with a gun, had been discovered prowling near his tent.[256] The man was arrested, but he turned out not to be armed (except with a German sausage).[257] The episode, however, indicates Te Kooti's extreme fear of assassination.

After Porter sent the message on the evening of 27 February that he would be coming to Waioeka the next morning, he 'secretly change[d] the hour of marching'.[258] He arrived with his reinforced column of 250 armed men at 5 a.m.: but Te Kooti was gone. Wi Pere, who came with Porter, learnt that Te Kooti had left for the Waikato. There

The composition of the 'Field Force' mustered on the East Coast to stop Te Kooti. On a draft version of this list it was noted that 'Mr Carrolls Contingent' was a 'Native' force: they were paid for one day. Most of the other volunteers were paid from 24 February to about 6 March. The Ngati Porou contingent was paid at cavalry rates, as were most of the men in the European militias.

AD1 1894/950, NA

were 300–400 people gathered on the road by the pa, all Te Kooti's followers: Porter seized the lot.

Bush had earlier warned the government that, in any encounter, they would find the women placed in front as a shield — a deterrent to any assaulting troops. He also said there would be about 100 women and, therefore, if the party was met on the move it would be impossible to pass them on a single-file track.[259] Boy Biddle narrated the story of the seizure of all the people at Waioeka, including the women. This event is still remembered with pain among the Ringatu:

> At Ōpōtiki, when they jailed them here, when they put them in the stockyards there, he [Te Kooti] put the women in front. He said, 'Put the women and children in front, and then the old people, and then the fighting type of person at the back.' I think his idea was, if you put the virile ones front, there's liable to be a confrontation, and when a confrontation occurs the reaction's going to be different. Whereas the women will warm them up a bit, a man may decide to react . . . . I think this was his strategy. To stop

giving the government any weapon to use on them. 'Cos he did this on several occasions. . . . They yard them all up, and put them in the stockyard, and put the police around them, and the army, and they tried to find him amongst them. But they couldn't. He'd cut across land to Waiotahe pā here.[260]

This confrontation is also remembered in song. Te Kooti composed two haka (songs of challenge) which are dated 27 February, the day before his own arrest. They were his response to Wi Pere's insistence that he must turn back. The gloss accompanying the songs tells that Te Kooti had said that they were going to Turanga, on the invitation of Rutene Hurahura, simply for a day's gathering of pipi on 12 March. Rutene had sent word, 'The day when we will see you, Father, will be the Turn of the year, and it will be good' ('Na he ra e kite ai matou i a koe, e pā, ko te Hurihanga tau, a e pai ana').[261] What annoyance was there, therefore, in such a visit? The two haka — or, more correctly, patere (replies to jealousies) — were bantering challenges to those assembled to block the way. The second patere begins:

> Pākia pākia pākia — kia rite. I ringa i torona kei waho, mau tonu. I uma tiraha.

> Strike, strike, strike — let us be prepared. Straight-stretched arms, held below. Strike home at an angle!

The text is not a threat: the people at Waioeka were all unarmed, and their 'challenge' lay only in the way they moved, as they held one another's hands, angled down by their sides. Thus were they 'armed' only by their unity.[262] The song continues:

> Aue. Hikohiko te uira papa te whatitiri i runga i te rangi whakahekeheke ana mai i runga o Turanga ra. I aha tera. Ko te mana o te Kuini pea e awhi ana ki te tikanga e. Ka korikori te ture whakarunga i aue, i tena i tukua iho. Ka mura te ahi. Huree!

> Alas. Lightning flashes and thunder rolls above in the heavens, descending over Turanga there. What is that? Perhaps it is the mana of the Queen, upholding the truth! The law moves upwards, alas from there it is released below. The fire bursts into flames![263]

In this famous patere, Te Kooti is being ironic about the Queen's law. Moreover, he suggests, and rightly so, that the law had been unleashed against him by popular prejudice.

This song is still sung. Some changes have been wrought in it, but it retains this scepticism about the form of law which hung over Turanga in 1889. In one modified version, chanted by the Whakatohea elder Himiona Kahika in 1982, Te Kooti asks quizzically if the thunder over Turanga could be the authority of the Queen, embracing himself and the truth of the Ringatu faith, 'e awhi ana ki ahau ki te tikanga'. This version laments the occasion in even stronger words, and inquires whose fault it was that feelings had become so strident there. The song ultimately defends the ascendancy of the law as the faith's protector.[264] It therefore stems from the fundamental teachings of Te Kooti; it asks about justice; and it retains the longer view (which Te Kooti himself upheld, despite these events) of sustaining the principle of law.

But it was the law as an instrument of colonising power that followed Te Kooti to Waiotahe on the afternoon of 28 February. The police had learnt about mid-morning

Labelled 'A reminiscence of old days — Te Kooti's whare at Waioeka', this house may have been the one in which Te Kooti was staying on 27 February 1889. It was described then as 'boldly gabled', decorated with 'Maori characters' and painted in bright colours. This was perhaps the house named Taramu, built for Te Kooti alongside Tane Whirinaki which, as oral tradition tells us, he never entered. (It is not the shelter standing on the Waioeka marae shown in the photograph on p.385.) The date of this photograph is unknown.   A 12437, APL

that he was there, and as soon as the news was confirmed by their scouts they set out.[265] Inspector Samuel Goodall now carried the warrant, and he was supported by the soldiers, the militia, and the Ngati Porou contingent under Ropata — altogether about 150 armed men. With them also came Wi Pere, who had been in constant communication with Atkinson. The forces first surrounded the pa; then the police advanced. They found Te Kooti seated under a poplar tree outside a whare, where a temporary brush awning sheltered him from the sun. He was dressed in tweed trousers, a striped vest and calico print shirt, and over his shoulders he wore the plaid shawl with which he is often associated in memory. He sat cross-legged on a fine flax mat, 'eating peaches and plums'.[266] Heni and Tamaku were seated near him, along with two other women, one or both of whom were also understood to be his wives.[267] These were the circumstances in which he was arrested for violation of the peace.

The police reports are curiously silent on the arrest. The question of duplicity in the tactics they adopted is certainly raised by the satirical cartoon published in the *Evening Press* on 13 March. It is also clear that more than one disagreement occurred between Porter and Goodall. Te Kooti greeted Porter uncertainly, asking whether or not they would shake hands. Porter voiced his indifference. Te Kooti then put his hand on

Labelled 'Fugitives' from Te Kooti, this photograph shows families coming into Gisborne, 24 February 1889. It looks northwards from Kaitaratahi hill towards Te Karaka. Photograph by William F. Crawford.

WFC A₁₃₈, GM

Porter's revolver, saying '"you have a weapon, see I have none, if you want to shoot me do so"'. He opened his shirt, and dramatically exposed his breast.[268] Porter and Wi Pere then spoke with Te Kooti at length, as they sat together under the awning for over half an hour. Te Kooti reiterated to them that he was returning to the Waikato. He had also sent a note to Ropata and Porter by Reihana, whom they had seized when he brought it to them as they rode towards Waiotahe. The letter referred to the arbitrary arrests at Waioeka and the fact that the people were still held prisoner, corralled in the yards at Opotiki. Te Kooti demanded their immediate release:

> Waiotahi 28 Febry 1889
> E hoa ma, tena korua. He kupu atu tenei ki a korua me hoki korua. Wehi mo ta korua mahi kino. Nga iwi katoa me tuku nai [*sic*] e koe inaeianei [*sic*].
>   Na Te Turuki

The volunteer troops returning to Gisborne in triumph in March 1889. A brass band leads the way.
Photograph by William F. Crawford.   WFC A182, GM

Waiotahi 28 Febry 1889
Friends, greeting. This is a word of mine to you two: both go back. I am startled at
your evil work. Let all the people come to me at once.
      Te Turuki.[269]

For all of them, the shadow of the past hung heavily over the present. Later, Porter
would boast that Te Kooti had predicted to his followers some months before his arrest
that '"When Porter and I meet face to face, my end will be near — Ka mate ahau."'[270]
If Porter had to wait a while yet for the fulfilment of these words, there was no doubt
that the atmosphere crackled with the unspoken thoughts of them all.

    Te Kooti asked Wi Pere to go back to Opotiki and get Mitchelson's approval for him
to return overland to Waikato. He also agreed to travel on to Auckland from Waikato. He
told them that he had no intention of 'running away', and that they could place a guard

over him if they were afraid of such an eventuality. But he did not wish to be arrested and forcibly taken. He was, he said, already complying with the government's request by returning to Waikato. It was at this juncture that the disagreements among the police, Porter and the Ngati Porou contingent surfaced. They were, at the very least, about using force to make the arrest. But the first point which should be made is that among the six policemen who had come with Porter and Pere were two constables, Edward Law and John Cavanagh from the Whakatane police. The two had been sent by Goodall to scout that morning; it was they who had found Te Kooti resting at Waiotahe when they followed up the report as to his whereabouts, first brought to the police by a Maori woman. Te Kooti had seemed not at all surprised to see them, and indeed asked them if they had come to escort him back to Waikato. Law galloped into Opotiki to alert the force, while Cavanagh stayed behind to watch the settlement.[271] While the version in the *New Zealand Herald* stated specifically that the constables had said that they did not intend to accompany him, the *Evening Press*'s cartoon certainly suggests that Cavanagh had persuaded Te Kooti that, if he waited, the police would escort him overland to Waikato.

It also seems clear that, during the long discussion, Porter was finally persuaded that Te Kooti should be allowed to remain at Waiotahe (as he had asked) while Wi Pere communicated with the government, and that if he gained its permission Te Kooti should set out for the Waikato the next day. This is certainly how the *Auckland Star* and *New Zealand Herald*, whose reporters were present, and also the *Press*, described the situation as it developed.[272] The *Gisborne Standard* reporter, who claimed to be present, implied the same, although he was not quite so explicit.[273] While Porter himself admitted in his official report that he had been seeking to achieve 'an amicable surrender instead of a forceable arrest',[274] he presented himself as being unmoved by all the persuasion. This was because of the row that developed between Porter and Goodall over the procedures Porter was adopting.

For Goodall suddenly intervened in the discussion, and with anger. He insisted that the warrant be executed immediately. Its terms were then read aloud by Michael Gannon, the interpreter whom Porter had hastily sworn in, and 'its imperative effect' noted.[275] Gannon (husband of Keita Wyllie, Wi Pere's half-sister) then suggested to Porter that he, as a JP, had the power to do as Te Kooti requested. He could bring Te Kooti before him there and then, and remand him until the following day in the charge of a constable, as Te Kooti had asked.[276] This procedure would achieve both the objectives of enforcing the warrant, as they were required to do, and equally giving them time to seek a rational and peaceful solution.

Again Goodall intervened. He insisted that the situation was not a matter of choice. The warrant for Te Kooti's arrest had to be executed, and its 'imperative' was that Te Kooti had to be apprehended immediately. There was no one there who had the power to alter the terms of the warrant.[277] As he himself was also a JP, there would, he argued, 'be a balance' and, as he also had 'the power', the 'balance' would be in his favour.[278] Goodall thus threatened force to make the arrest. On the advice of Pere and Porter, Te Kooti now consented to go with the police to Opotiki. He said, after having listened

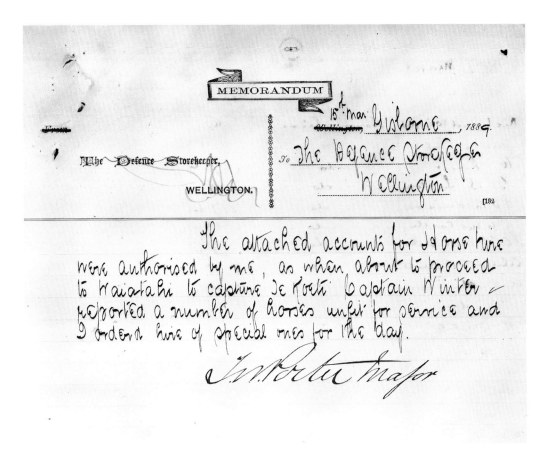

MEMORANDUM

15th Mar Gisborne, 1889

The Defence Storekeeper,
WELLINGTON.

To *The Defence Storekeeper*
Wellington

[182

The attached accounts for Horse hire
were authorised by me, as when about to proceed
to Waiatahi to capture Te Kooti Captain Winter
reported a number of horses unfit for service and
I ordered hire of special ones for the day.

J.W. Porter Major

Absurdities at the moment of imposing the authority of the law: how to get there! The total bill for the hired horses was £9 8s; about 12 were hired. AD1 1894/950, NA

closely to the terms of the warrant and the ensuing argument, '"Very well, I am going. I hope my people will not be dark."'[279]

Then a second huge row erupted. Goodall wanted to put Te Kooti in handcuffs; both Porter and Pere were determined to maintain his dignity, and Porter insisted that this was not necessary.[280] Te Kooti had consented to come with them; they would ride together into Opotiki. The troops were also to be called off.[281] Porter's retrospective account (while evading the first issue of dispute) is quite clear on this part of the disagreement: that Goodall's behaviour threatened all possibility of a peaceful arrest. Goodall is depicted by Porter as an angry and incompetent fool, in contrast with the experienced military men. Conversely, Goodall, in a later statement which greatly angered the Commissioner of Police, went so far as to claim that the government '"did not desire Te Kooti's capture and but for him he would not have been taken"'.[282] At the very least, the remark indicates that Porter and Pere attempted to find a rational and more dignified solution.

It was at this juncture that the Ngati Porou forces began to close in. They had been stationed about a quarter of a mile away at the rear of the settlement: 55 men, among

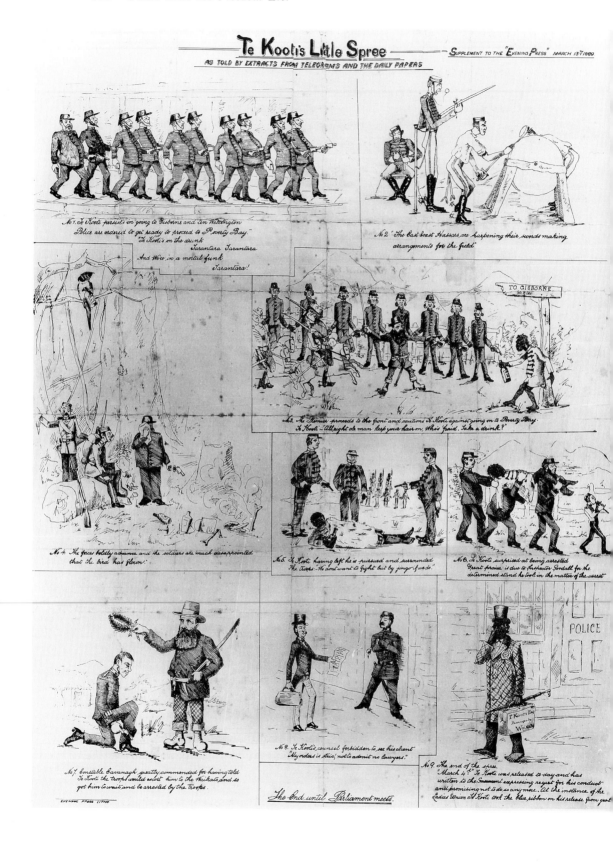

them Hapi Kiniha. Goodall was unexpectedly backed by this threatening movement. The contingent came to within 50 yards of the angry group of men. From all accounts this was an independent move on their part; but it is possible that Goodall had signalled to them.

The threat, however, was defused by the principal players in this charade of legality. Porter, Gannon and Pere all insisted that they would ride alongside Te Kooti into Opotiki. Te Kooti went into his tent to get ready, while the horses were saddled. As the party was making ready, Pere was subjected to 'much gesticulating and speechmaking' from those who were with Te Kooti:[283] undoubtedly he was seen as the Judas figure. Heni, who had been sitting beside Te Kooti, began to cry and 'make a hub-bub' but he cut her short, saying, '*Porangi koe?* "Are you mad?"'[284] Porter then ordered Ngati Porou to withdraw; Goodall immediately contested his authority to do so, panicking that he was going to be left without adequate protection.[285] Finally, Porter's will prevailed. The group rode into the town, followed by Te Kooti's wives and those who had sheltered him at Waiotahe — estimated variously as between 40 and 100 people. As they reached Opotiki they passed the stockyards, where those who had been arrested were still corralled: Porter noted their 'silent sadness . . . not a word being spoken and scarcely a movement being noticeable'.[286] Bush was waiting for the party to arrive, and he suggested that Te Kooti could stay in a hotel. Goodall refused. Te Kooti was taken to the local gaol for the night.

On the following day, 1 March, he was arraigned before Bush, acting in his official capacity as magistrate. Te Kooti was allowed no legal representation. A licensed interpreter was present but, as the *New Zealand Herald* reported, the evidence was 'not interpreted to the prisoner as it proceeded, but at its conclusion it was read over by the Magistrate in Maori, after which the prisoner was invited to cross-examine the Inspector'.[287] Te Kooti simply asked him what crimes he had committed. Richard Kemp, a settler at Waiotahe, had earlier given evidence about his fear for his family's safety. Te Kooti asked him whether he had, in fact, taken any of Kemp's stock or horses that he should be frightened, and Kemp had simply answered, 'No'. Te Kooti was given no opportunity to call any witnesses himself, although Bush would later claim that Te

Opposite: Te Kooti's Little Spree. Ironic cartoon from the *Evening Press*, 13 March 1889. No. 1 shows armed Wellington police being sent to Poverty Bay, and carries the ditty 'Te Kooti's on the drunk/ Tarantara Tarantara/And We're in a mortal funk/Tarantara!'; no. 2 shows the volunteer East Coast Hussars sharpening their swords; no. 3, the Premier, Harry Atkinson, carrying a sword, bars the way to Gisborne, while Te Kooti is presented as a drunken 'nigger' in an antiquated uniform; no. 4 shows the forces drowning their tears in rum, for the bird has flown; no. 5 shows Te Kooti, having turned back, being pursued and surrounded as he lies drinking at Waiotahe; no. 6, his arrest by Inspector Goodall; no. 7, Constable John Cavanagh receives a laurel wreath from Atkinson for having told Te Kooti he would be escorted back to the Waikato and so persuading him to wait — to be arrested; no. 8, Te Kooti's lawyer is prevented from seeing him; no. 9, the end of the spree: 4 March, Te Kooti is released from gaol in Auckland, wearing the Blue Ribbon of the Temperance movement, and carrying a suitcase addressed as 'T. Kooty Esq. Passenger to Waikato'. He is barefoot throughout. The sketch concludes 'The End until Parliament meets.' This last was a reference to an expected special Act of Parliament banning Te Kooti from the East Coast, which never eventuated. Lithograph attributed to J. S. Allan.

Kooti had said that he did not wish to. When Te Kooti lodged his appeal against the judgment given by Bush, he stated that he understood neither the evidence nor the proceedings which had been taken against him.[288]

Te Kooti was found guilty of unlawful assembly when he had ridden through Opotiki on 22 February, and elsewhere in the county. He was then bound over to 'keep the peace' for six months, on the payment of three sureties. One was for £500, which he had to find himself, and in cash. His bond 'was not good enough', Bush stated categorically.[289] The two other sureties, each for a further £500, had also to be found in cash. These sureties 'of the peace' had been demanded by Goodall on instructions from Atkinson.[290] This strategy had been planned in advance.[291] Te Kooti was sent immediately in custody to Auckland until he could raise the money. The only concession made was that Tamaku and his own interpreter, Hamiora Tuki,[292] were allowed to accompany him on the steamer. The law had entrapped Te Kooti despite the statements of good will from those who had executed it. This travesty of justice had, however, only just begun.

The people whom Porter had detained were held, under instructions from Atkinson, until the vessel taking Te Kooti to Auckland sailed early that evening. They had been kept for almost 48 hours in the stockyards. Porter's report to the Defence Department makes it clear that the danger which Te Kooti presented, in the opinion of the authorities, was the broad extent of the connections among his followers. The 400 — or more — who had been arrested[293] included representatives from 'almost every Tribe in the colony': Ngati Maniapoto, Waikato, Tuhoe, Ngati Awa, Te Arawa, Ngati Porou from Coromandel, Te Aitanga-a-Mahaki, Whakatohea and Te Whanau-a-Apanui. Porter and Bush now ordered them to disperse, and never again to 'reassemble in large bodies'.[294] As with the forced break-up of Te Whiti's pacifist community eight years earlier, it was the wide networks of Te Kooti's following which had brought the decision for confrontation at Opotiki. In Porter's eyes, the Ringatu were becoming intimidatory to other Maori, 'who were afraid to refuse hospitality'. They were, he said, fast 'becoming a formidable combination throughout the Tribes'.[295] This use of force was intended to check permanently the rapid expansion of their influence: it was the quintessential exercise of colonial authoritarianism.

Even as the law was being manipulated around them, and as a consequence of that manipulation, new stories of Te Kooti's powers grew in the Maori community. The local blacksmith at Opotiki (whom the people had visited as they prepared for the pilgrimage to Gisborne) commented, 'During the . . . month of February last, on several days between the 20th and 27th days of that month, I saw many of Te Kooti's followers. They brought horses to me to be shod, and conversed with me about Te Kooti. They said that Te Kooti was a god, and that they would do anything he told them to do. They said a bullet would not go through him; and after he was put in gaol at Opotiki they said the gaol would not hold him.'[296] Not one of these claims did Te Kooti make for himself. These stories grew because they asserted his ultimate triumph over the prejudice which had manipulated the law.

CHAPTER 13

HAPAINGA TAKU RONGO RITE RAWA I TE WHENUA
RAISE UP MY AGREEMENT OF PEACE OVER THE LAND
(FEBRUARY 1889–FEBRUARY 1893)

Ko te kupu nei na: Ka mutu te whawha o te ringa tangata ki a koe i tenei ra. Ko te whakapono ka nekehia ka nui haere.

This saying: From this day the laying hold of you by the hand of man is ended. The faith will advance and flourish.

THE WORD GIVEN TO TE KOOTI, MT EDEN GAOL, AUCKLAND, 3 MARCH 1889.[1]

Immediately after the court hearing at Opotiki, Te Kooti was bundled onto the steamer for Auckland. He went under police escort: travelling with him were all the returning naval volunteers. The voyage was not pleasant: Te Kooti, Tamaku and Hamiora Tuki were condemned to the elevated platform at the rear of the vessel, where they spent the night as the ship tossed and pitched in a wild sea. Tamaku was very ill. In the morning they were entertained (inconceivably) by 'a nigger minstrel party', formed from the volunteers.[2] As Auckland loomed in sight, Te Kooti became visibly more depressed. At North Head, a small vessel was sent out to take him directly ashore to avoid the excited crowd of onlookers waiting on the wharves. As soon as it made fast, he was brought out of the cabin and, the *Auckland Star*'s reporter wrote, 'He seemed very dejected, and leaned heavily upon a whalebone walking stick, in fact the old warrior seemed a feeble specimen of humanity to have caused all the commotion of the last few weeks.'[3]

Te Kooti was taken straight to Mount Eden gaol, while Tuki went to see Edwin Mitchelson. On the following morning, Sunday, 3 March, Mitchelson came to the gaol. He returned early the next day accompanied by James Mackay, who acted as the government's interpreter, and Tuki, who had seen Mitchelson again on the Sunday evening. Mitchelson set out the terms of an arrangement which would enable Te Kooti's early release. The required sureties would be raised from 'responsible natives' in Auckland, while Te Kooti agreed that he would not seek out a lawyer.[4] The whole deal rested on Te Kooti's understandable desire for freedom; it also connived at undermining the processes of justice. As the *Evening Post* soon recognised, the government's agents acted in this precipitate manner because they were becoming 'terribly alarmed at the impending exposure of the utterly illegal course they had adopted'.[5]

The implications of their procedure soon became apparent. On 28 February Rewi

Maniapoto had contacted the young Auckland lawyer, William Napier, in anticipation of Te Kooti's arrest. He asked Napier, who was Sir George Grey's solicitor, to act as Te Kooti's counsel. When Napier tried to visit Te Kooti on Monday morning, 4 March, he was told by the chief gaoler that Te Kooti had no wish to see him. Napier insisted that a written note be taken in informing Te Kooti that Rewi had hired Napier to obtain his discharge 'from what was an illegal imprisonment',[6] and to appeal the case to the Supreme Court. Te Kooti replied:

> To William Napier: Friend, your letter is good. But the Government has requested me not to see any lawyer, and they will release me from prison. I have consented to that. — From Te Kooti.[7]

Napier immediately replied in writing. He warned Te Kooti that the government was not to be trusted, and that his committal to gaol was unlawful. It was Rewi's wish, he said, that Te Kooti follow Napier's advice in appealing against the grounds on which he had been committed. Therefore, Napier needed to see him to get his signature for the papers necessary to set the appeal in motion. Napier concluded, 'Write to me and tell me whether you consent to see me for the above purpose. If not, I cannot set you free.'[8] At this juncture, the gaoler refused to bring a reply to Napier's letter — until a later time. He knew that Te Kooti was about to be released, and told Napier as much. The two sureties required had been raised by Mackay on Mitchelson's directive. Te Kooti later said (in his affidavit): 'I never asked or authorized any person or persons to become sureties for me'.[9]

The government was pulling the strings. The sureties were raised by two prominent Maori in Auckland: Kihirini (Kissling) Reweti, a nephew of the leading chief of Orakei, Paora Tuhaere (old Paora himself refused), and Hamiora Mangakahia. Hamiora was a major chief of Coromandel who, in the early 1860s, while staying with his father's people, had been taught at a tribal school of learning at Whareongaonga; he may well have encountered Te Kooti at that time. Like Te Kooti, Hamiora considered himself bound by the predictive teachings of old Toiroa to establish a lasting peace in the land, although he pursued this aim through the then evolving political association of the Kotahitanga under the Treaty of Waitangi.[10] Te Kooti stated categorically that he had asked neither man for the sureties. Mackay's account supports his testimony, in that Mackay admitted that it was he who had procured the bondsmen. He said it was at Te Kooti's request, but Hirini Taiwhanga MHR, who helped to negotiate the bonds, stated in Parliament that they had been raised from the two men because those requested from Rewi and Wahanui had not arrived.[11] Taiwhanga's motives were also duplicitous: he considered that, if Te Kooti were bailed out rather than being able to contest the legality of his imprisonment — Napier's intention — then his mana would be destroyed. Taiwhanga himself had initially offered to stand bail for Te Kooti in order to 'show the Te Kooti people afterwards that he had no power, and they could no longer look upon him as a god'.[12] The government also waived the requirement it itself had laid down for payment in cash, so as to expedite Te Kooti's release.[13] Mackay stated that the condition was set that Te Kooti should not return 'towards Opotiki' during the six months in which the bonds were in effect, and that Te Kooti had agreed to this in the presence of

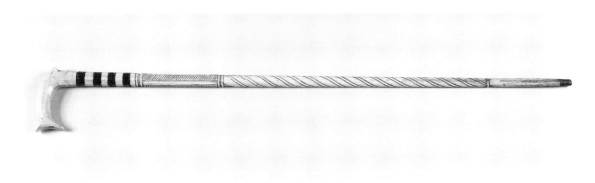

Carved whalebone walking-stick which Te Kooti gave to Edwin Mitchelson after the former's arrest. It is probably the whalebone stick noticed by the *Auckland Star* reporter. The inlaid bands are of coconut and turtle shell.   E5246, AIM

the bondsmen.[14] Hamiora, however, remembered differently. In reply to the question whether he would 'cease' to cause trouble, Te Kooti had said, '"Yes! for I was not causing trouble to the public in as much as I was accompanied by women and children."'[15]

While Napier was prevented access to Te Kooti, the women of the Ladies' Temperance Union were admitted. With Mackay again acting as interpreter and witness, Te Kooti was persuaded to take a pledge against alcohol. The 'blue ribbon' was pinned on his jacket, signed 'Na Te Kooti, March 4, 1889.'[16] It was reported that he also wrote to the government expressing his regret for his recent conduct, stating that it was 'the result of drink';[17] more certainly, he wrote that day stating that he would not, at any future time, attempt to go to Turanga again without first obtaining the government's consent.[18] The government had extracted a promise which it had no right to demand.

While in gaol on Sunday, Te Kooti attended the Anglican church service, where his presence startled the conducting minister, Reverend J. S. Hill. Hill changed his text from his intended admonition, Genesis 4:10: 'And he said, "What hast thou done? the voice of thy brother's blood crieth unto me from the ground"'; he feared that it might be seen as directed personally at Te Kooti. Hill's circumspection exposed the continuing existence of common, entrenched attitudes that Te Kooti was a murderer of innocents. The Ladies' Temperance Union was equally simplistic in its belief that alcohol was sufficient explanation for Te Kooti's resistance to the government's directives.

Te Kooti was released about midday on 4 March. He was taken by Mackay first to the home of a Maori clerk and then to the 4.15 p.m. train for Mercer. Tamaku accompanied him; Mitchelson farewelled them. The government had got Te Kooti out of town. He stayed the night in Mercer at a hotel, accompanied by Mackay. The government picked up the bill — it was, after all, a small cost compared with that of Atkinson's armed expedition. When Te Kooti passed through Hamilton on the train the next day, he was described as being in 'very low spirits' and suffering from chronic asthma.[19] Once again, he seemed to be a tired and defeated old man; once again, his appearance was deceptive.

His challenge to the government this time came through the law. Right from the beginning Napier had determined to attack the legality of Bush's findings. After Te Kooti's release, Napier pressed this issue. Te Kooti's appeal to the Supreme Court (under the Justices of the Peace Act 1882) argued that Bush had neither the authority to demand the sureties for peace nor the authority to imprison him until these had been raised. The section of the Act under which Te Kooti had been convicted allowed for the taking of sureties only if he had acted in an offensive or provocative manner, and was also deemed likely to repeat the offence.[20] None of these had been established by the court. Both the sureties and the imprisonment were, therefore, illegal. If the basis of the appeal rested on specific details of the legislation, Te Kooti himself was clear on the larger issue: '"The Government have treated me like a slave"' ('"I mahia taurekarekatia au e te Kawanatanga"').[21] He also told Wilkinson directly that he had been wrongfully arrested at Waiotahe, as he had already turned back towards Waikato, and that Bryce's promise to him — that the law would protect him — had been violated by Bush. He intended therefore to pursue the case to discover whether Bush was justified in using the law in this manner, and whether it was he, and not Te Kooti, who had broken the law.[22]

Almost as soon as Te Kooti returned to Otewa, his messengers began to travel the country to raise money for the costs of the appeal. Old Toha Rahurahu wrote early in April to warn Preece that Wairoa was beginning to raise funds. Tuki and Hoani Poururu were both reported at the same time to be travelling extensively — to Napier, to Whakatane, to Gisborne and to Wairarapa — undoubtedly for the same purpose.[23] By 25 April the money collected from the various Maori communities — Waioeka, Ruatoki, Te Whaiti, Wairoa, Waituhi and others — amounted to £207 19s.[24] On 14 June Te Kooti was able to give his formal instructions to Napier to appeal against Bush's order.[25] He also gave him two greenstone mere, which Napier would cherish.

It seems that Te Kooti hoped, as one tactic, to use the threat of his appeal to negotiate further with the government. At the end of July he told Wilkinson about the pending case; then, when Wilkinson asked him to come into Kihikihi again, Te Kooti told him that he was too unwell and, furthermore, that the matter was now out of his hands and rested entirely with Napier. But Wilkinson interpreted the letter in the light of his understanding that, if the government were to renew its efforts over Te Kooti's 'former requests' and to show him some consideration, he might not persist with the suit.[26] It becomes clear that what Te Kooti had in mind was the land grant at Ohiwa and also permission to journey to Gisborne with all his followers the following March.

The government was adamant that there would be no deal of any kind,[27] yet itself reopened the possibility later in August by approaching Te Kooti over the Tuhoe land. As a direct sequel to Te Kooti's arrest, a planned attempt to negotiate with Tuhoe for opening the Urewera to gold-prospecting had aborted: three surveyors turned back.[28] Now the government wanted Te Kooti to use his influence to dissuade Tuhoe from their opposition. Wilkinson broached the matter, and on 28 August Te Kooti wrote to him to say that he had contacted the Tuhoe chiefs, but as yet had had no reply.[29] On 5 September he made his own terms clear: although he had still not heard from Tuhoe, his reply to Mitchelson's request that he give up the legal proceedings was this:

Hamiora Mangakahia. Hamiora had connections with the Ringatu communities at Wharekawa, as well as with old Toiroa of Nukutaurua.

C5093, DAVIS COLLECTION, AIM

Me tuku ahau ki Turanga me aku hoa haere ano aha koa kotahi 100 nuku atu ranei wahine taane me whakaae e ia tena a te Maehe e haere ake nei i te 1890.

Allow me to go to Turanga, accompanied by 100 or more of my followers, male and female, in March 1890.[30]

That there were other terms also is made clear by Wi Pere's urgent telegram of 27 September, the day before Te Kooti recorded his affidavit in front of the Supreme Court solicitor in Auckland. Wi Pere, who was also in Auckland, said that he had asked Te Kooti to drop the case, but that Napier would not consent. To Mitchelson he wired, 'Friend, do you agree to Te Kooti taking up his residence at Ohiwa. If this agreed to Te Kooti will probably drop his case.' But again the government chose not to deal — at least not on those terms.[31] The following day Te Kooti made his lengthy, sworn affidavit, describing the circumstances of his intended visit to Te Karaka and Pa-o-Kahu, his birthplace in Gisborne, together with his account of the incomprehensible lower court hearing to which he had been subjected. He had set the tortuous processes of law in motion, although they would not end in his triumph.

The case was brought to the Supreme Court in Auckland on 4 December, but it was adjourned on technical grounds, a device adopted by the Crown's solicitor to gain time after Napier refused to desist from the case.[32] The hearing finally took place on 19 February 1890, by which time the Crown had gathered together many testimonies on its behalf. They included some of Te Kooti's old opponents from Turanga, such as George Goldsmith, Hapi Kiniha and Maria Morris, who described again the events at Poverty Bay in November 1868. The Crown even persuaded one of the former whakarau, Pera Kawenga,[33] to testify that Te Warihi was thrown overboard on Te Kooti's orders, even though all these acts were covered by the pardon, as Bryce had recently reminded the Native Minister.[34] These testimonies were intended to establish the 'state of terror' existing in the community, which Te Kooti's visit would have inflamed.[35] But Mr Justice Conolly would have none of it.

In a carefully reasoned judgment, Conolly stated that there had been no legal grounds for demanding sureties from Te Kooti. Te Kooti was entitled to go to Gisborne: 'No one had a right to stop him.' He had set out with only a small group from Kihikihi, including his 'four' wives and a number of children, but as the party travelled it grew enormously in size. In Conolly's view it had been ultimately a 'wise measure' to turn this large party back, even though it was unarmed. But the grounds of Te Kooti's commitment to gaol were not lawful. For 'it is clear that Te Kooti never did assemble to disturb the public peace to the terror and alarm of her Majesty's subjects; but they chose to be alarmed. . . . I am bound to say that . . . neither Te Kooti nor his followers did anything to justify that terror and alarm.' There was no single instance of 'misconduct' by any of those who travelled with Te Kooti; nor was there evidence of any unlawful act committed by Te Kooti, nor of any intention on his part to commit a breach of the peace. Consequently, the appeal was upheld, because there was no ground for the taking of sureties and no ground for Te Kooti's imprisonment. 'The order was bad'.[36]

Napier immediately indicated his intention to pursue the matter and to bring a charge of wrongful imprisonment against the government, and to seek substantial damages. It was therefore inevitable that the Crown would bring a counter-appeal against Conolly's decision. Notice was served on 14 March, and the hearing took place in Wellington on 12–13 May 1890. The judgment, postponed from 16 June, was finally given in July. There were questions at the time whether it was delayed because of ministerial pressure on the Bench for a favourable decision.[37] More certain is that the judges upheld the Crown's appeal and overturned Conolly's decision. Equally certain, their judgment was the result of the law flinching when confronted by hysteria and prejudice.

The Crown's case rested entirely on the affidavits it had. The appellate hearing was held before a full Bench of three justices. Christopher Richmond, elder brother of James, articulated the judgment, which was based on the view that the settlers' responses to Te Kooti's visit were not unfounded: Te Kooti's acts, he said, 'have left behind them amongst many of the European inhabitants and their Native allies bitter hatred and absolute distrust. The belief in his supernatural power gives him complete ascendancy over his followers, and makes him doubly dangerous. At the same time he is intemperate in his habits — a Maori prophet and a drunken one to boot.'[38] It therefore followed that, although nothing that Te Kooti or those who journeyed with him had done was unlawful, their 'assemblage' had generated fear 'on reasonable grounds'.[39] All three judges also considered that Bush was within his authority in demanding the sureties,

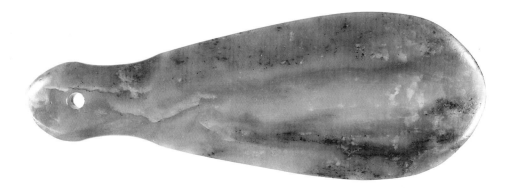

One of the two greenstone mere given to William Napier by Te Kooti. It is a relatively 'modern' mere, perhaps made for the presentation. It was donated to the Auckland Museum by the Napier family in 1928.

E1460, AIM

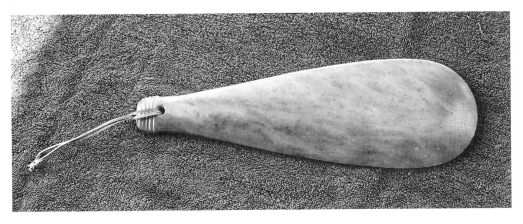

The other mere which Te Kooti gave Napier. It is slightly different, having a short carved handle. This mere is owned by David Napier, William's grandson. Photograph by Judith Binney.

for his powers rested in common law and not in the specific provisions of the Act under which Te Kooti had been charged. They rejected Napier's argument that Bush's authority as a justice of the peace had been limited and defined by the 1882 Act. Rather, it rested in the broader powers vested in the justices of the peace, which existed prior to the Act and which it had not abrogated.

The legal judgment as to the base of Bush's authority is not in question. What is at issue is whether the judgment of the case was 'on its merits', as Richmond expressed it.[40] Te Kooti was condemned because of the public state of mind; that state of mind was, very largely, fed on prejudice and misinformation. Certainly, the pilgrimage had swollen hugely in its numbers by the time it reached Omarumutu, but the police, who in their affidavits for the Crown speculated on hidden arms, knew at the time that there were none. The only piece of evidence that could actually be produced was a witness's statement that Te Whiu was carrying a mere. He tucked it back under his coat when Te Makarini warned him, '"The tongue of your *mere* is sticking out."'[41] But the justices were prepared to accept there was some reason for the police speculation, even though Napier stated that the police had detained about 70 of the party riding through Opotiki and searched their baggage in vain.[42] Even Atkinson had conceded this point in Parliament: he acknowledged the 'packages' with 'a suspicious appearance' had been innocent, and the travellers had borne no arms.[43] But the judges were prepared to state that there was good reason for the suspicion, because they believed, as Justice Williams put it, Te Kooti was 'returning in triumph in the guise of an inspired prophet to the scene of his bloody exploits, accompanied by those who assisted him in the massacre'.[44] Justice Denniston merely echoed his colleagues when he stated that the fear was understandably inspired in the minds of 'reasonable' people; and 'that the irruption of this drunken fanatic, with the instincts of a savage, and the prestige of a prophet' was 'in itself a menace to the peace'.[45] These are the opinions which underlay the legal judgments, and they are neither considered nor impartial.

Te Kooti's statement that he was going to Pa-o-Kahu, as well as Te Karaka, indicates that he intended to enter Gisborne itself (despite his lawyer's remarks to the contrary). He was indeed going home. His aim was, he said, 'to carry the Gospel there, to hasten the end of the troubles' ('ki te kawe i te Rongopai ki reira ki awe te mutu atu o nga kino').[46] The judges determined, however, that even if this was a journey of peaceful intent its feared effect made it into an unlawful assembly. This legal judgment was not unique,[47] although it was unjust in its premises, which legitimised and empowered the hysteria. There was no attempt to prosecute the armed vigilance committee, although they admitted at the time that they were an 'unlawful assembly'. The readiness to endorse the local hysteria indicates that there was another substantive issue at stake: that Te Kooti's pilgrimage would stop the process of land transfer to Europeans, then under way in the district. In this process Porter, for one, as the government land purchase officer, was playing a large part, as well as some of the Maori who spoke against Te Kooti's return. To these men Te Kooti indeed 'threatened to come down like an elderly wolf on the fold'.[48] But the burden of unlawfulness was borne only by the pilgrims, and Te Kooti was judged, finally, because he was labelled 'a Maori prophet and a drunken one to boot'. The very phraseology of the rulings of the Court of Appeal in 1890 reveals its bias.

For Te Kooti, working through the law had proved a harsh experience. He considered taking the appeal to the Privy Council.[49] But in the end, for him, the issue that mattered was resolved. As he said to his people, when they arrived at Otewa from Opotiki on 11 March 1889 to find him waiting:

> Na kua mutu te whawha o te ringa tangata ki au i tenei ra, mutu rawa. Kua tae hoki ahau ki te mate, a kua hoki mai nei ano i te mate. A, heoi ano whawhatanga o te ringa ki au.

> Now man's laying hold of me has ceased from this day, ceased altogether. I have come to death, and I have returned again from death. And there will be no more laying of hands on me.[50]

This promise, or kupu, was the product of a vision in Mount Eden gaol, brought, he said, by the 'spirit' ('wairua'). From this conviction sprang his final reorganisation of the faith. God's unconditional assurance to him had been renewed during this time of his second imprisonment. On 3 March the spirit told him that, 'The faith will increase, it will advance' ('Te whakapono ka piki, ka nekehia').[51] The people of the sword, who long ago had 'found grace in the wilderness', were bound to God, and he to them: these were the scriptural meanings of the hidden words which accompanied the kupu, 'Kei One Whirita'. 'Kei' was a reference to Jeremiah 31:2, 'One' to II Samuel 7:24, and 'Whirita' to Malachi 2:17. Te Kooti himself wrote down the interpretations.[52] The texts and the words in 'te reo ke' asserted the binding promise given to Israel, renewed again in this time of crisis.

Te Kooti had been battered by the rituals of the European legal system; now he continued with his efforts to strengthen the faith so that it would endure any further trials he might undergo. We have already seen that Te Kooti initiated some important changes after he left Te Kuiti in 1883. One was the Twelfths, introduced as a day of significance (along with the first of the month) on 28 December 1885. The Twelfths were, it is stated, intended 'for the manifestation of pain' ('ma nga putanga mamae mai').[53] The forms and procedures for this occasion were chosen by the committee of the church, and approved by Te Kooti on 5 March 1888. By then the Twelfths had replaced the first (representing the new moon) as the most significant day in the month. The importance of the Twelfths was both scriptural and historical, springing from key events in Te Kooti's life. The Twelfths also alluded to another cosmology.

At this juncture it must be reiterated that Te Kooti obscured many of his intentions, creating a necessary religious mystery. Many of the references within his teachings will be grasped only by the tohunga of the living faith, and it is not this book's purpose to explore that aspect. But the faith is itself historically constituted, and some of those elements may be touched upon. It is probable that the origins of the Twelfths lay in the past on Rekohu (Wharekauri). The Moriori had a unique calendrical cycle of 12 years, each possessing 12 months. This calendar was recorded by several European observers, including Alexander Shand, who was on the island at the time of Te Kooti's exile. Shand stated that the origin of the concept was a sacred tree called arapuhi, which once grew near Waitangi on Wharekauri, and which had a particular formation of 12 branches giving rise to a cycle of twelve.[54] Te Kooti certainly adopted this image of the beautiful tree with 12 branches; it was described in a visionary statement pronounced in 1880,[55] which will be discussed shortly. In the waiata he sang concerning the aborted journey to Te Karaka in 1889, he said that he had been invited for 12 March, the turning of the season or the year ('Ko te Hurihanga tau').[56] Similarly, in December 1887, he had written to Tiopira to tell him the sayings of the year: one on the 12th, one on the 16th: 'Nga kupu o te tau 12 tetahi te 16 tetahi'.[57] Such remarks suggest an independent calendar, based on the Twelfths as markers of the beginning of the month, and also the year. The Twelfths established another system of structuring and interpreting time, with which Te Kooti had always been fascinated; he was consciously reshaping Christianised time and the rhythms of its calendar to a cycle he had encountered on Wharekauri. This interpretation is supported from other sources. In a list of some of the practices of the Ringatu, Paora Delamere included the statement that the 12th was 'the beginning of the months. Numbers 28:11, 10:10' ('Ko te 12 . . . timatanga o nga marama. Tau 28:11, 10:10').[58] He also said that the Twelfths, or the appearance of the new moon, marked the beginning of all the months. He cited, as one of the several scriptural texts in support of the concept, Revelation 22:2, which refers to the Tree of Life with its 12 fruits.[59] This may well be the connection which Te Kooti found with the Wharekauri tradition of the sacred tree with 12 branches. Furthermore, Delamere began the list of the months of the year with April and concluded with March, and gave further scriptural references to explain this framework. March he equated with Adar, or the 12th month of the Old Testament lunar-based calendar.[60]

Thus it seems that Te Kooti introduced a new chronology for the Ringatu year, based on a combination of the Old Testament and the cycle of the Twelfths. The First of January, as the celebration of the passover, was understood to be, in one sense, the celebration of the month of Abib (following Exodus 13:4 and Deuteronomy 16:1), but Abib was also equated with April, the first month.[61] This new chronology for the year probably never became fully established. January still marked, in the orthodox manner, the 'turning' of the year, and 1 July the mid-point, the start of the seventh month. March was never traditionally the turn of the cyclic year for Moriori or Maori: both conceived of the year as beginning in early June — for Moriori with the pre-dawn rising of the bright star Rigel (Puanga) or, among most Maori tribes, by the rising of its rival, the constellation Pleiades (Matariki), in the eastern sky. This Polynesian calendar was confirmed by the huamata and the pure, the rites of planting and harvesting, which continued within the Ringatu church with new, evolved meanings attached to them. Three systems of reading time thus seem to have co-existed within the faith, including this underlying Polynesian stratum.

The name 'Ringatu', the 'Upraised Hand', for the faith first came into usage in the late 1880s. The earliest reference found to this as the commonly accepted name is February 1887, when the religion was being discussed at Pakirikiri. It seems to have been derived from the new instructions given by Te Kooti at Otewa on 19 July 1886, when the earth regenerated out of the waste created by the eruption of Tarawera. The fertile seed-bed was called 'the "new soil of God"' ('te "oneone hou a te Ariki"'), and in gratitude Te Kooti instructed the tohunga of the faith, and others of importance, to stretch forth both their hands to glorify the name of God in all their services. Matiu Paeroa was sent forth to demonstrate the practice, and it was said then that the custom ('ritenga') belonged uniquely to the church. Hamiora Aparoa's account of this new practice stated explicitly that the tohunga were to hold up both hands ('ara, te tu ake o nga ringaringa e rua').[62] In another account, also derived from Hamiora, the practice was explained:

> Te Tu o nga Ringa:
> Hurae 19 1886. Whakaarorangi: Ko te rā tenei i whakahaua ai e Matiu nga Tohunga kia tu nga ringa e rua: a kotahi ano ringa o te Haahi.

> The Raising of the Hands:
> July 19 1886. Whakaarorangi [Otewa]: This was the day when Matiu directed the Tohunga to hold up two hands: up until that time the Church used just one hand.[63]

The seal of the Ringatu Church, with the upraised hands. This seal was devised by the secretary Robert Biddle in 1926. In the centre is the bible: the Old Testament and the New. Around the open book are the words, 'Te Ture a te Atua me te Whakapono o Ihu' ('The Law of God and the Truth of Jesus'). Below, left, is the reference to the origin of the faith at Wharekauri in 1867; on the right is the reference to Te Wainui, the land given by the government to the trustees of the Ringatu Church, and the date of the seal, '26'. The eagle in the centre is a reference to Deuteronomy 32:11–12, where the eagle is compared to God, who protects and leads his children. By permission of Sir Monita Delamere.

Te Pukapuka o Nga Kawenata e Waru a Te Atua me Nga Karakia Katoa a Te Haahi Ringatu

The practice of the congregation's raising one hand had begun at the time of the landing at Whareongaonga, when Te Kooti told the whakarau to cease to kneel before their God and instead each to raise their hand. Or, as Ned Brown put it simply, 'He said to his people, 'Look, when we pay homage to God, let us not kneel. 'Cause the sand is wet, and the water — Let us pay homage to God with our hands upraised. And that's why it's called the Ringatū.'[64] Hamiora's textual reference of explanation in 1886 was to Ezra's faith (in Nehemiah 8:6), where the people responded by 'lifting up their hands'. Such hand-raising was, at least in its origins, a form of oath-taking as well as an act of prayer, and it had many scriptural precedents. The additional practice developed from 1886 was that, at the end of prayers, the tohunga raised up both hands, as depicted on the Ringatu seal, or, alternatively, brought them together in the form of 'the apex sign',[65] while the members of the congregation continued to raise their right hands in glorification of God. These gestures have been sustained by the faith into modern times. This decision of 1886 codified the practice begun at Whareongaonga 18 years earlier,[66] thus showing how the formalised faith evolved out of the historical events upon which it is based.

The celebration of the huamata and pure rites, the planting of the seeds and lifting of the first fruits, which had begun in 1879, was to remain integral to the faith. Te Kooti adopted the European calendar dates of 1 June and 1 November (or, variously, according to the region and its climate, 1 December) for their celebration, but, as two of the four pillars of the Ringatu year, these rites undoubtedly have their roots in the Maori cosmology. The planting of the sacred garden (mara tapu) on 1 June marked the beginning of the New Year with the pre-dawn heliacal rising of the Matariki, whose significance as the bright stars of fruitfulness was acknowledged among Tuhoe, Waikato and most East Coast peoples. The cycle of ripening or fructifying was completed at the taking of the first fruits in November or December, when the Matariki reappeared in the evening sky. This cycle of planting and harvesting is the traditional ceremonial cycle of Maori agriculture, whereby a small garden was set apart 'for the god', Rongo, and each person in the community contributed seeds for the special basket of the tohunga.[67] The planting of the land was accompanied by the 'planting' of the sea;[68] and the early summer rites opened the rivers and the sea for fishing, on the East Coast by the taking of the first kahawai of the season. But the meaning of these important ceremonies was to be transformed.

Now, the garden was set apart for God. Ultimately, the seed became the symbol of Christ, and of the resurrection. Out of the old seed came the new plant, as Paora Delamere's daughter, herself a Ringatu tohunga, has explained:

> They had to keep last year's seed in with the new seed, as well as keep seeds from those that went out to the sea. That's God's, to reach all parts of the world. In that garden they had to make certain that there were old seeds *and* the new seeds, and the inter-mingling of that growth. It is symbolic of society's growth, as well as the growth of a people, and the type of Christ — that new crop. He lived again after the Crucifixion. All that is in it, in that teaching, which he [Paora Delamere] was properly taught by his father [Te Kohi].[69]

Thus the lifting of the tapu on the sacred garden at the time of the first fruits, or the ripening of the year, came to symbolise the resurrection of Christ, as the modern Ringatu prayer-book clearly states.[70] This particular interpretation evolved from within the faith, and it probably developed during the last years of Te Kooti's teachings, at least in some regions.

From 1889, if not before, Te Kooti encouraged each 'Church' ('Haahi') of the grow-ing faith to follow its own particular forms of expression. When he farewelled Te Arawa at Otewa on 17 March 1889, telling them to return to their own places after the aborted pilgrimage, he told them to go home and create a new prosperity for the orphaned, the widowed and the poor. In particular he added:

> Kia pai te whakahaere kia ngawari nga Tikanga. Ko nga Tikanga o mua me whakarere atu. Ko tenei, kia ngohengohe nga Tikanga, kia pai te whakahaere i a taua Tamariki no te mea ko taua o ratau matua, no te mea kua mutu era Tikanga me era whakahaere. He timatanga tenei. Kia ngawari nga whakahaere inaianei.
>
> Organise well, and let the Rules be lenient. Give up the Rules of old. And let the Rules be easy. Direct our Children well, because we are their parents, and because those [old] Customs and methods have ended. This is a beginning. Let the organising be lenient now.[71]

Thus the faith was changing, evolving away from the strict laws and rules derived from the Old Testament, deemed appropriate in earlier days. The days of sacrifice, the times of Isaac and Moses, had been maintained particularly by the koha, the offerings of burnt coins in a sacred fire, which was a regular practice. 'Going to the fire' was among the most holy acts of the faith, and the sacrifice made there was understood to signify the offering of the land to God.[72] Now Te Kooti was attempting to take the people gradually into new and 'gentler' teachings. But he also indicated that it was up to each community to create its appropriate rules and practices.

As early as 1878, when Te Kooti was still living at Te Kuiti, he started to foretell the One who would come after him. There is no doubt that most of his followers understood his statements to refer to a real person. Some still do: 'In my mind, he's a real man, like you and I — now, to come, some time.'[73] The purpose of Te Kooti's journeys through the land after his pardon has also been explained as his search for Jeremiah, for him who could carry on his word.[74] In 1983, John Ihe, when explaining Te Kooti's prophecies about his successor, linked the evolution taking place within the faith with these predictions:

> When old Te Kooti [just about] died, he stand up and he told our people — everybody thinking what they are going to do when he passed away, nobody to — And Te Kooti called out, 'Don't worry. Everything's all right. The next one who is coming out, that's the One.'
>
> He should have finished everything. He wanted to cut the tapu out, and everything. Te Kooti. Well, he didn't finish that. . . .
>
> Oh, we was tapu before, when Te Kooti was on. Oh, we can't go to bed without diving in the cold water! Well, he wanted to cut all that off. For if you keep those tapus, and you make a little bit of a mistake — oh, die! And that's why Rua [who claimed to be Te Kooti's successor] don't like those [tapus]. That's why he went right round New Zealand to all those places, all those things there, and they're pointing out where it is, the koha. See, the Maoris make a fire and put money in there. If you go on that, where the fire has been — 'cos you don't know if it was there, just walk around — and you're finished [dead]! He [Te Kooti] wanted to cut all that out, but he couldn't do it. So when he passed away, and that One [Rua] come out, first thing he did was those tapus. Throw all that out.[75]

Te Kooti began a new series of utterances about his successor on 1 July 1878 at Te Kuiti. This was the beginning of the now well-known sequence of statements about the advent of two stars. In the first prediction, he referred only to the one large star in the east, which would bring enlightenment for the whole island. This particular kupu was understood to refer to two earlier predictions of 1868 and 1869, in which Te Kooti had looked to his successor; they have already been quoted.[76] The second saying of the new sequence was dated 25 March 1879. This text is taken from Hamiora's manuscripts:

> Whakarongo mai koutou ko te kupu tenei kua rite ke te *tangata* mo tatau, mo tenei motu i tenei ra ano. Ko te takiwa anake e tae mai ai ia kei te toe mai.
>
> Ki te puta mai taua Tangata he tohu ano tona e kore hoki e ngaro ki te pai te Kaihanga, kia kite ahau i a ia, ka kite ano ahau i a ia. Ahakoa toru aku waewae ka kite ano ahau, a tae atu ranei ki te ono oku waewae ka kite ano ahau i a ia, a ka tae ano ahau ki tona aroaro.
>
> A ki te tae ahau ki tona aroaro kia kite i a ia, ka koropiko ahau ki tona aroaro. Ko reira koutou mohio ai, O, ko to tatau Tangata tenei i whakaatutia ara i mua, a ka whakae koutou.
>
> Ki te pai ano hoki te Kaihanga kia kite ahau i a ia, a ka tae ahau ki tona taha ka tuohu

ahau i tona aroaro. No te mea he nui ake tana kaha, me tona mana i ahau, a ka takoto
ahau ki ona waewae a koia hei whakahaere tikanga mo tatau, me nga whenua hoki.

Listen to me. This is the saying. The *person* for us has already been arranged, for this
land, and on this day. Only the region in which he will arrive remains [to be seen].

When that Person comes he will have a sign, he will not be hidden. If it pleases the
Creator that I see him, then I shall see him. Although I have three feet I shall still see, or
even if I have six feet I shall still see him, and I shall come before his face.

And when I come into his presence to see him, I shall kneel before him. Thus you
will know — oh, this is the Person revealed to us in the past, and you will consent.

And if it pleases the Creator that I see him, then when I reach his side I shall bow
my head in his presence, for his strength and power will be greater than mine, and I
shall lie at his feet. He will be the one to organise the way for us, and for the lands
also.[77]

He said that the One who would appear could be Maori or Pakeha; he could even be a
grandchild of the Queen. Whichever, whoever, it would be as the Creator intended. His
words stressed love, unity and tolerance. Te Kooti concluded: 'The way for us will be
traced out, even for our descendants, and ever after' ('Te tikanga mo tatau, e whakataki
haere tae noa ki o tatau uri, a ake ake').[78] This vision can be understood in different
ways; and in these days of seeking a renewed Maori autonomy some will find it surprising. The prediction also implied that the successor would appear in Te Kooti's lifetime,
even if he was old and hobbling with a stick (three feet) or being carried on horseback
(six feet). The words also made it clear that Te Kooti did not see himself either as God
or as the Messiah.

The prediction which followed (in this sequence) was dated 10 August 1880, and it
too was uttered at Te Kuiti. Now Te Kooti mentioned two stars. He said that they had
been standing there all the time, but were now coming into conflict. The star in the east
was in the same position as it had always been, but a new star ('he whetu hou') in the
west, where the sun set, was stronger than it had been previously.

Engari ko te whetu i te Rawhiti nei kaore ano i ta matemate noa tona tū te totoro ona
hihi me te kaha tonu tona kororia.

No nga ahiahi o mua atu ra ka timata mai taku kite i taua whetu hou nei, me ona hihi
ano. . . . Kaati toku kitenga atu ano i taua whetu hou nei (*Rato*) tae tonu mai te mahara
ki ahau, O, kua tautohe enei whetu e rua. . . . Kati ko te Tikanga tenei o te whetu *hou*
nei (*Rato*) he uaua he kino kei roto.

But the star in the East had not diminished at all in its position, in the blazing of its
rays and the continuing intensity of its glory.

In the evenings before that I began to see that new star and its rays also. . . . Then,
when I looked out at that new star (*West*) the thought suddenly came to me, oh, these
two stars are contending with each other. . . . And this is the Meaning of the *new* star
(West), that there is difficulty and trouble within it.[79]

The star in the west, in this text, was the sign of evil. Thus Waioeka Brown, who was
considered a very knowledgeable old lady in Poverty Bay, a granddaughter of Hetariki
Te Oiikau, and who herself had lived with Te Kooti, 'always maintained that nothing

good comes from the west.'[89] Should the person (or idea) for whom the western star stood ultimately triumph, it would not save humankind; instead, evil would prevail. The island too would be overcome with evil. The text urged the people to remember their Creator in gratitude for this revelation, and to strive to ensure that the star in the east would be the one to which they consented. Thus the prediction warned and cajoled: the choice lay with the people.

Te Kooti expanded these sayings five years later, at Katikati. Here he made his first pronouncement (in this sequence) since his pardon, and he spoke just before he journeyed to the tangi of Rena Morgan, wife of the old chief of Te Aroha, on 26 June 1885.[81] For the first time, he defined the region from which his successor would appear.

> Whakarongo mai i whai kupu ake ai ahau ki a tatau i tenei waahi. . . . Ko nga whetu e rua nei kei te tu tonu raua. To te Rawhiti me to te Ratoo. E rua raua kai te tu katoa i naianei mai o mua 1880 e haere nei.
>
> Kati ko te kupu tenei: Ko te tangata mo tatau kai te Rawhiti. Timata i nga [*sic*] i Nga Kuri-a-Wharei ki Tikirau ka mutu kai kona te tangata mo tatau, mo te motu nei kai taua takiwa na.

> Listen to me when I speak to us all in this place. . . . These two stars are still standing, that of the East and that of the West. The two are still standing as they were, from before 1880.
>
> Well, this is the saying: The person for us will be in the East. Starting from Nga Kuri-a-Wharei and ending at Tikirau, there, in that region, will be the person for us, for this land.[82]

He went on to explain why it had taken so long, why their generation was still waiting for deliverance. The problems lay in the deeds of men — in the conduct of the chiefs, and, he added, in the conduct of the people. The conflict between the two stars remained unresolved. He urged them to return their support to the star in the east (implying a developing rivalry of faiths, probably at this time with reference to Te Whiti at Parihaka). The boundaries he had outlined were, on the west, the point of land on the coast near Katikati (thus near where the words were spoken), which now marked the western edge of the confiscated lands in the Bay of Plenty, and the hill Tikirau, on the eastern slope of Whangaparaoa (Cape Runaway). The two traditionally defined the coastal boundaries of the Mataatua canoe tribes.

These were his last words concerning his successor until he came to the Ohiwa harbour in 1892. There, on Hokianga island, which he had made a place of shelter, he delivered his penultimate prediction. This sequence will be concluded (for the moment) with this statement, dated 1 July 1892. The source is, as before, a transcript from Hamiora's manuscripts:

> 1. Tuori, 2. Waari, 3. Eeta.
> Kotahi kapua nui kei te rangi tona kororia mau tonu.
> *Whakarite.* 1. A ka puta mai he reo i te kapua e mea ana: Ko taku Tama tenei i aroha ai whakarongo ki a ia. Mark 9:7, M[atiu] 17:5. Ruka 9:34, 35.
> 2. He Atua tohu hoki a Ihowa tou Atua e kore ia e whakarere i a koe, e kore ano hoki e whakangaro i a koe a muri nei. He raruraru kei te hawhe o tenei tau. Tiu 4:31.

3. He whiu kai te haere.

1. Tuori, 2. Waari, 3. Eeta.
There is one great cloud in the sky, its glory is constant.
Parallel [saying]. 1. And a voice came out of the cloud saying: This is my beloved Son, hear him. Mark 9:7. Matthew 17:5. Luke 9:34, 35.
2. For the Lord thy God Jehovah is a merciful God; he will not forsake thee, neither destroy thee hereafter. There will be trouble for half of this year. Deuteronomy 4:31.
3. Punishment is coming.[83]

Thus he predicted the coming of the Messiah in the words of the New Testament evangelists, Matthew, Mark and Luke. He also linked those predictions with the promise of Deuteronomy, that God would not forget the covenant 'which he sware unto them'. And he also warned, with equal orthodoxy, of forthcoming punishment.

The Ringatu tohunga Boy Biddle has expanded on this prediction in a story which he has repeated to several inquirers, because it is of crucial importance. He tells how Te Kooti reminded his followers of an earlier prediction he had made in the Waikato in 1880, concerning a beautiful tree which grew in the Whangaehu valley. The tree 'spoke' with a soft appealing voice, and all who heard it flocked to it. It had 12 branches and six leaves to each branch.[84] The only thing he could think to compare it with in its beauty was 'a well-kept Pākehā garden, full of different kinds of flowers'. But now, he said,

> 'Do you remember me telling you about that beautiful tree I saw in the vision in the Whangaehu valley? Well, I saw a better vision here.' He said, 'It was a cloud.' It was so beautiful and it was above them. And after he looked at it for a bit, the same thing happened. A voice came out of the cloud and it said, 'This is my Son in whom I am much pleased. Listen to him.'[85]

The oral narrative, which ties this story directly to the Ra of July 1892 on Hokianga island, is understood as rejecting the tree in the west, which had once seemed so beautiful.

With these predictions, Te Kooti had taken the children of Israel into the days of the New Testament. As Boy Biddle commented, the parallels of the Maori situation with the Old Testament saga are obvious enough, for they, like the Israelites, 'were deprived of their land and also of their freedom. But the part that startles most people is Te Kooti's strong pull towards the New Testament.'[86] The written texts recorded by Hamiora certainly indicate an evolution in the faith, which Te Kooti was directing. The 'flexibility' he emphasised in his advice to Te Arawa in 1889 was a consistent element in his later teachings: 'kia ngawari' or 'hei ko te ngawari'. The meaning was: do not be tied by the rituals of the past;[87] rather, enter into the new and 'gentler' faith. The underlying emphasis in the word 'ngāwari', as John Ruru said explicitly, was to leave behind the days of the Old Testament and the harsh laws of the time of Moses. It was a direction into the doctrines of the New Testament, with their emphasis not on requital but rather on repentance and love. Hence Te Kooti's instructions to the people of Turanga to build the three houses named Ngawari, Aroha and Rongopai.[88]

Te Kooti also initiated the organisational structures which would enable the faith to survive after his death. On 27 January 1888 a committee, Te Roopu, was begun under his direction at Otewa. Its purpose was to establish the regulations and services for the sacred days. It confirmed as the four important pillars of the year 1 January, 1 July and the two days for planting and gathering the first fruits. The Twelfths were also formally established. They were often referred to at this time as the Po Takoto, or the night of preparation for the future, because they began with the night of fasting on the 11th, thus maintaining the lunar day, sunset to sunset, in accordance with both Maori and Old Testament practice. The committee deleted some prayers and arranged the prayer sequence for the Saturday sabbath. It was decreed that 'cooking food be abandoned' ('Ka whakarerea nga taonga kai') and that the prayers started ('i timatatia ai') in daylight, at three in the afternoon.[89] The people were to be called onto the marae by the slow ringing of the bell, rather than by a karanga (call by a person); this remains a Ringatu practice (although there is a suggestion in the 1888 text that the use of the bell might cease).[90] Then the house and its congregation were closed ('kati'), and the service took place, the people being in a state of holiness. Thus the order of the liturgy was developed by a committee, and this helped the institutionalisation of the faith.

A sequence of prayers unique to the Ringatu was established for all the services by this same committee. At the end of each service, whatever the occasion or purpose, there are always four prayers (inoi) whose order is invariable. They reinforce the fundamental teachings established by Te Kooti. The first of the final four is the inoi 'Tereina Whita', which always precedes the Lord's Prayer. Its name is taken from 'te reo ke', Te Kooti's secret language. 'Tereina' first appeared in his notebook of 1869–70, where he glossed it as the revelation given to Adam concerning the breath of life.[91] The kupu is also glossed in the Ringatu lists as referring to God's promise to Adam that the children of the primal pair would increase, but in the end should return to dust.[92] Thus it is the statement of the human predicament. The tohunga Wi Tarei of Te Teko explained that the prayer 'Tereina Whita' indicated a transition away from the holiness of the service. This prayer begins the movement from the tapu of the service back into ordinary life; Tarei compared it to drawing a curtain between two worlds. The prayer, in essence, commences the movement from the state of tapu to the state of noa; that is why, he said, 'it is never left out of the service, never'.[93] As the house and its congregation were closed at the beginning of the service, so the reopening rites allowed the flow of tapu to be reversed and the people to re-enter the unrestricted state of noa and 'te ao turoa', the wide world.

The prayer also appeals to God, 'let your right hand be near to save us' ('kia tata mai tou ringa matau ki te whakaora i a matou').[94] Thus it suggests that the gesture of raising the right hand by the congregation to glorify the Creator is reciprocal. 'Tereina Whita' is followed by a shortened version of the Lord's Prayer, and then by another important prayer, the 'Pōkaikaha'. This is the prayer for deliverance from confusion, doubt and sorrow: it asks God to listen to the people, 'lest you destroy us who sorrow here' ('kei whakangaro atu koe i a matou e tangi atu nei'). The final prayer, 'Whakatuwhera', opens the house and the people: it therefore asks God to open the doors of righteousness and faith and enlightenment and strength. This prayer concludes the sequence of the rites of passage back into the ordinary world. This sequence reverses the European conception of commencing with the 'opening' of a service and ending with the 'closing'. Its conceptual framework is derived from the traditional Maori world and the rites are used first to enter the state of being extremely tapu, and then to pass from that state into the unrestricted, and relatively unprotected, state of noa.

When Rua Kenana emerged among Tuhoe claiming to be the One whom Te Kooti had predicted, he removed the 'Pōkaikaha' as the penultimate prayer of the services. He replaced it with 'Maungārongo', thus saying that lasting peace had replaced division and the times of war, which had been the times of Te Kooti.[95] By so doing he was stating that the Iharaira, the Israelites who followed him, had reached the times of lasting peace and the times of the Messiah. Rua's decision, and its consequences, indicate the critical importance of the final prayers and their meaning. By removing 'Pōkaikaha' as the penultimate prayer of the service — thereby asserting his claim to be the Messiah who had removed the confusion and the doubts — Rua split the Ringatu world irrevocably.

Te Kooti established the form and sequences of the Ringatu services, which in some regions have since been modified. It is not the place of this book to depict the history and developments of the faith. The purpose here is only to trace the directions Te Kooti gave in their historical context. The texts from this period — the later 1880s — reveal his efforts to admit flexibility. At Otewa, in 1890, he reiterated that 'the Journey' ('te Haere') was difficult for the people and therefore, he said, the round of prayers used by each church could be according to its own wishes.[96] This very flexibility undoubtedly created some of the problems of division and conflict which developed after his death.

In anticipation of such conflict, and indeed partly as a consequence of its developing, he made preparations to modify the structures of authority within the church. At the beginning of February 1893, at Waihohonu, Taupo, he announced that the authority which had rested with Matiu Paeroa, as the 'Keeper of the Law',[97] was removed.

> Te tikanga i runga i a koe na, ka murua atu i runga i a koe, e kore koe e tu muri ake, a, ake tonu atu.

> The authority upon you is now taken away; never shall you be raised up in future for evermore.[98]

In his place, a wider base for authority was enunciated: the poutikanga, the pillars of authority; the ture atua, the scholars who announce the rules and procedures and who repeat the kupu whakaari; the tohunga, the ministers of the service; the takuta, or prayer-healers; the rangatira, the chiefs; the pirihimana or kaitiaki, the policemen, door-keepers and caretakers; and the haahi, the church, the congregation itself. Te Kooti stressed that each had a role, and none should usurp the others.

The authority of the tohunga he had already addressed in 1888, instructing that their food be not separated from that of others. Subsequently, in 1891, when he added instructions for the order of proceedings within the services, he emphasised that it was only the prayers which were tapu.[99] These strictures suggest that he was trying to move the attachment of tapu away from the person of the tohunga. Nor was a single Pouti-kanga appointed in Te Kooti's life-time — nor indeed for many years thereafter. It seems, in fact, that he never intended there to be only one; rather, he intended that there should be a head and spokesman for each branch (or segment) of the church, and the general practice for many years was that each area, or segment, had its own poutikanga.[100] The term was used in this way when the committee, Te Roopu, set up the rules in 1888 for the Twelfth, instructing all the congregation and the officers — that is, the tohunga, ture, takuta and 'nga Poutikanga' — to go into the house when the second bell was rung.[101] It was only much later that the title was awarded to a single leader, in an attempt to unite the different segments of the faith. Thus Paora Delamere became Poutikanga in 1938 and remained so until his death in 1981. No Poutikanga has replaced him. Indeed, as one kaumatua said in 1983, reflecting a truth about distinct tribal and regional identities, 'I [would] like the Poutikanga to end. I say we are all different.'[102]

Although unity has never been fully achieved, there is no doubt that Te Kooti established a distinct religion and a church which not only endured the loss of its founder but which still survives, more than 100 years after his death. It has survived because of what it offered: a vision which sprang from the harsh experiences of the 1860s but which also affirmed God's binding covenant. Among the many prayers Te Kooti composed there is one in his notebook of 1869 which states the roots of Maori pain, and the unconditional promise of God, which he linked precisely to the situation of a colonised people:

> A kua riro to matou wahi tipu i nga tangata ke ko koe tonu ia hei matua tipu moku. *Ake ake.*

> Our homeland has fallen to the foreigners but you indeed are the one to be my true parent. *For ever.*[103]

By 1890 this early vision had become a fully developed faith.

The basis for many of the rites is distinctly Maori. Going to the sacred water, which everyone brought up in the faith remembers, is one. Its purpose is to heal the sick and to prevent illnesses. It was practised in communities where the people's immunity to the common European viral infections was low. The practice was a rite of purification in running water:

> We used to get up, sick people and all, whether you were sick or not, and go to the creek at Wainui. One of our tohungas, whoever was in charge for that night, for this karakia, for the sick people — oh, sort of asking God to ward off illness and to make people better. We'd go out about 2 or 3 o'clock in the morning, to that creek, and whoever is in charge, would have a mānuka branch. He'd dip it into the creek and shake the water over everybody, to touch everyone, spraying the people with the water. Sort of blessing.[104]

This practice derived from pre-European Maori rites of protecting, cleansing and 'releasing' by sprinkling with water, the tohunga often standing with one foot on the land and one in the stream. In the Ringatu teachings, the meaning became transformed: 'That wai is the Holy Spirit. It becomes holy — holy water. Without God or the Holy Spirit the *water* is no good.'[105] With this meaning the ritual comes very close to the Roman Catholic rites of purification, the asperges: the sprinkling with holy water.[106]

The prophecies of the faith derived unquestionably from the sequence of promises contained in the scriptures. Equally, the secret codes Te Kooti adopted were derived from Anglican church practices. He is known to have possessed a copy of the 1859 Anglican prayer-book in Maori, containing alphabetically indexed tables ('A–g') for the lessons for each day of the month, and lists of the sacred days and movable feasts of the church. His prayer-book included the church's alphabetical reference system, called the Dominical or Sunday letters, as well as the tables and rules for the movable feasts for the years 1848–89. Commencing with 1848, the Sunday letters read BA (1848), G (1849), F (1850), E (1851), DC (1852), B (1853), A (1854), G (1855), FE (1856), D (1857), etc. The prayer-book thus contained a complete liturgical calendar, which included the epact, the means by which the ecclesiastical year was calculated in relation to the lunar year.[107] It was probably from this system that Te Kooti developed a similar code, used as a referential to the kupu whakaari. Puti Onekawa explained,

> Say if I stand up as a tohunga, to take a part in the church, and then I give out one word, say 'A', maybe that word 'A' is for Maketū or whatever — it's a special way of putting the whakaaris. That's a real staunch way of putting [it] in the Ringatū church. It's in a little book I had — it's only a little book but you couldn't understand what it is for. It's not really open to everyone to know — it's something like a code — just a secret code for him [Te Kooti], but all the Ringatū knows. That's when I used to go to the Twelfths. If I mention one alphabet like that, 'A' 'B' or whatever, well, everybody knows where it's leading to.[108]

Te Kooti had created a series of scriptural references and a hermeneutical account of Maori history, which reinterpreted both their past and the future in terms of the promises. As we have also seen, this vision was continued by Eria Raukura after Te Kooti's death; 'salvation history' is a particularly enduring conception of history.[109] Equally, narrative is a particularly enduring form of relating it, and parable a particularly enduring form of concealing it. Te Kooti's great skill was to weave history and Maori concerns for their land into the new world of the scriptures. He explained anew the meaning of the Maori past, linked it to the future, and built a new cultural and religious order for the believers. He thereby prevented (with others) a European control of time, space and history for Maori.

In 1889, after his return to Otewa, Te Kooti directed his energy into consolidating support for the faith, and also into carrying it to two new regions. For the First of July 1889, he went again to the Bay of Plenty, this time to Te Pahou, Whakatane, to open a meeting-house for the Kotahitanga of the faith.[110] This house was probably Awanui-a-Rangi, built by Ngati Pukeko, which certainly became associated with Te Kooti, although some accounts date its opening as earlier. The government did not oppose his journey, but the words Te Kooti spoke at the Ra warned of imminent conflict. He spoke obliquely — of parent against child and of chief against chief, calling it a time of punishment from God; he also referred to two 'hidden' leaders, and conflict over the land. He said simply that it was better that there should be only one leader, 'our father in the unseen place' ('ko to tatou matua i te wahi ngaro').[111] The two 'hidden' leaders of this prediction may have been the Ngati Pikiao chief Te Pokiha Taranui (Major Fox) and the prophet Himiona Te Orinui from Whakatane, who had recently developed a

A sketch of Te Kooti's seal. It is possibly the seal made by Matiu Paeroa in February 1890, and the letters '90' may be sketched at its base. This drawing was part of a folder of material relating to Te Kooti donated by Gilbert Mair to the Dominion Museum in 1924, and now held at the Alexander Turnbull Library.   MSS 390, ATL

rival faith centred at nearby Maketu. Its karakia were understood to be a challenge to Te Kooti's teachings in the eastern Bay of Plenty, if only because they were similar in both their forms and their emphasis. Te Pokiha had led the Arawa contingent against Tuhoe at Te Harema in 1869 and had received Te Kooti coolly on his earlier visits to Maketu in 1884 and 1887. One important objective of Te Kooti's journey to Whakatane was understood to be to find a means of resolving their rivalry.[112]

The first new area to which Te Kooti sent missionaries was the upper Whanganui. He was responding to a request from the carver, Te Ture Poutama, brought to Te Kooti in 1887 after a vision in which 'the spirit' ('te wairua') had appeared to Te Ture and commanded him to pray for a Ringatu tohunga for the district.[113] The news that Te Kooti was to come to Ranana to hold the Ra of 1 January 1890 was announced the preceding July. The government soon began to receive a trickle of protesting Maori letters from the district. Tohiora Pirato wrote from Hiruharama to object, saying that there were already too many preachers, and besides Te Kooti came from a people who had been conquered by Whanganui.[114] Henare Haeretuterangi wrote from Karioi asking that the visit be stopped.[115] In the event, Te Kooti did not go, although it is clear that he had intended to.[116] Instead, a party of ten of his followers went, travelling to Karioi and Ranana.[117] The First was held at Ranana, where a new meeting-house was opened[118] in direct challenge to Te Keepa Te Rangihiwinui's great carved meeting-house. Te Keepa, leader of the Whanganui forces fighting against Te Kooti during the wars, had become a formidable and notably autocratic leader of the movement for Maori control of their lands under the Treaty of Waitangi. To take the faith to Ranana was to penetrate the heart of Te Keepa's authority.

The Ringatu missionaries, who included Petera Te Rangihiroa and Rakuraku, came to introduce the new religion.[119] The song Te Kooti composed for this occasion was one of challenge, not of conciliation. It chastised the people of Ranana for their previous pursuit of him, and told them instead to take up in their hands 'the word of the law within the bible here' ('ko te kupu o te ture kei roto i te paipera naa'). The song asserted the sanctity and power ('Atu-te-ihi') of Te Kooti's missionaries, and urged that their triumphant chant should resound over Ranana ('e tangi te umere tupa whai ake ake ki runga o Ranana'). It told Te Keepa that the people who had arrived at his place were rare and to be valued. Finally it suggested that he, too, should drink of 'the waters of the Faith' ('nga wai o te Tikanga'), where he would find the great love of peace. In a final pun, Te Kooti called Te Keepa and his people the lame and sweaty ('Wai-totii, Wai-totaa'), or the kind of people whose thoughts and customs of heart would all be changed, as the gloss to the song comments.[120] Having thrown out this preliminary and successful challenge to Te Keepa, Te Kooti himself came for the celebrations of July 1890, which were held at Nga Mokai, Karioi, at the foot of Mount Ruapehu.

Here, again, a new house was opened for his Kotahitanga.[121] Te Kooti named the house 'Te Pou-o-te-Tikanga', the Pillar of the Faith. The scriptural basis for the name is cited as Revelation 3:12 ('I will make a pillar in the temple of my God'), which refers to the coming of the new Jerusalem and also the 'new name' for the One who will come. The chief and tohunga who had invited Te Kooti and who had built the house was Pouawha Te Riaki, famous for his school of learning which upheld the teachings of the god Io. It is recalled locally that Te Kooti said to Te Riaki:

> Kāti ki a tāua, e Ria, rauna ake tāua i te whare nei ā, waiho ake a waho kia wera atu i te ahi.

> Let us remain here, Ria, in the circumference of this house, and let outside be consumed by fire.[122]

Another version of the saying recorded Te Kooti's words as:

> E Ria, kaati iho i te taiepa o te whare nei kia taua. Ko taku tikanga, ka poua e au ki tenei whare.

> Ria, close the walls of this house around us. I shall pour my authority into this house.[123]

Both versions thus convey the importance of the house as a sanctuary for Te Kooti's faith. In another version, however, Te Kooti warned of a stranger who would occupy it:

> Tenei whare he tangata ke hei noho mo roto i a ia. Ki te manawanui a Te Riaki, he aha te kino o tena. He pai tonu hoki, ko te tino painga tena kia manawanui, hei whaka-aronga iho ki te Iwi. Tena, ki te kore e manawanui ki te pupuri i te whenua, ko tenei whare he tangata ke hei noho mo roto i a ia.

> As for this house, a stranger will occupy it. If Te Riaki is steadfast, what will be the harm in that? It would be very good, that would be the very best thing to be steadfast, in consideration of the People. So, if [you] are not steadfast in holding on to the land, then this house will have a stranger occupying it.[124]

Locally it was understood that Te Kooti was warning against the alienation of land when he spoke of the fire that would burn all around,[125] and his insistence on the need to retain the land is explicit in the longer statement. However these words have been —

Ranana, with Te Keepa's carved meeting-house and council house, Huriwhenua, at the centre of the community, 8 May 1885. The house built by the Ringatu believers was possibly named 'Nga Morehu' (The Survivors). But the issue is confused, for the name Te Morehu is attached to Te Keepa's house, which was partly swept away in a flood. It now stands, shortened by 20 feet, on a different site at Ranana. Another version states that the name remembers the survivors of the fighting on nearby Moutoa island in 1864. Photograph by Alfred Burton.   258, MONZ

or will be — interpreted, Karioi became a centre for the Ringatu with the conversion of Te Riaki.

Te Kooti's secretaries recorded at length his speeches at Karioi. Initially he said that they were a restatement of the sayings from January for Ranana: the January was the parent, the July the child. He warned of coming bloodshed over land — because of surveying, renting and selling. He also spoke of trouble within the gospel, when faith would fight faith. But then he also told those who followed the established churches, Anglican and Catholic, to maintain their beliefs, as his own followers would theirs. He urged not rivalry, but recognition: that their faith was, like that of the established churches, simply 'a calling on their three names, the Father, Son and Holy Ghost' ('he karanga ki o ratau ingoa e toru nei, ki te Matua ki te Tama ki te Wairua-Tapu').[126] The thrust of his speeches was therefore finally for reconciliation and co-operation. The battle had ended, he said, with his capture by the government, and although he was still seen by some to be 'the enemy' ('*Ko au te hoa riri*') and disturber of the peace, it was not so. Rather, the gospel and the several churches should provide the pathways for peace.[127]

The songs he composed for this occasion were also on these themes. They included his song of concern about the cutting of the land into pieces, already cited; another spoke of the governor's money, enticing people to leave their lands or to strip them for profit. And he sang, foreshadowing events and conflicts to come,

> Te riro noa mai he rongopai i te hau e hei whiu i a au, noho ana hoki au i te kei o te waka. Nou e Te Riaki, i, hei hautu mai mau e Taitoko e mo nga tau e maha a i e.

> The gospel is gently borne here on the wind so that I may be replete, sitting here in the canoe's stern. It is yours, oh Te Riaki, and for you, oh Taitoko [Te Keepa] to give time to the paddlers for many years to come.[128]

His song now hoped for unity, with himself quietly seated and the two great leaders of Whanganui being the kaituki for their district, under his spiritual guidance. In actuality, however, the contest with Te Keepa grew. The rivalry between the two culminated at a major gathering at Parikino, Whanganui, in January 1892.

Te Kooti had come to speak with increasing disparagement of the efforts of the leading chiefs to establish Maori unity. This was the Kotahitanga political movement, which sought a separate Maori Parliament under the Treaty of Waitangi. Its leaders included Te Keepa and Hamiora Mangakahia (who had earlier picked up Te Kooti's gaol-bond and who himself would be elected Premier of a separate Maori government at the first formal meeting of the Kotahitanga, held in June 1892). Te Kooti's challenge to Te Keepa was directed at the underlying premises of this movement.

Te Kooti's journey to Parikino for the First of January 1892 is recorded in detail by Hamiora Aparoa, as were the many statements he made as he travelled to the hui. Hamiora's account began with Te Kooti's vision:

> Nov. 8. 1891. Ka tangi nga reo: i te 12th ka whakaatutia e Te Kooti he whiu, he pakanga kai te haere, a he toto hoki.

> Nov. 8. 1891. The voices cried out: on the 12th Te Kooti directed attention to some affliction, a fight to come, and blood also.

The decision to travel was announced on 10 December, when Te Kooti said:

> 'Tatau ka haere nei kia mahara tatemea te hiahia o Taitoko he kohi moni mo te motu nei, ka haere atu i Otewa.'

> 'We shall go now. Remember, because Taitoko's [Te Keepa's] desire is to collect money for this land, [we] are going from Otewa.'[129]

On 20 December the party reached Tokaanu, at the southern end of Lake Taupo. They stayed for the tangi of the chief Herekiekie Paurini, who had fought alongside Te Kooti at Te Porere in 1869 and been so badly wounded there that he was reported dead. Te Kooti spoke at length, in the presence of Te Heuheu Tureiti, who had inherited the title of paramount chief of Tuwharetoa and who, as a little boy, had been with his father when he surrendered to Thomas McDonnell. Te Kooti reminded Tureiti that, although

Nini and Paurini and others had perished, they would not be forgotten. He then told him:

> Ko ratau nga tangata ko koe, e tama, te uri. I konei ano au i te ra takurua i kite ano au i a Paurini a whai ana ia i au. He kupu ano taku ki a ia e whawhai ana hoki ia mo tenei waahi. He ki atu naku hai aha waiho atu. Kaore, hei aha ma koutou ma te Rangatira.
>
> Haere tonu te Rangatira i ona whakaaro, a ina tatau e tangi wairua nei. Ko te mana tena o [o] tipuna tae mai ki a koe.

> They were the people, you, son, are the descendant. I was also here one winter's day when I saw Paurini again, and he followed after me. I had a word too for him — he also was fighting for this place. I said to him: 'Never mind that, leave it be. What possible good is it for you, for the Chiefs?'
>
> The Chiefs continue to go along according to their own thoughts, while we are weeping in spirit here. That is the mana of your ancestors and it reaches to you.[130]

From these uneasy words, which separated himself and his concerns from those of the high-born chiefs, even those who had given support to him, he moved into an attack on the Kotahitanga as formed by the chiefs. He stated unequivocally that it would never unite the land, nor could it be sustained, for the only bond which held it together was money. He concluded: 'This idle talk on our lips about the Kotahitanga' ('Ko tenei ki o tatou ngutu noa iho korero ai i te Kotahitanga') would end up as nothing more than the boasting of the chiefs.[131]

After this uncomfortable exchange, Te Kooti continued his journey, refusing Tureiti's invitation to travel with him as far as Patea. Next Te Kooti came to Waihohonu, at the foot of Ruapehu. He stayed the night there, but left in the morning, angry and impatient with this journey which, he said contemptuously, was not for him and those who were with him, but belonged to old men and women, or women and children. At Karioi, however, he met Te Riaki and also one of his most long-standing and loyal followers: Hirini Te Oiikau, who had come there especially to see him. To Hirini he spoke very differently:

> Ahakoa ahau koro-heke, mau tokotoko, noho i roto i te kawhena, ka tae ano ka tutuki ano, ka kite hoki: ko tenei haeremai ki te whakarite i karanga a Whanganui.

> Although I am an old man, carrying a walking stick, sitting in a coffin, it will still occur, it will be fulfilled and seen: this journey will be to confirm that Whanganui had called.[132]

The occasion at Parikino, he had predicted in July, would be the day when all the tribes would be seen to kneel before their Creator.[133] It was expected to be a major development for the faith.

An oral story told in Poverty Bay about Te Kooti's journey to Parikino, however, contains ominous premonitions. Like many of the oral narratives, its central concern is the difficulty of establishing peace. This particular story was told by the Ringatu tohunga Tawehi Wilson in 1968, at the centenary of Te Kooti's landing at Whareonga-onga, which was held at Muriwai in Poverty Bay. Wilson also wrote the story down in an abridged form. He recalled how, on the journey to Parikino, Te Kooti was given a greenstone slab 'to build the temporary shelter at the place which had not been be-smirched by blood' ('hei hanga i te whare tihokahoka ki te waahi kaore i paru i te toto'). Te Kooti chose Muriwai, the place where no blood had been spilt in 1868. He therefore told the elders to divide the piece of greenstone. One portion was to be the doorstep, the paepae (threshold) for the house. This act underlined his principle of making peace with former enemies, for the greenstone slab was the lintel, standing between one world and another. Greenstone is often associated with peace-making in the Maori world, and Te Kooti himself possessed a greenstone 'chair of peace', a large, uncut stone, which he carried with him on his journeys. The other portion of the greenstone slab was to be made into a candlestick ('hei teki kanara'). Its light would shine forth in the world. However, when the elders returned to Turanga, the greenstone slab vanished from a tangi held among Ngati Maru, and Te Kooti's word could not be fulfilled. The house was built at Muriwai, but it had to be constructed without its step. Then the elders returned to Te Kooti to call for the day on which he would open their imperfect house; significantly, they had decided on 12 March, the turn of the year. However, Te Kooti said the day for its opening would be 16 March, knowing already what the old men did not yet know: that their house had been burnt down.[134] It could never be opened — at least, not in their lifetime. It is a strange and grim story arising from the journey to Parikino.

On the way, Te Kooti made his first visit to Otoko marae, on the Mangawhero river. There, the people initially blocked their gateway and refused him entry. But in the end they opened their marae and their hearts to him, and thus he consecrated ('i tomokia') their beautiful little meeting-house, Tauakira,[135] built in 1870. The riddle he spun for the people on this occasion is recorded:

> Otoko . . .
> 1. Tenei whare ko Tauakira, me hua e ahau ko te Parakuihi, a ka tina ahau ki konei.
>
> Otoko . . .
> 1. This house is named Tauakira, but I shall name it the Breakfast, and I shall have dinner (repletion) here.[136]

It is remembered at Otoko how Te Kooti sat modestly in the corner of the porch of the house, where the karakia bell of the Ringatu now hangs, and suggested then that the Anglicans could retain one side of the meeting-house and the Catholics the other, while he would squeeze in the middle.[137] It is a parallel, but different, narrative to that already told for Kokohinau at Te Teko, where he had suggested he could tuck himself into the small side (taraiti) of the house. Today, Otoko is the most southerly Ringatu marae in the country and Tauakira stands there, painted with exquisite red and white kowhaiwhai panels which trace the people's genealogies. It also has two uncarved gable posts, seen as the means by which the prayers and korero from within the house, after ascending the kowhaiwhai lines and travelling along the tahuhu (the ridge-pole of the house), pass up to God. This teaching is attributed to Te Kooti.

On 28 December 1891 Te Kooti arrived at Parikino. There he instructed his people as to how they should enter the marae. They were 'to charge' ('e huaki') the pa, the women in front, the priests behind, and last of all the packhorses. He then raced his horse

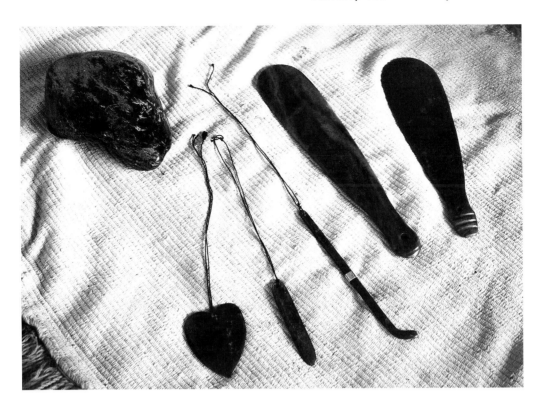

Greenstone taonga belonging to Te Kooti. He named the two mere Kapiti (Gabriel) and Mikaere
(Michael). Mikaere, the shorter mere on the right, was a fighting weapon, while Gabriel was a mere of
peace. In the drawing made in 1892, Te Kooti is wearing this long earring (p.189). At the top (left) is a
portion of the greenstone 'chair of peace', which Te Kooti took with him on his journeys. After his
death the 'chair' was said to have been cut into four quarters: one was returned to Wharekauri and one is
this portion. Stone 'chairs' were also used by Maori scholars in the highest schools of learning. The
greenstone heart belonged to Te Kooti's sister, Makaretu; the short pendant was his own teething
pendant. Photograph, by permission of Tihei Algie, by Gillian Chaplin, 1982.

around the large group, collecting them together. As he did this he pronounced a few
words in the strange language, holding his right hand up in glorification of God: it was
'like a prayer of protection' ('ano he inoi tiaki').[138] He then put on his hat, and they all
rode into the pa. The welcome sounded out and the local band burst forth in noisy
celebration. Thus the prophet and the people came to Parikino in their own ways and
for their own ends.

The meeting was a huge affair, with representatives from many tribes, and it would
last until 8 January. In the local newspapers the only references to Te Kooti's presence
seem to be that he had brought a large party with him (estimated as between 260 and
300 riders) and that he kept much to himself, staying apart in his tent and watched over
by his two wives — at least while the Europeans were there. He was described as
wearing a 'glaring check suit' and a large straw hat with a coloured ribbon, and carrying
a huge white umbrella (lined with green) to protect him against the sun.[139] This was an
outfit of which he was clearly fond, for it would be described again (and drawn) by

Portrait of Te Kooti painted on the lintel of the meeting-house Tuwhare, built at Galatea by Tuwharetoa for Ngati Manawa about 1890. Ngati Manawa became Te Kooti's followers after the wars. Te Kooti stands (on the far right) in what appears to be a line of prophets or scriptural figures, whose identity is uncertain. Not only his check suit identifies him; so does his mutilated left hand. This photograph was taken about 1905.   DETAIL, 7027 1/1, BIRCH COLLECTION, ATL

others later in 1892 (see illustration in Chapter 7). The same check suit was depicted in the portrait of him painted on the lintel above the doorway into the meeting-house Tuwhare, built about this time at Galatea. This is the only known contemporary Maori image of him.

In the newspapers, Te Kooti was reported as having nothing to say during the long public proceedings of the Parikino meeting. The Ringatu sources, however, record some remarkable exchanges, particularly between Te Keepa and Te Kooti. Te Keepa wrote to Te Kooti, from Putiki, on 31 December to welcome him to his district and to apologise for not being able to see him until after the end of the meeting. By then, he said cuttingly, Te Kooti would have had time to reflect on whether this was the time for living together, 'the owl and the hawk, the rat and the cat, the dog and the pig' ('te ruru raua ko te kaahu te kiore raua ko te ngeru, te kuri me te poaka').[140] Te Kooti replied with two waiata. In one he told Te Keepa to be swift, but he also said that he would wait

> mo te ua o te rangi, mo te makariri wero i nga po kino e, ki te kohi mai ano i te kakano e, hei oranga mo tama-a-roto kia ora ai e.

> for the rain of the sky, for the piercing cold of atrocious nights, to gather as well the seeds as sustenance for the inner man, so that life remains.[141]

The other waiata recorded his distrust of the whole occasion. He sang of the 'lack of substance' ('mo te kore e whai kiko') in the words of the chiefs, and also of the probability that they would remain divided.[142] On 1 January he made his pronouncements, which anticipated and remembered his conflict with the high chiefs:

Riewhe (Eriewhe) Tuokei Tuioewhe

Riewhe.	Whakamaori.
	1. Manaakitanga o tenei rā, o te whenua me te tangata. Ka toru hoki nga rā ki tenei taha he tohu tenei no te manaakitanga.
	E he ana hoki te haere o nga Rangatira.
	Ko nga Rangatira ano hei whiu i a tatau. . . .
	2. Ko te makutu me te toto, me nga whiu kei te haere tonu.
Tuokei Tauwira	Ka manaakitia e ia te hunga e wehi ana ki a ia te iti me te rahi, a ka tapiritia mai ano e ia he pai he ora.
Tuioewhe	1. E kore tenei waka e tahuritia, e kore e ara te take. Kei te whakaaro o Taitoko, kei te haere tena i taana haere i taana haere, me ahau hoki i taku haere. Otira ka hikoi i tetahi waahi iti nei heoi ano. Te mea i puritia ai te toto ko te Maungarongo.
	2. Ka haere tenei rangatira i taana haere i taana haere me era atu tangata i taana haere. Ta Taitoko a ki a ia anake te tika. Ki te rite te whakahaere a nga iwi katoa o te motu nei. He mea noa tenei. Kua riteā he Tamaiti noa nei maana e huri tenei waka. Ka ara te riu ki runga; a e pupuri hoki te Tikanga e kore e taea e Taitoko, e kore hoki e taea e au, ka paru hoki o maua ringaringa i te toto.

Riewhe (Eriewhe) Tuokei Tuioewhe

Riewhe.	Interpretation.
	1. Blessing of this day, of the land and the people. There are three days on this side, these are signs of the blessing.
	The way of the Chiefs is wrong.
	The Chiefs themselves are an infliction on us. . . .
	2. Sorcery, blood and afflictions continue.
Tuokei Example	He cares for those who fear him, the small and the great, and he provides prosperity and well-being.
Tuioewhe	1. This canoe will not be overturned; the keel will not rise up. The reason is with Taitoko's [Te Keepa's] thought — he went his way, and I went mine. But [I] step on one small place here, that's all. Peace is the means of restraining the blood.
	2. Each chief goes his way, and other people their way. Taitoko's [opinion] is that only he is correct. To arrange the organisation of all the tribes in this island, that's an easy thing. It is arranged that a mere Child will turn this canoe about. The bilge will rise up, and the Way will be held to. It will not be achieved by Taitoko, neither will it be achieved by me. Our hands have been soiled by blood.[143]

This prediction is one of the most famous of all those Te Kooti uttered. The last portion, concerning the prophesied Child who would achieve the unity which Te

Kooti's generation could not, is often quoted. It is this unknown Child who will turn the prow of the canoe around and, from this time, there 'will be a continuous upward movement of the faith: ka piki, ka piki te whakapono'.[144] This kupu is always included among the important sayings of the elders of the land:

> Te Kooti. 1892. Kia Meiha Keepa. 'He tamaiti noa nei mana e huri te riu o te waka ki runga, mana ano hoki e whakakotahi nga Iwi ki te Whakapono.'

> Te Kooti. 1892. To Major Kemp [Te Keepa]. 'There will be a child who will turn upright the bilge of the canoe, and he will unite the People through the Gospel.'[145]

The Ringatu records of this hui, however, are much more extensive. They trace the continuing debate, in which this statement was only an early salvo. Te Keepa replied to Te Kooti on 2 January. First, he ceremonially displayed the food and distributed portions to every tribe. Then he stood to speak. He stated directly:

> Ahakoa koe Te Kooti pokokohua mai ai ki au, kua riro kē i au to hereni, me Rakuraku raua ko Te Heuheu. Taku whakahē ki a Te Kooti — kaore ia i mea kia whiriwhiria e nga tangata matauranga te ahua o nga Pire, ara o nga ture a te Kawanatanga.

> Although you, Te Kooti, cursed me, I have taken your shilling and Rakuraku's and Te Heuheu's. My opposition to Te Kooti is that he did not intend that the form of the Bills, that is, of the laws of the Government, be chosen by knowledgeable people.[146]

The gulf between them was huge. Although at this hui Te Kooti's party had indeed contributed to the Kotahitanga (£15 7s by their own reckoning), Te Keepa was trying to do much more than fund-raise. He was, as he indicated, trying to organise a Maori Parliament, which would draft laws on Maori concerns. His objective was to prevent any further sales of Maori land. The authority he sought was through the inter-tribal co-operation of the senior chiefs. Te Keepa's purpose at Parikino was to set up a broadly representative committee of chiefs and of educated younger men in order 'to destroy' ('kia patua') the existing laws. Specifically, he opposed the legislation levying rates on Maori land, and the government's proposed land purchasing boards (established in 1893). On 8 January Te Keepa's committee of 70 (or 80) was chosen,[147] and again he spoke in reply to Te Kooti's objections to it:

> A ehara taku i te korero matauranga inaianei a mehemea koutou ka korero Atua kai kona ano au, a Karaipiture ranei, whenua ranei, a piki ranei ki te Rangi pena au. Engari ko te mauahara whakarerea atu. No reira, e Te Kooti, maku tenei Kingitanga e mau ki te motu, ara te Kotahitanga i raro i te maungarongo.

> And mine is not a learned speech now, if you speak of God I will be there too, or of the Scriptures, or land, or climb to Heaven, so will I. But do away with hate. Therefore, Te Kooti, I will hold to this Kingship in the land, that is, to the Kotahitanga in peace.[148]

In the evening, Te Kooti stood to make his farewell speech. His emphasis was on a different form of unity. The gap between the two men seemed unbridgeable. Te Kooti spoke as a religious leader, Te Keepa as a high chief. It could be said that Te Kooti was sabotaging the other's work, for he spoke of an entirely different Kotahitanga, a unity of spirit. He reiterated his opposition to everything which Te Keepa was trying to achieve.

Because this exchange sharply reveals the absolute nature of their differences, it is worth quoting in full.

> [Te Kooti:]   Mo te kupu a Taitoko maana e kawe te kingitanga o te maungarongo, ara te Kotahitanga. Kaore e taea e koe Taitoko, kua paru kē o taua nei ringa i te toto, he Tamaiti noa nei maana e whakatutuk[i] o taua nei hapa, te tahi e titiro atu ana ahau e rua o arero e korero mai nei koe.
>
> Taitoko: E Te Kooti, kaore i pena tena. Iana koe whakaae mai, moku tenei mea e kawe, a e ki mai nei hoki koe e rua oku arero ae engari kotahi ano to raua take, kotahi hoki ta raua e korero ai.
>
> Te Kooti: Tena koia hamama mai to waha kia kite atu au.
>
> Taitoko   Hamāmā tonu atu te waha. Ka purua atu e Te Kooti te pauna nooti ki roto, a ngau tomo mai hoki te rā.
>
> Te Kooti: Na koina te mahi ma tena waha me ena arero he apo moni mai a Te Kawanatanga.
>
> [Te Kooti:]   Concerning Taitoko's word that he would take the kingdom of peace, that is, the Kotahitanga. You will not achieve this, Taitoko, for both our hands have been soiled with blood. It is just a Child who will fulfil what we have neglected. Moreover, I see that you are talking with two tongues.
>
> Taitoko: Te Kooti, it was not like that. In the time it takes you to agree, I will bring this thing about. And you say that I have two tongues. Yes, but they have one aim, and they speak as one.
>
> Te Kooti: Well, then open your mouth so that I can see.
>
> Taitoko   As soon as he opened his mouth Te Kooti stuffed a pound note into it, and the day was fulfilled.
>
> Te Kooti: Now, that is the work for that mouth and those tongues, extorting money from the Government.[149]

An abridged version of this exchange notes specifically that it was the barrier erected by Te Kooti's words which prevented the fulfilment of the unification of the land by Te Keepa. This version states again that the hope rests with the next generation and the predicted Child.[150]

The speeches at Parikino starkly reveal the oppositional role of Te Kooti in a political context. He spoke as a spiritual leader; he sought the revitalisation of the wairua, the spiritual aspect of the people. He did not speak as a politician of the time. He kept himself apart during much of the feasting, remaining in his tent. He challenged the objectives of Te Keepa, suggesting that his activities were governed only by his interest in money. He accused him of raising money from the people, as well as from the government. He blamed the chiefs for many of the ills of the Maori, and he often labelled them 'the money rangatiras'.[151] The implication was that, while the chiefs lived in style, they ignored the real needs of the people. He placed emphasis, rather, on the needs of the poor, the widowed and the orphaned: those with little or nothing, 'te rawa kore'. In this he spoke firmly in the gospel tradition. The clash with Te Keepa was inevitable.

For all that, the sayings from Parikino also suggest the possibility of mutual tolerance. On 2 January Te Kooti said:

Kia ngohengohe nga Rangatira ki nga kuare, kia ngohengohe ano hoki nga kuare ki nga Rangatira, ara . . . kia ngawari a, tera e tapiritia mai he pai he tika mo tatau.

Let the Chiefs be tolerant of the ignorant, and let the ignorant also be tolerant of the Chiefs, that is . . . be accommodating, and then prosperity and justice will accrue for us.[152]

He spoke of working together, Anglican, Catholic and Ringatu, as they prayed. This unity would *then* underpin the Kotahitanga Parliament for the island. Always the unity he sought was spiritual, not through political associations created by the chiefs. He also sang of

Tera te Hurae ka rewa mai te runga he tohu no nga mahi no te Rangimarie.

The day the July is elevated, it [will be] a sign of the works of Peace.[153]

Here he urged recognition of the sacred days of the Ringatu as the basis for peace. To Te Keepa he said finally:

E koro Taitoko, whakarongo mai ra katahi ka heua te ara o te aroha aua atu te nui, kia iti noa oti. Engari te ngaringari, he kore te kore rawa, i te mea e mū ana ki roto o Whanganui i e.

Esteemed Taitoko, listen to me: why clear the path of compassion so large when a small one will suffice; no matter how small, something is better than nothing achieved. But as for unity, never, absolutely never [will it happen] because there is discontent within Whanganui.[154]

Wairarapa was the second new region to which Te Kooti sent his missionaries and then travelled there himself. Ngati Hikawera invited him to open their new meeting-house at Kehemane (Tablelands) on 1 January 1891.[155] This house, Takitimu, was the last of the meeting-houses which Matiu listed as being built for the Kotahitanga under God's words,[156] although it was certainly not the last house to be built, nor was it the last within Te Kooti's lifetime, as we shall see.

There is a persistent oral tradition that Takitimu was opened in 1887 by Te Kooti. His missionaries first went to Wairarapa in 1880, although earlier connections had been established during the wars, largely through Te Waru's kinship with the people there. Two kupu whakaari concerning the building of the house are dated August 1887; this suggests, at the very least, that the house was then being prepared for its opening. It is also known that the house was worked on by Ngati Porou carvers sent from Poverty Bay by Te Kooti between 1880 and 1886. However, there seems to have been some disagreement about the intended purposes of the house at that time.[157] It is probable, therefore, that the house was rededicated by Te Kooti on 1 January 1891; other houses certainly were rededicated.

In style, Takitimu is similar to Tokanganui-a-noho. Of particular interest are the large painted marakihau on the rear posts of the porch, which are similar to the two carved and polychrome marakihau on the side posts of the porch of the Te Kuiti house. At Te Kuiti, these two marakihau were originally placed confronting each other on the porch. They are named as two water-beings particularly associated with the Tainui canoe tribes. One, Kaiwhare, was dreaded; the other, Paneiraira, was a protective spirit. Paneiraira bore unique six-pointed 'stars', or perhaps 'spoke-wheels', on his curving tail, as did one of the pair of marakihau painted on the rear wall of the porch of Tokanganui-a-noho. Similarly, on the porch of the famous house built at Ruatahuna for Te Kooti, Te Whai-a-te-motu, which he also opened early in 1891, there were two carved and polychrome marakihau. They were Te Putaanga and Te Tahi o Te Rangi,[158] and they too confronted each other. Te Tahi o Te Rangi is considered to be the guardian of his descendants, the people of the Mataatua canoe, and his particular task is to protect them from the dangers of ocean taniwha. His role — certainly as adopted by Rua, who identified himself with Te Tahi o Te Rangi and flew a flag which bore his name — was to intervene against the vengeful forces of the old Maori world. Te Tahi was famous for saying, rather than destroy people, '"*Waiho ma te whakama e patu. Waiho hai korero i a tatau kia atawhai ki te iwi*" — Leave them for shame to punish. Let us acquire fame by means of mercy'.[159] When Timi Waata Rimini of Ngati Awa told the story of Te Tahi in 1899, he compared his marakihau–ancestor to Moses, and also to the 'apostle' ('āpotoro') and prophet Jonah, who rode upon (or, more correctly, inside) the whale.[160] The recurring images of marakihau in the early Ringatu houses acted as references to local narratives about sources of danger, old and new,[161] and also the protective guardians. It seems probable that underlying the use of these images was the principle of mercy, which Te Kooti had taken as his own from 1873. In turn, Rua accepted Te Tahi as the ancestor particularly appropriate for him, in the times of peace. The story of Te Tahi o Te Rangi is one of the great narratives of the Mataatua people, which Te Kooti adopted. The marakihau found on Takitimu and Tokanganui-a-noho are depicted in the Mataatua style of carving;[162] in other, later images they would acquire some of the European characteristics of the mermaid. These paintings and carvings affirmed the people's histories and local identities, but they also probably incorporated the moral principles of the faith.

The kupu whakaari concerning the building of Takitimu in 1887 are, once again, equivocal. Matiu recorded the phrases of 22 August:

> Ko te ra tenei i whakaputa ina ai nga Kupu whakaari mo te whare ki Wairarapa —
> > One Tuera
>
> One. Kupu whakarite. Ki te kore e hanga e Ihowa te whare he maumau hanga ta te tangata.
>
> Tuarua. Karangatia he huihuinga nui whakaminea mai nga kaumatua.
>
> Tuera. Ka hanga e ahau taku hahi ki runga ki tenei kamaka.
>
> Tuarua. Huihui mai e nga toenga o nga tamariki a Iharaira.

This was the day on which were revealed the predictive Words for the house at Wairarapa —
> One Tuera

One. Word of correction. If the house is not fashioned by Jehovah then it is pointless for man to build it.

Second. Call a large gathering and assemble the elders.

Tuera. I shall found my church upon this rock.

Second. Gather together the remnants of the children of Israel.[163]

A variant text, recorded by Tawehi Wilson, is dated Wairarapa, 28 August. It reads:

1 Tuiera.

Ka hangaa e ahau taku hahi ki runga ki tenei kamaka a e kore e taea e nga hau o Te Reinga te peehi.

2

Otira he atua tohu a Ihoa tou atua e kore ia e whakarere i a koe a muri ake nei.

1 Tuiera.

I shall found my church upon this rock and the winds from Te Reinga will not be able to trouble it.

2

But indeed Jehovah your god is a god of mercy, he will never forsake you hereafter.[164]

Hamiora's version, in turn, is dated 12 September and is identified as being said at Otewa. His statement is essentially the same as the first version, and Hamiora also gave the scriptural references for the kupu: Psalm 127:1 and Matthew 16:18.[165] It seems likely, therefore, that a division over the primary rationale for the house had emerged in the local community; moreover, Te Kooti did not travel there at this time. The opening (or probably rededication) of the house is dated in the Ringatu sources as 1891, when Te Kooti held the First of January at Kehemane. His remembered words for the house also suggest that there had been a conflict of purpose in its construction: '*Kai waho te mirimiri. Kai roto te rahurahu*',[166] that is, there was a roughness in its interior, which the exterior flattery of its fine decorations belied (see photograph, page 299).

Matiu Paeroa recorded Te Kooti's sayings for the gathering of the First of January 1891. They were largely words of faith taken from the scriptures. All that Te Kooti said now about the house was that it had been blessed, as had its people, and all their land. The fault had been on his side; the coming year would be a gentle one ('Ko te kino kei te taha ki au. Ko tenei tau he tau ngawari').[167] The conflict had apparently been resolved, and the house could be rededicated.

The one shadow which possibly lay across this assembly was Te Kooti's health. Alexander Shand wrote that a Maori woman, whom he knew from Wharekauri, had seen Te Kooti 'spitting quantities of blood'. Shand deduced from her description that he was suffering from tuberculosis. If her account is correctly dated to the visit to the Wairarapa (and there is some uncertainty),[168] it indicates that the disease had returned. Te Kooti may have been seriously ill before the accident to which his death is attributed. In the last letter he wrote immediately before this accident, his handwriting shows a marked deterioration (see pages 484–85).[169] However, his energies seemed undiminished in the months following the visit to Kehemane.

Upon his return to Otewa at the beginning of February 1891, Te Kooti renewed his search for a home for the covenant. The visit of the new Native Minister, A. J. Cadman, to Otorohanga on 1–2 April gave Te Kooti the opportunity to talk about the long-delayed land grant. Political memories being short, Cadman told him that 'if the records confirmed it, he would faithfully carry out the promise'.[170] The remark seems inconceivable: the previous government had received a series of well-supported petitions in November 1889 from Maori in the eastern Bay of Plenty, asking that Te Kooti be granted the land at Ohiwa, promised him by Mitchelson in place of Orakau. The petitions must have been orchestrated, for they came at the same time. Tamarangi and 104 others from the several hapu of Whakatohea wrote first from Opotiki on 12 November. On the following day, Heketoro Hikairo sent in a petition from Te Pahou, Whakatane, the community where the Ra for 1 July 1889 had been held. On 14 November, Te Whanau-a-Apanui drew up their request with 67 signatures, including those of the Maraenui chiefs Te Tatana and Paora Ngamoki. The next day, Rakuraku and Tutakangahau, leaders of Waimana and Maungapohatu, wrote their letter on behalf of all their people. On 18 November, Ngati Awa of Te Teko, led by the chief and famous carver Tiopira Te Hukiki, sent in their petition with 51 names. On 20 November, Makarini forwarded from Ruatoki another large Tuhoe petition. It included among its many signatories Te Whenuanui and Paora Kiingi, who were Te Kooti's followers, and also Numia Kereru (Numia Te Ruakariata) and Te Wakaunua, who were not. On 26 November, a second petition from Opotiki was sent by Hukanui, Reihana and 67 others representing the people of Ohiwa and Waiotahe, including Te Upokorehe, the hapu living on Hokianga island in the Ohiwa harbour, which Te Kooti would use as his last home and shelter. Nothing was done in response to the petitions; they were simply filed, with the accompanying note that, from the Atkinson government's point of view, Te Kooti was better located in the Waikato, as it was further from Poverty Bay.[171]

The new government of 1891, headed by Ballance, however, was prepared to reopen the issue, in the hope that a land grant might persuade Te Kooti to help with opening the Urewera for surveying. This was the unstated premise of the 'private' discussion between Cadman and Te Kooti at Otorohanga, which grew out of events in the previous month, when Te Kooti had been among Tuhoe and had helped to smooth the way for a successful visit by the governor, Lord Onslow, to Ruatoki.

Onslow had expressed an interest in visiting Tuhoe in 1890; he was the first governor to wish to do so. After an initial refusal, then much discussion and pressure, Tuhoe issued an invitation. It was sent from Ruatoki on 10 February 1891, and was signed by the major chiefs, Kereru Te Pukenui, Tamaikoha, Makarini and Tutakangahau, among others.[172] They invited Onslow to a gathering to be held at Ruatoki on 20–21 March. Shortly afterwards, at a hui at Ruatahuna on 2 March, where Te Kooti was present, the issue of the Tuhoe land was thoroughly discussed. Te Kooti was a central figure, and the hui confirmed unanimously that neither prospectors, nor surveyors, nor any Europeans were to be permitted to enter the Rohe Potae of Tuhoe. The only exception was to be the governor and his party.[173]

Undoubtedly, Tuhoe hoped to appeal to Onslow, particularly as he himself had stressed (when seeking their invitation) that there was 'much difference' between himself, as the representative of the Queen, and the representatives of the New Zealand government. It was on this ground alone, as Onslow later reported to Queen Victoria, that Tuhoe had been persuaded to invite him to the 'edge of their territory'. They had, he noted, 'said nothing about an expedition to the interior',[174] which was what he really

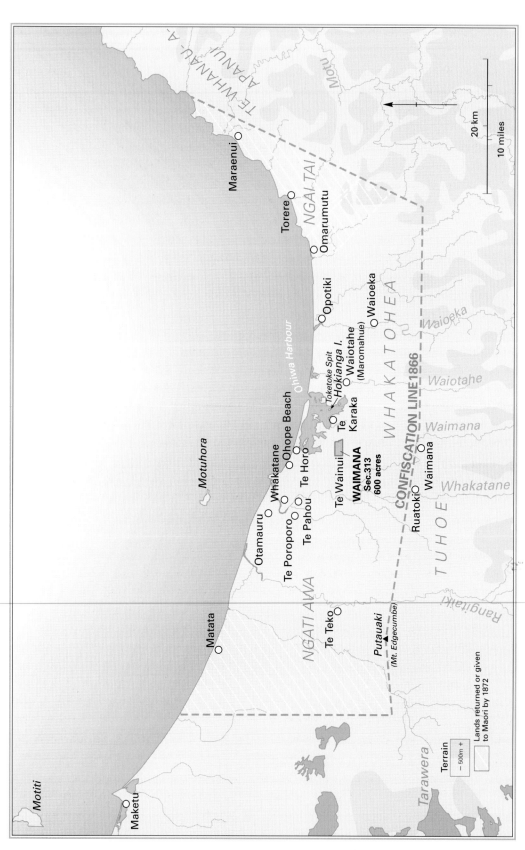

Map 8. Eastern Bay of Plenty

wanted. Onslow's political purpose was to test whether, in fact, an aukati, or line of demarcation against all the Crown's agents, had been established 'under the influence of Te Kooti', as had been represented to him.[175] Tuhoe's welcome for Onslow was thus intended as a manifestation of their loyalty and, equally clearly, of their determination to maintain their authority over their lands. In their view, and indeed, it should be noted, in Onslow's developed understanding, the two were not incompatible. At their meeting with Onslow, Tuhoe asked, among other requests, that land be found for Te Kooti at Te Wainui on the Ohiwa harbour. Numia, younger brother of Kereru Te Pukenui, urged that that land be given to Tuhoe, so that Te Kooti and members of the tribe who were with him might have a place to live. This reserve would also, Tuhoe hoped, give them access to kaimoana, which they had lost through the confiscations.[176] At the time Cadman, who had accompanied the governor, promised only to look into the matter.

Te Kooti himself had already met Onslow on this journey. Two days earlier, on 19 March, they had encountered each other when Te Kooti was journeying from Te Teko towards Rotorua for a large hui; this was, similarly, a gathering to petition the governor about Maori grievances. Onslow found Te Kooti camped by the Pakipaki creek near Putauaki mountain, in the company of 12 or 14 Maori men and two women. He was described as looking 'quite a respectable old gentleman', with a greying beard, and wearing a large straw hat. He was dressed in European clothing and carrying his 'green and white Sairey Gamp umbrella'.[177] When he was introduced, the governor expressed his gratitude for the welcome being accorded him, made possible by Te Kooti. To this Te Kooti simply replied, '"Aye, aye, aye!"'[178] He indicated that he had not come to see Onslow the previous year, when Onslow had visited Otorohanga, because he still faced the legal suit of the Atkinson government. According to the reporters, Te Kooti had little else to say beyond welcoming Onslow and hoping to see him again at Otorohanga (which Onslow said was unlikely). Yet there was a subtext to this accidental encounter, and to Te Kooti's relative silence.

Te Kooti had supported the decision to invite the governor as the 'one exception' to Tuhoe's ban on Europeans. He had been instrumental in setting up the meeting at Ruatoki, and indeed was expected to be there.[179] Instead, although he was in the district, he chose not to be present. This was Tuhoe's land, and Tuhoe's occasion. When he met Onslow he was coming from Te Teko — where the governor was going — and from a series of hui to prepare for Onslow's reception.[180] It is therefore clear that Te Kooti chose to absent himself. These preliminary meetings had certainly fired up some of the speakers, for they greeted Onslow at Te Teko as the representative of 'You people who are swallowing our land', who are bringing both 'good seed and bad seed'.[181] Onslow certainly did not forget this speech; it was the only one he quoted directly to Queen Victoria: 'we were designated as "Whales from Sea"' and '"you who have devoured the land"'.[182] When he encountered Te Kooti, the latter was on his way to Rotorua, where two petitions were being drawn up seeking an independent Maori mediator to be appointed directly by the Queen. They wanted someone who would watch over their interests.[183] Te Kooti was present at Rotorua while the initial drafts were composed, but again he left before Onslow returned there. In other words, Te Kooti was working ahead of the governor at each of these meetings; he was leading without being the visible leader. He was spiritually energising and cajoling each community, each area of mana.

Te Kooti had already voiced his concerns for Tuhoe. He chose to adapt an old song of theirs; his version tells of the wind blowing from Rotorua, hissing temptations in their ears:

> Whakarongo, whakarongo ra te taringa ki te hoko o te whenua e hau mai nei kei Rotorua. Hurihia, hurihia ra to kanohi ki Te Whaiti ki Ruatahuna ki Maungapohatu. Tikina, tikina ra te moni a te Kawana kei te peeke o Niu Tireni. He haonga na roto kia nohoia ai nga whare tiketike e te rangatira, kia noho noa atu ai nga rawakore i tahaki hei matakitakitanga ma te rau e pae nei e tangi ana ki tona whenua ka riro atu i te ringaringa o te Kawana, tangi kau ana te mapu e e.

> Listen, prick up your ears at the selling of the land, blowing in from Rotorua. Turn, direct your eyes towards Te Whaiti, towards Ruatahuna, towards Maungapohatu. Get, go get the money belonging to the Governor at the Bank of New Zealand. A greed within, for the stately houses to be occupied by the chiefs, and for the poor just to live on the shore, to watch for the hundreds who will be stranded, lamenting for their land taken away at the hand of the Governor; the sobbing resounds in vain.[184]

Te Kooti sang this song at the opening of Te Whai-a-te-motu, the great meeting-house Tuhoe had built for him at Ruatahuna. This was the occasion in late February from which he had just come, and it will be detailed in the next chapter. Suffice to say here that Te Kooti had startled Tuhoe with his bald statement that the house

> 'is good for nothing. It'll only be for playing with money.' 'Toroperepere': that's like when you play with marbles. 'And that's what you'll do — play with money in that house!'
>
> And that's true. That house was famous for a long time as a gambling den, days on end.[185]

Both the song and the words to Tuhoe feared for the loss of the land, even up to their sacred mountain, Maungapohatu. The song foresaw that even this might be sold to the government for the love of money, the love of gambling and the desire for 'stately houses' like the Pakeha. The song is still sung today as a warning.

During Onslow's visit to Tuhoe, Te Kooti had remained in the background and, clearly, had chosen not to see him. Instead, he emphasised that he was hurrying home to the meeting which Te Wahanui had called at Otorohanga to discuss Maniapoto's land. Cadman was due there. But Te Kooti left his 'secretary' at Ruatoki to watch and record all the events. He was described as a 'very smart young Maori in a mackintosh coat and policeman's hat', who 'took voluminous notes of all our doings'.[186] On 21 March, Onslow's party rode inland from Ruatoki a few miles up the river, escorted by some of the younger Tuhoe leaders. Te Kooti's secretary went with them. He is not named in any of these accounts, but again he was called Te Kooti's 'tout or spy . . . attached to the Governor's party so that Te Kooti be informed of the movements'.[187] He was from Tuhoe, and was described as being

> very smartly mounted and dressed in Te Kooti's uniform, top-boots, cord breeches,

over coat, and dark green velvet cap. He kept a most watchful eye on every movement of the party, wrote down the names of all those present, and was very attentive to all that was said about our future movements . . . .[188]

The government's caution about this kind of watchful eye, as well as Te Kooti's facilitation of the governor's visit, ensured that Cadman had the 'private interview' with Te Kooti at Otorohanga in April. The agreement they reached was that Te Kooti would 'give up all thought of going to Gisborne'. This was the pact he made, unpalatable though it was. In return, the government promised to keep gold prospectors out of the Urewera.[189]

Cadman described their discussion at some length.[190] He said Te Kooti had assumed that the previous government had abandoned its offer of Te Wainui, for which Te Kooti had been willing to exchange the land at Orakau. Orakau had proved to be only 'fit for birds and eels, and not suitable for human beings to live upon'. With the new administration, he hoped the offer of Wainui could be renewed. Te Kooti reminded Cadman of the ways in which he had shown his 'love to the Europeans' — by his 'protection' of Mackay at Te Kuiti (not quite accurate) and, ten years later, of Hursthouse. He reminded Cadman also that Bryce's pardon had been accompanied by the promise 'that the law would protect me in the future and that the Government would be my parent, and that I was to remain under the authority of the Queen'. This statement is the essential concept found in all Te Kooti's waiata from 1883. As the Whakatohea elder Jack Kurei said,

> wherever Te Kooti went — wherever he step foot from one area to another — he's singing. And one song he had — this concerns the whole of New Zealand, this song: 'Nei ka uru ahau i te ture ai mātua mo te pani mo te rawa kore' — I shall join the law to make it a parent for the poor people, for the orphans, for those without.[191]

Te Kooti told Cadman that the only time he had 'trampled on the *mana* of the Queen' was when he persisted in attempting to go to Gisborne, but that he had not intended his efforts to be seen in that light. 'In all my movements since then [the February 1889 interview with Mitchelson], I have never carried arms, but always trusted my protection to the laws and the *mana* of the Queen.' He promised to give up all thought of going to Gisborne.

The lever of influence that Te Kooti had with the government was his unique relationship with Tuhoe:

> 'As regards the Tuhoe (Urewera) people, I am the person that has the tying up of that district. I have always told them to be careful not to commit any wrong on the Europeans. There are two things objected to by that people — surveys and gold prospecting. I am very pleased to hear you say that you have refused to allow gold prospectors to go into that country. The natives place implicit confidence in me, and when I tell them to remain peaceable they will do so. I now ask you to let the matter of surveys and prospecting remain until it is seen what future action the Tuhoe will take. The Tuhoe are a good people and amenable to reason.'[192]

After consulting with the Premier, Cadman accepted these terms. He agreed that any future survey of Tuhoe's land must be carried out with their consent and in an open and clear manner.

The survey of Ruatoki had been determined upon by some of the Tuhoe chiefs, among whom were Numia and Tamaikoha. This decision was a direct consequence of Onslow's visit.[193] Later events were to show the extent of opposition which remained among many Tuhoe, and Te Kooti would soon be called upon to mediate. The offer of Wainui in 1891 was made, however, in exchange for the survey of Tuhoe land, and also for Te Kooti's promise never to go home.

Shortly after this interview, the government surveyor sent in a report about the land block at Wainui. Te Kooti asked immediately to see a copy.[194] However, once again — and unbelievably — the question of this land resulted in a protracted correspondence with the government, which would drag on for the next three years and continue unresolved until after Te Kooti's death. This time, the issue was complicated by the fact that Tuhoe had asked for the land at Wainui for themselves. Te Kooti stated firmly to Cadman that 'the Urewera had no authority from him to ask for this land'.[195] Subsequently, Tuhoe expressed a wish that Te Kooti should come to live with them at Ruatoki. This was, as Akuhata Te Kaha later explained to the Native Land Court, an attempt to fulfil Te Kooti's words at Te Whaiti in 1884: '"Let the Urewera be one people & one land"'. They had all begun to gather and settle at Ruatoki in consequence, and they wished him to join them there.[196] The long exchange of letters between Te Kooti and the government over the land grant (almost all of which, unfortunately, have been destroyed[197]) included one written in the midst of the developing dispute over the survey of Ruatoki. This letter of June 1892 expressed Te Kooti's desire to acquire a piece of land at Ruatoki, but from within the confiscated block.[198] Yet he had told Tuhoe firmly that he would not live with them. As Boy Biddle put it graphically, he said, '"No. In case you accuse me of pinching your poaka!"'[199] This desperate letter of 1892 seeking government land at Ruatoki was written because, by then, it had become clear that Wainui, just like Orakau, was virtually uninhabitable.

According to the records of the Ringatu church, Te Kooti first visited Te Wainui on 12 March 1891, on the journey during which he organised the hui for Onslow. He composed a song for Wainui, which it is said he sang on this occasion. In it he asked for 'the month to pass quickly' ('Tera te marama hohoro te kake mai') so that he could greet the land for which he longed.[200] It seems again to be a significant date, bearing the promise of a new dawn. However, it is clear that the particular block was not yet chosen, nor had it been properly examined. The surveyor's general report of the area followed, and in November 1891 Te Kooti met Cadman to select his particular piece. In actuality it was not until March 1892, when the survey of the precise block was organised, that the problems became obvious.

Shortly after their discussion at Otorohanga, Cadman had written to Te Kooti with Cabinet approval. He proposed that at the end of the current parliamentary session they reconvene in the district, and that they together choose the land. He also stated that this would be a grant which could never be leased nor sold, nor in any way alienated to Europeans, who might 'covet it when they see it under cultivation by your people'![201] The two met at Whakatane on 21 November. The meeting was formal; it was held in the

'The Expedition to the Urewera Country'. Photograph in Lord Onslow's album. Erueti Tamaikoha is kneeling, second from right in the front row. Alfred Cadman stands fifth from left in the back row; Onslow is beside him, sixth from left; Bush, the resident magistrate, is next to him. This photograph was taken at Onslow's camp at Opouriao on the morning of 22 March 1891. Tamaikoha at first refused to be photographed, saying that he did not wish to have 'his face for sale in the shops', but finally relented when it was explained that the photograph was for the governor's personal record. It was, however, published in the *New Zealand Graphic*, 2 May 1891.   Album W 14, Clandon Park, West Clandon

courthouse as a court session. A map of the Ohiwa harbour was displayed; the government's surveyor was present. Cadman told Te Kooti that he could mark out whichever piece he wished within the designated block of confiscated land. Then, because Te Kooti could not interpret the map, it was agreed that they would visit the area the following day and Te Kooti would point out the part he wanted.[202] The next day, Matiu, Cadman and the government surveyor went to the site; it seems, however, that Te Kooti himself did not. The choice then went 'for the second time to the Court at Whakatane. *Te Kooti* was there' ('Ka purua ki te Kooti i Whakatane. I reira *a Te Kooti*').[203]

In this manner, the block at Te Wainui was chosen and all seemed well. These November days in the early summer of 1891 are remembered among the happy times in the oral accounts: they are the days when Te Kooti and his followers celebrated with horse races on Ohope beach (the stake a sack of flour); the days when he sat on Whakatane's stone wharf on the old mill-stones, given by Ngati Pukeko after his attack on them in 1869, and chatted with friends.[204] This was probably about the time when he again met Gilbert Mair, who was living at Ohope and who joined in the beach races. It is also told how Te Kooti and a crowd of dusty riders arrived with a flourish to meet Mair at Ogilvie Ross's new home at Opotiki, where they tested each other's wits again in a cunning game of draughts.[205] (One would like to imagine that they played with real men on a life-sized board, as the Ngai Tahu chief Hone Taare Tikao once had with Te Keepa Te Rangihiwinui and Henare Tomoana!) It was only later that Te Kooti came to realise that — once again — the land he was to be given was almost uninhabitable.

Shortly after Te Kooti first talked with Cadman at Otorohanga, Matiu had recorded Te Kooti's preoccupation about where they all might live.

> Otewa Aperira 11 1891
>
> Ka puta te kupu whakaari mo te 12 apopo ake. . . . Whakahokia mai toku ora i tenei ra kia mahara mai ki ahau e tangi kopikopiko noa nei, a tae noa ki tenei ra ara ki te mutunga tonu. Kua riro to matou wahi tipu i nga tangata ke. Ko koe tonu ia hei matua tipu moku ake. Kati te whakahaerenga ai. E kore e tutuki te heke ki Ruatoki ara te haere atu i Otewa mo runga i te tono a Tuhoe. Otira kei te Hurae e mohiotia ai. Ka tuturu te noho i Otewa i te manenetanga ki te haere ko Matiu anake. Kua tuturu te noho. Ki te kore heoi ano.

> Otewa April 11 1891
>
> The prophetic saying came forth for the 12th, tomorrow. . . . Restore to me my well-being on this day; remember me who meanders about aimlessly weeping, even unto this day, that is, until the very end. Our own place has been taken by strangers. You yourself [God] shall be as my own father hereafter. Cease journeying about. The migration to Ruatoki shall not be achieved, that is, leaving Otewa according to Tuhoe's request. However, on the July it will be known. Remaining at Otewa is fixed because of [my] weakness. If [someone] goes it will be Matiu only.[206] [My] staying is settled. If not, so be it.[207]

The sadness is inescapable. The dilemma of homelessness, from which Te Kooti would never escape, is retained in the collective names by which he and those who lived with him are for ever known at Ohiwa: Te Heke, or the Exodus from Waikato, and Te Whanau-a-Pani, the Family of Orphans.[208]

Te Kooti — or rather, as it seems, Matiu — chose Wainui later that year. But the oral story which is told of the first sighting of the land itself is just as sad as Te Kooti's early fears. Te Kooti was living on Hokianga island when he sent Hoani Poururu up one of the estuaries of the Ohiwa harbour to try to look at the block which the government was proposing to give him:

> This chap just paddled his canoe up one of those estuaries, and he had a look in from out on the water there. And he said, 'Good gracious me!' He saw the massive timber then: just wild. So he came back and he said, 'Oh, not very good at all. Doesn't look habitable.' So Te Kooti sent Rakuraku up. He said, 'You go up there and have a look at it and see what this other fellow is talking about.' He trusted him. And Rakuraku came back: 'That man is right. That place is only fit for goats and crawly things. Not fit for human beings.' So Te Kooti said, 'Well, all right. That land God has given us — and you

turn round and say to me it is only good for goats and crawly things. Then I will go there, and stay with it.'[209]

And that is what he did.

Nevertheless, his dissatisfaction with the block, which proved to be quite landlocked, is made clear by the letters he wrote right up to his death. Although he met the surveyor, of whom he had approved, in March 1892[210] and the grant was certainly understood to be under way from that time, almost immediately Te Kooti tried to exchange some or all of the block for land on the coast, so that the people could have access to fishing. The government recognised the problem, and indicated that it was amenable to an exchange.[211] Then Te Kooti wrote again, as we have seen, trying to acquire some Crown land at Ruatoki, either by exchange or by purchase.[212] He was involved at precisely the same time in the offer being made to donate a section of Tuhoe land at Ruatoki for a native school, which Kereru Te Pukenui, Numia, Hetaraka Te Wakaunua and Tu-takangahau had proposed to Cadman.[213] The very last letter he wrote concerning Wainui, in April 1893, was received by the government four days after his death.[214] What exactly it said will never be known, for the letter is lost.

The block Te Wainui (Waimana 313), 600 acres, which now belongs to the Haahi Ringatu, was never formally transferred during Te Kooti's lifetime. Although it was certainly understood from early 1892 that Wainui had been granted to Te Kooti out of the confiscated lands, it was gazetted — and then as a general Crown land reserve for Maori — only in May 1895. This followed an agreement in May 1893, after Te Kooti's death, made at the request of Numia, that Te Kooti's followers be allowed to settle there. Their trek to Wainui was graphically recalled by Moerangi Ratahi: the women had to be lowered on ropes to the valley floor, so steep were the surrounding rock walls. It 'was a jungle, almost inaccessible, and the worst possible spot to found a marae', as Hoani Poururu had warned them, but they were obeying Te Kooti's will.[215] The reserve was then granted because the people had occupied it.[216] After yet another tortuous legal saga, the title was finally transferred from the Crown in October 1923, when it was vested in a trust of 12 Ringatu elders, set up under the guidance of Apirana Ngata.[217]

Despite all the difficulties, Te Kooti ultimately came to see Wainui as the home for the faith and the covenant. As Boy Biddle described it, he had come to recognise that each marae had its own ways and each was attached to one or another faith, but that the Ringatu themselves had no place which was their own. The first step Te Kooti took to rectify this was building a meeting-house on Hokianga island, where by 1892 he was more or less living permanently. Here he possibly held his last July gathering.[218] He named this house Te Here-o-te-Ra, the Binding of the Ra, with the underlying concept that the Ra would now be tied to one place. There would be no more travelling about the land. At one level, it was simply that Te Kooti was becoming older and more frail. At a more profound level, the idea of binding the faith and the days together was aimed at creating a permanent home for the Ringatu. This role of the nest of the faith was transferred to Te Wainui by Te Kooti in April 1893.[219]

Thus Te Wainui came ultimately to be seen as the 'promised land' of the Ringatu. As Boy Biddle said, Te Kooti's very act of accepting the land had 'cut out his ever going back to Gisborne'. Yet, as he also observed, Te Kooti's 'main thrust had been to get back to Gisborne'.[220] The decision to make Te Wainui the centre of the faith was taken out of necessity, and only in the last year of Te Kooti's life. But in the end Wainui would become, for the Haahi Ringatu, the 'eye of the island'. This is how Te Kooti described it in his last words.[221]

Te Kooti left Otewa in February 1893. The preparations for his departure had begun the previous year. At the beginning of August, he wrote to James White, the Opotiki agent for the steamer which traded from Auckland to the eastern Bay of Plenty, asking for an estimate of the cost per ton of shipping his goods to Ohiwa.[222] A second letter to White, dated 10 November, indicated that, although he had prepaid for a shipment which had already been despatched from Auckland, he had now received a bill for it. He was concerned that he was being deceived 'by this pakeha' ('a te pakeha nei').[223] A third letter, written from Hokianga island in a shaking hand only ten days before his death, forwarded £2 10s to the captain of the steamer for the cost of some telegrams; he also asked for the ten shillings to be reimbursed.[224] Dying, he was still wrestling with mundane details about his final move.

The Haahi Ringatu are certain that Te Kooti intended Te Wainui to be the final home for the faith, 'its roost' and its nesting-place. 'That's where Wainui will come into its own', said Boy Biddle.[225] The move was completed after Te Kooti's death. The ark of the covenant, which Te Kooti had intended to be placed there, arrived at Wainui at noon on 11 June 1893. As the text says, this was its final journey ('Ka tae tuturu te Aka o te Kawenata ki te Wainui').[226] The community of Ringatu which grew up around it were the inheritors of Te Kooti's vision, and of the land itself. But for Te Kooti the journey which he had begun to Wainui was never completed.

CHAPTER 14

THE JOURNEY TO MEET DEATH

'My word simply is: Save the land and the people.'

TE KOOTI AT OTOROHANGA, 15 APRIL 1891.[1]

There were still places to visit and journeys to make before Te Kooti began his final preparations to move to Te Wainui. In July 1891, although he knew now that he could never return to Turanga, he made his last visit to the East Coast. On the invitation of his old friend Areta Apatu, he travelled to Wairoa to hold the First of July there, this time at Kihitu, near the mouth of the river. As with every journey, there are different memories and different 'texts' from the occasion.

The story which has remained in the European imagination, to be told and retold, was the dispute on the new toll bridge over the river. Te Kooti's mounted party, 60 people, reached the bridge to discover that, unless they paid a shilling for every rider and horse, the gatekeeper refused to unbolt the entrance. After an argument, Te Kooti's 'secretary', who rode at the head of the party, angered at the expense, threw their money to the ground. The keeper demanded that he pick the money up and give it to him personally. At this juncture, Te Kooti rode up from the back and commanded courteous compliance. The story remembers Te Kooti as the man who rode quietly in the rear, and who came forward only to order that the law be observed.[2]

The party was bringing home the bones of some of the Wairoa people who had died during their long exile in the Waikato. The gathering was large, with visitors travelling from Poverty Bay and the Urewera to join it, and Te Kooti's words for both the occasion and the house were uncomfortably argumentative, but leavened with the promise of new possibilities.

For the old house, Te Poho-o-Tiakiwai, and for his former adversary, the Anglican minister the Reverend Tamihana Huata, Te Kooti said:

> Ka tiraha hoki te takoto o tenei whare. Ka maranga nga tara ki runga. Ka tau te taahu ki raro. Otira tera ano e tauria e te kohu. He wa tona, ka mahea atu te kohu i runga o tenei waahi.

> This house will lie open. The walls will rise up. The ridge pole will fall down. And, at the same time, mist will settle over it. After its time, the mist will clear away from this place.[3]

Kennedy Bay (Harataunga)

Auckland

Mercer

Nga Kuri–a–Wharei

Katikati

Whangaparaoa
(Cape Runaway)
Tikirau

Mokoia I.
Rotorua Rotoiti
Te Awahou
Waikuta Waiohewa
Ohinemutu

Te Houhi

Mangatu

Galatea

Puha Te Karaka

Gisborne

Taupo

Rotongaio

Tokaanu

Wairoa

Karioi

Petane Esk River

Ranana Parapara
Koriniti
Parikino Otoko

Napier

Kauangaroa

Waipukurau Waipawa

Motutawa

Aorangi

Porangahau

Kehemane

Wellington

Whanganui
Mangoihe / Northern
Whangaehu
Rangitikei
Rangitaiki

100 km

50 miles

Terrain
– 500m +

Map 9. Te Ika-a-Maui (North Island): the Journeys from 1883

For the people, the hidden words were 'Uperehi' (or, variously, 'Upereti') and 'Tai. Whaara'. As they were explained, they showed Te Kooti looking towards the future Ra at Parikino as the crucial occasion when it would be known whether his gospel had been accepted. Again it is clear that he was placing great importance on that gathering, and on his planned challenge to Te Keepa's work. He warned again of dissension, of the inner contempt of the chiefs for the low-born, of the destructive conflict which would occur when the commoners turned against them, destroying the chiefs, and of the practice of makutu. As for the land, he accurately predicted, 'Our pakeha friends are seeking reasons for making trouble for us' ('Kei te kimi tikanga o tatou hoa pakeha i naianei i etahi tikanga hei whakararuraru i a tatou').[4] But he also talked of two men who would emerge from the East Coast as organisers ('whakahaere') for the island, one of whom would be elected. The reference can be understood as anticipating the creation of the Maori Parliament, which took place at Te Waipatu, Hawke's Bay, in June 1892. Subsequently, when Te Kooti died, the Parliament was to adjourn for a day in his memory. Henare Tomoana, Te Kooti's former adversary, chief of Te Waipatu and now the Speaker of the Parliament, said that Te Kooti was one of the main people to support their movement.[5] His remark suggests that, despite all the friction with Te Keepa, and all Te Kooti's doubts about the effectiveness of the Kotahitanga, he had in fact been working behind the scenes (just as he had with Tuhoe) to help realise unity. He certainly shared with Hamiora Mangakahia, the first Premier of the Parliament, the view that Toiroa's words bound them to seek a lasting peace. In February 1892, after his return from Parikino, Te Kooti, despite stating firmly that he would participate in the Kotahi-tanga only when all the island was in agreement, had sent out three men to help gather signatures for its proposed Bills. Without the complete unity of the tribes, he said, there could be no benefit in it; and without unity it would indeed fail.[6] The recognition accorded him by the Parliament suggests that, for all his warnings about its worldly purposes and goals and the impatience and arrogance of its chiefly leaders, he had quietly given it some practical support. Even more certainly, although he had stood on the marae in rivalry with the chiefs, and had challenged them, they would naturally try to capitalise on his memory. They hoped to gather into their movement the religious enthusiasm he had generated among the people.

From Wairoa, in July 1891 the party travelled to Petane for what would be their last visit. The premonition that this would be so stands out in Te Kooti's words:

> Hurae 23. 1891. . . . A, e kore ai pea hoki ahau e hoki mai ki tenei wahi a mua ake nei. E hoki mai ranei e pehea ranei, ko wai ka mohio. No te mea ka he nei hoki tenei wahi me tenei marae, me nga tangata ano hoki. A ko wai hoki hei whakaaro? Ta te mea kua oti ake nei ano i au te korero o tenei waahi.
>
> Kai te papara rakau e tu nei te mutunga, ka riro katoa a konei, a ka noho nga tangata o tenei kainga i runga o tenei papara rakau nei.

> July 23. 1891. . . . And perhaps I shall never return to this place hereafter. Will [I] return, or how shall it be — who knows? For this place will fail too, and this marae, and the people also. And who will there be to plan? In fact I have completed the statement for this place.
>
> The end is at the poplar tree standing here. All from here will be taken away, and the

people of this village will remain living on top of this poplar tree [as all that is left to them].[7]

If the words foretell of the loss of their land (although a beautiful little meeting-house, Te Amiki, the Gathering-in of the People, stands there on a nearby site[8]), Te Kooti gave more lasting assurances to Petane. He spoke to them of Jehovah and his lasting promises: 'I am the Alpha and Omega, the beginning and the ending'. He said:

> Kei te toe mai nga rā e piko ai te tangata ki te aroaro o te Kaihanga, eke mai ai hoki ki runga ki te waka kotahi hoe ai. Kei te rā a Taitoko te mohiotia ai.
>
> Ko reira ano hoki a Te Whiti koropiko mai ai ki te tikanga kotahi.
>
> Kei muri mai i taua ra ka karangatia ano he rā ki reira. Kaore maku e karanga engari maana ano. . . .
>
> Ko reira tatau mohio ai, he rā tera no nga Poropititanga, mo nga matauranga, me nga Haahi; e hui ai ano kia kotahi te haere me te waka.

> The days remain when man will bow down in the presence of the Creator and climb onto the canoe to paddle as one. It will be known on the day for Taitoko [Te Keepa].
>
> Then also Te Whiti will bow down to the one faith.
>
> After that day another day will be called there. I will not call it but he himself [the Creator] will. . . .
>
> Then we will all know that that is the day of the Prophecies concerning the teaching and the Churches, on which [we] will come together, to be one in our direction and our canoe.[9]

The words illuminate Te Kooti's essential message of unity. His was a unity of spirit. The prophets, the chiefs and the churches would come together, and their journey would be as one. The warnings of conflict, and Te Kooti's challenges to rival Maori authorities, both secular and spiritual, were intended to make possible this ultimate harmony. The metaphor of the canoe in which they would all travel, and whose prow would turn towards the way, recurs in many of Te Kooti's speeches and songs. He never offered himself as the captain of that canoe; but he urged this collective search for Maori redemption.

The last great hui to which he journeyed, and where his messages concerning both rival prophets and his successor were elaborated, was the Ra held at Aorangi, near Te Awahuri, on 1 January 1893. He had been invited to carry the Ra there in the previous July, when a large delegation from Ngati Hau of Whanganui and Ngati Wairiki of Whangaehu had come to him. Their invitation arose out of Te Kooti's earlier visit to the Whanganui district, where he had disputed religious doctrines with the local minister, Arona Te Hana.[10] Now Arona, accompanied by the woman Te Ara o Rehua, who was known as a prophetess at Te Awahuri,[11] and Te Riaki and over 20 others had come to invite him to their marae. He accepted their call, and stayed a month in the district, travelling back slowly through Rangitikei, Whangaehu, Karioi and Taupo in the latter part of January and early February. Speeches from all these areas are recorded in the manuscript records of the Ringatu.

Te Kooti reached Aorangi on 31 December, where he kept himself apart and out of view. The newspaper accounts describe him remaining for lengthy periods in a separate tent;[12] it was the same pattern of separation which he always maintained at the great gatherings. He had brought his own 'native constable', Mokonui, whose role was commented upon supportively by the local police. Mokonui helped to distribute the provisions and also ensured that alcohol was not present among Te Kooti's people.[13] Te Kooti was also accompanied by three wives, all 'plainly dressed' and of differing ages. His eldest wife (probably Heni) was thought to be about 55, the second about 40, and the third was, in the predictable eyes of the local reporter, 'a rather pleasing-looking woman of about 25, and, judging from appearances, evidently the favourite'.[14] Te Kooti refused to go to Te Awahuri itself, where all the provisions for the hui had been gathered, 'alleging that evil awaits him there'. As a consequence all the facilities and supplies were moved, with considerable reluctance, to Aorangi and its tiny meeting-house.[15]

On 31 December Te Kooti first addressed the house in traditional fashion. Then, later in the evening, he made a lengthy speech. He stood up to pronounce the words for the day 'in the language of the "Atua"', as the local press described it.[16] They were, according to Hamiora Aparoa's records: '1. Tei 2. Umei 3. Pei 4. (Opera)'.[17] He then elaborated upon the first three of these words, but 'Opera' remained, as yet, deliberately unrevealed. The first is the famous saying which would subsequently be copied into many a family manuscript book:

> Tei 1. Ka torona atu toku ringaringa ki nga pito e whā o te ao, a, e kore tetahi ringa e kaha ki te peehi.
> Tokowhā nga kai whakararuraru.

> Tei 1. I shall stretch forth my hand to the four corners of the world, and no hand will be able to suppress [me].
> There will be four troublemakers.[18]

The remaining two were:

> Umei 2. Ka hoatu e ahau te toroona o te Ariki ki a koutou, ma te tangata e takahi.

> Pei 3. Ka waiho e ahau te Kotahitanga me te Maungarongo ki a koutou, a ka peke ahau ki te whakapono me te Rongopai noho ai, kei reira hoki tetahi waahi o to tatau mate. Wahanga kupu wahanga tangata, pakarutanga kupu pakarutanga tangata, a, e kore tenei Kotahitanga o te tangata e tere te ungutu, te take kai nga Rangatira.

> Umei 2. I will give the throne of the Lord to you; man will trample upon it.

> Pei 3. I will leave Unity and Peace to you, and I will go up to live with the faith and the Gospel; there too is one part of our trouble.
> Division of the word, division of man, breaking of the word will be the breaking of man, and this Unity of man will not come together quickly, the reason lies with the Chiefs.[19]

Thus he was renewing the warning that the Kotahitanga would not be achieved speedily, and that the fault lay with the chiefs. On 2 January he spoke more directly against his rivals:

> He kupu ake tenei. Tena koa, tikina wahia nga whare *whakakeke e toru* e tu mai ra, i te

motu nei. Te whare o Te Whiti me to Tohu, tae noa ki a Tawhiao. . . . No te mea kei enei whare-whakakeke e toru tetahi wahi e herehere roa nei i te ora mo tatau. E roa haere nei tetahi tika mo tatau. He whakaaro ake ki te pakaru enei whare whakakeke e toru, tera ano pea ka marama ake tetahi wahi ora mo tatau, me to tatau *Kotahitanga* hoki.

Here is another word. Now then, set to and break up the *three* houses of *resistance* standing in this land — the house of Te Whiti and that of Tohu and including Tawhiao's. . . . Because these three houses of resistance are one aspect of the long restriction on our well-being. A certain justice for us is a long time in coming. It is thought that if these three houses of resistance are broken then perhaps a safe place will come to light for us, and our *Kotahitanga* also.[20]

This attack on the Maori prophets can be explained by rivalries of mana. Te Kooti then also reiterated, as the koha was collected and some of it given to Arona, that their problems lay with the chiefs, Te Keepa, Wi Pere and others: 'What use is your money heaped up here?' ('Hei aha ra a koutou moni e whakahaupu nei?') he asked brutally.[21] Then Rakuraku spoke, under Te Kooti's instruction. He talked of the Kotahitanga which Te Kooti had brought, based only on his love for humankind ('mo te aroha anake ki te tangata'). Arona (whose song of opposition to Te Kooti, composed after the latter's previous visit in 1890, is included in Appendix B) then replied. He stated that unity between them had been established; their goals were as one. Thus the hui at Aorangi achieved, for those who were present, that which could not be won at Parikino. Nevertheless, Te Kooti's last words to Arona remained cautious: he instructed him to work with care 'so that it can be said later of you that you were a man' ('kia kiia ai ano koe a muri ake nei he tangata').[22]

On 8 January, the entire party, except for Te Kooti,[23] went to Awahuri. There they remained for the Twelfth, where Eria Raukura repeated Te Kooti's earlier sayings. But now Eria also explained the fourth, Opera:

'Opera.' Whakarite. Ko Tawhiao kua kopi tona mangai. Kahore ana mahi a muri ake nei.
Ko Te Whiti ko Tohu kua mutu ta raua.
Ko Te Kere kua tutaki taana.

'Opera.' Parallel [saying]. Tawhiao's mouth has closed. There will be no more of his work hereafter.
Te Whiti and Tohu's [work] has ended.
Te Kere's has come to a close.[24]

These words of Te Kooti hammered home the need for spiritual unity, by rejecting the rival prophets and their work. This was a time, to put it briefly, of severe friction within the leadership of the Kingitanga, which had established its own separate Parliament, the Kauhanganui, in 1892; moreover, Tohu and Te Whiti were deeply divided between themselves. Te Kere Ngataierua of Rangitikei was inevitably Te Kooti's main antagonist, once Te Kooti had stepped into his district of influence, the Wairarapa.[25] All these leaders claimed to be the mouthpiece of God. Unity demanded the rejection of their separate authorities in the search for the 'correct way' ('tikanga'). Where this was to come from, Te Kooti had said plainly to Arona: 'Look at me, I am the one' ('Titiro mai ko au tenei').[26]

The sayings from the journey home underline this continuing struggle for authority. On 17 January at Motutawa, on the Rangitikei river, Te Kooti spoke again of Te Kere, Tawhiao, Te Whiti and Tohu. He stood in the house Te Tikanga, which was associated with Te Kere and which had been built for an expected visit by Tawhiao that had failed to eventuate, and greeted the two by name, as if they were present:

> Tena koe, e te 'Kere', nou te whare. Tawhiao, tena koe, nou te whare. . . .
>
> Greetings to you, Te 'Kere', the house is yours. Tawhiao, greetings, the house is yours. . . .

Then he uttered his words of challenge. He spoke of his fear ('Kai te wehi ahau') of Te Kere, whose way ('tikanga') was different from his own. He called him his enemy ('he hoariri') and reiterated that Te Kere's work was finished. Te Kooti came now, he said, to bless him. He spoke in turn of Tawhiao, whose authority had been eroded and whose visit to England had been pointless. He described Te Whiti and Tohu as spent forces. He warned the people in the house, as he had warned Te Keepa (he told them), that the Kotahitanga of the Treaty of Waitangi would be to no avail. Impatience would destroy it and it would never succeed. The important thing, rather, was humankind.[27] This was the message he was preaching everywhere: the love of humanity. Unity would derive from following his pathway, not adopting the plans of the politician–chiefs, nor the failing hopes of the rival Maori prophets. For one who spoke of love, his words were barbed.

From Rangitikei, Te Kooti journeyed north to the Whangaehu river, where he stayed at Kauangaroa on 24–25 January 1893. This was his second visit; on the previous occasion (probably in December 1891), he had met with opposition from this predominantly Catholic community and had been forced to camp separately. Now, in the little house Kimihia, one of the most powerful dialogues recorded on this journey took place. Te Kooti was profoundly touched by the words of the chief Eruera Te Kahu (Edward Sutherland), who had invited him to return and who now greeted him in the house he had built for him. On the first day Eruera stood and explained that he had named the house Kimihia because he was searching for the life force and strength of his Maori ancestors, which had been usurped. 'Kimihia te mea ngaro' ('Search for that which is lost') was a phrase spoken by a number of Maori leaders at this time of power-lessness; it was, for example, a favourite saying of Tawhiao. Eruera said that, on this day, the life force had risen before him, and that Te Kooti himself had opened the door. 'Welcome, father, welcome. . . . Through the death of man and the land, it [this force] has come to you' ('Haere mai, e te matua, haere mai. . . . Na te mate hoki o te tangata me te whenua ka tae atu ki a koe'). In this manner the complete name of the house, Kimihia Te Maramatanga (Seeking the Clarity), emerged. On the following day, Te Kooti replied to him. He said that this was the first time, in all the marae he had visited, he had experienced anything like these words of Eruera:

> Ka tika to kupu e ki nei koe, naku i whakatuhera te tatau, maku ano e takahi tenei

marae. Ae, te take he aroha ake no te ngakau ki nga morehu tangata, koia i haereere ai kia kitekite. Ehara taku haere i te to tangata ki taku karakia, a he mea atu ranei, e tamā e, ina ke te oranga.

Ehara ano hoki i te haere he whakakahore i tou karakia i to wai ranei, kaore, engari he aroha. . . .

Ko taku kupu ano tenei, kia kaha nga Haahi nei ki te rapu tika mo tatau, nga whakapono ia e tika ana, ara, Mihingare, he Katorika.

Ko te kuhunga ke a nga Pakeha nei i te Atua ki roto i te moni, koia ahau i whakahē ai.

Ko taku ke e haere nei ahau, ko tau e korero mai na koe, ko te mauri me te mana kaha o [o] Tipuna e kimi na koe i runga i te aroha.

You are right in saying that I opened the door and that I too will tread on this marae. Yes, and the reason is love from my heart for the people who survive, this is why [I] travel to see them. My journeying is not to drag people into my faith, nor to say to them, friends, this is the way to salvation.

It is not a journey to oppose your prayers nor anyone's, no, rather it is love. . . .

This is my message: let the Churches persevere in seeking the right direction for us all, the faiths which are true, that is Anglicans and Catholics.

It is rather the Pakeha's hiding of God in money that I am opposed to.

Instead, the reason I have travelled about was, as you have said now, for the life force and powerful authority of your Ancestors, which you seek in love.[28]

After this revelation of his innermost purposes, Te Kooti journeyed to Parapara on the upper reaches of the Mangawhero river. There he stayed on 28–29 January, and there the exchanges were much more confrontational. Te Kooti's challenges derived, as he made clear, from the ambiguities of the people's earlier response to him. He referred particularly to Ngamokai, Karioi, on the upper Whangaehu river. Karioi had links with both Taupo and the upper Whanganui, and had seemed to commit itself to him, but this, he said, had become a false promise. He had therefore debated whether or not to visit that marae or to continue directly to Taupo. His speech at Parapara reveals the thrust of his teachings when challenged, and the energy with which he could respond. He reminded the people that they had promised him their land and their loyalty, and that he, in reply, had told them to remain in that place, steadfast, and to hold their land. There would be a day when the strength of the promise would be known. It had proved to be a false oath, and thus he added this third saying to those he had revealed at Kauangaroa:

No reira ko te toru tenei o nga kupu:
Tenei whenua ka mate ka riro katoa, a puta noa atu ka pau katoa tenei waahi. Te take he koha kore ki au, a he teka ano hoki ki toku aroaro . . . .

Thus this is the third of the sayings:
This land will be destroyed and all taken, and when that occurs this part will be completely consumed. The reason is that no offering was given to me, and there was deception in my presence . . . .[29]

He then repeated his condemnation of the chiefs Te Keepa and Wi Pere, uttered at Parikino. He described them as men who took government payment and who, as a consequence, had betrayed the cause of unity 'for the survivors of the Maori People'

'Te Koote's camp'. This lost photograph of Whanganui township bore this label on its obverse. It shows the camp on the riverbank near Pakaitore, and the long river canoes drawn up in front. It presumably dates from Te Kooti's visit in January 1893.　MISSING PHOTOGRAPH, AIM

('ki nga morehu o te Iwi Maori'). Then he spoke of his own loss, and of his lonely journeying. He identified himself tribally with Ngati Porou when he spoke, the people of the exiled communities of Coromandel and his own kin through his descent from Porourangi and Rongowhakaata. He spoke to the chief Hawira (Wira):

> Ko tatau Ngati Porou ma, he manene tatau nei, he aha hoki kei nga iwi? Ko Te Rangi-tahau, ko te Urewera he tangata whenua ena, tena ko tatau e kimi i tetahi ritenga mo tatau nei.
>
> [E] Hawira: 'Kia manawanui, tenei whenua kua mate, a, he ahakoa, kia manawanui ano. Kia mau ki tetahi wahi iti nei koa. Kati tonu hei whakaarohanga iho mo te kupu ki tenei marae.
>
> E Wira: 'Kia mau, ko te whare nei noa koa, ko te taiepa nei ranei ka mau. Kati tonu, hei taunga iho mo te kupu.
>
> Ko tenei whare hoki me te kupu ka tu tonu, ko te tangata anake e hē. Ka teka hoki te tangata ki te tangata, ara ki au, kaore ki te kupu . . . .

We, Ngati Porou, we are all strangers here. What do the tribes have? Te Rangitahau, and the Urewera, they are people of the land, but we are seeking some purpose for us here.

[Oh] Hawira: 'Be steadfast, this land is destroyed, but whatever happens, remain steadfast. Keep hold of even one small part here. That would be sufficient consideration for the saying at this marae.[']

Oh Wira: 'Hold on to this house even, or the fence should be held. That would be sufficient to establish the saying.[']

This house and the saying will remain, only man will go astray. Man will deceive man, that is, me, but not the saying . . . .[30]

The next evening, he spoke his final words for the house and the marae. He 'renamed' Te Poutikanga, the house, as 'O.A.I. Umera', and with it gave his warning that, if the people forsook God, then they would be forsaken by him. He spoke of troubles to come, and warned of two prophets, but, before them, two governors ('Nga Kawana e rua'), who would tempt the people. Finally, he said, and here he directed his words specifically at Eruera Te Kahu, who had travelled with him: be steadfast, hold firm to the purposes. He directed him to care for the remainder of the people and the land. Lastly, he reiterated to him to be wary of these two governors, who would rise from among them: two half-castes.

This last prophecy, or warning, is one of the best-known of Te Kooti's predictions. In its emphasis it plays on the doubts, sometimes expressed in the 19th century, of half-castes as ambivalent figures, manipulators and possessed of doubtful allegiances, particularly when placed in positions of power.[31] Wi Pere himself had acquired this reputation, partly because of the dominance he had created for his family over the East Coast tribal lands, which led eventually to a Maori loss of control.[32] Yet Te Kooti never spoke from a racist perspective and, indeed, he had already indicated that the One who would come after him could be a Pakeha. If he resorted to warning against people of mixed descent, his purpose was to alert local leaders to the need to control their own lands: this was the clear message he carried from marae to marae on this last journey. He urged all to be wary of the high chiefs and of men of doubtful allegiances: both could be pressured or bought.

From Parapara he decided to continue to Karioi, despite his cautions about its people's fidelity. He and old Te Riaki, who had travelled with him on this long journey homewards, arrived on 1 February. Now Te Kooti directed his words particularly at Te Maari, the daughter of his former supporter Nini, one of the most senior chiefs of Tuwharetoa, who had sheltered him after the fall of Te Porere but was now dead. Te Kooti told Te Maari to return to Taupo and guard her people's land:

> Ko Tongariro te maunga, ko Taupo te moana, ko Te Heuheu te tangata, a, ko koutou nga uri, ahakoa koe he uri wahine ka tika tonu koe. He waha mana tonu te waha wahine i nga rā i to Tipuna, engari me hoki ki Taupo.

> Tongariro is the mountain, Taupo the sea, Te Heuheu the man, and you are the descendants. Although you are a female descendant, you are still legitimate. The voice of women still had mana in the days of your ancestors; it is better to return to Taupo.[33]

Thus he urged leadership upon her, because of her high lineage.[34] His is a clear statement supporting a woman as an appropriate political leader, as women had been in the

The pretty little meeting-house Kimihia, decorated with mamaku (tree ferns) for a wedding, 1995. It stands by the Whangaehu river. There is also a monument to Eruera Te Kahu, tracing his whakapapa to eight ancestral canoes and to his Scottish father and grandfather. Eruera died on 9 October 1916, aged sixty-two. Photograph by Judith Binney, by permission of Val Kingi.

past. Taupo was not yet seized, he said plainly, but if she were to abandon it this could happen, and then she would be held in little esteem.

The second statement of advice to her was equally clear: never to deal with other gods, 'the Maori Gods, any stone or tree, or any other things' ('ki nga Atua Maori, ki te kohatu noa ki te rakau noa, ki nga aha noa'). He warned against 'the malevolent whistling Gods of the Maori' ('nga Atua kikokiko Maori whiowhio'), the ancestral atua who spoke in strange shimmering voices through a medium. He spoke again against the prophets, Te Whiti and Tohu, Te Kere, and Tawhiao, saying that their work was merely boasting and that they had abandoned the most important thing in the world, love: that which God desired for his people, and had created in the beginning. He warned also against charts to add up money, or money tables, as equally false guides. The only exceptions, institutions which could be used for guidance, were the Anglican and Roman Catholic churches. All others were false, given to Maori in their ignorance, to tempt them.[35]

This guidance to a 'daughter' makes Te Kooti's position very clear. He urged the power of one God, whose spirit alone could unite the tribes. His major rivals he considered to be spent forces, but he allowed a guiding role to the established churches. He also urged the caring for and retention of the land. He said:

Ko ahau e kiia nei etahi o koutou he Poropiti a he Atua hoki. E hika mā, whakarongo mai, ehara ahau i te Poropiti, ehara ano hoki i te Atua. Kaore ano koutou i matau noa ki te poropiti; kaore ano hoki te Atua e kai riwai. He tangata tonu ahau, kai raro tonu nei hoki e noho ana, kaore i runga o te rangi. Kaore ano tatau i kite noa i te Atua pehea ra tona ahua, pehea rā e karangatia nei e tatau i te ao. Ana kupu kai a tatau e korerotia ana, ara, ko te aroha, ko te pupuri i ana kupu me ana Ture, ko te atawhai ko te awhina tonu o tatau i a tatau ano, o tetahi iwi i tetahi iwi o tetahi tangata i tetahi tangata. . . . Ko ahau he kai mau ke au no te aroha ki te tangata me te Rongopai hoki.

Some of you say I am a Prophet and even a God. People, listen to me. I am not a Prophet, neither am I a God. You do not yet know the prophet; God would certainly not eat potatoes. I am just a human being, living right down here, not above in heaven. We have not yet seen God, what his appearance is like, how he is called by us into the world. His words as spoken are with us, that is, love, holding to his words and his laws, charity, and continual caring for each other, one tribe for another, one man for another. . . . I, I am rather a carrier of the love of man and the Gospel.[36]

The words could not be clearer, nor more orthodox. He claimed no divinity; he did not claim to be the one prophet, who was still to come, nor even to be a prophet at all: he was a mere 'human being, living right down here', eating potatoes.

Nevertheless, Te Kooti's followers thought of him as a prophet. The Ringatu church itself includes him in a carefully compiled list of the '*Prophets*' ('*Poropiti*') who emerged in the 19th and early 20th centuries.[37] His followers believed, and many continue to believe, that he had been entrusted with the gift of healing, which in their view is specifically bestowed by God.[38] For them, certainly, he was much more than the mere messenger he claimed to be. As Reuben Riki put it:

The Māoris live in the world of the spirits; they are today. When influenced [by] Te Kooti, [that is] the influence of the world of the spirits. Because Te Kooti was a god to them; there had to be a god — to be a god.[39]

By the final years of Te Kooti's life, the faith was developing autonomies of belief which transcended the claims of its founder. Quite possibly one of Hamiora Aparoa's purposes in transcribing Te Kooti's last speeches at such length was to document in detail the *man* with whom he journeyed. Most of the Ringatu tohunga today affirm the limited claims of the founder. They seek to maintain a separateness between the faith and the man. Te Kooti's last sayings certainly support their emphasis. But the faith has evolved and developed regionally under many different leaders. For most of Te Kooti's followers in the 1890s (and after), the Ringatu teachings have their roots firmly embedded in the soil of the Old Testament, and for them Te Kooti was *unquestionably* a prophet. He was seen as divinely inspired, a man whom the spirit of God had entered and through whom the spirit spoke. For some, he was 'a god himself (*he atua ano*)'.[40]

The moods of Te Kooti's speeches and songs on this long journey differ according to the audience. The advice to a 'daughter' was unassuming, while a chief could be chastised. But, for all the differences, the essential messages recur. Redemption lay with the people and the faith; mere political unity, proposed by the chiefs, would always betray. It was the task of each community leader to preserve the land and his or her own people, lest they should find that they were driven from it. Te Kooti spoke backed by the mana and life force of the ancestors. He spoke as a Maori spiritual leader to all the people in their time of great need.

The last stopping-point was Rotongaio, Tahau's home on the north-eastern shores of Taupo. Te Kooti arrived there on 5 February. Travelling with him in the same buggy all the way from Te Awahuri was Tahau himself: the old ties had been renewed. Te Kooti's speeches recorded at Rotongaio were primarily scriptural, and now his weariness becomes evident. He spoke of the long journeying from place to place, and from trouble to trouble. He told each of his followers, with the greatest simplicity, when they returned to their separate homes to think on the Creator and to hold to love. He said that the sayings of that day were finished. Nor would he return a second time 'to speak without omission of all those sayings, from the early days right to this day' ('ki te korero whakatepe ano i aua kupu ano, mai ano o nga ra o mua a tae noa mai ki o tenei ra ki ona kupu'). The sayings for 1893 begun at Aorangi were now completed. Each was said only once for its particular day; thereafter they belonged

> ki nga taringa o tena o tena taana whiwhi, taana pito, taana kore. Heoi ano a ko wai hoki hei kohikohi mai ano, a ka anga ka korero atu ano a mua ake nei, heoi ano, rato enei wa ka haere ake nei, he pupuri anake i aua korero, me te mahi, me te whakaaro ano.

> to the ears of each, [for] his possession, his end, his denial. And so, whoever gathers them up again and turns to speaking them again in the future — well — throughout the time ahead there will be only his retention of those sayings, together with the execution [of them], and consideration [of them].[41]

The journey was done, the task ended. What now followed remained to each and every one, according to their own understandings. This day, 5 February 1893, he said, was the last day of the sayings and all the talk. The year 1893 was the last year of the prophetic sayings of God ('ko te whakamutunga o nga kupu whakaari a te Atua'). There would be no more. The days of his predictions were complete. He spoke then of his frailty of body. He anticipated that he might not be able to attend the next Ra, called by Te Whanau-a-Apanui for 1 July at Waiorore, on the East Coast. The reason, however, would not be this body, for he told them that this frailty would pass, but, he said, through some trouble similar to that which had happened at Opotiki. His mind was undoubtedly on the developing tension at Ruatoki, which would soon lead to the arrests of some of the Tuhoe leaders close to him and in which he would be forced to intervene.

There seems little doubt that Te Kooti was exhausted at the end of this last journey back to Otewa. He was possibly ill with a recurrence of tuberculosis. He told the people sitting in the meeting-house at Rotongaio simply to remember the sayings, which remained. Then he left and retired to his tent. The text of his speech, recorded by Hamiora, tells us that the groups who had gathered to hear him speak stayed in the house, stunned and silent.

One major commitment remained in Te Kooti's life which must be examined before we can take the final journey with him to the Ohiwa harbour and his death: his long involvement with Tuhoe and their land. This commitment would lead also to his last political entanglements with the government's many agents — resident magistrates, politicians, surveyors and, once again, the police. It reveals what manner of man he was as he wrestled with the complexities of a survey of Tuhoe's land at Ruatoki, which brought terrible discord among them. What emerges is his unswerving determination to uphold the principle of law as the best instrument of government in a world in which Maori was divided against Maori.

Te Kooti's unique relationship with Tuhoe stemmed from the shelter they had given him in the years of war. Te Kooti's sayings for Tuhoe ('Tuhoe. Nga Kupu a T. Kooti') are recorded as beginning the night before the escape from Wharekauri. He spoke then to all the prisoners, and told them that the plans had been laid and they had their instructions. He added that he hoped they would reach Taupo, where the ark of the covenant would be raised up — if they arrived there without fighting. He concluded with the promise of Judges 2:1–5:[42]

> And an angel of the Lord . . . said, I made you to go up out of Egypt, and have brought you unto the land which I sware unto your fathers; and I said, I will never break my covenant with you. . . . And they called the name of that place Bo-*chim* (Pokimi): and they sacrificed there unto the Lord.

This text was confirmed with the offering of burnt sacrifices at Whareongaonga, and reaffirmed at Pokimi, the village beside Puketapu, the ancient sanctuary at the borders of Tuhoe's land where they rested in 1868. Then, in March 1869 at Tawhana, the further exchange of oaths took place. There, as we have seen, Tuhoe gave their land and themselves to Te Kooti. In return, he gave them the promise of Jehovah:

> 1869. *Tawhana*. Te owati ki a Tuhoe. Te kupu tenei a Ihowa.
>   Ko ahau hei Atua ki a ratau, a ko ratau hei iwi ki au.
>   Te Kawenata kai a Tuhoe.

> 1869. *Tawhana*. The oath to Tuhoe. This is the word of Jehovah.
>   I will be a God to them, and they will be a people to me.
>   The Covenant with Tuhoe.[43]

Te Kooti's relationship with Tuhoe remained unbroken through the long years of exile in the King Country. During this time they sent their carvers to work on a number of the houses of the Kotahitanga of the faith, including Tokanganui-a-noho. On 1 January 1884, after Te Kooti was free to travel, he came to Te Whaiti, where he renewed the oath:

> Ka mau taku pupuri i toku iwi me taku maunga, e kore e tukua e ahau te toenga o te tangata i hanga nei e toku ringa.

> I will maintain my hold on my people and my mountain, I will not let go the remainder of the people who were created by my hand.[44]

There, Tuhoe had built Eripitana for him, which from this date became the 'Holy of Holies'. It was from this time, too, that Te Kooti renewed his warnings to Tuhoe about their land, and reminded them that it was theirs to control.

Eripitana, March 1891. This engraving was derived from Thomas Ryan's sketch and published with his anonymous account of his visit to Te Whaiti, *NZ Graphic*, 2 May 1891. It can be compared with the photograph taken nine years later of the partly derelict house, p.327. Ryan annotated his sketch with the caption that the house was one of the most 'sacred worshipping whares in the Urewera country'. Tobacco, pipes and, significantly, watches were prohibited, and Ryan added that 'Te Kooti says the offence is punishable by the Atua.' Ryan's sketch-book was confiscated at Te Whaiti, because he had drawn Eripitana, but was returned.

Tuhoe had formed the Union of Mataatua, Te Whitu Tekau (The Seventy), at Ruatahuna in June 1872. Their purpose was to recover their confiscated lands, to prevent the sale and lease of their remaining lands, and to block the building of roads, knowing that roads led to access and ultimately 'conquest'. They also asserted their control over all the roads which led to their borders, and allotted the authority to guard these to the different chiefs.[45] Tuhoe also refused to allow any public officers or resident magistrates into their district.

The Union of Seventy was described at its foundation by Te Whenuanui as being the 'apportionment of chiefs among Tuhoe. There are this day seventy chiefs.'[46] It was not a union of chiefs; it was rather their collective shelter, their 'tawharau'. The resident magistrate at Opotiki, Herbert Brabant, who attended the gathering of Te Whitu Tekau at Ruatahuna on 23–24 March 1874, understood that the union 'excluded' the chiefs, which rather baffled him, as they were all present and spoke extensively.[47] The notion of the collective 'shelter' derived directly from Te Kooti's teachings and his distrust of autocratic chiefly authority. Oral histories seminal to Tuhoe tell that it was he who instructed Tuhoe to unite with the words: 'Kia tawharautia ai a Tuhoe' ('Let Tuhoe be sheltered'). The words themselves go back to the wars and beyond, in time, to the intertribal wars.[48] But Te Kooti told Tuhoe that they had God and the covenants: now they needed their union.[49] The prayers which protected the 1874 gathering of Te Whitu Tekau were described as 'Te Kooti's *karakia*' and they consisted of selections from the

Psalms and prayers from the Book of Common Prayer. They were conducted by a tohunga from Maungapohatu.[50] The flag of Te Whitu Tekau flew in front of the meeting-house at Ruatahuna throughout this gathering. It was said to be a portrait of a man, black on a red ground. This may have represented Te Kooti, for the flag was called 'the Te Kooti standard'.[51] The name Te Whitu Tekau was intended (in the minds of at least some of the Tuhoe leaders) to extend beyond Tuhoe into a union of all the Mataatua canoe tribes.[52] It was scriptural in its derivation, being based on Exodus 24:1 and 9, that is the instructions God gave Moses to choose 70 elders of Israel, who were 'to take some of the spirit' which he had placed on Moses.[53] Later, as will be seen, Te Kooti told Tuhoe that their shelter, 'tawharau', should more properly be 80 — perhaps to bring all Mataatua together.

At this feast in 1874, Tuhoe set apart ten great carved calabashes containing 1800 preserved birds. They were Tuhoe's 'repayment' for the food and clothing they had been given when they surrendered in 1870 and left their mountains, by government command, to stay at Napier, Whakatane and Opotiki for the duration of the last campaign. The taha were given so that no government claim could be placed on their lands for these 'debts'. Although Brabant tried to reassure them that such a claim would never be made, they remained, understandably, distrustful of his promises.

The Union of Tuhoe was never fully unanimous, even at its foundation. There was pressure on them to survey and lease part of their land in the eastern Bay of Plenty from the beginning. The issue of Tuhoe's closed Rohe Potae became ever more intense once speculations began as to the existence of gold in the Urewera country. A party of prospectors decided to turn back at Galatea in March 1889, because of the heightened tensions in the district after Te Kooti's arrest.[54] But the rumours of rich gold reefs continued to incite greed and, therefore, to place mounting pressure on Tuhoe.

The lands of Tuhoe had been closed to surveyors and prospectors since the wars. Very few Europeans were allowed to visit the interior during the 1870s and 1880s. In April 1889, Samuel Locke had met several of the Tuhoe chiefs at Ruatoki in an effort to persuade them to open the country, but had been firmly told that they would allow no one to wander in their country without their consent. As a consequence of this meeting, the Tuhoe leaders sent a collective statement to the government in which they defined their boundaries and listed the names of the chiefs who held the authority to defend their Rohe Potae against trespassers.[55] Only the year before Onslow's visit, the Minister of Lands and Mines in the Atkinson government, G. F. Richardson, was turned back at the confiscation line. This boundary was marked by carved posts, rahui — as well as settlers' fences. Tamaikoha had marked his post in the Waimana river valley, over which he had the recognised authority within Tuhoe, with the warning that any gold prospector or European who crossed it 'will make relish for my food'.[56] The invitation to Onslow had been an exception, and was known to be such at the time. Even the *New Zealand Herald* understood the issues, as it commented in its editorial on the governor's invitation: 'As for the Queen's writ, they [Tuhoe] carry out a better system of self-government than we could give them. There is no need for the policeman crossing the boundary line of the confiscated land.'[57]

Te Kooti's visit to Tuhoe in February 1891 had as its primary purpose the consecration (and reopening) of the great carved and painted house which Tuhoe had built for him at Ruatahuna, Te Whai-a-te-motu, The Pursuit across the Land. Its name recalls his long hunt by the colonial forces, and Te Whai-a-te-motu was built to remember the wars. The opening of this wondrous house is usually dated 11 April 1888, but it is certain that Te Kooti did not open it at this time. If the house was opened then, it may subsequently have been moved from its original site higher up Manawaru hill and re-erected. It had certainly been known for a long time as 'te whare tihokahoka', the unfinished house, for its construction began in 1872 and it had lain incomplete for many years. Then Te Kooti sent word that it must be finished, for an incomplete house had grave portents.[58] The reworking and extension of the house were under way in April 1889, when it was expected that Te Kooti would travel to open it on the following First of January.[59] In the event, the opening was late in February 1891.

A brief report described how the tapu on the house was lifted at three in the morning.[60] The scriptural text for the occasion, as Paitini Wi Tapeka told James Cowan when he took him through the house later, was, appropriately, Jeremiah 31:16–17:

> Thus saith the Lord; Refrain thy voice from weeping, and thine eye from tears: for thy work shall be rewarded . . . . And there is hope in thine end, saith the Lord, that thy children shall come again to their own border.

Te Kooti and 20 tohunga from Tuhoe entered the house, and at daybreak food was served for 1000 people. One oral tradition of Tuhoe tells that the people wished to make it a sacred house, like Eripitana. But Te Kooti said:

> 'Well, the only results you get from anything sacred or tapu, is spiders! That's the only people who'll live there. The house will be inhabited by air and spiders. But it will be remembered for the gambling of the people!' Te Kooti himself advised the people against making their houses tapu.[61]

His warning words for Te Whai-a-te-motu were

> Kupu tapu: Ereti Orete Ohuta
>
> Whakamāoritanga: Ka waiho koe hei whare toroperepere moni. Ko te kai mō roto i a koe he pūngāwerewere. Ka pau katoa te whenua, ko tēnei awa i mua i te whare nei ki tērā awa i muri i te whare nei, ka toe. Ka waiho te kotahitanga o te kupu, o te whaka-pono, o te tikanga, o te tangata ki a koe.
>
> Sacred word: Ereti Orete Ohuta
>
> Interpretation: You will be left as a house for gambling with money. Spiders alone will be your inhabitants. All the land will be consumed, and only this river in front of the house and that river at the back of the house will remain. The unity of the word, of the faith, of the way, and the people will remain with you.[62]

Rather than becoming a church-house, Te Whai-a-te-motu became 'the great Council Hall of Tuhoe'.[63] At times it would indeed be notorious for its gambling sessions. But it was also 'the shelter for Tuhoe' ('hei tawharau mo Tuhoe').[64] And with these words, Tuhoe were charged with the tasks of unity and fidelity.

Te Whai-a-te-motu, 1898. Just visible are painted and carved manaia and taniwha figures on the rear porch rafter (heke tipi) (right), similar in style to Tokanganui-a-noho. There were also two carved, polychrome marakihau on the porch. One was Te Tahi o Te Rangi, the ancestor of Tuhoe who was rescued by a whale and who, in his turn, protects his descendants. He is depicted with a long tubular tongue, enabling him to suck up fish and humans. The other was Te Putaanga. Photograph by Augustus Hamilton.   B1371, MONZ

This occasion was probably the first time Tuhoe had used the building for a large political assembly. One purpose of the hui was to confirm that the Rohe Potae of Tuhoe should remain closed to Pakeha. It was here that Te Kooti sang his song warning of the loss of their land. The *New Zealand Herald* described their meeting at Ruatahuna on 2 March, 'at which Te Kooti was the central figure' and where 800 people were estimated as attending: 'it was unanimously agreed that no gold prospectors, surveyors, or Europeans were to be allowed inside the Urewera boundary'.[65] It was there, too, that the one exception was reaffirmed: Onslow, who would be permitted to travel a short way up the Ruatoki valley. The gathering at Ruatahuna then dispersed, largely because of the shortage of food. It had originally been intended to continue the assembly until the

Interior of Te Whai-a-te-motu before its renovation in 1932. The realistically painted rafter (centre right) contained three images of people snaring or spearing birds in the Urewera forest, perhaps bearing reference to Te Kooti's means of survival during the wars, as the painted images in the houses often refer to larger histories. The pigeons are feeding on miro berries, the best time for catching them for their flavour. The two carved poutokomanawa (the upright posts supporting the ridge pole) are Whitiaua and (rear) Toroa (Albatross), captain of the Mataatua canoe. Hidden beneath Toroa's cloak and piupiu is a collar, tie and suit: thus he is portrayed as a navigator for the living.   C1007, MONZ

governor's visit, when the chiefs were expected to join him at Ruatoki, but this proved to be impossible.[66]

Te Kooti had also been expected to attend the hui at Ruatoki. It was reported from the Ruatahuna gathering that he would tell Tuhoe on that further occasion 'three things more, but what they are no one knows'.[67] Instead, as we have seen, Te Kooti chose to leave before the meeting eventuated. He orchestrated several hui, but decided to avoid the governor. After their accidental meeting and Te Kooti's subsequent compact with Cadman, in which it had been agreed that there would be no prospecting but that the surveying of Ruatoki could commence if Tuhoe agreed, Te Kooti seems to have felt that his contact with the governor had been significant. When Onslow left New Zealand, Te

Kooti wrote to him in February 1892 to wish him well. He added simply but plainly:

> Heoi te mihi he tono kia whai kupu iho koe ki te Minita mo te taha Maori me aroha ia
> ki te Iwi Maori tae noa ki nga whenua. Ara ki a Timi Kara otira ki tau tangata i
> whakarite ai.

> This is a request of ours, that you speak to the Native Minister, that he deal fairly with
> the Maori People, and with their lands. We refer to James Carroll, or to whomsoever is
> appointed to that position.[68]

But by the time he penned this modest request, the issue of the Tuhoe lands was erupt-
ing into a major political concern.

The problem was the division and conflict among the people over the intended Ruatoki survey. The leading chiefs there, Numia Kereru and Hetaraka Te Wakaunua, along
with Te Kooti, had agreed that it could take place. A meeting had been held at Ruatoki
on 22 November 1891 — the same day as Te Kooti's land at Te Wainui was picked out
in Cadman's presence. At Ruatoki, Te Kooti and the Ngati Rongo leaders met Cadman
and they reached a general agreement on the terms by which the survey of the Ruatoki
block could begin, on Ngati Rongo's application;[69] this was the preliminary to obtaining
their title of ownership though the Native Land Court. The survey papers were issued
in January 1892, and the survey was expected to start the following month, just as Te
Kooti was writing to Onslow.

However, it soon became apparent that there would be obstructions from among
Tuhoe. One problem which emerged was that an old application for the Urewera had
been made by Ngati Awa[70] — intended as a means of claiming the land, or at least to
ensure their inclusion in any grants of title. Other applications had followed — eight
in all by the beginning of 1892. The original Tuhoe application had been lodged by
Netana Te Whakaari, Numia Kereru and Tamaikoha in March 1891, following Onslow's
visit.[71] It was for the survey and establishment of title of the Ruatoki block. They then
discovered that they were not, in fact, the first applicants. Early in February 1892,
Numia wrote urgently to Cadman asking him on whose application the Ruatoki survey
had been authorised. Cadman thereupon informed him that, in fact, eight applications
(and 78 signatures) had been lodged for the survey of the Urewera, and that they were
acting upon them all.[72] Two of the applicants Cadman cited were the Ngati Awa chief
Wepiha Apanui and the Ngai Tai chief Wiremu Kingi Te Kawau, both of whom were
now dead. Te Meihana Koata of Ngati Pukeko of Whakatane had also sent in a petition
(as well as signing Wiremu Kingi's) and, despite Meihana's own query about it, his
petition had been included as one of those being acted upon.[73] Old Makarini Tamarau,
whose primary area of tribal authority had been at Waikaremoana but who was one of
the senior chiefs of Ngati Koura of Ruatoki and was now living there, also claimed the
land, to contest Numia.[74] In Numia's mind, Makarini became the major obstacle to the
Ruatoki survey, as he had been 'charged' by Tuhoe at the founding of Te Whitu Tekau
with carrying out their 'general policy': that is, 'to resist European customs'.[75]

All this was not just a clash of territorial ambitions, nor even a refusal to define
territorial boundaries among Tuhoe, whose family groups all had rights there of differing kinds and degrees. The problem was intensified because Ruatoki had assumed a

One of the original rafters from Te Whai-a-te-motu on an overturned truck on the road from Ruatahuna to Te Whaiti, 1932. They were being taken to the Dominion Museum (now Museum of New Zealand) in Wellington. Te Whenuanui II (Te Whenuanui Mihaka, who with his father was one of the carvers of the house) gave permission for the rafters to be moved but told Thomas Heberley, the curator, that 'I was taking a risk as the tapu would not be lifted until I passed through the gates of the Urewera.' All the work survived unscathed, although Heberley broke some ribs. Photograph by F. Corkill.   A630, MONZ

unique importance as the gathering-place of Tuhoe. It lay within the lands that Tuhoe had placed under the mana of Te Kooti in 1869. Following his directive to become 'one people & one land', they had decided to come to live together at Ruatoki. As Akuhata Te Kaha explained, it was soon after their union was reaffirmed at Te Whaiti in January 1884 that Tuhoe began to gather at Ruatoki, so as to live as one 'in consequence of the word of Te Kooti'.[76] All Tuhoe saw Ruatoki as their own, while for Te Kooti's followers that was where they had chosen to reside to fulfil their compact with him.

These doubts and concerns were the source of the spiralling conflict, which would continue long after Te Kooti's death. The decision to undertake a survey was, as Tuhoe had known when they made their original compact of the Seventy, the lever which would ultimately force open their control of their lands. Their power and their ability to set their terms with the government lay in their unity, but the very place they had determined to be the visible statement of that unity under Te Kooti, Ruatoki, was, tragically, to be the seedbed of their division.

Because of the developing tensions, another hui was held at Ruatoki on 20 February 1892. There, Ngati Rongo confirmed their decision to allow the Ruatoki survey, but only on their application. Their decision to go ahead had become, as Numia put it clearly, their statement that 'the land is ours'.[77] This survey was intended, by Numia,

specifically to shut out the claims of Ngati Awa and Ngati Pukeko of Whakatane.[78] But
the opposition grew, and it came from other senior Tuhoe chiefs with strong kinship
claims in Ruatoki, including some who had signed the original application and who
now no longer wanted it to go ahead. The mounting opposition was led by the younger
chief Paora Kiingi Paora (Paora Kiingi Te Urunga), who was a staunch follower of Te
Kooti, to whom he would appeal for guidance. It also included the senior leaders
Tamaikoha and Rakuraku, both of whom had kinship rights at Ruatoki, as did Paora
Kiingi. Indeed, those who wished to have the block surveyed and most of those who
did not were all leading figures within Te Hapu-oneone, the original people of the
Ruatoki and Waimana districts.[79] The conflict which grew derived from the fact that
they each had distinct family and hapu identities, which they did not want overriden by
the pre-eminent hapu, Ngati Rongo. Moreover, the two outspoken leaders of Ngati
Rongo who pushed for the survey, the young chief Numia and the older man Hetaraka
Te Wakaunua, were opponents of Te Kooti's teachings. They opposed the vision of turning their land into the gathering-place of Tuhoe and Te Kooti's 'place of residence'.[80]
Te Kooti's prediction of April 1891 (quoted in the previous chapter), in which he anticipated that Tuhoe's desire to bring him to join them at Ruatoki would not be achieved,
was based in this conflict.

These dissensions grew within Tuhoe. As a consequence they held another urgent
meeting at Ruatoki on 17 March 1892. Te Kooti, who had arrived in the district on 2
March to look over the government land at Te Wainui, came to the gathering. All those
who wished to survey, and all those who did not, were present. It seems clear that they
came to a general consensus to stop the survey going ahead. Paora Kiingi, Te Whenuanui, Tamaikoha, Te Whiu, Kereru Te Pukenui, Te Makarini and 73 other signatories
wrote to Cadman and to Percy Smith (the Surveyor-general) to inform them of their
decision. They told Smith that 'it was decided by Tuhoe, Ngatiawa and Te Kooti te
Turuki not to allow the survey, roads, lease, sale of land, prospecting for Gold and
mortgage within the Tuhoe Territory to trouble them.'[81] To Cadman they said the same:

> Te kupu i oti, te ruri kaore i whakaaetia. . . . Kua tukua ki te iwi ki nga rangatira katoa
> o Tuhoe ki a Te Kooti hoki tuturu te tuku a taua hunga tono ruri kua mau kei te iwi
> e pupuri ana nga rangatira pupuri.

> The word that was settled was that the surveys should not be agreed to. . . . They left it
> to the tribe, and to all the chiefs of Tuhoe, and to Te Kooti, these men who had applied
> for the survey have definitely left it to them and that it is now with the tribe, being
> kept by them.[82]

But these letters were written just as the Ruatoki survey started.

It had been authorised by Numia, despite the collective decision of Tuhoe.[83] The
consequent survey party, which set out on 29 March, was watched closely. No conflict
occurred because the surveyor himself was waiting on the government's instructions;
indeed, he had promised Tuhoe that he would not begin work for a few days, in order to
give the petitioners time to communicate with Cadman to 'ask that their "rights and
privileges" shall be regarded'.[84] Once he began surveying, however, he was quietly
escorted back to the confiscation line and his instruments removed. As a consequence,

Portrait of James Carroll from Kuramihirangi, Te Rewarewa marae, Ruatoki. This painting, by Rehu Kereama, was included in the house as a reminder that Carroll was involved in the alienation of Tuhoe land. Above him is a sinuous marakihau-type guardian, watching. Photograph by Gillian Chaplin, 1978.

James Carroll, MHR for Eastern Maori, was sent to discuss the matter with Tuhoe. He met the elders on 7 April and his stance (no doubt directed by Cadman's avowed interest in opening up the land) put the wedge in further. He told them that, as they had set the law in motion by requesting a survey in the first place, it would have to be undertaken. He was prepared to limit the area involved to only about 11–12,000 acres (about half the Ruatoki block), and also to give them a few weeks to think about it, but in the end the survey must go ahead.[85]

Throughout March, Te Kooti had stayed among Tuhoe and Ngati Awa wrestling with these issues. He went first to Awanui-a-Rangi at Te Pahou, Whakatane, where Tuhoe and Ngati Awa assembled under the authority of the man who was now the paramount chief of Ngati Awa, Te Hurinui Apanui, nephew of Wepiha. Hurinui had become a staunch Ringatu and he would, from this time, be a significant figure in the history of the faith. Among the senior Tuhoe chiefs present was Te Wakaunua, who still distrusted Te Kooti's teachings and who would continue to press for the original agreement to survey made by Ngati Rongo. Also present were old Te Whenuanui (who was the main carver of Te Whai-a-te-motu) and Te Ahikaiata, both of whom had been among the Tuhoe elders who had originally gifted the land to Te Kooti in 1869. At this gathering, Te Kooti spoke clearly to supporters and opponents alike:

> Tuhoe kia mau to whenua, kaua e rūritia kaua [e] hokona, ko te manawa hoki tena o te motu nei.

> Tuhoe, hold on to your land, don't let it be surveyed or sold, for it is truly the heart of this island.[86]

And he sang to them equally clearly, but now more sadly:

> Haere ra te whenua e huna i a koe, haere ra te whenua te ora o te tangata. Hoatu koe i mua ko au hei muri nei. Kore rawa te tangata i mahara ki a ahau, he kupu ka whanui ki te iti ki te rahi. Na te mahi whakatete nana i tiwara to te rangatira hemonga he ruri e i.
>   E Waka ma e, e ahu ki uta ra ki a Te Whenuanui e noho noa mai ra na Te Ahikaiata i pupuri te kupu o te Tikanga to te tangata iti tona oranga e i.
>   Moumou hanga noa taru nei a te kupu te whakatauria ki runga ki te whenua. He aroha noa ake noku ki te tangata, ko te manawa ora hoki tenei o te motu nei e i.

> Go, oh land, hide yourself. Go, oh land, the life of mankind. You go ahead, I will follow. No one remembered me, and everyone, whether leader or of the commoners, has been remiss. It was the quarrelling which caused the rift, surveying the demise of chiefs.
>   Oh Waka, you and the others, go inland to Te Whenuanui who remains there. It was Te Ahikaiata who retained the meaning of the Faith, the salvation of the ordinary person.
>   Wasted indeed is the deep contemplation if it is not concerned with the land. It is only my concern for mankind, for this [the land] is the heart of the well-being of this island.[87]

Tuhoe then pleaded with him to help them stop the troubles afflicting the people and the land 'within the Shelter of Matatua' ('ki roto i te Tawharau o Matatua'), that is, the Seventy ('kia 70 tekau nga Tangata'). Te Kooti replied:

> 'He Aitua he Tawhara he pouaru hoki — engari kia toopu, na ka whakaekea ki te 80 hei whakahaere mo nga raruraru. Ko Te Hurinui hei Tiaki.' A oatitia iho e Te Kooti taua whakahaere. Tu ana ia herea ana e ia tona tatua maurea ki te pou tokomanawa o taua whare.

> 'It was an Omen, an Odd number, a widow (a solitary branch left behind on a tree) — rather, when they do assemble, let the number be 80 to deal with the difficulties. Let Te Hurinui be the Guardian.' The planning was put under oath by Te Kooti. He stood up and tied his belt to the main post of that house.[88]

In this dramatic manner Te Kooti tied the tribes of Mataatua and the house together as one, with himself. And he gave them a new directive, to become the Eighty.

This narrative is one of the seminal stories of Te Kooti. There are now as many

Te Whenuanui at Te Whai-a-te-motu, 1902. His adopted daughter and his wife sit beside him.
Photograph by W. A. Neale.   117040 1/2, ATL

versions as there are elaborations of its meaning. What — or who — are the additional ten? As Boy Biddle tells it:

> Te Kooti decided that 70 was an uneven number. He said, 'No. You make it even. We'll take it to Eighty. I'll give you ten.' From that day to this, nobody knows what the ten is. It was a way to stop Tūhoe closing the door. The ten he put on so it could never be closed again to anybody. We term it 'He taha wairua tērā' ['that spiritual aspect']. It's just to keep it open, available to any person. So it could never be closed to anybody. It's open all the time.[89]

Thus the ten was seen as a device to allow others into the faith: 'never to lock it up'.[90]

Yet others have suggested it should be the proper number for the church committee (Te Roopu) which Te Kooti first set up in 1888, while other opinions suggest that the ten may rather be understood as the ten commandments, or the law of God, to provide the necessary unity when 70 men are not in themselves sufficient. Thus very different understandings now exist.

Another version of this narrative is recorded in a collection of texts kept by Te Haahi o Te Kooti at Te Teko. The narrative is part of a body of doctrine called there the seven Seals ('Ko nga Huri e (7)'), which, in their view, Te Kooti laid upon the land in the years 1891–93. There, it is told how Te Kooti instructed the Mataatua tribes to plait the binding with which he girdled the people and the house:

> Mataatua he maurea kia whiria, e toru (3) enei tangata. Ko te Mihingare, ko te Katorika, ko te Ringatu. Ka tatuaria e ahau ki tenei maurea ko Te Hurinui te kai haerere o runga o enei waka. Ko te tamaiti a Te Kooti tenei 'tawharau'.
>
> Mataatua, plait a binding. Let there be three (3) peoples: Anglican, Catholic, and Ringa-tu. I shall girdle Te Hurinui with this binding, as the helmsman for these canoes. The son of Te Kooti is the 'shelter'.[91]

From this powerful though enigmatic moment, new histories have sprung. Among Tuhoe, by the turn of the century it came to be understood that 80 was the proper number to complete the union of Mataatua and to represent all their different areas.[92] Consequently, when Rua, claiming to be the 'son' of Te Kooti and the 'shelter' of Tuhoe, took 80 chiefs of Tuhoe and Ngati Awa, including Te Hurinui, to Gisborne in 1906 to meet the King and recover the land, he was consciously seeking to complete the tasks which Te Kooti had set. This story has been told elsewhere.[93]

It was during this visit of Te Kooti to Tuhoe and Ngati Awa in March 1892 that the school inspector Henry Hill accidentally encountered him and, in his pocket notebook, drew the best-known sketch we have of Te Kooti (p.189). Hill happened by chance to attend a hui held at Kokohinau on 29 March, the day when the survey began. He was taken to meet Te Kooti, who was living apart in a separate whare. Hill described him in some detail, albeit crudely:

> Te Kooti at Te Teko. He wore a square plaid suit grey with black stripes.
> Hat — soft tweed.
> Height — 5' 8".
> Beard grey — very straggling.
> Fingers 1. 2. on left hand gone as drawn by me. They had slight appearance of nails forming at ends. 2 fingers on right hand broken. Portion gone but usuable [*sic*].
> Kindly face. Very intelligent. Suffers from asthma.
> He appears to be about 60 years of age.
> No adornment except Tau-Tau [greenstone ear pendant]. Thick knitted socks. Beard wiry & thick. Hair closely cut & showing dull grey.[94]

Some of these details Hill incorporated in his sketch. Later he recalled Te Kooti had concluded their conversation, when talking yet again about his exile to Wharekauri: 'All is over. I am done fighting. The Government has forgiven me and I have forgiven all the pakehas.'[95]

Hill also sketched the marae during his visit, showing that Te Kooti's separate whare had been constructed beside the meeting-house, Ruataupare. It was sited in the place of honour, facing north, like the house: the 'mana wairua', the spiritual authority over the people had been bestowed upon him.[96] Hill also observed how Te Kooti judged a case of alleged makutu, which was said to have caused the death of a man three months earlier and about which Te Kooti had already been informed when he was at Te Pahou. Because 'Te Kooti had the power of seeing & knowing mens thoughts' he was asked to determine the matter. The accused, Hikitene, was brought to the marae at Kokohinau and, when Te Kooti charged him with not only this death but that of two other men, he hid in fear. Then Te Kooti stated that Hikitene had also attempted to seek his, Te Kooti's, death when he had stayed in the district, but had failed. He told the people that Hikitene must be sent away within a week; if he refused to go he should be shot as the means of 'safeguarding themselves'.[97] But Te Kooti also urged the people to write to the government to obtain its confirmation of his sentence. This decision to place the final judgment in the hands of the law was a critical factor, which Hill failed to comprehend. If Te Kooti was judge on the marae, and used the power of threat, he acknowledged that he was under the law. The sentence — in practice, social banishment — was effective, but also limited. The narrative indicates Te Kooti's role as adviser and mediator in a world where the still unprecedentedly high Maori mortality was explained by the feared power of makutu; but he was also directing the community to abide by human law.

Te Kooti's stay among Tuhoe and Ngati Awa revived their joint determination to stop the survey of the Ruatoki lands. He acted as their guardian, and he had visibly reunited most of the people and the land. Carroll's visit in April now threatened this decision. Because of the 'promises [made] to Te Kooti',[98] Carroll wrote to him immediately after meeting with Tuhoe, to describe the situation as he perceived it and to state exactly what his intentions were:

> E koro, tena koe. He whakaatu ake tenei naku i etahi korero ki a koe. I hoki mai au i Ruatoki, i haere au ki te titiro i te raruraru a Tuhoe mo ta ratou ruri. Pono atu au e kaha ana tetahi taha ki te ruri, e kaha ana tetahi taha ki te whakakore.
>
> I mea atu au ki a ratou na ratou ano taua ruri, ara na etahi o ratou i whakaohooho te ture i runga i ta ratou tono kia ruritia te whenua.
>
> Ko tenei, kaore e taea e ratou te whakatete maori [i] taua Ruri. Kua hara ratou ki te ture, a me whakarite e ratou te taha ki te ture — Ko taku kupu atu ki a ratou me whakatutuki poro te ruri i te wa e iti ana, kia wawe te rite atu — Ki te oti tena i a ratou maku a muri atu. Katahi au ka kaha ki te whakamana i a ratou hiahia i te mea hoki kua rite mai te taha ki au ki te ture. . . .
>
> Ara, ahakoa oti taua ruri i te wahi iti i ki ake nei au, ka taea e au te whakatapu taua wahi, otira te rohe katoa o te Urewera. Ka whakahokia e au te kai-ruri, ka araitia e au nga ruri a muri atu me nga Kooti Whenua Maori. E kore e tukua e au kia mana nga tono a nga iwi o waho. Kia rite rano te whakaaro a te iwi nui tonu, otira ma te reo tonu o te iwi nui e whakakeukeu te ture, katahi ka pera. Kati tena.
>
> Katahi ano au ka mea atu ano — 'Ki te kore koutou e whakaae ki taku kupu ki te

tuku mai i ta koutou raruraru ki au maku koutou e awhina — heoi ka whakawatea au i
au ma koutou ano ko te ture e whakaoti a koutou raruraru. Ko tona mutunga ka puta
tena ruri ki te rohe nui katoa o te Urewera, kaore e taea te puru.'

Sir, greetings. This is my explanation of some news for you. I have returned from
Ruatoki [where] I went to look into Tuhoe's problem over their survey. I believe one
side insists on the survey and another is determined not to have it.

I said to them that they themselves caused the survey, that is, some of them invoked
the law by their order that the land be surveyed.

My [point] is this: they will not achieve that survey through a Maori quarrel. They
have broken the law, and they must put right the legal side. My advice to them was
that they should at once bring the survey to a final conclusion while it is [a] small [area]
so it can be settled immediately. If they complete that, it will be up to me thereafter.
Only then will I be able to sanction their wishes because my position with the law will
be justified. . . .

That is, although that survey over the small part which I mentioned above will be
completed, I will be able to restrict that part, that is, the whole region of the Urewera.
I will send back the surveyor and I will prevent surveys thereafter, and the Maori Land
Court [sittings]. I will not allow the demands of the tribes outside to be authorised
until the opinion of the whole people is the same, that is, the very voice of the whole
people will move the law, but only then will it happen like that. Enough of that.

Then I also said — 'If you don't agree to my suggestion to give your problems to
me, for me to help you — then I will free myself [of you] and it will be up to you
yourselves and the law to end your troubles, and the conclusion will be that that survey
will come out right over the vast region of the Urewera. Blocking it won't be
possible.'[99]

It was this understanding to carry out a limited survey only that made Te Kooti accept
Carroll's terms. Paora Kiingi had attempted to seek out Te Kooti — with Carroll's
encouragement — to discuss the matter further; however, ill health forced him to turn
back, and what he wished to urge remains unclear. On 2 May, Cadman met with Te
Kooti and Wi Pere at Otorohanga. Carroll had sent a telegram to the latter urging that
even the limited survey should not proceed until Te Kooti had had a chance to meet
with Tuhoe. Te Kooti agreed that he should try to bring about a satisfactory understanding between the parties, and it was understood that this survey would be postponed until that was achieved. It was also understood, however, that 'the matter is not
to stand over indefinately [*sic*]'.[100] As Cadman confirmed when he wrote to Numia, Te
Kooti had promised that he would do his best 'to bring about a satisfactory settlement
between the Maoris concerned in the matter' of the survey.[101] But by the time he sent
this letter, the survey had started — and so, too, had the obstructions.

The survey of part of the Ruatoki block began on 23 May 1892, on the instructions
of the Ngati Rongo chiefs. Te Kooti seems to have agreed to it; this was certainly
Cadman's understanding of the situation.[102] But the survey was obstructed immediately:
three trig stations were pulled down. After Cadman confirmed to Te Kooti that the
three stations were all within the boundaries of the area which they had agreed was 'all
that is to be surveyed at present',[103] Te Kooti cabled the leaders of the protest, Makarini

and Te Ahikaiata, urging them to desist. He also contacted Carroll, who was attending the first gathering of the Kotahitanga Maori Parliament at Waipatu.[104]

Tuhoe's messengers were also there. Among them was Paora Kiingi, who was chosen to represent the Urewera on the Council of Paramount Chiefs for the East Coast. Because of their shared concern, the two houses of the Kotahitanga assembly sent an urgent complaint to Cadman. They stated that they considered 'it is right that the survey should not be allowed to be proceeded with, without the consent of all' ('he mea tika kia kaua e tukuna taua ruri kia puta ma te whakaae o ratou katoa katahi ka tika kia ruritia'). They therefore asked the government to withdraw its surveyors.[105] They re-iterated this in a petition (with 400 signatures) to the Premier asking him to stop the survey.[106] Because of the mounting opposition, Cadman 'suggested' to the surveyor that it would be best if he wound up the survey for the present until he and Carroll could visit Ruatoki at the end of the parliamentary session, when they would discuss the whole issue again.[107] And there the matter rested until the following year. The revival of the conflict coincided with Te Kooti's tragic last journey to Ohiwa.

Ngati Rongo remained determined that the survey should proceed under their authority. From their perspective, it had become a test of their mana, on which they would not budge. When Cadman visited Ruatoki on 23 January 1893, those who were in favour of the survey as well as some of those who opposed it were present. At the end of the lengthy debate, Cadman spoke briefly. He gave the Tuhoe an ultimatum: one month in which to settle the matter among themselves. At the end of the month, if they had not reached any agreement, he would order the survey to recommence. And this is precisely what he did.

On 23 February he gave the surveyor his instructions. Cadman had received from Numia and Hetaraka several requests to act once the month was up,[108] but he had also received a petition from 'Tuhoe', dated 13 February, in protest. This petition was signed by six men: Te Ahikaiata as chairman, and including Paora Kiingi, Tamaikoha, Te Whiu and Hemi Kakitu. It claimed to represent eight hapu of the Urewera and told Cadman to wait for the meeting which they had called for March, when Te Kooti would be present. They said that all the people were opposed as 'This land has been given by us to Te Turuki (Te Kooti) and his people' ('Ko tenei whenua kua oti te tuku atu e matou ki a Te Turuki ratou ko tona iwi'). If Cadman chose to ignore their warning and persist, then, they said, 'you will be the cause of plunging the whole world into trouble' ('Mehemea ki te tohe koe nau i whakakino te ao katoa').[109] Makarini wrote in a similar vein a few days later, urging Cadman to delay just a little until Te Kooti reached them on 15 March. That was the day on which they would all assemble, he said, and he asked Cadman to come to meet them then.[110]

On the very last day he was at Otewa, 27 February 1893, Te Kooti wrote urgently to Wilkinson at Otorohanga, having heard that the survey was beginning. He had also heard, incorrectly, that 'soldiers' were protecting the surveyors. He was not incorrect, however, in his fear of the consequences of acting without general agreement. He said:

E hoa mau e whakaatu taku kupu ki te Minita mo te taha Maori. He mea wehi ki a au te hoia no te mea kua mutu te whakaheke toto.

Letter written by Te Kooti at
Otewa, 27 February 1893, the day
before his fatal accident.

J1 1893/515, NA

Kaore au e pai ki taua mahi kino me ata mahi marire. E haere ana hoki ahau ki reira.
A te tahi o nga ra o Maehe.

E hoa kia tere to whakaatu ki te Minita.

Friend, inform the Native Minister of my word. I am afraid of (do not like) the introducing of soldiers, because the shedding of blood has ceased.

I am not willing that that bad work (shedding of blood) should take place. Let the matter be dealt with carefully. I am going there on the 1st. of March (or early in March).

Friend be quick, and let the Minister know.[111]

On the same day, the survey commenced.

It was blocked by Makarini. The trig station was pulled down in the face of the younger chief, Numia, who had ordered it erected. At the same time, Makarini asked the surveyor to wait until Te Kooti arrived.[112] But Cadman determined to press on, and

e hoa kia tere to
whaka atu ki te
Minita heoi ano

na to hoa aroha

na Te Turuki

he instructed accordingly. He also sent a telegram to Te Kooti to this effect, and he warned him that, although there were no soldiers present, if necessary the survey would indeed be enforced by the police.[113] The second confrontation occurred when surveying recommenced on 6 March. Makarini, Paora Kiingi and Te Ahikaiata led a contingent of 100 protesters, who camped in front of the surveyor's tent. The local constable from Opotiki was present. Again Paora Kiingi and Makarini asked the survey party to wait until Te Kooti arrived. They said that they would be guided entirely by him.[114] But the surveyor refused to delay. The protests thus began, with the women taking away the instruments — a tactic adopted to prevent physical conflict. No resistance was offered, either; all parties were, in fact, seeking to avoid bloodshed. But from this point on, the conflict would escalate, as armed police were ordered into the area on 8 March.[115]

This was the explosive situation, engineered by the government to support Ngati Rongo's claim, in which Te Kooti left Otewa. On that day, 27 February, he spoke a 'saying for the abandonment of Otewa' ('te kupu o te mahue-tanga atu Otewa'):

Ari. Ope. Ekere.
'Ka moana tenei wahi.'
'Kaore e mohiotia te wahi mo tatau, otira kai te Kupu te Tikanga.'

Ari. Ope. Ekere.
'This place will become sea.'
'The place for us is not known, however the Way is in the Word.'[116]

Then this wanderer, who knew not for certain where he went, sang a waiata 'as a sign [of misfortune] — the third for him' ('he tohu ai — tuatoru mona').[117] The song begins,

E taia ana ahau e te mate anini,
E taia ana ahau e te mate aroha,

I am smitten by dizziness,
I am smitten by love,

and it continues, preoccupied with the troubles at Ruatoki,

No matamua ra te pounga mai manuka ra i roto i te hinengaro,
Me tuku taku tara kia kai haere ki nga ure haramai no te po,
He hanga hauā noa te hanga nei a te toto,
Te nei ka maringi e kai raro koe . . . .

Right from the start has my conscience been touched by anxiety,
Let my courage meet those warriors who come out of the night,
Fragile indeed is the property of blood,
For should it be spilt there, you fall . . . .[118]

The song is annotated sadly in the records of the church:

I titoa mai tenei waiata i Otewa Pepuere 27. 1893. Na te Wairua i homai ki a ia a me te
whakaatu ano i te whiu mona. I te awatea o te 28th ka pehia ia e te piringa kaata.

This waiata was composed at Otewa February 27. 1893. The Spirit gave it to him together with the revelation of the affliction for him. In the middle of the day on the
28th he was pinned down by the spring cart.[119]

It was on the first day of their journey, when resting in the shade of a dray while the party had stopped for lunch, that Te Kooti was struck when the dray suddenly up-ended. The laden cart had been jolted by a pair of squabbling dogs, and it tipped down heavily across his back. Although nothing seemed broken, it crushed him internally. This, then, was the 'insignificant accident' which Te Kooti had so long ago predicted would be the cause of his death.

While the people at Ruatoki waited anxiously for his arrival, and the government agents speculated cruelly that he was deliberately dragging out his journey, Te Kooti struggled to reach Ohiwa. He stayed at Kihikihi, trying to recover strength, until about 9 March. Then the party — 150 people with all their possessions — went to Rotorua, which they had reached by 16 March.[120] When the *Bay of Plenty Times* described him travelling north through Ngongotaha to Rotoiti on 21 March, he was 'packed in the buggy like an invalid with mattresses and pillows under him'. He had paused at the baths in Rotorua and had taken the waters, but it was obvious to all that 'He is far from being robust'.[121] He was, in fact, slowly dying.

As Te Kooti journeyed painfully towards Ruatoki, the first of the Tuhoe arrests occurred. Makarini, Paora Kiingi, Te Ahikaiata, another chief, Puketi, and 12 women, including Maata, wife of Netana Te Whakaari and sister of Paora Kiingi, were sentenced on 18 March to one month's imprisonment in Mount Eden gaol for their obstruction of the survey. Further police reinforcements arrived, but at a huge meeting held at Ruatoki on 21 March, it was decided to continue with the obstruction. On the following day, in the presence of a large party of protesters, the women again seized the survey instruments. The trig stations were removed that night.

Another gathering assembled on 24 March at Ruatoki, where a message was received from Te Kooti. He asked them to allow the survey to proceed, and to return the survey instruments.[122] The meeting continued to debate the matter, the Tuhoe leaders trying hard to work towards some compromise. Rakuraku and Tamaikoha, who had orchestrated the latest obstruction, offered to end the protest if an even smaller block was surveyed (about a quarter of that applied for by Ngati Rongo). George Wilkinson, who had been sent by the government, refused to accept any compromise. Instead, Cadman had instructed Wilkinson to threaten that 'persistent opposition to the Law' by Tuhoe could lead to the movement of the confiscation line 'further into their Country'.[123] He also used that favourite government device of indicating that he would cancel the opposing chiefs' pensions should they continue to protest. Wilkinson himself, however, could recognise that a genuine conflict of authorities underlay the issue. Ngati Rongo's insistence on the survey denied the shared guardianship of the land with the other major Ruatoki hapu, Ngati Koura, Hamua and Ngai Tawhaki, all of whom were involved in the renewed protests. It also denied the claims of the larger tribe to act in unity. The protesters, he said, were determined 'that the Maori law recognized by them shall not give way because of European law, if they can prevent it without bloodshed'. Those who had chosen to appeal to the European law to have their title established should 'not be able to exult over them', he observed correctly.[124]

On the same day as he wrote his report — 29 March 1893 — Te Kooti arrived at Otamauru,[125] the Ngati Awa settlement near Whakatane. There, he stayed with his old friend Hoani Poururu. On the same day, too, before Te Kooti could reach the Ruatoki gathering, the gift of the Tuhoe land to him was collectively renewed at Ruatoki: 'Ka whakahoutia te tuku whenua a Tuhoe ara i Ruatoki'.[126] But when Te Kooti arrived there the following afternoon, he came to 'acknowledge the dead' ('ki te mihi ki te mate'). The gathering had become a tangi, or more probably an uhunga, a wailing for the dead. It was for Paora Kiingi's elder brother, Tumeke, and another senior Tuhoe chief.[127] Death had intervened, and all debate was suspended.

In the minds of all those present, however, must have been the dying words of Tumeke's father, Paora Kiingi I. He was remembered for the lasting peace he had made between Tuhoe and the East Coast tribes, and his ohaki for Tuhoe was that binding phrase: '*Kia tawharautia a Mātaatua*' ('Let Mātaatua be sheltered').[128] It would also have been known to everyone present that Te Kooti had entrusted his sheathed sword to Tumeke's brother Paora, who had fought for the government during the wars in the

Urewera in 1870–71.[129] It was Paora who had brought the sword to Tuhoe from the King Country, and the oral narratives tell that Te Kooti sent him as a messenger of peace, 'so there would be no [more] bloodshed in New Zealand. To sign that treaty, to stick that sword into the ground, the point into the ground.'[130] Paora's guardianship of Te Kooti's sword was intended to seal Tuhoe's promise to maintain an everlasting peace.[131]

The survey was not discussed at all.[132] As the Ringatu text put it, Te Kooti 'did not stay. [He] went right on to acknowledge the dead' ('Kaore i noho. I haere noa mai ki te mihi ki te mate').[133] It was also clear to every observer that Te Kooti was in great pain.[134] Despite this, he did try to broach the subject later, having again indicated at Whakatane on 3 April that the survey should go ahead. But by then, according to the police report, the 'obstructionists declined to discuss the matter' further.[135] The dispute seemed to be deadlocked. But Te Kooti would not give up. He struggled to Hokianga island, where, as he lay dying, he wrote to Netana on 10 April commanding him to let the survey continue:

> Nathan salutations to you let the survey proceed until completed and better look to the law for redress in the future.[136]

As a consequence of Te Kooti's directive, the Ruatoki survey was completed. He would have preferred more unity and less authority but, once he took this unequivocal stance, the obstruction ceased.

The opposing chiefs, for whom warrants of arrest had been issued that very day, withdrew to Ruatahuna. Te Kooti's intervention stopped any further arrests. Old Makarini, who was still in Mount Eden gaol as a result of the first protest, told the government that there would now be no resistance 'seeing that Te Kooti had advised it to be gone on with'. He also blamed Te Kooti for not having made his position clear before they had been arrested.[137] Netana said the same, arguing that the land had been placed under Te Kooti's authority when he was opposed to surveying, and that he should have informed them when he changed his mind, before any arrests had been made. He, together with his wife Maata who had been imprisoned, felt very bitter.[138]

The Ruatoki survey began again on 13 April. Cadman telegraphed Te Kooti to thank him for the help he had given, particularly for his instruction to look to the law for any redress of grievance.[139] It was on this belief in the principle of law that Te Kooti's hopes rested; it was on this principle, too, that the integrity of the government rested. The subsequent tortuous legal history of the Tuhoe land and of the protesters lies outside the scope of this study. The hearings for the two land blocks at Ruatoki commenced in the Native Land Court in 1894, and then dragged their way through the Appellate Court in 1897, leading finally to the 'cutting of the land into pieces'. Some might argue that the remission of the fines of the Ruatoki protesters in 1895, combined with the passing of the Urewera District Native Reserve Act in 1896 (after the Premier's visit in 1894, and still further, strong, opposition to surveying within the Urewera in 1895), were ultimately honouring Te Kooti's principle of working through the law. In the history of Tuhoe's land, however, Te Kooti was betrayed. The authority of Tuhoe, which the 1896 Act recognised, was not upheld, and the promise to prohibit prospecting soon forgotten. It was in this betrayal that the roots of the new movement led by Rua

Netana Te Whakaari, 1921. Photograph
by James Cowan.   F10, 988 1/2, ATL

flourished and spread. From 1905 he, claiming to be the 'son' of Te Kooti, set out to redeem the land from the Crown, perhaps using Te Kooti's diamond.

In 1893, in the public world, the response was simply congratulations for Cadman. In the newspaper reporting of the issue, it was Cadman alone who was praised for success-fully obtaining the Ruatoki survey and for dealing firmly with 'malcontents'. The *New Zealand Herald*, which in March 1893 still referred to Te Kooti as the 'manslaughterer', and as the one whom Cadman had had to warn that any attempt on his part to stop the survey would be firmly dealt with 'according to law',[140] had nothing whatsoever to report concerning Te Kooti's last, and crucial, intervention. In this manner, stereotypes were publicly sustained and history distorted. The 'dominant' interpretation structured the meaning of all these events for the European public. They were given no chance to understand that the desperate mediation of Te Kooti had been central to Tuhoe's accept-ance of the Ruatoki survey. The newspaper had nothing to say either about the fact that he had laboured for 20 years to establish this principle of working through the law, and that it was he who had persuaded Tuhoe to submit to it.

The serious rifts in the Maori world, created largely by the dilemmas of dealing with the legal and illegal threats to their land, had helped to confuse Tuhoe's own collective decision-making processes. Te Kooti's spiritual authority became the one constant by which Tuhoe, in general, were prepared to act. In the end, despite all his personal experience of legal manipulation and chicanery, he chose the path of obedience to the European laws in order to avoid conflict and further imprisonments. He did so because he was honouring the compact he had made with Bryce in 1883. All his teachings from that time had been bound by the principle of upholding the law. It is clear that he equated the idea of scriptural law ('nga Ture') with the rule of law on earth, like many Maori of the generations taught by the missionary–teachers. But he also understood, as he said again as he lay dying on Hokianga island, that it is the law which must be pitched against the law:

> Ko te waka hei hoehoenga mo koutou i muri i ahau, ko te Ture, ma te Ture ano te Ture e aki.

> The canoe for you to paddle after me is the Law. Only the Law will correct the Law.[141]

These were the words he had first uttered at Te Kuiti in December 1882 while preparing to negotiate his pardon. Then he had been warned by Taratutu:

> E Koti, whakarongo mai, 'Pokokohua te Ture, koi nei te tahuna mo nga kuaka o te motu nei, hai aha tena Ture.'

> Oh Kooti, listen to me, 'Curse the Law, it is the sandbank for the godwits on this island, never mind that Law.'

And Te Kooti had replied then:

> Kia ngawari, e kore e hapa te Kupu.

> Be tolerant, the Sayings will not be passed over.[142]

To this commitment he remained constant. Yet, despite all his efforts and all the contacts he made with a succession of government ministers, that this was the guiding principle for all the actions of the last years of his life was never understood.

On his last journey to Ohiwa, Te Kooti had paused at Rotorua. On 16–17 March he stayed at Ohinemutu, where a large gathering assembled in Tama-Te-Kapua to greet him. On the second day there, Petera Tukino spoke for Te Arawa. He offered the gift of Mokoia island to Te Kooti, and also referred to the gift, made on his previous visit in 1883, of Te Pukeroa, the old pa and sacred site which overlooks the Ohinemutu settlement. Petera said:

> Mo te kohatu a o Tupuna, ara, mo Mokoia, me tuku rawa atu tena e au ki a koe, otira kai a koe tonu nei hoki i te tukunga ano i Te Pukeroa ki a koe i mua, ka tukua hoki tenei ki a koe, mau hoki e herehere rawa te kohatu a o taua Tipuna.

> Concerning the rock of your Ancestors, that is, about Mokoia, let me give this up completely to you. But indeed you still have [land] from the gifting of Te Pukeroa to

you earlier, then I give this to you also, you will secure firmly the rock of our mutual Ancestors.

Te Kooti replied. He referred first to his previous visit to Tama-Te-Kapua and the reconciliation effected at that time between the people of Ohinemutu and himself. He stressed that it was not he who had changed then, but rather they who had made that peace, out of their compassion for him — 'a lone man from the hills' ('he morehu tangata no runga i nga puke'), who had just come out from the shadow of the authority of the King. He talked of the heavy burdens he carried: 'When the Gospel began then I had a load for my back with which I went about this island' ('Ka timata ko te Rongopai a he pikau taku e haere nei au i te motu nei'). Then he came to the matter of the gifts. He reminded them that their last gift had not led to any place for their speeches — that is, they had not built a house for themselves, nor for the gospel. Rather, this gift had been gathered together and sold, he said. Pukeroa hill, with sites already donated to the government for a school and hospital, had been seized as a reserve in 1883, and the land for the township sold to the Crown by Ngati Whakaue in 1890. He challenged them with their own unfulfilled promises, which had left them without a meeting-house on Te Pukeroa in which to remember their chiefs, or himself and his pain. Through this speech he revealed the rationale for all the houses which he had requested be built, reinforcing this the more when he asked them: without Te Pukeroa, 'Where can your word be based?' ('Ko hea hoki te waahi e mana ai to kupu?').[143]

At the gatherings which took place around Rotorua lake over the following days, Te Kooti repeatedly challenged the people with their failure of guardianship. From Ohinemutu he went to Waikuta, a community like Te Awahou where the people had committed themselves to him. Here he again berated them for the loss of Te Pukeroa. But, as he also made clear, although he grumbled about their deeds and their treatment of him, he was not belittling them. Finally what would remain with them — for he himself could not stay — were his words, which would be the covenant between them:

> Ko tenei e haere ana ahau ki te ū kaipo, ko tena Kohatu ki a koe ano tauto ai.

> And this, I am going to the breast on which night feeds [that is, death]; that Rock [Mokoia] is for you yourself to tend.[144]

Directives were there, for those who could understand.

From Waikuta and Te Awahou he journeyed to Waiohewa (Te Ngae) on the north-eastern shore of Rotorua, where the road turns east towards Whakatane. There he rested on 22 March, and again Te Arawa gathered to greet him. The offer of Mokoia was repeated, as a place for him to live, as a place for him to hold — and by implication, which he himself touched upon in song, as his burial-place with the great Arawa chiefs. Tamati Te Kaharunga spoke, and he laid down a greenstone patu to seal the covenant between them. Te Kooti replied, saying again that they should remain, steadfast, on their land. The patu bound these words. But as for him, as he had told the people at Waikuta,

> Ka mohio me noho ahau ki whea? He noho nei hoki naku te waiho i nga Kupu.

> Who knows where I must live? I just stay to leave the Sayings.[145]

Sketch of the Ohiwa harbour looking south-west from the headland which overlooks Toketoke spit (seen in the foreground). It shows the south-east corner of Hokianga island (centre right). A detail from the drawing (opposite) shows Te Kooti's whare karakia. It is the long raupo building on the shore of the island. Sketch by James Forsyth, 1896.   WHAKATANE MUSEUM

Thus he journeyed, knowing that there would be no home now where he would rest. When he reached Otamauru on 29 March, he was to ask his friend Hoani Poururu:

> E 'Upe, he aha koe i whakatū ai i tō whare ki runga i te timutimu, wehewehe whenua, wehewehe tangata, wehewehe tikanga?

> O 'Upe [Taupe], why have you built your house on the stump, dividing the land, the people and their beliefs?[146]

Thus again he warned, using now the metaphor of the stump in the swamplands for division and discord. Indeed, shortly afterwards, as Otamauru became increasingly prone to flooding, the three meeting-houses of the shared community were, one by one, moved and separated.[147] Te Kooti's words at this time reflect his own sense of home-lessness and imminent death, but they insist on his desire for the unity of the people. The kupu whakaari for Otamauru must date from this sad last visit:

> Pū Oro Mei, Retiwōro

> Kua ōati a Ihoa ki ōna mano. Kua mea mai anō ia, 'Inā tāku i whakaaro ai, kei tēnā anō te otinga ō tāku i whakatakoto ai, ū tonu nei, āke āke. He rua tūpāpaku kei roto, he whare wehewehe, wehewehe tikanga, wehewehe tangata, wehewehe whenua.'

Pū Oro Mei, Retiwōro

Jehovah has made an oath to his multitude. He has said, 'In what I have spoken you will also find the fulfilment of what I have prescribed, and it will remain so forever. There is a grave within, a divided house, divided ways, divided people, divided land.'[148]

From Otamauru and Ruatoki, Te Kooti went to the island in the Ohiwa harbour, Hokianga. And there, as one elder from the area, Pat Aramoana, said quite simply, 'he was caught by death.'[149]

The Tuhoe elders gathered around Te Kooti on Hokianga island, and it was to them that he made his last predictions. On 10 April, in pain, he wrote to Netana and he spoke at length to Rakuraku and Hemi Kakitu. They were the chiefs of the 'two hearths' ('enei ahi e rua') which burnt on the island, that is Tuhoe and Te Upokorehe.[150] Te Kooti referred to his long and ambivalent associations with both men. His words recalled Hemi's involvement in the attempt to kill him in the last days of the fighting in the Urewera. He said dryly, 'I say someone else will kill me, not you two' ('E ki ana ahau ma te tangata kē au e patu, kaore ma korua'). He told them to continue to bring him food, and to 'continue coming to hurt me. There is no other road to the other side' ('haramai tonu hoki ki te patu i au. Kaore he ara atu ki tawahi nei') but death.

The song he then sang to them is described as a song of anger ('he waiata riri'), in which he 'struck' ('aki') Rakuraku and Hemi.[151] In it he spoke of the bullet ('te kariri') which had been sent against his people to afflict them. It had been sent against himself, but he had pursued it, as he said, 'until we were as one' ('whairawa atu au kia moe maua').[152] The anger was spent; the old warrior had defused the hatreds. He sang then

Hokianga island, c.1910. The island then still had a substantial Maori population.   Whakatane Museum

of the continuing fire of conversion, kindled by the flames of righteousness. But then he sang of desire, jealousy, betrayal, distraction, neglect and gossip. This is not the waiata of a man dying at ease. With the song he also bound Rakuraku in obligation to him: his was the task of 'tying the days to Te Wainui' ('Ko te herenga o nga rā ki runga i a Rakuraku ara ki Te Wainui').[153]

Just before Te Kooti was taken from the island, he requested that the local Anglican missionary, the Reverend George Maunsell, be brought to him. The dying man was carried on a litter into Te Here-o-Te-Ra, where Maunsell gave the last sacrament.[154] Then, on 12 April, Te Kooti was carried from the island across to Te Karaka, on the nearby shores of Ohiwa harbour; it was land which Te Upokorehe had recently gifted to him. Heni and Tamaku accompanied him. They watched over him until his death.

Te Kooti's ohaki — his dying speech and gift — is dated 12 April. It was uttered on his last Twelfth, and Hamiora recorded it in detail. Te Kooti spoke first about his successor. This kupu is, understandably, the best-known of all his predictions:

> E rua tekau ma ono nga tau e toe mai nei ka puta mai te Tangata mo tatau. Otira ki te pai te whakahaere ki te ngawari he nui rawa enei tau. Engari e toru ano tau ka puta mai te tangata mo tatau.
>
> Otira ki te uaua te whakahaere i runga i tenei motu ka nekehia ano, a, kore ake e tere mai. Heoi ano hei whakararuraru ko nga whakahaere a nga Rangatira, e mahi mai nei, mo te whenua i runga i tenei motu me era atu raruraru hoki.
>
> Tae noa hoki ki ta Tuhoe e mahi mai nei mo tona wahi, ara mo tāna Ruuri e mahi mai nei i Ruatoki. Ka poto nei te iwi ki te herehere ki Akarana. A, ka waiho ko te aroha kai roto i toku ngakau tangi ai ki te iwi. Na, ma konei anake e nekehia ai te wa, e kore ai.

Twenty-six years remain before the Person for us shall appear. But if everything goes according to plan, and runs smoothly, these years will be very important. But there will be three more years before the person for us appears.

But if there are difficulties with the organisation in this land [the time] will be moved again, and it will not come quickly. But that which will cause trouble will be the conduct of the Chiefs, who are working now for the land on this island, and other troubles as well.

This includes those of Tuhoe working here for their place, that is for the Survey being done at Ruatoki. The people will be lost to the prison at Auckland, and love will remain in my heart as I mourn for the people. So, only for these reasons will the time be moved on, and it will not [happen quickly].[155]

For all its enigmas, the framework of the ohaki is rooted in the immediate troubles about the land. Te Kooti's concern for the Ruatoki people explains his final intervention to permit the survey. He left ambiguous the time for the deliverance of the people by the One who would follow him. He spoke as a religious teacher in the gospel traditions. He then sang his last waiata:

Tera te ahi te kā mai ra
Kei nuku-wai.
Na to Ringa rawa koe i tahu mai
Kia mihi atu au.
Hohoro koe na te kau mai
Hei tokorua
Hei hoa ake ki te moenga
E tuohu nei.

There the fire glows
Across the vast waters.
It was kindled by your Hand alone,
It is there I cast my thoughts.
Hasten to me, cross those waters
Come again to be my friend,
Stay close with me
Until the end.[156]

The faith is the fire kindled by God across time and space. The song asks God to reach across these dividing waters to be with him at his end; and the words recall the hymn composed 300 years earlier by the Anglican divine John Donne:

I have a sinne of feare, that when I have spunne
My last thred, I shall perish on the shore;
Swear by thy selfe, that at my death thy sonne
Shall shine as he shines now, and heretofore;
And, having done that, Thou haste done,
I feare no more.[157]

Te Kooti's final spoken words followed the song that betokened his ultimate faith. They concerned Te Wainui as the home for the Ringatu:

Ki te mutu tenei Tekaumarua me noho a Te Wainui, ahakoa iti kati tonu. Ki te kore te Tangata e noho i Te Wainui, a kaati maku nei e noho.

Kua mutu nga rā ki te motu, kei au te rā kei Te Wainui. Ahakoa tau-Tahi tau-Rua, neke atu, Te Hanuere te Hurae kei au kei Te Wainui.

When this Twelfth ends occupy Te Wainui, although only a few, so be it. If no one stays at Te Wainui, well then I will stay.

The days on the island [Hokianga] have ended. I will have the day at Te Wainui, although one, two, or more years [pass], the January and the July will be with me at Te Wainui.

The people were sent again to look at Te Wainui, and Petera Te Rangihiroa exclaimed to him:

He ngarara, mokomoko hei noho i te Wainui ka rawe.

Ka mea a Te Turuki, 'Na whakarongo mai, kua kiia nei e te tangata he ngarara anake te tangata hei noho i te Wainui. He ahakoa, maku e noho, ka takoto ka takoto atu ahau ki Te Wainui. . . . Engari ano a Te Wainui e pai ana he mea hoki no roto i te mate. Koia au i ki ai me noho a Te Wainui, no te mea ki te nohoia a te Wainui tera e pata mai he tika mo te tangata i reira, a ma te *Wainui* e titiro atu tera waahi tera waahi.'

If reptiles and lizards were to live at Te Wainui, that would be fine!

Te Turuki said, 'Listen. Someone has said that reptiles will be the only creatures to occupy Te Wainui. Nevertheless, I will remain, I shall lie, I shall lie on at Te Wainui. . . . As for Te Wainui it is good, and it is also from the midst of misfortune. This is why I say to occupy Te Wainui, for if Te Wainui is occupied then justice will come for the people there, and Te *Wainui* will look to each place.'[158]

These last injunctions exist in Paora Delamere's manuscript too, where they are headed: 'Some words from Ariki-rangi from the time just before his death [when he was] carried to Te Karaka beside Hokianga, Ohiwa April 12. 1893' ('He kupu na Arikirangi no nga ra o mua tata o tona matenga, haria atu [ki] Te Karaka i Hokianga, Ohiwa Aperira 12. 1893'). This transcript, deriving from a different original source but clearly recording the same speech, incorporates some additional sayings about Te Wainui:

. . . engari ano a te Wainui he mea kuhu no roto i [te] pouri, i te mate, a, ka puta mai nei ko te Wainui. Ko tenei ka takoto, ka takoto ahau ki te Wainui. Kua mutu hoki nga ra ki te motu. Te Rā, te Hanuere, te Hurae, kei au kei te Wainui. Ka noho ahau ki te Wainui, a, ko te Wainui hei kanohi mo te motu nei, a, ma te Wainui e titiro atu tera waahi tera waahi. Ta te mea, ki te nohia a te Wainui, ka whiwhi mea ano te tangata i te Wainui. Ahakoa iti nei kaati tonu, tera ano e neke ake, a, ka puta mai he painga mo te tangata i te Wainui. Mehemea ka nohia, ka mahia hoki, ka puta mai he tika i te Wainui.

. . . but Te Wainui indeed was hidden in darkness, in death; and now Te Wainui has come forth. This is [where] I will lie, I will lie at Te Wainui. The days on the island are completed. The Days, the Januarys, the Julys, are with me at Te Wainui. I will remain at Te Wainui and Te Wainui will be as the eye for the island, and Te Wainui will look to each place. Because if Te Wainui is occupied, the people at Te Wainui shall possess things again. Although it may be small, it will be sufficient and it will increase, and prosperity will come for the people in Te Wainui. If it is occupied, work will be done also, and justice will come from Te Wainui.[159]

Hokianga island. The poplars, a symbol of renewal of life, stand by the site of Te Here-o-te-Ra.
Photograph by Judith Binney, 1994.

These were Te Kooti's last recorded words. Five days later, just as the evening tide turned and began to ebb away, at seven at night on 17 April, Te Kooti Arikirangi Te Turuki died at Te Karaka.

After his death the body was taken back to Hokianga island, which had remained free from the tapu associated with the end of life. As his body returned, his revolver was fired — and emptied — from the island: the shots flew over the deepest pool in the channel and smacked into the cliff face opposite. The waterway now bears the name 'Te Kōpua Tē Pū',[160] The Gun-Shot Pool. Te Kooti's tangi took place on the island. It goes without saying that there would be an emotional debate about where he should finally lie, and who could claim him. The argument is part of crucial Maori ethics concerning the last resting-place of those held in great esteem. In Te Kooti's case the debate was enormously heightened by the fact of his long exile. On 20 April, the senior Rongo-whakaata chief Heta Te Kani cabled from Opotiki to inform Cadman that,

> kua ona iwi me nga rangatiratanga i whiriwhiri ai kia tanumia tona tinana ki te whenua i homai e tona papa e te Kawanatanga ki a ia utua mai.

> we his relatives and the chiefs [assembled here] have decided that his body should be buried on the land given him by his parent the Government.[161]

But instead Te Kooti's body was secretly removed by Reihana's people, the exiles at Waiotahe who called themselves Te Whanau-a-Pani, the Family of Orphans, like himself. They took the following words to apply to them:

> Te Kupu tenei a Te Kooti ki a Te Whanau-pani: ki te mate (ara ki te Hē) ahau, Hunaia ahau.

> Te Kooti's Word to Te Whanau-[a]-pani: if I die (that is, am in Trouble), Hide me.[162]

The little whare in this rough sketch is where Te Kooti died — I don't have a very good light and I can do better work in pen & ink only I am very lazy at times

Rough sketch of the little whare at Te Karaka in which Te Kooti died. From a letter by the artist, James Forsyth, 2 June 1896.   WHAKATANE MUSEUM

It was they who 'stole' Te Kooti's body from the island and buried it secretly at Maromahue, their marae at Waiotahe, on 25 April.[163] Te Huinga (Jack) Karauna, an elder of this marae, related what they did. Reihana and others decided to steal the body of 'their younger brother' ('tō rātau taina'), so that he should lie for ever with them in the place of their exile, the place of his arrest. They came to Hokianga in the depth of night and fetched the corpse from where it lay, heaped with cloaks and overflowing with treasures.

> Ka tīkina atu ma muri o te whare o te tūpāpaku, ka tōia mai te tūpāpaku ki waho. Kāre he tangata i mōhio ka riro te tūpāpaku.
>
> [They] fetched the body away from the back of the house, and dragged the body outside. Nobody knew the body had been taken away.[164]

They took Te Kooti's body by canoe to a landing at Te Ruanui and then to Maromahue, where they buried him.

But today only an open grave remains there. Nearby there stood, until very recent times, a poplar tree. It grew, so they say, from Te Kooti's riding whip, which he thrust into the ground — at daybreak — when he came to Waiotahe to announce the long-abiding peace of 1883.[165] It grew, as poplar does, from an apparently lifeless stick. Beside this young poplar, it is remembered, Te Kooti was arrested in 1889; and indeed the rough shelter made from its branches was described at the time. The poplar stood for the years of war — the years of the so·nd of the whip; it stood for the covenant of peace; and it stood for Te Kooti's betrayal in 1889. It also marked his first grave. Today, at every place with which Te Kooti is associated there are poplars growing: on Hokianga

Remains of a boat said to have carried Te Kooti's body across the Ohiwa harbour. The elderly boatman is Chris Manuel. Photograph by Rone Vine, 1938.   WHAKATANE MUSEUM

island and at Te Wainui. In one narrative tradition of Tuhoe, and perhaps of others, the poplar tree is thought to be the wood from which Christ's cross was made.[166] Thus the poplar which grew at Waiotahe beside the grave was also the ultimate pledge of life from death: of sacrifice for renewal. But if you ask to see this poplar, you will be told it was cut down 'by an ignorant Pakeha only a few years ago'.

Te Kooti's body was secretly disinterred from Maromahue in June 1893. Jack Karauna told how Reihana stood watch over the grave but, one night, he heard the sound of thunder. He listened to the warning, but then the sky cleared and all seemed well; thus, he fell asleep. When he awoke the grave was open and the body gone. It had been taken by the elders of Te Wainui.

According to Hamiora Aparoa, who is named as one of the five men who carried Te Kooti to his last known burial-place, the body was first hidden by Matiu. This plan was devised by a group of 20 elders from Wainui, all of whom Hamiora listed by name. Matiu hid the body on 12 June, concealed in 'The Form of the Ark' ('Te Ahua o Te Aaka').[167] The body was then taken to Wainui and reburied, on 17 June, by five men from this group. This was done to fulfil Te Kooti's 'two words' ('aua kupu e rua') that he must lie at Wainui, and that, as Reihana's people had heard, if he were opposed or in trouble, then he must be hidden, lest his enemies seek to molest him. The five had exhumed the body from Matiu's hiding-place on the night of 16 June, and had carried it back to Wainui. There, the other 15 men (among whom was Matiu) were waiting. Then, as the Ringatu text states, 'On the 17th at 7.am. he was concealed again by us' ('I te 17. i te 7.am. ka huna ano e matou').[168] But only the five who had exhumed him and who reburied him knew the exact place. According to this account, which was carefully recorded by the Haahi Ringatu, they were: Hamiora himself; Awa Horomona, Wetini's son, who would become a significant follower of Rua;[169] Hera Tio; Kereti [Hawera] of Ngati Awa, who was married to Maiere, the daughter of Te Kooti's elder brother, Komene;[170] and Rikirangi Hohepa, who was the son of Te Kooti's younger brother, Hohepa, and whom Te Kooti had adopted and brought up at Te Kuiti. Thus Te Kooti's closest secretary and his two known brothers were represented among the five men; another was possibly, but not certainly, his grandson. A burnt offering was made that evening by Rikirangi Hohepa to bind for ever the sacredness of their act.

In this manner Te Kooti was protected and concealed by his very close followers and his kin. They concealed him for several reasons. They were afraid that there might be attempts to exhume him to practise that pseudo-science of the 19th century, phrenology.[171] When Wi Tamararo committed suicide in 1869 during the trials of Te Kooti's followers in Wellington, a cast of his head was put on public display for this precise purpose.[172] Te Kooti himself was examined when he was in Auckland in 1889. He submitted, it was claimed at the time, 'with great suavity', but he must have found it offensive — as was the newspaper item recording the occasion, headed 'TE KOOTI'S BUMPS'.[173] His followers hid him also out of fear that there would be further Maori attempts to claim him. Above all, the people at Te Wainui feared that there would be a concerted effort to take his body back to Turanga. As Boy Biddle acknowledged, there is an unresolved conflict in Te Kooti's statements, that he would 'lie on' at Te Wainui, and that he would, one day, return to Turanga. The one 'cuts across' the other — and 'this hurts'.[174]

From the original decision to conceal Te Kooti's body, many different narratives grew as to where he was, or is, buried. Some say he was hidden in a gully on the ferny slopes near Te Horo, a small Ngati Awa pa on the Ohope spit, directly overlooking the Ohiwa harbour. Many of his followers from Waikato, themselves known as Te Whanau-a-Pani, were living there. Other versions say that Te Kooti lay near Te Horo only briefly, after he was taken from Maromahue and before he was reburied near Te Wainui. One story tells how his body lay hidden near a tree at the outlet of the Waiotahe river, which flows into the sea from Maromahue. An elder came across it accidentally (his attention being drawn by the rank smell) when he stopped his cart by the pohutukawa under which he habitually rested on his ride home from Opotiki.[175] By 1910, a version was being circulated (and by one who claimed to have participated) that Te Kooti's body had already been taken back to Gisborne.[176] One source for this spreading belief is the fact that a tangi was held for Te Kooti at Whakato early in May 1893. A woman who attended, Louise Margaret U'ren, described how Te Kooti's hat and pipe were laid out on a woven mat, and his two little grandchildren, Rangi Rikirangi and Putiputi Miria, dressed in white with large black sashes, were placed beside the '"bier"'. Some of the men present had dramatically shaved one side of their faces;[177] this was, in fact, a statement of shame that the body was not there.[178] But the rumours began to spread from this date that Te Kooti's body had been returned.[179] This belief grew because of his affirmation that he would return to Turanga, even if in a wooden box. Thomas Lambert was told in the 1920s that Te Kooti was already buried in

Te Kcoti's poplar trees at the Tamatea Pa, taken in 1904. About 1880 Te Kooti visited the pa, carrying a poplar sapling as a riding whip. He said, "I have given up the ways of war, and would lead my people in the paths of peace," planting the sapling as a symbol. All the poplars in the valley have been grown from this tree.

The poplar tree at Waiotahe, 1904.   Whakatane Museum

Poverty Bay;[180] and the author was told (in 1991) that he is buried at a secret place at Te Karaka.

The church records confirm that the contest between Turanga and Te Wainui for Te Kooti's body began immediately. In January 1896 Hoani Ruru and Te Kani Pere (Wi Pere's elder son), neither of whom had been sympathetic to Te Kooti, wrote to say that they were coming to Wainui to claim him.[181] Whatever their motive — and perhaps it too was shame — it is remembered how, about this time, a party of 70 men came on a trading ship from Gisborne to claim Te Kooti. They landed on the western shore of the Ohiwa harbour and for hours performed a great haka of challenge on the sandy beach near Te Horo. 'All the people around the area decided they had better take to the bush . . . and the beach around here thundered, roared, and was absolutely churned up' by the protest. But the party still had to leave without him.[182] The issue of the return of Te Kooti's body would surface again and again thereafter.

In 1923 supporters of Te Kooti from Wairoa and the Mahia peninsula approached Heni Materoa Carroll, Paratene Pototi's granddaughter, for permission to bring Te

Kooti back, but she refused.[183] A second attempt was made in 1927 but again, as head of the family, she remained adamant. By 1932 the rift between Te Wainui and Manutuke over this issue had become so great that the Ringatu at Manutuke broke away from the registered Haahi. In 1934 James Cowan learnt, probably correctly, that the body was hidden at Te Wainui at a place known only to three surviving elders. He also described how most of Te Kooti's belongings — the ploughs, harnesses and harrows all brought from Otewa — had been buried on Hokianga island after Te Kooti's death. His buggy remained near Te Horo, where he had left it, and a surrounding shelter was built to allow it to decay quietly (although there is another tradition that it was taken away to the island and burnt). Te Kooti's 'day-book' and a large family bible, along with his saddle and bridle, and a mere, were kept in a small hut among the fern and manuka on a spur above Wainui. The hut was extremely tapu; no one went near it. But on one occasion two men did wander in; one took the stirrup leather and the other the mere. Cowan reported that both suffered consequential misfortunes of accident and death.[184] Small children of Wainui also knew about this hut, which was called the 'tabernacle'. Although they knew it was forbidden, they used to sneak in, as children will. The leather saddle was there and a tin box: once 'we used the tin box for a horse and mattress for a saddle, and the tin box burst open and inside the tin box there's quite a lot of books and other valuables. We did not dare touch them. We closed them up quickly, and put the burst mattress back in the corner, and ran off!'[185] All these personal objects kept in the tabernacle ultimately vanished. A large bible with metal clasps is still remembered: but it too was taken from Wainui.[186]

Both Hamiora and Rikirangi Hohepa spoke on different occasions about Te Kooti's secret burial-place. In 1902 Hamiora said that he was one of three men left who alone knew where Te Kooti lay (this was not quite accurate).[187] In 1938 Rikirangi told the *Poverty Bay Herald* that he was the last survivor of the original party of five who had buried Te Kooti in his 'last resting-place on the shores of the Ohiwa Harbour'.[188] Several years before, Rikirangi had attempted to take Wetini, Te Kooti's son, with Tihei, Wetini's granddaughter, to see if they could find the grave on the Ohiwa harbour. It was a test; and, as Tihei narrated it, it had to be 'one member of the family' who guided the elders to the site. The quest failed.[189] This search probably took place because, as it came to be widely understood, Te Kooti's body had been moved again by one of the five, who did not trust the others.[190] Rikirangi may no longer have known where Te Kooti was buried. Or perhaps it was simply, as he said in 1938, that the oath of secrecy, which they all had sworn on the bible, could never be broken. Rikirangi died in 1944. It seems that, as he had vowed, he never revealed what he knew.

In April 1948, the ban on Te Kooti's return to Turanga was finally lifted. At the tribal discussions preceding the Waiapu Maori pastoral synod in Gisborne, representatives of the Ringatu church listened silently as Apirana Ngata read a telegram from the family of Lady Carroll agreeing that now, after her death, they were prepared to relax the prohibition which had prevented Te Kooti from coming home.[191] Yet, while there is no certain truth, it seems that no one now knew where he lay.

Thus the words of the covenant made with Moses were confirmed for the people of another land and another time. The texts of Deuteronomy, the original promises

Te Kooti's buggy on the shores of the Ohiwa harbour, near Te Horo. This photograph was taken about 1900. The buggy had been allowed to stand just as Te Kooti left it, and a protective brush shelter built around it. Photograph by P. Keegan.   Whakatane Museum

revealed to Te Kooti on Wharekauri, themselves explain the essential story of Te Kooti's concealment. They remind that

> The Lord made not this covenant with our fathers, but with us, even us, who are all of us here alive this day.[192]

They also tell how Moses, the servant of God, died in the land where the covenant had been confirmed. For God took Moses into the hills above the plains of Moab, where he said:

> This is the land which I sware unto Abraham, unto Isaac, and unto Jacob, saying, I will give it unto thy seed: I have caused thee to see it with thine eyes, but thou shalt not go over thither.
>
> So Moses the servant of the Lord died there in the land of Moab, according to the word of the Lord.
>
> And he buried him in a valley in the land of Moab . . . but no man knoweth of his sepulchre unto this day.[193]

Thus it is that an empty grave still awaits Te Kooti in a hilltop cemetery at Turanga-nui.[194] His words for the people there may yet be fulfilled:

The monument erected by the Haahi Ringatu for Te Kooti at Te Wainui. This photograph was taken at the unveiling in 1908.   WHAKATANE MUSEUM

E kore Tūranga tāngata e kite i a au; e Tūranga whenua e kite i a au.

The people of Tūranga will never see me again; but the land of Tūranga will see me.[195]

For, as the living oral stories tell, it remains the task of Te Kooti's successor to find where he lies. In that way the One predicted will be known. It is the final test.

CHAPTER 15

EPILOGUE

In the oral traditions surrounding Te Kooti there are a number of seminal stories about the legacy he bequeathed. Any history of Te Kooti must conclude with some account of these traditions, for only then is the continuity of the Maori past in the present revealed. The stories narrate 'alternative histories'; they are statements made to change existing power relations. Born within the Maori world, they are particularly local stories: they relate to specific places, and to specific kin groups. They are stories with 'miraculous' content and thereby cut through the restrictions imposed on the narrators' lives by the quotidian structures of authority. Essentially, the stories deny that human authority, particularly secular government and European government, controls: they offer instead other sets of truths.

Most of the stories relate to tasks or quests set by Te Kooti for the generations to come. Before we consider these, however, there is one cluster of narratives which must be examined as they emphasise his message of lasting peace:

> There is a story in Gisborne. You know where Mākaraka is. Well, when you are going into Mākaraka, right on the corner, there's a vacant section there. Well, evidently that's where Te Kooti stuck a gun in — turned it upside down, and stuck it in the ground. And he prophesied that there would be no more war. He said, nothing would be built there, on that section. Well, whatever is the reason, the Ministry of Works declared that it is not to be built on — so they can keep the view open. But for the Gisborne people, it's because he poked a gun in there, and that's why they won't build on it.[1]

This story has been narrated in various forms. In one version, which may well be close to the original, Te Kooti buried his gun at Makaraka in November 1868 as his statement that he had drawn an aukati or boundary line. He would not attack Turanga; the crossroads define the limit of the 1868 reprisals.[2] John Mann's sled-house, located just north of Makaraka, was the furthermost homestead attacked in this direction, as was observed at the time.[3] It was the border of the contested land. The Ringatu elder Waioeka Brown showed the writer Leo Fowler the place where Te Kooti's 'pistol' was buried at the crossroads when she told her story.[4] The fact may have created the story; the story may have created the fact. Makaraka was where Te Kooti had sometimes lived as a young man, and it was at Makaraka that the monument, erected by public subscriptions raised in 1869, was built over the collective grave of the 'martyrs'. In 1889 Te Kooti intended to go to Makaraka,[5] where, as John Bryce himself commented, Te Kooti wished to 'bury' the remembrance of the past.[6]

When Ned Brown told the same story — though this time it was a sword Te Kooti plunged into the ground at Makaraka — he emphasised that it was the place where the roads meet: to Gisborne and the coast, south to Wellington, 'and this one to Tuhoe'. He stressed Te Kooti's words:

> He said, 'There'll be no more wars by the Māori people with the Europeans: the last will be with me. This is a promise from God to us.' Then he poked the sword in the ground. He took his hand off it, and the sword started going down, right into the ground — on its own accord. . . . At the crossroads at Mākaraka: that's where that sword is.[7]

This version echoes the Glastonbury legends, for the sword recalls King Arthur's Excalibur. Those earlier stories were themselves a Celtic–Christian fusion concerned with the recovery of autonomous power. Implicit in Ned Brown's story, like those concerning Paora Kiingi's trusteeship of Te Kooti's sword, is a once and future time when the Maori 'kingship' will be restored.[8]

The narrative of the buried sword at Makaraka has also evolved as a statement of the Ringatu commitment to peace. In 1915–16 many Tuhoe refused to volunteer for the First World War because they saw themselves as the children of the lasting peace, the Maungarongo of 1883. Their affirmation — that the sword had been thrust in — they linked with Te Kooti's prediction for his successor. As Mau Rua, Rua's son, told the story, their rejection of war was a commitment to Te Kooti's statement about the days that would come after him:

> Te Kooti prophesied before, 'War won't reach New Zealand. It is a holy land.' Te Kooti said, 'I've got a Son coming — after me. To finish what I have started.' They say he took the gun and pointed the barrel downwards, and he said, 'War won't reach New Zealand.' That's Te Kooti's prophecy; and Rua took that prophecy.[9]

While it is not this book's purpose to trace the religious movements which developed after Te Kooti's death (some of which I have already discussed elsewhere[10]), it is important to understand the narrative tradition which generated these histories. For events were set in motion by the very understandings which the narratives transmitted. Rua was one of the earliest claimants to be the 'Son' of Te Kooti, that is the One who would complete his work. In about 1905, he ascended Maungapohatu, the sacred mountain of Tuhoe, where the hidden diamond of Te Kooti was said to have been revealed to him. The oral narratives which I was told of this event derived from Pinepine, Rua's first wife, who accompanied him and who herself became a tapu woman because of her experiences. Heta Rua, Rua's son, told her story:

> So they [Rua and Pinepine] went to the top of that mountain. He went up to that diamond — there is a diamond there, I know. They were the last people to see it. And it's still there, to this day, still covered, when Te Kooti covered it up with that rug, 'rainbow shawl' they call it. A sort of travelling rug, with a lot of colours on it. And

that was still on it, 'cause he had a look at it and just covered it up again. Never took it. Never touched it.[11]

When Horopapera Tatu told the same story he, too, stressed that the shawl had been placed there by Te Kooti: 'He [Rua] went up to see the hōro: Te Kooti put the shawl on that mountain. Got to leave that thing on the mountain. Don't touch it! It looks after the mountain.'[12] Heta emphasised that this experience on the mountain was when Rua 'started off. That's how the gift was given to him.'[13] As Toiroa was the fount of Te Kooti's mana within the Maori world in his own lifetime, Te Kooti was the source of Rua's. At the same time, it was the Tuhoe ancestor Whaitiri, grandmother of Tawhaki, who revealed the hidden diamond to Rua on his ancestral mountain. Thus, simultaneously, the mana was transmitted to the new Tuhoe prophet from the most distant and the more recent pasts. Between the ancestral worlds and the world of the living, time itself is collapsed (unlike the time of Europeans, measured by watches and clocks).

One group of stories also links the transfer of mana to Rua from Te Kooti with Te Whiu Maraki, who had fought for Te Kooti and had been his swift messenger in the Urewera country. Te Whiu was known in later life as Kuku because, after one of his many absences from Te Waimana, he returned with a mussel shell (kuku) clamped to each ear, a sign of his changed status as a tohunga and medium of God.[14] Hillman Rua, Rua's adopted son, told the story this way:

> Te Kooti had this thing of God. This old man, Kuku — Te Whiu — Te Kooti said to him, 'I'll give you something to keep in your hand. Keep it for safe.' And Te Whiu says, 'What is that?' 'Oh — the life of the whole of the Waimana people. Something to look after them.' Te Whiu says, 'All right, I'll have it.' So he gave that thing to Te Whiu. And when Rua came, trying to be God, one day he decided to come over from Maunga-pōhatu out to Waimana. He told a man to go ahead of him and get Te Whiu to give this thing that Te Kooti gave him. So this man rode down and being all by himself he's faster on the track than the others coming behind him. So he came to Waimana and he went to Te Whiu and he asked him for that thing. Te Whiu said, 'No. I'm going to keep it for myself.' So this man rode back and met Rua at Tāwhana, that night. Rua says to him, 'Well, how you get on?' 'Oh, he won't let you have it. That's his own keep.' So, the next morning, Rua sent this man again, and the rest of the people came after. When they got to Matahī, they met there. Rua asked him, 'Well, what is it?' 'He won't give it to you. You're not the Son of God.' So Rua says, 'Oh well, I'll go in myself tonight.' And then, that very night, this old man [Te Whiu] told his daughters and his son, Te Maipi, 'That thing has gone out of my hand. That's the man all right, coming. Rua.'[15]

In some versions of the story the object which Te Whiu held in trust is a key. When Jeffrey Sissons was talking with Tuhoe elders from Te Waimana, he was told a version which linked the mana Te Whiu possessed with the diamond on Maungapohatu. Rua had seen the diamond, and thus, 'He had the knowledge but he needed that key to open the way so that he could achieve all the things he had to do.'[16] Heta Rua also told the story of Te Whiu's key. He said it was not 'a real key, it's a spirit. A lot of people think it's just an ordinary house key, well, it's not!' He stressed, also,

> the Law of God is still with that key. That is that gift. It was given by God to hand it

down, and that's how it is. . . . When he was just about dying Te Kooti gave him [Te Whiu] this key and told him there would be a certain person come to get it. And to give it to him. So he did, and when Rua came to ask for it, he handed it over. That's when *he* [Rua] started.

Heta added that no sooner had Te Whiu passed on the key than he died; that is the nature of the power.[17] It must be stated that Te Whiu died as late as 1922, but that is not the point.

The narrative of Te Kooti's diamond is known and told in several tribal areas. Each has its own version, and each narrator will tell the story with his or her own personal emphasis. In some accounts, the diamond was placed on the sacred mountain by Te Kooti; in other versions it has always been there. Heta said specifically, in answer to my question, that the diamond on Maungapohatu had always been there: 'That's how he knew it! So he just covered it up, so people won't be able to find it. It's still there from that day to this.'[18] Here the diamond is the mauri whenua of Tuhoe's land and its people; the covering shawl of Te Kooti conceals and protects the stone. In the old days, its bright light was clearly visible out to sea and 'the Europeans on big boats' saw it,

> but when they get closer, it disappears. So they knew quite well it wasn't a star. It must be something. Every boat that comes across, they see it, but as soon as they get closer they just can't see it again. I s'pose the land sort of — oh, I don't know. It's very much brighter than an ordinary star, but no sooner they get a bit closer, it disappears.[19]

The one constant in the narrative sequence of the diamond is that it is always hidden by Te Kooti, 'so people couldn't find it'.[20] The diamond is like the man himself, he who could never be found in the long years of fighting, nor after death. There is a version told by the Tuhoe elder Paetawa Miki to John-Erik Elmsberg in 1950, in which the bright light shines from one of the strangely coloured tarns on top of Maungapohatu. This light gleams from inside the world of the mountain. Its reflection in the sky had enticed Pakeha onto Maungapohatu, seeking the treasure they believed was there. Paetawa said that Te Kooti made this blue tarn smaller than it once was, but the light still shone forth at night. So then Te Kooti laid his cloak over it and all that was left was the piece uncovered by the neck hole of the cloak.[21]

In other versions, Te Kooti himself placed the diamond on the mountain. This is certainly how Ned Brown narrated the story of the diamond on Maungahaumi, his people's mountain, quoted in Chapter 10. Reuben Riki of Ngati Maru, formerly the assistant secretary to the Ringatu church in the Gisborne area, referred to one version which states that the diamond came from the *Rifleman*, when it was captured by the whakarau. Thus its implications stretch from the moment of Te Kooti's return to New Zealand, beyond the limits of his own life. As Reuben put it carefully:

> They say the diamond came from India, on the *Rifleman* itself. That's one story. The second story is — it refers again to the bible. One of those gems that used to go about, travel, with other people. They say this location of the diamond — if it's a diamond — some say it appears at night. People that go out opossum hunting, they could see this luminous light coming up from one area, only one area, at night. This one here, it's at

Pāparatū. . . . This one, here, it is a diamond. He [Te Kooti] came here with a purpose — as the story goes — that he came here to hide all the wealth. If they were to find the wealth of this country, they will ruin this country. He says, 'It's better to be hidden.' But there is a day coming. Some one, or somebody, will [be] bound to find this and there will be plenty for all.[22]

Mere Whaanga's version from inland Wairoa, which she published in 1990 as a children's story, also states that the diamond belonged to Te Kooti, and that he had used it as a bright light to guide his path at night. Because of its amazing powers, he determined to hide it 'so that one day it could be claimed by his successor' ('A tōna wā ka puta tōna kairīwhi ki te keremu').[23] This would be the person who would finally unite all the people and lead them into a new age of peace. Te Kooti placed the diamond in a waka huia (a carved box for the treasured huia feathers), which would not chip or rot. He hid it at the base of a matai tree, where a little spring of fresh water bubbled out. Then, a deep pool formed around it, cold and green, and you can still see the tops of the drowned forest trees within the lake, in a valley under Whakapunake mountain. The guardian of the treasure became a huge white eel, which grew as the lake grew.

> Kua mutu te wahanga kia ia. Taumaha ana tōna whatumanawa. Me tōna mōhio ake te wā e whakanuia ai tōna iwi kei te tino tawhiti tonu.

> Then, his task accomplished, Te Kooti left, his heart heavy with the realisation that his people's time of greatness was in the far distant future.[24]

The stories differ in many of their details. That does not matter: the stories belong to the place and to the local people. More important, they are essentially the same story. The water covers the inner light of the world, *lux mundi*; the diamond is hidden in water, or the lake itself is hidden. The diamond of Te Kooti may appear in the shape of the Lamb, *lux mundi* — as told in Ned Brown's narrative. The diamond, and the light, are hidden by Te Kooti's shawl. The diamond is Te Ao Marama, the Maori world of light and knowledge. It is the stone of light which holds and preserves the mana of the land and its people. All the mountains named in these regional narratives are specifically associated with Te Kooti's history of flight. Te Kooti is their guardian, until the right time comes around and the new leader emerges to redeem the land, the task Rua wished to undertake.

The age and origin of the story of the diamond, a stone not naturally found in New Zealand, is unknown. Possibly it derived from the Amerindian legend which was retold by Nathaniel Hawthorne in 'The Great Carbuncle', first published in 1851. This became a popular tale in the 19th century and was often reprinted. The story has many similarities with those about Te Kooti's diamond, for the carbuncle is the bright stone whose light overpowered the moon and could be seen far out to sea. It too was concealed in a mountain lake.[25] If this is indeed the origin of the Maori narrative of the diamond, the whole tale must have been given new life after Te Kooti's death by the discovery, in January 1905, of the largest diamond in the world, the Cullinan diamond. For the Boers this was 'God's stone' and, after much public discussion, the recently defeated Transvaal republic voted, in 1907, to present it to King Edward VII as a statement of their loyalty. It seems likely that the story of the diamond became a part of Rua's story because of the wide debate aroused by the Cullinan diamond.[26] The story expanded when Rua, in 1906, went to Gisborne to meet King Edward, taking with him, it is said, a large diamond (or in some versions gold). There, at Te Kooti's birthplace, he hoped — by exchange — to recover the land that had been ceded to Queen Victoria. The 'Son' of Te Kooti would redeem the land peacefully from the son of the Queen.

Stories of the 'hidden gold' of Te Kooti also stretch to encompass his potential successor. There are many versions, both Maori and Pakeha. Some say the gold is at Waikaremoana:

> Everybody that goes there gets killed. It's not a diamond, it's gold. He [Te Kooti] did say to the Waikaremoana people, 'You look for the spirit first. When you are deep in your faith, and hope, and charity, then that gold will naturally come out. Rāwiri Anderson, [the prophet] Tūtekohe's right-hand man, he told us where it was. There's a spirit there looking after that money.[27]

A different version tells that the 'hidden gold of Te Kooti' lies at Gisborne itself, and that Te Kooti sought to recover it when he tried to return there in 1889. In this, a Pakeha version, the gold was claimed by Rua, who took it back to Maungapohatu: greed becomes, therefore, a 'rationalisation' for Rua's pilgrimage, and the gold an explanation for Rua's apparent wealth.[28] In another version, the gold is buried at Te Rere falls, where the fighting of November 1868 occurred. Where the Makaretu river meets the Wharekopae river there is a little island, and the gold is said to be hidden there, at the joining of the waters. Some Pakeha narrators give this story a literal meaning and say the treasure consists of candelabra and valuables stolen from Matawhero. Indeed, a few abandoned objects taken from Matawhero, including a cast-iron cooking pot, have been found in the rifle terraces made by the defenders at Te Karetu. But all efforts to find the hidden gold at Te Rere — or anywhere else, including the Hauhau huts paddock on Wharekauri, or the bay at Whareongaonga where a bag of gold from the *Rifleman* is said to have been dropped by Te Kooti as a koha — have failed.[29] As Reuben Riki put it, referring to the hidden gold of Te Kooti understood to be in the cliffs behind Muriwai at Poverty Bay:

> It is said you walk between the solid gold, and you can't see it. You don't know where to look. See, I am of the opinion that there are some things which are hidden to us. . . . This is the place: but where is it? Is it a myth?[30]

All the Maori narratives are part of the extensive tradition of great wealth, shielded by Te Kooti, to which the proper person will one day be guided. Yet each narrative is local. The narratives are engendered from the community-based systems of knowledge in the Maori world. They stand as statements of the independent mana of the local people, as each area lays claim to its own relationship with Te Kooti. Each thereby also resists its subordination into a standard 'history', whether Maori or Pakeha.

Te Kooti's role as guardian of the land is stated in many other stories, too. His sign was the white lunar rainbow — not the rainbow of fire — and it was given to him on

Wharekauri, the island of rainbows. At Whareongaonga, it is said there is a spring of water which will never run dry; wherever Te Kooti went on his journeys, and on every Twelfth, he was blessed with a little shower of rain. It went before him, and those who travelled with him saw the rain falling and yet, as they said, 'you don't feel wet'. It was, rather, 'a shower of blessing'. Thus Te Kooti came also to be known as Patapataawha,[31] for like the rain which accompanied him he blesses and protects the land.

Hidden stones of power form yet another set of narratives surrounding Te Kooti and those who claimed his mantle. Hidden stones are biblical, but they are also, of course, part of pre-European Maori oral tradition. It is in the mingling of the different traditions that the appeal of a new story often lies. In the oral traditions from Muriwai, as narrated by Reuben Riki, it is said that Te Kooti, as he went inland from Whareongaonga in 1868, left behind seven tokens for the seven islands of the land: 'he whitu ngā mana whenua. Each token represented one island.'[32] These are the seven stones which have to be recovered to bring unity to the land. Similarly, in the records of Te Haahi o Te Kooti Rikirangi, which separated as a distinct church in 1937 and accepted the claims of Wi Raepuku (Ohana) to be the One foreseen, there is a body of written material concerning the 'seven seals' which are said, by this branch of the faith, to have been laid upon the land by Te Kooti between 1891 and 1893. They are seven sayings uttered by Te Kooti at various places on his last journeys. (Te Kooti himself did not refer to these kupu whakaari as the 'seven seals'; this is a construct of this church, as Wi Tarei, the tohunga, admitted.) The seven sayings were gathered together in the manuscript 'The Prediction of One to Follow' for a purpose: the quest to open the 'seven seals', which was undertaken by the prophet Wi Raepuku between 1921 and 1930.[33] In this compilation of statements, the 'seventh seal' concerns the hidden stone.

The 'seven seals' are all tasks and riddles set for the coming leader who, in unravelling them, will bring unity. Three (the fourth, sixth and seventh) are of particular interest because they are specific quests which Te Kooti set for his successor. The fourth seal is dated, in this source, as 1892, but in fact it refers back to an earlier occasion, on 15 January 1886, when Te Kooti visited Te Houhi, on the upper Rangitaiki river. He was returning from the January Ra at Wairoa, and at Te Houhi he reminded the Tuhoe people there of Jehovah's promise that he would not abandon them. This promise, called 'Te Umutaoroa', is referred to in other sources.[34] Boy Biddle narrated the story of Te Umutaoroa this way:

> Te Kooti was there, he slept at this particular pā, and where he did sleep he said to them in the morning, 'Now, I had a dream last night: the valley of the Rangitāiki here was just dense fog, right from the top of it to the other side, and I couldn't see through this fog, so the place where I slept, it will be known as Te Umutaoroa.' That's a hāngi — but it would perpetually be in that form until this person came and uncovered it. So this place became quite a gathering place for these false Christs, false prophets. They rush up there.[35]

It was this vision which Te Kooti recalled in 1892 at Te Poroporo, Whakatane:

> Te kupu ki te Umutaoroa — Te Houhi
> Ka taona e ahau tenei hangi ma taku tamaiti e hura.

> Tenei mea te hangi, ko nga kai o roto hei ora mo te tangata.

> The word concerning Te Umutaoroa [The Earth Oven of Long Cooking] — Te Houhi
> I am preparing this hangi for my child to unearth.
> The food inside this hangi will be for the salvation of the people.[36]

In Te Tupara's recollection of Te Kooti's dying words (ohaki) — in this account, said to have been uttered at Te Karaka on 17 April 1893 — the promise is again remembered. Only Wi Raepuku's followers have a record of this particular ohaki, which presumably derives from Te Tupara, who was one of the Ngati Koura mediators during the Ruatoki dispute.[37] When Te Tupara came to Te Kooti at Te Karaka he asked him about the coming Child:

> 'He aha te tohu ki au?'
>   Ka utua e Te Kooti, 'Ki te hukea, a Te Umutaoroa', koia tena, ko ta taua tamaiti.

> 'What will be the sign to me?'
>   Te Kooti replied, 'When Te Umutaoroa is opened', that shall be our child.[38]

From this tradition, Te Umutaoroa became, as Boy Biddle observed sardonically, a 'gathering place' for claimants. Consequently Wi Raepuku went there

> to exhume this thing and find out what was in it. But to be quite truthful there was nothing there, just bare ground. So, it's a symbolic thing; it was not an actual hāngi.[39]

The sixth seal concerns the hidden bones of Te Kooti. This tradition refers to his prediction that he would return to Turanga — whether on two, three or four legs, or in a wooden box. It becomes, therefore, the task of his successor to discover and carry his bones to the land promised to them — stated to be the same request as Joseph had made at his death to the children of Israel.[40] In one version, told in 1923, it is said that, if Te Kooti's bones are returned to Turanga,

> a diamond of considerable size would be discovered in the Whakapunake range, near Te Reinga. This statement . . . was made by Te Kooti in his last words to his people.[41]

Thus, in this version from upper Wairoa, the narratives of the diamond and the return of Te Kooti are linked. The elders who made this statement went to Wainui for the First of July 1923 to try to claim Te Kooti's bones and take them back to Gisborne.

The seventh and final seal in the manuscript 'The Prediction of One to Follow' concerns the hidden stone. No date or occasion is given for the following saying:

> Huri tua (7). Te Kupu a Te Kooti mo tona Kohatu.
> Ka whakatakotoria koe e ahau ki tenei waahi ma taku tamaiti ra ano koe e hura ake.

> 7th Seal. Te Kooti's Word, concerning his Stone.
> You are laid here in this place by me; it is for my child to unearth you.[42]

Juxtaposed with the statement are the scriptural texts of Isaiah 28:16 and Revelation 2:17, which are cited as confirmation. The first describes the precious stone laid as the foundation of Zion, or the corner-stone. The second is an even more famous text:

> To him that overcometh will I give to eat of the hidden manna, and will give him a
> white stone, and in the stone a new name written, which no man knoweth saving he
> that receiveth it.

From the first text has sprung the tradition of the lost corner-stones of the Maori world: 'Te Kohatu o te Kokonga'.[43] The search for these has created a host of local histories. The recovery of the sacred stones for the 'four quarters' has been undertaken by many different marae and different leaders — even as recently as 1984.[44] From the second text springs the lineage for Te Kooti's successor.

Those who emerged to claim the mantle of authority as Te Kooti's successor travelled to all the places associated with him, as did Rua. His daughter, Te Akakura, said, when revisiting Eripitana in 1978, 'Everywhere Te Tūruki was, our father was.'[45] Very early, Rua went to Te Here-o-te-Ra on Hokianga island, because he thought it was a source of the mana he sought. There he built his own meeting-house, Te Poho-o-Tuhoe (or Te Poho-o-Mataatua).[46] Then, on 12 March 1906, Rua went to Tawhana, the sacred place sworn to Te Kooti, and from there he journeyed to Te Waimana to commence, on 16 March, his first pilgrimage to Gisborne, the home to which Te Kooti had been unable to return. Rua must have been following a predetermined chronology, adopting 12 and 16 March as the start of the new year or cycle of time, as Te Kooti had apparently intended. At Repongaere, near Gisborne, Rua went into the sacred house Rongopai, and thus it was said 'the day was fulfilled' ('ka tutuki te ra').[47] The oral narratives relate how Rua entered that locked house. In some versions it is told how he rode through the rear of the house, re-emerging out the window at the front, the tapu part. In this manner, Rua established his lineage to be Te Kooti's 'Son', just as the ancestor Rangi Te Ao Rere had once revealed himself to his father,[48] and just as, in one version, Te Kooti himself burst through the rear wall of the meeting-house at Koriniti to claim his space. Rua's means of entry into Rongopai, in every narrative version, is the great white horse of Te Kooti, here named Te Ia. In some accounts, it is simply stated that 'The *horse* had the golden key'.[49]

From Gisborne, Rua went inland to Maungapohatu, where on 12 April he announced his second pilgrimage. He would go again to Gisborne, and on 25 June he would 'ascend the throne, the king will arrive at Turanga' ('i [te] 25 o Hune haere au ki runga i te torina, ka tae mai a te kiingi ki Turanga').[50] On this journey Rua took with him a large box or chest, which was guarded constantly, by day and night. The chest was probably the ark of the covenant, just as Te Kooti had once hoped to carry it to Gisborne, the 'seat of hatred'. But some believed that it contained the diamond, said to have been obtained from a secret place known only to Rua. Elsdon Best was told that Rua had gone to Paraeroa, on the upper Whakatane river, to unearth it.[51] On this second journey to Gisborne, Rua was accompanied by 80 chiefs in fulfilment of Te Kooti's words to Tuhoe and Ngati Awa in 1892. This quest, to find the Eighty, was itself called the fifth seal in the collated prophecies, 'The Prediction of One to Follow'. When King Edward failed to arrive at Gisborne, Rua then revealed the inner meaning of the pilgrimage: 'I am really that King' — 'Here I am, with all my people.'[52]

A contemporary of Rua, who also claimed to be the foreseen healer and prophet,

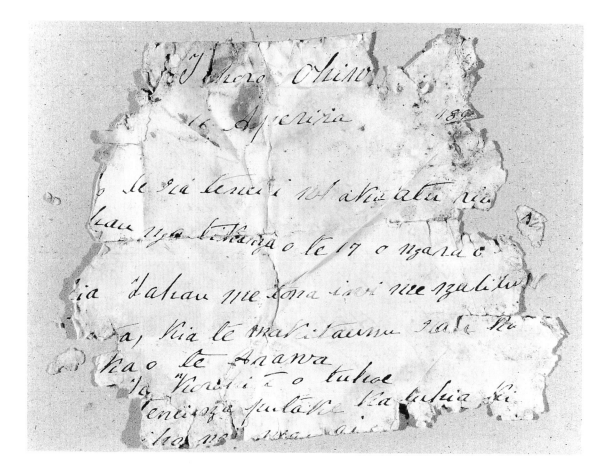

Fragment of a letter of instructions sent from Te Horo, Ohiwa, 16 April 1889. It sets out the rules for the new Ra of 17–18 of the month. The letter indicates that the rules were sent to Tahau for Tuwharetoa; to Tuhoe; to Te Arawa; and to the Ringatu community at Paritu, where it was found. The obverse lists the rules. The letter may be in Te Kooti's handwriting, and he is known to have returned to the eastern Bay of Plenty (after his arrest) for the Ra of 1 July 1889. By permission of Kati Wharepapa.

was Wi Wereta of Tokomaru. From about 1900 he too began his journeys to all the people and places associated with Te Kooti. He went from Gisborne to Te Kuiti and the Wairarapa, seeking in these places the power of healing ('mana whakaora') which he believed Te Kooti had possessed. When he arrived at Paritu on the Coromandel peninsula in the late 1920s, he came as a healer. The community there had built its unique church-house Hurae (July) to fulfil Te Kooti's 1892 directive from Parikino: to lift up the July as a sign of the works of peace.[53] The little wooden church, Hurae, still stands (albeit now derelict) and Rangimarie (Full of Peace) is the name of the later community hall. Hurae is unusual in that it was built like an Anglican church; it had tiered seats and a pulpit. It was unusual in another way, too: it was used by the community only for the sacred days of July, that is, the First and the Twelfth of July and, there, the Eighteenth. This last Ra was created on the instructions of Te Kooti, sent out

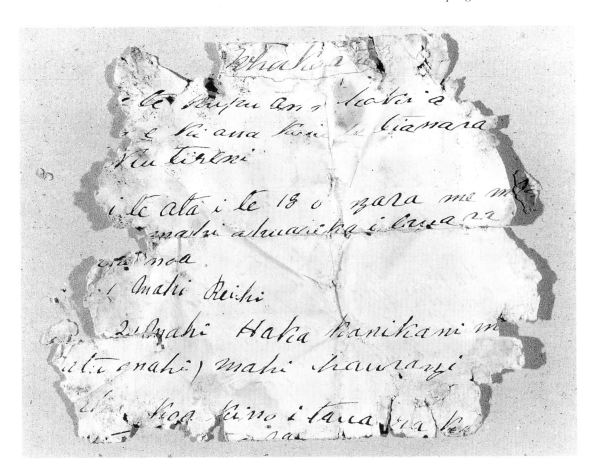

in April 1889. The 17th was set apart as the day for worship, the 18th for pleasure. His directions, surviving in a torn fragment of a letter, were

> i te ata i te 18 o nga ra me m[. . .] mahi ahuareka i taua ra [. . .] noa.
> 1. Mahi Reihi.
> 2. Mahi Haka kanikani m[e era] atu mahi, mahi haurangi . . . ka . . . koa kino i taua ra.
>
> in the morning of the 18th you are to . . . enjoy yourselves on that day . . . [whatever you like].
> 1. Races.
> 2. Haka and dances a[nd] other activities, drinking . . . [but don't] misbehave on that day.[54]

These gatherings at Paritu were maintained until the early 1930s. The people travelled by horseback and buggy from nearby marae at Puketui and Mataora to join the local community. Alongside Hurae there also once stood the community's meeting-house, which was used on all other months of the year, and for all other occasions, including the services held there by Wi Wereta to heal the sick. He healed by pressing the flat of his hand on the place of pain ('whakapā') and slowly 'pushing out' the trouble. Kati Wharepapa of Paritu, who remembered Wi Wereta attending him as a child, recalled that

Wi stayed with the sick person for about five or ten minutes and, during this time, 'he also churched over you'. Everyone was in the meeting-house, praying together. At the end, when the service was finished, 'the patient seemed to be good again. You had faith in him, that's why. . . . Wī Wereta was a good old man.'[55] The healing principles rested on faith and on the community's collective participation.

When that other claimant Wi Raepuku emerged from within the Whanganui district, he set out to open 'the seven seals'. He began his journey from Otoko, and the little meeting-house Te Kooti had re-named the Breakfast, on 1 July 1921. It was there that Wi Raepuku broke the first seal, declaring this house, Tauakira, to be a house of sacred knowledge and exposition, and himself to be the predicted child, 'te tamaiti a Te Kooti'.[56] On 1 January 1923 at Te Poroporo marae, Whakatane, he announced that he had opened the fourth seal, the hangi of long-cooking, Te Umutaoroa.[57] Then, at the Ra held the following July at Te Wainui, the hope of returning Te Kooti's bones to Gisborne was articulated. It was Rikirangi Hohepa who reminded the gathering of Te Kooti's prediction that he would, one day, return there, even if in a wooden box ('i roto i te papa rakau ka tae ahau ki Turanga'). Apirana Ngata was present on this occasion, when the trustees for Wainui were being established, and he replied sharply:

> Kaati ra. Whakatutukiria te kupu a te koroua, otira, waiho, kia mate te ahi e ka mai ra, i roto o Turanga.
> Na ka mea a Rikirangi, Waiho kia rua tau.

> That is enough. Let the statement of your uncle [Te Kooti] be put aside; drop this matter so that the fires burning in Gisborne may die out.
> Rikirangi replied, We will drop the matter for two years.[58]

When the two years had passed, Wi Raepuku came again to Wainui for the First of July, saying, 'I shall appropriate "the eye of the Island" so that I shall have two eyes' ('Ka tangohia e ahau "te kanohi o te Motu" hei rua mo oku kanohi').[59] But both he and Rua laid claim to Wainui at the same time, and consequently there was much dispute. Wi Raepuku moved the centre of his faith to Te Poroporo, and two years later, in 1927, he returned to Wainui, seeking permission to exhume the bones of Te Kooti and to return them to Gisborne. He was greeted by a stony silence from the assembled gathering.[60]

Te Kooti had foreseen the likelihood of such division. His often-told prediction concerning the meeting-house Tane Whirinaki at Waioeka, gnawed by rats from its rear, is mostly narrated in the context of the rift which occurred when Rua took the people away from the faith of 'Nga Morehu Tangata' (The Survivors), in 1906–7. The intention here is not to emphasise the issue of division; rather, it is to show how the *words* created living histories. The words set the events in motion. Thus prophecy can become self-fulfilling. This framework of thought is shared by many primarily oral societies because it enables the structuring of both history and memory amidst a myriad of human experiences. As Boy Biddle observed, 'What a prophet says, it will take time to prove if right or wrong.'[61] The words live through time and are not merely reinterpreted: they generate events. The Ringatu from the Whanganui district, for example, likened themselves to the children of Israel ('nga tamariki a Iharaira') when they undertook their pilgrimage with Wi Raepuku to find the Promised Land. Their journey from Otoko

Wi Wereta. Portrait from Te Rawheoro meeting-house, Tolaga Bay. Rephotographed, by permission of Sonny Kutia, by Gillian Chaplin.

took them to Kauangaroa and Karioi, places associated with Te Kooti, and along the Desert Road to Whakatane, where Ngati Pukeko and Ngati Awa sheltered them and gave them land on which to live. At every spot where they rested, they planted trees to mark the stages of their pilgrimage.[62] Much later, in 1940, a prayer–healer from Tolaga Bay, Wiremu Ritemana Rangi, who was known as Tutekohe, visited Te Raupunga and Mohaka, a district generally hostile to Te Kooti. One woman there who was attracted to Tutekohe's teachings described how a tradition reaching back to Te Kooti could appeal, even at Mohaka:

> Te Kooti left prophecies for the next one to carry on his work. Some of the kupu are only coming out now. It's the spirit that's passed down from generation to generation. The spiritual side is far greater, not the person. They were [only] the ones to uphold it for the time they were alive on earth. That's how we were told it. It passes down to another person. It's not the person, it's God.[63]

As with Te Kooti, Tutekohe's guiding angel was said to be Michael, and Tutekohe's task was to bring the people 'out of the Old Testament into the New'.[64] Tutekohe became

The church-house Hurae (July) at Paritu. The date of the house is given as 1894. Photograph by Judith Binney, 1993.

particularly influential among the Ringatu believers at Waikaremoana, and his role was understood to be to extend what Te Kooti had begun there.

This religious history has continued into the present. The Rastafarian leader among Ngati Porou on the East Coast, Christopher Campbell, shot dead in 1990, also claimed that the foundation of his teachings was scriptural: 'the King James bible'. He added, 'We are all believers in the teachings of the Māori prophet Te Kooti Arikirangi Te Tūruki'.[65] He joined this to his acceptance of the divinity of the Ras Haile Selassie, thereby identifying his particular cause, land occupations, with 'black Zionism'.

This religious history, therefore, is volatile. It can be constantly rewoven as well as renewed. As a lineage of ideas it may be seized upon as a way out of economic or political powerlessness. Its real dangers lie in the potential exploitation of the followers by the self-appointed religious leader. If he (more rarely, she) claims to be, in person, the answer to all the people's questions and choices, then the movement may become fanatical and obsessive, as well as violent. But if the leader is able to guide the people of a community to make mature considered judgments about the world, and their place in it, which was Te Kooti's ultimate objective, then the humanist principles which must underlie any religious belief in order to deserve that title — as distinct from mere sectarianism — may be regenerated within that community. So, also, may that community gradually regenerate itself.

To return briefly to the events that followed on Te Kooti's death. The land given to him at Te Wainui became a home for his followers. Their first act was to erect a 'whare maori' at the site where his tent stood when he first viewed the land on 12 March 1891. The earliest house built at Wainui, erected on Te Kooti's instructions within one day, was Te Tihokahoka: as its name indicates, it was a temporary shelter made of branches stuck into the ground.[66] The later raupo house was named Te Pou-whakatamore (The Sustaining Pillar) and was built between 13 and 18 May 1893, on land which turned out not to be part of the grant at all, indicating the confusion which still existed. Equally important, Hamiora constructed a house for copying all the books. This done, on 26 May, he wrote, 'we moved our things from Hokianga to Te Wainui' ('Ka whakahunu-kutia mai a matau mea i Hokianga ki te Wainui').[67]

Once settled, the community brought the ark of the covenant there on 11 June. The permanent tabernacle was completed on 23 May 1894, and the tapu-lifting ceremony was held that evening in Te Pou-whakatamore. The recorders Hamiora and Matiu were present. Then, in 1903, the wooden meeting-house, Te Ohaki, which stands today, was erected on the land grant. It was named for the dying words of Te Kooti, that the Ra should be tied by Rakuraku to Te Wainui. The name also conveys the broader meaning that the words compiled by Te Kooti 'shall live for ever'.[68] Te Ohaki was opened on 25 December, and it was then understood that the house would not be tapu but noa: that is, freed from the restrictions of the past while dedicated to the welcoming of people, and to the faith.[69] Thus the purpose of Te Ohaki is to sustain the teachings of Te Kooti at Te Wainui.

It was there that the texts of the faith were first transcribed. As Ned Brown said:

> My cousin was telling me, at Wainui, where Matiu was stationed — he's the secretary of Te Kooti, it was him that wrote up all the psalms, the hymns and the prayers — every time that old fellow went into his office, at Wainui, the rainbow always stood above it. He'd be looking at you, and his hand still going. Never went to a university: where he learnt his Hebrew from, nobody knows.
> *Heni Brown*: It's just a gift.[70]

Matiu, Petera and Hamiora were the three 'gospellers', the conscious recorders of Ringatu history. Hamiora remained at Wainui, a pivot of that community until his death in 1914. Matiu returned to the East Coast and became the centre of a growing Ringatu community at Waiomatatini, in the heart of the Waiapu valley. He became very influential in that district, despite the authority of Paratene Ngata's family.[71] Indeed, some attributed the mana of Paratene's son, Apirana, in part to the 'Apostle Matiu': he transmitted his power, which was derived from Te Kooti, to Apirana, some say.[72] Another pre-eminent figure on the East Coast was Eria Raukura, whom Te Kooti had baptised as his leading tohunga in the waters of the Manga-o-Kewa stream at Te Kuiti in 1881. Eria lived until 1938, and for a period he also acted as a guardian of Rongopai. He is spoken of with fear by all who knew him, because he was believed to possess the power of life and death, makutu. 'He can kill you!' warned Horo Tatu.[73] These elders transmitted some of their history to the following generations.

The oldest of the people with whom I have talked over the years were brought up by them, or remembered them.[74] This second generation learnt much of their history orally, and in writing this biography I have drawn on their knowledge, itself derived from these elders in both oral and written forms. I have attempted to maintain the integrity of form of both the oral stories and the Maori manuscript texts. I have, however, juxtaposed them with other sources. I have laid them openly alongside the military records, written by both European and Maori, the newspaper reports, and many private diaries and letters. Sound historical method cannot allow any single kind of recording to stand untested by other accounts, and that principle remains valid even as it is increasingly recognised that there are different cultural ways of transmitting, interpreting and structuring history. One purpose in bringing together what has previously been, on the one hand, mostly scattered and disparate — that is, the European sources — or, on the other, structured and purposeful — that is, the records of the gospellers held by the various branches of the church — is to show that very different understandings can co-exist about events which have taken place in our society.

Few Europeans have had any grasp of the consistency of Te Kooti's determination after 1883 to maintain peace, while still upholding the mana Maori. Only the Ringatu records bring this out. Hamiora recorded Te Kooti's speeches at length; that was his task. He was, as Boy Biddle said, 'the minute secretary', instructed to write down every word said. Matiu was, rather, the recorder of the wisdom that manifested itself in private personal discussion and communication, or 'the whakapā appproach', as Biddle described it.[75] Some of the earliest records were deliberately destroyed by Te Kooti. He ordered Hamiora to burn many of his sayings and songs from the times of war, particularly the karakia (like those cited in Chapter 5), which had been appeals to destroy their enemies. These were based in the Psalms of David, but 'he felt were not fitting for peace time'.[76] The times had moved on. Te Kooti also forced Hamiora to destroy all the records Hamiora had compiled, because of the sin of violence he had committed when once he struck his wife as they were all travelling home together.[77] Perhaps Te Kooti's reaction was so extreme because Hamiora's action reminded him of his own violence with Oriwia. Hamiora's book of waiata stops abruptly after recording the songs for July 1890 at Karioi. It is possible that this was when he was dismissed as secretary, although there is internal evidence that he compiled this manuscript book about 1907. There are also transcript copies of Te Kooti's last songs, 1890–93, some of which are directly attributed to Hamiora's original manuscripts. Nobody really replaced Hamiora, and he recommitted all the records to writing after Te Kooti's death. Many documents penned in his beautiful copperplate handwriting (which it is said he taught himself miraculously, overnight), covering the period from 1875 to 1913, survive.

Robert Biddle, secretary of the Haahi Ringatu, began the task of carefully transcribing from the manuscript books in his possession in 1927. He was scrupulous in sourcing his material, usually annotating in the margin the author and the particular manuscript book from which the copied text derived. He also kept an index of many separate correspondence files, from which he also transcribed. When he met the journalist Ronald

Te Ohaki, Te Wainui. The house was built in 1903 by Te Whenuanui, and renovated in 1942. In the foreground (right) is the marble monument erected for Te Kooti in 1908. Photograph by Gillian Chaplin, 1978.

Vine in 1938, he told Vine of the original papers he possessed, some written by Te Kooti and others by his three secretaries.[78] Most of these manuscripts Biddle hid during the Second World War, while his son, Boy, was away fighting. Biddle died in November 1945, just before Boy returned, and many of the original papers were lost.[79] Some survived, however, as well as the copies he had made. I have not seen all of Hamiora's originals, which are held by several families, but I have been privileged to have access to Biddle's transcripts. If the rainbow stood over Matiu while he worked, Biddle's care as a copyist was equally remarkable. Some of the original letters and records of speeches in Hamiora's handwriting exist along with Biddle's copies of the same documents, and they establish the care with which he transcribed them.

The importance of this source is that the texts and records have not been adapted to meet the claims of later prophets, which was the specific purpose behind the manuscript 'The Prediction of One to Follow', created by the followers of Wi Raepuku at Te Teko, particularly the family of the tohunga Wi Tarei. Similarly, the kupu whakaari published by the Ratana faith were chosen for their own purposes, that is, to demonstrate the legitimacy of Tahupotiki Wiremu Ratana's claims to be the predicted One. None of the Ringatu sources are neutral — nor should anyone expect them to be — but Biddle's compilation from first-generation texts are careful records of Te Kooti's words and teachings. They stand alongside Te Kooti's surviving letters and two diaries as good primary sources, along with the transcript of Matiu's notebook, made at Wharekawa in 1930.

Te Kooti often taught by parable, as Boy Biddle has observed.[80] He narrated stories whose meanings would be revealed in later interpretations. He gave out warnings whose outcome similarly remained contingent until it manifested itself. Thus he sustained a system of thought which is shared by many oral cultures: a prophetic tradition that allows understanding of the meaning in later events through analysis of the earlier, memorable spoken words. Far from paralysing initiative, as the linguist-turned-historian Tzvetan Todorov argued in his study of the 16th-century conquest of Mexico,[81] prophetic traditions may generate action and shift initiatives dramatically. They offer alternative understandings, as the language of allegory and symbol is the language of multivalence of meaning. We who claim to live in an age of signs tend to construct much more narrowly defined messages and forget the infinite variety of shadow and light which is maintained through a language of symbols. The names given to the meeting-houses, the paintings and carvings which shelter within them, and the songs and the oral stories, while the statements they contain may be condensed and mnemonic, all convey a multiplicity of reference and of possible interpretations. Thus many layers of experience were, and still are, transmitted in Maori culture.

This biography may appear to be an attempt to fix meaning by the very act of writing. That is not its intended purpose. Different understandings of the teachings of Te Kooti co-exist within the Ringatu world, and outside it. The stories and the sayings are not static. Among the Ringatu it is still understood of the sayings of Te Kooti that, 'though they are from 110 years ago, each one relates to *now*'.[82] In an oral culture, as a marae-based culture still is, the transmission of 'history' always reflects current concerns, and the Ringatu narratives have shifted widely according to local interpretations. It is not only the local details which shift; structural changes also occur in accordance with these larger concerns.

Having said this, I also believe that written history, based on a wide range of knowledge and sources, is of benefit to us all. In writing this biography, rather than finding the Maori oral narratives and songs incompatible with the European written sources, I have discovered that they are surprisingly congruent. That is to say, although their primary concerns and purpose may indeed be very different, if the context can be recovered then the message within the song and the narrative visibly flows from that context. The songs and the stories are spun from the occasion; their warnings and directives are derived from particular experiences.

The historical knowledge they contain is necessarily condensed, for oral memory needs mnemonic devices. Thus the critical messages are conveyed in pithy myth-narratives, or in sayings, or by songs. Indeed, on the marae, it is often the song which conveys 'the deadly point' and not the speech which preceded it.[83] The song carries the message from the past into the present; 'the song will tell you more than a person can'.[84] Te Kooti's adaptation of songs conveyed to his listeners subtle and complex messages from Maori ancestral history. A study of his waiata, and the political contexts for which

Robert Biddle, secretary
of the Haahi Ringatu
(left), and Te Whenuanui
II, 1938. Photograph
probably by Ron Vine.
WHAKATANE MUSEUM

they were adapted, is long overdue, and the appendixed songlist has been compiled for this reason. It is to be hoped that this biography has established the contexts for some of the songs, upon which Maori scholars can build. The songs are 'old' and the music to which they are sung is, as has often been stated, pre-European. Here, as in other ways, Te Kooti was consciously bringing values and knowledge from the past to give reference points for the future. The adaptation of the songs, like the construction of the meeting-houses and the paintings within them, was a part of his deliberate effort to sustain the Maori language, land and spirit, within the new vessel of his own creation: the protecting faith. That faith was itself a remarkable adaptation for his and his people's needs from ideas which had been only recently introduced to his generation by the early missionaries in the country.

In his history of the Tuhoe people of Te Waimana in the eastern Bay of Plenty, the anthropologist Jeffrey Sissons wrote that Maori oral history is essentially about mana. Therefore, it is almost always debatable, 'each narrative virtually requiring a counter-narrative if it is to remain within living tradition'.[85] I would not disagree with this judgment. Stories of conflict of mana abound in this biography. Nevertheless, it still seemed to be valuable to juxtapose the narratives — and some of the songs — in a sequential historical framework, rather than leaving them unattached, or placed only within a looser ordering of dialogue and personal narrative. Sissons' purpose in ordering the oral narratives that he was told within various 'domains' of local concern was to bring the Tuhoe dialogues to the fore, rather than to subordinate them to the perspectives and constructs of the historian. He wished to demonstrate the distinctiveness of the Tuhoe histories and the continual process of change which occurs within oral history.

This biography belongs much more to the Western European tradition of constructing written history. It is, after all, a biography of an individual, a particularly European approach based on the belief that individuals are important precisely because they break through and defy the structures and received truths of a particular time, place and culture. In a sense, it defends the validity of some established European forms of analysing the past — by constructing a life history of an individual who was not European either by birth or by cultural background. In this act of construction it argues, from the European tradition, that self-explanation does not present an adequate understanding of history. Thus it may seem to take the position of a 'meta-narrative', establishing over-arching analyses of events and their significance. Certainly, this book adopts the structure of an authorial narrative. But it defends the narrative form essentially because narrative is the method by which the colonised 'assert their own identity and the existence of their own history'.[86] Narrative is sustained in all human communities because it best demonstrates (as in this study) 'a progression from suffering to rage to redemption'.[87] This biography attempts, as well, to enter into 'the perilous space in-between' (as Anne Salmond has put it): the borderlands of thinking between cultures.[88] It is therefore infused with European traditions of the recovery and interpretation of the past, but it hopes to represent a Maori leader in ways that will illuminate him for Maori, as well as for Pakeha, by respecting Maori ways of seeing.

This book therefore seeks to establish not only 'what happened and why' (an orthodox historical goal), but also to show that different understandings and different truths co-exist. It tries to indicate by juxtaposition within sequential and thematic frameworks how different notions of 'what matters' — that is, history — are generated and transmitted. It attempts to demonstrate why misunderstandings arose, and why some events came to have a meaning for Maori which was quite different from Pakeha understanding. It shows how some of those events were memorialised — by the construction and naming of meeting-houses, for example. It also shows *why* the gaps in perception became entrenched in different sectors of society. It also tries to untangle some of the Pakeha misconceptions, usually engendered by fear but undoubtedly perpetuated by cultural and racial prejudice.

In this book I make no claims to have recovered or commented upon all the songs or all the religious texts. There are other songs concerning Te Kooti which are still sung, and I am aware of at least one for Heni Kumekume sung on the East Coast. Nor would I claim to have recovered all of the oral narratives, nor indeed told all of those I have heard. Equally, I have not seen, or cited, all of the texts and prophecies. What I have tried to do is demonstrate that, as with written documents, the oral histories and the songs stem from historical contexts which are at least partially recoverable. They can be better understood in those contexts although, by their nature, they will convey — and, certainly in the case of the stories, have evolved with — a multiplicity of meanings.

Nor would I pretend to have recovered all those contexts. Other writers will bring different knowledge to bear on both the oral and the written material — that, of course, is what the telling of history is about. There are Maori aspects to which some Maori will be able to respond more extensively, for the degree of understanding in those aspects relates to the degree of personal immersion in the Maori world: the meaning and closeness of a text varies according to what we already know. On Wharekauri, Te Kooti was called Tawhaki, the twice-born. In some senses he indeed became that ancestor, for, like Tawhaki, he had been the subject of the cruelty and jealousy of his 'brothers', and he was left for dead, his winding-sheet prepared; but, like Tawhaki, he returned from the dead. He brought with him knowledge — or a new way of seeing. Te Kooti was a master of disguise, changing his garments, appearing and disappearing, as he tested people — just like this ancestor. Sometimes, too, as is narrated in the story of Te Kooti's sudden appearance at Maraenui at night, his presence was revealed only by a flash of light about his cloak. Like Tawhaki, god of knowledge and light — and of ominous thunder as well — Te Kooti has been 'reborn' in the past, and will be in the future.

Thus Te Kooti sustained critical Maori concepts, providing a Maori environment for the new faith. It was a Maori understanding of tapu which he brought to the Hebraic idea of 'holy' ('qadosh'), and he gave it 'a physical content'.[89] Every bible was a tapu object. The printed texts of the scriptures were kept in separate whare, often built alongside the meeting-houses and called whare kawenata, houses for the covenant. People today recall how the elders kept their personal bibles apart from all other things, placed high in the rafters or up on a separate shelf. One woman recalled how the local tohunga (her uncle) refused to take his bible through the doorway when he left home, but instead placed it on the window sill and took it from there once he was outside. He returned it the same way. After re-entering the house, he put the bible back on its separate shelf in the house, and then washed, to lift the tapu upon him.[90] The burnt sacrifices, offerings to God, were made in places of tapu. Every Ringatu child grew up terrified of the power which inhabited such places. Finding the old coins, fire-blackened or green with verdigris, and being frightened by and also tempted to touch them, is a part of many of my informants' childhood memories. Going to the 'sacred water' in the very early hours of the morning to prevent or be cured of illness is another widely shared memory. This practice was Maori in its origins, although obviously reinforced by Christian baptismal and purification rites. In some communities, at least, the ritual adopted in the faith now demanded three immersions — for the Father, Son and Holy Ghost. The prohibitions against bringing cooked food and tobacco into meeting-houses, and against the use of hot water for washing, also derived from the Maori cosmology. Cooking transforms matter; cooked food belongs only to the human dimension of life. Therefore, all activities associated with cooking (by fire or heat) violated the state of being under tapu, that is divine influence, which makes possible creation and fruitfulness and achievement. This essentially Maori (and indeed Polynesian) concept was expressly maintained by Te Kooti.

Ancestral referentials from the Maori world run through all the songs and all the art created and inspired by Te Kooti. The great events in life in the Maori world conceptually reiterate the events of the past; thus tika, the appropriate and correct way, is conceived in terms of the traditions and acts of the Maori ancestors. The tipuna with whom Te Kooti explicitly compared himself in song was Mahaki, he who was banished from his own home, Turanganui. But he was also Te Tahi o Te Rangi, the ancestor who was taken away from the land by his own people, but who, on returning, possessed a new understanding of life: that mercy was a greater quality than revenge. And he became, in turn, the man-god Rongo-ma-Tane who, war-experienced, fetched the knowledge of peace from the afterworld, and whose ancient song Te Kooti is remembered as singing as he journeyed.[91] And I would suggest that he also became a transformation of Maui, the trickster-figure and the joker, the wild boy and the twice-born: thus, '*māna ano e whakamaui ake*'.[92] He captured the sun and light, and brought a new life for humankind, but was, indeed, finally mortal. Both the Maui myth-cycle and the Tawhaki cycle which extends it are about the acquisition of knowledge, and I am certain that Te Kooti was consciously acting by and transforming these myth-narratives for his own times. Maori history is embedded throughout Te Kooti's history. Perhaps it would be more correct to say that he was enclosing the new history within the old, and extending the old. Others will be able to explore these frameworks more fully. The korero exists in the songs and the houses, which are themselves complex systems of references and mnemonics to the ancestral world. It was by these means that Te Kooti both sustained and restructured the Maori past. The references were cosmological and historical, but he was also reshaping them.

A long time ago, J. Prytz Johansen observed that Maori views and experience of history are essentially different from those of Europeans. Maori did not, and probably still do not, acknowledge chance: each event has significance. Every deed, every occurrence thus possesses for Maori 'quite another depth than they do for us'.[93] Maori relive history in the meanings which they attribute to events. Maori ancestors appear to the living, and their words continue to exist in proverb and narrative; they are drawn upon, and reinterpreted, for guidance. Therefore, history re-emerges with them in the present and it shapes the present. The 'kinship I', the Maori conceptual identification with their ancestors, enables history to re-emerge and be actualised.[94] These Maori notions of history, conceived of as the days which lie not behind, but encompassing one — 'nga rā o mua' — underpin all of Te Kooti's acts and decisions. Conceptually, they may also explain his early dislike of watches, instruments which dictate notions of time as 'bearing all its sons away'. But every reproduction of the ancestral past is an alteration of it. 'Mua' (past and future), when carved as a god-figure, may be double-headed, Janus-like, looking both ways; he may possess a crooked leg, conveying the uncertainty of the past and future times that he simultaneously represents. He may stand, too, with one foot on the land and one on the sea; and his emblem is the rainbow, for he is the ancient god, Uenuku.[95] Thus Te Kooti too reworked the past, 'the days of Mua', inside a new framework of interpretation, by which he located Maori and their ancestral histories and referentials within a message of collective redemption.

In creating a biography of Te Kooti, I hope to open up a wider awareness of the issues surrounding one of the major figures in New Zealand's 19th-century history. It is not a definitive statement; it is not an act of closure. But I do hope that some of the worst stereotypes will vanish: primarily, Te Kooti the murderer, and the sole emphasis placed on Te Kooti as warrior and 'rebel'. In 1993, on the centenary of his death, some newspaper headlines were still of this nature: 'Te Kooti: the wily warrior'.[96] However, I believe that the historical experiences which engendered Te Kooti's vision — of being colonised, the loss of autonomy, and the pain that such loss brought — are now being recognised, and to some degree addressed.

The Ringatu faith today does not have a large following. In 1926, in the first census to include religion, 3837 people stated that they were Ringatu believers (six percent of the Maori population). Over time the number of its adherents has increased, but its proportional strength has declined: in 1981, 6117 people identified themselves as Ringatu, but they formed just two percent of the Maori population.[97] In the most recent census, 1991, 8052 people declared themselves to be Ringatu, a little over two percent of the Maori population and a mere 0.2 percent of the entire population.[98] The importance of the Ringatu faith does not lie in its numbers. Nor is it a mausoleum for 'Maoritanga', as some Maori (and also some Pakeha) would have it. Its importance lies in the fact that it is the oldest of the surviving Maori religions which understood the scriptural messages in the context of colonialism. Te Kooti emerged as a leader from the shards of the past urging that a new company of travellers — 'te tira hou' — be forged: a people of faith and peace.[99] He cajoled them and he challenged them, his purpose always to keep them alert, adaptive and thinking. He emphasised the importance of flexibility and of tolerance — 'haere ki te ngawari', his most recurrent statement in his later years. And, despite all his own experiences, he consistently urged resolution of dispute through the use of the law to challenge the savage bite of the law. Or, as he put it in song, 'I enter into the law which will be a parent for the orphaned' ('Ka kuhu au ki te ture hei matua mo te pani').[100] It was a vision which his followers — and others — may well argue is finally bearing fruit in the late 1980s and early 1990s.

Te Kooti's overall perception was religious. Many today would deny its validity, particularly the apparent emphasis on a predicted successor, a Davidic Messiah, a saviour for his times. But Te Kooti also sustained a way of thinking, derived from an oral world, whereby the knowledge of the past is brought to bear on the events of the present, so that problems can be confronted. If Te Kooti offered a hope of communal salvation, he also taught that the future of the people lay in their own hands and in their own collective decisions, mediated by the important quality of tolerance. This crucial message, evolved from Exodus, which he took as his own, is Te Kooti's lasting contribution.

THE DIARIES OF TE KOOTI

There are two known surviving diaries of Te Kooti written in his own hand. The first is the notebook he kept on Wharekauri. His earliest dated entry is 21 February 1867; the last entry is 4 November 1868, but this was probably made by a Maori soldier who had found the book. The diary is in a former police notebook and it still contains police entries from 1864. It appears to have been issued to a South Island provincial police-man,[1] Constable Brennan, who wrote his name and number (41) in firm clear letters on the front cover as a statement of ownership. Private John Brennan was dismissed from the guard on Wharekauri on 28 October 1867 (for petty larceny), and it seems probable that the notebook was once his.

The diary contains a variety of entries made by Te Kooti: scriptural texts from the Old and New Testaments, the record of his visionary experiences in 1867, and predictive statements or promises of God, each headed by a word in 'the strange language' ('te reo ke') and probably dated 1 January 1868.[2] It also lists names of men and women who were prisoners on Wharekauri, sums of money earned by various prisoners for work they had done on the island, two notes about the arrival and departure of ships, and what has been interpreted by some to be an entry for the birth of his child, written on 14 March 1868: 'Ko te marama tenei i whanau ai te tamaiti a Hana' ('This is the month in which Hana's child (son) was born'). On the back cover, written probably by Te Kooti, are the words 'Na Te Kooti'.

It is not clear where this diary was first found. Leonard Williams, in an undated note, described two notebooks found after the siege and evacuation of Nga Tapa, at the beginning of January 1869. One of these is clearly the Wharekauri notebook. The other was a book of prayers which had belonged to Renata Tupara, who was executed at Nga Tapa.[3] On 25 January 1869 William Atkinson, who was then at Turanga, copied out portions of what he called 'a few of Te Kooti's lucubrations [meditations]' for his brother Arthur Atkinson. He added that, if Arthur were interested in seeing more, 'I dare say James would let you see them'.[4] This was undoubtedly a reference to James C. Richmond, brother-in-law of the Atkinsons, who later told Arthur that he had obtained the original notebook at Nga Tapa.[5] William Atkinson had also shown the diary to the Reverend William Williams at Turanga on 22 January. This was the notebook 'which was got at or near Ngatapa, giving Kooti's account of his revelations'. Leonard Williams thereupon immediately borrowed it from William Atkinson and copied a portion of it.[6] William Atkinson also made a separate transcript of the entries for February–May 1867, which he headed 'Copy of a portion of a book belonging to Te Kooti found at Te Karetu December 1868', and sent this to his brother.[7] Arthur then sent his translation of these passages to the *Nelson Examiner*, where they were published on 5 May 1869.[8] He subsequently published a corrected translation of the same portions in March 1889, stating that he had made the first translation from a copy of the diary but that he had a 'week or two since . . . obtained sight of the original book, and has revised the translation with it'.[9] Late in August 1888 Richmond had written to the Native Department asking for the small book written by Te Kooti when he was imprisoned on Wharekauri to be returned; it was immediately sent to him.[10] Richmond, like Arthur Atkinson, was living in Nelson at this time and he presumably showed it to Atkinson. But the book then vanished again until it was found in a cupboard in the Police Museum at Trentham in 1979. With it now was a partial translation made by someone who had no idea of its origin, nor of the identity of the writer. The diary and translation were placed on loan in the Alexander Turnbull Library.

However, at some earlier date, a transcript copy, with another translation, had also been made. This transcript contained, in addition, a covering note by Richmond, the original of which can no longer be traced. Richmond was, in effect, Minister of Native Affairs for 1867–69 and was at the siege of Nga Tapa. This covering note, described as 'extract from Memorandum' and dated 27 November 1869, stated that the document was the 'Copy of a book', which 'was found in a whare in Tamihana Ruatapu's Pa which Te Kooti was known to have used'.[11] This memo suggests that the original note-book was found initially either at Whakato or, more likely, at Oweta in Poverty Bay. The two entries for 4 November 1868 in the original diary are in a different hand and seem to be those of a Maori soldier fighting for the government. One (entered upside down) reads:

> Turanui   Noema 4 . . . *1868*
> Okura i noho ai au i te mahi hoia o noa ki roto ki a Tihema.
>
> Tura[nga]nui   November 4 . . . *1868*
> [At] Okura I was occupied with work as a soldier from November [?] into December.

The other entry, written in pencil, lists his wages, commencing at 'Turanga' on 4 November. The rates of pay changed as the month progressed. The last date was 25 November. These two entries, along with the note, suggest that the diary was picked up initially *before* Te Kooti's attack on Poverty Bay on 10–11 November. However, as both entries are composite, running through November, they were probably backdated by the writer. It is possible, though, that the soldier first picked up the diary at Oweta, where Te Kooti went on 14 November to execute Paratene Pototi. If so, it seems that the diary was dropped again during the subsequent fighting at either Te Karetu or Nga Tapa. There are bloodstains on the back cover.

Richmond himself apparently got the notebook at Nga Tapa, but it is not clear how

The front and back covers of Te Kooti's diary.   C12472A, ATL

or from whom. He commented that Te Kooti had written in it 'some good words'.[12] That some of its words were fresh in his mind is evidenced by a quotation he made from it when speaking in the House of Representatives on 18 June 1869.[13] In August 1888, again when speaking (this time to the Legislative Council), he mentioned that, when he had picked up at Poverty Bay Te Kooti's 'memorandum-book' containing the laments and prophecies, he 'at once identified the writing in it' as Te Kooti's, because he had read letters written by him.[14] It would seem that Richmond then made a transcript — and probably the translation which accompanies this version. Richmond's memorandum of November 1869, the transcript and translation were in turn copied by George Davies into a manuscript book, which he lent to S. Percy Smith in 1896. He asked Smith to send it to Arthur Atkinson, and this Smith did.[15] This transcript volume, written in Davies' hand, together with his copy of Richmond's memorandum, are now in the Alexander Turnbull Library. However, the location of Richmond's original transcript is unknown. It does not appear to be among the Richmond papers in the Taranaki Museum, despite a published reference saying that it is.[16]

The second diary is a pocket notebook. The dated entries span 6 March 1869 to March 1870. This little book has been much handled: when it was found it was described as 'very much worn with constant usage and long carrying about his [Te Kooti's] clothes, and more than once repaired by stitching together with fibres of New Zealand Flax'.[17] This notebook is almost certainly the 'prayer-book' taken by Thomas Porter from Te Kooti's camp at Te Haupapa (Te Houpapa) on 30 March 1871.[18] There is a later reference to a prayer-book and diary which came into the hands of Gilbert Mair, when he was pursuing Te Kooti in the Urewera. This book may be the same notebook. It was described (in 1889) as containing many scriptural quotations, omens and interpreted dreams, as well as short jottings of incidents; that would be an appropriate description of the pocket notebook. But at that time, the whereabouts of the book, which had fallen 'into the hands of Captain Mair', was unknown.[19]

In 1871 the surviving notebook was given to William Colenso, the former Anglican missionary who was living in Napier. In December he published *Fiat Justitia* (Let There

Be Justice) as an urgent attempt to stop the trial of Kereopa Te Rau for the killing of the missionary Carl Volkner in 1865, and to bring the wars to an end. He also wrote to McLean, saying that he was appalled at the government's condoning of acts which he considered to be no better than murder and charging McLean with failure to honour an earlier promise to call off 'those mercenary bloodhounds'.[20] In a second letter, he urged McLean to read what he had written about 'our Maori Prisoner [Kereopa], & *why* he (*like others*) should be pardoned'.[21] This inserted statement was a reference to Te Kooti. As an appendix to his book Colenso published his translation of six of the prayers (inoi) from Te Kooti's notebook, to show that they 'are truly beautiful good and pious'.[22] He mistakenly called them Hauhau prayers. The notebook subsequently came into the possession of Henry Hill of Napier, who knew Colenso well. It was acquired by the Hawke's Bay Museum in 1958, along with other material from Henry Hill's collection. There is a covering note with it, written by Colenso.

The notebook has been used upside down: on its back cover the word 'NOTES' is embossed. It contains 50 inoi, some of which are duplicates. Colenso translated inoi [16], [27], [12], [30], [31] and [19], in that order. Inoi [16] is the most famous, because it expressed the sadness of the prisoners on Wharekauri:

Inoi
E te Atua, ki te hoki atu o matou mahara i runga i te whenua e noho whakarau nei matou, a ka repeneta, ka inoi atu ki a koe me te whaki atu ano i a matou hara ki tou aroaro, tena ra, e Ihowa, murua te hara o tou iwi i hara nei ki a koe. Kaua ra e whaka-ngaro atu i a matou, e te Atua. Koia matou e whakakororia nei i to ingoa tapu.

Amine

Prayer
O God, if our hearts arise from the land in which we now dwell as slaves, and repent and pray to Thee and confess our sins in Thy presence, then, O Jehovah, do Thou blot out the sins of Thy own people, who have sinned against Thee. Do not Thou, O God, cause us to be wholly destroyed. Wherefore it is we glorify Thy Holy Name.

Amen.[23]

The notebook also contains waiata, some jottings, a diagram of a predictive dream and 'kupu whakaari' (prophetic sayings). The earliest dated prediction is 6 March 1869, at Waioeka. But the book also contains, undated, the first kupu from Wharekauri, headed by the same three words in 'te reo ke' which Te Kooti used in the Wharekauri notebook, 'Aneko'; 'Iperene'; 'Utiera'.[24] The texts of the first two parts here, 'Aneko' and 'Ipereni', are essentially the same as those in the earlier notebook (with minor variations), but the text of 'Utiera' is not included here. The reference is simply to the uttering ('ka whiua') and then the confirmation ('ka mau') of that word on two success-ive days of a month, the 27th and 28th. The notebook contains several other entries which are glosses to words written in 'te reo ke'.

In a newspaper article published in April 1871, the notebook found at Te Haupapa was described in some detail.[25] The description lends support to the supposition that the Hawke's Bay notebook was the one found there, but it also raises doubts. The

A predictive dream, recorded in Te Kooti's second diary. It appears to show the stars, four choices or directions, and the rainbow. It reads:

		Te moe mo nga whetu
Kino	Hohepa	
Ko Pere		Na Rawiri i huihui enei whika
	Wi I	
Atua	Kohuru	Te hae o nga tuakana
Eripene		

		The dream concerning the stars
Evil	Joseph	
Rainbow		David assembled these symbols
	Wi I	
God	Killing	
	by treachery	The jealousy of the brothers
Eripene		(siblings)

The figure Wi I (or WI) was stitched on Te Kooti's flag captured at Te Porere in October 1869. It represented the Wairua Tapu (Holy Spirit), which was the original name of the faith. Eripene is a word in 'te reo ke', the strange language.   HBM

printed English translations of selected passages appear to be selections from the notebook; however, there are also some irreconcilable differences, which may be due to careless transcription. Three examples follow:

1. '*Tereina*': the prophetic word of God to Adam. In the published account *Tereina* is described as a Hebrew phrase, given to Te Kooti by inspiration from God. The interpretation given is: 'Be thou created out of my shadow.' In the notebook the text reads: 'Tereina, Ko te whakahanga o tona wairua' ('Tereina, The creation of his spirit').

2. '*Te Kipi*': the prophetic word to Abraham. The published account again states it to be a Hebrew word, and the interpretation given is: 'Go to Judea'. In the notebook the prophetic word to Abraham is 'Tiripe'. The text reads: 'Ko te tononga a te Atua i a Aperahama ki ura' ('God's calling of Abraham to Ura', Judea). The word to Abraham, 'Tiripe', is also transcribed in a list of prophetic words and their associated scriptural references, which was compiled by Petera Te Rangihiroa and transcribed by Robert Biddle into his collected documents of the faith.[26]

3. '*Te Kaumu*': the prophetic word to Christ. The published account again states it to be a Hebrew word, and the interpretation given is: 'Thou shalt be a king for ever'. In the notebook the prophetic word to Christ is the fifth in a series of six prophetic words listed (to Adam, to Abraham, to Moses, to David, to Christ and to Te Kooti). The word to Christ in the notebook is 'Epirinatai'. There appears to be no equivalent of 'Te Kaumu'. The text in the notebook reads: 'Ko te whakapumautanga Kingi' ('The establishment [of the] King'). 'Epirinatai' is also given as the word to Christ in Petera's list of the prophetic sayings.

The strange words were all said to be Hebrew, and Te Kooti's followers often say that Te Kooti could speak Hebrew by inspiration. The account of 1871 also reported this claim. The comparisons show the resemblances, which certainly suggest that the phrases were taken from the Hawke's Bay notebook. But the irreconcilable differences also raise the question of whether another, similar, notebook had been recovered.

The Hawke's Bay notebook contains the kupu whakaari uttered at Waioeka on 6 March 1869, which is one of Te Kooti's better-known predictions. The text is cited in Chapter 6. Te Kooti would reiterate it after the wars, and then, in 1886, indicate that it had been fulfilled. This text and its subsequent elaborations are discussed in their appropriate narrative contexts.

The notebook demonstrates a restatement and a reworking of the early kupu whakaari by Te Kooti. These are the basic texts of Te Kooti's developing 'theology of liberation'. Thus both surviving diaries contain the first bases of what would be extensively developed and recorded by Te Kooti's secretaries — the tradition of the kupu whakaari.

The second diary also records fragments of the war in 1869–70 — the places and people to whom Te Kooti looked for support, and also those whom he considered he could not entirely trust. One of the latter was the Tuhoe chief Rakuraku, who joined him, but whom he called here 'te Ngarara' ('the Monster'). Another was the unhappy Tuwharetoa leader Horonuku Te Heuheu, who, as Te Kooti wrote here, would be successfully caught ('ka mau') at Moerangi in June 1869.

The last dated entry is March 1870.[27] This, too, is a kupu whakaari, from the inland forests of Waioeka. The area, Te Tahora, was about a mile from Maraetahi pa where Te Kooti took shelter, and most of his people were staying at Te Tahora:

	Waioeka
Panui	
	Tetahora
tenei kupu	
	Maehe [?]1 –1870

1 Rapua a Ihowa, e te hunga mataki

2 Tiakina tou Arero.
 Ko wai te tangata e hiahia ana ki te ora

	Waioeka
Announcement	
	Te Tahora
this saying	
	March [?]1 –1870

1 Seek Jehovah, you watching crowd

2 Guard your tongue.
 Who is the person who desires life

There was one further notebook written in Te Kooti's hand which survived the wars. This was in the possession of the tohunga Eria Raukura in 1914 and was said to have come to him at Te Kooti's death in 1893. It contained the texts for 12 services, the original number that Te Kooti composed, each of which possessed ten portions. The text for the first service, which was composed on Wharekauri, was:

I Chronicles 16:28, 30.
Job 12:10–11.
Psalms 3:8
Jeremiah 31:16–17
Zephaniah 2:3
Proverbs 1:7
Proverbs 24:16–17.[28]

This service, 'Panui 1', with some slight extensions, is retained by the Ringatu today.[29] Eria showed the notebook to James Cowan at about the same time as he lent it to Porter in 1914,[30] and it was seen by a number of Europeans at this time. Porter published portions of scriptural texts from it in his serialised account of Te Kooti.[31] He also stated that the tapu had been lifted from the book, and that he would publish the complete text as an appendix. He made this statement in two of the three published versions of his history. It is significant that the remark is not included in the earliest published version. It would seem, therefore, to have been deliberately removed but then slipped through in the other two versions.[32] Certainly, the full text was not published. However, it is understood that the texts of the services were transcribed by Te Kooti's secretaries from this manuscript. The original also survived and was known about in the Gisborne district; it probably still exists. It awaits another time, and other writers.

SONGS FOR TE KOOTI

Te Kooti's life has captured the imagination of both Maori and Pakeha writers. This appendix includes some poems written for — or about — him; Appendix C summarises other imaginative evocations of him.

The first poem quoted was written by an Otago settler, Alan Clyde, and published in 1872.[1] It presents an ironic South Island perspective on the boasting of the northern military men and their claims to 'victory' in each and every encounter with Te Kooti. The poem challenges their assumption of inevitable victory over native forces, which 114 years later James Belich exploded through his cogent analysis of the Eurocentrism which had pervaded all accounts of the military history.[2]

TE KOOTI.
1870.

ONE day, in 'Northern files,' I read,
'Te Kooti's knocked upon the head,
It's pretty certain now he's dead.'

A week thereafter I peruse,
'Te Kooti his old way pursues,
Has killed and eaten Major Blues.'

Next day a telegram there was,
'We've captured all Te Kooti's squaws,
We've hanged himself and burnt his pahs!'

Great joyfulness such welcome news
Occasioned to the cockatoos,
Te Kooti now had got his dues.

A month or so, and then I hear,
'Te Kooti's fiends once more appear,
And all the land is full of fear.'

But then more cheering came the mail,
'This great event with joy we hail,
Te Kooti yesterday turned tail;

But not before he lost his nose,
Shot off just at the battle's close,
At a thousand yards, by Private Rose!

Reported too that Captain Pye
Has a bullet in his eye!
While Tompkins smote him on the thigh.'

Then, overjoyed, once more I read,
'Te Kooti certainly is dead,
They've brought to camp the traitor's head.'

This paragraph went on to say,
'The Government intend to pay
One thousand pounds reward to-day!'

Such tidings who on earth could doubt,
Te Kooti's pipe at last put out!
I called my friends and made them shout!

But then, a week or so at most,
Appeared Te Kooti or his ghost,
And with the nose which he had lost!

Fresh havoc made he 'mong the whites,
He had a taste for well-fed wights,
Who suffered badly from his bites!

'Thus runs the tale from day to day,'
Thus doth he eat whom he doth slay,
Yet still gets licked in every fray!

By post and press he loses right
And left his legs and arms in fight;
He must now be a (h)armless sight!

And frequent came the news by wire,
'Te Kooti riddled by our fire,
Cut off and ready to expire.'

While that tremendous gun, 'Our Own,'
Hast oft the rebel host o'erthrown,
And Kooti's self to atoms blown.

Strange fact! already he has lost
More lives than any cat can boast,
More legs than walk Tasmania's coast.

But still, for all this treatment rude,
His health and appetite are good,
Pakeha's his particular food,

When fail his basket and his store
Another raid must furnish more,
And he gets killed just as before.

The expedition of 1889 to block Te Kooti's return to Poverty Bay produced a number of poems written expressly for the local newspapers. This anonymous balladeer, writing in April 1889, mocked the Premier, Harry Atkinson:

Each warrior rode forth at the dawn of the day,
Bestriding his war-horse so proudly and gay,
His broadsword well-sharpened Te Kooti to slay —
    Hurrah for the warriors of Poverty Bay!

Brave General Redbeard*, his voice full of fate,
Addressed them in style, like Napoleon the Great;
He told them of honour and glory's bright ray —
    Hurrah for the warriors of Poverty Bay!

The bush next they entered in Indian array;
Their carbines and rifles a gorgeous display,
The swords of the Majors clink-clanking so gay —
    Hurrah for the warriors of Poverty Bay!

By the flare of the camp-fires what battles they fought —
What Maoris they slaughtered, as true heroes ought!
What Hauhau could ever such soldiers dismay? —
    Hurrah for the warriors of Poverty Bay!

They boldly marched onward the right to uphold,
And captured Te Kooti, that rebel of old;
'He sat on a mat in the heat of the day' —
    Hurrah for the warriors of Poverty Bay!

'He calmly ate plums while the war-chargers neighed;
'But the hearts of our heroes were nowhat dismayed,
'For his limbs were now feeble, his beard it was grey' —
    Hurrah for the warriors of Poverty Bay!

The campaign is over, the war's at an end;
And when they return who went forth to defend
Let's cheer them and fete them in a right royal way —
    Hurrah for the warriors of Poverty Bay!

        *Sir H. Atkinson.[3]

Arthur Desmond composed the following ballad for the Sydney *Bulletin*. It was published on 23 March 1889,[4] shortly after Te Kooti's arrest at Waiotahe. The heading described him as a 'kind of Robin Hood — an outlaw, who, for years, fought the invaders of his country, and eluded their cleverest generals by his knowledge of the bush.' Turning the Europeans into the 'others', the song purports to be a Maori voice. Desmond stated that, as the translator, he had 'done his best to turn the savage force and poetic fervour of a wild Maori chant into the rythmic [*sic*] swing of ordinary English verse.' He also claimed to have kept the meaning of the original but had been compelled to take 'some liberties with construction and metaphor'! It was Desmond's first published poem, the beginning of a series of revolutionary ballads for which he would become well known.

Te Kooti.

Exult for Te Kooti! Te Kooti the bold;
So fierce in the onset, so dauntless of old,
Whose might was resistless when battle-waves rolled,
    Exult for Te Kooti, yo-hoo!

The Pakehas come with their rum and their gold,
And soon the broad lands of our fathers were sold,
But the voice of Te Kooti said: 'HOLD THE LAND! HOLD!!'
    Exult for Te Kooti, yo-hoo!

They falsely accused him — no trial had he,
They carried him off to an isle in the sea;
But his prison was broken, once more he was free —
    Exult for Te Kooti, yo-hoo!

They tried to enslave us, to trample us down
Like the millions that serve them in field and in town;
But a sapling that bended is sure to rebound —
    Exult for Te Kooti, yo-hoo!

He plundered their rum-stores, he ate up their priests,
He robbed the rich squatters to furnish his feasts,
What fare half so fine as their clover-fed beasts?
    Exult for Te Kooti, yo-hoo!

In the wild midnight foray whose footsteps trod lighter?
In the flash of the rifle whose eyeballs gleamed brighter?
What man to our hero could match as a fighter!
    Exult for Te Kooti, yo-hoo!

They say it was murder; but what then is war —
When they slaughtered our loved ones in the flames of the pah?
O darker their deeds and more merciless far!
    Exult for Te Kooti, yo-hoo!

They boast that they'll slay him — they'll shoot him at sight,
But the power that nerves him's a power of might,
At a glance from his eye they shall tremble with fright,
    Exult for Te Kooti, yo-hoo!

When the darkness was densest he wandered away,
To rejoice in the charge of the wild battle-fray;
Now, his limbs they are feeble; his beard it is grey —
    Exult for Te Kooti, yo-hoo!

The Eternal's our father, the land is our mother,
The forest and mountains our sister and brother,
Who'd part with his birthright for gold to another?
   Exult for Te Kooti, yo-hoo!

We won't sell the land, it's the gift of the Lord,
Except it be bought with the blood drinking sword,
But ALL men are welcome to share in its hoard —
   Exult for Te Kooti, yo-hoo!

Yet, amid all thy gladness forget not the brave
Who in glades of the forest, have found a lone grave —
Whose choice it was Death than the life of a slave —
   Exult for Te Kooti, yo-hoo!

Exult for Te Kooti, Te Kooti the bold,
So sage in the council, so famous of old;
Whose war-cry's our motto — 'tis 'HOLD THE LAND! HOLD!'
   Exult for Te Kooti, yo-hoo!

Desmond's ballad had been written in riposte to 'The Settlers' Song', published in the *Poverty Bay Herald* at the height of the local hysteria at the prospect of Te Kooti's return to Gisborne:

Now's the day and now's the hour,
See the front of carnage lower,
See approach Te Kooti's power,
   As to victory!

Should the vilest murderer's hand,
Backed by that fanatic band,
Flaunt its power throughout the land,
   Britons are not free.

From the wrongs we have endured,
From such wounds as can't be cured,
We must be henceforth assured
   Safely in peace to be.

Shall we see our hearths and homes
Troubled as wide oceans' foams,
While the demon freely roams
   This fair country free?

Shall we coolly leave our wives
And our trusting children's lives,
While this dark-souled fiend contrives,
   To their destiny?

By the butchered babes of yore,
By the women bathed in gore,
Black Te Kooti must be evermore
   Backward hunted be.[5]

Hare Hongi (Henry M. Stowell), the part-Maori recorder of oral histories, composed a poem protesting at the abuse of liberty when Te Kooti was arrested in February 1889. He sent it to the *Evening Post*, which had run a series of editorials opposing the government's decisions and actions. Hare Hongi deliberately identified himself as a representative of 'both races', and he entitled the narrative of explanation which preceded his poem, 'JUSTICE, LIBERTY, FRATERNITY'. He asked why an 'aged Maori chief and warrior', who had been granted an 'unconditional pardon', should be prevented from revisiting his home by armed forces despatched 'with all the pomp and glorious circumstance of war'.

I sing of freedom's proud estate, of honour's cherished cause,
Of statesmen who by virtue frame a nation's righteous laws,
Of tyrants who usurp the right, and fell confusion raise,
Yet dare the scorn their acts awake in more enlightened days.

Dear liberty, thy glorious wreath is held aloft in vain
To guard the right, a shield to truth, and justice to maintain,
When, in their proud pre-eminence and temporary power,
Our legislators' ruthless hands despoil thy sacred bower.

And chivalry, blest shrine renowned, thy pure unsullied rights
Are in vile keeping when bestowed on 19th century knights.
Not now the heroic homage paid, pronouncing thee divine;
Nor earth the generous deeds proclaim, that once were truly thine.

Some hapless victim, now perchance, may quote thee with just pride
Anticipation, seek relief, a former age supplied:
But futile the appealing gaze that now uplifts to thee,
For them not stately honours march to notes of chivalry.

Go seek the graves of heroes where fame now slumbering lies,
And o'er their dust this message bear their virtues to despise;
Behold a hoar-head patriarch is hunted forth alone,
While Honour, Truth, and Justice sits unheeded on her throne.

Or, haply still, some monument might be upraised to tell
To all the world the direful spot where Truth and Freedom fell,
'Mid archives of barbarian Rome some meet inscription find,
Which, sad to think, a Christian age to dungeons deep confined.

Then shout along with lusty sound that triumphs in its power;
Come, slaves, your king invites you forth — it is his bridal hour;
And swiftly to the summons, as surging masses roll,
The foremost mark the column's base and gilded lettered scroll.

EPITAPH:

Here lies the form of Liberty, whom noble hearts have prized;
But foe to Persecution, by Autocrats despised,
Her votaries by Mammon wooed, did Freedom's gifts assign;
And justice was by Law entombed, A.D., eighteen eighty-nine.[6]

The following waiata was composed by Arona Te Hana. An Anglican cleric, Arona had objected to Te Kooti's visit to the upper Whanganui in July 1890. This song challenged the Whanganui leaders who came under Te Kooti's influence at this time, especially Te Riaki of Karioi and the chief Teki Kanara of Koriniti. Nevertheless, Arona joined with others to invite Te Kooti to return in 1893, and was reconciled with him at that time.

> Ka ura mai te rā ka kohi au e mahara,
> E Wiki mā ē, tirohia mai au.
> Ka mahara i taurite, tēnei ka raruraru,
> Te ngaru whakapuke e tere Raukawa.
> Ko te rite i taku kiri, ka ura mai te rā,
> Ka riro kau taonga i' Te Rīaki mā.
> Nō tawhiti a Te Kooti, nō Ngāti Kahungunu.
> Whakarongo mai e Teki i Pēpara,
> Te whare karakia o te iwi i te pō;
> I mahue mātou i te tira i a Titi.
> Nei whai kupu iho, e au ana tāku moe
> Ki tāku makau tuku iho.

> With the sun's glow I collect my thoughts,
> O Wiki, and the rest of you, look at me now.
> I thought all was well, but trouble stirs,
> Like the churning waves that swell across the Straits,
> My skin is like the blazing sun
> To see my followers stray with Te Riaki and his group.
> And Te Kooti who comes from afar because of Ngati Kahungunu.
> Listen well Teki, at Pepara,
> The church house of the people who have passed into the darkness,
> We have been abandoned by Titi and his companions.
> If the word had been given I would have slept on peacefully,
> Dreaming of my cherished one.[7]

In 1893, the *New Zealand Graphic* published a lengthy, well-informed obituary for Te Kooti. It began with a short but astute poem, whose author remains anonymous:

> He was the mildest-mannered man
> That ever scuttled ship or cut a throat;
> With such true breeding of a gentleman
> You never could divine his real thought.[8]

The remaining poems are of more recent composition. They reflect a renewed interest in the 19th century and the colonial experience. If the earlier poems belong to their times and evoke the truths as they were then perceived, the later works show how truth changes. The first two poems are part of a series written by Kendrick Smithyman on the Maori prophets. The first derives from Te Kooti's landing at Whareongaonga in 1868 and a half-buried textual note in J. A. Mackay's *Historic Poverty Bay*,[9] which

Smithyman's sharp magpie-eye observed. It is an account of an elderly Maori woman's memory of the landing. Tihei Algic, Te Kooti's great-granddaughter, herself talked of the part of the sea at Whareongaonga where the water is always disturbed, and where the waves rise without warning. It has a reputation for unexpected drownings.[10] The reefs at that spot are tapu — because of what Te Kooti saw in the water, it is said. He named the reefs the 'Tablets of the New Law' and said that when he returned to Whareongaonga in triumph he would touch these rocks with Aaron's rod, and the new revelation would spring from the earth.

PROPHET

He wasn't one of theirs although possibly
    a connection.
They heard about him, they read about him.
When he landed he called the hill ahead Mount Moriah,
reefs in the bay were Tablets of the New Law.
He was the Maori Moses.

God would, as already, guide them.
Later, when necks of the Egyptians were humbled,
he would return to the landing place
touching the reefs with Aaron's rod,
not for blood then in *vessels of* wood, and in *vessels of*
    stone
but filling that covenant to give them their land of Canaan
the land of their pilgrimage
wherein they were strangers

and his new revelation would spring from the earth
as sprang from Aaron's rod bud, blossom, and yield of almonds.

    An elderly woman remembered him at Whareongaonga
coming ashore from *Rifleman*, naming, proclaiming.
'He wore a perfect masher suit and patent leather boots.'

Smithyman's second poem refers to the occasion when Te Kooti and Gilbert Mair met, for only the second time in their lives, in January 1884. This poem is published in Smithyman's collection *Auto/Biographies*,[11] and was based on James Cowan's account of the episode, written in 1938.[12]

MEETING AT MATATA

After the amnesty it happened:
    Gilbert Mair had business at Matata.
Te Kooti rode in — a couple of wives,
thirty men in his bodyguard — to visit
at the village with the local faithful,
to do some healing if needed. All those years,
only once they'd met up face to face.

Captain Mair was praised for his shooting.
All those years! but never managed
to hit Te Kooti. People still think it strange.
Te Kooti heard Mair was at the Horseshoe Inn.

He marched his men across with borrowed weapons,
one or two rifles, some shotguns.
He paraded them. Mair was invited out
to inspect the guard of honour.
Such as had arms presented.

Te Kooti came to Mair. He hung a fine cloak
on him: '. . . my token of regard for you.
Wear this in memory of me. If it's not
big enough, let me clothe you with my love.'
He ordered his force Teihana! Pai te rewhi!,
quickmarched them back to their quarters.

    Make love, not war. Make peace, make friends.
These dim fond bromides, how they cling together
like album leaves, commonplace, a bit foxed,
yet what a sweet tune you can finger from them
on some old honey-brown Blüthner upright
      in a shadowy bar parlour.

Later that day a message from the kainga:
    Would the Captain be good enough to send over
a bottle of rum? Perhaps two?

The following poem was written by C. K. Stead for the sesquicentenary of New Zealand in 1990. It too relates to Te Kooti's journey of 1884. It is derived from the diary of an Athenree farmer's wife, Adela Stewart.[13]

January 24, 1884   The Visit

Up early, churning, I hope to sell my butter
tenpence per pound to campers on Waihi Beach.
A crowd, all Maori, gathers at our gate.
I'm told it is Te Kooti — a sort of royal tour.

I signal welcome and he steps from his buggy
flanked by armed protectors. My son Mervyn's
childish nightmares were all of this rebel prophet.
On the verandah Mervyn hongis with his dream.

My visitor asks for beer. All I can offer
is tea — a billyful — and scones for his party.
The rest I say can pick flowers from my garden.
They do, decorating their hair and horses.

The hard old killer, pardoned but never safe,
sits in my drawing room holding a china cup.
My house, he tells me, is ka pai — and he smiles
at something in his head I cannot guess at.

This night I have dreamed of the children of Israel.
Woken, I listen to the river rushing over rocks
under pines in the gorge. Somewhere above the rapids
inhuman voices are raised in lamentation.

Haare Williams, brought up at Ohiwa and Te Karaka within the Ringatu communities, published in 1980 a collection of poems entitled *Karanga*. Included was one for Te Kooti, in which Williams drew on the waiata 'Pinepine Te Kura', Te Kooti's song of protest about the misuse of the law to prevent him from returning home.

Te Kooti

The light cast
A shadow
On the good word
'Tidings of great joy'

Return to Te Rongopai
Turanganui
Put down the weapons
Of the Pakeha

The mouth
Twisted the law
Showing how men
Stand apart
From the Queen's law
And the Covenant
Of David

From Chathams
The mist did not
Lift
I yearned to return
But your banquet
Was bullets

The blood
The shame
Cannot be salved
In wine

Aue!
My people
Listen to the good word
Te Rongopai[14]

The younger Maori writer Apirana Taylor published 'Te Kooti' in 1979. This short poem has the stark quality of loss:

> Once the hāngi grew
> like melon pregnant bellies
> full of black and white flesh.
>
> Now the stones are cold.
> Te Kooti is dead
> under incubus earth.
>
> We are ashes of his fire
> dead a hundred years.
>
> Safe in our houses
> we have stripped him
> to a feather in the wind
> as distant as a morepork
> that calls in the night.[15]

This selection concludes with W. H. Oliver's new poem, previously unpublished. Thus it may be seen that the songs for Te Kooti continue:

A game of cards

> The prophet played a good hand at cards
> perhaps a skill they did not mean him to learn
> at Waerenga-a-hika between scripture lessons.
> Maybe he used to play with a greasy pack
> as the scow bent her slow way to Auckland.
> Maybe they occupied the long damp watches
> through nights in the bush on the run
> a break from the fighting and the preaching.
> Spades were for everyday use.
> Hearts were fine but you couldn't trust them.
> Diamonds were the suit he liked to bid.
> Clubs were trumps in the last hand and he lost.

FACTION, FICTION AND IMAGES

No biography would be complete without mention of some of the images which have been forged around Te Kooti, complementing the poems in Appendix B. Te Kooti has been portrayed in narrative fiction, in stage and voice drama, in film and in painted 'icons'. He has captured the imagination of many different New Zealanders, although he himself has remained largely elusive. The earliest stories and painted portraits appeared well before his death. This appendix gives a sampling of the portrayals of this man of many parts.

Of the paintings or drawings, apart from those attempted in his lifetime and reproduced elsewhere in this account, there are some of interest. The earliest of all images is an engraving by Thomas S. Cousins, based on an 1869 sketch by 'Captain Spiller'. Captain Harvey Spiller took up the command of the Wairoa district in January 1869 and went on Herrick's abortive expedition to Waikaremoana in June. His original drawing has not been located. However, he probably never saw Te Kooti and certainly not on that expedition. The engraving was quickly published: in the Nelson *Illustrated Examiner* for September 1869, and in the Christchurch *Illustrated Press* the following month.[1] The image and text are at variance, like so much that surrounds Te Kooti: the text (the same in both journals) calls him a '*parvenu*' and one whose power was circumscribed, but the engraving endows him with an heroic stature. This image would soon be redrawn, and not to Te Kooti's disadvantage. A version was reproduced as 'un guerrier de la Nouvelle Zélande' in the Paris journal *L'Univers Illustré* in 1872,[2] and republished in the *Church Missionary Gleaner* for June 1890, where it was labelled 'Te Kooti, a Maori chief of New Zealand'. In this redrawn engraving, an axe (replacing the earlier mere) is held inverted against Te Kooti's body, and a tree trunk replaces the glaring tekoteko (carved figure) on the gable of the raupo house on the right. The portrait was extensively modified too. The angle of Te Kooti's head is less challenging and his right leg, instead of being poised and bent, ready for action, is placed beside his other leg, his feet slightly angled. Other people have been introduced seated on the ground, and the weapons lying at his feet have vanished. Instead, the people sit near him, and one looks up towards him questioningly. The text in the *Missionary Gleaner* commented upon the change which had taken place among Te Kooti's followers of 'late years', as the 'cause of temperance' had increased (replacing 'licentiousness'), and as some 'have been won over to Christianity'.[3] Te Kooti's reformed image accorded better with this message.

Thomas Ryan's portrait of Te Kooti as an old man must have been painted shortly after Ryan's visit to Te Whaiti in 1891, the year it is dated. It is the best-known image of Te Kooti; his Maori clothing, the emphasis on his extreme old age, and the very full white beard are contradicted by most contemporary descriptions and by Henry Hill's sketch of 1892 (p.189). Hill added that Te Kooti's beard was 'thick', 'grey' and 'straggling'. The portrait may be considered imaginary but Ryan's painting has influenced other artists. For instance, Alan Taylor's recent oil painting (Plate 11b) evokes Te Kooti's escape from Wharekauri in 1868, and it portrays him as a man of two worlds, jauntily wearing a purloined guard's cap (from the 48th regiment, which was not sent to New Zealand); it is manifestly derived from Ryan's portrait of the old, full-bearded, white-haired man, which he was not — neither in 1868, nor even in 1891.

Another 19th-century oil painting portrays Te Kooti in the King Country. He wears a brown cloak, the second figure from the right here. He and the men with him are armed; however, his gun appears to be uncocked, while the open landscape behind them, together with their relatively relaxed demeanour as they stroll, suggests that the image was set in the time of Te Kooti's sanctuary there after 1872. The artist and date of the painting are not known, and therefore it is uncertain whether the painting derived from an actual encounter on a pathway. Nor are the painter's skills sufficient to enable us to read the image to find the man. J. Kerry-Nicholls's awkward sketch of Te Kooti, made from life in 1883 and in which Te Kooti is portrayed with a wide moustache and a thin pointed beard, similarly fails to evoke any of the personal qualities which had impressed the artist.[4] A better sketch (p.552), said to be of Te Kooti, never previously reproduced, may be drawn from memory. But the artist, whereabouts and provenance of the original are unknown.

It was not only Europeans who attempted to depict Te Kooti. The painted image on the lintel of the meeting-house Tuwhare, built about 1890, can be established as being his portrait because of its similarity with Hill's 1892 sketch (pp.438, 189). There is also a possible portrait of Te Kooti in the meeting-house Tutamure, built at Omarumutu in 1901. Roger Neich has written extensively about this house. The paintings narrate the history of the people, Ngati Rua of Whakatohea,[5] and Neich has been properly cautious about identifying the many individual portraits painted at the base of the rafter beams inside the house, because the Ngati Rua guardians are themselves no longer sure. Most are thought to be of the people who built the house. However, one is said, by some, to be of Te Kooti. It is possible: an unusual aspect of this image is the suggestion that he is wearing around his neck the little flax bag in which, in story, Te Kooti carried the diamond when he came to Opotiki in 1889. But there is no certainty. In more recent times, the carver Takerangi Smith completed a representation of Te Kooti for the meeting-house opened as part of Te Tari Maori at Victoria University, Wellington. The two upraised hands at the base of the carving, the paepae tapu, represent the change in beliefs from the old to the new teachings (te whakapono tawhito, te whakapono hou), and the spreading of the gospel and peace across the land.

No known photographs of Te Kooti exist. He refused always to allow his image to be

'Te Kooti, chief of the insurgent Maories',
Illustrated Press, Christchurch, 27 October 1869.

taken in this way (see Chapter 11). Various photographs have been mentioned at various times and all have proved to be false trails. Elsdon Best described elderly women of Tuhoe weeping copiously over the (false) image of Te Kooti reproduced by Thomas Gudgeon in 1879.[6] Best's story indicates both the frailties of human memory (for the picture is of a man possessing a full facial moko) and the hope that a portrait had been found. I have been told that a photograph of Te Kooti sitting with a group of people, taken without his knowledge, was returned to the earth with a Ngati Awa elder in 1969. Valued treasures are perceived as remaining active in the Maori world, and it can be decided that they should remain with their guardians, even at death, lest that object turn against the next generation. Such was understood to be the danger with this illicit photograph.

Even before his death, Te Kooti became the subject of narrative fiction written as history. Three examples appeal, and will suffice. One is the story, 'Kiore. A Tale of Ngatapa', written by Grace Whitelaw and published in the Christmas 1891 issue of the *New Zealand Graphic and Ladies Journal*.[7] It was well researched, and was accompanied by large images of Ropata and Renata Kawepo, derived from photographs of the war period. It also included Ryan's portrait of Te Kooti. The story is of two young lovers who were taken prisoner and brought to Nga Tapa, where they meet Te Kooti. He is described as being about 33 years old, without a facial moko, and wearing a mixture of Maori and European clothing, including huia feathers and top-boots. He is called a

Oil painting of Te Kooti by Thomas Ryan, 1891. This painting was included in a well-informed obituary of Te Kooti published in the *New Zealand Graphic* in April 1893. Interestingly, the writer (possibly Gilbert Mair) went on to state that Te Kooti's bent figure, his straggling, spare white beard and slouch-hat were familiar to many colonists whose business brought them into contact with him. The image may not be totally misconceived.

HBM

'mighty Sachem', a term for a North American fighting chief probably here borrowed from the tales of Fenimore Cooper, and he takes delight in using 'scriptural phraseology'. He welcomes Nikora Te Whakaunua, the whakarau who — in the narrative — captured the couple, as '"the beloved of Jehovah," "the thrice blessed of the Almighty"'. Te Kooti also jokes with his young prisoners, saying, '"Is the love of the pakehas so great that they also hasten to me?"' As the story develops so the surroundings become ever more reminiscent of the world of Victorian ghost tales: there is a row of 'baked human heads', 'a box of sacred bones', a lizard drops from the roof and tallowdip candles sputter out in the 'sacred whare', where the hero is intended to die at the hands of the 'hideous' and 'deformed' tohunga, Kiore (Rat). Te Kooti himself is portrayed as relaxed and as having 'by no means a repulsive appearance'. It is he who postpones the young couple's death sentence, first suggested by Nikora, as inappropriate, although it is also he who subsequently orders their deaths. Te Kooti states that Jehovah has cursed them 'to me, his servant, and has commanded me to slay you. You have been cursed by the Almighty, so you must die.' But this divine command, according to the narrative, has derived from Kiore, who communed with God and claimed second sight. Kiore is also outwitted by the lovers, who make their escape in disguise from Nga Tapa by turning the tohunga's skill at hypnotism against him. Te Kooti's image for this prize-winning Christmas story of 1891 is not of a crazed leader, nor even of a particularly ruthless one.

'Te Kooti in the King Country', oil on canvas, date and artist unknown. Te Kooti is the second figure from the right, dressed in a brown cloak and carrying an uncocked rifle. This painting probably derives from the late 1870s or early 1880s. It was acquired (in 1919) from the collector Alexander Thomson by the Otago Early Settlers Museum. Reproduced on the cover of a volume of *New Zealand's Heritage* in 1972 (no. 36), Te Kooti's cloak was recoloured red. This was a manipulation of the image to make a statement about mana. The painting is now damaged.   GM

Historical fiction in quite a different guise is that which purports to be a Maori voice, but is written by Pakeha. 'Kowhai Ngutu Kaka' (Flowering Kaka Beak) is presented as a Maori historian, and he comments, sensibly enough, 'You have written your side of the question many times, I have now written ours once.'[8] Ngutu Kaka gives a brief account of fighting alongside Te Kooti at Taupo in September and October 1869. He purports to have been there when Henare Tomoana arrived at Tauranga-o-Taupo: '"Oh," said Te Kooti, "Henare Tomoana is it? Ugh! a fat Leicester wether. Ngati Kahungunu are the dust under my feet."' The account is actually Thomas McDonnell's[9] and it remains in the vein of the *Boys' Own Paper*, although the heroes are in part reversed. McDonnell, while satirising, gives Ngutu Kaka an independent voice as a later convert to Te Whiti's teachings: 'we now await patiently the day when it shall please the god of Te Whiti and Tohu to cause the removal of all the pakehas, and the lands we have been plundered of will be returned to us, but without a renewal of bloodshed. How this is to be done none of us know, but we feel that it is sure and certain to come at last, for have not Te Whiti and Tohu said so?'[10] Ngutu Kaka is a narrative device, one already used by F. E. Maning to discuss the northern war; it allowed a limited presentation of Maori views by Pakeha authors, who could be simultaneously sympathetic to and distant from them. It also reserved the possibility of holding up the 'old men's voices' of another time to ridicule.

Another, much later tale of being captured and brought before Te Kooti was published by Katherine (Kitty) Morgan of Taradale, Hawke's Bay, writing under the name Kitty O'Sullivan. In a book entitled *The Curse of the Greenstone Tiki*, published in 1945, Kitty described how, aged ten, she was taken to Te Kooti at Waikaremoana. The narrative is extremely confused in its chronology; it jumbles together events of the wars and Kitty's own experiences. Nevertheless, there are elements in it which suggest the possibility of some small factual basis. Kitty dates their meeting as a few months after the death of her mother and just before her father's death, that is after October 1891 and before June 1892, when indeed she would have been ten years old.[11] Kitty may have seen Te Kooti about the time he met the surveyor at Ohiwa, in March 1892, the same time as Henry Hill, the school inspector from Hawke's Bay, met Te Kooti — or she may have heard Hill's story of their encounter when she was a pupil at Taradale school. Hill recorded the episode in his journals several times, suggesting that he could not stop talking about it. The encounter gave him the aspiration, never realised, to write a life of Te Kooti. Kitty's narrative, further confusing the chronology, states that Te Kooti died at Ohiwa many years after she met him. Kitty, like many other people, says she remembered Te Kooti as a man with compelling and 'fierce' eyes; the costume in which she dresses him — white robes — when he farewelled her, with his hand upraised, belongs to stories (undoubtedly recounted by father to child) from the period of the fighting, when just such a description of him was in circulation in Hawke's Bay.[12] Kitty depicts Te Kooti wearing a white robe when she gives what is ostensibly her father's account of seeing Te Kooti in 1868, when, according to her narrative, he joined the volunteers with Westrup.[13] Kitty writes that, when she was first brought before Te Kooti at Waikaremoana, he was wearing a long dogskin cloak, sandals, and the huia feathers of a chief. She calls him 'a sort of Moses', and the long speech which she attributes to him is of compassion, not anger. Te Kooti warns Tuhoe not to offer defiance to the law from 'this, my stronghold citadel of the mountains'.[14] Thus, rather than evoking the fearful bogeyman of a child's imagination, which the many references to events in the war period might suggest would prevail, Kitty creates an image of a kindly leader, who told her captor (here a woman) to take her home. Kitty adds, too, that Te Kooti carried no weapons. What is most interesting about this story, spun by a European girl from Hawke's Bay who was indeed left an orphan at the age of ten, is that it was not fabricated from the stuff of childhood nightmares. In this, as in other examples of imaginative creations of Te Kooti, the cruder stereotypes that one would have expected to find are not there. Instead, they vanish.

One of the earliest silent movies to be made in New Zealand was Rudall Hayward's drama–documentary, *The Te Kooti Trail*, filmed in 1927. Its narrative is based on Te Kooti's 1869 raid on Guerren's mill near Whakatane, and its cast consisted entirely of local people. The most illuminating casting was that of the Tuhoe carver, Te Pairi Tuterangi, a nephew of Te Whiu and then 70 years old, as Te Kooti.[15] Te Pairi told Hayward that, in the last phase of the Urewera fighting, he, aged 14, had on one

Crayon (or charcoal) sketch said to be of Te
Kooti. It was possibly drawn from memory.
The artist and location of the original drawing
are unknown.   15894 1/2, ATL

occasion carried Te Kooti's rifle. Te Pairi was also very insistent, said Hayward, that
he got certain details right, '"like the bridle on Te Kooti's horse"'.[16] Unfortunately,
Hayward seems not to have recorded any other directive Te Pairi gave him.

Hayward had also imbibed many colonialist stereotypes. His framework was based
on Rudyard Kipling's ode to the 'Lost Legion', seen in the film as the early pioneers,
colonists and soldiers of fortune. In this choice Hayward was echoing an earlier, entirely
fictionalised account of fighting alongside Whitmore against Te Kooti (and Titokowaru), entitled *With the Lost Legion in New Zealand*. This book was published as fact by
the fraudulent George Hamilton-Browne in 1911 and was for a while accepted as an
authoritative history; it was still cited by W. Hugh Ross in his biography of Te Kooti,
serialised in the *Auckland Weekly News* in September–December 1961.[17]

Hayward's film became the centre of attention for a different reason, however: the
issue of government censorship arising from a concern that the film meet the approval
of Ringatu elders. That this was a consideration in 1927 indicates a sensibility which
New Zealand's European society is not often credited with. The certificate for general
exhibition was withheld until elders from the Whakatane district had viewed it at a

This portrait, painted at the base of one of the rafters inside Tutamure meeting-house, Omarumutu, has sometimes been said to be of Te Kooti. Photograph by Roger Neich. Reproduced by permission of Te Riaki Amoamo, Opotiki.   CT 621, MONZ

private screening, shown the day that it had been intended to première the film. Hayward was outraged. He argued that objections were being raised because the '"superstitious Maoris still look on Te Kooti as something approaching a saint"', and that the Ringatu had opposed the film's portrayal of Te Kooti '"in his true character as a misguided patriot"' from the beginning. He also added that pique played a significant part because the objectors had not been invited to participate in the film.[18] The secretary of the Whakatane film company telegraphed his MP furiously: '"Directors emphatically object to natives viewing film. They consider it grossly unfair to allow Censor to be influenced."'[19] The film-makers' view was that the presentation must remain their creative work; the dilemma became that, in defending their freedom to interpret the story as they chose, they raised up the Europeans as the only capable defining authorities, regardless of any Maori concerns which might be aroused. After the viewing, the censor demanded that two subtitles, which referred to Te Kooti as '"resorting to faked miracles"' and to Peka Makarini as the '"torture master" and "stage manager of miracles"', be removed before the general certificate would be issued.[20] The film was returned to Hayward for these alterations to be made, and it was finally shown on 17

Te Pairi Tuterangi, portraying Te Kooti preaching. From Rudall Hayward's film, *The Te Kooti Trail*, 1927.

WHAKATANE MUSEUM

November 1927, six days after its intended première. The flyer now bore the legend, 'STOPPED BY THE N.Z. FILM CENSOR!' It also carried descriptions of the film as 'NOT FICTION − FILMED FACTS' and 'AN EPIC OF THE KING OF OUT-LAWS', showing its dual, and contradictory, purpose of being both thriller and history.[21] Hayward could now claim, however, that he had got it right in Maori eyes.

The film is a mixture of fiction and historical event. Its acknowledged sources are both. The titles credit Frank H. Bodle with 'a fiction version', published in the *Auckland Weekly News* and elsewhere, and James Cowan and Gilbert Mair with the historical base. Bodle joined Hayward as the scriptwriter. The central figure in the film is a young Englishman, who becomes somewhat marginalised when the film moves into its histori-cal heart. When the scene shifts from England to New Zealand, the film immediately introduces Te Kooti. Te Pairi's portrayal of Te Kooti is dignified, presenting him as a quick-moving and forceful speaker. There is a very close shot, shown at Te Pairi's first appearance, of his piercing eyes. This was probably derived from Te Pairi's knowledge; it is certainly an important moment in the film. Te Kooti rides the white horse, and its bridle appears to be hand-made from flax. Throughout the film Te Kooti wears an

Tipene Hotene, portraying Peka Makarini with his little dog. From the same film.　WHAKATANE MUSEUM

elegant 'looted' uniform and high boots, and he carries his sword at his left side. His hair is strangely cut, half-shaven up the back, which does not seem to be simply a style of the period of the film-making. The very first sight of Te Kooti is an emphatic rear perspective showing a roughly cut and close-cropped head and a full crown of hair. He is, in fact, seated on the porch of the meeting-house Tanenui-a-rangi at Maungapohatu, and he is preaching excitedly to his followers. His main adviser, Peka Makarini, is portrayed by Tipene Hotene as a crudely joking, whispering figure, a very rough diamond indeed, but the image is counter-pointed later by the introduction of the little dog which Peka carried in a wicker basket, bumping heavily on his back as he ran. The terrier escapes from its broken cage when Peka is shot in the flight from Ohinemutu on 7 February 1870, but returns to nuzzle his dead master lovingly. This last sequence in the film, showing the long-running fight in the scrub on the slopes of Tumunui (discussed at the end of Chapter 7), is one of the better episodes and must have derived from Mair. The film portrays Maori fighting against Maori with some humanity, despite its avowed colonial purpose of recording the struggles that made the 'pathway safe' for new settlers, ending with Te Kooti's 'dream of power' broken.

Other dramatisations have been created for stage, radio and opera. At least three plays about Te Kooti have been attempted, and two librettos. The earliest play is 'He Matakite', written by James Ritchie in 1967 and produced by Radio New Zealand. Its centre is a young boy and borstal inmate, Katu, and it is based on the visionary experiences of a young Tuhoe man who was held in Waikeria borstal for six months.[22] In the play, the boy dreams of Te Kooti riding the white horse along the cliff tops. Later, Te Kooti appears to the boy and tells him that his horse will carry the boy away to safety. He affirms, 'I am real. I am more than a vision. I am *your* vision.' He comments, 'A man has many names, one for every identity. Te Kooti the Christians called me . . . and history too reviles me by this name . . . Rikirangi before that, when I was a lad like you . . . a lad. But Katu, I was, Katu to those my first and faithful only friends. Katu, I am waiting for you and it is nearly time. Only time now lies between us.' The boy dreams the man; the man guides the boy. Katu asks of him, 'Be my first and only friend'. Te Kooti answers him at the end, 'Fear not thy cry hath reached unto God'.[23]

Two years later, Frank Davis directed a dramatisation entitled *Face to Face* in Gisborne. Created for the bi-centenary of the landing of James Cook at Poverty Bay, it focused rather on Te Kooti and the 'increasingly abrasive contacts' between Maori and European which, it was said, followed Cook's landfall. This multi-media exhibition and performance was the result of Davis's extensive research into Te Kooti, developing out of a pictorial saga of over 50 paintings connected with Te Kooti's life, which Davis had begun in 1965 and which he exhibited at the same time as his documentary–drama. This dramatisation included some of Te Kooti's waiata, as well as extracts from letters, journals and popular folk-songs, including Arthur Desmond's 'Te Kooti the Bold', which Davis was particularly fond of and loved to sing with gusto. My substantial debt to Davis's collation of research texts, and in particular his working translations of Te Kooti's waiata, will have become apparent.

At about the same time, Leo Fowler's verse play, *The Taiaha and The Testament*, was produced in Gisborne and broadcast by Radio New Zealand. The text was published, and with it the original cast-list of the (undated) Gisborne production, among whom were notable figures from the Ringatu Maori community, as well as the local Pakeha community.[24] In this play, Fowler gave Te Kooti a song remembering, with some bitterness, his younger trading days:

> There's no profit for the Maori whichever way it goes.
> If you insist on doing business sober
> you're cunning; slippery as an eel,
> too big for your boots.
> If you accept their invitation,
> quaff their raw spirits
> till your brain is numb —
> then they do you down. . . .
> So, you sink deeper in the ooze;
> but, because you've learned to think,
> your own nostrils recognize the stink. . . .[25]

Like Davis, Fowler collected historical material on Te Kooti — in his case mostly from

Portrait of Te Kooti, entitled 'Retreat from Ngatapa 1869', by Frank Davis, n.d., acrylic on board. Photograph by Gil Hanly.
DOROTHY AND LAURENCE BROWN

Poverty Bay, where he lived. His two-part article on Te Kooti, published in *Te Ao Hou* in 1957, was one of the earliest to challenge established opinions of Te Kooti as a 'veritable fiend',[26] although it did not halt writing in this vein by others. The three dramatists mentioned are Pakeha, although all have been personally involved in the Maori world.

The librettos are written by Maori. One is being composed as I write, by Hone Tuwhare. The other is Witi Ihimaera's opera, *Waituhi: The Life of the Village (Te Ora o te Whanau)*, first performed in Wellington in September 1984. While not directly concerned with the life of Te Kooti, it is based on the community which erected and preserved the great painted house Rongopai. The opera derived from Ihimaera's earlier novel *Whanau* and, in a sense, was a prelude to the book based on the history of his people, *The Matriarch*, published two years after the opera's performance. *The Matriarch* owes its origin to the conjunction of many strands of thought, not the least being a request made by one of Ihimaera's elder kinsmen, Whiro Tibble, at Rongopai in 1982, that he write about Te Kooti. This was on the occasion of the annual gathering of Maori writers and artists, which that year was held at Gisborne; the theme for the hui was the history and legacy of Te Kooti. Ihimaera began *The Matriarch* the following month.[27] I was present at this gathering, as was Frank Davis; thus, the different histories of Te Kooti that we each bore in our minds are linked by occasion, place and, for my part, the great generosity of the two men in sharing their knowledge.

The Matriarch contains much historical material as a deliberate stylistic device: summaries from commissioners' reports on the land confiscations at Poverty Bay, Te Kooti's 1879 letter to George Grey, Wi Pere's speech to the House of Representatives in 1884. For Ihimaera, 'what happened to Te Kooti is what happened to all of us and will continue to happen unless we fight on and hold to the truth.'[28] The 'factual' material is embedded in the narrative — that is, in the lineage of history transmitted from grand-mother to grandchild. Ihimaera also reworked this historical material. He took these texts, as well as portions from at least one contemporary historian, and cut or inter-polated passages to intensify his own narrative. He has been charged with plagiarism (because he did not acknowledge all his sources), but Ihimaera enclosed the texts as parts of a dialogue — a 'korero', a living discussion of a continuing history.[29] By so doing he was asking questions about the nature of recorded history: how it is constructed and what perceptions control and shape the established record. Ihimaera's framework is the whanau, his family, which provides an example of Maori experiences of colonisation; his purpose is 'to put Te Kooti back in front of us. To put Wi Pere' — 'the Maori with his own hands around his neck', as *The Matriarch* insists, but who Ihimaera knows was also the parliamentarian who sought Maori sovereignty — 'back in front of us. . . . And then to chart our course by heeding them.'[30]

The novel adapts history as the oral narratives convey it: woven around kinship and concerned with the vital sources of family mana. The living whanau today trace their relationships with Te Kooti through the oral stories. At the apex of the fan-shaped family narratives, which flow into the present like a river delta, there will be one or more which link the family's history to Te Kooti.[31] The narrative histories are structured like whakapapa: they are stories spun from the moment of junction — or fission — from which the hapu and the whanau take their identity and their name. *The Matriarch* is an oral narrative and an oral song about a young man's quest for mana; it is faithful to Te Kooti's ultimate purpose — that his spiritual descendants may cease to be 'slaves in the land of Pharaoh'.

In the same year as Ihimaera's novel was published, 1986, Maurice Shadbolt launched the first volume of a fictionalised trilogy based on the colonial wars, *Season of the Jew*. It focuses on the period of Te Kooti the warrior, although the central character is not Te Kooti but rather George Fairweather, an amalgam of several participants — George Preece, Thomas Porter, J. C. Richmond, Gilbert Mair. Te Kooti is largely absent; after his early trading days he becomes a deliberately shadowy presence in the background, but his life touches everyone. Shadbolt's method acknowledges that he cannot fully dramatise Te Kooti but, despite this sensitivity, Te Kooti remains not just an elusive figure but also a stereotyped one: prophet and warrior. The ambiguities of European colonialism are conveyed far better through the complexities of Fairweather. The two are linked across a large divide by the child Matiu Fairweather, who may be Te Kooti's — and who owes his historical origin to the recurrent story of Te Kooti's son born on the journey to Taupo in 1869 and who is said to have died at Gallipoli in 1915.[32] Many

Te Kooti, portrayed in the recent meeting-house Te Herenga Waka. The middle fingers on Te Kooti's left hand, destroyed at Te Porere in 1869, are missing. The two upright hands carved and painted at the base of the image refer to the old and new teachings. Carving by Takerangi Smith, 1987.

Te Tari Maori, Victoria University, Wellington

historical strands are adapted and rewoven in Shadbolt's novel, such as Te Kooti's letter left for Fairweather in his plundered kitchen which, in several of its phrases, directly copies the letter which Te Kooti left for Preece and Mair to find in August 1871.

The seedbed of Shadbolt's novel was the execution of Hamiora Pere for high treason on 16 November 1869. Pere and Wi Tamararo were the first to be tried under new legislation, the Disturbed Districts Act, passed in August 1869, which enabled the charge of high treason and with it the death penalty to be applied to Maori in the districts deemed to be in rebellion. The two young men were chosen as exemplars: both had joined the whakarau after the exiles' landing at Whareongaonga. Pere was tried for treason and for levying war; Tamararo was charged with the murder of Maria Morris's husband, Pera Taihuka, at Poverty Bay on 10 November 1868. One of the Crown's witnesses against them was Maata Te Owai. She stated then that 'the god was his (Te Kooti's) as well as the fight';[33] she was saying that these young men were not responsible.

At the time it was recognised that the trials, under this new (and temporary) legislation, were the first occasion on which the substantive sovereignty of the Queen had been asserted in law: at issue was the government's claim to an absolute authority over all regions.[34] Of those tried for high treason — 79 other prisoners in 1869, all from Titokowaru's fight on the west coast,[35] and in 1870 the 34 men captured at Maraetahi —

only Pere was finally executed. At his death he was described as extremely distressed and suffering 'intense mental agony'.[36] Tamararo hanged himself in prison two days after he was given his sentence of death. The remainder of the prisoners were tried in batches and most had guilty pleas entered against them or were persuaded to plead guilty, but their sentences were commuted. The society could not tolerate mass public executions. Nevertheless, the treason trials were a fulcrum in the extension of state power, and Shadbolt's novel arose from this history. 'Kooti' may be only a distant presence in his evocation of the war of the Israelites, but Fairweather's war for absolute power was 'not to be won',[37] either. Shadbolt and Ihimaera, Pakeha and Maori, examine history through fiction as a way towards our internal decolonisation. The roots of the two novels are different. They are like images reflected in two mirrors of the colonial experience, lying, like the glass taken from the *Rifleman*, across the bloody path to Nga Tapa. They demonstrate that there is more than one form of truth to be understood and remembered from the past, which also stretches before us.

AN INDEX OF WAIATA BY TE KOOTI

Te Kooti composed and adapted many waiata, singing them on many occasions so that the knowledge, perceptions and experiences from the ancestral past were brought to bear on the present. He is rightly remembered as a subtle and complex poet.[1]

This appendix is an alphabetical listing of first lines of his waiata. Its primary purpose is to indicate the extent of the song texts. It also locates the songs for scholars who may wish to study them in the context in which they were originally composed or adapted. This list includes only the songs which were written down during Te Kooti's lifetime and the songs collated by his secretaries. It does not attempt to include other song texts which are known and still sung, or which may have been recorded orally. The lines are transcribed as they were written.

The numbered references are to the manuscript book of waiata compiled by Hamiora Aparoa and donated to the University of Auckland Library by Sir Monita Delamere. This book includes only waiata composed up to 1890. 'B' preceding a number indicates that the text is also in the compilation of transcripts of the same waiata made by Robert Biddle. These transcripts contain also the last songs from 1890–93, which are not in the original manuscript book. A few more are contained in Biddle's collection of Ringatu texts, Volume I (B, I). Biddle's material is held by his son, the secretary of the Haahi Ringatu, who generously gave the author access to it. Two haka composed by Te Kooti were transcribed by Gilbert Mair into his field diary for 1871 (cited as GMD 92:46).[2]

Where an earlier version of the song has been located in the large collection of tribal waiata compiled and edited by A. T. Ngata as *Nga Moteatea*, the reference is cited as *NM*, with the volume and page numbers. For Sir George Grey's collection, *Ko Nga Moteatea*, the reference is *GNM*.

First line	Year of composition	Reference
Akuanei au ka piki ki Tongariro	1892	B81
Akuanei hoki ra	1884 for 1/1/1885	36/B36
Aue ka haere nga tangata	1889	[58a](i)/B60(i)
E Aro ma e Porokoru mā	1890	67/B69
E hine tangi kino kati ra te tangi	1889	57/B58
		NM, II, pp.130–33

E hoa ma	1889	56(ii)/B57(ii)
E koro ki nui e koro	1886 for 1/1/1887	48/B47
E muri ahiahi kia noho ia ake	1893	B, I, pp.46, 169
E muri ahiahi takoto iho ki taku moenga	c.1869	8, 9/B8, 9
E noho ana ano i o te kuare	1893	B89
E pa to hau he marangai	1885	37/B37
E pa to hau he wini raro	c.1871	14/B14
		NM, I, pp.236–39
E pa to hau ki te taha wai-hora	c.1869	7/B7
E pa to reo e Te Tai Rawhiti	1887	49/B50
		GNM, p.27
E riri ana a Tu raua ko Rongo	1884	32/B32
E rū ai moko puritia	1892	B85
(*incomplete*)		
E ta ma e ehara koutou	c.1870/1890	15, 62/B15, 64
E taia ana ahau e te mate anini	1893	B, I, p.169/B91
E taka putai (pitonga) he homai aroha	1889	60/B62
E tangi e te ihu e patukia iho	1872	16/B16
E too e te ra too atu ki te rua	1883	30/B30
		NM, I, pp.32–33
E tu Hurinuku e tu Hurirangi	1879	21/B21
E tu ra koutou i runga i te tikanga	1890	B72
(*incomplete*)		
E u ana oku whakaaro	1890	B73
(*incomplete*)		
E whiti e te rā parore ki te kiri	1884	34/B34
Haere mai tatau ka hoki	1890	B74
(*incomplete*)		
Haere ra Matahina	1882	28/B28
Haere ra te whenua	1892	B86
He aha ra kei toku ihu e pa tamaki nei	1864	4/B4
He aha ra kei toku ihu e waitohu noa nei	1884	33/B33
		NM, I, pp.28–31
He aroha noa no nga Pouriki	1893	B, I, p.93
He atua tonu nga iwi nei	1887	55/B56
He mahi (maki) taunu na te tangata	1878	19/B19
He mea mahue ia tenei nahau	1884	B[33a](v)
(*incomplete*)		
He moe po naku i konei tonu rangatira	1891	B79
(*incomplete*)		
Hei konei tonu au taritari atu	c.1879	23/B23
Hohoro mai e te hoa kauaka e	1884/1892	B83
Ka hua koe e Manga	1870	17/B17
(*second verse is waiata 10*)		
Ka mea e Timo	1880	25/B25
Ka riro raia nga tangata o te motu	1890	68/B70
Ka tu au ka korikori	1866	5/B5

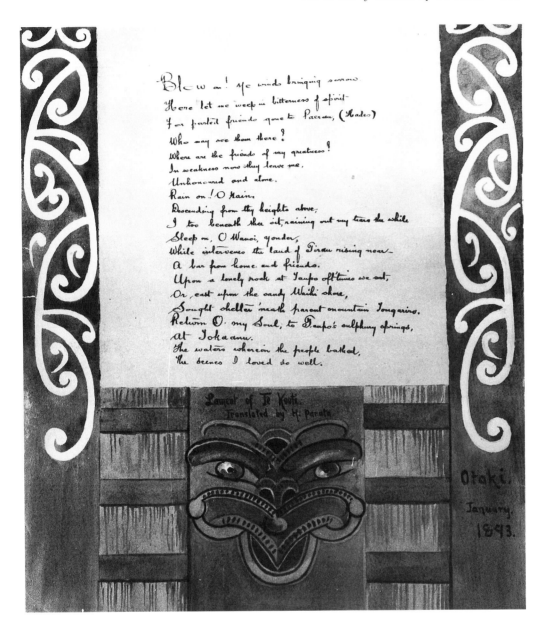

Blow on! Ye winds bringing sorrow
Here let me weep in bitterness of spirit
For parted friends gone to Paerau, (Hades)
Who may see them there?
Where are the friends of my greatness?
In weakness now they leave me,
Unhonoured and alone.
Rain on! O Rain,
Descending from thy heights above;
I too beneath thee sit, raining out my tears the while
Sleep on, O Wanoi, yonder,
While intervenes the land of Tirau rising near—
A bar from home and friends.
Upon a lonely rock at Taupo oft times we sat,
Or, east upon the sandy Waihi shore,
Sought shelter 'neath parent mountain Tongariro.
Return O. my Soul, to Taupo's sulphury springs,
at Tokaanu.
The waters wherein the people bathed,
The scenes I loved so well.

Lament of Te Kooti.
Translated by H. Parata

Otaki,
January
1893.

Lament of Te Kooti, translated by H. Parata at Otaki, January 1893. The song is Waiata 14 in Hamiora Aparoa's collection, 'E pa to hau he wini raro', dated about 1871. It is an adaptation of an earlier lament from Ngati Apakura hapu of Waikato. Painting by Margaret O. Stoddart.   STODDART ALBUM, CM

Kaore hoki e te kino nei	1889	56/B57
Kaore hoki koia te aroha mohukihuki	1870	11/B11
Kaore hoki koia te aroha noa	1890	64/B66
Kaore hoki koia te mamae	1884	35/B35
		NM, III, pp.72–73
Kaore hoki te manakonako	1868	6/B6

Kaore hoki te manukanuka	c.1871	13/B13
Kaore ra ia e hine he putanga	1888/1892	[54a]/B82
Kaore te aroha e awhea mai	1890	65/B67
Kaore te kohimu	c.1871	12/B12
Kaore te mamae ngau kino ki te hoa	1887	51/B52
		NM, I, pp.48–49
Kaore te po nei tuarua	1886	41/B41
Kaore te raro nei tuakiri	1886	40/B40
Kaore te whakamā e huri	1891	B78
Kaore te whakamā ko he ahi e	1890	69/B71
Kauaka range au e ngurunguru	1883 for 1/1/1884	31/B31
Kei te mitimiti rawa	n.d. (early)	3/B3
Ko nukutere ko nukutere	1766 [*sic*]	2/B2
Koi hua mai koutou	1870/1890	10/B10, 75
Mei penei ana te aroha i ahau e	1893	B, I, p.200
Moe hurihuri ai taku moe ki [te] whare	1884	B36[b]
		NM, I, pp.100–1
Na te tara ano te kati	1884	B[33a](iii)
(*incomplete*)		
Na te ure ano te whana	1884	B[33a](ii)
(*incomplete*)		
Noho noa e toku ngakau	1890	63/B65
Noho noa e toku tara	1886 for 1/1/1887	45/B46
Noho noa Whatitata	1885	38/B38
		NM, II, pp.64–67
Pākia pākia pākia	1889	[58a](ii)/B60(ii)
Pakipaki kau au ki te tau	1889	58/B59
Pinepine te kura hau te kura	1888	53/B54
		NM, III, pp.54–67
Popo popo e tangi ana tama	1886 for 1/1/1887	47/B49
		NM, II, pp.152–61
Pupu aku iwi e	c.1880	27/B27
Rangaranga, rangaranga taua i te Pahauwera e	1871	GMD 92:46
Takoto rawa iho ki te po	1883/1885	29, 39/B29, 39, 44
		NM, I, pp.226–29
Taku aroha ra e hika ki a	c.1880	26/B26
Taku noho noa taku tirotiro	1884	B36[a]
Taku taumata e noho ai	1891	B80
Taku turanga ake i te ihi o te whare	1884/1887/1893	B91
(*incomplete*)		
Te mahara i ahau te	1877 for 1/1/1878	18/B18
Te mokai puku nei nana rawa	1893	B, I, p.170
Te poho kapakapa noa	1871	GMD 92:46
Tera ia nga te po taua	1888	54/B55
Tera ia taku pu (putu) paukena	1879	22/B22
Tera koopu e whakakau (whakaū) ana	1889	61/B63

Tera te haeata	1887	50/B51
Tera te Hurae ka rewa mai	1892	B84
Tera te kakau c whakangaro atu ana	c.1879	24/B24
Tera te kotuhi auahi ana	1887	52/B53
		NM, I, pp.118-19
Tera te marama	1887/1892	B87
Tera te pukohu tairi ana	1886 for 1/1/1887	44/B45, 90
Tera te taiuru ka hura	1878	20/B20
Tirohia ki te rangi e parewaikohu ana	1890	66/B68
		NM, III, pp.238–41
Tiwha tiwha te pō	1766 [*sic*]	1/B1
Wewete atu ra koe e tau i a au	1886	42/B42
(*incomplete*)		
Whakapiri rawa atu ki te kiri	1891	B76
Whakarongo whakarongo ra te taringa	1886 for 1/1/1887	43/B43
		NM, I, pp.68–71
Whakarongo whakarongo ra te taringa	1891	B77
Whakatau rawa iho te mauri	1889	59/B61
Wharona hia ra te taura	1884	B[33a](i)
(*incomplete*)		

GLOSSARY
(HE KUPU MĀORI)

This list contains some common Māori words adopted into New Zealand English, which have not been translated. It also includes some words used frequently in this text. The long vowel is marked in this list. The meanings given are particular to this text; the reader should refer to Herbert W. Williams, *A Dictionary of the Maori Language* (first published in 1844 and revised in many editions subsequently), for further information.

ariki: high-born chief
atua: supernatural being, god

haahi: church
haere: come; go
haka: energetic dance of defiance
hāngi: earth oven
hapū: organised kin group, tribal or sub-tribal entity
heitiki: tiki (carved figure) made of greenstone, worn at the neck
hīnau: tree (*elaeocarpus dentatus*), with berries
hōiho: horse
hongi: to press noses in greeting
hōro: shawl
huamata: rites of planting
hui: gathering
huia: bird (*heteralocha acutirostris*), now extinct

inoi: prayer of the Ringatū
iwi: tribe, people

kahawai: fish (*arripis trutta*)
kāhui: assemblage, cluster
kaimoana: sea-food
kainga: village, settlement
kaituki: the man who gives the time to the paddlers in a canoe
kākā: New Zealand parrot (*nestor meridionalis*)
karakia: prayer
karanga: call, summon
kaumātua: elder
Kāwanatanga: government
kiekie: climbing plant (*freycinetia banksii*), whose flowers are considered a delicacy
kina: sea-egg
Kīngitanga: Māori King movement
koha: gift, offering
kōkiri: attacking party
kōpere: rainbow
kōrero: speech, dialogue, narrative
koruru: carved face on the apex of a house
kotahitanga: unity
kotiate: flat weapon with lobed blade

kōtukutuku: fuchsia
kōwhaiwhai: painted scroll patterns
kuia: old woman
kuku: mussel
kūmara: sweet potato
kūpapa: neutral
kupu: word, saying
kupu whakaari: prophetic saying

mākutu: cursing, sorcery, spiritual power
mana: authority, prestige
mana whenua: authority over land or a district
manaia: carved/painted twisting figure with face in profile
mānuka: tea-tree
māra: garden
marae: space in front of the meeting-house; also used for the complex of community buildings
marakihau: fabulous sea 'monster' portrayed with a fish-tail and often a tubular tongue
matakite: visionary
mate: sickness; death
mauri: the life principle, sometimes represented by a guardian stone on the land (mauri whenua)
mere: hand weapon usually made of whalebone or greenstone
miro: tree (*podocarpus ferrugineus*), known for its sweet berries
moko: tattoo
mokopuna: grandchild (used loosely and affectionately)
mōrehu: survivor; chosen few

nīkau: indigenous palm (*rhopalostylis sapida*)
niu: name for the great mast or flagpole used by the Pai Mārire at the centre of their worship, here probably a transliteration of 'news'; divinatory rod
noa: free from tapu, unrestricted

ngārara: lizard
ngāwari: tolerant, flexible

ōhākī: dying speech
ope: party of people travelling together

pā: fortified settlement; commonly used in the 19th century for a Māori settlement
paepae: sill, threshold
pai: good, fine
Pākehā: European New Zealander
papa: flat stone, slab
pātere: forceful song in reply to jealousy
patu: short weapon, often made of greenstone or whalebone
pāua: shellfish (*haliotis*)
pipi: cockle
piupiu: waist garment which moves with the body
poaka: pig
pōhata: wild turnip (*brassica campestris*)
pohutukawa: red-flowered coastal tree (*metrosideros excelsa*)
ponga: tree fern (*cyathea dealbata*)
poroporoaki: to farewell someone
pou (poupou): post, pillar
poutikanga: pillar of authority, leader
poutokomanawa: supporting post of the ridge-pole inside a meeting-house
pure: rites to lift the tapu at the Ringatū harvest

rā: day; the term Rā was adopted by the Ringatū for an occasion or particular gathering
rāhui: ban against entry; boundary marker
rangatira: chief
raupō: bulrush (*typha angustifolia*)
reo: voice, language
reo kē: different language
Ringatū: Upraised Hand
rohe pōtae: encircling boundaries
rongopai: good tidings; peace; gospel
rūnanga: council, assembly

tahā: calabash
taiaha: long wooden fighting weapon, carved with a face on each side
take: cause, reason
taniwha: fabulous water 'monster', sometimes a guardian
tangata: man, person; *plural* tāngata: people
tangata whenua: people of the land; hosts
tangi: funeral ceremony
taonga: valued possession, treasure
tapu: sacred, under divine protection
tekoteko: carved figure, usually for a front gable
tikanga: truth; plan; correct way
tipuna (tupuna): ancestor
tiwha: appeal for assistance in war
toetoe: sedge grass
tohunga: expert, commonly used in the sense of a priest
tōī: tree (*cordyline indivisa*), used for making heavy capes
tokotoko: staff, rod
tōtara: tall forest tree (*podocarpus totara*)
tukutuku: patterned raupō (bulrush) lining on the interior walls of a house
tuku whenua: gift or transfer of land
ture: law
tutu: shrub (*coriaria arborea*)

utu: requital

waiata: song
waiata tohutohu: song of instruction
wairua: spirit, soul
wepu: whip

whakapapa: genealogy
whakarau: prisoner
whakataukī: proverb
whānau: extended family
whare: house
whare kai: dining hall
whare karakia: house for prayer, church
wharenui: meeting-house
whare puni: meeting-house
whare wānanga: house of learning and study
whare whakairo: carved house
whenua: land

NOTES AND REFERENCES

Introduction

1 OS: Robert (Boy) Biddle, Ringatu tohunga, Kutarere, 5 December 1977, 14 December 1981.
2 James W. Stack, *Notes on Maori Christianity*, 1874, p.3. Stack was quoting Te Kooti's letter, which he had translated, written at the time of the escape from Chatham Island in 1868. See Chapter 4.
3 Waiata 68 contains a footnote reference to New Zealand as a colony, then in brackets 'Tominiona' ('Dominion'), with an added date, 1907. This book is in the neat and distinctive hand of Hamiora Aparoa. Te Kooti Arikirangi manuscript book of waiata, 1769–1890, MSS C-35, AU.
4 OS: Boy Biddle, 5 March 1983.
5 Matiu Paeroa's MSS book, copied 6 December 1930. This book can be found as Vol. 3 of the Frank Davis Dossier, ATL. Trans: based on Frank Davis.
6 OS: Boy Biddle, 7 December 1978, 15 October 1987.
7 OS: Wiremu Tarei, Te Teko, 13 February 1974, AK7/56, Radio New Zealand Archives.
8 *Te Kooti Rikirangi, General and Prophet*, p.9.
9 As narrated by Louise Margaret U'ren Sharp in 'Notes on Thomas U'ren', p.7, MSS, GM.
10 12 January 1884, Diary 1882–84, MSS 92:55, ATL.
11 W. J. Napier, probate 18453, NA Auckland. One mere remains with the family; the other was donated to the Auckland Museum in 1928. See Chapter 13.
12 T. W. Porter, *History of the Early Days of Poverty Bay*, 1923, p.54.
13 *AS*, 28 February 1914. The same biography was published in the *Otago Daily Times* and the *Canterbury Times* during February–July 1914.
14 *Stout Centre Review*, III, 2 (March 1993), pp.17–21.
15 OS: Muriwai, 16 May 1982.
16 OS: Boy Biddle, 14 December 1981.
17 OS: Boy Biddle, 14 December 1981, 6 July 1993.
18 Note written on behalf of the author, 17 January 1983.

Chapter 1: The Shadow of Prediction

1 MSS C-35, AU.
2 OS: Monita Delamere, Opotiki, 14 December 1981.
3 There are several versions in Delamere MSS, especially pp.11–12, 45–64. See following note.
4 Ibid., p.45. Paora Delamere was the Poutikanga of the Ringatu church from 1938 until his death in 1981. His book of narratives and other records was started in December 1931, and contains financial records for 1932–33.
5 Biddle MSS, I, p.239.
6 Hamiora Mangakahia, 10 May 1898, in *Te Puke ki Hikurangi*, 7 June 1898 (reference by courtesy of Angela Ballara). Hamiora Mangakahia attended a school of learning at Whareongaonga in 1862, and he must have known Toiroa about this time. In 1898 Hamiora stated that he was the person to whom Toiroa had told his predictions for peace.
7 Delamere MSS, p.59.
8 As told to Porter and published in *AS*, 7 March 1914.
9 Delamere MSS, p.66.
10 Biddle MSS, I, p.240.
11 Waiata 3, MSS C-35, AU.
12 Delamere MSS, p.66.
13 Ibid., p.67.
14 Te Kooti stated that he was born at 'Paoka', an abbreviation of Pa-o-Kahu, in his affidavit of 28 September 1889, J1 1890/407, NA. Ngati Maru oral tradition (narrated by Heni Sunderland, Gisborne, 26 January 1983) remembers that he was born at Paokahu (Te Pa-o-Kahu).

15　Photocopy of registered entry of marriage, 27 July 1867, Registry of Births, Deaths and Marriages, Waitangi, Chatham Island, by courtesy of Michael King.

16　Letter, published in *WI*, 21 September 1869.

17　Porter, *AS*, 7 March 1914. That Te Kooti opened his shirt and uncovered his breast was testified to at the time. See Chapter 12.

18　*Dominion*, 24 April 1937.

19　Te Kooti's elder brother Komene named his daughter Maiere. She married Kereti Hawera of Ngati Awa. I am indebted to Layne Harvey, a descendant, for this information.

20　Porter in reply to Tuke, *WI*, 23 September 1869.

21　Tawhai in F. Hamlin to J. Ormond, 23 June 1870, AGG HB7/5, NA (*AJHR* 1870, A-8B, p.84).

22　J. W. Harris to D. McLean, 7 April 1852, McLean Papers MSS 32:327, ATL.

23　J. Cowan, 'The Facts about Te Kooti', *NZ Railways Magazine*, 1 December 1938, p.18.

24　Annual Letter, 18 November 1877, Grace Papers, Box 1, MSS 583, AIM.

25　Photocopy of registered entry of marriage, 27 July 1867, Registry of Births, Deaths and Marriages, Waitangi, Chatham Island.

26　19 July 1886, Biddle Miscellaneous MSS.

27　Delamere MSS, pp.58, 71–72.

28　His signature appears on the Treaty text for Turanganui, and the fact that Te Turuki signed the Treaty was also noted in ibid., p.69. His mana was commented upon by Joseph A. Mackay, *Historic Poverty Bay and the East Coast, N.I.*, 2nd edn, 1966, p.466. The Ringatu oral narratives state that Te Turuki was a younger kinsman to Te Kooti's father.

29　Te Keepa Te Turuki's daughter Marara Te Kahukaone married Hirini Te Kani, who, as the adopted son of Te Kani a Takirau, became the senior chief at Turanga from 1856. That Te Kooti was directly associated with this family's land interests at Matawhero is demonstrated in Chapter 4.

30　pp.19–20.

31　Ibid., p.20.

32　Delamere MSS, p.72. Delamere noted in the margin that the 'Hāea' was the 'Tohi' ceremony using Maori prayers.

33　Ibid., p.73.

34　Ibid., p.75.

35　The *Queen* was slightly damaged in a storm off Mahia peninsula in May 1858, but was brought back to Turanga by its Maori owners and repaired. This could be the occasion remembered in Paora Delamere's narrative. The *Queen* was back trading with Auckland by June. Capt. George Read used it (although he also owned smaller vessels), and John Harris shipped goods in it (Harris to McLean, 22 January 1866, 66/687, HB4/7, NA).

36　M. N. Watt, *Index to the N.Z. Section of the Register of All British Ships 1840-1950*, [1963], Part 2, pp.164–65.

37　E. Baker to McLean, 21 May 1858, MSS 32:148, ATL; H. S. Wardell, Diary, 7 December 1858, MSS, ATL.

38　In 1870 Ropata Kaihau stated that he knew Te Kooti well 'at the Three Kings' (*AJHR* 1870, A-21, p.4). There are no surviving class lists of the Native Institution.

39　Maihi Pohepohe gave an account of Te Kooti reading passages from a book in English in 1869, *AJHR* 1870, A-8, p.5.

40　See Appendix A.

41　Samuel Williams taught briefly at Turanga in the latter part of 1847, during William Williams's absence in Auckland. Ngati Maru were keen that Samuel should remain at Turanga, but he was sent to Hawke's Bay in November 1847. This remembered association of Te Kooti with Samuel Williams, of which Leo Fowler was told at Turanga, gives a very precise date for Te Kooti's attendance at Whakato. Thomas Grace taught there from the latter part of 1850 through to 1853, during William Williams's visit to England. It was also remembered that Grace's son, Archdeacon Thomas Grace, knew Te Kooti as a boy: Edward Chudleigh to Henry Hill, 14 November 1912, MSS 146:2, ATL.

42　Manuscript dictated by Sarah Ross (née Dunlop), Leo Fowler Papers (uncatalogued, acc. no. 77-14), Box 2:5, ATL. (The first Anglican Maori deacon, Rota Waitoa, was ordained in 1853 and became a priest in 1860. He came from William Williams's diocese and his ordination as priest was held at Turanga. Williams was trying to develop a 'native pastorate'; Rota Waitoa provided a 'role model', which went sour for Te Kooti. Similarly, in 1858 another pupil of Williams's, Pera (Aperahama), stated that he had been 'dismissed' by Williams for drunkenness: Wardell, Diary, 21 May 1858, MSS, ATL.)

43　Journey to Taupo, 29 December 1853, marginal annotation, Grace Papers, Box 1, MSS 583, AIM.

44　'Early Taupo Days', unsourced obituary for John E. Grace, 4 August 1932, Maori Scrapbook, p.95, Elsdon Craig collection. (The meeting occurred at the Native Land Court at Cambridge and the date given there was 1882. This was one year before Te Kooti was able to travel outside the King Country, hence it is suggested the meeting occurred a year or so later.) See also John Te H. Grace, *Tuwharetoa*, 1959, p.401.

45 Grace to CMS, 7 January 1853, Box 1, MSS 583, AIM.

46 See E. J. Hobsbawm, *Bandits*, 1969, Chapter 1.

47 Rukupo to George Grey, 9 March 1852, MSS 32:327, ATL.

48 C. L. Nugent to Rukupo, 30 July 1853, Native Secretary's Office Letter Book, 1849–54, BAIE A646/9, NA Auckland.

49 Wi Pere, *GT*, 16 February 1916.

50 *NZM*, 8 April 1871, gives a very similar version to Wi Pere's account.

51 *GT*, 16 February 1916. The sum said to have been realised seems excessive for the times.

52 Wardell, Diary, 19 August 1858, MSS, ATL.

53 Ibid., 29 November 1858.

54 Ibid., 8 December 1858.

55 Ibid., 27 November 1858.

56 Sworn affidavit, 27 December 1889, *Court of Appeal, Goodall versus Te Kooti Rikirangi*, 1890, p.31, CL 19, NA.

57 'Notes on Thomas U'ren', p.5, U'ren Sharp MSS, GM. The U'ren family arrived in Poverty Bay in 1840.

58 As told to Henry Hill by William Heslop, Hill, Notebook 1889–93, MSS 146:9, ATL. Hill knew William Heslop (son of John Heslop) and he also met and drew a sketch of Te Kooti in 1892: see p.189.

59 Another early version from the Heslops is in the *Cyclopaedia of NZ*, VI, 1908, pp.404–5, where the name was spelt 'Hiroke'. William Greenwood also heard the name Hiroki from the Heslop family: 'Iconography of Te Kooti Rikirangi', *JPS*, 55, 1 (March 1946), p.10. The story is still narrated locally: Irene Lister of Taradale talking with the author, 18 April 1991; Mrs Nan Symons of Puketapu to the author, 19 April 1991. Also, Brian Makarell, a member of the Heslop family, *Dominion*, 1 November 1980.

60 Affidavit, 27 December 1889, *Goodall versus Te Kooti*, p.31, CL 19, NA.

61 The term is taken from the title of Nicholas Thomas's study of material culture and colonialism in the Pacific, published 1991.

62 *AS*, 7 March 1914.

63 Recounted in detail by James Cowan, *Canterbury Times*, 5 June 1912 and sourced to Tuta Nihoniho; and, more briefly, Nihoniho, *Narrative of the Fighting on the East Coast, 1865–71*, 1913, p.35.

64 Biddle MSS, I, pp.240–41.

65 Delamere MSS, inset at pp.72–73.

66 OS: Maaka Jones, Wellington, 28 August 1984 (and cited in Binney and Chaplin, *Ngā Mōrehu*, p.83).

67 OS: Bill Hook, Nukutaurua, 15 May 1982.

68 Biddle MSS, I, p.241.

69 OS: Boy Biddle, 7 December 1978, 15 October 1987.

70 Delamere MSS, p.75.

71 OS: Wiremu Tarei, in the Radio New Zealand programme, 'The Upraised Hand', compiled by Haare Williams, 1986.

72 Delamere MSS, p.76.

73 Biddle MSS, I, p.240.

74 Delamere MSS, p.80.

75 Ibid., p.82.

76 Biddle MSS, I, p.240.

77 Gustav Davidson, *A Dictionary of Angels*, 1967, p.194.

78 OS: Ned Brown, Ringatu elder, Whatatutu, 14 February 1982.

79 Manuscript notebook, n.d., p.139. Private collection, late Ned Brown.

80 See Chapter 5; also Binney and Chaplin, *Ngā Mōrehu*, pp.92–95.

81 Delamere MSS, p.85.

82 Eria Raukura, speech recorded in ibid., p.33.

83 Ibid., p.34.

84 Delamere MSS, p.43.

85 This line is also from Ruatapunui, born to Ruapani's second wife Uenuku-koihu. Turakau died at Whakato in October 1890.

86 Information from Rongowhakaata Halbert: Joseph A. Mackay Scrapbook, MSS 1006, Series 2:19, p.11, ATL. On Ngati Ruapani's claims extending to Waikaremoana, see the evidence of 4 November 1875, Napier Minute Book 4, pp.74, 78, MLC microfilm; H. A. Ballara, 'The Origins of Ngāti Kahungunu', PhD thesis, Victoria University of Wellington, 1991, pp.64–65, 181; and Rapata Wiri's

study of Ngati Ruapani, '"Te Wai-Kaukau o Nga Matua Tipuna": Myths, Realities, and the Determination of Mana Whenua in the Waikaremoana District', MA thesis, University of Auckland, 1994.

Chapter 2: The Hinge of Fate

1 MSS dictated by Sarah Dunlop, eldest daughter of James Dunlop, Fowler Papers, Box 2:5; Ted Bourke in ibid., Box 6:17, ATL. James Dunlop settled first at Makaraka and then moved to Te Arai. The Bourke family were neighbours of the Dunlops at Te Arai.

2 Evidence given by Greene, 26 July 1869, Wainui 2, Poverty Bay Commission Minute Book, p.224, MLC microfilm.

3 Henry Hill, interview with 'Mr King' at Makauri, 5 March 1892. King was living in Poverty Bay in 1868: Hill, Notebook 1889–93, MSS 146:9, ATL. Also, OS: Hei Ariki (Tihei) Algie, Manutuke, 17 May 1982.

4 *EP*, 7 July 1948; *NZ Women's Weekly*, 22 July 1948. These items concerned the possible return of Te Kooti's bones to Turanga, and the appropriate burial-place for them at his 'old home' there.

5 It seems clear that Maori at Turanga had, in their understanding, given the earliest European settlers 'tuku whenua' rights — that is, access to resources and land for their mutual benefit — which they were now attempting to withdraw, or renegotiate. It should be noted that, from 1840 until 1865 (except for a brief period, 1844–46), only the Crown could legally purchase Maori land. The practices which developed in Turanga were leasing (non-legal from 1841, and expressly prohibited from 1846) and 'gifts'. Some of the gifts, particularly those made to the part-Maori children of the first settlers, were genuine, but others were 'arrangements'. The early settlers' land tenures were, therefore, often extremely dubious. Most of their claims, and particularly those for transactions made after 1840, would not be upheld by the Old Land Claims' Commissioner in 1859.

6 Governor T. G. Browne to Duke of Newcastle, 22 February 1860, *AJHR* 1862, E-1, p.[3].

7 Wardell to Native Secretary, 20 September 1861, *AJHR* 1862, E-7, p.31.

8 Harris to McLean, 20 June 1860, MSS 32:327, ATL.

9 Harris to McLean, 15 September 1864, ibid.

10 Hervey to McLean, 3 March 1866, MSS 32:337, ATL.

11 Mackay, p.136.

12 Wardell to McLean, 12 June 1858, MSS 32:620, ATL.

13 Paratene Pototi, 21 May 1858, quoted, Wardell to Native Secretary, 20 September 1861, *AJHR* 1862, E-7, p.31; Kahutia, ibid., also in Wardell, Diary, 21 May 1858, MSS, ATL.

14 W. Leonard Williams, Diary, 21 April 1865, typescript, AIM.

15 Te Ua Haumene to Patara and Kereopa, 8 December 1864, Williams Family Papers, MSS 69:77B, ATL. Trans: William Williams.

16 William Williams, Diary, 7 March 1865, MSS 69:49, ATL, and a subsequent detailed account after Kereopa's capture, to Ormond, 6 December 1871, AGG HB1/3, NA.

17 Diary, 21 March 1865, MSS 69:49, ATL.

18 Quoted at length by William Williams to McLean, 26 December 1871, MSS 32:640, ATL.

19 Harris to McLean, 7 August 1865, MSS 32:327, ATL.

20 Te Waru's hapu is also given as Ngati Hinganga. Both names were used at this time, Hinganga being a son of Hinemanuhiri. The people lived in the upper Wairoa, with land claims on the Waiau and Ruakituri rivers.

21 W. Leonard Williams, Diary, 24 April 1865, AIM.

22 Te Teira Toheriri of Nukutaurua, to McLean, 5 August 1865, MSS 32:689h, ATL.

23 Te Kooti to Grey, 8 May 1879, 83/680, MA 23/8a, NA.

24 W. Leonard Williams, Diary, 12 July 1865, AIM; to William Williams, 12 July 1865, MSS 69:56A, ATL.

25 W. Leonard Williams, Diary, 17 July 1865, AIM.

26 Ted Bourke, whose family was a neighbour of the Dunlops at Te Arai, Fowler Papers, Box 6:17, ATL.

27 Harris to McLean, 7 April 1865, MSS 32:327, ATL.

28 10 April 1865, 'Records of Two Brothers Henry and William Williams', E. L. Gardiner and Fanny Marsh, typescript, p.124, Williams Family Papers, Series C, AIM.

29 Harris to McLean, 22 May 1865, MSS 32:327, ATL.

30 W. Leonard Williams to CMS, 22 May, 21 June 1865, CN/097, CMS microfilm; to William Williams, 23 May 1865, MSS 69:56A, ATL.

31 This argument, which I advanced in an earlier account, is contested in the biography of Mokena Kohere written by Rarawa Kohere, *The Dictionary of New Zealand Biography*, 1990, I, pp.230–31. But

the local support for Mokena's actions was limited, as this chapter demonstrates, and the view presented in the biography that Mokena was subsequently invited by Paratene Pototi to live there and look after Ngati Maru's lands indicates why Mokena (and Paratene) became contentious figures. This invitation was made at the time of the government's threat of land confiscation, and Mokena's claim to Hirini Te Kani's land (Rongowhakaata's land) was rejected by Reginald Biggs (the government's agent) in 1867. Mokena's involvement in disputed land sales at Matawhero is discussed in Chapters 4 and 5.

32 Wardell to McLean, 12 June 1858, MSS 32:620, ATL.

33 Delamere MSS, pp.86–87. This dream is also described briefly in Biddle MSS, I, p.240.

34 Waiata 4, MSS C-35, AU.

35 Delamere MSS, p.89. 'Porewarewa' means, literally, insane or giddy, but the word was used by Pai Marire for their leaders of community worship, underlining the ecstatic aspect of their rituals. The porewarewa spoke in many tongues during the services; hence the later reference in Te Kooti's dream to a language that he could not understand.

36 Ibid., pp.87–88.

37 Ibid., p.90.

38 Diary, 23 May 1865, AIM.

39 Paratene Pototi, Te Waaka Puakanga and three others to McLean, 25 May 1865, MSS 32:689e, ATL.

40 W. Leonard Williams, Diary, 5 June 1865, AIM.

41 Ibid., 7 June 1865.

42 Ibid., 20 July 1865; He Runanga no nga tangata Maori Kuini me nga Pakeha o Turanga, 22 July 1865, MSS 32:689g, ATL.

43 Harris to McLean, 7 August 1865, MSS 32:327, ATL.

44 W. Leonard Williams, Diary, 12 August 1865, AIM; to William Williams, 25 August 1865, MSS 69:56A, ATL.

45 W. Leonard Williams, Diary II, 6 September 1865, MSS, ATL.

46 W. Leonard Williams, 14 September 1865, ibid.

47 Mokena to McLean, 1 September 1865, MSS 32:689j, ATL.

48 W. Leonard Williams, Diary II, 2 November 1865, ATL.

49 W. Leonard Williams, 7 November 1865, ibid.

50 Terms issued at Turanganui, 10 November 1865, AGG HB2/1, NA.

51 Karen Neal, 'Maori Participation in the East Coast Wars 1865–1872', MA thesis, University of Auckland, 1976, p.41.

52 Oath of allegiance, 14 November 1865, AGG HB2/1, NA.

53 W. Leonard Williams, Diary II, 12–13 November 1865, ATL.

54 W. H. Oliver and Jane M. Thomson, *Challenge and Response*, 1971, p.94.

55 Talking with James Mackay at Te Kuiti, unsourced clipping 'Te Kooti and Mr. Mackay', E. Shortland MSS K, p.79, MSS 11, HL. Abridged versions in *PBH*, 4 March 1889, *EP*, 16 March 1889.

56 Fraser, 65/256, HB4/6, NA (*AJHR* 1866, A-6, p.4).

57 The reference is to Ensign Arthur Tuke, who (with Edmund Tuke) later served as a prison guard on Chatham Island in 1866. St George, Diary, MSS, ATL.

58 To McLean, annotation scribbled on the envelope, 21 November 1865, MSS 32:282, ATL.

59 Biggs to McLean, 6 November 1865, 65/203, HB4/6, NA.

60 Diary, 22 November 1865, ATL. The 'Gun' was the six-pound howitzer, brought up during the night of 21 November.

61 W. Leonard Williams, *East Coast Historical Records*, n.d. [1932], p.56.

62 St George, Diary, 19 November 1865, ATL; Harris to McLean, 25 August 1866, MSS 32:327, ATL.

63 Fraser, 21 November 1865, 65/256, HB4/6, NA (*AJHR* 1866, A-6, p.4).

64 Ngai Tahupo were the people of Muriwai. Diary, written 12 September 1924 (when Paratene was 75 years old). Précis and translation by Rongo Halbert. Fowler Papers Box 2:1C, ATL.

65 'Maori Account of the Campaign against the Hauhau on the East Coast, 1865–70', p.29, anonymous MSS copied by A. S. Atkinson, MSS 1187:6A, ATL.

66 *ECHR*, p.56.

67 16 November 1868.

68 W. Leonard Williams, Diary II, 12 November 1865, ATL.

69 Thomas W. Gudgeon, *Reminiscences of the War in New Zealand*, 1879, p.96; Porter wrote (supposedly especially) a history in 23 chapters for the *Otago Daily Times*, *Canterbury Times* and *Auckland Star*, February–July 1914.

70 *AS*, 28 February 1914.

71 W. Leonard Williams, Diary II, 18, 29 October 1865, ATL.

72 Wi Tako Ngatata wrote in concern about the safety of his 'child' ('tamaiti') Paora Parau at Turanga to McLean, 24 November 1868, MSS 32:692g, ATL. Paora Parau stated his tribal connections in his evidence, *AJHR* 1884, Sess. II, G-4, p.6; his whakapapa (given by Karaitiana Ruru in July 1903) is in the Tairawhiti District Minute Book 1, p.273, MLC microfilm.

73 *AS*, 28 February 1914.

74 Capt. A. F. Hardy later spoke of an inquiry by a 'court of officers', after which Te Kooti was released for lack of evidence. May 1898, unsourced clipping, Mackay Scrapbook, MSS 1006/2:19, p.180, ATL.

75 Ted Bourke narrative, Fowler Papers, Box 6:17, ATL.

76 Clipping 'Te Kooti and Mr. Mackay', Shortland MSS K, p.79, HL.

77 Te Kooti Te Turuki, 7 February 1873, MSS 32:549, ATL.

78 Manuscript dictated by Sarah Ross (née Dunlop), Fowler Papers, Box 2:5, ATL.

79 Fraser reported 39 'enemy' deaths on 21 November 1865, 65/256, HB4/6 (*AJHR* 1866, A-6, pp.[3]–4), but Biggs gave the final total in his census report, to Under-secretary Native Department, 23 May 1867, MA 62/8, NA.

80 14 April 1866, 66/587, HB4/7, NA.

81 To McLean, 16 April 1866, ibid.

82 Waiata 5, composed by Te Kooti, gives the date of his seizure precisely, although he could be stating the collective 'I'. See below.

83 Unsigned letter attributed to ?Fraser (more probably written by Capt. C. W. R. La Serre), dated 5 March 1866 at Napier, MSS 32:19, ATL.

84 Karaitiana and Renata Kawepo to McLean, 21 February 1866, HB4/13, NA.

85 *ECHR*, p.50; W. Leonard Williams to William Williams, 6 March 1866, MSS 69:56A, ATL.

86 ?Fraser [or La Serre], 5 March 1866, MSS 32:19, ATL; McLean to Colonial Secretary, 6 March 1866, IA1 66/724, NA (*AJHR* 1868, A-15E, p.4). Leonard Williams gave the figure of 44 men, to William Williams, 6 March 1866, MSS 69:56A, ATL.

87 W. Leonard Williams to William Williams, 6 March 1866, MSS 69:56A, ATL.

88 Sarah Dunlop MSS, Fowler Papers, Box 2:5, ATL; Hardy, May 1898, unsourced clipping, Mackay Scrapbook, MSS 1006/2:19, p.180, ATL.

89 Walter Mantell, speech to Legislative Council at time of passing of Amnesty Act, quoted *NZH*, 17 February 1883.

90 27 December 1889, *Goodall versus Te Kooti*, p.31, CL 19, NA. 'Taratukia' is presumed to be a misprint, possibly for 'Tahakahutia', inland in the Waikohu district, north-west of Te Karaka. (No manuscript original of the affidavit exists.) No one local (Maori or Pakeha) is able to identify 'Taratukia' as such.

91 O. G. Denton, 'Mohaka Raid Account', MSS, ATL. Based on the information from his mother, Joanna Sim of Mohaka.

92 Nihoniho, *Narrative*, p.35. The chief Hamiora is named in Nihoniho's account quoted by Cowan, *Canterbury Times*, 5 June 1912. Nihoniho told this account to Cowan in 1905.

93 In actuality, Biggs was not present on 3 March 1866. He was in Christchurch on long leave. But he had been at the siege of Waerenga-a-Hika, and was appointed resident magistrate for the East Coast from 1 April 1868.

94 See Chapter 5.

95 Best, manuscript biography of Te Kooti, Johannes C. Andersen scrapbook, AIM.

96 James Cowan, *The New Zealand Wars*, 2nd edn, 1956, II, pp.223–24. Preece had fought as a volunteer with Te Kopu Pitihera Parapara's contingent in Wairoa, 1865–66. The same account, by 'an officer' who had fought 'right through the war', was also given to Thomas Lambert, *Old Wairoa*, 1925, p.506.

97 W. Leonard Williams, Diary II, 16 January 1866, ATL; Williams to CMS, 2 February 1866, CN/097, CMS microfilm.

98 Diary II, ATL.

99 McLean to Colonial Secretary, 6 March 1866, IA1 66/723 and 724, NA.

100 McLean to Colonial Secretary, 30 May 1866, IA1 66/1728, NA.

101 George Worgan to McLean, 20 October 1866, 66/730, HB4/7, NA. See also Neal, p.73.

102 William Williams to McLean, 22 August 1863, MSS 32:640, ATL.

103 Anaru Matete to Paratene Titore, 7 June 1866, MSS 32:690d, ATL; also a copy in Williams Family Papers, MSS 190:18, ATL. See also *ECHR*, p.51.

104 Harris to McLean, 29 July 1866, MSS 32:327, ATL.

105 Biggs to McLean, 4 January 1866, MSS 32:162, ATL; Harris to McLean, 12 February 1866, MSS 32:327, ATL.

106 Biggs to McLean, 4 January 1866, MSS 32:162, ATL.

107 W. Leonard Williams to William Williams, 6 August 1866, MSS 69:56A, ATL.

108 *ECHR*, p.50.

109 An early written text collected by George Grey has 'Whanganui Whangaroa'. This is a textual adaptation of the Moriori form, 'Hanga'. Waiata [20], Miscellaneous Poems, GNZ Maori MSS 6, APL.

110 Waikawa is the name of Portland island, at the tip of Mahia peninsula.

111 Napier.

112 That is, the great lagoon on Wharekauri, Te Hanga.

113 Waiata 5, 1866, Biddle MSS, V, p.110. (Hamiora Aparoa's book contains only a shortened text of this waiata.) This song is still sung by the Ringatu, and is always attributed to Te Kooti (OS: Heni Sunderland, Gisborne, 26 January 1983).

    In 1925 Elsdon Best published a text of this waiata in *Tuhoe* (3rd edn, 1977), I, p.598. He said it had been composed by Tawapiko as a lament for his deported kin. Margaret Orbell took her text from this version, and translated it: *Waiata, Maori Songs in History*, 1991, pp.72–73. J. H. Kerry-Nicholls heard it sung at Ruakaka, in the King Country, in 1883 and his companion, J. A. Turner, wrote it down. Kerry-Nicholls was told then that it had been composed by Te Kooti; C. O. Davis translated this text for him: *The King Country*, 1884, pp.279–80. This translation, in turn, was copied by John Te H. Grace, *Tuwharetoa*, 1959, p.479. These texts all follow the Grey manuscript version in the line 'Whanganui Whangaroa', which Davis correctly assumed was on Wharekauri.

114 *Te Puke ki Hikurangi*, 7 June 1898; also (without the exact date) Te Huitau Te Hau in Delamere MSS, p.73.

115 Ibid., pp.90–91. The year given there was 1867, which is certainly wrong. Te Kooti dated his visit to Nukutaurua (narrated in Chapter 1) as being February 1865: Biddle MSS, I, p.241.

116 Names of Prisoners landed at Chatham Islands, 15 March 1866, AD 31:14, NA; McLean to Colonial Secretary, 26 March 1866, IA1 66/982, NA; W. E. Thomas to Native Minister, 19 March 1866, AD 31:14 (*AJHR* 1868, A-15E, p.4).

117 Harris to McLean, 14 April 1866, 66/587, HB4/7, NA.

118 McLean to Colonial Secretary, 26 April 1866, IA1 66/1352, NA (*AJHR* 1868, A-15E, p.6).

119 OS: Boy Biddle, 28 January 1983.

120 'Te Kooti and Mr. Mackay', Shortland MSS K, p.79, HL.

121 There are two lists of the prisoners sent in the second batch to Wharekauri: one dated 2 May 1866 and the other 16 June 1866, AD 31:14. There was a total of 48 males, 30 women and 11 children. One man, a part-Maori called Tiaki Jones, was listed as Rongowhakaata, but he was also described as Ngati Kahungunu.

122 W. Leonard Williams to William Williams, 25 April 1866, MSS 69:56A, ATL.

123 N.d., AGG HB2/1, NA.

124 St George, Diary, 22 May 1866, ATL.

125 McLean to Colonial Secretary, 30 May 1866, IA1 66/1726, NA.

126 HB4/13, NA.

127 Ibid.

128 Matenga Tukareaho was one of the first Maori Christian preachers on the East Coast. He came from Wairoa and signed the Treaty of Waitangi for that district in 1840.

129 OS: Heni Sunderland, Gisborne, 26 January 1983.

130 HB4/13, NA.

131 12 May 1879, 83/680, MA 23/8a, NA.

132 Ibid.

133 Anaru Matete, 17 May 1866, MSS 190:18, ATL..

134 The letter to Paratene exists in both the Williams Family Papers (in a copied version), MSS 190:18, and in the McLean Papers, MSS 32:690d, ATL. W. Leonard Williams told William Williams about a letter from Anaru which McLean had lent him that morning, 12 June 1866, MSS 69:56A, ATL.

135 MSS 190:18, ATL. He signed himself Anaru Matuakore, which was the name he had now taken (Harris to McLean, 18 June 1866, MSS 32:327, ATL).

136 Rongowhakaata to Anaru Matete, 23 June 1866, MSS 190.18, ATL.

137 Biggs arrived in Turanga, from Napier, on 8 June 1866. On 3 June, James Fraser wrote on the assumption that Biggs was in Napier: to McLean, 66/569, HB4/7, NA.

138 Roll of prisoners landed on the Chatham Islands on 10 June 1866, 16 June 1866, AD 31:14, NA.

Chapter 3: Exile (June 1866–July 1868)

1 A. H. Russell (Native Minister), instructions to Capt. W. E. Thomas, February 1866, AD 31:14 (*AJHR* 1868, A-15A, p.[3]).

2 Prisoners' Work List 1, March 1866–March 1867, AD 31:16, NA.

3 List of prisoners, 25 October 1866, AD 31:14, NA.
4 Return of Maoris taken in Arms and sent to the Chatham Islands, 11 February 1868, AD 31:16 (*GBPP*, Vol. 15, p.99). There is no list of names for the fifth group (unlike the other four) in the Army files AD 31:14–16; however, a letter from the Provincial Surgeon at Napier to McLean, 28 November 1866, names 21 men who were now sufficiently fit to 'be removed to the Chatham Islands at the earliest convenient time to the Government'. The letter is also annotated with the exact numbers of men, women and children who were finally sent on 22 December — 21, 12 and seven: 66/831, HB4/7, NA.
5 Russell to Thomas, 13 May 1866, AD 31:14 (*AJHR* 1868, A-15A, p.5).
6 W. Rolleston to Thomas, 28 January 1868, AD 31:16, NA.
7 *WI*, Supplement, 2 October 1869.
8 On an undated list of 'Wharekauri prisoners at large', compiled after the fighting at Nga Tapa, it is stated that 22 of the men had died on Wharekauri (AD 31:15, NA). An earlier list, compiled at the end of November 1867, listed 14 deaths, among whom were six children ('Return of Maoris taken in Arms and sent to the Chatham Islands', AD 31:16 (*GBPP*, Vol. 15, p.99)).
9 Russell, annotation on James Campbell to McLean, 12 May 1866, 66/531, HB4/7, NA; Major J. T. Edwards, Report, 8 May 1867, AD 31:15 (*AJHR* 1868, A-15E, p.17).
10 OS: Monita Delamere, Opotiki, 16 February 1982.
11 Diary, 29 May 1868, Z MSS 36/1/1, p.50, CPL.
12 Michael King to the author, 22 August 1991.
13 Medical report for the month ending 31 March 1867, AD 31:15, NA.
14 Lambert, p.521. This quoted narrative of Engst is different from his manuscript, 'Early History of Chatham Islands and its Inhabitants', R. S. Florance Papers, CM. Lambert's source is unknown.
15 OS: Monita Delamere, 16 February 1982.
16 Tuke's account in T. W. Gudgeon, *The Defenders of New Zealand*, 1887, p.269.
17 W. Leonard Williams, Diary, 9 August 1868, typescript, AIM.
18 OS: Monita Delamere, 16 February 1982.
19 The old woman was not named in the oral narrative but she was most likely Te Warihi Potini's wife, Wikitoria Topa. She was sent with her husband to the island, and she returned with the escaped prisoners in 1868. Te Warihi Potini (Paratene) would be killed on the return voyage, as is narrated later in this chapter.
20 He told the same narrative to the late Frank Davis on 19 October 1978, and on that occasion also he could not recollect the third and final test. Davis Dossier, Vol. 9, ATL.
21 OS: Monita Delamere, 16 February 1982.
22 See Lamentations 5:2.
23 See Lamentations 3:41. *Te Pukapuka o Nga Kawenata e Waru a Te Atua me Nga Karakia Katoa a Te Haahi Ringatu*, n.d. [1968], p.27.
24 OS: 16 February 1982. See also Chapter 13.
25 The list for the fourth batch of whakarau contains their ages. None of the others does.
26 *AS*, 7, 14 March 1914. See also Appendix A.
27 Lambert, p.513.
28 *School Songs, Sacred, Moral, and Descriptive designed to Aid Instruction in Schools and Families, and Connected with Appropriate Tunes*, ed. John Curwen, 1859. This book was donated, along with Te Kooti's Psalter and New Testament, to the Hawke's Bay Museum in 1958 by the family of Henry Hill of Napier.
29 The Hawke's Bay Museum possesses this book. It is stated to have belonged to Te Kooti and it came from Henry Hill of Napier, who also at one time owned Te Kooti's diary of 1869-70: see Appendix A. H. W. Williams, *A Bibliography of Printed Maori to 1900*, 1924, items 302, 346–47, gives a bibliographic description of the publications.
30 Diary, 9 August 1868, AIM.
31 *ECHR*, p.57.
32 Psalms 22, 134, 145; John 14, for example.
33 Diary kept on Wharekauri, MSS 3091, ATL. CT in G. H. Davies Maori Manuscripts III, ATL. This translation is used in all following quotations from the diary. For a discussion of the texts of this diary, see Appendix A.
34 See Revelation 1:12–16, but note also the differences.
35 Modified CT.
36 A. H. Turnbull, Scrapbook, ATL. This item apparently came from G. H. Davies, who had tentatively identified it as belonging to Te Kooti.
37 See Appendix A.
38 Wharekauri Diary, MSS 3091, ATL.

39 R. Biggs to McLean, 17 July 1867, MSS 32:162, ATL.

40 Thomas, Report, 2 August 1868, AD 31:16 (*AJHR* 1868, A-15, p.2).

41 To Under-secretary Defence, 1 July 1868, AD 31:16 (*AJHR* 1868, A-15B, p.4).

42 Te Kooti wrote 'Karamana' but in other letters he wrote Karanama, and this seems to be the more common spelling, although both occur. The name is the Maori transliteration of Cranmer; and it was particularly appropriate. For 'Karamana' was almost certainly Karanama Ngerengere of Ngati Porou, who was sent to Wharekauri with Te Kooti in June 1866. He became Te Kooti's staunch supporter, and at his trial in 1870 he was considered to be a 'priest' of Te Kooti's. He was of high rank, and was said to be able to punish by death. There was also, however, Karanama Te Whare (Moepuku), who was sent with the fourth group of prisoners and who also became a staunch follower of Te Kooti. Both men were part of the council of chiefs established by Te Kooti in November 1867.

43 Entry for 10 May 1867.

44 Modified CT.

45 Inoi [14], Te Kooti Diary 1869–70, p.18, HBM. See also inoi [16] in Appendix A.

46 Michael Walzer, *Exodus and Revolution*, 1985, pp.21, 78.

47 Deuteronomy 5:3.

48 Genesis 9:12–16.

49 The eight covenants were compiled by Paora Delamere in an effort to systematise the teachings. They were included, with the added scriptural references carefully collated by Boy Biddle, in the second edition of William Greenwood, *The Upraised Hand*, 1980, pp.93–95.

50 OS: 14 February 1982.

51 Biddle, in Greenwood, *Upraised Hand*, p.95.

52 Report, 8 May 1867, AD 31:15 (*AJHR* 1868, A-15E, p.17). This understanding had been set out right at the beginning: Russell to Thomas, February 1866, AD 31:14 (*AJHR* 1868, A-15A, p.[3]).

53 Colonial Defence Office to Thomas, 22 June 1867, AD 31:15.

54 Biggs to McLean, 13 June 1867, *AJHR* 1868, A-15E, p.19.

55 Biddle, in Greenwood, *Upraised Hand*, p.95. The covenant with Abraham is considered to be the fourth covenant.

56 Delamere MSS, pp.33–35. (Eria died 29 June 1938 and was said then to be 103 years old. Delamere's date for this speech (12 September 1948) is clearly wrong.)

57 The quotation is taken from the Kenyan novelist Ngugi Wa Thiong'o, who was writing of the Hebraic traditions adopted in precisely the same way by the Black West Indian resistance movements. *Homecoming*, 1972, p.89.

58 Te Kooti ('Tekoti'), and all of us, at Waitangi, to Te Ahipakura: to Heremaia [Rauwehe], AGG HB2/1, NA.

59 R. W. Rayner, Wharekauri Diary, 6 September, 23 October 1866, MSS 3694, ATL.

60 Edwards, Report, 8 May 1867, AD 31:15 (*AJHR* 1868, A-15E, p.17).

61 11 July 1868, *Diary of E. R. Chudleigh*, ed. E. C. Richards, 1950, p.226.

62 After the escape, the chest was taken by one of the guards, Michael Mullooly. It is now in the Auckland Museum. It is three feet long, 17½ inches wide and 16 inches high. A small lidded box and drawer are built within it; the chest formerly possessed an iron lock. It is said to have been given to Te Kooti by the government.

63 Clipping, n.s., February 1917, Elsdon Best Scrapbook 5, p.80, ATL.

64 Ritchie to W. E. Stafford, 2 April 1868, AD 31:16 (*AJHR* 1868, A-15B, p.[3]).

65 Ritchie to Stafford, 9 April 1868, AD 31:16 (*AJHR* 1868, A-15B, p.4).

66 OS: David Holmes, Waitangi, 6 December 1989.

67 Diary, 29 May 1868, Z MSS 36/1/1, p.50, CPL. (Tom Ritchie was a cousin of Thomas Ritchie senior.)

68 *Te Pukapuka o Nga Kawenata . . . a Te Haahi Ringatu*, p.144.

69 Delamere MSS, p.30.

70 Rotongaio, Taupo, 5 February 1893, Biddle, Miscellanous MSS. See Chapter 14.

71 Waiata 6, MSS C-35, AU. The text there is abridged. It was completed (at a later date and somewhat uncertainly) in the version in Biddle, V, p.110, quoted here. That text has 'punarua/manarua' bracketed as alternatives. This translation is hesitant: the text is not clear.

72 Tom Ritchie mss note in Scrapbook, Z MSS 36/3/3, CPL. I am indebted to Buddy Mikaere for this reference.

73 Engst, 'Early History', p.20, MSS Florance Papers, CM.

74 Ibid. This verbal confrontation is probably the origin of Christie's story, told to Lambert (Lambert, p.513) and thereafter much quoted (e.g. Ross, p.35), that Te Kooti stripped himself naked before Thomas, when the latter was questioning him about the reports. Christie also elevated himself to the centre of the stage as the man who intervened as Thomas panicked; but in fact Christie had been discharged and left the island in January 1868. This is typical of many of the stories which were put

into circulation and then became part of the standard histories of Te Kooti. It will suffice as an example.

75 These objections had been attributed (by some) to Grace's teachings. His 'peculiar opinions' in this respect were drawn to the governor's attention during his visit to Turanga in 1860: Browne to Duke of Newcastle, 22 February 1860, *AJHR* 1862, E-1, p.4. Rutene Piwaka's objections to the alterations in the prayer-book were quoted by Wardell to Native Secretary, 20 September 1861, *AJHR* 1862, E-7, p.31; Wardell also recorded the chiefs' objections at length in his diary, 21 May 1858, MSS, ATL.

76 Report, 2 August 1868, AD 31:16 (*AJHR* 1868, A-15, p.2).

77 Obituary for 'Taihuka', who had been one of the whakarau, October 1927. This man was probably Te Matenga Taihuka, who became a well-known figure in Poverty Bay. Te Matenga, his brother Hemi, and his father, Pehimana Taihuka, were all prisoners; Pehimana was released in 1868, and the other two escaped the island with Te Kooti. Clipping, n.s., n.d. [October 1927], Mackay Scrapbook, MSS 1006, Series 2:19, ATL.

78 Cowan, *NZ Wars*, II, p.226.

79 1 July 1868, AD 31:16 (*AJHR* 1868, A-15B, p.4).

80 Ibid.; Report, 2 August 1868, AD 31:16 (*AJHR* 1868, A-15, p.2).

81 Insert in diary, n.d., Z MSS 36/1/1, p.47, CPL.

82 Peneha Rakaihau, who was sent with the second batch of prisoners. Peneti, the next reference, is an affectionate form of his name.

83 OS: Ned and Heni Brown, Whatatutu, 14 February 1982.

84 OS: David Holmes, 6 December 1989.

85 *AS*, 28 March 1914.

86 He wrote '1878'.

87 For example, from Petera Te Rangihiroa's original MSS book, they are transcribed into Biddle MSS, I, p.23. (This text has the word 'riri', which was omitted in the original diary text of Utiera.) Tawehi Wilson MSS, p.139, has another version where the second word in 'te reo ke' has, through oral transmission, altered from 'Iperene' to 'Eprain'. The interpretation, or promise, is the same. 'Utiere' is the name of the third promise, and the text extends to include 'all things which creep, creep on the land' ('nga mea ngoki, ngoki o te whenua').

88 Report, 21 February 1868, AD 31:16 (*AJHR* 1868, A-15E, p.23).

89 3 February 1868, AD 31:16.

90 Diary, 24 January 1868, typescript, MSS 148:79, ATL; G. Mair to Cowan, October 1921, in Cowan, *NZ Wars*, II, p.234.

91 Letter to *Evening Post*, 14 March 1889, signed 'Wharekauri'. It was written in reply to an account given two days previously by Capt. W. H. L. Beamish, who had also been stationed on the island, in which he had argued that the prisoners had never been flogged. This debate had been stirred up by the arrest of Te Kooti in 1889.

92 Tom Ritchie, Diary, [April 1868], Z MSS 36/1/1, pp.47, 50, CPL.

93 Tuke to McLean, 21 July 1868, MSS 32:609, ATL.

94 Tuke, *WI*, 21 September 1869; *AS*, 7 March 1914.

95 Thomas, 1 July 1868, AD 31:16 (*AJHR* 1868, A-15B, p.4).

96 *AJHR* 1868, A-15, p.13 (modified CT).

97 *AS*, 7 March 1914.

98 There is an entry in Te Kooti's diary for 27 October which reads: 'This is the day on which God appealed to his people' ('Ko te ra tenei inoi ai te Atua ki tona iwi'), MSS 3091, ATL.

99 Rongowhakaata; Te Aitanga-a-Mahaki; Ngati Porou; Ngati Tu; Ngati Kurumoki; Ngati Hineuru; Waikato; Ngati Raukawa; Ngati Kahungunu; Ngati Matepu; Wairarapa; Taranaki; Ngati Matewai. Biddle MSS, I, p.52.

100 Ritchie to Stafford, 9 April 1868, AD 31:16 (*AJHR* 1868, A-15B, p.4)

101 Tom Ritchie Diary, 29 May 1868, Z MSS 36/1/1, p.50, CPL.

102 Ibid.

103 G. S. Cooper to Richmond, 4 August 1868, *AJHR* 1868, A-15, p.13.

104 OS: Monita Delamere, 16 February 1982.

105 *AS*, 14 March 1914.

106 The four signs Te Kooti gave were: first, misty drizzle; second, the arrival of the second ship; third, heavy rain; and, finally, a loud clap of thunder, the signal for action. OS: Monita Delamere, 16 February 1982. He told the same narrative to Frank Davis, 19 October 1978, Dossier, Vol. 9, ATL.

107 *AS*, 21 March 1914.

108 Thomas, Report, 2 August 1868, AD 31:16 (*AJHR* 1868, A-15, p.[1]).

109 Evidence given by Robert Hardie, carpenter, in Thomas, Report, 2 August 1868, AD 31:16 (*AJHR* 1868, A-15, p.4).

110 Tom Ritchie mentioned Te Kooti's red flag hoisted as 'the signal to begin', Diary, 5 July 1868, Z MSS 36/1/1, CPL; John Watson saw, to his surprise, a white flag with a red border raised over the prisoners' kainga and therefore went to the redoubt to investigate: W. Leonard Williams, Diary, 28 August 1868, AIM. It is possible that there were two flags, used for a sequence of signals.

111 OS: Monita Delamere, 16 February 1982.

112 Tom Ritchie, Diary, 5 July 1868, Z MSS 36/1/1, CPL.

113 Ibid.

114 Cooper to Richmond, 4 August 1868, *AJHR* 1868, A-15, p.13.

115 19 July 1868, S. Percy Smith Papers, MSS 281:17, AIM.

116 OS: Pat Smith, of Te Matarae, Wharekauri, who sheared there in the 1950s, 6 December 1989.

117 OS: David Holmes, 6 December 1989; also Michael King to the author, 22 August 1991.

118 OS: Lena Pohatu, great-granddaughter of Te Kooti, Manutuke, 17 May 1982.

119 Isabella Alexander's account is attached to Thomas's Report, 2 August 1868, AD 31:16 (*AJHR* 1868, A-15, p.6). The sum was reported at the time as being about £350 in sovereigns (Cooper to Richmond, 4 August 1868, *AJHR* 1868, A-15, p.13); S. Percy Smith, Reminiscences, p.57, MSS 281, AIM.

120 List of Arms and Ammunition taken 4 July 1868, in Thomas, Report, 2 August 1868, AD 31:16 (*AJHR* 1868, A-15, p.8).

121 Ibid., pp.8–11.

122 Report, 2 August 1868, AD 31:16 (*AJHR* 1868, A-15, p.2).

123 S. Percy Smith, Diary, 5 July 1868, MSS, ATL.

124 OS: Boy Biddle, 15 October 1987.

125 *AS*, 28 March 1914.

126 Account given to Cowan, 23 February 1921, MSS 39:41A, ATL.

127 'Te Kooti and Mr. Mackay', Shortland MSS K, p.79, HL.

128 Te Kooti to Grey, 8 May 1879, 83/680, MA 23/8a, NA.

129 Quoted by W. E. Gudgeon, 'The Tohunga Maori', *JPS*, XVI, 2 (June 1907), p.71.

130 Percy Smith commented on the fair south-west wind which sprang up from 6 July and which, he said, would ensure the *Rifleman*'s speedy passage to the East Cape. He anticipated, pretty correctly, that they would land near Te Mahia on 9 July: Diary, 6–9 July 1868, MSS, ATL.

131 *NZM*, 15 March 1889 (also *LT*, 1 April 1889).

132 Ibid.

Chapter 4: The Return (July–November 1868)

1 W. Leonard Williams, Diary, 12 July 1868, AIM.

2 Mackay Scrapbook, MSS 1006/2:19, p.223, ATL, and quoted in Mackay's *Historic Poverty Bay*, p.236. 'Masher' means stylish to the point of foppishness; perhaps the suit came from the captain's wardrobe. This image delighted the poet Kendrick Smithyman, who evokes it in his poem 'Prophet', quoted in Appendix B.

3 *NZM*, 15 March 1889.

4 The letter has not been found but it was translated by the Christchurch-based missionary, Canon James Stack: Stack, p.3, and letter written by Stack, quoted George Preece, 'Pursuit of Te Kooti through the Urewera Country', F. J. W. Gascoyne, *Soldiering in New Zealand*, 1916, p.190. Martin said that each of the five crewmen were paid £6. The mate got £10 (Biddle MSS, I, p.134). But by the time the story reached Biggs the sum said to have been paid to the mate had climbed to £100 (Biggs to McLean, 9 August 1868, MSS 32:162, ATL), and it would escalate further in the telling. Suspicion inevitably fell on the crew as to why they had not called at Napier and the extent to which they had been bought off. In the end, however, the mate's denials that he had received any significant payment were accepted.

5 See Genesis 22.

6 Biddle MSS, I, p.134.

7 Tutahi Pohatu from Te Mahia, speech recorded in Delamere MSS, p.31; OS: Reuben Riki, Muriwai, 16 May 1982.

8 OS: Rose Thompson, great-granddaughter of Wi Kaipuke, Tawatapu (Bartlett's), 28 November 1983.

9 OS: Reuben Riki.

10 Stack, p.3; Gascoyne, p.190.

11 OS: Boy Biddle, 15 October 1987.

12 Genesis 22:13.

13 OS: Reuben Riki.

14 OS: Reuben Riki.

15 Biddle MSS, I, p.135.
16 Mackay, p.236.
17 OS: Tihei Algie, Manutuke, 17 May 1982.
18 Biggs to McLean, 13 July 1868, MSS 32:162, ATL.
19 Biggs to Colonial Defence Office, 14 July 1868, AD1 68/2624, NA; Arthur Kempthorne, Journal of Events, 12 July 1868, HBM.
20 *AS*, 28 March 1914.
21 *WI*, 23 September 1869.
22 Biggs, 14 July 1868, AD1 68/2624, NA.
23 Diary, 14 July 1868, AIM.
24 Biddle MSS, I, pp.135–36.
25 Diary, 12 July 1868, AIM.
26 Kempthorne, Journal, 12 July 1868, HBM.
27 *WI*, 23 September 1869.
28 Evidence given by Riria Kaimare, one of the whakarau, *WI*, 21 September 1869.
29 Diary, 20 July 1868, AIM.
30 *AS*, 28 March 1914.
31 Whitmore to Haultain, n.d. [21 August 1868], AD1 68/2810, NA.
32 Diary, 20 July 1868, AIM.
33 Kempthorne, Journal, 12 July 1868, HBM; William Williams to McLean, 14 September 1868, MSS 32:640, ATL.
34 Statement of the prisoner Hotoma Kahukura, 15 August 1868, AD1 68/2810, NA; also Maata Te Owai, *WI*, 23 September 1869.
35 St George to H. T. Clarke, 23 March 1869, *AJHR* 1869, A-3, p.39.
36 Te Keepa Te Rangipuawhe to McLean, 11 March 1870, *AJHR* 1870, A-8B, p.5.
37 Biddle MSS, I, p.197.
38 Exodus 40.
39 *AS*, 28 March 1914.
40 W. Leonard Williams, Diary, 16 July 1868, AIM.
41 Biddle MSS, I, p.137.
42 *GT*, 16 February 1916.
43 W. Leonard Williams, Diary, 19 July 1868, AIM.
44 Ibid.
45 Biddle MSS, I, p.137.
46 Quoted by Frank Davis, Davis Dossier, Vol. 1, p.30, ATL. Davis does not name his informant, but Reuben Riki of Muriwai told the same story, 16 May 1982.
47 It goes further still, for it states that Hamuera's words anticipated the fact that Te Kooti would never be able to return to Poverty Bay, 'even after his pardon' of 1883. But that would be to look too far ahead: Te Kooti's return to Turanga in November 1868 was yet to come.
48 Kempthorne, Journal, 14 July 1868, HBM.
49 W. Leonard Willams, Diary, 19 July 1868, AIM; to William Williams, 20 July 1868, MSS 69:56B, ATL.
50 Paparatu was badly misplaced, by an editorial intrusion of which I was unaware, in my biographical entry for Te Kooti in the *Dictionary of New Zealand Biography*, I, p.464.
51 He had been sent to Wharekauri with the first group of prisoners.
52 *AS*, 4 April 1914.
53 Kempthorne, Journal, 20 July 1868, HBM.
54 Ibid.
55 Ibid., 30 July 1868; W. Leonard Williams, Diary, 31 July 1868, AIM.
56 Westrup to Colonel Commanding Field Force, 21 July 1868, *AJHR* 1868, A-15D.
57 W. Leonard Williams, Diary, 14 July 1868, AIM.
58 Ibid., 21 July 1868.
59 31 July 1868, MSS 32:222, ATL.
60 *AS*, 4 April 1914.
61 Kempthorne, Journal, 3 August 1868, HBM.
62 Statement by Maaka, 29 February 1872, AD1 72/325, NA. He had been sent with the fourth group of prisoners to Wharekauri. Maaka was also identified as belonging to Waikato, both on the Wharekauri prison list and by fellow whakarau.
63 *HBH, WT*, 27 August 1872, reporting the first hearing of Maaka's case. Also statement by Pera Uetuku and Hori Puru, n.d. [June 1870], MSS 32:25, ATL.
64 *HBH*, 10 December 1872.

65 Kempthorne, Journal, 5 August 1868, HBM.

66 *AS*, 4 April 1914.

67 Quoted in Lambert, p.529.

68 Whitmore, 9 August 1868, *AJHR* 1868, A-15C, p.[3]; S. Deighton to McLean, 14 August 1868, MSS 32:243, ATL.

69 Statement, enclosed in Porter to Defence Minister, 3 June 1870, AD1 70/2780, NA.

70 MSS copied by Arthur Atkinson, MSS 1187:6A, ATL. Also, Gudgeon, *Reminiscences*, pp.87–88. There is some confusion between Rukupo's son and adopted son in the various sources. Leo Fowler, in *Te Mana o Turanga*, 1974, after mentioning the death of Rukupo's 'only' son in the East Coast wars, stated that it was for the death of Rukupo's 'tukunga' (protégé), Pita, that the requital was sought (p.6). Hetekia Te Kani Te Ua, however, referred to the death of Rukupo's 'eldest' son at Pakairomiromi (mss annotations on William Greenwood, *Upraised Hand*, 1942, p.37, GM) and the events of these two conflicts have got confused in the telling. Rukupo's surviving son was, as has already been mentioned, Te Waaka Rongotu, who was sent to Wharekauri in the same group as Te Kooti in 1866 (Gisborne Minute Book 3, p.24, MLC microfilm; List of prisoners 66/1178, AD 31:14, NA). Rukupo died on 29 September 1873 without any living issue.

71 The reports of Pakairomiromi, which reveal that no male prisoners were taken in the pa, are Fraser, 3 August 1865, AD1 65/2470, NA, and Rev. Mohi Turei to McLean, 14 August 1865, MSS 32:19, ATL.

72 George Preece, Diary, 18 August 1871, MSS 249, AIM; [G. Mair and G. A. Preece], 'Expeditions against Te Kooti', in John Featon, *The Waikato War*, revised edn, 1923, p.220; Cowan, *NZ Wars*, II, pp.438–40. Oral tradition remembers that Ropata deliberately used this mere to execute some of the prisoners taken in the last stages of the Urewera war. See Chapter 9.

73 Biggs to Samuel Locke, n.d. [1867], Biggs to McLean, 12 August 1867, MSS 32:162, ATL; 'Confiscated Native Lands', *AJHR* 1928, G-7, p.24.

74 Ibid., p.26.

75 *AS*, 11 April 1914.

76 Ibid.

77 Walzer, p.54.

78 Best, *Tuhoe*, I, pp.201–3. OS: Taua McLean, who was brought up by Eria, Rotorua, 6 July 1981.

79 List of original owners, August 1890, Tahora 2F (Papuni), Gisborne Minute Book 19, pp.39–45, MLC microfilm. Te Kooti was listed as Turuki Rangipatahi (no. 331).

80 Deighton to McLean, 26 December 1867, MSS 32:243, ATL.

81 9 August 1868, *AJHR* 1868, A-15C, p.5.

82 W. G. Mair reporting the Maori messages to H. T. Clarke, 3 October 1868, Mair Letterbook 1868–69, MSS 1077, ML; Whitmore to Haultain, 7 October 1868, AD1 68/3383, NA.

83 W. Leonard Williams, Diary, 19 August 1868, AIM.

84 Russell Duncan, *The Fight at Ruakituri*, 1939, p.12.

85 Signed annotations by J. C. Richmond and E. W. Stafford (the Premier), to telegram Whitmore to Haultain, 7 October 1868, AD1 68/3383, NA; Haultain to Whitmore, 9 October 1868, AD8/1, NA.

86 Whitmore to Defence Minister, 9 October 1868, AD1 68/3494, NA.

87 W. Leonard Williams, Diary, 8 November 1868, AIM.

88 He had been sent to Wharekauri with the fifth batch of prisoners.

89 Whitmore to Haultain, 7 October 1868, AD1 68/3383, NA.

90 Ibid.

91 Frederick Helyar (at Runanga) to Commanding Officer Napier, 25, 29 October 1868, AD1 68/3761, 68/4128, NA.

92 Reignier to Commander of the Military Station, Napier, 17 October 1868, AD1 68/3585, NA.

93 A. Shand to S. Percy Smith, 9 April 1894, MSS 275, AIM; Elsdon Best, 'Notes on the Art of War', *JPS*, XII, 2 (June 1903), p.84, and ibid., 3 (September 1903), p.149.

94 Captain T. Withers to Haultain, 20 October 1868, AD1 68/3493, NA.

95 Reignier, 17 October 1868, AD1 68/3585, NA.

96 Called here 'karakia ohaoha'. W. G. Mair, 3 October 1868, reporting the message sent to Ahikereru, MSS 1077, ML.

97 Biggs to Colonial Defence Office, 1 September 1868, *AJHR* 1869, A-4A, [p.3].

98 McLean to Colonial Defence, 7 September 1868, AD1 68/3055, NA.

99 Riria Kaimare, one of the whakarau, and Maata Te Owai, *WI*, 21, 25 September 1869.

100 Hori Te Rangi (at Tukurangi) to Te Waru and others at Puketapu, 23 September 1868, AD1 68/4123, NA. (This letter itself was seized at Whataroa in November 1868, but presumably it had already been received.) Hori Te Rangi had also written to Te Kooti at Puketapu on 11 September, sending his greetings to 'the men of the loving God' ('nga tangata o te Atua i atawhai'), ibid.

101 Helyar to Officer Commanding Napier, 29 October 1868, AD1 68/4128, NA.

102 Information from Paora Hapi, one of the chiefs of east Taupo, F. E. Hamlin to McLean, 23 September 1868, MSS 32:322, ATL.

103 Helyar to Officer Commanding Napier, 30 October 1868, AD1 68/3762, NA.

104 J. D. Ormond to Defence Minister, 23 October 1868, AD1 68/3589, NA (*AJHR* 1869, A-4A, p.6).

105 W. G. Mair to Clarke, 3 October 1868, MSS 1077, ML.

106 The first reports of their refusal are in Deighton to McLean, 22 September 1868, MSS 32:243, and Biggs to McLean, 28 September 1868, MSS 32:162, ATL. This position seems to have been maintained throughout October.

107 Biddle MSS, I, p.173.

108 Sworn evidence, *WI*, 23 September 1869.

109 *AS*, 11, 18 April 1914. See Appendix A for a discussion of this notebook.

110 *AS*, 11 April 1914.

111 '[Official] Sketch Map . . . shewing the Confiscated Lands', 1869, in the possession of the author.

112 Hamlin to McLean, 23 September 1868, MSS 32:322, ATL.

113 *AJHR* 1867, G-1, pp.9–10, CT.

114 Biggs to McLean, 12 August 1867, MSS 32:162, ATL.

115 Hearing of the petition, 8 August 1867, Le1 1867/13, NA. Biggs to McLean, 14, 27 March 1868, MSS 32:162, ATL.

116 Richmond, evidence given concerning the petition, 26 July 1867, Le1 1867/13, NA.

117 W. Leonard Williams to William Williams, 29 February 1868, MSS 69:56B, ATL.

118 To F. E. Maning, the Native Land Court judge, 26 March 1868, MSS 32:11, ATL.

119 A useful account of the East Coast legislation, completed simultaneously with my assessment, is Vincent O'Malley, 'Report for the Crown Forestry Rental Trust on the East Coast Confiscation Legislation and its Implementation', 1994.

120 Wainui 2 lay next to Matawhero 4, which was Read's claim. In 1869, Wainui 2 would be awarded by the Poverty Bay Commission to Greene's children, and Matawhero 4 to Read. Matawhero 4 is discussed below.

121 Greene, evidence given 26 July 1869, Wainui 2, Poverty Bay Commission, p.222, MLC microfilm.

122 Te Kooti to Heremaia [Rauwehe] at Te Ahipakura, AGG HB2/1, NA. Heremaia was from Ngai Te Ika hapu of Rongowhakaata. He was not one of the owners but he had had cultivations in the old river bed at Wainui and he gave evidence at the 1869 hearing: Wainui 2, Poverty Bay Commission: Heremaia Rauehe [*sic*], pp.226–27; also Greene's evidence, ibid., pp.223–24.

123 Renata stated that he had been a party to the original gift, but then demanded this subsequent payment for the old river bed. He also stated that he had done this at some stage after the siege of Waerenga-a-Hika and that Mokena had gone with him when he went to Greene to make the demand, but that Mokena really had no right to the land: 22, 27 July 1869, ibid., pp.179, 227–28. Also, H. A. H. Monro (judge's notebook), Poverty Bay Notes, 1869, pp.132, 158–59, MSS 366:14, AIM.

124 Wainui 2, Award of title (B-13), MA 62/1; also OLC 4/21, NA.

125 Wainui 2, OLC 4/21, NA.

126 Greene mentioned particularly Te Watene, the third signatory, who (with others) pointed out the boundaries to him. 'Te Watene' is a Maori transliteration of the name of the former resident magistrate, Wardell; Te Watene was an elder kinsman of Hirini Te Kani, but his precise identity cannot be established. Greene stated that whereas the original boundary had been the southern river bank, Te Watene included the recently dried-up river bed. Greene's statement conforms with Te Kooti's understanding (expressed in his letter of 1867) that Greene now had this piece too. Greene's evidence, 26 July 1869, Poverty Bay Commission, pp.221–24, MLC microfilm.

127 Harata was the daughter of Paratene Te Mate, who signed the 1843 deed of 'sale' for the disputed portion of Matawhero 4, discussed below. See Whakapapa D (page 34).

128 Greene did not pay Piripi the full amount (£10) because of an existing debt owed to him by Harata and Piripi. Thus, all the ingredients of colonial land disputes exist in this convoluted transaction, including the indebtedness of the manipulating sellers.

129 Greene to Native Land Court Commissioners, 7 August 1867, MA 62/5, NA.

130 Dunlop MSS, Fowler Papers, Box 2:5, ATL.

131 *DSC*, 16 November 1868.

132 This was the amount awarded to Read by the Poverty Bay Commission in 1869.

133 Harris, in cross-examination by Read, 27 July 1869, Wainui 2, Monro, Poverty Bay Notes, p.157. (The clerk's transcript, that is, Poverty Bay Commission, p.226, omits this precise reference to Te Kooti.)

134 Read (cross-examining Harris), Monro, Poverty Bay Notes, p.157.

135 Read, giving evidence about the dispute, Wainui 2, Poverty Bay Commission, p.208, MLC microfilm; and in greater detail, Monro, Poverty Bay Notes, pp.148, 157.

136 Various witnesses referred to the disputed land as being at, or towards, Otoma (Te Toma). The exact portion was described best by a very old man, Te Koroneho, ibid., p.151. Otoma pa is marked on the 1869 survey map of Matawhero 4, ML 549, DOSLI, Gisborne. Harris himself described his entire block as 'my Matawhero, or Otoma, land, opposite to Mr. Greenes, and since sold by my sons to Capt. Read': Poverty Bay Commission, p.225, MLC microfilm.

137 The deed (in Maori) (also translated into English) was signed at 'Matawiro Turanga' and was presented to the Old Land Claims' Commission in 1859, OLC 1355(b), OLC Series 4/21, NA. (The texts are printed in H. H. Turton, *Maori Deeds of Old Private Land Purchases in New Zealand*, 1882, pp.520–21.) The gift was made to Harris in trust for his half-Maori son, Henry, and the boundaries were roughly described in the deed. No price or 'consideration' was mentioned in the deed. This property was sold by the Harris family to Read for £60 on 26 October 1864. This deed of sale was produced by Read before the Poverty Bay Commission and is now in OLC 4/21, NA.

138 A similar story — that is, of Harris's payment for land by a foaling mare — but pertaining to Papawhariki, a block Harris purchased on the coast, may be found in Mackay, pp.100–1. The fruitfulness of the mare in this case made for a different outcome. But the narrative is patronising and it clearly indicates that a similar resentment had for a while developed around the transactions there. However, Rawiri Te Eke, Hirini Te Kani's father, who was one of the three signatories to the deed of sale for Papawhariki, was reported as saying that finally he had a better deal than Harris. The Papawhariki deed was drawn up in July 1840 and it stated that Harris and his two sons had already been living on the land for 18 months. It is reproduced (in English) in Turton, pp.519–20.

139 The Old Land Claims' Commissioner in 1859 investigated some early purchases in Poverty Bay known to be illegal but which the Europeans argued were 'gifts', or sales made when no 'recognized rule' existed. Most of these transactions were repudiated by their Maori owners, who indicated their intention to repossess them. Matawhero 4 consisted of two blocks of land, both of which had been transferred to Europeans in 1843. The date of first 'purchase', as recorded on the award of title for all of Matawhero 4, was 4 December 1843 (Award B-14, MA 62/1, NA). This date was a reference for half the block, the sale made to J. H. King, who was an early Poverty Bay settler. He resold the land and this claim was lodged by Read with the Old Land Claims' Commission in 1858 (OLC 1/1320(b), NA). This block was said to be 150 acres and the date of original sale, according to the deed, was actually 8 December 1843. The deed stated that the price paid was a mare. The other half of Matawhero 4 was the 'Te Toma' claim, which was based on the gift of October 1843. This claim had been lodged separately by Harris before the Old Land Claims' Commission (OLC 1355(b), OLC Series 4/21, NA). King had been a witness to this deed and Harris stated later that King had accompanied him when the Maori sellers first pointed out the boundaries of the land (27 July 1869, Poverty Bay Commission, p.226, MLC microfilm). These Maori sellers pointed out its boundaries again when this land was resold by Harris and his two sons to Read. In 1869, Hemi Pukekore stated clearly that a balance of payment was owing on the Otoma portion of the block, and that 'those who received no payment still assert their claim' to the disputed land: 26 July, ibid., p.216; Monro, Poverty Bay Notes, p.152.

140 From the whakapapa records, it is clear that Paratene Te Mate was not the same man as Paratene Pototi. See Whakapapa D (page 34). The two signatories were the same men who, in December 1843, sold the other portion of Matawhero 4 to King.

141 The two men who burnt U'ren's house were named by Edward Harris in 1859 as 'Renata' (Leonard) and 'Hapapa'. This information is insufficient to identify them. Harris said he believed they were acting on behalf of others. In 1869, his father named Te Kooti as being involved in this incident: E. F. Harris, 31 December 1859, OLC 1355(b), OLC Series 4/21, NA; J. W. Harris, 27 July 1869, Monro, Poverty Bay Notes, p.157.

142 H. Harris to J. W. Harris, 3 October 1864, OLC 1/1320, NA.

143 F. Dillon Bell, Memorandum to the governor, 24 February 1860, OLC 4/21, NA (*AJHR* 1862, E-1, pp.5–6). In 1872, the Land Claims' Commissioner affirmed that Harris's 'Te Toma' claim had not been awarded in 1859 because of the dispute over the payment. However, by then, the title had been formally granted by the Poverty Bay Commission to Read. W. S. Moorhouse to Monro, 6 February 1872, MA 62/5, NA.

144 General survey map of 'Matawhero at Poverty Bay . . . Claimed by Harata ReParata, me etahi atu' ('Harata, Riperata [Kahutia], and others'), dated 21 January 1867, ML 446, GM. This map was produced at the Poverty Bay Commission hearings in July 1869. Read stated in his evidence that he surveyed his block in the winter of 1866.

145 W. F. McDonall, surveyor, evidence given 3 August 1869, Matawhero 4, Poverty Bay Commission, p.292, MLC microfilm. McDonall's survey map of Matawhero 4 is dated 17 July 1869: ML 549, DOSLI, Gisborne. Read's methods of illicit fencing-in and, thereby, piecemeal land acquisition are

well described in Mackay, p.188. No doubt this was how the extra acres were added to Read's title, turning an estimated 300 acres into 319.

146 Paora Matuakore, evidence given in the Matawhero 1, 5, and 6 hearing: Monro, Poverty Bay Notes, p.177.

147 'Reduced Copy of Plan of Surveys' showing the runs and the location of settlers' houses at Matawhero, 1868, SO 6392, GM; Map of Poverty Bay showing the Matawhero settlers' houses in 1868, *AJHR* 1872, D-6; original Poverty Bay Grants Roll Plan, DOSLI, Gisborne; Turanganui Survey District map, 1884, GM; Parts of the Counties of Cook and Wairoa, map showing the block names, 1889, GM.

148 Lt-Col. W. Moule to Army Defence, 27 September 1871, AD1 71/1113, Army Defence Register 1871, NA. (Original letter not able to be traced.) It is doubtful whether the redoubt was on Read's land (which Moule assumed). It seems rather to have been on the neighbouring block (Matawhero 6), which was recognised as Maori land in 1869.

149 'Expedition to Turanganui, Poverty Bay', December 1868, William Newland, MSS 018, Taranaki Museum.

150 The Poverty Bay Commission worked on the principle that the land had been ceded to the government in December 1868 (see Chapter 6). The commission's appointed task was to confiscate some land under the October 1868 legislation, and to award Crown titles for the rest. It chose to award some titles to the European claimants. In March 1871, when the grants of title were being formally issued, the Land Claims' Commissioner queried the 'extraordinary state of things' whereby the Poverty Bay Commission had validated some illegal European purchases. There was a brief legal flurry, but the position quickly adopted by the Attorney-general was that the 1868 deed of cession had stated that the completion ('whakaotia') of some gifts or sales ('kia hoatu kia hokona ranei') to Europeans would be carried out, subject to the Poverty Bay Commission's verification of the claims. The Poverty Bay Grants Act of September 1869 had then made it lawful for the governor to execute these awards. The specific question of Otoma was raised in 1872, but by then the grant of title had been made. The entire procedure seems shonky, to say the least. The Maori text of the deed of cession, 18 December 1868, together with the 1871 correspondence concerning the legal basis of the grant of titles to Europeans, is to be found in MA 62/8, NA.

151 Petition from Turanga, *AJHR* 1867, G-1, p.12, CT. The names of the signatories were not published, but Richmond stated in his report on the petition to the Native Affairs committee that Rukupo was the first in order of the eight petitioners: Le1 1867/13, NA (*JHR* 1867, p.100).

152 To Emily Richmond, 24 April 1867, *The Richmond–Atkinson Papers*, ed. Guy H. Scholefield, 1960, II, p.241.

153 Evidence given 22 October 1878, Petition 291, Le1 1878/6, NA.

154 Richmond, Le1 1867/13, NA (*JHR* 1867, p.100). And, as the original covering letter to Rukupo's petition about the land also made clear, Mokena pressed for the confiscation of all Poverty Bay, expecting himself to benefit: 10 July 1867, George Graham Papers, MSS 90:22/1, AIM.

155 Orakai-a-Pu hearing, 12 July 1875, Gisborne Minute Book 2, pp.271–73, MLC microfilm. The Orakai-a-Pu pa was then jointly claimed by Paora Kate (as younger brother of Rukupo) and Tamihana Ruatapu, chief of Ngati Maru.

156 Le1 1867/13, NA (*JHR* 1867, p.100).

157 In 1878 an additional £300 had been ordered to be paid to silence the second petition, lodged by Wi Pere: Le1 1878/6, NA. A detailed report on the house's acquisition was prepared by Sir Robert de Z. Hall, 1980, 1983 (amended), GM. The accord was announced in May 1994: *Kia Hiwa Ra: National Maori Newspaper*, 19, p.17.

158 Harris to McLean, 22 November 1866, MSS 32:327, ATL.

159 S. Deighton to Agent General Napier, 18 October 1868, AD1 68/3589, NA (*AJHR* 1869, A-4A, pp.6–7).

160 Iraia Tamarara to Paora Te Apatu, 17 October 1868, MSS 32:692d, ATL.

161 *AS*, 18 April 1914.

162 Ibid. I have here accepted Porter's chronology (although it is not always correct). Helyar's letter of 29 October 1868 gives support (AD1 68/4128, NA). Porter also stated that the scriptural text which follows was taken directly from Te Kooti's notebook.

163 Te Waru's wife was Horiana Arawhita. Their son Tipene Te Waru had also joined Te Kooti in 1868, and he would play a major part in the attack on Turanga. The genealogical data have been established from evidence given by Te Ia Te Waru, July 1899, Wairoa Minute Book 11, p.4, MLC microfilm. I am indebted to Russell Hargreaves of Palmerston North for this reference.

164 W. Leonard Williams, Diary, 8 November 1868, AIM.

165 See Appendix A.

166 Diary, AIM.

167 Biggs to A. Tuke, 6 November 1868, MSS 1296, ATL.

168 W. Leonard Williams, Diary, 8 November 1868, AIM.

169 22 August 1868. This letter was written by Paora Matuakore, Wi Pere, Himiona Katipa and two other chiefs of Te Aitanga-a-Mahaki to 'Warana Pirihi', J. Wathan Preece. Preece was a son of the Anglican missionary James Preece, and was a licensed interpreter acting on behalf of Te Aitanga-a-Mahaki in an attempt to protect their lands. He had acted as a mediator for Māori with the government in other regions previously. This letter has been translated by three different people. Rongo Halbert's 1946 translation was used by Mackay, *Historic Poverty Bay*, p.244. This translation stated that the chiefs supported the return of the whakarau 'fully armed'. But, as Lyndsay Head has noted in her translation, the Maori text is 'kaua e tonoa nga pu kia tae mai', which reads 'do not order the guns to come here'. It was a request to avoid bringing troops to Turanga, so that the matter could be left to the law to decide. Halbert's translation is in Mackay Scrapbook, MSS 1006, Series 2:19, p.242, ATL; the original letter, together with translations by Heni Sunderland and Lyndsay Head, is in VF 993, Box 3, GM.

170 Paora Matuakore and 'all of us', to J. W. Preece, published in *DSC*, 20 November 1868. It is presumed that the published text was Preece's translation.

171 Biggs to McLean, 13 October 1868, MSS 32:162, ATL.

172 Pera Punahamua in W. Leonard Williams, Diary, 25 January 1869, AIM.

173 Biggs to McLean, 13 October 1868, MSS 32:162, ATL.

174 Biggs to A. Tuke, 6 November 1868, MSS 1296, ATL.

175 H. Strong (who lived near the Patutahi ford) in *PBH*, 9 February 1903, and in Cowan, *NZ Wars*, II, pp.538–39.

176 [Mair and Preece], 'Expeditions against Te Kooti', in Featon, *Waikato War*, p.178.

177 [F. J. W. Gascoyne], 'Record of Services at Poverty Bay', K. A. Webster Papers 2:16, MSS 1009, ATL.

178 Withers to Colonial Defence, enclosing Helyar's letter, 4 November 1868, AD1 68/3914, NA. Samuel Williams received the news from Taupo on 1 November and told J. C. Richmond (who was in Napier) the next day. However, it was assumed the expedition to Whataroa (which had left on 31 October) would discover whether or not Te Kooti had left Puketapu, so nothing was done. The expedition returned to Wairoa on 6 November, and the information it brought reached Turanga on 8 November, including the news that Te Kooti was on his way to Turanga. McLean had written immediately to inform the Colonial Defence Office (6 November, AD1 68/4001, NA), but he did not write to Biggs. A lengthy defence by Major E. L. Green (McLean's secretary) called 'Reasons for not communicating with the late Major Biggs, relative to the intended attack by Te Kooti on Poverty Bay', tries to pass the buck, MSS 32:21, ATL.

179 Biggs to McLean, 9 November 1868, MSS 32:162, ATL. Wyllie told McLean that the confiscations would have been settled at that meeting: 5 December 1868, MSS 32:660, ATL.

Chapter 5: And Joshua Fit the Battle of Jericho (November 1868–January 1869)

1 The letter was from Teira Marutu of Te Mahanga, just south of Whareongaonga, to the chiefs of Whakatohea, 19 August 1868, *AJHR* 1869, A-10, p.25; Biggs to McLean, 13 October 1868, MSS 32:162, ATL.

2 OS: 16 May 1982.

3 W. Leonard Williams to William Williams, 6 November 1867, MSS 69:56B, ATL.

4 The prisoners Aperahama Uetuku and Hori Puru jointly stated in June 1870 that it was fulfilled, and that the four men from Ngati Maru had gone there: MSS 32:25, ATL. However, Leonard Williams had earlier heard that Te Kooti had complained that Karepa and his Ngati Maru companions had not been living there as planned: Diary, 16 January 1869, AIM. One of Williams's informants was Pera Punahamua; Pera would be named as one of the four men by Aperahama and Hori. Their statement was aimed deliberately at incriminating those who were being treated as 'loyal' at Turanga and it may be suspect.

5 *AS*, 18 April 1914.

6 Evidence, 1, 3 July 1869, Repongaere hearings, Poverty Bay Commission, pp.20–24, MLC microfilm.

7 Account given to St John, 2 April 1870, *AJHR* 1870, A-8B, pp.26–27.

8 Evidence given by Maata Te Owai, 3 July 1869, Poverty Bay Commission, p.25, MLC microfilm.

9 E.g. Harris to McLean, citing Maata Te Owai's evidence, 18 August 1869, MSS 32:327, ATL.

10 The contested part of the block which Read had bought from Harris and his sons was described as 'the whole from Wilson's house to Otoma': Hemi Pukekore, evidence given 26 July 1869, Wainui 2, Poverty Bay Commission, p.216, MLC microfilm. Wilson's home had previously belonged to George Poulgrain.

11 Fowler Papers, Box 2:5, ATL.

12 Statement enclosed in Porter to Defence Minister, 3 June 1870, AD1 70/2780, NA.

13 *AS*, 18 April 1914. It was said at the time that the attacking party was only about 25: McLean to Richmond, 13 November 1868, *AJHR* 1869, A-4A, p.25.

14 I Chronicles 12:28. Account given by Te Waaka Puakanga in W. Leonard Williams, Diary, 12 December 1868, AIM.

15 *AS*, 18 April 1914. Peita Kotuku, who was with this particular kokiri, gave a very similar account. He did not, however, mention the presence of Te Kooti in the party: MSS 39:41A, ATL.

16 Peppard and Dodd claimed the entire 9900-acre Repongaere block as their 'run' in 1868 (survey map SO 6392, GM). This block was brought to the Poverty Bay Commission in 1869 and was then awarded to Te Aitanga-a-Mahaki and Te Whanau-a-Kai. But among those named as owners were Ngati Maru leaders: Tamihana Ruatapu was the first name in the list of owners. Rukupo and Paora Kate were also included.

17 Te Kooti also stated accurately that 30 Pakeha were killed: to Wiremu Kingi Te Kawau, 10 December 1868, W. G. Mair Letterbook 1868–69, MSS 1077, ML.

18 James Belich is vague and suggests 20 were killed initially, and another 20–40 in the next few days, making the numbers double those of the European deaths (*The New Zealand Wars*, 1986, p.228). The estimates of the number of Maori killed varied considerably because some who were thought to have been killed had, in fact, been taken prisoner. Westrup compiled a list of 20, one of whom (Te Waaka Puakanga) is now known not to have been killed. Westrup's list also included four children (n.d., MSS 32:21, ATL). Another list, compiled in June 1869, of Europeans and 'Friendly Natives' killed 'not in actual warfare' also cited the figure of 20 Maori killed 10–14 November at Poverty Bay (and 32 Europeans) (MSS 32:23, ATL). Leonard Williams, writing on 27 November 1868 from Poverty Bay, gave precisely accurate figures for the European deaths and stated that 13 Maori were killed initially and another eight subsequently, making a total of 21 (to Rev. C. C. Fenn, CN/097, CMS microfilm, AU). These figures for Maori are lower than generally given thereafter by historians (usually around 30), but the known evidence suggests 18 adults, including one chiefly woman, Harata, and four of her children, making a total of 22. There is no evidence for any higher figure.

19 Cadle's former business partner said that Harata had sold Cadle two acres at Tauparapara (Taoparapara) in about February 1868 for £10: A. Blair to Poverty Bay Commission, 25 February 1869, attached to Tauparapara 1, Award of title (A-70), MA 62/2, NA. However, the title was awarded, without any discussion by the commission or any objections being offered, to Ngati Kaipoho. One of the four owners listed in the award of title in 1869 was Harata's surviving son, Hirini Taketake.

20 The Patutahi block was over 50,000 acres. One part of it, Kaimoe, was twice brought to the Native Land Court by Tutere (in July 1867 and in March 1868), but on both occasions the court was adjourned without a settlement. The first adjournment was due to the legal confusions and the second because of McLean's determination to get some land ceded before the court began to establish titles. Tamihana Ruatapu was a claimant in this block, as was Paora Parau, Ihimaera Hokopu (whom Te Kooti would also execute) and several others. Then the entire block was confiscated, still unsurveyed, in 1869; the co-operating chiefs lost everything, as well as those who had already been dispossessed by the law. (Confiscated block C-2, MA 62/1, and map MA 62/9, NA; Kaimoe block, Poverty Bay Commission, pp.2–4, MLC microfilm, and Monro, Poverty Bay Notes, pp.8–9; Wi Pere, evidence given 1 November 1882, *AJHR* 1884, Sess. II, G-4, p.19.) The connection with Te Kooti is made in Mackay Scrapbook, MSS 1006, Series 2:19, pp.222, 361, ATL.

21 Sworn statement, 10 February 1871, AGG HB1/5, NA. Renata was seized at Wairoa in March 1871 and sent to Napier for trial. He was committed to prison for 'rebellion', but was released in the amnesty for Maori political prisoners, proclaimed by the governor in March 1873: Cumming to Ormond, 21 April 1871, AGG HB1/6, NA; Lambert, p.549.

22 Te Kooti and Komene to McLean, 6 June 1866, HB4/13, NA.

23 Pera Taihuka was a son of Pehimana Taihuka. His father and two of his younger brothers were whakarau; he was clearly being singled out. Maria's account implies that Pera was one who, along with Ihimaera Hokopu, had named Te Kooti as supplying ammunition to the Pai Marire at Waerenga-a-Hika. In retaliation (as it would seem), Te Kooti named Pera. Ihimaera was also killed: see p.126.

24 Morris, sworn statement, 27 December 1889, *Goodall versus Te Kooti*, p.29, CL 19, NA.

25 Morris, p.[23], MSS 2296, ATL.

26 In 1869, Wi Tamararo was charged with the murder of Pera (and initially also of Piripi and Tutere, suggesting that he was being made a scapegoat, although the last two charges were subsequently dropped). According to Maata Te Owai, Wi joined Te Kooti when Te Kooti wrote to him on his return from Wharekauri. He pleaded not guilty, saying he had never touched any of them, but was sentenced to death for Pera's execution. This sentence was clearly intended to deter others from joining the whakarau. Wi tragically committed suicide in prison on 29 September 1869; a cast of his head was taken after death and publicly displayed in Wellington: *WI*, 7 October 1869.

27 Morris, p.[24], MSS 2296, ATL. The scriptural text is, again, Psalm 63:10.
28 W. Leonard Williams, Diary, 19 July 1868, AIM.
29 Morris, p.[26], MSS 2296, ATL.
30 Goldsmith owned the 17-acre block Huiatoa, which had been a gift in trust for his half-Maori children. Its south-western boundary was in dispute. He had extended this boundary by purchase from Mokena, who did not have the authority to sell the land: evidence from Te Koru hearing, Poverty Bay Commission, pp.156–57, MLC microfilm; Monro, Poverty Bay Notes, p.117. This disputed area is clearly marked on the original survey map of 1868: Te Koru, ML 462, DOSLI, Gisborne. The extremely ambiguous original deed of gift is dated 29 August 1854: it indicates that only two of the owners listed had consented to the gift. One was Renata Ngarangi who, it can be presumed, with Mokena later sold Goldsmith the old river bed. The deed of gift was presented to the Old Land Claims' Commission in 1859; the two donors upheld it at the time. It is reproduced, in Maori and English, in Turton, p.521. The title to Huiatoa was awarded to Goldsmith's son Robert (Rapata) in 1869, but the old river bed was not included.
31 W. Leonard Williams to McLean, 15 November 1868, MSS 32:22, ATL.
32 Riria Kaimare, one of the whakarau, *WI*, 21 September 1869, and Maata Te Owai, *WI*, 28 June 1870; cf. Peita Kotuku, who remembered that he got his first rifle from the ten captured at the Paparatu camp, MSS Papers 39:41A, ATL.
33 Ecclesiastes 9:12; 8:5. The source for the burning of watches is *DSC*, 23 December 1868. Nevertheless, Te Kooti himself had a watch and used it in 1870, and he also hid watches with other precious items, like rifles and notebooks, in caches during the war years.
34 Exodus 20:24.
35 Her estimate of Wetini's age makes him a little younger than the age given at his death in October 1928, 68 years.
36 W. Leonard Williams, Diary, 9 December 1868, AIM.
37 Hoera Kapuaroa, 1 July 1869, Poverty Bay Commission, p.21, MLC microfilm.
38 W. Leonard Williams, Diary, 8 December 1868, AIM.
39 Account given to W. G. Mair, 7 December 1868, MSS 1077, p.66, ML (*AJHR* 1869, A-10, p.30).
40 Hoera Kapuaroa, 1 July 1869, Poverty Bay Commission, p.21, MLC microfilm.
41 Even though Himiona had been one of the signatories (with Wi Pere) of the letter sent in August protesting about the government's pursuit of the whakarau, quoted in the previous chapter. He had, however, tried to co-operate with the government in its land schemes.
42 MSS 1077, pp.73–74, ML (*AJHR* 1869, A-10, p.31).
43 Morris, p.[34], MSS 2296, ATL; Maata Te Owai, 3 July 1869, Poverty Bay Commission, p.27, MLC microfilm.
44 Evidence of Aperahama Kouka, 1 July 1869, ibid., p.18.
45 Hoera Kapuaroa, 1 July 1869, ibid., p.21; *ECHR*, p.62.
46 Westrup to McLean, 15 November 1868, MSS 32:630, ATL.
47 Mere Kingi Paraone, who was herself taken prisoner at Oweta, *PBH*, 15 May 1937.
48 Nihoniho, p.36.
49 He escaped from Te Kooti in December. Waaka had been included in the lists of those shot at Oweta, and in previous writings the author incorrectly accepted those lists.
50 Sworn testimony, *WI*, 30 June 1870. Several other witnesses at the 1870 trials of Te Kooti's followers stated that he had been given powder at Oweta, but by whom, of course, is where the discrepancies lie.
51 Rukupo, 5 July 1869, Poverty Bay Commission, p.44, MLC microfilm.
52 5 July 1869, ibid.
53 James Hawthorne, *A Dark Chapter from New Zealand History*, 1869, p.15.
54 For the watch as a 'whakapatipati': Wiremu Kingi Te Paia, *AJHR* 1870, A-8B, p.26. This complex history of gift exchange continued: Rukupo then gave the watch and sword given to him by Te Kooti to Karepa, son of Tamihana Ruatapu (W. Leonard Williams, Diary, 19 November 1868, AIM). In turn, the watch was sent back to Robert Goldsmith in 'payment' for his wife, Karepa's daughter, who had gone with her father when he was taken prisoner: *GBPP*, Facsimile Vol. 15, p.303 (from *HBH*, 21 November 1868).
55 *AJHR* 1870, A-8B, p.26.
56 Evidence given by Katerina Kapapaki (Papaki), 1 July 1869, Poverty Bay Commission, p.18, MLC microfilm.
57 Ibid., pp.14, 20–21, 44. Also W. Leonard Williams, Diary, 3 July 1869, MSS, ATL; Harris to McLean, 18 August 1869, MSS 32:327, ATL.
58 Morris, p.[36], MSS 2296, ATL.
59 Gudgeon, *Reminiscences*, p.236.

60 Diary, 3 July 1869, MSS, ATL.

61 *EP*, 21 September 1869.

62 Editorial, *WI*, 2 October 1869.

63 *DSC*, 16 November 1868.

64 At the beginning of his diary he wrote, 'Maehe 14. 1868 Ko te marama tenei i whanau ai te tamaiti a Hana' ('March 14. 1868 This is the month in which Hana's child was born'), MSS 3091, ATL. There is no other entry on this page: it stands by itself as a proud statement. The doctor's monthly list of births to the prisoners for March 1868 recorded only one: 15 March, a son to the wife of Ratima Te Ami, AD 31:16, NA.

65 OS: Putiputi Onekawa, who was thus first named, 8 May 1984.

66 Statement made by Huhana Tamati, 5 August 1870, AD1 70/2668, NA. She was the widow of Meihana Te Whana, of Te Aitanga-a-Mahaki, one of the whakarau who had died on Wharekauri (List of Wharekauri prisoners killed and at large, n.d., AD 31:15, NA; W. S. Atkinson to Richmond, 9 February 1869, *AJHR* 1869, A-10, p.32).

67 *WI*, 30 June 1870.

68 W. S. Atkinson to Richmond, 9 February 1869, *AJHR* 1869, A-10, p.32.

69 Nepia Tokitahi was of Ngati Tu (Te Whanau-a-Tu) of inland Hawke's Bay, and had been captured at Omarunui. See also Chapter 6, n.43.

70 Morris, p.[30], MSS 2296, ATL.

71 *WI*, 23 September 1869.

72 Supplement, 2 October 1869.

73 To McLean, 22 November 1868, MSS 32:692f, ATL.

74 Morris, p.[33], MSS 2296, ATL.

75 OS: Heni Sunderland, 26 January 1983.

76 Taihuka, obituary October 1927, Mackay Scrapbook, MSS 1006, Series 2:19, p.369, ATL.

77 For example, he said this when he first came to the King Country in 1869: W. Searancke to Native Minister, 23 July 1869, *AJHR* 1869, A-10, p.91. G. Worgan's memo to McLean, n.d. [July 1869], also makes this point forcibly: MSS 32:25, ATL.

78 'Te Kooti and Mr. Mackay', Shortland MSS K, p.79, HL.

79 S. Locke to Richmond, 10 February 1869, Locke Letterbook, HBM (*AJHR* 1869, A-10, p.34).

80 Withers to Colonial Defence, 4, 10 November 1868, AD1 68/3914, 68/4128, NA. Also, St George, Diary, 9 November 1868, MSS, ATL.

81 St George (at Taupo) to McLean, 29 November 1868, MSS 32:21; McLean to Colonial Defence Office, 16 December 1868, AD1 68/4934, NA.

82 Joshua 6–8.

83 W. Leonard Williams, Diary, 24 November 1868, AIM.

84 Te Kooti called it 'Ngatapa wahi o Turanga' in a letter written from there on 10 December, MSS 1077, p.92, ML.

85 Westrup to McLean, 25 November 1868, AD1 68/4757, NA.

86 Information from Wi Pere, Maria Morris and others who escaped at Te Karetu, report of 30 November 1868, in *DSC*, 9 December 1868.

87 Diary, 25 November 1868, AIM.

88 Westrup to McLean, 25 November 1868, AD1 68/4302, NA (*AJHR* 1869, A-4A, p.16).

89 Pera Punahamua told W. Leonard Williams it was a party of 23, Diary, 25 January 1869, AIM; Westrup also reported privately to McLean that it was a party of only 20 mounted men, 27 November 1868, MSS 32:630. This estimate is more or less consistent with the information given on Te Kooti's preferred size for a kokiri (22).

90 The eight kegs were also reported as 9000 rounds of ammunition in G. Burton to Lambert, 1 December 1868, MSS 32:22, ATL. But W. Leonard Williams had written to McLean, on 28 November, saying that he understood it was more like 20–21 kegs of ammunition that had been taken, or nearly three times as much. He also estimated the raiding party at between 30 and 40 men: MSS 32:22, ATL.

91 Printed panui (circular) from Tawhiao, 29 January 1868, quoted in *DSC*, 28 December 1868; Tawhiao, panui dated 12 September 1868 [?1867], *AJHR* 1869, A-10, pp.24–25. This panui was being extensively debated in Hawke's Bay in September 1868, where a copy came into the hands of the resident magistrate. Also the King's panui taken to the governor in Wellington by Rapihana Otaota, 29 December 1868, *GBPP*, Vol. 15, pp.335–36.

92 In W. G. Mair, 7 December 1868, MSS 1077, p.72, ML (*AJHR* 1869, A-10, p.30).

93 Morris, p.[39], MSS 2296, ATL.

94 Richmond to Haultain, 5 December 1868, AD1 68/4634, NA.

95 Account written by Hukanui Watene, who fought for Te Kooti at Te Karetu, 13 August 1913, Elsdon Best, Maori Notes I, pp.102–3, MONZ; Porter, *AS*, 2 May 1914. Lambert disputed this story (p.554

n.19), but it is quite clear from the military letters that Nama was only wounded when he was captured. W. G. Mair referred to the belief that Nama had been threatened by Te Kooti 'but was received into favour by planning the death of Karaitiana and party': to Pollen, 28 December 1869, 69/50, AGG A1/4, NA.

96 Westrup to McLean, 4 December 1868, MSS 32:24, ATL.

97 Statement by Wi Tamararo, who fought at Nga Tapa for Te Kooti, 25 February 1869, MSS 32:23, ATL.

98 Hawthorne, p.32.

99 Information from a prisoner, W. Leonard Williams to McLean, 4 December 1868, MSS 32:22; Westrup to McLean, 4 December 1868, MSS 32:630, ATL.

100 Peita Kotuku, 23 February 1921, MSS 39:41A, ATL.

101 Richmond to Haultain, 8 December 1868, AD1 68/4711, NA.

102 [St John], [6 January 1869], Account of the siege of Nga Tapa, Whitmore MSS, Box D:5, HBM.

103 When Ropata made his first attack there were only rifle pits on the slope below the old pa (Unsigned report [Preece to McLean], 24 June 1869, MSS 32:23, ATL). St John watched the construction of the two great breastworks from Fort Richmond, on a ridge about one and a half miles away, but, as his view foreshortened the breastworks, his report is slightly misleading, for he placed the 'first line of defence' as being just in front of the 'large whare' (30 December 1868, Whitmore MSS, Box D:5, HBM). I am indebted to Kevin Jones, archaeologist, Department of Conservation, Wellington, for his analysis of the pa fortifications both from aerial photographs and on the ground. I would also like to express my gratitude to Major Chris Pugsley, who explored the pa with us both in November 1991 and analysed the strategies of both the siege party and the besieged with astuteness.

104 St John, 30 December 1868, Whitmore MSS, Box D:5, HBM.

105 St John, 27 December 1868, ibid.

106 Hawthorne, p.32.

107 Belich, *NZ Wars*, pp.231–33, is incorrect in his account of the fighting, for Te Karetu fell on 2 December (not 5 December); Ropata began his assault on Nga Tapa on 4 December and retreated the next day.

108 Richmond to Haultain, 5 December 1868, AD1 68/4635, and 8 December 1868, AD1 68/4711, NA.

109 Ibid.

110 McLean to Haultain, 8 December 1868, AD1 68/4748, NA. A different account, from Paora Parau, said that 30 guns, all in serviceable condition, had been recovered: W. Leonard Williams, Diary, 7 December 1868, AIM.

111 Fifty bodies were found before the first assault on Nga Tapa and seven (or ten) were killed then. The various estimates were all higher: both Preece and Gascoyne (then sub-inspector of the Armed Constabulary) suggested 'about sixty-five'. Richmond to Haultain, 8 December 1868, AD1 68/4711, NA; W. Leonard Williams, Diary, 5, 7 December 1868, AIM; Preece to Richmond, 11 December 1868, *AJHR* 1869, A-4A, p.18; Gascoyne, report, 11 December 1868, *AJHR* 1869, A-3, p.14.

112 W. Leonard Williams, Diary, 7 December 1868, AIM.

113 [G. Mair and Preece], 'Expeditions against Te Kooti', in Featon, *Waikato War*, p.191. This man could, in fact, be Komene; there appears to be no other contemporary reference to Rihari (Richard).

114 Richmond to Haultain, 8 December 1868, AD1 68/4711, NA.

115 Richmond to Haultain, 12 December 1868, AD1 68/4849, NA; W. Leonard Williams, Diary, 12 December 1868, AIM.

116 Information from a prisoner reported by Westrup to McLean, 4 December, enclosure in McLean to Haultain, 8 December 1868, AD1 68/4785, NA. When Ngati Kahungunu went to Puketapu at the end of December, they realised it had not been occupied for at least two or three months: S. Deighton reporting on this expedition to McLean, 1 January 1869 [*sic* 1868], MSS 32:24, ATL; W. Leonard Williams, Diary, 5 January 1869, AIM.

117 The text here reads 'whiangia' ('deceive'), but W. G. Mair's translation, 'spare', suggests that he made a transcript error in copying the letter.

118 Te Kooti Te Turuki, in W. G. Mair, MSS 1077, pp.92–94, ML. Trans: Mair. (The top copy is in 69/50, AGG A1/4, NA.)

119 In W. G. Mair, MSS 1077, pp.96–98, ML. Trans: Mair. Hori Te Aunoanoa joined Te Kooti and was taken prisoner in March 1870.

120 Te Kooti Te Turuki to Karanama (envelope dated 25 December 1868), MSS 32:692l, ATL. This letter had been placed for Karanama at Pokimi and was found by Samuel Deighton and the Ngati Kahungunu troops, who brought it to Napier where it was, as the envelope says, 'left with Mr Grindle' (James Grindell) for translation: Deighton to McLean, 1 January 1869 [*sic* 1868], MSS 32:24, ATL; W. Leonard Williams, Diary, 5 January 1869, AIM.

121   Richmond to McLean, 20 December 1868, MSS 32:534; Harris to McLean, 17 February, 18 August 1869, MSS 32:327, ATL.

122   Richmond to Haultain, 19 December 1868, enclosing report of 16 December, AD1 68/5014, NA.

123   Ibid. Richmond specifically mentioned the presence of Te Kooti's 'wife & child' (to McLean, 16 December 1868, MSS 32:534); W. Leonard Williams discussed Waaka Puakanga, Diary, 12 December 1868, AIM.

124   Whitmore to Haultain, 18 December 1868, *AJHR* 1869, A-3, p.15.

125   W. Leonard Williams, Diary, 8 December 1868, AIM.

126   Whitmore to Haultain, 18 December 1868, *AJHR* 1869, A-3, p.15. James Belich entirely overlooks this critical aspect of the campaign. Whitmore, rather than concentrating on the East Coast, as Belich has argued (*NZ Wars*, pp.258–59), was planning to leave.

127   Whitmore to Haultain, 19 December 1868, AD1 68/5016, NA.

128   Te Kooti Te Turuki, n.d., MSS 32:692l, ATL. The entire letter is reproduced in Greenwood, 'Iconography of Te Kooti Rikirangi', and roughly translated, p.12.

129   Aperahama Tutoko appears on the undated list of 'Wharekauri prisoners at large', AD 31:15, NA. However, he does not seem to be included (under that name) on any of the lists of prisoners sent to Wharekauri. He was held for a while at Napier in 1866 during an inquiry into his role in the killing of Volkner.

130   Hira and others, Waioeka, to Whakatohea. Trans: W. G. Mair, 69/50, AGG A1/4, NA. (No Maori original.)

131   Wiremu Kingi to W. G. Mair, 6 January 1869, 69/66, AGG A1/4, NA.

132   W. Leonard Williams, Diary, 12 December 1868, AIM.

133   Ibid.

134   Pera Punahamua escaped after Te Karetu: W. Leonard Williams, Diary, 16 January 1869, AIM.

135   Wilson MSS, p.141. The version in Lucky Tutua's MSS book has, more precisely, 'Ko nga tangata o te pa' ('The people of the pa'), instead of 'Ko nga tamariki katoa o te pae' ('The children of the region'), Davis Dossier, Vol. 3, ATL.

136   Kempthorne's chronology in his journal of the siege seems to be correct, and it has been adopted here. St John's account, which Whitmore used for his own report, states that the attack was begun on 31 December 1868, and all subsequent accounts have followed this. However, St John loses track of the dates, and he ends the siege one day too early. St John's and Kempthorne's chronologies were out of step by one day in the prelude to the siege as well, but William Newland's account (MSS 018, Taranaki Museum) supports Kempthorne for the later start of the expedition.

137   Kempthorne, 'Journal of the capture of Ngatapa', in MSS 69:49, ATL. St John said there were 702 men, all of whom marched to the pa on 31 December (Whitmore MSS, Box D:5, HBM); he estimated Ngati Porou at about 370 (ibid., Box B:15).

138   31 December 1868, Whitmore MSS, Box D:5, HBM.

139   Newland, 'Expedition to Turanganui', MSS 018, Taranaki Museum.

140   Kempthorne, Journal, 3 January 1869, MSS 69:49, ATL.

141   St John, 2 January 1869, Whitmore MSS, Box D:5, HBM.

142   Ibid., [5 January 1869].

143   MSS 69:49, ATL.

144   Ibid.

145   St John, [6 January 1869], Whitmore MSS, Box D:5, HBM.

146   Whitmore to Haultain, 30 December 1868, *AJHR* 1869, A-3, p.16.

147   Interview, 23 February 1921, MSS 39:41A, ATL.

148   Ibid.

149   Richmond to Colonial Defence Office, 20 December 1868, AD1 68/5057, NA.

150   St John, [6 January 1869], Whitmore MSS, Box D:5, HBM.

151   J. P. Ward, who was with No. 6 division of the Armed Constabulary at Nga Tapa, in Mackay Scrapbook, MSS 1006/2:19, p.387, ATL. William C. Tomkinson, who was with No. 3 division, also wrote, 'we . . . shot all the prisoners' (to his sister, 7 April 1869, MSS 1270, AIM). See also Porter, who was with Ngati Porou, *AS*, 2 May 1914.

152   To Robert Mair, 12 February 1869, MSS 93:4, ATL.

153   Richmond to McLean, 6 January 1869, MSS 32:534, ATL. The official figures of 'enemy losses', as collated by St John, differ somewhat: 136 killed; 22 males taken prisoner; 135 women and children taken prisoner. He added it was known that more men were killed but not reported to have been so (Whitmore Papers, Box B:15, HBM). Trooper Tomkinson told his sister that they had killed about 200 'rebels': 7 April 1869, MSS 1270, AIM.

154   1 August 1888, *PD*, LXII, pp.338, 345.

155   OS: Arnold Butterworth, former police constable at Gisborne, 19 May 1982. Butterworth joined the police in 1911: he saw five skulls, shot in the back of the neck or head, dredged from the river near the

Armed Constabulary base on Childers Road (now the police station). They were men shot at Nga Tapa, he stated.

156 W. Leonard Williams, Diary, 13 January 1869, AIM.

157 Kempthorne, Journal, [6 January 1869], MSS 69:49, ATL.

158 W. Leonard Williams, n.d., MSS 69:49, ATL. See also Appendix A.

159 Ibid. There is no Maori text given.

160 William Atkinson transcript, MSS 1187:12; trans: based on A. S. Atkinson, *Nelson Examiner*, 5 May 1869, MSS 1187:99, ATL.

161 William Atkinson, MSS 1187:12, ATL.

162 Daniel 5:25–26.

163 Biddle MSS, I, p.155; Lemuel MSS, p.31.

164 OS: 15 February 1982.

165 The book of Daniel is one of the later Jewish texts, which uses the Babylonian captivity as a setting for appeals against subsequent oppression. It was therefore being used in precisely the way that the text was originally created.

166 Maata Te Owai, sworn testimony, *WI*, 28 June 1870.

167 7 January 1869, MSS 69:49, ATL.

168 6 January 1869, ibid.

169 Hare Tauamanaia, who was one of them, said that at least 55 men got away, with 40 rifles: W. Leonard Williams, Diary, 20 January 1869, AIM.

170 H. T. Clarke to Native Department, 18 April 1870, *AJHR* 1870, A-8B, p.31.

171 *AJHR* 1870, A-8B, p.26. Also Karepa's account, in W. Leonard Williams, Diary, 8 February 1869, AIM.

172 OS: Ned Brown, 14 February 1982; Tihei Algie, 17 May 1982.

173 OS: 14 February 1982.

174 OS: Taua McLean, Rotorua, 20 December 1981.

175 Richmond to Haultain, 19 December 1868, AD1 68/5014, NA. Thomas Porter made the interesting observation that Te Kooti rode Captain Wilson's horse (taken at Paparatu) in the November attack on Turanga: *AS*, 18 April 1914.

176 Whitmore to Haultain, 18 December 1868, *AJHR* 1869, A-3, p.15.

177 Revelation 19:11–13.

Chapter 6: Covenants and a King (January–August 1869)

1 Waiata 8 and 12, MSS C-35, AU. Trans: based on Frank Davis.

2 Karepa's account given to W. S. Atkinson, 8 February 1869, in Atkinson to Richmond, 9 February 1869, *AJHR* 1869, A-10, p.31.

3 *AS*, 9 May 1914.

4 *AJHR* 1870, A-8B, p.27.

5 W. G. Mair to Pollen, 30 January 1869, MSS 1077, p.105, ML.

6 W. G. Mair to J. A. Wilson, 20 February 1869, MSS 1077, p.126, ML; Mair to W. S. Atkinson, 3 March 1869, *AJHR* 1869, A-10, p.32. Anaru was reported as passing through Taupo on his way to find Te Kooti at the end of January, W. Leonard Williams, Diary, 2–3 February 1869, AIM.

7 Wiremu Kingi Te Paia, *AJHR* 1870, A-8B, p.27.

8 These prisoners were taken at Maraetahi in March 1870. Porter published the account originally in the *Hawke's Bay Herald* in 1871 and quoted this at length in his serialised history, *AS*, 9 May 1914. A slightly fuller version (probably from the *Otago Daily Times*) is in Flotsam & Jetsam, X, p.130, HL, while yet another variant version is in the *Press*, 20 November 1871.

9 Psalm 32:7; Psalm 34:19.

10 Lemuel MSS, p.32; Biddle MSS, I, p.10.

11 Notebook, p.64, HBM.

12 Ned Brown, annotation in Wilson MSS, p.140.

13 Wilson MSS, p.140; Lucky Tutua MSS, Davis Dossier, Vol. 3. In Biddle MSS, I, p.138 the same reference is given for the nearby mountain, Puketapu.

14 I Samuel 15:6–8.

15 OS: Boy Biddle, 28 January 1983.

16 Maori text with 274 signatures, MA 62/8; English text, MA 62/9, NA.

17 This whole muddled process was discussed by the 1920 Native Lands Commission in its inquiry into the confiscated blocks of Poverty Bay, *AJHR* 1921–22, G-5, pp.15–17. Of course the Crown did not adjudicate all Poverty Bay titles at this time and Te Kooti would be included as a shareholder in some blocks that were determined later. See Chapter 12.

18 OS: Boy Biddle commenting on this text, 15 October 1987.

19 Biddle MSS, I, p.28. Wilson MSS, p.142 dates the text as 18 February. It is slightly more expansive in its third part but the sense is identical. The covenant is stated to be the Covenant of Jehovah.

20 Biddle MSS, I, p.28.

21 Hira Te Popo to Wepiha Apanui, 22 February 1869, MSS 1077, p.133, ML (*AJHR* 1869, A-10, pp.14–15).

22 Rakuraku (at Whakarae) to Wepiha Apanui, 26 February 1869, MSS 1077, p.134, ML (*AJHR* 1869, A-10, p.15).

23 They were seen in the attack on Rauporoa pa on 9 March: W. G. Mair to Clarke, 23 March 1869, *AJHR* 1869, A-3, p.38.

24 'Confiscated Native Lands', *AJHR* 1928, G-7, p.27; Wiri (op. cit.) re-establishes the connection of Ngati Ruapani of Poverty Bay and Waikaremoana with Tuhoe, along with the processes of their dispossession and their historical suppression: pp.100, 169–70, 217–24.

25 W. G. Mair to A. S. Atkinson, 3 March 1869, *AJHR* 1869, A-10, p.32; see also statement by Pauro [Paoro Te Amohau], Whakatane policeman, G. Mair, 5 March 1869, AD1 69/2609, NA. This rarely used full form of Tamaikoha's name comes from Te Keepa Te Rangihiwinui's report of 1870: AD1 70/2757, NA.

26 To McLean, 25 March 1869, MSS 32:693c, ATL.

27 Biddle MSS, I, p.173.

28 OS: Eruera Manuera, Te Teko, 25 May 1981; Boy Biddle, 29 January 1983.

29 Akuhata Te Kaha, 6 May 1897, Whakatane Minute Book 5, p.190, MLC microfilm.

30 OS: Horo Tatu, Tataiahape, 27 January 1978. Trans: based on Rangi Motu.

31 W. G. Mair to Clarke, 23 March 1869, *AJHR* 1869, A-3, p.36.

32 W. G. Mair to Wilson, 5 March 1869, MSS 1077, p.139, ML (*AJHR* 1869, A-10, p.15); extract from *Daily Southern Cross*, GBPP, Vol. 15, p.387.

33 To McLean, 9 March 1869, MSS 32:23, ATL.

34 GBPP, Vol. 15, p.387.

35 The island had been returned to Te Upokorehe by the government in 1867. This decision would be confirmed in 1872. Tuhoe would be given no lands at all.

36 Richmond set £500 in January; by March it had doubled: W. G. Mair to W. S. Atkinson, 3 March 1869, *AJHR* 1869, A-10, p.32.

37 W. G. Mair to Clarke, 23 March 1869, *AJHR* 1869, A-3, p.36.

38 Ibid.

39 Extract from *Daily Southern Cross*, GBPP, Vol. 15, p.388.

40 Mair to Clarke, 23 March 1869, *AJHR* 1869, A-3, p.37.

41 Ibid. This account is supported by statements made by three male prisoners who escaped from Ahikereru on 24 March. They made it clear that Te Kooti was with the party which went up the Rangitaiki river 14–19 March: *AJHR* 1869, A-10, pp.18–20.

42 St George, Diary, 24 March 1869, MSS, ATL; information from the three prisoners who escaped from Ahikereru, St George to Clarke, 26 March 1869, *AJHR* 1869, A-10, p.19.

43 Nepia Tokitahi of Ngati Tu had been sent with the fourth batch of prisoners to Wharekauri, and was still with Te Kooti after their escape from Nga Tapa. He died on 29 January 1888.

44 From Te Harema. The letter was intercepted at Taupo at the end of March: St George, Diary, 30 March 1869, MSS, ATL.

45 MSS 32:693c, ATL.

46 From Te Reneti, Tahau and others, ibid.

47 Account given by Tamati, a prisoner who escaped from Ahikereru, to G. Mair, 26 March 1869, *AJHR* 1869, A-10, p.20.

48 St George to McLean, 8 April 1869, MSS 32:557, ATL.

49 St George, Diary, 25 March 1869, MSS, ATL. By the time one of the prisoners, Tamati, had reached G. Mair, the number of skilled fighters had doubled: Tamati's report in Mair to Clarke, 26 March 1869, *AJHR* 1869, A-10, p.20. Tamati (himself from Ngati Porou) had been taken prisoner originally by the Ngati Porou party who joined Te Kooti at Waioeka.

50 *AS*, 9 May 1914.

51 Lambert, pp.612–13.

52 The map in Cowan, *NZ Wars*, II, p.326 is completely misleading, as are a number of his map reconstructions.

53 Diary, 14 January 1870, MSS, ATL.

54 This is clear in both versions told by Porter from Maori sources, *AS*, 16 May 1914; also Mere Scott, who was present at Mohaka, interview in Lambert, p.626.

55 Anne, wife of Nikora, who was present with Te Kooti at Mohaka: in E. Tuke, Report, 10 November 1869, *AJHR* 1870, A-16, p.28.
56 Rowley (George) Hill, who was among the party which fought its way into Hiruharama, account given to Ted Nepia in 1926, Te Reo o Te Maori, Radio NZ, 16 February 1972; Cowan, *NZ Wars*, II, p.329.
57 23 February 1921, MSS 39:41A, ATL.
58 G. Mair to Clarke, 26 March 1869, *AJHR* 1869, A-10, p.20.
59 See James Belich on 'Dutch' courage, 'War', *The Future of the Past: Themes in New Zealand History*, ed. C. Davis and P. Lineham, 1991, p.124.
60 Withers to Haultain, 14 April 1869, *AJHR* 1869, A-3C, p.10.
61 Whitmore to Defence Minister, 23 April 1869, *AJHR* 1869, A-3, p.44.
62 Eruera Manuera of Te Teko, 12 October 1978, recorded in Davis Dossier, Vol. 9, ATL.
63 Greenwood, *Upraised Hand*, p.71.
64 Biddle MSS, I, p.11. There are variant texts, particularly in the critical phrase 'me mate Hau-aitu'. All emphasise the insignificance of the manner of his death; thus Tawehi Wilson's text has 'me mate hauiti noa' ('natural death') (MSS, p.141). 'Hau-aitua', accidental death, is another variant.
65 OS: 14 December 1981.
66 Biddle MSS, I, p.11.
67 Whitmore to Haultain, 18 May 1869, *AJHR* 1869, A-3, p.48.
68 Whitmore to Colonial Defence Office, 11 May 1869, AD1 69/2913, NA.
69 Clarke to Native Department, 1 June 1869, *AJHR* 1869, A-10, p.65.
70 To Haultain, 18 May 1869, *AJHR* 1869, A-3, p.50.
71 *AJHR* 1870, A-8B, p.27.
72 George S. Whitmore, *The Last Maori War in New Zealand*, 1902, pp.165–66.
73 *WI*, 26 August 1869.
74 Gilbert Mair, Diary, 11 May 1869, MSS 92:43, ATL.
75 OS: Boy Biddle, 6 July 1993.
76 Evidence given 10 November 1890, Heruiwi No. 4, Whakatane Minute Book 3, pp.118–19, MLC microfilm. Peraniko was sent to Wharekauri with the fifth group of prisoners.
77 When Gilbert Mair transcribed the letter into his 1869 field diary, in his translation he glossed this date as being intended for 6 June: MSS 92:43, ATL.
78 St George, whose translation is adopted here, wrote 'to cruel'; Gilbert Mair chose, 'This therefore was the strength of my cruelty'. More literally it reads, 'prevailed upon to come [and do that]'.
79 St George, Diary, 10 June 1869, MSS, ATL. Trans: St George. As well as Mair's additional transcript (referred to above), there is a further good copy in AGG HB2/1, NA.
80 Locke to McLean, 14 June 1869, MSS 32:393, ATL.
81 St George, Diary, 25 March 1869, MSS, ATL.
82 Ibid., 12 April 1869.
83 Poihipi Tukairangi to James Grindell, 25 April 1869, AGG HB1/1, NA.
84 St George, Diary, 4 May 1869, MSS, ATL.
85 Thomas Hallett, who found the bodies at Opepe, account written 17 January 1893, MSS ZA 155, ML.
86 Diary, 9 November 1868, MSS, ATL. Paora Hapi and his people would also be given 500 acres from the confiscated land of Ngati Hineuru at Te Haroto in 1870.
87 Te Poihipi to St George, July 1869, original letter inserted in St George's Diary, MSS, ATL.
88 Proceedings of the Committee held at Oruanui, Taupo, 12 December 1868, St George, Diary.
89 Ibid., 20, 22 May 1869.
90 Henry Russell to Haultain, 14 June 1869, *AJHR* 1869, A-3, p.67.
91 Paora Hapi to Locke, 11 June 1869, AGG HB2/1, NA.
92 Hohepa Tamamutu to Henry Russell, 16 June 1869, ibid.
93 Hare [Tauteka], Te Oti, Ihakara, and others, to Major Charles Lambert, 13 June 1869, and Hare Tauteka, Te Oti, and Ihakara to Henry Russell, 24 June 1869, ibid.
94 Ibid.
95 Lambert to Haultain, 18 June 1869, *AJHR* 1869, A-3, p.68.
96 St George to Haultain, 24 June 1869, ibid.
97 Hallett, MSS ZA 155, ML. This account is more convincing than that adopted by Ken Gartner in his study of Te Kooti and Tuwharetoa. There Gartner argued, based on oral information, that the compact between the two was that Tahau should act as executioner on the East Coast and Te Kooti within the orbit of Tuwharetoa. The conflict arose, he suggested, because Tahau had forewarned his kinsmen, who fled, leaving Te Kooti with no one 'to slaughter'. But Te Kooti had not come to Taupo with the intention of execution. (See also Chapter 7.) Kenneth C. Gartner, 'Te Kooti Arikirangi Te Tūruki: His Movements and Influence within the Ngāti Tūwharetoa Region 1869–70', MA thesis,

Victoria University of Wellington, 1991, p.76 (and his biography of Te Rangitahau in the *Dictionary of NZ Biography*, II, pp.522–23).

98 Waiata 13, MSS C-35, AU (also Biddle MSS, V, p.111). Trans: adapted from Frank Davis.

99 Letters from Tukorehu, Paora Hapi, and Te Heuheu, all written before the Opepe attack, cited in Locke to McLean, 10, 14 June 1869, MSS 32:393.

100 Speech given to Ngati Tuwharetoa, MA 24:22, NA (*AJHR* 1870, A-8, p.23).

101 Major W. J. Birch to Russell, 27 June 1869, AGG HB1/1, NA. The five men got through to the Patea district, where Hare Tauteka had also fled, on 25 June.

102 St George reporting a hui held there, Diary, 23 April 1869, MSS, ATL.

103 Diary, pp.59–60, HBM.

104 *AJHR* 1870, A-8B, p.28.

105 W. Searancke to Pollen, 5 July 1869, 69/476, AGG A1/4, NA.

106 Letter in St George Diary, 7 July 1869, MSS, ATL.

107 Hitiri Te Paerata (at Titiraupenga) to Perenara [Tamahiki] of Taupo, 8 July 1869, in St George, ibid., 10 July 1869.

108 Information from a female prisoner captured by government soldiers, ibid., 8 July 1869.

109 Ibid.

110 Statement by Maihi Pohepohe, Hakaraia's nephew, to Ngati He, 20 August 1869, *AJHR* 1870, A-8, p.5. Pukerimu was in the same area as Kaiwha. The little villages Kaiwha, Pukerimu and Te Papa were all at the foot of Titiraupenga.

111 Hitiri had close connections with both Ngati Raukawa and Tuwharetoa. Ngati Te Kohera were a hapu of Tuwharetoa associated with the western side of the lake.

112 St George, Diary, 11 July 1869, MSS, ATL.

113 OS: Henare Tuwhangai, Te Awamutu, 19 January 1983. The same narrative about Paraharaha, but with a different defender of the mana of Maniapoto, is also recorded in F. L. Phillips, *Nga Tohu a Tainui: Landmarks of Tainui*, 1989, p.26.

114 Narrated by Robert Emery, 10 June 1979, Davis Dossier, Vol. 9, ATL.

115 OS: Henare Tuwhangai, 19 January 1983. Also told in Phillips, p.26. She married Topu Taioha of Paraharaha; and she had a son. Another version of this story was told to Frank Davis in 1979. It was about the same family, and the woman was called Te Iwa. However, the story was told as belonging to a later time, and at Otewa, Te Kooti's home from the mid-1880s. Robert Emery told a similar story from this later period, but he stressed that the woman's second marriage was barren. The stories have clearly become intertwined: Davis Dossier, Vol. 1, pp.[44–45]; Emery, 10 June 1979, ibid., Vol. 9, ATL.

116 One source for this story is *DT*, 29 November 1959. The boy is named 'Tohou' or 'Tahou' (therefore, possibly simply 'Newborn'). By 1915 he would have been 45 years old — thus, ten years too old for a volunteer, although his serving would not be without precedent. There are some candidates. One is Ngakepa Tahu, from upper Wairoa, who was killed on 6 August 1915, the first night of the Gallipoli attack. He had said he was born on 6 November 1884. The most probable, however, is Taiawhiao Te Whare, who was born at Waitahanui, Taupo, and whose mother was Miriama Te Whare, from Petane in Hawke's Bay. He died — from wounds received in action at Gallipoli on 16 July — in the Malta hospital on 31 July 1915; he was, therefore, the first Maori killed at Gallipoli. He had given his date of birth as 10 May 1884. In his personal file, held by the Ministry of Defence, Wellington, his father was not named; and he himself was unmarried. Tihei Algie, Te Kooti's great-granddaughter, mentioned the rumour that Wetini had one younger brother, the son of Te Kooti, possibly killed in World War I, but she knew no details.

117 'Te Miringa Te Kakara', unpublished typescript, Historic Places Trust, Wellington. Also narrated by Emery, 10 June 1979, Davis Dossier, Vol. 9, ATL.

118 This point was made in 1889, when Rewi secured the solicitor W. J. Napier for Te Kooti, after his arrest: *NZH*, 1 March 1889.

119 Maihi Pohepohe, *AJHR* 1870, A-8, p.5.

120 William Searancke to McLean, 12 July 1869, *AJHR* 1870, A-1, p.25.

121 Maihi Pohepohe, *AJHR* 1870, A-8, p.5.

122 Searancke to McLean, 12 July 1869, *AJHR* 1870, A-1, p.25; account of expenses and 'payment for secret service' during Te Kooti's visit, 10 August 1869, Maori Affairs Register of Inwards Correspondence, 1869, NA.

123 II Kings 9:18.

124 Clarke to Native Department, 25 June 1869, *AJHR* 1869, A-10, p.77.

125 OS: 19 January 1983.

126 Memorandum to the governor by McLean, 6 August 1869, *AJHR* 1870, A-1, p.32. His source is Searancke, 16 July 1869, enclosure in AD1 69/5950, NA.

127 II Kings 9:22–24.

128 St George to Clarke, 29 July 1869, Diary, MSS, ATL. St George's informant was from Hitiri Paerata's people.

129 To McLean, 12 July 1869, *AJHR* 1870, A-1, p.26.

130 Searancke to Native Minister, 23 July 1869, *AJHR* 1869, A-10, p.91.

131 Aihepene Kaihau to the government, 3 August 1869, *AJHR* 1870, A-21, p.4.

132 To Henare Pukuatua and Te Keepa Te Rangipuawhe (of the Arawa tribe), 9 August 1869, St George, Diary, MSS, ATL.

133 Mangatawhiri marked the original boundary of the King's country, which was crossed in 1863 by the government troops, bringing war. The Waikato lands from that point south to the Puniu river were then confiscated. Hangatiki was at Te Kuiti where Tawhiao was residing in exile in 1869: it was the King's 'capital'. St John's gloss, added at this point, 'i.e., to smite the Europeans from Hangatiki to Mangatawhiri', is therefore misleading. It is, however, a statement of the desire to re-establish the autonomous territory of the King from Mangatawhiri.

134 *AJHR* 1870, A-8B, p.28.

135 Ibid.

136 26 April 1869, *AJHR* 1869, A-15, p.5. CT.

137 Clarke to Cooper, 25 June 1869, *AJHR* 1869, A-10, p.77; Searancke to Pollen, 22 June 1869, ibid., p.81.

138 Henry Sewell (in London) reporting to Sir George Grey, 13 October 1869, GLNZ S18, APL; Henry Russell (in Napier), reporting Governor George Bowen's views favouring a 'separate principality' for Tawhiao, to Army Department, 29 May 1869, AD1 69/3283, AD Register of Inwards Correspondence, NA. (Original letter no longer extant.)

139 Sewell to Grey, 13 October 1869, GLNZ S18, APL. The argument had been mooted before, but Sewell was so outraged with the British government that he suggested the independence of New Zealand should be declared. Sir William Martin, the former Chief Justice in New Zealand, was also pushing for the recognition of the Kingitanga as an 'experiment in self-government' at this time, but neither McLean nor the Premier, William Fox, would have any of it: see Alan Ward, *A Show of Justice*, 1973, pp.232–33.

140 Reported by Searancke to Pollen, 30 July 1869, McLean Papers MSS 32:507, ATL; summary transmitted by Pollen to Colonial Defence, 1 August 1869, AD1 69/5952, NA, where James Mackay was named by Pollen as one of Searancke's sources.

141 Searancke to Native Minister, 23 July 1869, *AJHR* 1869, A-10, pp.90–91.

142 Searancke to Native Minister, 31 July 1869, ibid., p.87; St George, Diary, 11 August 1869, MSS, ATL.

143 Searancke, telegram [25 July 1869], quoted Pollen to McLean, 26 July 1869, *GBPP*, Vol. 16, p.119.

144 Searancke to Native Minister, 23 July 1869, *AJHR* 1869, A-10, p.91.

145 Pollen to McLean, 29 July 1869, MSS 32:507, ATL. Belich's account, *NZ Wars*, p.280, misunderstands Tikaokao's role.

146 Searancke to Pollen, 16 July 1869, *GBPP*, Vol. 16, p.120.

147 Searancke, 23 July 1869, quoted AD1 69/5947, NA.

148 *AJHR* 1870, A-8, p.6.

149 Letter in St George Diary, 28 July 1869, MSS, ATL.

150 To Native Minister, 31 July 1869, *AJHR* 1869, A-10, p.86.

151 To the government, 3 August 1869, *AJHR* 1870, A-21, p.4.

152 Searancke to Native Minister, 3 August 1869, *AJHR* 1869, A-10, p.86; Statement by Ropata Kaihau, 7 August 1869, *AJHR* 1870, A-21, p.4.

153 Searancke to Native Minister, 23 July 1869, *AJHR* 1869, A-10, p.91.

154 Ibid.; Searancke to Pollen, 19 July 1869, *GBPP*, Vol. 16, p.120.

155 Letters dated August 1869, 9 August 1869, in St George Diary, MSS, ATL.

156 To McLean, 3 August 1869, MSS 32:566, ATL.

157 Searancke to Native Minister, 28 July, 6 August 1869, *AJHR* 1869, A-10, pp.91, 85; to McLean, 3 August 1869, MSS 32:566, ATL.

158 St George, Diary, MSS, ATL.

Chapter 7: The Return to Babylon (August 1869–February 1870)

1 Petera, Teniwata and others, 18 August 1869, in St George Diary, 19 August 1869, MSS, ATL. St George obtained the letter from a 'spy'. CT in *AJHR* 1870, A-8, p.7.

2 Ibid. H. T. Clarke picked up the same phrase as now being on the lips of those at Taupo who had once been sceptical about Te Kooti, to McLean, 2 September 1869, MSS 32:217, ATL.

3 St George, Diary, 11–12 September 1869, MSS, ATL; Wiremu Kingi Te Paia, *AJHR* 1870, A-8B, p.29; T. McDonnell to J. D. Ormond, 18 September 1869, 29 March 1870, MSS ZA 155, ML; Henare Tomoana, evidence given 24 October 1882, *AJHR* 1884, Sess. II, G-4, p.10.

4 McDonnell to Ormond, 14 September 1869, MSS ZA 155, ML.

5 Belich seems to be incorrect in arguing that Te Kooti used all his men in the attack on Tauranga, and he is also incorrect as to the dates of that attack, *NZ Wars,* pp.281–82.

6 Ormond to Colonial Secretary, 20 September 1869, AD1 69/7112 *(AJHR* 1870, A-8, p.15).

7 Ormond to Colonial Defence, 22 September 1869, AD1 69/6044, NA.

8 McLean to the governor, 17 September 1869, *GBPP,* Vol. 16, p.157; McDonnell to Ormond, 21 September 1869, MSS ZA 155, ML.

9 McDonnell to Ormond, 26 September 1869, *AJHR* 1870, A-8, p.17.

10 Ibid.

11 McDonnell to McLean, 27 September 1869, MSS 32:412, ATL.

12 Wi Piro was one of the young men who had acted as 'social bandits' at Turanga in the late 1850s. He had been sent with the second batch of prisoners to Wharekauri. Maata Te Owai stated that Te Kooti had two brothers who were prisoners with him on Wharekauri (*WI,* 28 June 1870). Komene was one; the other was possibly Wi Piro. Wi Piro was present at the attack on Turanga in November 1868; he fled from the fight at Nga Tapa, along with his wife and three children, to rejoin Te Kooti. At the time of his death, one source described him as Te Kooti's 'own brother'.

13 Searancke to McLean, 7 August 1869, MSS 32:566, ATL.

14 McLean to the governor, 17 September 1869, *AJHR* 1870, A-1, p.45; Ormond to Dillon Bell, 5 October 1869, *AJHR* 1870, A-8, p.18.

15 Cowan, *NZ Wars,* I, p.139.

16 Wiremu Kingi Te Paia, *AJHR* 1870, A-8B, p.28. Thomas Gudgeon reported the episode with the very different emphasis that Te Kooti had wished to protect the old man, but that the Tuhoe shot him regardless: *Reminiscences,* p.302.

17 Wi Kingi Te Paia, *AJHR* 1870, A-8B, pp.28–29; McDonnell to Ormond, 18 September 1869, MSS ZA 155, ML; Wiremu Pukapuka to McLean, 23 September 1869, *AJHR* 1870, A-21, p.7; Mete Kingi at the hui at Ohinemutu, Whanganui, 19–20 November 1869, *AJHR* 1870, A-13, p.5; *WI,* 5 October 1869.

18 OS: Eruera Manuera, 1978, quoted in Davis Dossier, Vol. 1, p.[36]; Ranginui Walker, 2 April 1992, Auckland.

19 *AS,* 23 May 1914.

20 McDonnell to Ormond, 29, 30 September 1869, MSS ZA 155, ML.

21 Archaeological report by Colin Smart in Ormond Wilson, *War in the Tussock,* 1961, pp.65–66.

22 McDonnell to Ormond, 5 October 1869, MSS ZA 155, ML (*AJHR* 1870, A-8, p.22).

23 Te Keepa Te Rangihiwinui to Mete Kingi Te Rangi Paetahi, 7 October 1869, *AJHR* 1870, A-8, p.23.

24 McDonnell's dates are one day out: Monday, the morning of the attack, was 4 October, and not 3 as he stated.

25 MSS 39:41A, ATL.

26 Statement to Ngati Tuwharetoa, MA 24:22, NA (*AJHR* 1870, A-8, p.24).

27 Evidence from Kuare, who had been sent with the second group of prisoners to Wharekauri, and who surrendered in 1870, 5 October 1870, AD1 70/3308, NA.

28 Speech given by Poihipi Tukairangi, 15 November 1869, Locke, Diary extract, MSS 32:393, ATL.

29 OS: Hoani (Nick) Wall, Taupo, 8 October 1990, in Gartner, p.78.

30 Wi Kingi Te Paia, *AJHR* 1870, A-8B, p.29. This account names the place 'Reterake (a hill in Whanganui)'. The Retaruke river flows into the Whanganui river, and its headwaters are about 20 miles west of Tokaanu.

31 OS: Wiremu Karawana, Turangi, 2 October 1990, in Gartner, p.128.

32 G. Mair to W. G. Mair, after a visit to Te Porere, 27 July 1905, MSS 92:13B, ATL.

33 The source is G. Mair, 30 December 1869, *AJHR* 1870, A-8A, p.20. There may be a confusion with Wi Piro, Te Kooti's 'younger brother', who died at Te Ponanga. See n.12, above.

34 Te Waru's sister Mere and Te Mauniko, his daughter, were both sometimes called Mary, creating a confusion between them.

35 McLean to Ormond, 27 October 1869, AGG HB1/1, NA.

36 Horonuku's gift, or cession, arose from the claims being made by Te Keepa and the Whanganui hapu who fought at Te Porere. They stated they had conquered his lands; he was asserting his ownership by his gift: Grace, pp.497–500, describes the pressures placed on Horonuku.

37 Hare Tauteka to Colonial Defence, 29 October 1869, AD1 69/6656, NA. CT.

38 This flag was cut down in size by Ngati Tuwharetoa in order to remove the holes in it, which were possibly bullet holes. The flag was donated to the museum by F. J. Hayman of Tokaanu, to whom

Ngati Tuwharetoa had given it, in 1918: ME 3735, MONZ. It is depicted in *An Encyclopaedia of New Zealand*, 1966, I, p.701.

39 Preece to McDonnell, 20 October 1869, MSS ZA 155, ML.

40 'The Native Minister's interview with the leading Waikato chiefs', MA 24:22, NA (*AJHR* 1870, A-12, p.4).

41 Pollen, reminding McLean of Rewi's words to him, 30 December 1869, MSS 32:507, ATL.

42 James Booth, Report of the Upper Whanganui meetings, *AJHR* 1870, A-13, p.5.

43 R. Parris, reporting a hui held at Waitara which discussed the matter, 19 May 1870, *AJHR* 1870, A-16, p.21.

44 Hita Tarawhiti to Searancke, 5 October 1869, MSS 32:566, ATL.

45 *AJHR* 1870, A-13, pp.5–6.

46 Wi Pukapuka, quoted Pollen to McLean, 30 December 1869, MSS 32:507, ATL.

47 Horonuku's account in J. D. Ormond to Defence Minister, 5 November 1869, AD1 69/7118, NA (*AJHR* 1870, A-8, p.28).

48 G. Mair to Civil Commissioner, Auckland, 30 December 1869, *AJHR* 1870, A-8A, p.20.

49 OS: Henare Hemopo, Te Rena, 10 October 1990, in Gartner, pp.145, 179.

50 H. F. Way, Diary, 21 October 1869, MSS 32:622, ATL. Way was at McDonnell's Taupo camp at the time.

51 McDonnell to Ormond, 8 November 1869, MSS ZA 155, ML (*AJHR* 1870, A-8A, p.6).

52 As Hori Te Whetuki reported, guns, powder and shot were all available for purchase at Shortland (Thames) from Pakeha, 26 July 1869, AD1 69/5176, NA. Followers of Te Kooti among Ngati Porou were reported there at the beginning of August 1869 and again in early January 1870, that is at the start of the Taupo and then of the northern Bay of Plenty campaigns.

53 Te Oti Takarangi to Te Kooti, in McDonnell to Ormond, 11 October 1869, MSS ZA 155, ML.

54 Searancke to McLean, 3 September 1869, MSS 32:566. Searancke was told it was £600, which would have been the entire sum rounded upwards!

55 McLean to Ormond, 12 March 1870, AGG HB1/2, NA.

56 Horonuku's account in Ormond, 5 November 1869, AD1 69/7118, NA (*AJHR* 1870, A-8, p.28).

57 Sub-Inspector H. C. Morrison to Major J. M. Roberts, 2 December 1869, *AJHR* 1870, A-8A, p.11.

58 Lucy Grey to [McLean], 20 January 1870, MSS 32:48, ATL.

59 James Belich has read this letter very differently, apparently interpreting it as the evidence for Titokowaru's sending 30 men to Te Kooti ('*I Shall Not Die*', 1989, p.282, although no sources are cited in direct reference to statements in this book). What is certain is that no support came from Taranaki for Te Kooti.

60 Morrison to Roberts, 2 December 1869, *AJHR* 1870, A-8A, p.11.

61 Marino to Hare [Tauteka], 26 November 1869, ibid., p.15.

62 James Fraser to McLean, 9 December 1869, MSS 32:282, ATL.

63 G. Mair to Civil Commissioner, Auckland, 30 December 1869, *AJHR* 1870, A-8A, p.20. It is clear that this episode took place at Tuhua; probably, more correctly, it was the Ohura river.

64 Moule to Defence Minister, 16 December 1869, ibid., p.19.

65 Hetet to Defence Minister, 13 December 1869, ibid., p.18.

66 Three of the flags are held by the Auckland Museum (Ethnology nos 27291-1, 2; and 28933). The pair were deposited by the surveyor (later author) W. Hugh Ross, in 1944. They came from the area south-west of Mokai (that is, the southern slopes of Titiraupenga), and were associated with Te Kooti's flight through that district late in 1869. Ross deposited the third flag in 1945. This flag had been stored in a tin trunk in the derelict meeting-house, Te Kohera, at Te Kakaho, on the southern slopes of Titiraupenga. A fourth flag was brought to the Museum of New Zealand in 1995, as this book went to press. Accompanying it is an account of its history, which states that, in 1943, three flags were stored in a chest in Te Kohera, including or along with this flag. One (described as the best) vanished; this was presumably flag 28933, which was taken to Auckland with some carvings, which were subsequently returned. The fourth flag is associated in narrative with Te Kooti. The emblems on the four flags show distinct similarities, though each flag is unique. See Plates 4-5, 8.

67 Telegrams dated 16–28 December 1869, *AJHR* 1870, A-8A, pp.18–19.

68 A copy of the letter, dated 16 January/87 [1870], a translation and a commentary on it can be found in MSS 32:694a, ATL. A corrupt Maori copy exists in Staff-sergeant Samuel Austin's diary, 27 December 1869, MSS, QEIIAM. It has the same curious date, 16 January/87. The translation was published in *AJHR* 1870, A-8A, p.20.

69 Austin, Diary, 28–30 December 1869, MSS, QEIIAM.

70 Ibid., 10 January 1870.

71 OS: 19 January 1983. Honuku is the source of this family narrative. Henare Tuwhangai actually

placed this story in the sequence before Te Kooti's visit to Te Miringa Te Kakara and Paraharaha. This sequence is also upheld in the oral account of these same events told to Frank Davis by P. Tutaki of Paraharaha in 1979, cited in Davis Dossier, Vol. 1, p.[41]. Nevertheless, the documentary evidence of Te Kooti's journeys suggests that this story belongs to his second entry into the Rohe Potae, and his final flight from Taumarunui on 6 January 1870. Not that it matters: that is not the real point of the story.

72 Preece, 'Notes for Major Gascoyne', p.7, MSS 249, AIM.

73 Hitiri to Perenara and others, 16 January 1870, *AJHR* 1870, A-8A, p.31.

74 Statement made by Te Huare [31 January 1870], G. Mair, Diary 11, MSS 92:44, ATL. (The version of his statement which was published in *AJHR* 1870, A-8A, p.70, has been edited to distort, particularly with regard to one section of it, discussed below.)

75 Clarke to McLean, 15 January 1870, MSS 32:217, ATL.

76 Ibid.; Clarke to Native Department, 12 February 1870, *AJHR* 1870, A-8A, p.71.

77 *AJHR* 1870, A-8B, p.29.

78 18 January 1870, MSS 32:566, ATL.

79 Diary, 9 August 1869, MSS, ATL.

80 Firth to the chiefs of Turangamoana, 5 April 1869, *AJHR* 1870, A-24, p.6.

81 This description of Te Kooti compares closely with that given in July 1869, cited in the previous chapter.

82 Firth to Defence Minister, 20 January 1870, *AJHR* 1870, A-24, pp.5–6. The woman was most probably Heni Kumekume, who was reported at the time (by Te Huare) to be his favourite wife. The physical description fits.

83 Pollen to Firth, 17 January 1870, *AJHR* 1870, A-8A, p.35.

84 17 January 1870, Firth Papers, MSS 3808:1, ATL (*AJHR* 1870, A-24, p.6). No Maori original.

85 Te Kooti to Firth, 19 January 1870, Firth Papers, MSS 1491:1, ATL.

86 The Premier, William Fox, to Pollen, 24 January 1870, *AJHR* 1870, A-24, p.[3].

87 Ibid.

88 Ormond to McDonnell, 23 January 1870, MSS 35:7, ATL; Fox to Pollen, 24 January 1870, *AJHR* 1870, A-24, p.[3].

89 21 January 1870, MSS 3808:1, ATL. CT in *AJHR* 1870, A-8A, p.38.

90 Locke to Ormond, 27 September 1869, Locke Letterbook, HBM.

91 8 October 1869, AD1 69/7144, NA (*AJHR* 1870, A-8, p.22).

92 T. McDonnell, 'The War in New Zealand', *AS*, 11 June 1892.

93 Austin, Diary, 15 November 1869, MSS, QEIIAM.

94 H. F. Way, at Ohinemuri, to McLean, 10 August 1869, MSS 32:622, ATL.

95 [31 January 1870], G. Mair, Diary 11, MSS 92:44, ATL.

96 H. Andrews of Ohinemuri, reporting on contacts between Te Hira and Te Kooti, 29 July 1869, AD1 69/5953, NA.

97 Wi Kingi Te Paia, *AJHR* 1870, A-8B, p.28.

98 McDonnell to Ormond, 13 October 1869, MSS ZA 155, ML; also *WI*, 5 October 1869.

99 Te Huare in G. Mair, Diary 11, MSS 92:44, ATL.

100 Preece to McLean, 4 February 1870, MSS 32:514, ATL.

101 In the published version, dated 31 January 1870, Te Huare's narrative has been edited specifically to state that the event occurred 'past Peria in the direction of Matamata', and that Firth had handed over the ammunition to Te Kooti: *AJHR* 1870, A-8A, p.70. This meeting purported to be a second encounter between Te Kooti and Firth. McDonnell said that Te Huare had told him that Firth had had two meetings with Te Kooti and that he himself had been present at both. At the second meeting Firth had given Te Kooti a box of percussion caps: to McLean, 3 February 1870, AGG HB1/2, NA (*AJHR* 1870, A-8A, p.59). In his later published history of the wars, McDonnell dated this meeting as 28–29 January: *AS*, 2 July 1892. Firth was outraged by the published version of Te Huare's statement, and wrote immediately to the government in protest. He stated that he had met Te Kooti only on the one occasion, which he had documented fully in his original letter. He denied ever having given Te Kooti ammunition: 4 August 1870, *AJHR* 1870, A-24A, pp.3–4. In the published version, Te Huare (although he was present) is reported as saying that he was told about the conversation which occurred by 'the two or three men' who accompanied Te Kooti, indicating that he was out of earshot. The question which remains unanswered is: who edited this text to make these allegations against Firth? The published text is altogether a fuller statement than the version recorded in Gilbert Mair's diary, suggesting that Te Huare made a second, expanded statement at Rotorua, probably under pressure. He had come in voluntarily, having fled from the fight at Tapapa on 25 January, and surrendered at Rotorua. In the long obituary for Te Kooti published in *NZM*, 21 April 1893, Firth was exonerated and 'a lying Native' was blamed for the whole story.

102 Clarke to Native Department, 16 August 1869, *AJHR* 1870, A-8, p.[3]; Way, Diary, 13 January 1870, MSS 32:622, ATL.
103 E. Stokes, 'Pai Marire and the Niu at Kuranui', Occasional Paper No. 6, Centre for Maori Studies and Research, University of Waikato, 1980, p.3.
104 E. Stokes, 'Te Raupatu o Tauranga Moana: The Confiscation of Tauranga Lands', University of Waikato, typescript prepared for the Waitangi Tribunal, 1989, pp.118–27.
105 Waharoa [Tana Taingakawa] to Ngati He, *AJHR* 1870, A-8A, p.33.
106 Ngati Whakaue to Clarke, 16 January 1870, AGG HB7/3 (*AJHR* 1870, A-8B, p.89).
107 Tana Te Waharoa Tamihana to Bowen, 22 January 1870, *AJHR* 1870, A-21, p.15.
108 Te Waharoa Tana, 23 January 1870, *AJHR* 1870, A-8A, p.41. The insertion of Firth's name is by the government translator. It could, alternatively, be a reference to Isaac Featherston, the superintendent of Wellington province.
109 23 January 1870, *AJHR* 1870, A-21, p.15.
110 McDonnell at Camp Tapapa, to St John Branigan, 26 January 1870, AGG HB1/2, NA.
111 Despatch, 25 January 1870, in Branigan to Defence Minister, AGG HB1/2, NA (*AJHR* 1870, A-8A, p.44).
112 *AJHR* 1870, A-8A, p.70. This portion is not in G. Mair's diary entry.
113 G. Mair to Clarke, 11 February 1870, *AJHR* 1870, A-8A, p.68.
114 Branigan to Defence Minister, 5 February 1870, ibid., p.61.
115 Searancke to Defence Minister, 21 January 1870, ibid., p.39.
116 2 February 1870, ibid., p.57.
117 Fraser to Clarke, 3 February 1870, ibid., p.62.
118 *AJHR* 1870, A-8B, p.29. He named the place Kokohuranui.
119 Ibid.
120 G. Mair to Clarke, noon, 7 February 1870, MSS 32:441, ATL.
121 Mair described this letter when writing to Cowan, 6 June 1928, MSS 39:6, ATL. In the contemporary correspondence it is not specifically mentioned; only Baker's account is given. It is possible that Mair, in 1928, was confusing this episode with the letter he found left by Kepa Te Ahuru (see below).
122 Mair to Clarke, 11 February 1870, *AJHR* 1870, A-8A, pp.68–69.
123 7 February 1870, Diary 11, MSS 92:44, ATL.
124 *AJHR* 1870, A-8B, p.29.
125 11 February 1870, *AJHR* 1870, A-8A, p.69. (The manuscripts of these letters were probably contained in the file AGG A1/5, which covered the period July 1869–70, but was stolen from National Archives, Wellington, in the early 1980s.)
126 Kepa escaped later in the year and rejoined the forces against Te Kooti. He convinced the government that he had been taken prisoner, although for a time he had been Te Kooti's 'second in command'. See Chapters 8 and 9.
127 11 February 1870, *AJHR* 1870, A-8A, p.69.
128 St George, 22, 29, 30 November 1868, 23 January, 25 February 1869, Diary, MSS, ATL. Ihaia Te Mokomoko is also identified as belonging to Ngati Whaoa, a hapu from the same region of Waikato.
129 'Te Kooti's Bugler', [James Cowan], MSS 39:41A, ATL.
130 Peita Kotuku, MSS 39:41A, ATL; G. Mair to C. J. Hutchinson, 9 April 1886, Box II, MSS 1618, AIM.
131 Gilbert Mair described them as '200 fighting men', but Wiremu Kingi Te Paia said they were about 100 strong, with very few guns, having thrown most away in their haste.
132 Mair to Cowan, 6 June 1928, MSS 39:6, ATL.

Chapter 8: He Manu Tute Au kei te Ngahere (February–August 1870)

1 Waiata 9, MSS C-35, AU. Trans: Frank Davis. The chapter title is also taken from a waiata composed by Te Kooti. It refers to himself as a restless or turbulent bird, perhaps a 'sentry' bird, in the forest; it is also probably a statement that he is a leader, for that is a metaphor used: Waiata 17, ibid.
2 McLean to McDonnell, 11 February 1870, *AJHR* 1870, A-8A, p.74.
3 McLean to Ropata, 19 February 1870, *AJHR* 1870, A-8B, p.[3].
4 OS: 14 February 1982.
5 Mere Whaanga, *Te Kooti's Diamond*, 1991. Reprinted in Witi Ihimaera (ed.), *Te Ao Mārama: Contemporary Māori Writing*, 1992, I, pp.349–51.
6 OS: as told to John Sullivan, ATL, to whom the author is grateful for this story. Lena Te Kani was the daughter of Sir Apirana Ngata and his first wife, Arihia Tamate.
7 OS: Ned Brown, Mangatu, 30 November 1983.
8 John 1:29.
9 Sworn testimony, *WI*, 30 June 1870.

10 *AJHR* 1870, A-8B, p.30. Possibly Pera Te Uetuku who, like messenger Pera, was taken prisoner at Maractahi on 25 March 1870.

11 Preece, 'Notes for Major Gascoyne', p.10, and Diary, 4 April 1870, MSS 249, AIM. The letter was found after the attack on Maraetahi on 25 March. Te Ranapia said he was quite innocent; it is possible the letter was a forgery, made by Te Kooti, like that which was purported to have been written by Kepa Te Ahuru. St John said that the signature was not in Ranapia's normal hand: to McLean, 31 [March 1870], MSS 32:559, ATL.

12 Te Ranapia Waihaku and Piahana Tiwai, 17 March 1870, *AJHR* 1870, A-8B, p.21 (names misprinted); Way, Diary, 9, 23 March 1870, MSS 32:622, ATL.

13 Clarke to Native Department, 20 March 1870, *AJHR*, 1870, A-8B, p.19.

14 Diary, 25 March 1870, ibid., p.46.

15 Clarke to Native Department, 18 April 1870, ibid., p.33.

16 Porter, Diary, 25 March 1870, ibid., p.46.

17 Ibid.

18 Ibid.

19 The text of this prediction is quoted in full in Appendix A.

20 14, 16 March 1870, Porter, Diary, *AJHR* 1870, A-8B, p.44.

21 16 March 1870, ibid.

22 Keepa's report provides the chronology for his expedition: 13 March 1870, AD1 70/2757, NA; Austin, Diary, 4–12 March 1870, supports him, MSS, QEIIAM.

23 *AS*, 6 June 1914.

24 Porter, reported by Major St John, Opotiki, to Lt-Col. Lyon, 30 March 1870, AD1 70/1190, NA (*AJHR* 1870, A-8B, p.17).

25 *AS*, 6 June 1914.

26 He was variously named as Timoti (Timothy) and Tamati (Thomas), and is not therefore readily identifiable. Austin, Diary, 24–25 March 1870, MSS, QEIIAM.

27 Te Keepa to Defence Minister, 30 March 1870, *AJHR* 1870, A-8B, p.24. Austin cited almost identical figures: up to 28 March, 326 killed or taken prisoner, that is: 20 killed; prisoners: 24 men, 38 women, 26 children of Te Kooti's [88]; 57 men, 83 women, 78 children of Whakatohea [218] (Diary, 29 March 1870, MSS, QEIIAM). Topia Turoa said that they captured 86 belonging to Te Kooti (to Defence Minister, 30 March 1870, *AJHR* 1870, A-8B, p.25). Porter gave a slightly different break-down: 227 Whakatohea and 80 belonging to Te Kooti: 31 March 1870, AD1 70/2762, NA.

28 St John to Lyon, 30 March 1870, AD1 70/1190, NA (*AJHR* 1870, A-8B, p.17).

29 Austin, Diary, 28–29 March 1870, MSS, QEIIAM.

30 Porter, Diary, 25 March 1870, *AJHR* 1870, A-8B, pp.45–46; Porter, Report, 31 March 1870, AD1 70/2762, NA.

31 5 August 1870, AD1 70/2668, NA. This was one in the cluster of four pa in the area known as Wairata, about two miles up river. These were the pa which fell to Te Keepa and Topia on 24 March. Te Keepa (and others) called the main pa Waipuna, which was also the name of the nearby river: AD1 70/1349, NA (*AJHR* 1870, A-8B, p.25).

32 Diary, 25 March 1870, *AJHR* 1870, A-8B, p.46. In Porter's retrospective account he claimed to have recognised him on the ridge of the whare and fired at him, just missing! *AS*, 6 June 1914.

33 Austin, Diary, 28 March 1870, MSS, QEIIAM.

34 Entry in Te Kooti's notebook. see Appendix A.

35 Austin, Diary, 24 March 1870, MSS, QEIIAM.

36 Flotsam and Jetsam X, p.130, HL; the *Press*, 20 November 1871; *AS*, 9 May 1914.

37 *AS*, 18 April 1914.

38 At the trials Porter stated that he and Ropata 'captured' only two prisoners, neither of whom was in the dock: *WI*, 30 June 1870.

39 Diary, 31 March 1870, *AJHR* 1870, A-8B, p.46.

40 The story of their descendants, Heni and Ned Brown, I have recorded, in their own words, in an earlier book, *Ngā Mōrehu*. There, it was incorrectly stated that Aperahama had joined Te Kooti after his return from Wharekauri (p.10).

41 Statement, n.d. [June 1870], MSS 32:25, ATL. Also *WI*, 30 June 1870.

42 Governor George Bowen, 28 July 1870, Despatch No. 91, Colonial Office (CO) 209/217, microfilm, AU.

43 Ibid.; *WI*, 30 June 1870.

44 The prisoners were all released by governor's clemency in 1873.

45 A detail transmitted orally: Tairongo Amoamo, 9 December 1992.

46 OS: 15 December 1971, Te Reo o Te Maori, Radio NZ Archive.

47 The *Press*, 20 November 1871.

48 Diary, 11 March 1870, *AJHR* 1870, A-8B, p.43.

49 Mair to Pollen, 27 November 1868, AGG A1/4, NA.

50 Diary, 11 March 1870, *AJHR* 1870, A-8B, p.43.

51 Deuteronomy 20-21.

52 Diary, 11 March 1870, *AJHR* 1870, A-8B, p.43.

53 T. O. Ranger, 'Connexions between "Primary Resistance" Movements and Modern Mass Nationalism in East and Central Africa', *Journal of African History*, IX, 3 (1968), pp.449-52.

54 Flotsam & Jetsam X, p.130, HL. In the version he published in *AS*, 30 May 1914, Porter added his own translation. It differs slightly, but not in essence, from the one given here. The first words in Maori would read fully 'E aha te putake'.

55 Porter, Diary, 28 March 1870, *AJHR* 1870, A-8B, p.46.

56 OS: 28 January 1983. Eruera Manuera of Te Teko also narrated the same story, with the same implication for the family, to Frank Davis, Davis Dossier, Vol. 9, ATL.

57 OS: Rotorua, 20 December 1981. In April 1870, Gilbert Mair heard a rumour that Te Ahuru had been killed by Te Kooti: this may well be the context for this narrative. Taua McLean's father was Makarini Kepa (Makarini Te Ahuru), who was the son of Kepa Te Ahuru. Makarini became the secretary to Rua Kenana.

58 OS: Boy Biddle, 14 December 1981, 29 January 1983. See also Chapter 9.

59 OS: 20 December 1981. Taua also narrated this story on 22 October 1981, when he stated that the event occurred where Nama had been burnt. Elements in the story (particularly the broken belt) may have become blended with episodes from the later Urewera fighting (see Chapter 9).

60 OS: 28 January 1983.

61 Revelation 6:5. For the red horse, see Chapter 11.

62 F. E. Hamlin to Ormond, 18 April 1870, AGG HB7/3 (*AJHR* 1870, A-8B, p.37).

63 Statement recorded 21 May 1870, *AJHR* 1870, A-8B, p.65.

64 Clarke to McLean, 8 June 1870, MSS 32:217, ATL. Hoani and Hapurona were with Clarke in Tauranga, Bay of Plenty, at this time.

65 Statement recorded 21 May 1870, *AJHR* 1870, A-8B, p.65.

66 Ibid., p.66; also Preece to Defence Minister, 18 May 1870, ibid., p.62.

67 W. G. Mair to Clarke, 21 June 1870, ibid., p.88.

68 Ropata to Defence Minister, 26 July 1870, AD1 70/2609, NA (*AJHR* 1870, A-8B, p.94). CT.

69 Preece quoting a group of Ngati Whare from Tuhoe, who surrendered on 24 April 1870, 30 April 1870, *AJHR* 1870, A-8B, p.47.

70 Clarke to Native Department, 18 April 1870, ibid., p.33-34; Wi Kingi Te Paia, 2 April 1870, ibid., p.30.

71 McLean to W. G. Mair, 26 May 1870, ibid., p.72.

72 Clarke to Defence Minister, 2 May 1870, ibid., p.39.

73 18 April 1870, ibid., p.38.

74 Ibid., p.39.

75 Memorandum, J. A. Wilson, 7 May 1870, Whitmore Correspondence 1868-70, typescripts, ATL.

76 29 April 1870, *AJHR* 1870, A-8B, p.54.

77 To Defence Minister, 2 May 1870, ibid., p.39.

78 Tuhoe Potiki at Ruatahuna, to the Arawa, ibid., p.54.

79 'Notes for Major Gascoyne', p.10, MSS 249, AIM. Preece gave the date as 17 April but on 17 April, in the skirmish that he reported, the riders he encountered all got away. Preece's diary and the letter he wrote on 30 April (*AJHR* 1870, A-8B, p.47) clearly indicate that Paraone surrendered on 24 April and that the speech-making took place the next day.

80 Preece, Diary, 20 May 1870, MSS 249, AIM.

81 Te Meihana to Arama Karaka and Paraone Te Tuhi, 5 May 1870, *AJHR* 1870, A-8B, p.54.

82 Porter, Diary, 17 May 1870, AGG HB7/3, NA (*AJHR* 1870, A-8B, p.69).

83 Porter, Diary, 15 May 1870, ibid.

84 He was also known as Makarini Te Wharehuia. He was one of Elsdon Best's informants for *Tuhoe*. See Makarini's biography by Wharehuia Milroy in the *Dictionary of New Zealand Biography*, II, pp.499-500.

85 Clarke to Native Department, 25 June 1870, AD1 70/2477, NA (*AJHR* 1870, A-8B, p.87).

86 Hamlin to Ormond, 16 June 1870, *AJHR* 1870, A-8B, p.79.

87 Ibid.

88 G. Mair to Defence Minister, 22 July 1870, AD1 70/2608, NA (*AJHR* 1870, A-8B, p.91).

89 Te Whenuanui and all Tuhoe Potiki, *AJHR* 1870, A-8B, p.93.

90 Hamlin to Ormond, 23 June 1870, AGG HB7/5, NA (*AJHR* 1870, A-8B, p.84).

91 5 August 1870, AD1 70/2668, NA.

92 W. G. Mair to McLean, 29 July [1870], MSS 32:442, ATL.
93 List given by Huhana, 5 August 1870, AD1 70/2668, NA. Paora Tu (Paora Tu Te Rangiwhaitiri) had been sent with the second group of prisoners in April 1866. He was from Te Aitanga-a-Mahaki, but in a statement he made on 29 February 1872 he was also identified as belonging to Waikato (AD1 72/325, NA). Hirini Te Oiikau, of Ngati Kahungunu and Te Aitanga-a-Mahaki, was sent with the fourth group, in October 1866. Hoani Te Paiaka had mentioned a few others as still remaining in April, when he had left: *AJHR* 1870, A-8B, pp.65–66.
94 Huhana's statement in Locke to Ormond, 8 August 1870, AD1 70/2635, NA (*AJHR* 1870, A-8B, p.100).
95 Preece to Defence Minister, 30 April 1870, *AJHR* 1870, A-8B, p.47.
96 Statement made by Huhana, in Locke to Ormond, 8 August 1870, AD1 70/2635, NA (*AJHR* 1870, A-8B, p.100); Huhana, 5 August 1870, AD1 70/2668, NA.
97 Read to McLean, n.d. [1869–70], MSS 32:521, ATL.
98 Huhana named Oriwia as being with her at Opape and also at Uawa. She also said that she and three others of Te Kooti's wives had escaped from Maraetahi. One of these was Oriwia (although her name was badly garbled by the transcriber). Another was Nia, of whom only her name is known.
99 Her narrative is supported by the account given by Hohua Rawhea to Porter, AD1 70/2565, NA (*AJHR* 1870, A-8B, p.96).
100 Hohua Rawhea and Paora's statements, ibid.
101 Paora's statement, ibid.
102 AD1 70/2668, NA.
103 Porter to Defence Minister, 2 August 1870, AD1 70/2564, NA (*AJHR* 1870, A-8B, p.99).
104 See Chapter 10.

Chapter 9: The Shelter of Tuhoe (August 1870–May 1872)

1 Waiata 16, MSS C-35, AU. Trans: Frank Davis.
2 Te Keepa Te Rangipuawhe to Defence Minister, 11 March 1870, AD1 70/2755, NA (*AJHR* 1870, A-8B, p.5). CT.
3 31 March 1870, AD1 70/2465, NA. CT.
4 Preece, Diary, 17 March 1870, MSS 249, AIM; Preece to Army Defence, 17 March 1870, AD1 70/2759, NA.
5 G. Mair to Clarke, 5 May 1870, *AJHR* 1870, A-8B, p.53; G. Mair in Gudgeon, *Reminiscences*, p.333.
6 The argument that he had done so is a major theme of Gartner's thesis.
7 Mair to Clarke, 17 April 1870, MSS 32:441, ATL.
8 'Journal of a visit to Taupo', 13 November 1870, Box 1, MSS 583, AIM (S. J. Brittan et al. (eds), *A Pioneer Missionary among the Maoris 1850-1879*, n.d. [1928], p.217).
9 Gudgeon, *Reminiscences*, p.321.
10 Statement by Rewi (Porter's guide on the Urewera expedition), Porter, Diary, 14 May 1870, *AJHR* 1870, A-8B, p.69.
11 Preece to Defence Minister, 30 April 1870, ibid., p.47.
12 Keepa to Defence Minister, 13 March 1870, ibid., p.10.
13 St John to Ormond, reporting an intercepted letter from Rakuraku to Te Kooti, 11 May 1870, AGG HB7/3, NA.
14 W. G. Mair to McLean, 29 July 1870, MSS 32:442, ATL; Ropata to Defence Minister, letter begun 26 July 1870, AD1 70/2609, NA (*AJHR* 1870, A-8B, p.95).
15 W. G. Mair to G. Mair, 26 July 1870, MSS 32:48, ATL.
16 Tuhoe Potiki ('all the Tribe') to Preece, 16 May 1870, AGG HB7/3, NA (*AJHR* 1870, A-8B, p.63).
17 Hapurona Kohi and Hoani Paiaka to Te Keepa Te Rangipuawhe and the Arawa chiefs, 11 July 1870, *AJHR* 1870, A-8B, p.92.
18 McLean to Ormond, 27 June 1870, ibid., p.86.
19 7 June 1870, ibid., p.88.
20 Hamlin to Ormond, 11 June 1870, AD1 70/2037, NA (*AJHR* 1870, A-8B, p.78).
21 Te Harau and all the chiefs of Tuhoe, 7 August 1870, *AJHR* 1871, F-1, p.4. No Maori original.
22 Te Ahoaho, Te Whenuanui, Te Ahikaiata, Paerau . . . Tamaikoha and all Tuhoe, to the Wairoa, 15 August 1870, AGG HB2/1, NA.
23 Hamlin and the Wairoa chiefs to Te Harau and Te Paraone, 18 August 1870, *AJHR* 1871, F-1, p.5.
24 Hamlin and the Ngati Kahungunu chiefs, to Te Whenuanui and all Tuhoe, 18 August 1870, ibid.
25 Te Paea Tiaho's biography by Angela Ballara is in the *Dictionary of New Zealand Biography*, II, pp.520–22. This particular negotiation is not discussed.

26 Makarini, Paerau and others to Hamlin and the Ngati Kahungunu chiefs, 11 June 1870, AGG HB2/1, NA (CT in *AJHR* 1870, A-8B, p.82); Hamlin to Ormond, 18 June 1870, AGG HB7/5, NA (*AJHR* 1870, A-8B, p.81).

27 Clarke to McLean, 5 November 1870, enclosing an illicit copy (made by Louis Hetet) of Manuhiri's letter to Hare Reweti [C. O. Davis], 30 October 1870, MSS 32:217, ATL. Aporo had also been sent to Te Kooti by Tawhiao in July 1870, as will be discussed later, and was turned back in a second attempt, in November, by Ngati Whakaue at Rotorua: Clarke to McLean, 30 November 1870, ibid.

28 Ormond Papers, Box A:5, HBM.

29 Ibid., Box A:6.

30 To G. Mair, 13 October 1870, AD1 70/3387, NA (*AJHR* 1871, F-1, p.6). CT by Clarke.

31 Ibid. G. Mair had reported this epidemic, describing how the victims were seized with severe pain in the heart and throat and died within a few hours: 3 September 1870, AD1 70/3103, NA.

32 Preece to W. Moule, 4 September 1870, *AJHR* 1871, F-1, p.5.

33 Te Whenuanui to McLean, 27 September 1870, MSS 32:694d, ATL. No Maori original.

34 W. G. Mair to Clarke, 18 October 1870, *AJHR* 1871, F-6A, p.[3]; Erueti Tamaikoha's words of peace-making, ibid., p.4.

35 Preece to McLean, 31 December 1870, MSS 32:514, ATL.

36 Porter, Diary, 28 January 1871, AD1 71/776, NA (*AJHR* 1871, F-1, p.29).

37 Maika was from Tangoio in Hawke's Bay. He had been sent to Wharekauri with the fifth group of prisoners in December 1866.

38 30 January 1871, ibid. (The date of the letter is misprinted in *AJHR* 1871, F-1, p.30.)

39 G. Mair to Moule, 20 January 1871, *AJHR* 1871, F-1, p.11.

40 Ropata to McLean, reporting the evidence of a prisoner, Tamehana Te Wharehuia of Ngati Kurupakiaka of Wairoa (who had been with Te Kooti in the attack on Uawa), 7 September 1870, AD1 70/3105, NA.

41 When the original shareholders list was drawn up in 1890, Te Kooti (Te Turuki Te Rangipatahi) was included as one of the owners of Tahora 2C 1, 'Houpapa or Waimaha', Gisborne Minute Book 19, p.59, MLC microfilm.

42 Wepiha Apanui to McLean, 27 September 1870, MSS 32:694d, ATL.

43 Porter, Diary, 10 February 1871, AD1 71/776, NA (*AJHR* 1871, F-1, p.31).

44 Message and letter dated 12 February 1871, in ibid.

45 Diary, 13 February 1871, ibid.

46 Kereru and 'all of us' ('no matau katoa'), letter dated 14 February 1871, ibid.

47 Te Purewa to Te Turuki, n.d., Porter, Diary, 30 January 1871, ibid.

48 Porter, Diary, 18 February 1871, ibid.

49 20 February 1871, ibid.

50 28 February 1871, ibid. CT in *AJHR* 1871, F-1, p.34.

51 Preece estimated his age in his diary, 28 October 1871, MSS 249, AIM; note on Te Whiu Maraki by James Cowan, who met him in January 1921 at Ruatoki: MSS 39:41A, ATL.

52 Porter to Ormond, 23 March 1871, AD1 71/340, NA (*AJHR* 1871, F-1, p.18).

53 Talking with James Cowan. Cited Michael King, 'Moko of the Maori', *Face Value: A Study in Maori Portraiture*, n.d. [1975], n.p. Netana fought for Te Kooti, but after the agreement made with Te Keepa in 1870, he worked with Tamaikoha and Rakuraku to end the fighting in the Urewera. Netana bore a full facial moko incised, in his case, at Ruatoki before 1860. His photograph (taken in 1921) is reproduced on p.489; Cowan's crude sketch (also made in 1921) shows more detail: *NZ Wars*, II, p.445.

54 Porter, Diary, 30 March 1871, AD1 71/776, NA (*AJHR* 1871, F-1, p.35).

55 Porter to Ormond, 23 March 1871, *AJHR* 1871, F-1, p.18.

56 Statement made after his capture, enclosed in Westrup to Ormond, 13 May 1871, AGG HB1/5, NA.

57 Ropata to Ormond, 1 April 1871, enclosure in AD1 71/377, NA (*AJHR* 1871, F-1, p.21). No Maori original.

58 Porter, Diary, 30 March 1871, AD1 71/776, NA (*AJHR* 1871, F-1, pp.35–36).

59 See Appendix A.

60 Hirini Te Ratu was sent to Wharekauri in the same group as Te Kooti. (In Porter's published diary the name is printed as 'Te Kutu' in error.) Hirini was subsequently captured at Muriwai, near Turanga, in May 1871.

61 J. T. Large, *AS*, 26 July 1919.

62 Te Pukenui Kereru to Clarke, 10 April 1871, *AJHR* 1871, F-1, p.23. He wrote the same letter to G. Mair and Preece on the following day, ibid., pp.23–24.

63 Fox (the Premier) to Ormond, 19 April 1871, AGG HB1/3, NA.

64 Preece to Moule, 14 April 1871, *AJHR* 1871, F-1, p.23.

65 Diary for June 1871, concluding remarks, AD1 71/901, NA (*AJHR* 1871, F-1, p.44).

66 Tamaikoha to Ropata, 5 April 1871, AD1 71/655, NA; W. G. Mair to Clarke, 8 April 1871, ibid.; Wi Maihi statement, 19 May 1871, ibid.; Preece to Major J. M. Roberts, 3 July 1871, *AJHR* 1871, F-1, p.26.

67 Diary, 20 June 1871, AD1 71/901, NA (*AJHR* 1871, F-1, p.44).

68 Ormond to Defence Minister, 10 April 1871, AD1 71/377, NA (*AJHR* 1871, F-1, p.21).

69 Porter to Ormond, 9 March 1871, AGG HB1/6, NA.

70 Inspector G. J. Cumming to Ormond, 9 July 1871, AGG HB1/6, NA (*AJHR* 1871, F-1, p.40).

71 Cumming to Ormond, 16 July 1871, AGG HB1/6, NA. Makarini had been accused of taking a pouch of percussion caps from one of the Wairoa men when he was held at Napier (after his surrender) and of sending the caps back to Waikaremoana: Cumming to Ormond, 16 December 1870, AGG HB1/2, NA.

72 Porter (at Maungapohatu) to Ormond, 28 October 1871, AGG HB1/5, NA. His information came from Orupe, one of the Maungapohatu men who had recently been with Te Kooti; [W. L. Williams], undated note derived from Apikara's sworn deposition, made after she was taken prisoner, MSS 69:49, ATL.

73 W. G. Mair to Civil Commissioner Auckland, 10 November 1871, MA 23/2, NA.

74 Cumming to Ormond, 4 November 1870, AGG HB1/2, NA.

75 Cumming to Ormond, 27 July 1871, AD1 71/922 and AGG HB1/6, NA (*AJHR* 1871, F-1, p.45).

76 Ibid., and to Ormond, 29 September 1871, AGG HB1/6, NA; Tamihana Huata to Ormond, 28 August 1871, AGG HB2/1, NA.

77 G. A. McDonnell to Cumming, 23 April 1872, AD1 72/518, NA.

78 Hirini had apparently assumed that Te Kooti meant Tauranga in the Bay of Plenty, and referred to the people as 'Ngatirangi' (published as 'Ngaiterangi'). This may be a reference to Tahau, who was sheltering in the northern Bay of Plenty. But a later hint suggests that Te Kooti probably meant Tauranga-o-Taupo. The first reference is Cumming to Ormond, 16 July 1871, AGG HB1/6, NA (*AJHR* 1871, F-1, p.42). The later reference to Taupo, from Makarini, is Cumming to Ormond, 29 September 1871, AGG HB1/6, NA.

79 Cumming to Ormond, 27 July 1871, AD1 71/922 and AGG HB1/6, NA (*AJHR* 1871, F-1, p.45).

80 Preece to Ormond, [5] August 1871, AGG HB1/3, NA.

81 Cumming to Ormond, 1 August 1871, ibid. (*AJHR* 1871, F-1, p.47).

82 W. G. Mair to Clarke, 25 November 1871, Mair Letter and Telegram Book 1871–75, MSS A-31, AU. W. L. Williams had earlier identified him as Karanama Te Kani: Diary, 9 January 1869, AIM.

83 W. G. Mair to Civil Commissioner Auckland, 10 November 1871, MA 23/2, NA. Mair thought the name might be O'Connell, but it is presumably O'Connor, who was known to the government and from whom Te Kooti was said by Horonuku Te Heuheu to have obtained ammunition in 1869.

84 McDonnell to Ormond, 13 October 1869, MSS ZA 155, ML; also Fox to McLean, 20 October 1869, MSS 32:278, ATL.

85 Paora Toki was chief of Ngati Matepu hapu of Ngati Kahungunu. Turei Toki had been sent with the fourth batch of prisoners to Wharekauri. In November 1866 it was reported that Paora intended to try to capture a vessel at Napier and release his exiled kin: W. L. Williams, Diary, 9 January 1869, MSS, AIM; also statement of Wi Tamararo, 25 February 1869, MSS 32:23, ATL.

86 Ormond to G. Mair, 1 September 1871, MSS 32:48, ATL; W. G. Mair to Kemp, 20 September 1871, MA 23/2, NA; [Hitiri Te Paerata] to Ormond, 11 October 1871, AGG HB2/1, NA. A list of Te Kooti's followers, dated Napier, 7 November 1871, names Paora Toki, Tahau and nine others as being with Te Hira at Ohinemuri, AGG HB1/3, NA. (The covering letter, in which this list was originally enclosed, has recently gone missing from the file.)

87 Makarini to Cumming, 24 September 1871, AGG HB2/1, NA.

88 Pollen to McLean, 7 September 1870, MSS 32:507, ATL.

89 To H. T. Kemp, 31 October 1871, Mair Letter and Telegram Book 1871–75, MSS A-31, AU.

90 Pollen to McLean, 28 November 1871, MSS 32:508, ATL.

91 Ibid.

92 Wi Patene to Te Wheoro, 11 November 1871, W. G. Mair to Civil Commissioner Auckland, 10 November 1871, MA 23/2, NA.

93 W. G. Mair to Pollen, 25 September 1871, Mair Letter and Telegram Book 1871–75, MSS A-31, AU.

94 *AJHR* 1872, F-3A, p.18.

95 Manuhiri to McLean, 24 September 1871, ibid., p.17.

96 Manga (Rewi) to W. G. Mair, 31 (23?) October 1871, Mair Letter and Telegram Book 1871–75, MSS A-31, AU. (Mair received the letter on 24 October: Mair to Civil Commissioner, 24, 25 October 1871, ibid.) Manuhiri dissociated himself from the invitation: Wi Patene to Te Wheoro, 11 November 1871, Wi Te Wheoro to H. T. Kemp, 13 November 1871, MA 23/2, NA.

97 Preece, Diary, 9 August 1871, typescript, MSS 249, AIM. Also G. Mair to Cumming, 9 August 1871, AGG HB1/3, NA (*AJHR* 1871, F-1, p.51.)

98 In the contemporary published translation this phrase was given a significantly more potent reading: 'I sent my children to carry you a letter returning you (sending you back), but you persisted in chasing me': *AJHR* 1871, F-1, p.51.

99 AGG HB1/3. The translation here is based on that attached to this letter and published in *AJHR* 1871, F-1, p.51. There is also a transcript copy and translation in Preece's Diary, MSS 249, AIM. That translation was subsequently published by Preece in his account of the Urewera campaign, and he stated there that it was by Canon James Stack: Preece in Gascoyne, p.190. There are also copies of the letter in Gilbert Mair's field diary, Diary 12, MSS 92:46, ATL, and AD1 71/982, NA. Cowan, *NZ Wars*, II, pp.435–36 also publishes the text (with some errors) and yet another translation.

100 Patoromu Ruru was the younger son of the Te Aitanga-a-Mahaki chief Henare Ruru from Pakohai, near Repongaere at Turanga; Epiha was also from Turanga.

101 *Tuhoe*, I, pp.1097–98.

102 Elsdon Best, *Maori Religion and Mythology*, Part I, 1924, p.381.

103 Preece, in his diary translation, wrote 'the bread of Rua', which Gilbert Mair expanded upon in the published version with the addition '(hinau berries)': Preece, Diary, 9 August 1871, MSS 249, AIM; 'Expeditions against Te Kooti', in Featon, *Waikato War*, p.218. (The official published translation had 'the big eye of "Rua"'.) The hard kernel of the hinau was sometimes known as 'te whatu-o-Poutini', referring to greenstone.

104 Revelation 2:17.

105 G. Mair, Diary 12, MSS 92:46, ATL.

106 McLean, telegram to Ormond, 12 August 1871, *AJHR* 1871, F-1, p.51.

107 To Ormond, 13 August 1871, AGG HB1/3, NA.

108 Enclosure in G. Mair to Ormond, 29 August 1871, AGG HB1/6, NA. CT by Mair.

109 Preece to Westrup, 22 August 1871, AGG HB1/3, NA.

110 Curiously, in his retrospective account Mair dressed Te Kooti in a blue serge suit.

111 These items were retained by Preece and then given by him to the Palmerston North Museum. They were transferred to the Palmerston North Library in 1954 (*EP*, 13 July 1954).

112 The Spencer repeating rifle (invented during the American Civil War) was considered to be the equivalent of seven men armed with rifles. Snider-Enfields were superior breech-loaders using brass (instead of paper) cartridges. They became available to Preece only in March 1872, although other New Zealand Armed Constabulary forces acquired them earlier. The new military technology did not defeat Te Kooti in this last phase of guerrilla war in New Zealand.

113 Horonuku said that Te Kooti possessed Biggs's gold watch in October 1869.

114 Published in *NZM*, 21 October 1871.

115 Hamlin to Ormond, 18 June 1870, AGG HB7/5, NA. Portion removed from the published version in *AJHR*.

116 Wi Heretaunga, of Rongowhakaata and Tuhoe, had been sent with the fourth group of prisoners to Wharekauri in October 1866. According to Gilbert Mair's retrospective account, the troopers learnt the information about Wi Heretaunga's role at Poverty Bay from Mere Maihi. No contemporary evidence has surfaced. Mair described an elaborate court martial taking place, followed by a dramatic contest between several Maori troopers for the right to shoot their prisoner. Kepa Te Ahuru won the role, on the grounds that Wi Heretaunga was his uncle (his mother's full brother, from Tuhoe). Kepa's 'brother' (elder cousin) Makarini Te Waru had fought for Te Kooti, and this was given as the reason why Kepa had joined Te Kooti. This narrative of Kepa's role as executioner is counterpointed by the narrative told about his father, who tried to kill Te Kooti. That narrative remains in the oral tradition of Tuhoe (see Chapter 8 and later in this chapter). Kepa Te Ahuru's whakapapa may be found in Elsdon Best, 'Genealogies of the Tuhoe as of 1898', p.68, MSS, ATL; Kepa died on 9 January 1884.

  Neither Preece's official report (22 August 1871, AGG HB1/3, NA) nor his diary contains any account of Wi Heretaunga's execution. Neither does Mair's official report (29 August 1871, AGG HB1/6, NA), nor the account written by Mair and Preece and published in *Waikato War*, nor Preece's manuscript, 'Notes for Major Gascoyne', MSS 249, AIM, which he took directly from his diary. Mair's retrospective account was published in J. C. Andersen and G. C. Petersen, *The Mair Family*, 1956, pp.214–17. Their source is Mair's typescript (written in the third person and with much 'reconstructed' detail regarding both the encounter with Te Kooti and the trial), Cowan Papers, MSS 39:41F, ATL. Mair's MSS correction to a portion of this text, which he altered because of Preece's doubts about the legality of the court martial, is in Mair to Cowan, n.d., MSS 39:6; Mair's original typescript notes, made for Cowan, are in MSS 39:41E.

117 Hetariki was named by Maata Te Owai as one of the 12 Apostles, the young men under Te Kooti's direction when they landed at Whareongaonga. He fled from Nga Tapa and voluntarily gave himself up at Turanga, but was brought to trial and sentenced in 1869.

118 OS: Boy Biddle, 28, 29 January 1983. One account states that Te Kooti ordered the burning of all the songs and hymns of war after his pardon in 1883: Robin Winks, 'A Maori Form of Christianity: The Ringatu Church', p.22, MSS A-206, AU.

119 Diary 12, MSS 92:46, ATL. Trans: collaborative J. McRae, B. Woodard, J. Binney.

120 *AS*, 13 June 1914.

121 *AS*, 2 August 1919. Porter's retrospective account conversely said that the shot was fired at a woman who had gone to get some wood and had spotted the men lying in ambush: *AS*, 13 June 1914.

122 Porter to Ormond, 5 September 1871, published in *NZM*, 23 September 1871. Porter's diary entry for 1 September 1871 is very terse: 'Attacked Te Koote at Maungapohatu — killing 5 capturing 13 —', MSS, ATL. There is no report of this engagement in his military Letterbook 1871–73, AD 103/1, NA.

123 James Grindell (Napier) to McLean, 30 December 1870, MSS 32:30, ATL. Porter was also reported as having more than one female companion. His wife was Herewaka Porourangi Potai of Tokomaru, whom he married in 1873 but with whom he already had children. There was a persistent rumour of Porter's involvement with one of Te Kooti's wives, by whom he had a son. Irihapeti is sometimes named in this connection. The story was also attached to Herewaka herself (with whom he had at least eight children, including two sons) but this was probably tangled gossip. Herewaka's previous husband, by whom she had one child, was Hirini Kahua.

124 Diary, 3 May 1872, MSS 249, AIM.

125 Preece, ibid., 19 October 1871; 'Notes for Major Gascoyne', p.24, MSS 249, AIM.

126 Quoted in *NZM*, 9 December 1871.

127 OS: Boy Biddle, 14 December 1981. See also Chapter 8.

128 Makurata was the daughter of Himiona Te Pikikotuku from Te Rotoiti, who was living at Ruatahuna: Best, MSS annotation to her photograph, MONZ; *Tuhoe*, I, pp.627–28.

129 Ibid., pp.662–63.

130 OS: Boy Biddle, 29 January 1983.

131 Cowan, 'The Facts about Te Kooti', p.21.

132 This was noted by Henry Hill, who met Te Kooti on 29 March 1892. Hill commented on these two damaged fingers, as well as the missing fingers of his left hand, MSS 146:9, ATL. Also Johannes Andersen, MSS note appended to Elsdon Best's MSS biography of Te Kooti, Andersen Scrapbook, AIM; Best, *Tuhoe*, I, pp.662–63.

133 Preece, Diary, 28 October 1871, MSS 249, AIM.

134 Preece, ibid., 8 November 1871.

135 Cumming to Ormond, 27 July 1871, AD1 71/922, NA. This passage was understandably excised from the published version, *AJHR* 1871, F-1, p.46, as it made fools of the hunters. It is one of the rare acts of censorship found.

136 Ferris to Cumming, 12 March 1872, AD1 72/473, NA.

137 Anaru Matete's statement in W. A. Richardson to Ormond, 9 March 1872, AD1 72/471, NA.

138 Northcroft to Inspector D. Scannell, 23 January 1872, AD1 72/342, NA.

139 Hoani Wall, Taupo, 8 October 1990, cited in Gartner, pp.34–35. This story has also been amalgamated (in this version) with Te Kooti's first entry into Tuwharetoa territory in 1869, which cannot be correct.

140 It was first reported on 16 January, Scannell to Commissioner Armed Constabulary, 24 January 1872, AD1 72/342, NA.

141 Richardson to Ormond, 9 March 1872, AD1 72/471, NA. Northcroft reported that they took 200 pounds of flour and 50 pounds of sugar, as well as some potatoes, and the ammunition, which seems quite a lot for eight to 12 people to carry: to Scannell, 23 January 1872, AD1 72/342, NA.

142 Preece to J. M. Roberts, 7 February 1872, AD1 72/342, NA.

143 Richardson to Ormond, 9 March 1872, AD1 72/471, NA.

144 Preece, Diary, 14 February, 29 March 1872, MSS 249, AIM; Richardson to Ormond, 9 March 1872, AD1 72/471, NA.

145 Ferris report and notebook entries, 28 February 1872, in Cumming to Commissioner of Armed Constabulary, 1 March 1872, AD1 72/256, NA.

146 Narrated by the elder Bill Broughton of Mohaka: Patrick Parsons, evidence given at Mohaka River Conservation hearing, July 1989, corrected typescript in possession of the author.

147 10 March 1872, AD1 72/472, NA.

148 Statement of Hare Houwaka, n.d., in McDonnell to Cumming, 15 March 1872, AD1 72/473, NA; Ihaka Waanga and Paora Apatu to Cumming, 10 March 1872, AD1 72/472, NA.

149 Ferris to Cumming, 30 March 1872, AD1 72/477, NA.

150 Ferris to Cumming, 21 April 1872, AD1 72/518 and 570, NA.

151 Cowan, *NZ Wars*, II, p.453. The Ngati Porou redoubt built in 1871 at Maungapohatu was also known as Hinau-piwai, perhaps referring to the end of the killing. All signs of it were subsequently obliterated.

152 Makarini to Cumming, 22 September 1871, AGG HB2/1. CT; and to Ormond, 5 November 1871, AGG HB1/6, NA.

153 Te Purewa to Ormond, n.d. [November 1871], AGG HB2/1, NA.

154 Ormond to Porter, annotation dated 21 November 1871 on Porter to Ormond, 16 November 1871, AGG HB1/3, NA.

155 9 November 1871, MSS 32:222, ATL.

156 Statement to Te Arawa, 4 January 1872, AGG HB7/2(h), NA.

157 Ferris to Cumming, 24 April 1872, AD1 72/570, NA.

158 Te Kooti's comments at Arowhena and Te Waotu, reported in *NZH* Monthly Summary, 20 April–18 May 1872, p.4.

159 W. G. Mair, Diary, 25, 31 May 1872, MSS, ATL, describing the party on its way to and reaching Te Kuiti.

160 Preece, Diary, 23 May 1872, MSS 249, AIM.

161 [Hitiri Paerata] to Ormond, 11 October 1871, AGG HB2/1; Scannell to Commissioner Armed Constabulary, 20 May 1872, AD1 72/616, NA; *NZH* Monthly Summary, 20 April–18 May 1872, p.4.

162 Information from Huhana, Porter to Under-secretary Defence, 11 September [1870], AD1 70/3105, NA.

163 W. G. Mair to Manga [Rewi] Maniapoto, 11 November 1871, Mair Letter and Telegram Book 1871–75, MSS A-31, AU.

164 Diary, MSS 249, AIM.

165 Large to Ormond, 15 November 1871, AGG HB1/6, NA.

Chapter 10: The Shelter of Maniapoto (May 1872–February 1883)

1 Waiata 23, MSS C-35, AU. Trans: Frank Davis.

2 OS: Bruce Biggs, Auckland, 1990; Robert Emery, 10 June 1979, Davis Dossier, Vol. 9, ATL.

3 W. G. Mair to McLean, 16 June 1872, Mair Letter and Telegram Book 1871–75, MSS A-31, AU; *NZH*, 20 June 1872.

4 McLean to Governor Bowen, 8 June 1872, *AJHR* 1872, A-1, p.94.

5 Mair to McLean, 16 June 1872, Mair Letter and Telegram Book 1871–75, MSS A-31, AU.

6 Notes of interview between Aihepene and McLean, 29 June 1872, MSS 32:33, ATL.

7 Mair to McLean, 16 July 1872, MSS 32:442, ATL.

8 *NZH*, 24 April 1883.

9 W. G. Mair to McLean, 2 July 1872, Mair Letter and Telegram Book 1871–75, MSS A-31, AU.

10 R. S. Bush, resident magistrate at Ngaruawahia, 1 August 1872, *AJHR* 1872, F-3A, p.28; Bush to McLean, 12 August 1872, MSS 32:194, ATL.

11 W. G. Mair to G. Mair, 31 July 1872, Mair Letter and Telegram Book 1871-75, MSS A-31, AU.

12 W. G. Mair to McLean, 23 October 1872, ibid.

13 W. G. Mair to McLean, 14 January 1873, ibid.

14 Mair to Native Department, 12 June 1873, *AJHR* 1873, G-1, p.22.

15 Speech to John Bryce, 12 February 1883, Biddle MSS, I, p.145. The same speech is translated in *AJHR* 1883, A-8, p.5, but the 'tenth year' was there converted, erroneously, to 1874.

16 W. G. Mair to McLean, 1 July 1873, Mair Letter and Telegram Book 1871–75, MSS A-31, AU.

17 Memo on Sullivan murder, n.d., MSS 32:49, ATL.

18 Bush to Native Minister, 14 October 1873, *AJHR* 1874, G-2B, p.4 (corrected text). CT.

19 To Clarke, Letter and Telegram Book 1871–75, MSS A-31, AU.

20 Mair to Civil Commissioner Auckland, 26 September 1873, ibid.; the same to Under-secretary Native Department, *AJHR* 1874, G-2B, p.1.

21 Ibid.

22 Bush to Native Minister, 14 October 1873, *AJHR* 1874, G-2B, p.4; Bush to McLean, 7, 14 October 1873, MSS 32:194, ATL.

23 W. G. Mair to McLean, 25 October 1873, Letter and Telegram Book 1871–75, MSS A-31, AU; *NZM*, 25 October 1873, reporting that 'Tawhiao's house-warming' at Te Kuiti 'came off' on Wednesday, 22 October. The house from which the later name Tokanganui-a-noho would be taken was opened at Matakotako, Aotea, on 21 November 1873: Bush to Native Minister, 22 November 1873, *AJHR* 1874, G-2B, p.6. This house subsequently burnt down and the name was transferred (in 1883) to the house at Te Kuiti.

24 W. G. Mair to McLean, 27 October 1873, Mair Letter and Telegram Book 1871–75, MSS A-31, AU; Bush to Native Minister, 22 November 1873, *AJHR* 1874, G-2B, p.7.

25 Evidence given 18 June 1903, Wairoa Minute Book 13, pp.70–71, MLC microfilm.

26 Te Kuiti Manuscript, p.[89], MSS MP1990/3, Te Hukatai Library, AU. This text was quoted in this context by the Maniapoto elder Robert Emery, who holds the original mss, on the occasion of the centennial of Te Kooti's pardon, held at Te Kuiti. He also slightly misremembered it. He Rerenga Korero, 16 February 1983, Radio NZ Archives.

27 Biddle MSS, I, p.81. The source is stated there as being Hamiora's manuscript book. In a different document, File B No. 3, Biddle transcribed the same details from 'Te Kooti's papers'.

28 *Te Pukapuka o Nga Kawenata*, pp.125–26.

29 Ibid., p.[127].

30 OS: 16 May 1982.

31 OS: 29 January 1983.

32 Biddle MSS, I, p.81. The list of houses built for the Kotahitanga is sourced there to Matiu Paeroa.

33 Roger Neich, *Painted Histories: Early Maori Figurative Painting*, 1993, pp.107, 130.

34 The site of the Ringatu meeting-house which stood at Waiau (Athenree) has been tentatively identified by NZ Historic Places Trust. It is on the Waiau estuary; local oral memory recalls that Te Kooti visited this house. The site is N53/80 and, closely associated with it, N53/116. This marae complex stood at the northern boundary of the Mataatua canoe tribes.

35 OS: Eruera Manuera, Te Teko, 25 May 1981; 17 February 1982.

36 'Sketches in the King Country', by 'W.D.', *NZH*, Supplement, 26 May 1883.

37 Neich, *Painted Histories*, p.132.

38 *NZH*, Supplement, 26 May 1883.

39 *Painted Histories*, pp.132–33, 147–48.

40 Waiata 30, MSS C-35, AU. Trans: Frank Davis. The waiata is also published in *Te Pukapuka o Nga Kawenata*, p.121, where it is linked to the gathering held on 1 January 1883 at Te Kuiti. Biddle MSS, V, p.115 states specifically that this song was sung to Ngati Maniapoto at the opening of the whare whakairo at Te Kuiti on 2 January 1883. The source was Hamiora Aparoa's manuscript. The song is an adaptation of the Ngati Kahungunu song recorded in *Nga Moteatea*, 1959, Part I, p.32. The final lines were added to the original text by Te Kooti.

41 *Te Pukapuka o Nga Kawenata*, p.128.

42 Powhiri at Te Ngawari, Mangatu, 6 June 1982.

43 Preece, Diary, 6 November 1871, MSS 249, AIM.

44 Te Kooti to Ross, 7 February 1873, MSS 32:549, ATL.

45 Te Kooti to Teera Tanarapa, n.d., ibid.

46 W. G. Mair to Gilbert Mair, 22 May [1873], MSS 93:4, ATL; Diary entry for same date, transcript, Mrs Z. Craig, Auckland. (In the version of his mss diary for 1873 held in ATL, Mair does not mention Te Kooti's pardon, only that he himself wrote to Gilbert that day.)

47 Mair to McLean, 18 October 1873, Mair Letter and Telegram Book 1871–75, MSS A-31, AU.

48 Mair to McLean, 13 November 1873, MSS 32:442, ATL.

49 *PBS*, 26 November 1873.

50 Quoted in *Standard and People's Advocate* (Gisborne), 10 February 1875. Te Hata was known to be still with Te Kooti in August and November 1871 and may therefore have been one of the six men who accompanied him in the final flight to the Waikato in April 1872. In 1875 his mother, Tuatini, was living in Poverty Bay.

51 W. G. Mair to Gilbert Mair, 22 May [1873], MSS 93:4, ATL.

52 Report on the King Country, 10 July 1873, *AJHR* 1873, G-3, pp.5–8.

53 'Te Kooti and Mr. Mackay', Shortland MSS K, p.79, HL.

54 Mackay, 10 July 1873, *AJHR* 1873, G-3, p.8.

55 See Chapter 5.

56 'Te Kooti and Mr. Mackay', Shortland MSS K, p.79, HL.

57 *NZM*, 29 November 1873 (and an earlier abridged version, *NZH*, 20 November 1873). The *NZM* article establishes that the 'European' was not James Mackay; it is possible, however, that he was Ross.

58 W. G. Mair to McLean, 5 April 1875, MSS 32:442, ATL.

59 See Greg Dening, *Islands and Beaches: Discourse on a Silent Land: Marquesas 1774–1880*, 1980, p.165.

60 *Standard and People's Advocate*, 10 February 1875.

61 26 January 1875, AGG HB2/2, NA. Modified CT.

62 Brabant to McLean, 9 January 1875, MSS 32:171, ATL.

63 MSS 32:697f, ATL. The text quoted is Psalm 46:1–2.

64 Delamere MSS, p.30; Hamiora Aparoa's account of Te Kooti's explanation given at Taramakiri, Te Kuiti, 11 December 1875, Biddle Miscellaneous MSS.

65 OS: Monita Delamere, 16 February 1982; also *Te Pukapuka o Nga Kawenata*, p.[137].

66 Paeroa MSS, p.[80]; Biddle MSS, I, p.81.

67 Ibid.

68 OS: Dick Hauraki, Mataora, 19 April 1992.

69 Biddle MSS, I, p.81.

70 Ibid., p.53.

71 Bush to Native Department, 20 January 1885, 85/236, MA 23/8a, NA.

72 Hamiora Aparoa, Wharekawa, 31 March 1882, Biddle Miscellaneous MSS.

73 Biddle MSS, I, p.53.

74 Ibid., p.41.

75 Ibid., p.53.

76 *Te Pukapuka o Nga Kawenata*, p.144. (This page is not in all editions of the book.)

77 Davis Dossier, Vol. 6, ATL. *Te Pukapuka o Nga Kawenata* textually extends Panui 34, and also adds Panui 35, 36 and 38. Panui 35 and 36 are also understood to have been composed by Te Kooti and, with them, he completed his expansion. Panui 37 and 38 were added later. (There is no text for Panui 37 in the copy in the author's possession.)

78 *AS*, 14 March 1914.

79 Ibid.; *NZ Wars*, II, p.451.

80 Waiata 18, MSS C-35, AU.

81 Paeroa MSS, p.[1]. Trans: based on Frank Davis.

82 Ibid., p.[5].

83 Ibid., p.[80]. Trans: based on Davis.

84 Delamere MSS, p.30.

85 Quoted in Robin Lane Fox, *The Unauthorized Version: Truth and Fiction in the Bible*, 1991, p.41.

86 George Steiner, *Real Presences*, 1989, pp.40–41. (The author is indebted to Jane McRae for this reference.)

87 Delamere MSS, p.119. Biddle MSS, I, p.18 also records these texts in full, dates their first promulgation at Te Kuiti, 12 December 1877, and indicates that they were taken to Te Tahawai.

88 Paeroa MSS, p.[79].

89 Ibid., pp.[80–81]. Trans: modified from Davis.

90 Ibid., p.[81].

91 Delamere MSS, p.30.

92 Paeroa MSS, p.[83].

93 Frank Kermode, *The Genesis of Secrecy: On the Interpretation of Narrative*, 1979, pp.107–9.

94 Pollen to McLean, 21 July 1871, 31 January 1874, MSS 32:508, ATL.

95 OS: Martha Hakaraia, Moana Pouaka and others at Nga Tauiwi, Otaruru, 23 April 1984; Francis Bennett, *Tairua*, 1986, p.154; *Coromandel and Mercury Bay Gazette*, 7 February 1973.

96 27 May 1872, diary of Peneamene Tanui, Ngati Hei elder, MSS 671:2, AIM. The visit of Te Kooti to Mataora, Wharekawa, Tairua and Coromandel in July 1884 is also recorded in this diary, and the reference is supported by a dated saying from Wharekawa in Paeroa MSS, p.[11].

97 The 'elevation' of July (as the gathering for the church and, thereby, as the sign of the days of peace) was a prediction made by Te Kooti in 1892 (see Chapter 13). The house was named to fulfil these words. For other, earlier meeting-houses built and named in response to similar directives by Te Kooti, see Chapter 12.

98 OS: Kati Wharepapa, grandson of Wharepapa Perepe, Paritu, 13 February 1993; Faith Keenan, Paritu, 23 April 1984. Also Maree Wehipeihana, 'A Church Few Dare to Enter', *Dominion Sunday Times*, 24 May 1970. The invitation to Tuhourangi to come to Wharekawa, and the problems of Tuhourangi (many of whom stayed first at Te Awahou) are described in R. F. Keam, *Tarawera*, 1988, pp.295, 297.

99 L. P. Wheeler, *The Patchwork Quilt*, 1970, pp.130–32, 162–63. Pearl Wheeler was the daughter of an early settler in the district, W. Hugh Ross, who came there from Gisborne in 1895. Ross subsequently bought Maori land at both Whiritoa and Parakiwai. He was the source of his daughter's information, and was also a friend of Thomas Porter and his children. W. Hugh Ross, the author of the biography of Te Kooti published in 1966, is presumed to be Ross's son.

100 Major I. R. Cooper (at Shortland, Thames) to McLean, 5 February 1870, Militia Letters, Cooper MSS, Whanganui Museum.

101 OS: Heneriata (Nellie) Te Moananui and John Williams, Ngahu-toitoi, 30 November 1991. Also Laura Hiku (née Taupeki), Whiritoa, 19 April 1992.

102 OS: Nellie Te Moananui, 30 November 1991.

103 OS: Laura Hiku, 19 April 1992.

104 9 November 1870, MSS 32:338, ATL.

105 *NZM*, 14 December 1872, reporting the *Taranaki Herald*, 30 November 1872.

106 Letter to [J. D.] Ormond and [H. R.] Russell jointly, and letter to McLean, dated 4 December 1873, AGG HB2/2, NA.

107 Dandeson Coates.

108 18 November 1877, Box 1, MSS 583, AIM (Brittan and Grace, pp.285–86).

109 To CMS, 8 February 1878, CN/045, CMS microfilm.

110 *ECHR*, p.79.

111 Ibid., p.80; 'Notes on Ringa-tu', n.d. (written after April 1887), p.23, MSS, ATL.

112 *ECHR*, p.80.

113 Stack, p.3.

114 Annual report, 21 May 1879, *AJHR* 1879, G-1, p.6; also newspaper extract, no source, 26 February 1879, Mackay Scrapbook, MSS 1006/2:19, p.469, ATL.

115 F. Ormond to Native Department, 22 March 1877, 77/1470, Locke to Native Department, 26 May 1877, 77/2387, MA Register of Inwards Correspondence, 1877, NA.

116 Annual report, 10 June 1881, *AJHR* 1881, G-8, p.14.

117 30 April 1880, *AJHR* 1880, G-4, p.8.

118 p.5, MSS, HBM. Trans: adapted from Rev. A. Newman. A modern version of the Pokaikaha (showing very little alteration in transmission) is 'E te Atua tahuri mai ou taringa kia matou inoi, kei whakangaro atu koe i a matou e tangi nei. Anga mai titiro iho kia matou e pokaikaha noa nei e tangi nei hoki — kororia ki tou ingoa tapu. Amine.' This text, with Newman's translation, is in 'Nga Karakia me Nga Tikanga o Te Haahi Ringatu', compiled by Matarena Reneti, Te Teko, n.d., Davis Dossier, Vol. 8, ATL.

119 Binney and Chaplin, *Ngā Mōrehu*, pp.20–21, 81–82.

120 See Walzer, pp.78–81, 85.

121 Biddle MSS, I, p.1.

122 Waiata 22 and 25, MSS C-35, AU.

123 Porter to Defence Minister, n.d. [late 1870], MSS 32:25, ATL.

124 Biddle MSS, I, p.81. There were 19 numbered houses, with two others mentioned as part of the same complexes. Matiu's list stops at this time (1891), perhaps because he was dismissed as secretary shortly afterwards.

125 Reprinted from the *Daily Telegraph*, Napier, clipping n.d., Mackay Scrapbook, MSS 1006/2:19, p.465, ATL.

126 Ormond, enclosed in Locke to Native Department, 16 February 1877, 77/809, MA Register of Inwards Correspondence, 1877, NA.

127 11 May 1877, *AJHR* 1877, G-1, p.11.

128 *ECHR*, p.81.

129 Bush, Annual report, 30 May 1881, *AJHR* 1881, G-8, pp.12–13. The chief Apanui died on 30 October 1880.

130 Brabant to McLean, 6 March 1874, MSS 32:171, ATL.

131 Interview with Moerangi Ratahi, born c.1869, by Kotare [C. Kingsley-Smith], *Rotorua Daily Post*, 15 May 1971.

132 OS: Ned and Heni Brown, 14 February 1982. (A portion of this narrative is in Chapter 8.)

133 Wilson MSS, p.136.

134 McLean, Memorandum, 16 February 1875, MSS 32:33, ATL.

135 9 February 1878.

136 From *AWN*, reprinted in *AJHR* 1878, G-3, pp.3–4.

137 *New Zealander*, 7 May 1878, quoted in *AJHR* 1878, G-3, p.15.

138 Waiata 19 and 20, MSS C-35, AU.

139 King Tawhiao's meeting at Hikurangi, May 1878, Biddle MSS, I, p.146.

140 OS: 14 February 1982.

141 Te Turuki Te Kooti to Native Department, 14 May 1878, 78/3750, MA Index and Register of Inwards Correspondence 1878, NA. The originals of Inwards Letters to the Native Department, 1863–91 (except certain special files) were destroyed by fire in 1907. Only the indices and registers remain. This letter was destroyed because it had not been collated in the special file which concerned Te Kooti, MA 23/8a–c.

142 14 May 1878, quoted Alfred Saunders, *History of New Zealand*, n.d.[1899], II, p.392.

143 *WT*, 13 May 1879.

144 83/680, MA 23/8a, NA. CT.

145 13 May 1879, ibid.

146 12 May 1879, ibid.

147 Bush to Bryce, 10, 12 May 1882, MA 23/4b, NA.

148 12 September 1882, 83/680, MA 23/8a, NA. CT.

149 Bryce, Memorandum for the Governor, 13 February 1883, *AJHR* 1883, A-8, p.3.

150 Bryce, report of their meeting, 13 February 1883, ibid., p.5.

151 Paeroa MSS, pp.[84–85]. Trans: based on Frank Davis.

152 Ibid., p.[85].

153 *WT*, 13 February 1883.

154 Maori text taken from Matiu Paeroa's records, Biddle MSS, I, p.145; translation in *AJHR* 1883, A-8, p.5.

155 OS: 15 May 1982.

156 Davidson, *Dictionary of Angels*, p.193.

157 Daniel 12:1.

158 Biddle MSS, I, p.145. Some, but not all, of this text appears in the published version in *AJHR* 1883, A-8, p.5.

159 Quoted in *NZH*, 16 February 1883.

160 Speech given 9 September 1882, quoted *NZH*, 17 February 1883.

161 Quoted in *WT*, 17 February 1883.

162 Ibid., 20 February 1883.

Chapter 11: Hopes and Journeys (March 1883–June 1886)

1 MSS 32:33, ATL.

2 Waiata 36, MSS C-35, AU. Trans: Frank Davis. The song is annotated by Hamiora Aparoa stating that it refers to the amnesty of 1883.

3 G. T. Wilkinson to Native Minister, 21 March 1883, 83/1121, MA 23/5, NA.

4 Te Haere, who was imprisoned with Hursthouse, to the Speaker of the House of Representatives, 4 September 1884, 84/3893, ibid.

5 C. W. Hursthouse to Col. R. Trimble, 22 May 1884, MSS 408, AIM.

6 Hursthouse's account, reported in *NZT*, 29 March 1883.

7 *NZT*, *Taranaki Herald*, 21 April 1883; *NZH*, 23 April 1883.

8 Wilkinson to Bryce, 24 March 1883, 83/1126, MA 23/5, NA; *NZH*, 26 March, 23 April 1883.

9 *NZH*, 26 March 1883.

10 Wilkinson to Bryce, 25 March 1883, 83/1129, MA 23/5, NA.

11 Ibid.

12 Hursthouse, in *NZT*, 29 March 1883.

13 *NZH*, 27 March 1883. The text contains the misprint 'nia Ihowa' for 'ma Ihowa'. Also Wilkinson to Bryce, 26 March 1883, 83/1131, MA 23/5, NA.

14 *NZH*, 28 March 1883.

15 Biddle MSS, I, p.54.

16 *Taranaki Herald*, 21 April 1883.

17 *NZH*, 23 April 1883.

18 Ibid., 21 April 1883. Hoani Poururu (also known as Hone Taupe) had acted as a spokesman for Te Kooti at the meeting with Bryce in Alexandra the previous month.

19 Ibid.

20 Ibid., 23 April 1883.

21 *NZT*, 21 April 1883.

22 Ibid., 26 April 1883.

23 Annual report, 11 June 1883, *AJHR* 1883, G-1, p.4.

24 *AS*, 3 October 1889; *NZH*, 4 October 1889; unsourced clipping, Mackay Scrapbook, MSS 1006/2:19, p.21, ATL.

25 Annual report, 11 June 1883, *AJHR* 1883, G-1, p.4.

26 Paeroa MSS, p.[89]. Trans: Frank Davis. The same statement concerning a new start at Otewa, dated 28 April 1883, and copied from Hamiora's manuscripts, is in Biddle MSS, I, p.5.

27 Paeroa MSS, p.[90].

28 OS: Pei Te Hurinui Jones, 13 February 1974, AK7/56, Radio NZ Archives.

29 *The King Country*, p.335. This meeting took place 15–17 May 1883.

30 OS: Boy Biddle, 14 December 1981.

31 1 January 1883 at Te Kuiti, Paeroa MSS, p.[87].

32 Ibid., p.[90]. Trans: Frank Davis. The date of his arrival, 24 June, is supported by *WT*, 23 June 1883, which described his journey on the punt from Te Aroha to Ohinemuri.

33 Paeroa MSS, p.[89].

34 Statement of 30 June 1883, ibid., pp.[91–92].

35 Ibid., p.[93].

36 Ibid., p.[91].

37 Ibid., p.[93]. The identification of Ropata remains uncertain as there was an Ohinemuri chief called Ropata (Ropata Te Pokiha), who had been a major figure in opening the area for gold-prospecting in 1868. But Ropata Wahawaha also visited there. He maintained connections with his Ngati Porou kinsmen at both Mataora and Harataunga (Kennedy Bay).

38 *WT,* 28 June 1883.

39 *NZM,* 4 August 1883.

40 Ibid.

41 Inspector F. Swindley to Police Department, 11 December 1883, P1 1884/26, NA.

42 *BPT,* 20 December 1883.

43 Ibid.

44 *WT,* 11 December 1883.

45 *BPT,* 20 December 1883.

46 Waiata 31, MSS C-35, AU. Trans: based on Frank Davis. Tiki-tohua, in some traditions, was the creator of birds; the reference to clothing in feathers brings to mind Te Kooti's own 'wearing of feathers' on the night of his despair and renewal, narrated in the previous chapter. But Tiki is also an important ancestor for the people of Ohinemutu, and a double reference may well be intended here.

47 Delamere MSS, p.30.

48 Dated 29 December 1883/January 1884, Te Whaiti. Biddle MSS, I, p.11; also, in a slightly variant text, 29 December 1883, ibid., V, p.[5].

49 Waiata 32, MSS C-35, AU. Trans: based on Frank Davis.

50 Bush to Native Minister, 8 March 1884, 84/857, MA23/8a, NA.

51 Brabant, 25 May 1874, *AJHR* 1874, G-2, p.7.

52 Waiata tohutohu, sung by Puke Tari of Tuhoe, Mervyn McLean and Margaret Orbell, *Traditional Songs of the Maori,* 1975, pp.37–39. The waiata begins 'Alas for this unhappy night' ('Kaore te pō nei mōrikarika noa'); it is specifically dated here as being from Te Kooti's visit to Tuhoe in 1883.

53 Bush to Native Minister, 8 March 1884, 84/857, MA 23/8a, NA.

54 McLean and Orbell, p.38.

55 Waiata 33, MSS C-35, AU. The original waiata can be found in *Nga Moteatea,* I, pp.28–29, upon which this translation is based.

56 OS: Paetawa Miki of Maungapohatu, 26 January 1978; see Binney et al., *Mihaia,* p.61. There is a different tradition concerning the large bible from Whakarewarewa, given to Rua after an initial refusal. This was the family bible of the local storekeeper, Levuka Corbett. However, this bible reached New Zealand only in the 1890s. A further large illustrated bible, given to Te Kooti in 1880 by the Ngati Porou exiles living at Wharekawa, is discussed in Chapter 14, n.186.

57 Biddle MSS, V, p.[5].

58 S. M. Mead (ed.), 'Three Carved Houses at Te Whaiti: Part III, Eripitana', 1970, p.3, Dept of Anthropology Library, AU.

59 In one version of this kupu, dated 'Waioeka 1883', the words in 'te reo ke' were recorded as 'Eripitana': 'The Prediction of One to Follow', n.d., p.75, Davis Dossier, Vol. 10, ATL.

60 'Eripitana', p.3.

61 Rangiruru, Tuhoe elder, quoted in ibid. Another version of the word, recorded for 29 December 1883, was: 'I leave you (the house), you are the Holy of Holies' ('Rawaiho koe e ahau (te whare) ko koe te Tapu o nga Tapu'): Biddle MSS, V, p.[5].

62 OS: Te Akakura Rua at Eripitana, 21 January 1978; 'Eripitana', pp.15–18.

63 Biddle MSS, I, p.81.

64 *BPT,* 12 January 1884, reported him to be staying inland of Whakatane; Waiata 34 was sung at Kokohinau on 'perhaps' 12 January, MSS C-35, AU. Te Kooti went from there to Whakatane and Matata, which he reached on 12 January.

65 Delamere MSS, p.30. There is, of course, the popular belief that Te Kooti travelled secretly to these occasions before his pardon, but the Ringatu records deny it.

66 Waiata 28, 1 January 1882, MSS C-35, AU.

67 'Nga Korero a Te Kooti Rikirangi mo Nga Pahipoto me to ratou Whare, mo Ruataupare', 29 August 1981, in Hirini Moko Mead, *Te One Matua: The Abundant Earth,* 1982, p.83. Matiu dated the predictive words, Whakatane 1 January 1882: Paeroa MSS, p.[84].

68 OS: Monita Delamere, 16 February 1982.

69 OS: Wi Tarei, 13 February 1974, AK7/56, Radio NZ Archives.

70 Mead, *Te One Matua,* pp.84, 87.

71 Ibid.

72 The song text may be found in ibid., p.106, and Wi Tarei's comments on its hidden meaning, pp.85–87.

73 OS: Eruera Manuera talking with Frank Davis, n.d., Davis Dossier, Vol. 9, ATL.

74 Lane Fox, p.67.

75 Biddle MSS, I, p.81.

76 OS: Eruera Manuera, Te Teko, 25 May 1981. Also Wi Tarei in Mead, *Te One Matua*, p.82.

77 OS: Eruera Manuera talking with Davis, n.d., Davis Dossier, Vol. 9, ATL.

78 Kingi did not keep the mere. He gave it to Alma Baker, who sold it to the museum in 1890: Ethnology 331.

79 Kupu whakaari uttered at Ohiwa, 1893: *Te Whetu Marama o Te Kotahitanga*, 29 August–5 September 1931, p.9; included also in 'Nga Kupu Whakaari', p.9, typescripts compiled from the records of the Ratana church in the possession of Emma Lemuel, Raupunga. See Chapter 14, p.490.

80 Diary 1882–84, MSS 92:55, ATL. (See also Introduction.)

81 Mair to Hamilton, 20 February 1899, MSS, Rotorua Museum.

82 'The Facts about Te Kooti', p.21.

83 *BPT*, 15 January 1884.

84 Ibid., 29 January 1884.

85 Adela B. Stewart, 24 January 1884, *My Simple Life in New Zealand*, 1908, p.85.

86 Biddle MSS, I, p.161.

87 Ibid., p.204.

88 Wilkinson to Under-secretary Native Department, 28 August 1883, *AJHR* 1884, G-4A, p.[1].

89 Te Kooti to Bryce, 25 July 1883, ibid.

90 Wilkinson to Under-secretary Native Department, 28 August 1883, ibid.

91 Te Kooti to Under-secretary Native Department, 22 February 1884, ibid., p.5.

92 Te Kooti to Bryce, 22 November 1883, ibid., p.2.

93 Wilkinson to Under-secretary Native Department, 3 March 1884, ibid., p.5. A group of four maps published in *AJHR* 1873, G-3, shows Orakau pa, the confiscation line, and 'Ngamako No. 2' east of the confiscation line. The three blocks discussed here (Ngamoko No. 2 (DP 18514), Lots 55 and 55A respectively) are located clearly on the cadastral map of Otorohanga, N74 (1960).

94 Wilkinson to Native Department, 3 March 1884, *AJHR* 1884, G-4A, p.5; Bryce, 16 September 1885, *PD* 1885, LIII, p.836.

95 Wilkinson to Under-secretary Native Department, 3 March 1884, *AJHR* 1884, G-4A, p.5.

96 Te Kooti to Wilkinson, 3 November 1884, 84/3302, MA 23/8a, NA.

97 Native Department annotation, 12 November 1884, to Wilkinson to Native Department, 5 November 1884, 84/3302, ibid.

98 'Notes of a Meeting between the Hon. Mr. Ballance and Te Kooti and his People at Kihikihi', 3 February 1885, *AJHR* 1885, G-1, p.10.

99 See map, *AJHR* 1873, G-3.

100 Te Kooti to Native Department, 16 April 1885, 85/1335, MA Register of Inwards Correspondence, 1885, NA.

101 *PD* 1885, LIII, p.836.

102 *WT*, 19 September 1885; *JHR*, 16 September 1885, p.370.

103 Wilkinson to Native Department, 19 June 1886, 86/1731, MA Register of Inwards Correspondence, 1886, NA; Wainui Reserve, p.[1], Ringatu Church File 1923–39, ATL.

104 Te Kooti to Native Department, 14 November 1886, 87/29, MA Register of Inwards Correspondence, 1887, NA.

105 Ngamako [*sic*] No. 2, Uncertified Copy of Deeds, Index, 3W/299, Auckland Land Registry; Certificate of title, 382/140, Hamilton Land Registry.

106 'The Facts about Te Kooti', p.17. Cowan dated his first meeting as 1884.

107 Constable A. Berriman to Inspector W. A. Kiely, 31 October 1887, Kiely to Police Commissioner, 4, 15 November 1887, P1 88/213, NA. Exactly what land he had in mind is not known. But he was a shareholder in the large Mangapoike block (land which his great-granddaughter now helps to administer), and he would be listed among the original shareholders in Tahora 2F (Papuni) and Tahora 2C 1 (Waimaha). This huge block (Tahora No. 2) was heard in the Native Land Court 1889–90. See Chapter 12.

108 Wilkinson to Native Department, 16 November 1887, 87/2954, 7 December 1887, 87/3104, MA Register of Inwards Correspondence, 1887; Wilkinson, 7 December 1887, quoting Te Kooti's letter of 5 December 1887, 87/3105, MA 23/8b, NA.

109 Te Kooti is known to have visited the Coromandel settlements in March 1884, July–August 1884, and July–August 1885.

110 Wilkinson, enclosing letters from Te Kooti, 17 March, 6 May 1888, 88/555, 88/816, MA Register of Inwards Correspondence, 1888; Native Department to Wilkinson, 23 November 1887, Outwards Letterbook MA4/47, and 28 May 1888, MA4/48, NA.

111 Mead, *Te One Matua*, pp.45–46.
112 *DT,* 19 April 1884; *WT,* 26 April 1884.
113 Native Department to Wilkinson, 6 May 1884, 84/1505, MA 23/8a, NA.
114 John Brooking (Gisborne) to Preece, 13 February 1883, 83/501, ibid.
115 Preece to Native Department, 11 October 1884, 84/3046, ibid.
116 W. L. Williams to Native Department, 13 November 1884, 84/3372, ibid. The letter does not seem to have been published. *Te Waka Maori* published only a short note on 17 October stating that the government had said that Te Kooti would not come to Wairoa, and a longer piece on 14 November (its final issue) arguing against Te Kooti's visit but adding that Te Kooti himself had decided not to come because he would not break his agreement with the government.
117 84/3305, MA 23/8a, NA.
118 Preece to Native Department, 8 November 1884, and petitions dated 4 November 1884, 84/3316, ibid.
119 Porter to Native Department, 6 November 1884, 84/3297, ibid.
120 H. Williams to W. L. Williams, 5 October 1884, Williams Family Papers, MSS 190:20, ATL.
121 The government's letter to him, dated 25 October 1884, is reproduced in *PD* 1884, L, p.404, as is Te Kooti's initial reply, 25 [*sic*: 24] October (84/3188, MA 23/8a, NA). His decision not to go was sent to Wilkinson, 3 November 1884, 84/3302, and was reported in Wilkinson to Native Department, 5 November 1884, 84/3188, MA 23/8a, NA.
122 Te Kooti to Wilkinson, 3 November 1884, 84/3302, ibid. CT.
123 Areta Apatu and all Ngati Kahungunu, to Ballance, 6 November 1884, 84/3379, ibid. CT.
124 *DT,* 29 December 1884; Preece to Native Department, 3 January 1885, 85/43, MA 23/8a, NA.
125 Te Kooti to Wilkinson, 10 November 1884, 84/3386, ibid. CT.
126 To Wilkinson, 84/3640, ibid. CT. This lament is published in *Nga Moteatea,* I, pp.100–1. The variant 'tahu' for 'tau' is in Te Kooti's text, which is written in his own hand.
127 OS: 16 February 1982.
128 *PD* 1884, L, p.404.
129 Waiata 36 (3), MSS C-35, AU. Trans: Frank Davis.
130 *AJHR* 1885, G-1, p.10.
131 Ibid., p.11.
132 Ibid.
133 Waiata 38, MSS C-35, AU. It is an adaptation of the waiata recorded in *Nga Moteatea,* II, pp.64–67.
134 Mihi Takotohiwi, 'Ngā Marae ō Whakatāne', MA thesis, University of Waikato, 1980, p.3.
135 *BPT,* 28 May 1885.
136 26 May 1885, Diary, typescript, MSS A-31, Box 5, AU.
137 R. Donaldson to Education Department, 6 June 1885, Te Teko Maori School File, E44/4, I, BAAA 1001/615b, NA Auckland.
138 Ibid.
139 *AJHR* 1884, G-4A, p.[1].
140 Bush to Native Department, 29 June 1885, 1 December 1885, 85/2272, 85/3890, MA 23/8a, NA.
141 Bush to Native Department, 20 January 1885, 85/236, ibid., and Annual report, 1 May 1885, *AJHR* 1885, G-2, p.11.
142 Bush, Annual reports, 8 May 1884, *AJHR* 1884, Sess. II, G-1, p.15; 1 May 1885, *AJHR* 1885, G-2, p.11.
143 Ibid.
144 Wilkinson to Native Department, 16 December 1885, 85/4024, MA 23/8a, NA.
145 *DT,* 23 December 1885.
146 Preece to Native Department, 22 December 1885, 85/4132, MA 23/8a, NA.
147 Paeroa MSS, pp.[15–16].
148 Bullen to Police Commissioner, 23 December 1885, P1 85/3563, NA.
149 25 December 1885, 86/27, MA 23/8a, NA.
150 Te Waru died in April 1884.
151 Bullen to Police Commissioner/Minister of Defence, 28 December 1885, P1 85/3563, NA, and quoted verbatim, *WT,* 29 December 1885 (an interesting leak from the Wellington post and telegraph office).
152 O. G. Denton, 'Mohaka Raid Account', MSS, ATL. This account is based on the information of Denton's mother, Joanna Sim of Mohaka, who was present. It contains a number of verifiable details, giving it some weight.
153 Ibid.
154 Preece's account of the visit, *Free Lance,* 31 July 1924, Best, Scrapbook VIII, p.68, ATL.
155 He was described as a Rotorua chief, but it is more probable that he was Petera Te Rangihiroa.
156 Extract from 'the Wairoa paper', presumed to be the *Wairoa Guardian,* of which no known copies survive from this date: P. L. Porter, 'The Porter Family in New Zealand', p.13, MSS, ATL.

157 Biddle MSS, I, p.81. This second house is unnumbered and unnamed in the list of houses; the text simply reads 'Te Wairoa again' ('Te Wairoa ano').

158 P. L. Porter MSS, pp.13–14, ATL.

159 Bullen to Native Department, 29 December 1885, 86/27, MA 23/8a, NA.

160 E.g. Te Kooti to Ballance, 25, 31 December 1885, 86/27, 86/28, ibid.

161 P. L. Porter MSS, p.14, ATL: extract from *Wairoa Guardian*, n.d.

162 Bullen to Native Department, 29 December 1885, 86/27, MA 23/8a.

163 Greenwood, *Upraised Hand*, p.67.

164 OS: Eruera Manuera talking with Frank Davis, n.d., Davis Dossier, Vol. 9, ATL.

165 OS: 5 March 1983.

166 OS: Boy Biddle, 15 October 1987.

167 'Legend Translation', *Te Maori*, October–November 1979, pp.39–40. The translation (not the Maori text) correctly identifies Teki Kanara as Anglican. This story is told as referring to Te Kooti's visit to Koriniti in January 1893, after his visit to Aorangi, but more likely it took place in January 1892, after Te Kooti's visit to Parikino. A song of Te Kooti for Teki Kanara, which probably stems from the occasion, is recorded in 'Prediction', p.23. See Chapters 13–14 for Te Kooti's journeys to the Whanganui district.

168 OS: Niko Tangaroa, Ringatu tohunga at Otoko, 1 January 1995.

169 Greenwood, *Upraised Hand*, p.67. Also OS: Boy Biddle, 29 January 1983. (Biddle was Greenwood's source.)

170 J. H. Pope, 31 March 1882, *AJHR* 1882, E-2, p.3.

171 Bush, in Annual report of Inspector-general of native schools, 31 March 1886, *AJHR* 1886, E-2, p.6.

172 Annual report, 3 June 1889, *AJHR* 1889, G-3, p.7.

173 Report, 31 March 1889, Waioeka School File, E 44/4, II, BAAA 1001/706c, NA Auckland.

174 Annual report, 5 June 1890, *AJHR* 1890, G-2, p.7.

175 Such as Omaio school, memorandum 6 July 1887, E 44/4, I, BAAA 1001/388c, Te Awahou school report, [October] 1887, E 44/4, II, BAAA 1001/574b, Omarumutu school report, 27 February 1888, E 44/4, I, BAAA 1001/395c, NA Auckland. Also Pope, 31 March 1888, *AJHR* 1888, E-2, p.6.

176 Talking with Frank Davis, 1978. Cited Davis Dossier, Vol. 1, p.70, ATL.

177 Paeroa MSS, pp.[17–18]. Trans: adapted from Frank Davis.

178 Ibid., p.[15].

179 Biddle MSS, I, p.4. From Petera Te Rangihiroa's manuscripts.

180 Ibid.; Lemuel MSS (copied from a mss book held at Waikaremoana), p.4.

181 Matthew 13:13 and 35. Wi Tarei quoted Matthew 13 in explanation of Te Kooti's use of the 'sacred words' in 'te reo ke' for the house Ruataupare: Mead, *Te One Matua*, p.84.

182 Paeroa MSS, p.[18]. Trans: adapted from Frank Davis.

183 Biddle MSS, I, p.6.

184 Waiata 35, MSS C-35, AU. The first part of this waiata can also be found in Best, *Tuhoe*, I, p.600, where Best describes it as a lament composed by Te Kooti for his slain followers. This text was given to Best by Paitini Wi Tapeka. The original text, from which Te Kooti's is derived, is in *Nga Moteatea*, III, pp.72–73. It is said there to be a song of a woman from Wharekauri, lamenting her husband.

185 Waiata 37, composed 1885, MSS C-35, AU. Trans: based on Frank Davis.

186 Bullen to Native Minister, 29 December 1885, 86/27, MA 23/8a, NA.

187 Te Kooti to government, 23 October 1885, P1 85/3039, NA.

188 W. J. Phillipps, *Carved Maori Houses of the Eastern Districts of the North Island*, 1944, p.84.

189 Preece to Native Department, 28 December 1885, 86/27, Te Kooti, telegram to Native Department, 31 December 1885, 86/28, MA 23/8a, NA.

190 To Ballance, 22 January 1886, 86/236, ibid.

191 Wi Hapi Te Rangiheuea appears in D. L. Mundy's well-known photograph of a line-up of members of the Arawa flying column posing with Te Kooti's flag (captured at Te Porere) at Rotokakahi in February 1870.

192 *NZH*, 15 July 1886.

193 Te Kooti to Native Department, 8 August 1886, 86/2971, MA Register of Inwards Letters, 1886, NA.

194 Wilkinson to Native Department, 6 August 1886, loose item, MA 21/24, NA.

195 OS: 23 May 1982.

196 OS: Heni Brown, narrating the same story, 14 February 1982. Eruera Manuera also told the story: Te Kooti had asked for 'a penny or sixpence' from the people of Tuhourangi but they said to him, 'Oh, humbug': 17 February 1982.

197 OS: Paora Delamere narrating the same story, 15 December 1971, Te Reo o Te Maori, Radio NZ Archives.

198 The kupu is dated in the manuscript 6 May 1886; it is called the 'Second' ('Tuarua') prediction. It is then followed by a further revelation dated 9 June 1886. Paeroa MSS, pp.[21–22]. Trans: based on Frank Davis.

199 OS: Wi Tarei, 13 February 1974, AK7/56, Radio NZ Archives. Tarei was quoting closely from the predictive texts of 6 May, 9 June 1886, in Paeroa MSS, pp.[21–22], which manuscript he held.

200 Donaldson (Te Teko schoolteacher), to Rev. W. J. Habens, 26 June, 10, 18 July 1886, Te Teko Native School File, E 44/4, I, BAAA 1001/615b, NA Auckland.

201 OS: Heta Rua, 23 May 1982.

202 Witeri Whakahau, Tiopira [Te Hukiki] and others, Te Teko, 12 June 1886, 86/1671, MA 21/23, NA; also Reone Te Mahapapa, Te Awahou, 15 July 1886, 86/2186, Mehaka Tokopounamu, Karatia, 19 November 1886, 86/4043, MA 21/24, NA.

203 Arama Karaka Mokonuiarangi and others, to Native Minister, 16 June 1886, 86/2579, ibid.

204 Bush to Native Department, 4 August 1886, 86/2461, and Hamiora Pio to Native Department, 9 August 1886, 86/2774, ibid.

205 Wepiha Apanui, 30 July 1886, quoted in 86/2408, ibid.

206 Donaldson to Habens, 31 July 1886, Te Teko Native School File, E 44/4, I, BAAA 1001/615b, NA Auckland; Bush to Native Department, 4 August 1886, 86/2461, MA 21/24, NA.

207 Donaldson, Memorandum to Habens, n.d. (received 20 September 1886), Te Teko Native School File, E 44/4, I, BAAA 1001/615b, NA Auckland.

208 Quoted by F. K. B[roomfield], 'A History of Te Teko School', *Whakatane Historical Review*, XIII, 2 (1965), p.72. However, this sentence is not in the letter to which the author has attributed it. This letter, otherwise quoted accurately, is in the Te Teko Native School file. The original letter is intact; there are no pages missing. The sentence may have been taken from another letter and added in, but the source has not been located.

209 Hamiora Pio, 9 August 1886, 86/2774, MA 21/24, NA. CT. The name Hehuketo is difficult to transliterate with any confidence, because it is not found in the standard Maori bible or Maori concordance. If it is an unusual rendering of 'Jesus Christ', then Hamiora may be setting him against Te Kooti's prophecy.

210 *BPT*, 28 January 1886.

211 Paeroa MSS, p.[20]; Biddle MSS, I, p.44. (Misdated in the last by a copyist's error, and questioned there.)

212 27 January 1886, 86/321, MA 23/8a, NA.

Chapter 12: Where Does the Freedom Lie? (February 1886– March 1889)

1 Waiata 56, MSS C-35, AU. Trans: Frank Davis.

2 OS: Robert Emery, 10 June 1979, Davis Dossier, Vol. 9, ATL.

3 'The Facts about Te Kooti', p.17.

4 OS: Robert Emery, 10 June 1979, Davis Dossier, Vol. 9, ATL. The government had refused a petition to construct a road from Kihikihi to Otewa in 1887: Native Department to Wilkinson, 22 April 1887, MA4/46, NA.

5 *WT*, 4 April 1885.

6 Wilkinson to Native Department, 28 August 1883, *AJHR* 1884, G-4A, p.2.

7 Te Kooti to Hare Raupara [Hare Pati], 2 January 1885, Te Kooti to Hare, 4 January 1885, Te Kooti to Hare Pati, 14 November 1885, MSS 390, ATL. Elsdon Best, who translated these letters, apparently identified Hare as Te Kooti's nephew. Hare might therefore be Wi Pati (William Bird) of Ngati Porou, who married Taawhi Paraone, Te Kooti's great-niece, whom Te Kooti brought up. (Taawhi was the granddaughter of Te Kooti's elder brother Komene.) Te Kooti addressed Hare as 'son' ('tama') in the first two letters, while the third letter he wrote to Hare and all those staying at Ruatoki. The letters, by their style, appear to be written to a young Maori man under Te Kooti's patronage.

However, the identification of Hare Pati remains uncertain. He could be the Pakeha trader William Henry Bird (who was known to Maori as Hare Pati and to Europeans as Willie Bird), from Galatea. In 1885 Bird was living at Tarawera; after the 1886 eruption he returned to Galatea and became its storekeeper. He had already married into the Maori community there, and he acquired much land. Through his wife's family he was also connected with the Tuwharetoa carver Ngamotu who, about 1890, built the meeting-house Tuwhare at Galatea, which carried a portrait of Te Kooti on the lintel (see Chapter 13). However, Best knew Willie Bird, so it seems unlikely that he would have been mistaken. Nevertheless, it is clear from the fourth letter written by Te Kooti to Hare (17 February 1889) that Hare had been given access to extensive land blocks at Waiohau, which Te Kooti had made available to him (first 1000 acres, then 700,000 acres). In August 1889 James Carroll referred to a

Pakeha to whom Te Kooti had persuaded his followers to sell a portion of a large block of land that they had previously leased out near Whakatane, and from which transactions Te Kooti had benefited personally (*PD* 1889, LXVI, p.88). The block was probably Waiohau, or perhaps nearby Matahina, both of which were by then large, subdivided, Crown-titled land blocks, able to be leased and sold. Hare Pati also made an unsuccessful claim to Tuhoe land at Ruatoki during the survey dispute there in 1893 (see Chapter 14). Hare Pati's relationship with Te Kooti, therefore, remains equivocal, as do their transactions.

8 Te Kooti to Hare Pati, 14 November 1885, MSS 390, ATL.

9 Toha to Native Department, 19 November 1877, 78/675, MA Register of Inwards Correspondence, 1878, NA. Also, F. Ormond to Native Department, 21 February 1878, 78/694, ibid.; Lambert, pp.703–4.

10 Te Kooti to Native Department, 6 March 1882, 82/1211, Preece (enclosing Te Kooti's letter to Maaka) to Native Department, 29 June 1882, 82/1948, MA Register of Inwards Correspondence, 1882, NA.

11 She was with the party who, with Te Kooti, met Bryce on 27 March 1883 at Alexandra to negotiate for land for them to live on, Biddle MSS, I, p.161.

12 Wilkinson to Native Department, 22 June 1883, 83/214, MA Register of Inwards Correspondence, 1883.

13 Rangi was born about 1886; Putiputi on 31 June 1890.

14 Binney and Chaplin, *Ngā Mōrehu*, pp.93–94.

15 Waiata 41, MSS C-35, AU. Trans: based on Frank Davis.

16 Biddle MSS, I, p.5.

17 Waiata 41, MSS C-35, AU. Hamiora's gloss has one critical word missing in the instructions: 'kupu' (the word or sayings), but it is in the transcript in Biddle MSS, V, p.118. The two glosses are not identical, however, and must have been copied from different sources. But the song text is identical.

18 That is, Tareha Te Moananui of Ngati Kahungunu, who led a contingent against Te Kooti at Te Karetu in 1868. Tareha had close links with Tuhoe and had worked with them to form their anti-land-selling union, under the guidance of Te Kooti, in 1872-74 (see Chapter 14). (The other possibility here, Meha (Tanumeha) Te Moananui, a leading chief at Ohinemuri, was dead.)

19 Biddle MSS, I, p.8. From Hamiora's manuscripts.

20 Waiata 42, MSS C-35, AU; Biddle MSS, I, p.8.

21 Ibid.

22 OS: 15 February 1982.

23 OS: Mangatu, 6 June 1982.

24 Maungapohatu Notebook 1880–1916, pp.90–91, MSS C-22, AU. The same text (slightly shortened) is also in Biddle MSS, I, p.41.

25 Paeroa MSS, p.[57]. Trans: based on Frank Davis.

26 Bush, Annual report, 3 May 1886, *AJHR* 1886, G-1, p.13; also Memorandum on the census, 4 May 1886, ibid., G-12, p.8.

27 27 October 1886, 86/3551, MA 23/8b, NA. CT.

28 R. Bullen to Police Commissioner, 7 January 1887, P1 87/453, NA.

29 30 December 1886, 86/4239, MA 23/8b, NA.

30 *DT*, 23 December 1886; Bullen to Police Commissioner, 7 January 1887, P1 87/453, NA.

31 24 December 1886.

32 Hamiora Aparoa said there were eight songs composed for the journey to Porangahau, and then listed seven, numbered erratically as Waiata 43–47, MSS C-35, AU.

33 OS: 14 December 1981.

34 'Remembers Te Kooti as captive', *DT*, 2 September 1967, and an oral version retold by her daughter, Elsie M. Owens of Napier, in 1982.

35 23 December 1886.

36 *DT*, 29 December 1886.

37 Ibid., 28 December 1886.

38 Ibid., 30 December 1886.

39 The house at Porangahau is included in Matiu's list of houses built for the Kotahitanga of God's words, Biddle MSS, I, p.81. This was probably Poho-o-Kahungunu, whose timbers and carvings were included in the later house of the same name, which now stands at Porangahau. The name of the house was garbled in the newspaper reports of 1886 as 'Pohokangaau'.

40 *DT*, 30 December 1886.

41 Ibid., 28 December 1886.

42 Ibid., 30 December 1886.

43 24 December 1886.

44 Bullen to Police Commissioner, 7 January 1887, P1 87/453, NA.

45 *DT*, 30 December 1886.
46 OS: Boy Biddle, 15 October 1987.
47 *DT*, 28 December 1886.
48 Ibid., 4 January 1887; *EP*, 5 January 1887.
49 Paeroa MSS, pp.[29–30]. Trans: modified from Frank Davis.
50 Waiata 67, 1 July 1890, MSS C-35, AU. This observation is an annotation to the crucial question asked in the song, and it clarifies the thrust of an otherwise ambiguous text. The annotation places emphasis on a future leader, who will solve the problems.
51 *DT*, 6 January 1887.
52 Preece to Native Department, 1 January 1887, Renata Kawepo to Native Department, 5 January 1887, 86/3551, MA 23/8b, NA.
53 Bullen to Police Commissioner, 7 January 1887, P1 87/453, NA.
54 Telegram, 5 January 1887, 87/475, MA 23/8b, NA.
55 OS: Taradale, 18 April 1991.
56 Paeroa MSS, p.[31]. Trans: modified from Frank Davis. This interpretation rests on the reading of 'pakanga' as 'pākanga', relative. The alternative, 'a region in which a battle has not been fought', seems much less likely, for Petane, as Te Kooti knew, had been a centre of the East Coast fighting in 1866. The general intention is clear: it was a region which gave him support.
57 Wilson MSS, p.143.
58 Ibid.
59 Ibid.
60 Major W. E. Gudgeon (Police Commissioner) to Kiely, P1 87/453, NA.
61 Not only did Kiely say this about Te Kooti, it is stated by Ringatu. OS: Boy Biddle, 15 October 1987.
62 Kiely to Police Commissioner, 19 February 1887, P1 87/453, NA.
63 Ibid.
64 Jones to Kiely, 27 February 1887, ibid.
65 *PBH* (quoting *AS*), 16 February 1889; similarly, E. F. Sullivan, 'Memories of Kihikihi' (recollections of the 1880s), POM 43-3, Auckland Catholic District Archives.
66 Kiely to Police Commissioner, 2 March 1887, P1 87/453, NA.
67 Wilkinson, Annual report, 19 May 1887, *AJHR* 1887, Sess. II, G-1, p.7.
68 Bush to Native Department, 1 May 1885, *AJHR* 1885, G-2, p.11.
69 The house was listed by Matiu as part of the Kotahitanga, Biddle MSS, I, p.81.
70 Brabant to McLean, 3 June 1872, MSS 32:171, ATL.
71 A ridge pa on the coast to the east of Opape, occupied by Ngai Tai; it marks the boundary between Ngai Tai and Whakatohea and had been a source of dispute.
72 Waiata 50 (1) and (2), MSS C-35, AU. Trans: based on Frank Davis. Best published the text (slightly modified) as an example of a song of peacemaking, in 'Notes on the Art of War', *JPS*, XII, 4 (December 1903), p.202.
73 OS: 16 February 1982. Maaka Jones, Te Kohi's granddaughter, also narrated her version of this family story: Binney and Chaplin, *Ngā Mōrehu*, p.76.
74 Waiata 49, MSS C-35, AU. This song is an adaptation of a waiata aroha (love song) sung by Meroiti and recorded by Sir George Grey in *Ko Nga Moteatea*, 2nd edn, 1853, p.27. The lineation is taken from an essay comparing the two versions by Bob Pearson, written for Maori Studies, University of Canterbury, 1982. The names are of places along the journey: Maketu is in the Bay of Plenty, and the headland Kohi is the point at Whakatane from where the travellers would first see the mouth of the Motu river. See Binney and Chaplin, *Ngā Mōrehu*, p.194, n.1, for further comments on this song and translation.
75 Bush to Native Minister, 1 June 1887, 87/1705, MA 23/8b, NA.
76 P. B. Cahill to Inspector Goodall, 27, 28 June 1887, P1 87/1518, NA. Bush described the same event, but estimated the number accompanying Te Kooti as rather lower, 300: to Native Department, 27 July 1887, 87/2240, MA 23/8b, NA.
77 Wiremu Kingi Tutahuarangi [Te Kawau] to Ballance, 27 May 1887, 87/1705, ibid.
78 Ibid.
79 Bush, covering note to Wiremu Kingi's letter, 1 June 1887, 87/1705, ibid.
80 Biddle MSS, I, p.9. Matiu Paeroa quoted a variant of this kupu — 'Eneteri whota' — for 12 June 1887 (that is, just before the party set out for Maraenui), p.[34].
81 OS: Monita Delamere, 16 February 1982.
82 Te Turuki to Wiremu Kingi, 8 July 1888, 88/1310, MA 23/8b, NA. CT.
83 OS: Monita Delamere, 16 February 1982; Ema Rogers, Whitianga (eastern Bay of Plenty), 2 January 1985. On the hearing of 1898, see A. C. Lyall, *Whakatohea of Opotiki*, 1979, pp.14–15.

84 OS: Monita Delamere, 16 February 1982. A similar version, which Monita told Frank Davis in 1978, is in the Davis Dossier, Vol. 9, ATL.

85 OS: Maaka Jones, 20, 21 August 1984. Also quoted (with slight editorial differences) in Binney and Chaplin, *Ngā Mōrehu*, p.75.

86 Bush to Native Department, 27 July 1887, 87/2240, MA 23/8b, NA.

87 Ibid.

88 James Fox (for Police Commissioner) to Minister of Defence, 25 July 1887, P1 87/1518, NA.

89 To Police Commissioner, 30 July 1887, ibid.

90 Bush, 27 July 1887, 87/2240, MA 23/8b, NA.

91 Ibid.

92 OS: Tupae (John) Ruru, 15 February 1982. The gloss of the Maori is taken from his explanation.

93 Wi Haronga was the head of this family, who took their name from him. He was a kinsman and contemporary of Kahutia and Rukupo. The present house Whakahau bears the date 5 November 1926, and was derelict when seen by the author in 1982.

94 OS: John Ruru. The original Ngawari was destroyed by fire; the present house at Mangatu is the third of that name, and stands on a different site.

95 Te Aroha was moved from its original site in 1922, and stands today at Tapuihikitia Rd, Puha.

96 *PBH*, 9 February 1887.

97 *PBH*, 22, 24 October, 4 November 1887.

98 Witi Ihimaera, *The Matriarch*, 1986, p.183, has a modern reinterpretation.

99 See Chapter 10, p.291.

100 Biddle MSS, I, pp.132, 152–53: explanations of 'The prophetic sayings to Adam and up to Christ. By Te Kooti' ('Nga kupu whakaari ki a Arama tae mai ki a Te Karaiti. Na Te Kooti'). Not all the phrases in glossolalia are included in these explanations.

101 See Whakapapa B and C.

102 Wi Pere was MHR for Eastern Maori from July 1884 until July 1887 (and was re-elected in 1893).

103 Diary of Peneamene Tanui. His code started with the ace. MSS 671:2, AIM.

104 Ihimaera, *The Matriarch*, p.192.

105 23 May 1865, HB4/13, NA.

106 OS: Reuben Riki, 16 May 1982. The waiata referred to is Waiata 57 in Hamiora Aparoa's collection, MSS C-35, AU. It is dated 14 February 1889, and is an adaptation of an old waiata from the upper Whanganui (*Nga Moteatea*, II, pp.130–33). Te Kooti's adaptation refers in its last lines to 'the house of Wi Pere' ('te whare o Wi Pere'). The interpretation given is that the house — that is, the girl to whom the song is sung — would abide alone, because of the blockage at Turanga on the path of anger ('te puru ki Turanga ki te ara o te riri'). Thus she might cease to be cherished ('E kore pea koe e manakohia mai') and become abandoned.

107 'Rongopai', *AWN*, 12 October 1970 (article based on an interview with Turuki Pere, Moanaroa Pere's son); OS: Mahanga Horsfall, Waituhi, 1985.

108 *PBH*, 25 February 1887. The three other religions were Anglican, Methodist and Roman Catholic.

109 Quoted in ibid.

110 Wi Kingi Tutahuarangi [Te Kawau] to Ballance, 27 May 1887, 87/1705, MA 23/8b, NA. CT.

111 *PBH*, 25 February 1887.

112 Petition dated 16 February 1887, 87/674, MA 23/8b, NA.

113 Westrup and 17 others, 27 October 1887, 87/2783, ibid.

114 87/2886, ibid.

115 He actually wrote 'Pikirangi'.

116 14 October 1887, 87/2887, ibid. Based on CT. Apiata Parekahika was a chief of Ngati Ruapani and Te Aitanga-a-Mahaki at Turanga.

117 OS: Heni Sunderland, 11 May 1984. See Binney and Chaplin, *Ngā Mōrehu*, p.117.

118 Porter to Defence Department, 3 November 1887, AD1 1894/950, NA. (Tiopira Tawhiao's name was incorrectly written as 'Taiwaio' by the telegraph office.)

119 *Poverty Bay Independent*, 9 January 1886, transcript in Mackay Scrapbook, MSS 1006/2:19, p.[504], ATL.

120 Clipping [25 October 1887], in 87/2784, MA 23/8b, NA.

121 Porter to Defence Department, 3 November 1887, AD1 1894/950, NA.

122 Porter to Under-secretary Defence, 28 October 1887, ibid.

123 Native Department to Rewi, 11 November 1887, 87/2887, MA 23/8b, NA.

124 Rewi Maniapoto to Native Department, 14 November 1887, ibid.

125 Native Department to Wilkinson, 1 November 1887, Outwards Letterbook MA4/47, NA.

126 Te Turuki to Rawinia Ahuroa, 3 November 1887, AD1 1894/950; Rawinia's relationship with Te Kooti was described by Bullen to Police Commissioner, 8 November 1887, when he reported (and garbled) the telegram: P1 88/213, NA. He may have been confusing her with Mere Paraone.

127 Wilkinson to Native Department, 16 November 1887, 87/2910, MA 23/8b, NA.

128 Signed 'Te Turuki', 87/2976, ibid. Trans: based on Wilkinson, 18 November 1887, 87/2983, ibid.

129 87/2976, ibid.

130 Ropata to Native Department, 29 November 1887, 87/3036, ibid.

131 Biddle MSS, I, p.40. The original text here had 'rua toru' ('two, three'), which was then altered to 'toru wha' ('three, four'). This is a recurring phrase of Te Kooti, usually written as 'rua toru wha', and it will be seen in other predictions yet to be discussed.

132 Sergeant J. H. Bullen, Gisborne, to Inspector Bullen, 17 November 1887, P1 88/213, NA.

133 See, for example, *PBH*, 4 November 1887; *GS*, 1, 3, 5 November 1887.

134 Wilkinson's translation of letter by Te Turuki, 5 December 1887, 87/3105, MA 23/8b, NA. No Maori original.

135 R. Bullen to Police Commissioner, 17 December 1887, P1 88/213, NA.

136 Bullen to Police Commissioner, 9 December 1887, ibid.

137 Waiata 53, MSS C-35, AU.

138 Te Turuki to Tiopira, Maungapohatu Notebook, 1881–1916, pp.40–41, MSS C-22, AU. Te Kooti signed himself as 'tuakana', elder relation. The author has deduced from the context, and the fact that the letter has been copied into a Tuhoe notebook concerning Rua Kenana, that it is about Rongopai. The date on the letter could read 1881; it was sent from Te Kuiti; and as Tiopira (Theophilus) is a baptismal name, the recipient is also not absolutely certain.

139 Ibid., p.41.

140 A reference to the rifled muskets and breech-loading rifles firing the Minie bullet. The rifled musket, when used with the hollow lead bullet invented by Captain Claude Minié, created unprecedented gaping wounds, particularly if the practice of cutting a cross at the top of the bullet was followed. See also Chapter 9.

141 Waiata 53, MSS C-35, AU. The lineation and the translation are based on a version kindly prepared for the author by the late Wiremu Parker.

142 See *Nga Moteatea*, III, pp.54–61. For further comment in addition to the remarks here, see Binney and Chaplin, *Ngā Mōrehu*, p.188, n.61.

143 Waiata 54, MSS C-35, AU. Trans: based on Frank Davis.

144 Wilkinson (forwarding Te Kooti's petition) to Native Department, 13 February 1888, 88/368, MA Register of Inwards Correspondence, 1888, NA. The Native Affairs Committee rejected the petition on 15 June, Petition 64, *AJHR* 1888, I-3, p.8. (The petition is no longer extant.)

145 25 February 1888, Paeroa MSS, p.[45].

146 Bush to Native Department, 4 July 1888, 88/1322, MA 23/8b, NA.

147 Biddle MSS, I, p.81.

148 OS: Takerangi Smith, 17 November 1994. Te Ao Turoa Ramanui died in 1961; he was said to be 108 years old: obituary, *Te Ao Hou*, 37 (December 1961), p.3.

149 Bush to Native Department, 21, 22 June 1888, 88/1171, Wiremu Kingi [Te Kawau] to Ropata, 27 June 1888, 88/1673, Bush to Native Department, 4 July 1888, 88/1322, MA 23/8b, NA. Wiremu Kingi estimated a total of 1000 people, whereas Bush thought it was about 700, but both described a very similar composition for the gathering at Waioeka.

150 Bush to Native Department, 4 July 1888, 88/1322, ibid.

151 OS: Paroa (Jack) Kurei, Opotiki, 15 December 1981.

152 Biddle MSS, I, p.28.

153 *BPT*, 18 July 1888.

154 T. Rewiri and all of Te Patuai (Te Patuwai) of Whakatane, 14 September 1888, 88/1809, MA 23/8b, NA.

155 Hohepa Te Wharepu and others, Whakatane, 12 November 1888, 88/2116, ibid. CT.

156 18 July 1888, 88/1673, ibid.

157 12 November 1888, 88/2116, ibid. CT.

158 T. Rewiri (son of Rewiri Parera) and all Te Patuai (Te Patuwai) to Bush, 14 September 1888, 88/1809, Hohepa Te Wharepu to Parliament, 12 November 1888, 88/2116, ibid.

159 Bush to Native Department, 4 July 1888, 88/1322, ibid.

160 E.g. petition of Te Hautakuru and 38 others, Opotiki, to Parliament, 22 May 1888, 88/1141, ibid.

161 12 November 1888, 88/2116, ibid. CT.

162 Bush to Native Department, 4 February 1889, 89/333, MA 23/8c, NA.

163 Karauria Wiremu Kingi (Wiremu Kingi Te Kawau's son), and all Ngai Tai, 18 January 1889, 89/265, ibid.

164 Te Hata Te Kakatuamaro, 17 July 1888, Wiremu Kingi, 18 July 1888, 88/1673, MA 23/8b, NA.

165 Te Kooti Te Turuki to Mitchelson, 12 January 1889, 89/188, MA 23/8c, NA.

166 14 June 1888, 88/1312, MA 23/8b, NA.

167 The three ceded blocks — Te Muhunga (modern Ormond) (5000 acres), Te Arai (735 acres) and Patutahi (c.57,000 acres) — are listed in the Poverty Bay Commission records, 30 June 1869, pp.2–4, MLC microfilm. But the records there are extremely sketchy: the amounts of land taken appear to have been filled in later, and the records give no indication of the out-of-court discussions, which took place on 29 June between the government's agent and the agent acting for the tribes. Judge Monro's account included only the statement that Te Muhunga contained 5000 acres, and that the Patutahi block was 'unsurveyed' (Poverty Bay Notes, p.2). The only other contemporary record of the hearing appears to be in W. L. Williams, Diary, 29–30 June 1869 (MSS, ATL). There, he mentioned the 40,000 acres of the 'back country' which the government intended to be included. On 30 June he added that the amount ceded by the Maori was less than he had originally been informed, but then he changed his mind again. On 5 July, writing to his father, he mentioned 5000 acres each at Patutahi and Te Muhunga, and about '40,000 acres' 'up the Arai', commenting that no one actually knew where the last would extend (MSS 69:56B, ATL).

The surveyor first spoke to the commission on 4 August about two of the blocks (Te Muhunga and Te Arai), but significantly no acreage was then recorded (Monro, Poverty Bay Notes, pp.204, 209). In October, Samuel Locke viewed the three blocks and roughly described them: that is, the Muhunga block (5395 acres), the Patutahi block (now estimated at 57,000 acres) and c.1000 acres up the Te Arai stream, which Locke included in the 57,000-acre block: 25 October 1869, Letterbook, HBM. This description contradicted his earlier impression of what had been ceded: 30,000 acres of the rough hills and about 12,000 acres of good and fair land (writing from Turanga to McLean, 8 July 1869, MSS 32:393, ATL). Later, Locke stated in evidence that the Crown possessed about 47,000 acres in the Patutahi block (Patutahi Commission, *AJHR* 1884, Sess. II, G-4, p.7). The deposited copy of the survey map of the confiscations drawn in April 1873 marked the Patutahi block as 'about 50,746 acres' (MA 62/9, NA). It is clear that an appalling muddle existed.

The uncertainty as to what had been taken added to the distress of Rongowhakaata and Te Aitanga-a-Mahaki, the two tribes directly affected. In response to three petitions of 1914–17, the 1920 Native Land Claims' Commission investigated the Patutahi block and decided that (allowing for 5824 acres which had already been returned or compensated for) an excess of 20,337 acres had been taken: *AJHR* 1921–22, G-5, p.20. The matter then dragged its way painfully through the courts, with compensation finally being offered in 1930. The low value set by the government then had to be contested by the claimants. This long-drawn-out saga and muddle are only too typical of the confiscation histories.

168 Paora Parau, Eru Pohatu, evidence before the Patutahi Commission, *AJHR* 1884, Sess. II, G-4, pp.7, 20.

169 E. H. Ward, 6 July 1888 to Native Department, 88/1301, MA 23/8b, NA; Petition 390, *AJHR* 1888, I-3, p.29.

170 Annotation on Carroll to Native Minister, 27 August 1888, 88/1673, MA 23/8b, NA.

171 E. Morpeth, annotation on James Booth to Native Department, 13 February 1889, 89/372, MA 23/8c, NA.

172 R. Whititera Te Waiatua, Ohinemutu, 28 November 1888, 88/2637, ibid.

173 Biddle MSS, I, p.81.

174 Paeroa MSS, p.[50]. Trans: based on Frank Davis.

175 Neich has suggested that Te Kooti's house is probably Te Purei, which stands at Ngongotaha today (1994). Photographs reveal that extensive alterations were made to the porch and front wall of Te Purei before its move.

176 Paeroa MSS, p.[50].

177 Ibid.; Biddle MSS, I, p.44, contains Hamiora's text of this same kupu under the heading in 'te reo ke', 'Eri'. 'Eri' was the statement that God created heaven and earth, and this was also spelt out in Hamiora's version of the kupu. In Hamiora's text it was stated that this blood would be spilt for the land and the faith ('whakapono').

178 Bush to Native Department, 4 February 1889, 89/333, MA 23/8c, NA.

179 Paeroa MSS, pp.[49–50]. Trans: based on Frank Davis. Biddle MSS, I, p.44, contains Hamiora's version, and on p.45, a similar, but less complete version, derived from Petera Te Rangihiroa. The three words in 'te reo ke' in Hamiora's text for 1 January 1889 were 'Eri. Ote. Whata.' Matiu wrote for 3 January, 'Teraamu Hote.', while Petera wrote, also for 3 January, 'Tera. Amu. Ota.' The accompanying texts are recognisably from the same occasion and it is clear from Matiu's account that the sayings were delivered over three days.

180 Biddle MSS, I, p.44.

181 Hori Karaka, writing from Te Awahou, to Native Department, 3 December 1888, 88/2700, MA 23/8c, NA.

182 *AS*, 25 February 1889.

183 7 January 1889, 89/261, MA 23/8c, NA.

184 Pio Te Tuaina, Wiremu Te Haukakawa and others, 28 June 1897, Mill Hill Mission Papers, Auckland, Box II, 1897, 21-C-19a, St Joseph's Society of the Sacred Heart for Foreign Missions, Mill Hill, London. Trans: Father A. Ligthert.

185 Te Kooti Te Turuki to Mitchelson, 89/188, MA 23/8c, NA.

186 Te Turuki to Poata, 15 January 1889, AD1 1894/950, NA. CT.

187 To Native Department, 4 February 1889, 89/495, MA 23/8c, NA.

188 Maori Outwards Letterbook, MA4/95, NA.

189 P1 1889/559, NA.

190 As described by Mitchelson to Thomas Fergus MHR, 12 February 1889, ibid.

191 Mitchelson to Hursthouse, 4 February 1889, 89/495, MA 23/8c, NA; *PBH*, 9 February 1889.

192 Mitchelson to Native Department, 7 February 1889, 89/867, MA Register of Inwards Correspondence, 1889, NA; *PBH*, 9 February 1889.

193 Hursthouse to Native Department, 4 February 1889, 89/495, MA 23/8c, NA; *PBH*, 9 February 1889; Mitchelson to Fergus, 12 February 1889, P1 1889/559, NA — all quoting Te Kooti's statements in virtually identical words.

194 Affidavit by Te Kooti Turuki Rikirangi, 28 September 1889, J1 1890/407, NA.

195 Mitchelson donated the revolver to the Auckland Museum: Ethnology accession Nos 5244-45 (revolver and case).

196 Affidavit by Te Kooti, 28 September 1889, J1 1890/407, NA.

197 Waiata 56, MSS C-35, AU.

198 Bush to Native Minister, 18 February 1889, 89/495, MA 23/8c, NA.

199 Editorial, *PBH*, 19 February 1889, and 21 February: 'It is reported that at a meeting of Hauhaus Te Kooti had issued instructions that the sale of lands should be stopped, which would only result in establishing a system of Maori landlordism in this district.'

200 R. J. Seddon, 23 August 1889, *PD*, LXVI, p.85.

201 'Paokahu No. 3' hearing. The judgment (11 April 1889) stated that Hoani Ruru tried to set up Tarake, his immediate ancestor, as the recognised ancestor for the owners of this partition, instead of finding a shared descent line for all those who occupied the land in common beside the lagoon. It clearly stated that the land belonged to Ngati Maru and the descendants of Ruawhetuki, the common ancestor of Ngati Maru, acknowledged when this block was first separated in 1883 (see Whakapapa A and C). Te Kooti had not been included in the list of original owners presented to the court by Hoani Ruru in 1880; nor was he included in the partitions of 1883 and 1889: Gisborne Minute Book 6, pp.293-96; ibid., Book 9, pp.121-23; ibid., Book 13, pp.146-48; Judge Brabant's Minute Book 5, pp.121-24, MLC microfilm.

202 *EP*, 11 March 1889.

203 Westrup to Minister of Defence, 19 February 1889, P1 1889/559, NA.

204 W. K. Chambers, president of the committee, in *PBH*, 22 February 1889.

205 19 February 1889, 89/495, MA 23/8c, NA.

206 Bush to Mitchelson, 19 February 1889, 89/495, ibid.

207 Peneamine Tuhaka of Ngati Porou, and others to Native Department, 20 February 1889, 89/412, ibid.

208 T. W. Hislop (for Mitchelson), 21 February 1889, 89/495, ibid.

209 Kiely to Commissioner of Police, 8 March 1889, P1 1889/559, NA.

210 Ibid.

211 Kiely to Police Commissioner, 21 February 1889, ibid.

212 Kiely, 8 March 1889, ibid.

213 Porter to Under-secretary Defence, 15 March 1889, AD1 1894/950, NA.

214 Renata died 13 (14) April; Horonuku, 30 July.

215 To Native Department, 19 February 1889, 89/495, MA 23/8c, NA.

216 Tahora No. 2 was the vast inland block of land including Papuni, Te Haupapa (Te Houpapa), Waimaha, Nga Tapa and Te Wera — all Te Kooti's former sanctuaries. The hearing began on 11 January 1889. Wi Pere gave evidence from 18 February; the court was suspended 28 February–1 March because of the crisis over Te Kooti's arrest, and resumed again on 2 March. (Opotiki Minute Book 4, pp.18-25, 245-47, 257, 301-54; ibid., Book 5, pp.1-13, MLC microfilm.) Te Kooti's name (Te Turuki Te Rangipatahi) was included in the list of shareholders for Tahora 2F and 2C 1 when the block was subdivided, in 1890: Gisborne Minute Book 19, pp.45, 59, MLC microfilm; Tahora No. 2 block, lists of owners and payments, July 1890, AD 103/42, NA. Te Kooti owned two shares each in 2C 1 and 2F.

217 Michael Downey of Opotiki, sworn statement, 23 December 1889, *Goodall versus Te Kooti*, p.18, CL 19, NA; *AS*, 22 March 1889.

218 *AS*, *PBH*, 22 February 1889.

219 Goodall, sworn statement 27 January 1890, and Constable A. J. Sisam, 23 December 1889, *Goodall versus Te Kooti*, pp.13, 23, CL 19, NA.
220 See Chapter 14.
221 *PBH*, 22 February 1889.
222 25 February 1889.
223 Peneamine Tuhaka and others, 20 February 1889, 89/412, MA 23/8c, NA.
224 *AS, PBH*, 23 February 1889; *NZH*, 25 February 1889.
225 *PBH*, 25 February 1889; *NZH*, 25, 26 February 1889.
226 Biddle MSS, I, p.142, from Matiu Paeroa. Wi Paraone was Mere Kingi Paraone's eldest brother.
227 *NZH*, 26 February 1889.
228 This story ensured that the coat of arms would be recreated as a carving in the later house, Te Poho-o-Pikihoro, which now stands at Takepu marae, Te Karaka. Te Poho-o-Pikihoro became an Anglican meeting-house (and bears this statement of loyalty), it is said, in deference to Tiopira Tawhiao's wishes. *Gisborne Herald*, 1 February 1951, 8 March 1958.
229 To Native Department, 23 February 1889, 89/495, MA 23/8c, NA.
230 Ibid.
231 *BPT*, 25 February 1889.
232 *NZH*, 25 February 1889. The *Herald* had its own reporter at Opotiki by Sunday 24 February. *EP*, 25 February 1889, also carried the same report, telegraphed from Gisborne at 4 p.m., 24 February.
233 Waiata 58, MSS C-35, AU. Trans: based on Frank Davis. The word 'harirau' (wing of a bird) is annotated in the text to explain its usage as 'painful slapping'. This waiata is the first in a dated sequence concerning Te Kooti's arrest, which culminates on 28 February. The date for this waiata seems to be correct, although the song is said to have been composed at Waiotahe. Te Kooti went there on the night of 27 February.
234 Inspector Goodall to Police Commissioner, 24 February 1889, P1 1889/559, NA; Bush to Native Department, 24 February 1889, Native Department to Mitchelson, 24 February 1889, 89/495, MA 23/8c, NA; *PBH*, 25 February 1889; and Matiu's account in Biddle MSS, I, p.142. All agree on this.
235 Bush to Native Department, 24 February 1889, 89/495, MA 23/8c, NA; *GS*, 26 February 1889.
236 Bush to Native Minister, 27 February 1889, 89/495, MA 23/8c, NA.
237 *PBH*, 27 February 1889; the *Press*, 28 February 1889; *GS*, 5 March 1889.
238 OS: Ned Brown, 14 February 1982.
239 *EP*, 26, 27 February 1889.
240 1 March 1889.
241 *AJHR* 1889, G-8.
242 *AS*, 26 February 1889; *NZH*, 27 February 1889.
243 OS: 14 December 1981.
244 Bush to Native Department, 24 February 1889, 89/495, MA 23/8c, NA.
245 Bush to Native Department, 26 February 1889, ibid.
246 Bush mentioned this statement only later, but it seems very probable: Bush, sworn statement, 20 January 1890, *Goodall versus Te Kooti*, p.11, CL 19, NA.
247 Bush to Native Department, 26 February 1889 (9.26 p.m.), 89/495, MA 23/8c, NA. This cable from Bush was also published in *EP*, 27 February 1889.
248 Porter to Under-secretary Defence, 15 March 1889, AD1 1894/950; Bush, 20 January 1890, *Goodall versus Te Kooti*, p.11, CL 19, NA.
249 27 February 1889 (1.12 p.m.), 89/495, MA 23/8c, NA. The statement that he was leaving that day for Gisborne was also cabled through at 11.20 a.m. from Opotiki to the *Evening Post*, who printed it that evening.
250 Telegram quoted by Atkinson, 2 July 1889, *PD*, LXIV, p.149.
251 Biddle MSS, I, p.143.
252 Text in *AS*, 28 February 1889; also quoted (from memory) in Porter to Under-secretary Defence, 15 March 1889, AD1 1894/950; Bush to Native Minister, 27 February 1889 (9.54 p.m.), 89/495, MA 23/8c, NA.
253 *AS*, 28 February 1889.
254 Tamaku accompanied Te Kooti to Auckland after his arrest. This is the first known reference to her, but she is also remembered as going with him to Ohiwa in his last years and continuing to live there after his death: Mrs C. S. Armstrong, 'Some Reminiscences of Early Whakatane' (1957), *Whakatane Historical Review*, XIV, 1 (March 1966), pp.8–10.
255 Porter to Native Department, 28 February 1889, 89/495, MA 23/8c, NA.
256 *AS, EP*, 26 February 1889.
257 Seddon, 23 August 1889, PD, LXVI, p.83.

258 Porter to Under-secretary Defence, 15 March 1889, AD1 1894/950, NA; M. J. Gannon (the interpreter), in *PBII*, 11 March 1889.

259 [Bush to ?Native Department, 24 February 1889], 89/495, MA 23/8c, NA. (The first page of this telegram is missing.)

260 OS: 14 December 1981.

261 Biddle MSS, V, p.123. Also (but abridged) introduction to the two haka, waiata [58a], MSS C-35, AU.

262 OS: Monita Delamere, 16 February 1982, commenting on this patere.

263 Waiata [58a, (ii)], MSS C-35, AU. Trans: modified from Frank Davis.

264 OS: 16 February 1982.

265 Bush to Native Department, 12.24 p.m., 28 February 1889, 89/495, MA 23/8c; Porter to Under-secretary Defence, 15 March 1889, AD1 1894/950, NA.

266 *PBH*, 1 March 1889.

267 The reports vary as to whether there were three or four women with Te Kooti, who were his wives.

268 Porter to Under-secretary Defence, 15 March 1889, AD1 1894/950, NA; Gannon in *PBH*, 11 March 1889.

269 Enclosure (a copy) and translation in Porter to Under-secretary Defence, 15 March 1889, AD1 1894/950, NA. A slightly modified translation was published by Gannon in *PBH*, 11 March 1889, which Porter adopted for his retrospective account in 1914.

270 *AS*, 27 June 1914.

271 *NZH*, 1 March 1889; the *Press*, 2 March 1889; Porter to Under-secretary Defence, 15 March 1889, AD1 1894/950, NA.

272 *AS*, *NZH*, 1 March 1889; the *Press*, 2 March 1889.

273 GS, 2, 5 March 1889. The captain of the East Coast Hussars, who was present, soon attacked the *Standard*'s reporter for his account, arguing that he was 'never on the spot' but had instead obtained all 'his information from men on the opposite side – men at Opotiki who had proved themselves cowards'. *Opotiki Herald*, 15 March 1889.

274 Porter to Under-secretary Defence, 15 March 1889, AD1 1894/950, NA.

275 *PBH*, 2 March 1889. Gannon was a volunteer with the East Coast Hussars.

276 *NZH*, 1 March 1889; GS, 5 March 1889. Gannon's account, like Porter's, suppresses this aspect; both men's accounts are so much the same on the arrest that they suggest collusion against Goodall's public fury.

277 *PBH*, 2 March 1889.

278 *NZH*, 1 March 1889.

279 *PBH*, 2 March 1889.

280 Ibid.

281 The *Press*, 2 March 1889.

282 Commissioner of Police (quoting Porter's account of Goodall's words) to Goodall, 11 March 1889, telegram 57, P5/9, NA.

283 GS, 2 March 1889.

284 Gannon, *PBH*, 11 March 1889.

285 *NZH*, 1 March 1889; the *Press*, 2 March 1889. Porter, *AS*, 27 June 1914, conforms to these accounts on this aspect.

286 Porter to Under-secretary Defence, 15 March 1889, AD1 1894/950, NA.

287 2 March 1889. The *Herald*'s account supports Te Kooti's affidavit on this point. Bush and Goodall both stated, in retaliation for Te Kooti's account, that an interpreter was present. However, Bush admitted that it was himself who interpreted the actual evidence, and only at the end: *Goodall versus Te Kooti*, pp.11, 14, CL 19, NA.

288 Te Kooti, 28 September 1889, J1 1890/407, NA.

289 *AS*, 2 March 1889.

290 Goodall to Police Commissioner, 1 March 1889, P1 1889/559, NA.

291 *NZH*, 27 February 1889.

292 Hamiora was from Rotorua: ibid., 7 March 1889. The newspapers called him Te Kooti's secretary but in Matiu's account he was described simply as the interpreter ('kaiwhakamaori'), and it is clear from various other references that he spoke English. His full name was Tuki-haumene (Biddle MSS, I, p.143), suggesting that he had been a follower of Te Ua Haumene (Te Ua 'Wind-Man').

293 Porter stated in his report to the Ministry of Defence that he finally released the 400 people taken at Waioeka and 100 people from Waiotahe. This remark certainly implies that those who had ridden from Waiotahe were also corralled overnight. In Porter's first telegram concerning the arrests at Waioeka he estimated the numbers as 'upwards' of 300.

294 Porter to Under-secretary Defence, 15 March 1889, AD1 1894/950, NA.

295 Ibid.

296 W. Reece, sworn statement, 23 December 1889, *Goodall versus Te Kooti*, p.18, CL 19, NA.

Chapter 13: Hapainga Taku Rongo Rite Rawa i te Whenua (February 1889–February 1893)

1 Introduction to Waiata 60, MSS C-35, AU; also stated as a kupu in Biddle MSS, I, pp.143, 156. The title for this chapter is from Waiata 63, composed at Otewa, 27 April 1890, MSS C-35, AU.
2 *NZH*, 4 March 1889.
3 4 March 1889.
4 Te Kooti, affidavit, 28 September 1889, J1 1890/407, NA; Mitchelson, undated memo commenting on the affidavit [December 1889], 89/2834, MA 23/8c, NA; *NZH*, 5 March 1889.
5 *EP*, 11 March 1889.
6 *AS*, 4 March 1889.
7 *NZH*, 5 March 1889.
8 Ibid.
9 28 September 1889, J1 1890/407, NA.
10 Hamiora Mangakahia in *Te Puke ki Hikurangi*, 7 June 1898. See also Angela Ballara's biography of Hamiora, *Dictionary of New Zealand Biography*, II, pp.307–8.
11 *PD* 1889, LXIV, pp.147–48.
12 Ibid., LXVI, p.87. Taiwhanga said that he would also get Paora Tuhaere to join him; his reasoning may explain Paora's refusal.
13 *EP*, 11 March 1889.
14 Sworn statement, 9 January 1890, *Goodall versus Te Kooti*, p.15, CL 19, NA.
15 Mangakahia to Justice Department, 11 December 1889, J1 1890/407, NA.
16 *NZH*, 5 March 1889.
17 Ibid.
18 89/539, MA Register of Inwards Correspondence, 1889, NA.
19 *AS*, 6 March 1889.
20 Justices of the Peace Act, 1882, section 8(3).
21 Bush to Native Department, 20 April 1889, 89/922, MA 23/8c, NA.
22 Wilkinson to Native Department, 30 July 1889, 89/1959, ibid.
23 Toha to Preece, 5 April 1889, 89/1012, Bush to Native Department, 20 April 1889, 89/1198, ibid.
24 List of payments for the case of Te Kooti v. the Government, Biddle MSS, I, p.55. Annotated (in English) 'From Te Kooti's own *Book*'.
25 Te Kooti Te Turuki to Napier, *Goodall versus Te Kooti*, p.3, CL 19, NA.
26 Te Turuki [to Wilkinson], 7 August 1889, Wilkinson to Native Department, 8 August 1889, 89/1959, MA 23/8c, NA.
27 Annotation to Wilkinson's letter, ibid.
28 *NZH*, 9 March 1889.
29 Te Turuki, 28 August 1889, 89/2229, MA 23/8c, NA.
30 Te Turuki, 89/2229, ibid. Based on CT.
31 Wi Pere to Mitchelson, 27 September 1889, 89/2335, ibid. Annotated by the Native Department, 28 September.
32 C. E. Button to Justice Department, 6 December 1889, J1 1890/407, NA. It may not be immaterial to note that Button worked for the Attorney-general's own law firm, Whitaker and Russell.
33 Pera (of Rongowhakaata) had been sent with the fifth and final group of prisoners to Wharekauri.
34 18 December 1889, ibid.
35 Sworn testimony of John McCallion of Waioeka, 21 December 1889, *Goodall versus Te Kooti*, p.20, CL 19, NA.
36 Judgment of Edward Conolly, ibid., pp.33–34.
37 C. D. Whitcombe to Grey, 24 June 1890, GLNZ W30, APL. Whitcombe was a JP and former private secretary to Grey.
38 Goodall v. Te Kooti, Court of Appeal, *NZLR*, IX, 1891, p.46.
39 The findings of the court, ibid., p.26.
40 Ibid., p.41.
41 Michael Downey, 23 December 1889, *Goodall versus Te Kooti*, p.18, CL 19, NA.
42 *EP*, 13 May 1890. The police file P1 1889/559 contains nothing on this.
43 *PD* 1889, LXIV, p.149.
44 Goodall v. Te Kooti, *NZLR*, IX, 1891, p.51.
45 Ibid., p.57.
46 Te Kooti's words to Mitchelson, 7 February 1889, quoted Biddle MSS, I, p.142. From Matiu's account.
47 F. M. Brookfield, 'Maori Rights and Two Radical Writers: Review and Response', *New Zealand Law Journal*, November 1990, p.413.
48 Oliver and Thomson, p.165.
49 *NZH*, 9 July 1890.

50 Biddle MSS, I, p.7. These were also said to be the words uttered by 'the spirit [who] appeared to him' ('te wairua ki a ia ka whakaatu') on the evening of 3 March, in Mt Eden gaol, ibid., pp.143, 156.

51 Ibid., p.7.

52 Ibid., p.156. The source is Hamiora Aparoa, and the copy is annotated, 'Te Kooti himself wrote [this]' ('Na Te Kooti tonu i tuhi').

53 Ibid., p.41.

54 Shand to S. Percy Smith, 25 September 1891, MSS 275, AIM; Shand, 'The Moriori People of the Chatham Islands, Part XIV', *JPS*, VII (1898), p.85. Also, S. Deighton MSS, pp.19–22, in John White MSS 75:B27, ATL; Maud W. Makemson, *The Morning Star Rises. An Account of Polynesian Astronomy*, 1941, pp.79–80.

55 1 July 1880, Paeroa MSS, p.[96].

56 Extended introduction to two waiata, numbered 60, Biddle MSS, V, p.123. These are Waiata [58a], dated 27 February 1889, MSS C-35, AU.

57 Te Turuki (at Te Kuiti) to Tiopira, 21 December 1887, Maungapohatu Notebook, pp.40–41, MSS C-22, AU.

58 Delamere MSS, p.29. The scriptural references cited do not refer to the Twelfth, only to the celebration of the commencement of the month. Matarena Reneti also described the Twelfths as: 'Nga tekau-ma-rua o ia marama huri te tau': 'Nga Karakia me Nga Tikanga o te Haahi Ringatu', p.3, Davis Dossier, Vol. 8, ATL.

59 Delamere MSS, p.27. Among the texts were those from Numbers cited previously, and from the New Testament, Matthew 10:1, which refers to the 12 disciples.

60 Delamere MSS, p.26. This identification was based on Esther 3:7.

61 Delamere MSS, pp.26–27.

62 Biddle, Miscellaneous MSS. This document is in Hamiora's handwriting.

63 Biddle MSS, I, p.51.

64 OS: Ned Brown, 14 February 1982.

65 Ibid. Ned's grandfather, Te Hira Uetuku, was a Ringatu tohunga who adopted this practice, using the apex form.

66 OS: Boy Biddle, 29 January 1983.

67 See Marshall Sahlins, 'Hierarchy and Humanity in Polynesia', in Antony Hooper and Judith Huntsman (eds), *Transformations of Polynesian Culture*, 1985, p.203.

68 As in the planting karakia quoted in J. Prytz Johansen, *Studies in Maori Rites and Myths*, 1958, pp.165–66.

69 OS: Maaka Jones, Whitianga, 2 January 1985. Also quoted in Binney and Chaplin, *Ngā Mōrehu*, p.82.

70 *Te Pukapuka o Nga Kawenata*, pp.135, [137].

71 Biddle MSS, I, p.144.

72 OS: Monita Delamere, 16 February 1982.

73 OS: Himiona Kahika, 15 December 1981.

74 OS: Rose Okeroa Williams at Ngahu-toitoi, 30 November 1991. See Jeremiah 1:5–9.

75 OS: 28 January 1983. It should be noted that he spoke as a follower of Rua, who he believed had completed this task.

76 From Biddle MSS, I, p.13. See Chapters 5 and 6.

77 Biddle MSS, I, p.13.

78 Ibid.

79 Ibid., pp.13–14.

80 OS: George Brown (her son), 20 May 1982. He also stated that, for this reason, Waioeka would 'never condone Ratanaism', the faith of Tahupotiki Wiremu Ratana, which came to be interpreted by many Ringatu as the star in the west. On her mother's side, Waioeka was the granddaughter of Tamihana Teketeke, who killed Hartnett on Wharekauri. She died in November 1959, aged 86.

81 *WT*, 27 June 1885.

82 26 June 1885, Biddle MSS, I, p.14.

83 Ibid., p.15.

84 The reference here is to Te Kooti's sayings of 1 July 1880, ibid., p.12; Paeroa MSS, p.[96].

85 OS: Boy Biddle, 14 December 1981, 5 March 1983, and narrated in Greenwood, *Upraised Hand*, p.91.

86 OS: 14 December 1981.

87 OS: Boy Biddle, 5 March 1983.

88 OS: 15 February 1982.

89 Biddle MSS, I, pp.39, 165.

90 Ibid.

91 pp.62–63, HBM. See also Appendix A.

92 The prophetic sayings to Adam and up to Christ by Te Kooti, Biddle MSS, I, pp.132, 152.

93 OS: Wi Tarei, 13 February 1974, AK7/56, Radio NZ Archives.

94 Matarena Reneti, 'Nga Karakia', p.5, Davis Dossier, Vol. 8, ATL.

95 OS: Paetawa Miki, Ruatoki, 26 January 1978; Horo Tatu, Tataiahape, 27 January 1978.

96 10 September 1890, from Hamiora's records: Biddle MSS, I, p.157.

97 Ibid., V, p.108 (in English).

98 This text (and translation) is from 'Prediction', p.72. It is dated there both 5 March 1892 and 5 March 1893. Neither seems correct: but Te Kooti was at Waihohonu on 3 February 1893. The typescript, 'Offices and Rules of the Faith' of the Haahi o Te Kooti Rikirangi, p.9, Davis Dossier, Vol. 7, ATL, has the date 5 March 1892 for the organisational changes. If this date is correct, then the location cannot be. The last dated entry in Matiu Paeroa's manuscript book is Otewa, July 1892 [p.75]. Matiu makes no reference to this dispute nor to these structures, and he is thereafter silent. The weight of evidence, therefore, favours the correct date as being 3 February 1893.

99 Otewa, 13 February 1891, Biddle MSS, V, p.98.

100 OS: Boy Biddle, 14 December 1981, 13 May 1984. This structure was followed by Te Haahi o Te Kooti Rikirangi from its foundation in 1937. Hence it too kept these records among its texts.

101 Biddle MSS, I, p.42.

102 OS: Himiona Kahika, 6 March 1983.

103 Inoi composed by Te Kooti, Notebook 1869–70, p.54, HBM. Trans: based on Frank Davis.

104 OS: Heni Wiremu, who was brought up in the community at Te Wainui, the land given to Te Kooti (discussed later in this chapter), 25 January 1983.

105 OS: Monita Delamere, 16 February 1982.

106 Comment by W. H. Oliver to the author.

107 *Ko Te Pukapuka o Nga Ingoinga*, 1859, pp.9–24.

108 OS: 30 January 1983.

109 Michael P. Shirres, 'Beyond Religious Differences', 1985, cited Alan Newman, 'The Religious Beliefs, Rituals and Values of the Ringatu Church', MA thesis, Massey University, Palmerston North, 1986, p.64.

110 Biddle MSS, I, p.81.

111 Paeroa MSS, p.[55].

112 Bush, Annual report, 3 June 1889, *AJHR* 1889, G-3, p.6.

113 'Liturgy', p.117, Davis Dossier, Vol. 6, ATL. Te Ture carved the exquisite house Te Waiherehere at Koriniti, when it was reconstructed in 1921–22.

114 8 November 1889, 89/2834, MA 23/8c, NA.

115 21 November 1889, 89/2841, ibid.

116 The Ra is stated as having been held at Ranana, and that Te Kooti did not go, in both Delamere MSS, p.30, and Hamiora Aparoa's list of important events, 1868–93, Biddle, Miscellaneous MSS. Wi Tarei, narrating the story of calling this Ra, also said that Te Kooti did not, in the end, attend: cited Davis Dossier, Vol. 1, p.51. In the list of the Ra compiled in 'Prediction', p.119, it is stated clearly that the first occasion when Te Kooti's feet stood for a Ra within the Whanganui district was the following July gathering, held at Karioi.

117 *WC*, 28 December 1889.

118 Biddle MSS, I, p.81.

119 *WC*, 31 December 1889; 'Prediction', p.70.

120 Waiata 62, MSS C-35, AU. Trans: adapted from Frank Davis.

121 Biddle MSS, I, p.81.

122 'Legend Translation', *Te Maori*, October–November 1979, pp.39–40. The visit to Karioi is incorrectly dated there as 1891.

123 'Prediction', p.72. Trans: adapted from Frank Davis.

124 Biddle MSS, I, p.61.

125 *Te Maori*, October–November 1979, p.40.

126 Biddle MSS, I, p.63.

127 Ibid., p.62.

128 Waiata 68, MSS C-35, AU. Trans: Frank Davis.

129 Biddle MSS, I, p.207.

130 Ibid.

131 Ibid., pp.1, 208.

132 Ibid.

133 31 July 1891, Petane, ibid., p.25.

134 The words to Heemi Waaka on the journey to Parikino, 1891, Wilson MSS, p.134; OS: Tawehi Wilson, Muriwai, 26 June 1968, Radio NZ Archives. This story echoes Te Kooti's letter to Tiopira concerning Rongopai: one word for the 12th, and another for the 16th.

135 *Te Maori*, October-November 1979, pp.39–40; 'Prediction', p.8.

136 Ibid., pp.8, 72 (slightly variant texts). Trans: adapted from Frank Davis.

137 OS: Niko Tangaroa, 1 January 1995.

138 Biddle MSS, I, pp.208–9.

139 *Weekly Press*, clipping n.d., Mackay Scrapbook, MSS 1006/2:19, p.14, ATL.

140 Biddle MSS, I, p.210.

141 31 December 1891, Waiata 83, ibid., V, p.129. Trans: Betty Woodard.

142 31 December 1891, Waiata 76, ibid., p.127.

143 Ibid., I, pp.210–11. In the manuscript the alternative '(Eriewhe)' is annotated as being Petera Te Rangi-hiroa's version, as distinct from Hamiora's.

144 OS: Boy Biddle, 14 December 1981, 5 March 1983.

145 Published in *Te Whetu Marama o Te Kotahitanga*, 5 September 1931. Trans: based on Rev. J. G. Laughton. Another version of this text can be found in 'Prediction', p.38, where the prediction was interpreted as being fulfilled by 'Ohana', the prophet Wi Raepuku from Whanganui.

146 Biddle MSS, I, p.211.

147 Stated to be 80 in W. J. Butler to Native Minister, 11 January 1892, MA1 1892/232, NA. However, 70 names are listed in Biddle MSS, I, p.212 (and 71 mentioned in ibid., p.25). Te Keepa's circular from the hui (26 January 1892) also notes 70 as having been selected at Parikino (Important Native Circulars, Onslow Collection, Clandon Park, West Clandon, England). The issue of the 'appropriate number' for unity, 70 or 80, recurs in the next chapter.

148 Biddle MSS, I, p.213.

149 Ibid., p.214.

150 'Prediction', p.38.

151 *PBH*, 20 February 1889; *Report of the Waitangi Tribunal on the Orakei Claim*, WAI-9, 1987, p.42.

152 Biddle MSS, I, p.2.

153 Waiata 84, Biddle MSS, V, p.130. Trans: based on Betty Woodard. The house Hurae at Paritu was erected in 1894 as a consequence of these words. See Chapter 15.

154 Ibid. Trans: Betty Woodard and Wharehuia Milroy.

155 H. P. Tunuiarangi to Native Minister, 23 October 1890, 90/2306, MA 23/8c, NA.

156 Biddle MSS, I, p.81.

157 E. S. Maunsell, 25 April 1886, *AJHR* 1886, G-1, p.17; undated clipping, Best, Scrapbook I, p.1, ATL; Phillipps, *Carved Maori Houses of the Eastern Districts*, pp.70–72; Neich, *Painted Histories*, pp.303–4.

158 Best to [Percy Smith], citing Tutakangahau as his source, 19 February 1896, Best MSS 72:8, ATL.

159 Best, *Tuhoe*, I, p.962. Trans: Best.

160 Margaret Orbell, 'Two Versions of the Maori Story of Te Tahi o te Rangi', *JPS*, 82, 2 (June 1973), pp.135–7.

161 Marakihau who are sources of danger may be continually reborn. In the great house Mataatua (carved at Whakatane in 1874–75), one of two opposed marakihau was named Te Makarini, Donald McLean: H. M. Mead, *Nga Karoretanga o Mataatua Whare: The Wanderings of the Carved House*, Mataatua, 1990, pp.23, 26.

162 Neich, *Painted Histories*, pp.203–4.

163 Paeroa MSS, p.[38]. Trans: Frank Davis.

164 Wilson MSS, p.144.

165 Biddle MSS, I, p.141.

166 Phillipps, *Carved Maori Houses of the Eastern Districts*, p.71.

167 Paeroa MSS, p.[72].

168 Shand to Percy Smith, 24 September 1894, MSS 275, AIM. Shand did not know that Te Kooti was dead when he wrote this letter, in which he inquired after him. It is Shand's coinciding statement that Te Kooti was in the Wairarapa, rather than the woman's own remark, which locates her observation.

169 27 February 1893, J1 1893/515, NA. Reproduced in Chapter 14.

170 *NZH*, 3 April 1891.

171 Annotation to Makarini's petition, 89/2872, MA 23/8c, NA. All these petitions are in MA 23/8c.

172 Kereru Te Pukenui and others to the governor, 10 February 1891, GNZMA:230, APL. Trans: *NZH*, 26 February 1891.

173 *NZH*, 16 March 1891.

174 Onslow to Queen Victoria, 18 June 1891, MSS 2346, ATL.

175 Onslow to Secretary of State, 4 April 1891, *AJHR* 1891, A-1, p.21.

176 *NZH*, 23 March 1891; *AS*, 26 March 1891.

177 'The Urewera Trip', *NZH*, 30 March 1891.

178 *NZH*, 20 March 1891.

179 *NZH*, 16, 18 March 1891.

180 *AS*, 20 March 1891.

181 Ibid.

182 18 June 1891, MSS 2346, ATL.

183 *NZH*, 24, 26 March 1891.

184 The waiata is dated 17 March 1891, which is about the time Te Kooti was at Te Teko. (In the manuscript, the song is said to have been composed at Otewa after Te Kooti's return from the Wairarapa, which had been at the beginning of February.) Biddle MSS, V, p.127. Trans: Betty Woodard and Jane McRae. This waiata (in a variant and incomplete form) can also be found in Sam Karetu, 'Language and Protocol of the Marae', *Te Ao Hurihuri: The World Moves On*, 1975, p.47, where Karetu describes it simply as a recent composition, sung to a traditional tune. It is, in fact, Te Kooti's free adaptation of the predictive waiata (matakite) belonging to Tamakaimoana of Maungapohatu, found in *Nga Moteatea*, I, pp.68–71.

185 OS: Boy Biddle, 14 December 1981.

186 [T. Ryan], *NZ Graphic*, 25 April 1891.

187 *AS*, 23 March 1891.

188 *NZH*, 1 April 1891.

189 *NZH*, 2 April 1891; *AS*, 6 April 1891; Unsourced clipping, 7 April 1891, Mackay Scrapbook, MSS 1006/2:19, p.540, ATL.

190 *AS*, 6 April 1891. The official notes taken at the time, recorded as 91/631, MA Register of Inwards Correspondence, 1891, have been destroyed.

191 OS: 15 December 1981.

192 *AS*, 6 April 1891.

193 *NZH*, 2 April 1891. The other name mentioned in this report is Netana Te Whakaari. This application for the survey of Ruatoki would be the cause of later problems, discussed in Chapter 14.

194 Te Kooti to Native Department, 21 April 1891, 91/718, MA Register of Inwards Correspondence, 1891, NA.

195 *AS*, 6 April 1891.

196 6–7 May 1897, Ruatoki hearing, Whakatane Minute Book 5, pp.190–93, MLC microfilm.

197 All the correspondence concerning Te Wainui was transferred to a Lands and Survey file which cannot be located; it is presumed to have been destroyed in the accidental archival fire in Wellington in 1952. Only the Register entries for the inwards letters remain, summarising their contents. Copies of some of the outwards correspondence, however, exist in the Maori Affairs Outwards Letterbooks MA4/98 and 99, NA. Extracts from a few letters are also contained in the dossier 'Wainui Reserve', Ringatu Church File, ATL.

198 Te Kooti to Native Minister, 19 June 1892, 92/1066, and July 1892, 92/1365, MA Register of Inwards Correspondence, 1892, NA; Native Minister to Te Kooti, 19 July, 9 August 1892, Maori Outwards Letterbook MA4/99, NA.

199 OS: Boy Biddle, 14 December 1981, 15 October 1987, 6 July 1993.

200 Waiata 87, Biddle MSS, V, pp.128, 131.

201 Cadman to Te Kooti, 12 May 1891, 'Wainui Reserve', p.2, Ringatu Church File, ATL. The Maori text of the letter, setting out these conditions, is in the Maori Outwards Letterbook MA4/98, NA.

202 *NZH*, 30 November 1891.

203 List of events concerning 'Te Wainui', Biddle MSS, I, p.161. Cadman wrote formally to the Minister of Lands on 4 December 1891 stating that he had arranged with Te Kooti for a grant of 600 acres at Wainui: 'Wainui Reserve', p.2, Ringatu Church File, ATL.

204 It was there, beside the large pepper tree, that Rua also chose to meet the Premier, Sir Joseph Ward, in 1908 — probably because of its known association with Te Kooti. See *Whakatane Historical Review*, V (1957), pp.54–56.

205 Family story among the descendants of James Dunlop, whose daughter Sarah married Ross. OS: David Collier, Auckland, 1987. Gilbert Mair's diaries are silent.

206 An alternative reading is: 'Remaining at Otewa is fixed. If [someone] goes because of entreaty, it will be Matiu only.'

207 Biddle, Miscellaneous MSS.

208 OS: Boy Biddle, 29 January 1983.

209 OS: Boy Biddle, 14 December 1981, 17 February 1982. The account which names Hoani Poururu (Hone Taupe) is Moerangi Ratahi's, in *Rotorua Daily Post*, 29 May 1971.

210 Te Kooti to Native Minister, 29 January 1892, 92/151, MA Register of Inwards Correspondence, 1892, NA; *NZH*, 4 March 1892.

211 Native Minister to Te Kooti, 21 March 1892, Maori Outwards Letterbook MA4/99, NA; 'Wainui Reserve', p.2, Ringatu Church File, ATL.

212 Te Kooti's letter, sent on 19 June, was indexed as a request to 'buy' land; in the government's reply of

19 July, the term used was 'te hoko', which can mean either exchange or purchase: 92/1066, MA Register of Inwards Correspondence, 1892, and Outwards Letterbook MA4/99, NA.

213 Te Kooti to Native Department, 19 June 1892, 92/1067, MA Register of Inwards Correspondence, 1892, NA. This letter was written on the same day as his separate inquiry about land for himself at Ruatoki. Kereru Te Pukenui had, partly as a result of Onslow's visit, written to Cadman applying for a school in November 1891. The latter took up the issue, seeing it as a critical lever in opening the Urewera: Te Pukenui and 8 others, 10 November 1891, and Cadman's annotations to it, Ruatoki Maori School file, I, BAAA 1001/540a, NA Auckland. In the event, however, the issue of the school became caught up in the problem of the land survey and would not be resolved until the Native Land Court adjudicated the title in favour of Ngati Rongo in 1894.

214 Te Turuki, Opotiki, April 1893 (received 21 April), 93/558, J Register of Inwards Correspondence, 1893, NA.

215 *Rotorua Daily Post*, 22 May 1971.

216 'Wainui Reserve', pp.2–3, Ringatu Church File, ATL. It was formally gazetted under the October 1892 Land Act (sections 235–36) on 14 May 1895, *NZ Gazette*, 1895, II, p.1535. Biddle MSS, I, p.161 also cites correspondence from Justice Department, 9 May 1893, agreeing that Wainui should be occupied in accordance with Numia's request. This letter was a reply to Te Kooti's last letter of April 1893, J1 93/558 (recorded in J Register of Inwards Correspondence, 1893, NA, but original no longer extant). Also Cadman to Justice Department, 24 January 1895, 95/109, J Register of Inwards Correspondence, 1895, NA; Waimana 313, *Tai Whati: Judicial Decisions affecting Maoris and Maori Land 1958–1983*, [1983], pp.275–76.

217 The trustees were established under section 31 of the Native Land Amendment Act, 1921. The title was then transferred to the 12 trustees on 15 October 1923 (CT, 602/105, Hamilton Land Registry).

218 Biddle MSS, I, p.15 and Biddle Index, List of the Ra. However, both the Index and Delamere MSS, p.37, state that 1 July 1892 was held simultaneously at Hokianga island and Whakaarorangi, Otewa. Te Kooti was at Otewa when he wrote the two letters of 19 June 1892 to the government.

219 Biddle MSS, I, pp.15, 198. See Chapter 14.

220 OS: 14 December 1981, 17 February 1982.

221 OS: Boy Biddle, 7 December 1978. He was quoting Te Kooti's dying words of 12 April 1893, 'ko Te Wainui hei kanohi mo te motu nei' (Delamere MSS, p.16).

222 Te Kooti Turuki (at Otewa) to Timi Waiti, 5 August 1892, MSS 675, AIM.

223 Te Kooti Te Turuki, 10 November 1892, ibid.

224 Te Turuki, 7 April 1893, ibid.

225 OS: Boy Biddle, 14 December 1981.

226 Biddle MSS, I, p.59.

Chapter 14: The Journey to Meet Death

1 *AJHR* 1891, Sess. II, G-1, p.29.

2 Unsourced clipping, Teague Scrapbook, I; Geordie Wilson, aged 90, in *NZH*, 7 November 1970.

3 Biddle MSS, I, p.220.

4 Paeroa MSS, p.[73]. Trans: Frank Davis. Also Biddle MSS, I, p.3.

5 19 April 1893, *Paremata Maori — Waipatu, 1893*, p.2, ATL.

6 26 February 1892, Te Kuiti, Biddle MSS, I, p.2. He was referring specifically to Te Keepa's movement.

7 Ibid., p.4.

8 It was constructed from the home of the chief Henare Pohio after his death in February 1914. The house was moved to its present site in 1985.

9 Petane, 29 July 1891, Biddle MSS, I, p.183.

10 *WC*, 7 January 1893; Biddle MSS, I, p.215. The delegation is dated in the latter as having reached Te Kooti on 22 July 1892.

11 Te Ara o Rehua is carved on the porch of the modern meeting-house Te Herenga Waka at Victoria University, Wellington. The guide to the house states that she was included because of her role in inviting Te Kooti to Rangitikei, first seeing him at Koriniti in January 1892. An image of Te Kooti carved on an interior pou of the same house is reproduced in Appendix C.

12 *NZM, WC*, 6 January 1893.

13 Ibid.

14 *NZM*, 6 January 1893.

15 Ibid.

16 *WC*, 3 January 1893.

17 Biddle MSS, I, p.215. The text adds after '(Opera)', 'i waiho', that is, 'left out'. The text makes it clear that Te Kooti did not explain this word on this occasion. The source is given as Hamiora Aparoa.

18 Ibid. Wilson MSS, p.147, has the same text, dated Aorangi 1893; 'Prediction', p.71, has a slightly variant text, headed 'Taq', and dated from Aorangi, 1 January 1893.

19 Biddle MSS, I, p.215.

20 Ibid., p.6, and also p.216.

21 Ibid., p.215.

22 Ibid., p.216.

23 Ibid., p.217.

24 Ibid., p.218.

25 For a biography of Te Kere, see *Dictionary of New Zealand Biography,* II, pp.517–18.

26 Biddle MSS, I, p.218.

27 Ibid., pp.21, 98.

28 Ibid., pp.95–96.

29 Ibid., p.93.

30 Ibid.

31 See, for example, the story of 'te Awhekaihe' called 'He Tohutohu Tika' ('Good Advice'), originally published in Maori in 1912 and republished with a translation in *Te Karanga,* V, 3 (1989), pp.20–22.

32 See Binney and Chaplin, *Ngā Mōrehu,* p.190, n.21.

33 Biddle MSS, I, p.64. This speech is wrongly dated there as 1 February 1890, but the texts for Te Maari, which are also in ibid., pp.5, 9 are correctly dated there as 1893. They are all records of Te Kooti's speeches from the same occasion.

34 Nini (Matuahu) belonged to the Tuwharetoa kahui ariki lines: see the whakapapa in Grace, p.540, and his family's history, ibid., pp.257–58.

35 Biddle MSS, I, pp.9, 64. At the hui at Parikino in January 1892, Te Kooti included the Wesleyan church in this group of churches to be followed for guidance, ibid., p.213.

36 Ibid., p.64.

37 Listed in Biddle MSS, Index.

38 Such as Moerangi Ratahi, *Rotorua Daily Post,* 15 May 1971. Moerangi lived at Te Kooti's settlements at Te Kuiti and, later, at Te Horo, on the Ohiwa harbour.

39 OS: 16 May 1982.

40 Quoted in James Cowan, *The Maoris of New Zealand,* 1910, p.110.

41 The original text of this speech, in Hamiora's hand, is in Biddle, Miscellaneous MSS. (It is also copied (with some minor textual variations) in Biddle MSS, I, p.68.)

42 Cited in Biddle MSS, I, p.197.

43 Ibid. The full text of this oath (from ibid., p.173) is quoted in Chapter 6. There is a cross-reference in the source to this shorter text.

44 Biddle MSS, I, p.197. There is also a cross-reference to ibid., p.11, where the full text, with four accompanying words in 'te reo ke', and two prayers can be found. There, the kupu is dated 29 December 1883/January 1884.

45 Te Makarini and others to McLean, 9 June 1872, *AJHR* 1872, F-3A, pp.28–29.

46 Te Whenuanui and all Tuhoe to the government, 9 June 1872, ibid., p.29.

47 *AJHR* 1874, G-1a, p.3.

48 Best, *Tuhoe,* I, pp.494, 566.

49 OS: Paetawa Miki, 25 January 1978.

50 Brabant, 25 May 1874, *AJHR* 1874, G-2, p.7.

51 Robert Price, *Through the Uriwera Country* [March 1874], 1891, p.29. The flag was described by Brabant: *AJHR* 1874, G-1a, p.2. Elsdon Best also referred to the Tuhoe flag at Ruatahuna, with the black figure on a red ground, as being an image of 'Riki' (Ariki), whom he wrongly assumed to be the Pai Marire deity. It was, however, possibly an image of the archangel Michael. Best said that the same image of Riki 'in human form', stitched on a flag with a white ground (see photograph between pp.360–361), was flown at Te Whaiti: 'Notes on the Art of War', *JPS,* XI, 2 (June 1902), p.68.

52 *AJHR* 1874, G-1a, pp.3–4.

53 OS: Boy Biddle, 15 October 1987. The scriptural texts of the New Testament also reinforced this command: Luke 10:1, 17.

54 *NZH,* 9 March 1889.

55 Kereru Te Pukenui and others, 17 April 1889, *AJHR* 1889, G-6, pp.1–2.

56 *AS,* 24 March 1891; [Ryan], *New Zealand Graphic,* 2 May 1891.

57 18 March 1891.

58 Pou Temara, biography of its carver Te Whenuanui, *Dictionary of New Zealand Biography,* II, p.529. (The author has not seen Pou Temara's 1991 MA thesis, which is cited there and which discusses Te

Whai-a-te-motu, as the thesis is being prepared for publication.) That the house had been moved seems likely from information given by Temara Te Kaawa to Dr Allan North in 1952, cited by W. J. Phillipps, 'Report of a Visit to the Urewera', 1959, MONZ. However, North was told by other informants that the earlier house was only temporary, although it had been built as the 'shelter for Tuhoe'. It was not moved, they said, but abandoned, because it had become associated with makutu (North, notes collated 1 January 1965, MONZ). It is clear that some conflict had developed; the meeting-house itself was renewed 1889–91. The similarities with the tensions over Takitimu at Kehemane are striking, suggesting that again Te Kooti had insisted on changes before he would come to open the house.

59 Bush to Native Minister, 20 April 1889, 89/922, MA 23/8c, NA.

60 28 February 1891, unsourced clipping, Mackay Scrapbook, MSS 1006/2:19, p.539, ATL. Bush, in a letter of 4 June 1891, *AJHR* 1891, G-5, p.7, also explicitly linked the opening of the house and Onslow's visit to Ruatoki which, he said, took place 'three weeks' later. James Cowan, whose informant was Paitini Wi Tapeka, dated the opening as 1890 (thus he was one year out), and he stated that the house took three years to build and carve. He also said that Te Kooti opened it: 'Ringa-tu Temple', unsourced clipping, [1932], James Cowan Scrapbook, Mrs Z. Craig, Auckland; *The Maoris of New Zealand*, p.164; *The Maori Yesterday and Today*, 1930, p.123.

61 OS: Boy Biddle, 29 January 1983, 6 July 1993. Similarly, Eruera Manuera talking with Frank Davis, n.d., Davis Dossier Vol. 9, ATL.

62 'Voices: He Pūtahitanga', Museum of New Zealand exhibition with the original amo from Te Whai-a-te-motu, 1993.

63 Elsdon Best, *Waikare-moana*, 1897, p.7.

64 North, notes collated 1 January 1965, MONZ.

65 16 March 1891.

66 Bush, Annual report, 4 June 1891, *AJHR* 1891, G-5, p.7.

67 *NZH*, 16 March 1891.

68 Te Kooti Te Turuki to Onslow, 18 February 1892, Onslow Collection, Guildford Muniments Room, Guildford. Trans: based on James Mackay (CT).

69 *NZH*, 2 April 1891; Te Wakaunua to Percy Smith, 11 December 1891, Renata Numia [Numia Kereru] to Cadman, 24 February 1892, Wilkinson to Cadman, 6 June 1892, Le1 1893/165 (235G), NA. This file, which will be drawn upon extensively in the discussion of the survey conflict, is a transcript of correspondence from various government department files. Much of it can also be found (in original form) in J1 1893/515, NA, but each file contains material which is unique to it. Here, J1 1893/515 will be cited only when the material is not to be found in Le1 1893/165.

70 *NZH, AS*, 11 April 1892.

71 *NZH*, 2 April 1891. The application appears under Netana's name, signed as Netana Te Rangiihu.

72 The chief surveyor listed the eight petitions for survey in the Urewera, starting with the most recent; theirs was the third: to Cadman's private secretary, 9 February 1892, J1 1893/515, NA. Also Renata Numia [Numia Kereru] to Cadman, 6 February 1892, Cadman to Numia, 8, 10 February 1892, Le1 1893/165, NA.

73 Chief Surveyor to Cadman's private secretary, 9 February 1892, J1 1893/515, NA; Cadman to Meihana Koata, 10 February 1892, Meihana Koata to Cadman, 11 February 1892, Le1 1893/165, NA.

74 Numia to Cadman, 24 February 1892, ibid. Makarini was living at Otenuku, Ruatoki.

75 Numia, 28 April 1897, Ruatoki appellate hearing, Whakatane Minute Book 5, p.158, MLC microfilm.

76 6–7 May 1897, ibid., pp.190–91, 193.

77 Renata Numia to Cadman, 24 February 1892, Le1 1893/165, NA.

78 Numia to Bush, 10 February 1892, J1 1893/515, NA.

79 See genealogical table 5 in Best, *Tuhoe*, II. Tuhoe oral narratives indicate that Te Hapu-oneone ('The Earth-born People') were living in these valleys when the Mataatua canoe migrants, from whom Tuhoe trace their descent, arrived. These people intermarried, but as Jeffrey Sissons notes 'intermarriage is not absorption' (*Te Waimana*, 1991, p.8). When Tuhoe claim land they draw on these indigenous lines. The separate identities surfaced because of the decision initiated by Numia, a young but increasingly influential chief of Ngati Rongo, to survey the block.

80 Akuhata Te Kaha, 6 May 1897, Whakatane Minute Book 5, p.191, MLC microfilm.

81 Paora Kiingi and others to Smith, 29 March 1892, Le1 1893/165, NA.

82 Paora Kiingi and 78 others to Cadman, 29 March 1892, ibid. The Maori original is in J1 1893/515, NA. The translator commented that something seemed to be missing about the decision which had been left to Te Kooti and Tuhoe. The thrust, however, is quite clear. *NZH*, 4 April 1892, also referred to this petition asking for the withdrawal of the survey.

83 Renata Numia to Cadman, 31 March 1892, Le1 1893/165, NA.

84 *AS*, 5 April 1892.

85 Carroll to Cadman, 8 April 1892, J1 1893/515, NA; *NZH*, *AS*, 11 April 1892.

86 Biddle MSS, V, p.130.

87 Waiata 86, ibid. Trans: Betty Woodard and Wharehuia Milroy.

88 Ibid., p.131.

89 OS: 15 October 1987.

90 Ibid.

91 'Prediction', p.11; also p.33. Trans: based on Frank Davis.

92 OS: Paetawa Miki, 25 January 1978.

93 Binney et al., *Mihaia*, pp.28–30. The ritual significance of the number 80 was, however, not fully brought out in that account.

94 Hill, Notebook 1889–93, MSS 146:9, ATL.

95 Hill, Notebook 1926, p.151, MSS 146:5, ATL.

96 Hill, Notebook 1889–93, MSS 146:9, ATL; also Mead, *Te One Matua*, p.27.

97 Hill, Notebook 1889–93, MSS 146:9, ATL. The story seems similar to another episode told by W. E. Gudgeon in 1907 about the 'recent' death of the tohunga Te Uhi of Whakatane, who came to Te Kooti seeking the latter's death. In Gudgeon's version, Te Uhi died within a week, as predicted by Te Kooti, whose mana was thereby shown to be the greater: 'The Tohunga Maori', pp.72–73.

98 H. R. Burt to Cadman, 14 April 1892, Le1 1893/165, NA.

99 Timi Kara [James Carroll] to Te Kooti, 12 April 1892, Biddle Miscellaneous MSS.

100 Wilkinson, Memorandum of meeting, Otorohanga, 2 May 1892, J1 1893/515, NA.

101 Cadman to Numia, 14 June 1892, ibid.

102 T. Morpeth to Te Kooti Turuki, 8 June 1892, ibid.; Morpeth to Wilkinson, 8 June 1892, Le1 1893/165, NA.

103 Wilkinson to Cadman, 6 June 1892, ibid.

104 Ibid.; Timi Kara [James Carroll] to Te Kooti, 7 June 1892, Biddle Miscellaneous MSS.

105 Kipa Te Whatanui, Henare Tomoana and others to Cadman, 29 June 1892, Le1 1893/165, NA. Maori original in J1 1893/515, NA.

106 H. Tomoana to the Premier, 7 July 1892, ibid.

107 A. Baker (Cadman's private secretary) to Oliver Creagh (surveyor), 6 July 1892, Le1 1893/165, NA.

108 Te Wakaunua to Cadman, 18 February 1893, Numia and Te Wakaunua to Cadman, 21 February 1893, ibid.

109 13 February 1893, ibid. Maori original in J1 1893/515, NA.

110 Makarini (and others) to Cadman, 17 February 1893, ibid.

111 Te Turuki to Wilkinson, ibid. CT. The alternative given to the exact date of 1 March is suggested in Wilkinson's summary translation sent to Cadman, 27 February 1893, Le1 1893/165, NA.

112 Constable A. J. Sisam to Cadman, 27 February 1893, Creagh to Cadman, ibid.

113 Cadman to Creagh, Cadman to Makarini, n.d. [27 February 1893], C. J. Haselden (Department of Justice) to Wilkinson, 27 February 1893, ibid.

114 Sisam to Cadman, 9 March 1893, ibid.

115 *NZH*, 10 March 1893.

116 Biddle MSS, I, p.8.

117 Ibid., V, p.133.

118 Ibid., I, p.169. Trans: based on Betty Woodard.

119 Ibid. The source is Hamiora Aparoa.

120 Ibid., p.46. There is a conflicting report that suggests he left Kihikihi on 16 March (*BPT*, 20 March 1893), but it is probably a reference to the previous 'Thursday', that is, 9 March.

121 *BPT*, 27 March 1893.

122 Sisam to Cadman, 24 March 1893, J1 1893/515, NA. There seems to be a transcript error in the telegram, for the text reads 'message for Te Kooti', but the context indicates that it was a message 'from Te Kooti'. Wilkinson also reported to Cadman that such a message had been received from Te Kooti, 29 March 1893, as did Mehaka Tokopounamu, 30 March 1893, Le1 1893/165, NA.

123 Cadman, draft of instructions to Wilkinson, n.d. [24 March 1893], J1 1893/515, NA.

124 Wilkinson to Justice Department, 29 March 1893, Le1 1893/165, NA.

125 Ibid.

126 Biddle MSS, I, p.198.

127 Tumeke had been a Tuhoe applicant for the Ruatoki survey, with Netana. The second man was probably Iraia Te Toki (brother of Te Whenuanui), whose death was reported in the *Yeoman*, 6 February 1892. (The tangi, or probably uhunga, was described at the time as being for Paora Kiingi and Te Whenuanui.)

128 Best, *Tuhoe*, I, pp.493–94, 566.

129 Preece mentioned Paora Kiingi, a Urewera chief but who was one of 'my men'; this man became a sergeant (Diary, 9 June 1870, 25 October 1871, MSS 249, AIM). However, as Paora Kiingi's two elder brothers (Kepa and Tumeke) were also sometimes known as Paora Kiingi, it is a bit complicated as to just who was who!

130 OS: Heta Rua, 23 May 1982. Also narrated by Puti Onekawa, 30 January 1983.

131 For the extensions of this story connected with the arrest of Rua in 1916, see J. Binney, 'Myth and Explanation in the Ringatū Tradition', *JPS*, 93, 4 (December 1984), p.371.

132 Wilkinson to Cadman, 1 April 1893, Le1 1893/165, NA.

133 Biddle MSS, I, p.198.

134 Sisam to Cadman, 4 April 1893, Le1 1893/165, NA.

135 Sisam to Cadman, 5 April 1893, J1 1893/515, NA.

136 Quoted in J. Clendon RM to Justice Department, 11 April 1893, Le1 1893/165, NA.

137 Morpeth to Cadman, 13 April 1893, J1 1893/515, NA.

138 Morpeth to Cadman, 17 April 1893, ibid.

139 13 April 1893, Le1 1893/165, NA.

140 10 March 1893.

141 *Te Whetu Marama o Te Kotahitanga*, 29 August–5 September 1931, p.9. Trans: Rev. J. G. Laughton (see also Chapter 11, p.329). This text is one of the most famous of Te Kooti's sayings: it can also be found, for example, in Lucky Tutua's Notebook, p.[5], Davis Dossier, Vol. 3, ATL. It is usually dated Ohiwa 1893. A slightly variant text is in 'Prediction', p.75, where the emphasis is placed on the coming Child, rather than the people; it is he who is to paddle this canoe.

142 Biddle MSS, I, p.67. Boy Biddle also narrated this story, quoting Te Kooti's saying, to Frank Davis, 2 March 1979, Davis Dossier, Vol. 9, ATL.

143 Biddle MSS, I, pp.46, 169.

144 Ibid.

145 Ibid.

146 OS, quoted in Takotohiwi, p.22. The saying is there directly linked to the visit of 1893. It can also be found, abridged, in G. H. E. Kaiwhata and E. P. Leighton, *Descendants of Awanuiarangi and Moerangi Ratahi*, 1991, p.99, and in a variant version in 'Prediction', p.74.

147 The three houses (rebuilt) became three separate marae at Paroa, near Whakatane. This move began in 1904. The three marae today (1994) are trying to recover their unity. Takotohiwi, pp.20–40; Kaiwhata and Leighton, p.99.

148 OS: Wiremu Pakeha [Wiremu Tarei], quoted in Takotohiwi, p.21. Trans: based on Takotohiwi.

149 OS: at Kutarere, 22 May 1982.

150 Hemi Kakitu was one of the four Upokorehe trustees to whom Hokianga island was returned (after its confiscation) in 1872; Rakuraku's 'hearth' kept warm the claims of Tuhoe of Waimana and Ruatoki.

151 Waiata [92], Biddle MSS, V, p.134; ibid., I, p.200.

152 Ibid. Trans: Betty Woodard.

153 Ibid., p.198 in explanation of this song.

154 *Abbot Family Centennial Magazine 1875–1975*, 1975, p.39. Maunsell was stationed at Opotiki. The reliability of this account would seem to be confirmed by Paora Delamere's mention of the Abbot family's presence at Te Kooti's tangi: 15 December 1971, Te Reo o Te Maori, Radio NZ Archives. Unfortunately, there appear to be no surviving papers of Maunsell.

155 Biddle MSS, I, p.15. This text is of its nature ambivalent, and there are other possible interpretations. One reading of the last line suggests that the event, the coming of the One, will be moved forward to prevent the government's actions. This, however, seems to run counter to the middle paragraph. See also Greenwood, *Upraised Hand*, p.72, for a translation.

156 Biddle MSS, I, p.15. Lineation and translation based on Arapeta Awatere, in Greenwood, *Upraised Hand*, p.73.

157 'A Hymne to God the Father'.

158 Biddle MSS, I, p.15.

159 Delamere MSS, p.16.

160 OS: Mrs E. (Meri) Collier of Tuhoe, recorded talk on the Ohiwa harbour, n.d. [c.1960], Whakatane Museum.

161 J1 1893/551, NA. CT. Heta Te Kani was the son of Hirini Te Kani (see Whakapapa A). He was the whangai (adopted child) of Otene Pitau, who was himself the adopted son of Raharuhi Rukupo. Heta died in September 1903 after violating a warning, said to have been given by Te Kooti as he lay dying, that Heta must never journey on the East Coast beyond Whangara. The new prophet Wi Wereta encouraged Heta to defy Te Kooti's words; his urging was interpreted as an assertion of mana by Wi Wereta to show that his power was greater than Te Kooti's. Heta's death (from tuberculosis) came suddenly, and was the subject of police inquiry.

162 'The Body of Te Kooti' ('Te Tinana o Te Kooti'), Biddle MSS, I, p.56.

163 Ibid. Also *BPT*, 28 April 1893, which reported the secret removal of Te Kooti's body for burial by the 'Urewera'.

164 OS: 8 December 1978.

165 OS: Pat Aramoana, 22 May 1982.

166 Maungapohatu Notebook 1881–1916, pp.94, 100, AU. Early Anglican missionaries, such as William Colenso, taught that God had kept hidden the knowledge of the tree from which Christ's cross was made, so that it would not become an object of idolatry. Thus, Maori teaching of this 'hidden' knowledge sprang, in part, from the theological issue: possessing the knowledge became a statement of independent authority.

167 Biddle MSS, I, p.56.

168 Ibid.

169 Tawhaki Awa (Tawhaki Te Kaawa) said that her father, Awa Horomona, was the son of Wetini (OS: 28 January 1978). Whether this man was Te Kooti's son is unknown; the suggestion derives from the context. However, Awa Horomona's crucial importance is demonstrated by the arranged marriages of his two daughters: Tawhaki married Rua's second son, Toko; Te Ripo married the Ngai Tama chief of Matahi, Hori Hiakita. Their daughter, Te Paea, in turn married another of Rua's sons, Heta. Photographs of Awa Horomona, Tawhaki and Te Paea are in Binney et al., *Mihaia*, pp.102, 112, 186.

170 That is, Maiere (Te Warati) Komene Te Rangipatahi. Both she and her husband Kereti died in the influenza pandemic of November 1918. Kereti was the son of Hawera Te Hihira of Ngati Awa. Like Hoani Poururu, Hawera been imprisoned for the death of Fulloon, and after his release went to live with Te Kooti at Te Kuiti and Otewa. The evidence which confirms this line of Komene's family is from Wi Paati, who married Komene's granddaughter Te Taawhi Paraone, who was herself brought up by Te Kooti (see Whakapapa A). 15 October 1936, Gisborne Minute Book 62, p.349, MLC microfilm. The author is indebted to Layne R. Harvey for alerting her to this side of the family.

171 OS: Boy Biddle, 5 March 1983.

172 *WI*, 7 October 1869.

173 *NZM*, 9 August 1889.

174 OS: 14 December 1981, 15 October 1987.

175 OS: Tairongo Amoamo of Whakatohea, Wellington, 9 December 1992. Tairongo learnt this account from his father, Ngawai Amoamo.

176 *BPT*, 2 February 1910; *AWN*, 10 February 1910, p.21.

177 U'ren Sharp MSS, p.6, GM.

178 See II Samuel 10:4–5.

179 Cutting, 8 May 1893, Mackay Scrapbook, MSS 1006/2:19, p.553, ATL.

180 Lambert, p.149, n.8.

181 Biddle MSS, I, p.56.

182 OS: Meri Collier, recorded talk, Whakatane Museum.

183 *GT*, 10 October 1923.

184 *AS*, 22 February 1934. Written anonymously, but the style is Cowan's and there is a copy of the item in Cowan's Scrapbook II, Mrs Z. Craig, Auckland.

185 OS: Meri Collier, recorded talk, Whakatane Museum. She also told the story of a party of three people, two men and a woman, who later took these valuables. The woman, who was said in this account to have kept the mere, became ill with the palsy, the disease 'where the Maoris say she couldn't help shaking her taiaha'.

186 OS: Boy Biddle, 14 December 1981. He remembered that Te Kooti had asked for this particular bible as soon as he returned from Wharekauri; this seems likely, as the complete Maori bible was first published in 1868. An unusually large bible was also at Wainui in 1927. It was said to be a variant text, which Te Kooti had specifically asked for, one where 'some of God's words were missing' ('etahi korero a te Atua e ngaro ana') (Biddle MSS, I, pp.50, 54; Delamere MSS, p.103). This big bible was illustrated, and had brass hinges. It had been given to Te Kooti on 27 November 1880 by the Ngati Porou exiles at Wharekawa. This story seems to be a parallel to that of Tuhourangi's refusal to surrender up their big bible, which is told in Chapter 11.

187 *GT*, 20 May 1902. There were, in fact, at least three others of the original party still alive: Awa Horomona, Rikirangi Hohepa, Kereti Hawera.

188 5 August 1938. He stated that there were four men who were directed by a fifth, a tohunga, whom he does not name.

189 Tihei's account is in Binney and Chaplin, *Ngā Mōrehu*, p.95. By her account this event took place about 1927, which, given the rival claims to be Te Kooti's successor being put forward at exactly this time, seems likely to be correct.

190 OS: Jack Kurei, 15 December 1981. Also narrated by Te Onewhero in 'Tuhoe-Ringatu', directed Barry Barclay, Tangata Whenua series, NZTV, 1974; *Auto Age*, 14 July 1964.

191 Clipping, 'Bones of the Rebel Te Kooti', n.d. [c.April 1948], Whakatane Museum; *EP*, 7 July 1948; *NZ Women's Weekly*, 22 July 1948; Mackay, p.304; Grace, p.493.

192 Deuteronomy 5:3.

193 Ibid., 34:4–6.

194 OS: Boy Biddle, 14 December 1981.

195 OS: Ned Brown, 14 February 1982. Ihimaera, in *The Matriarch*, pp.195–96, also cites this kupu whakaari (somewhat loosely in both Maori and English).

Chapter 15: Epilogue

1 OS: Boy Biddle, 29 January 1983.

2 Leo Fowler, 'A New Look at Te Kooti', *Te Ao Hou*, 21 (December 1957), p.21.

3 Hawthorne, *Dark Chapter*, p.20. Noted also in Mackay, *Historic Poverty Bay*, p.259.

4 Fowler, 'A New Look at Te Kooti', p.21.

5 *NZH*, 25 February 1889.

6 *EP*, 28 February 1889.

7 OS: 14 February 1982.

8 See Binney, 'Myth and Explanation', p.371.

9 OS: at Whakarae, 19 May 1978.

10 See especially, Judith Binney, 'Ancestral Voices: Māori Prophet Leaders', in Keith Sinclair (ed.), *The Oxford Illustrated History of New Zealand*, 1990, pp.153–84; Binney and Chaplin, *Ngā Mōrehu*, particularly pp.18–24; and Binney et al., *Mihaia*.

11 OS: Heta Rua, Matahi, 18 May 1978.

12 OS: Tataiahape, 27 January 1978.

13 OS: 18 May 1978.

14 Sissons, p.225.

15 OS: Hillman Rua, Rotorua, 21 May 1978. A portion of this narrative (partly abridged but also continuing further) was published in Binney, 'Myth and Explanation', p.377.

16 Rev. Tamaheihei Takao, quoted in Sissons, p.224.

17 OS: 23 May 1982.

18 OS: 18 May 1978.

19 Ibid.

20 OS: Te Paea Hori Hiakita (Te Paea Rua), 18 May 1978.

21 John-Erik Elmsberg, *Islands of Tomorrow*, 1956, p.250.

22 OS: 16 May 1982. See also Binney, 'Myth and Explanation', pp.361–62, for these narratives. The slight differences in the quotations are due to editing of original, long narrations, in which digression and repetition inevitably occur.

23 Whaanga, pp.12–13.

24 Ibid., pp.22–23.

25 See Binney, 'Myth and Explanation', p.389, n.47.

26 I am indebted to Jeffrey Sissons, who drew my attention to this discovery, which both he and I had overlooked in our earlier discussions of Rua and the diamond on Maungapohatu. For Sissons' study, see *Te Waimana*, Chapter 9.

27 OS: Emma Lemuel, 20 April 1991. The visionary leader Tutekohe is discussed below.

28 Account by J. W. Witty in Mackay Scrapbook, MSS 1006/2:19, p.543, ATL. One source for these stories could be the caches of ammunition hidden in Poverty Bay in 1868. One was found at the time (see Chapter 5) and another, thought to have been hidden for Te Kooti in 1868, was found near Gisborne in January 1881.

29 Yet another story of Te Kooti's gold, also said to have been brought from Wharekauri and hidden in the Urewera, was reported in *EP*, 19 March 1960.

30 OS: 16 May 1982.

31 OS: Tihei Algie, 17 May 1982.

32 OS: 16 May 1982.

33 'Prediction', pp.1–25.

34 Biddle MSS, I, p.197.

35 OS: 5 March 1983.

36 'Prediction', p.10. Trans: based on Frank Davis.

37 *NZH*, 27 March 1893.

38 'Prediction', p.75. Trans: Frank Davis.

39 OS: Boy Biddle, 5 March 1983.

40 Genesis 50:25, cited in this context, 'Prediction', p.12.

41 *GT*, 10 October 1923.

42 'Prediction', p.12. Trans: Frank Davis.

43 Biddle MSS, I, p.197. This reference to the corner-stone is also linked there to the promise of Te Umutaoroa at Te Houhi, but without the accompanying narrative.

44 The recovery of the four 'stones' in 1984 with the help of a Pakeha clairvoyant, Dulcie Bolton, was documented in, for example, *NZH*, 10 September 1984; *AS*, 17 November 1984; *NZH*, 7 September 1992.

45 OS: 21 January 1978.

46 OS: Boy Biddle, 5 December 1977, 5 March 1983, 15 October 1987; Pat Aramoana, 22 May 1982. In one version it is said that Rua simply changed the name on the older house.

47 13 March–April 1906, Diary of Wi Te Pou, Tataiahape, quoted Sissons, p.189.

48 Best, *Tuhoe*, I, p.259; Sissons, p.200.

49 OS: Tumeke (Mac) Onekawa, Kutarere, 10 December 1978. See Binney et al., *Mihaia*, p.27.

50 12 April 1906, Diary of Wi Te Pou, quoted Sissons, p.190.

51 *The Maori*, 1924, I, p.127.

52 OS: Mangere Teka in 'The Mountain of the Lord', NZ Broadcasting Corporation, 1970; Kino Hughes, Ruatoki, 28 January 1978, quoted in Binney et al., *Mihaia*, p.30.

53 See Chapter 13.

54 Fragment of a letter, 16 April 1889, from Te Horo, Ohiwa, private collection. It appears to be in Te Kooti's handwriting. Kati Wharepapa also described the Eighteenths, OS: 13 February 1993. Te Kooti may have created this new Ra out of rivalry with Te Whiti, who, much earlier, had set aside the 'Eighteenth' (calendrically the 17th) of the month as the day for worship. Among other things, this day remembered the commencement of the wars in Taranaki in 1860.

55 OS: 13 February 1993.

56 'Prediction', p.13.

57 The January Ra for the Haahi Ringatu was held at Nukutaurua, Mahia; this was a splinter gathering.

58 Ibid., p.15. Trans: based on Frank Davis.

59 Ibid., p.16.

60 OS: Boy Biddle, 5 March 1983.

61 OS: Boy Biddle, 6 July 1993.

62 OS: Niko Tangaroa, 31 December 1994–1 January 1995.

63 OS: Ultima Te-Urupu, 20 April 1991.

64 OS: Emma Lemuel, 20 April 1991.

65 OS: interview by Erena Reedy with Campbell, *Mana News*, Radio New Zealand, 26 November 1990.

66 Mika Te Tawhao to Apirana Ngata, 13 April 1931, Ringatu Church File, ATL.

67 Biddle MSS, I, p.58.

68 OS: John Ruru, 15 February 1982.

69 'Te Oha-aki — whare', Biddle MSS, V, p.106.

70 OS: 14 February 1982.

71 OS: Eruera Manuera, 17 February 1982; Pinky Green, 'A History of northern Waiapu', 1960, p.67, MSS, ATL.

72 OS: Ned Brown, 14 February 1982.

73 OS: 27 January 1978.

74 Such as Taua McLean, who was brought up by Eria, and Himiona Kahika, who remembered Hamiora Aparoa at Wainui and Kutarere.

75 OS: 28 January 1983.

76 OS: Boy Biddle, 28, 29 January 1983.

77 OS: Boy Biddle, 7 December 1978, 15 October 1987.

78 *AWN*, 20 April 1938.

79 OS: Boy Biddle, 5 March 1983, 15 October 1987.

80 OS: 14 December 1981.

81 *The Conquest of America: the Question of the Other*, trans. Richard Howard, 1984.

82 OS: Boy Biddle, 17 February 1982.

83 OS: Boy Biddle, 15 October 1987.

84 OS: Boy Biddle, 14 December 1981.

85 Sissons, p.287.

86 Edward W. Said, *Culture and Imperialism*, 1993, p.xiii.

87 Ruth Bejar, commenting on the notion of narrative in the oral histories told by Esperanza, a woman of Mexico, in *Translated Woman*, 1993, p.12.

88 'Borderlands: Playing with the Past', paper delivered to the David Nichol Smith Seminar IX, University of Auckland, August 1993.

89 Maharaia Winiata, *The Changing Role of the Leader in Maori Society*, 1967, p.73.

90 OS: Rose Okeroa Williams talking about her uncle Apa Te Moananui, 30 November 1991.

91 Best, 'Notes on the Art of War', *JPS*, XII, 4 (December 1903), pp.197–98; *Tuhoe*, I, p.772.

92 Ibid., p.945.

93 *The Maori and His Religion*, 1954, p.152.

94 Ibid., p.162.

95 As in Pakariki Harrison's carving of lame Mua (Haere), created for the History Department at Auckland University in 1992. See also Best, *Maori Religion and Mythology*, I, pp.252, 272.

96 *NZH*, 14 April 1993.

97 Information supplied by the Department of Statistics, NZ Census of Population and Dwellings, 1971–81. Religious statistics for the Maori population, 1926–71, can be found in Hans Mol, *The Fixed and the Fickle: Religion and Identity in New Zealand*, n.d., p.42.

98 *Dominion Sunday Times*, 30 August 1992; *NZH*, 8 May 1993. No religious statistics were published from the 1986 census.

99 In the song, 'Pinepine Te Kura', waiata 53, MSS C-35, AU. Thus Tuhoe named their marae in Auckland city, Te Tira Hou.

100 Quoted by Mika Te Tawhao to Apirana Ngata, 21 March 1931, Ringatu Church File, ATL.

Appendix A: The Diaries of Te Kooti

1 'Te Kooti's Notebook', *Archifacts*, 13 (March 1980), p.285.

2 In the original the year is written as 1878. This is presumably a mistake.

3 Williams Family Papers, MSS 69:49, ATL.

4 Polynesian Society Papers, MSS 1187:9, ATL.

5 Richmond to A. S. Atkinson, 12 March 1869, *Richmond–Atkinson Papers*, II, p.283.

6 W. Leonard Williams, Diary, 22 January 1869, AIM.

7 Among A. S. Atkinson's Papers, in MSS 1187:12, ATL.

8 Cutting, with the initials 'ASA' [A. S. Atkinson] at the bottom, MSS Papers 1187:99, ATL.

9 *The Monthly Review*, I, 5 (March 1889), p.175.

10 30 August 1888, 88/1701, MA Register of Inwards Correspondence, 1888, Mitchelson to Richmond, 21 September 1888, Maori Affairs Outwards Letterbook, MA4/48, NA.

11 Davies Maori Manuscripts III, ATL.

12 Richmond to A. S. Atkinson, 12 March 1869, *Richmond–Atkinson Papers*, II, p.283.

13 *PD* 1869, V, pp.198–99.

14 1 August 1888, *PD* 1888, LXII, p.344. He referred there to an exchange of letters between them, 'three letters, at least'. The notion of exchange was possibly a distortion, but the mention of 'three' letters suggests that he may have read Te Kooti's three letters from prison in Napier.

15 Percy Smith to Atkinson, 26 March 1896, MSS 1187:9, ATL.

16 Barry Mitcalfe, *Maori Poetry*, 1974, p.120.

17 William Colenso (to whom this notebook was given), *Fiat Justitia*, 1871, p.23.

18 Diary, AD1 71/776, NA (*AJHR* 1871, F-1, p.36). See Chapter 9.

19 Anonymous article by an 'Old East Coast Campaigner', *AS*, 25 February 1889.

20 Colenso to McLean, 9 November 1871, MSS 32:222, ATL.

21 11 December 1871, ibid.

22 Colenso, *Fiat Justitia*, p.12. The six prayers are on p.23.

23 Diary, pp.19–20, HBM; Colenso's translation, *Fiat Justitia*, p.23.

24 See Chapter 3.

25 *NZM*, 15 April 1871 (taken from *HBH*, 11 April 1871).

26 Biddle MSS, I, pp.132, 152–56.

27 It could read 1 March 1870, but on 1 March Te Kooti was in the region of Ruatoki and Waimana and he would not return to the upper Waioeka until 7–8 March. See Chapter 8.

28 *AS*, 14 March 1914.

29 Panui 1, *Te Pukapuka o Nga Kawenata . . . a te Haahi Ringatu*, p.29; 'Nga Karakia me Nga Tikanga o te Haahi Ringatu' (Services and Articles of the Ringatu Church), mss composed by Mrs Matarena Reneti of Te Teko with an appendix by Rev. Alan Newman, Davis Dossier, Vol. 8, ATL.

30 *NZ Wars*, II, p.234.

31 *AS*, 18 April 1914.
32 This statement is not included in Chapter V, *Otago Daily Times*, 2 March 1914. It appears in Chapter V, *Canterbury Times*, 11 March 1914; *AS*, 14 March 1914.

Appendix B: Songs for Te Kooti

1 *'Te Kooti' and Other Poems.*
2 *The NZ Wars.*
3 Cutting, April 1889. A misprint had A. Atkinson. Kempthorne Scrapbook, p.3, GM.
4 p.8. It was republished, with minor textual changes, in the *Bulletin's Golden Shanty*, 1890. I am indebted to Bert Roth, and also his article, 'Te Kooti's Friend Desmond', *New Zealand Monthly Review*, August 1960, pp.10–11, for information on Desmond. Desmond's biography by Rachel Barrowman is in the *Dictionary of New Zealand Biography*, II, pp.116–17.
5 *PBH*, 22 February 1889.
6 Composed 4 March 1889, published *EP*, 14 March 1889.
7 *Te Maori*, October–November 1979, pp.39–40 (both text and translation corrected). Pepara is the Anglican whare karakia (chapel) at Koriniti.
8 29 April 1893.
9 p.236.
10 OS: 17 May 1982.
11 1992, p.79.
12 'The Facts about Te Kooti', p.21.
13 *Voices*, 1990, p.26; Stewart, pp.84–85.
14 p.25. Williams glossed Te Rongopai as the meeting-house and marae at Gisborne and also 'The good word'.
15 First published in *Eyes of the Ruru*. Republished, Ihimaera, *Te Ao Mārama*, I, p.283.

Appendix C: Faction, Fiction and Images

1 The engraving from the *Illustrated Examiner* is reproduced in Greenwood, 'Iconography of Te Kooti Rikirangi', portrait 7. Greenwood commented that Robert Biddle senior had shown it to an aged follower of Te Kooti, who could find no resemblance whatsoever! Greenwood's article discusses some mistaken images of Te Kooti published at various times, and the reader is referred there for these. A photograph recently reproduced as being of Te Kooti (in Bronwyn Elsmore, *Mana from Heaven: A Century of Maori Prophets in New Zealand*, 1989, p.[227]), and which is labelled on the negative 'Te Kooti', is rather of a startled Wesleyan minister, the Reverend Te Koti Te Ratou, who served on the Chatham Islands 1859–65.
2 Photograph 155205 1/2, ATL.
3 Clipping, *Church Missionary Gleaner*, p.89, Robert Mair Scrapbook, Mair Family Papers, Box II, MSS 1618, AIM.
4 Kerry-Nicholls, p.335. The sketch is reproduced in Greenwood, 'Iconography', portrait 1.
5 Neich, *Painted Histories*, pp.226–34 and plate 30.
6 *Tuhoe*, I, p.663. The image was from Gudgeon, *Reminiscences*, facing p.96. Gilbert Mair identified this portrait in 1911 as being of a Te Arawa chief: see Greenwood, 'Iconography', p.6.
7 24 December 1891.
8 [Thomas] McDonnell, 'A Maori History: Being a Native Account of the Pakeha–Maori Wars in New Zealand', in Gudgeon, *Defenders of NZ*, p.556.
9 Ibid., p.550.
10 Ibid., p.552.
11 Kitty was born in 1881; her mother, Bridget Morgan, died on 23 October 1891 and her father, James Morgan, on 11 June 1892, at Taradale, Hawke's Bay.
12 See Chapter 4, p.97.
13 O'Sullivan, p.17. Morgan was 40 (or 42) years old when he died so it is possible that he volunteered. However, it was stated at his death that he had migrated to New Zealand about 17 years previously, that is, in the mid-1870s.
14 Ibid., p.121.
15 Te Pairi Tuterangi was the son of Te Whiu's sister, Meri Maraki. The family whakapapa may be found in Best, 'Genealogies of Tuhoe . . . 1898', pp.22–23, MSS, ATL. Te Pairi died in November 1954.
16 Quoted in undated typescript, 'The Te Kooti Trail', NZ Film Archive file.

17 See *AWN*, 15 November 1961. It was also cited in the brief Bibliography in Ross's book, published in 1966.
18 *Sun* (Auckland), 11 November 1927.
19 *Whakatane Press*, 11 November 1927.
20 'Refusal of Censor to approve Film', sent to Hayward, 12 November 1927, photocopy by courtesy of S. R. Edwards. See Edwards, 'Docudrama from the Twenties', *Whakatane Historical Review*, 41, 2 (November 1993), p.59.
21 Flyer for the film, Whakatane Museum.
22 Ritchie to the author, 15 September 1993.
23 'He Matakite', typescript, pp.6, 18. Copy by courtesy of James Ritchie.
24 The author's copy of the text, a limited and undated edition published by the *Gisborne Herald*, is signed by Fowler in October 1970.
25 Ibid., p.11.
26 Nos 20–21, November–December 1957.
27 Witi Ihimaera, 'The Matriarch: Discussion: University of Auckland, 18 July 1990', unpublished typescript of a lecture.
28 Words of the matriarch to the child, *The Matriarch*, p.133.
29 Mark Williams, 'Witi Ihimaera and the Politics of Epic', *Leaving the Highway: Six Contemporary New Zealand Novelists*, 1990, pp.128–37; Ihimaera, 'The Matriarch: Discussion . . . 1990'.
30 Ibid. The author's interpolation is from *The Matriarch*, p.301.
31 See the discussion of these family narratives in Binney and Chaplin, *Ngā Mōrehu*, p.[1] and, deriving from it, J. Binney, 'Maori Oral Narratives, Pakeha Written Texts: Two Forms of Telling History', *NZ Journal of History*, XXI, 1 (April 1987), pp.20–21.
32 See Chapter 6, p.175.
33 *WI*, 28 September 1869.
34 *WI*, 25 September 1869.
35 Three other followers of Te Kooti, including Hetariki Te Oiikau, were tried for rebellion earlier in September, under different legislation. They were imprisoned.
36 *WI*, 18 November 1869.
37 *Season of the Jew*, 1986, p.379.

Appendix D: An Index of Waiata by Te Kooti

1 Margaret Orbell argued in *Waiata, Maori Songs in History*, p.74, that Te Kooti was not a poet, merely a clever adapter of songs. Yet the song text to which she appended this remark, and which she attributed to another composer, was created by Te Kooti, as she also somewhat reluctantly concluded. This song, 'Ka tu au ka korikori', is quoted in Chapter 2.
2 MSS 92:46, ATL.

SOURCES

This list collates and explains the references to manuscripts, unpublished theses, and published articles and books cited in the text. A few works of particular significance, although not cited, have been added. Oral sources recorded as radio interviews or as taped oral dialogues have also been collated. All other references — newspapers, artefacts, land deeds, maps, photographs, exhibitions, drawings — are itemised as they occur in the notes and captions.

I. MANUSCRIPTS AND UNPUBLISHED WORKS

(a) Manuscripts

— 'Maori Account of the Campaign against the Hauhau on the East Coast, 1865–70', anonymous manuscript copied by A. S. Atkinson, MSS 1187:6A, ATL.
— Maungapohatu Notebook 1881–1916, MSS C-22, AU.
— 'The Prediction of One to Follow', typescript, n.d., Frank Davis Dossier, Vol. 10, ATL.
— 'The Te Kooti Trail', typescript, n.d., NZ Film Archive.
— Te Kuiti Manuscript, MSS MP1990/3, Te Hukatai Library, AU.
Agent General Government, Auckland province:
    Inwards Correspondence, General (AGG A Series 1) (1865–71): 1/1–4, 6 (AGG A1/5 missing since 1985), NA.
Agent General Government, Hawke's Bay province:
    Inwards Correspondence, General (AGG HB Series 1) (1869–72): 1/1–6;
    Inwards Correspondence, Maori (AGG HB Series 2) (1865–75): 2/1–2;
    Miscellaneous (AGG HB Series 7): Maori prisoners of war 7/2b; Kereopa's Papers (1872) 7/2h; Te Kooti's Papers (1869–70) 7/3; Waikaremoana–Wairoa campaign (1870) 7/5, NA.
Army Department:
    Inwards Correspondence (AD1) and Registers: 1865–66; 1868–72; 1889–94;
    Outward Telegrams (AD8): 1868–72;
    Chatham Island prisoners (1866–68): AD 31:14–16;
    Thomas W. Porter, Papers, AD 103, NA.
Austin, Samuel:
    Diaries, 1869–70, MSS, QEIIAM.
Best, Elsdon:
    'Genealogies of the Tuhoe as of 1898', MSS, ATL.
    Manuscript biography of Te Kooti, Johannes C. Andersen Scrapbook, AIM.
    Maori Notes, 2 vols, MSS, MONZ.
    Papers 1869–1930, MSS 72, ATL.
    Scrapbooks, ATL.
Biddle, Robert:
    Manuscript Books compiled from the books of Hamiora Aparoa, Matiu Paeroa, Petera Te Rangihiroa, 1927, and Miscellaneous Manuscripts, Private collection, Robert (Boy) Biddle, Kutarere.
Biggs, R. N.:
    Letter to A. Tuke, 6 November 1868, MSS 1296, ATL.
Colonial Office:
    Governor's Despatches 1869–70, CO 209/217, microfilm, AU.

Cooper, I. R.:
  Militia Letters, MSS, Whanganui Museum.
Cowan, James:
  Papers, MSS 39, ATL.
Craig, Elsdon:
  Scrapbooks, including James Cowan's Scrapbooks, Maori Scrapbooks, and photographs from
    Elsdon Best, Private collection, Mrs Z. Craig, Auckland.
Crown Law Office:
  Court of Appeal, Goodall versus Te Kooti Rikirangi, 1890, CL 19, NA.
Davies, G. H.:
  Maori Manuscripts III, ATL.
Davis, Frank:
  Dossier on Te Kooti, Vols 1–10, ATL.
Deighton, Samuel:
  Manuscript on the Chatham Islands, in John White Papers, MSS 75:B27, ATL.
Delamere, Paora:
  Manuscript book, commenced 1931. Private collection, late Sir Monita Delamere, Opotiki.
Denton, O. G.:
  'Mohaka Raid Account', MSS, ATL.
Emery, Robert:
  'Te Miringa Te Kakara', unpublished typescript, n.d., NZ Historic Places Trust, Wellington.
Engst, J. G.:
  'Early History of Chatham Islands and its Inhabitants', R. S. Florance Papers, CM.
Firth, Josiah:
  Papers, MSS 1491; MSS 3808, ATL. (Some manuscripts transcribed in these files are in P. P.
    O'Shea Papers, MSS 306:89-043-11, 11A, ATL.)
Fowler, Leo:
  Papers (uncatalogued, acc. no. 77-14), MSS, ATL.
[Gascoyne, F. J. W.]:
  'Record of Services at Poverty Bay', K. A. Webster Papers 2:16, MSS 1009, ATL.
Grace, Rev. Thomas:
  Letters to CMS, 1864–79, CN/045, CMS microfilm, AU.
  Papers, MSS 583, AIM.
Graham, George:
  Letters, MSS 90:22, Folder 1, AIM.
Green, Pinky:
  'A History of northern Waiapu', 1960, MSS, ATL.
Grey, Sir George:
  Correspondence, GLNZ;
  Correspondence, Maori, GNZMA;
  Maori Manuscripts: Ua Rongopai (Gospel according to Te Ua), GNZ Maori MSS 1;
  Miscellaneous Maori Poems, GNZ Maori MSS 6, APL.
Hawke's Bay province, Inwards Correspondence (HB 4):
  Inwards (English) (1865–66): HB 4/6–7;
  Lists of people killed by Hauhau in various places in the province: HB 4/12;
  Inwards (Maori) (1861–67): HB 4/13, NA.
Hill, Henry:
  Papers and Notebooks 1889–1926, MSS 146, ATL.
Hursthouse, C. W.:
  Letter to Col. R. Trimble, 22 May 1884, MSS 408, AIM.
Internal Affairs Department:
  Inwards Correspondence (IA1) and Registers, 1865–93, NA.
Justice Department:
  Inwards Correspondence and Reports (J1): 1890/407; 1893/515; 1893/551;
  Inwards Registers of Correspondence, 1893–95, NA.

Kempthorne, Arthur:
    Journal of Events, 1868, HBM.
    'Journal of the capture of Ngatapa', in Williams Family Papers, MSS 69:49, ATL.
Laughton, Rev. J. G.:
    Papers on Ringatu, n.d., A. P. Godber Papers, MSS 78:47, ATL.
Legislative Department:
    Reports and Petitions (Le1): 1867/13; 1878/6; 1893/165, NA.
Lemuel Te Urupu, Emma:
    Transcript notebook of prophetic sayings, 1880–98;
    'Nga Kupu Whakaari', typescripts, Private collection, Emma Lemuel, Raupunga.
Locke, Samuel:
    Letterbook 1869–72, HBM.
McDonnell, Thomas:
    Manuscript notes and Letterbook, MSS ZA 155, ML.
    Papers, MSS 35, ATL.
Mackay, Joseph A.:
    Scrapbooks, MSS 1006, Series 2, ATL.
McLean, Donald: Manuscript Papers, MSS 32:
    Secretary, Native Department (1861–68): MSS 32:11;
    Superintendent, East Coast (1865–69): MSS 32:19–25, 25A;
    Native Minister (1869–73): MSS 32:30–31;
    Native Minister, Waikato affairs (1869–75): MSS 32:33;
    Minister of Colonial Defence, East Coast (1869–71): MSS 32:48;
    Minister of Colonial Defence, Waikato (1870–73): MSS 32:49;
    Inwards Private Correspondence: MSS 32:148 (E. Baker); 162 (R. N. Biggs); 171 (H. W. Brabant); 194 (R. S. Bush); 217–18 (H. T. Clarke); 221–22 (W. Colenso); 243 (S. Deighton); 278–80 (W. Fox); 282 (J. Fraser); 322 (F. E. Hamlin); 327 (J. W. Harris); 337 (J. Hervey); 338 (L. Hetet); 393–94 (S. Locke); 412 (T. McDonnell); 441 (G. Mair); 442 (W. G. Mair); 507–8 (D. Pollen); 510 (T. W. Porter); 514 (G. A. Preece); 521 (G. E. Read); 534 (J. C. Richmond); 549 (E. O. Ross); 557 (J. C. St George); 559 (J. H. H. St John); 566 (W. N. Searancke); 609 (E. Tuke); 620 (H. S. Wardell); 622 (H. F. Way); 630 (C. Westrup); 640 (W. Williams); 641 (W. L. Williams); 660 (J. Wyllie);
    Inwards Private Maori Letters: MSS 32:688–702 (1864–77, and undated), ATL.
Mair Family Papers:
    MSS 93, ATL.
    MSS 1618, AIM.
Mair, Gilbert:
    Diaries and Letters, MSS 92, ATL.
    Diary 1867–68, typescript, J. C. Andersen Papers, MSS 148:79, ATL.
    Letter to Augustus Hamilton, 20 February 1899, MSS, Rotorua Museum.
Mair, W. G.:
    Diaries 1872–75, MSS, ATL.
    Diary 1873, typescript, Private collection, Mrs Z. Craig, Auckland.
    Diaries 1876–85, typescripts, MSS A-31, AU.
    Letterbook 1868–69, MSS 1077, ML.
    Letter and Telegram book, 1871–75, MSS A-31, AU.
Maori Affairs Department:
    Inwards Correspondence (MA1) and Registers, 1865–94, (MA1 original Inwards Correspondence 1863–91 destroyed);
    Outwards Correspondence (Maori) Letterbooks (MA4), 1885–96;
    Miscellaneous, MA 24/22, 24/31;
    Poverty Bay Land Commission, MA 62/1–9 (MA 62/1–8 also photocopied in the Raupatu Document Bank, Vols 128–31, AU);
    Special Files: Te Kuiti Gathering 1869–72, MA 23/2; King Tawhiao's Papers, MA 23/3–4a,b; Te Mahuki's Papers MA 23/5–6; Te Kooti's Papers MA 23/8a,b,c;
    Tarawera Eruption, MA 21/23–24, NA.

Maori Land Court:
    Judge Brabant's Minute Book 5 (1889);
    Gisborne Minute Books 1–25, 62 (1868–96, 1936);
    Napier Minute Book 4 (1875);
    Opotiki Minute Books 4–5 (1889–94);
    Poverty Bay Commission Minute Book (1869–73);
    Tairawhiti District Minute Book 1 (1903);
    Wairoa Minute Books 11–13 (1899–1903);
    Whakatane Minute Books 3–5 (1890–97), microfilm, AU.
Maori School Files:
    Omaio, E 44/4, I, BAAA 1001/388c;
    Omarumutu, E 44/4, I, BAAA/1001/395c;
    Ruatoki, E 44/4, I, BAAA/1001/540a;
    Te Awahou, E 44/4, II, BAAA/1001/574b;
    Te Teko, E 44/4, I, BAAA 1001/615b;
    Waioeka, E 44/4, II, BAAA 1001/706c, NA Auckland.
Matuakore, P. (et al.):
    Letter to J. W. Preece, 22 August 1868, VF 993, Box 3, GM.
Mill Hill Mission Papers:
    Auckland, Box II, 1893–98, St Joseph's Society of the Sacred Heart for Foreign Missions, Mill
    Hill, U.K.
Monro, H. A. H.:
    Poverty Bay Notes, 1869, MSS 366:14, AIM.
[Morris, Maria]:
    Autobiography of a Maori Woman, MSS 2296, ATL.
Napier, W. J.:
    Probate 18453, NA Auckland.
Native Secretary's Office:
    Letterbook 1849–54, BAIE A646/9, NA Auckland.
Newland, William:
    'Expedition to Turanganui, Poverty Bay', 1868, MSS 018, Taranaki Museum.
North, Dr Allan:
    Notes on the Urewera collated 1 January 1965, MSS, MONZ.
Old Land Claims' Commission:
    Series 1, Case Files: OLC 1320;
    Series 4/21: Poverty Bay Claims, NA.
Onslow, Lord W. H.:
    Letter to Queen Victoria, 1891, MSS 2346, ATL.
Ormond, J. D.:
    Papers, MSS, HBM.
Paeroa, Matiu:
    Manuscript book, transcript made 1930–31, Frank Davis Dossier Vol. 3, ATL. Second copy, with
    additional page, Private collection, Te Riaki Amoamo, Opotiki.
Phillipps, W. J.:
    'Report of a Visit to the Urewera', 1959, MSS, MONZ.
Police Department:
    Inwards Correspondence (P1) and Registers: 1884–93;
    Outwards Telegrams (P5): 1886–93, NA.
Polynesian Society Papers:
    MSS 1187, ATL.
Porter, P. L.:
    'The Porter Family in New Zealand', MSS, ATL.
Porter, Thomas W.:
    Diary 1871, MSS, ATL.
    Papers 1868–1905, AD 103, NA.

Preece, George A.:
Diary 1870–72, annotated typescripts, MSS 249, AIM.
Diary 1870, MSS, APL.
'Notes for Major Gascoyne', typescript, MSS 249, AIM.
Papers, typescripts, HBM.
Rayner, R. W.:
Wharekauri Diary 1866–68, MSS 3694, ATL.
Ringatu Church:
Maori Affairs Department File 1923–39, MSS, ATL.
Ritchie, James:
'He Matakite', unpublished radio play, 1967, Private collection, James Ritchie, Hamilton.
Ritchie, Tom:
Diary 1866–68, Scrapbooks, and Drawings, Z MSS 36, CPL.
St George, J. C.:
Diaries 1865–69, MSS, ATL.
[St John, J. H. H.]:
Account of the siege of Nga Tapa, Whitmore MSS, Box D:5, HBM.
Shand, Alexander:
Papers, MSS 275, AIM.
Shortland, E.:
Clipping 'Te Kooti and Mr. Mackay', MSS K, p.79, MSS 11, HL.
Smith, S. Percy:
Diary 1868, ATL.
Papers, Reminiscences, and Sketchbooks, MSS 281, AIM.
Stafford, E. W.:
Papers, MSS 28, ATL.
Stoddart, Margaret O.:
Album of sketches and notes, CM.
Sullivan, E. F.:
'Memories of Kihikihi', POM 43-3, Auckland Catholic District Archives.
Tanui, Peneamene:
Diary, commencing 1871, MSS 671:2, AIM.
Te Keepa Te Rangihiwinui:
Circular, 26 January 1892, Important Native Circulars, Onslow Collection, Clandon Park, West Clandon, U.K.
Te Kooti Arikirangi Te Turuki:
Diary kept on Wharekauri, MSS 3091, ATL.
Diary 1869–70, HBM.
Letter to Lord Onslow, 18 February 1892, Onslow Collection, Guildford Muniments Room, Guildford, U.K.
Letter (fragment), 16 April 1889, Private collection.
Letters and other items, MSS 390, ATL.
Letters 1892–93, MSS 675, AIM.
Manuscript book of waiata, 1769–1890, compiled by Hamiora Aparoa, MSS C-35, AU.
Teague, Bernard:
Scrapbooks I–III, Private collection, Bronwyn Elsmore, Otumoetai.
Tomkinson, W. C.:
Letter to his sister, 7 April 1869, MSS 1270, AIM.
Turnbull, A. H.:
Scrapbook, ATL.
Tutua, S. Te Hau (Lucky):
Notebook, Frank Davis Dossier, Vol. 3, ATL.
U'ren Sharp, Louise Margaret:
'Notes on Thomas U'ren', MSS, GM.
Wardell, H. S.:
Diary 1858, MSS, ATL.

Whitmore, G. S.:
    Correspondence 1868–70, typescripts, ATL.
    Papers, HBM.
    Papers 1861–70, MSS 161, ATL.
Williams Family Papers:
    MSS 69; MSS 190, ATL.
    MSS, Series C, AIM.
Williams, W. Leonard:
    Diary 1865, typescript, AIM.
    Diary II, 1865–66, MSS, ATL.
    Diary 1868–69, typescript, AIM.
    Diary III, 1868–69, MSS, ATL.
    Diary IV, 1869–70, MSS, ATL.
    Letters to CMS, 1857–80, CN/097, CMS microfilm, AU.
    'Notes on Ringa-tu', n.d., MSS, ATL.
Wilson, Tawehi:
    Manuscript Book, n.d., Private collection, late Ned Brown, Whatatutu.
Winks, Robin:
    'A Maori Form of Christianity: The Ringatu Church', MSS A-206, AU.

(b) Theses and Research Documents

Ballara, H. A.:
    'The Origins of Ngāti Kahungunu', PhD thesis, Victoria University of Wellington, 1991.
Gartner, Kenneth C.:
    'Te Kooti Arikirangi Te Tūruki: His Movements and Influence within the Ngāti Tūwharetoa
    Region 1869–70', MA thesis, Victoria University of Wellington, 1991.
Ihimaera, Witi:
    'The Matriarch: Discussion: University of Auckland, 18 July 1990', unpublished typescript,
    Private collection of the author, Auckland.
Mead, S. M. (ed.):
    'Three Carved Houses at Te Whaiti: Part III, Eripitana', 1970, Department of Anthropology
    Library, AU.
Neal, Karen:
    'Maori Participation in the East Coast Wars 1865–72', MA thesis, University of Auckland, 1976.
Newman, Rev. Alan:
    'The Religious Beliefs, Rituals and Values of the Ringatu Church', MA thesis, Massey University,
    Palmerston North, 1986.
O'Malley, Vincent:
    'Report for the Crown Forestry Rental Trust on the East Coast Confiscation Legislation and its
    Implementation', [Wellington], 1994.
Salmond, Anne:
    'Borderlands: Playing with the Past', unpublished paper delivered to the David Nichol Smith
    Seminar IX, University of Auckland, 1993.
Stokes, E.:
    'Pai Marire and the Niu at Kuranui', Occasional Paper No. 6, Centre for Maori Studies and
    Research, University of Waikato, 1980.
    'Te Raupatu o Tauranga Moana: The Confiscation of Tauranga Lands', University of Waikato,
    typescript prepared for the Waitangi Tribunal, 1989.
Takotohiwi, Mihi:
    'Ngā Marae ō Whakatāne', MA thesis, University of Waikato, 1980.
Wiri, Rapata:
    '"Te Wai-Kaukau o Nga Matua Tipuna": Myths, Realities, and the Determination of Mana
    Whenua in the Waikaremoana District', MA thesis, University of Auckland, 1994.

II. Published Books and Articles

—— *Abbot Family Centennial Magazine 1875–1975*, Opotiki, 1975.
—— *Appendices to the Journals of the House of Representatives*, 1862–93; 1921–22; 1928.
—— *Cyclopaedia of New Zealand*, VI, Christchurch, 1908.
—— *The Dictionary of New Zealand Biography*, Vols I–II, Wellington, 1990, 1993.
—— *An Encyclopaedia of New Zealand*, 3 vols, Wellington, 1966.
—— Goodall v. Te Kooti, Court of Appeal, *New Zealand Law Reports*, IX, 1891.
—— *Great Britain Parliamentary Papers*, 1868–72, Facsimiles Vols 15–16.
—— 'He Tohutohu Tika' ('Good Advice'), [1912], trans. L. F. Head, *Te Karanga*, V, 3 (1989).
—— *Journals of the House of Representatives*, 1867–93.
—— *Ko Te Pukapuka o Nga Inoinga, me Era Atu Tikanga, i Whakaritea e Te Hahi o Ingarani, mo Te Minitatanga o Nga Hakarameta, o Era Atu Ritenga Hoki [a] Te Hahi: me Nga Waiata Ano Hoki a Rawiri, me Te Tikanga mo Te Whiriwhiringa, mo Te Whakaturanga, me Te Whakatapunga o Nga Pihopa, o Nga Piriti, me Nga Rikona*, London, 1859.
—— 'Legend Translation', *Te Maori*, October–November 1979.
—— *New Zealand Parliamentary Debates*, 1866–93.
—— *Paremata Maori — Waipatu, 1893.*
—— *Report of the Waitangi Tribunal on the Orakei Claim*, WAI-9, Wellington, 1987.
—— *Tai Whati: Judicial Decisions affecting Maoris and Maori Land 1958–1983*, Wellington, n.d. [1983].
—— 'Te Kooti's Notebook', *Archifacts*, 13 (March 1980).
—— *Te Pukapuka o Nga Kawenata e Waru a Te Atua me Nga Karakia Katoa a Te Haahi Ringatu*, n.p., n.d. [1968].
Andersen, J. C. and Petersen, G. C.:
  The Mair Family, Wellington, 1956.
Armstrong, Mrs C. S.:
  'Some Reminiscences of Early Whakatane' (1957), *Whakatane Historical Review*, XIV, 1 (March 1966).
Ballara, H. Angela:
  'Pakeha uses of Takitimutanga: who owns tribal tradition?', *Stout Centre Review*, III, 2 (March 1993).
Bejar, Ruth:
  Translated Woman, Boston, 1993.
Belich, James:
  'I Shall Not Die', Wellington, 1989.
  The New Zealand Wars, Auckland, 1986.
  'War', in C. Davis and P. Lineham (eds), *The Future of the Past: Themes in New Zealand History*, n.p. [Palmerston North], 1991.
Bennett, Francis:
  Tairua, Pauanui, 1986.
Best, Elsdon:
  The Maori, 2 vols, Wellington, 1924.
  Maori Religion and Mythology, Part I, Wellington, 1924.
  'Notes on the Art of War', *JPS*, XI–XIII, 1902–4.
  Tuhoe, 2 vols, 3rd edn, Wellington, 1977.
  Waikare-moana, Wellington, 1897.
Binney, Judith:
  'Ancestral Voices: Maori Prophet Leaders', in K. Sinclair (cd.), *The Oxford Illustrated History of New Zealand*, Auckland, 1990.
  'Maori Oral Narratives, Pakeha Written Texts: Two Forms of Telling History', *New Zealand Journal of History*, XXI, 1 (April 1987).
  'Myth and Explanation in the Ringatū Tradition', *JPS*, 93, 4 (December 1984).
Binney, Judith; Chaplin, Gillian:
  Ngā Mōrehu: The Survivors, Auckland, 1986, corrected edn, 1990.
Binney, Judith; Chaplin, Gillian; Wallace, Craig:
  Mihaia: The Prophet Rua Kenana and his Community at Maungapohatu, Auckland, 1979, corrected edn, 1987.

Brittan, S. J. et al. (eds):
  A Pioneer Missionary among the Maoris 1850–1879; being letters and journals of Thomas Samuel Grace,
  Palmerston North, n.d. [1928].
Brookfield, F. M.:
  'Maori Rights and Two Radical Writers: Review and Response', *New Zealand Law Journal*,
  (November 1990).
B[roomfield], F. K.:
  'A History of Te Teko School', *Whakatane Historical Review*, XIII, 2 (November 1965).
Clyde, Alan:
  'Te Kooti' and Other Poems, Dunedin, 1872.
Colenso, W.:
  Fiat Justitia, Napier, 1871.
Cowan, James:
  'The Facts about Te Kooti', *NZ Railways Magazine*, 1 December 1938.
  The Maori Yesterday and To-day, Auckland, 1930.
  The Maoris of New Zealand, Christchurch, 1910.
  The New Zealand Wars, 2 vols, 2nd edn, Wellington, 1955–56.
Curwen, John (ed.):
  *School Songs, Sacred, Moral, and Descriptive designed to Aid Instruction in Schools and Families, and
  Connected with Appropriate Tunes*, London, 1859.
Davidson, Gustav:
  A Dictionary of Angels, New York, 1967.
Davis, Frank:
  Face to Face, Gisborne, 1969.
Dening, Greg:
  Islands and Beaches: Discourse on a Silent Land: Marquesas 1774–1880, Honolulu, 1980.
Duncan, Russell:
  The Fight at Ruakituri, Dunedin, 1939.
Edwards, S. R.:
  'Docudrama from the Twenties', *Whakatane Historical Review*, 41, 2 (November 1993).
Elmsberg, John-Erik:
  Islands of Tomorrow, London, 1956.
Elsmore, Bronwyn:
  Mana from Heaven: A Century of Maori Prophets in New Zealand, Tauranga, 1989.
Fowler, Leo:
  Te Mana o Turanga, Auckland, 1974.
  'A New Look at Te Kooti', *Te Ao Hou*, 20–21 (November–December 1957).
  The Taiaha and the Testament, Gisborne, n.d. [1970].
Gascoyne, F. J. W.:
  Soldiering in New Zealand, London, 1916.
Grace, John Te H.:
  Tuwharetoa, Wellington, 1959.
Greenwood, William:
  'Iconography of Te Kooti Rikirangi', *JPS*, 55, 1 (March 1946).
  The Upraised Hand or The Spiritual Significance of the Rise of the Ringatu Faith, 1942, and 2nd edn,
  Wellington, 1980.
Grey, Sir George:
  Ko Nga Moteatea, 2nd edn, Wellington, 1853.
Gudgeon, Thomas W.:
  The Defenders of New Zealand, Auckland, 1887.
  Reminiscences of the War in New Zealand, London, 1879.
Gudgeon, W. E.:
  'The Tohunga Maori', *JPS*, XVI, 2 (June 1907).
Hawthorne, James:
  A Dark Chapter from New Zealand History, Napier, 1869.

Hobsbawm, E. J.:
   Bandits, Harmondsworth, 1969.
Ihimaera, Witi:
   Te Ao Mārama: Contemporary Māori Writing, Vol. I, Wellington, 1992.
   The Matriarch, Auckland, 1986.
Johansen, J. Prytz:
   The Maori and His Religion, Copenhagen, 1954.
   Studies in Maori Rites and Myths, Copenhagen, 1958.
Kaiwhata, G. H. E. and Leighton, E. P.:
   Descendants of Awanuiarangi and Moerangi Ratahi, Whakatane, 1991.
Karetu, Sam:
   'Language and Protocol of the Marae', in Michael King (ed.), *Te Ao Hurihuri: The World Moves On*, Wellington, 1975.
Keam, R. F.:
   Tarawera, Auckland, 1988.
Kermode, Frank:
   The Genesis of Secrecy: On the Interpretation of Narrative, Cambridge, Mass., 1979.
Kerry-Nicholls, J. H.:
   The King Country, London, 1884.
King, Michael:
   'Moko of the Maori', *Face Value: A Study in Maori Portraiture*, n.p. [Dunedin], n.d. [1975].
Lambert, Thomas:
   The Story of Old Wairoa and the East Coast District, North Island New Zealand, Dunedin, 1925.
Lane Fox, Robin:
   The Unauthorized Version: Truth and Fiction in the Bible, London, 1991.
Lyall, A. C.:
   Whakatohea of Opotiki, Wellington, 1979.
Mackay, Joseph A.:
   Historic Poverty Bay and the East Coast, N.I., 2nd edn, Gisborne, 1966.
McLean, Mervyn and Orbell, Margaret:
   Traditional Songs of the Maori, Wellington, 1975.
[Mair, G. and Preece, G. A.]:
   'Expeditions against Te Kooti', in John Featon, *The Waikato War*, revised edn, Auckland, 1923.
Makemson, Maud W.:
   The Morning Star Rises. An Account of Polynesian Astronomy, New Haven, 1941.
Maraenui Maori School:
   'Te Kooti Returns from the Dead', *Te Ao Hou*, 20 (November 1957).
Mead, Hirini Moko (S. M.):
   Nga Karoretanga o Mataatua Whare: The Wanderings of the Carved House, Mataatua, Whakatane, 1990.
   Te One Matua: The Abundant Earth, Te Teko, 1982.
Mead, Hirini Moko me Te Roopu Kohikohi o Ngati Awa:
   Te Murunga Hara: The Pardon, Whakatane, 1989.
Misur, Gilda Z.:
   'From Prophet Cult to Established Church: The Case of the Ringatu Movement', in I. H. Kawharu (ed.), *Conflict and Compromise: Essays on the Maori since Colonisation*, Wellington, 1975.
Mitcalfe, Barry:
   Maori Poetry, Wellington, 1974.
Mol, Hans:
   The Fixed and the Fickle: Religion and Identity in New Zealand, Dunedin, n.d. [1982].
Neich, Roger:
   Painted Histories: Early Maori Figurative Painting, Auckland, 1993.
Nihoniho, Tuta:
   Narrative of the Fighting on the East Coast, 1865–1871, Wellington, 1913.
Ngata, A. T.:
   Nga Moteatea, Parts I–III, Wellington, 1959–63.

Ngugi Wa Thiong'o:
  Homecoming, London, 1972.
Oliver, W. H. and Thomson, Jane M.:
  Challenge and Response, Gisborne, 1971.
Orbell, Margaret:
  'Two Versions of the Maori Story of Te Tahi o te Rangi', *JPS*, 82, 2 (June 1973).
  Waiata, Maori Songs in History, Auckland, 1991.
O'Sullivan, Kitty:
  The Curse of the Greenstone Tiki, Auckland, n.d. [1945].
Phillipps, W. J.:
  Carved Maori Houses of the Eastern Districts of the North Island, Wellington, 1944.
Phillips, F. L.:
  Nga Tohu a Tainui: Landmarks of Tainui, Otorohanga, 1989.
Porter, T. W.:
  History of the Early Days of Poverty Bay, Gisborne, 1923.
Price, Robert:
  Through the Uriwera Country, Napier, 1891.
Ranger, T. O.:
  'Connexions between "Primary Resistance" Movements and Modern Mass Nationalism in East and Central Africa', *Journal of African History*, IX, 3 (1968).
Richards, E. C. (ed.):
  Diary of E. R. Chudleigh 1862–1921, Christchurch, 1950.
Ross, W. Hugh:
  Te Kooti Rikirangi, General and Prophet, Auckland, 1966.
Roth, Bert:
  'Te Kooti's Friend Desmond', *New Zealand Monthly Review*, (August 1960).
Sahlins, Marshall:
  'Hierarchy and Humanity in Polynesia', in Antony Hooper and Judith Huntsman (eds), *Transformations of Polynesian Culture*, Auckland, 1985.
Said, Edward W.:
  Culture and Imperialism, London, 1993.
Saunders, Alfred:
  History of New Zealand, Vol. II, Christchurch, n.d. [1899].
Scholefield, Guy H. (ed.):
  The Richmond–Atkinson Papers, 2 vols, Wellington, 1960.
Shadbolt, Maurice:
  Season of the Jew, London, 1986.
Shand, Alexander:
  'The Moriori People of the Chatham Islands, Part XIV', *JPS*, VII (1898).
Sissons, Jeffrey:
  Te Waimana, Dunedin, 1991.
Smithyman, Kendrick:
  Auto/Biographies, Auckland, 1992.
Stack, James W.:
  Notes on Maori Christianity, Christchurch, 1874.
Stead, C. K.:
  Voices, Wellington, 1990.
Steiner, George:
  Real Presences, London, 1989.
Stewart, Adela B.:
  My Simple Life in New Zealand, London, 1908.
Tarei, Wi:
  'A Church called Ringatu', in Michael King (ed.), *Tihe Mauri Ora*, n.p., 1978.
Thomas, Nicholas:
  Entangled Objects: Exchange, Material Culture, and Colonialism in the Pacific, Cambridge, Mass., 1991.

Todorov, Tzvetan:
> *The Conquest of America: the Question of the Other*, trans. Richard Howard, New York, 1984.

Turton, H. H.:
> *Maori Deeds of Old Private Land Purchases in New Zealand*, Wellington, 1882.

Walzer, Michael:
> *Exodus and Revolution*, New York, 1985.

Ward, Alan:
> 'Documenting Maori History: The Arrest of Te Kooti Rikirangi Te Turuki, 1889', *New Zealand Journal of History*, XIV, 1 (April 1980).
> *A Show of Justice: Racial 'Amalgamation' in Nineteenth Century New Zealand*, Auckland, 1973.

Watt, M. N.:
> *Index to the N.Z. Section of the Register of All British Ships 1840–1950*, Part 2, Wellington, n.d. [1963].

Whaanga, Mere:
> *Te Kooti's Diamond*, Auckland, 1991.

Wheeler, L. P.:
> *The Patchwork Quilt*, Paeroa, 1970.

White, H. G. D.:
> 'Military Activities in the Opotiki District in 1870', *Whakatane Historical Review*, 20, 1 (May 1972).

Whitmore, George S.:
> *The Last Maori War in New Zealand*, London, 1902.

Williams, Haare:
> *Karanga*, Coromandel, 1980.

Williams, H. W.:
> *A Bibliography of Printed Maori to 1900*, Wellington, 1924.

Williams, Mark:
> 'Witi Ihimaera and the Politics of Epic', *Leaving the Highway: Six Contemporary New Zealand Novelists*, Auckland, 1990.

Williams, W. Leonard:
> *East Coast Historical Records*, Gisborne, n.d. [1932].

Wilson, Ormond:
> *War in the Tussock*, Wellington, 1961.

Winiata, Maharaia:
> *The Changing Role of the Leader in Maori Society*, Auckland, 1967.

III. Oral Informants

Copies of taped dialogues recorded by the author are, for the most part, held (for preservation) in the Archive of Maori and Pacific Music, University of Auckland. The originals will ultimately be transferred to a public collection. Only tape-recorded dialogues are listed here; all other oral references cited in this book are from interview notes.

(a) Dialogues tape-recorded by Judith Binney

Algie, Hei Ariki (Tihei):
> 26 November 1983, Manutuke.

Biddle, Robert (Boy):
> 14 December 1981; 17 February 1982; 28–29 January 1983; 5 March 1983; 13 May 1984; 15 October 1987, Kutarere.

Brown, George:
> 20 May 1982, Puha.

Brown, Ned and Heni:
> 14 February 1982; 6 June 1982; 30 November 1983, Whatatutu and Mangatu.

Butterworth, Arnold:
> 19 May 1982, Gisborne.

Delamere, Sir Monita:
    16 February 1982, Opotiki.
Horopapera Tatu:
    27 January 1978, Tataiahape.
Hughes, Kino:
    28 January 1978, Ruatoki.
Ihe, John and Waipiro:
    28 January 1983, Waiotahe.
Jones, Te Aomuhurangi Te Maaka (Maaka):
    20–21 August 1984, Wellington;
    and with Ema Rogers, 2 January 1985, Whitianga.
Kahika, Himiona:
    15 December 1981; 16 February 1982; 6 March 1983, Opotiki.
Karauna, Te Huinga (Jack):
    8 December 1978, Opotiki.
Kurei, Paroa (Jack):
    15 December 1981, Opotiki.
Lemuel Te Urupu, Emma:
    20 April 1991 (with Ultima Te-Urupu), Raupunga.
McLean, Taua:
    6 July 1981; 22 October 1981; 20 December 1981, Rotorua.
Manuera, Dr Eruera:
    25 May 1981; 17 February 1982, Te Teko.
Onekawa, Putiputi:
    30 January 1983; 8 May 1984, Kutarere.
Riki, Reuben:
    16 May 1982, Muriwai.
Rua, Heta:
    18 May 1978 (with Te Paea); 23 May 1982, Matahi and Whakatane.
Rua, Hillman:
    21 May 1978, Rotorua.
Rua, Mau:
    19 May 1978, Whakarae.
Ruru, Tupae (John):
    15 February 1982, Puha.
Sunderland, Heni Materoa:
    11 May 1984, Gisborne.
Thompson, Rose:
    28 November 1983, Tawatapu (Bartletts).
Williams, John, with Rose Okeroa Williams and Heneriata (Nellie) Te Moananui:
    30 November 1991, Ngahu-toitoi marae, Paeroa.
Wiremu, Heni:
    25 January 1983, Gisborne.

(b) Interviews tape-recorded by others

Campbell, Christopher:
    26 November 1990, interview with Erena Reedy, *Mana News*, Radio New Zealand.
Collier, Mrs E. (Meri):
    Talk to Whakatane Museum, c.1960, Whakatane Museum.
Davis, Frank:
    Transcribed oral statements of Ringatu elders, Davis Dossier, Vol. 9, ATL.
Delamere, Paora:
    15 December 1971, Te Reo o Te Maori, Radio New Zealand Archives.
Emery, Robert:
    16 February 1983, He Rerenga Korero, Radio New Zealand Archives.

Jones, Pei Te Hurinui:
    13 February 1974, AK7/56, Radio New Zealand Archives.
Nepia, Ted:
    16 February 1972, Te Reo o Te Maori, Radio New Zealand Archives.
Tarei, Wi:
    13 February 1974, AK7/56, Radio New Zealand Archives.
Wilson, Tawehi:
    26 June 1968, Muriwai, Radio New Zealand Archives.

(c) Recorded programmes of interviews

Simpson, Tony:
    'The Mountain of the Lord', New Zealand Broadcasting Corporation, 1970.
Williams, Haare:
    'The Upraised Hand', Radio New Zealand, 1986.

INDEX

N.B. Page numbers in *italic* indicate illustrations, maps or whakapapa. Page numbers in **boldface** indicate important references. TK = Te Kooti